1989

THE JEWS OF VIENNA
IN THE AGE OF FRANZ JOSEPH

THE LITTMAN LIBRARY OF JEWISH CIVILIZATION

FOUNDER
L. T. S. Littman

EDITORS
Albert Friedlander
Louis Jacobs
Vivian D. Lipman

For the love of God
and in memory of
JOSEPH AARON LITTMAN

'Get wisdom, get understanding:
Forsake her not and she shall preserve thee'

The Jews of Vienna
in the Age of Franz Joseph

ROBERT S. WISTRICH

PUBLISHED FOR
THE LITTMAN LIBRARY
BY
OXFORD UNIVERSITY PRESS
1989

Oxford University Press, Walton Street, Oxford OX2 6DP
Oxford New York Toronto
Delhi Bombay Calcutta Madras Karachi
Petaling Jaha Singapore Hong Kong Tokyo
Nairobi Dar es Salaam Cape Town
Melbourne Auckland
and associated companies in
Berlin Ibadan

Oxford is a trade mark of Oxford University Press

Published in the United States
by Oxford University Press, New York

British Library Cataloguing in Publication Data
Wistrich, Robert S. (Robert Soloman), 1945–
The Jews of Vienna in the age of Franz Joseph.—
(The Littman library of Jewish civilization).
1. Austria. Vienna. Jews, 1848–1916
I. Title II. Series
943.6'13004924
ISBN 0–19–710070–8

Library of Congress Cataloging in Publication Data
Wistrich, Robert S., 1945–
The Jews of Vienna in the age of Franz Joseph / Robert S.
Wistrich.
(The Littman library of Jewish civilization)
Bibliography: p. Includes index.
1. Jews—Austria—Vienna—History. 2. Jews—Austria—Vienna—
Intellectual life. 3. Vienna (Austria)—Intellectual life.
4. Zionism—Austria—Vienna—History.
5. Vienna (Austria)—Ethnic relations. I. Title.
II. Series: Littman library of Jewish civilization
(Oxford University Press)
DS135.A92V583 1988 943.6'13004924—dc19 88–6618
ISBN 0–19–710070–8

Set by Hope Services, Abingdon
Printed in Great Britain
at the Alden Press, Oxford

In Memory of My Grandparents
Salomon and Anna Wistreich
Simon and Helena Silbiger
Citizens of Cracow and Former Subjects
of the Austro-Hungarian Empire

Preface

Fin de siècle Vienna has in recent years exerted an extraordinary spell over historians, social scientists, and literary critics concerned with the cultural roots of modernity or with the origins of a variety of twentieth-century political pathologies. One of the missing links in our picture of Vienna around 1900 remains, however, the lack of a comprehensive study of its Jewish community, which played such a decisive role in the cultural, economic, and public life of the Habsburg metropolis. The galaxy of talents produced as a result of the process of Jewish acculturation and interaction with other national groups (primarily the Austro-Germans, Magyars, and Poles) under the benign umbrella of the polyglot Habsburg State has more than simply an academic interest. Can one conceive of twentieth-century culture without the contributions of Freud, Wittgenstein, Mahler, Schoenberg, Karl Kraus, or Theodor Herzl? Whether they were full-blooded Jews, half-Jews, self-haters, converts, or Zionists, this secularized Jewish intelligentsia changed the face of Vienna and, indeed, of the modern world. They helped transform a city which had not been in the forefront of European intellectual or artistic activity (except in music) into an experimental laboratory for the creative triumphs and traumas of the modern world.

My interest in the tremendous explosion of Jewish creativity in Central Europe and particularly in Vienna began some twenty years ago as a young student completing his first degree at Cambridge University. One of the most striking anomalies in those days for anyone doing modern European history was to observe the way in which the Jewish factor was largely ignored or marginalized, even where it had clearly helped to give much of modern intellectual life its special colour, tone, and vitality. Subsequently, during a postgraduate year spent at Stanford University, my interest in Central European intellectual history was greatly stimulated by coming into contact with the writings of Carl Schorske. Now, for the first time, some of the connections between politics, culture, and society in Habsburg Austria before the First World War began to fall into place. Yet already then, I felt that no comprehensive treatment of turn-of-the-century Vienna would be possible without a very detailed investigation of Habsburg Jewry and its history.

The first tentative step towards this forbiddingly difficult field was taken during 1969–70 which I spent as a student at the Hebrew University. At that time I had proposed doing a doctorate on 'The Jewish Intelligentsia in *fin de siècle* Vienna' to the late Professor Jacob Talmon, but for various reasons the plan fell through. But that year in Israel proved to be crucial in giving me a sense of the coherence of Habsburg Jewry and of a Habsburg Jewish tradition linking Austro-German, Hungarian, Czech, Polish, and South Slav Jews. As I began to master the necessary languages and see the possibilities of contrast and comparison between these diverse Jewries linked by their common citizenship in a vanished Empire, new horizons literally opened up. My year in Israel also led me to my thesis topic, undertaken in London under the supervision of Professor Chimen Abramsky, dealing with the attitude of German and Austrian Socialists to the 'Jewish Question' in Central and Eastern Europe.

It was during the years of research on my thesis in the early 1970s that I came to know better the city of Vienna and its archives. Indeed, the present work, whose theme finally crystallized about ten years ago, could hardly have been undertaken without that earlier (and at times painful) apprenticeship. In 1978 the Austrian Ministry of Science and Research offered me a scholarship to study in Vienna as the first stage in putting the materials for this book together. I divided my time between the rigours of the city archives, the Austrian National Library, and the Vienna University Library while trying to take in as much as possible of that café-society and museum-like atmosphere which still characterizes the Austrian capital. I was able to read much of the Viennese press—liberal, clerical, Pan-German, anti-Semitic, and socialist—as well as relevant pamphlet literature. A perusal of the proceedings in the Austrian Imperial Parliament, in the lower Austrian Diet and the Vienna Municipal Council transported me back into an era where anti-Semitism of an unbelievably crude and virulent strain was already rearing its head and threatening the tranquillity of Austrian Jews. This dark side of the cultural revolution in Austria was to assume increasing importance as I came to examine how the Jews in Vienna interacted with their non-Jewish neighbours and the socio-economic tensions which accompanied their rise in social status and intellectual creativity. It became increasingly clear that if Jews were indeed the 'intellectual cement' (Milan Kundera), the cosmopolitan leaven of the pre-Nazi world of Central European culture, their prominent role aroused the most morbid fears and anxieties in the hearts of the anti-Semites.

The next major stage in my research was undertaken in Jerusalem, still unquestionably the leading centre for the study of ancient and modern Jewish history. It was here that I began after 1980 to examine more closely the internal structure of the Viennese Jewish community, its social background, religious differentiation, and political orientations; to look at its reponses to anti-Semitism and Zionism, to the waves of immigration from the provinces, and to the process of adaptation and modernization in the big city. In Jerusalem I was able to use the Central Archives of the History of the Jewish People (which contain the surviving records of the Israelitische Kultusgemeinde), the holdings of the National and University Library, and the files of the Central Zionist Archives. The story of the established Jewish community (i.e. the core of Viennese Jewry which was conscious of its identity and organized in community bodies) began to fall into place. So, too, did the emergence of Zionism in Vienna and the reactions it provoked, a topic little studied apart from the extensive literature surrounding the charismatic personality of Theodor Herzl. Reading such sources as Smolenskin's *Ha-Shaḥar* and Birnbaum's *Selbsteman-zipation*, the early history of Austrian Zionism began to take on a different and more varied complexion.

Beyond the issue of Zionism, a careful study of the specifically Jewish press—from *Die Neuzeit* to Dr Bloch's *Österreichische Wochen-schrift* (a goldmine of information concerning Austrian Jewry in the pre-1914 period)—enabled me gradually to reconstruct the overall profile of Viennese Jewry with all its contradictions, tensions, and internal conflicts. In Vienna and Jerusalem I also found relevant primary materials for understanding the history of the Austrian Israelite Union, the operations of the Baron Hirsch Foundation, and the religious philosophy and outlook of Vienna's leading rabbis. These sources were supplemented by visits to the archives of the Alliance Israélite in Paris (important for correspondence relating to the Vienna-based Israelitische Allianz) and to the Leo Baeck Archives in New York with its valuable collections concerning the history of German-speaking Jews in Central Europe. It was here I consulted the diaries of Rabbi Moritz Güdemann (Chief Rabbi of Vienna) and the correspon-dence of Richard Beer-Hofmann.

The final and most testing stage in the genesis of the present book lay in attempting to synthesize this broad range of heterogeneous materials, in trying to connect the internal history of the Jewish community with broader themes in late Habsburg culture and society. The existing literature, particularly the older, impressionistic histories of Viennese Jewry like those of Ludwig Bato, Hans Tietze, or Max Grunwald, and even the highly readable *The Jews of Austria*, edited by Josef Fraenkel, were useful but clearly inadequate and out of date. The essentially demographic study by Marsha L. Rozenblit, *The Jews of Vienna, 1867–1914* (1983), was invaluable as a basic source of facts and figures but did not really address in depth what seemed to me such crucial questions as the nature of Jewish identity and self-definition, the impact of anti-Semitism, and the role of Jews in Viennese culture and politics. There remained, however, a growing literature (much of it highly specialized) dealing with prominent individual Jews discussed in this book, with anti-Semitism, with Zionism, and with the sociology of Austrian Jewry, which is indispensable to researchers in this area but had not previously been integrated into a single, systematic study of Viennese Jews.

This book, during its long period of gestation, greatly benefitted from the research of many scholars, friends, colleagues, and fellow toilers in the vineyards of Austrian, Viennese, and Jewish history. Among those from whose work I have learnt in Austria I should like to mention the late Professor Karl Stadler of Linz, Professor Gerhard Botz of Salzburg, and Professors Gerald Stourzh, Wolfgang Häusler, and Erika Weinzierl from Vienna. The writings of a number of American scholars, beginning with Professor Carl Schorske and including Professors William J. McGrath, Peter Loewenberg, Marsha Rozenblit, John Boyer, Harry Zohn, and Dennis B. Klein, have been an important source of stimulation. In England I benefited from the advice of Professors James Joll and Peter Pulzer (Oxford) and the friendship of Dr Arnold Paucker, Director of the Leo Baeck Institute in London, which kindly provided the illustrations to the book.

I also had the good fortune to be granted interviews by the late Dr Robert Weltsch, a true connoisseur of Austro-Hungarian Jewry and by Dr Anna Freud who patiently answered my many questions about her distinguished father Sigmund Freud, about psycho-analysis, and about Jewish identity in Vienna. Dr Solomon Birnbaum of Toronto (Canada) provided me with similarly valuable responses to questions relating to his father, the mercurial Nathan Birnbaum. Particular gratitude is due to my friend and colleague, the indefatigable Ivaar Oxaal of Hull

University, whose infectious enthusiasm for the *Soziologie der Wiener Juden* revived my interest in the topic whenever it showed signs of flagging. Others from whom I have learnt in conversations on related themes include Steven Beller (Cambridge), Michael Pollak of the CNRS (Paris), Dr Gerald Stieg (Rouen), and Allan Janik (Innsbruck). Walter R. Weitzmann (New York) was the first to draw my attention to the significance of Kultusgemeinde politics, for which I am very grateful.

Among institutions in Israel which contributed to this book, pride of place must go to the Institute of Advanced Studies at the Hebrew University of Jerusalem where I was a visiting scholar-in-residence during 1981/2. My thanks go to its Director at the time, Aryeh Dvoretsky, to his deputy, Shabtai Giron, and to Professor Shmuel Ettinger for having invited me to join the study group on modern Jewish nationalism. Among colleagues and friends in Jerusalem who helped clarify fundamental issues in Central European Jewish history, my particular thanks go to Professor Michael Graetz of the Department of Jewish History at the Hebrew University, with whom I taught a joint course in 1982/3 focused on this theme. I also discussed some of the themes of this book with Dr Steven Aschheim of the History Department, with Dr Shmuel Almog of the Institute of Contemporary Jewry, and with Professor Yosef Salmon of Ben-Gurion University in Beersheba. For guidance on sources concerning the history of Austrian Zionism, I should like to thank the Director of the Central Zionist Archives in Jerusalem, Dr Michael Heymann, and his assistants Dr Moshe Schaerf and Chaya Har-El as well as Professor Jehuda Reinharz (Brandeis) and Professor Julius H. Schoeps (Duisburg). Dr Alex Bein was also kind enough to share with me some of his encyclopaedic knowledge of Herzl and his entourage.

My research visits to Vienna were made possible by the generosity of the Austrian Federal Ministry of Science and Research, the Leo Baeck Institute in New York (particular thanks go to Dr Fred Grubl), and the Gustav Wurzweiler Foundation, also in New York. Dr Fred Lessing deserves my special gratitude for his financial support in the early stages of research. So, too, does the late Mr Louis Littman (who never lost faith in this long drawn-out odyssey) as does the editor of this series, Dr V. D. Lipman, whose moral encouragement was much appreciated at a time when the results seemed uncertain. Gratitude of a different order is due to my mother, herself a former citizen of Cracow and subject of the Emperor Franz Joseph, who (perhaps unconsciously) transmitted to me something of the lost traditions of Habsburg Jewry, and to my Grandparents who lived through the last act in the drama of Habsburg Jewry which I have sought to recapture in this book.

For exceptional stamina beyond the call of duty in typing an outsize manuscript, I commend Mrs Janet Lieber of Jerusalem. My thanks also to Anne Ashby of the Oxford University Press for helping the book through the press and to Mrs Alice Park, for her meticulous copy-editing.

Some important revisions and additions to the manuscript were made in the course of my sabbatical leave at the Oxford Centre for Hebrew Studies where I was Visiting Professor and Frank Green Fellow in Modern Jewish History. It is therefore a special pleasure for me to thank the Founder and President of the Centre, Dr David Patterson, for making my stay in Oxford such a pleasant and enjoyable experience. Far from the 'gay apocalypse' of Vienna and the messianic dreams of Zion, the green pastures of Yarnton provided exactly the right atmosphere for completing this book.

R.S.W.

Jerusalem/Oxford
1986–7

Contents

xiv   *Contents*

List of Illustrations

PART ONE

THE COMMUNITY

I

From Ghetto to Revolution

In future no Jew, as they are called, is to be allowed in Vienna without My written permission. I know no worse public plague than this people, with their swindling, usury, and money-making, bringing people to beggary, practising all evil transactions which an honest man abhors; they are therefore to be kept away from here and avoided as far as possible.

Empress Maria Theresa (1777)

. . . it is Our purpose to make the Jews more useful and serviceable to the State, principally through according their children better instruction and enlightenment, and by employing them in the sciences, arts, and handicrafts.

Emperor Joseph II, Vienna, 2 January 1782

Ever since the time of Pharaoh, governments which persecuted the Jews suffered for it.

Prince Felix Schwarzenberg

We have pleaded enough for thirty years on bended knee, and with hands raised up we have prayed for our rights and status as human beings.

Isaac Noah Mannheimer, 18 March 1848

Reactionaries denounce the Jews as the *perpetuum mobile* of the Revolution, progressives regard the Jewish money-men as obstacles to liberty.

Adolf Jellinek (1848)

The fate of Jews in East-Central Europe in the modern period was closely bound up with that of the multinational Empire ruled by the Habsburg dynasty from 1273 until its dissolution in 1918. The historic nucleus of their Empire was Austria though after 1526 it contained countries like Hungary, Bohemia, and Moravia with sizeable Jewish populations, as well as the Jews of the Italian territories in the eighteenth and nineteenth centuries. Following the partition of Poland and the annexation of Galicia (1772) and Bukovina (1775) the Habsburg dominions came to include the largest Jewish population in Europe, west of the Russian Empire. After 1867 this vast territory became a dualistic structure called the Austro-Hungarian Monarchy, constituting two distinct States (Austria and Hungary) under a single ruler, Emperor Franz Joseph I.

The history of Austria under the Habsburgs was not so much the history of a people or a country as the history of a State.[1] The real founder of the dynasty, Rudolph Habsburg, had established the patrimonial nucleus of the later empire at the end of the thirteenth century by defeating the Czech king Ottokar. Over the next 650 years the Habsburg domains continued to expand, through marriages, donations, and exchanges—*Bella gerant alii, tu felix Austria nube!* ('Let others make wars, thou, happy Austria, marry!') Since the late Middle Ages, the Habsburgs in addition to their family possessions on the Danube had also become Holy Roman Emperors and thereby supreme lords of the Empire's Jews—known as servants of the treasury (*servi camerae regis*). The imperial phantom of the Holy Roman Empire of the German Nation with its dream of universal dominion continued to haunt the dynasty until the nineteenth century when it was punctured by Napoleon and finally destroyed by Bismarck. Only in 1871 did the Habsburgs give up their dream of hegemony in Germany.

At the same time the Austrian State from the sixteenth century onward expanded eastwards, bringing the benefits of German colonization to the more primitive and backward social structures of East-Central Europe. Here it was to discover a new Habsburg mission, that of defending Christianity and Western civilization against the Turkish danger.[2] It was, however, during the period of the Counter-Reformation that the Habsburgs first emerged as the protagonists of a militant Catholicism and in alliance with the Jesuits defeated Protestantism in Central Europe. Following the historic battle of the

---

[1] See Oscar Jászi, *The Dissolution of the Habsburg Monarchy* (Chicago and London, 1971), 32, who notes that Habsburg rule was 'without a national character and it was far more of a private nature than that of the other unifying dynasties'. A. J. P. Taylor, *The Habsburg Monarchy, 1809–1918* (London, 1981), 12, even more scathingly describes the Habsburg lands as 'a collection of entailed estates, not a state, and the Habsburgs were landlords, not rulers . . . intent on extracting the best return from their tenants so as to cut a great figure in Europe'.

[2] On the rise of the Habsburgs in the 16th and 17th cent. see now R. J. W. Evans, *The Making of the Habsburg Monarchy, 1550–1700* (Oxford, 1979).

White Mountain (1620), the semi-independent kingdom of Bohemia was destroyed and the Czech nation submerged for nearly 300 years. Bohemia now became a 'hereditary land', its native nobility was exiled or expropriated, and on its ruins developed a grandiose Austrian Baroque civilization with its capital in Vienna.[3] The reconquest of Hungary from the Turks after the failure of the Ottoman siege of Vienna in 1683 heralded the consolidation of Austria and its emergence as a European great power in the early eighteenth century.

The history of the Jews in Vienna and the Habsburg lands is a complex and uneven one, marked by times of prosperity and also of bloody persecutions; by periodic protection from the Imperial rulers and hostility from the Estates, by blood libels and forced expulsions. Jews had lived in Austria as far back as the tenth century, the first settlers probably arriving with the Romans. As early as *c*.906 there is a document placing Jewish and Christian merchants on the same footing. The appointment of Shlom (Solomon) the mintmaster in 1194 is the first firm evidence of permanent Jewish settlement.[4] During the reign of Frederick I of Babenberg (1195–8) persecutions in Germany drove numbers of Jews to Austria.[5] In 1204 there is reference to a synagogue in Vienna and in 1238 the Emperor Frederick II granted a charter to the Jews of Vienna, taking them under his protection.[6]

In 1244 Duke Frederick II, the last of the Babenbergs, issued the charter known as the 'Fredericianum' to the Jews of Austria. This statute, which guaranteed the Jews inviolability of life and possessions, unlimited freedom of movement, the right to settle and carry on trade, was to become the model for similar *privilegia* conferred on the Jews of Bohemia, Hungary, and Poland in the thirteenth century.[7] Murder of a Jew was punishable by death and heavy fines were imposed for physical assault, for attacks on Jewish cemeteries, synagogues, or schools—itself a testament to the brutal norms of medieval Europe—

[3] Ernest Wangermann, *The Austrian Achievement, 1700–1800* (London, 1973).

[4] See Ludwig Bato, *Die Juden im alten Wien* (Vienna, 1928), 7: 'Der erste Wiener Jude, den wir namentlich kennen, ist *Schlom*, Münzmeister des Herzogs Leopold (1177–1194). Dieser Schlom geniesst überall grosses Ansehen und nennt auch die Grundstücke sein eigen, auf denen die Synagoge steht.

[5] 'Austria', in *Encyclopaedia Judaica* (Jerusalem, 1971), iii. 887–8.

[6] Bato, p. 8; also Max Grunwald, *Vienna* (Philadelphia, 1936), 1–14, on the political conditions of Jews under the Babenberg dukes.

[7] Grunwald, *Vienna*, 7 ff., emphasizes the liberality of this decree and remarks: 'Austria and Vienna became an oasis in the desert of Jewish suffering during the Middle Ages, until the time in 1420 when, at one fell blow, Austria became for them a "Land of Blood".'

while the abduction of Jewish children for baptism was strictly forbidden.[8] At the same time Frederick II restricted their economic role to money and credit transactions—a legal development that set an example for the economically underdeveloped lands of Eastern Europe where Jews were to remain a significant middle-class element for centuries to come. The charter was confirmed by the Holy Roman Emperor Rudolph of Habsburg in 1278 and ratified again by his successors in 1330 and 1348.

In this period Austria and the Habsburg lands became Jewish sanctuaries, centres of Jewish learning and leadership for the German and western Slavonic lands. The Jews of Vienna, who had already been granted extensive autonomy in the charter of privileges dating back to Frederick II of Hohenstaufen in 1238 (*Judeos Wienne servos camere nostre*), were increasingly recognized in the fourteenth century as the leading German Jewish community in Europe. The influence of the 'Sages of Vienna' spread far beyond the confines of the city. Significantly, Vienna was spared the Black Death persecutions of 1348–9 during which Jews were butchered in virtually every town in the German-speaking countries and it even became an asylum for Jewish refugees from other lands. During the late Middle Ages, however, the situation of the Jews rapidly deteriorated under pressure from the rising Christian middle classes in the towns. The Jewish population became not for the last time the lightning conductor of social conflicts which had little to do with them. Thus towards the end of the fourteenth century there was an increasingly marked hostility to the Jews among the burghers of Vienna, admittedly aggravated by the Catholic Church. Confiscations of Jewish property, cancellation of debts, and economic restrictions led to their gradual impoverishment.[9] In 1421 Duke Albert V, hoping to replenish his empty coffers, ordered their arrest after the blood libel in Enns. In that year no less than 214 Jews died as martyrs at the stake charged with desecrating the sacramental host—the calamity known as the *Wiener gezerah* (Evil Decree of Vienna) in medieval Jewish history.[10] The community was

[8] Gerson Wolf, *Geschichte der Juden in Wien (1156–1876)* (Vienna, 1876), 5.

[9] Bato, p. 9.

[10] Grunwald, *Vienna*, 32–8: 'Thus ended the Jewish community of Vienna of the Middle Ages, with its population of from fourteen hundred souls—one of the largest of its times.' Also Bato, pp. 10–11, and Wolf, *Geschichte der Juden in Wien*, 18–19, who passes very rapidly over this episode. A Latin inscription in the first district of Vienna, Schulhof No. 2, malevolently recalled the *auto-da-fé* as 'the expiation for the terrible crimes committed by the Jewish dogs who paid the penalty upon the stake' (Grunwald, *Vienna*, 37).

destroyed, its property was confiscated by Albert V, and those children who were not expelled were forcibly baptized. Following this disaster, Austria became notorious among Jewry as 'the bloodstained land' (*Erets ha-Dammim*) and Vienna as 'the city of Blood' (*Ir ha-Damim*).

Jewish settlement in Vienna was subsequently renewed on a small scale in the sixteenth century and continued in spite of the hostility of the Estates, the Church, and the threat of periodic expulsions. Under the tolerant cosmopolitan Holy Roman Emperor Rudolph II (1576–1612) the spectacular rise of Prague Jewry began and a number of Jewish families enjoying special privileges (*hofbefreite Juden*) were also permitted to move to Vienna and subsequently to build a public synagogue for the first time since 1421. In 1624 Ferdinand II, disregarding local protests, allocated the Jews to a ghetto outside the city walls in the *Unterem werd* on the site of the present-day Leopoldstadt quarter. By 1632 there were 106 houses in the ghetto. The Jewish inhabitants, mainly merchants and petty traders, could circulate during business hours in the 'inner city' and own shops in other parts of town.[11] The *Judenstadt* was placed directly under the Imperial Chancery, free of control by the Vienna city council. From some fifty families in 1625, Viennese Jewry had reached approximately 2,000 by 1650, augmented by refugees who had fled from the Chmielnicki massacres of 1648 in Poland.

The population growth testified to the increased importance of Vienna's Jewish community in the mid-seventeenth century and the gratitude of the Emperor Ferdinand at its services in raising subsidies from the other Jews of his territories during the Thirty Years War against Protestant rebels and foreign adversaries. Though personally committed to the ideology of militant Counter-Reformation Catholicism, Ferdinand II had come to recognize that the Jews were an indispensable local asset in the years 1618–20 when the Habsburg Monarchy had confronted its greatest crisis. It was the Jews who provided cash in advance, food, and munitions to the soldiery at the critical moment, an act of co-operation which had found its reward when the Prague *Judenstadt* was spared by Imperial troops during the ransacking of the city in 1620.[12]

The economic potency of Jews as financiers, military suppliers, and

[11] G. Wolf, *Die Juden in der Leopoldstadt im 17. Jahrhundert in Wien* (Vienna, 1864), 4–15.

[12] Jonathan I. Israel, *European Jewry in the Age of Mercantilism, 1550–1750* (Oxford, 1985), 88–9.

masters of mints, a potency highlighted during the Thirty Years War, increasingly aroused the envy of the Christian business community of Vienna. Moreover, once the back of Protestantism in Austria and Bohemia had been broken after 1648 and the Habsburg lands were at peace, the Emperor, who had previously protected the Jews with his favour, no longer depended on their assistance. The inherent logic of Counter-Reformation militancy, whipped up by a triumphant Catholic Church, was now free to turn against the Austrian and Bohemian Jews. Popular demonstrations against the *Judenstadt* by burghers and handcraftsmen, incited by the clergy and in particular by Jesuit students, became a feature of the new anti-Semitism that seized the Austrian lands in the 1650s and 1660s.[13] The inexperienced young Emperor Leopold I, influenced by the bigotry of the implacable Bishop Kollonitsch of Wiener Neustadt, by the religious fanaticism of his Spanish wife, and by the promise of financial gains for his treasury as well as the ceaseless pressure of the Vienna city council, finally decided to expel the Jews from Vienna in 1669.

Not even the offer of a 100,000 florins or the intervention of Queen Christina of Sweden could prevent the execution of the decree.[14] By early 1670, some 3,000–4,000 Jews had been forced out of Vienna, the largest Jewish expulsion in Europe for a whole century.[15] For the second time the historic continuity of Jewish settlement in Vienna was violently interrupted. Yet the cruel expulsions did not prevent the Viennese court from remaining a veritable hotbed of Catholic anti-Judaism, which was exacerbated still further in 1683–4, at the time of the Turkish siege of Vienna, and then once again at the beginning of the Austrian advances into Hungary. At this time of crisis a wave of anti-Jewish violence swept Central Europe (especially Bohemia and Moravia) while the fiery Augustinian court preacher in Vienna, Abraham a Sancta Clara (1646–1709), inflamed the populace with his violently anti-Semitic tracts and sermons denouncing the Jews as Christendom's worst enemy.[16]

Nevertheless, the financial losses to the city following the expulsion and the hazardous disorder in the Austrian State finances, at a time

[13] Israel, pp. 146–7; on the social and economic background see G. Wolf, *Die Juden in der Leopoldstadt*, 37 ff.; also Bato, pp. 14–17.

[14] David Kaufmann, *Die letzte Vertreibung der Juden aus Wien und Niederösterreich: Ihre Vorgeschichte (1625–1670) und ihre Opfer* (Vienna, 1889), 105–53.

[15] Israel, p. 147.

[16] Robert A. Kann, *A Study in Austrian Intellectual History: From Late Baroque to Romanticism* (London, 1960), 74–9.

when the Habsburgs were engaged in a confrontation on two fronts with France and the Ottoman Empire, led by 1693 to a proposal to readmit the Jews. However, the numbers remained small compared with those of the *Judenstadt* before the 1670 expulsion and for nearly 200 years there was to be no provision for an *organized* Jewish community. Only the wealthiest Jews were permitted to reside as 'tolerated subjects' in Vienna, in return for a payment of 300,000 florins and an annual tax of 10,000 florins. Prayer services were allowed to be held only in private homes—a situation which continued to prevail in Vienna over the next century.

During the late seventeenth and early eighteenth centuries the leaders of the community were prominent 'Court Jews' (*Hofjuden*) like Samuel Oppenheimer, his nephew Samson Wertheimer, and Baron Diego Aguilar (Moses Lopez Pereira), who founded the Sephardic 'Turkish community' in Vienna in 1736 which grew as a result of commerce with the Balkans.[17] On the surface the Court Jews appeared to lead a glittering existence while the majority of their poorer co-religionists in Central Europe continued to live constricted lives in ghettos. Nevertheless, though outwardly assimilated in their way of life or mode of thinking, and at times egotistical and despotic towards their co-religionists, many *Hofjuden* remained committed Jews, who interceded with the authorities on behalf of their brethren. Not infrequently they founded synagogues and Jewish schools, studied Torah and Talmud, printed religious books and the works of Jewish scholars at their own expense.[18] As a result of their efforts, Vienna became a centre of Jewish diplomatic activity on behalf of the Jews of the Habsburg lands as well as a centre of philanthropy, including support of the poor of Erez Israel.

[17] On Diego d'Aguilar and the Sephardic community of Vienna, see Bato, pp. 64–8, and Grunwald, pp. 130–4. D'Aguilar was probably the son of a proselyte or of a Marrano who returned to Judaism. Because of his tobacco trade he received a Portuguese barony and even enjoyed the favour of the fanatically anti-Jewish Charles VI and Maria Theresa. In 1718 he had intervened on behalf of the Sephardic community of Temesvar, threatened with expulsion by the Austrian army command. Similarly, he intervened on behalf of the Jews of Prague during the Silesian wars when they were accused of treason. The Sephardic community of Vienna, as subjects of the Turkish Sultan, enjoyed a privileged position and considerable wealth during this early period. Its vernacular language was Ladino.

[18] On Oppenheimer, Wertheimer, and the Court Jews see Max Grunwald, *Samuel Oppenheimer und sein Kreis: Ein Kapitel aus der Finanzgeschichte Österreichs* (Vienna and Leipzig, 1913); also F. L. Carsten, 'The Court Jews. A Prelude to Emancipation', *Leo Baeck Yearbook*, 3 (1958), 140–56; and Heinrich Schnee, *Die Hoffinanz und der moderne Staat*, iii (Berlin, 1955), 191–2, 239–45.

Furthermore, the Court Jews were often the pacemakers in gaining permission for other Jews to join them, wherever they had already settled with their large families and retinues, thus opening up a small breach in the tight restrictions on Jewish residence.[19] They were also sometimes effective as *shtadlanim*, ready among other things to exert their influence against the new anti-Semitism that had emerged in Central Europe at the end of the seventeenth century. Thus it was to the *Judenkaiser* in Vienna, Samson Wertheimer, that the Frankfurt Jews turned to stop the publication of Johann Andreas Eisenmenger's vicious defamatory libel *Entdecktes Judentum* (Judaism Uncovered) (1699)[20]; thanks to the Court Jews Oppenheimer and Wertheimer, this massively 'learned' work by a Heidelberg Professor of Hebrew that was to inspire future generations of European anti-Semites was duly banned in the Habsburg lands by the Emperor Leopold and his successor Joseph I as being prejudicial to the public and the Christian religion, and especially to the unlearned'.[21] Eventually Eisenmenger's book was to be reprinted in Berlin under the patronage of Frederick I, King in Prussia.[22]

The beginnings of the Court Jews' influence can be traced to their crucial function of supplying garrisons and ready cash during the Thirty Years War. From that time onwards the big Jewish bankers effectively provided the essential sinews of war for the Habsburg armies, thanks to their international network of credit in Central and Eastern Europe. Though the Habsburg emperors were of course strict Catholics, they preferred to employ Jewish financiers because, as one historian has put it, 'they [the Jews] could supply their needs more cheaply, and above all, because they were prepared to wait longer for their payment'.[23] Moreover, the Court Jews were indispensable as long as the Habsburg emperor 'did not possess the administrative machinery to pay and supply the army', a situation which persisted down into the nineteenth century. They could play such a vital role in the seventeenth and eighteenth centuries in financial and business affairs, precisely because in Central Europe (unlike France or England) there was no efficient native bureaucracy, no well-oiled

---

[19] Grunwald, *Vienna*, 135 ff.; Schnee, pp. 215–16, 220–4; *Encyclopaedia Judaica*, xvi. 123; and Nikolaus Vielmetti, 'Vom Beginn der Neuzeit bis zur Toleranz', *Das österreichische Judentum*, ed. Vielmetti *et al* (Vienna, 1982), 78.

[20] Grunwald, *Vienna*, 127; Eisenmenger, see Jacob Katz, *From Prejudice to Destruction: Anti-Semitism, 1700–1933* (Cambridge, Mass, 1982), 13–22.

[21] Israel, pp. 234–5.

[22] Katz, p. 14.

[23] Carsten, p. 144.

machinery of taxation or prosperous, developed bourgeoisie capable of raising the necessary money so effectively on the rulers' behalf.

In the Habsburg territories it was above all Samuel Oppenheimer of Heidelberg (1630–1703), the leading Jewish army contractor of his time, who fulfilled this need, supplying the whole Austrian army on the Rhine during the war with France between 1673 and 1679; it was, moreover, Oppenheimer who organized the logistics of Vienna's defence against the Turks during the desperate siege in 1683 and who had provisioned the advancing Austrian troops in Hungary, which now came definitively under Habsburg dominion. During the Nine Years War (1689–98) Oppenheimer was again supplying the Austrian armies in both Germany (against the French) and in Hungary, while simultaneously providing the Viennese court with luxury items and costumes for its coachmen and hangers-on.[24] Repeated attempts by the bigoted anti-Semite Bishop Kollonitsch to supplant him failed since virtually no 'Catholic factors' had the necessary capital or were willing to extend such massive credit to the over-extended Habsburg State with its proverbially empty Treasury. By 1694 the Imperial Treasury owed Oppenheimer the huge sum of 3,000,000 florins. When he died in 1703, the Habsburgs refused to honour their debts to his heir Emmanuel Oppenheimer, and the consequent bankruptcy of his firm provoked a major financial crisis not only in the Monarchy but also in Europe among those rulers to whom the Austrian State still owed money.[25]

Samuel Oppenheimer had ultimately derived his monopolistic position as military contractor to the Austrian army from unusual business acumen and organizational skills. The first Jew to be permitted to resettle in Vienna after the expulsion of 1670, he had achieved his power and prestige by bearing a large part of the cost of the wars against the Turks, which could not otherwise have been brought to a successful conclusion. Though he was too powerful to be ever dislodged by the local anti-Semites, his Vienna mansion was none the less attacked and plundered by a frenzied mob in 1700, three years before his death.[26] Oppenheimer was succeeded at Vienna by his

---

[24] Grunwald, *Oppenheimer und sein Kreis*, 78–9.

[25] Schnee, iii. 239 ff.; Grunwald, *Vienna*, 120–1.

[26] On the anti-Jewish riots of 1700 see Grunwald, *Vienna*, 119–20, who claims it was the 'discontent of the upper circles with the alleged usurious practice of Oppenheimer, and the destitution of unpaid officers and soldiers, often without food or clothing', which incited the deep-rooted mass feeling against the Jews.

protégé Samson Wertheimer (1658–1724) who now became the senior Jewish *Hoffaktor* (chief agent) of the Habsburg Empire. Wertheimer, who came originally from Worms and studied at the Frankfurt *yeshivah*, had been introduced to the Emperor Leopold I by Samuel Oppenheimer himself. From 1694 to 1709 he was to act as the chief administrator of the financial affairs of three successive Habsburg emperors. During the War of the Spanish Succession and the war against Turkey, Wertheimer was primarily responsible for financing military operations; he undertook the payment of generals, officials, and ambassadors as well as of princes of the Empire, who received Imperial subsidies.[27]

The wealthiest Jew of his age, the resourceful Wertheimer excelled in the speedy supply of cash with the assistance of a well-organized international network of Jewish money-changers, merchants, and brokers. Having already saved the Austrian Treasury in the aftermath of the Oppenheimer crisis in 1703, he again came to the rescue of the Habsburgs by advancing huge sums to the Emperor until the end of the War of the Spanish Succession, which alone enabled Austria to wage war on two fronts against France and the Hungarian rebels.[28] Indeed, such was their influence that one might argue that, between them, Oppenheimer and Wertheimer did as much as the generals and statesmen to enable the Austrian Monarchy to maintain its Great Power position in the early eighteenth century. Wertheimer was also entrusted with a number of important diplomatic missions and paid the expenses of the peace conference at Utrecht which finally brought an end to the War of the Spanish Succession. Court Jew, philanthropist, and *shtadlan*, Wertheimer was in addition a scholar and patron of scholars who built a large synagogue in Eisenstadt and received the title of *Landesrabbiner* (Chief Rabbi) of Hungarian Jewry for his role in restoring the Jewish communities there, which had been destroyed by war.[29]

[27] Carsten, p. 144.

[28] See David Kaufmann, *Samson Wertheimer, der Oberfaktor und Landesrabbiner (1658–1728) und seine Kinder* (Vienna, 1888).

[29] It was the Emperor Charles VI, as King of Hungary, who appointed Wertheimer Hungarian Chief Rabbi, and ordered his officials to look to him as the highest authority in all Jewish lawsuits. Wertheimer retained the good will of the anti-Jewish Emperor until his death in 1724 (Grunwald, *Vienna*, 128–9. In Vienna itself, though social intercourse between Jews and Christians had increased, agitation against the Jews intensified among the local merchants *c.*1721. Wolf, *Geschichte der Juden in Wien*, 62, comments: 'Die Verhältnisse der Juden unter Carl VI. waren überhaupt schlecht, insbesondere aber für die Wiener Juden. Man hatte den besten Willen, die Juden mit

In 1725 he was succeeeded in his position by his son-in-law Issachar Berush Eskeles (1692–1753) a scholarly orthodox Jew of Moravian descent who was simultaneously active as a Viennese court purveyor, providing arms and other commodities to his patrons. His son Bernhard Eskeles (1753–1839), ennobled in 1797, was to become one of the leading financiers in the Monarchy, founding the Austrian National Bank in 1816 and, along with his great rival Salomon Rothschild, pioneering the promotion of railways in Austria. Bernhard's wife Cecily, the daughter of the wealthy Berlin banker Daniel Itzig, made their home a renowned centre of high society during the Congress of Vienna. Like her sister Fanny von Arnstein—from another leading Viennese banking dynasty—Cecily Eskeles belonged to a less traditional, far more assimilated, aesthetically conscious generation than that of the original Court Jews.[30] No longer bound to any cultural tradition, they adopted the values of German *Bildung* and artistic beauty with a freedom, passion, and openness that was truly remarkable.

The Arnstein banking dynasty had been founded by Isaac Aaron (1682–1744) who arrived in Vienna in 1705, had risen in the service of Samson Wertheimer, and eventually became court purveyor to the Emperor Charles VI and his military establishment. His financial influence helped avert the expulsion of Jews from Vienna in 1736, while it was his son Adam Isaac Arnstein (1721–85) who secured the diplomatic intervention to help reverse the Empress Maria Theresa's banishment of Prague Jewry in 1744–5. Another son, Nathan Adam Arnstein (1748–1838), husband of Fanny, together with Bernhard Eskeles (his business partner and brother-in-law), was later to provide large-scale loans to the government of Joseph II; at the beginning of the nineteenth century it was the Arnstein–Eskeles banking firm who financed the Tyrolese peasant revolt against the Napoleonic armies.[31] The Court Jews were therefore not only instrumental in the growth

Stumpf und Stiel auszurotten, und wenn die nicht geschah, so zeigt sich eben darin, dass die Verhältnisse stärker waren, als die Menschen.'

[30] For a lively description of this circle see Hilde Spiel, *Fanny von Arnstein oder die Emanzipation: Ein Frauenleben an der Zeitwende, 1758–1818* (Frankfurt, 1978); also Bato, pp. 166–80.

[31] Spiel, pp. 335 ff., on the enthusiastic support of the Arnsteins and Eskeles for the Tyrolese uprising against Napoleon. On Fanny von Arnstein's passionate loathing of the French and the romantic, idealized 'Prussian patriotism' of her salon (in spite of the fact that the French had been the first European nation to emancipate the Jews) see ibid. 198–9. Her hatred of Napoleon, in whose wars one of her nephews died and another was wounded, was even more pronounced.

and consolidation of the centralized absolute state—they provided the foundations for the emergence of several important Jewish bankers who were to play a key role in the nineteenth-century Austrian economic history.

The significance of the Court Jews and their successors for the future of the Jews of Vienna and for the history of the Empire as a whole was to prove considerable. For the symbiotic relationship that developed in the seventeenth and eighteenth centuries between the wealthy Court Jews and the Habsburg State left a profound mark on the political orientations of Austrian Jewry. On the one hand, it was in the economic interests of the absolutist State to grant individual Jews certain privileges, to treat them as a separate group, and to discourage their full assimilation into a Catholic population that was openly hostile to them; at the same time from the Jewish side there developed a tendency to look to the absolutist State as a protective guardian, even when its power was decaying and its policies were seemingly inimical to the mass of Jewry. The bargain that was struck presupposed the exceptionality and indispensability of the Jews' economic function. The absolutist State was ready to grant Court Jews rights and liberties which it denied not only to the mass of semi-destitute Jews but even to the contemporary Christian middle class. Nowhere was this more true than in the Habsburg Monarchy, where as Heinrich Schnee and others have argued, Jewish finance played a decisive part in ensuring Austrian Great Power status.

The exceptional character of such arrangements was heightened by the fact that the Jews, unlike other groups in the early modern period in European society, did not belong to any clearly defined class of society. They were neither landowners, nor peasants, neither soldiers, bureaucrats, middle-class people, petty bourgeois, nor artisans. To quote Hannah Arendt

. . . their status was defined through their being Jews, it was not defined through their relationship to another class. Their special protection from the state (whether in the form of open privileges, or a special emancipation edict which no other group needed and which frequently had to be reinforced against the hostility of society) and their special services to the governments prevented their submersion in the class system as well as their own establishment as a class. Whenever, therefore, they were admitted to and entered society, they became a well-defined, self-preserving group within one of the classes, the aristocracy or the bourgeoisie.[32]

[32] Hannah Arendt, *The Origins of Totalitarianism* (New York, 1958), 13.

Official policies of various Habsburg governments since the seventeenth century were of course much less consistent, unwavering, and clear-cut than such a theoretical model might suggest. Thus the policy of the Empress Maria Theresa (1740–80) wavered between the mercantilist desire to exploit the benefits of Jewish participation in economic life—which found expression in a special decree of 1749 encouraging Jews to establish manufacturing establishments—and harsh restrictive legislation which reflected a deep religious antipathy.[33] The total expulsion of the Jews of Prague after the Second Silesian War (in which Silesia was formally ceded to Prussia) clearly contradicted the more general policy of her government to encourage commerce and industry, though it was consistent enough with her Catholic prejudices.[34] These did not admittedly extend to the phenomenal Joseph von Sonnenfels, a baptized Jew and one of the Empress's leading advisers who established a German national theatre in Vienna and made it a citadel of enlightened taste.[35] Nevertheless, such exceptions aside, under Maria Theresa draconian restrictions on the residence rights of her unbaptized 'tolerated subjects' prevented any rapid growth of the Jewish population in Vienna.

In 1752 there were no more than 452 Jews living in the city and by 1777 the number had risen only slight to 520 out of a total of some 350,000 Austrian Jews. Yet, one year later the Archbishop of Vienna, Migazzi, complained to the government about growing social contacts between Christians and Jews. A conservative member of the Council of State in the ensuing deliberations declared himself appalled that young Jews could be seen in public 'in the company of young Christians', dressed indistinguishably, 'some even with swords at their side'. No less disturbing to him was the sight of a Jewish women

[33] On Maria Theresa, whose emotional antipathy was best characterized by her remark, 'I know no worse plague for the State than this nation, because of its deceitfulness, its usury, its ability to drag people down to beggary . . .', see Bato, p. 26, and Grunwald, *Vienna*, 139 ff. For a Jew to be 'tolerated' in Vienna, he had to prove that he possessed property, would be useful to the State, and would pay an annual toleration tax. Every three months the head of a household had moreover to present a list of all its members to the authorities. Periodic checks were made on the servants and everything was done to reduce the number of Jews permitted to live in the capital. Residential segregation, religious discrimination, and social degradation were the norm. Thus Jews had to keep out of sight of religious processions, married men were obliged to let their beards grow, the building of synagogues was prohibited. Jews could not even appear on the street before noon on Sundays and Christian holidays.

[34] See G. Wolf, 'Die Vertreibungen der Juden aus Böhmen in Jahre 1744 und deren Rückkehr im Jahre 1748', *Jahrbuch für Geschichte der Juden*, 2 (1896), 145–334.

[35] Wangermann, pp. 117–20, 132–4 and Kann.

'dressed in a manner little different from a lady of rank, walking in the company of Christian men and women . . .'. The Jewish people, the Councillor complained, 'now frequent inns, ballrooms and theatres, and mix with the Christians who are there'.[36]

This process of integration was to be greatly accelerated by the enlightened legislation of Maria Theresa's son, Joseph II (1780–90), whose *Toleranzedikt* of 1781, though attacked in some Jewish circles, was in many ways the herald of future emancipation. Joseph did not share his more fanatical mother's contempt for Jews, nor was he ready cautiously to await a change in popular anti-Semitic prejudices among the urban and rural poor. In May 1781 he made clear in a letter to the Court Chancellor that he was considering the admission of Jews to public education, agriculture, industry, and the professions, once they had the necessary training. The objective of the Josephinian policy was to make his increasingly numerous Jewish subjects (the annexation of Galicia in 1772 following the first partition of Poland had more than doubled the Jewish population of the Monarchy) more *useful* to the State. Joseph saw his proposed reform as part of a wider endeavour to modernize and centralize the Empire, to provide it with uniform, administrative laws, and in this aim he had the support of his more enlightened councillors and advisers.

The *Toleranzpatent* finally issued in 1782, in which he summed up his previous proposals, made a few inevitable concessions to popular prejudice (and the hostility of the Lower Austrian government) but none the less removed many existing restrictions on the Jews.[37] Thus the wearing of the yellow badge and the poll-tax hitherto levied on Jews were abolished.[38] Jews were encouraged to engage in agriculture and to learn trades, and permitted to attend schools and universities. They were to be allowed to set up factories and large-scale businesses and to compete on equal terms in commerce. They were instructed to establish German language elementary schools for their children (or else to send them to State schools) as part of the new drive to ease Jewish contact with the general culture. Another important move towards removing segregation was the induction of Jews into the army

---

[36] Wangermann, p. 112.

[37] For a summary of its main points see Wolf, *Geschichte der Juden in Wien*, 84–7. For the full documentation see A. F. Pribram (ed.), *Urkunden und Akten zur Geschichte der Juden in Wien* (Vienna and Leipzig, 1918), 440–500 (Part I, no. 205); also Paul P. Bernard, 'Joseph II and the Jews: The Origins of the Toleration Patent of 1782', *Austrian History Yearbook*, 4/5 (1970), 101–19.

[38] Hans Tietze, *Die Juden Wiens* (Vienna and Leipzig, 1933), 117–20.

in 1787, where at least in the lower commissioned ranks they would eventually enjoy equal opportunities.

At the same time Joseph's reforms led to the abolition of Jewish judicial autonomy (1784). Jews were ordered in 1788 to cease using Hebrew and Yiddish for public and commercial purposes and to adopt German-sounding family names. Such measures—especially the ending of their autonomy and separatism—which were intended to change Jewish social mores, to reform economic practices, and above all to end the *national* distinctiveness of Austrian Jewry were resented by the majority of traditional Jews (outside Vienna) as an ominous threat to their culture and way of life. The integration of the Jews into Austrian society, education, and the army entailed, as one historian of early modern Europe has recently put it, 'sweeping away Jewish self-rule and the autonomy of Jewish society'.[39] First the Jewish community organizations were to be stripped of their fiscal powers and then the juridical autonomy of the Bohemian and Moravian communities numbering some 69,000 Jews in the 1780s was abolished altogether under the decrees of 1785 and 1788.

In Galicia, which already had a Jewish population of 212,000 when Naftali Herz Homberg (1749–1841) was appointed in 1787 as superintendent of the German-language Jewish schools (and assistant censor of the Jewish books), the conflict between Josephinian modernization and traditional culture became particularly intense. Homberg, a former collaborator of Moses Mendelssohn and a pioneer of the Berlin *Haskalah*, who had been born in Lieben near Prague, had moved to Vienna in 1782, attracted by educational activities initiated by Joseph II's government, after the toleration edicts. Following his official appointment in 1787, Homberg was to set up no less than 107 classes and schools in Galicia, including a teachers' seminary at Lemberg. In Galicia he collaborated closely with the Austrian authorities to force acceptance among local co-religionists of his notions of 'enlightenment', and was ruthless in denouncing religious Jews who refused to submit to his requirements.[40] In official memoranda he castigated the rabbis and the Talmud for discouraging Jews from fulfilling their patriotic duties to the Christian State (significantly Homberg's four sons all converted) and he insistently proposed that Jewish literature be purged of its superstitious and

---

[39] Israel, p. 250.
[40] Meir Balaban, 'Herz Homberg in Galizien', *Jahrbuch für jüdische Geschichte und Literatur*, 19 (1916), 189–221.

allegedly anti-Gentile bias. Among his more radical proposals, Homberg argued for the disbanding of most traditional Jewish education, strict prohibition on the use of Hebrew, the abolition of distinctive dress and beards, and obliging Jews to take up productive occupations.[41] Homberg's pedagogical programme with its ruthless drive to adapt Jewish education to contemporary European (and especially German) culture was certainly in line with the ethos of the Josephinian Enlightenment, and for his services to the government in reorganizing Jewish life he eventually received an Imperial gold medal. But his attempts to impose a German school system upon Galician Jewry, entirely manned by teachers from Central Europe, met with fierce local resistance that forced his resignation in 1806.[42]

It is not surprising that from the outset broad traditional strata of Habsburg Jewry centred in Galicia and Hungary had regarded the edicts of toleration of Josephinian absolutism as a *gezerah* (oppressive decree)—especially the calling up of Jews for military service. The religious leaders feared moreover the open hostility of the Enlighteners to the Talmud, their resolve to transform the educational system and destroy community self-rule (leaving only religious matters and charity in the hands of the community), not to mention the Josephinist determination to abolish the national languages of Yiddish and Hebrew. Moreover, the Jews of Galicia were explicitly required after 1785 to change their business activities in radical fashion so as to be of benefit to the State. The Jewish masses had indeed good reason to resent the oppressive special 'Jewish' taxes and the bungled efforts of Josephinian officialdom aimed at their 'productivization' which simply led to the loss of livelihood of much of the rural Jewish population in Galicia and its growing 'proletarianization'.[43]

In the lands of the Bohemian Crown, on the other hand, Joseph II's efforts to integrate the Jews into the economic and cultural life of the Empire met with a more positive response.[44] Admittedly a number of discriminatory provisions remained in force. These included Maria Theresa's notorious family law (*Familiantengesetz*) designed to prevent the natural growth of the Jewish population by permitting only the

---

[41] See Raphael Mahler, *A History of Modern Jewry, 1780–1815* (London, 1971).

[42] Kurt Schubert, 'Der Einfluss des Josephinismus auf das Judentum in Österreich', *Kairos*, NS 14 (1972), 91 ff.

[43] Gottfried Schramm, 'Das Ostjudentum als soziales Problem des 19-Jahrhunderts', in Heinz Maus (ed.), *Gesellschaft, Recht und Politik* (Neuwied-Berlin, 1968), 371.

[44] Ruth Kestenberg-Gladstein, *Neuere Geschichte der Juden in den böhmischen Ländern, i. Das Zeitalter der Aufklärung, 1780–1830* (Tübingen, 1969), 357–9.

oldest son of a family to marry; a taxation system which imposed a threefold burden on Jews as against non-Jewish taxpayers; and the continuing exclusion from State citizenship. However, the Emperor's order to permit Jews to establish *Manufakturen* (factories and industrial workshops) outside the restrictions of the artisans' guilds was of great importance for the future. So, too, was the opening up of the universities to the children of more wealthy Jewish families and the fact that Josephinian assimilation was necessarily German in culture and language. This process of Germanization was an integral part of the unitary *imperial* patriotism of the reformed Austrian State—founded as it henceforth was on a unitary system of education and relying as it did on a single *Staatssprache*.

While religiously conservative elements among Bohemian Jewry no less than their counterparts in Galicia rejected Josephinian German-style secularization, Joseph's policy did meet with some success in the Czech lands.[45] The appeal of German literature and its humanistic mission to educated Bohemian Jews was considerable at this time; not only did it appear in line with Mendelssohnian rationalism and with other liberal trends in the Jewish and non-Jewish worlds; it offered the most convenient vehicle for cultural and socio-economic progress, one which was particularly attractive to Jews, as an urban population who already spoke a language close to German (i.e. Yiddish) even when living in a Czech peasant milieu. Josephinism seemed to offer a universalist, secularizing model of modernity to Bohemian Jews, which was eagerly seized on in the nineteenth century even though it helped stamp them in the mind of rising Czech nationalism as an alien pro-German element.

If Joseph II subsequently became the idol of Jewish *maskilim* throughout the Monarchy, nowhere was his *Toleranzpatent* received more enthusiastically than among the 'tolerated' Jews in Vienna, even though it did not alleviate any of the legal restrictions on Jewish residence there.[46] Nor, for that matter, did it grant the Vienna Jews

[45] Eduard Goldstücker, 'Jews Between Czechs and Germans around 1848', *Leo Baeck Yearbook*, 17 (1972), 61–71.

[46] The official historians of Viennese Jewry invariably reflect the older attitudes of gratitude and admiration for Joseph II. See, e.g., Wolf, *Geschichte der Juden in Wien*, 78: 'Auch die Juden in Oesterreich bewahren dem grossen Monarchen ein dankbares Angedenken, und sie haben allen Grund dazu, denn er hat ihre Fesseln gesprengt. Während sie noch überall unter dem tiefsten Drücke schmachteten, dürften sie in Oesterreich aufathmen.' Grunwald, *Vienna*, 156, goes even further, describing Joseph as 'the first truly liberal monarch, one of the noblest men who ever lived', and as being 'among the greatest humanitarians in the history of human progress'. According to this

citizenship of either the State or the communes. They had in effect all the duties of citizens but *not* all the rights. They were rigorously excluded from civil service, from a variety of retail trades and professions, from the acquisition of land and peasant holdings. Viennese Jews could not even construct a house without a permit, and they were still subject to tedious bureaucratic controls. Nor could they yet organize their own community (*kehilla*) with its recognized statutes, its own public synagogues, and recognized rabbis. Against this there were admittedly no more restrictions on the dwelling rights of 'tolerated' Jews who could live wherever they pleased in the city and its suburbs. They could now also appear on the streets before middays on Sundays and Christian holidays.

Moreover, the 'tolerated' Jews and the *maskilim* realized that Joseph's policy, for all its limitations, was none the less a revolutionary departure from the purely exploitative attitude of mercantilist absolutism adopted by his predecessors; they could see that it was animated by relatively tolerant, enlightened principles and a genuine desire to break with the more ignoble humiliations of past servitude. The betterment of the Jews was after all a declared goal of the Enlightenment, though holding down their numbers was still seen by the Austrian government as its necessary accompaniment. From the Viennese perspective this did not, however, detract from the fact that Josephinian policy seemed to open up new economic opportunities for a rising merchant class, especially in the wholesale trade. At the same time it provided for the beginning of a secular Jewish intelligentsia educated in German-language schools and free to attend university.[47]

Moreover, Joseph's reforms, precisely because they sought to guide Jewish culture into German channels for the first time, were to forge new weapons in the long drawn-out Jewish struggle for emancipation in Austria. The edict of Tolerance, besides setting an important precedent in Austria itself, was after all the first legal act of *any* European State granting Jews the right to regard themselves as permanent residents of the country they lived in. It implied that the

view, the Emperor Joseph 'believed in Man, and saw him in the Jew,—a "product of that unfortunate people" as he characterized them'.

[47] See Wolfgang Häusler, 'Toleranz, Emanzipation und Antisemitismus. Das österreichische Judentum des bürgerlichen Zeitalters (1782–1918)', in Vielmetti *et al* (ed.), *Das österreichische Judentum*, 84: 'Den Wiener Tolerierten, durchwegs wohlhabenden Familien, brachte das Gesetz die rechtliche Sicherung, ihrer vorragenden wirtschaftlichen Stellung. Wie die aufgeklärten christlichen Zeitgenossen begrüssen sie im Reformwerk Joseph II. den Beginn einer neuen Epoche'.

ruler saw the Jews of his lands as subjects for whose welfare he was responsible no less than he was for the subjects of other religions or national groups. The Jews to be sure, in return for the right to participate in the common culture, were expected to abandon previous group loyalties. But this, too, seemed only part of the *general* price exacted by the modern, unitary, bureaucratic State which was out to level old restrictions, prohibitions, and corporate particularisms wherever it found them.

Joseph II, the tireless chief bureaucrat of the State, accepted that it was the duty of his administration to concern itself with the welfare of *all* his subjects, just as he optimistically believed in the sovereignty of reason and the malleability of man and society. This Heavenly City of the eighteenth-century *philosophes*, translated into an Imperial model of enlightened absolutism, made such a deep impact on educated nineteenth-century Austrian Jewry not only because of its rationalism, cosmopolitianism, and practical humanism; even more pertinently it promised a synthesis of the almost religious faith of many Jews in the strong paternalistic hand of the supranational State and their steadily growing commitment to German *Bildung* and *Kultur*. This was to be one of the most important legacies bequeathed by the new epoch in Austrian Jewish history introduced in the 1780s through legislative fiat from above by the Emperor Joseph II. As the Austrian Jewish notable Joseph von Wertheimer wrote in 1842, Joseph was 'a despot, like the springtime, which breaks apart the winter's ice'.[48]

In other respects the Josephinian era transmitted an ambivalent legacy. The road to social and cultural integration was unquestionably opened up to the Jewish upper classes who were only too eager to be assimilated. The situation of the Jewish masses, on the other hand, deteriorated even further as they lost their traditional cohesion and their old self-governing institutional framework. The Viennese Jewish social and intellectual élite of the late eighteenth century seemed indeed to be melting into their surroundings. Among the 'tolerated' in Vienna, the more socially integrated their manner and life-style, the more estranged they became from Jewish society as a whole. A number of these privileged families, in spite of the severe legal restrictions they still suffered, were actually elevated to the titled nobility. In this respect the Habsburgs were far more generous than the other German dynasties. Thus in 1820 out of 135 'tolerated' families in Vienna there

---

[48] Joseph von Wertheimer, *Die Juden in Österreich* (Leipzig, 1842), i. 137.

were nine (bankers, industrialists, and big merchants) with various titles of nobility—Rothschild, Arnstein, Eskeles, Herz, Neuwall, Wertheimstein, Honigsberg, Lamel, and Leibenberg—at a time when *no* Austrian Jews enjoyed any *civil* or *political* rights.[49] The social élite were clearly the bankers, suppliers, and monopoly leaseholders; next in prestige came the wholesale merchants in grain, wool, and hides, who also exported the finished products of textiles, silk, and dry-goods factories in and around Vienna to the provinces. They pioneered new methods of production and marketing as well as promoting the development of industry in the capital. This class of exceedingly rich financiers and merchants dominated Jewish society in early nineteenth-century Vienna.

The wars against the French Revolution and Napoleon had meanwhile provided new opportunities for Jewish banking families, often connected by marriage like Arnstein and Eskeles, to expand their business activities. Some of these Jewish notables were to achieve spectacular successes in Viennese society, and in contemporary cultural and intellectual cirlces. Many leading personalities of the age, ranging from the Emperor Joseph II and the aristocracy, through to the Varnhagens, the Schlegels, Madame de Stael, and the great Austrian poet Franz Grillparzer, frequented the luxurious salon of Fanny von Arnstein (1757–1818). At the Congress of Vienna (1814–15), the leading diplomats of the age including Metternich, Talleyrand, and Hardenberg were present at her splendid receptions and 'the congress danced' mainly in her ballrooms. Though the Arnsteins adopted the mores and life-style of upper-class Christian circles and showed little interest in Judaism, Fanny's husband Nathan Adam along with Eskeles, Herz, Lämel, and Auspitz did sign a petition to the Emperor requesting civil rights for Austrian Jews during the congress of Vienna, a request which not surprisingly proved to be abortive.[50]

The sparkling and graceful culture of Vienna at the beginning of the nineteenth century was much more aristocratically orientated and lacked the critical intellectuality of its Berlin counterpart, typified by Rahel Varnhagen's salon.[51] Nevertheless the close family connections

[49] See Hanns Jäger-Sunstenau, 'Die geadelten Judenfamilien im vormärzlichen Wien' (Univ. of Vienna diss., 1950); also H. G. Reissner, 'Daniel Lessmann in Vienna and Verona', *Leo Baeck Yearbook*, 14 (1969), 203–14; Schnee, iii. 249.

[50] Spiel, pp. 446–9; Salo Baron, *Die Judenfrage auf dem Wiener Kongress* (Vienna and Berlin, 1920), 130 ff.

[51] See Hannah Arendt, *Rahel Varnhagen: Lebensgeschichte einer deutschen Jüdin aus der Romantik* (Munich, 1959).

with Berlin (Fanny von Arnstein was the daughter of the Berlin Court Jew, Daniel Itzig) and the tremendous intellectual influence of such leading figures of the German Enlightenment as the philosophers Kant and Lessing, Wilhelm von Humboldt and Hardenberg (Prussian representatives at the Congress of Vienna who displayed a sympathetic attitude to Jews) provided much common ground.[52]

As in Berlin the baptismal movement also made rapid progress among this generation of *arriviste* upper-class Jews, who went over to Christianity for a variety of reasons. For some it was primarily the promise of economic opportunity, social status, and the chance to reach coveted positions of influence. For others it was, in Heinrich Heine's cynical dictum, their 'entry ticket to European culture'; for others still, it was a matter of religious conviction, a product of idealistic romanticism, of genuine if complex inner spiritual needs. Thus Dorothea Mendelssohn-Veit (eldest daughter of Moses Mendelssohn), after marrying the hot-headed Friedrich Schlegel in Berlin, subsequently ended up after 1808 as 'the advocate of counter-reformatory Catholicism during the Restoration period in Vienna'.[53] Catholicism, such a dominant element in medieval, Counter-Reformation, and Austrian Baroque culture, exercised a certain seduction on those Jews and Jewesses of the wealthy, cultured élite who had been cut adrift from their spiritual moorings. Lacking as they did, in contrast to Berlin, the reinforcement of a legal, organized Jewish community or the example of a strong rabbinical leadership, and being already quite remote from the world of the ghetto and orthodox Judaism, they were more easily drawn to the well-springs of Catholic mysticism. On the other hand, many converts were not Christians in any deeper sense at all but simply saw the abandonment of Judaism as a convenient step towards complete assimilation in their new surroundings. It has been estimated, for example, that three-quarters of the *ennobled* Jewish families in Vienna between 1787 and 1847 converted to Christianity. For this élite, conversion did not necessarily stand in contradiction to the ideals of tolerance and the religion of reason proclaimed by the Enlightenment; rather it expressed their desire to accommodate to the spirit of the age. Fanny von Arnstein may be taken as a typical intermediate case. Though she had the first

---

[52] See Grunwald, *Vienna*, 194–5; also Jacob Allerhand, 'Die Rabbiner des Stadttempels von J. N. Mannheimer bis P. Z. Chajes', *Studia Judaica Austriaca*, 6 (Eisenstadt, 1978), 9.

[53] Friedrich Heer, *God's First Love* (London, 1970), 178.

Christmas tree known in Vienna among her co-religionists, none the less she did not convert, retaining a residual, sentimental loyalty to aspects of Judaism which she tried in vain to pass on to her baptized daughter.[54] In her final testament she endowed equally the local Jewish hospital and a Catholic priests' old-age home in Vienna.

What probably saved the 'progressive', if structurally weak, community of Viennese Jewry from complete disintegration in the pre-1848 (*Vormärz*) period was the founding of a Jewish school (1812), the construction of an impressive neo-classical synagogue (*Stadttempel*) in the Seitenstettengasse (1826), and the calling of the young Danish rabbi Isaac Noah Mannheimer (1793–1865) from Germany to be spiritual leader of the community. It was Mannheimer who subsequently prevented a split in Vienna between 'orthodox' and 'reformers' by establishing together with the musically gifted cantor, Salomon Sulzer his own 'Vienna ritual', an aesthetically pleasing form of service replete with a choir in which a central place was taken by the uplifting German-language sermon.[55] Mannheimer had served his apprenticeship in the Reform Temples in Germany, though in Vienna he was careful to tone down the radical aspects of German Reform (such as the use of an organ, of priestly clothing, or the imitation of church songs), and to avoid any changes that contradicted the *Shulḥan Arukh*. In particular, Mannheimer accepted that the religious service be conducted in Hebrew and that prayers of a messianic or national character be retained. This moderation and relative conservatism of the Viennese Reform had a profound impact on Hungarian Neology—it was adopted in Pest (1826) and spread rapidly to Austrian provincial centres such as Prossnitz (1832), Prague (1833), Lemberg, Cracow, and Brody in the 1840s, and eventually on to Warsaw and Odessa.

The driving force behind the Viennese Reform and indeed the man who invited Mannheimer to the city was the energetic *Vorsteher* Michael Lazar Biedermann (1769–1843), a wealthy wholesale merchant from Pressburg in Hungary, who in the early nineteenth century had transformed Vienna into the centre of the wool industry in the Empire.[56] Biedermann had settled in Vienna as a youth, taking up engraving and being commissioned to work on the imperial seal in

---

[54] 'Fanny von Arnstein', in *Encyclopaedia Judaica*, iii. 490–1; Grunwald, *Vienna*, 195.

[55] Moses Rosenmann, *Isak Noa Mannheimer: Sein Leben und Wirken, zugleich ein Beitrag zur Geschichte der israelitischen Kultusgemeinde in Wien in der ersten Hälfte des 19. Jahrhunderts* (Vienna and Berlin, 1922), 50 ff.

[56] Ibid. 52–3.

1798. After a number of years in jewellery and antiques he entered the wool business along with L. A. Auspitz, where he made his fortune. Biedermann played a crucial role in organizing a congregation in Vienna, of which he was a representative (*Vertreter*) from 1806, at a time when the conditions of Jews had steadily deteriorated. His initiative as a community leader, using his influence with the Emperor as a successful financier and self-made entrepreneur (he had founded one of the first banks in Austria), was central in the struggle of Viennese Jewry for some kind of official recognition and social respectability.[57]

Encouraged by his bookkeeper Leopold Harzfeld (who also served as the Viennese Hebrew book censor), Biedermann strove to introduce educational reforms and religious services modelled on those in Hamburg and Berlin. It was largely thanks to his efforts that the foundation stone of the first city Temple (which accommodated a school, a home for the aged, and a ritual bath as well as a synagogue) was finally laid on 12 December 1825—providing a new focus of religious and communal life for the cultured Viennese Jewish *Grossbürgertum* of the Restoration period.

Mannheimer, for his part, supplied the spiritual inspiration, leaving a profound imprint on the ethos of the new *Stadttempel* over the next forty years, astutely adapting traditional Judaism to the standards of decorum, dignity, ennoblement (*Veredelung*), and *Bildung* required by his patrons, without sacrificing either religious content or the unity of the congregation.[58] In the *Vormärz* period, this harmony was not yet endangered by a mass migration of poor, orthodox Jews from the provincial ghettos of the Empire, to whom Vienna was firmly barred by government policy.[59] Nevertheless the orthodox element could not be ignored, either in Vienna or in the provincial perhiphery, and this was one factor which held in check Mannheimer's own reformist inclinations.[60]

Even before 1848 several thousand Jews would enter Vienna on business each year from the far-flung corners of the Empire—Bohemia, Moravia, Hungary, Galicia, Trieste, and Gorizia—especially for the great fairs.[61] Though they were subjected to constant police surveillance by the *Judenamt* (Jewish Office) and if found without a

---

[57] Sigmund Mayer, *Die Wiener Juden: Kommerz, Kultur, Politik, 1700–1900* (Vienna and Berlin, 1917), 139, 283–4; Grunwald, *Vienna* 214–15.

[58] Allerhand, pp. 10–11; Rosenmann, pp. 65–74.   [59] Raphael Mahler, p. 233.

[60] Rosenmann, pp. 63–4.   [61] Raphael Mahler, pp. 236 ff.

134 368

'ticket' of entry, summarily expelled, a few thousand Jews escaped the repressive net and defeated all the government's efforts to seal off Vienna to Jews and prevent any increase in its 'tolerated' Jewish population. One of the inadvertent consequences of this steady infiltration of Bohemian, Moravian, Hungarian, and Galician Jews in the *Vormärz* period was to restrain the accelerating process of assimilation among Viennese Jewry. Eventually the authorities began to turn a blind eye to these illegal residents who did not register as required by law but were active in the upsurge of Austrian commerce and industry (whether by opening workshops or peddling manufactured products), preferring in classic Austrian fashion a posture of 'slovenly despotism' to reform or changing the laws.

The Jewish policy of the Emperor Francis I (1792–1835) was indeed full of such inconsistency and contradictions, both in its legislation and administrative praxis—a mixture of tolerance and repression, protection and illegality, the encouragement of assimilation and its hindrance by endless bureaucratic restrictions on Jewish rights.[62] The granting of special privileges for *grossbürgerlich* Vienna Jews alongside humiliating repression of the Jewish masses in the provinces continued therefore to characterize Austrian policy before 1848.[63] Where Joseph II had been manifestly ahead of his time, his more conservative successors ensured that Austrian Jewry remained frozen in the same position in which the 1782 edict had placed them, while the Jews of France (1791), Holland, Prussia (1812), and other German States steadily moved forward towards emancipation and full legal integration.

Between 1782 and 1848 Revolution, however, fundamental changes were taking place in Jewish life of which Austrian legislation took no account, thus creating a dangerous gap between *le pays légal* et *le pays réel*. In this period, the expansion and first steps of modernization in Austrian industry, commerce, banking, and transportation were carried out with the crucial assistance of a number of enterprising Jewish financiers and businessmen.[64] The textile industry was developed by Lazar Auspitz, Michael Biedermann, and Simon von

---

[62] Allerhand, p. 9; Grunwald, *Vienna*, 168–71.

[63] Häusler, 'Toleranz, Emanzipation und Antisemitismus', 89.

[64] Ibid. 94. Häusler points out that although the Jewish bankers and big merchants through their *de facto* alliance with the State outwardly stood in opposition to the popular aspirations for constitutional freedom, 'mit der Schaffung der Grundlagen einer kapitalistischen Wirtschaftsordnung die Voraussetzungen für eine bürgerliche Revolution gegeben waren'.

Laemel; Salomon Mayer Rothschild (1774–1855), who had moved to Vienna in 1816 and was ennobled six years later, built Austria's first railroad and subsequently established the Österreichische Creditanstalt (which later became Austria's State bank). Salomon von Rothschild's participation in the floating of government bonds and his intimate relations with the all-powerful Chancellor Clemens von Metternich, gave him *de facto* political as well as enormous economic power in pre-1848 Austria. The fact that Salomon Rothschild still needed exceptional permission to acquire an estate because Jews lacked civil equality, truly exemplified the curious modern-conservative ambiguity of the Metternich era.[65] In addition to the Rothschilds, Arnstein, Eskeles, and the Königswarters were among the leading Austrian bankers and sat on the board of the newly created National Bank.

The period between the *Toleranzpatent* and the 1848 Revolution also saw the entry of many Jews to University and their growing prominence in German literature and journalism. Though none attained the epoch-making importance of Heine, Börne, and Marx in Germany, they included talented writers, poets, and journalists like Ludwig August Frankl, Leopold Kompert, Moritz Saphir, Ignaz Kuranda, Hermann Jellinek, and Moritz Hartmann—some of whom were to participate actively in the 1848 Revolution. Already in the *Vormärz* period the *rapprochement* of these Jewish intellectuals with their Christian counterparts had begun. The gap between the cultural attainments of this numerically modest but growing intelligentsia, already a significant proportion of the Jewish population, and their humiliating status was a source of much resentment. It was one important reason why these younger Jews began openly to identify themselves with the rising liberal, democratic, and nationalist ideologies in Central Europe.

Though the revolutionary year of 1848 found no united Jewish community in Vienna (or in Austria as a whole), growing numbers of the new generation, chafing under the Metternich system, were now ready to fight openly for the ideals of freedom and equality. Most of these young men had come to Vienna from the provinces, and studied in the Habsburg capital under very difficult material conditions. They included two of the best-known victims of the Revolution, both of them from Moravia, the twenty-five-year-old radical democratic

---

[65] Robin Okey, *Eastern Europe 1740–1980: Feudalism to Communism* (London, 1982), 64.

journalist Dr Hermann Jellinek (executed in November 1848 by the military tribunal established by General Windischgrätz) and the Jewish technical student Karl-Heinrich Spitzer; two prominent Bohemian Jews, the poet Moritz Hartmann and the Pan-German journalist Ignaz Kuranda; and two Hungarian Jews, the *Sekundarartz* (assistant physician) Adolf Fischof (1816–93) and the chemist Josef Goldmark, who both played a decisive role as spokesmen of the liberal-revolutionary movement during the events of 1848.[66]

The newly elected Reichstag, which met in July 1848, also included among its four Jewish deputies, in addition to Fischof and Goldmark, the preacher Isaac Mannheimer from Vienna and the Cracow rabbi, Berusch Meisels. The question of Jewish emancipation was on the agenda of this constitutional Reichstag though it was never dealt with, due to the dissolving of the assembly in the course of the counter-revolution. But the election of Jews in Austria (and other German States) to parliaments and legislative bodies in 1848, unprecedented as it was, remained secondary compared to the role of individual Jews on the many revolutionary committees. Indeed the popular movement itself was ignited on 13 March 1848, at its very beginning, by a courageous impassioned speech calling for the overthrow of the old system made by Dr Adolf Fischof—who was to emerge as the leading personality of the Revolution—before the surging crowds gathered in front of the Lower Austrian Landhaus.[67] In Vienna, where students generally were to play a decisive role as the vanguard of the liberal-democratic Revolution, Jewish medical and law graduates were especially prominent in the common cause.

The Chairman of the student committee formed at the end of March 1848, which played an important part in the Revolution, was Joseph Goldmark. Its Jewish members included, apart from Fischof and Frankl, Boch, Flesch, Kapper, Mannheimer, Tausenau, Taussig,

[66] See 'Das Judentum im Revolutionsjahr 1848', *Studia Judaica Austriaca*, 1 (Vienna and Munich, 1974), esp. the contributions by Häusler, 'Die Revolution von 1848 und die österreichischen Juden; Eine Dokumentation', 5–63, and also pp. 64–77, 92–111. Also Grunwald, *Vienna*, 253 ff.

[67] Richard Charmatz, *Adolf Fischof: Das Lebensbild eines österreichischen Politikers* (Stuttgart and Berlin, 1910), 20–5. Fischof gave voice to popular demands for freedom of the press, of conscience, and of public assembly and called for a fraternal unification of the peoples of Austria. His speech, which includes the famous words 'Wer an diesem Tage keinen Mut hat, gehört in die Kinderstube!' is described by his admiring biographer as the first truly free one given in Austria in the 19th century. See also Werner Cahnmann, 'Adolf Fischof als Verfechter der Nationalität und seine Auswirkung auf das jüdisch-politische Denken im Österreich', *Studia Judaica Austriaca*, 1. 78–91.

and Unger. In May 1848 when the Security Committee was established—the most important political body in Vienna before the Reichstag's convocation—Fischof was appointed Chairman and one of his two deputies was also a Jew. There were also not a few Jews serving in the Akademische Legion and the National Guard, originally established to defend the Revolution against its enemies though it was later to be used against the Viennese proletariat as well. There were even Austrian Jews, like the radical Hermann Jellinek and the Polish Jew Adolf Chaizes, who stood in the forefront of 'socialistic' agitation among the working class.[68] During the bloody conflicts and armed resistance of October 1848 some Jews died at the barricades and others were forced to emigrate.

Both quantitatively and qualitatively this heavy Jewish involvement in the Austrian upheaval during 1848 had no real parallel elsewhere in Europe, not even in Germany and Hungary, which also provided examples of a significant commitment by Jews to the revolutionary movement.[69] To be sure, this remained mainly a Viennese phenomenon and the mass of orthodox Jews in Galicia, Bohemia, and Moravia were by and large untouched by the democratic struggle. But the effects of this unprecedented Jewish revolutionary participation were far-reaching, not only on the Jews themselves but also on their adversaries.[70]

Jacob Toury has emphasized that during 1848 for the first time in European history a very close identity emerged between Jewish and wider liberal and patriotic middle-class objectives in the German lands.[71] Hence Jewish demands for emancipation were no longer presented as separate or particularist issues but rather in the framework of general political aspirations. There was seemingly no

---

[68] Wolfgang Häusler, 'Hermann Jellinek (1823–1848): Ein Demokrat in der Wiener Revolution', *Jahrbuch des Instituts für deutsche Geschichte*, 5 (Tel Aviv, 1976), 125–75.

[69] See Reinhard Rürup, 'The European Revolutions of 1848 and Jewish Emancipation', in Werner E. Mosse, Arnold Paucker, Reinhard Rürup (eds.), *Revolution and Evolution: 1848 in German-Jewish History* (Tübingen, 1981), 1–53, for an excellent overview of the subject. For Germany, the classic work remains Jacob Toury, *Die politischen Orientierungen der Juden in Deutschland: Von Jena bis Weimar* (Tübingen, 1966), 47 ff.

[70] See Jacob Toury, 'Die Revolution von 1848 als inner jüdischer Wendepunkt', in Hans Liebeschutz und Arnold Paucker (eds.), *Das Judentum in der deutschen Umwelt 1800–1850: Studien zur Frühgeschichte der Emanzipation* (Tübingen, 1977), 359–76.

[71] Ibid. 363. Toury quotes the claim of a rabbi in Frankfurt, reported by the *Allgemeine Zeitung des Judentums* (1848): 'Wir haben und wünschen kein anderes Vaterland als das deutsche! Nur dem *Glauben* nach sind wir Israeliten, in allem übrigen gehören wir aufs Innigste dem Staate an, in welchem wir leben!'

further justification for a specifically Jewish struggle for equality.[72] This was powerfully expressed by the preacher Isaac Noah Mannheimer in an inter-denominational graveside ceremony for the first victims of the Viennese Revolution (who included the Moravian-born Jewish student hero, Karl-Heinrich Spitzer) and repeated by him a week later on 24 March 1848 in a synagogue sermon in Vienna.[73]

Mannheimer warned Austrian Jews not to place their own problems first. 'Not a single word about Jewish emancipation unless it be spoken on our behalf by others!' For thirty years Jews had pleaded 'on bended knee, and with hands raised up' for their rights. Now the Jews must act on the assumption that 'first comes the man, the citizen, and only then the Jew. No one must be able to accuse us of always thinking of ourselves first.'[74] For Mannheimer and the majority of Viennese Jews in 1848, including Isidor Busch and Meir Letteris, the editors of the newly established journal *Österreichisches Central-Organ für Glaubensfreiheit, Cultur, Geschichte und Literatur der Juden*, Jewish equality was held to be inseparable from the general emancipatory struggle for political freedom, human and civic rights. Mannheimer emphasized that the Jews would henceforth have to take their place solely as a religious community (*Religionsgemeinschaft*) in the context of a reformed liberal Austrian State.

This new *confessionalization* of Jewish identity and rejection of any organized Jewish movement for emancipation went together with a strengthened feeling of identification with the German-Austrian people and their struggle for full constitutional freedom and equality. Henceforth, through the nineteenth century, Viennese Jews would proudly identify themselves not only as Austrians but as *Germans* in the cultural, national, and humanistic sense. The depth of this ardent identification with German *Kultur* which was greatly strengthened by the experiences of the 1848 Revolution was even more emphatically expressed by Adolf Jellinek, the Moravian-born preacher from Ungarisch-Brod who eventually succeeded Mannheimer as Viennese Jewry's spiritual leader. In a major article published in Leipzig in July 1848 Jellinek stated that the Jews of Austria demanded their emancipation as an integral part of the *German* people in the Habsburg Empire. It was as Germans that they (the Jews) were also bearers of education, culture, commerce, and industry to the non-German

---

[72] Toury, 'Die Revolution von 1848', 364–5.

[73] *Österreichisches Central-Organ* (1848), no. 1, p. 1, quoted in Rosenmann, p. 147.

[74] Grunwald, *Vienna*, 274–5.

peoples of the Empire; 'to feel German means to feel free' since the German spirit was identical with the spirit of liberty.[75] The centres of industry and science in the Empire were all German; German nationalism unlike that of the Czechs, for example, did not seek to impose itself upon others. It was, according to Jellinek, liberal, humanist and imbued with a well-founded confidence in its own cosmopolitan, spiritual mission rather than dedicated to brute force and numbers. The salvation of the Jews 'can only come from a liberal government', declared Jellinek, and from an alliance with *Deutschtum* (Germandom) against the fanaticism of 'Czechomania, Pan-Slavism and the law of the fist'.[76]

Many years later, the Austrian Zionist leader Isidor Schalit, commenting in his memoirs on this Austrian Jewish commitment to the national cause of *Deutschtum* which had its origins in the struggle of 1848, wrote:

Throughout the Nineteenth century the Jews as a whole were German. They were German through their education since the German *Kultur* dominated the multilingual Empire. They learned and taught in German schools. The Jews were German because the German nation in Austria was the symbol of freedom and progress . . . The Jews remained not only the bearers of German culture, they were also the most conspicuous defenders of German policy.[77]

This generalization can be applied broadly to Bohemian Jewry, and to the dominant trend among Jews of Vienna during the liberal era before the tension between a universalist cultural paradigm of *Deutschtum* and late nineteenth-century *völkisch* definitions of German nationality had become manifest.[78] It clearly cannot be upheld with

---

[75] Adolf Jellinek, 'Die Juden in Oesterreich XIII', *Der Orient*, 8 July 1848, 217–18.

[76] Ibid. 218; see also ibid., 17 June 1848, p. 193–4, and 1 July 1848, 209–10. According to Jellinek the 'Slavization' of Austria would be a disaster for the Jews since the Slav peoples lacked the basic requisites of a rich history—the culture, enlightenment, literature, commerce, and industrial skills of the Germans. There could be 'no alliance with barbarism and fanaticism'. Czech nationalism was intolerant and a palpable physical threat to Jewish existence. Only the bayonets of the imperial soldiery stood between the Jews and peasant pogroms in Bohemia and Moravia.

[77] Isidor Schalit, 'Kadimah: Aus meinem Erinnerungen' (MS, Central Zionist Archives, A 196/25, Jerusalem).

[78] On Bohemian Jewry see Goldstücker, pp. 66–71, who also discusses the rejection by the leading Czech journalist of the day, Karel Havlíček (1821–56), of the idea that Jews might claim Czech nationality. According to Havlíček, it would have been highly dangerous for the Czech bourgeoisie to assimilate the Jews before they had established their own position. This helps place the Jewish identification with the Germans in Bohemia, a legacy of the Josephinian era and of socio-economic developments, in a somewhat different perspective.

regard to Hungarian Jewry, where the growing attraction of Magyar nationalism already obvious in the 1840s went hand in hand with the Jewish movement for religious reform.[79] The ardent participation of many Jews in the Hungarian fight for independence against the Austrian armies was 'rewarded' indeed by the extreme harshness with which they were treated by the imperial troops. Similarly, in Austrian Galicia the growing national self-consciousness of the Polish struggle for freedom and independence in 1848 exercised considerable attraction on the more enlightened urban Jewish circles striving for emancipation. In Italy, too, the Jews significantly sided with the Italian cause against Austrian rule. Since they could not simultaneously espouse the cause of Hungarians, Poles, Italians (or for that matter Czechs), *and* that of the German-Austrians, conflicts were unavoidable and often provided a fertile terrain for anti-Jewish prejudices that grew out of what was an objective clash of national interests.[80]

It was one of the most fateful paradoxes of the 1848 Revolution in Austria that in liberating the Jews from their ghetto existence, it confronted them for the first time in European history not only with the forces of nationalism but with the seeds of the *modern* anti-Semitic political movements that developed later in the nineteenth century.[81] While building on traditional Christian and popular prejudices that had accompanied Jewish settlement in the Habsburg lands since the early Middle Ages, the emerging anti-Semitic ideology clearly responded to the novel phenomenon of a secular, acculturated, and politicized participation of the Jews in the events of 1848.[82] Significantly, the most violent reactions against Jews occurred in those Habsburg territories like Bohemia, Moravia, and Hungary (though not Galicia) where the pre-1848 conditions of Jewry had been even more oppressive than in Vienna or Lower Austria, where as we have seen few Jews were in any case permitted to reside—or for that matter in ethnic German areas like Upper Austria, Styria, Carinthia, and Carniola where *no* Jews were tolerated at all.

The popular disturbances and anti-Jewish excesses reflected in part the social and national crisis that had given rise the to revolutionary outbreak of 1848. Economic and national issues had played, for

[79] Wolfang Häusler, 'Assimilation und Emanzipation des ungarischen Judentums um die Mitte des 19 Jahrhunderts', *Studia Judaica Austriaca*, 3 (Eisenstadt, 1976), 33–79.

[80] For the effect of the nationality problem on the position of the Jews, see the comprehensive essay by Salo W. Baron, 'The Impact of the Revolution of 1848 on Jewish Emancipation', *Jewish Social Studies*, 11 (1949), 195–248, esp. 234 ff.

[81] Toury, 'Die Revolution von 1848', 375–6.   [82] Katz, pp. 227–9.

example, a significant part in attacks on Jewish enterprises in Prague and other Bohemian cities since the mid-1840s. Violent anti-Jewish riots in Prague triggered by a Jewish firm's introduction of new machinery into their textile factories even had to be put down by the army.[83] In the spring of 1848 Prague workers again attacked Jewish merchants and dealers at a time of price rises and unemployment.[84] In Pressburg (Hungary), too, there was looting and destruction of Jewish shops and the large synagogue was actually razed to the ground during Easter 1848. The ugly popular mood, whipped up by an intense anti-Jewish press campaign and economic unrest, persuaded the Hungarian Parliament to abandon for the time being any emancipatory measures.[85] Similar propaganda in other Hungarian localities produced further anti-Jewish disturbances and even in Pest it succeeded for a while in diverting popular discontent.[86]

In Vienna, however, though there were no pogroms, the connection between anti-Semitic agitation and the course of the Revolution was clearest of all. To some extent, as in the anti-Jewish petition submitted by Viennese tradesmen and shopkeepers in July 1848, this agitation against Jewish emancipation was guided by narrow social and economic interests.[87] The fear of free competition and Jewish 'usury' was no less conspicuous among the artisan guilds. Even more significant, however, was the *political* dimension which reflected itself in the link between anti-Semitism and reactionary opposition to the radical and democratic currents in the Viennese Revolution.[88] Those who rejected the liberal and democratic principles of the Revolution tended to focus on Jewish participation in the popular movement in conspiratorial terms.[89] This was especially true of conservative and clerical commentators who singled out the prominent role of Jews like Fischof, Goldmark, Hermann Jellinek, and others as revolutionary protagonists, agitators, and 'subverters' of the Monarchy and of the Christian social order.

One reactionary Viennese newspaper, *Schild und Schwert*, even

---

[83] Goldstücker, p. 66.

[84] S. Dubnow, *Weltgeschichte des jüdischen Volkes*, 10 vols. (Berlin, 1925–9), i.x. 467 ff.

[85] Ibid. 370 ff.; see also Häusler, 'Assimilation und Emanzipation', 62–5.

[86] Rürup, p. 38.   [87] Ibid.

[88] R. John Rath, *The Viennese Revolution of 1848* (New York, 1969), 303.

[89] On the general theme of conspiracy see Johannes Rogalla von Bieberstein, *Die These von der Verschwörung 1776–1945: Philosophen, Freimaurer, Juden, Liberale und Sozialisten als Verschwörer gegen die Sozialorduung* (Berne, 1976); also Jacob Toury, *Turmoil and Confusion in the Revolution of 1848* (Hebrew) (Merhavia, 1968) 42–4, 138–43, on the use of this theme against the demand for Jewish equality.

denounced the Jews on 10 November 1848, 'and *chiefly the Jews* as the misfortune of our fatherland, that is to say, the misfortune of *all* of us'.[90] Gustav Otruba's detailed inventory of the often scurrilous pamphlet literature in 1848 vividly reveals that the fear of *Juden herrschaft* (Jew-rule), supposedly manifested by Jewish 'money-power' and control of the press, was a powerful factor in conservative and lower middle-class circles during the Revolution itself.[91] The prospect of equal rights being granted to Viennese Jews after decades of far-reaching restrictions imposed by the *Vormärz* regime also alarmed many sincere Catholics. The founding father of modern Austrian anti-Semitism, Sebastian Brunner, Catholic priest and editor of the *Wiener Kirchenzeitung*—a newspaper launched during the 1848 Revolution— became obsessed with the threat of the Jews as a symbol of everything harmful and destructive in modern society. Jews were already perceived by Catholics as being in the forefront of the rationalist, secular, and anti-clerical forces of liberalism. The 1848 Revolution, and Jewish emancipation as its by-product, epitomized to Brunner and his followers the *de-Christianization* of the Austrian State and society— a process which they were determined to reverse.[92]

It was the historic task of the Catholic Church to set its face against the subversive free-thinking mask' of Jewry, against its sinister 'Talmudic' spirit and animosity to time-honoured Christian truths and values. The control of finance and domination of the press was in Brunner's view simply the latest manifestation of an age-old 'Jewish' war against Christianity which had now brought the weapons of liberalism and modernity into its service. Brunner and his successor Albert Wiesinger, who became editor of the *Kirchenzeitung* in 1866, provided the link between the traditional theological anti-Judaism of the Catholic Church and the modern political anti-Semitism of the Christian Social movement that arose in Vienna during the 1880s.

Even racial arguments were not absent in the anti-Semitic pamphlet war against the democratic and liberal movement of 1848. Thus, in the writings of the former artillery officer Johann Quirin Endlich, the 'Jew' appears as the embodiment of all evils—as capitalist exploiter *and* revolutionary democrat—as the subverter *par excellence* of the Christian

[90] Rürup, p. 48.

[91] Gustav Otruba (ed.), *Wiener Flugschriften zur Sozialen Frage 1848* (Vienna, 1980), pp. xl–xlii, and 120–1, 212–13, 225–30, 336, 341–9.

[92] Erika Weinzierl, 'On the Pathogenesis of the Anti-Semitism of Sebastian Brunner (1814–1893)', *Yad Vashem Studies*, 10 (Jerusalem, Yad Vashem, 1974), 217–39; also Katz, pp. 227–8, 282, 286.

State and its shameless plunderer.[93] Anti-capitalist themes, too, nourished anti-Jewish propaganda during the 1848 Revolution and these came from the Left as much as the Right. Partly this was a response to the spectacular role Jewish banking firms had played in Austrian history between 1815 and 1848—'the age of Rothschild' as much as it was the age of Metternich.[94] The close connections between the Austrian Chancellor and *la haute finance juive* was hardly a secret to European radicals. Though Jews in the *Vormärz* period could not serve in the government, practise law, teaching, or any political functions, though they had to pay poll-tax and report regularly to the *Judenamt*, the House of Austria remained as dependent on Rothschild's State loans as in the heyday of the Court Jews.

Even the Habsburgs had to abandon some of their traditional *hauteur* and eventually make Salomon von Rothschild, the pioneer of the Nordbahn railway system, into a fully fledged citizen. In 1843 Salomon was finally granted permission to acquire inheritable agricultural real estate, so essential had he meanwhile become to the Austrian State's shaky finances. In the same year the German Left Hegelian radical, Bruno Bauer, doubtless with the Metternich–Rothschild alliance in mind, could write in his *Die Judenfrage*: 'The Jew, who is merely tolerated in Vienna, for example, determines the fate of the whole empire through the financial power he possesses.'[95] The founder of Communism, Karl Marx, who approvingly quoted these lines in his essay *Zur Judenfrage* (1844), claimed that this was not an isolated fact. 'The Jew has emancipated himself in a Jewish way', he added, 'not only by acquiring financial power but also because through him and apart from him *money* has become a world power and the practical Jewish spirit has become the practical spirit of the Christian peoples.'[96]

During the 1848 Revolution in Austria the Jewish 'aristocracy of money' became not merely a philosophical issue but a target of popular wrath, of mixed anti-feudal and anticapitalist tendencies which reflected the crisis of modernization overtaking Central European society. Among lower middle-class Viennese tradesmen and

---

[93] Johan Quirin Endlich, *Der Einfluss der Juden auf unsere Civilisation mit besonderer Rücksicht auf Industrial-Anstalten in Österreich* (Vienna, 1848).

[94] See Egon Caesar Conte Corti, *Der Aufstieg des Hauses Rothschild* (Vienna, 1953), and Frederic Morton, *The Rothschilds* (London, 1964), 76–85.

[95] Bruno Bauer, *Die Judenfrage* (Brunswick, 1843), 114.

[96] Karl Marx, 'On the Jewish Question', in Karl Marx, *Early Writings* (London, 1975), 237.

shopkeepers, among the local tailors and shoemakers, it was not difficult to invoke the spectre of Rothschild and the 'money power' of the Jewish bankers—remote though their life-style might be from the impoverished mass of Austrian Jewry. This was consistently done by the Vienna correspondent of Karl Marx's *Neue Rheinische Zeitung*, Eduard von Müller-Tellering, who wrote in a vitriolically anti-Semitic 1848 pamphlet published in the Habsburg capital: 'At the root of tyranny is money, and the money is in the hands of the Jews.'[97]

In his despatches from Vienna for Marx's newspaper (which were much appreciated by the editors and published without any editing out of their malicious invective) von Müller-Tellering indulged in an orgy of rabid anti-Jewish rhetoric against 'Israel's satanic cunning' which had supposedly prostituted the Austrian freedom movement of 1848. Monarchs, soldiers, and bureaucrats were mere tools of the Jews who had buried Austria and were now sucking its blood. A truly democratic order, this fanatic radical insisted, would only be possible through 'the destruction of Jewry' (*Vernichtung des Judentums*) in Austria. As long as the Viennese democracy was led by 'cowardly Jewish hucksters [*Schacherjuden*] and phrase-mongerers' it could only deliver up Austria to a million blood-sucking capitalists! Hence the task of the Central European revolution was not merely to sweep away feudalism but first and foremost to drive out the Jewish exploiters.[98]

The 1848 Revolution and counter-revolution thus brought in its wake a complex fusion of traditional religious and more modern anticapitalist, nationalistic, and racial anti-Semitic motifs emanating from both Right and Left. As Reinhard Rürup has pointed out, these diverse stands were directed more 'at a Jewry which was taken as having achieved emancipation' than at traditional, unemancipated Jewry.[99] The numerous and ugly anti-Semitic caricatures of 1848 with their antiliberal, anticapitalist motifs and fear of 'Jewish domination' reflect this fact, as indeed does the backlash against the prominent Jewish participation in the Revolution.[100] To quote Rürup again:

Thus the post-emancipation propaganda theme, basic to modern antisemitism, was already present in the antisemitic utterances of the revolutionary period.

---

[97] Eduard von Müller-Tellering, *Freiheit und Juden: Zur Beherzigung an alle Volksfreunde* (Vienna, 1848), 9.
[98] Ernst Hanisch, *Der kranke Mann an der Donau: Marx und Engels über Österreich* (Vienna, Munich, Zurich, 1978), 77–82.
[99] Rürup, p. 48.
[100] Wolfgang Häusler, 'Toleranz, Emanzipation und Antisemitismus', 100.

Even in 1848, then, that ominous compound of contradictory sentiments—contempt for traditional Jewry coupled with fear of the modern Jews—was strongly in evidence. The new antisemitism was in essence a manifestation of these incongruous reactions, an amalgam of arrogance and anxiety. The malignant potential of this explosive mixture became apparent for the first time during the period of Revolution. Yet the new antisemitism could not flourish during the immediate post-revolutionary era when, in spite of the political defeat of the Liberal and Democratic forces, bourgeois-liberal ideas continued to be dominant.[101]

Viennese Jews could indeed take comfort from the fact that the new anti-Semitic ideologies had failed to set off a genuine mass movement in 1848/9 capable of fusing with the political reaction, and that they were unable to turn Austrian Jewry back to the *Vormärz* ghetto, in spite of the victory of the Habsburg dynasty and the counter-revolution. Hence the Viennese Jewish bourgeoisie was able to integrate the revolutionary year of 1848, in spite of its more disturbing features and setbacks, into that liberal optimism and faith in *Deutschtum* which would characterize its world-view through to the end of the nineteenth century. Jewish poets like Ludwig August Frankl, famous preachers like Isaac Noah Mannheimer and Adolf Jellinek, publicists and liberal politicians like Adolf Fischof or Ignaz Kuranda, and Austrian Jewish notables like Joseph von Wertheimer could in subsequent years synthesize such seeming contraries as the cult of 1848 liberalism (suitably stripped of its revolutionary dynamic) with veneration for the ruling Habsburg dynasty that it had nearly toppled. Even the late nineteenth-century Austrian Zionists looked back nostalgically to the stirring heroism of the Akademische Legion and the German national enthusiasm of the Viennese revolutionary students as one of the models for their own movement.

Hence the 1848 Revolution, in spite of its apparent contradictions and ambiguities, did mark in the consciousness of Viennese Jewry a new stage of self-awareness and self-confidence.[102] The bourgeois revolution had failed in Austria but its spirit was not so easily extinguished and the promise of liberal emancipation still shone brightly for the majority of Viennese Jews.

---

[101] Rürup, pp. 48–9.
[102] See Mayer, pp. 310–26.

2

Migration to the Kaiserstadt

Wien, l'unique syllabe du nom de la capitale impériale avait toujours, dans ce village du fin fond de la monarchie, une résonance prestigieuse. Pour nous tous, et pas seulement pour mes frères et moi, Vienne signifiait splendeur et magnificence ... Combien parmi nous rêvaient alors de vivre un jour dans la ville impériale, où ils pourraient, comme de vrais Viennois s'émerveiller chaque matin à voir passer François-Joseph 1ᵉʳ dans son magnifique carrosse attelé de chevaux blancs.

Manès Sperber, Porteurs d'Eau (1976)

I was already second-generation Viennese, and Viennese-born Jews felt resentment towards the less assimilated Jews from the East. We were, or rather thought we were quite different from that bearded, caftaned lot. We were not just Austrian, but German-Austrian.

George Clare, Last Waltz in Vienna (1980)

On the eve of the 1848 Revolution there were according to official estimates only 179 'tolerated' families in Vienna, though as we have seen a steady flow of illegal immigrants had in fact infiltrated the capital during the *Vormärz* period. They had tended to come mainly from Bohemia, Moravia, and Hungary—especially from the Pressburg ghetto and the smaller Jewish communities in the Burgenland, just east of Vienna, and through appropriate bribes to local officials, these immigrants could often prolong their sojourn in the city.[1] Sigmund Mayer, himself such a newcomer from the Pressburg ghetto (later to become one of Viennese Jewry's most respected community politicians), vividly recalled in his memoirs the sharp contrast between the dark, overcrowded, and dirty ghettos of the Austro-Hungarian provinces and the clean, airy, bright streets of *Vormärz* Vienna which had left their imprint on the ethos of its Jews. Modern, elegant, free-thinking,

---

[1] Sigmund Mayer, *Ein jüdischer Kaufmann, 1831 bis 1911* (Leipzig, 1911), 107 ff.; Hans Tietze, *Die Juden Wiens* (Vienna and Leipzig, 1933), 138–9.

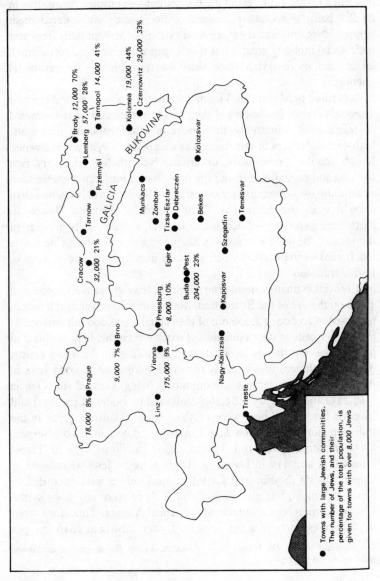

Austria-Hungary, 1910

● Towns with large Jewish communities.
The number of Jews, and their
percentage of the total population, is
given for towns with over 8,000 Jews

Prague 18,000 8%
Linz
Brno 9,000 7%
Vienna 175,000 9%
Cracow 32,000 21%
Tarnow
Brody 12,000 70%
Lemberg 57,000 28%
Przemysl
Tarnopol 14,000 41%
Kolomea 19,000 44%
Czernowitz 29,000 33%
GALICIA
BUKOVINA
Pressburg 8,000 10%
Munkacs
Zombor
Eger
Tizsa-Eszlar
Debreczen
Buda-Pest 204,000 23%
Bekes
Kaposvar
Szegedin
Kolozsvar
Temesvar
Nagy-Kanizsa
Trieste

they had already grown accustomed to 'enjoy the beautiful surroundings of Vienna just like the rest of the population—to indulge themselves in its élite balls, aristocratic restaurants, coffee-houses, and entertainment centres.[2] Not only was their personal existence incomparably freer and their social mobility greater but they engaged in commerce on a much larger and more lavish scale than was possible in the provincial ghettos.[3]

According to Mayer, the Vienna Jews in the *Vormärz* period enjoyed a special prestige in the eyes of their less fortunate and more backward co-religionists. Admittedly, there were no real aristocrats, diplomats, high-ranking offiers or bureaucrats among them; nor, as yet, renowned Jewish scholars, professors, or artists. Nevertheless, the very rich banking and capitalist élite and the new class of intellectuals were seen as standing on a much higher material and literary level in Vienna than elsewhere in the Monarchy.[4] The wealth of Viennese Jewry, in particular, inspired confidence and respect, enhancing its prestige in the eyes of the Jewish masses in the provinces even if its élite had a much shakier reputation when it came to religiosity and fidelity to Jewish tradition.

If official estimates numbered Vienna's Jews at between 2,000 and 4,000 on the eve of the Revolution, Mayer considered the real figure to be closer to 10,000–12,000 out of the capital's 400,000 inhabitants[5]— i.e. 2.5 per cent of the population. To place even this high estimate in perspective, one needs to recall that according to the 1846 census (unreliable though it is in many respects) there were 729,005 Jews in Austria—the two largest communities being centred in Galicia (317,225) and Hungary (265,260), followed by Bohemia (70,037) and Moravia (37,169). There were 11,581 Jews in Bukovina, 7,725 in the Italian regions of Venetia and Lombardy, 7,000 in Siebenburgen, 3,530 in Istria, Gorz, and Trieste, 2,895 in Silesia, 978 in Tyrol/ Vorarlberg, and 410 in Dalmatia. There were no Jews whatsoever in Upper Austria, Styria, and Carinthia, and only 2 were recorded in Krain (Carniola).[6] It also is doubtful if there were any Jews in the Lower Austrian region outside of the capital, Vienna. Thus if we taken the official estimate of 4,296 Jews for Lower Austria in 1846 (0.9 per

---

[2] Sigmund Mayer, *Die Wiener Juden: Kommerz, Kultur, Politik, 1700–1900* (Vienna and Berlin, 1917), 207–9.

[3] Ibid. 214.   [4] Ibid. 281–2.

[5] Ibid. 219, 245.

[6] Heinrich Jacques, *Denkschrift über die Stellung der Juden in Österreich* (Vienna, 1859), p. xl.

cent of Austrian Jewry as a whole) we can see that a dramatic geographical displacement in the foci of Jewish demography took place within the Habsburg lands during the long reign of Franz Joseph I.

TABLE 2.1   Distribution of Cisleithanian Jews by Provinces 1846–1910: Total Number of Jews in Austria (excluding Hungary) (%)

Province	1846	1857	1869	1880	1900	1910
Lower Austria	0.9	1.1	6.3	9.4	12.8	14.1
Galicia	73.3	72.3	70.0	68.2	66.2	66.4
Bohemia	15.6	13.9	10.9	9.4	7.6	6.5
Moravia	8.9	6.7	5.2	4.3	3.6	3.1
Bukovina	—	4.7	5.8	6.7	7.8	7.8
Silesia	—	0.5	0.7	0.8	0.5	1.0

Sources: These figures are based upon Jacob Thon, *Die Juden in Österreich* (Berlin, 1908), 6–8; Anson G. Rabinbach, 'The Migration of Galician Jews to Vienna, 1857–1800', *Austrian History Yearbook*, 11 (1975), 44; and *Die Ergebnisse der Volkszahlung vom 31 Dezember 1910 in den im Reichsrat vertretenen Königreichern und Ländern* (Vienna, 1912), 57, Table XXX.

The central feature of the redistribution of population as shown in Table 2.1 was clearly the spectacular growth of Jewish population in Lower Austria (i.e. overwhelmingly in Vienna) which leapt from 1.1 to 6.3 per cent of the total number of Austrian Jews by 1869 and to a peak figure of 14 per cent by 1910. At the same time the concentration of Jews in Galicia, Bohemia, and Moravia declined somewhat in the same period—most noticeably in the Czech provinces. Galicia remained the demographic centre for Austrian Jewry throughout the nineteenth century (even in 1910 it still represented 66.4 per cent of the total population) but there is no doubt that once the gates of the Imperial capital were open to mass migration in the 1850s, the *Ostjuden* from the Polish provinces began slowly to abandon this economically backward region and to converge on Vienna or else emigrate overseas. They were joined and initially, at least, outpaced by a steady stream of Jewish immigrants from Bohemia, Moravia, and above all Hungary, which swelled the Viennese Jewish community from less than 10,000 in the 1850s to a high point of 175,318 by 1910—making Vienna numerically the third largest Jewish city in Europe after Warsaw and Budapest.

TABLE 2.2   Growth of the Jewish Population of Vienna
1857–1910

Year	Total Population	Jews	Total Population (%)
1857	476,220	6,217	1.3
1869	607,510	40,227	6.6
1880	726,105	72,543	10.0
1890	827,567	99,441	12.0
1890*	1,364,548	118,495	8.7
1900	1,674,957	146,296	8.8
1910	2,031,498	175,318	8.6

* Includes enlarged boundaries of Vienna in 1890.
Source: Figures taken from Table 1 in Ivar Oxaal and Walter R. Weitzmann, 'The Jews of Pre-1914 Vienna: An Exploration of Basic Sociological Dimensions' in *Leo Baeck Yearbook*, 30 (1985), 398. There are a few minor discrepancies between these figures and those given by Rabinbach, 'Migration of Galician Jews', 46, but the general trend is clear enough.

From Table 2.2 it is evident that by 1910 the Jewish population in Vienna had increased twenty-eight times over what it had been in 1857, though in the same period the total population had only increased by a factor of five. This extraordinary rate of growth was unparalleled after 1860 anywhere in the Habsburg Empire or on the European continent. Though Budapest Jewry grew even more rapidly in absolute numbers from 44,890 (16.6 per cent) in 1869 to 203,687 (23 per cent) in 1910, its take-off point was much higher than that of Vienna Jews as a percentage of the total population.[7] In the German Imperial capital Berlin, where there were 36,015 Jews in 1871 and 144,007 by 1910, the percentage of Jews as part of the total population actually declined from 4.4 to 3.7.[8] A similar trend was visible in the smaller cities of Prague (13,056 Jews, i.e. 8.2 per cent in 1869 as against 18,041 in 1910, i.e. 8.1 per cent), among Lemberg Jews (down from 30.6 per cent in 1869 to 27.8 per cent of the population in 1910),

[7] P. G. J. Pulzer, *The Rise of Political Antisemitism in Germany and Austria* (New York and London, 1964), 346–7.
[8] Ibid.

and in Cracow, where the number of Jews fell as a percentage of the general population from 35.5 to 21.3 in the same period.[9]

Thus Vienna, unlike other provincial capitals in the Empire, continued to expand and maintain its hold after the 1860s as a magnet for Habsburg Jewry, and in this respect it was rivalled only by Budapest. As Table 2.2 shows, the fastest rate of growth was achieved in the years between 1857 and 1869, a period in which the remaining governmental restrictions on Jewish freedom of movement and the purchase of real estate were removed (1859–60) and which also witnessed the passing of the *Grundgesetz* of 21 December 1867 that finally granted civic equality to all Austrian Jews. In the same year Vienna's Israelitische Kultusgemeinde (IKG) received its definitive statutes—the climax of a long, frustrating development from Joseph II's *Toleranzedikt* through the 1848 Revolution to the provisional recognition granted by the authorities in 1852. It should be no surprise, then, that the first mass convergence on Vienna coincided with the breaking down of the legal barriers to full emancipation in Austria and the golden age of liberal hegemony.

Interestingly enough, according to a sample study of the social structure of Viennese Jewry in the year 1857 (based in particular on the Leopoldstadt), 25 per cent of its Jews were born in Hungary (mainly Pressburg), 20 per cent in Vienna itself, 15 per cent in the many small Jewish communities of Moravia, 10 per cent in Galicia, and only 4 per cent in Bohemia.[10] From this it would appear that in 1857 the migration *en masse* of the traditionally structured East European Jewish communities of Galicia had not yet begun and it is doubtful if it was really these *Ostjuden* who were the main source of immigration to Vienna in the period before 1880.[11] However, there is data to show that by 1880 Galician Jews had proportionately increased more than any other regional component in Viennese Jewry since 1857 (from 10 to 18 per cent) though they still lagged behind those born in Vienna (31 per cent), in Hungary (28 per cent), and the Czech lands (20 per cent).[12]

---

[9] Ibid. 346–7.

[10] Peter Schmidtbauer, 'Zur sozialen Situation der Wiener Juden im Jahre 1857', *Studia Judaica Austriaca*, 6 (Eisenstadt, 1978), 62.

[11] See Rabinbach, 'Migration of Galician Jews', 43–54, who claims Galicia was the main source of migration to Vienna; and the remarks by Scott Eddie, 'Galician Jews as Migrants: An Alternative Hypothesis', *Austrian History Yearbook*, 11 (1975), 59–63; Oxaal and Weitzmann, 'Jews of Pre-1914 Vienna', 398 ff.

[12] Oxaal and Weitzmann, p. 400.

The impression of a high percentage of Hungarian Jews in the first waves of migration to Vienna, no doubt favoured by their geographical proximity, is reinforced by the census of December 1869 which shows that out of 40,227 Jews in Vienna, no less than 17,500 according to the father's place of birth came from the Hungarian lands (i.e. 42.3 per cent).[13] To some extent, this was not surprising since in 1857, at the outset of the migration process, 40 per cent of all Jews in the Habsburg Monarchy lived in Hungary. On the other hand, it is interesting to note that only when the Hungarian influx began noticeably to decline in the 1890s, did the mass migration of Galician *Ostjuden* to Vienna really take off, representing the last substantial wave of Jewish immigration to the Imperial capital before 1914.[14] It would appear that the increased pull of Magyarization and the attractions of Budapest as a major urban centre explain this decline in Hungarian Jewish migration to Vienna in the same period.

The Hungarian immigration came predominantly from medium or large Jewish communities in regions geographically proximate to Vienna like western Hungary and western Slovakia rather than from the heaviest areas of Jewish concentration in the central and eastern district of Hungary. Though many of the earlier Hungarian Jewish immigrants came from a traditional background and some of them reinforced the orthodox community in Vienna, there is no doubt that in comparison to Galician Jewry they were far more Germanized—the Herzl family being only one of the more famous examples. This trend reflected the profound impact of German *Haskalah* in Hungary which occurred well before the *Ausgleich*.[15] The Hungarians also tended to be relatively prosperous though much less so than the Bohemian Jews. Most probably, the majority were either members of the middle class

---

[13] Marsha Rozenblit, *The Jews of Vienna, 1867–1914: Assimilation and Identity* (Albany, NY, 1983), 22. The earlier study by Israel Jeiteles, *Die Kultusgemeinde der Israeliten in Wien mit Benutzung des statistischen Volkszählungsoperatus vom Jahre 1869* (Vienna, 1873), 67–7, concluded that in terms of origins, in 1869 46.3 per cent of Jews in Vienna were Hungarian, 20.9 per cent Moravian, 13 per cent Galician, 11.3 per cent, and only 3.4 per cent Viennese!

[14] Rabinbach, 'Migration of Galician Jews', evidently placed the bulk of the Galician migration too early and overlooked not only the scale of the earlier Hungarian immigration but also the fact that more Jews left Bohemia and Moravia (despite their smaller Jewish populations) than Galicia. See the criticisms of Eddie, pp. 60–1.

[15] See Michael K. Silber, 'Roots of the Schism in Hungarian Jewry: Cultural and Social Change from the Reign of Joseph II until the Eve of the 1848 Revolution' (in Hebrew) (Hebrew Univ., Jerusalem, unpub. Ph.D. thesis, 1985). On their general political orientation see the article by Robert A. Kann, 'Hungarian Jewry during Austria-Hungary's Constitutional Period (1867–1918)', *Jewish Social Studies*, 7 (1945), 357–86.

before they migrated to Vienna or else succeeded in achieving a respectable position fairly rapidly.[16] No doubt there were also pockets of poverty among the immigrant Hungarian Jewry, but far more striking in the economic, cultural, and political life of Vienna was the number of enterprising, dynamic, and creative Jews who had originated from the Hungarian lands.

Bohemian and Moravian Jews had been among the first to flock to Vienna following the lifting of residential restrictions in the 1860s. As we have seen, the decline in the numbers of Austrian Jews residing in the Czech lands was most dramatic after 1846 and the pull of Vienna for geographical, economic, and cultural reasons was especially strong for the Bohemian and Moravian Jews.[17] In the case of Bohemian Jewry, they migrated from all five regions of the province (nearly a third from Prague and central Bohemia) and predominantly from southern Moravia in the case of Moravian Jews. Having suffered cruelly from the onerous eighteenth-century Austrian restrictions on their population growth and freedom of movement, it is not surprising that Moravian Jewry rapidly abandoned their small *Gemeinden* to seek greater economic opportunities in the urban centres, especially Vienna.[18]

Moreover, both Moravian and Bohemian Jews felt threatened by the rise of a competing Czech bourgeoisie which was undermining the semi-monopolistic position of Jewish traders and shopkeepers in the rural economy.[19] The formation of local consumer co-operatives to eliminate the Jewish middleman and the organizing of anti-Jewish boycotts became features of the Czech national movement. As we have seen, economic and national issues were already prominently interwoven back in the 1840s during the anti-Semitic riots in Bohemia. Furthermore, as Czech nationalism in the late nineteenth century assumed a more stridently anti-German character, seeking to weaken and even eliminate local German economic and political influence, so, too, the pressure on the Jews as a 'Germanizing' element intensified.[20] Similar trends were observable in Hungarian-ruled Slovakia and

[16] Rozenblit, *Jews of Vienna*, 35.   [17] Eddie, pp. 60–1.

[18] Hugo Gold (ed.), *Die Juden und Judengemeinden Mährens in Vergangenheit und Gegenwart* (Brünn, 1929).

[19] Ruth Kestenberg-Gladstein, 'The Jews between Czechs and Germans in the Historic Lands, 1848–1918', in *The Jews of Czechoslovakia*, 2 vols. (Philadelphia, 1968), i. 32–7, 43 ff.

[20] Gary B. Cohen, *The Politics of Ethnic Survival: Germans in Prague, 1861–1914* (Princeton, 1981), 237–42.

Austrian Galicia towards the end of the nineteenth century, as Slovak, Polish, and Ukrainian nationalists sought to squeeze out Jewish merchants, traders, and middlemen from their traditional roles in the agrarian economy. The combination of threatened loss of livelihood, exposure to local nationalist cross-currents, and economic anti-Semitism were all powerful inducements for Jews to seek the relative security of Vienna or else to emigrate abroad, mainly to the United States.

In the case of Bohemian and Moravian Jewry the choice of Vienna was natural enough, since no other provincial Austrian Jewish communities had undergone such an intense process of Germanization since the time of Joseph II. Moreover, by the second half of the nineteenth century they were already increasingly urbanized, a fact which made the move to the metropolis easier to contemplate and smoothed the process of adaptation to the *Weltstadt*.[21] Bohemians were also the wealthiest Jewish immigrants to Vienna, a fact reflected in their over-representation among the tax-payers to the Kultusgemeinde.[22]

The residential pattern of Bohemian and Moravian Jews in Vienna itself was, significantly enough, quite different from that of Gentile Czech immigrants to the capital, who constituted the largest *national* minority in the city.[23] The 100,000 Viennese Czechs were mainly concentrated in working-class areas such as Favoriten (X District), Ottakring (XVI District), or the lower middle-class Landstrasse (III). They worked for the most part in factories, spoke Czech as their everyday language, and attended Viennese trade-schools rather than Gymnasien. On the other hand, Bohemian and Moravian Jews in Vienna, clustered in the typically 'Jewish' areas (the Inner City, Leopoldstadt, and Alsergrund), practised middle-class occupations, spoke only German, and focused their energies on sending their sons to the most prestigious schools of Vienna.[24] In other words, Bohemian Jewry behaved very much like Viennese-born Jews once they had become acclimatized to the city, and like other Jewish immigrants they lived in the predominantly 'Jewish' neighbourhoods. Remarkably enough, they had virtually no contact with Gentile Bohemian immigrants—the largest comparable minority in the city—from whom

---

[21] Rozenblit, *Jews of Vienna*, 38.   [22] Ibid. 35.

[23] See Monika Glettler, *Die Wiener Tschechen um 1900: Strukturanalyse einer nationalen Minderheit in der Grossstadt* (Munich and Vienna, 1972), for a detailed study of the assimilation process undergone by Czechs in Vienna.

[24] Rozenblit *Jews of Vienna*, 95–6, 116–17.

they felt divided by religion, class, culture, and occupational structure in spite of a common regional origin.

Marsha Rozenblit in a detailed study has argued that this phenomenon was part of a wider pattern of adaptation to the metropolis in which immigrant Jews created Jewish neighbourhoods where 'Jews of all social classes lived near each other rather than with gentiles with whom they shared economic interests'.[25] This pattern of residential concentration which applied equally to Hungarian, Galician, Bohemian, Moravian, and native-born Viennese Jews tended in her view to reinforce Jewish self-consciousness and identity while restraining the impact of environmental forces of assimilation.

The comparison between Vienna and Prague is instructive in this respect with regard both to residential patterns and to the integrative process into Gentile society.[26] Admittedly, the migration of Jews into Prague came principally from other areas of Bohemia and was not a multinational, multilingual phenomenon. There were virtually no *Ostjuden* in pre-1914 Prague and assimilation took place as a minority *within* another (i.e. German) minority. Notwithstanding these significant differences and the fact that Viennese Jews were never seriously faced with a comparable problem of cultural alignment (i.e. that between Czechs and Germans), there were common problems arising out of religious differences, distinct occupational and class structure as well as political orientations. Gary Cohen's study suggests, for example, that in the *private* sphere (family relationships friendships, social contacts, and intermarriage) German Jews and Gentiles in Prague generally avoided each other, in spite of the high degree of Jewish participation in the *public* life of the German community.[27] They tended, as in Vienna, to prefer other Jews rather than Germans as their neighbours.[28] Though they did not cluster in specific neighbourhoods except to some extent in Josefov, within individual apartment buildings 'Jewish households, particularly the German Jews, tended to be gathered together with few if any German Gentiles in the same building'.[29] In spite of high acculturation, Cohen concludes, German Jews in Prague retained 'something of a separate existence', a distinct body of Jewish values and habits, a sense

[25] Ibid. 94.
[26] See Gary B. Cohen, 'Jews in German Society: Prague, 1860–1914', *Central European History*, 10 (1977), 28–54; repr. also in David Bronsen (ed.), *Jews and Germans from 1860 to 1933: The Problematic Symbiosis* (Heidelberg, 1979), 306–37.
[27] Cohen, *Politics of Ethnic Survival*, 322–3.
[28] Ibid. 323.   [29] Ibid. 324.

of group identity based on intimate family and social links in the private sphere with other Jews.[30]

The pattern of Gentile–Jewish residential interaction was clearly different in Vienna from that in Prague, with the community boundaries less clearly defined in the Austrian capital. In spite of the Jewish concentrations in certain areas of the city, Vienna with its metropolitan character, faster growth, and larger population offered a wider potential range of social contacts and avenues of assimilation than Prague.[31] Significantly, there was not the same degree of residential segregation within individual apartment buildings as could be found in Prague.[32]

This was particularly the case in the more affluent areas of the *Innere Stadt* (Inner City) where prosperous Jews, engaged in wholesale trade and in the liberal professions, tended to congregate. In the Leopoldstadt, the heaviest area of Jewish concentration, there was predictably a greater tendency for Jews to live together, especially in the inner sections of the district. But as Ivar Oxaal and Walter Weitzmann have recently pointed out, even here Jews lived in the midst of a Christian majority. Moreover, housing shortages and the practice of subletting sections of apartments to apprentices and lodgers encouraged a certain degree of Gentile–Jewish living together.[33] Clearly in cosmopolitan Vienna—in spite of the existence of distinctively Jewish neighbourhoods—there was more social interaction between Jews and Gentiles than existed in Prague, let alone in the old Moravian *Gemeinde* or the ghettos of Hungary and Galicia.

However, in this framework, the *Ostjuden* represented something of a special case among the new immigrants to Vienna, once the advent of the railways and the abolition of the *Vormärz* restrictions had made possible their arrival *en masse* in the capital. By 1914 they constituted around a quarter of Viennese Jewry and their presence was magnified by differences in manners, dress, speech, and religious customs. The Josephinian interlude and its sequel had not succeeded in westernizing the *Galizianer* or eroding the ethnic cohesion of the Jewish masses on

[30] Cohen, p. 326. For a critical review of Cohen's book see Hillel J. Kieval, in *Studies in Contemporary Jewry*, ed. Jonathan Frankel (Bloomington, Ind., 1984), i. 424–7. Kieval argues that Cohen ignores the presence of 'ethnicity' before 1848 and subsumes Jewish distinctiveness into the narrow framework of their place in German or Czech public life.

[31] Oxaal and Weitzmann, p. 405.

[32] See the analysis, based on the 1857 census, of Peter Schmidtbauer, 'Zur sozialen Situation der Wiener Juden'.

[33] Oxaal and Weitzmann, pp. 405–11.

the north-eastern fringes of the Empire. Their share in the Jewish population of Vienna was steadily growing after the 1880s as conditions in the Polish province deteriorated.

Between 1857 and 1900 the Jewish population of Galicia had in fact grown from 448,973 to 811,183 (11.1 per cent of the total population).[34] Like the rest of the non-Jewish population, they had suffered their fill from the harvest failures, cholera epidemics, overcrowding, and the pauperization in the cities which increasingly made itself felt from the early 1850s. Of even greater long-term significance was the gradual loss by Galician Jews of their traditional position as mediators between the large Polish landowners (*Schlachta*) and the peasantry—a trend aggravated with the beginning of anti-Jewish economic boycotts and the formation of agricultural co-operatives which openly excluded Jews by the 1890s. Towards the end of that decade, growing Polish middle-class and peasant anti-Semitism, incited by the Catholic priest Father Stojalowski, exploded in the pogroms of 1898 which undermined still further the already precarious condition of Galician Jewry.[35] Thus a combination of factors—the economic backwardness of the region, endemic poverty, malnutrition, population pressures, Polish nationalism, and anti-Semitism—together contributed to driving Galician Jews towards Vienna.[36]

The material resources of this migration were much poorer than those of immigrants from other regions of the Empire and relatively few Galicians were listed among the Vienna *Gemeinde* (IKG) taxpayers. Marsha Rozenblit has, for example, calculated that although 20 per cent of Vienna Jews were probably Galician in origin between 1870 and 1910, only 8 per cent of all IKG taxpayers were from Galicia. The poverty of the last wave of Jewish immigrants (between 1900 and 1910) was particularly striking, with only 4 per cent of new *Gemeinde* taxpayers being Galician.[37]

The Galicians were differentiated from other Jews not only by their

[34] Abraham Korkis, 'Zur Bewegung der jüdischen Bevölkerung in Galizien', in *Jüdische Statistik* (Berlin, 1903), 314; Max Rosenfeld, 'Die jüdische Bevölkerung Galiziens von 1772–1867', *Zeitschrift für Demographie und Statistik der Juden*, 10 (Sept.–Oct. 1914), 140 ff.

[35] Robert S. Wistrich, 'Austrian Social Democracy and the problem of Galician Jewry 1890–1914', *Leo Baeck Yearbook*, 26 (1981), 89–124.

[36] Siegfried Fleischer, 'Enquête über die Lage der jüdischen Bevölkerung Galizien', *Judische Statistik*, 217–20; Rosenfeld, 'Die jüdische Bevölkerung'; Rabinbach, 'The Migration of Galician Jews', 50 ff.

[37] Rozenblit, *Jews of Vienna*, 36–7.

poverty but also by their greater attachment to orthodox religion, establishing either their own decorous synagogues according to the Polish rite or else the more noisy *stieblach* where they could pray in the traditional manner. They did not feel comfortable with the formalism, decorum and restraint of the German Jews and the pomp of the official Wiener Kultusgemeinde. The ultra-orthodox Hasidic Jews, too, though not especially numerous in the Austrian capital before 1914 (their numbers were to increase dramatically during the First World War as a result of the Russian advance into Galicia), organized to protect their interests, opening a branch of the Galician *Machzike Hadath* in Vienna in 1903.

In addition to religious interests, Galician Jews established a whole network of *Landsmannschaften* in Vienna, providing welfare benefits, mutual aid, and social contacts to help the new immigrants. Vienna did not, however, provide a fertile ground for the emergence of a working-class, Yiddish-speaking subculture such as existed in the far-flung Russian and Polish Jewish diasporas at the turn of the century—from Vilna and Minsk to London's East End, the Lower East Side of New York, the Paris *Pletzl*, or Amsterdam. The dominance of the German language and *Kultur* in Vienna and the absence of a Jewish proletariat economically rooted in the clothing industry and the sweatshops seemed to preclude this development.[38] Moreover, there was no Yiddish press or theatre comparable to that of London and New York and no ideologically committed Jewish socialist movement such as already existed in embryonic form in Galicia itself at the turn of the century.[39]

Immigrant Galician Jews did, however, participate more actively than other Viennese Jews in the rise of Zionism, autonomism, and 'diaspora' nationalism in the Habsburg Monarchy during the closing decades of the nineteenth century. This political involvement reflected their strong sense of ethnic identity and separatism which derived from demographic, economic, and cultural factors operating in Galicia itself—a trend that was reinforced by their sense of alienation and exclusion from the German Jewish establishment in Vienna. Galician Jews acutely felt the animosity directed at them not only by the anti-

---

[38] See Jonathan Frankel, *Prophecy and Politics: Socialism, Nationalism and the Russian Jews, 1862–1917* (Cambridge, 1981), 3, for a characterization of this subculture.

[39] See Wistrich, pp. 89–124; also John Bunzl, *Klassenkampf in der Diaspora; Zur Geschichte der jüdischen Arbeiterbewegung* (Vienna, 1975), 119–25.

Semitic parties in Austria but also by the Germanized Jewish élite in the capital.[40]

At the root of this animosity lay the embarrassment of the native-born and the more settled, assimilated Bohemian, Moravian, or Hungarian Jews of the capital at their 'backward' brethren from the East who obstinately insisted on preserving their group particularism. Nothing was more guaranteed to arouse their ire than the sight of a beared, caftan Jew in the streets of Vienna with his 'Yiddish singsong intonation', reminding them of their own not so distant past in the pre-emancipation ghettos.[41] The *Ostjuden* were widely seen to be loud, coarse and dirty, immoral, and culturally backward in the eyes of their more modern Westernized brethren—a symbolic construct that was particularly widespread among German and Austrian Jews by the end of the nineteenth century.[42]

The origins of this split within Jewry date back, as we have seen, to the Enlightenment. In Austria such stereotypes had been rife among the Josephinist bureaucrats who ruled Galicia with an iron hand, openly seeking to stamp out Hasidism in the *Vormärz* period.[43] With the breakdown of traditional Jewish society and self-understanding, such attitudes were increasingly internalized by German-Austrian Jews in a more systematic fashion. The fragmentation of Jewry into 'western' and 'eastern' branches was inevitably accelerated by mod-ernization and the impact of *Haskalah*. Local and regional differences between Jews became more pronounced as a consequence of the uneven socio-economic development and varied stages of cultural assimilation that characterized Jewry in Central and Eastern Europe.

In the case of Austro-Hungarian Jewry this fragmentation and erosion of solidarity had become explicit ever since the Josephinian reforms. Following emancipation and the migration of Jews from the different corners of the Empire to Vienna, the problem became even more acute. The distasteful idea of the 'ghetto' Jew with its associated

---

[40] Rozenblit, *Jews of Vienna*, 152.

[41] See George Clare, *Last Waltz in Vienna: The Destruction of a Family, 1842–1942* (London, 1982), 31, for an entertaining and perceptive personal account.

[42] See Steven E. Aschheim, *Brothers and Strangers: The East European Jew in German and German Jewish Consciousness, 1800–1923* (Madison, Wis., 1982), for a detailed and illuminating analysis of the ramifications of the cultural antithesis.

[43] Wolfgang Häusler, *Das galizische Judentum in der Habsburgermonarchie: Im Lichte der zeitgenössischen Publizistik und Reiseliteratur von 1772–1848* (Vienna, 1979), provides some revealing documentation on the prejudices of enlightened Austrian bureaucrats confronted with the 'alien' world of Galician Jewry at this time.

images of isolation, compulsion, narrowness, obscurantism, and an ethos of mutual distrust and antagonism had come home to roost.[44] It was physically embodied, so to speak, in the Galician Jewish immigrants. For the nineteenth-century liberal mind (Jewish or Gentile), the *Ostjude* was little more than a medieval remnant who symbolized 'the distinction between progress and reaction, Enlightenment and superstition, even beauty and ugliness'.[45]

All the values which Viennese (and other German) Jews cherished —beginning with the key concept of *Bildung* which radiated an aesthetic and ethical ideal of the self-cultivated personality emphasizing purity of expression, manners, refinement—seemed to find their polar antithesis in the *Unbildung* of the East European Jews.[46] In Vienna the encounter between these two worlds tended to be more direct, both physically and intellectually, since geographical proximity and common citizenship brought them together in one melting pot. In the Habsburg capital, the caftan Jew, with his Talmud and sidelocks, was no 'foreigner' who could be easily denied his equal rights as an Austrian citizen and loyal subject of the emperor in a constitutional State, a fact of which the anti-Semites were only too aware. Moreover, the Germanized Jews of Austria, however much they might secretly blame the 'Polish' Jews for impeding the own assimilation and exacerbating anti-Semitism, could not ultimately renounce responsibility for their co-religionists. Traditional forms of mutual aid and a sense of responsibility for the fate of their less fortunate brethren would have somehow to be reconciled with the fundamental assumption of the emancipation—that Jewish *national* solidarity was a thing of the past.[47] The Kultusgemeinde of Vienna, for instance, tried to achieve this accommodation in its own way (not always successfully) through the framework of charitable institutions, philanthropic organizations like the Wiener Israelitische Allianz, and by encouraging the Baron Hirsch network of schools in Galicia designed to bring Western Enlightenment to the superstitious Jewish masses. This charitable work was not without its magnanimous aspects but it scarcely went to the roots of the problem or was able to provide a cure for the social and economic ills afflicting Eastern Jewry.

[44] Steven E. Aschheim, 'The East European Jew and German Jewish Identity', *Studies in Contemporary History* (1984), 3–22.   [45] Ibid. 5.
[46] George L. Mosse, *German Jews beyond Judaism* (Hebrew Union College, 1985), rightly stresses the tremendous impact of the German Enlightenment ideal of *Bildung* on the post-emancipatory Jewish identity.
[47] Aschheim, 'East European Jew', 8–9.

No liberal writer reflected the post-emancipation dilemmas created by the cultural gulf that had opened up between the Jewries of the Empire better than Karl-Emil Franzos (1848–1904). The extraordinary popularity of this Austrian novelist and journalist born in Czortkow (on the Russo-Galician border), who regularly contributed his tales and sketches on East European Jewry to Vienna's greatest daily paper, the *Neue Freie Presse*, was a testament to the sensitive nerve he had touched. Those tales entitled *Aus Halb-Asien* (Out of half-Asia), published in two volumes in 1876, ostensibly described the border regions of the Austro-Hungarian Empire (Galicia, Bukovina, Romania, western Russia). In fact they were 'not merely a geographical designation but a condition of the mind', a metaphor for Europe as the realm of light and love, in opposition to its polar opposite, Asia, a jungle of darkness, barbarism, and violent hatreds.[48] The *Ostjuden* were 'half-Asian' precisely because they lived within these social and cultural boundaries. They were an unfortunate *product* of this unredeemed world of religious fanaticism, national oppression, superstition, and backwardness.[49] It was in this special sense that Franzos coined his famous formula 'Every country gets the Jews it deserves'.

Though often describing East European Jewry with its strange customs and superstitions in compassionate terms, notably in such tales as *Die Juden von Barnow* (1877) or *Der Pojaz* (posthumously published in 1905), Franzos was uncompromising in his call for *Bildung*. The Jews of *Halb-Asien* would have to be remoulded in the image of German liberal humanism, according to the cultural standards of a *Deutschtum* whose moral superiority was self-evident and incontestable. It was the duty of all Western Jews in the name of the 'community of faith' (*Glaubensgenossenschaft*)—of the 'denationalized' Judaism of the emancipation—to carry out this sacred cultural mission.[50]

Franzos was careful to differentiate sharply between Germanization of the East which he rejected ('ein undeutsches Wort für ein undeutsches Thun') and the extension of German culture—above all productive, physical labour, selflessness, and *Gründlichkeit*—to the

---

[48] See Mark H. Gelber, 'Ethnic Pluralism and Germanization in the Works of Karl-Emil Franzos (1848–1904)', *The German Quarterly*, 56, no. 3 (May 1983), 376–85.

[49] Aschheim, 'East European Jew', 9–10.

[50] Karl-Emil Franzos, 'Die Kolonisationsfrage', *Allgemeine Zeitung des Judentums*, 55 (Nov. 1891).

backward and indolent Slavic nationalities of the East. In this context he could only regard Yiddish, the language of the *Ostjuden*, as a corrupt and vulgar jargon that obstructed the assimilation[51] which in his view was the only long-term solution to the socio-economic misery of Eastern Jewry. Not surprisingly, Franzos's didactic stories mercilessly attacked traditional Galician Jewish notions of marriage, ridiculing irrational superstitions and customs in the classic Enlightenment fashion. Writing in German for a middle-class Western audience, this Austrian novelist proposed an image of the *Ostjuden* which exactly mirrored and corresponded to its liberal expectations.[52]

The somewhat patronizing vision embodied by Franzos and enthusiastically accepted by his readers from the Jewish *Bildungsbürgertum* of Vienna, ignored for the most part the strengths of Galician Jewish culture, especially its enduring retention of ethnic and religious pride.[53] The sense of separateness which extended into private life (Galician Jews tended to choose one another as marriage partners and not to mix socially with Gentiles) protected them against the erosion of identity that was the inevitable concomitant of assimilation.

Even as they began to move more frequently into clerical, sales, and managerial positions in Vienna at the turn of the century—thereby coming into greater contact with Viennese Gentiles—Galician Jews retained their sense of belonging to a distinct group. Moreover, coming as they often did from lower-class backgrounds, they attended *Gymnasien* in Vienna much more rarely than Jews from other immigrant backgrounds. Thus the powerful factor of early socialization into German culture through the élite school-system of Vienna played a less decisive role in shaping their outlook.[54] Not surprisingly, too, very few Galician Jews or Jewesses converted to Christianity. Here again they represented the polar opposite of Viennese-born Jews.[55] In the light of this fact the presence of a large Galician Jewish component in Vienna must be considered to have acted as a counterweight to baptismal attrition which claimed over 9,000 Viennese Jews between 1868 and 1903.[56]

The great migration of Austro-Hungarian Jewry to the *Weltstadt* after 1848 was not therefore a uniform story of assimilation to Gentile

---

[51] *Aus Halb-Asien*, i (Berlin, 1901), 183.
[52] Gelber, pp. 383–4.   [53] See Rozenblit, *Jews of Vienna*, 44.
[54] Ibid. 116.   [55] Ibid. 140–1.
[56] For statistics on conversion from Judaism in Vienna between 1868 and 1903, see Jacob Thon, 'Taufbewegung der Juden in Österreich', *Zeitschrift für Demographie und Statistik der Juden*, 3 (May 1908).

culture or of linear adaptation to the ethos of a modern secular society. Environmental and cultural pressures did indeed lead to a growing integration of the Jews into the Viennese economy and in the case of many immigrant Jews to a high level of acculturation and social integration with Gentiles.[57] But 'structural assimilation' in the sense of a group fusing with the majority (and the consequent disappearance of its ethnic character and culture) did not take place in Vienna any more than it did in other provincial capitals with large Jewish populations such as Budapest, Prague, Lemberg, Cracow, or Czernowitz (Chernovtsy).[58] Jews clearly began to behave, dress, and speak like other Viennese but they still retained their own modes of social integration, their own network of Jewish organizations, and—especially among Galician Jews—a strong sense of ethnic identity.[59]

It is undoubtedly true that past urban experience, literacy, and business skills enabled Jews to adapt more quickly than many Gentiles to the challenges of urban life. Their well-documented social mobility, thirst for education, and drive to make successful careers did not, however, mean that they wished to or could simply dissolve as individuals into the anonymity of the big city.[60] Urbanization in Vienna did nevertheless exercise a significant impact on its new Jewish population. In the big city there were far greater social, economic, and educational opportunities.[61] Jews were no longer bound by the restrictions of their traditional life-style in the small towns and *shtetlach* of the provinces. They began to enter new occupations, became arbiters of taste in the arts and sciences, transformed the face of

[57] Oxaal and Weitzmann, pp. 428–32.

[58] For relevant discussions of 'structural assimilation', see the work by Milton Gordon, *Assimilation in American Life: The Role of Race, Religion and National Origins* (New York, 1981); also the remarks by Rozenblit, *Jews of Vienna*, 2–12; Cohen, 'Jews in German Society', 306–22; George Barany, '"Magyar Jew or Jewish Magyar?" Reflections on the Question of Assimilation', in Bela Vago and George L. Mosse (eds.), *Jews and Non-Jews in Eastern Europe, 1918–1945* (Jerusalem, 1974), 51–98; Victor Karady and István Kemény, 'Les Juifs dans la structure des classes en Hongrie: essai sur les antécédents historiques des crises d'antisémitisme du XX. siècle', *Actes de la recherche en sciences sociales*, 22 (June 1978), 25–59.

[59] Robert S. Wistrich, 'Remaining outsiders', *Times Literary Supplement*, 28 June 1985.

[60] Oxaal and Weitzmann seem to me slightly to overstate the degree of assimilation of the *mass* of Viennese Jews into the life of the capital.

[61] See the fine chapter in Rozenblit, *Jews of Vienna*, 99–126, on education, mobility, and assimilation. By way of comparison see Victor Karady, 'Jewish Enrollment Patterns in Classical Secondary Education in Old Regime and Inter-War Hungary', *Studies in Contemporary Jewry*, i. 225–52.

Viennese and Austrian journalism, actively participated in politics.[62]

Coming as they did from heterogeneous Jewish societies in the provinces, at different levels of development and adaptation to modernity, Jews did not experience Vienna uniformly. Nor, being a distinct group who often migrated to the capital for reasons quite different from those of Gentiles, did they react to the metropolitan environment in the same way.[63] Unlike Gentile immigrants, they did not come predominantly from Bohemia, Moravia, or Lower Austria but rather from Hungary and Galicia; they were not peasants unfamiliar with city life, nor did they come as single individuals or as workers in transit, looking primarily for better wages. They came mainly in families hoping to escape the poverty, provincial stagnation, and anti-Semitism of their native regions. Typically, they moved into commercial or white-collar occupations, the liberal professions and managerial positions, rather than working in industry.[64] For second-generation Jews, the sons of small traders and merchants, Vienna offered the enticing prospect of more wealth, security, and social status than they had ever enjoyed before. However, the Austrian capital attracted Jews not only as a Mecca of financial opportunity and personal freedom but also as the major cosmopolitan and German-speaking city in the Empire; moreover, it was the supranational centre of Habsburg power and of its major institutions, which in the liberal era came to be seen as more benevolent toward Jews than local nationalisms. Thus there was also a cultural and ideological as well as an economic dimension to the prestige and attraction of Vienna in the eyes of Austro-Hungarian Jewry.

The spectacular rise of Viennese Jewry in social status and prestige in the post-1848 era was an integral part of the *emancipatory* process which had opened up a window of opportunity and social mobility for

[62] Josef Fraenkel (ed.), *The Jews of Austria: Essays on their Life, History and Destruction* (London, 1967).

[63] See Rozenblit, *Jews of Vienna*, 18–19.

[64] Ibid. 49. Rozenblit argues that the 'restructuring of the professional profile of Viennese Jews did not lead to growing similarity between Jewish and non-Jewish occupational distribution. On the contrary, the statistics show that Jews continued to practise occupations which made them distinct from the society in which they lived'. In particular, she singles out the high percentage of Jewish clerks, managers, and salesmen as a 'new typically Jewish pattern of occupational preference'. This is probably overstated. For a contrary view, see Oxaal and Weitzmann, pp. 428 ff. They, too, point however to a major occupational discrepancy between Jews and Catholics in Vienna—namely 'that the vast majority of Jewish men were either salaried or self-employed, while to have been a Catholic male in Vienna would usually have meant being an *Arbeiter* in some capacity'.

enterprising Jewish immigrants, encouraging their rapid embourgeoisement. It was significant, for instance, that very few Jews lived in the proletarian areas of the city such as Ottakring (XVI), Hernals (XVII), or Favoriten (X), and only a small percentage of the most wealthy were to be found in the villa districts of Döbling (XIX), Währing (XVIII), or Hietzing (XIII)

TABLE 2.3 Jewish Population of Vienna 1869–1910

District	Jewish Population			% of Total Population		
	1869	1880	1910	1869	1880	1910
I Inner City	9,256	12,452	10,807	14.4	17.8	20.3
II Leopoldstadt	19,657	35,061	59,722	23.2	34.6	33.9
IX Alsergrund	1,943	6,872	21,615	3.2	10.1	20.5
XX Brigittenau*	—	—	14,144	—	—	14.0

* Brigittenau was part of the Leopoldstadt (II) until 1900.

Sources: Statisches Jahrbuch der Stadt Wien für das Jahr 1910 (Vienna, 1912), 45; Leo Goldhammer, *Die Juden Wiens: Eine statistische Studie* (Vienna, 1927), 10; Rabinbach, 'Migration of Galician Jews', Table XII. For the percentage of all Viennese Jews living in each district, Rozenblit, *Jews of Vienna*, 76.

As Table 2.3 indicates, the Jews of Vienna lived primarily in three districts; the Inner City (a centre of government, banking, and commerce), the Leopoldstadt (the oldest Jewish area of settlement with a mixed class composition), and Alsergrund, which was the district of middle-class, professional people. In 1880 these three districts accounted for 75 per cent of all Viennese Jews though by 1900 this figure had dropped to 55%.[65] By 1910 the Jewish population in the middle-class business and shopping districts of Josefstadt, Neubau, and Mariahilf had grown significantly, accounting for a greater dispersal of Viennese Jewry.[66] Thus in 1910 there were six districts of Vienna where Jews represented more than 10 per cent of the population—Leopoldstadt (34 per cent), Alsergrund (20 per cent), the Inner City (20 per cent), Brigittenau (14 per cent), Mariahilf (13 per cent), and Neubau (11 per cent).[67]

[65] Rozenblit, *Jews of Vienna*, 76.
[66] Goldhammer, p. 10.   [67] Ibid.

The important factor in this distribution was that Viennese Jews of all social classes tended to cluster in certain specific areas, and therefore to form a definable ethnic enclave, despite the general trend to acculturation.[68] In Leopoldstadt, the 'Mazzesinsel', where orthodox Galician Jews were particularly visible because of their distinctive dress and appearance, the immigrant ghetto syndrome was evident. But even in middle-class Alsergrund, the home of Freud, Victor Adler, Herzl, and many other intellectual luminaries in Vienna, there was something of a distinctively 'Jewish' *bürgerlich* character. The Jewish communal élite, especially the wealthiest *Gemeinde* members, tended for their part to cluster in the Inner City as did some of the more successful Jewish doctors, lawyers, and other professional people. On the other hand, they could also be found in the Leopoldstadt, living in different sections of the same district inhabited by poor Jews.[69]

This residential pattern appears to support Marsha Rozenblit's assertion that in pre-1914 Vienna, though Jews may have divided along class lines within Jewish areas, 'Jewishness and not class was the major criterion by which Jews selected a neighbourhood'.[70] In residential terms there was, for example, no conspicuous segregation between German and East European Jews such as existed in other European and American cities during the same period, even though comparable social, cultural, and political tensions were similarly present.[71] When, as happened elsewhere in European cities, Viennese Jews became more wealthy or successful and moved out of their old areas of residence, they did not simply disperse or assimilate into the general mainstream but tended to form new Jewish clusters within the middle-class districts of the city. In other words, there were no rigidly definable 'uptown' and 'downtown' Jews in Vienna, divided though Jews were by social class, cultural background, and place of origin.

In the field of education, where Jewish aspirations for upward social mobility were especially striking, the differences between Jews and Gentiles were in fact more evident than those between different classes of Jews. Nearly one-third of all Gymnasium students in Vienna

    [68] Rozenblit, *Jews of Vienna*, 75.
    [69] Mayer, *Ein jüdischer Kaufmann*, 463.   [70] Rozenblit, *Jews of Vienna*, 94.
    [71] For comparative purposes see the fine article by David Weinberg, ' "Heureux comme Dieu en France": East European Jewish Immigrants in Paris, 1881–1914', *Studies in Contemporary Jewry*, i. 26–54; Michael R. Marrus, *The Politics of Assimilation* (Oxford, 1971); William J. Fishman, *East End Jewish Radicals 1875–1914* (London, 1975); and Irving Howe, *The Immigrant Jews of New York 1881 to the Present* (London and Boston, 1976).

were Jews and approximately one-fifth of all students in the Realschulen.[72] The determination with which Viennese Jewish middle-class parents ensured an élite education for their children was unique, reflecting both traditional Jewish respect for learning and their post-emancipatory striving for successful acculturation and professional mobility. In the *Innere Stadt*, two-fifths of all Gymnasium students were Jews, in the Alsergrund the proportion was two-thirds, and in Leopoldstadt it reached three-quarters.[73]

Though the poorer new immigrants from Galicia had greater financial problems in sending their children to the élite schools, they did so significantly more often than Viennese Gentiles in a comparable social position. The class barriers in Gentile Austrian society were perpetuated within the educational system in a way that did not apply to the Jewish population, where a certain proportion among the sons of artisans, shopkeepers, or businessmen could still be expected to attend Gymnasium. Similarly in the Austrian universities, but above all at Vienna, Jews used the higher educational system as an avenue of social mobility far more effectively than non-Jews.[74] Statistics show that between 1800 and 1890 Jews averaged exactly one-third of all students at the University of Vienna though by 1900 this figure had dropped to 24 per cent.[75] In the technical high schools of Vienna there was a comparable trend, with Jews representing 30 per cent of the student body in the early 1880s and 27 per cent around the turn of the century.[76] At the University of Vienna the medicine and law faculties were generally the most popular choices of Jewish students. In the peak year of 1885, Jews constituted 41.4 per cent of the medical students though by the 1900s they averaged only about one-quarter of those studying medicine.[77] The impact of the anti-Semitic movement and agitation in *fin de siècle* Vienna was probably one of the main causes for this relative decline.

Since the 1880s the University of Vienna had turned into a veritable hotbed of nationalist and anti-Semitic hostility, and this agitation centred on the Pan-German *Burschenschaften* (student fraternities) which became increasingly violent towards the turn of the century.[78] The racist campaign left an indelible mark on Jewish students in

---

[72] Detailed tables in Rozenblit, *Jews of Vienna*, ch. 5.   [73] Ibid. 102–3.
[74] Thon, *Die Juden in Österreich* (Berlin, 1908), 100–4.
[75] Ibid. 104.   [76] Ibid.   [77] Ibid. 100.
[78] Marsha L. Rozenblit, 'The Assertion of Identity. Jewish Student Nationalism at the University of Vienna before the First World War', *Leo Baeck Yearbook*, 27 (1982), 181–3.

Vienna, who after 1900 came increasingly to identify *en masse* with the Zionist ideology of Jewish nationalism. Significantly, students from Galicia and Bukovina were in the forefront of this militant response (about a quarter of all Jewish university students at Vienna originated from Galicia) though it extended to and embraced, to a somewhat lesser degree, even Viennese-born and Bohemian Jewish students.[79] Sigmund Freud's son Martin, who joined the Zionist student corporation, Kadimah, vividly recalled the atmosphere at the University of Vienna at the turn of the century. He described how German nationalist students would break into lecture-halls, 'shouting "*Juden hinaus*", and kept it up until the Jews, and the very few Jewesses, had gathered up their books and filed out in despondency'.[80] The advent of Zionism, however, provided the Jewish students with a new will to resist submission to insults and intimidation. The resistance was shown, initially at least, 'by boys from Galicia and Bukovina, the despised and spurned "Polish Jews" '.[81]

Fifty years after the great migration to the *Kaiserstadt* had begun, some of the golden lining on the dreams of assimilation had clearly faded, especially for the younger generation of Jews. Though Vienna had emerged as the largest Jewish city in the Austrian half of the Empire and as a dynamic, creative centre of Jewish life, the success story had already been somewhat tarnished by the strength of political anti-Semitism in the city since the 1880s. The mass exodus to Vienna had opened up a new world of secular modernity and unprecedented opportunities to thousands of Jews but in its wake it also brought new problems of identity and the ominous rise of a raucous mass politics, one of whose primary vehicles was Judaeophobia.[82]

The character of the political struggles in *fin de siècle* Vienna was, then, to be inextricably intertwined with the far-reaching demographic shift that resulted from the great nineteenth-century trek of the Jews to the Habsburg capital. Their concentration, urbanization, and spectacular ascent within its confines changed the face of the city and the nature of

[79] Martin Freud, 'Who was Freud?', in Fraenkel (ed.), *The Jews of Austria*, 206–7.
[80] Ibid. 207.
[81] On Viennese anti-Semitism, see Dirk van Arkel, 'Antisemitism in Austria' (Univ. of Leiden, Ph.D. diss. 1966); Pulzer, *Rise of Political Antisemitism*; Andrew G. Whiteside, *The Socialism of Fools: Georg Ritter von Schoenerer and Austrian Pan-Germanism* (Berkeley and Los Angeles 1975); and John W. Boyer, *Political Radicalism in Late Imperial Vienna: Origins of the Christian Social Movement, 1848–1897* (Chicago and London, 1981).
[82] See Carl E. Schorske, 'Politics in a New Key: An Austrian Triptych', *Journal of Modern History*, 39 (1967), 343–86.

the Jewish community as well as its social interaction with the Gentile population. The history of the Viennese Jews in the era of emancipation and assimilation could no longer be detached from that of the Empire as a whole. Nor was government policy a decisive factor to the same degree as in the pre-1848 era when the fate of the Jews was largely decided by the whims of the Emperor and his entourage of officials and advisers. Complex social, economic, and political processes were now at work which would more materially shape the dialectic of Jewish–Gentile relations from below.

The Jewish community, too, was exposed in unprecedented ways to the vicissitudes of modernization, secularization, and social change. Caught between the vice of tradition and modernity, orthodoxy and reform, liberalism and nationalism, assimilation and anti-Semitism, Viennese Jews had to develop new responses and ideologies to meet the challenge. The central leadership of wealthy notables and rabbis had to confront the dilemmas of representing a heterogeneous community of immigrants from widely different backgrounds who no longer defined themselves in traditional terms.

The Jewish intelligentsia, too, had to face the agonizing possibility that their claim to be Germans would not be accepted by growing numbers of their Austrian fellow-citizens. The rise of Zionism raised a no less troubling possibility—that of a new mass migration of the Jews to their own State in order to resolve the ubiquitous 'Jewish question'. Viennese Jewry found itself confronted with a bewildering multitude of cross-currents and rival ideologies even before it had fully crystallized its own group character and identity.

None the less, in spite of these tensions and conflicts, late nineteenth-century Vienna continued to attract Jews, to provide a fertile ground for their talents and for their hope of successful integration as respected and cultured members of society. Within the whirlpool of contradictory tendencies and hostile currents, elements of accommodation and compromise were to be found which would permit the maintenance of a unique and vibrant Jewish community through the rest of the century.

3

Philanthropy, Politics, and the Ostjuden

The fault lies in Hassidism! This Jewish Jesuitism, which for more than a century has ruled Polish Jewry, is responsible for the darkness in which it lives, for its superstition, fanaticism, contempt and loathing for civilisation . . .

Adolf Jellinek (1889)

We feel Jewish only through our faith, not our nationality: we sacrifice our money, our energy to save our unfortunate brothers in faith . . .

Karl-Emil Franzos (1891)

You are breeding *schnorrers*. It is symptomatic of the situation that no other people shows so high an incidence of philanthropy and so much beggary as the Jews. Plainly there must be a close connection between these two phenomena.

Theodor Herzl to Baron Maurice de Hirsch (1895)

I regard the Rothschilds, judging from the local head of the family, as a limited, and snobbish family, bent on plunder, against whom I want to have free hands in the interests of the movement.

Theodor Herzl to Max Nordau (20 June 1896)

Men who have turned grey in honourable disinterested labour on behalf of the Jewish people . . . were suddenly accused of corruption and graft before the whole world. They [the Zionists] in incredible emulation of anti-Semitic paradigms, have adopted as their own these tactics of political struggle.

Österreichische Wochenschrift (1902)

Viennese Jewry during the second half of the nineteenth century was distinguished by the diversity of its regional and cultural background. The mass migration from the more Germanized areas of Bohemia and Moravia, from Hungary and the Eastern provinces (especially Galicia), not only altered the social structure of the Jewish community but generated new tensions between established Viennese Jews and the newcomers as well as between Jews and Gentiles. These tensions were indeed a microcosm of the wider social gulf within Austrian Jewry as a whole and a reflection of the varied tempo of acculturation in different parts of the Monarchy. Even after the emancipation, the great mass of Austrian Jews (nearly 70 per cent) were still concentrated in the economically backward, densely overcrowded, and unhygienic conditions of Polish Galicia—their traditional religious observance, folk customs, Yiddish language, and socio-economic structure resembled that of Romanian and Russian Jewry; while the Jews of western Austria (Bohemia, Moravia, and Lower Austria) in their social character remained much closer to German than to East European Jewry.[1] Hungarian Jewry, itself split to some extent along a similar east–west axis, provided something of an intermediate case in terms of its immigration to Vienna.

As a result of these contrasts, by the end of the nineteenth century the Jewish population of the Habsburg capital embraced social and cultural characteristics of both western and eastern Jewries within the context of one community.[2] At the apex of the social pyramid stood the wealthy, sophisticated Jewish banking clans, industrialists, and merchants who dominated the community institutions. After them came the increasingly acculturated, Germanophile bourgeoisie well-represented in commerce, manufacturing, and the liberal professions. In retailing areas like the ready-made clothing industry, furniture production, leather goods, food processing, and department stores, the Jewish bourgeoisie came to play a crucial role in the city's economy.[3] In journalism, the theatre, the opera, and the concert-hall, their presence was no less striking. The most powerful organs of liberal middle-class opinion in the Monarchy—above all the *Neue Freie Presse*—were owned, edited, and largely written by Viennese Jews.[4] In law and medicine, Jewish students formed sizeable proportions of graduates

[1] Jacob Thon, *Die Juden in Österreich* (Berlin, 1908), 4.
[2] Ibid. 4: 'Nur dürfte Wien, dessen jüdische Bevölkerung hauptsächlich durch Zuwanderung in einigen Jahrzehnten stark angewachsen ist und das eine zahlreiche jüdische Proletarierklasse besitzt, eine etwas abgesonderte, zwischen diesen beiden Ländergruppen vermittelnde Stellung einnehmen.'
[3] Max Grunwald, *Vienna* (Philadelphia, 1936), 393–4.
[4] Henry Wickham Steed, *The Habsburg Monarchy* (London, 1913), 187 ff.; also Adam Wandruszka, *Geschichte einer Zeitung: Das Schicksal der 'Presse' und der 'Neuen Freien Presse' von 1848 zur Zweiten Republik* (Vienna, 1958), 101–6.

from the University of Vienna and in 1889 as many as 394 out of the capital's 681 practising lawyers were reputed to be Jews.[5]

On the other hand, the petty-bourgeois and semi-proletarian immigrants from Galicia and Bukovina with their Yiddish dialect, their Talmudic heritage, and their traditional Jewish culture provided a pointed contrast to the Germanized middle-class Jews of Vienna. Many of them eked out a meagre living as pedlars, old-clothes-dealers, and petty tradesmen. In the Leopoldstadt and Brigittenau district, not a few of these *Ostjuden* belonged to the wage-earning class, though significantly more Jews in industry, trade, and the professions were independent than their Gentile counterparts.[6]

The Galician immigration, especially after 1870, left its mark on Gentiles as well as established Viennese Jews—popular anti-Semitism frequently reflecting fears that the poor Galician peddlar-Jew would dislodge local shopkeepers, small tradesmen, and artisans from their already tenuous economic positions. At another level, the famous Viennese surgeon Theodor Billroth was not above arguing in 1876 that medical studies in Vienna were being corrupted by an influx of 'proletarian Jews' from Galicia and Hungary 'who are absolutely without resources and have conceived the insane notion that they can earn money in Vienna (by teaching, through odd jobs at the Bourse, peddling watches or taking up employment as post office or telegraph clerks . . .) and simultaneously study medicine'.[7] Between 1857 and 1885, it should be noted, the proportion of Jewish students enrolled in the Faculty of Medicine had risen from 22.7 to 41.4 per cent and most of this increase was indeed due to the Hungarian and Galician immigration.[8]

It is not surprising then that the anti-Semitic movement in Vienna should have had its strongholds among those social groups like university students, petty traders, and artisans who felt most threatened by 'Jewish' competition and were most likely to come into direct contact with the Eastern Jews. The Österreichische Reformverein, founded in 1880, which advocated the protection of local artisans and small businessmen, specifically singled out the problems posed by the

---

[5] Hans Tietze, *Die Juden Wiens* (Vienna and Leipzig, 1933), 212; also H. Gold, *Geschichte der Juden in Wien* (Tel Aviv, 1966), 36.

[6] Leo Goldhammer, *Die Juden Wiens: eine statistische Studie* (Vienna, 1927), 56.

[7] Theodor Billroth, *Über das Lehren und Lernen der medizinischen Wissenschaften an den Universitäten der deutschen Nation* (Vienna, 1876), 148.

[8] Jacob Thon, 'Anteil der Juden am Hochschulen in Oesterreich seit dem Jahre 1851', *Zeitschrift für Demographie und Statistik der Juden*, 3, no. 3 (Mar. 1907), 34.

Galician (and Hungarian) Jewish pedlars. At their first mass meeting in the Dreher Beerhall in November 1880, the clock-maker Joseph Buschenhagen exclaimed: 'They, the pedlars, damage the artisans and not one of them has ever learned a trade.'[9] The negative stereotype of Polish Jewish pedlars was to be effectively manipulated in later years by the Christian-Social movement and the German nationalist anti-Semites, along with the spectre of a mass immigration of poor Hungarian and above all Russian Jews flooding Austria from across its East Galician border.

In Vienna itself, the Galician Jews who settled in the overcrowded poor districts along the Danube canal did to a certain extent compete with the lower middle-class artisans. Mostly engaged in petty trades as tailors, shoemakers, jewellers, turners, upholsterers, locksmiths, bookbinders, and carpenters, they were the obvious target for popular xenophobia.[10] Easily identifiable in their East European garb, sidelocks, and caftans, frequenting their own synagogues, they were clearly differentiated from the German Jews. N. H. Tur-Sinai recalled that 'every Rosh Hashana, you could see thousands of them in the *tashlich* procession. In other parts of the city you could see a different type of Jew and the farther one went from those centres of Jewish mass settlement, the less genuine a Jewry did one find. Jews were no longer recognisable as such.'[11]

The Galician Jews who lived in the Leopoldstadt and Brigittenau districts confronted the worst housing conditions in the city, with as many as six Jews to each room in these areas.[12] They helped swell the numbers of Viennese Jews involved in some form of commerce to 43 per cent as against 28 per cent of the Catholic population.[13] Much of this commerce was in fact in small-scale merchandise, concentrated in textiles in the garment trade. On the other hand, in industry and workshops the ratio between Gentiles and Jews was almost inverted. Fifty per cent of Viennese Gentiles were engaged in factory or manual labour of some type as against 28 per cent of Jews, who were involved by and large in domestic industry.[14] The Jewish semi-proletarian element in Vienna remained as much outside the primary processes of

[9] E. Pichl, *Georg von Schoenerer und die Entwicklung des Alldeutschtums in der Ostmark* (Oldenburg, 1938), ii. 25.

[10] See Ernst Waldinger, 'Darstellung einer jüdischen Jugend in der Wiener Vorstadt, in Josef Fraenkel (ed.), *The Jews of Austria: Essays on their Life, History and Destruction* (London, 1967), 259–81; also Franz Borkenau, *Austria and After* (London, 1938), 107.

[11] N. H. Tur-Sinai, 'Viennese Jewry', in Fraenkel (ed.), *Jews of Austria*, 313.

[12] Goldhammer, p. 64.   [13] Ibid. 53–4.   [14] Ibid.

production as it had been in Galicia.[15] Hence their economic function appeared rather marginal to the Viennese economy as a whole.

The overall stastistics for the employment of Catholic and Jewish males in Vienna show that three-quarters of the non-Jewish males in the workforce, engaged in trade and industry, were in fact *Arbeiter*; only 9 per cent were salaried and 14 per cent were self-employed. On the other hand, among the Jews almost exactly one-third of the Jewish males were to be found as 'either self-employed, or salaried or as a worker'.[16] To what extent, however, was the Jewish preference for self-employment, petty commerce, or small-scale artisan employment a 'deviant' phenomenon?[17] Did the successful Jewish avoidance of 'proletarianization' really represent an anomaly in the broader Viennese context of slow modernization, the survival of significant numbers of small retail shops and workshops, and the modest scale of industrial organization? Oxaal and Weitzmann, looking at this problem in the macro-context of both the Viennese and the Austrian social structure, have concluded that 'the everyday Jew did play a peculiarly fitting and integral role . . . in the economic life of his beloved [*sic*] Wien';[18] in spite of Jewish 'over-representation' in some major economic sectors, occupational differences between Jews and Gentiles were perhaps less significant than has been widely assumed.

This view seems 'objectively' persuasive though it does not dispose of the fact that both anti-Semites and many Jews themselves thought otherwise at the time. The conviction was widespread in the late nineteenth century that Viennese Jewry was excessively represented in areas like banking, entrepreneurial roles, department stores, the liberal professions, and cultural life; similarly, anti-Semites and to some extent even Jews responded negatively to what they perceived as a changing economic profile of the Jewish community at the end of the century. Peter Pulzer summed up this shift over twenty years ago when he hypothesized: '. . . as the number of Galician Jews increased in Vienna the Jewish *haute bourgeoisie* became less and less representative of Viennese Jewry as a whole, while the pedlar, the old-clothes dealers,

---

[15] Goldhammer, pp. 53–4. For the occupational structure of Jews and Gentiles in Galicia itself, see Samuel Josephs, *Jewish Immigration to the United States from 1881 to 1910* (New York, 1969), 36 ff.

[16] See Table IX in Ivar Oxaal and Walter R. Weitzmann, 'The Jews of Pre-1914 Vienna: An Exploration of Basic Sociological Dimensions', *Leo Baeck Yearbook*, 30 (1985), 425, based on the *Berufsstatistik nach den Ergebnissen der Volkszählung vom 31. Dezember 1910*, NS 3, no. 1, *Österreichisch Statistik* (Vienna, 1916), 132.

[17] Oxaal and Weitzmann, p. 428.   [18] Ibid. 432.

and the *Lumpenproletarier,* scraping an irregular existence on the periphery of the economic system became typical.'[19]

Recent research has reminded us of one of the more sordid aspects of this social marginality—the part played by Galician Jews in commercial prostitution—which proved a real windfall for German and Austrian anti-Semites.[20] The involvement of Jewish men and women in Galicia and Bukovina in brothel-keeping and procuring led to a great trial in Lemberg during the winter of 1892. The anti-Semitic deputy Schlesinger introduced a parliamentary question on 11 November 1892, signed by fourteen of his Christian-Social colleagues, calling for effective measures against 'the shameful outrages of the Jewish people in Austria'.[21] The ensuing scandal led to a disciplining of the anti-Semitic deputy but even the socialist *Arbeiterzeitung* was prompted to comment unfavourably on the excessive proportion of crooks, swindlers, smugglers, and 'white-slave merchants' among Galician Jews: 'It happens to be true that the exploiters in Galicia and many other places are Jewish, and that it is they who come up with the sort of cunning and deviousness which the Germans or Slavs lack.'[22] Several years later, writing in *Die Welt* (24 June 1898) following the outbreak of pogroms in Western Galicia, Theodor Herzl attributed this phenomenon to the 'almost subhuman conditions' under which Galician Jews lived. Observing that 'in recent years large numbers of Galician Jewesses have become prostitutes', he added:

They have come to all parts of the world as merchandise in the most horrible human trade. If one considers the traditional purity of Jewish family life, such a fact makes one heartsick. And those who are thus weakened in their moral power of resistance are exposed not only to the most severe hardships but also to persecution and abuse from the mob.

The connection between Galician Jews and prostitution had indeed become notorious in Vienna by the time Herzl wrote these lines and

[19] P. G. J. Pulzer, *The Rise of Political Antisemitism in Germany and Austria* (New York and London, 1964), 14.
[20] Edward Bristow, 'The German-Jewish Fight against White Slavery', *Leo Baeck Yearbook*, 28 (1983), 301–28; also Bristow, *Prostitution and Prejudice* (Oxford, 1982). For an eyewitness account see Bertha Pappenheim and Sara Rabinowitsch, *Zur Lage der jüdischen Bevölkerung in Galizien* (Frankfurt, 1904), 47 ff.
[21] *Stenograpisches Protokoll über die Sitzungen des Hauses der Abgeordneten des österreichischen Reichsrats in den Jahren 1892 und 1893*, 9 Session, Vol. 7 (Vienna, 1893), 11 Nov. 1892, pp. 7638 ff.; also *Neue Freie Presse*, 15 Nov. 1892.
[22] 'Der Sklavenhändlerprozess in Galizien', *Arbeiterzeitung*, 22 Nov. 1892, pp. 2–3.

was one more factor envenoming anti-Semitic feeling at the end of the century. Rabble-rousers like the Christian-Social deputy Ernst Schneider continued to refer in Parliament to 'countless cases in which Christian servants employed by Jews disappear without trace, carried off to a dreadful fate in the brothels of Hungary, the Orient and South America'.[23] Schneider and other Austrian anti-Semites characteristically linked 'white slavery' to ritual-murder fantasies; they quite falsely charged Jews with organizing a *mass* traffic in Christian women though most of the victims were in fact Jewish girls. It was these distorted racist fantasies that Adolf Hitler echoed when he wrote in *Mein Kampf* that 'in no other city of Western Europe could the relationship between Jewry and prostitution . . . be studied better than in Vienna . . .'—a connection that was already solidly anchored in the public mind by the time he arrived in the Austrian capital in 1907.[24]

The problem of Jewish prostitution also aroused the concern of major Jewish organizations in Germany and Austria who had long recognized their need for social reconstruction in Galicia. The Israelitische Allianz in Vienna, which soon after its foundation in 1873 began to sponsor schools and relief work in the Polish province, approached the Paris central body with the proposal to concentrate 'all efforts to come to the aid of the miserable population of Galicia'.[25] In 1901 a group of Viennese philanthropists laid the groundwork for the Relief Society of Galicia, providing employment for vulnerable Jewish females. The Austrian lodges of the B'nai B'rith joined forces with German and Czech lodges for a comprehensive plan of Galician rehabilitation. Above all, in 1904 the Viennese Jewish feminist Bertha Pappenheim founded her Jüdischer Frauenbund, which placed the whole issue of prostitution near the top of the agenda of women's issues.[26] The organization initiated kindergartens, girls' clubs, and dormitories and recruited 'the awakened women of Galicia and Bukovina for anti-slavery committees'.[27] Even some of the orthodox rabbis of Galicia were won over to co-operation with the cause in spite

[23] Quoted in Bristow, 'The German-Jewish Fight', 311.

[24] Adolf Hitler, *Mein Kampf*, trans. Ralph Manheim (Boston, Mass., 1943), 59: 'If you walked the streets and alleys of Leopoldstadt, at every step you witnessed proceedings which remained concealed from the majority of the German people until the war . . .'

[25] *Files Austriche IDI Galicie*, Alliance Israélite Universelle Archive, Paris. See Bristow, 'German-Jewish Fight', 321–2; also Siegfried Fleischer, 'Enquête über die Lage der jüdischen Bevölkerung Galiziens', in *Judische Statistik* (Berlin, 1903), 209–31.

[26] Sara Rabinowitsch in *Zur Lage der jüdischen Bevölkerung*, 67–98.

[27] Bristow, 'German-Jewish Fight', 323.

of local indifference and their own proverbial suspicion of outside interference.

The struggle against 'white slavery' was, of course, merely one item in a much vaster problem of improving the material and cultural conditions of Galician Jewry which had increasingly engaged the attention of the Viennese Jewish establishment in the nineteenth century. For reasons of self-interest as well as charity it was apparent to Viennese Jewish notables that intervention was essential to correct what they regarded as serious moral and vocational defects among their less assimilated co-religionists. The need to find ways and means of transforming the miserable condition of Galician Jewry by engaging them in productive activities and turning them into 'respectable Westernized Jews' had indeed been on the agenda of the Vienna community before 1848.

In 1840 the Viennese-born philanthropist, pedagogue, and merchant Joseph Ritter von Wertheimer (1800–87) had organized the Verein zur Förderung der Handwerk unter den inländischen Israeliten, which was designed to train thousands of Jewish children to useful occupations.[28] The man who was to become President of Vienna's Jewish Community and first President of the Israelitische Allianz zu Wien (1872–87) had already grasped in the *Vormärz* period the connection between the productivization of Austrian Jewry and their struggle to achieve equal social and political status.[29] By encouraging the vocational training of poor Jewish youths he intended 'to break the prevailing prejudice that the Jews were work-shy'.[30] The programme initially encountered government resistance (the authorities were not

[28] Wertheimer's general humanitarian services were recognized by Franz Joseph I who ennobled him in 1868 and conferred on him the order of the Iron Crown. He had founded the first kindergarten in Vienna in 1830 and subsequently established a society to aid released criminals and juvenile delinquents. In 1843 he established a Jewish kindergarten and in 1860 a society for the Care of Needy Orphans of the Israelite Community. Wertheimer's anonymously published work in 1842 *Die Juden in Österreich* (2 vols.) was a pioneering landmark in the struggle for Austrian Jewish emancipation. His pamphlet *Die Stellung der Juden in Österreich* (Vienna, 1853) condemned the civil degradation of 800,000 loyal Israelites by imperial decree. Between 1855 and 1865 he edited the *Jahrbuch für Israeliten* in Vienna. See G. Wolf, *Joseph Wertheimer:Ein Lebens- und Zeitbild* (Vienna, 1868); Adolf Jellinek, *Gedenkrede auf Herrn Josef Ritter von Wertheimer am 25 März 1887 im israelitischen Bethause der innern Stadt Wien* (Vienna, 1887); *Die Neuzeit*, 25 Mar. 1887, pp. 113–14, and 8 Apr. 1887, p. 131.

[29] See G. Wolf, *Geschichte der Juden in Wien (1156–1876)*, (Vienna, 1876), 143, 146 ff., for details on the history of the Verein which, he points out, 'hat auch viel dazu beigetragen, die sociale Stellung der Juden im Allgemeinen zu Verbessern'.

[30] Wolf, *Joseph Wertheimer*, 36.

interested before 1848 in encouraging Jewish apprentices to settle in Vienna) but after the liberalization of the trade regulations in 1859, it became rather more successful.[31]

By 1875 the Verein financially supported 258 apprentices in such crafts as carpentry, lockmaking, turning, and machine production—placing them at its own expense with Gentile artisans. By 1890 the association was annually sponsoring over 1,300 Jewish apprentices in the craft trades of Vienna, including shoemaking and carpentry where artisanal anti-Semitism was traditionally most prominent.[32] This training programme was encouraged by leading Jewish financiers such as Baron de Hirsch (who provided an annual subsidy of 14,000 florins in the early 1880s) and the industrialist David Ritter von Gutmann.[33]

Its effects were admittedly paradoxical. On the one hand it did act, as originally intended by Wertheimer, to erode older myths and stereotypes of the Jews as usurers, old-clothes-dealers, speculators, and petty merchants, incapable of honest labour. It also provided the kind of occupational diversification which the leaders of the Vienna Jewish community recognized was crucial if Jews were to become integrated among the Gentile population.[34] At the same time the vocational training of Jewish apprentices increased the fear of economic competition among precisely that sector of Viennese society most susceptible to anticapitalist and anti-Semitic rhetoric. The master artisans under the influence of racist demagoguery now became alarmed that Jewish immigrant apprentices and artisans might destroy their livelihoods and hence they redoubled their call for 'tests of competence' designed to exclude Jewish competition from the craft guilds.[35]

Nevertheless, Wertheimer's concept of Jewish 'productivization' and self-help, first developed in Vienna, remained the dominant model to be applied to the social problems of the *Ostjuden*. Artisanry and productive labour on the land were regarded by Wertheimer and the Jewish leadership as a method of 'completing the work of self-emancipation'.[36] Jews, it was argued, must work tirelessly to develop the virtues of industriousness and eliminate the vices of laziness,

---

[31] Wolf, *Geschichte der Juden in Wien*, 216.

[32] John W. Boyer, *Political Radicalism in Late Imperial Vienna: Origins of the Christian Social Movement, 1848–1897* (Chicago and London, 1981), 86–7.

[33] Ibid. 86–7.

[34] Sigmund Mayer, *Die Wiener Juden: Kommerz, Kultur, Politik, 1700–1900* (Vienna and Berlin, 1917), 452.

[35] Boyer, pp. 87–8.   [36] Jellinek, p. 6.

physical weakness, and isolation which were consequences of past oppression. To be worthy of equal rights, they had to avoid both the extremes of exaggerated displays of wealth and the *Luftmensch* syndrome; manual work and learning a trade would help inculcate patriotic virtues, turning them into honest, loyal, law-abiding subjects fit for social intercourse with their Christian fellow-citizens.[37] This self-emancipation would obviate the resentment and prejudice of the Gentile lower classes and free Eastern Jews from the stigma of pariahdom and the legacy of the ghetto. Legal egality and civic freedom would thus be completed by full social emancipation.[38]

According to Wertheimer the 'tolerated' Viennese Jews in the *Vormärz* period had shown the way. Long before receiving equality they had proved their economic usefulness to the city of Vienna and to the Austrian state. They had acquired the requisite social graces, introduced elevated religious services, and established impressive charitable institutions which had won the respect of Gentiles.[39] While warning against ostentatious behaviour, luxurious living, and flashy parvenu manners, Wertheimer constantly emphasized the values of civility, urbanity, and politeness carefully cultivated by the established Viennese Jewish élite.[40] By contrast he pointed to the deleterious effects of traditional Jewish behaviour-patterns which he associated with the ghetto: arranged marriages, excessive fertility, the huckstering mentality, and contempt for manual labour as a degrading occupation.[41] The improvement of morals could best be achieved by character-building activity based on the time-honoured Latin formula, *Mens sana in corpore sano*. More concretely, he pushed the need to develop a network of educational institutions in Galicia and Bukovina on the Viennese model which would counteract the harmful influence of rabbinical orthodoxy and Hassidism.[42]

Partly towards this end the Israelitische Allianz of Vienna was established as an independent Jewish society in Vienna in 1873 with Joseph von Wertheimer as its first President. Originally intended to

[37] Ibid. 5.

[38] Joseph Ritter von Wertheimer, *Zur Emancipation unserer Glaubensgenossen* (Vienna, 1882), 2–5.

[39] Ibid. 13: 'Es ist daher kein vaterstädtischer Eigendünkel, sondern ein gerechter Stolz auf die Verdienste unserer Altvordern, wenn ich sage, dass die Juden Wiens zur Erwirkung der socialen Emancipation mit Glaubenseifer, Umsicht und Opfermuth in der vordersten Reihe der Vorkämpfer gestanden sind.'

[40] Ibid. 14–15.   [41] Ibid. 17–21.

[42] File 4408, IA 1–3, Alliance Israélite Universelle Archive, Paris, letter of 22 Jan. 1873 from J. Wertheimer to the Comité Central de l'Alliance Israélite Universelle, p. 9:

operate as a branch of the Alliance Israélite Universelle in Paris[43]—an affiliation opposed in the 1860s by the Austrian authorities for political reasons—it initially focused on assisting the Jews of Romania and Serbia. During its early years it helped the Jewish victims of the Russo-Turkish war of 1877 and supported the French central organization in campaigning for Jewish civil rights in the Balkans. At the Congress of Berlin in 1878 the Viennese Allianz co-operated with international Jewish organizations to ensure the rights of Romanian Jewry.[44] This diplomatic activity enhanced its prestige and strengthened its links with the Alliance Israélite Universelle, which had originally been downplayed for fear that these might be exploited by Austrian anti-Semites to cast aspersions on the loyalties of Viennese Jewry.[45]

Both Wertheimer and Adolf Jellinek firmly believed that the Vienna Allianz must be a universal organization working together with the Paris Alliance, rather than a purely Austrian national body.[46] The protection of Jews, persecuted for their religious beliefs and denied their civic rights, was perceived and explicitly defined as an *international* humanitarian task that transcended national, separatist, and confessional

---

'C'est là [en Galicie] que l'Orthodoxie et le Chassidisme ont encore en grande partie le dessus et sont ennemis de tout progrès; les synagogues, les écoles, les institutions bienfaisantes ne s'en repentent que trop. Néanmoins l'émancipation complète influe partout favourablement en ce que les professions utiles, se trouvent bien plus fréquenment embrassés . . .'

[43] N. M. Gelber, 'Die Österreichische Polizei und die Alliance Israélite Universelle', in *Aus zwei Jahrunderten* Vienna and Leipzig, 1924), 131–77, deals extensively with government regulations and police suspicions which forbade foreign organizations to conduct activities in Austria. In particular he details the opposition of orthodox Austrian Jews led by Ignaz Deutsch who feared that the Alliance would strengthen Reform Judaism. See also N. M. Gelber, 'Die Wiener Israelitische Allianz' (*Publikationen des Leo Baeck Instituts Bulletin*, no. 11, 1960 Sonderdruck), for more details on the suspicions of the authorities regarding the 'revolutionary' and pro-Polish affiliations of the Alliance Israélite as well as its role as an instrument of French foreign policy.

[44] On the importance of this episode and the diplomatic background, see Fritz Stern, *Gold and Iron: Bismarck, Bleichröder and the Building of the German Empire* (London, 1977), 351–93. 'In the history of Jewry, July 1878 stands out as a moment when because of its own power and influence and by virtue of universally held principles, the fate of Jews in East and West seemed at last safe and propitious. The principle of equality had been formally enshrined; Rumanians had been forced to swallow it, and the presumption of most Western Jews that emancipation would win over new ground received clear confirmation'.

[45] Zosa Szajkowski, 'Conflicts in the Alliance Israelite Universelle and the Founding of the Anglo-Jewish Association, the Vienna Allianz and the Hilfsverein', *Jewish Social Studies*, 19 (1957), 29–50.

[46] Adolf Jellinek, *Der israelitische Weltbund: Rede, am I. Tage des Hüttenfestes 5639 gehalten* (Vienna, 1878), 12.

boundaries.[47] The Viennese Allianz was not intended to become an 'Austro-Hungarian *Hilfsverein*' confined to succouring Galician Jewry or smaller communities in Bohemia, Moravia, Upper and Lower Austria but to be as global in its scope as the Jewish people itself. Like its French prototype, its aim was to combine patriotism and humane cosmopolitanism in spreading the blessings of 'modern culture' and emancipation to less favoured co-religionists.[48] To this end it could not be confined to any one community, to a mere province or even to a whole Empire but had to spread its activities on behalf of Jewry wherever civic rights, religious needs, or training to productivization required its intervention.[49]

By spreading the message of *Bildung* and *Kultur* to the backward Jewish masses, the Viennese organization along with its Parisian model believed it was thereby helping to uproot ancient prejudices against Jews as well as remaining faithful to humanitarian and Mosaic principles. It was striking a blow against all forms of national separatism, narrow religious and provincial particularism, barbarism, intolerance, and inhumanity from which Jews had suffered over the centuries.[50] No dual loyalties were involved since it was argued that Judaism, patriotism, and *Weltbürgertum* formed an indissoluble unity.[51]

Both Wertheimer and Jellinek were profoundly influenced by the universalist model of the French emancipatory creed that had inspired the Alliance Israélite Universelle. They regarded this organization in quasi-Messianic terms as the modern secular expression of Hebraic monotheism.[52] In the French ideals of 1789—liberty, equality, and fraternity as they had been incorporated in the humanitarian ideology of the Alliance Israélite—they saw that Wertheimer called 'l'institution la plus mémorable du judaisme de nos temps'.[53] The liberal, civilizing ideals adopted by modern French Jewry, its universalist patriotism and

[47] Wertheimer, *Zur Emanzipation*, 28–9.

[48] A. Jellinek, 'Stimmen über den verewigten Herrn Joseph Ritter von Wertheimer. IV. Die Worte eines Sterbenden', *Die Neuzeit*, 8 Apr. 1887, pp. 131–2, quotes its founder's last words on the Allianz: 'International muss sie sein.'

[49] Jellinek, 'Stimmen', 131.

[50] 'Die israelitischen Allianzen', (Dec. 1884), in Adolf Jellinek, *Aus der Zeit: Tagesfragen und Tagesbegenheiten* (Budapest, 1886), 130–6.

[51] 'Doppelte Zeitrechuung', ibid. 140.

[52] 'Die Israelitischen Allianzen', ibid. 131.

[53] J. de Wertheimer to the Comité Central d l'Alliance Israélite Universelle, 26 June 1879 (Vienna, 1B 1–10); also, ibid., letter of 20 July 1878 praising the initiative of the Alliance on behalf of Romanian Jewry at the Congress of Berlin.

opposition to all forms of religious prejudice, intolerance, and obscurantism, were taken as a worthy model of imitation.

Cosmopolitan leaders of Viennese Jewry like Wertheimer, Jellinek, Ignaz Kuranda, and Leopold Kompert recognized the element of self-preservation involved in this broad perception of Jewish interests. As long as Jewish rights were infringed upon with impunity in remote far-flung parts of the globe, there would be no real security for the Jews among the civilized nations. Hatred and persecution of Jews could not be easily quarantined and the rise of modern anti-semitism had underlined its epidemic character.[54]

The fight against discrimination was therefore indivisible and not simply a narrow 'Jewish' interest. Far from espousing a bloodless ideal of cosmopolitanism, the Alliance claimed to be engaged in strengthening the *Heimatgefühl* of Jews in their adopted fatherlands, in overcoming the traditional barriers that separated them from non-Jews. It was educating Jews to true patriotism and citizenship in Austria-Hungary as in other continental countries and in the more backward extra-European territories. Its 'civilizing' mission, expressed through secular schooling, training in civility, raising the standard of living, and modernizing religious instruction, reinforced the ties that bound Jews to the countries in which they lived.[55] In Vienna the Allianz had moreover a special mission operating in what Jellinek called the 'metropolis of East European Jewry' and in a centre serving the needs of over a million Austrian Jews. Furthermore, it was in Austria alone, so *Die Neuzeit* optimistically claimed in an editorial of 26 August 1881, that the Archimedean point for combatting anti-Semitism could be found;[56] from Vienna, too the call for assistance to the Russian Jews fleeing the Tsarist pogroms had first gone forth and it was only from the Austrian capital that the plight of Galician Jewry could ultimately be alleviated.[57]

In reality the policy of the Viennese Allianz was considerably more ambivalent than this humanitarian rhetoric might suggest. Worried by the predictable Gentile backlash in Vienna, the Allianz had in fact sought to protect Austrian Jewry from an inundation of Russian Jewish

[54] 'Ein Wort an die isr. Allianz zu Wien. II', *Die Neuzeit*, 2 Sept. 1881, p. 279.

[55] Ibid. 280.

[56] 'Ein Wort über die isr. Allianz zu Wien', *Die Neuzeit*, 26 Aug. 1881, p. 271.

[57] Archives of the Alliance Israélite Universelle, Paris IA 3, 'Von der israelitischen Allianz zu Wien', no. 8757 (2), 8 Feb. 1884, esp. Wertheimer's remarks on 'den dringenden civilatorischen Bedürfnissen im eigenen Vaterlande, namentlich in Galizien, Rechnung zu tragen'.

refugees who since 1881 had been massing at the East Galician border town of Brody, and it opposed any suggestion that they should settle in Austria.[58] The leaders of Viennese Jewry were willing to contribute financially to the emigration of Russian Jews to America but not to endanger their own position or that of their Austrian co-religionists. In a letter to Baron Edmond de Rothschild in Paris in July 1882. Wertheimer explained that Austria could not receive the Russian refugees because 'the Jews in the Dual Monarchy already had enough on their hands in their struggles against the wave of antisemitism' in their own country.[59] Common Austrian citizenship precluded, however, the Viennese Jewish leaders from encouraging the repatriation of the Galician *Ostjuden* in the Habsburg lands, growing numbers of whom had in any case already settled in the capital. However unpalatable their customs and culture, nurtured by centuries of rabbinic and Talmudic indoctrination, were to Viennese Jews they were not only co-religionists but fellow-citizens of a common Empire who had yet to be fully 'enlightened' and civilized by German *Bildung*.

In its fight to modernize these Eastern Jews, the Allianz was fortunate in finding a powerful ally in the great philanthropist and financier, Baron Maurice de Hirsch (1831–96).[60] Descended from a family of Court Jews in Bavaria, Hirsch was not only an outstanding railroad-magnate and industrialist but also the first Jewish benefactor to conceive and plan large-scale resettlement of Jews. He had personally initiated and supervised the railway scheme linking Vienna and Constantinople begun in the early 1870s—a daring project that earned him the nickname 'Tuerkenhirsch'.[61] Through the success of these and other enterprises in the sugar and copper industries, Hirsch's fortune had accumulated to an estimated $100 million by 1890. He was already a familiar figure in the highest strata of the

---

[58] Zosa Szajkowski, 'The European Attitude to East European Jewish Immigration (1881–1893)', *Publications of the American Jewish Historical Society*, 41, no. 2 (Dec. 1951), 139–40; *Die Neuzeit*, 1 June 1883, p. 207.

[59] Szajkowski, 'European Attitude', 140; see also 'Rechenschaftsbericht des Vorstandes der Israelitischen Allianz zu Wien über die Thätigkeit im Jahr 1881', *Die Neuzeit*, 9 June 1882.

[60] See Kurt Grunwald, *Türkenhirsch: A Study of Baron Maurice de Hirsch, Entrepreneur and Philanthropist* (Jerusalem, 1966); S. Adler-Rudel, 'Moritz Baron Hirsch. Profile of a great Philanthropist', *Leo Baeck Yearbook*, 8 (1963), 29–69.

[61] Kurt Grunwald, 'Railways and Jewish Enterprise', *Leo Baeck Yearbook*, 12 (1967), 163–209. This article also contains important information on the role of other Austrian Jewish financiers like Salomon Rothschild, Königswarter, and Leopold von Lämel in laying the foundations of Europe's railway revolution.

European aristocracy, included among the intimates of the Austrian Crown Prince Rudolf, the Prince of Wales, and King Edward VII. A devotee of horse racing, he gave all his winnings on the track to philanthropic causes.

By the late 1880s Hirsch had recognized the need to alleviate the dire poverty and distress of East European Jewry, in particular by facilitating their mass emigration and resettlement in countries like the United States, Canada, Argentina, and Brazil. To this end he set up the Baron Hirsch Fund in New York and the Jewish Colonization Association in 1891. Hirsch's central idea, reminiscent of the French Physiocrats in its emphasis on land as the source of all values, was to rehabilitate the Jews as an agricultural people, as free farmers in their own colonies, which would he believed enable them to regain the virtues of their biblical forefathers. Hirsch was, however, negative towards resettlement in Palestine, preferring that the Jewish Colonization Association direct its land purchases to North and South America, especially Argentina.[62]

Baron de Hirsch, the proverbial *Weltbürger*, was at the same time a naturalized Austrian citizen who owned vast estates in Moravia and Hungary. After the Congress of Berlin (1878) he had made Vienna a centre of his activities. He had been closely associated since the early 1880s with the efforts of the Viennese Allianz to improve the situation of Austrian Jewry by providing a network of primary and technical schools and encouraging vocational training. In 1888, to mark the fortieth anniversary of Francis Joseph's accession to the throne, he established his own organization, the Baron Hirsch Foundation, with a capital of 12 million gold francs, for educational work in Galicia and Bukovina.[63] Its first President, the wealthy Viennese industrialist and benefactor David Ritter von Gutmann (1834–1912), had meanwhile succeeded Joseph von Wertheimer as President of the Israelitische Allianz of Vienna, which further strengthened co-operation between

---

[62] Haim Avni, 'Mifalo ha-Hityashevuti shel ha-Baron Hirsch be-Argentinah' (Hebrew Univ. of Jerusalem Ph.D. thesis, 1969), 56 ff., 336–42. See Grunwald, *Türkenhirsch*, 76–85, for the Baron's views on Zionism. For Theodor Herzl's letters to Hirsch and his critical perspective on philanthropy, see *The Diaries of Theodor Herzl*, ed. and tran. Marvin Lowenthal (London, 1958), 13–28. The interview with Hirsch had a considerable influence on Herzl.

[63] On the difficulties of obtaining permission from the Austrian government and the hostility of orthodox Jewish circles in Galicia to a project sponsored by assimilated Western Jews, see Adler-Rudel, pp. 40 ff., and Grunwald, *Türkenhirsch*, 69; also 'Baron Moritz von Hirsch', *Die Neuzeit*, 6 Sept. 1889, p. 341, and 'Die Millionen-Stiftung des Baron Hirsch', ibid., 1 Feb. 1889.

the two organizations. The trustees of the Hirsch Foundation were mainly wealthy Viennese Jews who believed that the *Ostjuden* of Galicia must be retrained, productivized, and gradually assimilated to their Gentile environment.

One of Hirsch's closest advisers on the Galician issue was the preacher Adolf Jellinek who since its foundation had been the chief ideologue of the Vienna Allianz.[64] Both men shared the view that Russian and Galician Jews could best be rehabilitated through manual labour and appropriate schooling to become either artisans or agriculturists. The relief of poverty and suffering, the improvement of living conditions and educational standards, were not therefore merely acts of charity but rather designed to transform the East European Jews into free, self-supporting, and useful human beings. A new breed of Jew would then arise who would put paid to anti-Semitic stereotypes of huckstering and usury.[65] For this purpose the Baron Hirsch Foundation established kindergartens, primary schools and recreation grounds, free supplies of schoolbooks, food and clothing for poor school children, subsidies for teachers, interest-free loans to Jewish artisans and agriculturists as well as assistance to Jewish pupils at commercial and other professional schools in Galicia and Bukovina. Hirsch's object—not so different from the radical Zionist idea of *Berufsumschichtung*—was to show the world that the Jews were after all 'fitted for agriculture' and manual crafts and did not only produce a surplus of pushy businessmen, clever lawyers, successful doctors, and university-educated intellectuals. As he impatiently told Theodor Herzl in their interview of 2 June 1895 which strikingly underlined the anti-intellectual element in the Baron's credo: 'I do not want to raise the general level. All of our misfortunes come from the fact that the Jews want to climb too high. We have too much brains. My intention is to restrain the Jews from pushing ahead. They shouldn't make such great progress. All of the hatred against us stems from this.'[66]

What wealthy Jewish financiers like Baron de Hirsch, the Roths- childs, and their advisers conveniently overlooked was the role which their own enormous wealth and influence behind the scenes played in

[64] See A. J., 'Ein Wort über Herrn Baron Hirsch', *Die Neuzeit*, 22 Feb. 1889, p. 74; 6 Sept. 1889, p. 31.

[65] Ibid., 22 Feb. 1889: 'Er will Arbeit, nichts als Arbeit unterstützen, will den armeren Classen es möglich machen, das sie durch ihrer Hände Arbeit sich ernähren und überlasst es Anderen die höheren Universitätsstudien zu fördern'. See also 'Ein Interview mit Baron Moritz Hirsch', ibid., 1 Sept. 1893.

[66] *The Diaries of Theodor Herzl*, 18.

exciting the economic envy and fear behind so much of *fin de siècle* anti-Semitism. Even more curious was the fact that urbane cosmopolitan Jews like Hirsch and Edmond de Rothschild in Paris who stood in the vanguard of modern capitalism should have embraced a romantic pre-capitalist philosophy which regarded agriculture as the key to Jewish rehabilitation. As Kurt Grunwald has suggested, their urge towards a 'Return to the Soil' was perhaps due 'to the yearning of the Wandering Jew, just escaped from the ghetto, to become rooted, *"bodenständig"* '.[67]

Hirsch's notions were surprisingly close to the philosophy of Zionism in spite of their lacking an explicitly national or ideological foundation and despite the Baron's well-known scepticism concerning the economic viability of Palestinian settlement. What linked together his activities in Austrian Galicia and his efforts on behalf of Russian and Romanian Jews was the realization that mere philanthropy would *not* solve the problem of Jewish economic marginalism: that mass emigration and auto-emancipation in a new territory were indispensable for Russian and Romanian Jews and could be realized only by settlement on the land.[68] This, too, was his panacea for Galician Jews whether they emigrated or remained in Austria—a doctrine with more than just an echo of the labour Zionist credo of *'avodah azmith'* (agricultural self-labour).[69] Only such a redemption through labour and contact with the soil would put to an end—according to Baron de Hirsch—to the demoralization of Eastern Jewry and to persecution by Jew-baiters.[70]

The Baron Hirsch Foundation of Vienna was not therefore just another 'charitable' or 'philanthropic' institution but a kind of development agency, a pilot plant for relieving the economic poverty and cultural backwardness of Galician Jewry. As Kurt Grunwald has observed, it aimed to set up an educational system which would

---

[67] Grunwald, *Türkenhirsch*, 7.

[68] For Hirsch's views on self-emancipation and the re-establishment of oppressed Jews as productive, independent citizens, see 'My views on Philanthropy', *North American Review*, 416 (July 1891); 'An Asylum for the Russian Jews', *Forum* (Aug. 1801); Lucien Wolf, 'Glimpses of Baron de Hirsch', *Jewish Chronicle*, 8 May 1896.

[69] Grunwald, *Türkenhirsch*, 84–5.

[70] *Jewish Chronicle*, 8 May 1896, Baron de Hirsch to Lucien Wolf: 'The time will come when I shall have three or four hundred thousand Jews flourishing on their homesteads in the Argentine, peaceful and respected citizens, a valuable source of national wealth and stability. Then we shall be able to point to them and contrast them with their brethren who have been demoralised by persecution. What will the Jew-haters have to say then?' Similarly, he believed that the return to the soil of Galician Jewry would take the wind out of the sails of Austrian anti-Semitism.

transform the economic structure of Galician Jews by overcoming their traditional resistance to 'alien' culture, providing them with modern elementary schooling and a knowledge of the language of the country—basic prerequisites for occupational reconstruction.[71] The standard of teaching was high enough to secure equivalence between the certificates of the Hirsch schools and those of the State schools. By the end of the century there were fifty Hirsch schools in Austria with a total of 9,934 pupils (among them 93 non-Jews) and the number of pupils attending evening classes had reached almost 1,500.[72] This rapid expansion necessitated the establishment by Hirsch's widow in 1898 (the fiftieth anniversary of Franz Joseph's reign) of the Baronin Clara von Hirsch-Kaiser Jubiläums-Stiftung zur Unterstützung von Knaben und Mädchen in Österreich (Baroness Clara von Hirsch Emperor's jubilee foundation for the support of boys and girls in Austria). The supplementary foundation with its 1.5 million florin endowment provided school-lunches and clothing for needy pupils of the Hirsch schools, grants for further training abroad for its graduates, financial aid to establish vocational schools and commercial colleges, as well as scholarships for learning a trade. Last but not least, it provided special training for handicapped children.

The Hirsch schools characteristically emphasized instruction in handicrafts and manual skills (woodwork and cardboard work) and tried to promote gynmastics and hiking excursions alongside the regular curriculum. Following completion of elementary schools, apprenticeship in a trade was encouraged and many youngsters were apprenticed in Vienna under the supervision of the Society for the Promotion of Crafts among local Jews. There were also trade schools for girls where they learned dressmaking, how to make a living in

[71] See the annual reports of the board of trustees of the Hirsch Foundation at the National and University Library in Jerusalem (*Bericht des Curatoriums der Baron Hirsch Stiftung zur Beförderung des Volksschulunterrichtes im Königreich Galizien und Lodomerien mit dem Grossherzogthume Krakau und Herzogthume Bukowina* (Vienna, 1891/2–1911/12)). The 1908/9 Report noted that eventually thousands of orthodox and even Hasidic Jews in Galicia and Bukovina did send their children to the Hirsch schools, whose combination of Jewish character and modern education made them preferable to both the traditional *heder* and the Christian school system. In Galicia the language of instruction was Polish with German as a second compulsory language. In Bukovina the first language was German.

[72] See the table in Kurt Grunwald, 'A Note on the Baron Hirsch Stiftung Vienna, 1888–1914', *Leo Baeck Yearbook*, 17 (1972), 227–36. The statutes of the foundation provided that subject to limitations of space, up to 25 per cent of Gentile children were to be admitted where no other schools existed in a given area. Education was free for poor children.

domestic service, etc. Apart from this vocational emphasis, the scholastic standards were considered relatively high though not all fifty Hirsch schools or their 230 teachers were of the same level. In the context of the prevailing ignorance in Galicia and the uncompromising hatred of most Hasidim for any kind of 'secular' eduction, the social and cultural impact of the Hirsch schools was particularly important.

In spite of the *ḥerem* (ban) initially pronounced by the Hasidic rabbis and the violence sometimes practised by Hasidic ruffians on pupils who went to the 'goyische school', they soon became an accepted part of Galician Jewish life.[73] Writing in 1904, the Viennese Jewish feminist leader Bertha Pappenheim noted that 'each one of these schools is a stronghold, often conquered in battle, in the fight against the malaise from which Galician Jewry suffers as from a hereditary disease'.[74] Pappenheim, like the bankers, industrialists, rabbis, and lawyers who sat on the board of the Hirsch Foundation in Vienna, saw the schools as waging a battle to 'reduce and eliminate the influence of the *ḥeder* on families or communities'.[75] Though by no means purely secular (Hebrew lessons were provided as well as religious instruction in Polish), the Hirsch schools could not altogether avoid a *Kulturkampf* in Galicia against the predominantly conservative and orthodox community though this had certainly not been the Baron's intention.[76] One could not after all encourage the gradual disappearance of Yiddish and of those outward characteristics which differentiated Jews from Gentiles without arousing orthodox suspicions of an assimilationist intrigue to modify religious customs and beliefs.[77] It was essentially the practical orientation and success of the Hirsch schools along with their

[73] Quoted in Grunwald, 'Note', 235.

[74] Bertha Pappenheim (under the pseudonym P. Berthold), *Zur Judenfrage in Galizien* (Frankfurt, 1900) 23, and id., with Sara Rabinowitsch, *Zur Lage der jüdischen Bevölkerung*, ii: 'Dennoch ist jede Schule ein zum Teil schwer eroberter Befestigungspunkt im Kampfe gegen alle jene Schaden, an denen die jüdischen Einwohner Galiziens wie an einer schweren, sich stetig forterbenden Krankheit leiden.'

[75] Pappenheim, *Zur Lage der jüdischen Bevölkerung*, ii.

[76] 'Baron Moritz von Hirsch', *Die Neuzeit*, 6 Sept. 1889, p. 341: 'Er mische sich nie in religiöse Angelegenheiten, weder im Orient, noch im Abendlande; das Einzige was er wolle, sei, dass die Juden die nöthige Bildung erhalten und so erzogen werden, das sie arbeitstüchtig werden, um sich durch ihrer Hände Arbeit, durch Handwerk und Ackerbau zu ernähren.'

[77] Ibid. The glowing editorial on Hirsch's philanthropy remarked that it would give him great pleasure 'wenn der jüdisch-deutsche Jargon aus Galizien verschwinden werde . . .'.

conservatism in matters of Hebrew and religious instruction which eventually attenuated some of this opposition.[78]

Nevertheless, in Vienna itself the issue of welfare, poor relief, and religious education for the *Ostjuden* continued to be a source of division between orthodox and liberal Jews in the 1880s and 1890s. From the orthodox side criticisms were sometimes heard of mismanagement, bureaucratic highhandedness, and heartless indifference towards the poor Jews by the responsible Kultusgemeinde authorities.[79] It was suggested that the honorary officers of the board were less than conscientious in actively seeking out cases of poverty and that their tendency to complacency and self-congratulation was altogether out of place.[80] The community leadership was openly accused by the editor of one orthodox newspaper in Vienna of constituting a self-interested 'autocratic clique' who were mainly responsible for the widespread 'religious indifferentism' in the capital.[81] The wholly inadequate remuneration for religious teachers and the neglect of Hebrew instruction in Vienna as opposed to the excessive administrative and cultic expenses were singled out for particular criticism by conservatives.[82] It was argued that the community should give more money to Jewish education and the rehabilitation of impoverished families in Vienna than to the beautification of its synagogues.[83] Orthodox critics also

---

[78] 'Für die Baron Hirsch-Stiftung', ibid., 6 Nov. 1891, p. 433. See also 'Das Kulturwerk der israelitischen Allianz in Galizien', *Oesterreichische Wochenschrift*, no. 33, 20 Aug. 1886, pp. 387–8, for the attitudes of a member of the Galician 'Machzike Hadas' to Viennese philanthropic activity in the province.

[79] 'Ein Capitel. über die Verwaltung der isr. Cultusgemeinde in Wien. I. Die Armenpflege', *Jüdisches Weltblatt*, 1 Apr. 1883. The editor of this orthodox weekly was Joseph H. Waltuch and its subtitle was 'Social-politisches Organ für das gesetzestreue Judenthum'. According to Jacob Toury, *Die jüdische Presse im österreichischen Kaiserreich, 1802–1918* (Tübingen, 1983), 54, it was originally founded in Pressburg (Bratislava) in 1878 or 1879. The orthodox critique was sharpened by the Zionists at the turn of the century; see 'Die Wahlen in den österreichischen Cultusgemeinden', *Die Welt*, no. 46, 16 Nov. 1900, pp. 1–4.

[80] 'Öffentliche Vorstandssitzung der isr. Cultusgemeinde in Wien', *Jüdisches Weltblatt*, 15 Jan. 1884, p. 2.

[81] 'Ergänzungswahlen in den Wiener Cultus-Vorstand', ibid., 1 Dec. 1884: 'Protection und Coteriewirtschaft ist aber der Fluch, der auch auf der Wiener israelitischen Cultusgemeinde lastet'.

[82] Ibid., see also 'Zur Consistorial-Verfassung', *Österreichische Wochenschrift*, 2 Jan. 1885, p. 4.

[83] Wertheimer, *Zur Emancipation*, 23, seemed to echo some of these criticisms when pointing to the modesty, simplicity, and '*Schmucklosigkeit*' of the Protestant churches in Vienna as a desirable model for the Jewish community. Wertheimer also put his finger on the weakness of the community in matters of Jewish education, quoting the saying: 'Der Kultus hat den Unterricht erschlagen'.

warned that a Jewish youth which was not instructed in its own sources, which remained unfamiliar with the Hebrew language and Torah values, would be left defenceless against the enemies of Jewry and religion. This was a line of argument adopted by Dr Bloch's *Oesterreichische Wochenshcrift* and by the Chief Rabbi of Vienna, Moritz Güdemann, in the 1890s.[84]

With regard to Galicia, orthodox strictures were more severe and the claims of the Viennese Allianz leadership to be promoting a 'cultural mission' in the province were angrily dismissed.[85] It was pointed out that traditional Galician Jewry who had remained true to the faith of their fathers had no need of such patronage, least of all from the 'irreligious' Jews of Vienna. The wealthy salon Jews who preached the gospel of 'pure humanity' and agitated themselves about the decadence of traditional *heder* education could scarcely provide a desirable model for Galician Jewry. Orthodox opponents insinuated that the Viennese reformers were more concerned with theatre, ballet, and dancing than with the conscientious promotion of religious education and values. Indeed, it was suggested that irreligiosity and moral slackness were rife even in the heart of the Allianz itself.[86] In their misguided arrogance the leaders of Viennese Jewry had confused the ability to read and write German correctly with those religious virtues which characterized the real *Kulturmensch*.

The liberal Jews of Vienna continued for their part to fulminate against the zealotry, 'ultramontanism', and *Bildungshass* of the Galician rabbis and Hasidim as being among the worst enemies of Jewry.[87] They insisted that the *heder* and traditional Talmud Torah education had become wholly anachronistic; that Jewish religious teaching had to take account of secular learning, modern culture, and the changed political circumstances brought about by civil emancipation. In order to fully participate in public life, in the spectacular achievements of science, industry, and the arts, Galician Jews would have to free

[84] Dr M. Güdemann (*Oberrabbiner*), *Was bedeutet das Hebräische für de israelitischen Religions-Unterricht* (Vienna, 1893), 18.

[85] 'Galizien und die Wiener isr. Allianz', *Jüdisches Weltblatt*, 15 Nov. 1884. The editorial ironically asked: 'Wie kommt das isr. Allianz in Wien dazu, sich um den religiösen Unterricht in einem Lande zu kümmern, in dem die Religiosität noch zu Hause ist und die religiöse Erziehung das Alpha-Omega des Unterrichtes bildet?'

[86] Ibid.: '. . . in der nächsten Nähe der Allianz, in Wien vor Allem, ja in den Kreisen vieler Wortführer der Allianz selbst.'

[87] 'Wiener Briefe', *Die Neuzeit*, 2 July 1880, 11 June 1880; 'Analphabetischer Obscurantismus', ibid., 24 May 1889, p. 204; 'Briefe aus Galizien', ibid., 24 Mar. 1893, p. 112.

themselves from the yoke of orthodox obscurantism as their co-religionists in the West had long since done.[88]

Hasidim and Polish orthodoxy in liberal eyes were the hoary products of centuries of suffering, persecution, and oppression, of the sombre resignation and isolationism encouraged by ghetto conditions.[89] The blind fanaticism and superstition encouraged by the *Wunder-rabbiner*, by the *Machzike Hadath* and other orthodox bodies in Galicia, were denounced as a rearguard action that contradicted the interests of Polish Jewry itself, reinforcing its economic misery, social backwardness, and lack of modern hygienic facilities. The unfortunate result was that the Polish Jew had become in the Gentile mind a veritable prototype of dirt, ugliness, parasitism, *Schnorrertum*, and dishonest business dealings.[90] The aim of the Allianz and Viennese Jewish philanthropy was to overcome this social pathology, to improve, refine, and productivize the Galician Jews by liberating them from this tragic ghetto inheritance. Above all, it was hoped to inculcate them with a modern work ethic.[91] As a result of this activity, a new generation of Jewish youth would gradually be freed from the curse of beggary and the *Luftmensch* syndrome.[92] Exposed to German *Bildung* and enlightenment they would acquire human dignity, self-confidence, and the means to stand on their own feet. The response of the Viennese Jewish leadership to the plight of their own *Ostjuden* was not couched therefore in purely philanthropic terms nor was it simply designed to prevent mass migration to Vienna, which was both legal and in any case inevitable in Austrian conditions.

The scale of the problem increased significantly, however, in the 1890s with the deterioration of the economic situation of Galician Jewry.[93] This was a period when bourgeois philanthropy came under

---

[88] 'Beschauliches über Galizien', ibid., 6 Apr. 1883, p. 130; also 'Ein Wort über die galizisch-jüdische Deputation und deren Wünsche', ibid., 4 Jan. 1889, p. 3.

[89] 'Die Juden in Galizien und in der Bukowina', ibid., 23 Jan. 1885, pp. 33–5; also 'Zur Lage der Juden in Polen, I', ibid., 7 June 1889, p. 224.

[90] 'Die Juden in Galizien', p. 33.

[91] 'Die Wiener Allianz und Galizien', ibid., 2 Oct. 1883, p. 366: 'Galizien ist das Arbeitsfeld der Wiener Allianz; dass aber dort in keiner anderen Richtung gearbeitet werden kann, als indem man die Jugend zu Handwerk und Ackerbau heranzieht, ist eine Thatsache . . .' Also, 'Die zwölfte ordentliche Generalversammlung der Israelitischen Allianz zu Wien', ibid., 1 May 1885, pp. 169–71.

[92] 'Die Thätigkeit der Allianz in Galizien', ibid., 13 Feb. 1885, pp. 61–2; also ibid., 21 Jan. 1881.

[93] 'Vorschlag zu einer Enquête über die Nothlage der galizischen Juden', ibid., 11 Jan. 1895, p. 14; Fleischer, 'Enquête über die Lage der jüdischen Bevölkerung

challenge from new movements like Zionism and Social Democracy and when the Israelitische Kultusgemeinde in Vienna was subjected to growing pressures to democratize communal institutions. In Galicia itself general economic pressures led to the gradual pauperization of Jewish petty traders and merchants; growing numbers of Poles entered urban occupations previously occupied by Jews; new credit associations and local agricutural co-operatives began to exclude the Jewish middlemen.[94] These factors, allied to the boycott movement and outbreaks of violent anti-Semitism in the Polish province, swelled the Jewish migration to Vienna, severely straining the welfare facilities of communal institutions.

At the same time the Austrian and Polish Social Democrats, the Galician Jewish socialists, and the burgeoning Zionist movement began to compete for the support of the Jewish 'proletariat' in Galicia.[95] In Vienna, too, the cultural and organizational needs of the Galician migrants became an issue both in internal Jewish politics and in general elections. The Austrian and Polish socialists were highly antagonistic towards the separatism of the Jewish masses and their religious leadership; they constantly attacked the harmful social role of the Galician Jews as exploiters of the peasantry.[96] At the same time they also blamed the Jewish bankers and businessmen in Vienna and Galicia for abandoning the Jewish proletarians and victimizing those who joined socialist organizations. According to the Marxist analysis, the 'national solidarity' of the Jewry, 'forged through centuries of persecution', had been torn to shreds by capitalism.[97] Viennese Jewish philanthropy was nothing but a hypocritical mask for the naked realities of the class struggle.[98]

The Zionists were no less aggressive in their attacks on the politics of middle-class philanthropy and sought to build a base of electoral support among *Ostjuden* threatened by 'proletarianization' in Galicia and in the Leopoldstadt district of Vienna.[99] Since the early 1890s the

---

Galiziens', 217 ff.; also Abraham Korkis, 'Zur Bewulgung der jüdischen Bevolkerung in Galizien', ibid. 311–16.

[94] See Robert S. Wistrich, *Socialism and the Jews: The Dilemmas of Assimilation in Germany and Austria-Hungary* (Littman Library, London and Toronto, 1982), 310–11; also 'Einiges aus Halbasien', *Dien Neuzeit*, 23 Aug. 1895, pp. 376–7; 'Der Nothstand unter den Juden in Galizien', ibid., 10 May 1895, p. 196.

[95] Wistrich, *Socialism*, 313–14.

[96] Max Zetterbaum, 'Nach den Judenexzessen', *Arbeiterzeitung*, 11 Sept. 1898, pp. 6–7.

[97] Wilhelm Ellenbogen, *Wer lügt? Ein Mahnwort an die Wähler* (Vienna, 1897), 12.

[98] 'Der Streik der Talesweber in Kolomea', *Arbeiterzeitung*, 11 Dec. 1898, pp. 8–9.

[99] For a detailed description of the conditions of the *Ostjuden* by a leading socialist-

founder of political Zionism, Theodor Herzl, had wanted 'to bring the suffering, despised, and worthy mass of poor Jews into contrast with the rich', whom he held mainly responsible for anti-Semitism.[100] Herzl was no less convinced than the liberal Viennese Jewish leadership that the ghetto had seriously damaged Jewish character, demeaning Jewry and leading it into dishonourable occupations. But he held the principle of philanthropy to be altogether mistaken, one more factor which 'debases the character of our people'. In his interview with Baron de Hirsch on 2 June 1895 he reproached his interlocutor with dragging 'would-be Jewish farmers across the seas' to no avail. Exporting fifteen to twenty thousand Jews to Argentina would not solve the 'Jewish question'—'more than that number live in one street of the Leopoldstadt in Vienna'.[101] What the Jews needed was not phil-anthropy but united political leadership, a collective vision, an organized mass exodus inspired by a national idea. If necessary, the Jewish masses would even have to be mobilized against the Rothschilds and the wealthy Jewish élite, if they continued to oppose Zionism.[102]

With regard to the *Ostjuden*, Herzl repudiated certain features of the nineteenth-century liberal attitude of his milieu and class, especially after his encounter with the Russian Jews at the First Zionist Congress in Basle (1897). To his mind, they were indeed 'ghetto Jews' but at the same time integral, authentic, and still uncorrupted by assimilation. Initially, it is true, he had looked upon the role of the Eastern Jews in the Zionist movement as purely subordinate: the masses of 'unskilled labourers' in Russia, Romania, Hungary, and Galicia would supply the rank and file of his future army.[103] They were miserable, oppressed, poverty-stricken *schnorrers* whom Zionism had come to redeem from an 'abnormal' life-style and return to physical labour on their ancestral soil.[104] This somewhat patronizing attitude towards the *Ostjuden* was not so different from that of Baron de Hirsch and the

Zionist activist in Austria, see Saul Raphael Landau, *Unter jüdischen Proletariern: Reiseschilderungen aus Ostgalizien und Polen* (Vienna, 1898).

[100] *The Diaries of Theodor Herzl*, 5 (diary entry c. Apr. 1895).

[101] Ibid. 17.

[102] Ibid. 36: 'If I can't do the thing together with the Rothschilds, I shall do it in opposition to them', 7 June 1896. In a letter to the Chief Rabbi of France, Zadok Kahn, on 26 June 1896, Herzl described the House of Rothschild as 'a national misfortune for the Jews' (p. 193) though he still felt some sympathy for Edmond de Rothschild as a 'philanthropic Zionist', in spite of their disastrous personal encounter.

[103] Herzl, 'The Solution of the Jewish Question', *Jewish Chronicle*, 17 Jan. 1896.

[104] See Jacques Kornberg, 'Theodor Herzl: A Re-evaluation', *Journal of Modern History*, 52 (1980), 229 ff.

assimilated Jewish leadership who were no less concerned with
productivizing the East European Jewish *Luftmensch* through a return
to the land. Nevertheless, Herzl insisted that his Zionist approach to
the Jewish question as a *national* issue was fundamentally different
from that of bourgeois philanthropy. As he told a large audience of
over 1,000 listeners in Berlin in February 1898: 'If philanthropy is
practised on an entire people it is called politics, and the philanthropy
which a people attempts to practise for its own prosperity is the politics
of that people'.[105]

The emergence of political Zionism in Vienna in the mid-1890s
reflected not only a crisis of assimilation generated by anti-semitic
electoral successes but also the increasing impotence of the Kultusgemeinde and its philanthropic networks in coping with the problems
of the *Ostjuden*. Moreover, though the Jewish masses in Galicia were
on the whole still tied to the coat-tails of rabbinical orthodoxy and to
the assimilationist Polish political parties, Zionism did make an
immediate impact on Galician immigrants in Vienna, especially on the
students and intellectuals. Their sense of national identity had existed
long before the coming of Herzl and had if anything been intensified
by their sense of exclusion from the Jewish community in Vienna.

In Galicia, too, the Zionist movement had been attracting elements
of the educated Jewish middle-class, university, and high-school
students as well as commercial employees since the mid-1880s. Even a
maverick Hasidic scholar like Aron Marcus (1843–1916), an orthodox
German Jew born and educated in Hamburg who had enthusiastically
embraced the spiritual world of the Polish ghetto, warmly supported
Theodor Herzl and his *Judenstaat*.[106] Writing to Herzl from Cracow-
Podgorze on 27 April 1896, Aron Marcus spoke glowingly of his
'wonderful pamphlet' which in his view altogether transcended the
outdated polemics between assimilators and orthodox Jews in Galicia.
He also expressed his full identification with Herzl's critique of
capitalist philanthropy, reserving his sharpest barbs for the recently
deceased Baron de Hirsch:

We are angry with this man, Baron Hirsch, who with his money and his
Turkish connections could have brought about the colonization of Palestine in
your sense, but who allowed himself to be convinced by the spineless Rabbi

[105] Herzl, 'Who Fears a State?', *Zionist Writings: Essays and Addresses*, trans. Harry
Zohn (New York, 1973), i 213–14; originally appeared in *Die Welt*, 18 Feb. 1898.
[106] On Aron Marcus, see Marcus Markus, *Ahron Marcus: Die Lebensgeschichte eines
Chossid* (Basle, 1966).

Jellinek that it was necessary only to lower the Polish Jew's mental level, his disgusting mania for thinking, to turn him into a peasant and a lowly manual labourer, in order to make the Jewish question disappear, to liberate our Aryan brothers—that monstrosity of Christian-Germanic stupidity—from the trouser-selling youths who cannot, it is true, fulfil their task as men but do at least know how to fulfil it as bank directors.'[107]

The religious Zionism of this German-born propagator of cabbalistic teachings was of course far from typical of hasidic Galician Jews but his strictures against the assimilationist ideology of the Allianz and the Viennese Jewish establishment were indeed representative of orthodoxy in both Galicia and Vienna. Such support from a religious quarter was moreover of great value to Herzl in refuting the charges of the Chief Rabbi of Vienna, Moritz Güdemann, that Zionism stood in express contradiction to Jewish orthodoxy. To prove the contrary, Herzl was able to quote from a pamphlet by Marcus showing that 'The movement for agricultural settlements was started over 50 years ago in Orthodox circles by some of the most respected rabbis with the express purpose of forming a state'.[108] Aron Marcus had argued that 'even the most Orthodox Jews are willing to accept proposals for a political regeneration of Jewry which are being made by some of the most modern freethinkers'.[109] The views of this unconventional Hasid gave some substance to Herzl's conviction that Zionism would embrace 'all the members of the Jewish nation', orthodox, reform, and free-thinkers, Eastern and Western Jews. They also encouraged him to suggest that Chief Rabbi Güdemann of Vienna was being manipulated by the wealthy lay leaders of the Vienna community and was not expressing an authentically Jewish religious viewpoint. Herzl's hostility to the capitalist and philanthropic élite now found increasingly bitter expression:

These are the people [i.e the wealthy Jews] about whom one hears constantly, whether it be scandals involving their mistresses, or the winnings of their race horses, their stock exchange manœuvres with which they turn middle-class traders into proletarians, or the corruption which they spread around

[107] For extensive extracts from Marcus's letter of 27 Apr. 1896 to Herzl, see *Herzl Year Book*, 1 (New York, 1958), 187–90.

[108] The quotation was taken from a pamphlet published in Hamburg in 1897, containing the text of a lecture by Aron Marcus on Herzl's *Der Judenstaat*, originally delivered in Cracow: *Dr. Theodor Herzl's Judenstaat, besprochen in der Generalversammlung der 'Chowewe Erez Israel' in Krakau am 10 Januar 1897, von Ahron Marcus.*

[109] Reproduced in Herzl's reply to Güdemann's *Nationaljudentum, Österreichische Wochenschrift*, 23 Apr. 1897, Eng. trans. in Herzl, *Zionist Writings*, i. 65.

themselves like a pestilential stench. Let these people, who are seen everywhere, except where poor Jews are engaged in a hard struggle, watch out lest a second popular movement arise against them behind their backs, weaker in numbers but for that reason all the more desperate than the first. Oh yes, there are among them so-called 'philanthropists'; this means they breed *schnorrers* and harm the Jewish people by making charitable donations from their fortunes, some of which were amassed in dubious ways.[110]

During Herzl's own lifetime, the threat to unleash a popular movement, based in part on the poverty of the *Ostjuden*, against the Viennese Jewish establishment was not in fact translated into operational terms. Herzl saw his movement as essentially global in scope, and in spite of his call to 'conquer the communities' devoted far more energy to international diplomatic activity than to winning support in internal elections of the Israelitischen Kultusgemeinde (IKG). Only after his death in 1904 did an all-out frontal confrontation for communal power between the Zionists and the IKG leadership develop. Nevertheless, Herzl was by no means indifferent to the campaign waged against Zionism by Jewish community officials, both directly and indirectly, during internal elections and in the local Viennese Jewish press. In his own journalist organ, *Die Welt*, he scathingly castigated what he saw as the petty-mindedness, mediocrity, and underhand tactics of the *Gemeinde* leaders when faced with the challenge of Zionism and the larger issues facing Jewry.[111] He pointed to the extraordinarily low turnout in the Vienna *Gemeinde* elections of 1898 as a sign of their political bankruptcy—a mere 2,000 voters out of nearly 140,000 Viennese Jews participated in the selection of candidates to the Board.

This apathy reflected the extreme conservatism of the communal structures in Vienna which had permitted the uninterrupted domination of its assimilationist leadership of wealthy notables throughout the nineteenth century.[112] Ever since 1852 when it was first authorized as the sole agency for supervising the cultic, religious-educational, and charitable needs of Viennese Jews, the *Gemeinde* had been run by an oligarchy of rich bankers, industrialists, merchants, and lawyers. According to the 1867 statutes (revised in 1890) its functions were

---

[110] *Zionist Writings*, 69–70.

[111] Herzl, 'Ein Armutszeugnis (Zu den Wiener Cultuswahlen)', *Die Welt*, 2 Dec. 1898 (no signature); included in the Hebrew edn. of his *Zionist Writings: Essays and Addresses (1895–1899)* (Jerusalem, 1976), 285–8; also 'Die Wahlen in die Wiener Kultusgemeinde', *Die Welt*, 21 Nov. 1902, no. 47, pp. 1–2.

[112] For a denunciation of this system, see *Die Welt*, 9 Nov. 1900, p. 6.

predominantly religious and charitable:[113] to establish Jewish synagogues, cemeteries, and ritual baths, to preserve a network of welfare
institutions (including hospitals, old-age homes, institutes for orphans,
for the blind, deaf, and dumb, and poor relief) and to supervise Jewish
religious education. This legally mandated *Religionsgenossenschaft*
(religious association) had no ostensible political functions though it
was internally autonomous and held its own elections to the Board.

Traditionally, the focus of community energies had been concentrated
on cultic matters designed to raise the prestige of the community in the
eyes of Gentiles and to ennoble the outward forms of the religious
service.[114] This was of special concern to the upper-class Viennese
Jews who wished thereby to mark themselves off from what they
considered the unaesthetic forms of East European Judaism.[115]
Serving the community was through most of the century a matter of
honour for this Jewish élite—many of them ennobled—and the
longevity of tenure encouraged by the anachronistic voting structure
made the Board (*Vorstand*) virtually its private preserve. The wealth,
social status, family connections, and renown of the lay élite had
rendered it virtually impregnable to challenge until the end of the
century. Even in purely religious matters Board leaders could exercise
a decisive influence whenever they chose to do so, putting the rabbis in
their place by using the broad powers given to them by the statutes.[116]
Their success in the Gentile world, their frequently close ties with
court, aristocratic, banking, and big business circles, gave them a
special prestige which seemed to make the Jewish notables indispensable. In community elections before 1900 close connections
with the higher strata of society were invariably considered an asset

---

[113] Israel Jeiteles, *Die Kultusgemeinde der Israeliten in Wien* (Vienna, 1873); 'Die
Organisation der israel. Cultusgemeinden', *Die Neuzeit*, 30 May 1884, p. 206; 'Regelung
der ausseren Verhältnisse der israelitischen Religionsgesellschaft', ibid., 21 Feb. 1890,
pp. 72 ff.

[114] 'Die Tradition der Wiener Cultusgemeinde', *Die Neuzeit*, 23 May 1884, pp. 195–
6.

[115] Ibid., 23 May 1884: 'Der alte Singsing, das mittelalterliche Tohu wa-Bohu in der
"Judenschul" konnte in der Residenz [Wien] nicht aufrecht erhalten bleiben; es musste
etwas geschehen, damit das Judenthum in der Hauptstadt Oesterreichs so erscheine,
dass es nicht den Spott der Nichtjuden mit Recht verdiene.'

[116] See the letter of Rabbi Güdemann protesting at the criticisms made of him for
overstepping his competence by Joseph Ritter von Wertheimer over the question of a
'Jewish Gymnasium' in Vienna; the lay leadership disapproved of rabbis involving
themselves even in such matters: 'Die Autonomie des Cultusgemeinde-Vorstandes',
Die Neuzeit, 16 July 1886, p. 272.

rather than a liability.[117] Similarly, good relations between the Kultusgemeinde and powerful Jewish families like the Rothschilds were looked upon as essential to the interests of the community.[118]

In this respect, pre-emancipation norms of *shtadlanut* continued to govern the political responses of the community élite even as anti-Semitism began to threaten the achievement of civil equality. Intense loyalty to the State, hunger for titles, honours, and social acceptance in the highest circles, the unconscious aping of feudal, aristocratic values, and excessive attention to outward form were all part of this parvenu syndrome that left its mark on the tone of Jewish community life in Austria as in other Central European countries. Wealth, social success, and position, so it was believed, were the best antidote and shield against anti-Jewish attacks from below; by the same token the *Ostjuden*, sunk in poverty and lacking status or any obvious 'usefulness' to the Jewish community and the State, were a source of embarrassment and danger. They had therefore to be banished from the Jewish political arena. Philanthropy in the Jewish sphere acted here as conscience—money, a reinforcement of the class system, and a form of self-glorification; apart from fulfilling a recognized obligation of the rich, it was also held up in public as a tribute to the unique humanitarian virtues of the Mosaic faith.

But in a community where in 1895 only 12,797 Jews (out of 133,397) paid taxes to the *Gemeinde*, neither its total income nor additional philanthropy could resolve the economic problems of the poorer Jewish immigrants to Vienna. With a total budget that was exceeded four times over by Berlin Jewry, the Vienna Kultusgemeinde was working with constant deficits after the turn of the century.[119] In 1907 through the number of tax-payers had risen to 21,164 the deficit was 96,000 kronen and in 1908 it had increasd to 175,848. The famed wealth of the community as a corporate body was indeed a myth though some of the individual families who particpated in its administration were exceedingly rich, prestigious, and distinguished.[120]

---

[117] 'Eine ausgezeichneter Bürger', *Die Neuzeit*, 29 Feb. 1884, p. 81; also ibid., 28 Nov. 1884, p. 452; 'Zu den Wahlen in den Wiener israelitischen Cultusvorstand', *Österreichische Wochenschrift*, 23 Nov. 1888, pp. 728, 731.

[118] *Österreichische Wochenschrift*, 23 Nov. 1888, p. 728.

[119] Berlin with 86,152 Jews in 1895 had 17,261 financial contributors to the *Gemeinde*, producing an income of 564,362 florins as against the sum of 190,979 florins for Vienna with its much larger Jewish population but smaller pool of tax-payers. Berlin did not have nearly so significant an influx of impoverished *Ostjuden* in this period. See John Boyer, *Political Radicalism in Late Imperial Vienna*, 452, for the figures.

[120] 'Die Schatzkammer der Wiener Cultusgemeinde', *Die Neuzeit*, 15 Feb. 1884. This

The established liberal élite had insisted, ever since the 1867 statutes were drawn up, that voting rights within the community were conditional on paying an annual community tax of at least ten florins.[121] Although lowering the minimum level to five florins would have increased the pool of tax-payers and helped improve community finances, it would also have widened the number of voters—something the leadership was definitely not prepared to do. Thus, only 11,000 Jewish households in Vienna were taxed at all in 1893 and nine-tenths of these contributors paid the minimum ten-florin tax.[122] As a critic of this policy pointed out three years later in the *Österreichische Wochenschrift*, the Jewish leadership evidently feared that lowering the tax-rate and thereby enfranchising lower middle-class and poorer Jews would undermine its power and authority.[123]

Hence, the anomaly that in an age of growing democratization in Austrian politics (the five-florin artisans and small traders had been enfranchised in general and local elections in Vienna since 1882) the Jewish community remained more oligarchichal in its internal tax and voting structure than the wider community. The retarded political awareness of most of the poorer *Ostjuden* in Vienna, primarily concerned with gaining a livelihood and adapting to a new environment, reinforced this trend to oligarchy. Not until the first decade of the twentieth century did a serious movement for democratization within the Jewish community begin to acquire momentum. Even organizations like the Österreichisch-Israelitische Union, which had been created in 1886 in opposition to the established Jewish leadership and initially aspired to raise the political consciousness of the Jewish masses, avoided any attempt to overhaul the IKG voting structure. Admittedly the Zionist movement, which was considerably more militant than the Union, did challenge the IKG leadership at the turn of the century but it was severely handicapped by the great difficulty in changing community statutes and by its own lack of material resources.

editorial underlined the fact that 'die Wiener Cultus-Gemeinde als solche, als Corporation, ist nichts weniger also begütert'. It admitted that there was no comparison with the much greater resources of Berlin Jewry but singled out the uniqueness of the Viennese community as residing in its harmonious unity and the immense contributions of its members to the parliamentary, financial, business, legal, medical, philanthropic, and educational institutions of Vienna as a whole. 'Die Wiener israel. Cultus-Gemeinde kann mit einem Gefühl von freudigem Stolze über diese Männer, die in ihren Reihen zu finden sind, Revue halten', p. 61.

[121] See G. Wolf, *Geschichte der Juden in Wien*, 165 ff., on the 1867 statutes.
[122] *Österreichische Wochenschrift*, 15 Dec. 1893, p. 974.
[123] See Hermann Fialla on the revised 1896 statutes in ibid., 25 Sept. 1896, pp. 765 ff.

Until the end of the 1890s only a very small percentage of Jews had been actively involved in the internal affairs of the *Gemeinde* in spite of the massive campaign of anti-Semitic slander which had been going on for more than a decade and a growing dissatisfaction with the administration of the community. The prevailing apathy in many respects suited the existing leadership.[124] Its spokesman consistently argued that community affairs were in any case best left in the hands of the *Besitzbürgertum*, whose superior wealth, social position, connections, and expertise entitled them to the leading role. Property was widely considered a guarantee of independence and objectivity while the prestige and renown of the élite would ensure necessary access and influence with the authorities.[125]

These assumptions were somewhat modified in the first decade of the twentieth century with the budgetary crisis and a substantial rise in the number of tax-payers in the community.[126] From 19,045 in 1904 the number of contributors increased to 25,276 in 1909, a leap of 33 per cent. Similarly the number of enfranchised members of the community rose from 13,111 in 1902 to 18,632 Jews in 1912.[127] Nevertheless, in terms of the Viennese Jewish population as a whole these figures were far from impressive, never embracing even 15 per cent of the total population.[128] In voting terms, this is even more striking when on looks at the number of enfranchised Jews who actually utilized their rights to vote: from 4,700 in 1902, the number declined to 4,421 in 1906, briefly rose to 5,019 in 1908, evened out at 4,446 in 1910, and then fell to a new low point of apathy in 1912 with only 1,960 out of 18,657 enfranchised voters (10.5 per cent) bothering to register their preference in internal elections to the Jewish Community Board.[129]

[124] See 'Die Elemente eines Cultusvorstandes in einer Gross- und Residenzgemeinde', *Die Neuzeit*, 28 Nov. 1884, p. 451: 'Das Wort eines Diplomaten: "Pas trop de zèle", sollte man an den Eingang des Saales hinschreiben, wo jüdische Cultusvorstande ihre Sitzungen halten. Denn der jüdische glühende Thateneifer, der immer sich und Anderen zu schaffen gibt . . . kann mehr Unheil in einer Cultusgemeinde stiften, als der vornehmste Indifferentismus'.

[125] Ibid.; see also *Österreichische Wochenschrift*, 16 Feb. 1900.

[126] Central Archives of the History of the Jewish People (Jerusalem), File A/W 98–102. Internal reports by the Board of the Israelitische Kultusgemeinde for the years 1902, 1904, 1906, 1908, 1910, and 1912.   [127] Ibid.

[128] See Avraham Palmon, 'The Jewish Community of Vienna between the Two World Wars, 1918–1938: Continuity and Change in Internal Political Life' (Hebrew Univ., Jerusalem, unpub. doctoral diss., 1985), p. 47.

[129] Ber Borochov, 'Kehillat Vina ve-ha-behirot le-hanhala' (Dec. 1912), *Ketavim* (Tel Aviv, 1955–66), iii. 147–53.

Criteria for eligibility in these elections had been modified by the 1896 statutes which no longer made the right to vote contingent upon the privilege of residency in the city. In 1869, for example, fewer than 8,000 out of Vienna's 40,000 Jews had even possessed the residence permits required to belong to the official community. In that liberal era, when the gap between the upper strata and the Jewish masses was very striking, only a few hundred voters participated in the annual elections to select a quarter of the members of the Community Council.[130] After 1896, to be eligible as a candidate for IKG elections one had to be thirty years old and a taxpayer for three consecutive years. Women were of course excluded from being candidates or from voting, as were the mass of poor *Ostjuden*. Orthodox Jews, who were prevented by the Austrian legal statutes from seceding to form separate communities as they had wished, generally refused to participate in elections and to put up their own candidates.[131] The 1896 statutes stipulated elections every two years with one-third of all seats on the Board up for election each time. The members of the council were increased from 20 to 24, and then in 1900 from 24 to 36. The additional twelve seats were elected *exclusively* by members paying the highest rate of community taxes (more than 200 kronen per year)—i.e. they were elected by about 1,000 persons. Thus while the general trend after 1900 was towards the democratization of politics in the Habsburg Monarchy, the Kultsgemeinde was moving in the opposing direction towards a reinforcement of its 'plutocratic' structure.

Not even the numerical growth of the Jewish population and the rise of a powerful Zionist challenge within community politics between 1900 and 1914 could make a real change in leadership feasible, as long as there were no universal voting rights. Similarly, the great debates of the day could not find a proper reflection or representation in the official community while the leadership continued to resist demo-cratization and any challenge to the old notable politics.

The Zionist movement, in particular, did its best to raise such important issues as the position of the Jews in the nationality conflicts of the Empire or the struggle for the recognition of the Jewish 'nationality' and its rights to cultural autonomy; it focused attention on attitudes to the *Ostjuden*, to combatting student anti-Semitism, towards

[130] See Palmon, pp. 10–50, for a summary of the changes in statutes and in the structure of the community with their effect on the right to vote and on internal elections before 1914.

[131] Ibid., p. 23.

general politics and the colonization of Palestine; in general it tried hard to relate internal elections to these national and global issues, as well as to the wider question of the character, fate, and future of Viennese Jewry as a whole. But the leadership of the Kultusgemeinde persisted in hiding behind its official status as a religious body with no political functions. This was largely a fiction, since in the early 1880s it had in practice been obliged to take a position on wider economic and political issues, partly as a result of the rise of organized anti-Semitism.

The emergence of Zionism and, especially, its call after August 1898 for the 'conquest of the communities', were undoubtedly profound irritants and challenges to the traditional notable leadership. For the Zionist opposition manifesto of 1900 directly raised the central issue of democratization and the banner of struggle against 'plutocratic' rule. It demanded remedies for the poverty of the Jewish masses, for the discrimination exercised by the Christian-Social municipal administration against Jewish teachers, employees, and immigrant pedlars from Galicia, and generally called for an active political stand in defence of Jewish national rights.[132] It was moreover apparent that the Zionists drew their support from electors of more modest means in the Viennese Jewish community and that their call for universal suffrage would probably mean the eclipse of the old community power-structures.

This democratic stance thrust the official leadership of the Kultusgemeinde into a defensive position. However, it was clear to all that the Zionists would win no truly significant victory as long as the community maintained its pre-democratic voting statutes. The IKG tried for a while to ignore Zionism, to kill it by silence and indifference; when this failed it accused the Zionists of upsetting the traditional harmony and communal consensus, of introducing the raucous politics of the street into Jewish life. By November 1900 the President of the Jewish community, Heinrich Klinger, had sharply attacked the intolerant tone and style of Zionist agitation.[133] The new opposition was condemned for adopting the mannerisms and methods of the Christian-Social anti-Semites, for its rowdyism and militancy as well as its nationalist ideology.

For their part the Zionists castigated the Jewish leadership for supporting a 'liberal' and 'democratic' orientation in general politics while preserving bureaucratic and oligarchic rule within the Jewish

---

[132] Palmon, p. 41.
[133] *Österreichische Wochenschrift*, 17 Nov. 1900; also 30 Nov. pp. 853–4.

community for its own economic benefit. They denounced the high incidence of conversion to Christianity among the wealthiest families and the assimilationist character of their leadership style;[134] their indifference to the plight of the *Ostjuden* and their depoliticization of vital Jewish community concerns.[135] They even accused the Community Board of having 'nothing to do with Judaism', of 'de-Judaizing' and betraying the democratic values of the Jewish people.[136]

Again and again, the Zionists polemicized against a rotten electoral system which excluded over 125,000 Viennese Jews from participation in community affairs and lashed out against the two-class voting system slated in favour of the rich assimilatory 'clique'.[137] They claimed that if elected they would transform the castrated 'Israelite' Kultusgemeinde—a pathetic caricature of Jewish self-determination—into a truly representative *Volksgemeinde* (people's community) serving the needs of all Jews and energetically defending its vital interests.[138] At the peak of their success in 1906 the Zionist lists received 42 per cent of the vote and two of their candidates gained enough support to force a run-off election, in which they were defeated.[139] But despite their respectable showing in community elections after 1902 the Zionists still had no realistic prospect before the First World War of being elected to the *Gemeinde* Board, let alone of conquering the community institutions. The disenfranchisement of most Viennese poor Jews reduced their following to a sector of the new Jewish middle class in those districts of Vienna where members of the liberal professions were concentrated.[140]

---

[134] *Die Welt*, 16 Nov. 1900, pp. 2–4; also 4 Nov. 1904, pp. 6–7.

[135] For an example of the type of Zionist programme intended to transform and democratize the Kultusgemeinde, drawn up by Herzl, see 'Das Gemeindeprogramm der Wiener Zionisten', *Die Welt*, no. 41, 10 Oct. 1902, pp. 5–7. It called *inter alia* for the centralizing of charitable institutions, the productivization of the community, the development of credit, co-operative, and insurance funds, assistance to the victims of pogroms, to workers and commercial employees' organizations, and the establishment of national schools. The Zionist programme insisted on putting an end to the 'plutokratisches Kuriensystem', the preferential treatment of Jewish *Hochfinanz*, and castigated the exclusion of the Jewish masses from voting rights as an insult to the democratic traditions of the Jewish people.

[136] 'Die Wahlen in den österreichischen Cultusgemeinden', *Die Welt*, 16 Nov. 1900, p. 2.

[137] *Jüdische Zeitung*, 12 June 1908, pp. 1–2; also Borochov, 'Kehillat Vina'.

[138] *Die Welt*, 16 Nov. 1900, pp. 2–4.

[139] Central Archives of the History of the Jewish People, A/W 53/10, 'Wahlprotokolle 1906'.

[140] Marsha Rozenblit, *The Jews of Vienna, 1867–1914: Assimilation and Identity* (Albany, NY 1983), p. 188, observes that 'by 1906 between 50 and 60% of the voters in Mariahilf-Neubau as well as Alsergrund (IX) and Wahring (XVIII) voted for the

Before 1914 therefore, the IKG notables were able to resist successfully the Zionist challenge without making any substantive reforms in the undemocratic structure of the communal system.[141] They managed with some success to present themselves as the loyal guardians of Jewish interests, as tireless, dispassionate administrators of community affairs and selfless philanthropists concerned only with the welfare of Jewry as a whole. Their essentially confessional definition of Jewish identity prevailed before 1914 as did their credo of 'noblesse oblige' with regard to the Jewish poor.[142] They could point proudly to an impressive network of religious, charitable, and humanitarian organizations subsidized by the Kultusgemeinde which undoubtedly contributed to easing the burdens of the impoverished, the sick, the old, and the orphaned. Through their support for vocational training and their financial help to Jewish artisans in Vienna, as well as through the efforts of the Vienna Allianz and the Hirsch Foundation to establish modern schools in Galicia, they did contribute substantially to ameliorating Jewish poverty and suffering in the Empire. Moreover, the Viennese Jewish élite did much to assist pogrom victims in Russia and in Austria itself, while through quiet diplomacy it also intervened on behalf of persecuted Jews in the Balkans and the Middle East.[143] These were by no means negligible

Zionists'. These were middle-class districts with the largest number of Zionist Shekel-payers in Vienna.

[141] Even the militant Dr Joseph Samuel Bloch, who earlier in his career had clashed with the Jewish establishment, supported its opposition to universal suffrage on the grounds that since poor Jews paid no taxes to the *Gemeinde*, they had no right to vote. Moreover, he believed that internal democracy would ruin the community financially. *Österreichische Wochenschrift* (Oct. 1893), 826 ff.; 23, no. 50 (Dec. 1906), 856–7.

[142] See *Bericht des Vorstandes der israelitischen Cultusgemeinde in Wien über seine Thätigkeit in der Periode 1896–1897* (Vienna 1898), 3. The report characteristically praised the exemplary nature of the community's philanthropic institutions while expressing some concern at the growing problem of Jewish mass poverty: 'Der Pflege der Wohlthätigkeit, an der Spitze von Vereinen und humanitären Instituten, widmen sich edle Frauen und hochherzige Männer, deren mustergiltiges Wirken weit über die Grenzen unserer Stadt hinaus bekannt ist. Gleichwohl konnte der Vorstand, angesichts der an ihn tagtäglich und in immer steigenderem Masse herantretenden, durch die zunehmende Armuth in der jüdischen Bevölkerung begründeten Ansprüche, welche durch die herrschenden Verhältnisse ihre Verschärfung finden, sich der Nothwendigkeit nicht entziehen, der Armenpflege erhöhte Beachtung zu geben . . .'.

[143] Letter of David von Gutmann to the Alliance Israélite Universelle in Paris, 6 Nov. 1895, in *Archives of the Alliance Israélite Universelle*, IIA4, enumerating the numerous interventions of the Vienna Allianz on behalf of persecuted co-religionists abroad. These included actions on behalf of Romanian Jewry in the 1870s; assisting the emigration of Russian Jews in the 1880s, intervening for Bulgarian Jews, and assistance to Jews in Corfu and Salonika. Between 1897 and 1905 the Allianz established new

achievements. But in an age of rising anti-Semitism which also witnessed the sharpening of social and national antagonisms, the old notable politics appeared to younger, more militant spirits in Vienna as the outworn relic of an assimilationist mirage.

relief emigration projects for Romanian and Russian Jews, together with the 'Esra' Association of Berlin and the Jewish Colonization Association (ICA).

4

Three Viennese Preachers

> With philosophical doctrines one builds neither nations nor
> sacred institutions . . . Judaism is not a philosophical doctrine but
> a historical institution, sanctified by divine revelation, and firmly
> established and unified by ancestral tradition and filial piety and
> devotion . . .
>
> Isaac Noah Mannheimer (1843)

> Since the days of Moses Mendelssohn and particularly since the
> great historic revolution in France the Jews have sent out their
> best men to fight for their recognition and equality in the
> European states and they have marshalled their intellectual
> resources in numerous writings, on the speaker's platform and
> in the pulpit for the goal of emancipation.
>
> Adolf Jellinek (1882)

> I have always believed that we are not a nation, or rather more
> than just a nation: I believe we had the historic mission to
> propagate universalism among the nations and that we were
> therefore more than a territorial nation.
>
> Rabbi Moritz Güdemann (1895)

In 1826 Isaac Noah Mannheimer had consecrated the stylish newly
built synagogue in Vienna's Seitenstettengasse over which he was to
preside until his death on 17 March 1865.[1] The son of a Hungarian
ḥazzan, this preacher who was to be Viennese Jewry's spiritual
shepherd for forty years had been born and educated in the freer
atmosphere of Copenhagen where he had been head teacher of
religion since 1816. The Jews had been completely emancipated in

[1] See Gerson Wolf, *Isak Noa Mannheimer, Prediger: Eine biographische Skizze* (Vienna,
1863); and above all M. Rosenmann, *Isak Noa Mannheimer: Sein Leben und Wirken*
(Vienna and Berlin, 1922) for biographical details; Jacob Allerhand, 'Die Rabbiner des
Stadttempels von J. N. Mannheimer bis P. Z. Chajes', *Studia Judaica Austriaca*,
6 (Vienna, 1978), 10–13; and Rabbi Dr Alfred Willman, 'Famous Rabbis of Vienna', in
Joseph Fraenkel (ed.), *The Jews of Austria: Essays on their Life, History and Destruction*
(London, 1967), 322 ff.

Denmark since 1814.[2] In Copenhagen Mannheimer had preached in the Danish language and held weekly services for Reform Jews to the accompaniment of the organ and music written by Christian composers. Hebrew was totally eliminated, to the dismay of the traditionalists in the community. Before arriving in Vienna, he had also preached in the synagogue in Berlin and Hamburg and at the Leipzig fair, where he had come to the attention of Michael Lazar Biedermann who invited him to officiate in the new synagogue in Vienna.[3] Since the Viennese Jews were still not permitted at that time to constitute a community, Mannheimer was not given the title of rabbi or even preacher but of 'Director der Wiener K.K. genehmigten öffentlichen israelitischen Religionsschule'—in other words he was officially designated as the 'religious teacher'.[4] As headmaster of the religious school, Mannheimer, though he was a man of wide secular culture and classical education as well as Jewish learning, determined to ensure the primacy of Hebrew in religious instruction in order that his pupils could read the Bible in the original text and follow the Hebrew prayers.[5]

In contrast to his earlier practice in Denmark and Germany he also maintained Hebrew as the language of worship in the synagogue services and came to oppose the use of the organ as a Christian innovation, alien to the spirit of Judaism.[6] From the mid-1820s Mannheimer's tireless dedication and organizing energy made him the main point of crystallization of community life.[7] He determined the liturgy, seeking to preserve as much of the traditional service as possible despite the more sophisticated tastes of his wealthy congregation and his own personal inclinations towards a more far-reaching reform.[8] His exemplary German translation of the prayer-book and the festival prayers which appeared in 1840 proved to be of permanent importance. In addition to his pedagogical, religious, and social duties, Mannheimer in accordance with the requirements of the Imperial authorities kept the record of all births, marriages, and deaths. In his pastoral work he displayed remarkable selflessness and concern for

---

[2] On the Danish background and the influence of the Mendelssohnian *Haskalah* in Copenhagen, see Rosenmann, *Mannheimer*, 22–7.

[3] Ibid. 52–3.   [4] Wolf, *Mannheimer*, 17.   [5] Ibid. 18–19.

[6] See Max Grunwald, *Der Kampf um die Orgel in der Wiener israelitischen Kultusgemeinde* (Vienna, 1919), 27 ff. 30–3, on Mannheimer and Sulzer's opposition as well as the internal debates in the community; also Rosenmann, *Mannheimer*, 68, 93–4, for Mannheimer's disagreement with Jellinek over this issue.

[7] G. Wolf, *Geschichte der Juden in Wien (1156–1876)* (Vienna, 1876), 132.

[8] Ibid. 135 ff.

every aspect of community affairs.[9] Whether it involved advising wealthy notables or helping the poor through charitable institutions, he demonstrated a practical intelligence that enhanced his influence and prestige.[10] Mannheimer was a prime mover, together with Joseph Ritter von Wertheimer, in the foundation of many of Vienna's Jewish social institutions which were the envy of much wealthier communities beyond Austria's borders.

Perhaps Mannheimer's greatest service to Viennese Jewry was the moderate spirit behind the liturgical reforms he introduced into the community, which helped prevent an open split between Orthodoxy and Reform, such as was later to occur in Germany and Hungary. Mannheimer in his mature years rejected a reform based on systematic rationalism, on the discarding of revelation and tradition, the elimination of Hebrew, or the exclusion from the prayer book of messianic passages concerning the return to Zion.[11] With regard to public worship he was closer to positive, historical Judaism as pioneered by the Breslau school of Zacharias Frankel than to the more radical German reformers like Samuel Holdheim and Abraham Geiger.[12] Thus he strongly opposed mixed marriages, transferring the Sabbath to Sunday, and the abolition of ritual circumcision.[13] After the mid-1840s he rejected any further experimentation in the religious life (*Kultusleben*) of the community. While not against reform as such, he insisted that it should not tamper with the historic core of Judaism.[14]

This religious conservatism which Mannheimer saw as appropriate to the ethos of the Habsburg capital and its Jewish community enabled him to work closely with Rabbi Lazar Horowitz, the spiritual head of the orthodox Jews in *Vormärz* Vienna, who officiated in accordance with the Polish rite. Horowitz was a pupil of the Pressburg Rabbi Moses Sofer (Schreiber), leader of Hungarian ultra-orthodox Jewry, whose consent he had received to work with Mannheimer. Horowitz advised Mannheimer in drawing up the by-laws of the First Temple,

---

[9] Rosenmann, *Mannheimer*, 106–11.

[10] See G. Wolf, *Joseph Wertheimer: Ein Lebens- und Zeitbild* (Vienna, 1868); Rosenmann, *Mannheimer*, 124–5.

[11] Max Grunwald, *Vienna* (Philadelphia, 1936), 376.

[12] See Michael A. Meyer, 'Jewish Religious Reform and The Wissenschaft des Judenthums—The Positions of Zunz, Geiger and Frankel', *Leo Baeck Yearbook*, 16 (1971), 19–44. On the wider issues, see Max Wiener, *Jüdische Religion im Zeitalter der Emanzipation* (Berlin, 1933), and David Philipson, *The Reform Movement in Judaism* (Cincinnati, 1967).

[13] Rosenmann, *Mannheimer*, 74–5.   [14] Ibid.

in the choice of *Piyyutim* for its prayer-book, in minor modifications of the circumcision ceremony, and in all ritual questions.[15] In spite of his strict orthodoxy Horowitz participated in Temple services, placing the unity of the congregation above all other considerations.[16] His influence and co-operation with Mannheimer delayed the open and deep religious conflict which began to emerge after 1849, pitting the more liberal Viennese and Bohemian Jews against the orthodox Hungarian and Galician immigrants.

For all his caution and tact in religious matters, Mannheimer was none the less determined to adapt Judaism to the spirit of modernity, to raise the level of decorum, dignity, and refinement (*Veredelung*) in the synagogue. Not for nothing did the great Jewish historian Heinrich Graetz describe him as the personal embodiment of the spiritual 'ennobling of the Jews'.[17] The modernity of his sermons was not just a matter of satisfying the craving for social status and respectability of his listeners, predominantly from the Viennese Jewish *Grossbürgertum*, or of improving their image in the eyes of Gentiles. For Mannheimer genuinely believed, as he indicated to Zunz in 1826, in the 'rebirth of a decayed and disintegrated people' through the restoration of a purified divine service.[18] Even though the restraints of his Viennese environment had obliged him to temper his fervent idealism, he never abandoned the passionate faith of his youth in the purity and sublimity of the 'idea' of Judaism when fused with the aesthetic side of German *Bildung*.

This belief achieved vivid expression in his inspirational German-language sermons and addresses, models for their time, often infused with a searing prophetic power and eloquence. Alexander Altmann has even called him 'the most vigorous and most endearing of the early preachers and undoubtedly the outstanding figure in the nineteenth-century Jewish pulpit'.[19] Mannheimer's oratorical gifts ensured his success in Vienna, where they left a deep imprint on Christian as well as Jewish contemporaries. He belonged to the new academically trained generation of Central European preachers—influenced by classical and Christian examples—who regarded the raising of

---

[15] Grunwald, *Vienna*, 376–7.   [16] Rosenmann, *Mannheimer*, 69.

[17] Ibid. 106. According to Rosenmann, 'Die Triebkraft seines Wesens war die absolut restlose Hingabe an die Idee der Veredlung des damaligen Judentums durch Kultur und Kultus.'

[18] Ibid. 63.

[19] Grunwald, *Vienna*, 347–8; Philipson, pp. 87, 135. Altmann, quoted in Robert Weltsch, Introd. *Leo Baeck Yearbook*, 11 (1966), p. xiii.

standards of decorum and civility, beauty and order in the synagogue service as a necessary prelude to emancipation.

In this task Mannheimer was greatly assisted by the gifted cantor Salomon Sulzer (1804–90), who had arrived in Vienna in 1825 to take charge of the synagogal music. In later years Sulzer's school of religious music was to exercise a powerful influence on synagogal services all over the Western world and he was widely admired for his outstanding singing voice and dignified, uplifting way of rendering the prayers. Hundreds of *hazzanim* came to Vienna to sing in his synagogue choir and learn their art at his feet. His *Shir Zion* became, for example, a basic book for Jewish liturgical music. In his preface to the first volume he wrote: 'I thought it my duty to consider, as far as possible, the traditional tunes bequeathed to us, to cleanse the ancient and dignified ones of the later accretions of tasteless embellishment, to bring them back to their original purity, and to reconstruct them in accordance with the text and rules of harmony.'[20]

This conservative approach was very much in the spirit of Mannheimer with its insistence on reconciling traditional Jewish characteristics with the new standards of artistic form. The traditional melodies were to keep their place in the liturgy but they were to be 'improved, selected and adjusted to the rules of art'. New music, too, was introduced for psalm texts by Viennese non-Jewish composers such as the great Franz Schubert (1797–1828), who contributed *Tov lehodot* (Psalm 92) for unaccompanied choir. Upon hearing Sulzer sing some of his German songs, Schubert commented: 'Now for the first time I understand my own music and what it is that gives significance to the words of my songs.'

The composer Franz Liszt (1811–86) was another great admirer of Sulzer, recalling that 'the vibration of the chords of divine worship and of human sympathy' heard in the Vienna synagogue when Sulzer sang, was an overwhelming spiritual and aesthetic experience. '. . . One seemed to see the psalms floating aloft like spirits of fire, and bowing as suppliants at the feet of the All Highest.'[21]

Jews and non-Jews alike came to the Temple to hear Sulzer's majestic renderings and the cantor received the highest awards of the city of Vienna as well as enjoying the esteem of the Jewish community. In 1868 he was decorated with the Order of Franz Joseph and even the

[20] Quoted in Peter Gradenitz, 'Jews in Austrian Music', in Fraenkel (ed.), *Jews of Austria*, 19.

[21] Grunwald, *Vienna*, 335.

Russian Emperor bestowed on him a mark of distinction. Sulzer's music was perhaps too assimilated and un-Jewish for the tastes of East European Jewry but its dignity, exaltation, and artistic character exercised a profound influence on the more Westernized Jews of Germany. Sulzer's 'mediatory mission' between Hebrew melodies and Western music was the aesthetic equivalent of Mannheimer's adaptation of the rabbinical *modus operandi.*

Mannheimer had no pretensions to being a traditional 'Rav', learned in Talmud Torah. The religious regeneration of Jewry for Mannheimer and his successors in Vienna implied the integration of Judaism with the world of modern European culture, the improvement of Jewish education, and the intellectual justification of faith and observance. Defence of the Jewish past and of Jewish honour against its detractors, insistence on the unconditional loyalty of Jews to the adopted fatherland, and enlightenment of public opinion regarding Jewish values would become for Vienna's preachers highly significant aspects of their activity as spiritual leaders.

Mannheimer insisted that Judaism was 'an indivisible unit like any organism, in which the body and soul are inseparable'; in his eyes it represented a *historical* institution unified by divine revelation, ancestral tradition, and filial piety rather than by philosophical doctrines, though he was not unsympathetic to the more 'scientific', systematic ideology of German religious reform. Thus he did not object *on principle* to the use of German in the prayer-books of the Hamburg Temple and even invited its *Prediger*, Dr Gotthold Salomon, to preach in the Seitenstettengasse synagogue. But in contrast to some of his German and Hungarian counterparts, the preservation of the outward unity and well-organized consistency of the faith was more important to Mannheimer than any metaphysical idea of Judaism or theory of its historical evolution. While clearly influenced by the *Wissenschaft des Judentums* he could no more be described as one of its leading lights than he could be regarded as a great Talmud scholar. It was rather in his inspiring oratory, in his finely tuned sense of Judaism as a synagogal and congregational *form*, in his combination of the roles of *Seelensorger*, preacher, communal organizer, and pedagogue that Mannheimer stood out among his contemporaries.

This was all the more striking since he operated in a community framework dominated not by rabbis but by a wealthy lay élite of notables. Mannheimer's synthesis of innovation and tradition, liberal enlightenment and conservatism, the values of German reform and

East European orthodoxy, reflected not only his own diplomatic skills but something of the *genius loci* of Vienna. He was all too aware of the need to take into account the sensitivities of the far more pious, traditionalist population in the provinces of the Empire; in particular, he had to reconcile the views of Polish and Hungarian orthodoxy with the more refined needs of his liberal constituency in Vienna. As he wrote from Vienna in 1842 to the Haham Bernays in Hamburg, precisely as 'a teacher and spiritual guide of one of the most important communities in Germany, which with all due respect to tradition and ritual, devotes its efforts to the improvement and refinement of the religious service among Jews', he [Mannheimer] could accept neither the orthodox, schismatic tendencies of Eastern European Jewry nor the religious nihilism of radical Reform Judaism. This balancing-act lay at the heart of his community concerns and constituted his most important legacy. To quote Mannheimer's optimistic speech of 19 April 1863, in Vienna, 'the Orient with its thousand year old traditions meets the Occident with its modern views—rigid observance of the past, alongside the searching and constructive spirit of the new Age'.[22] This attempted blending of heterogeneous elements, of acculturated, Westernized Jews with the orthodoxy of the provinces was indeed one of the great challenges facing the Viennese community. It was a test that stretched to near breaking-point the harmony of the formal community structure (Israelitische Kultusgemeinde) following the arrival of the first permanent settlers from the East.

Before 1848 the patrician Jewish élite of Vienna had opposed orthodoxy from within the context of their often humiliating dependence on the Habsburg rulers and on the conditional 'toleration' of the Austrian bureaucracy. Mannheimer was acutely aware of this dependence and very active in the long and hard struggle for Jewish emancipation. In the 1840s he had successfully resisted the attempt of Professor Rosas to establish a *numerus clausus* in the study of medicine by Jews, and together with a group of Austrian rabbis, including Lazar Horowitz, he helped achieve in 1846 the abolition of the degrading medieval *more judaico* ('Jewish Oath').[23]

On occasion Mannheimer did not hesitate boldly to confront the social and political problems of Austrian Jewry in his sermons, nor to denounce the arbitrary despotism by which they were deprived of elementary human rights before 1848. This increasingly political

[22] Wolf, *Mannheimer*, 43.
[23] Rosenmann, *Mannheimer*, 73.

stance which reached its peak during the 1848 Revolution, when Mannheimer passionately identified himself with the popular cause of constitutional freedom, was radical enough to alarm some community leaders.[24] They tried indeed to restrict his liberal activity and even to censor his utterances in the Reichstag for fear that his outspokenness would rebound on their position. In a sermon on 18 March 1848 Mannheimer had proclaimed to his co-religionists in ringing terms that their time of liberation from the yoke of servitude was coming.[25] The age of Amalek and Haman and other more contemporary oppressors was fading fast, to be replaced by the reign of law, justice, truth, and the rights of man.[26] For more than thirty years, he declared again on 24 March, 600,000 Austrian Jews had waited in vain for the implementation of civil rights promised them at the Congress of Vienna in 1815. They served loyally in the army, shed their blood for the fatherland, participated in the freedom struggles of the German nation since 1813, yet an arbitrary absolutist regime had denied them their due.[27]

With the Revolution of 1848, the liberal doctrine of the Rights of Man had finally penetrated into the Habsburg Empire proclaiming freedom of conscience, speech, assembly, and thought. Yet already the '*Krämergeist*' of petty shopkeeper interests and popular prejudice had raised its ugly head, challenging the premisses of Jewish emancipation. Mannheimer vigorously denounced and refuted the arguments and claims of the new anti-Semitic literature, then beginning to surface in Vienna. He sought to appeal to the nobler instincts, the sense of justice and fair play of the German-Austrian people.[28] Elected to the Austrian Reichstag to represent the Galician city of Brody, he delivered two stirring speeches, one calling for the repeal of the 'Jews' tax' (5 October) and the other for the abolition of the death penalty as contrary to law, justice, and humanity.[29] Jewish radical politicians like Adolf Fischof and Joseph Goldmark, as well as the Polish Rabbi Meisels, supported his impassioned and successful campaign to annul the special Jew-tax. The ruthless crushing of the October 1848 rising in Vienna (the most radical in a year of revolutions) aroused Mannheimer's bitter indignation at the scale of the repression and at

[24] Ibid. 84–5.
[25] 'Predigt, gehalten am 18. März 1848 beim Dankfeste für die bewilligte Konstitution im israelitische Bethause in Wien', ibid. 140–5.
[26] Ibid. 140.
[27] 'Erklärung bezüglich auf die Judenfrage' (24 Mar. 1848), ibid. 152 ff.
[28] Ibid. 155.   [29] Ibid. 204 ff.

the same time his satisfaction that no Jews were involved in the acts of vengeance, pillage, and barbarism.[30] On the other hand, Mannheimer did not disguise his distaste at the subservient attitude of the Viennese community leaders towards the Habsburg government.

The victory of the dynasty and the counter-revolution had brought to the throne the eighteen-year-old Franz Joseph, whose future policies were to be dominated in part by the experiences of 1848, when the Empire appeared to be crumbling before his eyes. In many ways the last monarch of the old order, he was to reign for sixty-eight years and preside over the golden twilight of the Habsburg Empire, which collapsed two years after his death in 1916. The Jews of the Austrian Monarchy would in time develop a veritable cult of the Emperor Franz Joseph who simply by remaining immovably in place for so long could create a sense of security and permanence that appeared to guarantee them their physical existence, their civil rights and prosperity. Yet in the decade after 1849, following the Habsburg recovery and the defeat of revolutionary liberalism, the internal situation appeared in a much gloomier light. The new abolutism that underlay Imperial policy, the renewed domination of Austria by the military, by the most caste-conscious landed aristocracy and perhaps the most reactionary Church in Europe, effectively rescinded all the liberties granted in 1849 and quashed Jewish hopes for emancipation.

The new Emperor and his advisers quickly reneged on the 1848 Constitution, which included the implicit promise of civil equality of Jews, and restored earlier prohibitions on the acquisition of landed estates which were not to be lifted for over a decade.[31] The medieval law forbidding Jews to employ Christian servants was re-enacted and the celebration of marriage was once more contingent on the consent of government officials. Jews were again excluded from public office and teaching posts.[32] The Concordat with the Catholic Church in 1855 which restored its monopoly on education and the efforts of the clerical Minister Count Leo Thun to create Jewish denominational schools further alarmed the Jewish community. A few anti-Semitic articles began to appear in Viennese newspapers, seemingly with the encouragement of some government officials.[33] No doubt these negative trends were aggravated by the suspicion of the authorities

---

[30] 'Predigt, gehalten am 11 November 1848 in Tempel zu Wien', ibid. 183–92.

[31] Wolf, *Geschichte der Juden in Wien*, 155 ff.

[32] Hans Tietze, *Die Juden Wiens* (Vienna and Leipzig, 1933), 201; Grunwald, *Vienna*, 289–9.   [33] Grunwald, *Vienna*, 301.

concerning the new 1848 generation of Jews and their liberal opposition to the *ancien régime*. Driven by this fear and resentment, the authorities found it expedient in the 1850s to support the claims of the poorer orthodox Jews against the more liberal tendencies of the *Gemeinde* leadership. It was not that Habsburg officialdom was enamoured of Jewish traditionalism but it did appreciate the monarchist, *Kaisertreu* component implicit in the political stance of orthodoxy whereas reform Jews were viewed as among the most zealous representatives of the modern levelling spirit.

Nevertheless, not all the achievements of 1848 could be reversed by the neo-absolutist regime. Freedom of movement was only partially restricted and Jews no longer had to conceal themselves or receive a special dispensation to live in Vienna. Hence the official Jewish population of nearly 4,000 in 1846 rapidly increased to 9,000 by 1849 and to 14,000–15,000 by 1854. Liberty of immigration extended even to areas like Styria, Carinthia, Upper Austria, and the Tyrol which had been virtually *judenrein* before the Revolution. Moreover, in spite of the revocation of Jewish legal rights, the leading banking and merchant families continued to play a crucial role in developing Austrian industry and in making Vienna a centre of commerce.[34] Jews dominated the Stock Exchange, the money-markets, and the development of the Austrian railroad network. In areas such as the textile industry, the trade in alcoholic liquors, the manufacture of articles as diverse as underwear and umbrellas, in shipping and iron-working industries and coal, Viennese Jews were already prominently represented. They had virtually created the ready-made clothing industry and the wholesale export business in Austria and continued to control them after 1848. In 1855 Anselm, who had succeeded his father Salomon Rothschild, organized the Austrian Creditanstalt. In 1861 at the dawn of the liberal era he was admitted to membership in the Upper House of the Austrian Parliament. The Kaiser-Ferdinand-Nordbahn railroad —financed by his father—which linked Vienna and Galicia via Moravia and Silesia, led to the development of the coal-mining works of Witkowitz, founded by the Rothschilds together with the Moravian-born Gutmann brothers. Since the early 1850s the Directors of the Nordhbahn had been investigating the oil possibilities of Galicia and were to contribute much to its future development.

[34] Sigmund Mayer, *Die Wiener Juden: Kommerz, Kultur, Politk, 1700–1900* (Vienna and Berlin, 1917); George Franz, *Liberalismus: Die deutschliberale Bewegung in der Habsburgischen Monarchie* (Vienna and Munich, 1955), 198 ff.

But for the community structure of Vienna Jewry, of much more immediate importance was the 'provisional' recognition by the authorities of the by-laws of the Israelitische Religionsgemeinde (Israelite religious community) on 14 January 1852, for which Mannheimer and his colleagues had worked so tenaciously.[35] Already on 3 April 1849 the Emperor Franz Joseph in receiving representatives of the Jewish Community of Vienna in an audience had accepted 'the expression of the true devotion and loyalty which you extend to me in the name of the Israelite community'.[36] This was the first time that the hitherto taboo word 'community' had been *officially* used to describe the Jews of Vienna. Though their equality of rights was quickly revoked, the Emperor Franz Joseph and his officials did not from this time forth go back on their recognition of the Viennese 'Israelites' as a legally constituted *religious* community with complete autonomy.

According to the by-laws which remained in force throughout the reign of Franz Joseph (and beyond), the executive of the board (*Vorstand*) consisted of five representatives (*Vertreter*) and fifteen councillors (*Beiräthe*) who were not remunerated for their work.[37] These officials had full power over the community and could regulate all matters of religion according to their judgement. The role of rabbis and preachers, in contrast to their colleagues in Eastern Europe, was purely advisory and they had no real control over community affairs or even right to vote.[38] Indeed, in the Jewish community—in contrast even to the grossly undemocratic elections to the Vienna city council, the Austrian Landtag, or the Imperial Parliament—the Jewish *Intelligenz* (i.e. professors, teachers, doctors, civil servants) were discriminated against unless they paid the stipulated religious tax (*Kultussteuer*), the minimum amount being ten florins per year.[39] This tax and voting structure gave the Kultusgemeinde leadership a manifestly oligarchic character. The lay leaders of Viennese Jewry consistently opposed any attempt to widen the franchise, rejecting even government wishes to give the rabbis more voice in the running of the community. As late as the 1890s when the Austrian government itself introduced a proposal to this effect in the Upper House, the leaders of the community mobilized all their political influence to defeat the plan.[40] By the end of

[35] Rosenmann, *Mannheimer*, 88.
[36] Grunwald, *Vienna*, 293; A. F. Pribram (ed.) *Urkunden und Akten zur Geschichte der Juden in Wien* (Vienna and Leipzig, 1918), 549.
[37] Wolf, *Geschichte der Juden in Wien*, 154.
[38] Ibid.   [39] Ibid. 168–9.
[40] Grunwald, *Vienna*, 419 ff., who also points out that 'the leaders of the Jewish

the century the issue of the *Kultussteuer* and voting rights had become bound up with the internal challenge of Jewish nationalism. For the first time there was open debate over the issue of the domination of organizational life exercised by the affluent leadership of the community and the strain placed on its resources by the need to care for a large number of poorer immigrants.[41]

In the 1850s and 60s, however, the central question facing the community was still the conflict between orthodoxy and reform, which also had its political dimension.[42] The Kultusgemeinde had become more liberal in its general outlook and was regarded by some Ministers of State as potentially subversive. Its leaders, including Mannheimer, were suspected of liberal-democratic and even 'revolutionary tendencies' dangerous to the State (*staatsgefährlich*).[43] The government had found an unexpected ally in the orthodox money-changer Ignaz Deutsch (1808–81), a native of Pressburg and *gabbai* (manager) of the Polish *schul* in Vienna since 1848. Deutsch submitted a series of memoranda in the 1850s to the Minister of Religious Affairs confirming his conviction that whereas Reform Jews favoured radical political change, orthodoxy was loyal to Habsburg rule. Deutsch even requested orthodox rabbis not to support the Kultusgemeinde's protests against the revocation of Jewish rights, and appealed instead to the government to invest the rabbis with the same powers enjoyed by Catholic clergy under the Concordat of 1855. In 1857, with the encouragement of Count Thun, Deutsch sought to persuade the government to permit orthodox communities to secede from the established *Gemeinde* and found their own central synagogue.[44] This demand was later to be repeated a number of times by other Austrian Jewish orthodox leaders. Deutsch tried to organize the orthodox Jews from Hungary and

Community . . . made it a matter of a cavalier dignity for the Community to meet its own needs' rather than requesting a government subsidy for maintaining Jewish charitable institutions.

[41] Ivar Oxaal and Walter R. Weitzmann, 'The Jews of Pre-1914 Vienna: An Exploration of Basic Sociological Dimensions', *Leo Baeck Yearbook*, 30 (1985), 417–18.

[42] See Wolf, *Geschichte der Juden in Wien*, 164–6; Rosenmmann, *Mannheimer*, 93–6.

[43] N. M. Gelber, *Aus zwei Jahrhunderten* (Vienna and Leipzig, 1924), 145 ff., 170; also Wolfgang Häusler, 'Orthodoxie und Reform in Wiener Judentum in der Epoche des Hochliberalismus', *Studia Judaica Austriaca*, 6 (Vienna, 1978), 35.

[44] See Tietze, pp. 217–20, who observes that services in the First Temple were anathema to Deutsch's followers among the Galician and Hungarian Jews but his efforts to mobilize them failed politically. See also I. Oehler, 'Geschichte des "Leopoldstadter Tempels" in Wien', in H. Gold (ed.), *Zeitschrift für Geschichte der Juden*, i (Tel Aviv, 1964), 22–4.

Galicia against the building of a second synagogue in the Leopoldstadt, utilizing their well-known revulsion at the 'frivolous' services in the Seitenstettengasse.[45] But for all their antipathy towards the *Daytsch Yidn* (German Jews), the orthodox could not be so easily organized against the liberal Jews by an extremist leader like Deutsch and his efforts to erect a separate central synagogue for the 'old believers' (*Altgläubige*) failed.[46] Finally, Ignaz Deutsch's readiness to approve the Pope's standpoint in the notorious Mortara case (which virtually entailed condoning Catholic kidnapping of Jewish children), the public exposure of his collaboration with the clerical Ministry of Education, and the failure of his bank finished his career.[47]Even his successor Solomon Spitzer (1826–93), another Hungarian-born leader of the Viennese orthodox, refused to co-operate with him.

Spitzer, son-in-law of the Hatam Sofer, the ultra-orthodox leader of Hungarian Jewry, had in fact been appointed in 1853 at Deutsch's suggestion to be rabbi of Vienna's Pressburger *schul*, serving a small community of orthodox Jews primarily from Pressburg and the Hungarian provincial communities. In 1858 he had been named assistant rabbi to Lazar Horowitz and ten years later he was offered the position of Chief Rabbi in Vienna providing he would modify his strict orthodoxy. Spitzer refused to do this and in 1871 he was to lead the orthodox opposition to efforts by the renowned liberal politician Ignaz Kuranda, the new President of the Kultusgemeinde (and by other members of the Board) to introduce more radical reforms in the order of the services.[48] The protest meeting, attended by approximately 500 people—a quarter of Vienna's entire synagogue membership— eventually led to a compromise. The introduction of the organ into services was indefinitely delayed and instead of excising from the liturgy references to Zion and to the reinstitution of the sacrifices (as

[45] Tietze, p. 217.

[46] Ibid. 218.

[47] G. Wolf's *Beitrag zur Geschichte juedischer Tartuffe* (Vienna, 1864), written under the pseudonym of Israel Levi Kohn, which exposed Deutsch's applications to the Ministry of Religious Affairs after he had denied writing them, helped destroy his credibility.

[48] These included the introduction of the organ and the elimination of all references in the prayer-books to an ultimate return to Zion, to belief in the Messiah, and to the reinstitution of sacrifices. The Viennese reformers, represented at the Augsburg synod (1871) by Joseph von Wertheimer, Leopold Kompert, and the influential editor of *Die Neuzeit* Simon Szántó, saw such changes as an appropriate response to the granting of full emancipation and the liberal ideology of the new era. See 'Beschlüsse der beiden israelitischen synoden im Jahre 1869 und 1871', in *Die Neuzeit* (20 Oct. 1871), pp. 497–500.

the *Gemeinde* leaders desired) these prayers were to be silently recited by the congregation.[49] This characteristically Viennese accommodation succeeded in cooling the heated atmosphere, especially as the few minor changes introduced in the services were diplomatically termed 'modifications'. Nevertheless, Spitzer resigned from the rabbinate of the Kultusgemeinde and henceforth devoted his energies solely to the Adass Yisroel synagogue in the Grosse Schiffgasse (better known as the *Schiffschul*) and its subsidiary institutions.

The antagonism between orthodox and reform Judaism which had surfaced in the 1850s with the new immigration from Hungary and Galicia, the intrigues of Deutsch, and the controversy surrounding construction of a second Temple in the Leopoldstadt, was if anything exacerbated by the arrival in 1856 of a new *prediger* in Vienna, Adolf Jellinek (1821–93). No less eloquent than Mannheimer but closer to reform Judaism, he was even more determined than his predecessor to bring the traditional faith into line with modern developments.[50] Jellinek was somewhat lax in ritual matters. For example, during his ministry he omitted the reading of the *Ketubah* (marriage contract) at the wedding ceremony. He also ignored the mandatory immersion of a proselyte to Judaism and abandoned the rite of *ḥalizah*, by which the levirate marriage of a widow whose husband was without offspring could be avoided. Even Jellinek's observance of the dietary laws was considered suspect. But by general consent he was the outstanding preacher of the age and far more of a scholar in the tradition of *Wissenschaft des Judentums* than Mannheimer.[51] He was one of the pioneers, for example, of the study of cabbala, having translated Adolphe Franck's *La Cabbale* from French into German as a young man of twenty-three.[52] This was only the starting-point for his own original researches in the field of Jewish mysticism which began with *Moses ben Schemtob de Leon und sein Verhältnis zum Sohar* (1851)— subsequently in his 1887 edition of Abraham Abulafia's *Sefer ha-Ot*, Jellinek demonstrated that de Leon and not Abulafia was the author of

[49] For a critical view of the 'compromise' and the position of the orthodox by a contemporary, see Wolf, *Geschichte der Juden in Wien*, 201–4. On Spitzer's campaign, see Häusler, pp. 52–3.

[50] The standard biography is by M. Rosenmann, *Dr Adolf Jellinek: Sein Leben und Schaffen* (Vienna, 1931); see also Grunwald, *Vienna*, 360–5; Alfred Willman, 'Famous Rabbis of Vienna' in Fraenkel (ed.), *Jews of Austria*, 323–4; and Allerhand, pp. 14–17. Allerhand's characterization of Jellinek as 'Apologet eines blutleeren Judentums' is, however, one-sided.

[51] Rosemann, *Jellinek*, 121, 124, 129, 194.   [52] Ibid. 36–7.

the *Zohar;*[53] works such as *Beiträge zur Geschichte der Kabbala* (1852), *Auswahl Kabbalistischer Mystik* (1853), *Philosophie und Kabbala* (1854), and his publication of many largely unknown Midrashim also proved of great value for the study of early cabbala.[54]

The preacher who dominated the spiritual life of Viennese Jewry in the liberal era had been born in the Slovakian village of Drslavice, near Ungarisch-Brod (Uhersky Brod) in Moravia on 26 June 1821. His forefathers had been Czech peasants of Hussite background who probably converted to Judaism in the eighteenth century, an ancestry of which Jellinek was very proud. His mother, who died when he was only five years old, came from a distinguished rabbinical family (her grandfather had been the celebrated Hungarian rabbi and Talmudist, Hirsch Broda) and young Adolf Jellinek was sent in his early years to the Prossnitz *yeshivah* of the orthodox Hungarian rabbi and Talmudist, Menahem Katz, one of the outstanding disciples of the Hatam Sofer, with whom Jellinek also became friendly. Already in Prossnitz, in addition to his Talmudic expertise, Jellinek began to learn modern languages and secular subjects on his own initiative. In 1838 he moved to Prague where he was exposed to the lectures of Salomon Judah Rapoport and the classical sermons of Dr Michael Sachs.[55]

But his secular education began after 1842 in Leipzig, where he graduated from university, having studied philosophy, philology, and Oriental languages (especially Arabic and Persian). Among his teachers was the renowned Christian Semitologist Professor Heinrich Fleischer. Jellinek also studied rhetoric at Leipzig University with great enthusiasm (he was especially enamoured of Cicero and Bossuet)—which stood him in good stead in later years.[56] His polished presentations, plasticity in forming ideas, mastery in description, and talent of fitting everything into place were carefully acquired and studied skills.[57] It was his ability to combine the rich sources of the Bible and Midrashim with the classical culture which he had studied at university that made Jellinek's addresses such masterpieces of artistic

---

[53] Rosemann, *Jellinek*, 58.

[54] Ibid. 59–60. His *Beit ha-Midrash*, 6 vols. (1853–78), was perhaps Jellinek's major contribution to modern Jewish scholarship. He not only collected, classified, and edited rare Midrashim and wrote commentaries on them but used them with rare effect in his speeches and sermons. His reconstitution of the Midrashic literature showed the influence of the critical methods he had learned from Zunz, Steinschneider, Rappoport, and Munk; his rhetorical application of this treasury reflected the more artistic side of his temperament.

[55] Rosenmann, *Jellinek*, 25–7.   [56] Ibid. 28–33.

[57] Grunwald, *Vienna*, 360–1; Rosenmann, *Jellinek*, 44.

construction.[58] In Max Grunwald's words, he was 'an innovator, not so much in creating a new style of homiletics as in bringing to life the ancient meaning of the Midrash. Jellinek did not follow the latest form of preaching which, modelling itself upon Christian methods, banished the Midrash and even avoided a Hebrew citation. He made use of the *derashah* (lecture, sermon) of the former days, but impregnated it with a modern spirit.'[59] In his blending of biblical, Midrashic, and rabbinical sources with the aesthetic requirements of edification (*Erbauung*), their skilful interpretation and in the novel and unexpected turns of meaning given to the old texts, Jellinek continued (though in a more brilliant and extravagant fashion) the examples of Michael Sachs in Prague and Mannheimer in Vienna.[60]

In 1845 Jellinek was appointed preacher at Leipzig's small Berliner synagogue which had been established under the guidance of the Dresden rabbi and *Wissenschaft* scholar Zacharias Frankel. Though somewhat overshadowed during these years by Frankel's formidable personality, Jellinek's fame as a preacher and scholar steadily grew. He shared his patron's opposition to drastic reforms of the liturgy but did not hesitate to create a choir using Christian singers from the local school for services in the synagogue. In a similarly liberal spirit, he co-founded with Christian clergymen the Kirchlicher Verein für alle Religionsbekenntnisse, an interdenominational association which he would have represented at the German National Assembly in 1848 had this not been prevented by the Saxon Minister of Religious Affairs. Thus already in his formative years at Leipzig, Jellinek espoused a dynamic and libertarian model of Judaism, opening out towards the Christian world.

The young preacher enthusiastically greeted the freedom resulting from the 1848 Revolution, though opposing the radical quasi-socialist

---

[58] Grunwald, *Vienna*, 361.

[59] Ibid. 361–2; see also 'Adolf Jellinek ist ein moderner Prediger, *par excellence*, ein jüdischer Kanzelredner der unmittelbaren Gegenwart', 'Dr Adolf Jellinek', *Die Neuzeit*, 6 Oct. 1882.

[60] On Jewish homiletics and sermons in this period, see the instructive article by Alexander Altmann, 'The New Style of Preaching in Nineteenth-Century Germany', in A. Altmann (ed.), *Studies in Nineteenth-Century Jewish Intellectual History* (Harvard, 1964), 65–116. Altmann discusses extensively the concern of the reformers for decorum and beauty in the mode of worship and the belief that 'edification' was the central purpose of preaching as being two of the dominant characteristics of the 'new style'. Rosenmann, for his part, praises Jellinek's synthesis of 'deutscher Sprachgewalt und jüdischer Geistigkeit', seeing him as the classic exponent 'der neuzeitlichen jüdischen Kanzelberedsamkeit' (*Jellinek*, 6).

views of his young brother Hermann Jellinek, who was expelled from Germany for his political convictions. Though he rarely referred to it subsequently, the traumatic impact on Adolf Jellinek of Hermann's brutal execution at the age of twenty-five (for his role in the Viennese Revolution) must have been considerable. One exceptional reference was a moving eulogy in 1867 following the execution of Franz Joseph's own brother, the Emperor Maximilian of Mexico, which prompted Jellinek to propose the abolition of the death penalty for political offenses. Adolf Jellinek's reticence on the subject of his brother reflected their tense relationship. Hermann despised his elder brother as a 'lousy phrasemonger' and hypocritical theologian; Adolf Jellinek, for his part, had not been attracted by an overt political role, preferring to keep in the background, though subsequently he always acknowledged the importance of the 1848 Revolution in the destiny of German and Austrian Jewry. But even at that time he already strongly identified with the German cultural nationalism of 1848, joining for example the board of an association established to support German interests in the Slav countries.

In an article published in *Der Orient* in April 1848 Jellinek forcefully argued that in language, culture, and education Jews represented 'Germandom' in the mixed population areas of the multinational Habsburg Monarchy and that in Austria, Bohemia, Moravia, Hungary, Silesia, and Galicia they were German to the core. Hence the cause of German freedom could be strengthened only by collaboration with the 'Israelites' and by their full emancipation; 'the freedom of the Jews is at the same time the freedom of Germandom'—this maxim was his youthful credo.[61]

Jellinek's Leipzig years, on the borders of the Slavic world, at the crossroads of Western and Eastern European Jewry, between the realms of *Haskalah* and Talmud, liberal Christian scholarship and the *Wissenschaft des Judentums*, prepared him well for his future role in Vienna.[62] In 1856 he was called in as preacher to the Leopoldstadt Temple and nine years later, when Mannheimer died, he succeeded him at the Seitenstettengasse synagogue. His oratorical brilliance and skill as an apologist of Judaism—first nurtured in Leipzig—would make a great impact in Vienna, with its well-known love of theatrical

---

[61] A. J., 'Die Juden In Österreich', *Der Orient*, 22 Apr. 1848, pp. 129 ff. Since moving to Leipzig, Jellinek had helped Julius Fuerst to edit the *Orient*, putting to good use his knowledge of Romance languages, Arabic, and Persian.

[62] 'Dr. Adolf Jellinek', *Die Neuzeit*, 6 Oct. 1882.

performance, its appreciation of poetry, feeling for pathos, gesture, and atmosphere.[63]

In Vienna, Jellinek rapidly established himself as the most eloquent preacher of the era, spreading the fame of the community beyond the borders of the Monarchy and across the world.[64] Many of his sermons were published in various languages and his captivating addresses with their spiritual elevation, their Jewish learning, original use of *aggadah*, and appeal to the emotions as well as the intellect, reached into the hearts of his listeners. For all the studied pauses, the leaning on the pulpit, 'the stretching out of his hand to be kissed after the sermon', Jellinek's style was lucid, simple, and persuasive. There was a prophetic spark in his glorification of Judaism and its spiritual uniqueness, reminiscent of Mannheimer, though after failing to be elected to the Lower Austrian Diet in 1861 he was less directly involved than his predecessor in political affairs. But like Mannheimer, Jellinek strove above all to preserve unity in a community constantly threatened by the possibility of orthodox secession: he, too, opposed the omission of references to Zion in the prayer-book, in spite of his resolute opposition to any shade of Jewish political nationalism.[65] Equally he rejected the hostility of the reformers to the Talmud, regarding it on the contrary as the embodiment of the Jewish love of study and learning for its own sake.

Jellinek regarded the Talmudic dedication to the Holy Word, to knowledge and religious faith without thought of profit or recompense, as an admirable Jewish trait and one that had encouraged and developed the virtues of self-control, self-sufficiency, and sacrifice for the sake of higher spiritual values that characterized the Jewish people.[66] The Talmud exemplified the realm of truth and peace, inspiring the cultivation of brotherly and divine love, and far from being esoteric, it was open to all classes of the people. It did not differentiate between rich and poor, the powerful and the powerless,

---

[63] See the appreciation by Julius David, 'Zum ersten Jahrzeitstage Dr. Adolf Jellinek's', *Die Neuzeit*, 11 Jan. 1895: 'Jellinek war ein rednerischer Dichter oder dichterischer Redner, weil man an seinen Reden nicht nur die Tiefe des Denkers und den Lichtglanz des Idealen, sondern auch die heilige Gluth der Phantasie, die fesselnde Form und die gewählteste Sprache des Dichters beobachten kann.' Also Grunwald, *Vienna*, 362: '. . . his eloquence burst like a lava from the crater of his soul.' He could be plagiarized 'but never imitated, let alone equalled'.

[64] Willman, p. 324, even called him 'the most talented Jewish preacher that modern Judaism has produced'.

[65] Rosenmann, *Jellinek*, 47–8.

[66] Jellinek, *Der Talmudjude: Vier Reden* (Vienna, 1882), 8–9, 15.

but instead affirmed the superiority of intellectual and moral values above all else. Thus the traditional prestige of Talmud scholars, of Talmud schools and teachers in Jewish communities, was a testament to the egalitarian spirit of Judaism. Jellinek's defence of Talmudic learning was all the more notable in view of the fact that it was viewed by many 'enlightened' Viennese Jews with open distaste and by the early 1880s had again become a central target of the Austrian anti-semites. Denouncing these prejudices, Jellinek sought to demonstrate that Talmudic morality was in fact profoundly 'cosmopolitan' and that it proclaimed the unity of the human race, descended from one common root and one stem since the time of the Creation.[67]

Jellinek also passionately opposed striking the messianic idea out of Judaism. Nevertheless he gave it an openly liberal and enlightened colouring. The Hebrews, he claimed, had been the first to teach humanity the 'knowledge of God, love of mankind, loving-kindness, the purest morality'; to be a Jew therefore meant in the *ideal* sense to be 'loving, helpful and benevolent to all men'.[68] In contrast to the pagan cult of beauty, Israel's mission had been and remained the removal of idolatry, force, arbitrariness, chaos, and madness from the face of the earth, and the proclamation in its place of the unity of creation and mankind on the foundations of morality, justice, and truth. Israel's war on the pagan gods was a tough, tenacious, and unbending battle against cruelty and barbarism. It was for this messianic mission as a light among the nations that it had been chosen.[69] In spite of the dispersion and constant persecution, Israel had maintained its inner cohesiveness, its uniquenes and unity throughout world history, thanks to the power of this messianic vision.[70]

At the same time, in the spirit of the Enlightenment, Jellinek gave a liberal humanist and universalist interpretation to this Jewish mission, speaking in the name of religious tolerance, the equality of all faiths, the brotherhood of man, and freedom of conscience. On the hundredth anniversary of Moses Mendelssohn's death, he stressed that the message of spiritual ennoblement, the perfection of humanity, and the cultivation of *Menschenfreundlichkeit* lay at the heart of the *Aufklärung* (Enlightenment). Mendelssohn had heralded the coming of

[67] Jellinek, *Talmudjude*, 8–9, 15; 'Die Rede und Vortragsweise der Talmudlehrer, zunächst Adam betreffend'.

[68] *Die letzten Reden des verklärten Predigers Dr. Adolf Jellinek gehalten an den Freitag-abenden des abgelaufenen Winters im Tempel der Seitenstettengasse in Wien*, ed. D. Löwy (Vienna, 1894), 37–40.

[69] Ibid. 48.   [70] Jellinek, *Talmudjude*, 5–6.

the 'Heavenly City' of freedom of conscience at a time when Jews were not only oppressed, humiliated, despised, and hated by their fellow men but subject to religious compulsion, arbitrary rule, and penalties of excommunication within their own communities.[71] Mendelssohn's call for the separation of state and religion, for an end to clerical sanctions or to doctrines of heresy and exclusion, as well as his appeal to persuasion, reason, and toleration contained a profound universal truth for Jews and Christians alike. Hence he remained a relevant figure of light, wisdom, and justice not only for Israel but all civilized mankind.[72]

It was in the spirit of the Mendelssohnian Enlightenment that Jellinek glorified Judaism as a torch of humanity, intellectual progress, and moral elevation for the nations. At the same time it was also destined to be the messianic religion of the future.[73] Hebraic monotheism was therefore not merely an instrument for the ethical refinement of mankind, it would prove to be the original prototype for a new purified *Weltreligion* which would finally bring peace and reconciliation to all humanity.[74] In contrast to Catholicism, which Jellinek firmly believed was in decay and whose never-ending polemical attacks against Judaism were a constast bone in the throat of Austrian Jews, Israelite monotheism proposed the glorious vision of a Third Temple, beyond all divisive confessionalism—a true religion of *Humanität* open to all classes and races.[75]

Jellinek did not however ignore the 'tribal consciousness' (*Stammesbewusstsein*) of Jews in the name of a bloodless, cosmopolitan conception of the Messianic role of Judaic monotheism.[76] On the contrary, he sought to blend its universalist aspirations with the particularism embedded in Jewish life and law, to synthesize its 'ideal

[71] Jellinek, *Denkrede auf Moses Mendelssohn am 4 Januar 1886 im israelitischen Bethause der innern Stadt Wien* (Vienna, 1886), 1–8.

[72] 'Moses Mendelssohn war ein Weiser des Judenthums, ein Kämpfer für Geistesfreiheit, ein Erlöser der Gewissen, ein Lehrer der Menschheit, der Erbauer der Welt- und Gottestadt Jerusalem, der Stadt der Freiheit und des Friedens!'

[73] Rosenmann, *Jellinek*, 86.

[74] Ibid. 132–40.

[75] Ibid. 138–40; see Jellinek, *Schma Jisrael: Fünf Reden über das israelitische Glaubensbekenntnis* (Vienna, 1869); *Bezelem Elohim: Fünf Reden über die israelitische Menschenlehre und Weltanschauung* (Vienna, 1871); *Zur Feier des fünzigjährigen Jubiläums des israelitischen Tempels in der innern Stadt Wien* (Vienna, 1876); Dr. Adolfo Jellinek, *Dio, il mondo e l'uomo secondo le dottrine del giudaismo* (Trieste, 1890).

[76] See Jellinek, *Studien und Skizzen. Der jüdische Stamm: Ethnograpische Studie* (Vienna, 1869), in which a sense of modern tribal consciousness does appear alongside, though firmly subordinate to, universalist humanitarian ideals.

of *Humanität* with a strong sense of ethnic identity.[77] Jellinek's *Stammesbegriff* was not so much a precursor of secular Jewish nationalism as an attempt to harmonize Hebraic universalism with 'tribal' particularism in such a way as to ensure the continuity of Jewish tradition and identity in the modern age. He disliked both the exclusivist insularity of the Eastern orthodox ghetto as well as the superficial 'formless universalism' of a reform lacking 'any inner content'.[78]

For Jellinek, the Jewish *Stamm* was a historic category, rooted not so much in biological or unchanging natural characteristics but in the essence of Hebrew religiosity and a Messianic idea of Judaism compatible with modern liberal aspirations for the universal progress of mankind.[79] While the Jewish *Volksgeist* was indeed a reality expressed in the medium of language, literature, religious genius, history, morality, and above all the 'character' and ethos of the Jewish people, Jellinek was careful to distinguish between 'national' and 'tribal' peculiarities' (*Stammeseigentümlichkeiten*).[80] In *Der jüdische Stamm* (1869) he explained that Jews did not have any national characteristics as such but 'thanks to their universalism they adapt and absorb qualities from the nations in whose midst they are born and educated'.[81] In the ghetto, Jewish particularism based on *Halakhah* and ritual observance had been dominant, as a result of oppression and lack of social intercourse with other nations; in conditions of emancipation and individual liberty, of cultural openness and progress, the universalist polarity in Judaism would gain the upper hand along with its predominantly prophetic, moralistic strain.[82]

Both the Talmudic-Rabbinical era with its legalism and avid scholasticism, as well as the cabbala with its mystical supernaturalism, had reflected the one-sided polarities created by the challenge of

---

[77] Altmann, 'The New Style of Preaching', 87, referring to Jellinek's sermons on the idea of 'Zion (*Predigten*, ii (Vienna, 1863), 155 ff., 167 ff.), argues that 'he preached a pre-Zionist humanistic Zionism'. This may be overstretching a point.

[78] Jellinek, *Der jüdische Stamm*, 14.

[79] Ibid. 10–11; *Schma Jisrael*. Jellinek sharply rejected the antitheses first developed by the French liberal scholar Ernst Renan in his *Histoire générale des langues sémitiques* (Paris, 1855) concerning 'Aryan' and 'Semitic' characteristics. See A. J., 'Eine neue Judenfrage', in *Jahrbuch für Israeliten* (1865/6), p. 140.

[80] See however *Der jüdische Stamm*, 6: 'Die Art und Weise wie ein Volk denkt, zeigt seine Sprache; wie es fühlt, seine Religion; wie es schafft, sein Schriftum; wie es sich entwickelt, seine Geschichte; wie es handelt, sein Charakter; wie es lebt, seine Sitten.' These and other passages show the influence of the German romantic school on Jellinek's thought.

[81] Ibid. 47–8.   [82] Ibid. 11.

Christianity, by external pressures and enforced isolation. But Jellinek was convinced that the modern era of enlightenment and toleration was opening vast and limitless perspectives, enabling the Jewish *Stamm* to overcome its historical weaknesses and contradictions through contact with other nations. The sharp intellect, wit, fantasy, receptivity, practicality, and enthusiasm of the Jews, their openness as a dispersed people to countless influences—as well as their 'feminine' qualities of liveliness, rapidity of thought, mimicry, and adaptability—had already found creative expression in countless fields.[83] They would surely become 'the predestined mediators' between East and West, whose reconciliation in a higher unity would be the inspiring future mission of Diasporic Jewry.[84]

Jellinek's glowing optimism concerning the beneficial effects of enlightenment and emancipation had already found passionate expression in a famous Passover sermon, *Schir ha-Schirim* (The Song of Songs); it was delivered in 1861 in the Leopoldstadt synagogue following the proclamation of the February Patent by the new liberal Ministry of Anton von Schmerling. The Austrian defeats in northern Italy (1859) and the burgeoning signs of rebirth of the Italian nation heralded indeed the end of the absolutist era and sparked off Jewish hopes for a final release from its immemorial fetters. Jellinek made himself the spokesman of those aspirations for 'Israel's resurrection to new life', trenchantly evoking the visions of the Prophet Ezekiel.[85] The year 1861 heralded the beginning of a new epoch for Viennese Jewry; the medieval chains and antiquated restrictions on Jewish freedom of movement, on their right to own landed property, on liberty of expression and the right to vote, were beginning to fade away. Significantly, too, on 30 August 1861 *Die Neuzeit* (*Wochenschrift für politische, religiose und Cultur-Interessen*) was founded as the organ of

---

[83] Ibid. 220–10n 'Die Zukunft des jüdischen Stammes'. Jellinek was fascinated by the 'femininity of the Jewish people' (see ibid. 89 ff., esp. pp. 92–5), constantly drawing parallels in his sermons and writings between what he felt were 'Jewish' and 'feminine' characteristics. On the whole, he admired women but among the more negative qualities he listed as being common to both groups (i.e. Jews and females) were vengefulness, jealousy, the capacity for intense hatred, a tendency to vanity and superficiality, lack of true originality and creativity in the sciences, and a love of luxury and show. In the hands of German and Austrian anti-Semites (many of whom were also misogynists) these stereotypes were often used to quite different and macabre purpose.

[84] Ibid. 222: 'Er [Der Jude] ist der prädestinirte Vermittler zweier Welten: des Orients und Occidents, deren Versöhnung zu einer höhern Einheit im Schosse der Zukunft ruht!'

[85] Jellinek, *Predigten*, i (Vienna, 1862), 156.

liberal Viennese Jewry, edited by Simon Szántó and the Bohemian-born writer, Dr Leopold Kompert.[86] It was to be Adolf Jellinek's mouthpiece and main literary weapon for over thirty years in his exertions to adapt Judaism to the requirements of the dawning liberal age.[87]

In a stirring dithyrambic hymn to 'the new, great and glorious era' delivered in yet another Passover sermon (1863), Jellinek effusively greeted the signs that Austria was throwing off the yoke of the Middle Ages; that the Empire was at last entering the realm of justice, freedom, and light in which Jews, too, would fully participate as equal citizens before the law. His sermons of the 1860s can be seen as a faithful mirror of the aspirations and ideas of liberal Austrian Jewry which gratefully hailed the 1867 Constitution as 'the crowning work of centuries' and a victorious consummation of their arduous striving for emancipation.[88]

Internal dissatisfaction with Jellinek's religious liberalism continued to manifest itself, however, among orthodox circles in Vienna, irritated at his latitudinarianism in ritual observance and ostentatious identification with the cause of reform. Their proportion of the synagogue membership, especially in the Leopoldstadt, continued to grow as Viennese Jewry climbed towards the 40,000 mark by the end of the 1860s. At the beginning of the decade Mannheimer was already an old and sick man whose moderating influence on the community was declining with his strength; Jellinek, for all his wonderful articulateness and scholarly achievements did not have the same interest or command a similar degree of authority in community affairs. The orthodox felt the time had arrived to counterattack and their sense of urgency was, if anything, aggravated by the triumph of liberalism in most areas of Austrian public life and the growing self-confidence of the Kultusgemeinde lay leadership in pushing for changes in the liturgy.[89]

The orthodox were vigorously opposed by Jellinek's most radical supporter, Simon Szántó (1819–82), the Hungarian-born editor of the *Neuzeit*, who had participated in the Reform synods of Leipzig and Augsburg. Szántó, the son of a rabbi, had received a strict religious

---

[86] On *Die Neuzeit* and its journalistic importance, see Jacob Toury, *Die jüdische Presse im österreichischen Kaiserreich, 1802–1918* (Tübingen, 1983), 669 ff., 39 ff.

[87] Rosenmann, *Jellinek*, 92.

[88] Grunwald, *Vienna*, 407.

[89] On the class background to the conflicts between orthodoxy and reform, see Häusler, p. 49.

upbringing in Talmudic schools during his youth. In 1849 he had established in Vienna a boys' elementary and secondary school teaching Jewish and secular subjects, which became the first of its kind in Austria entitled to issue officially valid diplomas. Szántó was subsequently appointed inspector for Jewish religious instruction at public schools and official interpreter of the Hebrew language. He also taught Bible and Hebrew literature at the *Beth Hamidrash* in Vienna, founded by Jellinek as a centre of Jewish *Wissenschaft* in 1862. This background allied to his forceful literary style gave added weight to Szántó's campaign in the *Neuzeit* and other journals against the religious conservatives. Yet even Szántó was careful to wrap calls for change in the mantle of concern for tradition and for the restoration of the historic principles of Judaism.[90]

Szántó's co-editor, Leopold Kompert (1822–86), internationally celebrated for his evocative descriptions of the Bohemian ghetto of his youth, was another driving-force behind the reform campaign.[91] Having become active during the 1850s in Viennese civic life, and an official of the Kultusgemeinde, Kompert threw his influenced solidly behind the liberal trend which was now gaining ground. In 1863/4 he earned the enmity of the orthodox Jews of Vienna for his views, as a result of a lawsuit brought by the Austrian government against him as publisher of the *Jahrbuch für Israeliten*. The *Jahrbuch* had published an article entitled 'Die Verjüngung des jüdischen Stammes' (The Rejuvenation of the Jewish Race) by the renowned German Jewish historian Heinrich Graetz, in which he referred to Israel as the suffering Messiah-people and made some scathing remarks about Christianity and the concept of a personal Messiah. Kompert as the publisher was accused by the government (with the encouragement of

---

[90] Simon Szántó, 'Staat und Synagogue in Österreich', *Jahrbuch für Israeliten* (1862/3), p. 220. Szántó also edited the *Jahrbuch* from 1865 to 1868.

[91] Kompert's first collection of ghetto stories, *Aus dem Ghetto*, appeared at the outbreak of the 1848 Revolution, which he greeted enthusiastically. Distressed however by the anti-Jewish riots of the same year, he had urged Austrian Jews to emigrate to America: see his 'Auf, Nach Amerika!', *Österreichisches Central-Organ*, 1, no. 6 (6 May 1848). Kompert himself none the less settled in Vienna, publishing further collections of tales such as *Boehmische Juden* (1851), and *Neue Geschichte aus dem Ghetto*, 2 vols. (Vienna, 1860), which gave him an international reputation as a sympathetic, masterful narrator of ghetto life based on his own childhood memories of Bohemia. A recurring theme in many of his tales was the confrontation of Jews and Gentiles and the writer's liberal attitude to the problem of intermarriage. See 'Dr. Leopold Kompert's Schriften', *Die Neuzeit*, 5 Oct. 1883; also Grunwald, *Vienna*, 327–8, 351–3; Guido Kisch, *In Search of Freedom* (London, 1949), 215–29, for the 1848 text of 'Auf, Nach Amerika!', and Paul Amann, *Leopold Komperts literarische Anfänge* (Prague, 1907).

Ignaz Deutsch and his zealous followers in Vienna) of degrading
orthodox Judaism—for which he was eventually acquitted—and also of
insulting Christianity, for which he was fined.[92] Although Mannheimer
and Lazar Horowitz testified on his behalf, claiming that there were no
sects or divisions in Judaism, the affair aroused the orthodox rabbis to
sharp refutations and protests against what they saw as a Reform-
inspired abandonment of belief in a personal Messiah. Jellinek's own
stance on religious questions came under increasing criticism from
orthodox circles.

The position of the conservative forces was temporarily strengthened
by the election in 1868 of the wealthy banker and orthodox Jew, Jonas
Freiherr von Königswarter (1807–71), as President of the Kultusgemeinde.[93] It was partly his influence and the increasing orthodox
pressure which brought the conservative rabbi Moritiz Güdemann
(1835–1918) to Vienna in 1866 to officiate at the Leopoldstadt
synagogue.[94] His appointment and installation as rabbi in 1869 (the
first religious leader in Vienna to bear this title since the 1670
expulsion) contributed in the long run to placating orthodox resentment,
since it clearly served to offset and balance Jellinek's influence.[95] The
decision to appoint Güdemann, no less importantly, reflected the
demographic impact of the more traditionalist Jewish immigration
from Hungary and Galicia which was gradually changing the character
and structure of Viennese Jewry.[96]

Shortly after Moritz Güdemann's arrival in Vienna, he became
involved in a dispute with Jellinek over the validity of a conversion
ceremony performed without ritual immersion. The case concerned
the Christian fiancée of a Viennese Jewish neurologist, Dr Moritz
Benedikt (later to become a very famous professor), who had been

[92] 'Der Prozess Kompert', *Die Neuzeit*, (1 Jan. 1864); see also Grunwald, *Vienna*,
351–2; Tietzte, *Die Juden Wiens*, 220.

[93] Königswarter was ennobled by the Emperor and appointed to the Upper House in
1870. Director of a major banking firm, he had helped the Rothschilds establish the
Creditanstalt, Austria's largest bank, in 1855. He also played a part in developing the
Austrian railways, which was continued by his son Moritz Baron von Königswarter
(1837–93), one of Vienna's leading financial figures; see *Jüdisches Weltblatt*, 15 July
1882, p. 3.

[94] By 1868 there were eleven orthodox ritual-bathhouses in the Leopoldstadt and it is
estimated that orthodoxy comprised about 25 per cent of dues-paying *Gemeinde*
members; see Tietze, *Die Juden Wiens*, 222.

[95] Though Jellinek and Güdemann did not agree on some important religious issues,
they generally avoided open confrontation; see Ismar Schorsch, 'Moritz Güdemann;
Rabbi, Historian, Apologist', *Leo Baeck Yearbook*, 11 (1966), 46–7.

[96] Ibid. 46; Rosenmann, *Jellinek*, 121–2; Häusler, pp. 48–9.

converted without immersion by the German reform rabbi Abraham Geiger. The neo-orthodox rabbi of the doctor's home congregation in Eisenstadt, Dr Israel Hildesheimer, had refused to confirm the marriage, so the ceremony was performed instead by Jellinek in Vienna. Güdemann, however, not only supported Hildesheimer's position but made it clear that he regarded the innovations of the Reform movement as a distressing symptom of the religious decadence of the age.[97]

Moritz Güdemann's stance on matters of Jewish law was much stricter than that of Jellinek, though he was liberal enough in his approach to scholarly research. A classic product of the *Wissenschaft des Judentums* and the embodiment of the new type of German scholar-rabbi, Güdemann had been born of middle-class parents in Hildesheim, Prussia, near Hanover, on 19 February 1835. After attending Jewish elementary school he entered an episcopal institution at the age of eight, where he was taught by Catholic priests, two of whom exercised a lasting influence on the boy. This easy mixing with non-Jews and the lack of anti-Semitism in his childhood environment probably strengthened his sense of rootedness in German soil.[98] In 1854 he went to study at the Breslau Jewish Theological Seminary under Dr Zacharias Frankel, the historian Heinrich Graetz, and the scholar Dr Jacob Bernays. He also attended lectures at the University of Breslau on Arabic, Syrian, and Persian literature.

Güdemann's rabbinic and scholarly career was decisively shaped by the character of the Breslau seminary which first developed his interest in historical research, gave him a critical method and also a sense of how Judaism had responded over centuries to the challenges of a non-Jewish environment. His training in philology, Oriental languages, and Islamic studies subsequently enabled Güdemann to reconstruct the Arabic and Hebrew literature of the Spanish Jewish Golden Age in his first major scholarly work, *Das jüdische Unterrichtswesen während der spanisch-arabischen Periode* (1873). As Ismar Schorsch has pointed out, studying the achievements of medieval Jewry within the framework of Islamic civilization sharply pointed up the contrast with the intolerance

---

[97] See his anonymous contributions 'Reform und Reformschwindel' and 'Die Gebetmacherei' published in Zacharias Frankel's *Monatsschrift für Geschichte und Wissenschaft des Judentums*, 18 (1869, 81–8, 122–30).

[98] Josef Fraenkel, 'Between Herzl and Güdemann' (Hebrew), *Shivat Zion*, 4 (1956–7), 100–13 (esp. pp. 100–1). For the revised English versions of this important article, see 'Moritz Güdemann and Theodor Herzl', *Leo Baeck Yearbook*, 11 (1966), 67–82, and *Jews of Austria*, 111–30.

of the Christian Middle Ages and was intended to enhance the self-image of German Jewry. The fascination of *Wissenschaft* scholars with this field was clearly not unrelated to the struggle for recognition, self-respect, and emancipation on German soil.[99] Similarly, Güdemann's interest in the local and communal history of German Jewry also had a broader, appologetic function—to demonstrate that Jews were not 'aliens' on German soil but that their roots went back over many centuries to the early Middle Ages.

Güdemann's most important scholarly work, *Die Geschichte des Erziehungswesens und der Cultur der abendländischen Juden* (3 vols., 1880–8), was a pioneering study of the underlying trends and institutions of medieval Jewish life conceived against the background of their non-Jewish milieu.[100] It placed him in the front rank of nineteenth-century German Jewish scholarship and his volumes marked an important turning-point in the direction of social and cultural history, going beyond the reliance of his mentor Heinrich Graetz on literary and biographical material. Güdemann succeeded in reconstructing the internal life of medieval Franco-German and Italian Jewry by approaching history from below and examining Jewish customs, manners, superstitions, morals, language, and literature in terms of the society in which they lived.[101] He demonstrated a hitherto unsuspected degree of harmonious co-existence and cross-fertilizing influences between Jews and Christians, which forced the revision of many accepted notions concerning the Middle Ages. At the same time, in spite of his grasp of the importance of socio-economic factors, of pedagogy and community organization, Güdemann insisted on classifying Jewish history as primarily *religious* and denying it any national or political character. This was consistent enough with his ideological conception of Judaism but in many ways conflicted with his critical methods and some of his own scholarly findings.[102]

Güdemann had been ordained at the Breslau seminary in 1862 and in the same year he was appointed rabbi in Magdeburg. Four years later he became Vienna's second preacher after the reformers on the Board of the Berlin Jewish community had prevented his appointment

[99] Schorsch, p. 45.   [100] Ibid. 42.

[101] Güdemann, *Die Geschichte des Erziehungswesens und der Cultur der abendländischen Juden*, i (Vienna, 1880), 109–13, 128 ff., 161.

[102] Schorsch, p. 61, quotes Güdemann from an 1898 article: 'Our history is itself religious. Not only did our internal life at one time revolve and today revolves in part about religion as its centre, but also our external life exhibits the same relationship.' Güdemann was convinced that only the adversaries of the Jews labelled them as a nation.

there, on the grounds of his known conservatism in religious affairs.[103] It was precisely this cautious approach to Jewish law and observance which made him acceptable, however, to the moderately liberal Vienna community leaders after the death of Mannheimer. In view of the growing pressure of orthodox Jews, it was hoped that a conservative, pious German-trained rabbi, familiar with the modern, critical methods of *Wissenschaft*, could provide the best bridge between the two hostile camps.[104] During his fifty years of active service, the scholarly Güdemann gave ample proof that this expectation was justified, though his tenure was not without its tensions and conflicts.

During the community crisis of 1872, he was, for example, adamant about *rejecting* the proposed introduction of the organ or the suggestion to cut out the Zion passages (which he argued dealt not with a political but a spiritual return of Israel to Zion); he particularly castigated the desire to excise references to sacrifices as an unacceptable tampering with the Torah itself.[105] Güdemann was prepared to resign over these issues along with Salomon Spitzer and the rabbi of the Sephardi community in Vienna, Reuben Baruchy, until the Community Board eventually backed down.[106] In subsequent years Güdemann played an active role in developing community institutions such as the Öster-reichisch-Israelitische Union (1886) and helped to found the Israelitisch-Theologische Lehranstalt (1893).

His association with the Austrian Israelite Union partly reflected what was to become a central concern in the life of Viennese Jewry towards the end of the nineteenth century, namely the fight against anti-Semitism. Güdemann himself devoted a growing part of his scholarly output to the refutation of academic anti-Semitism. Even his purely scholarly works reveal this apologetic element, virtually forced on him by the presence of palpable external danger and the persistent distortion of Jewish teachings by Christian scholars as well as by anti-Semitic demagogues. Thus even in his introduction to the monumental *Geschichte des Erziehungswesens* he wrote that the need to refute the modern anti-Semitic myth of the *Verjüdung* ('judaization') of German society had spurred him to demonstrate that already in the Middle

---

[103] In Güdemann's 4-vol. memoirs, 'Aus meinem Leben' (n.d.), in the Archives of the Leo Baeck Institute, New York, this episode is dealth with in some detail and clearly still grated on him.

[104] Allerhand, p. 12.

[105] Güdemann, *Jerusalem: Die Opfer und die Orgel* (Vienna, 1871); Rosenmann, *Jellinek*, 129; Fraenkel, 'Between Herzl and Güdemann', 112–13.

[106] Rosenmann, *Jellinek*; Hausler, p. 53.

Ages there were strong cross-fertilizing influences between Jews and Christians.[107] In the second volume, he added a long footnote to his opening remarks, designed to answer the charges of the German anti-Semitic Orientalist, Paul de Lagarde, concerning the allegedly cosmopolitan, mercantile, and conspiratorial character of the Jews.[108]

Like Jellinek before him, Güdemann was extremely sensitive to Christian caricatures of rabbinic and Talmudic Judaism and the tendentiousness of much of the 'higher criticism' (Harnack, Wellhausen, Kuenen, etc.) in this field.[109] In 1906 he devoted a whole treatise to this subject, calling it *Jüdische Apologetik*; it was consciously intended as a defence of Judaism against its detractors.[110] Güdemann had some harsh things to say about 'scientific' Christian theology and its negation of the unity, continuity, and integrity of Judaism as a living tradition. The failure of Christianity to understand Judaism in its own terms, to grasp the central role of oral tradition and the praxis of a whole community over centuries, along with its Pauline misunderstanding of the Torah as rigid legalism were recurring themes in his critique.[111]

No less important for Güdemann was the need to emphasize the universalism, humanism, and idealism of the monotheistic Hebrew faith;[112] there was no place here for particularism, for pride in origins, ethnic self-assertion, or exclusivism, since Judaism, he insisted, was not a *national* religion in the modern sense. Israel had always been a religious community (*Religionsgemeinschaft*) not a nation (*Volk*), he pointedly wrote in an obvious allusion to the racial ideology of contemporary anti-Semites seeking to strip Jews of their rights.[113] Zionism, too, stood in open contradiction to Güdemann's one-sidedly idealized and *anational* interpretation of the Torah which stripped it of any particularist, ethnic, or historical character, let alone any physical link to the Promised Land of Israel.[114] The national history of Israel had no meaning in itself; it was simply a prelude for the recognition by the nations of the one God, a preparation for the reign of universal brotherhood and Divine Kingship over all humanity.

Güdemann's apologetic works, for all their obvious weaknesses, none the less fulfilled an important and necessary function in Jewish self-defence against anti-Semitism. Since 1891 he had held the post of

[107] *Geschichte des Erziehungswesens*, i. 1 ff.
[108] Ibid. ii. 4.   [109] Schorsch, p. 63.
[110] Güdemann, *Jüdische Apologetik* (Glogau, 1906), p. vii.
[111] Ibid., 40, 124–5, 133, 139.   [112] Ibid., 50–1, 74, 205 ff., 211–12.
[113] Ibid., 88–90.   [114] Ibid., 205–18.

Chief Rabbi of Vienna and following Jellinek's death three years later, he had become the spiritual head of a community numbering well over 100,000 souls, which in spite of its social and cultural diversity, he managed to keep intact and formally unified. Nevertheless, the problems created by the Empire's explosive nationality conflicts, by the overwhelming success of political anti-Semitism in Vienna, and by the rise of militant Jewish nationalism clearly transcended his competence. Essentially an apolitical figure, extraordinarily reticent on most of the burning public issues of the day, Güdemann felt out of his depth in this area. Though a fine speaker he did not, unlike Mannheimer and Jellinek, possess a charismatic presence or polemical flair and in the open fight against the new *völkisch* anti-Semitism he gladly vacated the arena to the more pugnacious and militant Galician rabbi, Dr Joseph Samuel Bloch.[115]

On the one occasion on which Güdemann did involve himself in a major internal political controversy in the Jewish community—namely in his complex dealings with Theodor Herzl and the Zionist movement—the result was a comi-tragedy of misunderstandings, errors, and mutual recriminations. This episode will receive separate treatment, but a comment in Herzl's diary on 26 March 1896, following his disillusionment with Rabbi Güdemann, is perhaps appropriate at this point. Herzl caustically observed:

The publisher Breitenstein tells me that Güdemann has declined to give an address on my *Jewish State*. My standpoint is political, whereas his is religious. From his point of view, then, he must deplore my attempts to forestall Providence. In other words: he doesn't dare; he no longer finds it opportune; he is afraid of the rich Jews who oppose it . . .[116]

In his Memoirs, Güdemann fiercely denied that he was subjected to any pressure by the leading figures of the Viennese Jewish community to reject Zionism. Be that as it may, it is evident from his own account that Güdemann had great difficulty in making up his mind. He was for a time mesmerized by Herzl's charismatic personality and by the grandiose vision he unfolded which temporarily seemed to eclipse even Güdemann's longstanding dislike of nationalism. The Chief Rabbi

[115] Allerhand, p. 19: 'Die Gabe des Polemisierens im wissenschaftlichen sowie im praktischen Bereich war Güdemann nicht gegeben'.

[116] *The Diaries of Theodor Herzl*, ed. and trans. Marvin Lowenthal (London, 1958), 107. For the full story see Fraenkel, 'Güdemann and Herzl', 67 ff., and from the other side, Mordechai Eliav, 'Herzl und der Zionismus aus der Sicht Moritz Güdemanns', *Bulletin des Leo-Baeck-Instituts*, no. 56/7 (1980), 135–68, based on Güdemann's own memoirs.

was not after all a political animal but an orthodox Jew and a *Wissenschaft* scholar of the German school. To the extent that he did have political views, they scarcely differed much from those of most of the Viennese Jewish bourgeoisie—namely, they were liberal, anti-Zionist, pro-German, and loyal to the Empire.[117] As long as he believed that what Herzl had in mind was simply action 'on behalf of the Vienna Jews' against anti-Semitism, he was indeed sympathetic; once the international dimensions of Herzl's plans for the exodus of the Jews from Europe became clearer to him, he felt by his own account confused and out of his depth.[118]

Güdemann could not accept that Jews in Germany or Austria should feel anything but German. As he confessed in his Memoirs, he could not understand how Herzl, as a product of German culture, should regard himself as belonging to the Jewish *nation*. Why should any Jew, especially one who had been fortunate enough to acquire a German education, 'uproot himself from his native soil?'[119] This was a point of view shared by most German Jews in *fin de siècle* Vienna, though they did not necessarily rationalize it in terms of the spiritual 'mission' of Jewry in the Diaspora and the transcendent universalism of the Hebraic monotheistic faith.

The activities of Mannheimer, Jellinek, and Güdemann, three of the greatest modern rabbis of their age, spanned almost the whole of the nineteenth century and largely determined the spiritual profile of the Israelitische Kultusgemeinde of Vienna. The passing of each of these defenders of the Jewish faith symbolized the turning of an era. Mannheimer devoted his life to the fight for Jewish emancipation and died in 1865 on the eve of its consummation. Jellinek presided over the transformation effected by emancipation and assimilation, adapting Judaism to the demands of a new liberal epoch of civic equality, freedom, and religious toleration. His death in 1893 occurred just before Viennese liberalism succumbed to the onslaught of Lueger's anti-Semitic cohorts. The more conservative Güdemann held the community together in the closing years of the Empire and his passing in 1918 coincided with the death-rattle of the Habsburg Monarchy.

These great figures successively achieved fame as preachers and rabbis in the capital city of a Roman Catholic State, where protection of the dominant religion was a matter of great public prestige. They had to fight to assert the dignity of the Jewish faith not only against

---

[117] Schorsch, p. 53.
[118] Fraenkel, 'Güdemann and Herzl', 74–75.   [119] Ibid. 80.

official prejudice and popular anti-Semitism but also against growing Jewish indifference and ignorance of its cardinal principles. They had to serve a lay leadership which was determined to maintain exclusive control of the community and to reduce the role of the rabbis to instruments of its social pretensions and guardians of its 'cult'. The splendid synagogues, the sumptuous cemeteries, the well-organized burial society, the hospitals, the homes for the aged, the institutes for the blind, deaf, and dumb were a tribute to the efficiency of this 'official' Judaism and the ability of Viennese Jews to distribute charity in the grànd style.

But in spite of a multitude of teaching establishments including several kindergartens, a Talmud Torah school, a *Beth Hamidrash* (1862), and a Jewish theological college (1893), religious education made little impact on the mass of Viennese Jews. In spite of the valiant efforts of Mannheimer, Jellinek, and Güdemann to introduce the scholarly traditions of German *Wissenschaft* to their more easy-going co-religionists, Vienna did not ultimately prove a very fertile soil for modern Jewish education and learning.

The officials of the Kultusgemeinde and its many rabbis, great and small, were already fighting a losing battle of attrition in the liberal era against the seductions of the larger society and of secular European culture. For a time the fiery oratory and religious ardour of Vienna's renowned preachers could stem the tide. However as one shrewd observer of the scene recalled: 'large and interested audiences flocked to these sermons as if they were theatrical shows, but for all that, Jewish Vienna, cultured Vienna, educated Vienna, was not really interested in rabbis or Judaism at all. Viennese Jews were interested in rabbis or Judaism at all. Viennese Jews were interested in—and extremely actively and prominent in—general culture, not Jewish culture.'[120]

There is much truth in this assessment though it is not the whole story. The dilemmas with which Mannheimer, Jellinek, and Güdemann contended and the seemingly trivial conflicts between orthodox and reform tendencies which they faced were part of a deeper, more universal problem confronting all Jews in the modern era. How could Jewish culture and identity best be preserved in a pluralistic, free, and open society under conditions of emancipation, acculturation, and secularization? What was the meaning of Judaism and its traditions in

[120] N. H. Tur-Sinai, 'Viennese Jewry', in Fraenkel (ed.), *Jews of Austria*.

the context of enlightenment and civil equality? How could the Jewish community, defined solely in 'confessional' terms, survive the stresses and internal conflicts generated by the uneven pace of the modernization process among its component parts, divided as they were by class, culture, and regional background? Finally, what did Judaism have to say concerning the various political options open to Jewry in a modernizing Central European society, itself torn apart by religious, class, and ethnic conflicts? Mannheimer, Jellinek, and Güdemann sought in their various ways to provide some spiritual guidance and moral leadership in facing these issues but they could no more solve them than could their more secular-minded contemporaries among Austrian Jews. It is to them that we must now turn.

5

Liberalism, Deutschtum, *and Assimilation*

Because I was born without a fatherland, my desire for a fatherland is more passionate than yours, and because my birthplace was not bigger than the *Judengasse* and everything behind the locked gates was a foreign country to me, therefore for me now the fatherland is more than the city, more than a territory, more than a province. For me only the very great fatherland, as far as its language extends, is enough.

Ludwig Börne (1832)

The Jews who are German by language, disposition and outlook should remain so and prove themselves as the bearers and guardians of German *Volksthum.* Germandom in Austria stands first among all nationalities in its education, manners, civilisation, science and its connection to a rejuvenated Germany awakened to liberty. To fraternize with fanatics of Czechdom, Slavdom, and Magyardom means to secede from *Kultur* and *Bildung.* The Germans in Bohemia, Moravia, Hungary, and Galicia should moreover also consider that through the fraternization with the Israelites they will receive a powerful increase in their national strength and that it is in the interests of Germandom to draw the Jews into their orbit and work for their liberation with all their might. The liberty of the Jews is at the same time the liberty of Germandom.

Adolf Jellinek, Der Orient (May 1848)

Centralism in Austria is an anachronism, a sin against the spirit of our time. The German does not have any need of this sin. He stands above his non-German countryman without placing himself upon the pedestal of special privilege. His moral superiority offers him more lasting guarantees than artificially contrived parliamentary power. He should not be a guardian but a model to the nations.

Adolf Fischof (1869)

The Jews, whose culture in Bohemia is German and whose

formative years coincided with the time when liberal ideals
predominated, attached themselves to the German nation with all
their hearts . . . too closely, it would seem. Then all of a sudden
they found themselves shaken off. All of a sudden, they were told
that they were parasites . . . One jerk only, and they were no
longer Germans but Jews.

Theodor Herzl (1897)

Who created the Liberal movement in Austria? The Jews! By
whom were the Jews betrayed and abandoned? By the Liberals.
Who created the German nationalist movement in Austria? The
Jews. Who left the Jews in the lurch—worse yet, who spat on
them like dogs? The German nationalists.

Arthur Schnitzler, *Der Weg ins Freie* (1908)

Ever since the reforms of the Emperor Joseph II towards the end of the
eighteenth century, Austrian Jewry had increasingly identified with
German language and culture. The language decree of Joseph II,
compelling Jews, wherever they lived in the multi-ethnic polyglot
Empire, to establish German-language schools and conduct their
internal affairs in German, had far-reaching effects. Not only Viennese
but also large numbers of Bohemian, Moravian, Bukovinan, and
Hungarian Jews became culturally German and thereby separated
themselves still further from the local population in whose midst they
lived. Even in Galicia with its predominantly Polish and Ukrainian
character there were significant enclaves of German-speaking educated
Jews and cultural assimilation on the German model made substantial
progress among the *maskilim* in the first half of the nineteenth century.
Austrian Jews generally came to identify with an enlightened,
cosmopolitan, late eighteenth-century paradigm of *Deutschtum* modelled
on Goethe, Kant, von Humboldt, Lessing, and Schiller;[1] with an ideal
vision of Germany and the power of *Bildung* which expressed their
optimism, their faith in culture and in humanity. *Bildung* and

---

[1] For a typical example of this cult among Austrian Jews, see Heinrich Jacques,
Denkschrift über die Stellung der Juden in Österreich (Vienna, 1859), pp. cxvii–cxviii, where
he calls for a powerful, united, free Austria strong enough to resist its neighbours and
based on the closest union (*Anschluss*) with Germany—'because all that Austria must
attain in the briefest possible time is and always will be exclusively the native product and
flower of the German spirit. Our pride and our comfort are that great treasury of
German science and literature, Lessing and Schiller, Goethe and Alexander von
Humboldt'.

Enlightenment joined together on the German model were the keys to Jewish emancipation in Central Europe and the central myth sustaining Jewish existence and identity after its achievement.[2] Indeed as George Mosse has pointed out, the concept of *Bildung* became for many Jews 'synonymous with their Jewishness' as well as the essential means to integrate themselves into German middle-class society.[3]

Furthermore, German culture and German schools were clearly the gateways to economic advancement and rising social status in the Austro-Hungarian Monarchy, a crucial factor which influenced Jews as far apart as Bohemia and Hungary, Bukovina and the Adriatic port of Trieste. In Bohemia and Moravia, the far-reaching impact of the Josephinian reform led Jews to ignore or refuse to accept for a long time the process of Czechization going on around them, especially in cities like Prague and Pilsen during the second half of the nineteenth-century.[4] Before 1914 the great majority of Prague Jews preferred German to Czech primary and secondary schools; they generally adopted the values and ideals of their German neighbours and the culture of Austria's German-speaking bourgeoisie:[5] the predominance of German as the *Staatssprache* (language of State) throughout the Monarchy, as the language of business, public education, and secular learning, seemed to provide ample incentive for nineteenth-century Austrian Jewry to identify with the German *Bürgertum* of the Monarchy.

Even in Hungary this was the case, for all its intense linguistic-national consciousness and despite the readiness of its ruling gentry to improve the status of the Jews and encourage their assimilation to the Magyar nation. As late as 1870 Hungarian Jewry, because of its size, was virtually the largest German-speaking Jewish community in Europe. German had been the language of great Hungarian thinkers and poets in the early nineteenth-century before the Magyar literary renaissance. German was indeed spoken by every educated Hungarian. Both Theodor Herzl and Max Nordau, though born in Budapest, wrote naturally in German, which offered far more openings to the

---

[2] George L. Mosse, *German Jews beyond Judaism* (Hebrew Union College, Cincinnati, 1985), 3–4.

[3] Ibid. 4–8.

[4] Ruth Kestenberg-Gladstein, 'The Jews between Czechs and Germans in the Historic Lands, 1848–1918', in *The Jews of Czechoslovakia* (Philadelphia, 1868), i. 32–5; Guido Kisch, *In Search of Freedom* (London, 1949), 58–66.

[5] Gary B. Cohen, 'Jews in German Society: Prague, 1860–1914', in *Central European History*, 10 (1977), 28–54.

wider European culture.[6] Even in 1890, after the Magyarization process had been firmly established, German was still the mother-tongue for nearly two-thirds of the Jews in the western regions of Hungarian-ruled Slovakia. This adherence to the German language was all the more remarkable, given the close link between the cause of Jewish emancipation and liberal Magyar nationalism since the 1830s and the demographic strength of the Yiddish-speaking orthodox Hasidic element in Hungary.[7]

In the case of Galicia, the modernizing Jewish élite also looked to Vienna as the cultural capital, though after 1867 there was a significant shift to a Polish orientation, especially among Jews in the eastern part of the province.[8] Assimilationist tendencies, whether of a German or Polish character, were restrained however by the greater strength of Hasidic orthodoxy and the more cohesive East European structure of the Galician Jewish community.[9] In Bukovina, on the other hand, with its mutually cancelling multi-ethnic balance of Romanians, Ukrainians, Germans, Poles, and Jews (who in 1910 represented one third of the total population in the provincial capital of Czernowitz), German retained its centrality as the language of administration, communication, and public education. The Jewish *Bildungsbürgertum*, in particular, saw itself as the bearer of German culture in this remote north-eastern periphery of the Empire, whose character was symbolized by the German-language State Gymnasium and the Franz-Joseph University in Czernowitz founded in 1875.[10] The Austrian writer

[6] Hans Kohn, 'Before 1918 in the Historic Lands', *Jews of Czechoslovakia*, 17. Herzl did, however, also speak and write flawless Hungarian. Some of his adolescent essays reveal 'great enthusiasm and profound understanding of Hungarian nationalism, its literary bases and its political objectives'; see Andrew Handler, *Dori: The Life and Times of Theodor Herzl in Budapest (1860–1878)* (Univ., Alabama, 1983), 72–5.

[7] Nathaniel Katzburg, 'Assimilation in Hungary during the Nineteenth Century: Orthodox Positions', in Bela Vago (ed.), *Jewish Assimilation in Modern Times* (Boulder, Colo., 1981), 49–55: also George Schöpflin, 'Jewish Assimilation in Hungary: A Moot Point?', in ibid. 75–87, who lays stress on the central role played by Jews along with the highly urbanized Germans in the capitalist transformation of 19th-cent. Hungary, which altogether lacked an indigenous bourgeoisie.

[8] Ezra Mendelsohn, 'A Note on Jewish Assimilation in the Polish Lands', in ibid. 141–9. By 1869 Polish had become the official language of Galicia and in 1873 the province received full autonomous status.

[9] Ibid. Mendelsohn points out that Jewish society in Galicia was on the whole much less assimilated than in Hungary. The size of the Jewish community in eastern Galicia was in this respect a retarding factor. So, too, was the fact that the Polish élite, the rising middle classes, and the peasantry were more openly anti-Semitic than in Hungary and did not regard the Jews as equal partners.

[10] Hugo Gold (ed.), *Geschichte der Juden in der Bukowina*, 2 vols. (Tel Aviv, 1958–62);

Karl-Emil Franzos characteristically regarded the Bukovina Jews as flourishing models of Western culture and the German *Geist* in the 'half-Asiatic cultural desert' of the Imperial hinterland, even though they had retained their Jewish nationality.[11] Only at the end of the nineteenth-century did this enthusiastic 'Germanism' with its liberal political orientation begin to give way to a strong Jewish nationalist movement.[12]

Long before 1848 German culture had indeed become for Jewish *maskilim* throughout the Habsburg lands the normative expression of Europeanism and Enlightenment. German *Bildung* and the Berlin *Haskalah* in the field of Jewish learning were widely accepted as an ideology and a model to be imitated. Indeed, the whole *Jüdische Moderne* in Austria, the transition from a traditional to a modern society, from the narrow confines of the ghetto to wealth, status, culture, and social acceptance in the non-Jewish world, was mediated primarily through the gateway of a cosmopolitan *Deutschtum*.[13]

In the case of Viennese Jewry the reasons for the pro-German orientation were largely self-evident. Though the capital and hub of a multinational Empire, Vienna was still a predominantly German city and the major centre of German power and cultural influence radiating outwards to the most remote areas of the Habsburg lands. The Jews of Vienna were the natural embodiment of the Austro-German pattern of modernization for their co-religionists in Budapest, Prague, Cracow, Lemberg, Czernowitz, Trieste, and the outlying areas of the Monarchy, even if the centrifugal forces of local nationalism partially weakened this cultural bond in the course of the nineteenth century.

We have already noted the impact of Mannheimer's Viennese 'rite' and his modern adaptation of German reform on the religious services and liturgy of the Austrian provinces.[14] No less remarkable and at first

Martin Broszat, 'Von der Kulturnation zur Volksgruppe—Die nationale Stellung der Juden in der Bukowina im 19. und 20. Jahrhundert', *Historische Zeitschrift*, 200 (1965), 572 ff.

[11] Karl-Emil Franzos, *Aus Halb-Asien: Culturbilder aus Galizien, der Bukowina, Süd Russland und Rumanien*, i (Leipzig, 1876), 113.

[12] Gerald Stourzh, 'Galten die Juden als Nationalität Altösterreichs?', *Studia Judaica Austriaca*, x, *Prag–Czernowitz–Jerusalem* (Eisenstadt, 1984), 73–116.

[13] Robert S. Wistrich, 'The Modernization of Viennese Jewry: The impact of German culture in a multi-ethnic State', in Jacob Katz (ed.), *Towards Modernity: The European Jewish Model* (Rutgers, NJ, 1986).

[14] See the dissertation by Kopel Blum, 'Aufklärung und Reform bei den Wiener Juden' (Univ. of Vienna, 1935).

sight contradictory was the fact that Vienna in the 1820s also became the centre of a Hebrew-language *Haskalah* and its diffusion in the Habsburg territories, especially Galicia.[15] More than any other German city, Vienna nurtured a Hebrew literary culture inspired by the Berlin *Haskalah* and established itself after the 1790s as a centre for publishing Hebrew books—the Bible in various editions, the Talmud, Midrash, *Shulḥan Arukh*, and prayer-books, but also the works of Maimonides, Nahmanides, Rashba, Eybeshütz, Wesseley, and others. It was here that the first Hebrew periodical in the Austrian Empire and a major forum of the Galician *Haskalah*, *Bikkurei Ha 'Ittim* (The First Fruits) (1820–31), was launched by the Polish-born Shalom ben Jacob Cohen, who had arrived in Vienna in 1810.[16] Cohen, a central figure in early modern Hebrew poetry after Naftali Herz Wessely (in whose Berlin circle he had participated), had previously published and edited the last three volumes of Mendelssohn's *Ha-Meassef*—the cradle of the *Haskalah* movement.

Moreover, in addition to *Bikkurei Ha'Ittim*, the Hebrew-language annual of the Galician *Haskalah*, *Kerem Hemed* (Delightful Vineyard) (1833–56) was also published in Vienna, reflecting all its diverse aspects—humanistic and scientific studies, the revival of Hebrew, caustic criticisms of the Hasidic movement and of Jewish mysticism. Among its contributors were such leading *maskilim* as S. D. Luzzato, Josef Perl, Solomon Judah Rappoport, and the pioneers of German *Wissenschaft*, Zunz and Geiger.[17] Significantly, a chapter from Nachman Krochinal's celebrated philosophical-historical work, *Moreh Nevukhei Ha-Zeman* (Guide of the Perplexed of the Time) was first published in *Kerem Hemed*.

Most of the early Viennese *maskilim* originated from Galicia and were employees of the capital's printing establishments, or private teachers who tutored in the homes of wealthy 'tolerated' Jews. As typesetters and proof-readers familiar with Hebrew, Aramaic, and Yiddish, these literati found a livelihood in Vienna and helped make it

---

[15] Bernhard Wachstein, *Die Hebräische Publizistik in Wien. In drei Teilen* (Vienna, 1930): M. Gilboa, *Nitzanei ha'itonuth ha'ivrit 1691–1856*, (Tel Aviv University, 1977); R. Mahler, *A History of Modern Jewry, 1780–1815* (London, 1971), 240–1.

[16] For further details on the twelve consecutive volumes of *Bikkurei Ha'Ittim*, see Wachstein, pp. xiii–xx (introd.). See also Max Grunwald, *Vienna* (Philadelphia, 1936), 244–6; and on Cohen, Eisig Silberschlag, 'Parapoetic Attitudes and Values in Early Nineteenth Century Hebrew Poetry', in A. Altmann (ed.), *Studies in Nineteenth Century Jewish Intellectual History* (Harvard, 1964), 122–4.

[17] Grunwald, *Vienna*, 250.

a centre for the diffusion of Hebrew culture in the Monarchy. Judah Leb Ben-Zeev (1764–1811), one of the earliest of these Galician migrants, was the first to teach Hebrew as a living language.[18] A pioneer of modern Hebrew grammar and lexicography, his two major works, *Talmud Leshon Ivri* (System of the Hebrew language) and *Otzar Ha-Shorashim* (Dictionary of Roots), were milestones in the application of Western research methods to the study of Hebrew.[19]

Ben-Zeev, like other Viennese *maskilim*, was employed in the Hebrew printing establishment of the Austrian imperial-royal publisher Anton von Schmid, who profited by the regulation which excluded Jews from the publishing business while obliging them to buy only books published in Austria.[20] His Hebrew printing press, taking advantage of this monopoly, reached a wide Jewish market in the Monarchy, with Hebraist scholars and poets, from Prague, Lemberg, and Brody to Padua, Trieste, and Gorz, sending their manuscripts to Vienna for publication.

Thus, early nineteenth-century Vienna became the crossroads between Western and East European Judaism with Hebrew as its lingua franca of literary activity, in a way that was no longer possible in Germany or Western Europe. The forum which the Viennese periodicals provided, especially for Galician Hebrew scholars and writers, encouraged in the long run an increased influx of educated Jews from Galicia and their exposure to modern European culture. As Meir Henisch has pointed out, 'they worked towards a synthesis of historical Judaism and the new sciences, thus creating a basis for the revival of the Hebrew language and Hebrew literature'.[21] Thus, when the Russian *maskil* Perez Smolenskin founded his Jewish nationalist periodical, *Ha-Shaḥar* (The Dawn), in Vienna in 1868, the foundations of a Hebrew-language culture already existed in the imperial capital.

Nevertheless, the early Viennese-based *Haskalah*, like its Berlin model, was not at all national in inspiration but sought rather to mediate between the Jewish and German cultures. A typical product of the Galician-Austrian *Haskalah* was the Hebrew poet and author Meir Letteris (1800–71), who also worked as a copy-reader in Anton von Schmid's printing house (as well as in Prague and Pressburg). An

[18] Ibid. 503; also Meir Henisch, 'Galician Jews in Vienna', in Josef Fraenkel (ed.), *The Jews of Austria: Essays on their Life and Destruction* (London, 1967), 362 ff.

[19] R. Fahn, *Tekufat ha-haskalah be-Vinah* (1919), 38–46.

[20] Grunwald, *Vienna*, 248; Also A. Mayer, *Wiens Buchdruckergeschichte,* ii (Vienna, 1887).

[21] Henisch, p. 362.

extraordinarily prolific translator of European literature into Hebrew (including cosmopolitan German classics like Goethe's *Faust* and Lessing's *Nathan the Wise*), Letteris thereby contributed to the implanting of German alongside a modernized Hebrew culture in Austrian Galicia. Letteris was also the co-editor with Isodor Busch of the *Österreichisches Central-Organ für Glaubensfreiheit, Cultur, Geschichte und Literatur der Juden*, which first appeared in March 1848 and espoused the radical-liberal emancipatory demands of Viennese Jewry.[22] Subsequently, Letteris abandoned this radicalism, editing the German-language *Wiener Mitteilungen* (1854–69) and a number of other periodicals in Vienna directed at the more general public. His attempted synthesis of Austrian patriotism, German and Hebrew culture, though rewarded by an imperial gold medal, became however increasingly irrelevant in the freer atmosphere of the 1860s which saw the emergence of civil equality and the domination of liberal German values among Habsburg Jewry, especially in Vienna.[23]

The literary activity of the Viennese and Galician *maskilim* did not exercise a noticeable direct influence on the Jews of Vienna, who could not have constituted at any time more than a minority of the subscribers to their periodicals. Nevertheless, the spiritual leaders of Viennese Jewry—Mannheimer, Jellinek, and Güdemann—did seek to encourage the love of the sacred language and the spread of Hebrew culture, seeing it as being complementary, rather than in contradiction to the spirit of German *Wissenschaft* and *Bildung*.[24] Jellinek in particular vaunted the merits of the Hebrew language as a loyal ally in the holy struggle for Israel's good name, honour, and freedom.[25] Harnessing it to the needs of apologetics, he declared in a speech in Vienna in 1881 that the sacred language provided a rich armoury of concepts to refute the slanders of Israel's enemies. Since every language mirrored 'the soul of a people', so too Hebrew reflected the freedom-loving character, the high moral concepts, the seriousness, dignity, and humanity of the Israelites in their historic fight against slavery and oppression.

It should be studied not in order to be spoken 'as is being attempted in our Jewish schools in Jerusalem', or to 'enrich our divided

---

[22] On Letteris's journalistic activity in Vienna see Jacob Toury, *Die jüdische Presse im österreichischen Kaiserreich, 1802–1918* (Tübingen, 1983), 12 ff.

[23] Ibid. 21.

[24] Grunwald, *Vienna*, 251.

[25] Jellinek, *Die hebräische Sprache: Ein Ehrenzeugnis des jüdischen Geistes* (Vienna, 1881), 12.

fatherland with yet another language', but rather 'to promote, nurture, fathom, esteem and honour the Jewish spirit with a glittering badge of distinction'.[26] The efforts of Jewish secular nationalists like Smolenskin or Ben-Yehuda to revive Hebrew as a living language were dismissed by the Viennese rabbis as of little consequence. For Jellinek, Hebrew, though faithfully mirroring the original character of the Jewish people in its pristine purity, was primarily a literary and historical weapon of enlightenment in the battle to assert the human and civil rights of Jewry. It might serve as the jewel in the crown of Jellinek's flashing rhetoric but as the vehicle of a Jewish national revival it could provoke only the most summary reprobation.

No less decisively did Vienna's leading preacher repudiate the 'phantom' of a 'Jewish nationality' put forward in the 1870s and 1880s by such East European Hebrew-language journals as *Hamagid* (Lyck), *Hameliz* (St Petersburg), or *Hazefirah* (Warsaw). 'A community, which lives dispersed in all parts of the globe and speaks the languages of all nations, which possesses no separate territory nor forms an independent political commonwealth, has forfeited through the power of time all those elements which make up the attributes of a nationality.'[27] Jews admittedly formed a distinct *Stamm*, they professed the same religion, they shared a common past and common ideals for the future, but they were *not* bound by national ties.

As long as the Hebrew journalism of Eastern Europe sought to spread *Kultur* and *Bildung* among Jews who did not read European languages, they were performing a necessary task. But to fight assimilation and to seek to strengthen a 'fictive' Jewish-national consciousness, could, according to Jellinek, only 'embarrass their co-religionists in Europe and through encouraging national illusions make more difficult the struggle against anti-Semitism'.[28] Assimilation for Jellinek did not in the least imply the abandonment of Jewish religious teachings, historic festivals, or traditional ceremonies, nor the renunciation of the glories of the Jewish past and its hopes for the future; rather it meant that 'the Jews should not differentiate themselves from their non-Jewish fellow citizens in speech, clothing, manners, social behaviour';[29] that they must adopt the interests and welfare of the states to which they belong as 'true, loyal and selfless sons of the fatherland'. They could 'learn Hebrew, write the biblical language in

---

[26] Ibid. 4.
[27] A.J., 'Assimilatio', *Die Neuzeit*, 19 Dec. 1884, p. 482.
[28] Ibid.   [29] Ibid. 481.

prose and verse, only they must not deform the national vernacular of
their adopted fatherland through incorrect and peculiar accentuation,
thereby making themselves and Judaism look ridiculous'.[30] Austrian
Jewry must follow the examples of the Jews of France, England, Italy,
Belgium, and the United States who were 'fully assimilated and
identified with their fellow-citizens of non-Jewish origin yet had
preserved their loyalty to Judaism'.[31]

This classical Central European ideology of Jewish emancipation
was, however, complicated by the polyethnic, multilingual character of
Austria—a factor which Jellinek like most Viennese Jews tended to
oversimplify. With which exactly among the myriad nationalities of old
Austria were Jews expected to assimilate? Who in fact were the 'hosts'
from the viewpoint of assimilating Jewry?[32] How did one define who
was 'Austrian' and 'un-Austrian' in an Empire divided into a multitude
of regions, provinces, districts, political societies, warring ethnic
groups, and linguistic entities? Even in class terms, the problems of
social integration into such an inherently centrifugal and heterogeneous
structure were multiple.

Under the *ancien régime* before 1848 these dilemmas had been less
acute since the Metternichian censorship of free expression and lack of
basic human rights gradually drove the developing Viennese Jewish
intelligentsia into the German liberal-democratic camp. In such
circumstances it was difficult to espouse an Austrian dynastic
patriotism. Opposition to the regime naturally encouraged a Pan-
German orientation since Germany was seen as being more liberal,
dynamic, and progressive than the repressive Habsburg State.[33] At the
same time the beginnings of a commercial and industrial bourgeoisie
in the Habsburg lands during the 1840s (which had an important
Jewish component and sought to modernise Austria in its own image)
encouraged the liberal Pan-German trend.

The Prague-born Jewish publicist and politician Ignaz Kuranda
(1812–1884), who was to lead the German Liberal party in Austria
for twenty-three years and represented it in the Vienna *Gemeinderat*
(city council) and the Imperial Parliament, tried to synthesize this
orientation with Austrian patriotism throughout his long career.[34] The

---

[30] A. J., 'Assimilatio', *Die Neuzeit*, 19 Dec. 1884, p. 481.   [31] Ibid.

[32] W. O. McCagg, 'The Assimilation of Jews in Austria', in Bela Vago (ed.), *Jewish Assimilation*, 127–40.

[33] Michael Pollak, *Vienne 1900: Une identité blessée* (Paris, 1984), 38 ff.

[34] On Kuranda's political career, see 'Dr. Ignaz Kuranda', *Die Neuzeit*, 29 Apr. 1881, pp. 133–5, and the obituary notice in ibid., 11 Apr. 1884, pp. 139–40; A. Kohut,

autodidact Kuranda was a skilful journalist who had first attracted attention for his lectures on German literature in Belgium during his years in exile after 1838. In 1841 he founded the periodical *Die Grenzboten* (The Frontier Messengers) in Brussels. This popular newspaper, forbidden in Austria, became the organ of the pre-1848 liberal opposition under Habsburg rule, being smuggled over the border from Leipzig, where Kuranda had moved in 1842. Advocating a modern constitutionalism, its sharp criticism of Austrian internal policy helped prepare the path for overthrowing the Metternich regime. Arriving in Vienna in 1848, Kuranda was promptly elected to the German National Assembly in Frankfurt, after having assumed the leadership of the Committee of Fifty which had originally issued the call for an all-German national Parliament. He headed the unsuccessful negotiations in Prague with Czech politicians whom he sought to persuade to attend the Frankfurt Assembly. Kuranda's intense political activity at this time aroused the ire of the Czech nationalists who saw in it an expression of Bohemian Jewry's identification with the German cause. Indeed, Kuranda was forced to flee the town of Kolin (Bohemia) at the time of his wedding in 1848, when personally threatened by Czech hotheads.[35]

After the defeat of the 1848 Revolution, Kuranda was under police surveillance like his colleague, Adolf Fischof, as one of the recognized leaders of the liberal-democratic opposition. He nevertheless succeeded in establishing the *Ostdeutsche Post* in Vienna as a leading political journal and successor to the *Grenzboten*, continuing to espouse the cause of Pan-Germanism, constitutionalism, and Greater Austrian centralism. An ardent supporter of continued German liberal hegemony in Austria, he energetically opposed what he regarded as a fratricidal war with Prussia in 1866. The victory of the Prussian forces which effectively removed Austria from German affairs destroyed the *raison d'être* of Kuranda's *grossdeutsch* programme, which in the post-1866 climate could not but alienate Austrian patriots among his readers.[36] Kuranda remained, however, a deputy of the Lower Austrian Diet (he had been elected in 1861), whence he progressed to the Reichsrat

Allgemeine Zeitung des Judentums, 76 (1912), 273–5, 282–4, 292–4; Georg Franz, *Liberalismus: Die deutschliberale Bewegung in der Habsburgischen Monarchie* (Munich, 1955); and Grunwald, *Vienna*, 365–71.

[35] 'Dr Ignaz Kuranda', *Die Neuzeit*, 29 Apr. 1981, p. 134.

[36] Richard Grunberger, 'Jews in Austrian Journalism', in Fraenkel (ed.), *Jews of Austria*, 86.

(Parliament), rising to the leadership of the Liberal party. He was highly respected not only as a veteran freedom-fighter of 1848 but as a parliamentarian of wide experience (in earlier years he had lived in exile in France, Belgium, and Germany) with expert knowledge of international affairs.

Kuranda's dedication to German cultural ideals and to the cause of *Deutschtum* through his liberal, Pan-German political stand did not however alienate him from Jewish affairs as was later to be so frequently the case in Austria. Since 1860 he had been on the board of the Jewish community—the same year in which he won a famous libel case in Vienna against the Catholic anti-Semite Sebastian Brünner— an event which struck an important blow for Jewish emancipation. At the trial Kuranda compared the case with the earlier emancipatory struggle of Protestants in Germany and of Catholics in England. 'Just as we were the first to carry the banner of civilization as a people or nation or tribe so we are the last', Kuranda declared, 'to knock at the portals of Humanity asking for admittance and equality of rights.'[37] He skilfully succeeded in presenting his clerical opponent as 'the representative of a lost cause' who relied solely on hate and prejudice in the fight 'against the general feeling for justice which is struggling for utterance, against the course of history'.[38] Kuranda's victory uncannily presaged the coming of civil equality for Austrian Jewry which was to be closely bound up with the triumph of liberalism over clerical reaction.

A year earlier, in 1859, the Jewish publicist and lawyer Heinrich Jacques, in his *Denkschrift über die Stellung der Juden in Österreich* (Memorandum on the Status of the Jews in Austria) which went through four editions in a few weeks, had made out the case for Jewish emancipation in typically pragmatic terms which appealed to the same liberal bourgeois *Zeitgeist* on whose wave Kuranda would rise to such heights. Jacques argued not so much as a Jew but as an Austrian patriot concerned with 'general political' questions. He pointed out the economic as well as the intellectual loss to the Fatherland entailed in maintaining the pariah status of Austria's most excluded religious minority:

Austria allows a substantial part of its material and spiritual national capital to go unused when it deprives its Israelite inhabitants of the rights of free

[37] Grunwald, *Vienna*, 368–9.
[38] Ibid.; see also Wolfang Häusler, 'Orthodoxie und Reform in Wiener Judentum in der Epoche des Hochliberalismus', *Studie Judaica Austriaca*, 6 (Vienna, 1978), 39–40.

enterprise, ownership of property, and the opportunity of civil and political office. It turns its Jews into unproductive consumers rather than socially useful producers. Austria harms itself by driving Jewish capital into cosmopolitan commerce instead of identifying it with the fate of the Fatherland.[39]

Jacques recalled 'the blessed year of 1848' during which patriotic reformers had sought to break down class barriers and had promised in Paragrah 17 of the Constitution (25 April 1848) 'complete freedom of faith and conscience, as well as personal freedom'.[40] He reviewed the steady regression in imperial laws after 1849, arguing strongly that civil and national rights must be made independent of a religious belief.[41] He freely acknowledged that civil equality entailed the disappearance of the Jewish nationality—'. . . the Jewish Bohemian, Pole etc. is a Bohemian, Pole, Austrian like any other'.[42] The fact that some Jews spoke Yiddish or wrote in Hebrew script, Jacques dismissively compared to 'a private language of freemasons or Trappist monks', which had no significance from a constitutional viewpoint. The task of a liberal Constitution must be to sweep away all caste privileges and corporate particularism in one blow as the antiquated remnants of medieval feudalism.[43]

Jacques appealed on the intellectual plane to the free-thinking, Enlightenment tradition of German humanism (Lessing, Schiller, Humboldt) against the clerical obscurantism of the ultramontane opponents of Jewish emancipation.[44] It was a deformed Christianity which had ghettoized the Jews and driven them into usurious occupations. The clericals were, however, sworn enemies of economic and political progress who sowed division, enmity, and discord in the Empire. Their victory would not only be at the expense of individual liberties, plunging Austria once more into the dark age of the Inquisition, wars of religion and witchhunting. It would also be harmful to the interests of the State. Ultramontanism failed to grasp that, because of its linguistic, confessional, and national diversity, the Austrian State had to pursue policies that would preserve imperial unity.[45]

The Jews as patriotic, loyal, and industrious citizens could only benefit the State in achieving this objective, if careers were fully opened to their talents.[46] They would continue to modernize Austrian finance and industry as before, to develop new enterprises, raise

[39] Jacques, p. ix.   [40] Ibid., p. xiii.   [41] Ibid., pp. xiv–xv.
[42] Ibid., p. xxii.   [43] Ibid., pp. xxix–xxx.   [44] Ibid., pp. cix–cx, cxiv.
[45] Ibid., p. c.   [46] Ibid. 1–10.

agricultural productivity, and stimulate commerce.[47] Experience had demonstrated that only where they were deprived of their rights and of any stake in the country did the Jews join the forces of subversion against the State, as had indeed happened in 1848. In terms reminiscent of Disraeli, Jacques wrote: 'The Jews have often been called unpatriotic and revolutionary; if they are allowed to be property-owners and citizens, I believe one will discover that they are patriotic and conservative'.[48]

Jacques insisted that the Jews saw themselves as 'aliens' only where the modern State excluded them as pariahs and provided them with no alternative but to seek personal enrichment rather than the public good.[49] In West European countries like England, France, Belgium, and Holland on the other hand, examples like Crémieux, Goudechaux, Disraeli, and others proved that Jews were suited to high public office and that their moral code was no different from that of Christians. Emancipation was therefore a necessity if the Austrian State did not want to endanger its own existence by creating a class of people whose only hope of bettering their position was through revolution. At the same time emancipation was also necessary if Austria were to modernize itself, become economically competitive and strong enough to deter its enemies. Already, Jacques warned, it was lagging behind Germany and France and threatened by the superior demographic and military resources of the Russian Empire.[50]

The liberal ideology put forward by Heinrich Jacques, Kuranda, and other Austrian Jewish spokesmen in the 1860s looked to a combination of strong central authority, free political institutions, and economic development based on *laissez-faire* capitalism, as the key to Jewish emancipation.[51] Following the disastrous defeat by Prussia in 1866 and the accession to power of a new administration, the so-called *Burgerministerium*, Jewish expectations were finally fulfilled in the *Staatsgrundgesetz* (21 December 1867), which represented the high watermark of liberal constitutionalism in Austria. Article 2 stated: 'All citizens of this State are equal before the law.' Article 3 declared that public office was open to all citizens of the State. Article 14 guaranteed complete freedom of faith and conscience. Civic and political rights

---

[47] Jacques, pp. 14–15.   [48] Ibid. 26.   [49] Ibid. 37.
[50] Ibid. 50 ff.
[51] See Dennis B. Klein, 'Assimilation and the Demise of Liberal Political Tradition in Vienna: 1860–1914', in D. Bronsen (ed.), *Jews and Germans from 1860 to 1933: The Problematic Symbiosis* (Heidelberg, 1979), 234–61, for a useful survey.

were made independent of religious belief. Freedom of occupation, the right to own property, and the rights of residence were all guaranteed by the Constitution. Article 17 even provided that the pursuit and teaching of science should be free.[52]

The 1867 Constitution was from the standpoint of Austrian Jewry the culmination of the long struggle for emancipation, for it effectively guaranteed them both their equality before the law and their civic rights on the basis of general liberal principles upheld by the central government. Not surprisingly, the combination of faith in the centralized Austrian Monarchy, in liberalism, and in the hegemony of the Austro-German bourgeoisie henceforth became the bedrock political credo of Viennese Jewry. When these principles came under attack from the late 1870s onward, with the rise of local particularisms, Slav and German nationalism, economic protectionism, political anti-Semitism, and the mass movements of Christian Socialism and Social Democracy, Viennese Jews were thrust on the defensive but they never abandoned their dominant credo.

Both Joseph II's *Toleranzedikt* (1781) and the 1867 Constitution had emanated from a strong central power whose protective hand was seen as essential to safeguarding Jewish rights. As Adolf Jellinek put it in June 1883, Austrian Jews 'want a strong Austria because they cannot forget that it was the central parliament . . . which voted for the *Grundrechte* (Bill of Rights)'.[53] It was not after all the provincial Diets, the Slav nations, or the aristocratic Federalists who had initiated this enlightened legislation. Similarly, economic and political liberalism was seen as being more compatible than any other creed with the Jewish role as mobile innovators of the capitalist system—as bankers, railroad-pioneers, coal and iron industrialists, founders of the textile industries, owners of great metropolitan newspapers, and barons of the Stock Exchange.

The capitalistic classes in the Habsburg Empire, among whom Viennese and Budapest Jews played a central role, were after all 'a very efficacious force in the unification and cohesion of the monarchy'.[54] The societal backwardness of both Austria and Hungary, the strength

---

[52] Grunwald, *Vienna*, 406–7.

[53] A.J., 'Jüdisch-Österreichisch', *Die Neuzeit*, 15 June 1883.

[54] Oscar Jászi, *The Dissolution of the Habsburg Monarchy* (Chicago and London, 1971), 171. Ch. VII deals with Capitalism and Jewry as a centripetal force in the Monarchy. For the alliance between the Magyar feudal aristocracy and Jewish financial capitalism in the modernization of Transleithania, see William O. McCagg, jun., *Jewish Notables and Geniuses in Modern Hungary* (New York, 1972).

of the feudal traditions that despised industry and banking (which were largely in the Jewish hands), and the absence of a fully developed indigenous bourgeoisie inevitably thrust the Jews forward as pioneers of capitalism. Even in the 1860s major sections of the Empire were still very backward compared to Western Europe in terms of their economic development and, even in more advanced regions, commercial capitalism was relatively retarded.[55] Since the main pillars of the dynastic regime—the aristocracy, the Church, the bureaucracy, and the army—were not interested in rapid modernization, this task had devolved on the Austro-German bourgeoisie, led by the Viennese bankers and Jewish capitalists.[56] Their partnership with the supranational State, which reached its high point in the liberal era, could not however, encourage a *rapid* modernization since the forces endangered by industrialization were simply too strong, and no resolute 'national' policy could be seriously envisaged in the framework of the Monarchy.[57] Objective institutional and structural difficulties rooted in the multinational character of the Empire and its anachronistic class structure made the free-trade ideology of liberalism something of an artificial plant in Austria-Hungary.[58]

The political weakness of Austrian liberalism was even more apparent, and it has been admirably summarized by Carl Schorske.

Austrian liberalism, like that of most other European nations, had its heroic age in the struggle against aristocracy and baroque absolutism. This ended in the stunning defeat of 1848. The chastened liberals came to power and established a constitutional regime in the 1860s almost by default. Not their own internal strength, but the defeats of the old order at the hands of foreign enemies brought the liberals to the helm of the state. From the first they had to share power with the aristocracy and the imperial bureaucracy. Even during their two decades of rule, the liberals' social base remained weak, confined to the middle-class Germans and German Jews of the urban centers'.[59]

Given this weak social base and their dependence on the German nationality, it is not surprising that the Austrian liberals ultimately

[55] See N. T. Gross, 'The Habsburg Monarchy 1750–1914', in Carlo M. Cipolla, *The Fonatana Economic History of Europe* (London, 1980), 228–78.

[56] Ibid. 250–1.

[57] See Bernard Michel, *Banques et banquiers en Autrîche au début du XXe siècle* (Paris, 1976), for a comprehensive account of the decisive part played by banking in Austrian *fin de siècle* economic life. Michel underlines the importance of the Jews in the world of Viennese finance.

[58] Gross, p. 250.

[59] Carl E. Schorske, *Fin-de-siècle Vienna: Politics and Culture* (London, 1980), 5.

failed to transform the Habsburg Empire into a genuinely constitutional State; that they lacked the strength to replace the aristocracy as a ruling class; and, even more fatally, that they resorted to maintaining their parliamentary power by preserving an undemocratic restricted franchise.[60] The German centralism of the liberals was increasingly resented by the awakening Slav nationalities. Equally, their identification with capitalist oligarchy (especially in Vienna) made them the natural target of exploited social classes excluded by the electoral system—the lower middle class, the peasantry, and the proletariat— and their raucous anticlericalism ensured the undying enmity of the Catholic Church.[61]

These weaknesses of Austro-liberalism were in the long run to have a seriously detrimental influence on the position of Jews in Vienna and other parts of the Empire. From the end of the 1870s the warning signals were already apparent. The great Stock Exchange crash of 1873 which contributed much to discrediting both the ruling Liberal Ministry and *laissez-faire* capitalism in Austria were pointers to what still lay in the future. The Jewish dimension, though less in evidence than in Berlin, was also present. Victor Ritter von Ofenheim, Chairman of the bankrupt Lemberg–Czernowitz railroad, and a Jew, was accused in court proceedings that began in January 1875 of having criminally neglected his shareholders' interests and of having made illegal profits. Though he was acquitted, the trial provoked a scandal and implicated members of the Liberal Cabinet. Though the Stock Exchange crash in Vienna did not provoke any immediate anti-Semitic backlash in Austria (unlike Germany), given the prominence of Jews in finance, industry, in the liberal press and politics, disenchantment with the morality of economic liberalism was bound to have a deleterious effect on the position of Jewry.[62]

---

[60] See John W. Boyer, *Political Radicalism in Late Imperial Vienna: Origins of the Christian Social Movement, 1848–1897* (Chicago and London, 1891), 1–40, on Austrian liberal politics. Boyer surveys both the détente which the liberals arrived at with the imperial bureaucracy and their betrayal of the ideals of 1848—especially that of the unitary *Bürgertum.*

[61] Ibid. 136 ff. for the secularism and anti-clericalism of liberal Viennese culture, which in turn exacerbated the antagonism of Catholic politicians towards Austro-liberalism.

[62] On the Ofenheim case, see Richard Charmatz, *Oesterreichs innere Geschichte von 1848 bis 1907* (Leipzig, 1909), 118. For a differentiated analysis of the connection between the 1873 crash and the rise of anti-Semitic movements in Germany and Austria, see Jacob Katz, *From Prejudice to Destruction: Anti-Semitism, 1730–1933* (Cambridge, Mass., 1982), 245 ff.

By 1879, the crucial year which saw the demise of the brief liberal era in Austrian politics, a reassessment of unconditional Jewish allegiance to liberalism and German hegemony in the Empire was certainly feasible. Nevertheless, in that crucial electoral campaign Adolf Jellinek restated once more the central credo of emancipated Austrian Jewry in uncompromising terms: 'The Jews of Austria must adhere to the Constitution and the forces of liberalism in accordance with their most vital interest. In respect of their background and education they incline to the German nationality, sympathizing with a grandly conceived Austria founded on strong central government'.[63] Jellinek went on to enumerate a lengthy list of the 'political enemies' of the Jews—all of them predictably adversaries of German liberalism. They included the clerical ultramontane element, the feudal aristocracy resentful of mercantile capitalism, the pro-Slav federalists, and even the nascent labour movement.[64]

This stance was, as we have seen, not without historical justification. The German Liberals in Austria did oppose clericalism, absolutism, and the 'historic rights' of the provincial Diets.[65] It was also true that they represented the most educated, the wealthiest, and the most 'enlightened' nationality in the Empire, whose language was also that of the Imperial administration, of business life, and of the dominant culture. Furthermore, the German Liberals stood for representative government, secularism, and free-trade capitalism—values with which Viennese Jews naturally tended to identify. On the other hand, their enemies—the Catholic Church, the feudal élites, and the Slav nationalities—clearly seemed to represent the illiberal forces of reaction and counter-revolution, which had defeated the 1848 uprising and were considered hostile to Jewish emancipation.

Nevertheless, despite these basic facts the Jewish commitment to the Verfassungspartei (German Liberal party) could be judged as one-sided in certain respects. Even during the liberal era, Jews continued to be excluded from the bureaucracy, from diplomatic posts and the upper reaches of the judiciary;[66] they were still discriminated against for teaching positions in universities and Gymnasien and only converts like Julius Glaser and Joseph Unger—who between them laid

---

[63] A.J., 'Zur Wahlkampagne', *Die Neuzeit*, 6 June 1879.

[64] Ibid.

[65] P. G. J. Pulzer, 'The Austrian Liberals and the Jewish Question, 1867–1914', *Journal of Central European Affairs*, 33 (1963), 131–42.

[66] Sigmund Mayer, *Die Wiener Juden: Kommerz, Kultur, Politik, 1700–1900* (Vienna and Berlin, 1917), 376, 477.

the foundations of modern Austrian jurisprudence—actually became Ministers of State.[67] As baptized Jews, they could have astonishing careers altogether unattainable by their former co-religionists. Thus Julius Glaser served as Minister of Justice in the Liberal Cabinet from 1871 to 1879 along with Joseph Unger, the Minister without Portfolio. A year later Unger was appointed President of the *Reichsgericht*, the highest legal instance in the Empire.[68]

But such examples merely underlined the point that even under liberal hegemony, conversion to Christianity was a condition for exercising the highest offices of State. Moreover, the German Liberals, under growing pressures to defend their *Deutschtum* against the Slavs and their liberalism against the reactionary elements among the Germans, were scarcely 'philo-Semitic'. In no circumstances did they wish to appear as a 'Jewish party' and thereby to endanger their position with the German lower classes in the country districts. Thus their press 'carefully avoided referring to the Jews', preferring not to nominate too many Jewish candidates, let alone appoint any of them to office.[69] More serious than this liberal ambivalence were, however, the political implications of the Jewish involvement in the fight of Germanism against the Slavs and the social repercussions of their identification with capitalist oligarchy. These dangers had been foreseen by the most far-sighted Jewish politician of the century, Adolf Fischof (1816–93), whose reflections on Habsburg nationality problems exerted a seminal influence on the most diverse currents in Austrian public life.[70] No other Jew, with the possible exceptions of Ignaz Kuranda and the founder of the Austrian Social Democratic party, Viktor Adler, had such an impact on nineteenth-century Austrian politics and none enjoyed a comparable moral authority.

Born in Budapest where he attended Gymnasium, Fischof came to Vienna in 1836 to study medicine. After years of material hardship, which delayed his obtaining of a medical degree, Fischof was

[67] Franz Kobler, 'The Contribution of Austrian Jews to Jurisprudence', in Fraenkel (ed.), *Jews of Austria*, 29.

[68] Ibid. 30–1.   [69] Grunwald, *Vienna*, 414–15.

[70] On Fischof's career and political outlook the most important sources are Richard Charmatz's biography, *Adolf Fischof: Das Lebensbild eines österreichischen Politikers* (Stuttgart and Berlin, 1910); Werner J. Cahnman, 'Adolf Fischof and his Jewish Followers', *Leo Baeck Yearbook*, 4 (1959), 111–39; Grunwald, *Vienna*, 255–64; and N. M. Gelber, *Aus zwei Jahrhunderten* (Leipzig, 1924), 126–31. See also R. A. Kann, *The Multinational Empire*, 2 vols. (New York, 1950) for the background to the nationality problem; Rabbi Joseph Samuel Bloch, *My Reminiscences* (Vienna and Berlin, 1923), 55–60, for the Jewish aspect; and *Die Neuzeit*, 31 Mar. 1893, pp. 1–2.

appointed *Sekundarzt* (assistant physician) at the Vienna General Hospital in 1846.[71] Nearly two years later on 13 March 1848, in front of the *Landhaus* court, Adolf Fischof stepped out of his anonymity and in a fiery, enthusiastic, and impromptu speech stirred the Viennese crowds to the cause of press freedom, popular sovereignty, ministerial responsibility, liberty of conscience, and union of the Austrian nations.[72]

Even more than his co-religionists—Ludwig August Frankl, composer of the best-selling lyric *Die Universität* (the 'Marseillaise' of the Viennese rising), Joseph Goldmark, or Hermann Jellinek—Fischof emerged as the hero of the Revolution, respected by contemporaries for his sober, tactful, and statesmanlike behaviour. By March 1848 he had been made head of the *Sicherheitsausschuss* (Committee of Public Security), the highest governing body of the Revolution, and in the coming months was active as a parliamentarian and in various administrative capacities. During 1848 there were times when his moral authority extended over the most of the Monarchy and he came to symbolize its democratic aspirations.[73]

Following the defeat of the Revolution, Fischof refused to flee for his life and had to face trial for high treason, but was acquitted after all witnesses testified in his favour. He was however deprived of political rights until an amnesty in 1867, earning his living with some difficulty as a physician in private practice. In 1861 he published anonymously (together with Joseph Unger) *Zur Lösung der ungarischen Frage*, which anticipated many features of the *Ausgleich* with Hungary six years later. It sharply criticized the centralistic repression by Vienna of Hungarian constitutional traditions and rights.[74]

Between 1867 and his death in 1893 Fischof became something like the 'moral conscience' of Austria, a much sought-after figure visited by numerous Austrian politicians in his village retreat in Carinthia. In these years he tried to develop and systematize reflections on the national question which he had first enunciated in 1848 when he called for a 'brotherly alliance' of the peoples of Austria to achieve strength in unity.[75] The consequences of the 1866 defeat by Prussia and the compromise with Hungary had exposed the fragility of the

---

[71] Charmatz, *Fischof*, 10–11.   [72] Ibid. 20; Grunwald, *Vienna*, 256–7.
[73] Grunwald, *Vienna*, 262.
[74] See Dr Ferdinand Kronawetter. Speech of 9 Apr. 1898 in honour of Fischof, *Mittheilungen der Österreichisch-Israelitischen Union*, 10, no. 104, p. 6.
[75] Ibid. 7.

Monarchy, reinforcing Austro-German fears of the internal Slav danger. Fischof, though a German by education, feeling, and culture, sought to allay these fears by stressing the need for peaceful reconciliation between the different ethnic groups, based on developing the national rights anchored in the 1867 Constitution.[76]

In that year he first put forward the federalist model as a possible solution for the Czech–German conflict, arguing that if the peoples of Austria were permitted a free development on Swiss lines, 'Moscow will cease to be the Mecca of the Slavs'.[77] By 1868 he was advocating extensive administrative decentralization and broad municipal autonomy as the best guarantee for the preservation for individual and national liberties.[78] Without self-government, Fischof argued, parliamentarism would remain a hollow word. The free municipality must be the foundation of the constitutional State.

These premises were elaborated at greater length in *Oesterreich und die Bürgschaften seines Bestandes* (Austria and the Guarantees for its Existence), published in Vienna in 1869 and widely recognized as a classic of Austrian political literature. In this work Fischof put his finger on the central contradiction of the 1867 Constitution—that Austria-Hungary was a multinational State (*Nationalitätenstaat*) masquerading under liberal German hegemony as a national-state on the West European model. It had a dual personality, liberal with regard to the rights of the individual but oppressive in its relation to the Slav nationalities who were still treated as 'servant peoples' (*Bedientenvölker*).[79]

Austria could no longer be defined however as a German state when its German inhabitants barely exceeded one-third of the total population in Cisleithania (excluding Hungary). Only in the Alpine lands did the Germans form an overwhelming majority, particularly in Lower Austria, Upper Austria, Vorarlberg, and Salzburg. In the most industrially developed region of Bohemia, Germans compromised only 37 per cent of the population while the Czechs were in a majority; Austrian Silesia was 44 per cent German as against 32 per cent Poles and 24 per cent Czechs; Moravia was predominantly Czech with a German minority of 28 per cent. Galicia, divided between a Polish majority in the west, with a Ukrainian majority and a large Jewish minority in the eastern sector, had barely any Germans at all. In Bukovina the Germans were a more substantial minority among Poles,

---

[76] Ibid.; see also Charmatz, *Fischof*, 198. [77] Charmatz, *Fischof*, 205.
[78] Ibid. 214; Kronawetter, *Mittheilungen*, 8.
[79] See the admirable discussion of this contradiction by Cahnman, pp. 111 ff.

Ukrainians, Romanians, and Jews. The southern parts of the Tyrol were Italian as was Trieste. Carniola was overwhelmingly Slovene (there were also important Slovene-speaking minorities in Styria and Carinthia) and the Adriatic regions of Dalmatia, Istria, and the Austrian Littoral were predominantly Serbo-Croat.[80]

The nationality problem was not, however, merely demographic but constitutional, economic, political, and moral, affecting all aspects of Austrian life. The Slav nationalities in the course of the nineteenth century had developed their own intelligentsia, literature, cultural-national consciousness, and political demands. They were no longer prepared to accept the political leadership role of the Germans as the exclusive *Staatsnation* or even their post-1867 subordination to a triumvirate of 'master-races', the Germans, Hungarians and Poles.[81] By 1910, moreover, the Slavs made up 23.5 million inhabitants (45 per cent) of the total population of Austria-Hungary.[82]

It was therefore a far-sighted act of political realism on Fischof's part to recognize as early as 1869 that none of Austria's nationalities was strong enough to dominate the others, though each one of them through its opposition could endanger the overall structure.[83] Austrian statesmen, he argued, should accordingly abandon the fiction of a 'unitary state' (*Einheitsstaat*) and develop new constitutional forms to satisfy the neglected non-German nationalities and their aspirations for social justice and national equality.[84] The Habsburg tradition of centralistic absolutism had created centrifugal tendencies among the newly awakening nationalities. But only if Austria were decentralized could it become truly centripetal.

The era of national privileges had long since passed along with that of Josephinian absolutism, which, progressive in its time, had now become a fetter on the free development of the Austrian peoples. Swiss-style federalism was the only rational solution for, according to Fischof, 'Switzerland is a republican Austria *en miniature* just as Austria is a monarchical Switzerland writ large'.[85] The examples of

---

[80] For the statistics of Austrian population figures see Robert A. Kann, *The Multinational Empire*, ii. 299 ff.

[81] For the ramifications of the Austrian nationalities' question see Kann, *The Multinational Empire*; A. J. P. Taylor, *The Habsburg Monarchy, 1809–1918* (London, 1891); C. A. Macartney, *The Habsburg Empire, 1790–1918* (London, 1969); also the multivolume official history, Adam Wandruszka and Peter Urbanitsch (eds.), *Die Habsburgermonarchie, 1848–1918* (Vienna, 1981).

[82] Taylor, p. 286.   [83] Charmatz, *Fischof,* 223 ff.

[84] Ibid. 235–6; Kronawetter, *Mittheilungen,* 11.   [85] Charmatz, *Fischof,* 227.

Switzerland, Belgium, Canada, Britain, and the United States proved that federalism, extensive local government, and the decentralization of education increased the prosperity, liberty, and patriotism of the inhabitants.

The mistake of the Austrian liberals lay in their failure to see that, in Central and Eastern Europe, individual liberties and the integrity of the state could be guaranteed only by recognizing the fact of nationality. This appeared to Fischof as a logical extension to the liberation of the individual effected by the French Revolution. But it had to be applied equally to the non-German 'nationalities'. Hence his warning to the liberals of the Verfassungspartei that the Austro-Germans could maintain their leading role in the Empire only 'if we respect with German humanity the rights of the other nations and promote their linguistic and cultural development'.[86] The Austro-Germans could afford to and should become more generous in their national policy, relying on their industrial, commercial, scientific, and cultural superiority instead of institutional repression and electoral chicanery to preserve their hegemony.

Thus, Fischof supported universal, equal, and direct suffrage without property qualifications along with the idea of the 'curia-vote' to protect minorities against majorities in areas of mixed population.[87] In Austrian conditions, territorial autonomy would not be sufficient, for the boundaries of the historic crown lands did not coincide with those of ethnic groups. Voting in national curias would ensure that in matters of education and culture, no measures could be taken which were detrimental to or against the will of a national minority. Fischof also favoured legal guarantees for the use of the mother tongue in schools, courts, local and general administration. Though German would remain the language of central authority, the mother tongue of each nationality in a given territory would be taught as a compulsory subject, and instruction in the languages in everyday use (*Umgangssprachen*) would also be given in schools.[88]

Fischof envisaged, therefore, not only a system of local self-government in the counties, districts, and communities of Austria but a comprehensive programme of cultural-national autonomy. Once

---

[86] Ibid. 225.

[87] Ibid. 237, 270. In a letter to the Czech leader Rieger, Fischof explained: 'Die nationale Kurie ist die Festung, innerhalb welcher die nationale Minorität sich erfolgreich gegen die Angriffe der nationalen Majoritat verteidigen kann . . .'

[88] Cahnman, pp. 120–1; Kronawetter, *Mittheilungen*, 14–15.

equilibrium was re-established between the nationalities, and once national minorities were guaranteed the free development of their cultural individuality, the 'social question' too would be open to constructive solutions. Fischof recognized the socio-economic dimension to the nationality conflict but rightly saw that only if the latter was attenuated would the economic grievances of the working classes and rural masses be seriously dealt with.

Though far removed from Marxian socialism, Fischof's programme anticipated by exactly three decades many of the ideas that underlay the Austrian Social Democratic party's national programme formulated at the Brünn Congress (1899). The influence of his federalism and his theories on the reorganization of the multinational State are clearly to be found in the works of the outstanding Austro-Marxist thinker and Chancellor of the First Republic, Karl Renner.[89] In 1918, on the eve of the Habsburg Empire's collapse, Renner appropriately wrote that 'alone among all the Austrian politicians of German nationality, Fischof understood the conditions of life of the Austro-Germans and of the Empire'.[90]

Even the future Christian-Social leader Karl Lueger, shortly before he placed himself at the head of the anti-Semitic movement in Vienna, honoured Fischof, with whose efforts to secure the cohesion of the Austrian State by reconciling the nationalities he strongly identified. In 1886, on the occasion of Fischof's seventieth birthday, after the liberals on the Vienna City Council had vetoed a proposal to convey their congratulations, Dr Lueger declared: 'Not one of the gentlemen present in this hall is fit to carry water for Fischof and there is no one living who can equal him in political experience, in service to the city of Vienna, and in integrity of character.'[91]

It was one of the bitter ironies of Austrian history that Lueger should have paid homage to Fischof whereas the liberals and their Viennese Jewish supporters were among his sharpest adversaries. This was all the more remarkable since Fischof was not only the acknowledged leader of the 1848 liberal Revolution but a self-conscious, proud Jew with a well-developed sense of Jewish solidarity acquired during his upbringing and early years of schooling in

---

[89] See Karl Renner (Rudolf Springer), *Staat und Nation* (Vienna, 1899); also his *Der Kampf der österreichischen Nationen um den Staat* (Leipzig, 1902).

[90] Renner, *Das Selbstbestimmungsrecht der Nationen* (Vienna, 1918), 232.

[91] Quoted in Grunwald, *Vienna*, 304, and Charmatz, *Fischof*, 298–9.

Budapest.[92] He could write in Hebrew script and felt a powerful identification with the teachings of Judaism, with its vocation as the 'ethical instructor of a great part of mankind' and with the Jews as a martyred nation.[93]

In spite of his political differences with Adolf Jellinek, Fischof wrote him a letter on 26 June 1891 praising in the warmest terms his 'flaming eloquence' and passionate defence of Jewish values, on the occasion of the Vienna preacher's seventieth birthday. In his letter Fischof stressed his consciousness of a high and ennobling moral mission contained in the Hebrew Bible, which had profoundly shaped the religions of civilized humanity. He affirmed his pride that the Jews had displayed throughout their history an unparalleled spiritual strength which enabled them to resist centuries of persecution; that in spite of oppression, discrimination, and exclusion they had never bowed to their enemies, nor would they now yield to the anti-Semitic witch-hunt in Vienna. 'They wish to reduce us to helots, to humiliate us as pariahs but we are not the national material out of whom slaves can be made.'[94] The 'drive to education and knowledge', the respect for science, the urge to civilize humanity, were collective virtues of which not even 'the cannibalistic greed of anti-Semitism' could deprive the Jewish people.[95]

Already in 1848 Fischof had taken a clear stand in favour of political equality for Jews, along with the preacher Mannheimer whose demand to abolish the 'Jew-tax' he strongly supported.[96] This battle for Jewish rights was an integral part of his general campaign for constitutional freedom, national equality, and social justice. He also concerned himself with the economic misery of Galician Jewry. In 1851, following a study visit to Galicia, he prepared a model statute of association for the establishment of a Jewish agricultural association (Israelitischer Ackerbauverein) designed to improve the conditions of the Galician Jewish proletariat through encouraging farming colonies.[97] Another testament to Fischof's profound sense of Jewishness came in 1870. After the granting of the Constitution and the achievement of

---

[92] Charmatz, *Fischof,* 262. At Gymnasium in Budapest, every classroom at that time had a special 'Jew-bench'. See Dr Ferdinand Kronawetter, 'Adolf Fischof und die Verfassungskämpfe der Gegenwart', *Mittheilungen der Österreichisch-Israelitischen Union,* 10, no. 104 (Apr. 1898), p. 4.

[93] 'Gratulationsschreiben des Herrn Dr. Adolf Fischof an Herrn Dr. Adolf Jellinek', *Die Neuzeit,* 3 July 1891, p. 262.

[94] Ibid.   [95] Ibid.

[96] Grunwald, *Vienna,* 262–3.   [97] Charmatz, *Fischof,* 278–81.

Jewish emancipation in 1867, the amnestied Fischof was offered a post
in the Austrian Cabinet which he turned down. Apart from health
problems and political disagreements with the German liberals, his
refusal almost certainly stemmed from reluctance to compromise his
Jewish faith. For even in liberal Austria no Jew could accept a
ministerial position without taking an oath of office 'in such terms as
only a professing believer in Christianity could assume'.[98]

The extent of Fischof's Jewish identification came even more
sharply into focus with the rise of an organized Viennese anti-
Semitism in the early 1880s. In 1882 he enthusiastically supported the
efforts of the maverick Galician rabbi Dr Joseph Samuel Bloch—at
that time the *enfant terrible* of the Viennese Jewish establishment—to
defend the Talmud by carrying the fight into the proletarian suburbs of
Vienna. Bloch, who regarded Fischof as a moral guide and political
mentor (and later sought to apply his theories on national autonomy to
Galician Jewry), sent him a copy of his address on ' The workers in the
time of Jesus' given to a social-democratic gathering in Florisdorf.[99]
Fischof not only warmly approved Bloch's 'excellent lecture' but
backed his successful parliamentary candidacy for a Galician constituency
in 1883, seeing in him a courageous defender of Jewish civic rights
against anti-Semitic slander. Bloch became a regular guest at
Fischof's Carinthian home in the village of Emmersdorf, seeking his
advice on parliamentary affairs and on ways to defend the civic status
of Jews against mounting anti-Semitism.[100]

The Galician rabbi shared Fischof's views on the priority of
national reconciliation in Austria, his advocacy of federalism, and his
scepticism concerning exclusive Jewish identification with the German
national cause. Both politicians agreed on the need to assume an active
posture of collective self-defence against anti-Semitism, which resulted
in Rabbi Bloch's drive to create the first Jewish defence organization in
Austria, the Österreichisch-Israelitische Union (1886).[101]

Though Fischof was not directly involved in its creation and took no

---

[98] Grunwald, *Vienna*, 303; also Kronawetter, *Mittheilungen*, 10, for Fischof's earlier
rejection of an offer to sit in a clerical-conservative Cabinet.

[99] Joseph S. Bloch, *Erinnerungen aus meinem Leben* (Vienna and Leipzig, 1922), 25 ff.,
53; *My Reminiscences* (Eng. trans.), 55–60.

[100] For references to his correspondence with Fischof, see Bloch, *Erinnerungen*,
i. 53 ff., 79, 270; *My Reminiscences*, 55 ff.

[101] Bloch, *Erinnerungen*, 197 ff. For the background see Jacob Toury, 'Troubled
Beginnings: The Emergence of the Österreichisch-Israelitische Union', in *Leo Baeck
Yearbook*, 30 (1985), 475–75.

active part in its deliberations, he sympathized with its objectives and his memory was later invoked by its members. Shortly after his death, at the annual meeting of the Union in April 1893 a speaker recalled that Fischof's work for progress and humanity had been in the best traditions of Judaism.[102] According to the report in Dr Bloch's weekly, the speaker observed: 'The people from whom Fischof stems will survive. When the enemies and persecutors of our community have been forgotten and the anti-Semitic movement will have become an object of social psychiatry, Fischof's name will glow into the faraway future.'[103] Four years later the Union recommended a return by Austrian Jewry to the national reconciliation programme of 'the unforgettable Fischof', based on justice and equality before the law, as the only rational solution to the chaos facing Jews and the Austrian fatherland.[104] Most poignant of all, in an address to the Union in April 1898, a close non-Jewish political associate of Fischof, the Viennese democrat Dr Ferdinand Kronawetter, pointedly asked his listeners why Fischof had found no communal support among his co-religionists when in 1882 he had sought to create a Deutsche Volkspartei to rally liberals from all nationalities.[105]

This reminder of a historic missed opportunity in the history of Viennese Jewry highlights the differences between mainstream Austroliberalism and the radical-democratic variety espoused by Fischof and his circle. These differences focused in equal measure around the 'social question' and the resolution of the nationalities' conflict, both of paramount importance not only for the future of the Monarchy but also for that of Austrian Jewry. Since 1848 Viennese liberals had systematically sought to exclude the lower *Bürgertum* from the privileged curia voting system and had built their power on a solid middle and upper *Mittelstand* of property-owners, officials, wealthy artisans, and prosperous shopkeepers.[106]

This heavily capitalist, interest-orientated politics which unashamedly betrayed the radical democratic ideals of 1848 emerged as a hallmark of Viennese liberalism. It became a major target of the lower middle-class protest movement of the 1880s and it was slyly used by opportunist anti-Semitic politicians who focused attention on the role

[102] Cahnman, pp. 128–9.
[103] *Österreichische Wochenschrift*, 28 Apr. 1893. The speaker was Dr Marcus Spitzer.
[104] *Mittheilungen der Österreichisch-Israelitischen Union*, 9, no. 92 (Mar. 1897).
[105] Kronawetter, 'Adolf Fischof und die Verfassungskämpfe der Gegenwart', *Mittheilungen*, 3 ff.
[106] Boyer, *Political Radicalism*, 16–17.

of the Jews in Viennese banking and commercial capitalism. Only a small group of left-liberal Viennese democrats who had remained faithful to the radical 1848 ideal of a unitary *Bürgertum* stood up against both the oligarchic tendencies of the liberals and the anticapitalist anti-Semitism of the excluded artisans and their demagogic tribunes. The leader of the Viennese democrats, Kronawetter, was not by chance one of Fischof's closest collaborators in the abortive attempt to create a Deutsche Volkspartei in 1882.

Among the Jewish participants in this effort, attracted by Fischof's social reformism as much as by his national programme were the publisher and editor of the *Wiener Allgemeine Zeitung*, Theodor Hertzka (1845–1924), the economist and social statistician, Professor Isidore Singer, the internationally celebrated neuropathologist, Professor Moritz Benedikt, and the architect Wilhelm Fraenkl.[107] Politically the most influential of these collaborators was undoubtedly Hertzka (born like Fischof in Budapest), an economist by training and a social reformer who became famous as the author of the lengthy utopian tract, *Freiland*.[108] Hertzka, who composed the economic reform programme of the Deutsche Volkspartei and advocated a moderate liberal socialism based on 'mutualism' and co-operation, was the closest in spirit to Fischof's social thought. Both Fischof and Hertzka opposed the *laissez-faire* capitalism advocated by the classical liberals as well as Marxian socialism based on class war, which unduly restricted personal initiative and individual liberties. On the other hand, they saw clearly enough the urgency of raising the living standards of the proletariat and extending the suffrage to the working classes.

Like Kronawetter and his Viennese radicals, Fischof's Jewish disciples argued the need for a moderate German national party which would regenerate the forgotten ideals of 1848 on a democratic basis by co-operating with like-minded liberals of other nationalities. In a letter to Hertzka, published in the *Wiener Allgemeine Zeitung* on 28 May

---

[107] Cahnman, p. 122 ff.

[108] See Theodor Hertzka, *Freiland: Ein soziales Zukunftsbild* (Leipzig, 1890) His social utopian vision may well have influenced Theodor Herzl, the founder of political Zionism, who mentions *Freiland* in the intro. to his *Der Judenstaat* (Vienna, 1896). Both Hertzka and Herzl grew up in Budapest, came to Vienna as young men, and initially made their careers in journalism. Both were proud of their Jewishness, deeply troubled by anti-Semitism and espoused similar conceptions of economic justice and social organization. For Hertzka's notions on the middle road between capitalism and socialism see his *Sozialdemokratie und Sozialliberalismus* (Dresden and Leipzig, 1891).

1882, Fischof explained that electoral reform and constitutional guarantees for the Slav nationalities were vital in order to prevent an open clash between the Austrian State and its constituent peoples. The latter should not be driven to choose between Austrian patriotism and their own national-political interests. Liberalism, in order to become viable, would have to be freed from the hitherto justifiable reproach of intolerance towards non-Germans.[109]

Neither Fischof nor Hertzka supported the policy of the new Austrian Prime Minister, Count Taafe, who since 1879 stood at the head of a Slav-clerical-conservative coalition which openly favoured the Slavs at the expense of the Germans.[110] None the less they were vehemently attacked by the Verfassungspartei and the radical German nationalists for betraying the German cause. Similarly the liberal Viennese Jews deplored Fischof's espousal of federalism and greater national autonomy as a desertion of German liberal centralism and therefore as detrimental to Jewish interests.[111] In spite of their pride in Fischof as an Austrian patriot and symbol of 1848 liberalism, Jewish communal leaders were profoundly unnerved by his social and political programme. They saw Count Taafe and his conservative Cabinet as the immediate adversary of Jewry and the return of the Verfassungs-partei to government as their primary task.

In the great debate between centralism and federalism, liberal capitalism and social reform, German hegemony or national equality, most Viennese Jews opposed Fischof, remaining true to the spirit of the 1867 Constitution which had guaranteed their emancipation. They were ready to risk the wrath of the Taafe government by denouncing its national policy as 'treason to the German cause', though he had offered (for political reasons of his own) to collaborate with them to suppress the anti-Semitic movement.[112] Even though anti-Semitism was mounting daily in Vienna and Liberal opposition leaders remained conspicuously silent, the President of the Kultusgemeinde, Joseph Ritter von Wertheimer (himself a veteran liberal), told Rabbi Bloch, '*Zum Taafe gehen wir nicht*'.[113] Bloch had to turn to Hertzka's

---

[109] Charmatz, *Fischof*, 382–4.

[110] Ibid. 342–4 on the deep distrust in German Liberal circles for Taafe's government and the growing radicalization of the Austro-Germans after 1880.

[111] Cahnman, p. 121.

[112] Grunwald, *Vienna*, 429. In order to wean Viennese Jews away from their support of the Verfassungspartei, Taafe financed the printing of Joseph Bloch's 1886 pamphlet, *Der nationale Zwist und die Juden in Österreich* (The Strife of the Nationalities and the Jews in Austria).   [113] Bloch, *Erinnerungen*, 167; also Grunwald, *Vienna*, 429.

Wiener Allgemeine Zeitung to publish his militant counter-attack against the clerical anti-Semite August Rohling, since the community leaders and the great liberal newspapers (owned mainly by Jews) preferred to guard a low profile.

In a private meeting in 1882—probably at Hertzka's home—Fischof warned some of those Kultusgemeinde leaders who were present that they faced a clear choice: either the nationalities of Austria were reconciled or they would turn anti-Semitic.[114] The warning was disregarded along with Fischof's prophetic advice that the efforts of 8 million Austro-Germans to dominate 14 million non-Germans would create a remorseless *Rassenkampf*, poison all public debate, and eventually destroy the Austrian State itself.[115]

Instead, the Liberals and the radical German nationalist movement under Georg von Schoenerer carried on a tumultuous agitation against the creation of the Deutsche Volkspartei. At its first meeting on 16 July 1882, two of von Schoenerer's leading followers, the future Social Democrat Engelbert Pernerstorfer and the Jewish-born ideologist of Austrian Pan-Germanism, Heinrich Friedjung (1851–1920), disrupted proceedings.[116]

Fischof's new party never recovered from this false start and the determined efforts of the German Liberals and radical nationalists to render it stillborn.[117] Thus evaporated what may have been one of the last opportunities to reconcile the nationalities in Austria. The pro-Germanism of the leaders of Austrian Jewry was, however, to bear a bitter fruit. For the envenoming of the national struggle speedily brought in its wake the emergence of a racial anti-Semitism that threatened the very existence of the Jewish community. By the mid-1880s the Pan-German movement had expelled even such ardent Jewish collaborators as Heinrich Friedjung from its ranks. It now openly called for 'the removal of Jewish influence from all sections of public life' as a central and indispensable plank in its programme.[118]

The fate of the Moravian-born Heinrich Friedjung was indeed a paradigm of the one-sided nature of Jewish pro-Germanism and its unrequited love-affair with *Deutschtum*. Friedjung, the man who was to become the greatest of all nineteenth-century Austrian historians, had recognized like Fischof that the shock of 1866 necessitated a

---

[114] Cahnman, p. 128; Charmatz, *Fischof*, 386; Isidor Schalit, 'Kadimah: Aus meinem Erinnerungen' (MS, Central Zionist Archives, A 196/25, Jerusalem).

[115] Charmatz, *Fischof*, 391.   [116] Ibid. 385.

[117] Grunwald, *Vienna*, 426.   [118] Pulzer, p. 153.

fundamental revision of German-Austrian aspirations. They could no longer hope to have a leading position in both Germany and the Habsburg Empire. The pre-1866 Austro-liberal dream of a Germany united under Austrian rule while still preserving German hegemony inside the Danubian Empire itself had irremediably faded.[119] The time had come, so Friedjung believed, for a clear choice in favour of German rather than Austrian identity.

Friedjung unlike Fischof did not regard a federal solution to the national question as in any way desirable, favouring on the contrary a more centralized and German-dominated commonwealth which would seek to reduce the number of Slavs within its borders. He blamed the 'reactionary' dynasty for the 1866 defeat and sharply criticized the half-heartedness on the national question of the older generation of Austrian liberal leaders like Dr Eduard Herbst.[120]

Their 'Austrianism' seemed to him an artificial, self-alienated effort 'to close off' their deeper emotional feelings as Germans in favour of a nebulous supranational fiction. It was the young Friedjung's conviction that on the contrary 'the highest duty of the political writer was to exert an influence on that obscure first cause of the history of all peoples, on the national character . . .'. It was the task of the younger Germanocentric generation to create a new *Nationalgefühl* (national feeling) among the Austro-Germans. As he wrote in 1877: 'The only party which will be able to breathe new life into our fatherland is the one which rules Austria from a nationalistic point of view, which brings into being an alliance with Germany, which holds down the nationalities and which reaches an agreement with Hungary that both states will rule themselves separately and independently of each other'.[121]

Friedjung's Pan-German nationalism had a strong *völkisch* flavour though his definition of membership in the German nationality was essentially cultural rather than racial in character. The failure of the Slav nationalities to share his enthsiastic and almost mystic belief in the superiority of German *Kultur* and its educational mission was something difficult for him to comprehend. A. J. P. Taylor's psychological explanation clearly touches the heart of the problem:

[119] See Heinrich Friedjung, *The Struggle for Supremacy in Germany, 1859–1866*, trans. A. J. P. Taylor and W. C. McElwee (New York, 1966).

[120] William J. McGrath, *Dionysian Art and Populist Politics in Austria* (New Haven and London, 1974), 75.

[121] Quoted in ibid.

Friedjung regarded himself as a German, but he was only a German by adoption: he had become a German, because he valued German culture, and the process was no less deliberate for being subconscious. He therefore tended to expect a similar subconscious recognition of German superiority from the other races and he could not understand the reluctance of the Czechs, the Slovaks, or the Croats to follow his example.[122]

According to Taylor, 'Friedjung's race did in fact influence and warp his political career, for it made him overrate the ease with which the Germans could dominate and control the other races of the Empire'.[123] The dynamic of extreme assimilationism, which argued that Jews should be completely absorbed into the nationalities among whom they lived, sometimes worked in the direction of encouraging an exaggerated German chauvinism.[124]

Friedjung during his years as editor of the *Deutsche Wochenschrift* (1883–6) and subsequently as editor-in-chief of *Deutsche Zeitung* (the major publication of the Deutschnationale Partei) continued to espouse a vigorous, elemental nationalism, constantly recalling the glories of the tribal past and medieval Germanic greatness. Favourably contrasting 'the mighty Chancellor' (Bismarck) with the 'hoary' Austrian Emperor Franz Joseph, Friedjung claimed that a succession of feeble and reactionary Austrian regimes since 1848 had repressed the vital life-forces of German nationality. But tribal feeling was now undergoing a mighty resurgence for as Friedjung wrote in January 1885, 'We are of *one blood*, and of *one tribe*, the children of the one mother Germania', an ideological conviction to which he remained faithful to the bitter end.[125]

Friedjung, though personally insulted by von Schoenerer's extreme anti-Semitism, initially regarded it as an unfortunate diversion from the common central task of consolidating the German national rebirth against the Slav menace. Like other Jewish Pan-Germans, Friedjung had undoubtedly internalized a certain degree of cultural anti-Semitism as part of his embrace of the *völkisch* ideology.[126] But

---

[122] Taylor, introd. to Friedjung, p. iv.

[123] Ibid., p. xiv.

[124] For parallel phenomena in Hungary see Jászi, p. 171.

[125] *Deutsche Wochenschrift*, 18 Jan. 1885. See also Taylor, introd. to Friedjung, p. xxviii, who quotes from Friedjung's preface to the *Historical Essays* (one of the last things he wrote), reaffirming his youthful Pan-German credo and belief that 'in the end we shall return to the mother-country [i.e. Germany] whence one of the best stocks has migrated to the south-east in the pursuance of a historic mission'.

[126] See George L. Mosse, 'The Influence of the Völkisch Idea on German Jewry', *Leo Baeck Yearbook*, 12 (1967), 84–6.

von Schoenerer's turn to uninhibited racism placed him and other Jews in the movement in an untenable and ultimately impossible position.[127] Friedjung could perhaps accept that Jews were too intellectual, too mercantile, rootless, or cosmopolitan and he insistently demanded that they dissolve completely in the German nation.[128] But the new racial anti-Semitism cut the ground from under his feet for it implied that even the most assimilated Jews could not hope to play an active role in the German national rebirth. The longing for community and acceptance which underlay the assimilationist drive was thus dealt a cruel blow while the already split German nationalist forces were divided still further.[129] Friedjung's efforts to create a new party between the liberals and the radical Pan-Germans were temporarily successful but even in this more moderate grouping (the Deutscher Klub) his Jewish origins provoked a bitter anti-Semitic controversy which split the Klub down the middle.[130] Friedjung's political career was not only undermined as a consequence but he had to suffer the humiliation of insults directed at him as the representative of a Judaism he had repudiated—delivered in the name of a German culture which he continued to defend passionately. As the case of Friedjung suggests, the ideology of radical assimilation, intended to ease the merger into non-Jewish society, had clearly backfired by the mid-1880s. The rise of an aggressively illiberal and racist *Volksdeutschtum* in Austria whose prime target was modern, emancipated, Germanized Jewry already cast its dark shadow over the whole strategy of assimilation in Central Europe.

[127] For the reaction of Friedjung's closest collaborator, the young Victor Adler, to anti-Semitism, see Robert S. Wistrich, *Socialism and the Jews: The Dilemmas of Assimilation in Germany and Austria-Hungary* (Littman Library, London and Toronto 1982), 232–61.

[128] *Deutsche Wochenschrift*, no. 43, 25 Oct. 1885: 'Der einzige Ausgleich liegt . . . in dem vollständigen Verlassen der Sonderstellung, welche die Juden vielfach einnehmen, in dem radikalen Aufgehen in dem modernen Völkern (verstehe in das Deutschtum), unter denen sie leben. Denn die weltgeschichtliche Aufgabe, welche ihnen zugeteilt wurde, haben sie gelöst.' Friedjung's 'assimilationism' was bitterly attacked as a form of 'Semitic anti-Semitism' by Dr Joseph Samuel Bloch in *Österreichische Wochenschrift*, 16 Jan. 1885, 16 July 1885, 14 Nov. 1885.

[129] See Pulzer, pp. 137 ff., on the changing attitudes to Jews in the nationalist ranks. On the question of Friedjung's editing of the *Deutsche Zeitung*, see ibid. 134–6.

[130] McGrath, pp. 206–7.

6

Parvenus, Patriots, and Protected Jews

The Israelite Community in Vienna is a religious Community and not a political association.

Gerson Wolf (1868)

The Jews of Austria are Austrians first and last, they feel and think Austrian, they want a great, strong and mighty Austria . . . They know and remember in boundless gratitude what the Emperor of Austria has granted them . . . From father to son and in Jewish prayer-houses it is loudly proclaimed that Franz Joseph I made his Jewish subjects into real human beings and free citizens. Hence the Jews are thoroughly dynastical, loyalist, Austrian. The Double Eagle is for them a symbol of redemption and the Austrian colours adorn the banners of their freedom.

The Jews in Austria also cannot forget that it was the central Parliament, representing the whole of Austria, which voted for the Bill of Rights thanks to which all earlier laws of exception were abolished and Jews attained the precious possession of civil equality . . . The Jews of Austria are therefore a very important constituent part of the multinational Empire. For they are the standard-bearers of the Austrian idea of unity . . .

Dr Adolf Jellinek (15 June 1883)

The Austrian Israelite Union shall be the central headquarters for the successful defence of our positions. It seeks to arouse interest among our co-religionists in public affairs and will work ceaselessly to make each Jew into a fighter for this sacred task.

Mittheilungen der Österreichisch-Israelitischen Union (October 1889)

The government alone will concern itself with the question as to whether it can be considered appropriate for the good name and interests of the Empire that Vienna be the only great city in the world administered by an anti-Semitic agitator.

Neue Freie Presse, 30 May 1895

At the end of the nineteenth century the material prosperity of Viennese and Austrian Jewry as a whole appeared in the eyes of many Gentiles as an indisputable fact. These legendary riches were to a large extent mythical. Jewish wealth and power was invariably exaggerated by anti-Semitic demagogues who ignored the far greater assets and influence of the great feudal landowners as well as the poverty of the mass of Austrian Jewry.[1] It was however true that famous Jewish family clans like Rothschild, Todesco, Auspitz, Lieben, Wodianer, Gustav Springer, and Königswarter continued to play a major role in the expansion of Austrian industry and commerce, in State finances and securing funds for the major railway lines. The virtual Jewish monopoly of Viennese high finance was underlined by the palatial residences of some of these leading families along the Ringstrasse.[2] Moreover, Jewish industrialists played a major part in developing the textile industry in Prague, Reichenberg, and Brünn, the beer industry in Pilsen, as well as the sugar-refining and malt industries of Bohemia. Jewish entrepreneurs opened up the Moravian–Silesian coalfields and the giant Witkowitz steel works; the lignite fields of North Bohemia were first developed and exploited by the Petschek and Weinmann families who handled 75 per cent of the output.[3] The millionaire industrialist and patron of the musical arts Karl Wittgenstein, (father of the linguistic philosopher Ludwig Wittgenstein), dominated the steel cartel of the Habsburg Empire.[4] Some of these industrialists and bankers as in the case of Wittgenstein had severed their connections with Judaism and Jewry, but others including the Rothschild family, the Königswarters, the Gutmanns, and Theodor von Taussig were active in varying degrees within the Israelitische Kultusgemeinde.[5]

[1] See the careful statistical analysis by Sigmund Mayer, 'Der Reichthum der Juden', *Die Neuzeit*, 2 Apr. 1886, pp. 129–31, who pointed out the misleading character of an economic analysis focused on the Rothschild family or 'die Handvoll in Wien concentrirter jüdischer Financiers . . .'.

[2] Hans Tietze, *Die Juden Wiens* (Vienna and Leipzig, 1933), 231.

[3] Joseph C. Pick, 'The Economy', in *The Jews of Czechoslovakia* (Philadelphia, 1968), i. 372–4.

[4] Allan Janik and Stephen Toulmin, *Wittgenstein's Vienna* (New York, 1973), 169–74. The Wittgensteins thought of themselves 'as entirely *Jewish* by extraction' though the father had thoroughly absorbed the Protestant work-ethic and had no religious connection with Jewry (p. 172).

[5] Among the most prominent ennobled members of the Israelite Community Board after 1880 one finds names such as Wilhelm Ritter von Gutmann, David Ritter von Gutmann, Julius Ritter von Goldschmidt, Theodor Ritter von Goldschmidt, Arthur Edler von Mises, Leopold von Lieben, Dr Philipp Ritter von Mauthner, Ignaz Ritter von Ephrussy, Moritz Ritter von Borkenau, and Theodor Ritter von Taussig.

A few of these financiers, like Jonas Freiherr von Königswarter, had been profoundly religious God-fearing Jews in the orthodox mould.[6] Some like Moritz Ritter von Goldschmidt had distinguished themselves by the purity of their family life and devotion to the welfare of their co-religionists.[7]

The most outstanding example of simultaneously combining industrial success and dedication to Jewish causes was the firm of Gutmann Brothers, established in 1853 by Wilhelm and David Ritter von Gutmann. They were eventually to emerge as Austria's leading coal magnates and as philanthropists on a grand scale.[8] Wilhelm Gutmann (1825–95) had been born in the Moravian town of Lipnik, where he studied for several years in a *yeshivah*. As a youth he had suffered all the familiar humiliations of pre-1848 Austrian Jewry, aggravated by the severity of legislation in Moravia.[9] He had started out as a commission agent in the coal trade before founding with his brother the firm which developed the seams in the Ostrava basin and Galicia, thereby coming to control most of the Austro-Hungarian coal business. In 1865 he had entered into partnership with Anselm von Rothschild and two years later established a sugar factory. In 1872 Gutmann joined forces with the Viennese Rothschilds in setting up the Witkowitz iron and steel works, of which his firm acquired half a share.[10] A founder in 1874 of the Austrian industrialists' club and Board member of the Rothschild-controlled Creditanstalt, Gutmann was duly elected to the Lower Austrian Landtag where he supported the German Liberals. In 1878 'the coal-king' had been knighted for his

[6] See Moritz Güdemann, *Grabreden während der letzten fünfundzwanzig Jahre in der Wiener Israelitischen Kultusgemeinde* (Vienna, 1894), 5.

[7] 'Moritz Ritter von Goldschmidt', *Österreichische Wochenschrift*, 13 Apr. 1888, pp. 230–1; also 'Galerie berühmter Männer des Judenthums', *Jüdisches Weltblatt*, 15 June 1882, p. 3.

[8] See 'Die vierzigjährige Jubelfeier des Geschäftshauses der Herren Wilhelm und David Ritter von Gutmann', *Die Neuzeit*, 8 Jan. 1892, p. 11, which praised 'the extraordinary humanitarian deeds of the firm' in the area of general philanthropy. See also the editorial 'Wilhelm und David Ritter von Gutmann', ibid., 20 Oct. 1889, pp. 397–8, which saw in this *non-denominational* generosity an expression of 'Jewish' values and a vindication of the 'modern principle of the equality of all confessions'.

[9] See 'Erinnerungen von Herrn Wilhelm Ritter von Gutmann', *Die Neuzeit*, 1 Jan. 1892, where the famous industrialist recalled: 'Das Leben eines damaligen Israeliten war ja ein fortläufendes Martyrium . . .' Gutmann emphasized the importance of his religious upbringing, especially the early study of 'scientific works of Hebrew literature' and the value placed on charity to the poor and compassion for one's fellow man, as motivating his later philanthropic activity and patronage of Jewish scholarship.

[10] Max Grunwald, *Vienna* (Philadelphia, 1936), 499.

services to Austrian industry, with his brother being ennobled the following year.[11]

Elected President of the Vienna Kultusgemeinde in 1891, Wilhelm Ritter von Gutmann founded a children's hospital in Vienna, a home for the crippled at Krems, a girl's orphanage in the Doebling district and together with his brother the Viennese Israelitisch-Theologische Lehranstalt in 1893.[12] David Ritter von Gutmann (1834–1912) was no less intensively involved in Jewish affairs as head of the Vienna Israelitische Allianz and the Baron Hirsch foundation for Galicia. Since the early 1880s he had been concerned at the rise of Austrian anti-Semitism, helping to cover Rabbi Joseph Bloch's expenses in the extended court-case against the Catholic Judaeophobe, August Rohling.

In the story 1890s this concern with anti-Semitism found frequent expression in his correspondence with the leaders of the Alliance Israélite Universelle in Paris.[13] David von Gutmann emphasized, for example, in a letter to his Parisian colleagues on 6 November 1895 that the Vienna Allianz had to proceed with great caution in a hostile Viennese climate where the anti-Semites at every opportunity lashed out against the 'internationalism' and disloyalty of the Jews. The community could not close its eyes to the 'extraordinary appeal of precisely this accusation to the anti-Semitic and nationally aroused masses in Austria and to the depressing circumstances surrounding us'. In spite of its feelings of solidarity with the cosmopolitan aims and humanitarian objectives of the Alliance Israélite, the Austrian sister organization could not therefore afford to take any risk which 'might promote the charge of lack of patriotism' (*Vaterlandlosigkeit*).[14]

David von Gutmann, therefore, rejected the pressure of the French

---

[11] Ibid. See also the obituary of Wilhelm Ritter von Gutmann, *Die Neuzeit*, 24 May 1895, p. 120.

[12] This seminary was partly inspired by the importance which Gutmann and other Jewish philanthropists in Vienna attached to Jewish cultural defence and apologetics against the tidal wave of anti-Semitism. It included many leading Jewish scholars such as Meir Friedmann and Adolf Schwarz among its teachers. Most of the students came from outside Vienna, in particular from Galicia.

[13] Autriche IA1–3 Vienne, also IIA 4–7, Archives of the Alliance Israélite Universelle, Paris. See e.g. a letter of 24 Oct. 1895, where David von Gutmann writes on the situation in Vienna: 'Die sociale und politische Lage unsere Glaubensgenossen hier ist derzeit eine derart penible, dass man es sich sehr wohl überlegen muss, Situationen zu schaffen, die der gehässigen Deutung der Internationalität des Judentums neue Nahrung geben könnten'.

[14] Autriche IIA 4, David von Gutmann to the Alliance Israélite Universelle in Paris, 6 Nov. 1895.

organization for financial assistance and collaboration in creating new Alliance schools in Galicia as politically imprudent. The Hilsner ritual-murder affair in Bohemia at the end of the 1890s strengthened this reticence and the long struggle for a revision of the verdict was constantly hamstrung, according to Gutmann's testimony, by the virulence of Austrian anti-Semitism; this made any overt public campaign by an official Jewish body on behalf of Hilsner extremely delicate, since it might encourage the anti-Semites to divert attention from the specific case itself to 'Jewish machinations' behind the scenes.[15]

Furthermore, Gutmann himself, along with the Rothschilds, was a favourite target not only of the anti-Semites but also of the rising force of Austrian Social Democracy which remorselessly attacked him as a coal-baron and 'blood-sucking exploiter' of the workers. For the Viennese socialists, he symbolized the power of the big Jewish capitalists whom the Christian-Social party attacked in words but collaborated with in deeds. According to the Marxist analysis, the Catholic anti-Semites had been led by the logic of capitalist profiteering to unite with Gutmann and Rothschild against striking miners and railwaymen.[16] For all its demagoguery and tinge of leftist Judaeophobia there was a grain of truth in this picture of capitalist class solidarity.

Vienna was after all the undisputed financial centre of a vast Empire of 50 million people and its leading banks were decisively important for the industrialization of the Monarchy. Their privileged relations with the Austrian State, their control of long-term investment, and the supply of capital to industry gave them a pivotal position in economic development.[17] Industrialists like Gutmann or financial potentates like Albert de Rothschild and directors of his Boden Creditanstalt bank— especially Theodor von Taussig and Rudolf Sieghart (1866–1934) —did exercise some influence behind the scenes on governmental ministers, though they were reluctant openly to enter the political

[15] Autriche IIA 6, 'Für den Vorstand der "Israelitischen Allianz zu Wien" [Gutmann] an die Alliance Israélite Universelle', 11 May 1908.

[16] Robert S. Wistrich, *Socialism and the Jews: The Dilemmas of Assimilation in Germany and Austria–Hungary* (Littman Library, London and Toronto, 1982), 283–5, 287, 290.

[17] See Bernard Michel, *Banques et banquiers en Autriche au début du XXe siècle* (Paris, 1976), 52–4, on the importance of the two big banks of the Rothschild group, the Creditanstalt and the Boden Creditanstalt, in issuing state loans, managing the private fortunes of the Habsburgs, of princes, archdukes, and aristocratic families as well as in furthering the growth of industry.

terrain.[18] Sieghart, in particular, acted as the *éminence grise* of successive Austrian governments during the first decade of the twentieth century—a fact which convinced the heir to the throne, Franz Ferdinand, that he was running a secret 'Jewish conspiracy'. Moreover, Jewish bankers and entrepreneurs received the highest decorations of the Emperor and generally enjoyed the confidence of higher administration circles. In banking and the big business sector they suffered no visible discrimination and their quasi-monopoly of *la haute banque* in Vienna was never seriously undermined before 1914. According to the French economic historian Bernard Michel, Jews accounted for over half of the major German bankers in Austria in the late nineteenth century and in the key positions their proportion was as high as 80 per cent.[19]

The fidelity of the Jewish financial élite to the Emperor, their fervent dynastic patriotism, and their commitment to the multinational State was beyond doubt. However, powerful opposition to their influence came from the conservative landowners, the Catholic Church, and from the anticapitalist forces of both Right and Left, embodied in the Christian-Social anti-Semitic party and the Social Democrats. In a semi-feudal Austrian State still dominated before 1914 by the nobility, Church, and agrarian interests—where the capitalist mentality had never percolated down into broad strata of society—this was a serious limitation on their power. Nevertheless, their indispensability to the economic modernization of the Empire and their role as patrons of culture were understood and appreciated by more educated Austrians. Even the ruling anti-Semitic administration of Vienna was obliged after 1897 gradually to tone down its attacks on the great Jewish banking firms and did not seriously threaten the economic base of the Jewish financial bourgeoisie.[20] Admittedly, the leading Viennese families never quite dominated Austrian industry, banking, and the Stock Exchange to the extent of their counterparts in Budapest.[21] Nor did they enjoy the special protection given to

[18] See Rudolf Sieghart, *Die letzten Jahrzehnte einer Grossmacht* (Berlin, 1932); Michel, pp. 140 ff., 344; also W. O. McCagg, 'The Assimilation of the Jews in Austria', in Bela Vago (ed.), *Jewish Assimilation in Modern Times* (Boulder, Colo., 1981, 127 ff.

[19] Michel, p. 312.   [20] Ibid. 351.

[21] William A. Jenks, 'The Jews in the Habsburg Empire, 1879–1918', *Leo Baeck Yearbook*, 16 (1971), 155–62, writes: 'Fifty great families, the majority Jewish by origin, dominated Hungarian industry, banking, and, in reality, the marketing or agricultural commodities. Thanks to their ties with Vienna and Germany, they were a most necessary part of Hungarian society, a fact realized by the magnates rather than by the gentry and peasantry'.

Hungarian Jews by the Magyar landowning aristocracy. They were none the less relatively secure in face of the anticapitalist rhetoric that began to sweep Austria in the closing decades of the nineteenth century.

At the height of the liberal era in 1873, what Joseph Ritter von Wertheimer described to the Alliance Israélite in Paris as 'Jewish preponderance in *la haute banque*, commerce and industry', the ennoblement and the distinctions which they received, had been a cause for much satisfaction and self-congratulation in the Jewish community.[22] Not only in banking but also in sectors like leather goods, furniture, ready-to-wear clothing, and food processing, Viennese Jews had already consolidated a strong economic position. In the relatively enlightened 1870s baptized Jews like Julius Glaser and Josef Unger were appointed Cabinet members. In the German Liberal party men of Jewish origin played a prominent role. By the 1880s a majority of Viennese doctors and lawyers were Jews.[23] In literature, theatre, and the entertainment sector, the sons of the new Jewish bourgeoisie began to influence public opinion and taste, a trend that was never seriously upset until the end of the Monarchy.

Above all, Jews were prominent among the great press tycoons. They owned, edited, and very extensively contributed to most of the leading newspapers of Vienna. Though somewhat exaggerated, it was significant that Henry Wickham Steed, *The Times* correspondent in the Austrian capital, could write that 'economically, politically and in point of general influence they—the Jews—are, however, the most significant element in the Monarchy'.[24] Wickham Steed particularly singled out the liberal *Neue Freie Presse*—the most important newspaper in the Empire—whose pro-capitalist orientation and German chauvinism he thoroughly disliked: '. . . owned, edited and written by Jews it appeals in the first instance to a distinctively Jewish community of readers, many of whom, like the bulk of its non-Jewish readers, suspect it of aiming constantly at influencing the stock-exchange . . .'[25] Like many hostile observers, Wickham Steed regarded the *Neue Freie Presse* as essentially an organ of 'Jewish' financial interests and sensed behind its exaggerated Germanism a rationalization of Jewish assimilationist

---

[22] Joseph Ritter von Wertheimer, letter of 22 Jan. 1873 to the Alliance Israélite Universelle, Archives Autriche IA 1–3 Paris.
[23] Tietze, pp. 232–3.
[24] Henry Wickham Steed, *The Habsburg Monarchy* (London, 1913), 145.
[25] Ibid. 187.

drives. None the less its editor-in-chief, the autocratic, irrepressible Moritz Benedikt (of whom it was said that 'next to him the Emperor is the most important man in the country'), had indubitably succeeded in making it the representative organ of liberal-bourgeois opinion, in spite of the endemic anti-Semitism of so many Austro-Germans.

Benedikt's main rival, the *Neues Wiener Tageblatt*—edited and owned by a Francophile Galician Jew, Moritz Szeps—appealed to the more 'democratic' trend among the Viennese *Bürgertum* and lower middle class.[26] It was to this semi-populist paper that Szeps' close friend and confidant, the Austrian Crown Prince Rudolf, contributed many of his anonymous articles on social and political topics in the early 1880s. Significantly both the Crown Prince and Szeps extensively discussed the threat posed to liberal values by the new anti-Semitism in both Austria and Hungary. They were in full agreement that the anti-Jewish agitation of the 1880s was not only an outrage against religious tolerance, humanity, and civilization but also a movement which could menace the stability of the Monarchy itself.[27]

Another 'Jewish'-owned newspaper was the Marxist *Arbeiterzeitung*, which Wickham Steed unstintingly praised in spite of its 'narrow-minded Marxist orthodoxy' as constituting a refuge of common sense and 'the only protection against the tide of semi-officialism and financial interestedness that pollutes the German press of Austria'.[28] Its founder and editor, Victor Adler—the leader of the Austrian Social Democratic party—was depicted in rather positive terms as 'a Jew of the prophetic, self-sacrificing, zealous type that has so often saved the people of Israel from the reproach of worshipping solely the Golden Calf'.[29] The principled stand of the Austrian Social Democrats against capitalist egoism, racial rivalries, and brute force and in favour of international brotherhood made them appear somewhat exceptional in the late Habsburg context. Though the *Arbeiterzeitung* clearly did not serve Jewish capitalist interests, its contents displayed according to Wickham Steed the 'quickness of Jewish intelligence', the 'power of

[26] Ibid. 189: 'Edited and mainly, though not exclusively written by Jews for a public chiefly Christian, it defends Jewish interests by omission rather than commission'.

[27] See *Kronprinz Rudolf, Schriften*, ed. Brigitte Hamann (Vienna and Munich, 1979), 107–12, for Prince Rudolf's article on Hungarian anti-Semitism published by Szeps in Aug. 1883. In her introduction Brigitte Hamann comments: 'Kronprinz Rudolf verteidigte die Rechte der Juden so lange, bis er selbst in den schmutzigen Kampf als "Judenknecht" hineingezogen wurde und einen Gutteil seiner früheren Popularität verlor'.

[28] Wickham Steed, p. 135.

[29] Ibid.

abstract ratiocination', the concentration and purposefulness typical of the Jews as a race. In its efforts to educate and uplift the proletarian masses, the Social Democratic press had evidently inherited something of the liberal-bourgeois tradition of *Bildung* in the best cosmopolitan sense of the term.

Wickham Steed's observations on the ubiquity of Jews in Viennese journalism (they played a similarly dynamic role in Hungary and some other parts of the Monarchy) were well founded if at times unduly acidic. Already in 1848 Jewish intellectuals like Ludwig Frankl, Ignaz Kuranda, and Hermann Jellinek had thrown themselves into an activity well suited to redrawing the outlines of a society that still denied them admittance.[30] In the post-emancipation liberal era their example was followed by other Jewish newspaper editors and journalists like Leopold Landsteiner, Max Friedländer, Alexander Scharf, Moritz Szeps, Moritz Benedikt, Eduard Bacher, and Theodor Hertzka. It was also in Viennese journalism that such diverse talents of the *fin de siècle* as Theodor Herzl, Victor Adler, and Karl Kraus first made their mark. However, it was not any special 'Jewish interests' or motivations which characterized these journalists but rather their highly developed critical faculties, their polemical talent and gift for observation. These qualities were sharpened perhaps by inherited Jewish intellectual traditions, by the sense of release from a burdensome ghetto inheritance and the need to find an outlet for repressed energies bursting to be expressed.[31]

It was this intellectual mobility, restlessness, and ubiquity of the Jewish presence—symbolized in many ways by their control of the press—which particularly struck contemporary observers. The German Jewish writer Jakob Wassermann, on moving from Munich to Vienna in 1898, felt something akin to culture-shock. However, it was not the elegant and attractive exterior of the metropolis, the exaggerated pleasure-seeking of its inhabitants, or the perverse malice of Austrian politics that stunned him but rather the fact that 'all public life was dominated by Jews'.[32] They controlled 'the banks, the press, the theatre, literature, social organizations . . .' and their omnipresence seemed to determine the very tone and colour of Viennese life. It was

---

[30] See Richard Grünberger, 'Jews in Austrian Journalism', in Josef Fraenkel (ed.), *The Jews of Austria: Essays on their Life and Destruction* (London, 1967), 83–95.

[31] Sigmund Mayer, *Die Wiener Juden: Kommerz, Kultur, Politik, 1700–1900* (Vienna and Berlin, 1917), 398 ff.

[32] Jakob Wassermann, *My Life as German and Jew* (New York, 1933), 186.

not that Jewry held actual political power but their spirit animated commercial, intellectual, and artistic circles, from which the Austrian aristocracy, officialdom, and military families maintained a disdainful distance. 'The court, the lower class and the Jews gave the city its stamp. And that the Jews, as the most mobile group, kept all the others in continuous motion is, on the whole, not surprising. Yet I was amazed at the hosts of Jewish physicians, attorneys, clubmen, snobs, dandies, proletarians, actors, newspapermen and poets.'[33]

Not all Viennese Jews were successful, of course; but the general trend was disernible enough. Jews were making their mark everywhere in banking, commerce, manufacturing, the liberal professions, the press, and politics. In the universities too, the expansion of the Jewish bourgeois élite was well under way by 1880. Jewish enrollment in Vienna secondary schools was exceedingly high. In the classical Gymnasien it reached 31 per cent in 1885 and in the science-orientated Realschulen it stood around 20 per cent throughout the later nineteenth century.[34] At the end of the 1880s the Jewish presence in the faculties of medicine (48 per cent), law (22 per cent), and philosophy (15 per cent) was impressive enough and as we have seen constituted a powerful factor in Austrian student anti-Semitism.[35] It was this massive thrust towards higher education that also provided the backbone and reservoir of recruitment to Vienna's cultural élite and accounts for the strikingly 'Jewish' character of the capital's liberal intelligentsia.

Since non-baptized Jews frequently found their path to full professorships barred, and advancement within the judicial system was similarly blocked, this tended to reinforce further the Jewish trend to independent careers in journalism, the letters and arts, or the liberal professions.[36] In spite of political emancipation, Jews also had extremely limited access to civil service jobs at state, regional, or local government level.[37] Their exclusion from higher state service in

---

[33] Ibid.

[34] Marsha Rozenblit, *The Jews of Vienna, 1867–1914: Assimilation and Identity* (Albany, NY, 1983), 107.

[35] See Jacob Thon, *Die Juden in Österreich* (Berlin, 1908), 93–8; Tietze, p. 232.

[36] Tietze, p. 232, points out that the great majority of Jewish university teachers were *Privatdozenten*. Rabbi Joseph Bloch in a parliamentary speech refuted the assertion of the German nationalist deputy Türk that there were 55 Jewish professors in medicine and law at Vienna; according to his reckoning 21 of these professors were converts, and of the remainder only 2 were full professors (*My Reminiscences* (Vienna and Berlin, 1923), 246).

[37] *Österreichische Wochenschrift*, 31 Aug. 1894, p. 673.

general, even during the liberal era, reflected the wide gulf between administrative praxis and the premisses of civil equality.[38] On the other hand, in accessible areas such as commerce, the professions, and white-collar employment in banking, commerce, and private industry, the economic competition which Jews represented for Gentiles tended greatly to exacerbate anti-Semitism.[39]

One sector which was relatively free of discrimination was the Austro-Hungarian army, in which Jews had served since the Josephinian reforms of the 1780s. The first Jewish officers had probably been commissioned into the Austrian army between 1800 and 1810. In spite of the general distrust and reserve with which they were still regarded, the number of Jewish soldiers steadily rose and it has been reliably estimated that between 10,000 and 20,000 Jews served in the Imperial Army during the wars of 1859 and 1866. By 1902 their number had reached 60,000 (4 per cent of the ranks) which roughly corresponded to their percentage of the general population.[40] Jews formed only 1 per cent of the professional officers in the regular army—tending to be concentrated in the medical and service corps—but they represented about 18 per cent of the one-year reserve officers due to their high proportion among high school and university students.[41]

Though the military held little attraction for them as a career option, the proportion of Jews in the Austro-Hungarian army was none the less exceptional, compared to German and most other European armies. In striking contrast to the Prussian regiments, there was no deliberate exclusion of Jewish officers and anti-Semitic prejudice was not officially tolerated.[42] Indeed anti-Semitism appears to have been

[38] Mayer, *Die Wiener Juden*, 471.

[39] See Rozenblit, *Jews of Vienna*, ch. 3, 'From Trader to Clerk: The Occupational Transformation of Viennese Jewry', pp. 48–70, for the statistical background. On the Gentile reaction, see John Boyer, *Political Radicalism in late Imperial Vienna: Origins of the Christian Social Movement, 1848–1897* (Chicago and London, 1981), 82, who argues that 'antisemitism found enormous support among thousands of Gentile employees, who competed with their Jewish colleagues for appointments, promotions, salary raises, and positions in institutions like the *Handelsakademie*'.

[40] Lecture by Erwin A. Schmidl, 'Jews in the Austro-Hungarian Army', delivered on 28 Oct. 1984 at a Conference on Jews in Habsburg Politics and Culture, Hebrew University, Jerusalem. I have drawn here on the careful information contained in his paper. See also Wolfgang von Weisl, *Die Juden in der Armee Österreich-Ungarns* (Tel Aviv, 1971).

[41] Schmidl, p. 9.

[42] Joseph Ritter von Wertheimer, letter of 22 Jan. 1873 to the Central Committee of the Alliance Israélite Universelle, favourably contrasts attitudes in the Austrian army towards Jews with those in Prussia. See also *Jewish Chronicle*, 20 Nov. 1891, p. 14.

notably weaker in the army than in many other sectors of Austrian society in spite of persistent nationalist agitation and the fact that most officers were Roman Catholic Germans. There was nothing like a Dreyfus affair in the Austrian army before 1914, nor was there any parallel to the humiliating *Judenzählung* carried out in the German army during the First World War.[43] In this supranational institution *par excellence* which was loyal to the Emperor and the dynasty alone, Jews were by and large treated on equal terms with other ethnic and religious groups.[44] The army could simply not tolerate open racial or religious discrimination which would only undermine morale and patriotic motivation.[45]

Austrian Jewry as a supranational group within the multinational State felt a close identification with the Emperor as the supreme warlord and symbol of unity. As the *Österreichische Wochenschrift* put it on 23 August 1901: 'For us the Imperial Army is the symbol of the unity and power of the state, it embodies the pure state idea without national, political, and confessional disfigurement . . .' To the civil patriotism which had become the bedrock of post-emancipation Judaism throughout Europe, Austrian Jews added the dimension of unshakeable dynastic loyalty and devotion, which grew into a veritable cult after 1867. Religion, fatherland, and the Kaiser became sacred values for the Austrian Jews. This imperial patriotism was nourished from the pulpit, in the Jewish press, at public gatherings, and on commemorative occasions. The imperial-royal loyalty of the Jews stood moreover in sharp contrast to the centrifugal forces of Slavic nationalism and feudal particularism.[46] Most significant of all, the civil religion of dynastic patriotism became a central feature in the defence strategy of the Jewish establishment, threatened as it was after 1880 by the new force of organized political anti-Semitism. When on 26 September 1891 the Emperor received representatives from the Board

[43] Schmidl, p. 10.

[44] '27,945', editorial by Adolf Jellinek on the Jewish soldiers in the Austrian army, *Die Neuzeit*, 5 June 1885, p. 215. According to Jellinek, Austrian Jews had to thank their co-religionists in the army for the fact 'dass der Antisemitismus in dem massgebendsten und einflussreichsten Kreise öffentlich verdammt wurde'.

[45] Ibid.: 'Da fragt man nicht, ob das Blut arisch oder semitisch, deutsch oder slavisch, sondern ob es bereit sei, auf dem Altar des Vaterlands zu fliessen'. See also 'Die Juden in der Armee', *Österreichische Wochenschrift*, 23 Aug. 1901, p. 564.

[46] 'Sie [Die Juden] sind kaiserlich und königlich gesinnt, wollen nicht, das die Machtfülle unseres Monarchen auf den König von Böhmen, den Herzog von Steiermark, auf ein slovenisches und polnisches Reich vertheilt werde, sondern dass sie in einer Hand concentrirt bleibe' (*Österreichische Wochenschrift*, 23 Aug. 1901).

of the Prague Jewish community and informed them that he knew that 'the Israelites are good patriots', *Die Neuzeit* and its editorialist Adolf Jellinek were beside themselves with joy. Was this not a stinging rebuke from the highest authority in the land to Prince Liechtenstein, Dr Lueger, Ernst Schneider, and their anti-Semitic colleagues? Did it not show that the exalted Monarch had indeed grasped how 'the hearts of Jewish Austrians beat patriotically for the Emperor and Empire'?[47]

Nearly ten years earlier, in 1882, when the Austrian anti-Semitic movement was celebrating its first Jew-baiting orgy, the Emperor had indeed declared to his Ministers: 'I will tolerate no *Judenhetze* in my Empire.'[48] In 1883 during the Habsburg festivities in Styria he had told a Jewish deputation in Graz: 'I am fully persuaded of the fidelity and loyalty of the Israelites and they can always count on my protection.'[49] In the same year, receiving another Israelite deputation at Szegedin he had assured the Hungarian Jews of his fatherly protection and that of the dynasty in return for their loyalty to throne and fatherland—this at a time when anti-Semitic agitation was spreading like a forest fire in Hungary.[50] In June 1885 he had clearly hinted at his disapproval of the prospect of an anti-Semitic success in the Austrian elections and in September of the same year he declared his firm resolve to ensure that all denominations would freely exercise their religion without fear or hindrance.[51] Again, in September 1887 Franz Joseph insisted before two separate Jewish delegations that 'unconditional equality is in every respect a command of justice'; and that the patriotic and loyal Israelites could continue to be assured of his 'royal protection' and sympathy.[52]

In the Jewish press during the closing decades of the nineteenth century such statements were quoted with exuberant satisfaction to demonstrate the nobility, sincerity, mildness, and sense of justice of

[47] Jellinek, 'Der Patriotismus der Juden in Österreich', *Die Neuzeit*, 2 Oct. 1891, p. 331: 'Die Worte des Kaisers sind unsere Burg, eine kaiserliche Burg, der wir vertrauen . . .'; see also *Jewish Chronicle*, 2 Oct. 1891, p. 18.

[48] 'Franz Joseph I. und das Judentum in Oesterreich', *Österreichische Wochenschrift*, 28 Dec. 1888, p. 817.

[49] Ibid.

[50] 'Das Wort des Kaisers', *Die Neuzeit*, 19 Oct. 1883, p. 399. The editorial closed with the lines: 'Unter der Regierung Franz Josef I. wird den Ausschreitungen des Antisemitismus immer ein Damm gesetzt sein durch die Menschenliebe und Milde unseres Kaisers, welche die Lippen von Tausenden segnen!'

[51] 'Ein Wort unseres Kaisers', *Die Neuzeit*, 3 July 1885, p. 251; *Österreichische Wochenschrift*, 28 Dec. 1888, p. 818.

[52] *Österreichische Wochenschrift*, 28 Dec. 1888.

the Habsburg Emperor. Franz Joseph I increasingly appeared to Austrian Jews as their guardian angel, custodian, and patron saint against the swelling tide of anti-Semitism from below.[53] It was recalled that granting civil equality to Jews was one of the earliest acts of his regime in 1849; the fact that it was the 1848 Revolution so hated by the Habsburgs which had first placed emancipation on the political agenda was discreetly played down. Instead, the chaos, the disorder, and the anti-Jewish excesses of that stormiest of years in Austrian history were dutifully highlighted. Similarly, the fact that Jews were so quickly stripped of their promised rights by the new ruler and had to wait almost nineteen years, until Franz Joseph accepted their full equality at the very height of the liberal era, was conveniently overlooked.

By the 1880s it must be said that the darkening situation of Austrian Jews had begun to encourage a more positive view of the Habsburgs as uniquely benevolent custodians and patrons of Jewry, under whose blessed sceptre they had always enjoyed protection against medieval blood-libels, clerical fanaticism, and mob rule.[54] Franz Joseph I now became, in Jewish eyes, an inheritor of this gracious, merciful, and benign Habsburg tradition, a monarch who outshone not only his illustrious predecessors but also all contemporary princely rulers of Europe in his respect for religious tolerance and justice.[55] In a heart-warming toast to his Majesty the Emperor at the *Chewra-Kadisha* celebration in Vienna on 22 February 1885, Adolf Jellinek enthusiastically declaimed:

No Prince of the glorious House of Habsburg has so graciously stood by our brothers in Austria as our beloved Monarch. What progress has been made in the liberty of our co-religionists under the exalted sceptre of our sublime Monarch! . . . the chains which oppressed the Jews in Austria fell at the word of deliverance pronounced by our lofty Regent . . .'[56]

In Jellinek's peroration, the Habsburg double-headed Eagle was transformed into a symbol of the dual commitment of the Emperor to

[53] Ibid. The rabbi from Baden who wrote this article took comfort from 'the benevolent attitude of the Emperor Franz Joseph I to the Israelite confession' in 'this dangerous time, when we Israelites are especially endangered by the darkness of the Middle Ages'.

[54] Adolf Jellinek, *Rede zur Feier des sechshundertjährigen Habsburg-Jubiläums im israelitischen Bethause der innern Stadt Wien* (Vienna, 1883), 4–5.

[55] Ibid. Jellinek suggested that History would remember the Emperor 'als den edelsten, den erlesenen und auserwählten unter den Fürsten Europas'.

[56] 'Zwei Toaste', *Die Neuzeit*, 13 Mar. 1885, pp. 104–5.

freedom and justice for his Jewish subjects.[57] It was also suggested that Austrian Jews suffered less from anti-Semitism than their Hungarian co-religionists, thanks to their Emperor's special protection.[58]

The forty-year jubilee of Franz Joseph's accession to the throne was the occasion of a further outpouring of gratitude and affection for the Habsburg ruler and an optimistic celebration of what Austrian Jewry had accomplished in terms of industry, culture, politics, and civil freedom during four decades under his rule.[59] A year later the Vienna correspondent of the London *Jewish Chronicle*, observing the Empire-wide Jewish celebrations on the Emperor's fifty-ninth birthday in August 1889, affirmed that they were personally indebted to him 'for the liberty which they have enjoyed during the last 40 years'.[60] The same source reported that in the wake of anti-Semitic excesses in Vienna the Emperor 'is said to have spoken very unfavourably of the attitude taken up by the authorities' in failing firmly to curb them.[61] If this was not enough, in September 1890 while attending military manœuvres at Grosswardein Franz Joseph I wished the Jewish deputation the peace and prosperity 'which the protection of the law and my own unalterable favour assure to them'.[62] On 7 October 1892 Austrian and foreign newspapers again reported the Emperor's condemnation of anti-Jewish agitation 'in the most emphatic words'. His remarks at a reception of the Delegations in Budapest were mainly devoted to the previous week's scandals in the Lower Austrian Diet, where anti-Semitic deputies had slandered Jewish doctors—accusing them of wanting to kill off the Christians by sending them to the cholera hospitals![63] His Majesty reportedly told Professor Eduard

---

[57] 'Zwei Toaste', *Die Neuzeit*, 13 Mar. 1885, p. 105. In this speech, Austrian conditions were favourably contrasted with those of Hungary, and the presence of an orthodox Jewish financier, Baron Moritz Freiherr von Königswarter, in the Austrian Upper House, was taken as tangible proof of the Emperor's goodwill.

[58] For a detailed comparison of Austria and Hungary from the liberal-Jewish viewpoint, see 'Der Dualismus in Oestereich-Ungarn', *Die Neuzeit*, 3 Apr. 1885, p. 131. Here the liberal Hungarian government was criticized for contenting itself with merely verbal condemnations of anti-Semitism in contrast to Count Taafe, the Austrian Prime Minister, who had allegedly acted more firmly. The truth of the matter was probably the reverse of this claim.

[59] 'Zum Regierungs-Jubiläum Sr. Majestät des Kaisers', *Österreichische Wochenschrift*, 30 Mar. 1888, p. 196.

[60] *Jewish Chronicle*, 6 Sept. 1889, p. 5.

[61] Ibid., 25 Apr. 1890, p. 6, 'The Anti-Jewish Excesses in Vienna'.

[62] Ibid., 19 Sept. 1980, p. 15.

[63] Ibid., 7 Oct. 1892, p. 8, 'The Emperor of Austria on Anti-Semitism'. See also *Die Neuzeit*, 7 Oct. 1892, 'Der Kaiser über den n.-ö. Landtag'.

Suess, the eminent geologist and a liberal member of the Lower Austrian Diet: 'It is a shame and a scandal. One scarcely knows what to say to it.'[64] Needless to say, such statements did not endear the Emperor to the Austrian anti-Semites, who were already infuriated by his tolerant appointments policy, his willingness to receive Jewish deputations, his occasional visits to synagogues, and the decorations he conferred on distinguished Jews.[65]

There can be little doubt that Franz Joseph I was sincere in his desire to see anti-Semitism stamped out, and his periodic references to the patriotism, bravery, and devotion of the Jews were certainly more than mere rhetoric.[66] In a letter to his wife at the height of the Lueger agitation in 1895 he wrote significantly: 'Anti-Semitism is an illness spread by now in the highest circles and the propagation of it is incredible. . . . Its excesses are awful.'[67] The Emperor's refusal on four successive occasions to confirm Karl Lueger in his mayoral office was at least in part connected to his repugnance at the mob character of the Christian-Social anti-Semitic agitation, though Hungarian pressure to use the Imperial veto was probably a weightier factor. The more fanatical anti-Semites responded to this intervention from above by nicknaming Franz Joseph the *Judenkaiser*.[68] For Austrian Jews, however, the Emperor's obvious distaste for the upstart Lueger and his cohorts was one more confirmation of their trust in his basic sense of decency. Lueger's eventual confirmation as Mayor made them even more conscious than before of their dependence on Franz Joseph's paternal benevolence.

The Vienna correspondent of the *Jewish Chronicle*, on the occasion of the Austrian Emperor's jubilee in December 1898, commented:

The Jews owe a great deal to their Emperor Francis Joseph; and if a drop of

---

[64] Ibid.
[65] See 'The Emperor of Austria and the Jewish Theological Seminary', *Jewish Chronicle*, 5 Jan. 1894, p. 17; also ibid., 18 Aug. 1893, p. 13, which reported the anger of Prince Alois Liechtenstein, a leading Christian-Social anti-Semite, at the conferring of the Order of the Iron Crown First Class on Baron Albert de Rothschild for his assistance in carrying out the Austro-Hungarian currency reform. See also ibid., 4 Aug. 1893, p. 7.
[66] Adolf Kessler, 'Die Juden in Österreich unter Kaiser Franz Joseph I' (Univ. of Vienna diss., 1932), p. 125: 'Die Juden sind tapfere und patriotische Männer und setzen ihr Leben mit Freuden ein für Kaiser und Vaterland.'
[67] Georg Nostitz-Rieneck (ed.), *Briefe Kaiser Franz Josephs an Kaiserin Elizabeth, 1859–1898* (Vienna and Munich, 1966), ii. 111.
[68] Arthur J. May, *The Habsburg Monarchy, 1867–1914* (Cambridge, Mass., 1951), 310.

anguish should fall into their cup of happiness in thinking of the various political retrogressive measures which they have to endure, they do not in the least blame the Emperor for it. Francis Joseph is strictly a constitutional monarch, who does not interfere with the right or the responsibility of the Minister president, to whom he leaves fully and completely all executive responsibility and activity. Thus we see that in Hungary, where there is at present a liberal government, the Jews enjoy the fullest political freedom and often receive from the Emperor the highest compliments for their loyalty and their patriotism. On the second of December heartfelt prayers will be offered up in the Jewish places of worship, not because, as is probable, several heads of Jewish congregations will receive decorations or titles, but because the noble attitude of this upright monarch is a guarantee for the maintenance of our rights.[69]

Rabbi Moritz Rosenmann of Florisdorf echoed similar sentiments in a speech on 2 December 1898 in Vienna that reflected more directly the background of the personal calamity which had recently befallen the Emperor (the assassination of his wife by an Italian anarchist) and the turbulent domestic political atmosphere in Austria. In the midst of confusion and despair, parliamentary obstruction, rabid nationalism, and anti-Semitism run amok, the dynasty and its supreme head stood out as a bastion of piety, patriotism, and hope for eventual harmony among the warring peoples of Austria-Hungary.[70] Once more, on this jubilee occasion, the Jewish press was full of superlatives for 'the conciliatory mildness and wisdom of our Emperor' and attributed to his graciousness alone the transformation of Jewry from the step-children of Austrian society into free and legitimate sons of the fatherland, equal in all respects to their Christian fellow-citizens.[71]

This equality had indeed been punctured by the anti-Semitic movement, mainly 'promoted by the high aristocracy and the clerical party' which had been conducting a remorseless campaign of defamation and slander against the Jews for nearly twenty years. The medieval superstitions and barbarity of the anti-Semites stood in glaring contrast to 'the noble virtues' of the Habsburg Emperor whose

---

[69] 'The Emperor of Austria's Jubilee', *Jewish Chronicle*, 2 Dec. 1898.

[70] *Zwei Jubiläums-Reden gehalten am 2. December 1898 anlässlich der Feier der 50 jährigen Regierung Sr. Majestät des Kaisers Franz Joseph I. von Dr. M. Rosenmann* (Vienna, 1898).

[71] Dr A. Schmiedl, 'Zum 2 December', *Die Neuzeit*, 2 Dec. 1898, p. 502; also 'Kaiserliche Worte', ibid. 502–3, which evoked the Emperor Franz Joseph as the liberator of Austrian Jewry 'der die Ketten gebrochen, welche unsere Glaubensgenossen noch fesselten, als allen Völkern des Reiches die Sonne der Freiheit aufgegangen war'.

warm-hearted recognition of Jewish loyalty to the throne constituted 'a powerful dam' against this corrupt and subversive agitation.[72] Both Francis Joseph and the murdered Empress Elizabeth—his beautiful, artistic wife who so admired the poetry of Heinrich Heine—came to represent for many Jews the divine, unspoiled grace of royalty against the racial and confessional zealotry of a troubled and increasingly anti-Semitic era.[73]

Royalty could arouse almost religious feelings in patriotic Austrian Jews especially when it was presented as the ultimate guardian of the Constitution and civil equality. The young Habsburg Emperor who in 1849 had supposedly removed 'the curse of Egypt' from the Israelites with his powerful 'outstretched arm' could indeed appear in some Jewish sermons as a latter-day Moses liberating his chosen people.[74] The new tablets of the law were the statutes of civil equality and the promised land was now Imperial-Royal Austria under the benign sceptre of his Apostolic Majesty, transposed into 'a mighty warlord of freedom and justice'. In this idealized image, Franz Joseph seemed to be imperiously calling to order the enemies of Israel 'who attack our status and wish to drive us from the soil of equality'.[75] He was the supreme bulwark against the raw and brutal hand of wicked seducers of the people sowing only disharmony and strife in his Empire.

Franz Joseph's history of family tragedy (which included the violent deaths of his wife, brother, and only son) if anything reinforced the existing feelings of identification by a spontaneous release of compassion among the Jewish subjects of the Empire for the lonely suffering ruler. The unexpected suicide of his son, the promising and talented Crown Prince Rudolf (1859–89), had provoked a deep sense of shock in the Jewish community of Vienna, saddened by the loss not only of one of the brightest hopes of the Monarchy but also of an outspoken friend of the Jews. At a funeral ceremony address delivered in February 1889 in the Inner City synagogue, Adolf Jellinek eulogized the young Crown Prince for rising above his time as 'a pillar of equality

---

[72] 'Zu des Kaisers 70 Geburtstag', ibid., 17 Aug. 1900, p. 343.

[73] 'Kaiserin und Königin', ibid., 23 Sept. 1887, p. 355; also 'Ein Wort der Kaiserin', ibid., 13 May 1887, p. 181. The magic word of the Empress Elizabeth to her daughter, according to this somewhat obsequious editorial, was: 'Sie möge religiös, aber nicht zelotisch werden!' See also ibid., 11 Nov. 1898, on the qualities of the Empress, p. 469.

[74] A. T. Jellinek, *Das vierzigste Passahfest unter der Regierung Sr. Majestät Franz Josef I.: Rede am I. Tage des Passahfestes im israelitischen Tempel der inneren Stadt Wien gehalten* (Vienna, 1888), 5.

[75] Ibid. 7.

in this age of racial and religious hatred—he shone forth as a model of confessional tolerance and noble humanity'.[76] Prince Rudolf's moderation, his physical courage, his sense of justice, and love of the arts and sciences had won the hearts of all patriotic Austrians; his passing had filled them with melancholy, pain, and apprehension at the future.[77] Jellinek also singled out for praise Rudolf's sharp words of condemnation for anti-Semitism, which the Prince had denounced in classic liberal terms as the 'disgrace of the century'.

He did not, however, discuss the Crown Prince's controversial political views—his fierce opposition to clericalism, to aristocratic arrogance, and sterile Habsburg traditionalism, his loathing of modern nationalism, of mass democracy, and the Austro-German alliance.[78] Franz Joseph's only son was in truth a political loner at the Habsburg court, out of step with his more authoritarian father on most important political issues except for their common devotion to the army and their commitment to the strengthening of the supranational Monarchy. Though both father and son despised anti-Semitism as a vulgar form of mob politics, Prince Rudolf's more passionate response derived from a consistently liberal-progressive outlook that informed his thinking on most issues. He fully identified himself with the ideals of cosmopolitan humanism, progress, and enlightenment, modern science and liberal rationalism. Hence he detested the Catholic Church and the Jesuits 'who are closely connected with all the influential members of the Imperial family'. Not surprisingly he also despised the clerical-conservative regime of Count Taafe which had ruled Austria since the demise of the German Liberals in 1879, as an 'inveterate enemy of modern culture' and the educated middle classes. In truth, the Taafe regime inspired in him sentiments shared by most liberal Viennese Jews. 'Elements have been brought into motion and ghosts evoked which it is impossible to banish. How much has the proud, liberal and hopefully developing Austria changed within a few years. These are dismal times and yet it is only the first step on the path of reaction.'[79]

---

[76] 'Rede auf den durchlauchtigsten Kronprinzen Erzherzog Rudolf am 5 Feb. 1889 bei der Trauerfeier im Bethause der inneren Stadt Wien gehalten von Dr. Ad. Jellinek', *Die Neuzeit*, 15 Feb. 1889, p. 62.

[77] 'Kronprinz Rudolph', ibid., 8 Feb. 1889, p. 53: 'Ein Winter ist über Oesterreich hereingebrochen, ein Winter, wie ihn grausiger und eisiger die Natur nicht zu erzeugen vermag . . . die Herzen aller Oesterreicher sind zu Eis erstarrt . . .'

[78] For further details see Oskar Freiherr von Mitis, *Das Leben des Kronprinzen Rudolf* (Vienna, 1928) and Brigitte Hamann, *Rudolf: Kronprinz und Rebell* (Vienna, 1978).

[79] Richard Berkeley, *The Road to Mayerling* (London, 1958), 121–2.

The anti-Semitism of the Schoenerites was a particularly ugly symptom to Prince Rudolf of these 'ghosts of the past'—a product of the endemic brutality of modern nationalism.

. . . it is indeed the victory of the carnal instincts and sympathies over the spiritual and cultural advantages which cosmopolitanism, the idea of the equality of all nations brings to humanity. I consider the enmity of nations and races a decisive step backwards, and it is characteristic that just those elements hostile to progress in Europe indulge in these principles and exploit them.[80]

In contrast to the Pan-Germans and even to liberal advocates of the Austro-German alliance, Rudolf identified with the western ideals of parliamentary democracy and espoused a Francophile orientation in foreign policy.[81] On this and other related issued, the rebellious Rudolf found a willing and powerful ally in his friend and political adviser, Moritz Szeps, editor-in-chief of the radical-liberal newspaper *Neues Wiener Tageblatt*.[82] A confidant of the French politicians Léon Gambetta and Clemenceau, Szeps tirelessly advocated an Austro-French *rapprochement* which made him a *bête noire* of Count Taafe as well as of Pan-German and anti-semitic circles. Twenty years older than the Crown Prince, the highly cultured, well-connected Szeps supplied Rudolf with inside information on domestic and foreign affairs, and reinforced his republican pro-Western sympathies and his distrust of both Bismarckian Germany and Tsarist Russia. At the same time his newspaper provided an outlet for anonymous articles by the Crown Prince.

Rudolf's intimate association with a liberal bourgeois journalist like Szeps (who was in addition an *Ostjude* by background) offered a ready-made target for constant abuse in the anti-Semitic press. As a result of this friendship and of gestures like his willingness to lunch openly in a famous Viennese restaurant with the cosmopolitan Jewish financier Baron de Hirsch, Rudolf was shamelessly accused by German nationalists and Catholic anti-Semites of being in the pay of the 'Golden International'. *The Times* of London in an obituary of 8 February 1889 coolly noted that 'several of the anti-Semite journals have behaved with great indecorum in abstaining from all words of respect for the Crown Prince's memory'.[83] In effect, with his suicide perhaps the last hope for a more liberal Central Europe animated by

[80] Ibid. 124.
[81] Berta Szeps, *My Life and History* (London, 1938), 110 ff.
[82] On Szeps, see Grünberger, pp. 91–2. [83] Berkeley, p. 200.

enlightened, progressive principles had disappeared and in that as well
as in other respects the year 1889 was undoubtedly significant for the
subsequent fortunes of Viennese Jewry.

The signs of social and political deterioration in Austria were soon
to become apparent. In the spring of 1889 a deputation of Viennese
Jews from the Board of the religious community drew the attention of
the Prime Minister Count Taafe to the anti-Semitic movement's
excesses. A copy of the 27 page memorandum dated March 1889,
preserved in the community archives, reviewed in detail the vicious
campaign of anti-Jewish slander in such Viennese newspapers as the
Catholic *Das Vaterland*, the *Österreichische Volksfreund*, the German
nationalist scandal-sheet *Deutsches Volksblatt*, etc.; it documented the
mounting ferocity of anti-Semitic agitation in local and national
elections, in the municipal council, in schools, professional associations,
and craft guilds—stressing its 'anarchist', subversive, and revolutionary
character.[84] Taafe assured the deputation that his government
supported the equality of all citizens based on the Constitution and
promised to look into the matter.

The fact that at this very time anti-Semitic agitators were taking
advantage of the strike among Viennese tramcar employees to foster
their cause, gave the Jewish community protest a more topical
character.[85] Whereas some foreign observers like the correspondent of
the London *Jewish Chronicle* asserted 'there is no fear whatever that the
authorities will fail to protect the Jews against overt acts of hostility',[86]
others like *The Times* of London and the French daily *Le Matin* were
less sanguine.[87] Reporting violent demonstrations and the pillaging of
Jewish shops in some Viennese districts against a background of anti-
Semitic successes in the recent municipal elections, *Le Matin* reproved
the Austrian government for the mild manner in which it had hitherto
applied existing laws against racial and religious incitement. It noted
with sympathy the protest of the Jewish community that similar insults
'ne seraient jamais tolérés par le gouvernement s'ils étaient dirigés
contre des catholiques romains'.[88] *Le Matin*, like *The Times* of London,

---

[84] Central Archives of the History of the Jewish People (Jerusalem), A/W 315, File on
Anti-Semitism. Also the personal file of the future President of the community, Dr
Alfred Stern, A/W 744.1; handwritten draft of Mar. 1889.

[85] 'The Jews in Austria', *Jewish Chronicle*, 19 Apr. 1889, p. 14.

[86] 'Notes of the Week', ibid., 26 Apr. 1889, p. 5.

[87] *The Times*, 24 Apr. 1889.

[88] 'Les Désordres de Vienne', *Le Matin*, 25 Apr. 1889, pp. 14 ff., commented on the
Jewish community memorandum as follows: 'Les auteurs du mémoire faisaient ressortir

speculated that Count Taafe 'qui se montrait jusqu'alors indifférent à ce mouvement, a dû certainement entretenir à ce sujet l'empereur, et les juifs devront à cette intervention d'être protégés un peu plus contre leurs fanatiques adversaires'.[89]

British and French reports particularly underlined the refusal of Jewish and Christian firms from Budapest, Prague, Pressburg, etc. to attend the international Corn Market in Vienna, because of the growth of anti-Semitism, as the one economic factor which might encourage firmer government intervention. On the other hand, it was conceded 'that the Government, in allowing the anti-Semites a free hand, acts in harmony with the view of nine-tenths of the non-Jewish population'.[90] Rather pessimistically, a *Jewish Chronicle* report in May 1889 concluded: 'Recent elections, whether parliamentary or civic, show incontestably that the Jews committed a great mistake in failing to assert their Constitutional rights five years ago, when the movement was set on foot. It is now too late'.[91] However, subsequent reports suggested that though the Austrian Prime Minister believed anti-Semitism was just a passing phase, 'a cloak for other agitations', he had given clear instructions to repress attempts to sow hatred and discord among different citizens of the State.[92] This less equivocal policy, it was initially hoped by Jews in Austria and without, would lead to a decline in the anti-Semitic movement.[93] But the Taafe government, absorbed 'by the ever-widening breach between the different nationalties' and the problem of maintaining a parliamentary majority in a highly complicated and confused domestic situation, had little time to devote to curbing anti-Semitism.[94] The Christian-Social anti-Semites, reinforced by the patronage of distinguished aristocratic figures like Prince Alois Lichtenstein, were in fact constantly gaining in strength and even expanding their influence to other parts of the Monarchy.[95]

les dangers sociaux de la croisade déplorable engagée contre eux, et insistaient sur le préjudice considérable qui résulterait pour l'Empire de la disparition des capitalistes juifs.'

[89] Ibid., 20 Apr. 1889.

[90] 'The Jewish Question in Vienna' ('Standard' Telegram), *Jewish Chronicle*, 10 May 1889, p. 7.   [91] Ibid.

[92] 'The Austrian Premier on Anti-Semitism', ibid., 14 June 1889, p. 7; 6 Dec. 1889, p. 18; 28 Feb. 1890, p. 11.

[93] 'The Anti-Semites in Vienna', ibid., 25 Mar. 1892, p. 11; 25 Dec. 1891, p. 6, for the condemnation by Taafe in the Austrian Parliament of anti-Semitism as 'unpatriotic'.

[94] 'The Anti-Semitic Agitation in Vienna', ibid., 14 Dec. 1892, p. 9.

[95] Ibid., 21 and 28 Aug. 1891, noted young Czech nationalist support for the Viennese anti-Semite, Ernst Schneider, quoting him as saying 'that anti-Semitism is the only bond that has kept all the races of the Austrian Monarchy together'.

One of the few brighter spots in this increasingly gloomy picture was the formation of a society in Vienna to combat anti-Semitism (Verein zur Abwehr des Antisemitismus) composed of prominent Christian and aristocratic personalities from the highest social circles.[96] They included Baron von Suttner, Counts Edmund Zichy and Rudolf Hoyos, Baron Friedrich Leitenberger, Baron Heisenauer and Baroness Marie Ebner-Eschenbach, Professors Theodor Billroth, Chrobak, Hermann Nothnagel, Eduard Suess, and Victor Tilgner, Prince and Princess von Metternich, the city council deputies, Frauenberger, Uhl, and Constantin Noske, the Mayors of Döbling, Nussdorf, and Heiligenstadt as well as Michael Matscheko, President of the Tradesmen's Association.

The creation of this Christian association in June 1891 was warmly welcomed in the Jewish press as a counterweight to the 'brutal and dangerous' anti-Semitism which was sweeping Vienna, though it was soberly recognized that to cleanse the city of this 'poisonous weed' would be an uphill task.[97] The Verein like its German model, sought to fight anti-Semitism with the weapons of reason, intelligence, culture, and decency: its orientation was humanistic rather than towards political action; stressing the common universal ideals which Christian and Jews shared against the 'brutal force' and 'moral barbarity' of the anti-Semites.[98] Anti-Semitism was depicted as a 'scandal' with its roots in 'the impurest and ugliest traits of human nature';[99] its principles were 'the abolition of justice and humanity'— therefore it could best be combatted through a reassertion of *Menschlichkeit* combined with an intensive pedagogic and publicistic activity.[100]

The Verein founded a weekly organ, the *Freies Blatt*, for this purpose, closely monitored the meetings and publications of the anti-

[96] 'Ein neuer Verein in Wien', *Die Neuzeit*, 20 Mar. 1891; 'Verein gegen den Antisemitismus', ibid., 22 May 1891; *Jewish Chronicle*, 29 May 1891.

[97] Ibid., 20 Mar. 1891. The editorial in *Die Neuzeit* acknowledged that Viennese anti-Semitism was more virulent and 'gemeinschädlicher als in irgend einer Stadt in der österreichisch-ungarischen Monarchie oder in Deutschland'. See also 'Die Nichtgewählten', ibid., which described anti-semitic electoral successes in Vienna as 'eine Schmach für die Stadt, welche das Haupt der Österreichischen Monarchie ist'.

[98] 'Verein gegen den Antisemitismus', ibid., 22 May 1891, p. 202. In his opening speech Professor Nothnagel emphasized: 'Was wir vorhaben, hat mit der Politik absolut nichts zu thun; es ist nur ein Act der Menschlichkeit und der Humanität, welcher nicht auf irgend einem Partei-Standpunkte basiert'. See also 'Zur Abwehr des Antisemitismus', 2 Feb. 1894, p. 45.

[99] Ibid., 22 May 1891, p. 202; 20 Apr. 1894, p. 158; 1 June 1894, p. 222.

[100] Ibid., 24 July 1891, p. 290.

Semites, and sought to expose their falsehoods.[101] By March 1893 its membership had passed the thousand mark[102] and reached 4,520 by 1895 which was about one-third of the size of the equivalent Berlin Verein. Headed by the novelist Baron von Suttner and the distinguished Professor of Medicine at the University of Vienna, Dr Hermann Nothnagel, the Vienna Verein was more aristocratic and intellectual and less overtly political in its social composition than its German prototype.[103] Nevertheless it did organize protest meetings against anti-Semitism which stressed its harmful social, cultural, and political character and the need to struggle actively against 'this poisonous element in our society'.[104]

The intellectual inspiration of the Viennese Verein had come from Professor Dr Hermann Nothnagel, a world-renowned stomach specialist and man of extraordinarily noble human qualities whose philosemitism was legendary among the poor Polish Jews of Galicia and Vienna. A sincere believing Christian, Nothnagel despised Lueger's movement as being neither religious nor truly 'social' and refused to accept the title of 'honorary citizen' of Vienna from the reigning Christian-Social administration.[105] A favourite target of Pan-German student heckling at the University of Vienna,[106] Nothnagel regarded nationalism as an 'incurable malady', as the 'most dangerous sickness of humanity'. His detestation of Schoenerer's Pan-Germans was intensified by the latter's vociferous campaign against him for having betrayed German national interests as the co-founder of the 'Society to Combat Anti-Semitism'.[107]

Nothnagel and his colleagues in the Verein consistently regarded the Austrian Jews as fellow citizens and members of a religious community, just like Catholics and Protestants. Hence they also strongly opposed Jewish nationalism as undermining the defence of civic equality and as a movement encouraging the German-Nationals.

---

[101] See *Jewish Chronicle*, 1892, p. 16.

[102] 'The Anti-Semitic Agitation—Vienna', ibid., 24 Mar. 1893, p. 10.

[103] See Ismar Schorsch, *Jewish Reactions to German Antisemitism* (New York, 1972), 83.

[104] 'Die Protestversammlungen gegen die Antisemiten', *Die Neuzeit*, 21 Oct. 1892, p. 417. Baron von Suttner in his speech stressed the importance of the Emperor's condemnation of anti-Semitism and the need to sanitize the Austrian Parliament by electing deputies who opposed the anti-Semites.

[105] Chaim Bloch, 'Herzl's First Years of Struggle. Unknown Episodes and Personal Recollections', *Herzl Year Book*, 3 (New York, 1960), 83.

[106] 'Die Demonstrationen an der Universität', *Volkstribune*, 6 July 1894, p. 1.

[107] Bloch, 'Herzl's First Years', 86–7.

Nothnagel told Herzl bitterly on one occasion: 'You have made a deal with the German-Nationals to disrupt my fight against anti-Semitism. You are creating conditions for the Jews of Austria and Germany beyond imagination to envisage'.[108]

In a long letter to Baroness von Suttner, Nothnagel again pointed to 'an affinity' between the Jewish nationalists and the Pan-Germans. He particularly emphasized 'how closely allied they are also in their fight against the Society to Combat Anti-Semitism'. Professor Nothnagel considered both movements inimical to the cosmopolitan Austrian State, and like other European nationalisms he denounced them as representing 'a negation of humanity and pure culture', which would in the future produce only 'chaos, destruction, divisiveness, strife and war'.[109] He felt that Jewish nationalism had given a strong impetus to German nationalism.

Schoenerer maintains that, in the monarchy, the Germans are a people of martyrs. Herzl, too, speaks of the Jews as a nation of martyrs. Both maintain that they are preparing better days for the Germans and for the Jews. I am worried lest they prepare a tragic future and hopelessness. Both ideas, Pan-Germanism and overriding Jewish nationalism, are a misfortune for the world. Both seem bent on destroying the divine world order. If it depended on me I would treat the leaders of these unfortunate movements as mentally ill.[110]

Herzl's own view of both Jewish and Christian defence activity (*Abwehr*) against anti-Semitism was equally scathing. It was very clearly articulated in a letter of 26 January 1893 from Paris to the Viennese industrialist and sponsor of the Verein, Baron Friedrich Leitenberger. While acknowledging in principle 'the influence which the example of distinguished, aristocratic and wealthy people can have on the large public in our good Austria', Herzl pointed out that the Verein had appeared about 'ten or twelve years too late'.[111] The anti-Semitic movement had grown too strong to be countered simply by well-intentioned pedagogic efforts. The only practical alternative was to create another movement like Social Democracy to counter its influence. Nothing could be politically accomplished, according to Herzl, by 'moderate publications' like the *Neue Freie Presse* or *Das Freie Blatt* which preached to the already converted.

Herzl cogently criticized the Verein's organ as 'a circular which does not circulate', suited to the needs of a small town, of a club, or of a

---

[108] Bloch, 'Herzl's First Years', p. 88.   [109] Ibid. 89.   [110] Ibid.
[111] For the full text of the letter see ibid. 78–82.

group of notables rather than to an age of mass politics.[112] While he did not object *per se* to the German-liberal orientation of the *Freies Blatt*, Herzl insisted that to succeed it would have to get rid of the monotony and boredom engendered by the established liberal press. It would have to be moderately 'socialist' and attractively presented to the public. The potential readership, he warned, would not stand for 'being lectured, corrected and educated'—one of the reasons for Herzl's deep scepticism about the very possibility of conducting any journalistic struggle against anti-Semitism. Interestingly enough, in January 1893 Herzl still shared the older Jewish establishment position that the war on anti-Semitism was most effectively waged (if at all) by Christians. Hence, as he wrote to Baron Leitenberger, 'the paper to combat anti-Semitism must not have a single Jew on its editorial staff'—neither Jews nor 'servants of Jews' (*Judenknechte*).[113]

Essentially, however, Herzl had by the end of 1892 come to the conclusion that self-defence activities were an exercise in futile posturing, based on false premises. Educational and propagandist efforts would never be effective in dissolving the age-old antagonism to the Jews. This summary rejection of apologetics and of the tempered optimism of the Jewish establishment regarding future integration into Gentile society was later to become almost a dogma in the Zionist movement. Herzl's clash with the first editor of *Die Welt*, Saul Raphael Landau, came in part over the founder of Zionism's insistence that it was not the task of the paper 'to engage in polemics against anti-Semitism'.[114] On the principle of 'the worse the better', Herzl even came to see in the intensification of anti-Semitism a factor which would increase support for the Zionist movement and be ultimately beneficial to Jewry.[115] The Christian *Abwehr* method of Baron Leitenberger and Bertha von Suttner was based in Herzl's view on a

[112] Ibid. 80.

[113] Ibid. 81.

[114] Saul Raphael Landau, *Sturm und Drang im Zionismus: Rückblicke eines Zionisten* (Vienna, 1937), 79 ff. See also *Die Welt*, 1 June 1897, pp. 4–5, for a critique of *Abwehr* strategy.

[115] As early as April 1895 Herzl remarked in his diaries: 'Anti-Semitism has grown and continued to grow—and so do I' (*The Diaries of Theodor Herzl*, ed. and trans. Marvin Lowenthal (London, 1958), 7). In his record of a conversation with Viennese Chief Rabbi Moritz Güdemann in Munich, Herzl observed on 18 Aug. 1895 that 'antisemitism no doubt has within it something of the divine Will to Good, for it forces us to close ranks, unites us under pressure, and through our unity will bring us to freedom'.

[116] Ibid. 6 Herzl stresses that it was in Paris that he came to recognize 'the emptiness and futility of trying to "combat" anti-Semitism'.

misunderstanding of the historical phenomenon of anti-Semitism, on a failure to grasp the dynamics of mass movements, and on a small-scale approach to the Jewish problem.[116]

How far were these strictures justified with regard to Jewish self-defence in *fin de siècle* Germany and Austria? In both countries there had been before the 1880s a deep aversion from the kind of defence activity which would involve a public affirmation of Jewish identity. Generally preferred were such traditional methods as appealing for special protection through influential Court Jews to the seat of power, playing down anti-Semitism, relying on dignified silence, or else calling for the suppression of unpleasantly distinctive 'Jewish' traits.[117] Thus during the first anti-Semitic tidal-wave in Germany (1879/80) the Board of the Berlin Jewish community had contented itself with timid requests for intervention from the Prussian Ministry of the Interior and a policy of quiet accommodation. It was widely believed in Jewish establishment circles that this outburst of anti-Semitism was only the final epidemic of a medieval plague which could not seriously danger Jewish legal status.[118] Why then give it free publicity? Why, the notables reasoned, exacerbate its popular appeal by provocative actions or confrontation tactics?

This policy of quietism and passivity adopted in the early 1880s by German Jewish leaders had its parallels in France and Austria. In all three countries Jewish establishment leaders waited for the storm to pass, bolstered by their confidence in the ideology of emancipation, in the strength of political liberalism, by their trust in the support of the authorities (not always justified), and by the conviction that anti-Semitism was essentially an ephemeral phenomenon. In Germany, special prudence was dictated by Gentile rejection of any form of separate Jewish activity—social, cultural, educated, or religious.[119] This attempted homogenization of Jewry by the Prusso-German State and by political parties, who expected the abandonment of Jewish identity to be the price of emancipation, did not exist to the same degree in the pluralistic multinational environment of Imperial Austria. Nor did republican uniformity and political reflexes deriving from Jacobin and Bonapartist centralist traditions, which had made most French Jews assert their inalienable Frenchness and 'their

---

[117] Schorsch, pp. 65–6.
[118] Ibid. 68.
[119] Sanford Ragins, *Jewish Responses to Anti-Semitism in Germany, 1870–1914* (Cincinatti, 1980), 17.

devotion to the Republic' during the Dreyfus affair, have an exact parallel in *fin de siècle* Austria.[120]

Nevertheless, the behaviour of Jewish Community Boards or of the Consistoires and their equivalents in Paris, Berlin, and Vienna, when faced with the rise of anti-Semitism, was not so dissimilar. Their apolitical legal status in itself virtually precluded community leaders from taking a strong public stand on the 'Jewish question'. They either acted bureaucratically as if there was no crisis at all, or they deferred to the authority of the State and to established institutions, or else they emphasized even more insistently than before the patriotism of the Jews.[121] Invariably anti-Semitism was depicted as a foreign excrescence on the historic traditions of the particular country and State (both French and Austrian Jewish leaders liked to portray the modern Jew-bait as a 'German' import); moreover, the disruptive, anarchic, and subversive character of anti-Semitism for the State and its enmity to liberal civilization was underlined no less strongly than its threat to the Jews.[122] In this way it was evidently hoped to isolate the anti-Semites and solidify the support of Gentiles against this 'alien' phenomenon. As far as possible Jews were not to fight their war qua Jews against these enemies of humanity and it was liberal Gentile opinion that in the first instance had to be mobilized. At the same time, though a specifically Jewish policy towards anti-Semitism was frowned upon as separatist and contrary to the spirit of emancipation, it gradually became acceptable, at least in Austria, to equate 'Jüdische Politik' with the liberal principles of religious tolerance, social harmony, progress, *Bildung*, and free individual development.[123]

Even more commendable was to defend the 'honour of Judaism' through apologetic writings, though orthodox and reform Jews could never agree on how this should best be done. Liberal Judaism had traditionally seen in 'the social isolation of the Jews' and the unaesthetic 'outer garb' of the traditional orthodox religion one of the major sources of mob prejudice.[124] Hence in Austria as in Germany,

[120] Michael R. Marrus, *The Politics of Assimilation: The French Jewish Community at the time of the Dreyfus Affair* (Oxford, 1971).

[121] Ibid. 200, 225, 231.

[122] For an Austrian variation on this theme see J., 'Anarchismus und Antisemitismus', *Die Neuzeit*, 22 Dec. 1893, p. 507, which compared anarchist bombs, dynamite, violence, and terror to its 'elder brother'—the racial hatred, witch-hunts, lies, slander, and persecution mania of the anti-Semites. Both were branded as sworn enemies of European civilization, of liberalism, social peace, and morality.

[123] 'Unsere Politik', *Die Neuzeit*, 16 Oct. 1891, p. 391.

[124] Jellinek, 'Die Juden in Oesterreich', *Der Orient*, no. 17 (22 Apr. 1848), 129–30.

liberals advocated both internal and external reform of the 'cult' in order to help overcome Gentile antagonism. Hungarian, German, and Polish ultra-orthodoxy, on the other hand, regarded Reform Jews as an even greater threat than Gentile anti-Semitism, which it blamed on enlightenment, assimilation, and the progressive abandonment of Torah Judaism. Not surprisingly orthodox Jews tended therefore to be more sceptical than their reform adversaries concerning the value of self-defence, especially if they held to the 'theological' explanation of Jew-hatred as divine chastisement for Israel's sins.

It was only in the 1890s that any serious reappraisal of these traditional postures took place in France and Germany, where anti-Semitic electoral successes shook Jews out of their earlier lethargy and began to challenge the assumptions of the liberal order. Thus the Centralverein in Germany turned the fight against anti-Semitism into one of the strongest components of a new form of Jewish self-consciousness;[125] it called from its foundation in 1893 for energetic, systematic self-defence activity in place of the old tactics of *Schutzjuden* (protected Jews), held to be anachronistic in an age of civil equality. Though it still tied the future of German Jewry to the survival of the Rechtsstaat and of German liberal *Kultur*, emphasizing unconditional loyalty to the Emperor and fatherland, nevertheless there was a new willingness to battle for Jewish interests and to organize Jews within a single, united body.[126]

Though the 'Jewish question' was held to be a *Rechtsfrage* (rather than a *Parteifrage*), though in Germany no independent Jewish political representation was created, and though in contrast to Austria the self-perception of Jews as a national minority group remained an unacceptable fantasy, the Centralverein nevertheless constituted a new post-emancipation phenomenon.[127] It represented what Ismar Schorsch has termed a kind of surrogate Judaism for Jews who had abandoned the Torah and also rejected Zionism, yet still retained a secular Jewish identity that was being badly bruised by the new racial anti-Semitism.[128] By the 1890s they no longer saw Jewish interests as best served by acting through exclusively German channels nor were they ready passively to continue the degrading self-renunciation required by the politics of assimilation.[129]

---

[125] Schorsch, pp. 207–8.   [126] Ragins, p. 89.
[127] Ibid. 64   [128] Schorsch, p. 208.
[129] Ibid. 104 ff.; see also M. R. Marrus, 'European Jewry and the Politics of Assimilation: Assessment and Reassessment', in Vago (ed.), *Jewish Assimilation*, 5–23.

Austrian Jews had in fact preceded their German co-religionists in the Centralverein by nearly a decade in such a public defence of specifically Jewish interests, by fighting against animosity without and massive 'indifference' within and by seeking to revitalize religious and national consciousness in response to anti-Semitism. Indeed it was precisely in Vienna during the mid-1880s that the first concrete effort to establish a Jewish self-defence organization was successfully implemented. Here, for perhaps the first time in Central European history, Jews as a collective body broke with the clandestine methods of notable politics and *shtadlanut* to form a well-organized pressure group on a religious and ethnic basis.

The emergence of the Österreichisch-Israelitische Union in 1886 did not represent a total rupture from tradition nor a revolution in Jewish politics.[130] But it was decidedly original in its early formulation of an organized programme of Jewish self-help and in its militant, public struggle against anti-Semitism. The Union proposed a middle road between assimilation and Jewish nationalism, seeking a positive definition of Jewishness in terms of religion, common descent, a shared historic fate, and the reality of ethnic ties alongside a devoted Austrian patriotism. At the same time the Union sought to mobilize Jews in defence of their civic rights and vital interests against anti-Semitic agitation from outside, as well as to fight apostasy and the religious 'indifferentism' of a new generation of emancipated Jews from within. It aimed to heighten Jewish pride and consciousness in an era of communal apathy and psychological demoralization.

In this respect the Union was very much in harmony with the Viennese Jewish establishment which also saw as one of its main goals the battle against Jewish anti-Semitism. As *Die Neuzeit* phrased it on 30 December 1881:

Jewish youth is beginning to be ashamed of its Jewishness, it attaches importance to not being recognized as Jews—it looks at the small weaknesses of the race through a magnifying glass and has no eye for its shining merits. Jews have become the most bitter enemies of Jewry and the most stubborn anti-Semites are the chosen, baptized offspring of the pious old tribal Father Shem, founder of the Hebrew nation.[131]

---

[130] See Jacob Toury, 'Troubled Beginnings: The Emergence of the Österreichisch-Israelitische Union', *Leo Baeck Year Book*, 30 (1985), 457–75, who seems to me to overstress the conservatism of the organization in its original phase, though its subsequent move to the Right can hardly be doubted.

[131] *Die Neuzeit*, 30 Dec. 1881, p. 417.

Community leaders and rabbis saw the phenomena of apostasy, religious indifference, and self-hatred among Viennese Jewish youth as related consequences of 'the anti-Semitic poison which has insinuated itself into the emotions'.[132] Thus they were prepared to support the programme of strengthening Jewish consciousness advocated by outsiders like the Galician-born Rabbi Joseph Samuel Bloch (1850–1923), the driving-force behind the creation of the Union.[133] They were not opposed in principle to Bloch's declaration of war against 'the rapidly spreading semitic anti-Semitism', nor his programme to improve religious instruction and Jewish historical knowledge and to strengthen the consciousness of a common racial origin (*Stammesbewusstsein*). Nor was Bloch's insistence that Jews in Austria, confronted by rabid anti-Semitism and national chauvinism on all sides, should 'again become *Jews, Austrian Jews*', in itself, a cause for concern;[134] what worried the community leadership was less Bloch's supranational Austrian patriotism (which they had been advocating for many years) than his support for Eduard Taafe's clerical-conservative Iron Ring Coalition and his sharp rejection of Austro-German liberalism.[135]

Not only did Joseph Bloch attack the liberal Jewish–German alliance but he also gave a clear anti-assimilatory orientation to his critique of Jewish involvement in the Austrian nationality struggles. Again and again, he emphasized that the Jews should not allow themselves to be pulled in tow by the German national cause—or indeed that of the Magyars, Poles, Czechs, and other nationalities. The Jews were 'neither Germans nor Slavs' but 'Austrians *sans phrase*', the 'foundation' of an Austrian nationality, as yet to be constituted.[136] Founded in 1884, Bloch's weekly *Österreichische Wochenschrift* (a title deliberately chosen as the antithesis to Heinrich Friedjung's pro-Prussian and assimilationist Pan-German *Deutsche Wochenschrift*) proposed a veritable cult of loyal pro-Habsburg Austrianism.[137] But

---

[132] *Die Neuzeit*, 30 Dec. 1881, p. 417.

[133] 'Jüdischer Bürgerverein', *Österreichische Wochenschrift* (1885), no. 14, p. 1.

[134] See Joseph Bloch, *Der nationale Zwist und die Juden in Österreich* (Vienna, 1886), 28, 40, 45–53. In another variation Bloch wrote: 'Wir sind weder Germanen noch Slaven, sondern österreichische Juden oder jüdische Österreicher'.

[135] See William A. Jenks, *Austria under the Iron Ring, 1879–1893* (Charlottesville, Va., 1965), on the political alignments of this period. Also *Österreichische Wochenschrift*, 30 Apr. 1886, pp. 193–4, and Bloch, *My Reminiscences*, 182.

[136] Bloch, *Der nationale Zwist*, 41.

[137] For Bloch's attacks on Friedjung's Germanism as a form of 'Semitic anti-Semitism', see *Österreichische Wochenschrift*, 16 Jan. 1885, 16 July 1885, 14 Nov. 1885.

this ideology of supranational *Österreichertum* went together with a militant, public opposition to anti-Semitic calumny that contradicted the strategy of avoidance then adopted by the Kultusgemeinde and the financial magnates of Viennese Jewry.

Bloch's determination to defend the Talmud in public against anti-Semitic demagogues like August Rohling, Ernest Schneider, and Franz Holubek, even to the extent of addressing Social Democratic meetings in the industrial Viennese suburb of Florisdorf (where he was the *Bezirksrabbiner*) clearly embarrassed community leaders.[138] Bloch's attempt to modernize and humanize the teachings of the ancient Talmudists, presenting them as defenders of 'socialist' theories in ancient Palestine, was unequivocally rejected by the *Neue Zeit*.[139] The spectacle of this militant Galician rabbi from Dukla defending Talmudic Judaism as a model of social justice for the exploited Gentile working classes of Vienna was also too much for Joseph Ritter von Wertheimer, who revealingly reproached him: 'You defend the Talmud too much, we do not know it—and do not want it anymore'.[140]

Dr Bloch's intense Jewish self-consciousness aroused the opposition of the established German-speaking liberal Jews in Vienna. Except for the more perspicacious among them, like the ageing Ignaz Kuranda, who felt keenly the reawakening of anti-Semitism in Austria and therefore encouraged him, Bloch found himself initially cold-shouldered by the established Jewish leaders.[141] As Max Grunwald has written:

They could take their Judaism only in small doses. Indeed, they were fearful that the carrying out of his [Bloch's] views would lead to a loss of civil status. The Jewish upper classes and the intellectuals regarded Judaism as something to be practised during religious service either on holidays or at family functions. The Jewish local politicians failed to see where the enemy was . . . The communal leaders even opposed an open issue with anti-Semitism on the

Friedjung's extreme assimilationist position and his loathing of the Talmud was expressed on a number of occasions; see *Deutsche Wochenschrift*, no. 43, Oct. 1885.

[138] See Bloch, *Aus der Vergangenheit für die Gegenwart* (Vienna, 1886), 13–23; also *My Reminiscences*, 33. See the critical though respectful comments in *Die Neuzeit*, 3 Dec. 1886, p. 459, 'Literarische Nachrichten'.

[139] *Die Neuzeit*, 3 Dec. 1886, p. 459–60.

[140] Isidor Schalit, 'Erinnerungen' in *Festschrift zur Feier des 100. Semesters der akademischen Verbindung Kadimah* (Mödling, 1933), 53.

[141] See Grunwald, *Vienna*, 370, 441. On Kuranda's attitude to the new anti-Semitism see Naama Magnus, 'Ignaz Kuranda', *Die Gemeinde* (Vienna), 7 June 1984, p. 19. As early as 1881 Kuranda was warning that the anti-Semitic movement might destroy 'all das, was wir ingesamt geschaffen haben . . .'.

ground that it would aggravate the opposition. In fact, in the City Council of Vienna, the Jews had taken a pledge to each other to ignore the worst ravings of the anti-Semites. The Jew was to appear before the public as a man and not as a Jew.[142]

It was primarily against this politics of silence practised by the liberal assimilationist leadership and as a protest against the steady advances being made by Austrian anti-Semitism, that Rabbi Bloch founded the Union in 1886. By 1910 it had 7,935 members in 501 Jewish communities throughout Austria and through its *Rechtsschutzbureau* had established itself as an effective Jewish self-defence organization in legal matters. But for all its commitment to Jewish rights the general orientation of the Union was none the less assimilationist. Bloch had originally argued for a united cultural-religious and political organization based on the consciousness of common ancestry and fate, which would transcend the old divisions between orthodoxy and reform in a national direction.[143] He suggested that Viennese and Austrian Jewry faced a dangerous common enemy in anti-Semitism which necessitated not only self-defence but an autonomous Jewish political representation.

Such a militant defence of specifically Jewish interests still remained anathema to most community leaders of Viennese Jewry in the early 1880s. They rejected Rabbi Bloch's strictures against *Deutschtum* and the German Liberal Verfassungspartei, just as they disliked his populist appeal to the Jewish masses, and his insistence on direct confrontation and controversy with the Austrian anti-Semites. More-over, they resented the fact that since 1884, as a deputy for the preponderantly Jewish Galician constituency of Kolomea, he had become a member of the Polish Club in the Austrian Parliament. This seemed to give concrete expression to Bloch's pro-Taafe, pro-Slavic, and conservative 'clerical' orientation, thereby disqualifying him in the eyes of the Viennese Jewish leadership.

Behind these party-political frictions which made Rabbi Bloch the *enfant terrible* of the religious community in the 1880s lay profound cultural differences. Many of the sophisticated Jewish notables, the business and intellectual élites of Viennese Jewry, probably felt closer to their German Gentile middle-class neighbours than to unassimilated orthodox Jews from Hungary, Galicia, or Bukovina, to Czech immigrants from Bohemia, or to the simple working-men of Vienna. They felt that Rabbi Bloch overemphasized the importance of racial

---

[142] Grunwald, *Vienna*, 441–2.

[143] See *Österreichische Wochenschrift*, 15 Oct. 1884, pp. 1–3; also 10 Apr. 1885, p. 1.

ancestry, the past glories of the Talmud, and the cultivation of Jewish national-religious consciousness. Hence, when the Prime Minister Count Taafe sought to nominate him to a Professorial chair in Jewish Antiquities and sounded out the Kultusgemeinde, they vetoed the initiative, stating: 'The appointment of Dr. Bloch, a member of the Polish club, to Professor of Hebrew Antiquities at the University of Vienna would be a provocative act against the Viennese Jews.'[144]

Nevertheless, the resentment of the centre against the periphery, of the *Schutzjude* against the *Staatsbürger*, of the *Westjude* against the *Ostjude*, of the parvenus against the pariahs of society, could not long survive the anti-Semitic landslide of the 1890s. The establishment of the Union in 1886 and Bloch's courageous public stance against anti-Semitism provided the seeds in the last decade of the nineteenth century of a significant reorientation in the politics of Viennese Jewry. The irrefutable evidence that the great mass of the Viennese Gentile *Bürgertum* and lower middle classes were voting for the anti-Semites and that the German Liberals were impotent to prevent this defection could not be swept under the carpet. The vision of harmonious social integration slowly but surely began to crumble in a post-liberal climate of nationalism, class struggle, parliamentary paralysis, and populist demogogy.

By February 1891 Adolf Jellinek had even mellowed his opposition to Bloch enough to advocate strongly his re-election to the Reichsrat from the Kolomea–Buczacz–Sniatyn constituency as essential for defending the status of Austrian Jewry.[145] Disillusionment with the consequences of a one-sided commitment to *Deutschtum* and growing emphasis on the need for Jewish self-defence and independent political representation against anti-Semitism had begun to make headway even among the German-orientated leaders of the community.[146] Much of the old resentment had faded against the maverick

---

[144] *Festschrift des Kadimah*, 54; Bloch, *My Reminiscences*, 155–6.

[145] 'Kolomea–Buczacz–Sniatyn', *Die Neuzeit*, 13 Feb. 1891, pp. 62–3. See also 'Dr. Bloch hat das Wort!' 2 Dec. 1892, p. 477, which concluded that the voters of Kolomea 'haben sich durch ihre Wahl des Dr. Bloch in den österreichischen Reichsrath um die gesammte österreichische Judenheit verdient gemacht. Er vertritt und vertheidigt die Sache der Juden muthig und mit rednerischer Gewandtheit'.

[146] 'Kolomea–Buczacz–Sniatyn', ibid., 13 Feb. 1891, p. 62. Even Jellinek now argued that Austrian Jewry had to be represented in the Reichsrat, 'durch einen Mann unseres Glaubens . . . welcher die Fähigkeit und die Kraft besitzt, für das Judenthum, dessen Lehre und Ehre zu kämpfen und der antisemitischen Frechheit, Verlogenheit, Verfolgungs- und Verleumdungssucht entgegenzutreten'. Jellinek supported Bloch's candidacy against Leon Meisels, a wealthy Jew and nephew of the Warsaw rabbi of the

Galician rabbi, parliamentarian, and politician who had dared to make Jewish affairs his main concern. The importance of his defence of Judaism against the blood libel which had been demonstrated in 1882 during the Rohling affair was again underlined in the 1890s when he initiated proceedings against further ritual-murder charges by the Catholic priest Father Deckert and the baptized Jew Paulus Mayer.[147] Again, during the Hilsner blood libel he was active together with other community leaders—especially Alfred Stern and the directors of the Israelitische Allianz—in seeking to revise a case which more than any other underlined the power of medieval superstition in undermining the fabric of modern civilized states.[148]

The Hilsner affair was indeed a good illustration of the change which had taken place in the attitudes of the Jewish community leadership. Sixteen years earlier at the time of the Tisza-Eszlar blood libel in Hungary and the simultaneous agitation against the Talmud in Vienna, the Kultusgemeinde had feared to send its leading rabbis, Jellinek and Güdemann, into the fray against Rohling's followers.[149] It was this excessive official caution which had permitted Bloch, then an obscure, uninhibited *Bezirksrabbiner* in Florisdorf, to become a hero overnight by intellectually clubbing Professor Rohling into submission and proving him to be a forger, liar, and ignoramus.

In the Hilsner case, the community Board, the rabbinate, and the Israelitische Allianz did not wait for outside prodding to make their representations to the government. The lawyer, Alfred Stern, a member of the IKG Board and later its President (who had already been active for fourteen years in the city council as a member of the German Progressive Party) took the initiative in organizing an IKG meeting attended by thousands on 7 October 1899 to protest at 'the greatest judicial murder of our time'.[150] Stern was tireless in conducting the fight against the ritual-murder fable and in urging every Jew in Austria to stand up for his human rights, civil status,

same name. See Dr M. Rosenmann, *Dr Adolf Jellinek: Sein Leben und Schaffen* (Vienna, 1931), 176 ff.

[147] On the Deckert–Mayer affair see Bloch, *My Reminiscences*, 382 ff., 563 ff., for the comments of the leading Viennese newspapers on the court case which created something of a sensation.

[148] See Dr Alfred Stern, 'Der Hilsner Prozess', *Ost und West*, 10, no. 10 (1910), 615–20. Also the personal files of Stern in the Central Archives of the History of the Jewish People (Jerusalem), A/W 744.1 for valuable further materials.

[149] Rosenmann, *Jellinek*, 160–1.

[150] Stern, p. 615; also *Die Neuzeit*, 2 Oct. 1899.

honour, and dignity against anti-Semitic defamation—a line which Bloch's *Wochenschrift* warmly approved.[151] Even the *Neue Freie Presse*, normally reticent on Jewish affairs, praised this aspect of Stern's activity in a long and highly complimentary article on his seventieth birthday. The leading liberal newspaper of Vienna emphasized with some satisfaction that 'Dr. Stern had indeed often damaged the Antisemites . . .', and in addition to his administrative efficiency in Religious Community matters had proved to be one of the most energetic political opponents of anti-Semitism in the Vienna city council.[152] Even if this compliment was not wholly deserved, the fact that it was made at all is in itself significant.

The higher profile involvement of Stern and other Jewish representatives during the Hilsner affair, though it bore no fruit, underlined their sensitivity to the damage already done by recurring ritual-murder charges in the heated atmosphere of *fin de siècle* anti-Semitic agitation. The leaders of the Vienna Allianz were also concerned by the affair and with the encouragement of the Kultusgemeinde and of the Paris Alliance prepared pamphlets and other literature to counter the blood-libel propaganda.[153] In this activity they had the full and wholehearted support of Rabbi Bloch and his *Österreichische Wochenschrift* which by the end of the century had become part of that same Jewish establishment whose complacency he had badly shaken two decades earlier.

Indeed, from its very inception in 1886 the Österreichisch-Israelitische Union which Bloch had created (without ever officiating in the organization) had a rather pronounced middle-class character and integrationist aspirations which suggested that it might readily be co-opted in the future by the IKG leadership.[154] By 1900 it was clear that just as the Union was somewhat less militant in its ethnic assertion

---

[151] *Österreichische Wochenschrift*, 23 Aug. 1901, pp. 562–3; also *Die Neuzeit*, 2 Oct. 1899; 'Dr. Alfred Stern', *Die Wahrheit*, no. 34, 30 Aug. 1901, p. 3.

[152] *Neue Freie Presse*, 29 Aug. 1901, pp. 2, 3, and 5.

[153] Archives of the Alliance Israélite Universelle, Autriche IIA 4, (Hilsner affair). Letters from Kuranda to the Alliance . . . Paris, 29 Sept., 4 Oct., 15 Oct., 10 Nov. 1899. See also 'Der Mord in Polna', *Die Neuzeit*, 19 May 1899, p. 197.

[154] See Rozenblit, p. 155, who observes that the Union was 'composed primarily of businessmen and industrialists from the same circles which provided leadership for the IKG (minus the nobleman) . . .'. Also Toury, pp. 474–5, who notes that in 1886 the Board of the Union 'reflected a predominance of the professions' and writes that 'a new, culturally orientated, politically liberal, but not over-active club had been formed, which consisted of the newer, upward-moving strata of the Vienna Jewish middle classes'. Toury suggests that this sociological profile may have inhibited their willingness 'to tangle in the open with the antisemitic enemy'.

of Jewish identity than Bloch had originally intended, so too the communal establishment had become considerably less pusillanimous in its expression of Jewish pride, consciousness, and self-defence against anti-Semitism. The fact that after 1900 both the IKG and the Union rejected Jewish political nationalism and were attacked in similar terms by the Zionists as treacherous 'assimilationists' was a further sign of the overlap between the old centre and the periphery; they had now virtually merged under the familiar banner of a fairly benign 'Austrian patriotism' and a fight for the human rather than the national rights of the Jews.[155] The sharpening of anti-Semitism and the challenge from within had indeed forced the Jewish establishment into a more active defence posture in which the Union became the favoured instrument of organizational and ideological unity.[156] Whether in legal battles combating anti-Semitic boycotts, press defamation, or blood libels, the Union stood in the very forefront of 'safeguarding the general and political rights of Jews and helping those practising the Jewish religion to these rights'.[157] Thus the gospel of self-reliance preached by Dr Bloch and by the early Jewish nationalists, which had seemed so provocative in the 1880s to the Jewish community leadership, had become widely accepted by the first decade of the twentieth century. This transformation of previously passive assimilated middle- and upper-class Jews into conscious defenders of their heritage and rights was a direct outcome of radical Austrian anti-Semitism.[158] As Sigmund Mayer, President of the Union after 1905, recalled in his memoirs: 'I had in fact forgotten that I was a Jew until

---

[155] See *Österreichische Wochenschrift*, 30 Apr. 1886, pp. 193–4. Already at the opening meeting of the Union in Apr. 1886, Dr Sigmund Zins had proposed an open-ended Habsburg loyalism which could be reconciled with the German, Czech, or Polish identification of Jews and their preservation of Jewish consciousness. This was virtually identical with the classic liberal position.

[156] On the collaboration between the Union and the Community Board, at the end of the century, see e.g. 'Zu den Cultuswahlen', *Die Neuzeit*, 11 Nov. 1898.

[157] *Monatsschrift der Österreichisch-Israelitischen Union*, Feb./Mar. 1903, pp. 9–10; also 2 Feb. 1910, pp. 1–3. By 1910 the legal rights bureau had acted in some 5,000 cases on behalf of Austrian Jews. See Ber Borochov, 'Soher yehudi naor', *Ketavim* (Tel Aviv, 1966), iii. 95–6 for a surprisingly sympathetic sketch of Mayer and the Union from a left-wing Zionist viewpoint. The article was originally written in Vienna and published in Dec. 1911.

[158] An example of this new Jewish consciousness was the sharp protest of the Union against the involvement in 1906 of Theodor Ritter von Taussig, a leading member of the Kultusgemeinde and one of Vienna's most important bankers, in arranging a loan to the anti-Semitic Russian government. In the autumn of 1906 von Taussig failed to be re-elected to the Community Board as a result of the Union's campaign. See Borochov, p. 96.

Kandidatenliste

des

ZENTRAL-WAHLKOMITEE

für die israel. Kultuswahlen in Wien 1906.

Mit sechsjähriger Funktionsdauer (weisser Stimmzettel):

Dr. Alfred Berger, Hof- und Gerichtsadvokat, I., Judenplatz 8

Emanuel Hoffmann, Brauhauskassier, XVIII., Karl Ludwigstrasse 27

Dr. Gustav Kohn, Hof- und Gerichtsadvokat, IX., Hahngasse 25

Dr. Josef Pollak, Universitätsprofessor, I., Annagasse 1

Adolf Schramek, Kaufmann, II., Novaragasse 21

Kommerzialrat Leopold Simon, Kaufmann, I., Freisingergasse 1

Dr. Maximil. Steiner, Generalrepräsentant, I., Graben 16

Dr. Alfred Stern, em. Hof- u. Gerichtsadvokat, II., Unt. Donaustr. 27

Mit vierjähriger Funktionsdauer (grüner Stimmzettel):

Kais. Rat Leopold Langer, Bankier, I., Kärntnerring 1

Mit zweijähriger Funktionsdauer (blauer Stimmzettel):

Max Frank, Handelsgesellschafter, IX., Berggasse 19

Dr. Hermann Löwi, prakt. Arzt, II., Novaragasse 20

Samuel Steiner, Bauunternehmer, VII, Burggasse 72

List of Candidates for the Jewish Community Elections in Vienna (1906)

the anti-Semites brought me to this unpleasant discovery.'[159] Like many assimilationist and patriotic Jewish liberals, anti-Semitism brought him back into the fold, as a defiant reaction of injured pride. Defence activity against anti-Semitism thus became an important element in the new secular Jewish identity that developed in Habsburg Austria at the turn of the century.

[159] Sigmund Mayer, *Ein jüdischer Kaufmann, 1831 bis 1911* (Leipzig, 1911), 289.

PART TWO

SELF-DEFENCE AGAINST ANTI-SEMITISM

7

The New Austrian Anti-Semitism

... More and more the Christian social order is being dissolved by Jewry. Workers and craftsmen are drifting into the Jews' factories, landed property into the Jews' hands, houses into their possession, and the wealth of the peoples into their pockets. Through electoral laws they dominate elections, politics and the *Reichsrat* ... a few more years of such 'progress' and Vienna will be called New Jerusalem and old Austria Palestine.

> *Das Vaterland* (1871)

But if you ask yourself: why has the liberal press sunk to such depths? There is only one answer. It sunk to this depth because the party it serves had long since disappeared, and was replaced by lies and hypocrisy, corruption and thirst for power. That is how it is with the '*Presse*'. In addition, it mostly belongs to Jews, and all events, therefore, are treated solely on the basis of whether they are useful or damaging to the Jew.

> Speech draft (*c.*1886), *Nachlass*, Karl Lueger

... Our antisemitism is not directed against the religion, but against the racial traits of the Jews which have not been changed either by the earlier pressure or through the freedom that now prevails ...

> Georg von Schoenerer (1887)

A man next to me said with tender warmth but in a quiet voice: 'That is our *Fuehrer* (leader). Actually, these words showed me more than all declamation and abuse how deeply antisemitism is rooted in the hearts of these people.

> Theodor Herzl (1895) on Karl Lueger's electoral campaign.

The multi-ethnic Habsburg Empire was the cradle of the most successful modern political movement based on anti-Semitism to emerge anywhere in nineteenth-century Europe. In spite of parallels that can be drawn with events in neighbouring Germany and Russia, the main components of Austrian anti-Semitism, its multinational character, agitational techniques, and mass impact, were distinctly novel.[1] It was no accident that the Berlin movement of Adolf Stoecker failed to register the kind of electoral success or popular mobilization comparable to that of Karl Lueger's Christian-Social party in Vienna.[2] Nor did the myriad *völkisch* anti-Semites in *fin de siècle* Imperial Germany ever achieve the kind of decisive and seminal influence on public life which was enjoyed for a time by the Austrian Pan-German leader, Georg von Schoenerer (1842–1921).[3] Thus, despite the rather sharp dichotomy that developed between clerical and Pan-German varieties of anti-Semitism in Austria, the movement as a whole achieved an astonishing resonance. This was not the case before 1914 either in neighbouring Germany or in Hungary.

Before examining the specifically Viennese variant of Judaeophobia, it is important to bear in mind the multinational character of anti-Semitism in the Habsburg Monarchy. During the 1848 Revolution the connection between the national question and anti-Semitism had already become apparent. Pogroms occurred in Pressburg (Bratislava), riots in Prague, and disturbances in other Czech towns which reflected the nationalist enthusiasm, economic distress, and local resentment of Bohemian Jewry as a pro-German element.[4] But the Germanocentrism of Austrian Jewry was only one side of the problem. When in the second half of the nineteenth century Jews in Hungary and Galicia began to adopt a Magyar or Polish rather than a German orientation, the situation was scarcely improved. The Jewish realignment towards Magyars and Galician Poles almost immediately provoked the anti-Semitism of submerged, 'historyless' nationalities, oppressed by the Hungarian and Polish aristocracy.

There was, for example, a Slovak anti-Semitism, partly economic in

[1] See Jacob Katz, *From Prejudice to Destruction: Anti-Semitism, 1730–1933* (Cambridge, Mass., 1982), 245–91 for a valuable comparison of Germany, Austria, and Hungary. I cannot agree however with Katz's view that Austrian anti-Semitism 'lacked a central principle' as in Germany, or that it developed more slowly (pp. 290–1).

[2] On Stoecker see Walter Frank, *Hofprediger Stöcker und die christlichsoziale Bewegung* (Hamburg, 1935), and Uriel Tal, *Christians and Jews in Germany: Religion, Politics and Ideology in the Second Reich, 1870–1914* (New York, 1975), 223 ff. On the electoral weakness of German anti-Semitism before 1914 see Richard S. Levy, *The Downfall of the Anti-Semitic Political Parties in Imperial Germany* (New Haven, 1975).

[3] For this influence see Adam Wandruszka, 'Die drei Lager', in H. Benedikt (ed.), *Geschichte der Republik Österreich* (Vienna, 1954), 292 ff.

[4] Gary B. Cohen, *The Politics of Ethnic Survival: Germans in Prague, 1861–1914* (Princeton, 1981), 82; Guido Kisch, *In Search of Freedom* (London, 1949), 42–3.

character but which probably owed more to the ardent identification of Hungarian Jews with Magyar nationalism.[5] Slovak nationalists resented what they saw as a Jewish 'jingoist' participation in journalism, business, and politics on the side of the Magyars. In the same way, the excessive Germanophilia of most Jews in Bohemia and Moravia nettled the Czech nationalists, some of whom came to see in the Jews 'the worst opponents of the Czech people in political matters'.[6] Czech anti-Semitism peaked at the end of the 1890s with the Hilsner affair. (Leopold Hilsner, a Jewish shoemaker's assistant, had been falsely accused of murdering a young Christian girl for ritual purposes.)[7] The case aroused a flood of anti-Semitic articles throughout the Empire. Anti-Jewish riots broke out, aggravated by Czech national strife with the Germans and the industrial unrest in the Bohemian crown lands.[8]

In Galicia, too, there was a nationalist and economic anti-Semitism coming from the Ukrainian side. Mostly, it was directed at Jewish 'collaboration' with the dominant Poles. More significant, however, was the anti-Semitism periodically encouraged by some of the great Polish landowners, by the rising Polish bourgeoisie, and elements in the Catholic Church. This anti-Semitism, especially when directed at the Jewish middleman role in the agrarian economy, found a strong echo in the Galician peasantry. Exacerbated by the demagogy of the Christian People's party and its Polish leader Father Stojalowski, it flared up in 1898, resulting in devastating pogroms.[9] Polish anti-Semitism also had a markedly nationalist aspect (both anti-German and anti-Russian) which found expression in the National Democratic party of Roman Dmowski.[10]

[5] See Oscar Jászi, *The Dissolution of the Habsburg Monarchy* (Chicago and London, 1971), 174–5.

[6] See P. G. J. Pulzer, *The Rise of Political Antisemitism in Germany and Austria* (New York and London, 1964), 140, for the remark made by a Czech deputy in a debate on anti-Jewish riots in Moravia.

[7] See Thomas G. Masaryk, *Die Notwendigkeit der Revision des Polnaer Prozesses* (Vienna, 1899). Masaryk, then Professor at the Czech University in Prague, took an outspoken position against the ritual-murder fantasy and the conduct of the Hilsner trial.

[8] Michael Riff, 'Czech Antisemitism and the Jewish Response before 1914', in Robert S. Wistrich (ed.), *European Antisemitism 1890–1945* (special issue of *The Wiener Library Bulletin*, 29 (1976), NS nos. 39/40, pp. 8–19. Riff points out that increasing Czech anti-Semitism undermined efforts at Czech–Jewish assimilation which had been under way since the 1880s.

[9] On the 1898 riots in Galicia see 'Die Judenverfolgung in Galizien', *Arbeiterzeitung*, 18 June 1898, p. 1; also 'Die Judenhetze in Galizien', 26 June 1898, p. 2.

[10] Wilhelm Feldman *Geschichte der politisch Ieen in Polen seit dessen Teilungen* (Munich, 1917), 348 ff.

Some of the nationalist anti-Semitism in Central and Eastern Europe was perhaps the result of Jewish patterns of assimilation to the dominant nationality in their environment. In Austria-Hungary, the Jews tended to gravitate naturally towards the 'historic' nations. Germans, Magyars, and Poles seemed to represent greater political security as well as higher standards of culture, education, and commercial life. The prospect of acculturation with predominantly peasant peoples like the Slovaks, Serbo-Croats, Ukrainians, or Romanians was scarcely even contemplated. Nor did the more cultured and industrially advanced Czechs offer a particularly tempting target for integration. It was not merely that they were a smaller, less developed nation as compared to the Germans of the Empire. Assimilation with the Czechs would have involved complete devotion to the declared objectives of Czech nationalism which were openly antagonistic to those of the Germans. There was, moreover, no guarantee that such a commitment from the Jews would have been welcomed or even accepted.[11]

Jewish identification with the *de facto* 'master races' of the Empire undoubtedly exacerbated the antagonism of the oppressed nationalities. Austrian Jews appeared in their eyes as adversaries in a dual sense. They were 'assimilators' to the ruling nation (German, Hungarian, Polish) and capitalistic allies of the powerful land-owning classes who exploited the Slav peasantry.[12] But the anti-Semitism of the dominant 'historic' nations, especially of the Germans and Poles, was potentially far more dangerous. Only in Hungary was this reaction moderated by the tacit alliance between the great Magyar aristocracy, the smaller gentry and the Jewish business classes. Nevertheless, even in liberal Hungary after 1875, the parliamentary deputy Gyözö von Istóczy succeeded for the first time in Europe in organizing an explicitly anti-Semitic political movement. By 1882 the Hungarian anti-Semites had five members in Parliament and the elections two years later they reached their peak total of 17 out of 157 deputies.[13]

The Tisza-Eszlar blood libel (1882) greatly aggravated anti-Jewish

[11] See Riff, p. 18. The difficulty was exposed already before 1848 by the Czech national leader Karel Havlíček, who doubted whether Jewish declarations of love for the Czechs could be considered sincere and accepted. See Eduard Goldstücker, 'Jews between Czechs and Germans around 1848, *Leo Baeck Yearbook*, 17 (1972), 67–71; also Kisch, pp. 36–42.

[12] Pulzer, *Political Antisemitism*, 142.

[13] Nathaniel Katzburg, *Ha-Antishemiut be-Hungaria, 1867–1914* (Tel Aviv, 1969), 86–90.

sentiments in Hungary. There were disturbances in Pressburg and other towns, including the capital city of Budapest. Only the strong stand of Prime Minister Tisza and his government against this agitation kept the movement in check. As a result, von Istóczy, who had played a major part in organizing the first international anti-Semitic Congress in Dresden (September 1882), gradually fell into eclipse.[14] Hungarian Judaeophobia, after a flying start, proved to have less stamina than its German counterparts in the Austrian half of the Monarchy.

The new Austrian Pan-German anti-Semitism which surfaced at the end of the 1870s had a more paradoxical character. It was ostensibly nationalist, vehemently denouncing the 'anti-German' policies of the ruling Slav–clerical government coalition which came into office in 1879. At the same time, Pan-Germanism was explicitly disloyal and unpatriotic, since it openly called for the dissolution of the Habsburg dynastic State.[15] Both the nationalist and the anti-dynastical components in its programme contributed to envenoming Pan-German attitudes to the Jews. Above all it was the revolutionary, disintegrative character of the Pan-German movement that would give its anti-Semitism such an extremist edge.

There was a deep and bitter irony in this development, for Pan-Germanism in Austria was partly a creation of liberal-nationalist Jews. From Ignaz Kuranda and Moritz Hartmann in 1848 to Heinrich Friedjung in the 1870s, Austrian Jews had been among the leading promoters of the *grossdeutch* idea. The turning-point came with the Prussian victory of 1866. Pan-Germanism began to assume an explicitly anti-Habsburg, anti-Austrian flavour. Initially, this shift did not deter more radical Jews of the younger generation from sympathizing with its programme. The predominantly Jewish circle around Victor Adler (future leader of Austrian Social Democracy) was, for example, enthusiastically pro-Bismarck and anti-Habsburg after 1870. 'The Austrian Jews were at that time the most ardent representatives of the *Anschluss* idea',[16] the socialist Karl Kautsky recalled in his memoirs. The 'pronounced, intense German nationalism' of this Viennese bourgeois milieu of Jewish lawyers, doctors, journalists, and artists was the 'one thing which divided them all from

---

[14] Katz, pp. 276–80.
[15] See Hannah Arendt, *The Origins of Totalitarianism* (rev. edn., London, 1967), 238.
[16] Benedikt Kautsky (ed.), *Karl Kautsky: Erinnerungen und Erörterungen* (The Hague, 1960), 530–1.

me'.[17] Compared with the loyalist Prague Germans, Karl Kautsky shrewdly observed, 'the [Vienna] Jews were all decidely oppositional, anti-Habsburg, anti-aristocratic, social-liberal. They were enthustiastic nationalists, many of them downright chauvinists. But it was not Jewish nationalism which inspired them . . . No it was German nationalism, Pan-German nationalism'.[18]

'Jewish' Pan-Germanism in Austria still claimed to be republican and anticlerical in the best traditions of 1848. It was in that spirit in 1882 that Heinrich Friedjung and Victor Adler joined with Georg von Schoenerer in formulating the Linz programme of the *deutschnational* movement in Austria.[19] This radical nationalist programme envisaged an end to Austro-Hungarian dualism, calling for the incorporation of Dalmatia, Bosnia, and Herzegovina into Hungary. It demanded autonomy for Galicia and Bukovina. Above all, it advocated the integration of all the German-speaking parts of the Empire into an autonomous German commonwealth to be joined by a customs union to the neighbouring Bismarckian Reich. The size of the Slav population in this commonwealth would be diminished to more manageable proportions. Austro-Germans would none the less be ruling over substantial non-German populations in Bohemia and Moravia, Silesia, Carniola, Istria, Tyrol, and Trieste. The Linz programme also developed a series or radical social demands. These included extension of the suffrage, a tax on Stock Exchange transactions, nationalization of the railways and insurance companies, obligatory trade unions, a progressive income tax, inheritance tax, and the protection of labour by factory laws.[20]

For secularized, emancipated Jewish intellectuals like Adler and Friedjung, democratic Pan-Germanism initially seemed to offer an attractive political option.[21] This new generation already saw themselves as *Germans* in every sense of the word.[22] None the less, the break between von Schoenerer and his assimilated Jewish collaborators came within only a year of the publication of the Linz programme. Already in

---

[17] Kautsky (ed.), *Karl Kautsky*, pp. 530–1.   [18] Ibid.

[19] According to his chief lieutenant, Engelbert Pernerstorfer, 'Aus jungen Tagen', *Der Strom*, no. 2 (July 1912), 98, von Schoenerer was not yet openly anti-Semitic in 1882.

[20] For the Linz programme see E. Pichl, *Georg von Schoenerer und die Entwicklung des Alldeutschtums in der Ostmark* (Oldenburg, 1938), i. 111 ff.; also Klaus Berchthold (ed.), *Österreichische Parteiprogramme 1868–1966* (Munich, 1967), 198–203.

[21] See William J. McGrath, 'Student Radicalism in Vienna', *Journal of Contemporary History*, 2, no. 3 (July 1967), 183–201.

[22] Heinrich Friedjung, *Der Ausgleich mit Ungarn* (Vienna, 1877), 28.

July 1883, in the first issue of his *Unverfälschte Deutsche Worte* (Undiluted German Words), von Schoenerer made it clear that 'if some of the Jews want to join our ranks, they may do so for all I care, but only as simple privates, not in any leading position'.[23] A few years later he openly declared that anti-Semitism was 'the mainstay of our national ideology . . . the most essential expression of genuine popular conviction'.[24]

By 1885 anti-Semitism had become officially enshrined in the Austrian Pan-German programme in spite of the fact that Jews continued to help the Deutsche Schulverein, and Jewish schools in Bohemia, Moravia, Bukovina, and Galicia remained important outposts of the German language.[25] Von Schoenerer's call for an uncompromising racial policy (excluding Jews) did not pass unchallenged in the German National camp. In 1886 it became an issue between the Deutscher Klub (50 members in the Parliament) and the more moderate nationalists of the Deutsch-Österreichischer Klub with 81 deputies. The 'moderates' led by the schoolmaster Otto Steinwender disagreed with von Schoenerer over the 'Jewish question'. However, they also resented having Heinrich Friedjung as their chief spokesman and editor of the *Deutsche Zeitung*, a post from which he was ultimately forced to resign.[26] By 1891 the fiercely nationalist Friedjung was already disillusioned enough to inform Rabbi Joseph Bloch that he had broken with organized German nationalism since it 'was coquetting with anti-Semitism'.[27]

The central issue between von Schoenerer and mainstream German nationalism in Austria did not involve anti-Semitism but rather attitudes towards the Habsburg Monarchy. The Austrian Pan-Germans totally rejected the multinational framework of the Empire. They owed their chief loyalty to the Germanic *Volk*, not to the Austrian State. It was their call for the dismemberment of the Monarchy which would divide them, not only from moderate German nationalists, but also from the clerical anti-Semites in Austria.[28] Hatred of the

---

[23] *Unverfälschte deutsche Worte*, 1 July 1883.   [24] Pichl, i. 316–17.

[25] On the prominence of Jews in the Deutsche Schulverein and its increasingly anti-Semitic policy see P. G. J. Pulzer, 'The Austrian Liberals and the Jewish Question, 1867–1914', *Journal of Central European Affairs*, 33 (1963), 137 ff.

[26] See Erich Zailer, 'Heinrich Friedjung unter besonderer Berücksichtigung seiner politischen Entwicklung' (Univ. of Vienna, Ph.D. diss, 1949), 51–2; William J. McGrath, *Dionysian Art and Populist Politics in Austria* (New Haven and London, 1974), 74–7, 198–207, 310 ff.   [27] *Österreichische Wochenschrift*, 20 Mar. 1891.

[28] Robert S. Wistrich, 'Georg von Schoenerer and the genesis of modern Austrian antisemitism', in Wistrich (ed.), *European Antisemitism*, 20–9.

supranational Habsburgs was closely linked to the ideological world-view of Pan-German anti-Semites. In their eyes the Jews appeared as a 'state-people' in Austria, as the group whose fortunes were most closely tied to the central power, to the Habsburg Emperor, and to the corrupt liberal system.[29] Precisely because the Jews could be seen as 'the supra-national people of the multi-national state' and therefore as one of the centripetal symbols of the Monarchy, they were almost predestined to become a target for Pan-German secessionists. Carl Schorske's summary hits the nail on the head: 'If the emperor was supra-national, the Jews were subnational, the omnipresent folk substance of the Empire, whose representatives could be found in every national and every creedal grouping. In whatever group they functioned, the Jews never strove to dismember the Empire.'[30] Once the disintegration of the dynasty became a crucial element in von Schoenerer's political creed, anti-Semitism was its inevitable corollary. It was, moreover, extraordinarily functional, enabling Pan-Germans 'to be simultaneously anti-socialist, anticapitalist, anti-Catholic, anti-liberal, and anti-Habsburg'.[31]

The uncompromising nature of von Schoenerer's opposition to the Habsburgs proved however to be a political liability to his movement. Open disloyalty to the dynasty and to the Austrian fatherland made it difficult for the 'Knight from Rosenau' to maintain his earlier position as leader of the democratic opposition in Austria. It was primarily his unpatriotic extremism that repelled the provincial German-speaking middle class in Austria which remained this main electoral constituency. Von Schoenerer's authoritarian personality also played a considerable role in his demise by alienating former collaborators like Pattai, Lueger, Schneider, Vergani, Steinwender, Wolf, Friedjung, Adler, and Pernerstorfer.[32] They eventually turned to Christian Socialism, Social Democracy, or moderate German nationalism. Each in his own way understood that open war on the Habsburgs was not a great vote-catching formula. The Deutsche Volkspartei, under the Carinthian

---

[29] Arendt, ch. 2.

[30] Carl E. Schorske, *Fin-de-siècle Vienna: Politics and Culture* (London, 1979), 119. The radical nationalists like Friedjung and Adler were ambiguous on this point though *Anschluss* with Germany was clearly their ultimate goal.

[31] Ibid. 130.

[32] See Andrew G. Whiteside, *The Socialism of Fools: Georg Ritter von Schoenerer and Austrian Pan-Germanism* (Berkeey and Los Angeles, 1975) on these splits. Also P. G. J. Pulzer, 'The Development of Political Antisemitism in Austria', in Josef Fraenkel (ed.), *The Jews of Austria: Essays on their Life, History and Destruction* (London, 1967), 435–6.

schoolmaster Otto Steinwender, remained loyal to the Empire and confined itself to vague generalities about 'liberation from Jewish influence'.[33] It consistently did better than von Schoenerer's Pan-Germans at the polls.[34] Nevertheless, Steinwender, like the Christian-Socialists and even the Austrian socialists, felt obliged to engage in a conventional mode of anti-Semitic rhetoric. This was itself an indirect tribute to von Schoenerer's success in transforming the 'Jewish question' into an unavoidable political issue.

Von Schoenerer's biological anti-Semitism was undoubtedly the most radical of the many existing varieties in pre–1914 Austria. It was an uninhibited racial ideology which distinguished sharply between 'Aryans' and 'Semites'. Even the despised Czechs and Slovenes were regarded as 'Aryans'. With them the conflict was only temporary, unlike the 'eternal', biological necessity of combating the Jew.[35] In the first issue of his new journal *Unverfälschte Deutsche Worte* in 1883, von Schoenerer proclaimed that from a 'brutal racial point of view', the mixing of Jews and Germans was inadmissible: '. . . we must on the contrary declare that we rather consider possible a mixing . . . with Slavs and Latins than any intimate connection with the Jews. For the former are related to us as Aryans, while the latter are totally alien to us on account of their origin . . .'[36]

Von Schoenerer regarded the war on the Jew as 'a basic pillar of the national idea, as the principal means of promoting genuine national [*volkstümlich*] convictions, and therefore as the greatest national achievement of this century'.[37] Anti-Semitism thereby became a major yardstick for differentiating between *authentic* German nationalism and liberal betrayers of the *Volk* who 'consciously support Jewry and its agents'.[38] The war against 'International Jewry' clearly implied an assault *within* the German national camp against inauthentic 'Judaized liberalism' and its subservience to the 'supra-national money-power'.

Since 1879 a more conventional anticapitalist anti-Semitism directed against 'the Semitic rule of money and the press' had also been part of

[33] Whiteside, *Socialism of Fools*.
[34] Pulzer, 'Development of Political Antisemitism', 435; Wistrich, 'Georg von Schoenerer', 26–8.
[35] E. v. von Rudolf, *Georg Ritter von Schönerer: Der Vater des politischen Antisemitismus* (Munich, 1936), 33–4.
[36] Quoted in F. L. Carsten, *Fascist Movements in Austria: From Schönerer to Hitler* (London, 1977), 15.
[37] Rudolf, p. 34.
[38] Ibid.; also Pichl, i. 316–17.

von Schoenerer's national-social program.[39] In 1882, at the first meeting of the Österreichische Reformverein (a Reform association founded to relieve the economic distress of Viennese artisans) von Schoenerer fiercely attacked the Jew as 'the sucking vampire . . . that knocks at the narrow-windowed house of the German farmer and craftsman'.[40] At first, a regular speaker at the Reformverein, von Schoenerer broke with the new organization because of its Austrian dynastic patriotism.

In 1884 von Schoenerer was still the recognized leader of radical opposition in Austria to the clerical-conservative Taafe regime. He led the fight for the nationalization of the Rothschild-owned Kaiser-Ferdinand-Nordbahn railway, accusing Jewish bankers, the Habsburg court, and Ministers of 'transport usury' at the expense of the public. His populist campaign which achieved wide notoriety and coverage in the press was regarded by the liberal *Neue Freie Presse* as 'communistic'.[41] Only in May 1885 did von Schoenerer finally add the infamous *Judenpunkt* to the Linz programme. This made the 'removal of Jewish influence from all areas of public life' a necessary prerequisite to achieving any national-social reform programme.[42]

Following his adoption of anti-Semitism and the extension of the franchise to those who paid a minimum annual tax of five florins, von Schoenerer at first increased his electoral support. By 1887 six of his followers sat in the Austrian Reichsrat, all of them elected in the lower income Third and Fourth Curias.[43] In the same year, von Schoenerer introduced an anti-Semitic bill in the Austrian Parliament, designed to prohibit the immigration of Russian Jews into the Empire. A classic document of late nineteenth-century Austrian anti-Semitism, it began with a short preamble about the need to 'protect the rights and interests of the honest working classes', in view of the fact that 'Jewry . . . is already obtaining a position of supreme power in our country'.[44] The parliamentary bill for which von Schoenerer had

[39] Pichl, i. 84–7.

[40] Ibid. ii. 25–6; Schorske, p. 128.

[41] *Neue Freie Presse*, 22 Apr. 1884. Schoenerer's father had counselled the Rothschilds in the construction of the railway many years before. For the psychoanalytic implications—i.e. anti-Semitism as a form of Oedipal rebellion—see Schorske, pp. 121–8. For details of the campaign, William A. Jenks, *Austria under the Iron Ring, 1879–1893* (Charlottesville, Val., 1965), 141–57.

[42] Pichl, i. 115; Rudolf, p. 56.

[43] Pulzer, *Rise of Political Antisemitism*, 154.

[44] For the text of this bill see Rudolf, p. 58; reproduced in L. Graf von Westphalen (ed.), *Geschichte des Antisemitismus in Deutschland* (Stuttgart, 1967), 49–50.

obtained 37,068 signatures openly described 'these foreign people, the Jews', as:

enemies of Christian culture and of nations of Aryan descent, not only of the Germans but of the other Austrian nations as well, considering that as a result of the continuous increase of the Jewish element, Jews are obtaining more and more monopoly positions in important branches of business and that in particular, the Jewish owned press fosters corruption, so as to jeopardize the public order'.[45]

The Pan-German proposals demanded 'strict regulation of immigration and settlement of alien Jews in Austria', predicting that 'it cannot be long before the indigenous Jews are placed under a special law'.[46] Georg Ritter von Schoenerer was now at the peak of his political career. Since the early 1880s he had enjoyed ardent support among German university students in Vienna, Graz, and Prague.[47] He was clearly the acknowledged leader of German nationalism in the eyes of German gymnastics clubs in Vienna, Lower Austria, and the Alpine lands. Following his example, they no longer accepted Jewish members.[48] Schoenerer was no less of a hero figure for German nationalist elements in the professional middle classes (doctors, lawyers, teachers, and accountants), resentful of Jewish competition. Above all, in the rural Alpine areas and among border-Germans in Silesia and Bohemia (where the Slav challenge was more acute) von Schoenerer maintained a strong popular constituency.[49]

The university students were from the beginning the most aggressively racist and anti-Semitic of all the Pan-German supporters.[50] Since 1878, the *Burschenschaften* (student fraternities) in Vienna had begun to exclude Jews from their membership. The trend spread rapidly throughout the Empire, affecting school associations, gymnastic clubs (*Turnvereine*), and German societies.[51] Like von Schoenerer, the university students took their cue from Berlin. In the student

[45] Ibid.   [46] Ibid.

[47] On the racial anti-Semitism among Austrian university students see Karl Beurle, *Beiträge zur Geschichte der deutschen Studentschaft Wiens* (Vienna, 1892), 50 ff.; O. Scheuer, *Burschenschaft und Judenfrage: Der Rassenantisemitismus in der deutschen Studentenschaft* (Berlin, 1927), 45; Paul Molisch, *Die deutschen Hochschulen in Österreich und die politisch-nationale Entwicklung nach 1848* (Munich, 1922).

[48] Carsten, pp. 10–11, 15–16.

[49] For a detailed occupational breakdown of von Schoenerer's constituency, see Dirk van Arkel, *Antisemitism in Austria* (Leiden, 1966), 136 ff.

[50] Pichl, i. 85 ii. 320; also Paul Molisch, *Geschichte der deutsch-national Bewegung in Österreich von ihren Anfängen bis zum Zerfall der Monarchie* (Jena, 1926).

[51] Carsten, pp. 37–8; Pulzer, *Rise of Political Antisemitism*, 223; Pichl, vi. 314.

community, pro-Prussian sentiment had been strong since the Austrian defeat of 1866. Nothing had underlined the decadence of the Habsburg Monarchy in the eyes of the younger generation more than this débâcle. Its immediate consequence was the exclusion of Austria from the new German Empire built by Bismarck. This greatly intensified German feelings of isolation and Slavophobia in Austria. The *Wacht am Rhein* now became the rallying-cry for German students at Austrian universities. Veneration for Bismarck and pride in the neighbouring Hohenzollern Reich was transformed into an article of faith. In these circles, insulting the Austrian flag and mocking the national anthem became commonplace. It is scarcely surprising that in this milieu von Schoenerer's enmity to the Habsburgs and to Slavdom as well as his racial anti-Semitism acquired an irresistable resonance.

Anti-Semitism in the Austrian student corporations was motivated by mundane fears of Jewish competition no less than by ultranationalist fanaticism. At the University of Vienna in 1880, 22.3 per cent of the law students and 38.6 per cent of those reading medicine were Jews. By 1889–90 the proportion of Jewish teaching staff in the faculty of medicine reached 48 per cent.[52] The fact that many poor Jewish students from Hungary and Galicia flocked to the medical faculty had already aroused apprehensions in 1876. The distinguished Viennese surgeon Theodor Billroth (later prominent in the Austrian association *against* anti-Semitism) anxiously observed in that year that 'a Jew is as little able to become a German as can a Persian or a Frenchman, or a New Zealander, or an African'.[53] Racial anti-Semitism, by stressing the ineradicably 'alien' character of the Jews, promised to exclude them from the liberal professions where they were becoming serious competitors for the sons of the German-Austrian *Mittelstand*. The influx of Jews was seen by this stratum as a dangerous threat to their future prospects as an élite group. Economic competition undoubtedly heightened the attraction for Austro-German students of the 'non-confessional' *völkisch* anti-Semitism pioneered in Bismarckian Germany by Richard Wagner, Wilhelm Marr, Eugen Dühring, and Paul de Lagarde.[54]

---

[52] Carsten, p. 11.

[53] Theodor Billroth, *Über das Lehren und Lernen der medizinischen Wissenschaften an den Universitäten der deutschen Nation* (Vienna, 1876), 152–3.

[54] On German racial anti-Semitism there is a huge literature. See in particular Fritz Stern, *The Politics of Cultural Despair: A Study in the Rise of the Germanic Ideology* (Berkeley and Los Angeles, 1961); Uriel Tal, *Christians and Jews in the 'Second Reich'*

According to this racial ideology, even Germanized Jews were not only 'alien' to the German spirit but responsible for the mammonization of European society and culture. In the writings of Dühring and de Lagarde, the call for *Entjudung* (de-Jewification) was explicit. It clearly implied the abolition of Jewish emancipation. Henceforth, eradication of the Jewish *Geist* (spirit) from the culture of the Germanic peoples would become an irresistable slogan for the nationalist student fraternities in Germany and Austria. If anything, the Austrian students were even more radical than their German counterparts in the Reich.[55] The Austrian student convention at its Conference in Waidhofen (1896) formulated the ideology of Germanic racism in inimitable prose:

In full appreciation of the fact that there is so deep a moral and physical difference between Aryans and Jews, and that our special character [*Eigenart*] has already suffered so much from Jewish trickery [*Unwesen*]; in full appreciation of the many proofs which the Jewish student has also provided of his lack of honour [*Ehrlosigkeit*] and character, and since he in any case is wholly destitute of honour according to our German concepts, today's conference of German student fencing corporations resolves: no Jew is to be given satisfaction with any weapon'.[56]

Alarmed at the prospect of losing their élite privileges, the Pan-German fraternities fervently advocated biological racism. No doubt, as Henry Wickham Steed observed, they had also become apprehensive of duelling with Jewish nationalist fencing corporations like Kadimah which were more than capable of meeting their challenge: '... presently the best fencers of the fighting German corps found that Zionist students could gash cheeks quite as effectively as any Teuton and that the Jews were in a fair way to become the best swordsmen of the University'.[57] In the closing decades before 1914, the *deutschnational* students directed their increasingly violent and racist agitation not only against Jews but also against Catholic, socialist, and Italian students in Vienna.[58] Their hatred for the sclerotic Habsburg state and its

(1870–1914) (Hebrew edn., Jerusalem, 1969), 205–24; Jacob Katz, *From Prejudice to Destruction: Anti-Semitism, 1700–1933* (Cambridge, Mass., 1982), 260–9.

[55] Wistrich, 'Georg von Schoenerer', 26–7.
[56] *Unverfälschte deutsche Worte*, 1 Apr. 1896.
[57] Henry Wickham Steed, *The Habsburg Monarchy* (London, 1913), 176.
[58] See John Haag, 'Blood on the Ringstrasse: Vienna's Students 1918–33', in Wistrich (ed.), *European Antisemitism*, 29 ff.

Catholic supporters were especially marked, echoing von Schoenerer's vehement denunciations of Rome. The Pan-Germans suspected Catholic students of dual loyalty. Enthustiastically, they adopted von Schoenerer's slogan: '*ohne Judah, ohne Rom wird gebaut Germaniens Dom.*'[59] Revulsion against Austrian clericalism was nothing new among German nationalist students. Indeed it had a long history going back to the *Vormärz* period. Before 1848 the Catholic Church had been identified in student circles with absolutism, censorship, and Metternich's repressive Carlsbad decrees.[60]

The romantic, revolutionary, and anticlerical spirit of 1848 never wholly disappeared in the German-Austrian *Burschenschaften*. Memories of 1848 when the students' Academic legion fought the absolutist Habsburg regime carried over into the Pan-German agitation fifty years later against the Habsburgs and Rome.[61] Georg von Schoenerer and his followers campaigned tirelessly in favour of civil education and lay marriage. They even organized a *Los von Rom* (Break with Rome) movement which aimed at the mass conversion of all Austro-Germans to Lutheranism, in order to facilitate *Anschluss* with the Prusso-German Reich. From the end of the 1890s von Schoenerer called for the break with Rome 'in the hope of the final victory of Germandom over the un-German, quarrelsome, Roman Church'.[62] The campaign to uproot totally the Jesuit 'spirit of intrigue', along with the fight against the supranational power of 'Judah' and the Slav threat, became one of the central planks in the Austrian Pan-German programme after 1900.

Though von Schoenerer publicly embraced Lutheranism, his personal religion was in reality much closer to Teutonic paganism with its cult of 2,000 years of Germanic tribal history. Not for nothing did the Pan-Germans install a new Germanic calendar with the year One (113 BC) to commemorate the victory of the Cimbri and Teutonic tribes over the Romans.[63] Von Schoenerer even tried to resurrect old Germanic names for the months of the year. Many of the *Turnvereine*, cycling clubs, and other para-political organizations associated with his movement adopted names evocative of Germanic tribal history. This neo-paganism sharpened still more the gulf between Austrian

---

[59] Rudolf, p. 87.

[60] Pulzer, *Rise of Political Antisemitism*, 248 ff.

[61] Wistrich, 'George von Schoenerer', 26.

[62] For the original 'Los-von-Rom' Manifesto of Nov. 1898, see Pulzer, *Rise of Political Antisemitism*, 343–4.

[63] Ibid. 208.

Pan-Germanism and the Christian-Social party which anchored its appeal in popular Catholic tradition.

Though twenty-one of his followers were elected to the Imperial Parliament in 1901 following a wave of German national unrest in Bohemia, von Schoenerer ultimately failed to build a great mass movement in Habsburg Austria. His paranoid political style turned him into his own worst enemy. The raid which he led in 1888 on the editorial offices of the liberal newspaper *Neues Wiener Tageblatt* (owned by Moritz Szeps) proved to be the most fateful case in point. It led to his conviction on charges of assault and battery, a brief prison sentence, loss of title, and a five-year suspension of political rights.[64] By his own intemperate behaviour, von Schoenerer had provided the Austrian authorities with a convenient pretext to curb a movement whose extremism was clearly perceived as a danger to public order and to the Habsburg State itself. Von Schoenerer's virtual disappearance from the political scene for five crucial years enabled his arch-rival Karl Lueger (1844–1910) to take his place as leader of the antiliberal, anticapitalist, anti-Semitic movement in German Austria.

The Viennese-born Lueger, in contrast to von Schoenerer, did not come from the Austrian backwoods. Nor did he attempt to reduce his homeland to a mere appendage of Greater Germany. Lueger had never been a Pan-German, let alone an enemy of the Habsburg dynasty, though in the early 1890s his Christian-Social movement spoke a social-revolutionary language which alarmed court circles and the Austrian ecclesiastical establishment. However, Lueger's anti-Semitism always lacked the rigid ideological consistency and racial fanaticism that characterized von Schoenerer's Pan-Germans.[65] As the leader of a 'patriotic' (*schwarzgelb*) party which aspired to become the backbone of a regenerated Austrian State, Lueger was bound to clash with Pan-Germans and to distance himself from their radical anti-Semitism.[66] The Christian Socialists had never indulged in the Pan-German idolization of Bismarck or of the powerful Hohenzollern Reich. Above all, von Schoenerer's *Los-von-Rom* movement threatened one of their most cherished goals, namely the *re-Christianization* of

---

[64] See 'Die Affaire Schönerer', *Gleichheit*, 17 Mar. 1888, p. 1.

[65] John Boyer, 'Karl Lueger and the Viennese Jews', *Leo Baeck Yearbook*, 26 (1981), 137–40; Robert S. Wistrich, 'Karl Lueger and the Ambiguities of Viennese Antisemitism', *Jewish Social Studies*, 45 (1983), 251–62.

[66] For one of the earliest critical surveys of the differences between the two movements, see Oskar Karbach, 'The Founder of Political Antisemitism: Georg von Schoenerer', *Jewish Social Studies* 7 (1945), 3–31.

Austria through a popular mass movement allied to the Catholic Church.

These differences sharpened, once the Christian Socialists achieved their dream of conquering Vienna (to which end they had briefly collaborated with the Pan-Germans) and then began to expand their support into the Austrian countryside. However, during the formative period of the Lueger movement between 1889 and 1897, parallels between Pan-Germanism and Christian Socialism had been much more striking. Carl Schorske has already noted some of the similarities in political style between von Schoenerer and Lueger, the two leading Austrian tribunes of anti-Semitism:

Both men began as liberals, both criticized liberalism initially from a social and democratic viewpoint, and both ended as apostates, espousing anti-liberal creeds. Both used anti-Semitism to mobilize the same unstable elements in the population: artisans and students. And—crucial for our purposes—both developed the techniques of extra-parliamentary politics, the politics of the rowdy and the mob'.[67]

As early as 1883, when he was a radical Democrat, Lueger had still identified himself with von Schoenerer's campaign to nationalize the Nordbahn railroad, owned by the Rothschilds. He supported the Pan-German leader in Vienna's city council and in political agitation among the lower middle-class strata in the capital.[68] Like von Schoenerer he also participated in the anti-Semitic Austrian Reform Verein, appearing with him at various meetings and public platforms in the early 1880s. Despite a certain reluctance fully to commit himself to anti-Semitism, Lueger supported the Pan-German bill in May 1887 to stop foreign Jewish immigration. This was the decisive step which presaged his final break with the radical wing of Austro-liberalism. In the late 1880s the 'Jewish question' would provide common ground between the Pan-Germans and what came to be known as the *Vereinigte Christen* (United Christians). A decade later, the Christian Socialists still tolerated a brutal variant of anti-Semitism in their own ranks, exemplified by plebeian demagogues such as Ernst Schneider (1845–1913), Ernst Vergani (1848–1915), or the Catholic priests Joseph Deckert (1843–1901) and Father Abel (1843–1926), which scarcely lagged behind that of von Schoenerer.[69]

[67] Schorske, p. 133.
[68] Kurt Skalnik, *Dr. Karl Lueger: Der Mann zwischen den Zeiten* (Vienna and Munich, 1954), 43.
[69] See, e.g., Joseph Deckert's pamphlets, *Der ewige Jude 'Ahasver'* (Vienna, 1894), and

This is less than surprising, when one recalls that key figures in the Christian-Social party like Schneider, Vergani, or the parliamentary deputy Robert Pattai had once been nationalist anti-Semites who frequently shared a common platform with von Schoenerer. They had split with him out of opportunism or impatience at his personal intransigence.[70] The *Deutsche Volksblatt*, edited by Ernst Vergani, once a close colleague of von Schoenerer, was indubitably a *völkisch*, racist newspaper. It went over to the Christian-Socialists when it was evident that Karl Lueger would emerge as Vienna's leading anti-Semitic politician.[71] Vergani exemplified that variant of Christian-Social *Geschäftsantisemitismus*, which exploited Jew-baiting to accumulate private wealth and gain political influence.[72] His semi-pornographic scandal-sheet reflected the blurring of frontiers in the 1890s between 'Christian' and racist anti-Semitism in the world of Viennese gutter journalism. The philosophy of the beercellar which animated this 'Christian-Social' newspaper scarcely differentiated between Jews and converts. Nor, for that matter, did the parish priest Joseph Deckert, who tirelessly proclaimed from his Vienna pulpit in the 1890s that Jews murdered Christian children for ritual purposes. This popular Catholic preacher openly disseminated racialist anti-Semitism.[73]

The dividing-line between 'Christian' and racial anti-Semitism was even more difficult to trace in the case of the mechanic Ernst Schneider. An effective organizer of the craft guilds and one of Lueger's most trusted lieutenants, his knowledge of artisans' conditions in Vienna was probably unrivalled among party colleagues. Schneider regularly indulged in the most blood-curdling threats against Austrian Jewry. During a parliamentary debate in 1901 he declared:

The Jewish question is a racial question, a question of blood, a culture question, which can be solved only by blood and iron as hundreds of thousands of years of ancient history has taught not only our people, but all peoples, and you will not escape this truth. I am not engaged in any discussion of Jewish baptism, but I will say this: if I had to baptize Jews, then I should follow though

---

Semitische und antisemitische Schlagworte in Doppelbeleuchtung (Vienna, 1897); also Arkel, pp. 88–90, and Joseph S. Bloch, *My Reminiscences* (Vienna and Berlin, 1923), 383–5, 564–8.

[70] Wistrich, 'Georg von Schoenerer', 28.   [71] Arkel, pp. 88–90.

[72] 'Ein Streit über "Rassenantisemitismus" und "christlichen Antisemitismus"', *Arbeiterzeitung*, 9 July 1897, p. 2; 25 July 1897, p. 2; 15 Aug. 1897, pp. 4–5; also 'Gessmann, Vergani und Friedmann', 9 June 1911, pp. 1–2.

[73] I. A. Hellwing, *Der Konfessionelle Antisemitismus im 19. Jahrhundert in Österreich* (Vienna, 1972), 185 ff.

in somewhat improved fashion, the method of St John, he held them under water for baptism, but I should immerse them for the duration of five minutes.[74]

It should be noted that in the course of debates in the Austrian Parliament in 1898 and 1899, Schneider made speeches which called in all seriousness for bounties (*Schussgeld*) to be paid for shooting Jews, as if they were harmful birds of prey.[75]

Karl Lueger, more refined and intelligent, generally avoided such language. Nevertheless his anti-Jewish discourse was by no means immune from the bloodthirsty idiom of the Viennese streets. In a Reichsrat debate on 13 February 1890 Lueger spoke in terms that recalled the diatribes of Ernst Schneider.

Wolves, panthers, and tigers are human compared to these beasts of prey in human form. The chief generator of anti-Semitism was the Jewish liberal press. Its corruption and monstrous terrorism was bound to give rise to a counter-movement from within the nation . . . We do not shout 'Hep, Hep', but we object to Christians being oppressed and we object to the old Christian Austrian Empire being replaced by a new Jewish Empire. It is not hatred for the individual, not hatred for the poor, the small Jew. No, gentlemen, we do not hate anything except the oppressive big capital which is in the hands of the Jews.[76]

In the early 1890s Lueger constantly harped on the theme that the Christian *Volk* of Vienna were no longer the 'masters in their home'. Exploited by 'anti-Christian' Jews who monopolized industry, commerce, and banking, the 'little man' was threatened with economic disaster. Lueger's movement also echoed the language of an Austrian clerical tradition of Judaeophobia dating back to the populist rhetoric of the seventeenth-century preacher, Abraham a Sancta Clara.[77] Medieval superstition and modern social protest fused together in the new movement constantly energized by the resentment of the *Spiessbürger* against Jewish capital and high finance. Racial and religious conflicts generated by the slow industrialization of the Habsburg lands, by the economic crisis of the Viennese petty

[74] 'Stenographische Protokolle über die Sitzungen des Hauses der Abgeordneten des Reichsrates', XVII Session, VII–VIII, p. 7044, 22 Oct. 1901.
[75] See Gustav Kolmer, *Parlament und Verfassung in Österreich*, 6 vols. (Leipzig, 1902–14), vi. 408.
[76] Quoted in Richard Kralik, *Karl Lueger und der christliche Sozialismus* (Vienna, 1925), i. 52 ff.
[77] On Abraham a Sancta Clara see Robert A. Kann, *A Study in Austrian Intellectual History: From Late Baroque to Romanticism* (London, 1960), 78 ff.

bourgeosié, and by the prominent role of Jews in Austrian capitalism fuelled the concrete *social* demands represented by Lueger's party. But it was the existence of a deeply rooted religous tradition of popular anti-Semitism which virtually ensured that the Jews would become the primary target of the Viennese petty-bourgeois masses.[78] The constantly recurring blood libels in German Austria, Hungary, Bohemia, and Galicia before 1914 testify to the potency of Catholic traditions in modern anti-Semitic agitation.

Ever since 1848 Catholic circles had been the chief instigators in Austria of hostile propaganda against the Jews. In the 1860s and 1870s Sebastian Brunner and his successor as editor of the *Wiener Kirchenzeitung*, Albert Wiesinger, had carried on a persistent though unsuccessful campaign against the liberal social order and Jewish emancipation. Brunner argued that the 'Jewish question' was not just a religious but also a national question, for the Jews 'according to their morals, language and customs form a special oriental nation, separate from us, which itself regards us as aliens and explicitly recognizes that it does not belong to us . . .'.[79]

The conservative Brunner served as the bridge in Austria between traditional Christian anti-Judaism and its modern transformation into an anticapitalist, antiliberal, and racist ideology. An ordained priest and preacher, he consistently presented the Jews as the symbols *par excellence* of a destructive modernity, inimical not only to the Church but to Austrian society and culture as a whole. His successor, Albert Wiesinger, was more radical, seeking to influence the unsophisticated masses through popular brochures which denounced 'Jewish capitalists and spendthrifts' as exploiters of 'poor Christians and starvelings'.[80] This social demagogy juxtaposing Jewish capital and Christian labour anticipated a central motif of Christian-Social propaganda. But in an era of liberal-rationalist hegemony, the time was not yet ripe for its popular acceptance.

Similarly, the scandalous work, *Der Talmudjude* (1871), written by the Catholic Professor of Semitic languages at the University of Prague, August Rohling, achieved a significant impact in the

[78] Erika Weinzierl, 'Antisemitismus als österreichisches Phänomen', *Die Republik* (Vienna), 3 (1970), 28–35).

[79] 'Wo wird die Judenemanzipation enden?', *Wiener Kirchenzeitung*, 25 Jan. 1860, p. 59.

[80] See the pamphlet by Albert Wiesinger, *Arme Christen und Hungerleider, jüdische Kapitalisten und Geldvergeuder* (Vienna, 1870).

Monarchy only at the beginning of the 1880s.[81] Rohling's diatribe against Talmudic Judaism was essentially a vulgar rehash of the earlier German work by Andreas Eisenmenger, *Entdecktes Judentum* (1701). It was the Tisza-Eszlar affair in Hungary (1882) and the anti-Semitic electoral campaign of the Hungarian politician, Victor von Istóczy, which first ensured the dissemination of Rohling's ideas to a wider public in the Monarchy.[82] In 1882 the Viennese journalist Franz Holubek exploited Rohling's academic authority for his own incitement against the Talmud. Holubek was arrested but duly acquitted of causing religious and racial incitement at a sensational trial in Vienna.[83] The ritual-murder charges in Hungary were proved to be without any foundation and Rohling was eventually exposed in a Viennese court in 1885 by the indefatigable Rabbi Joseph Bloch as a liar and forger. Yet the damage to Jewry was considerable, encouraging Austrian anti-Semites to persist in their blood-libel allegations. Rohling's charges that the Talmud required Jews to oppress Christians mercilessly found many willing listeners among the impoverished Viennese artisans, craftsmen, and small businessmen.

If Rohling represented the vulgar, disreputable side of Catholic anti-Semitism in Austria, Baron Karl von Vogelsang (1818–90) was its more human face. The chief ideologue of Christian socialism, this North German Protestant convert to Catholicism lived in Vienna from 1859 until his death in 1890. Since 1875 he had edited the Vienna-based *Das Vaterland*, the organ of clerical-conservative circles in Austria, using it to promote his romantic, neo-feudal vision of a corporate state based on Christian moral principles.[84] The main targets of his newspaper were liberalism, the Jews, capitalist society,

---

[81] On the Rohling affair, see Hellwing, pp. 71–183, for relevant documents and Bloch, *My Reminiscences*, 30 ff.

[82] Arkel, p. 20; Hellwing, pp. 105–9. Rohling volunteered to testify in the Hungarian trial that Jews required Christian blood for the Passover festival.

[83] See Bloch, *My Reminiscences*, 61 ff. At a gathering in Vienna in Apr. 1882 attended by some 500 participants, Holubek, after claiming that Jews had proved themselves unworthy of emancipation, told his audience: 'Judge if such a people [the Jews] has any right of existence amidst civilized society . . . This book, the Talmud! Do you know what this book contains? The Truth! And do you know how you are described in this book? As a herd of pigs, dogs, and asses!' At the trial he was defended by the German nationalist lawyer, Dr Robert Pattai, and his acquittal seemed to confirm the charges he had made against the Talmud.

[84] The most important source for Vogelsang's teachings is the work by his son-in-law Wiard Klopp, *Die sozialen Lehren des Freiherrn von Vogelsang: Grundzüge einer christlichen Gesellschafts-und Volkswirtschaftslehre* (St. Pölten, 1894).

materialism, atheism, and nihilism. For von Vogelsang these were the deleterious results of the dechristianization of state and society.

There was a certain similarity between von Vogelsang's critique of economic activity as an end in itself and that of Karl Marx, which also extended to their views on the 'Jewish question'. Von Vogelsang even quoted from Marx's *Zur Judenfrage* (1844) to buttress his conviction that the victory of capitalism had meant the emancipation of the Jews, who had no God but Mammon.[85] He agreed with Marx that modern Christians had become 'Jews'; that capitalism and the 'Jewish spirit' were essentially synonymous. Baron von Vogelsang gave a specifically *Christian* tinge to such concepts, thereby staking out the ideological divide between Christian Socialism and Marxism. Similarly, he rejected the assumption of Germanic racism that Jews as a group had a special monopoly on godless behaviour, materialism, or capitalist greed. In 1875 von Vogelsang wrote in *Das Vaterland*: 'If by some miracle all our 1,400,000 Jews were to be taken from us, it would help us very little, for we ourselves have been infected with the Jewish spirit'.[86] It was insights such as these which won the respect of the Austro-Marxist theoretician Otto Bauer, a Jewish intellectual who admired von Vogelsang's critique of *laissez-faire* capitalism, though rejecting his Christian corporatist panaceas.[87]

Das Vaterland constantly deplored the dissolution of organic, Christian-feudal values as a result of commercial capitalism and the influence of the big-city press. Though not a systematic anti-Semite, von Vogelsang believed like Brunner before him that the capitalist 'spirit' of Judaism had undermined the traditional social order. Only a restoration of Catholic morality could save Austria from 'Jewish tyranny'.[88] Von Vogelsang did not conceal his anxiety at the 'Judaization' (*Verjudung*) which had overtaken European society since the Enlightenment and French Revolution. In his view, this trend had reached its peak in the 1870s, the era of triumphant, 'Jewish' materialism and liberal permissiveness. He argued that only a truly Christian people would be able 'to receive and absorb the Jew without becoming Judaized [*verjudet*]; but a people which has fallen away in its faith, morality and law from Christianity must crawl . . . and expect to be dominated, robbed and reduced to a pariah by the Jews'.[89]

[85] Ibid. 631. [86] *Das Vaterland*, 10 Oct. 1875.
[87] Otto Bauer, 'Das Ende des Christliche Socialismus', *Der Kampf* (1910–11, iv. 393–8.
[88] Klopp, p. 194. [89] Ibid. 187.

In contrast to the racial anti-Semites, von Vogelsang stressed the centrality of the religious factor. In his view, *re-Christianization* was the only solution to the 'Judaization' of Austrian society and culture. For the *völkisch* prophets of race, the Catholic faith itself was a source of 'Judaization', a symbol of the 'enemy within'. To von Vogelsang's mind it was the key to redemption. Nevertheless, the aristocratic *Das Vaterland* under his editorship contributed greatly to the diffusion of a negative dualistic stereotype of the Jew in Vienna and Lower Austria: that of the wealthy Jewish manufacturer, banker, and capitalist exploiting the honest Christian artisans and tradesmen[90]—and his counterpart—the anticlerical, subversive, Jewish revolutionary seeking to destroy the foundations of traditional society. Lueger's populist movement inherited these powerful negative stereotypes and effectively disseminated the myth of an 'incredibly insolent *Judenpresse*', regarded by Vogelsang as an insidious enemy of the Christian masses.[91]

Probably the most important political legacy of von Vogelsang was the creation of the Christlich-sozialer Verein in 1887, implemented by his Tyrolese Catholic disciple, Ludwig Psenner (1834–1917), together with Adam Latchka. This association was to become the focus of antiliberal agitation in Austria and the nucleus of the future Christian-Social party.[92] It included, among its top leadership, aristocrats like Prince von Liechtenstein, Viennese artisans like Ernst Schneider, the nationalist lawyer Robert Pattai (1846–1920), the theologian Franz Schindler, and the 'democrat' Karl Lueger. The motley alliance was assembled into the formidable Vereinigte Christen in 1889. It was this organization, later transformed under Lueger's dynamic leadership into the Christlich-soziale Partei, that would overthrow the bastions of liberal hegemony in the Vienna municipal council and the Lower Austrian Diet during the late 1890s.

The United Christian manifesto of 1889 was explicitly anti-Semitic, reflecting the growing radicalization among the Viennese lower middle classes. It called for the exclusion of Jews from the professions (medicine, law, etc.), from teaching in Christian schools, from the civil service and the judiciary, as well as demanding restrictions on Jewish immigration.[93] The 'Jewish question' had emerged by 1889 as a central political theme in the United Christian alliance of clerical conservatives, German nationalists, racial anti-Semites, social reformers, disillusioned

---

[90] Klopp, p. 436.   [91] See Pulzer, *Rise of Political Antisemitism*, 133–4.
[92] Friedrich Funder, *Von Gestern ins Heute* (Vienna, 1952), 95.
[93] Pulzer, *Rise of Political Antisemitism*, 171–5.

ex-liberals, and radical democrats. It was the one issue which could unite the heterogeneous class constituency of the new movement while at the same time ensuring the crucial support of impoverished Viennese artisans.

Christian Socialism as a quintessentially *Viennese* movement appealed from the outset to the economic fears of local artisans. One of its prime targets was the post-1859 institutionalization of the free-trade principle in Austria.[94] Nearly a decade before the creation of the Christian-Social party, artisan anti-Semitism had already emerged in Vienna as a spontaneous response to economic distress. Initially, in 1880, it had been directed against foreign immigration and the 'unfair' competition of Jewish pedlars from Poland, Hungary, and Russia. The artisans called for a return to the restrictions on Austrian Jews operative before 1848. They demanded a system of economic protection that included a restoration of the guild-system and of 'special certificates of competence' (*Befähigungsnachweise*) to protect artisans from the unwelcome blasts of free competition.

Artisan anti-Semitism enjoyed a particular weight in Vienna because of the traditional framework of pre-capitalist organization which the city had preserved into the second half of the nineteenth century. Vienna remained a residential capital of the Habsburg court, dominated by the aristocracy, officialdom, and a large petty bourgeoisie rooted in small-scale production. According to the industrial census of 1902, 90,714 out of 105,570 industrial and commercial establishments employed from 1 to 5 persons only. In the industrial sector, these tiny workshops employed almost a third of all wage-earners—115,505 out of a total of 373,424 persons.[95] Another third of the labour force worked in small and medium-sized factories. This predominance of small producers, shopkeepers, craftsmen, and small tradesmen threatened by new capitalist techniques of production increased the likelihood of a strong *kleinbürgerlich* movement emerging in Vienna. Ilsa Barea has evoked the desperate struggle of this class to avoid 'proletarization':

The survivors fought for their existence with redoubled acrimony on two fronts: politically—through Lueger's party—against the liberals, as the advocates of free enterprise, and the 'Jews' as their own main competitors and/ or financial overlords; and economically against their workers. They were a

---

[94] M. Weiss, 'Der politische Antisemitismus im Wiener Kleinbürgertum 1867–1895', *Emuna*, 8, no. 2 Mar./Apr. 1973), 94–103.
[95] *Österreichischen Ingenieur- und Architektenverein* (Vienna, 1910), 563.

powerful lobby, and gradually obtained measures of protection for small crafts against the encroachments of modern industry . . .'[96]

The economic crisis of the Viennese *Kleinbürgertum* coincided with the dramatic rise in social status after 1867 of immigrant Jews. This coincidence provided a fertile terrain for anti-Semitic agitation. So, too, did the widening of the franchise in 1882 which effectively ended the conservative-liberal monopoly of Austrian politics. The electoral reform ensured that power in Vienna would in future depend on winning the discontented lower middle class. The newly enfranchised Five-Guilder Men (payment of five florins a year in tax was now a qualification for the vote), composed mainly of small proprietors, artisans, petty officials, and shopkeepers, would become a decade later the social base of Lueger's victorious Christian-Social movement. Their enfranchisement strengthened those forces in Vienna who were increasingly embittered by liberal indifference towards their plight. The anticapitalist mood in the intermediate social strata of the Viennese population opened the way to a political alliance between the clerical Conservatives and the representatives of the 'little man' at the Liberals' expense.[97]

The antiquated Austrian electoral system, with its divisions into various curias according to property and income, still excluded the working classes from the vote in the 1880s. Thus, the potential counterweight of Social Democracy (which in Imperial Germany opposed anti-Semitism) did not enter into the picture until the electoral reforms of the 1890s. Not until the Reichsrat elections of 1907 (based on universal male suffrage) would the Austrian labour movement be able to confront the Christian-Social party on equal terms.[98] This vacuum, created by the persistence of a backward electoral system, the lack of a strong bourgeois-democratic tradition, the decline of Austro-liberalism, and the exclusion of the Social Democrats, clearly encouraged a petty-bourgeois Catholic social protest movement in Vienna. As John Boyer has shown, the *curia* system operative in late Imperial Vienna was in many ways ideally suited to the ideology and structure of the Christian-Social Party as an antiliberal protest movement of the Austro-German *Bürgertum*.

Anti-semitism became the integrative ideology of the Christian-

[96] Ilsa Barea, *Vienna: Legend and Reality* (London, 1966), 332–3.
[97] Ludwig Brügel, *Geschichte der österreichischen Sozialdemokratie* (Vienna, 1922), iii. 293.
[98] See William A. Jenks, *The Austrian Electoral Reform of 1907* (New York, 1950).

Social party, the binding cement which enabled it to bridge successfully over class contradictions within the Viennese *Bürgertum*.[99] Lueger and his lieutenants sought to present the Jews of Vienna as a single monolithic enemy with international connections against which *all* Christians had to unite if they wished to survive in the struggle for existence.[100] Economic liberalism would otherwise ruin all classes of the 'labouring Christian *Volk*' while Jewry profited in order to consolidate its 'alien rule' (*Fremdenherrschaft*) in the Imperial capital.[101] Christian Socialism claimed to be saving the people of Vienna from this crushing yoke of 'Jewish' capital and its handmaiden —the 'terrorism of the Jewish-liberal press'.[102] It proposed a united front of the indigenous population against the drive of Jewry to 'world-domination', based on a revival of Christian values and the return of the Catholic Church to its popular foundations.[103]

Christian Socialism also offered an alliance between the German and Czech *Mittelstand* in Vienna against 'Jewish' capital. It even proclaimed the reconciliation of the Austrian nationalities at the expense of the common Jewish enemy on an Empire-wide basis. The Christian peoples of the Balkans could be reconciled (so Lueger seemed to believe) to Greater Austrian Imperial ambitions by evoking the spectre of 'Jewish domination'.[104] The political uses of anti-Semitism were further underlined in Lueger's attacks on the 'Judaeo-Magyars', which skilfully exploited Viennese resentments against the Hungarians. They provided a useful adjunct to the Imperial Austrian 'patriotism' of the Christian-Social party.[105] Lueger, in contrast to von Schoenerer, was thereby able to combine Habsburg dynastic loyalty with populist anti-Semitism. He successfully singled out 'Jewish liberalism' as the enemy of *all* Austrians irrespective of nationality or class.[106]

Once the liberals had been vanquished in Vienna, Lueger used similar tactics no less effectively against the Austrian Social Demo-

---

[99] See Heinrich Waentig, *Gewerbliche Mittelstandspolitik: Eine rechtshistorisch-wirts-chaftspolitische Studie auf Grund österreichischer Quellen* (Leipzig, 1898), 136 ff., for a contemporary account that focuses on the *Mittelstand* character of the Viennese movement.

[100] Lueger's speech of 23 Sept. 1889, quoted extensively in Kralik, i. 42–3.

[101] Lueger's speech to the Christian-Social Verein in Währing on 26 Sept. 1889, ibid. 43.

[102] Ibid. 53.   [103] Ibid. 54.

[104] Lueger speech of 27 July 1891, ibid. 75–6.

[105] Ibid. 141; Pulzer, *Rise of Political Antisemitism*, 184.

[106] Kralik, pp. 162, 175.

crats. By the end of the century they had emerged as the most serious political rival of the Christian-Social party.[107] Lueger recognized and articulated deep-rooted status anxieties in the Viennese *Mittelstand* fuelled by the rise of Social Democracy. His anti-Semitic rhetoric after 1897 sought to tap petty-bourgeois fears of 'proletarization' and the 'Red Menace'. His social traditionalism expressed classic *Bürger* cultural values of order, hierarchy, paternalism, and a complex of class superiority which despised the proletariat as much as it feared big capital.[108] The Catholic Mayor's conservative style served however to defuse partially the racial anti-Semitism exhibited by some of his followers and rivals. By focusing on pragmatic issues he sought to soothe the status insecurity of his *Bürger* constituency. Lueger's socio-economic anti-Semitism, cleverly dressed up in a pseudo-religious façade, achieved an ideological and cultural respectability which none of his adversaries could match.[109]

Christian-Social religiosity provided a source of social solidarity, a sense of stability and of authority which corresponded to the traditional values of lower *Bürgertum* and of artisan voters. Religious deference was frequently the obverse side of artisanal anti-Semitism re-creating the sense of a social community with which the medieval guilds had once imbued their members. Not surprisingly, Catholic clerics played a central role in the propagation of this ideology, combining the cult of paternal authority and family solidarity with thunderous invectives against 'Jewish' domination.

Activist priests like Joseph Scheicher who came from a poor peasant background were especially effective in spreading the Christian-Social message to the plebeian masses. A disciple of Sebastian Brunner, Scheicher's anti-Semitism flowed logically from his commitment to the hegemony of Catholic culture in Austria.[110] He explicitly repudiated the traditional dependence of the Austrian Church on State power. Younger clerics like Scheicher and Schindler dreamed of creating a religious revival by democratizing a corrupt ecclesiastical establishment. Among the more malevolent of the clerical anti-Semites, some even linked the decadence of the Church to the alleged 'Judaizing' influences of liberalism. According to Father Joseph Deckert, for

---

[107] Kralik, pp. 190–1.

[108] See John Boyer, *Political Radicalism in Late Imperial Vienna: Origins of the Christian Social Movement, 1848–1897* (Chicago and London, 1981), 110–12 on the antisocialism of the master artisans.

[109] Ibid. 113 ff.

[110] Ibid. 140 ff.

example, Judaism had eroded the character of the Austrian State and society in which Christian culture was no longer supreme.[111]

The clergy's growing involvement in political agitation aroused the consternation not only of the higher bishops but also of leading court circles.[112] The Austrian government vainly tried through the mediation of the Prague Cardinal Schönborn to secure Papal condemnation of the Christian-Social movement in Vienna.[113] The radicalism of Luegerites profoundly shocked the Emperor, the Conservatives, and the old-guard Catholic hierarchy. The *Neue Freie Presse* and other liberal newspapers joined in the chorus of outrage though to no avail. The Christian Socialists merely increased their strength in May 1895, achieving for the first time an absolute majority in the municipal elections. The imminent prospect of Karl Lueger as the new Mayor of Vienna now set off a major constitutional crisis. Only an Imperial veto still stood between Lueger and the fulfilment of his supreme ambition. On 30 May 1895 the *Neue Freie Presse* expressed the feelings of most liberals: 'The government alone will occupy intself with the question whether it considers it in keeping with the interests and reputation of the Empire that Vienna should be the only great city in the world whose administrator is an anti-Semitic agitator.'[114]

The Austrian government of Count Badeni was not insensitive to such objections. The protest to the Emperor by Baron Banffy, the Hungarian Prime Minister, who had been outraged by the anti-Magyar insults of Lueger, must have carried special weight.[115] But the successive Imperial vetos merely strengthened popular support for Lueger. As a result, opposition to the government, to the liberals, and to the Jewish community grew in intensity. Were they not seeking to prevent the confirmation of the people's mandate by illegitimate means? That was certainly the view of the man in the street. Lueger skilfully manipulated the situation, proclaiming his party's patriotism while at the same time insisting that the Crown had to respect urban autonomy and the rules of the constitutional system.[116]

By 1896 Karl Lueger had clearly outmanœuvred the Imperial government and his Liberal adversaries. He had even won over to his

---

[111] Joseph Deckert, *Türkennoth und Judenherrschaft* (Vienna, 1894), 15.
[112] Boyer, *Politicial Radicalism*, 162.   [113] Schorske, pp. 143–4.
[114] *Neue Freie Presse*, 30 May 1895. For Social Democratic satisfaction at liberal disorientation and their disapproval of the Imperial veto, see Robert S. Wistrich, *Socialism and the Jews: The Dilemmas of Assimilation in Germany and Austria-Hungary* (Littman Library, London and Toronto, 1982), 255–8.
[115] Boyer, *Political Radicalism*, 375–6.   [116] Ibid. 381 ff.

side a substantial proportion of the upper-middle-class *Hausherren*
voters in the First Curia. The Christian-Socialists cleverly 'refrained
from using heavy antisemitic rhetoric on First Curia voters, and
instead approached these men with the argument that they should
support the party which would restore autonomy and propertied virtue
to the municipal regime'.[117] Lueger realized that the Viennese
Hausherren were unlikely to respond to anti-capitalist rhetoric or to the
street-corner Jew-baiting of Ernst Schneider and his artisan constituency. As John Boyer has suggested, the need to win over big property-
owners 'did not destroy antisemitism in the party as a functional device
for political mobilization, but it did lessen the dependence of the elite
upon Jew-hatred as an issue'.[118]

In their final march to power, the Christian Socialists therefore
presented themselves less as 'anti-Semites' and more as a traditionalist
middle-class party. Their immediate goal was to unite the voters of all
three curias into a unitary *Bürgertum* against the rising threat of Social
Democracy. Lueger now openly appealed to a united front of big
capitalists and the lower-middle-class *Bürgertum* against the common
enemy on the egalitarian left. The consequences were not insignificant
for the future of the Viennese Jewish community. Karl Lueger's
election did not herald its demise but instead led to a *modus vivendi* that
left essential Jewish interests intact. To quote John Boyer again:

In Vienna political antisemitism in a formal sense never disappeared since by
their very nature the Christian socials were an 'antisemitic' party. But the real
effectiveness of the antisemitism issue did suffer a decline nonetheless, which
was ultimately similar to what occurred in Germany. Antisemitism became a
mere subsidiary issue, directed more against the Social Democrats than
against the Jewish community as such.[119]

After 1897 the Christian Socialists would concentrate most of their
energies on effective interest-group representation for the Viennese
Bürgertum. Their anti-Semitism was diluted although it still remained
an important weapon in the political battle against the Left.

Thus, within the course of two years, Lueger's movement abandoned
its social radicalism. It turned into a middle-class dam against the
rising tide of socialist demands. Its programme and symbolism had

[117] Boyer, *Political Radicalism*, p. 402.
[118] Ibid. 403.
[119] Ibid. This judgement, while broadly valid for the Christian Social party before
1914, is not however applicable to Austrian anti-Semitism as a whole.

become consciously *staatserhaltend* ('state-conserving').[120] The Social Democrats were quick to spot his metamorphosis in the nature of Viennese anti-Semitism and to pass over to the counter-offensive. At an electoral meeting on 28 February 1897, their leader Victor Adler reacted to aspersions on his ancestry by attacking Lueger's party for associating with wealthy Jews: 'even though the anti-Semites have recently invited the richest Jews to the annual ball of the City of Vienna they maintain that the Socialist Party is led by Jews'.[121]

The Socialist press would regularly brand Lueger after 1897 as an ally of the Rothschilds. The class interests of Christian Socialism were declared to be identical with those of the Jewish banking bourgeoisie. The Catholic Mayor was ridiculed for reducing anti-Semitism to a hollow phraseology and making his party dependent on the goodwill of the Jewish business community.[122] At the Social Democratic Party Congress of 1897, Adler put his finger on the duplicity of Vienna's new masters:

When Lueger, when the antisemites, wish to ingratiate themselves, do they still talk about liberation from the yoke of Jewish capital? Damned little . . . Dr Lueger fancies himself as the general of the Austrian working class, to demonstrate how good he is at breaking them in, at making them trot in time *against* Jewish capitalism, but *for* Christian capitalism, which is just as Jewish as the other. (Laughter).[123]

The Socialists mocked Lueger—the so-called 'dragon-slayer' of Jewish capital—for delivering his beloved 'Christian people' to 'Stock Exchange Jews' and for doing business with *Bankjuden* 'against whom he made such violent and justified attacks in his radical days'.[124] The Viennese Mayor had even remained on cordial terms with the Jewish press magnates and with journalists like Moritz Szeps and Alexander Scharf. Wilhelm Ellenbogen, a leading Jewish intellectual in the Socialist party, concluded that 'the leading party in Vienna today has really so little to do with antisemitism that a politician was once able to

---

[120] Pulzer, *Rise of Political Antisemitism*, 187: 'Never had poacher become gamekeeper so quickly and so successfully'.

[121] 'Christliche und judische Ausbeutung', in Victor Adler, *Aufsätze, Reden und Briefe*, 11 vols. (Vienna, 1922–9), xi. 106.

[122] *Arbeiterzeitung*, 1 May 1897, p. 2; also 14 May 1897.

[123] *Verhandlungen des sechsten österreichischen Sozialdemokratischen Parteitages, abgehalten zu Wien vom 6. bis einschliesslich*, 12 June 1897 (Vienna, 1897), 77.

[124] 'Vom Tage', *Arbeiterzeitung*, 5 Jan. 1898, p. 1; also 'Herr Lueger als Verteidiger Rothschild's', 15 May 1898.

joke that no party apart from the Liberals has so many Jews among its membership as the antisemitic party'.[125] Socialist propaganda constantly harped on the *Scheinantisemitismus* (sham anti-Semitism) of the Christian-Social administration and its alleged subservience to 'Jewish capital'. According to the *Arbeiterzeitung* on 6 April 1900: 'Herr Lueger has spent his whole life among Jews; if there is anyone to whom one can apply the word "Judaized", it is to the Viennese Mayor'.[126]

Exposure of the 'Judaized' Christian-Social leaders who socialized with rich Jews like Rothschild, von Taussig, or Ritter von Gutmann was thus an object for endless barbs in the workers' press. Already outraged by Lueger's own tirades against the 'Jewish Social Democracy', the Left responded by suggesting that never had Jewish finance flourished as it now did under Christian-Social municipal administration.[127] Poor Jewish pedlars and immigrants from Galicia were still subject to harassment. But the influence of rich Jews in economic life, in the press, and in the universities had grown. Jewish civil rights had not been touched.[128] The Viennese Mayor even demonstrated a notably solicitous attention to the religious needs of the Jewish community while discriminating against the class-conscious workers.[129] Far from damaging bourgeois economic interests, Lueger's party had been led by the logic of capitalist profiteering to unite with Jewish entrepreneurs against striking miners and railwaymen.[130] According to the Marxist Left, the clerical and Jewish 'exploiters' were motivated by a common fear of social democracy.[131] In the same spirit, the socialist *Volkstribune* denounced Lueger's municipal contract with Theodor Ritter von Taussig (Jewish head of the Boden Creditanstalt) as 'a new edict of toleration for Jewish *Grosskapital*'—a final surrender to *la haute banque*. 'Now Taussig (!!) is their man, the Jews have never done better in Vienna than under Lueger, and "foreign rule" has arrived— Taussig as the source of money in the Christian city of Vienna!— Lueger's anti-semitism has been unmasked as a pack of lies'.[132]

---

[125] Wilhelm Ellenbogen, 'Der Wiener Antisemitismus', *Sozialistische Monatshefi*, no. 1 (Sept. 1899), p. 421.

[126] *Arbeiterzeitung*, 6 Apr. 1900.

[127] 'Der Antisemitismus der Luegerei—Um das goldene Kalb—das jüdische Grosskapital—tanzen nun die Parteifreunde Luegers', *Volkstribune*, 1 July 1908, p. 2.

[128] 'Antisemitische Praxis', *Arbeiterzeitung*, 3 June 1900, p. 2; 'Antisemitisch—jüdische Solidarität', 23 Nov. 1900, p. 4.

[129] 'Jüdische und christlicher Klerikalismus', ibid., 15 May. 1900, p. 2.

[130] 'Rothschild, Gutmann und Vergani', ibid., 31 Jan. 1900.

[131] 'Die Lüge des Antisemitismus', ibid., 18 Mar. 1907, pp. 1–2.

[132] *Volkstribune*, 1 July 1908, p. 2.

The Socialist critique of Lueger's administration noted the sharp distinction which it seemed to draw between rich and poor Jews. While eager to solicit the loans of big Jewish bankers, Lueger did not hesitate to pension off minor Jewish officials, to harass illicit Jewish pedlars, or unscrupulously to sack Jewish municipal employees. But those converted Jews 'who were well disposed to the one and only Holy Church . . . were entrusted with key decisions'.[133] The half-Jewish Dr Julius Porzer (1847–1914) even became deputy Mayor of Vienna in 1904 while one of the leading lawyers in the Christian-Social party was Max Anton Löw, grandson of a rabbi.

This half-hearted anti-semitism of Lueger's party did not escape the attention of the young Adolf Hitler (1889–1945) when he arrived in Vienna in 1907. Hitler soon recognized that Christian-Social principles did not constitute a major inconvenience for Viennese Jewry. In *Mein Kampf* he recalled: 'If the worst came to the worst, a splash of baptismal water could always save the business and the Jew at the same time.'[134] Von Schoenerer's ideological anti-Semitism based on Pan-German race principles left a much more lasting impression on the young Hitler. But Pan-Germanism had never really struck root in Vienna. Von Schoenerer's supporters in the Habsburg capital tended to be either university students, schoolteachers, Gymnasial professors, disgruntled journalists, or the occasional small businessmen of nationalist inclinations. The Pan-German style was far too extreme for the easy-going Viennese temperament. Moreover, nationalism had little relevance to the economic distress of Viennese artisans. Lacking any insight into the problems of building a political movement in the specific local conditions of Vienna, von Schoenerer's supporters remained outsiders, 'an ill-integrated group of quasi-sectarian professionals'.[135]

Lueger, on the other hand, had always been a quintessentially Viennese politician. He knew exactly how to make his skilful mix of Catholic tradition and modernity acceptable to broad strata of the Viennese middle-class population. He intuitively grasped the impracticality of racism in its purest form in Vienna, though he continued to tolerate extremist anti-Semitism on the fringes of the party even after he had destroyed liberal hegemony in the city. But this rhetoric had

[133] 'Die Christlich-Sozialen und die Beamtenschaft', 24 May 1911, p. 4.
[134] Hitler, p. 120; See also Robert Wistrich, 'Karl Lueger', pp. 251–62, and *Hitler's Apocalypse: Jews and the Nazi Legacy* (London, 1985), 12–26.
[135] Boyer, *Political Radicalism*, 93.

little influence on his practical policies once in power. As a sophisticated municipal leader, he evidently recognized the need after 1897 to reach an accommodation with the Jewish business élite in Vienna. More importantly, he understood the indispensability of the Jews to the everyday functioning of a city where they were occupationally enmeshed in all its activities. Viennese finance, business, industry, and education could not operate effectively on the scale that he wished without the Jewish contribution. This reality was acknowledged in a revealing aside to Sigmund Mayer, a leading Jewish community politician: 'I like the Hungarian Jews even less than the Hungarians but I am not an enemy of our Viennese Jews; they are not so bad and we really cannot do without them . . . The Jews are the only ones who always feel like being active.'[136]

Such cynical pragmatism was typical of a politician who could describe Jew-baiting as 'an excellent means of propaganda and of getting ahead in politics' but as being altogether useless in office. This opportunism in no way excuses Lueger's willingness to condone brutal anti-Semitic slander in order to achieve political goals. His initial successes had depended on harnessing the coarse instincts of the mob.[137] Even under his relatively benevolent rule, Viennese Jews could scarcely feel comfortable with the demonic image of their activities fostered by many of his followers. Nor could the geniality of the Catholic Mayor disguise the fact that he had helped to make anti-Semitism seem both normal and respectable. For all his lack of ideological fanaticism, Lueger had given cultural and political legitimization to the most tenacious popular prejudices.[138]

Lueger's party had expertly manipulated the base motivations of professional envy, fear of Jewish competition, xenophobia, anti-intellectualism, and religious intolerance in order to achieve municipal power. It had made the 'Jewish question' into a norm of Austrian public life, which frequently lowered the tone of debate in the Reichsrat, the Vienna city council, or the lower Austrian Landtag to that of the

---

[136] Sigmund Mayer, *Die Wiener Juden: Kommerz, Kultur, Politik, 1700–1900* (Vienna and Berlin, 1917), 475.

[137] See Richard S. Geehr (ed.), *'I Decide who is a Jew!' The Papers of Dr Karl Lueger* (Washington, DC, 1982), 321–5, who provides some evidence that Lueger was himself a convinced anti-Semite since the early 1880s, though to what extent remains an open question.

[138] Ibid. 323. Geehr points out that as leader of a party of imperial Stature, Lueger was a 'respectable politician', so that his responsibility in legitimizing anti-Semitism was so much the greater.

cattle-market. Nevertheless, in spite of its vulgarity, Christian-Social anti-Semitism did not generate any pogroms in Vienna. It remained within the limits of a conciliatory, supranational Habsburg state with a political culture based on respect for the law and mutual accommodation between ethnic groups. Even the more sinister features of this popular anti-Semitism were still containable by the Austrian Rechtsstaat, as long as the Emperor Franz Joseph lived. With his demise the flood-gates of barbarism would be thrown wide open.

8

Adolf Jellinek and the Liberal Response

The moral earnestness with which the Jew-baiter Istóczy was repelled and reprimanded in the Hungarian house of Deputies by the Ministerial and opposition benches and the open manner in which the Minister President Tisza honoured truth and justice will undoubtedly increase still more the ardent patriotic feelings manifested at every opportunity by Hungarian Israelites. But on this Austrian side of the Leitha, too, anti-Semitism finds no soil and we believe ourselves to be well informed when we say that it is rejected by all the leading circles . . .

Josef Ritter von Wertheimer (1882)

Anti-Semitism negates nationality and places race alone in the foreground—hence it is a great danger, an element of decomposition and disintegration in a state like Austria which consists of many different nationalities. The Austrian anti-Semites do not recognize the German Austrians—that is Germans whose historical development on Austrian soil has been consummated by living together with other nationalities—they acknowledge only the German race and feel themselves to be a mere fragment of Germany, where the German race alone feels at home and powerful.

Adolf Jellinek (1888)

But what did we do against anti-Semitism when it first arose? Some of us practised an ostrich-like policy and believed that anti-Semitism would disappear on its own as a result of our silence; some indulged themselves in aesthetic humility; they listen to its insults without reply; others did not care at all about anti-Semitism since it had not yet directly affected them. Today, on the other hand, there is no profession or class in Jewry where anti-Semitism is not felt. The academic, the employee, the businessmen, whether rich or poor, great or small, all suffer from it—the one from its blows, the other from its pin pricks; to some it threatens their existence, to others their honour and dignity. But, the growth of latent anti-Semitism will abolish all differences

in Jewry and expose us altogether to social atrophy if we do not at
least begin once more to feel solidarity with each other . . .

Österreichische Wochenschrift (8 June 1888)

It was a historical moment, when in 1880, Count Taafe
approached the leaders of the Jewish community in Vienna, with
the request that the Jews should separate from the Germans and
form a separate party, friendly to the Government. This request
was refused, and thus there arose the anti-Semitic movement
which was provoked and favoured by the Government, and from
which the entire body of Jews in Austria is still suffering. The
Germans rewarded the Jews for their loyalty by becoming the
principal representatives of anti-Semitism in Austria.

The Jewish Chronicle (December 1898)

The liberal leaders of Viennese Jewry did not face the challenge of
an *organized* anti-Semitic mass movement in Austria until the early
1880s. During the long struggle for emancipation they had, however,
frequently been obliged to defend Jewry and Judaism from defamation
by its enemies.[1] Prominent community leaders and publicists like Ignaz
Kuranda, Joseph von Wertheimer, or Heinrich Jacques centred their
defence of Jewish rights around liberal Enlightenment principles such
as freedom of religion, equality before the law, or the civic patriotism
of the Jews.[2] In the first years of the Constitutional Era the hegemony
of liberal principles encouraged most Austrian Jews to believe that
clerical and Conservative anti-Semitism had little prospect of attracting
popular support. Other problems—such as the conflict between
orthodoxy and reform, the migration of *Ostjuden* to Vienna or the
'enlightened' struggle against Polish Hasidism in Galicia—continued
to be the main preoccupations of the community leaders. These
themes found frequent expression in the community organ, *Die
Neuzeit*, during the editorship of Simon Szántó.[3] By the time of his
death in 1882, the outlook for Jews throughout the Habsburg Empire
had changed significantly following a series of unexpected events of
international importance.

---

[1] See Central Archives of the History of the Jewish People (Jerusalem), A/W 315,
File on Anti-Semitism.

[2] Hans Tietze, *Die Juden Wiens* (Vienna and Leipzig, 1933), 239 ff.; P. G. J. Pulzer,
The Rise of Political Antisemitism in Germany and Austria (New York and London,
1964), 130–1.

[3] Jacob Toury, *Die jüdische Presse im österreichischen Kaiserreich, 1820–1918* (Tübingen,
1983), 69–70.

The most dramatic of these events were the Russian pogroms of 1881 which provoked the start of a massive migration of Jews from East to West. This emigration passed across the Austrian border and its scale necessitated the co-operation of many international Jewish philanthropic organizations. The pogroms which had inspired the mass exodus gave rise to the Russian Hibbat Zion movement (advocating emigration to Palestine) and to a new Jewish nationalism which soon found an echo in Vienna. At the same time, the brutal discrimination of the Russian regime coincided with the emergence between 1880 and 1883 of Jew-baiting movements in neighbouring Germany and Hungary as well as inside the Austrian half of the Monarchy. The confluence of these diverse though related phenomena boded ill for the future. Furthermore, they occurred at a time when the German Liberal Verfassungspartei had been relegated to ineffectual opposition in Austria. This was a serious blow to Viennese Jews who had seen in German Liberalism their natural political home.

One of the first Austrian Jews to perceive the seriousness of the new anti-Semitic wave was the Viennese preacher Adolf Jellinek.[4] Fifteen years earlier, he had already foreseen the dangerous implications of modern race-theories (as developed by the French scholar Ernst Renan) which postulated the inherent inferiority of 'Semites' to 'Aryans'. This racial world-view was liable, Jellinek realized, to encourage brutal nationalist hatreds and to threaten the physical existence of Jewry. 'Here, in this Jewish question, it is not a matter for the Jews of a greater or lesser measure of political rights but of the whole man, of his innermost essence and his world-historical honour.'[5]

Jellinek's commitment to the humanist principles of German Jewish *Wissenschaft* did not blind him to the dangers of the new gospel of anti-Semitism being preached in Berlin and Vienna. Since the 1860s he had spoken out in powerful sermons against clerical intolerance, aristocratic reaction, and the revival of medieval *Judenhass* in the German-speaking world. In 1880 he had published an anthology of philo-Semitic statements by prominent French statesmen, jurists, scholars, writers, and scientists in order that they be used 'as a shield

---

[4] Toury, p. 71, rightly mentions that Jellinek's contribution to the struggle against anti-Semitism has not been sufficiently recognized but unfortunately does not analyse it in any detail.

[5] Jellinek, 'Eine neue Judenfrage', *Jahrbuch für Israeliten* (1865–6), 143; see also M. Rosenmann, *Dr Adolf Jellinek: Sein Leben und Schaffen* (Vienna, 1931), 113.

against Teutonic offensive weapons'.[6] He clearly believed it to be his task to forge both the intellectual weapons and a political strategy to counteract the anti-Semitic flood unleashed across Europe and now rapidly finding imitators in Austria itself.[7]

Jews could not leave the defence of their honour solely in the hands of well-meaning Christians. It was their personal duty to unmask the falsifications of Jewish sources and to correct the accumulated Christian prejudices that had developed over the centuries against Judaism.[8] According to Jellinek, Jewish apologetics must spread the truth about the sublime faith of Israel and demonstrate the profound universalism of the Talmud. It must make Jewish achievements in the natural sciences, medicine, law, literature, the fine arts, commerce, industry, philanthropy, and politics more widely known. Above all, in the battle against anti-Semitism, rabbis must stand firmly in the front line to defend the honour of the Jewish name, the grandeur of Judaism, and the nobility of its teachings.[9] Jellinek believed it to be essential to refute the charge that 'Biblical Judaism is an exclusive, nationally limited [faith]' and to demonstrate that the gospel of universal love had been Jewish teaching centuries before Christ.[10]

In a long-running polemic with the leading conservative newspaper in Vienna, *Das Vaterland*, Jellinek emphasized that the foundations of Talmudic ethics were in no way inferior to Christian morality.[11] Indeed, the teachings of the Talmud, contrary to the claims of its detractors, had provided a unique pedagogical instrument for maintaining the high level of Jewish morality. Jellinek contrasted Jewish qualities of learning, compassion, and devotion to their faith nurtured by the Talmud with the heartless cruelty of their anti-Semitic persecutors. Jew-baiting, with its unscrupulous unleashing of mob instincts and its encouragement of blind passion, represented a profound sickness of Christian civilization which it now seemed singularly impotent to restrain.[12] 'Christian' virtues of humility, charity,

---

[6] See Rosenmann, p. 155, on Jellinek's major contribution to the creation of modern Jewish apologetics; also Jellinek, *Franzosen über Juden: Urteile und Aussprüche berühmter französischer Staatsmänner und Gelehrter über Juden und Judentum* (Vienna, 1880).

[7] See 'Ein Wort über unsere Publizistik', *Die Neuzeit*, 30 Dec. 1881, pp. 415–16, which deals with the wider issue of the *raison d'être* of the Jewish press in the modern age.

[8] *Die Neuzeit*, 30 Dec. 1881, p. 416.

[9] Jellinek, *Aus der Zeit: Tagesfragen und Tagesbegebenheiten* (Budapest, 1886), 7.

[10] See Jellinek's open letter to Rabbi Joseph Samuel Bloch, 5 Oct. 1892, ibid. 8–9.

[11] Ibid. 23 ff. This was in response to an article in *Das Vaterland* on 29 July 1883.

[12] Jellinek, *Aus der Zeit*, 24–5.

vows of poverty, and love of one's neighbour had too rarely been carried out in practice. Traditional Christianity lacked genuine freedom of belief, insisting on the conversion of Jews and other non-believers, according to the principle *extra ecclesiam nulla salus*.

For centuries Christianity had nourished anti-Semitism through its religious instruction, its prayers, sermons, and festivals, and a popular folklore that blamed the Jews for the crucifixion of Jesus.[13] Emancipation would remain a dead letter until the Christian peoples abandoned these inherited prejudices, deeply-rooted in their collective 'unconscious'. Civic equality would remain a chimera until Judaism was at last recognized by Christians as 'a religion which educates those who profess it to justice and love of one's neighbours, to being virtuous human beings and loyal citizens through the purity of its monotheism and ethics as well as through the beautiful and noble example of its believers'.[14] Without recognition of the integrity of Judaism by the Christian world, there could not be any effective struggle against anti-Semitism.[15]

Jellinek, as a convinced liberal, also regarded the separation of religion and State as essential to overcoming the persistence of denominational prejudices. The status of the Jews was to his mind determined by the degree to which the revolutionary ideas of liberty, fraternity, and equality succeeded in penetrating the modern State. It was no accident that anti-Semites rejected these liberal premisses, calling instead for a restoration of the Catholic social order or advocating a homogeneous national community that would exclude Jews from the body-politic.[16] Modern anti-Semitism, as 'a legitimate descendant of medieval barbarism', demonstrated that millions of European Christians had yet to overcome 'the rage for persecution and plunder of the Middle Ages'.[17] Against the weight of such inherited prejudice, it was a Jewish task 'to educate the Christian nations for the victory of liberal ideas', which represented 'the most developed, progressive and refined religious-ethical consciousness'.[18]

Liberal ideas were presented here as a modern version of the Mosaic Law and the prophetic teachings of Israel. Austrian Jews were

---

[13] Jellinek, *Aus der Zeit*, pp. 8–9.

[14] Ibid. 53, 'Das Judenthum den Juden, das Christenthum den Christen'. Jellinek recognized Christianity's historic contribution as having been the 'overcoming of paganism'. But Christian missionizing of the Jews was bitterly rejected.

[15] Ibid. 60–1, 68. He stressed the ignorance of Jewish religious teachings among Austrian statesmen, soldiers, professors, and intellectuals.

[16] Ibid. 10.   [17] Ibid. 19.   [18] Ibid. 33.

expected to commit themselves to this 'sacred' civilizing mission, undaunted by the pseudo-religion, the envy and blind fanaticism displayed by the anti-Semites. 'Antisemitism has become a religion, not a religion of peace, of love, humanity and brotherhood', Jellinek declared in April 1884, but of 'virulent campaigns, racial hatred, and inhumanity'.[19] The intensity of the new Judaeophobia demonstrated the immaturity of the Christian peoples of Europe, not the guilt of the Jews. Attacks on Jewish wealth, 'exploitation', ostentation, and other alleged faults were merely a pretext. The intolerance of German students in Berlin and Vienna, the barbaric plunder of Jewish homes in Tsarist Russia, or the violent agitation in Hungary had nothing to do with Jewish behaviour.[20] Anti-Semitism was essentially a question of national pedagogy. 'It is not the Jews but certain individual peoples, especially German and Slav, who are not yet ripe for so-called emancipation, they are not sufficiently advanced in their culture of feeling, their intellectual education and their ethical thinking to be capable of unprejudiced and just behaviour towards the Jews . . .'[21] Jellinek clearly sensed in the early 1880s that civil equality without a solid ethical foundation was vulnerable to the assaults of a new generation of anti-Semites in Central and Eastern Europe. The problem was that neither Germans nor Slavs manifested the Latin or Anglo-Saxon capacity for assimilating foreign peoples. Liberalism had not yet become an integral part of their political culture.

This recognition of the limits of formal emancipation did not bring Jellinek closer to Jewish nationalism. In a fascinating account of his encounter in Vienna (April 1882) with Leo Pinsker, Russian founder of the Hibbat Zion movement, Adolf Jellinek rejected the pessimistic prognoses and conclusions of his anguished visitor from the East.[22] The Viennese preacher was not prepared to renounce the liberal ideas of emancipation that had guided Austrian Jewry for over forty years. Nor could be accept Leo Pinsker's contention that his co-religionists were mere 'vagrants' or aliens in their homelands.

We are at home [*heimisch*] in Europe and feel ourselves to be children of the lands in which we were born, raised and educated, whose languages we speak

---

[19] Ibid. 37. [20] 'Völker-Pädagogik', ibid. 3–18.
[21] Ibid. 6.
[22] See 'Ein Zwiegespräch', ibid. 70–80; *Die Neuzeit*, 31 Mar., 7 Apr., and 14 Apr. 1882. See also 'Leo Pinskers Begegnung mit Adolf Jellinek: zur Wiederkehr des 100. Geburtstages Pinskers', in N. M. Gelber, *Aus zwei Jahrhunderten* (Vienna and Leipzig, 1924), 193–201.

and whose cultures constitute our intellectual substance. We are Germans, Frenchmen, Englishmen, Hungarians, Italians etc, with every fibre of our being. We long ago ceased to be genuine, thoroughbred Semites [*echte Vollblut-Semiten*] and the sense of a Hebrew nationality has long since been lost.[23]

Jellinek assured Leo Pinsker that 'almost all Jews in Europe', if put to the test, would vote against the proposed plan for an independent Jewish territory. Patience was vital in confronting the anti-Semites. Was it reasonable to expect 'that the Jews should conquer within a single century the prejudices against their faith and descent harboured and promoted for so long a time?'[24] Nor, despite his own 'partiality for the theory of heredity', could Jellinek agree with Pinsker's contention that Judaeophobia 'has become an immutable heritage of the nations' (*ein unabänderliches Erbstück der Völker*).[25] It was conceivable that instincts, passions, talents, and even predilections might be inherited 'but not complex psychic processes like hatred of a specific religion or race'.[26] Furthermore, Jellinek accused Pinsker of exaggerating the threat of German and Russian anti-Semitism. 'This poisonous plant which has been nurtured on the banks of the Spree [in Berlin] has no roots in the soil of history.'

This did not mean that Viennese Jewry was not 'deeply distressed by the sad situation of our co-religionists in Russia and that we are not constantly thinking of ways to change their lot'. Indeed, Jellinek confessed that rarely in his life 'has anything shaken me so profoundly as the emigration of Russian children to Jaffa through Vienna'.[27] But the suffering of these migrant boys 'torn from their parents', singing mournful Russian dirges for the homeland they had left, did not prove Pinsker's case. There was no urgent reason to found 'a small state like Serbia or Romania outside Europe, which would most likely become the plaything of one Great Power against another, and whose future would be very uncertain'.[28]

Jellinek affirmed his conviction that a continuation of the cruel Ignatiev decrees of 1881 against Russian Jewry was inconceivable. The problems of Russian Jewry derived mainly from their massive concentration in the Pale of settlement. The only rational solution was 'a large-scale, prudently planned, and well-organized emigration' to a free democratic country like the United States. Though there was no

---

[23] 'Ein Zwiegespräch', *Aus der Zeit*, 76.
[24] Ibid.   [25] Ibid. 77.   [26] Ibid.   [27] Ibid. 78.
[28] Ibid.

denying their traumatic impact, the Russian pogroms did not constitute grounds for surrendering to black despair. Public opinion in the West and the new means of communication made any recurrence highly improbable. In the future, news of events in Russia would be disseminated 'with the greatest speed'. This would deter the Russian authorities from permitting a repeat performance.[29] Jellinek explicitly criticized Pinsker's obsessive fixation with the scale and significance of the disaster that had overtaken Russian Jewry. His visitor had been overcome to the point that everywhere he saw 'only hatred and hostility, anti-Semites and pan-Slavists'. For Jellinek, Pinsker's views could most charitably be understood as 'symptoms of the *pathological* conditions in Russia'.[30] They had no universal significance or lessons for Western Jewry.

Jellinek's response to the pogroms was typical of most liberal German or Austrian Jews at that time.[31] It was not so much that they were complacent about the new political anti-Semitism. But in their eyes there was still an immense difference between semi-barbarous, pogromist Russia and German Central Europe. Russian Zionists like Pinsker had been traumatized not only by the savagery of the peasant masses but by the cold hostility of the Tsarist government and the indifference of the Russian revolutionary movement. They perceived Germany and Austria through a Russian prism, concluding that Western-style emancipation would not solve their problem. The gap in perceptions was evident when Pinsker explained to Jellinek the meaning of German anti-Semitism for Russian Jewry:

. . . if a nation as highly civilized as the Germans can tolerate anti-Semitic scenes in the capital of the German Reich—if a court chaplain [Stoecker] agitates and rages against those who profess Judaism and arouses the most brutal hatred against equal citizens of the same Reich, and a brilliant and all-powerful statesman [Bismarck] permits them to be reviled and stigmatized as pariahs etc . . . why then should the Russian press not denounce Russian Jewry as aliens and intruders?'[32]

The diagnosis of anti-Semitism made by early Russian Zionists like Pinsker emphasized the endemic, *pathological* character of the phenomenon. It was viewed as the inevitable consequence of the homeless,

---

[29] Ibid. 80.

[30] 'Ein Zwiegespräch', *Die Neuzeit*, 14 Apr. 1882, p. 124.

[31] See Robert Wistrich, 'Anti-Semitism and the Origins of Jewish Nationalism', *Midstream* (Nov. 1982), pp. 10–15.

[32] 'Ein Zwiegespräch', *Aus der Zeit*, 74.

extra-territorial status of the Jewish people. This perception of anti-Semitism which stressed its resistance to all reason, logic, or enlightenment was much too disturbing for most emancipated Western Jews to contemplate. To be defined as members of a 'ghost people', as foreigners or mere guests in the lands of their residence (Pinsker), appeared to cut the ground from under the feet of emancipated Jewry.

Nevertheless, in 1882 there were Jewish students at the University of Vienna, deeply shaken by the Russian pogroms, who *did* seek to apply to Pinsker's teaching to their own situation.[33] Having been born in Russia, Romania, or Galicia, where they had grown up with an ethnic-traditional sense of Jewish peoplehood, these students found themselves isolated from the existing community framework in Vienna.[34] As university students they suffered directly from the anti-Semitic policy of the Pan-German nationalist fraternities in Austria in the 1880s. This racism had spread to school associations, gymnastic societies, and German cultural societies. The humiliating reminders of Jewish 'racial' inferiority at high school and university helped to convince a small group of East European Jewish students that assimilation was a cul-de-sac.[35] Pinsker's dictum that '*legal* emancipation is not *social* emancipation' spoke to their own marginal situation which led them to experience social discrimation as a form of national oppression.

The result was the creation at the University of Vienna on 23 March 1883 of the first Jewish national student organization in Europe, Kadimah.[36] The early Zionist ideology of auto-emancipation which animated Kadimah represented an unmistakeable challenge to the political orientation of the Viennese Jewish establishment. Thus it is no surprise to find that Kadimah's militant response to anti-Semitism, its ideological assault against assimilation, and its openly nationalist

[33] N. Birnbaum, 'Gegen die Selbstverständlichkeit', in Ludwig Rosenhek (ed.), *Festschrift zur Feier des 100. Semesters der akademischen Verbindung Kadimah* (Mödling, 1933), 30.

[34] Birnbaum (ibid.) pointed out that 'die jungen Leute aus dem Osten noch aus einem lebendigen jüdischen Volksmilieu kamen, wo es schon eine Bewegung der Selbstemanzipation oder der nationalen Wiedergeburt gab . . .'. Those nationalist students who came from a German cultural background had no living *Volksjudentum* to serve as their inspiration.

[35] See Nathan Birnbaum, *Die Assimilationssucht: Ein Wort an die sogenannten Deutschen, Slaven, Magyaren mosaischer Confession* (Vienna, 1884), 9–10.

[36] Julius H. Schoeps, 'Modern Heirs of the Maccabees: The Beginnings of the Vienna Kadimah, 1882–1897', *Leo Baeck Yearbook*, 27 (1982), 155–70.

appeal received a decidedly cool reception from the leaders of the Kultusgemeinde.[37]

Nevertheless, it was difficult for communal leaders to deny that the rise of an aggressive, racist *Volksdeutschtum* in Austria after 1880 had cast a heavy shadow over their liberal dream. Particularly traumatic was the realization that the new wave of anti-Semitism had been inspired by German models from Berlin. Its acknowledged prophets were Richard Wagner, Wilhelm Marr, Adolf Stoecker, Heinrich von Treitschke, and Eugen Dühring. Writing in 1899, Theodor Herzl recalled the impact of Berlin anti-Semitism on him at a time when he was still a liberal German nationalist student at the University of Vienna:

I am still aware what an impression it made upon me when I, in the year 1882, read Dühring's book on the Jewish question *Die Judenfrage als Rassen- Sitten- und Kulturfrage*, a book which is as full of hate as it is brilliant. I think that prior to it I really no longer knew that I was a Jew. Dühring's book had an effect on me as if I had received a blow on the head. And that same thing probably happened to many a Western Jew who had already forgotten his peoplehood. The anti-Semites awakened it . . .[38]

In 1882 the young law student Theodor Herzl had already noted in his diary the thought that if a serious German scholar like Dühring insisted on racial segregation between Jew and non-Jews, then one could not expect anything better of the uneducated masses. German *Wissenschaft* now appeared in the new and unfamiliar guise of organizing a vicious assault on the principle of Jewish emancipation. The shock was profound though it would remain repressed in Herzl's unconscious for nearly fifteen years. Serious questions were also being raised among Austrian Jews concerning the coldly neutral attitude of the Prussian authorities towards the anti-Semitic agitation.[39] In private conversation with Jellinek in 1882, Leo Pinsker had already pointed to the ominous implications of the government authorities' lack of response to anti-Semitism in the capital of the German Reich. In 1886 the Jewish-born Austrian engineer and social philosopher Josef

---

[37] See Dennis B. Klein, *Jewish Origins of the Psychoanalytic Movement* (New York, 1981), 16–20.

[38] Theodor Herzl, 'Zionismus', in his *Zionistische Schriften*, i (3rd edn., Tel Aviv, 1934), 373. The article first appeard in the *North American Review* (1899).

[39] See Fritz Stern, *Gold and Iron: Bismarck, Bleichröder and the Building of the German Empire* (London, 1977), 494–531, for a fascinating discussion of the 'New Antisemitism' in Germany and Bismarck's ambiguous response to it.

Popper-Lynkeus (1838–1921) went further, openly blaming Chancellor Bismarck for complicity in encouraging the spread of German anti-Semitism.[40] He indicated that the German anti-Semites regarded Otto von Bismarck 'as their silent but most helpful chief'.[41] Despite their lawless agitation, 'until now to the best of our knowledge there has appeared not a single authentic utterance of the German Chancellor, that condemns all this, certainly not a public disavowal'.[42]

The ambiguous response of the German authorities to the rise of anti-Semitism convinced Popper-Lynkeus—ten years before the publication of Herzl's *Judenstaat*—that only a Jewish State could eliminate anti-Semitism. Its main cause, he wrote prophetically in 1886, was the lack of respect which the nations felt for a minority unprotected by any existing political power, military force, or State institutions.[43] The Jews were everywhere perceived as wandering nomads, vagrants, or even 'bastards' among the peoples because they lacked a homeland. An independent State recognized by the international community had become in the modern era the *sine qua non* of national virility and legitimacy.[44]

The majority of Austrian Jews, though rattled by the intensity of Russian, German, and Hungarian anti-Semitism in the 1880s, could not accept such radical conclusions. In a speech in January 1881, Kultusgemeinde President Ignaz Kuranda enunciated the view that the Jews of Austria 'had nothing to fear in the immediate present', thanks to the 'good nature of the Viennese population and the prestigious positions which Jews occupy in this country'. Though concerned about the future, Kuranda still believed that the patriotism and mutual solidarity of the Austrian Jews would help to prevent such 'brutal outbursts as have taken place in Berlin'.[45]

Joseph Ritter von Wertheimer expressed a similar optimism in 1882 that Viennese Jewry would be spared anti-Semitic excesses on the Berlin model. He noted with approval that Hungarian Minister-

---

[40] Josef Popper-Lynkeus, *Fürst Bismarck und der Antisemitismus* (2nd edn., Vienna and Leipzig, 1925), 146. For his discussion of Wagner see pp. 42–3 and on Dühring, pp. 46–74. Ingrid Belke, *Die sozialreformerischen Ideen von Josef Popper-Lynkeus (1838–1921)* (Tübingen, 1978), 111–120, has a useful discussion of his attitude to Jews, Judaism, and Zionism.

[41] Popper-Lynkeus, p. 145.   [42] Ibid. 146.   [43] Ibid. 124–6.

[44] Ibid. 126: 'Nichts anderes als das Bewusstsein, das hinter den in der Welt versprengten Juden kein sich ihrer annehmender jüdischer Staat steht, der völkerrechtlich zu respektieren wäre, machte alle bisherigen judenfeindlichen Bewegungen möglich . . .'

[45] 'Kleine Chronik', *Die Neuzeit*, 7 Jan. 1881, p. 4.

President Koloman von Tisza (1830–1902) had strongly condemned von Istoczy's anti-Semitic movement. He felt confident that leading circles in German Austria would never encourage or countenance such agitation.[46] By contrast, von Wertheimer sharply rebuked the veteran Czech national leader Rieger for an anti-Semitic remark made during a budget debate in the Imperial Parliament.[47] This preoccupation with the rather marginal Czech anti-Semitism in Vienna seems surprising. *Národní listy*, organ of the Young Czech party was attacked for encouraging immigrant Czech artisans in Vienna to vote for a German nationalist candidate in the Mariahilf district during the 1884 elections.[48] *Die Neuzeit* warned that Jews would turn their backs on the Czech nation if it made common cause with anti-Semitism. At the same time it ridiculed the 'linguistic chauvinism' of the Czechs. The authenticity of Czech nationalism and its 'narrow-minded', intolerant struggle against the inroads of German culture in Bohemia was unreservedly criticized.[49] Jellinek, for example, unfavourably compared Czech attitudes to the Jews with those of Germans, Hungarians, and Poles in Austria. He castigated Czech national 'assimilationism' for supposedly depriving Bohemian and Moravian Jews of their alienable right to be Germans[50] This was the same language which he had used in the 1840s to discredit the Czech national movement.

Die Neuzeit still assumed in November 1884 that 'in Vienna anti-Semitism will never strike root in the hearts of the [German] *Bürgertum*'.[51] The vehement Pan-German propaganda of von Schoenerer was presented with some justification as alien to the temperament of the Viennese common man. Much less convincing was the assumption that the middle classes could be trusted to remain impervious to the 'import of North German and South Russian barbarism'.[52] The Jewish press still drew comfort from the fact that official public opinion in Vienna was hostile to anti-Semitism, with the exception of Vogelsang's *Das Vaterland*.[53] Vienna was even presented in

[46] Joseph Ritter von Wertheimer, 'Zur neuen Zeit an die "Neuzeit"', letter dated 20 Feb. 1882, published in *Die Neuzeit*, 24 Feb. 1882, p. 61.

[47] Ibid. See also Kuranda's reference to Czech resentment of 'die deutsche Gesinnung der vaterländischen Juden', ibid., 7 Jan. 1881, p. 4.

[48] 'Czechischer Antisemitismus in Wien', ibid., 7 Nov. 1884, p. 421.

[49] 'Jüdisch-czechisch', ibid., 8 June 1883, pp. 215–16.

[50] Ibid. 216. Jellinek's pro-German position on the nationality question in Bohemia had never deviated since his articles in *Der Orient* during the 1848 Revolution.

[51] 'Czechischer Antisemitismus in Wien', ibid., 7 Nov. 1884, p. 421.

[52] 'Wiener Stimmen', ibid., 14 Apr. 1882, pp. 124–5.   [53] Ibid. 125.

the early 1880s as a haven of reconciliation, peace, and tolerance—free from the raging national conflicts that divided the Monarchy as a whole.[54] It was optimistically pointed out that no prominent establishment figures like the Prussian historian Heinrich von Treitschke or the court-preacher Adolf Stoecker in Berlin had sought to legitimize Jew-baiting in Vienna.[55]

For most Austrian Jews, at this early stage anti-Semitism seemed to be a specifically Prusso-German excrescence. It was no accident, Jellinek observed in *Die Neuzeit* (October 1882), that Austrian anti-Semites looked to Germany as their true fatherland, to Chancellor Bismarck as their idol, and to Berlin as their intellectual capital. 'They identify themselves as sons of *Germania*, not as Austrians.'[56] It was from Berlin, symbol of Prussian discipline, austere Protestant morality, and military obedience, that the poisoned fruit of modern Judaeophobia had gone forth into the world. Its midwife had been the Lutheran court-preacher Adolf Stoecker.[57] Encouraged by the very highest circles, the new racial anti-Semitism had spread out from the Prussian capital, leading to the barbarism that had climaxed in Russia and Hungary.[58] According to Jellinek, there could however be no doubt that anti-Semitism was a 'specifically German national sickness to which the Teutons are always disposed and which always breaks out whenever conditions are propitious'.[59] Unlike the more primitive parallels in Russia and Hungary, German anti-Semitism was seen as especially malevolent because of its 'scientific' form. Unfortunately, as Jellinek noted, even among German intellectuals 'the Lessings were exceptions and Richard Wagner the rule'.[60]

For all his bitterness at the Berlin movement, Jellinek did not abandon his faith in the superiority of German culture. In April 1881 he seemed reassured by the fact that *only* 255,000 Germans had signed the anti-Semitic petition to Chancellor Bismarck, calling for a revocation of Jewish equality![61] Adolf Stoecker's defeat in Berlin by the

---

[54] 'Wiener Briefe', ibid., 21 Oct. 1881, p. 328: 'Im Ganzen und Grossen bleibt aber Wien die Schutzstadt des Friedens und der Duldung.'

[55] Ibid.

[56] 'Zur Naturgeschichte des Antisemitismus: I. Anti-semitisch-Antiösterreichisch', ibid. 20 Oct. 1882, p. 367.

[57] 'Der Mann von Blut und Thränen', I, ibid., 6 Oct. 1882, pp. 338–9, for an assessment of Adolf Stoecker's pernicious influence.

[58] 'Berlin's Ehrenrettung und Wien's Beschimpfung', ibid., 21 Nov. 1884, p. 442.

[59] Ibid., 21 Oct. 1881, p. 328.   [60] Ibid.

[61] 'Diese 255,000 Unterschriften, welche ihm einige Tage vor Ostern übergeben wurden, sind das untrüglichste Zeugniss, dass das deutsche Volk durchaus nicht gegen

distinguished liberal physician Rudolf Virchow during the 1884 Reichstag elections appeared to salvage German honour in his eyes.[62] Jellinek correctly observed that working-class votes had defeated anti-Semitism in Berlin in contrast to the representatives of high society who had quietly abetted its poisonous spread. In Vienna during the early 1880s the disenfranchised workers had no less spontaneously demonstrated opposition to von Schoenerer's racism. *Die Neuzeit* approvingly reported in April 1882 the resolutions and speeches against anti-Semitism made at a popular rally attended by 600 workers in Vienna. The speeches revealed that the Austrian workers refused to be used as the 'foot-soldiers of anti-Semitism'; that they abhorred national and confessional discrimination; that they supported civil equality, regarding the anti-Semitic movement as 'a scandal in the century of Enlightenment'.[63] For all the hostility of the Jewish establishment to socialist principles, it was not ungrateful to this unexpected ally.

The resistance of Viennese workers to the appeals of Pan-German demagogues like Georg von Schoenerer and Robert Pattai was also the object of approving comments by the Austrian Jewish journalist Isidore Singer (1859–1939). In a pamphlet published in 1882, Singer depicted anti-Semitism as a German import from Berlin which had no prospects of success in 'tolerant', cosmopolitan Vienna. Singer was convinced that it could not strike roots in the Austrian capital for 'no genuine citizien of Vienna or of Austria, would lend himself to the advancement of this disgraceful movement'.[64] This confidence was directly related to the 'outstanding part played by the Viennese workers in the recently raised question of anti-Semitism, through which the workers have gained the respect and regard of the whole civilized world. They may now fully expect the warmest gratitude of the Jews.'[65] Another pamphlet, published in 1885 by the free-lance Jewish

seine Mitbrüder jüdischen Bekenntnisses antipathisch gestimmt ist . . .' See 'Deutsche Ostern', ibid., 22 Apr. 1881, p. 125.

[62] 'Berlin's Ehrenrettung, ibid., 21 Nov. 1884, p. 442. In the background to Stoecker's defeat, see Robert S. Wistrich, *Socialism and the Jews: The Dilemmas of Assimilation in Germany and Austria-Hungary* (Littman Library, London and Toronto, 1982), 90–7.

[63] Ibid.

[64] Isidore Singer, *Berlin, Wien und der Antisemitismus* (Vienna, 1882), 31.

[65] Ibid. 26. Singer favourably contrasted the 'healthy, unadulterated kernel of pure humanity' displayed by the workers with the attitudes of the Austrian aristocracy and Catholic clergy.

publicist Dr Friedrich Elbogen, also praised the opposition of the Austrian working class to anti-Semitic incitement. The pamphlet was unstinting in its admiration for socialism: 'Thousands, hundreds of thousands of my fellow Jews welcome this movement with boundless enthusiasm', Elbogen wrote, 'a movement whose object it is to realize the most elevated tasks of civilization.'[66]

Austrian socialism could not, however, solve the problem of Jewish self-defence against anti-Semitism. The Austrian Social Democrats, unequivocally rejected the role of being used (in Victor Adler's words) 'as a battering-ram either for or against the Jews'.[67] Equally, reliance on the 'gentle, mild and conciliatory' nature of the Viennese population and its 'dislike of extremes' no longer seemed a very convincing posture by the mid-1880s. Earlier editorials in the local Jewish press contrasting the tolerance and moderation of the Viennese *Bürgertum* with Prusso-German fanaticism soon began to acquire a somewhat faded look.[68]

More persuasive was the claim made by Jellinek that anti-Semitism in the Habsburg State was 'anti-Austrian through and through' because it endangered the viability of a political system dependent on concord between its nationalities.[69] To support this hypothesis, Jewish communal spokesmen could point to Pan-German efforts to break up the Habsburg Monarchy; to von Istoczy's campaign to separate Hungary from Austria; and to secessionist trends in the Young Czech movement which evoked anti-Semitism 'as a spectre to compel the Jews to join their ranks and fully embrace Czech national aspirations'.[70] Jellinek, in particular, believed that such arguments with their appeal to dynastic patriotism offered the best strategy for reaching out to the non-Jewish population.

It was, however, evident to *Die Neuzeit* that attempts to combat the flood of anti-Semitic slander still lacked any systematic organization, planning, or seriousness. 'To leave everything to the course of time, to the police and military—that is the sum of all wisdom for a great number of Jews', Jellinek observed, 'especially for those who thanks to

[66] Friedrich Elbogen, *Ein Mahnruf an das arbeitende Volk: Die Arbeiter und der Antisemitismus* (Vienna, 1885), 13.

[67] See *Gleichheit*, 17 May 1889, p. 1. For a detailed analysis of Austrian socialist 'neutrality' on the Jewish question, see Wistrich, *Socialism and the Jews*, 242 ff.

[68] See, e.g., 'Die Kaiserstadt', *Die Neuzeit*, 10 Feb. 1882, p. 45: 'Nein, in Wien ist für derartige perverse Bestrebungen kein Boden.'

[69] Antisemitisch—Antiösterreichisch', ibid., 20 Oct. 1882, p. 367.

[70] Ibid.

their social standing are less exposed to the poisoned arrows of anti-Semitism.[71] The passivity and silence of the wealthy Jewish élite was a great obstacle to effective action. While German, Austrian, and Hungarian anti-Semites prepared to organize an International Congress in Dresden (March 1883), the Jews in Central Europe had decided nothing as yet for their own protection and defence.[72] Their enemies displayed fanaticism, energy, and resolve in pursuing their infamous agitation. Unfortunately this had not been matched by a similar motivation or determination, necessary if the Jews of Central and Eastern Europe were successfully to beat back the anti-Semitic challenge.

Events in Hungary were followed in the Jewish press with particular interest and anxiety. Adolf Jellinek and his associates regarded the Magyar Kingdom as especially vulnerable to the impact of anti-Semitic agitation in the early 1880s. Like Galicia, it exhibited what to the liberal mind represented a particularly unholy Trinity—'semi-Asiatic' backwardness, a powerful Hasidic community, and a retarded process of acculturation.[73] The blood libel of Tisza-Eszlar, quite apart from its sensational character, seemed to confirm these fears. The trial provided the pretext for an alarming extension of anti-Semitic violence in Transleithania.[74] Jellinek did not however deviate from his belief that the frenzied gang of Hungarian anti-Semites led by von Istoczy and von Simonyi had been contaminated primarily by the influence of racial doctrines imported from Germany.[75]

It was widely held that anti-Semitism in Hungary during 1883 had assumed a more threatening character than elsewhere in the Habsburg Monarchy.[76] On the other hand, nowhere in Europe was it so quickly suppressed by the intervention of government troops. Its anarchic, lawless, and disloyal character was unequivocally rejected by the dominant political establishment.[77] The firm use of the gendarmerie,

---

[71] Ibid., 15 Dec. 1882, p. 536.

[72] Jellinek, 'Die Jahresbilanz des Antisemitismus', ibid., 22 Dec. 1882, pp. 543–4.

[73] 'Zurückweisungen des Antisemitismus', ibid., 11 May 1883, p. 177.

[74] Ibid. Also 'Der Tisza-Eszlarer Process', ibid., 20 July 1883, p. 278.

[75] 'Die Filiation der Ideen', ibid., 17 Aug. 1883, pp. 313–14; 'Die Anarchie im Osten', ibid., 31 Aug. 1883, p. 330.

[76] 'Der Antisemitismus in Ungarn', ibid., 24 June 1886.

[77] See 'Herr von Tisza in Wien', ibid., 31 Aug. 1883, p. 330: 'Allerdings hat Herr von Tisza sowohl durch entschiedene Erklärungen im ungarischen Reichstag als durch sein thatkräftiges Einschreiten gegen die wilden Ausbrüche des Antisemitismus bewiesen, dass es ihm nicht an Willen und Kraft fehlt, der Schande des Jahrhunderts mit allem Nachdrucke entgegenzutreten.'

army, and police by the Hungarian Minister-President to nip anti-Semitic agitation in the bud was warmly praised by Jewish leaders in Austria who saw it as a model for solving their own problems in Cisleithania. Speeches and declarations would not be sufficient against a movement which (as Jellinek constantly remarked) was essentially immune to reason and argument.[78]

In the Austrian half of the Monarchy, anti-Semitic agitation had not immediately seemed to present a serious threat. *Die Neuzeit* claimed in September 1883 that the Austrian Minister-President Count von Taafe 'loathes the demagogic and revolutionary activity of the anti-Semites and has given the strictest directives to the authorities not to tolerate anti-Semitic public meetings and demonstrations.'[79] However it also noted that August Rohling still retained his post as University Professor in Prague despite his outrageous distortions and calumnies against the Talmud. Austria was none the less still being compared favourably to Prussia for its humanism and tolerance, for the common sense of its citizens and the antipathy of its government to inter-confessional hatred.[80] Similarly, Austrian 'tolerance' was contrasted to the situation in Hungary where the malevolent agitation of von Istoczy, Onody, von Simonyi, and Verhovay made even the Berlin movement seem decidedly moderate.

But the theory that Austria would remain immune to the insidious spread of German anti-Semitism was clearly difficult to maintain. Already in July 1883, Jellinek had sensed the growing influence of economic anti-Semitism in the 'socialistic' propaganda of Dr Karl Lueger, directed against 'Jewish big capital'.[81] Conditions were becoming more propitious among Viennese artisans for anticapitalist Judaeophobia as Carl Löwy pointed out in *Die Neuzeit* (June 1884). The candidacy of the Pan-German lawyer Dr Robert Pattai, in the VI District of Vienna (Mariahilf) in 1884 seemed to prove that 'in many

---

[78] 'Ein probates Mittel gegen den Antisemitismus', *Die Neuzeit*, 17 June 1887, p. 230.
[79] Ibid., 14 Sept. 1883, p. 350.
[80] J., 'Unser Oesterreich', ibid., 5 Mar. 1886, pp. 89–90, contrasts the humane treatment of Russian-Jewish émigrés by the Austrian government with the brutal expulsions of *Ostjuden* from East Prussian territory by the German authorities. See also J., 'Die wahre, Alles versöhnende Humanität', ibid., 10 Dec. 1886, p. 466, praising remarks made by Crown Prince Rudolf to the academic youth of Austria; also 'Von unserem Kronzprinzen', 3 Dec. 1886, pp. 455–6.
[81] 'Verschämter Antisemitismus', ibid., 20 July 1883, pp. 277–8. Jellinek characterized Lueger as follows: 'Derselbe ist ein Wiener Kind, hat Bekannte, Freunde und Studiengenossen unter den Juden, mit denen er verkehrt und ist von der antisemitischen Krankheit unserer Zeit angesteckt.'

circles today it is part of the *bon ton* to declare oneself an opponent of the fundamental law of equality'.[82] Initial hopes that Viennese voters in the 1885 Reichsrat elections would reject the 'confused' programme of the anti-Semites and their primitive message proved premature.[83] Appeals by Old Czech leaders to Czech immigrant artisans not to support Ernst Schneider in the Leopoldstadt or similar declarations by German Liberal politicians gave rise to an exaggerated optimism that would soon be dashed.

In 1885 Dr Robert Pattai's unexpected election in the Mariahilf district with 5,554 votes and Schneider's near-success in the Leopoldstadt (where Jewish residents voted massively for his Liberal opponent, Professor Eduard Suess) were lamented in the Jewish press as 'a victory of barbarism over culture, of blind passion over superior reason'.[84] The attempted exclusion of Jews from the Deutsche Schulverein and the opting for moderate anti-Semitism of Otto Steinwender (leader of the German Club in the Reichsrat) were yet other disappointments.[85] Nevertheless, *Die Neuzeit* tried to maintain a tone of qualified optimism. It insisted that von Schoenerer, Pattai, Türk, and the other Pan-German deputies were 'totally superfluous in Austria'; their 'holy mission to save Germandom in Austria' had passed to others who no longer looked to Berlin or 'grovelled in the dust before their idol Bismarck'.[86]

In Jellinek's assessment at the end of November 1885, anti-Semitism was visibly declining as an 'organized army', or even as an important political factor.[87] The so-called 'pure, unadulterated Germandom' of Georg Ritter von Schoenerer had merely split the German national cause into rival camps. It was not Austrian Jewry but the Pan-Germans who had shown themselves to be an 'alien' element of disintegration in the Austrian Monarchy.[88] Von Schoenerer had

[82] Carl Löwy, 'Zur Beleuchtung der Mariahilfer Reichsratswahl', ibid., 13 June 1884, p. 224. See also 'Der Antisemitismus vor der Wahlurne', 30 May 1884, pp. 207–8.

[83] 'Zu den Wahlen', ibid., 8 May 1885, p. 180, included such optimistic predictions as: 'Kein Candidat kann in Wien einer Niederlage sicherer sein, als einer, der sich zum Antisemitismus bekennt.'

[84] Ibid., 5 June 1885, p. 216.

[85] J., 'Der deutsche Schulvereine,' ibid., 10 July 1885, p. 261, also 'Die deutsch-nationalen Antisemiten. Fremde in Oesterreich', ibid., 25 Feb. 1887, p. 71.

[86] 'Der Niedergang des Antisemitismus', ibid., 27 Nov. 1885, p. 441.

[87] Ibid.

[88] 'Das unverfälschte Deutschtum im österreichischen Reichsrath' ibid., 18 Feb. 1887, pp. 61–2; also 'Antisemitisches Feuerwerk', 3 June 1887, p. 212, which underlined the German Club's opposition to von Schoenerer's parliamentary bill proposing eventually to place Austrian Jews under 'exceptional legislation'. Jellinek

consistently displayed his contempt for the Austrian fatherland and its Habsburg ruling house, sowing the seeds of disloyalty in an entire generation of Austro-German students. But he had turned to a 'brutal, bloodthirsty Jew-hatred', as the 'motor which would make him popular among the masses' at the very time when the racist tide was ebbing in Germany and Hungary.[89] Jellinek reaffirmed that Austrian Jews opposed on principle all forms of national chauvinism which sought to belittle or disparage other nationalities. The ridiculous nationalist quarrels in Austria-Hungary over the language in which menus, price lists, traffic signs, or railway tickets should be printed were thoroughly alien to Jews. They had no possible interest in the endemic nationalist struggles for hegemony and privileges in the Habsburg State.

As *Die Neuzeit* never ceased to proclaim, Jews were 'Austrians through and through'; neither 'German-Jewish' nor 'Czech-Jewish' but 'Jewish-Austrians who love Austria and desire a national flag that extends over all the kingdoms and lands, tribes and nations'.[90] In Jellinek's own words, the Jewish dream was Imperial-Austrian, that of a 'strong, concentrated Austria', neither German, Polish, nor Czech, but under the firm rule of a head of State 'to whom they thankfully and reverentially look up'. 'The Jews are Austrians, proud of naming Austria their fatherland', he wrote in 1890, 'they are true to emperor and empire'. Nothing could be further removed from this dynastic patriotism than Pan-German anti-Semitism whose racial principles undermined the existence of the Habsburg State. 'The anti-Semite in Austria and especially in Vienna is neither an Austrian nor a dynastic patriot', wrote Jellinek in May 1888, 'but a son of the German race, whose centre of gravity is in Germany'.[91] The Austrian authorities had belatedly recognized the seriousness of this threat to State interests, condemning von Schoenerer in 1888 to a short term of imprisonment and loss of his parliamentary privileges. But official attitudes to anti-Semitism still left much to be desired.

Count Taafe had promised in May 1889 that where law and order were clearly infringed (as in the tramway-drivers' strike) the Austrian government would take firm measures to protect property. Yet the

noted, however, the support of 11 clerical deputies and of the so-called 'Democrat', Dr Lueger, for the racialist legislation.

[89] 'Der Process Schönerer', *Die Neuzeit*, 11 May 1888, pp. 184–5.

[90] J., 'Die Juden und die Nationalitäten in Oesterreich-Ungarn', ibid., 22 Aug. 1884, pp. 313–14; also 14 Feb. 1890, p. 62.

[91] J. 'Der enthüllte Antisemitismus in Wien', ibid., 25 May 1888, p. 204.

Minister-President proposed no specific measures against anti-Semitic harassment though this has been requested not only by the Kultusgemeinde but also by a high-powered delegation from the Wiener Verein für Stadt-Interessen und Fremdenverkehr.[92] Led by its President, the parliamentary deputy Freiherr von Pirquet, the non-Jewish delegation had pointed to the damage done to Vienna's international reputation and commercial interests by the activity of various anti-Semitic groups. The cool government response and the successes of the new clerical–anti-Semitic alliance in the 1889 elections scarcely reassured the Jewish community.

The Vereinigte Christen, under Lueger's charismatic leadership, promised to be a formidable threat to both Jewish and liberal interests. By the late 1880s the climate of opinion which it had created, reflected 'the mean and brutalized anti-Semitism which dominates Vienna and its environment, soils the city and country, stains the beauty of the *Kaiserstadt* and the charm of its surroundings'.[93] The nationality struggle had become equally envenomed with Czech nationalists imitating the Germans and openly striving for the 'domination of the Slavs' in Austria. According to Jellinek, Czech national egoism made them subordinate everything to their racial interests.[94] The resurgence of clericalism and its alliance with the anti-Semites in favour of confessional schools were disturbing symptoms of the retreat from liberalism.[95] Anti-Semitism in each case was perceived by liberal Viennese Jews as part of a general assault on the modern constitutional State and its most sacred principles—equality before the law, freedom of conscience and religious toleration.[96] Already it had penetrated into the Viennese educational system where teachers were widely held to be among the strongest supporters of the anti-Semitic movement.[97]

In Vienna, Graz, and other strongholds of the *deutschnational* movement, anti-Semitism in the 'zoological sense' had become the 'unadulterated' core of German national identification.[98] Its growing viciousness prompted the veteran liberal Adolf Fischof to denounce it

---

[92] 'Graf Taafe über den Antisemitismus', ibid., 10 May 1889, pp. 183–4.

[93] 'Wien und seine Umgebung', ibid., 29 June 1888, p. 253.

[94] 'Religion und Race', ibid., 24 Sept. 1888, pp. 359–60.

[95] Ibid., 20 Jan. 1888, p. 22: 'Die Clericalen wollen in der Schule herrschen und die Antisemiten sollen die Juden verdrängen. Um dieses erhabene Ziel zu erreichen, gehen sie ein Bündniss mit einander ein. Dahin also führen Herrschsucht und Racenhass!'

[96] Ibid.; also J., 'Die Vaterland-Christen', 16 Mar. 1888, pp. 104–5.

[97] See Sigmund Mayer's 'Offener Brief an den Herrn Dr. Joh. Nepomuk Prix, Bürgmeister der Stadt Wien!', ibid., 24 Jan. 1890, p. 33.

[98] J., 'Deutschnationale in Berlin und in Wien', ibid., 27 Feb. 1891.

in a letter of 28 February 1891 to *Gemeinderat* Dr Alfred Stern (one of the leaders of the Jewish community) as an affront to enlightenment, reason, and Austrian patriotism.[99] What would become of a country, Fischof asked, in which such doctrines were daily preached in the schools and churches? What would become of Vienna when its major political forums—the Parliament, the Lower Austrian Diet, and the city council—were ceaselessly besmirched by the mindless ranting of anti-Semitic deputies?[100] No other city in Europe was privy to such disgraceful scenes in its legislative bodies, such rawness of tone and unrestrained verbal violence. Yet this scandal was permitted to go unchecked by the seemingly impotent authorities.

An editorial in *Die Neuzeit* on 28 August 1891 unequivocally condemned the timidity and silence of Ministers and government officials in Austria. It unfavourably compared such lethargy to the firm repression undertaken by the Hungarian State several years earlier against a similar challenge to its authority. Magyar statesmen had acted speedily against this plague precisely because they recognized the crucial economic role which Jews played in Hungarian society. More importantly, they immediately grasped the harmful implications of anti-Semitism for the multinational structure of the Hungarian State. Austrian statesmen had not yet displayed a similar foresight and resolution even when confronted by the openly subversive character of Pan-Germanism.[101] The anti-Semites deliberately undermined the respect for authority, for law, order, and property. They were challenging the foundations of civilized values and morality.[102] 'How can a government passively look on', *Die Neuzeit* asked in May 1893, 'while this moral unruliness spreads further and further?'[103] Not a single government Minister in Austria had spoken out energetically against the monstrosity of anti-Semitism, in contrast to the clear stand taken by Magyar political leaders or more recently by the new German Chancellor, Count Caprivi.[104] This official Austrian silence cast a curious light on anti-Semitic obsessions with Jewish wealth and power.

---

[99] Text of Fischof's letter under the heading 'Ein scharfes Urtheil', in *Die Neuzeit*, 6 Mar. 1891.

[100] J., 'Die Stadt der Scandale', ibid., 1 Apr. 1892, pp. 133–4.

[101] 'Antisemitische hohe Politk', ibid., 28 Aug. 1891.

[102] 'Caveant!' ibid., 5 May 1893. In this editorial Jellinek once more emphasized the effectiveness of the measures undertaken by the Hungarian government, as a model for the Austrians.

[103] 'Vom niederösterreichischen Landtage', ibid.

[104] 'Reichskanzler Caprivi gegen den Antisemitismus', ibid., 8 Dec. 1893.

Although anti-Semites demagogically exploited the 'social question' to claim constantly that most Jews were rich, this was far from being the case. The majority of Austrian Jews, who lived in Galicia, were floundering in a vicious circle of poverty, unemployment, and discrimination. Elsewhere Jews still found themselves excluded from government service, the teaching profession, and state-owned industries.[105] In spite of formal equality before the law, as Adolf Jellinek pointed out, non-baptized Jews continued to suffer from a discriminatory administrative praxis. Furthermore, their economic opportunities were being constricted by a reactionary guild legislation which sought to appease artisan demands.[106] This situation had not improved despite the fall of the Taafe Ministry and the presence of two Liberal Ministers in the Windischgrätz Cabinet.

In the early 1890s, anti-Semitism also began to assume alarming dimensions at the University of Vienna, where liberal Christian professors like Hermann Nothnagel (known for their opposition to Jew-baiting) were subjected to vitriolic oral abuse by German nationalist students.[107] Pan-German teachers in the Austrian universities and high schools publicly denounced Jews as 'Asiatic invaders'.[108] Catholic priests in Vienna like Father Joseph Deckert lashed out against the 'Semitic exploiters' and even indulged in blood libels without being cautioned by their ecclesiastical superiors.[109] Parliamentary immunity enabled rabble-rousers like Ernst Schneider to call publicly for the expropriation and expulsion of the Jews 'by legal means', without fear of prosecution.[110] Ernst Schneider's party colleagues, led by Lueger, Liechtenstein and Gessmann, sought for their part to discredit the handful of politicians who dared to challenge their vile calumnies as being 'servants of the Jews'.[111]

The Christian-Social party could even surreptitiously engage in 'race-anti-Semitism' under the benign protection of clerical-conservative circles associated with the newspaper *Das Vaterland*. Yet the Catholic clergy officially maintained that Christianity and anti-Semitic racialism were incompatible.[112] Their argument seemed plausible in so

---

[105] J., 'Sociale Fragen', I., ibid, 3 Apr. 1891, pp. 132–3.
[106] 'Ein Jahr Coalition', ibid., 16 Nov. 1894, p. 459.
[107] Justus, 'Antisemitische Jugend', ibid., 6 July 1894, p. 270.
[108] Emes, 'Asiatische Eindringlinge', ibid., 9 Nov. 1894, p. 449.
[109] 'Aus dem antisemitischen Lager', ibid., 14 Sept. 1894, p. 370.
[110] 'Auf gesetzlichem Wege', ibid., 16 Nov. 1894, p. 461.
[111] Emes, 'Die Partei der Verleumder', ibid., p. 461.
[112] Emes, 'Eine Absage', ibid., 18 Jan. 1895.

far as Christianity based itself on the Old Testament. Jesus Christ and the apostles had sprung after all from Judaism. Moreover, racial anti-Semites had openly declared their hostility to both the Old and New Testaments. On the other hand, the most dangerous Austrian adversaries of Jewry like Prince Liechtenstein, Dr Karl Lueger, Ernst Schneider, Father Deckert, or Joseph Scheicher were unreservedly backed by the Catholic Church. They also enjoyed the sympathy of the influential papal Secretary of State, Cardinal Rampolla. Hence, *Die Neuzeit* remained highly sceptical about any papal condemnation of the Austrian anti-Semites, though this had been requested by some leading bishops in the Monarchy.[113]

The municipal elections of late March and early April 1895 for the Second and Third Curias in Vienna provided a further breakthrough for the anti-Semites and another setback for Jewish hopes. Lueger already dominated the Third Curia. He now added another mandate, this time in the Leopoldstadt district where Jewish artisans boycotted the Liberal candidate out of resentment at his party's indifference on the Jewish issue. This prompted some angry comments from the liberal politician Dr Richter in a speech to the Österreichisch-Israelitische Union on 30 March 1895. He pointed out that such electoral abstinence would mean political suicide for Viennese Jews.[114] An anti-Semitic victory in the coming parliamentary elections could threaten the foundations of Jewish economic existence. More serious still was Lueger's victory in the Second Curia on 1 April 1895 (24 seats against 22 for the Liberals)—a spectacular shift in favour of the Catholic anti-Semites since 1894. This triumph in the curia of teachers, civil servants, and professional people meant that only Liberal domination of the (capitalist) First Curia still preserved their narrow overall majority of 72 seats against a solid phalanx of 66 anti-Semites. Vienna was already ungovernable. New elections were inevitable but as the Jewish press realized, they were unlikely to check the Christian-Social surge.[115] In September 1895 Lueger's cohorts controlled the municipal council of the Austrian capital by a two-to-

---

[113] 'Papst und Antisemitismus', *Die Neuzeit*, 1 Mar. 1895, p. 81. On the role of Rampolla and the papal nuncio in Vienna, Antonio Agliardi, in supporting the Christian-Socialists, see Joseph S. Bloch, *My Reminiscences* (Vienna and Berlin, 1923), 165–75, and also John Boyer, *Political Radicalism in Late Imperial Vienna: Origins of the Christian Social Movement, 1848–1897* (Chicago and London, 1891), 340–9.

[114] 'Die Wiener Gemeinderathswahlen', *Die Neuzeit*, 5 Apr. 1895, p. 143.

[115] See Boyer, pp. 359 ff.; Pulzer, *Rise of Political Antisemitism*, 179–84.

one majority (92 anti-Semites against 46 Liberals), having received 43,776 votes in Vienna against 22,868 for the Liberals.[116]

Adolf Jellinek did not live to see this crushing anti-Semitic victory or to experience the demoralization which came in its wake.[117] Nor did he witness the silence of most Austro-German liberals in face of the Christian-Social flood, despite the massive Jewish support which the Liberal party had previously enjoyed in Vienna. His successors had to wrestle with the *de facto* collapse of the German liberal tradition in Austrian politics. They had to face the seemingly permanent loss of Vienna to the anti-Semites after the mid-1890s.[118] When on 8 April 1897 the Emperor Franz Joseph reluctantly confirmed Karl Lueger as Mayor of Vienna, they confronted a new reality in which Christian Socialism ruled the city and the Social Democrats were gradually emerging as the leading opposition party. Circumstances now dictated a reassessment of Jewish political alignments. The result was a more critical attitude to the Liberal party, a more active policy of self-defence, and a bolder assertion of Jewish interests.

The shape of things to come was glimpsed even before the electoral disasters of 1895 by 'assimilationist' Jewish politicians like Sigmund Mayer, Siegfried Fleischer, and Heinrich Friedjung during discussions in the Österreichisch-Israelitische Union.[119] In the Jewish press, after April 1895, criticism of the Austrian government and German liberal progressives (the Vereinigte Linke) became increasingly uninhibited.[120] Far from defending 'Jewish' interests it was now argued that the Liberal party had 'with incomprehensible, deplorable indulgence allowed anti-Semitism to wax strong' in Vienna.[121] They had made no serious effort to protect Jewish rights or even allowed Jews to exercise a political influence commensurate with the electoral support they had

---

[116] *Neue Freie Presse*, 18 Sept. 1895.

[117] 'Coalition und Judenthum', *Die Neuzeit*, 15 Feb. 1895; also X.Y., 'Das Judenthum und die verschiedenen Parteien Oesterreichs', ibid., 26 Apr. 1895, p. 177, which argued in favour of a 'new social-liberal *Volkspartei*' that would replace the bankrupt *Scheinliberalismus* which Jews had hitherto supported.

[118] See P. G. J. Pulzer, 'The Austrian Liberals and the Jewish Question 1867–1914', *Journal of Central European Affairs*, 33 (1963), 131–42; also Albert Fuchs, *Geistige Strömungen in Österreich 1867–1918* (Vienna, 1949), 5–12.

[119] See 'Coalition und Judentum', *Die Neuzeit*, 15 Feb. 1895, p. 64, for critical comments by Mayer, Friedjung, and others concerning the passive liberal response to anti-Semitism; also 'Generalversammlung der "Oesterreichisch Israelitischen Union"' ibid., 26 Apr. 1895.

[120] 'Der Regierungswechsel', ibid., 28 June 1895; 'Das Judenthum und die verschiedenen Parteien Oesterreich's, VI, ibid., p. 284.

[121] '"Das Vaterland" für und gegen den Antisemitismus', ibid., 18 Nov. 1895, p. 459.

given to the party. The failings, weaknesses, and endemic splits in German 'progressive' ranks were now the object of much critical Jewish comment.[122] Distinctions were drawn between the enlightened liberal *principles* to which Jews had remained faithful and the German Liberal party which no longer adequately represented them. At a general meeting of the Union on 25 April 1896, its secretary Josef Fuchs openly suggested that the 'passivity' of the Liberals in defence of Jewish rights required a revision of the traditional alliance. Jews should look to the creation of a new Social-Liberal party, genuinely committed to 'progressive' ideals.[123]

Sigmund Mayer in an address to the Union on 23 May 1896 analysed the significance of the anti-Semitic victory in Vienna and its deleterious consequences for Austrian Jews. He called for a return to the traditions of 1848 and the liberal-democratic programme of Adolf Fischof. Mayer observed that 'today the idea of the leadership of Austria by the German Liberal party has become illusory'.[124] The traditions of German centralism which Austrian Jews had long supported for cultural and political reasons were no longer valid. They conflicted both with the multinational structure of the Habsburg State and with the awakening of the non-German nationalities. Since there was no other bourgeois party which Jews could feasibly support, Mayer recommended a policy of political abstinence. Austrian Jews should vote only for those Liberal candidates 'who were liberal not because but in spite of their being German' and who supported universal suffrage as a just solution to the nationality struggles in the Empire. Adolf Fischof, he argued, had been correct in his perception of the connection between the sharpening of the nationality conflict and the rise of Austrian anti-Semitism. Fischof had demanded 'freedom and equality for all, nationality within the context of liberty. He demanded freedom for us not as Jews, but as men. Our proposal is to fight under the banner of Fischof.'[125]

Mayer's suggestion was supported by the *enfant terrible* of the Jewish establishment, Rabbi Joseph Bloch, who maintained that 'when the Jews reneged on the democratic principles of freedom, equality and fraternity, the result was anti-Semitism'. The Jews were now paying a

---

[122] 'Secession in der Vereinigten Linken', *Die Neuzeit*, 29 May 1896, pp. 230–1; 5 June 1896, pp. 238–9.
[123] 'Oesterreichisch-israelitische Union', ibid., 1 May 1896, p. 185.
[124] 'Versammlung der österr.-israel. Union', ibid., 29 May 1896, pp. 227–8.
[125] Ibid.

heavy price for having served the idols of German national chauvinism in the past. Had Austrian Jewry supported the efforts of the conservative Count Taafe to solve the nationality conflict in the early 1880s then anti-Semitism would never have attained such resonance in Austria. Another speaker, Dr Schnabl, echoed Bloch's criticism of the German Liberals. He argued that in present circumstances there was 'no party which we can join'. However, other speakers suggested that there was no alternative political home for Vienna's Jews. Hence, to break ties with the Liberals would be unwise. As one speaker put it: 'We live in a German culture, we think and feel German.' The answer to anti-Semitism was not to abandon German progressive ideals but to reform the Liberal party to insist on more Jewish candidates and to mobilize effectively voters in constituencies that had a substantial Jewish population. This attitude was echoed in *Die Neuzeit* which began to hint that Jews would have to organize, to stand up more resolutely for their rights and increase pressure on the German 'progressives' to fight against anti-Semitic discrimination.[126]

But the division of opinion among Viennese Jews in the Union over political tactics could not disguise the narrowness of the available options. The formation of a specifically Jewish party was generally considered as impractical. Even in those areas of Vienna where there was a significant Jewish concentration like the Inner City or the Leopoldstadt there seemed to be no chance of defeating Christian-Social anti-Semites at the polls.[127] The Democratic party of Dr Ferdinand Kronawetter, though attractive to liberal Jews on account of its leader's decidedly courageous stand against anti-Semitism, was far too small to represent a serious counterweight to Lueger. Confined to Vienna, it could scarcely provide a solution to the dilemmas of Austrian Jewry as a whole.[128]

The Social Democrats did express a powerful current in Austrian politics but their demand to socialize the means of production hardly appealed to most bourgeois Jews before 1914.[129] A Marxist class party of the industrial proletariat, intransigently opposed to free competition, the Social Democrats were manifestly unsympathetic to the Jewish role in Austrian commerce, finance, and the manufacturing industry. This

---

[126] 'Nach den Wahlen und vor den Wahlen', ibid., 13 Mar. 1896.

[127] 'Zu den Landtagswahlen', ibid., 2 Oct. 1896, pp. 405–7.

[128] 'Das Judenthum und die verschiedenen Parteien Oesterreichs', V, ibid., 7 June 1895, p. 248.

[129] X.Y., ibid., 10 May 1895, pp. 198–9.

was not a very attractive prospect to leaders of the Viennese Jewish community.[130] The strident hostility to Austro-liberalism in the Social Democratic press unpleasantly recalled certain features of Christian-Social rhetoric. Though anti-Semitism was not a central feature of the socialist critique of the capitalist system, their enmity towards the middle classes in Vienna was not without an anti-Jewish tinge.[131] This tendency was scarcely diminished by the presence of Jewish intellectuals in the Austrian Socialist leadership driven by the messianic vision of a classless society based on economic justice and inter-racial harmony. These Jewish Marxists were invariably alienated from Judaism, antagonistic to organized religion and indifferent to the specific interests of the Jewish community. They sometimes attacked the wealthy Jewish bourgeoisie of Vienna with a zeal that exceeded that of their Gentile comrades.

Confronted by aspersions against their own ancestry, some of the 'Jewish' Socialist leaders responded by unconsciously internalizing the language of the anti-Semites. The leader of the Austrian Social Democrats, Victor Adler (a converted Jew), answered his Christian-Social adversary in a public debate in Vienna on 2 March 1897 by claiming that 'there are among the anti-Semites more Jews than among us, yet they never speak of the great mass of leading Aryan [*sic*] comrades'.[132] Such ambivalent responses and the generally anticapitalist thrust of the Austrian workers' movement did not suggest to most middle-class Viennese Jews that the Social Democrats constituted a reliable bulwark against anti-Semitism. Moreover, working-class resentment against the domination of the Socialist party by Jews was felt to be growing.

Die Neuzeit noted, for instance, that within the Socialist party 'there is today an anti-Semitic undercurrent making itself felt against the Jewish academics and students pushing forward in its ranks'.[133] The 'Jewish' intellectual leadership of the Social Democrats would merely exacerbate rather than restrain anti-Semitism among the masses. In any event, the official Jewish community of Vienna could scarcely be expected to sympathize with left-wing attacks on financial capital. It was proud of the prominent part that had been played by Jewish bankers and entrepreneurs such as Arnstein, Eskeles, Rothschild,

---

[130] X. Y., *Die Neuzeit*, 17 May 1895, pp. 213–14; also pp. 248–9.
[131] See Wistrich, *Socialism and the Jews*, 250 ff.
[132] Victor Adler, *Aufsätze, Reden und Briefe*, 11 vols. (Vienna, 1922–9), x, 109.
[133] *Die Neuzeit*, 10 May 1895, p. 199.

Wertheimstein, Todesco, and Königswarter in the economic development of Austria. Hence, Socialist agitation against banking capital and
the Stock Exchange hardly seemed less threatening than the *Mittelstand*
anti-Semitism of the Christian-Social party.[134]

The tidal-wave of illiberal forces in *fin de siècle* Vienna emanating
from both Right and Left confronted the Jewish community with an
insoluble dilemma which merely underlined its powerlessness. The
absence of an organized Jewish political representation outside Vienna
further aggravated the scale of the problem. In Galicia, for example,
there were more than 800,000 Jews who formed just over a tenth of the
entire population. A number of Jewish deputies had been elected to
the Austrian Parliament but these representatives remained firmly
under the thumb of the aristocratic Polish Club.[135] Nothing significant
had been achieved in the Polish province to alleviate the misery of the
semi-proletarianized Jewish masses or to soften socio-economic
discrimination, least of all by the election of a few assimilationist 'Poles
of the Mosaic confession'.[136]

Still worse, according to *Die Neuzeit*, orthodox Jewish community
leaders in Galicia had helped to elect anti-Semitic candidates, thereby
demonstrating their complete lack of political acumen and inability to
utilize the suffrage in defence of Jewish rights.[137] The stranglehold of
Hasidism in Galicia had always been a thorn in the flesh of Viennese
Jewry. They tended to blame orthodox fanaticism for the economic
disintegration of Galician Jewry in the late 1890s. Polish and
Ukrainian economic boycotts of Jewish traders as well as the agitation
of Father Stojalowski now added new and more alarming dimension to
Galician Jewish misery.[138] Violent pogroms in western Galicia in the
summer of 1898 were an especially painful reminder to the Viennese
Jewish community of the vulnerable position of their co-religionists in
more backward parts of the Habsburg Monarchy.[139]

---

[134] 'Ueber den wirtschaftlichen Einfluss der Juden in Oesterreich', ibid., 9 Oct. 1896,
pp. 417–18.
[135] 'Das Parlament und die jüdische Wählerschaft', ibid., 5 Feb. 1897, p. 54; also 'Ein
Mahnwort in letzter Stunde', pp. 54–5.
[136] Ibid., 12 Feb. 1897, pp. 65–6.
[137] 'Die Führung der galizischen Juden', ibid., 10 Apr. 1897, pp. 151–2.
[138] See the speech of Polish Club Deputy Dr Emil Byk in the Austrian Parliament on
24 Nov. 1897, reported in *Die Neuzeit*, 6 Jan. 1898, pp. 3–4.
[139] 'Die antisemitischen Excesse in Galizien', ibid., 17 June 1898, p. 251; 'Das
Standrecht in Galizien', 1 July 1898; 'Das Judenelend in Galizien', 23 Dec. 1898, p.
538; 'Vollkommen gleichberechtigt', 25 Nov. 1898, pp. 489–90; 'Die Judenhetzen in
Oesterreich', 17 Nov. 1899 (excerpts from Dr Byk's parliamentary speech of 16 Nov.).

In Bohemia and Moravia, too, the spread of Jew-baiting against the troubled background of the Czech–German national conflict, darkened the closing years of the nineteenth century. The collapse of German liberalism seemed imminent in the Czech lands with the rise of racist Pan-Germanism, extreme Czech nationalism, and Social Democracy. Caught in the cross-fire of these contradictory forces, Bohemian Jews faced irresolvable dilemmas, no less agonizing than those of their Viennese co-religionists.[140] According to reports in *Die Neuzeit*, many Jews in Bohemia had turned in desperation by the late 1890s to the Social Democrats. The paper was sceptical of this trend, claiming that Czech Social Democrats had failed to take an unequivocal stand against anti-Semitism.[141]

It was argued that Jewish voters would inevitably suffer the same disappointment which they had already experienced with German Liberals. The 'Jewish leaders of Social Democracy' would simply provide a new scapegoat for Czech and German anti-Semitic agitators. The Hilsner ritual-murder trial of 1899 which whipped up Czech anti-Semitism to a fever pitch was especially disturbing, since it provided a fertile soil for Jew-baiters throughout the Monarchy.[142] It underlined the exposed position of the Czech Jews, caught in the vice of an intense ethnic conflict seriously exacerbated by the persistence of blood-libel superstitions.[143]

Although they were increasingly trapped within an inextricable knot of clerical, reactionary, and nationalist hatreds, many Austrian Jews still believed in the 'protection' provided by the benevolent despot on the Habsburg throne.[144] But prudence suggested avoidance of a clear identification with political or national groupings. Such abstinence by no means implied any relaxation of the need to protect Jewish legal equality.[145] Austrian Jews were encouraged instead to vote according to

---

[140] 'Die Juden in Böhmen und der Nationalitätenstreit', *Die Neuzeit*, 15 Oct. 1897, pp. 423–4; 22 Oct. 1897, pp. 432–3, 454–5.

[141] Ibid., 22 Oct. 1897, p. 432.

[142] 'Der Mord in Polna', ibid., 21 Apr. 1899, p. 155; 'Das "Geständniss" Hilsner's', 29 Sept. 1899; 'Die Judenhetzen in Oesterreich', 17 Nov. 1899; 'Professor Masaryk über den Mord in Polna', ibid.; and the reprint of an article by Masaryk, 'Das Wesen und die Entstehung des Ritualaberglaubens', 30 Mar. 1900, pp. 125–6.

[143] 'Aus dem Protokolle', *Mittheilungen der Oesterr:- Israel. Union*, no. 111, 14 Jan. 1899, pp. 4–5, on the efforts of Dr Fleischer, head of the Union's *Rechtsschutz- und Abwehrbureau*, to counter the spread of ritual murder agitation to Galicia.

[144] 'Die Stellung der Juden in Oesterreich in den letzten fünfzig Jahren', ibid., no. 110, 29 Dec. 1898, pp. 10–11; see also 'Goldene Worte', *Die Neuzeit*, 31 Aug. 1900, p. 364; 'Das Wort des Kaisers', ibid., 15 Dec. 1899, p. 495.

[145] See the remarks of Dr Fialla, 'Plenarversammlung des politischen Volksvereines',

integrity and character of individual candidates and to pay less attention to party-political labels or national affiliations.[146] By the turn of the century, there was indeed a growing consensus that no identification of Jews with existing Austrian political parties was possible. Though only a minority advocated the need for an independent Jewish political party or a unified self-defence organization representing the whole of Austrian Jewry, these propositions were no longer rejected out of hand.[147] This development was itself an indication of how far the principle of an organized struggle against anti-Semitism had gained ground even in liberal Jewish circles.

The notion that Viennese Jewry passively resigned itself to anti-Semitic rule, blindly clinging to 'assimilationist' politics or to traditional German-liberal loyalties, therefore, requires some revision. Jewish liberals in Vienna did not simply despair, accept their fate with equanimity, or else flee from reality into an idealized image of the past. They protested vehemently at the discrimination practised by the Christian-Social administration in Vienna against Jewish teachers, municipal employees, pedlars, and other social groups.[148] Liberal Jews were outraged at the bigoted, intolerant speeches of anti-Semitic deputies in Austrian legislative bodies. They denounced proposals to confessionalize schools, or to introduce racial segregation. They also protested strongly against any economic boycott of Jewish businesses.[149] The Jewish press was by no means deceived by Lueger's pious protestations that the Christian-Social party opposed only rich Jewish capitalists.[150] Moreover, *Die Neuzeit* reacted with undisguised contempt to the ravings of Gregorig or Schneider against Jewish entrepreneurs, lawyers, and intellectuals. It remorselessly exposed the malevolence of the Austrian anti-Semites who had turned against all civilized values,

Die Neuzeit, 29 Oct. 1897, pp. 443–4; 'Zur politischen Stellung der Juden', ibid., 6 Apr. 1900, p. 135.

[146] J. F., 'Reflexionen über die Reichsrathswahlen', ibid., 19 Mar. 1897, p. 116.

[147] 'Jüdische Politik', ibid., 5 Nov. 1897, pp. 452–3; also 'Jüdische Realpolitik in Oesterreich', ibid., 2 Feb. 1900, for a sympathetic review of a brochure of the same name by the Florisdorf rabbi, Dr M. Rosenmann, advocating the creation of a Jewish political party. Rosenmann's criticism of Palestinocentric Zionism was particularly emphasized. See also 'Nochmals die Frage der Organisation', ibid., 19 Oct. 1900, p. 434.

[148] 'Die Antisemiten und die Lehrer', ibid., 17 Mar. 1899, pp. 106–7; also the remarks of Dr Alfred Stern and Landtag deputy Julius Ofner, 'Eine Protestversammlung', ibid., 28 May 1897, pp. 225–6.

[149] Ibid., p. 226; also 'Die Machthaber im Rathause', ibid., 2 Apr. 1897, p. 142; 'Aus der antisemitischen Gemeindewirtschaft', ibid., 10 Mar. 1899, pp. 95–6.

[150] 'Der politische Seilkünstler', ibid., 15 Oct. 1897, pp. 422–3.

including education, progress, and elementary respect for human decency.[151]

Lueger was sharply attacked for tolerating the brutal Jew-baiting of his more plebeian associates, allowing them free rein to drag not only Jews but also political opponents into the mire.[152] His more redeeming features were not permitted to gloss over the cynicism and offensiveness of his political opportunism.[153]None the less, the Jewish press acknowledged by 1900 that Lueger was more amenable than most of his followers. The consensus of opinion among the Jewish leadership was that the Mayor would not permit an overt attack on the civic and religious rights of Viennese Jewry.[154]

The dramatic events in France at the time of the Dreyfus affair also seemed to strengthen optimism that the *fin de siècle* morass of anti-Semitism was only a temporary phenomenon. *Die Neuzeit* passionately followed the twists and turns of the Dreyfus Affair, pointing at times to pertinent analogies with the political situation in the Habsburg Monarchy. The shameless defamation, lies, and intrigues indulged in by the French anti-Semites and clerico-military efforts to overthrow the French Republic seemed to have obvious lessons for Austria. The Dreyfusard victory over their reactionary adversaries was seen as a hopeful sign that liberalism might yet prevail in Europe. In France, at least, the forces of clerical obscurantism had been defeated.[155]

There were admittedly no champions of justice like Zola, Clemenceau, Bernard Lazare, Picquart, and Scheurer-Kestner on the horizon in Vienna. The Austrian people showed no obvious signs of rising against the medieval legacy of Jesuitism and clerical anti-Semitism. Viennese Jew-baiters continued to slander with impunity not only the 'Semites' but also the Throne, the judiciary, the working classes, and other adversaries of their political aims.[156] None the less, the Dreyfusard campaign in France, cradle of human rights and emancipatory ideals, did provide a fleeting source of consolation for Viennese Jews.[157] The rehabilitation of the martyred Jew, Alfred Dreyfus, seemed to

---

[151] 'Die Vorgänge der jüngsten Zeit', *Die Neuzeit*, 26 Nov. 1897, pp. 482–3; 'Dr. Lueger contra Dr. Stern', ibid., 24 Dec. 1897, p. 523; 'Das Kind des Volkes', ibid., 7 July 1899, p. 266; 'Die antisemitische Pest', ibid., 28 Oct. 1898.

[152] 'Anarchisten in Amt und Würden', ibid., 12 May 1899.

[153] 'Kronawetter und Lueger', ibid., 4 Mar. 1898.

[154] 'Lueger ein Ausnahms-Antisemit', ibid., 7 Jan. 1898, p. 1; 'Dr. Lueger und die confessionelle Gleichberechtigung', ibid., 14 Sept. 1900, p. 384.

[155] 'Der Triumph der Gerechtigkeit', ibid., 2 June 1899, p. 217.

[156] 'Paris und Wien', ibid., 9 June 1899, p. 227.

[157] 'Der Sieg der Unschuld, Wahrheit und Gerechtigkeit', ibid., 23 June 1899, pp. 246–7.

demonstrate that progressive principles might eventually overcome the forces of calumny, injustice, and inhumanity in a modern, civilized state.

The Dreyfusard victory could not however disguise the depressing truth that Austria was not France. The liberal emancipatory optimism of 1848 to which Viennese Jews looked back as their own birthright appeared seriously dented five decades later. On the eve of the new century, an editorial in *Die Neuzeit* recalled: 'More than fifty years ago the Jews Fischof and Goldmark carried forward the banner of liberty and our noble co-religionists [Hermann] Jellinek and Becher died a martyr's death—today we are thanked for this with Dreyfus and Polna!'[158] Austrian Jewry had once believed that the revolutionary storm of 1848 might deliver them from slavery into freedom. Since then, Jews had contributed mightily in all areas of human thought and endeavour to the progress of civilized mankind. They had more than repaid their debt to their emancipators. Yet their reward had been the revival of clericalism, feudalism, and 'a shameless falling back into the old Jew-hatred'.[159]

Did this mean that the revival of anti-Semitism was 'a proof that we will never be digested?' For the editorialist of *Die Neuzeit* such gloom was a 'Zionist dogma'. It could only be justified had the 'Aryan' world relapsed into Judaeophobia while at the same time remaining faithful to libertarian ideals on all other issues. But the reaction against liberalism had been general. Anti-Semitism was merely a temporary, though in Vienna 'an effective lever which feudalism and clericalism had exploited with virtuosity'.[160] This was perhaps no cause for optimism. But in the eyes of the official Jewish leadership, anti-Semitism was above all a reproach to 'our Christian fellow citizens', who, blinded by cheap catchwords, had fallen victim to clericalism— the deadliest enemy of progress. 'Not Jew-hatred but the humiliation of the *Bürgertum* is the disgrace of the nineteenth century', *Die Neuzeit* concluded, 'and with it begins the twentieth century!'[161]

---

[158] 'Das Judenthum und die Jahrhundertwende', ibid., 29 Dec. 1899, p. 517.

[159] Ibid.

[160] For a similar analysis, see *Mittheilungen der Österr.-Israel. Union*, no. 114, 22 Apr. 1899, pp. 3–4. This suggested that only in Vienna, the city of the 'little man', with its socio-economic and intellectual backwardness, had the clerico-feudal conspiracy succeeded. In Hungary, anti-Semitism had quickly collapsed, in Germany it was already a political anachronism, and in France clericalism was on the point of going down to defeat. It was unlikely therefore that 'eine überall versiegte Strömung sich in Wien wie in einer Insel aufrecht erhalten sollte'. On the other hand, the Union warned against the illusion 'diesen Zusammenbruch in Wien bald zu erhoffen'.

[161] 'Das Judenthum und die Jahrhundertwende', ibid., p. 517.

9

Joseph Bloch: Rabbi, Parliamentarian, and Publicist

If one could construct a specifically Austrian nationality, then the Jews would constitute its foundation.

Dr Joseph S. Bloch,
Der nationale Zwist und die Juden in Österreich (1886)

You may try ever so hard and ever so cunningly—you will never succeed even in extracting from the German language and literature the Semitic spirit which took part in the creation of the language as far back as Luther's translation of the Bible. If you win power you will be able to suppress some individual Jews, you can worry them, but you will not get rid of the 'Jewification.' (Laughter.)

In this fight against 'Jewification' you resemble some funny fellow who swimming in a pond continually wards off the waves with his arms so as not to get wet. (Laughter.)

Parliamentary speech of Dr Bloch (2 April 1886)

We have fought for Germanism in all countries of Europe. (Herr Hevera: 'Unfortunately!'—Great mirth.) Herr Hevera is right: yes, unfortunately. Even in Poland where we have been received in the greatest hospitality, where kings and princes have dealt out favours and benefits to us, we continue to remain true to the German language. We were the martyrs of the German language, we have brought upon ourselves dislike and doubt . . . because in spite of our living in the country for centuries, we have not yet given up this foreign language. I repeat: For the national interest of the Germans there exists nothing so valuable and so sacred as hospitality, and the Germans ought to be the very last to discredit this hospitality. However, the German nationalist of Austria praises the wisdom of the Tsar, because he oppresses the Jews although he not only hits the Jews but the Germans as well.

Parliamentary speech of Dr Bloch (11 February 1890)

Kindly accept my heartiest congratulations for your brilliant speech. You have exposed the meanness of anti-Semitism with a profusion of knowledge, acumen, spirit, wit and sarcasm, and also the necessary pathos was there, when you wished to voice the indignation of the insidiously calumniated. You have merited the thanks of all our co-religionists by your annihilating fight against Rohling and the heavy blows you dealt his followers in your philippic against his disciples . . .

Dr Adolf Fischof to Dr Joseph Bloch (14 February 1890)

We who profess to be Jews must be represented in Parliament by a man of our faith who has the faculty and power to fight for Judaism, its doctrines and its honour, and to oppose anti-Semitic impudence and lies, persecutions and calumnies. This man must be thoroughly acquainted with the teaching of Judaism and with the brutal ways in which our adversaries fight, he must know their catchwords, arguments, and commonplaces. Such a man represented us in the Parliament now dissolved . . . he was the representative of the electoral district Kolomea–Buczacz–Sniatyn, Dr J. S. Bloch, he must be re-elected. It is not a question of personal sympathies but of a common concern of the Jews of Austria.

Dr Adolf Jellinek (1891)

Ever since the Austrian government first gave provisional approval to its by-laws in 1852, the Viennese Kultusgemeinde had defined itself as a religious body, not as a political association.[1] It was originally intended to provide solely for the religious, welfare, and Jewish educational needs of its members in Vienna. Unlike Catholic and Protestant bodies, the Jewish religious community was self-financing and did not turn to the government for assistance, even for the maintenance of its purely charitable institutions.[2] Under the 1890 statutes (which had settled the legal status of the Jewish communities in Austria) it became compulsory for all Jews to belong to the community in their place of residence.[3] Only one religious community was permitted in each locality, much to the resentment of the orthodox. Their efforts to secede and form their own autonomous

---

[1] See G. Wolf, *Vom ersten bis zum zweiten Tempel: Geschichte der israelitischen Cultusgemeinde in Wien (1820–1860)* (Vienna, 1861), 93–8.

[2] Max Grunwald, *Vienna* (Philadelphia, 1936), 420–1.

[3] For the various formulations of communal statutes, see the files A/W 24, 1–5; 24, 7; and 26, 1–14 in the Central Archives of the History of the Jewish People, Jerusalem.

communities were a continuous source of communal friction during the nineteenth century.[4]

Though the orthodox had their own Talmud-Torah schools which were recognized by the authorities, attempts at full-scale secession were successfully blocked by the Gemeinde board, with the support of the Austrian government. But Jewish orthodoxy never truly reconciled itself to the leadership of the community by liberal 'Reformers'. It consistently accused them of neglecting Jewish religious education and the Hebrew language, disregarding the needs of poor Jews and consciously furthering assimilation.[5] Orthodox criticisms were usually focused on the handling of religious and educational welfare issues (including discrimination against the poor in the matter of burials) by the communal bureaucracy.[6] They did not seek to challenge the traditional power-structure of a community still led by a narrow élite group of wealthy Jews who were generally older residents. Nor did they try to mobilize the mass of immigrant newcomers by calling for a democratization of the electoral system within the Gemeinde. Unlike the Zionists, community power-struggles were not one of their main preoccupations. This did not mean, however, that they were indifferent to political issues or 'Reform' influences in the community. There were orthodox Jews in Vienna who saw an intimate connection between their goal of strengthening Jewish religious consciousness in 'the strict conservative sense' and larger political questions affecting the future of Austria as a whole.[7]

The orthodox did share at least one assumption with the liberal leadership of the community regarding the political interests of Austrian Jewry. Like their rivals, they saw 'in the person of his Holy Majesty Franz Joseph a guarantee of our protection'; hence their cult of dynastic patriotism.[8] An orthodox newspaper like the *Jüdisches*

---

[4] See Avraham Palmon, 'The Jewish Community of Vienna between the Two World Wars, 1918–1938: Continuity and Change in Internal Political Life' (Hebrew Univ., Jersualem, Ph.D. diss. in Hebrew, 1985), 10 ff. for a summary of changes in the statutes before 1914 and the background to some of these tensions.

[5] See *Jüdisches Weltblatt*, 9 Dec. 1885, 'Dr. Maximilian Steiner, Vorstand der isr. Cultusgemeinde'. The editorial claimed that the poor Jews of Vienna had scarcely benefited from communal philanthropy and deplored the fact that 'Wien hat kein Waisenhaus für judische Knaben, Wien hat kein jüdisches Versorgungshaus, Wien hat kein Asyl für jüdische Obdachlose, Kurz und gut, Wien hat keine einzigen jener jüdischen Armeanstalten, die in anderen Geimeinden sich vorfinden.'

[6] Ibid.; see also 'Jüdische Gymnasien', *Österreichische Wochenschrift*, 2 July 1886, pp. 302–3.   [7] See 'Unser Programm!', *Jüdisches Welblatt*, 1 June 1882.

[8] Ibid. For the liberal cult of Franz-Joseph, cf. *Mittheilungen der Osterr.-Israel. Union*, no. 100, 30 Nov. 1898, pp. 3 ff., 'Heil dem Kaiser!'

Weltblatt glorified the 'noble and chivalrous monarch' on the Habsburg throne no less effusively than its liberal counterparts. It had nothing but praise for Franz Joseph's efforts to uphold concord and harmony among the nations of Austria. The old Latin motto, *justitia fundamentum regnorum*, was, so it believed, 'the firm foundation of this throne'.[9] The Emperor's declaration of 1882 was frequently quoted: 'I will tolerate no Jew-baits [*Judenhetze*] in my Empire, every anti-Semitic movement must immediately be nipped in the bud.' Franz Joseph uttered these noble words as soon as 'symptoms of this disgraceful movement began to appear in the Imperial capital of Vienna'.[10] The God-fearing Jew had every reason 'to be a patriot and faithful subject of the Emperor' for his Sovereign had proven not only that he desired 'equal rights for the Jews but that this civil equality would be maintained in practice'.[11] Orthodoxy, no less than liberal Austrian Jewry, regarded dynastic patriotism, loyalist *Österreichertum*, concord among the nationalities, as corresponding to its fundamental needs.

Austrian orthodoxy also recognized the need to combat rising anti-Semitism by a sustained campaign of persuasion directed at Christian fellow-citizens. Such a campaign would have to explain the true aims of Judaism, defend its honour, and correct the baseless reproaches against its teachings.[12] However, beyond this minimal area of consensus, orthodox Jews viewed the new political constellation in post-1879 Austria in terms diametrically opposed to those of the community leadership in Vienna.

The Kultusgemeinde leaders persisted until the mid-1890s in their traditional alliance with German liberalism. They remained vehemently opposed to the Slav, conservative, and clerical coalition headed by Count Taafe. Neither the willingness of the German Club under Otto Steinwender to enter into an agreement with von Schoenerer nor Taafe's own overtures to the Jews, could weaken the loyalty of Viennese community leaders to the leading German opposition party.[13] The orthodox camp, on the other hand, regarded Count Taafe's conservative regime as highly beneficial to the long-

[9] 'Jahresrevue 5643–5644', *Mittheilungen*, no. 31, 14 Sept. 1883.
[10] Ibid.
[11] 'Die Versöhnungs-Aera und die Juden', ibid., no. 79, 4 Oct. 1885.
[12] 'Unser Programm!', *Jüdisches Welblatt*, 1 June 1882.
[13] See 'Politische Wandlungen', *Österreichische Wochenschrift*, 2 July 1886, p. 302. Also Grunwald, *Vienna*, 429: 'The Jewish communal leaders rejected every proposal that they address themselves to Taafe, as "treason to the German cause"; *'Zum Taafe gehen wir nicht*,' they said.'

term interests of Austrian Jewry.[14] The *Jüdisches Weltblatt* constantly emphasized the 'resolute opposition to Schönerer's anti-Semitic movement' of the Austrian Prime Minister and the broad support which he enjoyed among the population.[15] It rejected liberal criticisms that Count Taafe had been less energetic than his Hungarian counterparts in condemning anti-Semitism. The orthodox newspaper claimed that under Taafe's government there had been fewer anti-Jewish 'excesses' than under any previous Austrian regime.[16] It argued that the new anti-Semitism derived not from Conservative government circles but from the German national opposition.[17] Count Taafe's record was irreproachable: 'The nations of Austria are content with the government system of the Taafe Ministry, the Count has energetically declared his opposition to anti-Semitism, whever it disturbs public order and hence it is only natural that the people obeys the voice of the man who stands at the head of a government which is sympathetic to its needs.'[18]

The orthodox weekly insisted that the Jews of the Habsburg Monarchy had every reason to be grateful to the Taafe government for the failure of the anti-Semitic movement to strike root in Western Austria. As a result, growing numbers of Jews in Galicia 'were turning from opponents into friends of the present government system'. This was particularly gratifying to the Jewish defenders of Taafe since they believed it to be in the interest of Austrian Jewry to support a regime 'which had made the reconciliation of the nationalities its primary goal'. In the opinion of Austrian orthodoxy, liberal Jewry 'should be less pushy in its eagerness to march at the head of this or that political party'; it should be less ostentatious in its display of wealth and stop advertising its oppositional stance.[19] Orthodox circles also observed that those Jews who protested loudest against Austrian anti-Semitism 'had pushed their progressiveness in religious matters so far that they feel positively wounded when not just Judaism but religion in general is even spoken about'.[20]

According to the *Jüdisches Weltblatt* this embarrassed stance was typical of the 'assimilationist' illusions of *Reformjuden*. Liberal Jews

---

[14] 'Das Ministerium Taafe und die Juden', *Jüdisches Weltblatt*, 1 June 1882, begins by quoting a remark of the leading Viennese orthodox rabbi, Salomon Spitzer, to this effect: 'Wir Juden sind die glücklichsten unter allen Juden der Welt.'

[15] Ibid.

[16] 'Die Stellung der Juden dem Anti-Semitismus gegenüber', ibid., 1 Sept. 1883.

[17] 'Rückblick auf das Jahr 1883', ibid., 1 Jan. 1884.   [18] Ibid.

[19] 'Die Stellung der Juden', ibid., 1 Sept. 1883.   [20] Ibid.

invariably blamed the rise of anti-Semitism on the laxity of the Conservative Taafe government or even on orthodox Judaism itself. They based themselves on the false assumption that observance of the Torah or fidelity to Jewish customs and traditional dress provoked Gentile hostility. Anti-Semitism was not, however, a reaction against Jewish orthodoxy but rather to the irreligiosity and self-seeking materialism of backsliders who had abandoned the traditional faith.[21] Liberal *Reformjuden* in Budapest or Vienna, eager to imitate the Gentiles by displaying their impeccable assimilation to Magyardom and Germandom, were the real culprits responsible for Austrian anti-Semitism. On the other hand, 'precisely in the Slavic provinces where Jews are mostly concentrated', where they had preserved their traditional mode of life unchanged, anti-Semitism had made the least impact.[22]

The Galician Poles, in particular, had demonstrated throughout their history a remarkable tolerance and hospitality towards Jews, despite Poland being a Catholic nation. Their reception in 1881 of Jewish refugees fleeing from the Russian pogroms was a recent illustration of this generosity of spirit. It was not members of the Polish Club but German nationalists in the Austrian Parliament who had sought to ban Russian Jewish emigration into the Habsburg territories. Poland was 'the only land which had not known the persecution of Jews', the *Jüdisches Weltblatt* confidently affirmed; small wonder then that Jews had enthusiastically participated in Polish struggles for freedom since the 1790s.[23]

The pro-Polish orientation of orthodox Jewry was accompanied by warnings to Viennese community leaders (especially to the Israelitische Allianz) to keep their fingers out of Galician affairs. No Viennese-inspired attempts to 'Germanize' or rather to 'de-Judaize' Galician Jewry would be tolerated. Galician Jewry was not about to sacrifice its faith on the altar of a German culture responsible for the poisoned fruit of modern anti-Semitism. Galician Jews already enjoyed full civil equality and identified themselves with the Polish nation. They would give their political support only to those parliamentary candidates who guaranteed the religious-conservative interests of Jewry, not to those

---

[21] Ibid. See also 'Juden und Judenthum in Berlin und Wien', *Österreichische Wochenschrift*, 5 Dec. 1884, pp. 1–2, for a similar analysis evoking 'the spiritual decay of Viennese Jewry'.

[22] Ibid. See also 'Seien wir einig!', ibid., 25 May 1885.

[23] 'Das Ministerium Taafe und die Juden', *Jüdischen Weltblatt*, 1 June 1882.

recommended by the 'reformers' and 'pseudo-Jews' in Vienna.[24] Viennese religious and lay leaders liked to accuse Galician orthodoxy of religious obscurantism and seeking to confine Jewry in a backward ghetto. But orthodox Jews proudly refused to betray their ancient faith for the 'false' freedom and emancipation from religion ultimately advocated by the reformers. 'It is self-evident that the orthodox [*gesetzestreue*] Jew cannot make common cause with such liberalism just as it is obvious that he prefers to support the Party which does not see faith as an anachronism but like the present governmental party makes one of its tasks the strengthening of faith.'[25]

In the perceptions of orthodox Jewry, the tacit alliance with the Taafe government and the Polish Club was seen as embodying the true interests of those who had remained faithful to Torah Judaism. Viennese liberalism of the 'Kuranda school' contradicted these interests. It was based on the assumption that social equality could best be achieved by religious reform and the stripping away of 'outdated' customs.[26] But for the orthodox it was clear that the abandonment of *heder* and *Kashrut*, the increase in intermarriage, and the efforts of the Israelitische Allianz to apprentice Jewish artisans to Viennese master-craftsmen merely exacerbated anti-Semitism.[27]

According to orthodox spokesmen, the growing religious indifference among Viennese Jews was logical consequence of the 'Reform' programme.[28] From their own standpoint there was little to choose between liberal Judaism and a completely deJudaized humanism (*Konfessionslose Nurmenschenthum*). Laxity in matters of religion could only undermine Jewish solidarity and cohesion. It was no surprise therefore that many Viennese Jews 'know nothing about the *Cultusgemeinde* and also do not wish to pay the necessary contributions to its upkeep'.[29] Orthodox Jews in Vienna regarded this 'indifferentism' as the inevitable consequence of a community structure whose spiritual leader preferred the Christian designation of 'preacher' (*Prediger*) to that of Rabbi which was considered too 'Jewish'.[30] Polish orthodoxy had little time for the universalist religion preached by Adolf Jellinek,

---

[24] 'Hände weg!' *Jüdischen Weltblatt*, 18 Feb. 1885.

[25] 'Die Politische Aufgabe der Juden Oesterreichs', ibid., 1 Feb. 1883.

[26] See 'Die Reformbestrebungen auf dem Gebiete des Judenthums und deren Wirkung', I, ibid., 15 Apr. 1884, for a critique of Ignaz Kuranda and 'die ganze fortschrittliche Judenschaft Wiens'.

[27] 'Seien wir einig!', ibid., 25 May 1885.

[28] 'Dr. Maximilian Steiner, Vorstand der isr. Cultusgemeinde', ibid., 9 Dec. 1885.

[29] 'Die Versöhnungs-Ara und die Juden', ibid., 4 Oct. 1885, p. 2.   [30] Ibid.

who in their eyes had dissolved Torah Judaism into a vague gospel of humanist ethics.[31] The long-term result could only be the encouragement of *Konfessionslosigkeit*, of conversion, or even of a 'self-hating' German nationalism among Jewish youth. The logic of Jellinek's integrationist philosophy would erode the foundations of Jewish survival.[32]

The *Jüdisches Weltblatt* effectively exploited the Rohling–Bloch affair to place Jellinek and the Viennese community leaders in an unflattering light. It fully supported the courage of the young Galician-born rabbi and expert in Talmud, Dr Joseph Samuel Bloch, who had dared to expose the Catholic Professor August Rohling as a forger and charlatan. At the same time it sharply denounced Jellinek for blocking Bloch's nomination (which had Count Taafe's warm support) as Professor of Jewish Antiquities at the University of Vienna. The Community Board in Vienna had in fact done everything to prevent the appointment.[33] The orthodox weekly accused Adolf Jellinek not only of selfishness, envy, and megalomania but of deliberately sabotaging Count Taafe's pro-Jewish policy. For the appointment of Rabbi Bloch to a professorial chair might have increased Taafe's popularity among the Jews and 'exposed the identification of the present government with anti-Semitism, so beloved in the Seitenstettengasse, as a shameless lie'.[34]

Dr Bloch (1850–1923) the rabbi, publicist, and Austrian politician who played such a decisive role in exposing Rohling, was a rather unconventional representative of Galician orthodoxy. Born in Dukla (East Galicia), the son of a poor baker, he had attended *yeshivot* at Lemberg and Eisenstadt where he acquired his expertise in the Talmud. He had completed his education at the universities of Munich and Zurich. This gave him a broad knowledge of European culture and reinforced his mastery of German, a language he came to wield with formidable polemical skill.[35] After a period officiating in provincial communities, Dr Bloch was appointed rabbi in the

---

[31] 'Ergänzungswahlen in den Vorstand der Wiener Cultusgemeinde', ibid., 20 Nov. 1885.

[32] 'Die Neuzeit über das orthodoxe Judenthum', ibid., 8 Jan. 1885.

[33] 'Dr. Jellinek contra Dr. Bloch', ibid., 23 June 1884.

[34] Ibid. See also Isidor Schalit in Ludwig Rosenhek (ed.), *Festschrift zur Feier des 100. Semesters der akademischen Verbindung Kadimah* (Mödling, 1933), 53, on Taafe's subsidising of Bloch and an orthodox Jewish newspaper 'Der Wiener Israelit' as a counterweight against the German Liberal party.

[35] See Joseph S. Bloch, *My Reminiscences* (Vienna and Berlin, 1923), 20. At the age of seventeen, Bloch could not yet read German.

industrial Viennese suburb of Florisdorf. He also served as a teacher at the *Beth Hamidrash* in Vienna where he lectured for two years alongside distinguished Jewish scholars like Eisig Hirsch Weiss and Meier Friedmann.[36]

Bloch displayed an unusual sensitivity to the labour question and the social needs of the Gentile lower classes in his early Florisdorf period. Reacting to the agitation against the Talmud carried on by Franz Holubek in meetings of Christian tradesmen in Vienna, he decided to launch a counter-offensive and began by initiating a series of lectures on Jewish social history to the workmen of Florisdorf and other districts of Vienna.[37] On 12 August 1882 the Rabbi gave, for example, a lecture on the theme 'The Workmen at the Time of Jesus Christ' before an enthusiastic audience of proletarians in the largest hall of Florisdorf.[38] His purpose was to refute current assertions that the Talmud trained Jews to become 'pillars of capitalism' and exploiters of the labouring masses. Dr Bloch shrewdly emphasized to his proletarian audience the 'socialist' humanist values developed by Palestinian Jews in antiquity.

Neither the Greeks, art-loving and philosophically skilled as they were, nor the cunning Romans, well versed in jurisprudence, wanted workers—they only wanted slaves. But the Palestine Hebrews, called Semites, knew nothing of slavery and only had free workmen, and this alone makes it possible for me to speak to you tonight of a working class in ancient times.[39]

The Hebrews had 'abolished the institutions of castes and slavery'. In Palestine 'it was the workman who led the political parties, who was consulted in affairs of state and who controlled the legislative'. Labour had been elevated in ancient Palestine to the highest status as the supreme expression of personality and human mastery. It was 'the greatest teacher, tutor and benefactor of man, the mother of our culture, the sister of morality, the friend of progress'.[40] Mosaic law had

[36] Bloch, *My Reminiscences*, p. 26.

[37] J. S. Bloch, ' "Der Arbeiter bei den alten Völkern," Vortrag, gehalten am 12. 8. 1882 vor den Arbeitern der Lokomotiv-Fabriken in Florisdorf und am 28. 8. 1882 vor den Eisen- Metall- und deren Hilfsarbeitern Wiens und Niederösterreichs im Saale "zum Grünen Jäger," V. Bezirk in Wien'. Reprinted in J. S. Bloch, *Aus der Vergangenheit für die Gegenwart* (Vienna, 1886), 13 ff. See also 'Das Recht auf Arbeit', *Österreichische Wochenschrift*, 1 Oct. 1884, pp. 1–4.

[38] See *My Reminiscences*, 32–51, for the full text of his speech. For a critical review of Bloch's speeches on the 'social question' and the Talmud, see *Die Neuzeit*, 3 Dec. 1886, pp. 459–60.

[39] Bloch, *My Reminiscences*, 35.

given the Sabbath day of rest to civilized mankind. This amounted to nothing less than 'the legal regulation of working-time by the State'. Four thousand years ago the Palestinian Jewish legislators had already planted the seeds of contemporary socialism 'without society having ever recognized or even wished to recognize the importance of their work'.[41] It was a tragic misfortune for the contemporary proletariat that not the Jews but the Greeks and Romans, 'the ancient classical nations who so shamefully misunderstood the worth and dignity of labour degrading it even to slavery are now the model and prototype of our modern Europe'.[42]

Dr Bloch hinted that current Bismarckian 'persecutions in Germany of Catholics, Socialists and Jews succeeding each other in wild disharmony' were ultimately a continuation of this Roman slave tradition. On the other hand, modern socialism could draw inspiration from the ancient Mosaic and Talmudic legislation which had been designed to protect the interests of the labouring classes.[43] With vivid examples Bloch illustrated the humane and far-sighted concepts of social justice contained in the Talmud, skilfully evoking great sages (including Hillel and Akiba) who in everyday life were simple woodcutters, blacksmiths, and labourers:[44] 'in the Talmud the workmen appear as learned encyclopaedists with great knowledge of the world and its nations and with a profusion of rare erudition.'[45] In ancient Jewish society differences of rank and class did not have any bearing on the communitarian democracy of learning. In the words of the Talmud: 'A bastard of some learning is superior to and has the precedence of a High-priest, if he be ignorant.' On the other hand 'modern exploitation of the worker by fortunate owners is not Palestinian but Aryan: it is the tradition of the Roman empire with its army of slaves.'[46]

Dr Bloch had cleverly turned the assumptions of modern anti-Semitism on their head. He explained to the workmen of Vienna that it would be to their benefit 'and would also promote the welfare of the State, if they did not fight against, but much rather for Semitism'.[47] Bloch repeated these arguments in the hall at the Grüner Jäger in Vienna on 20 August 1882 but was eventually 'obliged to refuse invitations from other Workers' Associations, because the Police Head

[40] Ibid. 38.   [41] Ibid. 42.   [42] Ibid. 37.
[43] Ibid. 39, 41. 'Ferdinand Lassalle found predecessors congenial in mind in his ancestors of 2000 years ago.'
[44] Ibid. 45–9.   [45] Ibid. 49.   [46] Ibid.   [47] Ibid. 51.

Quarters gave me a hint not to lecture any more to workmen'.[48] His lectures were nevertheless distributed in thousands of copies, reprinted in the socialist press, and helped to dissuade Viennese workers from being manipulated by anti-Semitic agitators. They also impressed contemporaries like his mentor Adolf Fischof, who warmly thanked Bloch immediately after receipt of his 'excellent lecture'. In a letter to his Galician disciple Fischof enthusiastically wrote:

Your comparative survey of the estimate of labour and the social position among the Greeks, Romans and Palestinians opens perfecty new and surprising views as to the high ethic importance of Mosaism and its adherents. The workers who are even now bravely resisting the allurements of anti-Semitism will in consequence of your enlightenment most certainly turn away with loathing from people who preach hatred of those whose religion, like no other, appreciates the moral and cultural importance of labour, and, like no other, demands an honorable social position for the worker.[49]

The influence of Adolf Fischof on Dr Bloch's political outlook at this stage in his career was of considerable importance. Both men challenged in their different ways the perception that Jewish interests were identical with those of German centralism, political liberalism, or *laissez-faire* capitalism. They were equally sympathetic to the demands of the Slav nationalities, advocated a constructive solution to the social question, and favoured the reconstruction of Austria as a federalist State based on the principles of cultural-national autonomy.[50] Both Fischof and Bloch fearlessly criticized the chauvinistic narrowness of the German Liberals in the Empire (supported by the powerful Jewish-owned press of Vienna) who opposed a democratic solution to the demands of the Austrian nationalities. A disillusioned Fischof told Bloch in 1882: 'the Viennese Jews do not guess what an awful reaction will break out and that it will certainly be accompanied by furious anti-Semitism; my efforts to form a democratic party would probably have

[48] Bloch, *My Reminiscences*, p. 51.

[49] This letter of Fischof is quoted in Bloch, *Reminiscences*, 54. See ibid. 54–9, for Bloch's immense admiration for the moral authority of Adolf Fischof, his identification with the latter's efforts to solve the nationality question in Austria, and his social-reformist programme. Bloch deplored the fact that the inaugural meeting of Fischof's Deutsche Volkspartei on 16 July 1882 had been broken up by young German nationalists and 'by a band of Jewish students with their leader Dr Heinrich Friedjung'. Bloch observed that not only the German liberal Press 'but the Jewish population of Vienna as well spoke of Fischof's attempt to prejudice the *soi-disant* privileged position of the Germans in Austria with the greatest animosity' (ibid. 58–9).

[50] See Werner J. Cahnmann, 'Adolf Fischof and his Jewish Followers', *Leo Baeck Yearbook*, 4 (1959), 126 ff.

prevented all that. Now the Jews themselves prevented this attempt to save them.'[51]

Dr Bloch, the Galician *Ostjude* and orthodox rabbi, strongly sympathized with Fischof's autonomist programme which was designed to overcome national egotism in Austria. His own originality lay in his attempt to apply such ideas to the Jewish situation within the Habsburg Empire. Bloch, like other orthodox rabbis, regarded the encouragement of national harmony as vital to the interests of Austrian Jewry. He also saw this policy as being consistent with the best historic traditions of Jews as 'mediators' between the nations. This was a role classically exemplified in Fischof's own life and teachings.[52]

With Fischof's tacit encouragement, Bloch launched into an energetic campaign against Rohling's *Der Talmudjude*. The Catholic Professor had attested on oath during the Tisza-Eszlar blood-libel trial in 1883 that Jews practised ritual murder. Boldly denying Rohling's scholarly competence (his adversary was at the time Professor of Ancient Hebrew at Prague, the oldest of German universities) he accused him of deliberately falsifying Jewish texts. Bloch even offered Rohling the sum of 3,000 florins if he could successfully translate a random page of the Talmud. The extraordinary publicity surrounding the affair obliged Rohling to sue the young Florisdorf rabbi for libel. But after a two-year investigation Rohling withdrew his action in October 1885, two weeks before the trial was due to open.

Bloch's vitriolic articles against Rohling were originally published as a series by Theodor Hertzka, the chief editor of the *Wiener Allgemeine Zeitung*, a well-known publicist and political ally of Adolf Fischof. They created an instant sensation, suddenly transforming the Talmud into a major topic of conversation in the cafés, hotels, streets, and

---

[51] Bloch, *My Reminiscences*, 59 In a lecture in 1898 to the Austrian Israelite Union, Dr Ferdinand Kronawetter, the Gentile leader of the small Viennese Democratic Party and another disciple of Fischof, recalled the fateful decision of Austrian Jewry to oppose the creation of a new party in 1882: 'I must, however, openly state, that the Deutsche Volkspartei did not meet with any encouragement on the part of the Israelites and that we had to submit to vehement attacks precisely from that side. Whether they acted wisely or not, you may judge better today . . . I suppose you have a different view of the matter today than you had in 1882' (ibid. 60).

[52] See 'Der Antisemitsmus in Nöthen', *Österreichische Wochenschrift*, 7 Nov. 1884, pp. 2–3, and Bloch's article, 'Dr. Adolf Fishof', ibid., 4 July 1888, pp. 419–20. 'Aus Adolf Fischof spricht unbewusst das Judenthum mit dessen Mission, wenn er seit vierzig Jahren bei jeder Gelegenheit seine Stimme für die Versöhnung der Nationalitäten in Oesterreich erhebt. Er will dass der Nationalitätenkampf in dem Kampf um die gesetzliche Freiheit aufgehe. Er verkündet damit nur das ewige Wort Moses! Ein Recht und Ein Gesetz soll Allen sein.'

public houses of Vienna.[53] In his preface to the articles, Bloch fiercely criticized the leading liberal Viennese newspapers and established Jewish politicians for their silence in face of 'the Hydra of anti-Semitism'. The Jews, he admonished, had done 'nothing but trust to the Government' while the poisoned arrows were being directed at their heads and a strong popular movement was beginning to take shape.

Our clever politicians and able parliamentary men whose task it should have been to be the protagonists in the fight against the medieval ghosts and revenants of obscurantism, they who ought to have made fiery speeches with ardent words against savagery and ever spreading brutality, who ought to have unrolled the glorious flag of Jewish humanity in the public assemblies of the representatives of nations—they seem to have other business on their hands. Their eyes are blinded by the fatal national strife which makes men unfit to see or judge events correctly. They do not protect the cause of Judaism, on the contrary, they perhaps made matters worse, they forgot that they were Jews and thought their enemies would not remember it either; instead of coming out to the front with their banners, they preferred to retire from the line of battle in affected superiority, leaving to others the hard and bitter day's work.

The writers and professional journalists of our race and blood proved to be even worse. I do not speak of several who were dishonourable enough to stand in secret pay and employment of our adversaries, nor of those who openly have gone over to the enemy's camp—but even the distinguished and great daily papers belonging to Jews or under Jewish lead used to do nothing, or next to nothing, in perpetual fear of being labelled as 'Jewish papers'.[54]

Only Hertzka's *Wiener Allgemeine Zeitung* had 'sent its ablest editors to fight anti-Semitism and had readily opened its columns to all enunciations directed against this pack of liars'. Hence Bloch advised Viennese Jews to support Hertzka's newspaper. This appeal and the tone of Bloch's preface not surprisingly angered certain members of the Kultusgemeinde Board and of the Israelitische Allianz. In any case, they scarcely welcomed criticisms made by an unknown upstart from Galicia, presuming to meddle in communal affairs. The community leaders had been notably reluctant to send their leading rabbis into the fray though they were best placed to expose the forgeries of Rohling, derived from an earlier work by Eisenmenger. Jellinek apparently told Rabbi Bloch: 'I cannot possibly refute Eisenmenger's whole book.'[55] Both Jellinek and Moritz Güdemann contented themselves with a categorical denial of the ritual-murder

---

[53] Bloch, *My Reminiscences*, 64 ff.　　　　[54] Ibid. 74–5.　　　　[55] Ibid. 65.

charges against Judaism. Rohling arrogantly dismissed their remarks as 'arrant knavery'. The establishment rabbis did not respond again, at least in public. They were evidently reluctant to become further involved in the cesspool of anti-Semitic politics for fear of aggravating the situation. Such considerations did not worry Dr Bloch.

Three editions of 100,000 copies of his first article (which appeared as a supplement of Hertzka's newspaper) were sold out in a single day. Ignaz Kuranda, the ageing President of the Kultusgemeinde, clearly disturbed by the mounting anti-Semitic campaign proved to be surprisingly supportive.[56] Joseph Ritter von Wertheimer was more critical of Bloch's aggressive tone in defending the Talmud. He also reproached him for having chosen to publish his counterattack in the *Wiener Allgemeine Zeitung*, a paper disliked by Board members because of its opposition to the German Verfassungspartei. Emmanuel Baumgarten, another leading member of the Board with excellent connections to the great Jewish bankers, gave Bloch a verbal lashing in the street and subsequently became his 'mortal enemy'.[57] For their part, Jellinek and Güdemann were initially reserved though the latter later co-operated closely with Rabbi Bloch in the establishment of the Austrian Israelite Union. The response in the provincial communites was unequivocally enthusiastic in sharp contrast to the cool reaction in Vienna. Overnight, Dr Bloch became a hero of the Jewish cause, the recipient of hundreds of grateful telegrams. The Austrian provinces did not share the reluctance of the Vienna board to 'make too much noise about the Rohling case' for fear of ruffling Christian sensibilities.[58] They evidently desired a more militant Jewish representation in Parliament. Following the death of the Chief Rabbi of Cracow, Simon Schreiber, Dr Bloch was promptly invited to become a candidate for the Galician constituency of Kolomea, Buczacz, and Sniatyn. In spite of the pressures exericised by Polish Jewish assimilationist circles, Bloch was duly elected to the Austrian Parliament in 1884, in 1885, and again in 1891. During the next decade he would remain the one

[56] Ibid. 66, Grunwald, *Vienna*, 434.
[57] Bloch, *My Reminiscences*, 76.
[58] In his memoirs Bloch somewhat bitterly recalled the ingratitude of the Kultusgemeinde board following his long struggle against Rohling: 'not even a line of appreciation was dedicated to me by the Congregational Board of the Vienna community' (*My Reminiscences*, 135). Wertheimer was 'still burdened with the spiritual inheritance of the epoch of enlightenment and the "Haskalah" and he, therefore, felt uncomfortable about the way I treated the anti-Semites' (pp. 137–8). Baumgarten and Baron Königswarter (who hated Eastern Jews) were outright enemies but 'Kuranda liked me and I could always count on his approval of my writings'.

parliamentarian in Austria who made Jewish affairs his predominant concern and consistently defended Jewish values from the tribune of the Reichsrat.

In 1884 Dr Bloch founded the weekly *Österreichische Wochenschrift*, dedicated to combating both anti-Semitism and assimilationist tendencies among Austrian Jewry. The militant Jewish self-consciousness which he expressed in this weekly and his strong support for Count Taafe's Cabinet (echoing the orthodox Jewish consensus in Galicia) increased tensions with the community leaders in Vienna.[59] Faithful to the inspiration of Adolf Fischof, Dr Bloch continued to link the struggle for Jewish rights in the Empire with the principle of equality for all nationalities.[60] At the same time, like the bulk of orthodox Jewry in the Empire, he glorified Habsburg dynastic patriotism, developing this into a veritable cult in his *Der nationale Zwist und die Juden in Österreich* (1886). This collection of essays was printed at the expense of the Taafe government.[61]

In this pamphlet Rabbi Bloch appealed to his co-religionists to remain neutral in the nationality struggle. They should avoid assimilation to Germans, Czechs, Poles, or Hungarians, regarding themselves solely as 'Austrian Jews' or 'Jewish Austrians'. This was certainly a position popular among orthodox Jewry in Galicia but decidedly antithetical to that of most West Austrian Jews, who regarded themselves as Germans.[62] 'National ostracism excludes the Jews from its circles', Dr Bloch argued, a fact which simply could not be ignored.

As soon as the people are permeated with the conviction that racial kinship is paramount, the bravest preacher of tolerance will not succeed in making the people accept Jeiteles or Kohn as their kindred. We cannot put on German-national or Czech-national airs without becoming a political caricature; it

[59] Bloch, *My Reminiscences*, p. 79. 'The upper circles of the Viennese Jewish society were highly indignant at my unhesitatingly putting myself at the disposal of Count Taafe's government, and I felt that I had forfeited their sympathies.'

[60] Bloch saw in Taafe's policy the implementation of Fischof's principles, noting that because the latter was free of national intoxication 'he was treated like a coin that was no longer current and was often abused by the "Neue Freie Presse" ' (ibid. 80).

[61] Cahnmann p. 127; Isidor Schalit, 'Erinnerungen', in Rosenhek (ed.), *Festschrift*, 53.

[62] See J. S. Bloch, *Der nationale Zwist und die Juden in Österreich* (Vienna, 1886), 28–33; see also pp. 45–53 for his polemics against Heinrich Friedjung on this issue. Bloch regarded Friedjung's German nationalism as political suicide and even as a form of 'Semitic anti-Semitism'. See also *Österreichische Wochenschrift*, 21 Nov. 1884, 9 Jan. 1885, 16 Jan. 1885, 16 July 1885, and 14 Nov. 1885.

follows, then, as a logical conclusion as well as a command of political wisdom, that we must take up a position outside all national parties.[63]

Bloch did not mince his disapproval of the role of Westernized Jews in Austria in 'the spreading and intensifying of the German national sentiment', though it was now boomeranging against them.[64] This highly critical stance allied to his membership of the 'Polish Club' in the Austrian Reichsrat and consistent support for the Taafe coalition deeply antagonized the Viennese Jewish leadership.[65] It ensured that the Community Board would respond negatively to Count Taafe's proposal in 1884 to appoint Dr Bloch, 'a member of the Polish Club', as Professor of Hebrew Antiquities at the University of Vienna. In the words of the reply drafted by Dr Jellinek and Emannuel Baumgarten to the Minister of Public Instruction, such an appointment 'would be no less than a provocation of the Viennese Jews'.[66]

Dr Bloch continued to defend Count Taafe's nationality policy despite the government's persistent passivity during the 1880s in face of the rising anti-Semitic agitation. He blamed this official indifference on Viennese Jewry's obstinate opposition to the Conservative government at a time when even the 'clerical' anti-Semites were supporting the men in power. According to Dr Bloch, Count Taafe's neutrality was inevitable 'the more so, as the Jews went over to his strictest political opponents and condemned every endeavour to make the Slav nations concessions of any kind, proclaiming them to be harmful for the German interests'.[67] Taafe, he pointed out, had no prejudices against the Jews as such and 'accepted with great goodwill numberless Jewish appeals against unjust decisions of the Governor of Galicia or in West-Austria'. But given justified conviction that 'the Viennese Jews were his implacable opponents' and sought his political downfall, Taafe

---

[63] From *Der nationale Zwist*, quoted in *My Reminiscences*, 159.

[64] Ibid. 90.

[65] Symptomatic in this regard was the attitude of the coal-baron David Ritter von Gutmann who 'considered the political dogmas of the German Liberal upper middle class holy and unassailable'. Though Gutmann initially financed the court case against Rohling, he baulked at paying the lawyer's fees and spoke of Bloch 'in a disparaging manner'. He was especially displeased by the rabbi's lectures to Viennese workmen. Above all, Dr Bloch recalled, 'my political connection with the Galician and Slav deputies was a crime in his eyes' (*My Reminiscences*, 88).

[66] Schalit, p. 54. For Bloch's own assessment of this affair, see *My Reminiscences*, 153–7. Bloch notes the orthodox Rabbi Güdemann's 'undisguised sympathy' for his position and Jellinek's subsequent efforts to make amends. The appointment had also been opposed by clerical and German chauvinist elements.

[67] *My Reminiscences*, 152.

could not be expected to suppress forcibly anti-Semitic agitation. The Austrian government could at most informally commit itself to preserving law and order against violent 'excesses'.[68] The real answer to anti-Semitism would have to be organized self-help by the Jewish community.

In the very first issue of the *Österreichische Wochenschrift* (15 October 1884) Dr Bloch had appealed to the Jewish public to create a political organization devoted to self-defence. He pointed to the impotence of the existing Jewish leadership in the face of anti-Semitism. 'All parties are in a state of war against us, none will show us any consideration, our alliance has become troublesome and compromising. In our own ranks despondency is spreading, cowardly renegades are multiplying daily, and our leaders are sitting with folded arms leaving the rest to providence.'[69]

Racial intolerance had become a destructive passion 'revealing itself in an awful brutality of all the lowest insticts', painting the life, thoughts, and religion of Jewry in the most lurid colours. Most Jews did not see the danger clearly since they did not generally read the anti-Semitic speeches and pamphlets that were daily poisoning the climate of opinion in the Austrian population. Worse still, Jewish leaders, confronted by the explosive elements of racial, religious, and class hatred in contemporary anti-Semitism, displayed a shameful weakness, political impotence, and failure of moral energy. They supplicated the government to protect their civil rights while opposing its general policies.[70] Disorganized, fragmented, and powerless, Austrian Jews would have to learn from their enemies. Their task must be to establish 'a defensive alliance [*Schutzbündnis*] and start the formation of an Israelite society of citizens!' Rabbi Bloch called on Austrian Jews to hold their heads high, to stand up for their rights and 'take up all the intellectual weapons at our disposal to fight the battle'.[71] The militant thirty-four-year-old rabbi concluded with a stirring appeal to form a

---

[68] See *Österreichische Wochenschrift*, 14 May 1886, p. 223; also *My Reminiscences*, 159–60. Bloch observed that only in 1889 had Dr Alfred Stern in the name of the Kultusgemeinde officially and belatedly presented a memo to the government on this issue, by which time the flood of anti-Semitism had grown enormously 'in view of the inactivity of the Jews and the passiveness of the Government'.

[69] 'Unsere Situation. Ein Mahn- und Weckruf,' *Österreichische Wochenschrift*, 15 Oct. 1884, pp. 1–3.

[70] Ibid. 2.

[71] Ibid. See also *My Reminiscences*, 188 ff., on 'The Foundation of the Austrian Union of Israelites'.

Jewish Bürgerverein 'for the defence of our seriously threatened political and social rights!'[72]

Dr Bloch envisaged a central role for his new weekly ('a fighting organ for rebutting all hostile attacks against Judaism') in the campaign against 'the torpor of fatalistic indolence' which had 'until now tied down even the most intelligent of our race'.[73] The *Österreichische Wochenschrift* would provide 'the spiritual armoury in the fight for the honour of the Jewish name'. Its aim was to conduct an unremitting offensive against the propagation of German national ideas among the Jewish youth so that they should not 'be degraded into helots in the vile welter of nationalist party struggles'.[74] Severely reprimanded for his politics by Baron Moritz von Königswarter (a prominent Jewish member of the *Herrenhaus* and opponent of the Taafe Cabinet), Rabbi Bloch pointedly observed that it was not the patricians but 'the small Jewish tradesmen and defenceless pedlars in the Prater' who were 'the prey of the anti-Semitic mob'.[75]

The marked anti-assimilatory tone of Dr Bloch's programme was inevitably seen by detractors like Emannuel Baumgarten and Dr Heinrich Friedjung as a 'retreat into the political ghetto'.[76] The Galician rabbi's intense Jewish militancy aroused resentment among many liberal Germanophile Jews who felt that he emphasized his racial affiliation too strongly. Dr Bloch himself admitted in his memoirs that he had conducted the *Wochenschrift* 'in a Jewish-national spirit' though he was at no time committed to Zionist 'party-dogma'. It is therefore no surprise that Kadimah already in 1884 expressed warm sympathy for this 'organ of loyal and self-conscious Judaism, which was scoffed at by non-Jews and abused by Jews'.[77] Rabbi Bloch was a welcome guest of honour on 17 December 1884 at the Maccabean function of the Jewish student fraternity, with which he had established friendly relations from the outset.[78] His address on that occasion celebrated the story of the Maccabees as a victory of the weak over the mighty, of liberty over tyranny and spirituality over brute force. He also reminded

---

[72] *Österreichische Wochenschrift*, 15 Oct. 1884, p. 3: 'Bilden wir eine jüdischen Bürgerverein zur Vertheidigung unser arg bedrohten politischen und sozialen Rechte!' See also Gerson Wolf's 'Jüdische Burgervereine' in ibid., 7 Nov. 1884, pp. 3–4, and the subsequent polemics.

[73] *My Reminiscences*, 185.   [74] Ibid. 182.   [75] Ibid. 179.

[76] *Der nationale Zwist*, 29; Gerson Wolf, 'Jüdische Burgervereine', also argued in this vein.

[77] *My Reminiscences*, 182, 185.

[78] Central Zionist Archives (CZA ZI/I) Jerusalem. Letters of Dr Bloch to Kadimah, 10 May, 1883, 28 April, and 5 June 1884.

the students of Kadimah that the celebration of military victories was a profoundly un-Jewish practice. The duty of Jewish students was to dedicate themselves to 'the great cultural tasks facing mankind' rather than 'to confront other peoples, in enmity'.[79]

Rabbi Bloch's reputation as a fearless fighter against anti-Semitism, his determination to make Jews conscious 'of their inescapable common fate' and to arouse their pride in a common past of 4,000 years 'unparalleled alike in suffering and glory' linked him to the aspirations of Kadimah. Like the youthful founders of Kadimah he was committed to strengthening Jewish self-respect and to the fight 'to counteract treason and aspostasy' in Jewish ranks.[80] It was only natural that his electoral success in June 1885 against Dr Emil Byk (the Polish Jewish assimilationist leader in Austrian Galicia) was hailed as a day of honour for the whole Jewish people' by the organ of Kadimah.[81] Its editor, the twenty-one-year-old Nathan Birnbaum, described Dr Bloch as 'the first non-assimilated Jew in the Austrian Parliament, the first Jewish parliamentary deputy who has approached so closely to the Jewish national idea from which hopefully he will no longer distance himself'.[82]

By 1885 the thirty-five-year-old district rabbi was no longer an unknown outsider but already a serious force for change within Viennese communal politics. His initiatives had been acclaimed by Austrian provincial communities, by the Jewish 'man in the street', and by Jewish nationalist students in Vienna. Though the Florisdorf community had been obliged to dismiss him as their *Bezirksrabbiner*, Dr Bloch had rapidly established a solid base of electoral support in Galicia. He was widely respected by orthodox and nationally-minded Jewish constituents as well as enjoying the confidence of some influential Galician politicians who had helped him to found the *Österreichische Wochenschrift*. These Polish Gentile friends included Franz Smolka, the President of the Austrian House of Commons (an admirer of Adolf Fischof) and Count Alfred Potocki, a leading statesman of the Galician aristocracy.[83]

[79] Quoted in Julius H. Schoeps, 'Modern Heirs of the Maccabees: The Beginnings of the Vienna Kadimah, 1882–1897' *Leo Baeck Yearbook*, 27 (1982), 159.

[80] *My Reminiscences*, 182.

[81] See 'Chronik' (Die Wiederwahl des Dr. Bloch), *Selbstemanzipation*, 1, no. 10, 17 June 1885, p. 3.

[82] Volkswille,' ibid., p. 3. See also 'Correspondenzen', *Österreichische Wochenschrift*, 1 May 1885, for the warm letter of greetings to Dr Bloch from the Akademische Verein Kadimah for his courageous defence of Jewish interests.

[83] *My Reminiscences*, 211–13.

From the Polish base and his parliamentary platform in Vienna, the pugnacious little rabbi single-handedly carried on a remarkable guerrilla war against the growing phalanx of Austrian anti-Semites. Between 1883 and 1895 he established himself as the foremost public defender of Jewish constitutional rights in Austria. He was the first Austrian Jew to put forward a coherent defence strategy predicted on Jewish political organization and the consciousness of common ancestry and fate. Bloch's proposal of a *Bürgerverein*, first enunciated in October 1884, did not pass unheeded. It led after a year a half of negotiatons to the founding on 24 April 1886 of the Österreichisch-Israelitische Union (Austrian Israelite Union). Its declared aim was 'to elevate and foster Jewish consciousness [*Stammesbewusstsein*], to create a front against the rapidly spreading "semitic anti-Semitism" and as much as possible, to suppress all tendencies which seek to sharpen religious and racial antagonisms'.[84] Composed mainly of a younger generation of middle-class Jewish businessmen, academics, and professionals, the Union was both a political club and a forum for the promotion of Jewish religion and culture, designed to win young Jews back to the fold.

The Union officially announced that it would engage in an 'internal struggle against the shameful self-surrender and degradation and the retrieval of the younger generation, which is practically totally estranged from us, from our glorious . . . tradition'.[85] Improving the quality of Jewish education and religious instruction came to be anchored in the Union's statutes as the first line of defence against disaffection. The fight against 'self-hatred' in the Jewish camp was transformed into a necessary prelude for the defence of Jewish rights against anti-Semitism. At the same time, under Dr Bloch's guidance, the Union also organized protest meetings against the electoral advances made by anti-Semitism. In the 1890s it established legal bureaux to defend Jews whose political rights had been infringed.

The preparatory meeting of 4 April 1885 in a Leopoldstadt restaurant had been attended by Dr Bloch, by the lawyers Dr Friedrich Elbogen and Dr Sigmund Zins, the University *Docent* Dr Josef Grünfeld, the physician Dr Emil Pins, the bankers, S. G. Fischel, Bernhard Kanitz, and J. H. Singer, the barrister-at-law Dr Jacob Kohn, and others.[86] It had spoken of founding a Jewish society 'with

---

[84] *Österreichische Wochenschrift*, 10 Apr. 1885, p. 1.
[85] 'Das Vereinsprogramm', ibid. 17 Apr. 1886, pp. 1–2.
[86] *My Reminiscences*, 188–9.

the object of bringing about united political action in all questions referring to Judaism'. Dr. Zins was elected chairman of the provisionary committee, Fischel as vice-chairman, and Dr Jacob Kohn as secretary. The new society issued a proclamation to the public in May 1885, addressed to 'co-nationals' rather than 'co-religionists', deploring the alienation of Jewish youth from its own history. It also criticized the inadequacy of the Kultusgemeinden in confronting external threats, emphasizing in particular the need for a concerted, vigorous fight against anti-Semitism.[87]

The draft-programme of the Union was initially rejected by the Austrian government for reasons that remain obscure. The statutes had moreover to be considerably watered down before they became acceptable to the moderate elements of the Jewish community, who in respect of anti-Semitism still 'preferred the policy of silent disregard to an open confrontation'.[88] By the time of the constituent general meeting of the Union in the festive hall of the Lower Austrian Chamber of Commerce in April 1886, the society could no longer be described as a fully-fledged civic association. The aim of protecting 'all special Jewish interests' in Austria and creating a militant political self-defence organization had clearly been muted.[89] The founding meeting was the epitome of respectability, including several Jewish town-councillors, the President of the Kultusgemeinde, representatives of the Israelitische Allianz and other established Jewish institutions.[90]

Dr Zins's keynote speech expressly denied that there were any 'separatist' tendencies motivating the creation of the Union. He emphasized the 'duties of the Austrian Jews to a staunch Austrian patriotism' whether they regarded themselves as Germans, Czechs, or Poles. The chairman also downplayed the dangers of Judaeophobia, affirming that: 'if anti-Semitism is to be fought we must begin with Jewish anti-Semitism. Our first task is to raise Judaism in the eyes of

---

[87] *My Reminiscences*, 190–1. Dr Bloch declined the presidency of the new society in view of his 'pronounced political position which was exposed to many attacks'. See ibid. 189.

[88] See Jacob Toury, 'Troubled Beginnings: The Emergence of the Österreichisch-Israelitische Union', *Leo Baeck Yearbook*, 30 (1985), 467. Toury's comparison of the original aims of the *Bürgerverein* as envisaged by Bloch and the final statutes of the Union, emphasizes the downgrading of its political thrust and of the dangers of anti-Semitism.   [89] Ibid. 472–5.

[90] *Österreichische Wochenschrift*, 30 Apr. 1886, p. 193. *My Reminiscences*, 191–2, also gives a list of dignitaries present at the meeting. They included among others town-councillor Dr Alfred Stern, *Landesschulrat* Dr Fürth, and Professor Adam Politzer of the University of Vienna.

others and in our own . . .'[91] Furthermore, Dr Zins made it clear that the Union was not defending 'Jewish rights' but 'the human rights of the Jews', not simply Judaism but the universal values of 'truth, freedom and justice'.[92]

The evident dilution of Dr Bloch's militant idea of a *Bürgerverein* was reflected not only in the statutes but also in the middle-class composition of the board members. No less significant was the official invitation to the conservative rabbi Moritiz Güdemann to wind up the proceedings with a lecture on ' The Importance of Jewish Science for Judaism'.[93] Jacob Toury's caustic verdict that 'a new, culturally orientated, politically liberal, but not overactive, club had been formed, which consisted of the newer upward-moving strata of the Vienna Jewish middle classes' is unduly harsh but not altogether wide of the mark.[94]

It should not be forgotten that the Union did come to play a very important role in Jewish community life and in practice exercised a key influence in gradually politicizing certain sectors of middle-class Viennese Jewry.[95] This role could not be played by the Kultusgemeinde because under its official statutes it manifestly lacked the legal-political authority to conduct any counter-offensive against anti-Semitism. In1885, there was no other Austrian Jewish body equipped to take up the defence of endangered Jewish rights. The Union stepped into the vacuum. However, it did not seek to operate outside the parameters of Jewish self-definition as laid down by the 1890 government statutes. Like the Community Board, it too maintained that the Jews were a religious rather than a national community in Austria. Moreover, within a few years of its foundation most of the top offices in the Kultusgemeinde were undeniably held by Union members. More than anything, this fact symbolized its peaceable merger with the older Jewish establishment. Yet, the emergence of the Union also signified a rupture with older patterns of Jewish passivity in the face of external pressure, provocation, and incitement. Not only did it provide a new organizational framework for middle-class Viennese Jews; the Union became a major forum for the expression of a more forceful sense of Jewish pride and identity.[96]

[91] *My Reminiscences*, 192.
[92] *Österreichische Wochenschrift*, 30 Apr. 1886, p. 194.
[94] *My Reminiscences*, 193; Toury, p. 475.   [94] Toury, p. 475.
[95] See Palmon for a useful account of the Union's internal history and subsequent impact on Viennese Jewry.
[96] Marsha Rozenblit, *The Jews of Vienna, 1867–1914: Assimilation and Identity*

Although the Union was notably less assertive and more 'assimilationist' than Dr Bloch had originally intended, this did not prevent him from being a regular speaker at its general meetings and advising its board of directors.[97] Moreover, since the early 1890s as Dr Bloch pointed out in his memoirs, 'the desire for and the necessity of political activity grew stronger; the hatred of Jews in the lower and middle classes of the population became more and more aggressive, and so it was necessary to pay continual attention to the defence against hostile attacks.'[98] The more passive posture of the Kultusgemeinde board symbolized in the past by such influential members as Emmanuel Baumgarten gradually made way for an activist stance that owed much to the impact of the Union.[99] As for Dr Bloch himself, having somewhat moderated his earlier oppositional tendencies, he was gradually co-opted by the Jewish establishment of Vienna after 1889.

Not only the orthodox circles in Galicia or Vienna but even the assimilationist lay leaders of the Kultusgemeinde slowly came to see Rabbi Bloch as their most effective representative in the Reichsrat. His powerful, hard-hitting speech in the parliamentary sitting of 11 February 1890, defending the Talmud against its detractors and exposing the bad faith of the Austrian anti-Semites with devastating irony, made a tremendous impression on both Jews and Gentiles.[100] In his speech, Dr Bloch wittily exposed the double standards on which anti-Semitism thrived:

Gentlemen, in dealing with us [Jews] all ideas of right and wrong, of virtue and vice are turned into the reverse of what they are . . . That which is virtue in everybody else, when noticed in Jews becomes a vice (Cries: Hear, hear!) You think this is an exaggeration on my part? Gentlemen, the aspiration towards culture is acknowledged to be a virtue . . . you praise the paterfamilias who

(Albany, NY, 1983), 155 ff., describes the ideology of the Union as essentially 'integrationist' while underlining its 'principled and assertive struggle against anti-semitism' and its commitment to strengthening Jewish identity.

[97] *My Reminiscences*, 193. According to Bloch, until 1896 'the Society had been a help and support to me against animosities on the part of the Jews'. Subsequently 'the board of the society considered it necessary to emancipate themselves from my influence, and I gradually lost touch with the Society I had myself founded.'

[98] Ibid. 196.

[99] Ibid. 161. Bloch in his memoirs argued that the victory of Union candidates in the Congregational Board elections of 1889 (where Baumgarten lost his seat) was, 'one of the first symptoms of a change of opinion among the majority of Jews in Vienna'. But this change came too late to stem the tide of clerical anti-Semitism in Austria.

[100] For the extraordinary impact on his Galician electors see Bloch, *Auswahl aus seiner Briefsammlung*, ed. Max Grunwald (Vienna, 1930), 4, 20–1.

spends his last on giving his children a higher education. In the Jews, on the contrary, it is considered a crime: we are accused of sending a disproportionate number of children to school. The honorable member Türck has made it his particular care to find out how many Jewish children attend elementary schools, how many secondary schools, how many universities. You see, what is a virtue in Christians, in Jews becomes a vice. If you were consistent at least in this, that the yearning for education is a vice in Jews! But, no. Our accusers say that in Galicia Jewish children keep away from school. This is also a vice. (Loud laughter) . . . Nothing can help the Jew. He will never give satisfaction no matter what he does. If he spends too much, he is ostenstatious, a spendthrift; if he spends too little, he is called stingy, a miser. If he keeps aloof from political life, he is lacking in public spirit; if he takes part in political life, he is an impertinent intruder. (Laughter.) If he joins the government, you say, of course, the Jew is always on the side of the powers that be (loud laughter), if he joins the opposition he is an element of dissatisfaction in political life. (Renewed laughter.) In a Vienna meeting, the discovery was made that Czech nationalism was an invention of the Jews. (Resounding laughter.)[101]

In the concluding section of his speech, Dr Bloch insisted 'that xenophobia and anti-Semitism constituted a pathological degeneration of the national sentiment and that it would backfire against the Germans in particular, as the only great nation in Europe 'enjoying more hospitality in all countries of the world than they offer'.

And therefore I say, Gentlemen, national anti-Semitism is madness [*ein Wahnwitz*], for it turns against the essential national interest. There is nothing so sacred to the national interest of the Germans as hospitality [*Gastrecht*] and they should be the last to give Europe the example that a race because it is different should be vexed and oppressed! What fate is awaiting the Germans in France, England, and Italy if the world succumbs to a mood of hate against foreigners?'[102]

Dr Bloch ended up by dramatically juxtaposing the *Gastfreundschaft* (hospitality) practised by the Palestinian Jewish State in antiquity with the modern anti-Semitic idea of 'extermination of foreigners' (*Ausrottung des Fremden*).

The cumulative impact of this speech was extraordinary. For the first time in Austrian parliamentary history, a Jewish deputy had thrashed the anti-Semites on their own chosen ground.[103] When

---

[101] Quoted in Bloch, *Israel and the Nations* (Berlin and Vienna, 1927), xiii–xiv.

[102] 'Sitzung des Österreichischen Abgeordnetenhaus am 11 Februar 1890', included in *Dokumente zur Aufklärung: Talmud und Judenthum in der Oesterr. Volksvertretung* (Bloch's Parlamentsreden, Vienna, n.d.), 26–7, 29.

[103] Dr Bloch himself had of course taken on the anti-Semites since his first

reports of the parliamentary debates reached the provinces, Dr Bloch received more than a thousand telegrams of thanks from Austrian and Hungarian congregations, some of them containing masses of signatures. His old rival Adolf Jellinek was moved to write in *Die Neuzeit* that it was 'a sacred duty' for Jewish voters in Kolomea–Buczacz–Sniatyn to re-elect Dr Bloch in the forthcoming parliamentary elections.

It is certain that however the elections may turn out, the anti-Semites of the lowest and meanest sort will appear in the future Parliament, and as they are incorrigible they will again attack the Jews on every occasion—suitable or not,—they will be impudent and scornful towards them . . . they will fall upon and cast dirt upon them and their belief, their morals and their way of living and disgrace the Austrian Parliament and the name of Austria. In such a case a representative of Judaism must stand there prepared for battle to smite our enemies to the ground.[104]

Following a tough but successful electoral campaign, Dr Bloch continued to justify the faith of his Galician Jewish constituents in his polemical abilities. In a stormy parliamentary debate in June 1891, replying to Prince Liechtenstein, he exposed with facts and figures to hand the myth that Jews exercised a monopolistic control over Austrian banks, the Stock Exchange, the wholesale trade, or the manufacturing industry.[105] On 20 October 1891 he defended Jewish physicians against the slanders of Christian-Social deputies with characteristic bluntness.

Let us speak openly and honestly! Gentlemen! How do matters really stand? The anti-Semitic gentlemen here among us insult Jewish doctors and instigate

parliamentary appearances in 1885, and in the *Österreichische Wochenschrift* he regularly gave them a drubbing. See esp. his brilliant polemical analyses, 'Das Problem des Antisemitismus', 2 Jan. 1885, pp. 1–4, and 'Assimilation und Antisemitismus', 16 Jan. 1885.

[104] Quoted in *My Reminiscences*, 265. See also the preface to Bloch, *Israel and the Nations*, p. xi, including a letter from Jellinek of 11 Aug. 1893 which referred to Bloch as 'the Hercules of the anti-Semitic Augean stable', appealing him to work up 'the subject-matter of Jewish apologetics into literary shape' and to expose the anti-Semitic leaders 'in all their wretched nakedness'. Jellinek added that every Jewish minister, especially in the smaller congregations, 'ought to be in a position without much trouble to refute anti-Semitic slanders, and this would be possible only if there is a work at hand to give him the necessary information with which to take up the inglorious fight. Dr Bloch is in possession of the necessary literary ability; he is well versed in the tactics and strategy of warfare. Let us hope that he will not be lacking in ammunition or literary means.'

[105] For his contribution to this debate in the parliamentary sitting of 22 June 1891, see *Dokumente zur Aufklärung: Talmud und Judentum*, 92–4.

the people against Jewish doctors, but when they themselves are ill they don't call in the anti-Semitic quack but a capable Jewish doctor. I even believe that there, on the extreme Left, quite close to Dr Lueger, people are sitting who are being treated by Jewish doctors.[106]

Replying to Ernst Schneider's claim that in the General Hospital of Vienna 'only Christian corpses are dissected and never a Jewish one', Dr Bloch calmly explained the humanitarian role of the *Chewra Kadishah* and Jewish religious beliefs concerning burial and the immortality of the soul.

Among us Jews there exists a burying brotherhood in every community, even the very smallest. It is their bounded duty to bury every corpse in a separate grave, also that of the poorest Jew. We have such an association in Vienna, too, and they consider it their most sacred duty to bury every Jewish corpse from the hospital. You may see the Town Councillor Gustav Simon at every funeral, also at the funeral of the very poorest, he never tires of fulfilling his duty. These societies are older than our congregations, they are as old as the Jewish Diaspora.

Well, you call yourself a 'Christian-Social' party; imitate the Jews in this (Dr Lueger: 'We have not got the money for it!') There are plenty of rich people among you, for instance His Highness the Prince Liechtenstein; you ought to start such a society; practise Christian charity! Instead of spending the money on anti-Semitic agitation do as the Jews do; perform a work of Christian mercy, found such a society.[107]

During the parliamentary sitting of 25 November 1892, Dr Bloch crossed swords with another Viennese anti-Semitic deputy, Dr Schlesinger (professor at a veterinary school) over Jewish responsibilies for the white slave traffic in Galicia. While condemning 'this shameful and dishonest trade' Rabbi Bloch quickly pointed out that brothel-owners all over Upper and Lower Austria, Silesia, Styria, Bohemia, and Moravia were 'thoroughbred Aryans of the same race and the same faith as the interpellant' (laughter). Yet Herr Schlesinger had not bothered to enquire 'how many of these Aryan houses there are in *Vienna*' nor had he mentioned that 'an anti-Semitic idol', Georg Ritter von Schoenerer, had transformed the house he inherited from his father in Vienna 'into a Temple of Venus so as to force his mother and

---

[106] Ibid. 75 ff.; see also *My Reminiscences*, 290–2.

[107] *My Reminiscences*, 292–3. See pp. 300–7 for the positive responses of Viennese newspapers like the *Presse*, the *Deutsche Zeitung*, the *Wiener Tageblatt*, and even the clerical *Das Vaterland* to Bloch's speech. See also Jellinek's commentary in *Die Neuzeit*, 6 Nov. 1891.

sister to clear out'. Not mincing his words, Dr Bloch informed the House: 'I once asked a German nationalist student, one of Herr Schönerer's worshippers, how it happened that Schönerer had made his house in the Krugerstrasse a brothel? And he said: "That is an ancient German institution". Well, a few Jews have Germanized themselves, that's all.'[108]

In the same pugnacious style Rabbi Bloch defended Jewish beliefs concerning animal slaughter (*Schechita*) from the aspersions of deputies like Dr Pattai, sweeping aside the Pan-German's efforts to portray Jews as a criminal element in Austrian society.[109] With particular gusto he led a public campaign against the ritual-murder fable preached by Dr Joseph Deckert, bringing a lawsuit in Vienna which provoked an instant sensation.[110] Father Deckert, basing himself on the false testimony of a baptized Russian Jew, Paulus Meyer (recommended to him by Dr Rohling), had published an article in the influential Viennese newspaper *Das Vaterland*. In this article, Deckert asserted 'that the blood-ritual is handed down as a secret tradition among the Chassidim' and that it could be proved 'by reference to the Talmud and the Kabbala'.[111] According to the parish priest, these murders were *still* taking place among the Hasidim, and Meyer even purported to have been an 'eye-witness of more than one ritual slaughter of Christian children'.

The lawsuit was brought by Dr Bloch at a time when Christian-Social rabble-rousers like Ernst Schneider were assiduously spreading the fable of ritual murder among the lower classes in Vienna and in the German provinces. Father Deckert was defended in court by leading anti-Semitic deputies such as Dr Pattai and Dr Porzer (himself a baptized Jew). According to Bloch's own account, seldom did 'the poisonous hatred against the Jews display itself so nakedly and hideously as at this trial'.[112]

The three accused, Paulus Meyer, Dr Joseph Deckert, and Franz Doll, (the responsible editor of *Das Vaterland*), were eventually found guilty by the Vienna High Court 'of defamation of character'. Meyer

---

[108] *My Reminiscences*, 308–9; *Dokumente zur Aufklärung: Talmud und Judentum*, 54–5.

[109] 'Sitzung des Österreichischen Abgeordnetenhaus am 5. 11. 1894', *Dokumente zur Aufklärung: Talmud und Judentum*, 40 ff.

[110] Ibid. 48 ff.; also *My Reminiscences*, 383 ff., 561 ff.

[111] The article entitle 'Rabbi Bloch and the Ritual Murder' was published in *Das Vaterland*, 5 May 1893.

[112] For details of the lawsuit and all the documents relating to the case, see *My Reminiscences*, 362–570.

was sentenced to four months' imprisonment, Deckert to a fine of 400 florins, and Franz Doll was fined 200 florins. In a leading article on 16 September 1893, Moritz Szeps's *Wiener Tagblatt* commented that the trial ought to 'open the eyes of those who are wont to look on the anti-Semitic question as a purely academic one', especially those establishment circles who speak of the movement 'with a certain indulgence and approbation'. The *Wiener Tagblatt* hopefully concluded that the trial would be 'a lesson to these high circles not to pander to the low instincts of the mob; for passion, once loosed, does not inquire into the origin of the victim, and will not, of a surety, stop at the Jews'.[113]

Dr Bloch's victory in the Deckert case underlined once more the extent to which he had become a thorn in the flesh of the Viennese Jew-baiters. They now redoubled their efforts to remove him from the Reichsrat. Prince Liechtenstein, Ernst Schneider, and other anti-Semitic deputies assiduously sought to persuade the public that Dr Bloch had been illegally elected. At the same time they pressured the Polish Club to force him to resign his seat.[114] Eventually Bloch was sacrificed by the Galician Poles for the sake of a coalition agreement with the Christian-Socialists. Hence after 1895, Austrian Jewry was deprived of its foremost parliamentary representative.[115] Out of the twelve Jewish deputies who sat in the Austrian Parliament following the 1891 elections, Dr Bloch had been the only one to defend specifically Jewish interests. The other Jewish members of the Polish Club, with the occasional exception of Dr Byck, tamely followed the orders of their aristocratic patrons. Similarly, Czech and German deputies of 'the Mosaic confession' kept a low profile on Jewish issues.[116] Even an eloquent spokesman of the German Progressives such as Dr Heinrich Jacques, who represented the Inner City (an important Jewish concentration in Vienna) generally avoided mention of the 'Jewish question'. A speech by Dr Jacques to the Union on 7 February 1891 on 'the duties of an Austrian Parliamentary deputy' suggested that this silence reflected more than anything the reluctance

---

[113] Ibid. 565–6.

[114] Ibid. 340 ff.

[115] 'Freiherr von Chlumecky, Dr. Bloch und die Antisemiten', *Die Neuzeit*, 29 Nov. 1895, pp. 520–1. Bloch had resigned his seat but unsuccessfully sought re-election in the Kolomea–Buczacz–Sniatyn constituency against powerful Polish and assimilationist opposition. See also Isidor Schalit, 'Erinnerungen', in Rosenhek (ed.), *Festschrift*, 63–4, on the betrayal of Dr Bloch by the Polish Club.

[116] Schalit, pp. 61–2.

of his own Party to confront squarely what was regarded as an embarrassing issue.[117]

Despite his defeat in the parliamentary elections of 1895 Dr Bloch could still continue his pedagogical campaign against anti-Semitism in the *Österreichische Wochenschrift*. Ever since its foundation in 1884 this periodical had taught the Jews of Austria to bear their Judaism with honour and pride. Every week it reached readers in the most distant parts of the Habsburg Monarchy, helping to guide their thoughts on Jewish affairs and providing a platform for reflection on all the main issues affecting Austrian Jewry.[118] Like the liberal *Neuzeit* it emphasized the 'ideal mission of the Austrian imperial State' based on national and confessional equality, whose prosperity and survival represented a major Jewish interest.[119] In its pages, the Emperor Franz Joseph was depicted in glowing terms as a Solomonic ruler, a Prince of peace and justice, seeking only harmony and concord among his subjects.[120]

From its earliest issues, the *Österreichische Wochenschrift* systematically exposed the dangers of racial anti-Semitism (which had sprouted from the soil of German nationalism) not only for the Jews but for the survival of the Austrian State itself. The two issues were inextricably linked in Dr Bloch's mind.[121] As the *Österreichische Wochenschrift* pointed out, the Pan-Germans in Austria were also the party of national treason (*Vaterlandsverrath*).[122] In the last analysis, they were tools of Prussian policy, who owed their first allegiance to Berlin. For them Austria was merely the Germanic *Ostmark*.

The university youth in Vienna had been poisoned by nationalist anti-Semitism, turning against the Habsburg State and participating

---

[117] See 'Dr. Jacques', *Österreichische Wochenschrift*, 1 May 1885, for a hostile and even offensive editorial, depicting Heinrich Jacques as wholly indifferent to Judaism and 'ashamed of his descent'. According to Dr Bloch his re-election 'would be a shameful certificate of poverty for all the Jews of the Austrian capital', Dr Jacques's lecture of 7 Feb. 1891 in *Mittheilungen der Österr.-Israel. Union*, no. 10, pp. 2–11, suggests the need for a modification of this picture. The much more respectful obituary in the *Wochenschrift* on 2 Feb. 1894 seemed to take account of this change and avoided any such criticism.

[118] Grunwald, *Vienna*, 444.

[119] See the article by Dr Bernhard Münz, 'Die ideale Mission des österreichischen Kaiserstaates', *Österreichische Wochenschrift*, 20 Feb. 1885, pp. 1–2.

[120] 'Zum 2 December 1888', ibid., 30 Nov. 1888: 'er nur ist der wahrhafte, der einzige Friedensfürst Europas'; also, 'Eine Jübelschrift zum Kaiser-Jubiläum', ibid., 9 Nov. 1888, pp. 696–7.

[121] 'Der Antisemitismus in Deutschland und Oesterreich', ibid., 6 Jan. 1888.

[122] 'Die Stellungnahme der Regierung', ibid., 5 Oct. 1888, pp. 611–12.

regularly in anti-Austrian demonstrations.[123] Discarding old liberal ideals of academic freedom, the new generation had become hypnotized by the basest passions of national intolerance and race-hatred. Barbaric anti-Semitism had irredeemably infected university professors, high-school teachers, and students alike.[124] By his violent lawlessness von Schoenerer had obliged the State to react but as Bloch's weekly suggested, his temporary eclipse in 1888 was no cause for rejoicing.[125] Anti-Semitism in the liberal professions, the aristocratic salons, clerical circles, or among Habsburg officials was more dangerous precisely because it was more respectable. There was still a hidden but no less effective exclusion of Jews in the State service, the universities, the army, commercial associations, and other areas of public life.

In May 1888 the *Wochenschrift* pointed to the dangers of the clerical-patriotic (*schwarzgelb*) anti-Semitism promulgated by *Das Vaterland* and the disciples of Karl von Vogelsang.[126] This Catholic anti-Semitism, sponsored by the feudal nobility and supported by the Church, was no less subversive to the interests of the State than its German-national rivals. Feeding off *Mittelstand* resentment against Liberalism, capitalism, and Jewry, the 'United Christians' aimed to build a mass movement which would expropriate Jewish capital. They skilfully used 'Christian' catchwords to increase their popular electoral appeal.[127]

This cynicism found its perfect incarnation in the character of their leader, Dr Karl Lueger, who was 'pious in the same sense as he was anti-Semitic'. According to Dr Bloch, Lueger 'knew how to twist every matter of public interest somehow into the neighbourhood of the Jew-question, and then he could be sure of having touched his audience to the quick'.[128] In the art of 'varying the Jew-theme Dr Lueger was an unrivalled master, and thus he made his greatest hits'. Bloch by no means trivialized Lueger's anti-Semitism but he did recognize its essential ambiguity. Dr Bloch recalled that as a student Lueger had associated a great deal with Jewish comrades. His political mentor had

[123] 'Wie lange noch?', ibid., 21 Dec. 1888; 'Antisemitismus und Hochverrath', 28 Dec. 1888.

[124] Leo Hutschneker, stud. med., 'Der Antisemitismus an den Wiener Hochschulen', ibid., 19 Dec. 1884, p. 3; 'Die deutsch-nationalen Blüthen', ibid., 20 Apr. 1888; 'Arische Studenten als jüdische Erzieher', ibid., 25 May 1888.

[125] 'Die Katastrophe Schönerers', ibid., 23 Mar. 1888; also 'Glossen zum Prozess Schönerer', ibid., 11 May 1888: 'Dem Judenthume jedoch war Schönerer in seiner Vollkraft, wenn auch eine widerliche, doch aber keine gefährliche Erscheinung.'

[126] 'Das "Vaterland" in Nöthen, ibid., 25 May 1888, p. 324.

[127] 'Eine Felonie', ibid., 13 Apr. 1888, p. 228.   [128] *My Reminiscences*, 235.

been a radical Jew, Dr Ignaz Mandl, whom he later sacrificed for careerist reasons. Lueger had also been a great admirer of Adolf Fischof. Bloch speculated that if the latter had succeeded in creating a democratic German Party, Lueger might well have remained faithful to his liberal ideals. Even after his accession to power, the Viennese Mayor 'remained on the same intimate terms with his friends of former times'. But as Rabbi Bloch observed, Lueger never had the courage to stand up publicly for what he was willing to do privately and without fuss. Ambivalence was too deeply rooted in the nature of the man, his culture, and his society. 'Lueger fought the Jews as a race, as one fights in war, in a brutal, inhuman way, without conviction, merely from a tactical point of view; but when he had to tell some Jewish municipal employee who was complaining of his lack of advancement that there was no chance for him, he would show his genuine sympathy and respect.'[129]

Bloch acknowledged Lueger's leadership skills, his personal incorruptibility and achievements as an efficient municipal administrator who had modernized Vienna. But he did not ignore the negative balance—Lueger's responsibility 'for the sufferings of a minority persecuted and crushed with hatred'.[130]

The central question for the *Österreichische Wochenschrift* remained, however, the appropriate Jewish response to Austrian anti-Semitism. On this point, Dr Bloch's weekly differed from the liberal perspective. It outspokenly rejected the social 'assimilationism' of the Jewish bourgeoisie as well as the 'reform' tendencies of the Viennese Kultusgemeinde leadership. Anti-Semitism was not a consequence of the inability of Jews to assimilate. It reflected the incapacity of the Central European nations in the post-emancipation era to digest such a large number of newcomers.[131] The efforts of Austrian Jews to strip off their national, cultural, and religious characteristics in order to diminish anti-Semitism were therefore doomed to failure. Every acceleration of these efforts simply accentuated the tensions between Jews and Gentiles.

Neither Germans nor Slavs would admit even the most selfless, self-sacrificing Jews to be their equals despite their chauvinistic devotion to the adopted national cause. Jews would always remain 'adoptive children', a heterogeneous element among the nations of the Empire.

---

[129] *My Reminiscences*, 230.   [130] Ibid. 236.

[131] 'Assimilation und Antisemitismus', *Österreichische Wochenschrift*, 16 Jan. 1885, pp. 1–2.

Neither self-mockery, denial of Jewish decent, or indifference to their religious traditions could change this basic fact.[132] The 'suicidal contempt for their religion and *Stamm*' of many Viennese Jews merely increased the suspicions of Gentiles.

The *Wochenschrift* disapproved of efforts by certain co-religionists to imitate the easy-going hedonism of the Viennese, condemned the ostentatious display of jewellry by Jewish women, and satirized the social climbing of weatlhy Jews who sought entry to the aristocratic salons. Such behaviour provoked the envy of their Christian fellow-citizens.[133] Even more vexatious was the prevalence of the 'Jewish braggarts of national chauvinism, who have developed the peculiarly fanatical immoderation of renegades in all the national parties', thereby abandoning the most sacred Jewish traditions.[134] Alienated from their Jewish heritage, with no sense for Jewish history, they played into the hands of nationalist anti-Semites. For Dr Bloch the symbol of this political pathology was the great historian and ideologue of Austrian Pan-Germanism, Heinrich Friedjung, who had argued in his *Deutsche Wochenschrift* that 'Judaism is condemned to die out'.[135] When Friedjung sought political support in the Österreichisch-Israelitische Union at a discussion held on 14 March 1891 Bloch firmly opposed his candidacy.

Friedjung and other Germanized Jews were regarded by Bloch as having encouraged excesses of political nationalism. The neurotic fears, passions, and hatreds nourished by national exclusivism lay at the root of contemporary European anti-Semitism. Rejection of Jewish 'aliens' in their midst was built into the logic of nationalist fanaticism as the examples of Germany, Hungary, Russia, and Romania demonstrated. European liberalism, for over a generation 'the spiritual asylum' of the Jews, their 'protective haven after a millenium of homelessness', was everywhere surrendering without resistance to the siren-call of nationalism.[136] Jews who ill-advisedly took sides in the national conflicts opposing Czechs and Germans, Poles and Ukrainians,

---

[132] 'Zum Jahresschlusse', ibid., 7 Sept. 1888, pp. 563–4.

[133] 'Ein Erfolg des Antisemitismus', ibid., 30 Nov. 1888, p. 749: 'Aber die Wiener Juden liessen sich von dem Strudel der Vernügungen mitreissen, assimilirten sich mit dem Volke der Phäaken. Und was war der Dank? . . . Die Ballsäle wurden Brutstätten des Antisemitismus, weil die Frauen sich der Hass gegen Andersgläubige mit grösserer Schärfe als bei Männern entwickelt.'

[134] 'Semitische Antisemitismus', ibid., 9 Jan. 1885, pp. 1–2; see also 'Aus dem Protokolle', *Mittheilungen der Österr.-Israel. Union*, no. 12, 14 Mar. 1891, pp. 2–4.

[135] 'Das Problem des Antisemitismus', ibid., 2 Jan. 1885, pp. 1–4.

[136] Ibid. 3.

Hungarians and Slavs, soon found themselves trapped between the hammer and the anvil. The bitter national struggles of the Monarchy, Dr Bloch persuasively argued, 'leave us no other choice—but to become Jews again, Austrian Jews'.[137]

But Austrian Jews could not rely solely on the benevolence of the Emperor or the legal protection of the government. The increase in anti-Semitism at every level of Austrian society, the growth of incendiary propaganda, and the deteriorating situation of the Jewish poor demanded a more concerted response based on time-honoured principles of Jewish solidarity and self-help.[138] By the early 1890s this demand began to crystallize into a call for more organized, systematic *Abwehr* activites to prevent the violation of basic civil rights.[139]

The fact that a new coalition government, despite containing several Liberal ministers, had proposed discriminatory legislative measures against Jewish pedlars was one disturbing symptom of the *Zeitgeist*.[140] The inability of the authorities to curb inflammatory anti-Semitic articles or restrict rabble-rousing speeches at public meetings, in the municipal council, the Lower Austrian Diet, or the Parliament was another source of growing concern.[141] The witches-Sabbath in the legislative bodies and the press was blamed on this troubling laxity of the Austrian government. Like the liberal Press, Dr Bloch's weekly deplored the open violations of the Constitution and the failure to punish public slander of Jewish citizens.[142] The claim of the Austrian authorities that they could deal only with explicit infringements of law and order was dismissed as bad faith. Official neutrality merely encouraged the apostles of race-hatred to renew their calumnies with redoubled force.[143] Austrian Jews, it was now felt, had been abandoned both by the Government and the Liberal party, from fear of the mounting popular strength of the anti-Semitic parties.[144] Not surprisingly, voices were now heard advocating an organized self-defence for Viennese Jews on the lines of the German Centralverein. This

[137] Ibid. 4.

[138] 'Denken wir an uns', ibid., no. 23, 8 June 1888, pp. 355–6.

[139] See 'Der Conferenzvorschlag', ibid., 5 Jan. 1894, with its call for concerted action by the Jewish communities of Vienna, Prague, Lemberg, etc. to undertake more decisive steps against anti-Semitism and the infringement of Jewish rights.

[140] Eduard Beer, 'Der Gesetzentwurf gegen die Hausirer', ibid., 2 Mar. 1894.

[141] 'Wie lange noch?', ibid., 19 Jan. 1894.

[142] Ibid.; also 'Pan Verganew gegen die "Oesterreichische Wochenschrift"', ibid., 2 Feb. 1894, p. 83.

[143] 'Die Enunciationen der Regierung', ibid., no. 6, 9 Feb. 1894.

[144] Ibid.; also 'Wo bleibt der Staatsanwalt?', ibid., 23 Feb. 1894.

appeared to be the best way to counter feelings of communal impotence and despair in the face of anti-Semitism.[145]

The Österreichisch-Israelitische Union was the one available forum in the 1890s for organizing such a concerted action. Its internal discussions provide perhaps the best indicator of the mood of middle-class Viennese Jewry in this period.[146] Already in April 1891 it had warned Jews of the possible consequences of an anti-Semitic majority in the Viennese municipal council—unjustified tax increases, restrictions on Jewish businesses, refusal to channel public funds to Jewish institutions, and the deleterious effects on Jewish children of growing anti-Semitism among Catholic teachers. It therefore urged Jewish voters to give massive support to German Liberal candidates, sponsored by the Union, at the polling-booths. The Union leadership pointed out that this was 'a question of existence not only for our religious community but for any civilized society'. Out of civic patriotism and in the name of liberal values, Vienna's Jews were called upon to prevent an anti-Semitic victory.[147] The energetic defence of Jewish interests went together, it was asserted, with those of 'free citizens of a free state', whose exercise of the right to vote was a civic responsibility of the first order.[148]

The Union also tried to work for the development of a feeling of solidarity among Jewish parliamentary deputies, though to little avail. As its Vice-President Dr Marcus Spitzer pointed out, Jewish solidarity had hitherto been sadly lacking, with Dr Bloch generally left to battle alone against Ernst Schneider and his Christian-Social colleagues.[149] The passive attitude of Jewish parliamentarians and the low profile of the Liberal party on 'Jewish questions' was the object of growing criticism within the more activist circles of the union. On the other hand, reproaches that the Kultusgemeinde Board had undertaken no effective action against anti-Semitism were rejected by the Union leadership.[150] The co-operation and overlap between the two bodies

---

[145] See S. Hammerschlag, 'Organisirte Abwehr', ibid., 9 Mar. 1894, for a discussion of the confusion in Viennese Jewish circles.

[146] See, e.g. the call for a massive turn-out of Jewish voters in the municipal elections for the Third Curia in Vienna, 'Glaubensgenossen!', *Mittheilungen*, 3, no. 13, Apr. 1891, pp. 1–2.

[147] 'Glaubensgenossen', ibid., no. 14, Apr. 1891.

[148] 'Aus dem Protokolle', ibid., no. 15, 25 Apr. 1891, pp. 3–4.

[149] 'Aus dem Protokolle', ibid., no. 16, 9 May 1891, pp. 2–3.

[150] Herr Maximilien Steiner, 'Einiges über die Geschäftsfahigkeit des Cultus-Vorstandes 1890–1896', ibid., no. 89, 12 Dec. 1896, pp. 2–12. Steiner detailed the numerous interventions of the Board in the 1880s with government circles which he felt

were perhaps too close to permit a rigorous self-examination in this matter.

The central political issue which preoccupied the Union in the 1890s remained the extent to which it could still advocate unconditional support for the German Liberals. The address of the Deputy Mayor and liberal leader Dr Grübl to the Union on 4 February 1893 touched directly on this issue. Dr Grübl, aware of the rumblings of discontent among Viennese Jews, stressed the political difficulties which his party faced and the need to solidify ranks in the face of anti-semitic challenges.[151] Well aware of the sympathy many Jews felt for Dr Kronawetter's radical Democratic party, he warned that communal support for this rival could be a divisive force, preventing the Liberals from returning to power. To this claim, another speaker objected that the German Liberals seemed to have abandoned their principles. In a recent debate on education they had not even energetically opposed Christian-Social proposals for 'confessional schools'. Such criticism provoked sharply negative responses from successive speakers including Dr Heinrich Friedjung, Dr Alfred Stern, and town-councillor Constantin Noske—a prominent non-Jewish member of the Liberal party.[152] Dr Bloch, for his part, opposed any attempt to reproach either the Liberals or Democrats for anti-Semitism, emphasizing the need for a united struggle against the common enemy.

In subsequent debates held in the Austrian Israelite Union during the 1890s Dr Bloch adopted a conciliatory line. The central issue in this mind was not whether Jews should vote for the Liberal party, for the Sozialpolitiker (a radical-liberal grouping) or even for the Social Democrats. Austrian Jews would have to mobilize all available forces against anti-Semitism.[153] Dr Bloch was generally sceptical concerning Jewish alignments with the three 'progressive' parties in Austrian politics while recognizing that Jews had no alternative but to support them in confrontations with the anti-Semites. But he stressed the fact that the unparalleled sacrifices which Austrian Jews had made in the past for the defence of the German culture and language in Slavic lands had been poorly rewarded by the Liberals.[154] Their betrayal, the

---

were ultimately counter-productive. Discretion, tact, and well-thought-out quiet protests were in his view more effective.

[151] 'Aus dem Protokolle', *Mittheilungen*, 3, no. 48, 4 Feb. 1893, pp. 11–12.

[152] Ibid., pp. 15–17.

[153] 'Vereinsversammlung der Oesterreich-Israel. Union', ibid., 8 Feb. 1896.

[154] Ibid., no. 85, p. 12.

political weakness of the Sozialpolitiker and the latent anti-Semitism in the Social Democratic Party underlined to Rabbi Bloch that Austrian Jews could have no illusions about the gravity of their situation.[155]

Bloch's attitude to the Zionist movement was initially ambiguous. There had always been a strong national component in his own political ideology which he had sought to synthesize with elements of religion and tradition. In the mid-1880s he had for a time been regarded as a Jewish national leader by the founders of Kadimah. Indeed, he never altogether abandoned his sympathy for the moderate, practical Zionism, proposed by the Hovevei Zion.[156] In 1896 he had at first encouraged Herzl's efforts, publishing one of his articles and introducing him to the Austrian Finance Minister, Leon Ritter von Bilinski (1846–1923), a leading member of the Polish Club.[157] Like the Polish aristocrat, Bloch was impressed by Herzl's magnetic personality, by his integrity, vision, and political insight, but sceptical of his nationalist ideology. He feared the long-term implications of Zionism for Jewry.[158]

The first encounter between Dr Bloch and Herzl had taken place at a meeting of the Austrian Israelite Union held in a Vienna restaurant on 5 November 1895.[159] Herzl, as Bloch later recalled, was known as a consummate man of the world and witty conversationalist 'whose *feuilletons*, with their air of ironic superiority, very rarely touched upon the fate of the Jews and then only to shower icicles of delicate ridicule upon it'.[160] Rabbi Bloch's first reaction was one of pleasant surprise that such a man should be at all interested in Jewish affairs. Five days

[155] Ibid., no. 92, 20 Feb. 1897, pp. 6–7.

[156] See his remarks in the debate 'Zur Reform der Armenpflege in der Wiener Cultusgemeinde', *Die Neuzeit*, 19 Nov. 1897, p. 474.

[157] See N. M. Gelber, 'Herzl's Polish Contacts', *Herzl Yearbook*, i (New York, 1958), 211–19. Bilinski was a Catholic of Jewish origin. Brought up in Galicia and educated at Lemberg, he had been elected to the Austrian Parliament in 1883. His meetings with Herzl at a time when he was Finance Minister of the Monarchy were strictly confidential. Subsequently he gave 1,200 typewritten pages dealing with these contacts to Dr Bloch, who had been their intermediary.

[158] See *Österreichische Wochenschrift* (1904), p. 455, for Bloch's obituary of Herzl which acknowledged him as a 'historic figure' in spite of their differences. On Herzl's side this alienation was caused by his dismissal of Bloch's fight against anti-Semitism (which he privately characterized as a modern form of 'theological' disputation) and by his anger at the readiness of the *Wochenschrift* to publish criticisms of political Zionism.

[159] See Chaim Bloch, 'Theodor Herzl and Joseph S. Bloch', *Herzl Yearbook*, i. 154–64.

[160] Ibid., p. 156.

later, on 10 November 1895, Bloch was invited to the home of his friend, the wealthy architect Wilhelm Stiassny (a leading community figure), to listen to Herzl's reading of what would soon become known as *Der Judenstaat*.[161] Bloch was impressed by its literary style and relieved that Palestine was not mentioned during the session. Because of its geo-political position, Bloch felt that '. . . we Jews should not lay our heads in this sickbed once again'. A few days later Herzl paid a surprise visit to Dr Bloch, informing him that he had been convinced by friends that the Jews had a historic claim to Palestine and that 'the Jewish soul clings to these regions'. Bloch immediately warned him against messianic pretensions (recalling the disastrous episode of Sabbatai Zvi's movement of return in the seventeenth century) and advised his visitor of the history of the Holy Land which spoke against attempting to revive an independent Jewish State.

Bloch also lent Herzl two speeches on the Talmud by the recently deceased Adolf Jellinek, which had been published in Vienna almost three decades earlier. The speeches contained an implied disapproval of any attempt to rebuild the Temple, and reflected the prophetic spirit of supranational Judaism. 'Be generous to the poor, for to aid a single father and sustain his children is worth more in the eyes of God than if you slaughtered a hundred bulls in his honour; do philanthropic deeds; study the Torah and stamp its spirit of justice and love upon your actions, and then you will never have need of a blood sacrifice.'[162]

Dr Bloch also described to Herzl the historic encounter between Adolf Jellinek and Leo Pinsker, which had taken place fourteen years earlier in Vienna. Evidently, when confronted with political Zionism, Dr Bloch took up many of the misgivings of his old rival, Adolf Jellinek, concerning the dangers of a return to Zion. He pointed out to Herzl that Judaism forbade a *mass* return to Palestine and the restoration of the Jewish State until the advent of the Messiah,

---

[161] See Central Zionist Archives, A 80/8 Stiassny, for an article by Klothilde Benedikt (a friend of Stiassny's wife) entitled 'Erinneurungen an Theodor Herzl', published on 26 May 1918, to the effect 'dass Baurat Wilhelm Stiassny erst in Herzl die zionistische Idee entzündet hat, während dieser ursprünglich weit Praktischer an ein anderes Land für Verwirklichung seines Judenstaates gedacht hat'. *Gemeinderat* Stiassny was a prominent member of the IKG Board for many years and had been one of the founders in 1888 of the Verein zur Unterstützung jüdischer Handwerker und Kleingewerbe-treibender in Vienna. See also his lecture 'Wienerisches, Jüdisches', *Mittheilungen der Österr.-Israel. Union*, no. 102, 5 Mar. 1898, pp. 3 ff., for an illuminating account of the Vienna city council under Christian-Social domination and its petty discrimination against Jews.

[162] Chaim Bloch, pp. 158–9.

although he acknowledged that residence in the land was considered a great virtue in the Talmud. Dr Bloch cautiously supported a religious and humanitarian rather than a national-political variant of Zionism.[163]

On 7 November 1896 Herzl delivered a skilful speech on 'Judaism' at the Österreichisch-Israelitische Union, before an enthusiastic audience, which Dr Bloch subsequently published in his weekly.[164] The subject of this speech was cleverly tailored to its audience, eschewing utopian flourishes as far as possible, while depicting a philanthropic 'Zionism' that even members of the Union could be expected to approve. The agricultural settlements encouraged by Sir Moses Montefiore, Baron Hirsch, and Edmond de Rothschild were put forward as precursors of what Herzl had in mind; the possibilities of modern technology and communications were outlined; so, too, were the financial difficulties of Ottoman Turkey, the nature of the new post-emancipation anti-Semitism, and the need to find a solution for the material misery of Russian and Romanian Jews. Only on one point might Herzl's approach have disturbed the equanimity of Union members—namely his insistence on defining the Jews as a secular nation—as 'a historical group of people who clearly belong together and are held together by a common foe'.[165] This was indeed a central point at issue between Rabbi Bloch and the Zionists. The Jews were not a nation like other nations in his mind. Their sense of community was based on the Mosaic faith.[166] On the other hand, Bloch ever since the early 1880s had sought to arouse a sense of tribal kinship in the Jewish race, to make his co-religionists more conscious of their common past and fate. This was a *national* sentiment on which political Zionism deliberately sought to build.

Even in their attitudes to anti-Semitism and its impact on the Jews there were some curious parallels between Bloch and Herzl. In a lecture on 18 October 1890 before the Austrian Israelite Union Bloch had argued that anti-Semitism was bringing many alienated Jews back to Judaism. Renewed persecution was strengthening the dissipated bonds of Jewry and checking the previously rampant process of conversion and de-Judaization.[167] 'The consciousness of belonging together is today once again alive in the Jewish soul and the credit for

---

[163] Ibid., p. 161.

[164] See Th. Herzl, 'Judentum', *Österreichische Wochenschrift*, 13 Nov. 1896. For an Eng. trans.; see Theodor Herzl, *Zionist Writings: Essays and Addresses*, trans. Harry Zohn (New York, 1973), i. 44–58.

[165] Ibid. 52.   [166] Chaim Bloch, pp. 154–5.

[167] See *Mittheilungen*, no. 3, 18 Oct. 1890, pp. 2–13, for the text of Dr Bloch's lecture.

this is entirely due to the antisemites; they exercise the function of that force which seeks Evil, but constantly creates the Good,' Dr Bloch confidently informed his listeners on that occasion. Like Herzl after him, Bloch clearly believed that anti-Semitism was uniting the Jews. In some respects it had exercised an educative function. By a process of natural selection it was even improving the qualities of the race.[168]

For example, Rabbi Bloch held that the remarkable intellectual attainments of Jews were a consequence of the hard school of discrimination which Christian anti-Semitism had imposed on them. In posing a permanent moral and intellectual challenge to the Jews, their adversaries unwittingly created the foundations for their survival and for the preservation of their uniqueness. In the era of assimilation, anti-Semitism 'had brought us back to ourselves and to the consciousness of our task'. Anti-Semitism had exercised this providential role throughout history, reminding Jews of their mission among the nations, obliging them to abandon the worship of false gods and forcing them to reaffirm the highest ideals of humanity.

. Over four years later in Paris, Herlz, still groping his way towards political Zionism, also held that anti-Semitism was 'a movement useful for the development of Jewish character'. In his diaries he wrote that external pressure had to a great extent determined the persistence of Jewish qualities. But Herzl had little time for Bloch's 'medieval, theological tussle with the anti-Semites'. He was convinced since the early 1890s of the inherent 'emptiness and futility of trying to "combat" anti-Semitism'.[169] In his mature Zionist phase, anti-Semitism came to serve a much more functional purpose for Herzl. As he wrote to Chief Rabbi Güdemann of Vienna, it was part of the natural force of 'Jewish misery' that would give life to his project 'and set a people in motion'; like the power of steam which lifts the kettle lid, anti-Semitism and *Judennot* would transform the Zionist utopia into social reality.[170]

This was a pragmatic conception that Dr Bloch could never accept and which reinforced his growing reservations about political Zionism. After 1900 he increasingly embraced the philosophy of the Austrian

---

[168] *Mittheilungen*, no. 3, 18 Oct. 1890, p. 6: 'Nach dem harten Gebot der eisernen Nothwendigkeit, welchem der Kampf um's Dasein eine Race unterwirft, entwickeln sich die Qualitäten ihrer Gehirnmassen.'

[169] See 6 Aug. 1895 entry in *The Diaries of Theodor Herzl*, ed. and trans. Marvin Lowenthal (London, 1958), 58, on Bloch's weekly. Also entry begun in Paris around Pentecost 1895, ibid., p. 6.

[170] Herzl-Güdemann, 22 Aug. 1895, in ibid., pp. 65–6.

Israelite Union and identified with its endemic anti-Zionism. Unlike the Zionists or the Jewish Nationalists in Austria Dr Bloch had never regarded the Jews as a separate political nation. In the domestic context of the Habsburg Empire he saw Zionist demands for such recognition as harmful. As the Austrian Zionists began to engage more intensively in *Landespolitik* after Herzl's death, the rivalry between them, Dr Bloch, and Union-sponsored candidates in local and national elections grew sharper. These tensions climaxed in the run-up to the 1907 Reichsrat elections in the Loepoldstadt district of Vienna, where Dr Bloch was originally one of four Jewish candidates (including a Zionist), though he subsequently withdrew.[171] Bloch initially resented Zionist politicking in Austrian parliamentary elections. He evidently believed that Jewish nationalist ideology stood in sharp contradiction to his own vision of supranational Austrian Jewry as a mediating element in the multinational State. Nevertheless, Dr Bloch welcomed the election of four Jewish national deputies (Benno Straucher, Heinrich Gabel, Arthur Mahler, and Adolf Stand) in the 1907 elections, who constituted the first independent Jewish Club in the Austrian Parliament. Playing down their Zionist programme, the Galician Rabbi focused instead on the novel fact that Austrian Jewry had finally voted for a group of representatives who were wholly committed to defend Jewish honour and opposed the 'false' path of assimilation.[172] The proud affirmation of Jewish identity, which Dr Bloch had first introduced into Austrian politics twenty-five years earlier during his battle with August Rohling, had found an unexpected consummation in the elections of 1907.

[171] *Österreichische Wochenschrift*, 22 Feb. 1907, pp. 121–7; 29 Mar. 1907, pp. 213–17.
[172] Ibid., 21 June 1907, pp. 405–6.

IO

The Austrian Israelite Union

Our first task is to raise Judaism in the eyes of others and in our own, to battle against the inner humiliation and abasement and to win back the younger generation which has been almost entirely estranged from us . . . then to ward off the agitation which is being led against tolerance and humanity, to keep down all endeavours tending to heighten religious and racial contrasts.

Dr Sigmund Zins (24 April 1886),
Constituent Assembly of the *Union*

Jews band together, unite in defence against the shameless attacks! This is the watchword of the *Oesterreichisch-Israelitische Union*!

Mittheilungen der Österreichisch-Israelitschen Union
(October 1889)

What qualities ought a candidate to possess who is specially suitable and willing to represent the interests of Jews? First of all, that which makes up the deepest kernel of each and every kind of genuine liberalism: a just heart! He must have the ability to feel the injustice from which another suffers. Indeed 'Justice' is the oxygen without which we Jews cannot breathe. But secondly, this deputy, this representative of Jewish interests, if he is a good German—and a non-German candidate is quite impossible in Vienna—must not be a national chauvinist. National chauvinism is the nutriment of Antisemitism, a necessary symptom of the sickness of overstrung, national nerves. That is true everywhere. But especially here in Austria, the baiting of nationalities creates for us Jews the most dangerous of atmospheres.

Vice-President Sigmund Mayer,
report to the Osterreichisch-Israelitische Union
(26 September 1896)

The Jew must stand up for a social order in which all are equal and free, without discrimination. (Bravo! Bravo!) Not just when it concerns the struggle against the anti-Semites, but always and everywhere he must stand up with conviction for those who like him strive for nothing else than to be men and citizens . . .

Julius Ofner, lecture to the Oesterreichisch-Israelitische Union
(29 April 1897)

Jews who were disappointed by liberalism and were scornfully rejected by the nationalistic parties began to seek refuge among the Socialists, and in the process Socialism became Judaized. Suddenly every place was teeming with little Marxes and Lassalles; the workers' movement can hardly tolerate these beyond a certain limit. Is Socialism already saturated with Jews? Was the limit reached all of a sudden during the lively influx caused by anti-Semitic pressure? It would almost seem that way if one reads the reports of the Austrian Social Democratic Convention.

Theodor Herzl, *Die Welt* (18 June 1897)

The creation of the Austrian Israelite Union in 1886 had been the response of a younger generation of middle-class Jewish notables in Vienna to the challenge of anti-Semitism. Its aim had been to defend Jewish political rights, improve the quality of Jewish education, and encourage the pride of Austrian Jews in their own distinctive identity. While espousing Habsburg dynastic patriotism and seeking the integration of Jews in the supranational State, the Union consciously worked against the dissolution of Jewish group identity by stressing the common origins and fate of Jews as a people (*Stamm*). The Union had inherited from its founder Dr Joseph Bloch a sense of the need for Jewish political representation. It hoped to become the organizational centre which would enable Jews to act as an ethnic-religious pressure group in defence of their own interests.[1] Since its establishment the Union had been deeply concerned with countering anti-Semitism, though its members were divided as to the most effective way of achieving this goal.

In the early years of its existence the Union did admittedly play down the political side of its activity. Preferring to avoid a frontal confrontation with the anti-Semites, it concentrated on the issue of Jewish education and on combating self-hatred among the younger generation. It was also keen to underline that it had no separatist

---

[1] Jacob Toury, 'Troubled Beginnings: The Emergence of the Österreichisch-Israelitische Union', *Leo Baeck Yearbook*, 30 (1985), 461.

goals.[2] But the continuing defeats of the German Liberals and the growing danger that Lueger's Christian-Social party would gain power in Vienna obliged the Union to clarify its stand on political issues that affected the Jewish community. In the 1890s these issues included the workability of the Austrian political system as a whole, the growing pressure for franchise reform, the nationality struggles, the rise of mass movements, and the future of liberalism in Austria. The attitude which the Union adopted on these questions was closely bound up with its assessment of anti-Semitism and its position on Jewish self-defence.

The fall of the Taafe coalition and the return of the United German Left (the new name for the old Liberal party) to power in October 1893 briefly aroused hopes for better days in the Vienna Jewish community. For fourteen years the Liberals had been in opposition. Now they found themselves with a share of power, ruling in a new Coalition Ministry together with the Clericals and the Polish Club. Their leader, Ernst von Plener, had the Finance Ministry and hoped to push through a progressive programme of tax and commercial measures as well as a moderate franchise reform that would not damage Liberal political privileges.[3]

It was the issue of franchise reform which had finally brought down the Taafe coalition. The German Liberals were determined to prevent any further erosion of the traditional position, by obstinately maintaining the link between tax levels and voting rights on both the national and local level. The 1867 Constitution, historically the supreme liberal achievement, had been deliberately weighted in von Plener's words 'to secure the historic and political position of the German nation, which, as is well known, does not make up the majority of the Austrian population, but which as a result of its historic labours, education, prosperity and tax burden, towers above all others'.[4]

The Liberals had deeply resented the Taafe suffrage reforms of 1882 and 1885 which had given the vote to the lower *Bürgertum* (the five-florin men), thus permitting the rise of anti-liberal bourgeois parties and weakening their own electoral strength. Depending as they

[2] Marsha Rozenblit, *The Jews of Vienna, 1867–1914: Assimilation and Identity* (Albany, NY, 1983), 156 ff.

[3] See J. Boyer, *Political Radicalism in Late Imperial Vienna: Origins of the Christian Social Movement 1848–1897* (Chicago and London, 1891), 321 ff., on the coalition and the decline of Austrian liberalism after 1893.

[4] Ernst von Plener, *Erinnerungen* (Stuttgart and Leipzig, 1911–21), iii. 90–1.

did on the big Liberal landowners, the Chambers of Commerce and Industry, and the privileged curial voting system, the Liberal party had no political interest in a further extension of the suffrage.[5] This would not only further undermine the hegemony of the Germans in Austria but threaten their very existence as a loosely organized party of notables in an age of mass politics. Ever since their exile from power in 1879 they had lost much of their halo as a *Regierungspartei*, closely aligned with the *Verwaltung* (adminstrative power) and the traditions of German centralism. Increasingly, they had become a 'conservative' party which grimly defended its national and class property interests (*Besitzstand*) while turning a blind eye to the poverty of the propertyless masses.[6]

But a Liberal party based on the narrow capitalist interests of the *Grossbürgertum*, if it ignored the demands of the non-German nationalities, of the lower middle classes, and of the proletariat, was bound to become isolated from new currents of popular opinion in the 1880s. The franchise reforms and protectionist *Sozialpolitik* initiated by the Conservative government further weakened the Liberals. The radicalization of Austrian politics in the 1890s—symbolized by the rise of the Christian-Socials, the Social Democrats, and the Young Czechs—announced their imminent demise. By the time they joined the coalition in 1893 the Liberal party was clearly on the defensive.[7]

The Vienna Jewish community, one of the most loyal and influential backers of Austro-liberalism, suffered more than most from its precipitous decline. Though the powerful Viennese press, which was mainly in Jewish hands, continued to support the Liberal party until the end of the Monarchy, it was impotent to prevent the triumph of anti-Semitism in Vienna. The Jews of the Habsburg capital became scapegoats of a massive revolt of the Viennese *Bürgertum* against the traditional Liberal hegemony.

Jews had traditionally provided a solid phalanx of voters for the Liberal party in its Viennese bastions (the I and II districts). But by the early 1890s they increasingly felt that the United German Left was

[5] Herbert Matis, 'Sozioökonomische Aspekte des Liberalismus in Österreich 1848–1918', in Hans-Ulrich Wehler (ed.), *Sozialgeschichte Heute: Festschrift für Hans Rosenberg zum 70. Geburtstag* (Göttingen, 1974), 243–65; Georg Franz, *Liberalismus: Die deutschliberale Bewegung in der Habsburgischen Monarchie* (Munich, 1955; Richard Charmatz, *Deutsch-österreichische Politik: Studien über den Liberalismus und über die auswärtige Politik Österreichs* (Leipzig, 1907).

[6] Albert Fuchs, *Geistige Strömungen in Österreich 1867–1918* (Vienna, 1949), 6 ff.

[7] Boyer, p. 321.

ignoring their interests and seeking accommodation with the clerical anti-Semites. Even influential members of the Union felt that the Liberal party was niggardly in allowing Jews a fair share of seats in various legislative bodies.[8] The inadequacy of the German Liberal response to anti-Semitism was especially galling as Jews often bore the brunt of the Christian-Social onslaught against liberalism.

The disappointment in the Union at the attitude of their allies was already apparent at a plenary meeting addressed by the Liberal parliamentary deputy, Carl Wrabetz, on 9 December 1893.[9] On speaker critized the Liberal party for ignoring the working classes. Another, Siegfried Fleischer, cautioned against its coalition with the Clericals, 'the worst enemies of Jewry'.[10] Much to Wrabetz's irritation, it was suggested that he owed his seat to the support of Kronawetter's small Democratic party, who had taken a much firmer line in the defence of Jewish civil equality.[11]

New frictions were provoked by the need to replace Heinrich Jacques, following the death of this distinguished Jewish lawyer who had represented the Liberals in the Inner City for many years. Should Jacques be replaced by another Jewish candidate? Siegfried Fleischer argued that 'the Jews can only compel the respect of their opponents when they demonstrate that they wish to maintain a position they have hitherto held'. He insisted that Jacques must be succeeded by another Jew, sponsored by the Union.[12] This view was rejected by Heinrich Friedjung (now a candidate of the Liberal Left) for whom firm opposition to the anti-Semites could only be successful on the basis of the Constitution. According to Friedjung, its best protectors were still the German Liberal party. Their fidelity to the *Staatsgrundgesetze* which they themselves had initiated was second to none. The key issue was not one of religion but the union of all progressive (*freisinnige*) parties around a single candidate.[13] Friedjung's view was echoed by

---

[8] Boyer, p. 334.

[9] Carl Wrabetz had the reputation of being sympathetic to Jewish interests. In the 1897 Reichsrat elections to the Inner City, he was one of three successful Liberal candidates, having been recommended to voters by the Union; see *Neue Freie Presse*, 23 Mar. 1897, p. 2. In the 1901 elections he was reelected with 3,021 votes in the I district, along with 2 Liberal (*deutschfortschrittlich*) colleagues and one *Sozialpolitiker*; see Julius Ofner, ibid., 15 Jan. 1901, p. 2.

[10] 'Aus dem Protokolle', *Mittheilungen der Österreichisch-Israelitischen Union*, no. 57, 9 Dec. 1893, p. 3.

[11] Wrabetz replied by reproaching the Democrats 'es sei durch ihre Schuld der einzige Jude aus dem Stadtrathe eliminert worden . . .', ibid., p. 3.

[12] 'Aus dem Protokolle', ibid., no. 59, 13 Jan. 1894, p. 13.   [13] Ibid., p. 14.

most of the other speakers. They felt that the Jewishness of a candidate was secondary to his liberal political convictions which must include strict observance of Jewish constitutional rights.[14]

The withdrawal of Friedjung's candidacy in favour of the non-Jewish Liberal city councillor and Landtag deputy Konstantin Noske (nominated by the German Progressive Central electoral committee) sharpened the confessional issue. Noske was widely considered to be a friend of the Jews. He told Union members that he had accepted nomination only after consultations with its Board. He had no desire to 'drive a wedge among Jewish voters', agreeing to stand once he was assured that Jews would above all support the candidate who 'will promote the interest of humanity and justice'.[15] Noske insisted that the United German Left had cause gratefully to recognize and draw the proper conclusions' from the fidelity of Jewish voters to its cause. He recalled that his party (supported by the Democrats) had been alone in opposing anti-Semitism. But as long as they remained in opposition there was little that Liberals could do to ameliorate the situation. Now that they had Ministers in the Coalition Government, they would do everything to ensure the strict maintenance of civic equality. Noske warned his listeners that 'it would be political suicide for the Jewish voters to abandon them [the Liberals]'.[16]

Konstantin Noske's supporters in the Union clearly agreed with his closing remarks. Above all, they wished to avoid a divisive and embarrassing dispute with the German Liberals over the issue of a Jewish or non-Jewish candidate. Noske, it was recalled, had proved his readiness in the past to stand up energetically for Jewish rights. He was a candidate of personal integrity and honourable character. Moreover, as Herr Isidor Popper suggested, a Christian might be preferable to a Jew in the current climate of animosity. Since Noske had a powerful party behind him, he might also do more for his Jewish constituents than an independent candidate, even if he were a Jew.[17]

Noske's rival was indeed an 'independent' the Bohemian-born Jewish lawyer, Julius Ofner (1845–1924).[18] A disciple of Fischof, he

[14] Ibid., p. 15.

[15] 'Aus dem Protokolle', ibid., no. 60, 14 Mar. 1894, p. 3.

[16] Ibid., p. 4.   [17] Ibid., pp. 6–7.

[18] On Ofner, see Fuchs, pp. 133 ff.; Werner J. Cahnman, 'Adolf Fischof and his Jewish Followers', *Leo Baeck Yearbook*, 4 (1959), 125–6; and Eva Holleis, *Die Sozialpolitische Partei: Sozialliberale Bestrebungen in Wiem um 1900* (Vienna, 1978), 22 ff. Ofner was elected to the Lower Austrian Diet in 1896 and to the Reichsrat in 1901 as a Sozialpolitiker. Later he joined the Austrian Liberal party. A distinguished jurist, he

was known as a militant campaigner for comprehensive social legislation, women's rights, and the humanizing of the penal code. Ofner had been one of the founders of the Viennese Fabian Society in 1893.[19] Out of this intellectual circle emerged the nucleus of the Sozialpolitiker, a non-Marxian, radical progressive association devoted to the cause of social reform. Closely allied with the Viennese Democratic Party (Kronawetter was elected to the Lower Austrian Landtag on their platform in 1896), the Sozialpolitiker unfortunately lacked solid roots in either the old middle classes or in the Lower *Bürgertum*. Despite their defence of working-class interests, the Sozialpolitiker also made little impact in the proletarian districts of Vienna dominated by the Social Democrats. They were a progressive (*freisinn*) party representing 'neo-liberal' ideas against the Liberal party while appealing to a similar constituency.[20] The Sozialpolitiker insisted that the 'social question' be dealt with seriously by bourgeois society in its own interests. They sought to awaken the *Bürgertum* out of its political stagnation and to build an alliance of the radical bourgeoisie with the working class against the privileged Parliament and the forces of clerical reaction.[21] The demand for universal suffrage (the core of democratic radicalism in the 1890s) and a comprehensive *Sozialpolitik* formed the heart of their political platform.

More consistently than any other progressive politician Ofner epitomized this liberal-socialist programme of social reform. An enlightened, humanitarian free-thinker, his ethnic background reflected the strikingly Jewish composition of the new party as well as its voting constituency, concentrated in the old Liberal strongholds of the

---

initiated the *Lex Ofner*—a law preventing criminal prosecution for petty larceny—and advocated the abolition of ecclesiastical jurisdiction in matters of marriage and divorce. The fact that a Jew pressed for such a measure was of course exploited to the full by Catholic anti-Semites in Vienna.

[19] Cahnmann, p. 124. Among the Viennese Fabians were a number of Jewish intellectuals including the inventor Josef Popper-Lynkeus (a friend and mentor of Ofner), the philosopher Wilhelm Jerusalem, the socialist Victor Adler, the poet Siegfried Lipiner, etc. Its most prominent Gentile members were Engelbert Pernerstorfer, Michael Hainisch, Otto Wittelshofer, Professor Max von Grüber, and the economist, Professor Eugen von Philippovich.

[20] Holleis, p. 37: '. . . sie war eine freisinnige Partei, die zwar die Grundgedanken des Liberalismus vertrat, aber in Opposition zur Liberalen Partei stand.'

[21] Ibid. 36–7. The Sozialpolitiker sought to neutralize the anxiety and fear of the *Bürgertum* at the rise of Social Democracy. They argued that the main enemy of the people was not socialism but reaction and creeping clericalism in the mask of anti-Semitism. The latter was a danger not only to the Jews but to the moral and educational level of the masses.

I, II, and IX districts. In his appearance before the Union on 14 March 1894 Ofner linked his support of franchise reform in Austria with an explicit appeal to Jewish values: 'in the course of my social science studies', he told members, 'I have always been filled with patriotic pride by the fact that the ancient Jewish legislation stood far above all other legislations of the time in that it did not discriminate between nobles and commoners, rich and poor.'[22] Attacking the United German Left from a radical position, Ofner described its coalition with the Clericals as a crime against liberal principles. The 'old' Austrian Liberals had allied themselves to ultramontane, feudal reaction. In order to please their new partners they had even proposed legislation against immigrant pedlars. They were following the path of the National Liberals in Germany, namely capitulation and renunciation of their progressive principles. This was also visible in their passive attitude to anti-Semitism.[23]

Defending his radical social principles which had previously been criticized in the Union, Ofner also protested against the outmoded curial system which heavily penalized the Social Democrats.[24] Pointedly appealing to Jewish compassion, Ofner asked his audience how they could remain indifferent to the exploitation and the humiliating status of the workers as second-class citizens?[25] The theme of universal suffrage and social justice was to find a conserable echo in later discussions with the Union. A growing number of Viennese Jews were sympathetic to Ofner's democratic principles and determination to apply them on behalf of all classes. Some members like Dr Weiss and Siegfried Fleischer regarded Ofner's independence and freedom from party discipline as a distinct advantage from the Jewish standpoint. Others, like Dr Elias, supported him simply because they

[22] 'Aus dem Protokolle', *Mittheilungen*, no. 60, 14 Mar. 1894, p. 5. Similar statements on the socially progressive character of ancient Hebrew legislation can be found in the writings of Joseph Bloch and Josef Popper-Lynkeus. On the latter see Ingrid Belke, *Die sozialreformerischen Ideen von Josef Popper-Lynkeus (1838–1921)* (Tübingen, 1978); Also Israel Dorion, *Popper-Lynkeus* (Jerusalem, 1981) in Hebrew, pp. 112–35.

[23] The social-liberals frequently repeated this charge, which went down well with Jewish voters. See *Österreichische Wochenschrift*, 29 Mar. 1895, pp. 235–7; 5 Apr. 1895, p. 249; 2 June 1896, pp. 785–8. Also Boyer, pp. 334–5.

[24] See, e.g., *Mittheilungen*, no. 59, p. 15, for the remarks of the liberal *Gemeinderath*, Dr Alf. Mittler: 'Dr. Ofner selbst stellt nicht in Abrede, dass er ein ausgeprägter Socialist ist, dass er ausgesprochen socialistischen Ideen huldige. Wenn wir die Wahl haben, so wählen wir den, der uns in wirtschaftlicher Beziehung am nächsten ist.'

[25] *Mittheilungen*, no. 60, p. 5.

wanted a Jewish candidate in the Inner City and felt that this was also the consensus among Jewish voters.[26]

In his parliamentary campaign, Dr Ofner made the introduction of universal suffrage a central issue. Despite his radicalism, he won a respectable 27 per cent of the vote among its prosperous electors as against 58 per cent for his successful Liberal rival Konstantin Noske, and 14 per cent for the Christian-Social candidate.[27] Notwithstanding Noske's victory, dissatisfaction with the German Liberals did not diminish among Jewish voters or members of the Union. Indeed, it increased, the clearer it became that the Liberals in the governing Coalition were incapable of arresting or even restraining the *Hetzreden* against Jews in schools, courts, public meetings, and the anti-Semitic Press.

The liberal lawyer, Dr Heinrich Steger, addressing the Union in February 1895, had to admit that the situation had spun dangerously out of control. The conspicuous silence and indifference of the German Liberal party to the brutal terrorism of the anti-Semites had become intolerable.[28] The disgraceful scenes in the Landtag and city council, the public insults to which a community of over a million loyal Austrian Jews were daily subjected, the poisoning of German youth, and the growing contempt for authority were all symptoms of the same political disintegration.[29] Liberal deputies had remained silent in face of this barrage, despite the debt they owed to their Jewish electors. This timidity had encouraged the insolence of Christian-Social demagogues like Gregorig and Schneider.[30]

What then could be done? A special law against anti-Semitism was not insisted upon but Jews did expect that 'the existing *Staatsgrund-gesetze* be observed and strictly maintained'. Above all, Jews must awake from their lethargy and insist on their inalienable rights as equal citizens (*Staatsbürger*). They could no longer be satisfied with mere 'toleration' as in the pre-emancipation era. They should not wait

---

[26] *Mittheilungen*, no. 60, pp. 6–7.

[27] *Neue Freie Presse*, 16 Mar. 1894, p. 3; 30 Mar. 1894, pp. 2–3; for electoral results, ibid., 3 Apr. 1894, p. 3.

[28] 'Aus dem Protokolle', *Mittheilungen*, no. 68, 9 Feb. 1895, 'Herr Hof—und Gerichtsadvocat, Dr. Heinrich Steger, "Die politische Situation in Oesterreich und die Stellung der Juden"', pp. 2 ff. The first part of Steger's speech was a typical liberal defence of the privileged curial system, i.e. an electoral system based on the representation of interest groups for preserving the German national *Besitzstand*. In dealing with the laxity of the Liberals on the 'Jewish question', the speaker became much more critical.

[29] Ibid., pp. 6–7.   [30] Ibid., p. 8.

passively for a kind word to be spoken on their behalf. Austrian Jews must defend their own cause while pressuring the German Liberal party to act more decisively against the anti-Semites.[31]

In the ensuing debate condemnation of Liberal behaviour in the coalition government was virtually unanimous. Sigmund Mayer was appalled that Liberal deputies in the Lower Austrian Diet had remained 'silent as fishes' while Ernst Schneider advocated the expropriation and expulsion of the Jews. Such cowardice in face of the physical threats to the security and rights of the Jewish community was inexcusable. Mayer's resolution of censure was unanimously adopted.[32] Dr Alfred Kanitz called on all Jewish communities to pass a similar resolution against the Landtag and the club of the United German Left. Siegfried Fleischer pointed out that if the Liberal party 'has allied itself with Feudalism, then its hands are tied in the struggle against the Antisemites'. Even Dr Heinrich Friedjung attacked the government for failing to guide public opinion and criticized his Liberal party colleagues for responding so weakly to the anti-Semitic barrage.[33]

Sigmund Mayer elaborated at greater length two weeks later on the crisis of confidence between the Liberal party leadership, the Union, and Jewish voters. Anti-Semitic bravado and the fragility of the Liberals had obliged him to reassess the political situation 'specifically from the standpoint of a Jewish voter'. It was not just the indifference but the calculations behind Liberal silence on the 'Jewish question' which were disturbing. Jews had a right to expect that once the Liberals reached the 'Promised Land' of governmental responsibility after fourteen years in opposition, they would use their influence to guarantee the constitutional rights of all citizens. A government which included liberal ministers should have acted firmly and decisively to stop the policy of official connivance that had enabled anti-Semitism to thrive.[34]

---

[31] Ibid., p. 9: 'Wir müssen uns aufraffen und unsere Sache, wo und wie wir es können, selbst führen. Wir dürfen in der Folge nicht mehr den Eindruck machen, dass wir uns feige verkriechen und zufrieden scheinen—wie im Zeitalter des gelben Flecks—noch geduldet zur werden . . .'

[32] Ibid., pp. 10–11.   [33] Ibid., p. 12.

[34] *Mittheilungen*, no. 69, 23 Feb. 1895, p. 12. On the development of Mayer's convictions, see his autobiographical *Ein jüdischer Kaufmann, 1831 bis 1911* (Leipzig, 1911), 317 ff. In 1890 he had suggested that Jews abstain from all activities in municipal bodies, educational committees, civic organizations, and chambers of commerce, until the anti-Semitic storm blew itself out. By 1894 he had modified this position and favoured organized political action against anti-Semitism.

Mayer insisted that Jewish self-defence would be ineffective as long as Christians believed the anti-Semitic movement to be quietly approved from above or that its aims could be realized in practice. The Viennese tailors, shoemakers, carpenters, locksmiths, upholsterers, bricklayers, small retailers, and school teachers who had voted for Lueger's party hoped to drive the Jews out of industry, commerce, and the professions.[35] They would not be disabused except by firm government action. Yet, Mayer revealed, the German Liberal leadership had rejected Union requests to undertake such a campaign, claiming that they lacked the power to implement such a policy.

Mayer strongly condemned this hypocrisy. He reminded his listeners that the German Liberals had acted vigorously over the Celje language dispute in Styria during 1894. They had refused to allow Slovene classes in the local grammar school at Celje on the grounds that this would be a betrayal 'of German culture in the south'. Indeed the Germans had threatened to leave the Coalition Ministry over what was a relatively minor issue. Similarly, in other cases involving petty linguistic quarrels, they had used their influence on behalf of party comrades. But when the *Besitzstand* of the Jews was being threatened, together with State authority and the credibility of liberal principles, they invoked their powerlessness. This was worse than Count Taaffe's ambiguous policy especially since the ex-Minister President had no pretensions to liberalism. Von Plener, leader of the United German Left, had no right to call himself a Liberal while remaining in the government. He had always acted purely as a party man. From that narrow standpoint he had evidently decided to sacrifice the Jews despite their past loyalty.[36]

Mayer observed that Jews still consistently supported German candidates in Bohemia and Moravia. Facing fierce Czech resentment and economic boycotts, they risked their physical existence and livelihoods in defending the German cause. In Vienna, too, they had paid a heavy price for their fidelity to the German Liberal party. In 1894 they had voted in the parliamentary elections to the Inner City for the non-Jewish Liberal Gentile Konstantin Noske rather than the Jewish Sozialpolitiker, though Julius Ofner was the more attractive

---

[35] *Mittheilungen*, p. 13.

[36] Ibid., pp. 14–15: 'Herr v. Plener ist ganz und durchaus Parteimann—ihm steht die "deutschliberale Partei" weit über den Liberalismus, und wenn es das Interesse der "Partei" verlangt, so müssen sich die Juden eben damit begnügen, für die Partei geopfert zu werden.'

candidate to enlightened Christians as well as Jews. This election would be the last in which Jews would unconditionally defend the Liberal party. Fifty years of *Kampfgenossenschaft* (fighting union) now stood on the line.[37] Jews demanded a clear answer from the Liberal party. If they supported the clerical call for the return of confessional schools, then liberalism was truly dead. The Jewish demands on this and other related issues would be shortly submitted to Liberal political leaders by the Union. If they were ignored, the Union proposed to mobilize Jewish support for the Sozialpolitiker in those Viennese districts where Jews represented a significant voting bloc. Mayer intimated that a government based on universal suffrage with all its risks from the standpoint of Jewish interests was still preferable to the existing situation.[38] Mayer's viewpoint was not unanimously shared by all Union members. Some felt that Viennese Liberalism had by no means exhausted its strength. Moreover, Ofner's social-liberal alternative, with its radical fervour, was not universally popular with the wealthier sections of the Jewish bourgeoisie.[39] But the disillusionment of many Viennese Jews with the Liberal party was none the less manifest. Following a defection of Jewish voters, the anti-Semitic candidate defeated his Liberal rival in the Leopoldstadt by-elections to the III Curia in late March 1895. The Liberals only narrowly prevented a similar desertion by Jewish voters in the II Curia of the Leopoldstadt in early April 1895.[40] It was during these months that Lueger succeeded in winning over the capitalists of the First Curia to the anti-Semitic cause. The Christian-Social party cleverly profited from Liberal mistakes and the unpopularity of the Badeni government to constantly extend its mass support.

In the summer months preceding the scheduled elections of September 1895 the atmosphere in Vienna became increasingly hostile

[37] Ibid., p. 15.

[38] Ibid., p. 16. See also Mayer, *Ein jüdischer Kaufmann*, 310, where he reveals the negotiations between the Union and the Sozialpolitiker on the eve of the Lower Austrian Diet elections of Nov. 1896. The Union promised to mobilize eligible Jewish votes in the I district in return for a commitment by the Sozialpolitiker to fight both the anti-Semites and the old Liberal party.

[39] *Mittheilungen*, no. 69, pp. 17–18. Ofner was not present at the debate on 23 Feb. 1895 but his democratic ally, Ferdinand Kronawetter, intervened to declare that 'Jews will never achieve their rights if they continue to turn to the privileged classes'. Kronawetter's advocacy of the working classes and universal suffrage as the only guarantee of Jewish rights met with some resistance within the Union, in spite of his personal popularity among Viennese Jews.

[40] Boyer, p. 350.

to Jews. The personality-cult of Lueger and the efforts to portray him
as a victim of Imperial, Hungarian, and Jewish pressures seemed to
aggravate popular anti-Semitism.[41] Lueger's crushing victory in
September 1895 was, however, irrevocable. Another Imperial veto and
the ineptitude of the new Minister President, Count Badeni, played
into his hands. In November 1895 even 'Christian women' were
mobilized on the streets of Vienna to demonstrate the overwhelming
popular support that Lueger enjoyed. A major demand at Christian-
Social rallies during this period was for the boycott of Jewish
merchants and shopkeepers. This was presented as an act of revenge
for 'Jewish' attempts to prevent Lueger's confirmation as Mayor of
Vienna.[42] The spring elections of 1896 gave the Christian-Social party
a decisive majority of 92 seats against 42 liberal mandates in the City
council. Lueger was received by the Emperor in an audience on 27
April 1896 and gracefully agreed to stand down for a year so that his
deputy, Strobach, could be officialy sworn in on 19 May. His victory
was officially complete when he formally took office on 20 April 1897.

Internal discussions in the Union during this tense period reflected
a mood oscillating between grim determination and despair. The
ominous results of the April 1895 municipal elections pointed to the
need for uniting a fragmented Austrian Jewry in concerted action to
defend any threat to its legal rights. But the Union, as of 20 April
1895, still embraced only 1,200 members out of a Viennese Jewish
population of 130,000. It might require at least three or four such
associations to exert real countervailing pressure.[43] Another blow, as
the publisher Dr Max Breitenstein reminded members on 7 December
1895, was Dr Bloch's electoral defeat in Galicia. This removed
Austrian Jewry's most effective spokesman from the parliamentary
arena at a critical moment.[44]

Dr Bloch continued however actively to participate in Union
debates. On 8 February 1896 he warned against pinning too many
hopes on the Austrian Social Democratic party as a counterweight to
the anti-Semites in forthcoming elections. The Viennese Social
Democrats, he remarked to general applause, were already tainted by
anti-Semitism. Attempts to mobilize Liberal' voters on their behalf
would most likely play into the hands of the Christian-Socials.[45]

---

[41] Boyer, p. 367.   [42] Ibid. 378–9.
[43] 'Aus dem Protokolle', *Mittheilungen*, no. 72, 20 Apr. 1895, p. 5.
[44] Ibid., no. 76, 7 Dec. 1895, p. 7.
[45] 'Aus dem Protokolle', ibid., 8 Feb. 1896.

Another speaker, the industrialist Herr Brod, criticized Socialist hostility to the Liberal party in the current electoral campaign. To great applause he declared that 'when Social Democrats claim to welcome anti-Semitism because it helps to fight liberalism, then they are ripe for the madhouse'.[46] Sigmund Mayer also attacked the decision of the Sozialpolitiker to support Social Democratic rather than Liberal candidates as helpful only to the anti-Semites—a point that was echoed by other speakers.[47]

Although the Union was unhappy with the Liberals, the political alternatives still seemed too discouraging to encourage a clean break. Moreover, all hope had not yet been abandoned that the existing German Liberal party might be won back to the progressive ideals espoused by many Viennese Jews. But Liberalism would have to represent something more than defence of the German *Besitzstand* and its traditional privileges. Their long history dictated in the words of the Union's secretary, Josef Fuchs, that Jews 'everywhere intercede for liberty and equal rights'.[48] German liberals had once acted in accordance with this principle to which Austrian Jewry owed their civic liberties and constitutional rights. Unfortunately, in an age of racial hatred and religious intolerance Liberal resolve had weakened.[49]

Fuchs warned that anti-Semitism was not a temporary aberration in public opinion but a conscious movement encouraged by the forces of reaction to reverse Jewish political rights. He told his audience that threatening perspectives and 'unpredictable final goals' of the anti-Semites demanded an energetic response which the Liberals had thus far failed to provide. The Union had pointed this out on several occasions to the German Liberal leadership, warning them that continued passivity on this issue would destroy the basis of Jewish collaboration with the party. The aim of the Union's political activity must now be to encourage the unity of Liberals, Democrats and

[46] Ibid.

[47] Ibid. For a valuable contemporary discussion of the contradictions between Jewry and the Social Democratic party, see Dr M. Rosenmann, *Jüdische Realpolitik in Oesterreich* (Vienna, 1900), 12–15; Rosenmann was district rabbi in Florisdorf.

[48] 'Aus dem Protokolle', *Mittheilungen*, no. 81, 25 Apr. 1896. In the first half of his speech Fuchs reviewed briefly the history of the Union and its efforts to foster the feeling of *Zusammengehörigkeit* and Jewish solidarity in the face of external assaults. The Union existed to provide a common framework for Jews of different political persuasions to unite and resist their adversaries. Current developments in Austria had vindicated the need for this political forum against those who had argued that existing laws were sufficient to protect Jewish rights.

[49] Ibid., p. 5.

Sozialpolitiker, mobilizing Jewish voters for this purpose through electoral committees in those districts where they were influential.[50]

Four days after the swearing-in of the new Mayor the Union held its first post-mortem on the anti-Semitic triumph in Vienna. Vice-President Sigmund Mayer in a sober speech attempted to assess the significance of Lueger's success. It was essentially a victory of the *kleiner Mann*. The Third Curia had triumphed over the First and Second Curias, the lower over the upper *Bürgertum*, clerical reaction over intellectual and material progress. Anti-Semitism was the specific form of this social reaction because this was the simplest way to mobilize the popular masses. Even without the Jewish presence in Vienna, Mayer seemed to feel that Lueger might have triumphed.

Since the Mayor and the anti-Semitic *Gemeinderat* were subordinate to the Austrian government and its ministers, there was probably no immediate danger of a reversal of legal equality. The real threat was the possibility that the new administration might try to destroy the foundations of Jewish economic existence.[51] But this, too, was considered unlikely. Should the government make concessions to anti-Semitic demands there was always the option of recourse to the Imperial Courts of Justice to protect constitutional rights.[52]

The central political question still remained the relations of the Union with the German Liberal party. Mayer recalled in some detail the strong linguistic, cultural, and political ties that had bound the Jews to German liberalism. Austrian Jews were traditionally centralists who looked to the protection of a strong state against the recrudenscence of medieval persecution. They recalled with nostalgia the constitutional achievements of the Liberal party in its golden period.[53] But ever since the late 1870s it had become evident that the dream of exclusive German hegemony was moribund in Austria. This had already been foreseen by 'an excellent Jew', the far-sighted sage of Emmersdorf, Adolf Fischof.

[50] *Mittheilungen*, no. 76, 7 Dec. 1895, p. 6: 'Als unsere Hauptaufgabe haben wir es aber betrachtet, ausserhalb unserer Tätigkeit in den einzelnen Bezirks-Comités eine Einigung zwischen allen freisinnigen Vereinen herbeizuführen.'

[51] Sigmund Mayer, 'Die Stellung der Juden zu der actuellen "Wiener Frage"', *Mittheilungen*, no. 83, 23 May 1896, p. 4.

[52] Ibid. At this point in his speech, Mayer emphasized the importance of the newly created *Rechtsschutzbureau* (legal rights office). The office undertook legal action on behalf of Jewish individuals or the Jews as a collectivity subject to attack in newspapers, public meetings, or legislative bodies. '*Hier beginnt für das von Ihrem Vorstande seinerzeit eingesetzte Rechtsschutz-Comité jene Bedeutung, welche dasselbe, wenn die rechten Männer in seiner Mitte sitzen, erlangen muss*' (underlined in the protocol).   [53] Ibid., p. 5.

The German Liberal leader Ernst von Plener had shown by his actions that he was ready to sacrifice 1.25 million Austrian Jews without hesitation. The party's provincial German interests in Bohemia or Styria were far more important to him than the plight of small-town Jews in the Czech lands who had loyally defended the German cause. Precisely since they were a narrow *national* party, the German Liberals in Austria had abandoned the principles of equality and justice.[54] Their bankruptcy was moral as well as political. In Mayer's opinion they were beyond regeneration.

The only possible conclusion was that Jews cease to serve as cannonfodder in Austrian nationality struggles. They must forthwith abandon the bankrupt Liberal party, returning to the programme of Fischof's Volkspartei in 1882 which they had mistakenly opposed fifteen years earlier.[55] They would have to support universal suffrage despite the risks, not just because it was politically inevitable but also in order to defuse the dangerous *Nationalitätenhetze* which promised to destroy the Habsburg Empire.

Mayer insisted that universal suffrage would not be the 'end of the world' as many Liberals and German nationalists claimed. Its main effect would be to bring the new class of the urban industrial proletariat into the political arena as an equal actor. Its recognition by the Austrian State and society was both necessary and inevitable. Universal suffrage and greater proletarian influence would have the advantage for Jews of highlighting socio-economic issues rather than the nationalist squabbles within the bourgeois classes which were always accompanied by anti-Semitism. Austrian Jews should not undermine their own future in opposing universal suffrage out of consideration for that very same German *Bürgertum* which had already betrayed them. The bourgeoisie no longer deserved to exercise political hegemony in Austria. By implication, there could not therefore be any objection to middle-class Jewish voters supporting either the Radical Progressives or the Social Democratic party. The economic disadvantages of Socialism in the long term were a remote

---

[54] Ibid., pp. 6–7: 'Was ist der innerste Kern alles und jedes Liberalismus? Nichts weiter als die "Gerechtigkeit," die Gerechtigkeit für Jeden und gegen Jeden. Keine *"nationale"* Partei aber kann gerecht sein oder bleiben.'

[55] Ibid., p. 8 Mayer summed up Fischof's programme as one of freedom and equality for all nationalities and above all other considerations. '*Jede* Nationalität muss ihr Recht und ihre Entwicklung innerhalb des weiten Rahmens der Freiheit und Gleichheit suchen und finden.'

consideration compared to the immediate danger of a victorious anti-Semitic movement.[56]

In an address to the Union on 26 September 1896 Mayer elaborated on this analysis. Austrian Jews were described as an integral part of the *Bürgertum*, distinct only in their religious denomination.[57] They had none the less been sacrificed without compunction by the Liberal party which had recently allied itself in Moravia with German nationalist anti-Semites. Yet the administration in Moravia would have been in Czech hands were it not for Jewish votes.[58] The lesson to be drawn was that Jews must cease to support any form of national chauvinism whether in Vienna or in the provinces.[59] Nationality conflicts had been the main source of anti-Semitism in Austria. They had encouraged barbaric instincts to flourish and created 'the most dangerous atmosphere' for Jews.[60] They must therefore support only candidates who were committed to national and social justice on a democratic basis. This was not a 'Jewish' politics but it was consonant with historic Jewish traditions of sympathy for 'disinherited' classes and nationalities.[61]

Mayer argued that universal suffrage and social reform were the only rational solution to the chronic disintegration of Austrian political life.[62] The endless bickering between Germans and Slavs had resulted in excessive Magyar and Polish influence within the Austrian State. Linguistic quarrels continued to obstruct social and economic progress. Extending the suffrage to the working classes would bring a fresh wind of change to Austrian commercial and industrial life. It would provide a vital counterweight to the madhouse of bourgeois

[56] *Mittheilungen*, no. 83, 23 May 1896, p. 10: 'Dass der Sohn der letzten Arbeiters das ganz gleiche Recht hat, die gleiche Fürsorge des Staates geniesst wie der Sohn des reichsten Juden, das ist wahrlich zu ertragen. Nicht zur ertragen ist, dass das bravste unserer Kinder weniger Recht haben soll wie jenes des letzten Vagabunden, dass wir Kinder zeugen sollen, die schon bei Geburt einen gelben Fleck mitbringen.'

[57] Sigmund Mayer, 'Die politische Stellung der Juden', 'Aus dem Protokolle', *Mittheilungen*, no. 85, 26 Sept. 1896, p. 3.

[58] Ibid., p. 4 'Ohne die Juden wird die Verwaltung slavisch. Jetzt eilen diese braven Juden zu Hilfe, jetzt wird die Verwaltung mit ihrer Hilfe antisemitisch!'

[59] Ibid., p. 5.

[60] Ibid.: 'Aber speciell bei uns in Oesterreich ist die Nationalitätenhetze jene für uns Juden allergefährlichste Atmosphäre.'

[61] Ibid. Mayer made it clear that 'eine solche specielle jüdische Politik darf es nicht geben und gibt es auch nicht'.

[62] Ibid., p. 7: 'Ein Staat, in dem keine einzige Partei mehr Staatspartei, keine mehr die Partei des Staates nehmen will, ist kein Staat mehr, sondern thatsächlich ein politisches Narrenhaus.'

nationalism and reduce the appeal of anti-Semitic demagogy. At the same time, Mayer recommended that Jews support the creation of a Radical party more congenial to its *freiheitlich* aspirations.[63]

Not all Union members sympathized with Mayer's conversion to a democratic stance on general Austrian issues. Some members still opposed a break with the Liberals, emphasizing that Vienna was predominantly a German city and that the cause of liberty in Austria was identical with that of Germandom.[64] Concern was voiced at the prospect of the Liberals losing six secure municipal seats in the Inner City and two in the Leopoldstadt, if Jews failed to support the Liberal candidates.[65] Others were simply nervous at the prospect of universal suffrage. Nevertheless, a slightly more radical tone was discernable in internal discussions. In a Union debate on 12 December 1896 Dr Friedrich Elbogen sounded a quasi-socialist note, commenting that 'the Jews made the mistake of recognizing an economically reactionary programme, namely that of the Liberal party, instead of marching at the head of Progress in accord with their historic tradition'.[66]

On 20 February 1897 Dr Gustav Kohn reviewed once again the question of how Jews should cast their votes in the forthcoming parliamentary elections. Evoking Sigmund Mayer's advocacy of a democratic programme of national reconciliation, he conceded that the Sozialpolitiker stood closest to this platform.[67] Dr Kohn contended that their entry into Austrian political life had not fulfilled Jewish expectations.[68] The Union had therefore decided not to ally itself with

[63] Ibid., p. 11.

[64] Ibid. *Gemeinderath* Dr Alfred Mittler declared : 'Deutschthum und Freisinn seien immer Hand in Hand gegangen. (Rufe: Niemals.) Deutsche Männer seien as gewesen, die diejenigen Gesetze schufen, welchen die Juden ihre heutige Gleichberechtigung, verdanken.'

[65] See remarks of *Hof- und Gerichtsadvocat* Dr Elias, ibid., p. 12.

[66] 'Aus dem Protokolle', *Mittheilungen*, no. 89, 12 Dec. 1896, p. 13. Dr Elbogen was reacting to a somewhat complacent defence of the Kultusgemeinde's policies over the past six years by Maximilian Steiner. The latter had argued that internal communal affairs and combating 'indifferentism in our own camp' was much more important than external *Abwehr* activities against anti-Semitism. The two central problem areas of Viennese Jewry, he asserted, were lack of Jewish education and inadequate poor relief. Elbogen retorted that the Gemeinde board had always been evasive on the question of anti-Semitism and had failed to implement a practical welfare policy for the Jewish poor.

[67] 'Aus dem Protokolle', *Mittheilungen*, no. 92, 20 Feb. 1897, p. 3.

[68] See S. Mayer, *Ein jüdischer Kaufman*, 322, for a critique of the naïvety of the Sozialpolitiker: 'Diese Leuten waren brav, aber keinen praktischen Politiker. Sie kannten weder die Psychologie der Massen, noch hatten sie überhaupt Menschenkenntnis . . . Zwiespältig in ihrem Herzen und schwankend nach aussen hatten sie keine Haltung und gelangten zu keiner Stellung.' The socialist *Arbeiterzeitung*, 5 Nov. 1896,

either the Liberals or the Sozialpolitiker but to work instead for a reconciliation of the two progressive parties. Decisions would be made on a personal basis, with the Union backing all eight *freiheitlich* candidates in the I district (4 Liberals, 4 Sozialpolitiker), especially Konstantin Noske and Ferdinand Kronawetter.[69] In the Fifth Curia, the official attitude of the Union seemed to be one of passive sympathy with the Social Democrats.

The ensuing debate revealed a division of opinion over Union attitudes to the Social Democrats. Dr Bloch sternly warned against any electoral pact with the Socialists. Those renegades who had fled to the Social Democrats out of a momentary panic 'can scarcely expect a hospitable welcome there'.[70] Jewish flirtations with the labour movement were liable to have negative repercussions on both sides. Jews might be tempted to vote for Social Democratic candidates for the same reasons as they favoured universal suffrage—namely to help the oppressed and underprivileged classes. But they should also be aware of anti-Semitic trends in the Social Democratic party which must arouse in 'every Jewish patriot the greatest caution'.[71]

Other speakers like Siegfried Fleischer rejected these admonitions, contending that only the workers in the Fifth Curia could provide a counterweight to the small trademen, artisan, and businessmen who supported the Christian-Social party. The liberal Dr Elias also insisted that 'in this curia anti-Semitism can be effectively fought only by Social Democracy'.[72] Dr Schnabl, one of Julius Ofner's most enthusiastic supporters in the Union, went even further, calling on Jews to join the Workers' party. 'Social Democracy is called to realise the ideals of liberty, equality and fraternity', he boldly declared, 'which the other parties shamefully deny.'[73]

In a report to the Union on 29 April 1897, the secretary Josef Fuchs, referred to this issue while reiterating the vital importance of Jewish neutrality in Austrian nationality struggles.[74] Fuchs stated that the

---

p. 1, struck a typically anti-Jewish note. It claimed that the Sozialpolitiker owed their votes in the I district during the Nov. 1896 Landtag elections solely to the Israelite Union and the 'Stock Exchange'. It was not their social policies but merely the hope that they would counter anti-Semitism which had attracted Jewish voters. The *Neue Freie Presse*, on the other hand, was enthusiastic and supportive of the new party; see 1 Nov. 1896, p. 4.

[69] *Mittheilungen*, no. 92, pp. 4–5.   [70] Ibid., pp. 6–7.
[71] Ibid., p. 7. See also Rosenmann, pp. 14–15.
[72] *Mittheilungen*, no. 92, p. 6.   [73] Ibid., p. 6.
[74] Ibid., no. 96, 29 Apr. 1897, p. 4.

hopes placed in the Sozialpolitiker as a force that could counteract anti-Semitism had proven illusory. The Union was now working with some success to unify the entire progressive camp. It therefore supported the Social Democrats as the sole factor capable of breaking the monopoly of the anti-Semites, who obviously presented the most immediate danger to Jews.[75] The appearance of Socialist deputies in the Austrian Parliament was a hopeful sign. The secretary of the Union believed that they might offer new orientations which could rescue the Empire from the twin evils of nationalist strife and political irrationality.[76]

A similar note of optimism was sounded by Dr Julius Ofner in a lecture on anti-Semitism before the Eleventh General Assembly of the Union. Ofner observed that contemporary anti-Semitism unlike its feudal and clerical forerunners in the Middle Ages had 'a pronounced democratic character'.[77] The Christian-Social party in Austria was the first to have involved the popular masses in politics. Its rise was essentially a result of the franchise reform initiated by Count Taafe in the mid-1880s. For this reason, Ofner believed, the anti-Semitic movement could not afford to renounce its promises of modern democratic reform nor allow itself to be wholly identified with clericalism.[78]

Ofner interpreted anti-Semitism primarily as a symptom of the struggle between modern and medieval forces in Austrian society. Liberalism and Social Democracy represented political modernity against its bittest enemies—the established forces of the court, the feudal nobility, and the Catholic clergy.[79] These reactionary elements had exposed the class egoism of the Liberal party and its identification with 'plutocratic' interests to mobilize the discontent of the lower middle classes. Anti-Semitism had consequently spread among all those social strata economically endangered by the new industrial system. Because it rested on ancient religious prejudices anti-Semitism was more effective as a political slogan than 'antiliberalism', 'clericalism', or the fight against capitalist corruption.[80] Ofner pointed out that it had been particularly nourished by the great Jewish

---

[75] Ibid., p. 6: 'Wir sind keine Bundesgenossen der Sozialdemokraten, aber wir halten fest an dem allgemeinen Wahlrechte, weil es das einzige Mittel ist, um diesen politischen Monopolbestrungen entgegenzuwirken . . .'
[76] Ibid., p. 9.
[77] 'Vortrag des Herrn Landtags Abgeordneten Dr. Julius Ofner über "Das Wesen des Antisemitismus"', ibid., no. 97, 29 Apr. 1897, p. 9.
[78] Ibid., p. 10.   [79] Ibid., p. 11.   [80] Ibid., p. 12.

immigration to Vienna after 1848. The economic success of the Jews in a modernizing, capitalist society and their prominent role in the Liberal and Social Democratic parties had reinforced this blind reaction. Everything 'modern' in Austria was branded as 'Jewish'. Political reaction had temporarily succeeded in channelling the backlash against industrial and political modernity 'into a struggle against Jews and supporters of the Jews'.[81]

Ofner concluded by stating that the key issue for Jews in the future would be their relation to the 'social question' and the demands of the proletariat. It was not enough for Jews to view the Austrian workers only from the standpoint of 'the struggle against anti-Semitism'. They had to develop a positive interest in the fate of the propertyless classes. Ofner believed that such an involvement corresponded to the great ethical demands of Mosaic legislation, to the long history of persecution and exile suffered by Jews, and to their own long-term interests.'The Jew must stand up for a social order, in which all are free and equal, without discrimination', he proclaimed to enthusiastic aplause.[82] Jews who followed this principle had nothing to fear from anti-Semitism which in spite of its democratic pretensions was ultimately a backward-looking reaction against the new social order that was dawning. Christian Socialism could not succeed for long in delaying the advent of a 'free society' where the Jew would finally enjoy full equality with his fellow-citizens.

Ofner's liberal socialism with its strong humanitarian and ethical impulses undoubtedly had a certain appeal for Jewish voters in Vienna.[83] His personal integrity and idealism, in conjunction with his firm stand against both clericalism and anti-Semitism, impressed many Austrian Jews. Unfortunately, enlightened bourgeois radicalism seemed to have little prospect of affecting the whirlpool of the early twentieth-century Austrian politics, increasingly divided between the nationalist parties, the Christian-Socialists, and the Social Democrats. After 1901 the Sozialpolitiker virtually disappeared as an electoral force. Thus, Ofner's intense activity as a parliamentary deputy was reduced to that

[81] *Mittheilungen*, no. 97, 29 Apr. 1897, p. 13. 'Alles, was modern denkt, wird Jude genannt; deshalb spricht man von Judenliberalen und Juden-socialen.'

[82] Ibid., pp. 14–15.

[83] See Cahnman, p. 125, who writes that 'the poor *Galizianer* of the Leopoldstadt adored him'. At a mass meeing of Jewish voters on 25 Feb. 1907 in the Leopoldstadt, Ofner affirmed: '. . . as in the past, I will defend the interests of the Jews with all my strength. You have seen me wherever the poor and disinherited needed protection. It is my belief that we Jews owe it to ourselves to stand up for full equality of rights for all.'

of a lone outsider, though he did collaborate at times with the Social Democrats.[84] Without the loyalty of his Jewish constituency in Vienna it is perhaps doubtful whether Ofner could have been consistently re-elected to Parliament or the Lower Austrian Landtag.

Jewish attitudes to the Austrian Social Democratic Party before 1914 were generally much cooler than towards leftist bourgeois radicalism. Anxiety at the tidal-wave of Christian-Social anti-Semitism had admittedly made the workers' movement seem more inviting to some Jews in the 1890s. This was a party in which Jewish intellectuals like Victor Adler, Friedrich Austerlitz, and Wilhelm Ellenbogen had played an important role since the early 1890s. After 1900 the party would become increasingly attractive to a new generation of theoreticians, journalists, party activists, and organizers from a middle-class Jewish background.[85] Many of these intellectuals like Otto Bauer, Friedrich Adler, Robert Danneberg, Julius Braunthal, and Julius Deutsch would attain great prominence in 'Red Vienna' between the wars.[86]

Austrian Socialists of Jewish origin rarely retained any connections with the organized Jewish community, usually defining themselves as *Konfessionslos*. Marxist Social Democracy provided them with a substitute for the lost faith of their fathers. Once they had adopted the new secular faith they tended to dissociate themselves from anything 'Jewish', especially in the anti-Semitic climate of *fin de siècle* Vienna. Their frequent attacks on the Liberal 'Jewish' press in the Habsburg capital, on the bourgeois 'monied Jews' of the Union, the Jewish religion, or the 'Judaized' Stock Exchange scarcely endeared them to the average Jewish voter.[87]

This hostility did not pass without comment. On the eve of the 1897 parliamentary elections, Jakob Brod, a Moravian-born Jewish trade union official, wrote to Karl Kautsky, complaining that 'in Vienna, Lower Austria and all the Alpine territories, as well as in all of Moravia and Galicia, only pure "Christians" were put up'. Apart from the party leader Victor Adler (a convert) and Wilhelm Ellenbogen, who stood in a remote Silesian constituency, there were no Jews in the socialist list of candidates. Brod blamed this policy on Adler's bias in 'Jewish

---

[84] Holleis, pp. 93–104.

[85] Robert S. Wistrich, *Socialism and the Jews: The Dilemmas of Assimilation in Germany and Austria-Hungary* (Littman Library, London and Toronto, 1982, 332 ff.

[86] In the inter-war period there was also a far more massive Jewish vote for the Social Democrats in Vienna than was ever the case in the Habsburg period. See Walter B. Simon, 'The Jewish Vote in Austria', *Leo Baeck Yearbook*, 16 (1971), 97–123.

[87] Wistrich, pp. 254 ff.

questions'.[88] At the June 1897 Party Congress he asserted that socialist propaganda readily identified 'Jews' with capitalists but ignored the Jewish proletariat—'the most oppressed, miserable and backward of all'.[89] The Austrian Socialists were consistently more severe on Liberalism than in their reproaches against anti-Semitism, whose electoral successes had even been welcomed in the workers's press.

An undercurrent of suspicion towards Jews in the Austrian Socialist party was indeed unmistakable. One Bohemian delegate declared that:

the Jews are today crowding into the Social Democratic party not in order to become Social Democrats, but because they believe that social democracy will protect their interests. In saying this I mean only bourgeois Jews. If we attack the Schwarzenbergs, everyone approves, but if we get hold of the Jewish exploiters, then these bourgeois pseudo-Social Democrats come along and begin to complain that it was not necessary to attack these people so fiercely, (Laughter and agreement) . . . It has simply become part of the contemporary *bon ton* to pose as being at least interested in social policy, or as a protector of social democracy. If we need to inspect every bourgeois who arrives in our party with the greatest care, then each bourgeois Jew who comes into the party must be examined three times over.[90]

Prominent Social Democratic leaders like Engelbert Pernerstorfer, Franz Schuhmeier, and Victor Adler himself echoed this suspicion. Pernerstorfer openly complained about 'the point of view of some Jews who at once raise a hue and cry about the violation of equal rights if they do not immediately achieve what they want'.[91] Schuhmeier called for ruthlessly eliminating 'Jews who pretend to be Social Democrats and might perhaps have the intention of making the Social Democratic party a Jewish protective guard' (*Judenschutztruppe*). Adler concluded that 'the special feature of the Jewish question as it manifests here in Vienna, is that the capitalist bourgeoisie has a Jewish complexion'.[92] If many Jews were joining the Socialist movement then they were not 'really guided by such ideal motives'. Adler reaffirmed his policy that 'we will not permit the Social Democratic party to be diverted into anti-Semitic or philo-Semitic channels'.[93]

Following this Socialist Party Congress, the Zionist leader Theodor Herzl noted in *Die Welt* that 'the Jewish question' had become 'a

[88] Brod to Kautsky, 9 Feb. 1897, Kautsky Nachlass, Amsterdam, K (DVI), no. 675, quoted in ibid. 260–1.

[89] *Verhandlungen des sechsten österreichischen Sozialdemokratischen Parteitages* (Vienna, 1897), p. 87.

[90] Ibid. 91–2.   [91] Ibid. 89.   [92] Ibid. 103.   [93] Ibid.

source of embarrassment for the Social Democrats'.[94] The sudden influx of Jews into its ranks as a result of anti-Semitic pressure had created an unexpected problem. Herzl felt little sympathy for the 'pseudo-Socialists of recent vintage', though rather more for those who had 'joined the movement in its early difficult period'. He predicted that Socialism would one day slough off 'the pinko Jews' as a matter of self-preservation. This elimination, he anticipated, 'will be of an anti-Semitic character'.[95] Herzl's comments on Jewish participation in the Austrian Socialist movement summed up the Zionist view:

Now, the last thing that these gentlemen, the Social Democrats . . . want to be is an army for the protection of the Jews; they would rather not be reminded that there are Jews in the world. Well, are the comrades so blind that they cannot see the inevitable consequences of the sudden influx of so many Jews into their movement? In the long run, whom will they get to believe that they are not Jews? Not even their poor comrades, who are no gentlemen; in fact, these will believe it least of all. Surely they, the Jewish members, must be afraid of a simple statement pointing out their growing numbers and disproportionate power in the party. There is something tragic about this, for many of them have invested their good will and their best talents, even their very lives in this cause.[96]

The Union had its own reasons for distrusting the Austrian Social Democrats, who had consistently portrayed bourgeois Jews as a homogeneous class of wealthy 'exploiters'. In a lecture to the Union on 14 November 1899, Vice-President Sigmund Mayer angrily repudiated the myths of Jewish wealth, class solidarity and 'exploitation' propagated by a number of Social Democratic Deputies.[97] Like the anti-Semites, Austrian Social Democrats attacked Rothschild, Baron von Gutmann, and other great Jewish magnates as if they represented the mass of Jews. But Jewish society was not a monolithic entity.[98] Sharp cleavages existed between rich and poor, between *la haute banque*, the middle classes, the small tradesmen and workers in the Jewish world. It was the small Jewish artisans, traders, and pedlars in Vienna, Bohemia, Moravia, or Galicia who suffered most from the

---

[94] *Die Welt*, 18 June 1897 [The Social Democrats and the Jewish Question], repr. in Theodor Herzl, *Zionist Writings: Essays and Addresses*, trans. H. Zohn (New York, 1973), i. 86–7.
[95] Ibid. 87.   [96] Ibid. 86–7.
[97] 'Aus dem Protokolle', *Mittheilungen*, no. 115, 14 Nov. 1899, Herr Sigmund Mayer, 'Die Lage der österreichischen Judenschaft', pp. 3 ff.
[98] Ibid., pp. 8–9.

economic anti-Semitism supposedly directed at big Jewish capitalists.[99] It was the task of Jewish self-defence to explain this differentiation to the Christian population. The Jewish and Christian lower classes, so Mayer believed, shared common economic interests.[100]

This liberal emphasis on class solidarity seemed remarkably close to the Marxist analysis of the 'Jewish question'. It seemed to derive mainly from a desire to refute anti-Semitic attacks on 'Jewish' solidarity which might serve as a pretext to suspend civic equality.[101] At the same time, while sharply criticizing Socialists for ignoring the existence of poor Jews, Mayer himself bitterly reproached wealthy Viennese Jews for not giving financial support to the activities of the Union.[102] The millionaires in the Jewish community had provided paltry sums for the maintenance of its major defence organization. It was only thanks to 'the participation of our Jewish middle class and the sums willingly paid by many of our small people in Vienna and the provinces' that the legal bureau had covered its normal budget.[103] The efforts of the Union to obtain additional funds for its 'guerrilla-war against the anti-Semites' had demonstrated that Jewry was divided into two classes; the rich 'who had not the slightest interest for the mass of their co-religionists' and the middling Jews who paid the bill for anti-Semitism.[104]

The cost of defence activities and the financial deficits which the Union incurred through its legal office were a perpetual source of

[99] *Mittheilungen*, no. 115, 14 Nov. 1899, 'Wenn die Kohlen theurer geworden sind, haben diese kleinen Juden, die Kleider-, Leder- und Schnittwaarenhändler, die jüdischen Handwerker die Montanwerke? Oder bekommen sie die Rothschild-Gutmannschen Kohlen billiger als jene des Grafen Larisch? . . . wenn in Nachod die Arbeiter der grossen jüdischen Spinner und Weber Striken, um bessere Löhne zu erzielen, hatten die kleinen jüdischen Händler, Handwerker, Hausirer in Nachod und Umgebung vielleicht das geringste Interesse an dem Siege der Fabrikanten? Im Gegentheile!'

[100] Ibid.

[101] Ibid., p. 10: 'Fürchten Sie nicht die Socialisten! Fürchten Sie nicht das Unmögliche . . . Aber fürchten Sie die Antisemiten! Die Gesetze der Gleichberechtigung—die können aufgehoben werden, fürchten Sie das Mögliche! Alles was schwarz und reaktionär ist in Oesterreich, ist gegen uns. Die Socialisten sind nur mehr die einzige Kampfpartei gegen diese Mächte.'

[102] Ibid., pp. 5–6. For a different viewpoint, which criticized the Union for its secrecy and defended 'die jüdischen Grossen', see Rosenmann, pp. 18–19.

[103] Mayer, p. 6.

[104] Mayer's critique was echoed in the discussion by the Jewish nationalist deputy from Bukovina, Dr Benno Straucher, ibid. 12: 'Als er nach Wien kam, glaubte er, dass die Wiener Judenschaft der ganzen Judenschaft voranleuchten könne. Er habe sich aber bitter getäuscht. Die grossen Juden, die in ihren Salons keine jüdischen Gesellschaften empfangen, haben kein Herz für die Leiden ihres Volkes.'

anxiety.[105] In 1900, out of 13,000 tax-paying members of the Kultusgemeinde, just one-tenth were members of the Union paying the minimal annual contribution of two florins.[106] The organization was not willing to contemplate a compulsory increase of this sum for fear of losing its poorer supporters. Initial attempts to expand membership were, however, only modestly successful. Three hundred new members joined the Union between 1896 and 1899. But the mass of community tax-payers, especially the wealthiest strata in the community, made it clear that they had no 'money for such [defence] goals'. Even the Israelitische Allianz, which had generously supported the legal office from the beginning, was obliged to cut its assistance for financial reason.[107]

The *Rechtsschutz und Abwehr-Büro* (Legal Aid and Defence Bureau) had been founded officially on 15 December 1897. It was headed by an energetic secretary, Siegfried Fleischer, who two years later was to become secretary of the Union as a whole. He had at his disposal a small number of devoted officials, committed to 'safeguarding the political rights and economic interests of our co-religionists not only in Vienna but also throughout Cisleithania'.[108] According to Joseph Fuchs the legal office was a 'vigilant protector of the personal honour of every Jew even though he lead a wretched and obscure existence in the most forlorn Galician village'. The Bureau was a 'battle-ready organ of defence against anti-Semitic lies and malevolence'.[109] It was the institutional answer of the Union to the outdated politics of silence, resignation, and abstinence.[110] If Jews were not to be reduced to second-class citizenship following the rise of Christian-Social anti-Semites to power in Vienna, then 'a new system of defence' was essential.[111] It was vital, Fuchs argued, 'to speak up loudly and decisively and to bring all legal means to bear which exist for the defence of our rights'.[112]

---

[105] *Mittheilungen*, no. 114, 22 Apr. 1899, pp. 14–15. The current deficit at this date was 2,000 florins.

[106] Ibid., p. 15. By 1910, however, the organization claimed 7,000 members; see Rozenblit, p. 158.

[107] *Mittheilungen*, no. 114, p. 15.

[108] Ibid., no. 105, 23 Apr. 1898, p. 4, from the report of Union secretary, Joseph Fuchs, at the XII General Assembly. [109] Ibid.

[110] See ibid., p. 3, for an example where the Union did abstain, recognizing that the national struggles threatened the existence of Austria. Fuchs regarded any Jewish commitment to one or the other side in these conflicts to be 'einen Act der Selbstvernichtung'.

[111] Ibid., p. 4. [112] Ibid.

The Defence Bureau did not interpret its work in a narrow, formalistic manner nor was it confined simply to repelling anti-Semitic attacks in Vienna. Early on, it recognized that the defence of Jewish rights must be extended to the mass of Jews in the Austrian provinces who were physically more exposed than their co-religionists in the Imperial capital. Already by March 1897 the Bureau declared that it had recruited trustees in over sixty Austrian towns. Its research and monitoring network extended throughout the Austrian half of the Monarchy, receiving valuable assistance from its variegated contacts in Bohemia, Moravia, and Galicia. One of the main duties of the Bureau, according to Fuchs, was to collect evidence and intervene whenever the Jewish people (*das Gesammtjudentum*) was defamed in Austria—whether in the press, public meetings, or in representative institutions.[113] Its most important single task was, however, to supply free legal aid 'in all cases where the constitutional rights of the Jews as such are discriminated against'.[114]

How effective was the Bureau in its legal battles against the seemingly endless flood of Austrian anti-Semitic activity between 1897 (the year of its foundation) and 1914? If the claims of its secretary are to be believed (in a report of 1910 in honour of the Union's twenty-fifth anniversary) no less than five thousand cases dealt with by the Bureau were brought to a successful conclusion.[115] This claim is difficult to test but presumably depended on a very broad definition of 'successful' defence activity. It appears to have deliberately obscured the fact that many files dealt with by the Bureau never received sustained treatment, never went to the courts, nor became the subject of political mediation. Nevertheless, the Bureau had a vested interest in regarding any file that was opened—even for information only—as a demonstration of its indispensable and successful intercession. From a close examination of its own internal documentation a more modest and variegated picture emerges. Thus, of the files actually handled between 15 December 1897 and April 1898, less than half of the eight-two cases involved intervention with government departments, petitions, audiences, or legal counsel in the courts. The main achievement, according to Fuchs, was that in more than a quarter of the cases the anti-Semitic press—much to its annoyance—had to print

---

113 '*Mittheilungen*, no. 105, 23 Apr. 1898.

114 Ibid., p. 4, and no. 107, Oct. 1898, p. 2.

115 '25 Jahre Österreichisch-Israelitische Union', *Monatsschrift der Österreichisch-Israelitischen Union*, 17 Apr. 1910, p. 20; see also *Monatsschrift*, Feb. 1910, pp. 1–3.

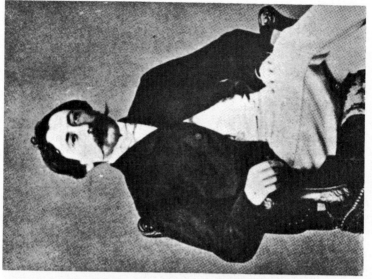

2 Baron Maurice de Hirsch (1831–1896)

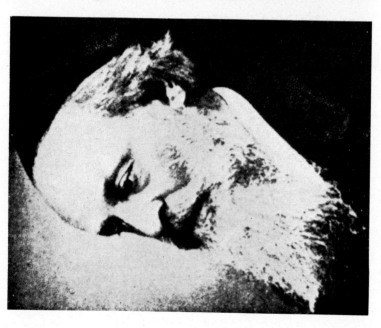

1. Chief Rabbi Mortiz Güdemann (1835–1918)

3. Dr Joseph Samuel Bloch (1850–1923)

4. Four students from the Viennese Kadimah Fraternity, *c.*1895

5. Dr Nathan Birnbaum (1864–1937), who coined the term Zionism

6. Dr Theodor Herzl (1860–1904) *c.*1897

8. Dr Victor Adler (1852–1918), leader of the Austrian Social Democratic party

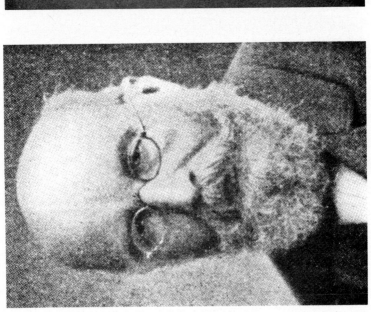

7. Dr Julius Ofner (1845–1924)

10. Gustav Mahler (1860–1911)

9. Sigmund Freud (1856–1939) in 1891

12. The young philosopher Otto Weininger (1880–1903) on his deathbed

11. Arthur Schnitzler (1862–1931)

rectifications or even humble apologies for its calumnies against Jews.[116] This ability to force retractions from its anti-Semitic adversaries in the press, was undoubtedly a source of satisfaction for the Bureau, especially when the courts imposed fines on the offenders. But it must remain a moot point whether this part of its legal work (as Sigmund Mayer firmly believed) significantly reduced the level of anti-Semitic attacks in Vienna or in the rest of Cisleithania.[117] A certain deterrent effect cannot be denied when in the period between April 1898 and March 1899 fifty-four of the 114 files acted on (i.e 47 per cent) did lead—according to Bureau statistics—to retractions in the anti-Semitic press.[118] But events proved that it was not too difficult to circumvent legal suits by avoiding the specific naming of Jewish persons, addresses, or names of firms while continuing to publish anti-Semitic slogans with impunity. Moreover, there was a serious obstacle to successful legal action in the immunity from prosecution of Christian-Social deputies in the Reichsrat or the Lower Austrian Diet like Schneider, Gregorig, or Schlesinger, whose anti-Jewish diatribes were regularly reproduced in the party press. Having made their slanderous accusations from within the safety of Austrian legislative bodies where their party was already in a very strong position, these deputies could not easily be brought to book. Nor could the press be indicted for reporting their words. Thus when the Defence Bureau sought to petition the President of the Lower Austrian Diet following a notorious speech by Gregorig against the sexual malpractices of Jewish employers, its protest was easily voted down by the anti-Semitic majority.[119]

A more successful intervention by the Defence Bureau was the detailed memorandum delivered to the Austrian Prime Minister, Baron Paul von Gautsch, on 6 January 1898, concerning the anti-Semitic riots in Prague.[120] The memorandum had been prepared by Siegfried Fleischer following the visit to Prague in the wake of the Jew-baiting that had begun in December 1897. Czechs on the rampage had attacked Jewish shops, homes, and synagogues following German–

---

[116] *Mittheilungen*, no. 105, p. 8: 'Der Werth dieser Berichtigungen liegt in dem Umstande, dass der antisemitische Leserkreis selbt allmälig und unausgesetzt auf die Presse aufmerksam gemacht wird . . .

[117] S. Mayer, *Ein jüdischer Kaufmann*, 314.

[118] 'Aus dem Protokolle', *Mittheilungen*, no. 114, 22 Apr. 1899, p. 10.

[119] *Österreichische Wochenschrift* (1898), no. 6, pp. 101–2.

[120] See '25 Jahre', *Monatsschrift*, 17 Apr. 1910, p. 32.

Czech clashes in Prague and other parts of Bohemia.[121] This agitation, originally provoked by the Badeni language ordinances, was serious enough to encourage von Gautsch to act on the Defence Bureau's memorandum. On 7 February 1898 he dissolved the anti-Semitic Národní Obrana (National Defence) for its role in instigating the riots. This success may have pushed the Bureau to demand financial compensation from the authorities for further damage inflicted on Jewish property when striking workers went on the rampage in the Bohemian town of Nachod in the spring of 1899.[122]

Between April 1898 and March 1899 the *Rechtsschutzbureau* provided legal aid in thirty-three of the 114 cases it actually handled (29 per cent) and intervened in a further twenty-seven cases with the political authorities 'for the warranted interests of individual co-religionists'.[123] Sometimes its reports on illegal discrimination or its willingness to undertake legal action were restrained by political considerations or respect for the family and business interests of individual Jews. But whatever the practical limitations, both the Defence Bureau and the Union were convinced that the perceptible improvement in Jewish morale in Vienna and the provinces was due mainly to their new policy of assertive self-reliance and vigorous intercession with the authorities.[124] Intensive defence activity, it was claimed, had revived the courage and 'contributed to strengthening the civic consciousness of our co-religionists'.[125] According to the Union, silence and apathy in the face of illegal discrimination and the increasingly frequent attempts to exclude Jews from craft guilds or from professional and commercial associations were giving way to a new optimism in the fight to preserve civic equality.

With regard to the more serious manifestations of anti-Semitism—such as the pogroms which swept western and central Galicia in the summer of 1898—they afford an insight into the kind of irresolvable problems confronting Jewish self-defence organizations like the *Rechtsschutzbureau*. The first response of the Bureau was to try and mobilize Jewish members of the Polish Club to intervene with their

---

[121] Michael A. Riff, 'Czech Antisemitism and the Jewish Response before 1914', *The Wiener Library Bulletin*, ed. Robert S. Wistrich, 29, nos. 39, 40 (1976), p. 12.

[122] *Mittheilungen*, no. 114, 22 Apr. 1899, pp. 8–9.

[123] 'Aus dem Protokolle', ibid., 22 Apr. 1899, p. 10.

[124] *Mittheilungen*, no. 105, p. 8: 'Das Gefühl der Schutzlosigkeit und Rechtsunsicherheit schwindet in dem Masse, als die Erfolge unserer Thätigkeit öffentlich, sichtbar und auch in der Provinz mehr und mehr bekannt werden.'

[125] Ibid., pp. 8–9.

Gentile colleagues and with the Polish Governor of Galicia but with little practical result.[126] More successful was the appeal to the Austrian Prime Minister, Graf Leo Thun, promptly to despatch military reinforcements and to declare martial law in the affected areas. Two Board members of the Union had been received by Graf Thun in June 1898 and he was also the recipient of a petition by the Union's President, Wilhelm Anninger.

The Union sponsored a major sociological investigation into the background of the riots in which opinions were solicited not only from Jews but also from leading Polish politicians and intellectuals.[127] Siegfried Fleischer also carried out a very extensive *Enquête* on behalf of the Defence Bureau into the economic and political causes of the pogroms.[128] Along with these investigations, the Union also sought to promote constructive change within the Polish province, especially the development of industry and educational reforms. But the requisite funds from foreign Jewish organizations were never forthcoming and 'scientific' studies did not bring a cessation of pogromist propaganda in Galicia. In 1903 and again in 1906 under the influence of pogroms in the neighbouring Tsarist Empire, anti-Semitism revived and the Bureau was powerless against the prevalence of economic boycotts against the Jews by Polish nationalists. In Galicia, as elsewhere in the Monarchy, efforts to arouse public opinion against anti-Semitism or to undertake 'constructive' measure to productivize the Jews had little prospect of success. Self-defence based on appeal to higher authority or to the courts was somewhat more promising as a strategy and may have exercised a temporary deterrent effect. But it could scarcely provide a cure for such an endemic phenomenon as popular anti-Semitism in the late Habsburg Monarchy. In the years between 1898 and 1905 alone, there were no less than thirty blood libels recorded in different parts of the Empire, especially in the rural Slavic (and Catholic) regions of Galicia, Bohemia, and Moravia. The Defence Bureau meticulously investigated most of these cases, appealing on occasion to the Ministries of Justice or Education. But there were no tangible results.

In the Hilsner case of 1899 the Bureau made perhaps its single most

---

[126] *Mittheilungen*, no. 108, Nov. 1898, pp. 3 ff.

[127] 'Unsere Rechtsschutz- und Abwehr-Action. Bericht erstattet vom Vorstande in der Plenarversammlung vom 29 October 1898', *Mittheilungen*, no. 108, pp. 7–8; see also Siegfried Fleischer, 'Enquête über die Lage der jüdischen Bevölkerung Galiziens', in A. Nossig (ed.), *Jüdische Statistik* (Berlin, 1903), 219 ff.

[128] *Mittheilungen*, no. 108, Nov. 1898, pp. 3 ff.

intensive effort—both before, during, and after the trial—to stem the tide of defamation encouraged by the revival of the medieval blood libel. It provided free legal aid to Hilsner and constantly sought, even after his conviction, to have the case reopened. At the same time, the Bureau vigorously protested against booklets in the Czech or German languages seeking to propagate the ritual-murder fabrications and subsidized a compilation containing Christian refutations of the blood libel.[129] The counter-propaganda of the Bureau and the noticeably greater readiness of the Austrian courts after 1905 to convict perpetrators of the blood libel may account for the decline of this plague in the closing years of the Monarchy. Nevertheless, the conviction of Hilsner and the boost which this gave to anti-Semites in Prague, Vienna, and the Galician hinterland of the Empire more than neutralized the value of the Bureau's efforts.

If the Defence Bureau could do little against racial, religious, or economic anti-Semitism which enjoyed mass popular support, it was no less disadvantaged by the persistence of bias against Jews in the upper and lower reaches of the Austrian bureaucracy. It had reacted with a sharp protest to the Ministry of the Interior over the chilling call of Professor Dr Joseph Sturm in a Christian-Social electoral meeting in Vienna simply to 'shoot the Jews'.[130] The Bureau warned the Ministry that its passive behaviour in this instance risked encouraging 'scenes in Vienna such as we experienced to the disgrace of the fatherland in Galicia'.[131] The Union in a separate memorandum that significantly received no response from the Ministry observed that in no other modern, civilized State would a paid civil servant be permitted to engage in such blood-curdling threats against a group of his fellow-citizens. However, precisely in cases where the anti-Semitism of civil servants (or government officials) was in question, there was little hope of gaining redress.

Nevertheless, the Bureau did succeed in blocking the renewed efforts of Lueger's party to introduce denominational separation of Jews and Christians in Vienna's city schools.[132] This 'clerical' demand threatened to reverse the long tradition of Jewish attendance in general schools dating back to the time of the Emperor Joseph II. It was guaranteed to arouse the passions of Viennese Jewry. The IKG

[129] '25 Jahre', *Monatsschrift*, 17 Apr. 1910, pp. 34 ff.
[130] *Mittheilungen*, no. 108, p. 15.
[131] Ibid.
[132] Ibid., pp. 17–18.

promptly petitioned the Education Ministry while the Defence Bureau of the Union helped organize protest meetings and political opposition to the segregationist measures proposed by Vienna's municipal board. The combination of lobbying the Ministry of Education (which was committed to upholding the principle of non-segregation in the schools) and mobilizing support from anticlerical political parties was in this instance successful in checking a dangerous precedent for undermining Jewish civil equality. The Union could, for once, point to an indisputable achievement in the defence of Jewish rights. It was a rare example of the ability to use public opinion (in a society that was not yet fully democratized) along with an appeal to the authorities, in order to frustrate a central anti-Semitic goal. No doubt the fact that 'clericalism' as an issue could also be counted on to arouse the passions of Liberal, Progressive, and Social Democratic politicians, helped the Jewish cause. Equally important was the ability and willingness of the Union (and the Bureau) to put together such a 'democratic' coalition in order to protect Jewish rights in terms of wider general interest.

The Union was, however, notably less liberal in internal Jewish affairs than in its general orientation towards Austrian politics. It did not, for example, oppose the decision of the Viennese Community Board to introduce a two-class voting system in 1900, by means of which the wealthiest community taxpayers (over 200 Kronen per annum) would elect an additional twelve members to the *Vorstand*.[133] This reactionary franchise reform handed weapon to anti-Semites to contend in the words of one critic that 'while we stand up for the most far-reaching equality in political life, in our ranks we practice class discrimination and this hurts the moral prestige of the Jews'.[134] Other critics, like *Gemeinderat* Wilhelm Stiassny, opposed the oligarchical content of the new system as being 'against the *Zeitgeist*, and the spirit of Judaism'.[135] The Union was none the less reluctant to oppose formally the Community Board. After 1900 it increasingly defended the plutocratic structure of community elections attacked by the Zionists.[136] It was one of the great internal contradictions of the Union

---

[133] See the fierce critique by *Gemeinderat* Lucien Brunner of this new caste-system 'nach dem Masstabe des Geldsackes', published under the heading 'Zur Wahlreform der Cultusgemeinde', *Die Neuzeit*, 19 Jan. 1900, p. 23. See also the free debate in the Union on 12 Feb. 1900, 'Aus der Protokolle', *Mittheilungen*, no. 117, pp. 2–6.

[134] Ibid., p. 3.   [135] Ibid., pp. 2–3.

[136] It is true that the Union in 1896 wanted a more representative board and greater attention paid to Jewish education by the Kultusgemeinde. See 'Wahlprogramm der

that it should have advocated universal suffrage in Austria from the turn of the century while failing to encourage the democratization of the Jewish community.

The Union had vehemently rejected political Zionism from its first appearance on the scene in Vienna, convinced that it could only aggravate anti-Semitism and undermine the struggle of Jews to maintain their civic rights in their countries of residence. Sigmund Mayer (President of the Union after 1905) regarded Zionism as a particularly perverse attempt to reverse the trend of social integration since the Enlightenment. For Mayer, the idea of transforming Austrian Jews into a Hebrew-speaking 'political nation' like the Germans, Czechs, Poles, Ukrainians, Slovenes, or Romanians, seemed the height of folly.[137] No less 'fantastical' was the call for a 'special voting curia' on a national basis, proposed by Zionists in Moravia in 1905.[138] This would play into the hands of the anti-Semites by sabotaging Jewish legal rights, encouraging a self-imposed pariah-dom, and bringing about disastrous economic consequences for the Jewish population.

Like other assimilationist critics of Zionism, Mayer regarded its programme as completely utopian. He insisted that Jews were not a nationality (since they lacked any common territory, language, or culture) though the Zionist successes in mobilizing this non-existent 'nation' in Austria seemed to belie the assertion.[139] Indeed the 1907 parliamentary elections in which Zionists conducted a vigorous campaign, provided the Union with a tactical problem that could not simply be wished away. In particular, a position had to be adopted on the Zionist proposal to establish an independent Jewish political group in the new Parliament. Some members of the Union like Siegfried Fleischer and Joseph Bloch favoured this option despite their opposition to Zionism as an ideology. This faction favoured candidates whether in Vienna or in the provinces who represented specifically Jewish interests.[140] Their candidates included Dr Gustav Kohn in the

OIU, 1896', Central Archives of the History of the Jewish People, A/W 48/3. But this did not prevent it from supporting IKG candidates.

[137] Mayer, *Die Wiener Juden: Kommerz, Kultur, Politik, 1700–1900* (Vienna and Berlin, 1917), 464 ff.

[138] Ibid. 467; also *Ein jüdischer Kaufmann*, 348 ff., and 'Die Agitation für die judische Kurie', *Monatsschrift*, Jan. 1906, pp. 1–2.   [139] *Die Wiener Juden*, 480–1, 490.

[140] S. Fleischer, 'Die Juden und das allgemeine Wahlrecht', *Monatsschrift*, Dec. 1906, pp. 1–2; also Dr. Alexander Mintz, 'Die politische Lage der Juden', ibid., Nov. 1906, pp. 1–11.

Leopoldstadt who faced no less than three Jewish opponents, and Kamillo Kuranda in the Inner City.[141] The attempts to present these Union candidates as representatives of a distinct 'Jewish point of view' was surprising in view of their undeniably assimilationist outlook. The fact that the powerful Mayer faction in the Union favoured the social reformer Julius Ofner over Dr Kohn as the best 'Jewish' candidate for the Leopoldstadt underlined the confusion. No less curious was the fact that some Union members like Dr Bloch interpreted the victory of four 'Zionist' candidates in the 1907 parliamentary elections as being consistent with their long-standing views on the political representation of Austrian Jewry.[142]

Within the context of the Jewish community the conflict between the Union and the Zionist movement remained for all that uncompromising. The Zionists were frequently identified by Union officials with the Viennese anti-Semites, especially in their use of 'rabble-rousing' tactics.[143] The Union and members of its Central Electoral Committee saw their chief rivals for community power as a radical nationalist element, ignorant of Judaism and destructively bent on undermining the foundations of Jewish civic equality.

The Union remained as adamantly opposed as ever to any national definition of Jewish identity. It especially resented the 'anti-Semitic' concept of the Jews as a *Gastvolk* (guest nation) in the Diaspora, provocatively adopted by many Zionists. This notion seemed to undermine any effort by Austrian Jews to integrate themselves in the supranational Austrian State. The existence of such deeply-felt objections to Zionism within the Union should not however blind one to the parallel process of reinforcing Jewish identity that was taking place among the rival organizations. Something of the pride and self-assertion associated with the Jewish national renaissance did influence the Union leadership and helped to shape its activity after 1900.[144]

[141] *Die Wahrheit*, 22 Mar. 1907, pp. 3–4; 14 May 1907, pp. 43–4. This newspaper had replaced *Die Neuzeit* as the quasi-official organ of the IKG. The veteran social-political candidate Julius Ofner, who was a native of the Leopoldstadt and very popular among the Galicians, was depicted by *Die Wahrheit* as insufficiently 'Jewish'. However his victorious candidacy was supported by Sigmund Mayer precisely for this reason; see *Monatsschrift*, May 1907, pp. 1–2. A prominent socialist, Friedrich Austerlitz, the Jewish-born editor of the *Arbeiterzeitung*, also stood as a candidate and strongly attacked Zionism as a 'return to the ghetto'. See 'Wiener Wahlversammlung: die erste Wahlversammlung in der Leopoldstadt', *Arbeiterzeitung*, 28 Mar. 1907, p. 6. His *Konfessionslosigkeit* and hostility to religion made him quite unacceptable to the Jewish leadership.

[142] *Österreichische Wochenschrift*, 21 June 1907, pp. 405–6.

[143] Ibid., 7 Nov. 1902, pp. 723 ff.; 2 Oct. 1908, pp. 697–8.

[144] This point is well made by Rozenblit, p. 192.

PART III

THE RISE OF ZIONISM

Kadimah and Jewish Student Nationalism

Yet, in our midst, was the divinely inspired writer Smolenskin . . .
He meditated for a moment, his pale lips pursed in readiness,
and when I called on him to speak he suggested that the society
be called Kadimah. The word signified the eastward direction of
our strivings, but also at the same time a forward progression. All
those who were present accepted the name by acclamation . . .

Reuben Bierer,
Letter to Akademische Verbindung Kadimah (*c.*1898)

Comrades! For eighteen centuries, ever since the Jewish people
lost their independence, they have been subject to continuous
persecutions whose aim is the destruction of Jewry.

Unfortunately, in this endeavour our enemies have been aided
all too often by members of our own race. Indifference at the core
of Jewry competes with external animosities to achieve this goal.
As far as our enemies are concerned, we can only defend
ourselves; but we must also counteract indifference. The newly
formed academic society 'Kadimah' has set this as its goal.

First proclamation of Kadimah in Vienna
(Spring 1883)

The card with which you honoured me was an auspicious sign
that the idea of our national self-awareness [*Selbstbewusstein*] has
struck root among Vienna's academic youth. The generation that
is currently setting the tone, a generation which you will soon
replace, cannot renounce those principles implanted in it for
decades; while at present you yourselves still lack social influence.
On the other hand, the future belongs to you. The men of
superior rank cannot take this away from you and the time is
coming when the noble dream of your youth will be turned by
your strong hands into deeds . . .

Leo Pinsker, Letter to the President of Kadimah
(11 December 1884)

At the end of the 1880s a significant change occurred in the functioning of Kadimah. If previously its recruits had come from the great Eastern reservoir of Russia and Poland, now there were students from Vienna, Moravia, and Bukovina who immediately upon their entry strove to introduce new methods. When I came into Kadimah, I already found several Viennese students . . . whereas the founders brought their conscious Jewishness with them, we, the new freshman recruits who came from an assimilationist milieu, were seeking our Jewishness in Kadimah . . .

Dr Isidor Schalit,
'Memoirs, 1890 to 1914' in Kadimah Festschrift

The Jewish students assembled today, 4 March 1896, in Robitschek Restaurant regard it as their duty to express their heartfelt appreciation to Dr Theodor Herzl for the courage and resoluteness with which he is championing the Zionist idea. The Jewish students declare their readiness to answer Dr Herzl's call and to fight at his side for the realization of this great and lofty idea.

Resolution of the Jewish Association,
Gamalah (Vienna 1896)

Fin de siècle Vienna has been widely recognized as the birthplace of Herzlian political Zionism. It is less generally known that Vienna had been the centre of gravity of Jewish nationalism in the German-speaking world since the early 1880s. The bearers of this national idea were a small group of Jewish students at the University of Vienna who in 1882 had organized the Akademischer Verein Kadimah, the first Jewish national student society in Western Europe.[1] Kadimah subsequently provided the model for the foundation of a variety of new Jewish nationalist student organizations in the Austro-Hungarian Monarchy. By the late 1890s its influence had spread to Germany and

---

[1] There is no authoritative history of Kadimah in existence. The most valuable single sources are the *Festschrift zur Feier des 100. Semesters der akademischen Verbindung Kadimah* (Mödling, 1933), ed. Ludwig Rosenhek, and the archival material in the Central Zionist Archives (CZA) in Jerusalem. In addition there is an article by Harriet Z. Pass, 'Kadimah: Jewish Nationalism in Vienna before Herzl', *Columbia University Essays in International Affairs: The Dean's Papers* (1969), 119–36, and useful information in G. Kressel's Hebrew essay, 'Selbstemanzipation', *Shivat Zion*, 4 (1956), 55–99. The best attempt at synthesis to date is by Julius H. Schoeps, 'Modern Heirs of the Maccabees. The Beginning of the Vienna Kadimah 1882–1897', *Leo Baeck Yearbook*, 27 (1982), 155–70, to which Marsha L. Rozenblit's 'The Assertion of Identity. Jewish Student Nationalism at the University of Vienna before the First World War', ibid. 171–86, provides a valuable accompaniment for the decade after 1900.

parts of Western Europe.[2] In Vienna itself, it would supply the backbone of Theodor Herzl's support in the mid-1890s, providing a well-tested group of devotes cadres that enabled him to build the first centrally organized Zionist movement.[3] One of the most important leaders of Austrian Zionism, Isidor Schalit, recalled in his memoirs by the 1890s that Kadimah had emerged as the 'centre of agitation throughout Western Europe for the Palestinian idea, a vital centre of energetic activity. We were not only the standard-bearers of the Jewish national idea in Western Europe, we were its only orators, its agitators, propagandists and journalists: we were the movement.'[4]

The origins of Kadimah can be traced to the encounter of two young students at the University of Vienna, Moritz Schnirer (1861–1941) and Nathan Birnbaum (1864–1937), with the forty-six-year-old Reuben Bierer, who had recently moved to the Habsburg capital with his family.[5] Reuben Bierer (1835–1931), a physician from Lemberg, had been one of the earliest Ḥovevei Zion activists in Galicia.[6] In 1882 Bierer had helped found the Viennese chapter of the Ahavat Zion society for the colonization of Ereẓ Israel together with Rabbi Salomon Spitzer, the leader of Viennese orthodoxy.[7]

[2] See, e.g., N. M. Gelber's Hebrew article, 'The First Organization of the Russian-Jewish students in Berlin', *Heawar*, iv (1956), 47–55; Jehuda L. Weinberg, *Aus der Frühzeit des Zionismus, Heinrich Loewe* (Jerusalem, 1946), 98 ff.; Richard Lichtheim, *Die Geschichte des deutschen Zionismus* (Jerusalem, 1954); Moses Landau, 'Der Zionismus in Österreich-Ungarn' (Univ. of Vienna diss., 1932). Also *Festschrift*, 'Kadimah. iv. 1890 bis 1904: Erinnerungen von Ehrenburschen Medizinalrat Dr. Isidor Schalit, Wien' (henceforth, Schalit, 'Erinnerungen'), 49 ff.

[3] Schalit, 'Erinnerungen', 106: 'Ohne "Kadimah" kein Zionismus in Westeuropa, ohne diesen kein Herzl, ohne Herzl kein Judenstaat.'

[4] Ibid. 41.

[5] See '25 Jahre Kadimah', *Die Welt*, no. 6 (1908), pp. 6–8: 'Festrede, gehalten von M. T. Schnirer auf dem Jubiläumskommers des "Kadimah"'. Also, Dr. M. T. Schnirer, 'Gründung der Kadimah', *Festschrift*, 15 ff.

[6] On Bierer, there is unfortunately no detailed study or scholarly article. See however *Die Welt*, no. 11 (1897), p. 6) G. Kressel, 'Selbstemanzipation', and his brief entry in the *Encylopaedia Judaica* (Jerusalem, 1971), iv. 984–5; N. M. Gelber, *Toldot Ha-Tnuah ha-Ziyyonit be-Galitsiah* (Tel Aviv, 1958) for the Galician background and Bierer's letter to the Akademische Verbindung Kadimah (n.d.) CZA Z 1/1. Bierer, interestingly enough, contributed a number of Zionist articles from Sofia to the liberal and anti-Zionist *Die Neuzeit* in the 1890s. See, e.g., 'Nationale Lebensreichen', 23 July 1897, pp. 304–5, which criticizes the A.I.U. and anticipates the creation of a Hebrew University in Jerusalem; and 'Der projectirte Gemeindebund der Juden Oesterreichs und seine Separatisten im Lichte des Zionismus', 21 Jan. 1898, pp. 24–5, a sharp polemic against the Polish Club and the 'pseudo-Polish chauvinism' of its Jewish representatives against the background of the economic decay of Galician Jewry.

[7] Bierer maintained his links with orthodox and Ḥovevei Zion circles even after becoming a devoted supporter of Herzlian Zionism. He was active after 1896 in

Another founder-member of the Viennese Ahavat Zion was the Russian *maskil* Perez Smolenskin (1842–85), in many ways the spiritual father of Kadimah. His initial influence on the movement would be difficult to exaggerate. At the founding meeting in December 1882 in the backroom of the Café Gross in Vienna's Obere Donaustrasse, it was Smolenskin who provided the evocative Hebrew name Kadimah for the new association.[8] As Isidor Schalit pointed out: 'In this one word Smolenskin revealed his life's goal, for the word "Kadimah" has two meanings: "Eastward", against assimilation and for national work, and "forward" against Orthodoxy and for progress.'[9]

Perez Smolenskin was the editor of a Hebrew monthly *Ha-Shahar*, which he founded almost immediately after settling in Vienna in 1868. The twelve volumes which he edited single-handedly until his death provide a key documentary source for the transition from East European *Haskalah* to modern Jewish nationalism.[10] Born in the Russian Pale of Settlement and educated in the *yeshivah* of Shklov, Smolenskin had revolted against orthodoxy in his adolescent years. He then began a life of wandering which took him in 1862 to the more secular environment of Odessa where he was to spend the next six years and to crystallize a radical enlightened outlook.[11] Already in 1867 he decided for *maskilic* reasons to write in Hebrew, hoping through

promoting Herzl's ideas in Bulgaria, where he worked as a court physician. Herzl sent him the first copy of *Der Judenstaat*, dedicated 'to the first pioneer of Zionism' (Kressel, in *Encylopaedia Judaica*, iv. 985).

[8] Bierer's letter, CZA Z 1/1. On the founding meeting to draft statutes, called by Bierer and attended by about 15 persons (mainly students from Galicia, Romania, and Russia) see Schoeps, pp. 156–7. Also 'Statuten der akademischen Vereines "Kadimah" 19 Januar 1883' (CZA Z 1/1), A/368/8–1, and Schnirer, 'Gründung der Kadimah', *Festschrift*, 16–17.

[9] Quoted in Schoeps, p. 156. Schnirer, in *Festschrift*, 16, saw in the name 'eine Synthese des Fortschrittsgedanken und der zionistischen Idee'. See also the long obituary by Nathan Birnbaum, 'Perez Smolenskin', *Selbstemanzipation*, 17 Mar. 1886, pp. 6–9.

[10] See Arthur Hertzburg (ed.), *The Zionist Idea: A Historical Analysis and Reader* (New York, 1973), 142–57, for translated extracts from articles Smolenskin published in *Ha-Shahar*: 'It is Time to Plant' (1875–7), 'Let Us Search our Ways' (1881), and 'The Haskalah' (1883). *Kol Sifrei Perez Smolenskin*, 6 vols. (1905–10), including a biography by Reuben Brainin, and *Ma'amarim*, 4 vols. (Jerusalem, 1925–6), are the most important collections of Smolenskin's Hebrew writings. For an evaluation of his contribution as a novelist, see David Patterson, *The Hebrew Novel in Czarist Russia* (1964), and the latter's admirably succinct article in the *Encylopaedia Judaica*, xv. 7–11.

[11] Smolenskin's longest work his autobiographical novel, *Ha-Toeh Be-Dareche Ha-Hayim* (The Wanderer in the Paths of Life) (1876), vividly reflects his *Wanderjahre* and contemporary Jewish life, especially in Eastern Europe. Parts of it were originally published in *Ha-Shahar*, (1868/9) and 2 (1871).

this medium to transmit European culture and literature to the Jews of the Pale. Before finally settling in Vienna, Smolenskin travelled through Bohemia and the German states. His encounter with Reform Judaism in Central Europe shook him profoundly, especially its pronounced German patriotism and contempt for Hebrew, which in his eyes amounted to a betrayal of Jewish tradition. In the Austrian capital, poverty obliged the young Smolenskin to abandon his original project of studying at the University. Instead, he took a job as proof-reader (later as manager) in a printing-house, while devoting most of his energies to the writing, publishing, editing, and distribution of *Ha-Shaḥar*. This journal soon emerged as a leading Hebrew literary organ of the *Haskalah* and subsequently of modern Jewish nationalism.[12]

Smolenskin was a severe critic of the many shortcomings of both rabbinical orthodoxy and Hasidism in Russia and Poland which he viewed from the standpoint of a modern *maskil*. At the same time, he was even more condemnatory of the assimilationist tendencies in the Mendelssohnian *Haskalah*, emanating from Berlin. Since the late eighteenth century, this Enlightenment trend had gradually taken root in Vienna, the Habsburg provinces, and Eastern Europe.[13] Smolenskin particularly reproached Adolf Jellinek and the Kultusgemeinde leaders in Vienna for their neglect of the Hebrew language. He deplored the attempts to divorce religous education from the national spirit of Judaism and the marked hostility of many community leaders to the *Ostjuden*.[14] Smolenskin felt that the source of these aberrations lay in

---

[12] Birnbaum's obituary in *Selbstemanzipation*, p. 7, correctly points out that, from the first number of *Ha-Shaḥar*, Smolenskin proclaimed his clear-cut opposition to assimilation and belief in the Jewish national rebirth. His cultural nationalism was not a product of the new anti-Semitism or the Russian pogroms of 1881 but rooted in a deep loyalty to Hebrew language and literature, the real basis in his eyes of Jewish national identity, in the absence of either state or national territory. In Smolenskin's words: '. . . die Sprache fasst in sich die Festigkeit einer Nation [*ha-le'om*] und wenn die Sprache in Vergessenheit gerath, dann verschwindet das Andenken des Volkes selbst von der Erde.' Already in 1868 Smolenskin had written: 'Die Liebe zu unserem Volke sei die Leuchte unserer Schritte und unter dem Banner unserer Sprache mögen wir wachsen!'

[13] *Selbstemanzipation*, 17 Mar. 1886, p. 8: 'In allen seinen Werken aber, selbst in den Romanen und Novellen, erscheint eine Tendenz und diese Tendenz ist der Kampf gegen die "haskalah berlinith", die "Berliner Aufklärung", gegen die Mendelssohn'sche Schule, gegen diejenige Richtung, die dem Judenthume als Volk Vernichtung geshworen hat.'

[14] Of the Viennese Jewish leaders, Smolenskin felt close only to Dr Ignaz Kuranda, who at the end of his life seemed half-convinced by his arguments against 'assimilationism'. See *Ha-Shaḥar* (1884), pp. 135–42. For his criticisms of the Mannheimer–Jellinek school see e.g. 'Beit-Sefer le-rabbanim be-Austria', *Ha-Shaḥar*

'the vicious and corrupt doctrine' espoused by the Berlin *Haskalah*, which had cast off the bonds of Jewish group solidarity. Reform Judaism explicitly abandoned all hope of a return to Zion, seeking 'utterly to eradicate the Hebrew language, the tongue which united us and enabled us to hear one another's cries of woe to the ends of the dispersion'.[15] In the first issue of *Ha-Shahar* (1868) Smolenskin recounts how he felt like a mourner while walking among the populace (including many Jews) in Vienna's famous Prater Park during the Schutzen Fest. 'All the peoples ascend and the daughter of your people descends. The nations unite and your brethren remain separated. Since they walk in exile they have forgotten their land. They have violated the covenant of brothers and neglected peace and unity . . .' The Reformers were responsible for undermining the unity and memory of the nation. In their efforts to uproot Hebrew they were striking at the last surviving remnant of a holy culture.

Smolenskin reproved the efforts of the German enlighteners as an ill-disguised attempt to cast off the national heritage in pursuit of false hopes of assimilation. The Berlin *Haskalah* ultimately encouraged Jews 'to accept on our heads all the sins ever ascribed to us by our enemies, to justify our persecutors, and, instead of seeking ways of saving ourselves, to seek only to "mend our ways" and to redress wrongs we have not committed'.[16] Attempting to seek the favour of the Gentiles was a delusion that merely fragmented Jewry into sects and parties; by seeking to remove 'all the bonds of love and solidarity' which united Jewry, such a policy could only 'serve to estrange our people from its own spirit'.[17] Still worse, the Berlin *Haskalah* unwittingly encouraged the Jews to 'go on being wretched and rootless wanderers for all eternity', instead of seeking to return to their land and 'living there in dignity, as all peoples do'.[18]

Smolenskin unceasingly castigated 'enlightened' efforts to de-

(1877), pp. 57–61. For the extraordinary impact of *Ha-Shahar* on the *yeshivah* students in the Russian Pale and the resulting hostility to Smolenskin among the orthodoxy in Eastern Europe, see the memoirs of Samuel Leib Citron, 'A Pilgrimage to Peretz Smolenskin', in Lucy S. Dawidowicz (ed.), *The Golden Tradition* (London, 1967), 138–42.

[15] 'The Haskalah of Berlin' (1883), in Hertzberg, p. 156.
[16] Ibid.   [17] Ibid. 156.
[18] After the trauma of the 1881 pogroms, as Smolenskin's nationalism became more concrete, tangible, and Palestinocentric, so too, did his declaration of war against assimilation. 'Only a dog neither has nor wants a home. A man who chooses to live his whole life as a transient, without a thought for the establishment of a permanent home for his children, will forever be regarded as a dog' (Hertzberg, 157).

nationalize Jewry, abandon Jewish patriotism and renounce prophetic hopes of redemption. He had nothing but contempt for any philosophy that implied apelike mimicry of the Gentiles. Smolenskin did not, however, reject *en bloc* the values of Western civilization.[19] His objective was to modernize Jewish life through self-criticism. Thus, in his essay *Am Olam* (The Eternal People), Smolenskin was no less disapproving of East European orthodoxy than of the German religious Reformers. Nevertheless, the view of radical Reformers like Abraham Geiger that Israel had ceased to be a *people* once it lost its statehood in Palestine was anathema to Smolenskin. In this respect he remained closer to Ḥatam Sofer and the outlook of the East European orthodox camp.

In Smolenskin's philosophy, the Jews represented a supremely 'spiritual nation' whose separate identity had been sustained over the centuries by the Torah, by its messianic hopes, and loyalty to the Hebrew language. Above all, Israel existed through the power of historical memory.

Jews of different countries regard and love another as members of the same people because they remember that the tie that binds them did not begin yesterday; it is four thousand years old. Four thousand years! This sense of history alone is a great and uplifting thought, an inspiration to respect this bond and hold it dear. Any sensitive person must feel: For four thousand years we have been brothers and children of one people; how can I sin against hundreds of generations and betray this brotherhood?'[20]

From this nationalist perspective which defined the Jews in terms of fraternal feelings and a common history extending over four millennia, Smolenskin insisted that '*every Jew belongs to his people so long as he does not betray it*'.[21] Neither rejection of religious authority nor the lack of Torah observance could be considered grounds for exclusion from the community in the post-emancipation era. The supreme 'betrayal' was

---

[19] Baruch Kurzweil, 'The German Jew in Modern Hebrew Literature', *Leo Baeck Yearbook* (1961), pp. 173–5, praises Smolenskin's differentiated, complex view of Western Jews—perhaps 'promoted by his long residence in Vienna and other centres of Western European culture'—for avoiding one-sided oversimplifications of 'the Western-Jewish problem.' While disliking the innovations of Western Jews he did not reject the need for reforms.

[20] 'Et Lata'at' (It is Time to Plant), in *Ha-Shaḥar*, 6, 8, 9 (1875, 1876/7, 1878); short translated extracts in Hertzberg, pp. 145–7. For Smolenskin's general view of the importance of language, common historical memories, and emotional subjective factors in nationalism, see *Ha-Shaḥar* (1877), pp. 359 ff.

[21] Hertzberg, p. 146 ('It is Time to Plant', 1877).

assimilation since this amounted to a form of national suicide that broke the continuity of the generations.[22] As a character in Smolenskin's novel *Gemul yesharim* puts it (albeit in a religious context): '. . . we would then be responsible for the deaths not merely of ourselves, but of hundreds of generations, of four thousand years of existence. At one stroke we would erase ourselves from the pages of history, as though we had never been.'[23]

The Russian pogroms of 1881 added a more urgent note to Smolenskin's sense of Israel as a 'spiritual nation', whose Torah had been the historic foundation of its statehood. He had long felt that the roots of anti-Semitism lay in the inferior national status of the Jews which could only be countered by a concrete affirmation of Jewish nationhood. The terrible pogroms in Russia underlined that cultural nationalism alone would no longer suffice.[24] The pillaging of Jewish homes by Russian peasant mobs 'with a cruelty unheard of since the Middle Ages' was not just a temporary aberration. It could not have happened 'without considerable and prolonged preparation'.[25] These outrages were the product of 'the anti-Jewish venom which has filled most of the Russian press and periodicals for the last twenty years', an invective that constituted a constant incitement to plunder, pillage, and murder. The time had therefore come for Russian Jewry to draw the necessary conclusions and concentrate its efforts on establishing agricultural settlements in Erez Israel for the homeless Jewish masses.[26]

Smolenskin never believed that all Jews could or would go to the Holy Land. But he was convinced that Erez Israel had considerable advantages over alternative lands of emigration in North and South America. In the first place, 'those who cherish the memory of their ancestors will gladly go there, if they can be assured that they will make a living'; the country was 'not too distant from their former homes' and emigrants could live there in accordance with their accustomed traditions; Jews in the land would acquire a new spirit which would turn them away from idleness to a life of productive labour; finally

[22] See David Vital, *The Origins of Zionism* (Oxford, 1975), 47.

[23] Quoted in Patterson, p. 164.

[24] The last three volumes of *Ha-Shahar* (1880/2, 1883, 1884) contained 25 articles on the need for a physical return to Zion and the establishment of an economic and political as well as a spiritual centre in Erez Israel. This was essential as a refuge for gathering in all the dispersed tribes of Israel, menaced by a palpable and physical danger.

[25] 'Let us Search our Ways' (1881), in Herzberg, p. 148.

[26] Ibid. 152.

commerce and industry as well as agriculture would develop, for scientific explorations had revealed the economic potential of Palestine, if the land were 'cultivated with skill and diligence'.[27]

Smolenskin's visionary nationalism had a profoundly galvanizing effect on Reuben Bierer, Moritz Schnirer, and other founders of Kadimah. Like Smolenskin they, too, had come from the East—from Russia, Galicia, or Romania to pursue their secular studies in Vienna.[28] As *Ostjuden*, they were attracted by the call for a struggle on two fronts—against the 'counterfeit' assimilationism of Western Jewry and the 'reactionary' orthodoxy of the East.[29] Their national consciousness had been aroused by the Russian pogroms and the new German anti-Semitism originating in Berlin, which had found such a powerful echo at the University of Vienna. The founders of Kadimah responded enthusiastically to Smolenskin's call for a Hebrew-based national renaissance and his warnings that assimilation was leading to the self-destruction of Jewry. They shared his intense sense of Jewish pride and ardent belief in the imminent end of the exile (*Galut*). His programme of colonizing Palestine, made tangible by the first settlements of Russian and Romanian *Biluim* in Rishon Le Zion, Zichron Yaacov, and Rosh Pina, provided a practical focus for their national aspirations.

Smolenskin's nationalist ideology fitted perfectly the needs of this small circle of 'Easterners', leading a marginal existence on the fringes of Viennese society. As typical 'men of transition' suspended between traditional and modern society, they were groping towards a new secular identity to achieve their ideological reintegration.[30] Excluded from the mainstream of both Jewish and German society in Vienna, their detachment enabled them to take a more radical view of their existence. The attempts of parvenu Jewry in Vienna to imitate the life-style of the aristocracy or the educated German middle classes aroused their derision and disgust.

This reaction against assimilation was particularly vehement in the writings of the young Nathan Birnbaum, the only Viennese-born member among the original founders of Kadimah. He regarded the assimilationist 'mania' of Viennese Jewry as an unmistakable sign of

---

[27] Ibid. 153.

[28] See Kressel, 'Selbstemanzipation', 57 ff.; also Ludwig Rosenhek, 'Die Juden zu Anfang der Achtzigerjahre', *Festschrift*, 14.

[29] Schnirer, 'Gründung der Kadimah', 15 ff.

[30] See Joachim Doron, 'The Impact of German Ideologies on Central European Zionism, 1885–1914' (Univ. of Tel Aviv, Ph.D. diss., 1977) [in Hebrew], 346 ff.

moral inferiority and weakness of character.[31] Like the more sophisticated anti-Semites, he attacked the materialist, hedonist ethos of modern Jewry for its singular lack of idealism and desertion of spiritual values. This uncompromising critique of 'assimilation' paradoxically reflected the impact on the young Birnbaum of German *Kultur* and its romantic, anti-capitalist proclivities.[32]

Such an emotional backlash against the smug complacency of the Jewish bourgeois élite in Vienna was common enough among other Jewish nationalist students.[33] Ludwig Rosenhek, recalling his impressions of Viennese Jewry in the early 1880s evoked above all the vanity, frivolity, and inauthenticity of the assimilated mileu, its inner uncertainty, and absence of moral principle. According to Rosenhek, the rootlessness of the newly emancipated Jews encouraged an excessive identification with alien nationalisms.[34] The Romanian-born Moritz Schnirer (who began his medical studies in Vienna in 1880 at the age of twenty) also felt a 'deep shame over the undignified obtrusiveness of the Vienna Jews and of most Jewish students', concluding that what 'grew up here under the cover of liberalism and freedom was nothing other than spiritual servitude and self-abnegation which must lead to self-destruction'.[35]

These remarks recall Max Nordau's famous speech to the First Zionist Congress (1897), depicting the emancipated Western Jew as 'a cripple within, and a counterfeit person without, so that like everything unreal, he is ridiculous and hateful to all men of high standards'.[36] According to Nordau, the best powers of the Jew were dissipated in the effort of concealing his true character. The greatest fear of the emancipated Western Jew was to be recognized as 'Jewish' so that as a consequence he became 'insecure in his relations with his fellow man, timid with strangers and suspicions even of the secret feeling of his friends'.[37]

---

[31] Nathan Birnbaum, *Die Assimilationssucht: Ein Wort an die sogenannten Deutschen, Slaven, Magyaren etc. mosaischer Confession von einem Studenten jüdischer Nationalität* (Vienna, 1884), 10. Also, N.B., 'Pflege der geistigen Güter unseres Volkes', *Selbstemanzipation*, 1 June 1893, p. 1.

[32] See Vital, *The Origins of Zionism*, 221–2. Vital aptly describes Birnbaum as a young man 'in process of emerging into the educated bourgeoisie, but not yet of it'. Also Joachim Doron, 'Social Concepts Prevalent in German Zionism: 1883–1914', *Studies in Zionism* (Apr. 1982), pp. 1–31, on the general intellectual background to Central European Zionism.

[33] *Festschrift*, 40.   [34] 'Die Juden zu Anfang der Achtzigerjahre', ibid. 12 ff.

[35] Schnirer, 'Gründung der Kadimah', ibid. 15.

[36] Max Nordau, 'Speech to the First Zionist Congress', in Hertzberg, p. 23.

[37] Ibid.

In Vienna this problem of assimilation and Jewish identity had been exacerbated by the inexorable racial conflicts within the multinational Empire. The convergence of ethnic and social antagonisms in the Empire had found its stormiest focal point in the German student agitation at the University of Vienna.[38] The intensity of this German nationalism would in the long run destroy the prospects of Jewish social integration. Already in the 1880s it encouraged, as we have seen, the appeal of a specifically Jewish nationalism. The Zionist synthesis emerged here not only as the response to an exclusivist German nationalism but also because Vienna was a natural bridge between Eastern and Western Jewry which could provide the axis for a new Jewish self-understanding.

It was a Russian Jew, Leon Pinsker (1821–94), who played the decisive role in crystallizing the ideology of Kadimah with his German-language pamphlet *Autoemancipation* (1882). The pogroms of 1881 had turned Pinsker away from his earlier assimilationist position towards the view that Jews must emancipate themselves politically as a nation. In 1882 he visited Central and Western Europe in order to advocate his Zionist ideas, but initially found little support. Adolf Jellinek, as we have already seen, suggested that he needed medical attention. Nevertheless, Pinsker persisted, publishing his views anonymously in September 1882 as 'an appeal to his People by a Russian Jew'. The pamphlet was prefaced with a quotation from the first century Palestinian Jewish sage, Hillel, that became a motto for Kadimah: 'If I am not for myself, who will be for me? And if not now, when?'

Autoemancipation provided a stark, pitilessly clinical examination of the Jewish condition, one which emphasized both the failure of liberal emancipation and the intractable nature of Jewish homelessness in the *Galut* (exile).[39] It analysed Judaeophobia as a 'psychic aberration', a 'form of demonopathy' which had become rooted and 'naturalized among all the peoples of the earth with whom the Jews have had intercourse'.[40] For centuries Judaism and anti-Semitism had been wandering and inseparable companions, to the point that the Jews had become 'the people chosen for universal hatred'. They remained eternal aliens 'who can have no representatives because they have no fatherland'; they were treated in the *Galut* as adopted children whose

---

[38] Doron, 'The Impact of German Ideologies', 343 ff.
[39] For a summary of Pinsker's ideas, see Vital, pp. 126 ff.
[40] L. Pinsker, 'Auto-Emancipation', in Hertzberg, pp. 184–5.

rights could always be questioned—never as 'a legitimate child of the fatherland'. Legal emancipation should not therefore be confused with *social* emancipation. In spite of formal equality, Pinsker noted that even in the West 'the Jews are still far from being emancipated from their exceptional *social* position'.[41] He concluded that civil and political emancipation would be unable to raise the Jews in the estimation of the peoples; nor could humanity and enlightenment provide 'radical remedies for the malady of our people'.[42] The only solution would be 'the creation of a Jewish nationality, of a people living upon its own soil, the auto-emancipation of the Jews; their emancipation as a nation among nations by the acquisition of a home of their own'.[43]

Pinsker looked to a Congress of Jewish notables to pave the way for this national regeneration of the Jews. Eastern Jewry lacked organizational experience, the freedom of action, or the men of requisite political stature; hence, Pinsker believed that the co-operation of Western Jews would be vital to the national project and wrote his pamphlet in German specifically to appeal to them.[44] Auto-emancipation meant in effect anticipated rescue of Eastern Jewry by the Western part of the nation.[45] But the bulk of Western Jewry, intent on social integration, did not respond to this appeal, least of all in cosmopolitan Vienna. Only the students of Kadimah identified with Pinsker's demand that the Jews abandon their vain efforts at 'fusion' and seek to establish their own national state. Like Pinsker, they were convinced by their own experience that the Jews were 'organically' incapable of assimilation. The frantic efforts of the Jewish bourgeoisie at Germanization, Magyarization, or Slavicization were doomed to failure.[46] Like the physician from Odessa, the students of Kadimah looked to the creation of a Jewish nationality settled on its own soil as the only way to bring anti-Semitism to and end.

Pinsker had placed 150 copies of his *Autoemancipation* at the disposal of Kadimah in the autumn of 1883. In a letter sent from Odessa on 11 December 1884, he praised the Viennese fraternity's commitment to the raising of Jewish national self-awareness.[47] Pinsker expressed

[41] Pinsker, 'Auto-Emancipation', in Hertzberg, ibid. p. 187.
[42] Ibid. 198.   [43] Ibid.   [44] Vital, p. 132.
[45] See ch. 4 in S. Aschheim, *Brothers and Strangers: The East European Jews in German and German Jewish Consciousness, 1800–1923* (Madison, 1983), 80 ff., which discusses some of the complex ambiguities in the relationship between Zionism, Western Jewry, and the *Ostjuden*.
[46] Birnbaum, *Die Assimilationssucht*, 8 ff.
[47] Letter of Pinsker to Kadimah, 5 Sept. 1883 (CZA Z 1/1), A 368/8, and letter of Pinsker to the President of Kadimah, 11 Dec. 1884, repr. in Schalit, 'Erinnerungen', 38.

his firm conviction that the future belonged to a Jewish nationalist youth, proud of their own identity and committed to the new gospel of practical self-help.[48] In these early years, Pinsker gave frequent advice to the founders of Kadimah, supporting their efforts to found a weekly that would work 'for the general interests of the Jewish nation . . . .'.[49] His influence on the young Nathan Birnbaum was particularly strong and it was no accident that the latter's periodical was named *Selbstemanzipation*, recalling Pinsker's earlier pamphlet.[50] Birnbaum's view of assimilation clearly owed a great deal to Pinsker's sociological and political analyses of the 'Jewish question'.[51]

Only the Lithuanian Rabbi Isaak Rülf of Remel, author of *Aruchas Bas-Ammi: Israels Heilung* (1883), exercised an intellectual influence on Kadimah at all comparable to that of Smolenskin and Pinsker.[52] Rülf's synthesis of national consciousness and the return to traditional Jewish values complemented the more secular approach of the two Russian Jews. These diverse influences which crystallized their own experience of social marginality into a coherent ideology motivated the students of Kadimah to form their nationalist association. Though at first only a tiny minority within the Jewish student body of Vienna, the members of Kadimah were united by their common belief that only through the conscious fostering of Jewish peoplehood (*Volkstum*) could they avoid the destruction of Judaism. Each new member was secretly committed to uphold this principle and to support the settlement of Erez Israel as a practical step towards future Jewish independence.[53]

[48] Ibid. 38. Pinsker added: 'Möge der Jude seinem nichtjudischen Brüder in Treue beide Hände reichen, sein Blut für ihn vergiessen, nur tue er es als Jude. Denn dass er einer anderen Nation als der jüdischen angehört, wie ihm zu sagen zugemutet wird, wird ihm von niemandem geglaubt werden.'

[49] See Pinsker's letter to Kadimah on 10 Dec. 1883 and 26 Jan. 1884 (CZA Z 1/1), A 368/8.   [50] Kressel, 'Selbstemanzipation', 61–2.

[51] See Josef Meisl, 'Selbst-Emanzipation', in A. E. Kaplan and Max Landau (eds.), *Vom Sinn des Judentums: Ein Sammelbuch zu Ehren Nathan Birnbaums* (Frankfurt, 1925), 20 ff.; also *Selbstemanzipation*, no. 1 (1892), on Pinsker's death, and the supplement of *Davar* (1937), no. 25.

[52] Isaak Rülf, *Aruchas Bas-Ammi. Israels Heilung: Ein ernstes Wort an Glaubens- und Nichtglaubensgenossen* (Frankfurt, 1883); Kressel, 'Selbstemanzipation', 61; Schoeps, p. 163. Also the older article by Reuwen Michael, 'Israels Heilung, Isaak Rülf und die Anfänge des Zionismus in Deutschland', *Bulletin des Leo Baeck Instiuts*, 6, no. 22 (1963), 126–47.

[53] Schnirer, 'Gründung der Kadimah', *Festschrift*, 17. Nathan Birnbaum defined the programme of the association in similar terms in *Selbstemanzipation*, 16 Feb. 1886, p. 1: 'Kampf gegen die Sucht, sich mit anderen Völkern zu assimilieren; Pflege der eigentümlichen Literatur und Sprache; Ansiedlung von Stammesgenossen in Palästina; Schaffung eines Jüdischen Ackerbaustandes.'

In order to avoid difficulties with the police regulations in Vienna, the official statutes of Kadimah were obliged to disclaim any political tendency. The purpose of the association was defined simply as the creation of a centre for the 'cultivation of Jewish literature and the sciences of Judaism'.[54] These statutes were submitted to the Austrian authorities and finally approved on 23 March 1883. At the first official meeting of the new association on 5 May 1883, Moritz Schnirer was elected President and its major ideologues, Smolenskin and Pinsker, were elected honorary members.[55]

The first public act of Kadimah consisted in pasting up posters on the walls of Vienna University, boldly proclaiming the new message of Jewish nationhood. This gesture shocked the official Jewish community and aroused the derision of most Jewish students.[56] The declaration, in German and Hebrew, had been penned by Schnirer and Birnbaum. It began with an evocation of the persecutions which had plagued Jewry since its loss of political independence in Palestine. Confronted for nearly two millennia by a world of oppressors, Jews had no choice but to defend themselves. But the existing 'indifference at the core of Jewry' would first have to be overcome as a prerequisite to national revival. The newly founded society of Kadimah was designed to prepare the path.

Its purpose is to treasure and sustain the spiritual wealth of our people. Only from the abundant riches of Jewish literature can the young generation learn to love the Jewish people and only from the inexhaustible sources of Jewish history can it draw useful and fruitful lessons for the future of the Jewish people. To attain this sublime goal the young Society will need all the moral and material support of those in whose breast a Jewish heart still beats. Fellow Jews! [*Stammesgenossen!*] Give us your helping hand in the firm conviction of contributing towards a sublime and lofty purpose: the regeneration of the Jewish nation!'[57]

Such an open appeal to Jewish nationalism embarrassed those students and bourgeois circles in the Viennese Kultusgemeinde who feared any aspersions being cast on their German nationality.[58] The Jewish religious establishment was especially upset by the patriotic cult

---

[54] 'Statuten der akademischen Vereines, "*Kadimah*", 19 Januar 1883' (CZA Z 1/1), A 368/8–1; also Kressel, 'Selbstemanzipation', 58; Schnirer, p. 17.

[55] Kressel, 'Selbstemanzipation', 58.

[56] See M. T. Schnirer, '25 Jahre "Kadimah"', *Die Welt*, no. 6 (1908), p. 7.

[57] *Festschrift*, 18.   [58] Schnirer, '25 Jahre "Kadimah"', 8.

of the Maccabees which developed in Kadimah, constituting the climax of its official programme in December of each year. The invocation of the Maccabean struggle against the tyranny of Syrian rule nearly 2,000 years earlier was clearly intended as a historic model for Jewish national regeneration. 'The spirit which inspired Judah Maccabee to his unforgettable deeds has been revived', declared Nathan Birnbaum during the first Maccabean celebrations of Kadimah on 22 December 1883. 'This spirit will create a free Israel, united in brotherhood.'[59]

The celebration of Maccabean heroism synthesized those historical elements which inspired the ethos of Kadimah: the critique of 'Hellenizing' tendencies which encouraged a 'process of disintegration' and self-contempt within Jewry; the liberation struggle against foreign oppression; the fight for a free autonomous identity; and the dream of restoring an independent Jewish State in Erez Israel.[60] The Maccabees had demonstrated how to conquer freedom with the sacrifice of their blood against a numerically superior adversary. They had shown the way to break the chains of slavery by their uncomprising defence of Jewish national identity. Rooted in the popular resistance of the countryside, the Maccabean rising had been a victory of Judaism over Hellenism, of self-sacrificing idealism over materialism, of the National idea over assimilationism.

This transformation of the ancient religious festival of *Chanuka* into a modernized national cult predictably aroused the ire of the preacher Adolf Jellinek who denounced the un-Jewish cult of military glory and victory in battle. Judaism, he insisted, did not celebrate the deeds of individual heroes nor did it idolatrize prowess in war. Kadimah had introduced 'a neo-pagan element into Judaism' and falsified its pure ethical monotheism in the spirit of secular nationalism.[61] What

---

[59] See Nathan Birnbaum, 'Jehuda Makkabi', *Selbstemanzipation*, no. 21 and 22 (1885).

[60] See 'Festrede gehalten von Dr. med. Max Rosenthal am 15. Dezember 1890 bei der Makkabäer-feier des akademischen Vereines "Kadimah"', *Selbstemanzipation*, no. 1, 2 Jan. 1891, p. 4. Also the speech by A. Horwitz on 21 Dec. 1891 in ibid., no. 1, 5 Jan. 1892, pp. 13 ff.

[61] See Schnirer, 'Gründung der Kadimah', 25. For a good example of Jellinek's view, see his editorial 'Weihfest oder Makkabäerfest?', *Die Neuzeit*, 18 Dec. 1891, pp. 491–2. In this polemic he argued strongly against Zionist political amibitions while defending the right of Jews to settle in Palestine. He accused the supporters of the Maccabean celebrations of being 'enthusiasts without any political understanding', who distorted Jewish history for their own purposes. For Birnbaum's defence against the charge of 'neo-paganism', see *Selbstemanzipation* no. 1 (1892), pp. 3–6, and no. 5 (1893), p. 6; also 'Chanukah', *Jüdische Volkszeitung*, 26 Dec. 1894.

disturbed Jellinek was not only disapproval of its militant 'love of Zion' or a pacifist distaste for Kadimah's Maccabean enthusiasm.[62] The new gospel of self-reliance, anchored in a secularized nationalist vision of history, seemed to threaten the foundations of traditional Jewish messianism. The founders of Kadimah regarded the nation (*Volk*) as the true subject of history and saw in the glories of the Jewish past the instrument for rehabilitating Jewish self-respect and honour in the present. In this Zionist vision the Jews were destined once again to become a factor autonomously shaping their own destiny.[63]

An eloquent address by Kadimah's President, Moritz Schnirer, on 20 December 1883 at the inaugural Maccabean commemoration in Vienna crystallized the profound didactic importance which the association attached to the glorious deeds of the biblical past.[64] For Schnirer, historical consciousness was the *sine qua non* of all patriotic feeling, 'the counsellor, teacher and leader of mankind and the nations'.[65] It bound the generations in a single chain, illuminating their deeds and encouraging emulation. History embodied the spirit of the nations, it instructed and inspired individuals to bold acts on behalf of the fatherland; it gave them the courage to believe that freedom and national independence were possible. History represented in Hegelian terms 'continuous self-awareness of humanity and the peoples'.[66]

The commemoration of the Maccabees was for Kadimah a celebration of *national* history, of 'the heroes of the Jewish people'. Its purpose was to reawaken national sentiment, to remind Jews that 'our spiritual heritage never ceased to be alive, never ceased to pulsate in millions of human hearts'.[67] The messianic hopes of Jewry could not be revived by passive indifference to the disintegrating tendencies operating in an era of assimilation. Schnirer recalled the classical models of Greece and Rome that had inspired the Renaissance, the humanist ideas of the European enlightenment and French revolutionary nationalism. He called on Jewish youth similarly to honour and emulate the glorious spirit of its own ancestors. Quoting the enthusiastic response of the German Jewish historian Heinrich Graetz

[62] Schalit, 'Erinnerungen', 19, records that Jellinek had told Birnbaum and Schnirer in 1883 that 'es sei seine politische Ueberzeugung, dass die Juden einst Zion haben würden, aber sie mögen warten, bis Moschiach komme. Dessenungeachtet entliess er die jungen Studenten mit Segenssprüchen und der Versicherung seines Wohlwollens.'
[63] See Shmuel Almog, *Zionut ve-historia* (Jerusalem, 1982), 36–7, for a general discussion of the uses of Jewish history in shaping Zionist nationalism.
[64] See Schalit, 'Erinnerungen', 20–5, for the text of Moritz Schnirer's speech.
[65] Ibid. 20–1.   [66] Ibid. 20.   [67] Ibid. 24.

to the founding of Kadimah, Schnirer concluded: 'We have the pride and the joy to be the first to have ignited the remnant Jewish sparks in the hearts of our Jewish students. In Vienna first resounded the cry: "I am a Hebrew" and from Berlin, Paris, St. Petersburg echoed the cry "We are Hebrews".'[68]

This feeling of pride and mission had been inspired by a sense of the vital significance of Jewish history and the belief that the very survival of Jewry as a nation was at stake. It led Kadimah to execrate assimilation as a cowardly act of betrayal and the prime cause of anti-Semitism.[69] In their idealistic search for authenticity, self-awareness, and a new national identity, the angry young men of Kadimah had revolted against the efforts of their fathers' generation to pass as Germans, Poles, or Czechs.[70] Nevertheless, in spite of their war on assimilation many of the rules and habits of the traditional German student fraternities in Austria were institutionalized in Kadimah. These customs, as Julius Schoeps has pointed out, included 'the institution of *Kneipen*, regular ritualised beer-swilling sessions, and their more solemn variant, the *Kommers*, reserved for festive occasions such as the annual Maccabean function. The songs sung at those gatherings were mostly taken from the *Kommersbuch*, a collection of traditional German student drinking songs.'[71] Thus, by a curious paradox, the movement to halt the denationalization of Jewry found itself borrowing its expressive forms and modes of behaviour from the German culture against which it reacted.

This trend was strengthened in the late 1880s by the entry of Viennese students from assimilated families into Kadimah. Within a few years they had transformed the association from an 'academic society' into a 'duelling fraternity' (*farbentragende, schlagende Verbindung*). By contrast, the original nucleus of Kadimah had been predominantly *Ostjuden* from Russia, Romania, and Galicia with only a tiny sprinkling of Viennese students. They had come from the heartland of the Jewish masses, already imbued with a strong sense of ethnic Jewish consciousness. The newer recruits like Siegmund and Julius Werner, Karl Pollak, Max Rosenthal, or Isidor Schalit came from an

---

[68] Ibid. 24–5.

[69] See *Selbstemanzipation*, 1 Feb. 1885, p. 1; also 'Assimilation', *Jüdische Volkszeitung*, 12 Dec.1894.

[70] Alois Gaisbauer, 'Eine Jugendbewegung. Zur Geschichte der jüdisch-nationalen Studentenbewegung in Österreich 1882–1914', *ZEIT GESCHICHTE*, 2, no. 6 (Mar. 1975), 135 ff.

[71] Schoeps, p. 161.

assimilated milieu, influenced by the ideals of German liberal nationalism and utopian socialism.[72] Disillusioned by the rampant anti-Semitism of the German nationalist students at the University of Vienna, they had turned to Kadimah out of defiance.[73] No less westernized were the new recruits from Moravia, already steeled in the provincial struggle between Germans and Czechs. Most militant of all were the Jewish students from Bukovina.[74] A microcosm of Habsburg ethnic conflicts with its Germans, Romanians, Poles, Ukrainians, Armenians, and Jews, this small Crownland provided a powerful reinforcement of robust academic youth for the ranks of Kadimah. By the end of the 1880s, Jewish student nationalism in Austria had already begun to reflect the multi-ethnic character of the Monarchy and its internal political cleavages.

The significance of the new recruits in reshaping Kadimah can be seen from the essentially literary and social nature of the association in its earlier phase. During its first decade of existence, Kadimah had concentrated mainly on educational activities such as deepening the knowledge of Jewish history, culture, and literature among Viennese Jewish youth. By the end of 1884 the club library had a stock of 970 volumes, 700 of them in German and 150 in Hebrew.[75] It subscribed to thirty-two newspapers, including four in Hebrew—*Hazefirah, Haibri, Hameliz,* and *Hamagid*—which were translated by Josef Bierer from Czernowitz for the benefit of other members.[76] In addition, there were also English, Spanish, and Italian newspapers but German-language material naturally predominated. The association had been helped in its acquisition of these reading materials by donations from its scattered sympathizers and supporters. Those who contributed sums of at least 50 gulden were known as 'founders' (*Stifter*) while those who paid an annual sum of at least 2 gulden earned the title of 'sponsors' (*Förderer*).

In 1884, only 17 out of 40 'sponsors' actually lived in Vienna, 13 came from Galicia, 5 from the Ukraine, 3 from Hungary, 1 from

---

[72] Schalit, 'Erinnerungen', 38–9: 'Wir lebten in der Glanzzeit des Liberalismus. Zwischen den Idealen des deutschen Liberalismus vom Jahre 1848 und dem neuaufstrebenden sozialistischen Evangelium suchten wir tastend ein Lebensziel.'

[73] Ibid. 39.   [74] Ibid. 40.

[75] *Bericht über die am 17 Dezember 1884 vom akademischen Verein 'Kadimah' veranstaltete Makkabäer-Feier, Sammt Ansprache des Reichsraths-Abg. und Rabbiners Dr. J. S. Bloch: Anschliessend Jahres-Berichts des Vereines* (Vienna 1885), 14 ff.; also Doron, p. 350, Schoeps, p. 158.

[76] Schalit, 'Erinnerungen', 41.

Trieste, and one was unknown.[77] Among the 'corresponding members' of Kadimah at this time the best-known were Dr Reuben Bierer, Dr Joseph Bloch, and Rabbi Isaak Rülf. The special status of honorary member was granted to Sir Moses Montefiore, alongside the ideological guides of the society, Smolenskin, Pinsker, and Rülf. At the end of 1884 there had been 60 regular members (*wirkliche Mitglieder*) of Kadimah, of whom 25 studied medicine, 15 engineering, 14 law, 3 philosophy, 2 chemistry, and one forestry.[78] The predominance of medical over law students, and the relatively high number of those in engineering was a characteristic reflection of social differences between Habsburg Austria and the German Reich.[79] Nevertheless, the general orientation of Kadimah members tended towards the Humanities.

Although Kadimah was in its early years a comparatively poor and small society, its Maccabean functions had from the outset aroused a considerable echo among the Viennese Jewish public. According to a report in Dr Bloch's *Österreichische Wochenschrift*, as many as 500 people participated in the Maccabean celebrations on 17 December 1884.[80] Over the next decade its influence steadily increased with the spread of the national idea in Vienna and Kadimah's ability to involve itself in struggles that directly affected Jewish students at the University.[81]

Following the radicalization of the German nationalist student body and its systematic anti-Semitic policy, Kadimah emerged in the early 1890s as the principal defender of Jewish honour in the university arena.[82] It also began to challenge the dominance of the 'liberal' oligarchy in the Jewish community, publicly opposing its political orientation.[83] For example Kadimah condemned the passive response of the community leadership and of the Union to the expulsion of Jews from Moscow in 1891. It contrasted unfavourably the silence of the Kultusgemeinde over the oppression of Russian Jewry with vociferous Gentile protests in Britain and America.[84] The openly Zionist tendency of Kadimah with its propaganda for a Jewish Palestine

[77] *Bericht*, 17.   [78] Ibid. 16 ff.   [79] Doron, p. 349.

[80] *Österreichische Wochenschrift*, 20 Dec. 1884, p. 7.

[81] Schalit, 'Erinnerungen', 43 ff.

[82] See William J. McGrath, 'Student Radicalism in Vienna', *Journal of Contemporary History*, 2 no. 3 (July 1967), 183–201 on the general intellectual background.

[83] Schalit, 'Erinnerungen', 66.

[84] See ibid. 67 for the text of a sympathetic letter sent in Mar. 1891 by the British Cabinet Minister Lord Aberdeen to Kadimah on the persecution of Russian Jews.

aggravated still further its conflict with the Board of the religious community and the Union.[85]

The central issue which confronted Kadimah in these years remained, however, the need to adopt an active stance of self-defence against the rising tide of anti-Semitism at the University of Vienna. A growing number of Jewish students came to realize that the 'power of the idea' (*die Macht des Geistes*) might not suffice in face of the 'mindless brutality, the aggressiveness of drunken louts, and the barbaric treatment of the Jews as a race of worthless slaves'.[86] The resort to clenched fists and the sabre came more easily to the new generation of Kadimah recruits from an assimilated milieu, exasperated by German taunts of Jewish 'cowardice'.[87] It was these students who resolved to adopt the 'un-Jewish' practice of duelling and to transform Kadimah into a fighting fraternity on the German-Austrian model.[88] Already in 1890 Siegmund Werner (future editor-in-chief of *Die Welt*) had engaged in a duel at Vienna University. A year later the Hasmonea fraternity in Czernowitz formally introduced the practice.[89] At a stormy General Meeting of Kadimah on 15 May 1893 the association decided to oblige every member 'to give satisfaction' whenever an insult could not be settled by a formal apology (*Ehrenerklärung*).[90] Seven members who were skilled fencers (Bierer, Schalit, Caleb, Pollak, Gach, Neuberger, and Kreisling) were selected by the executive in 1893 to defend the 'honour' of the fraternity. In the autumn of 1893 six duels were fought by Kadimah with the Waidhofen German national fraternity, Philadelphia. Their results caused something of a sensation in Vienna.[91]

The issue of duelling provoked considerable controversy not only

---

[85] Schalit, 'Erinnerungen', 69. The Viennese Kultusvorstand withdrew its subsidy for the library of Kadimah on the grounds 'dass er die zionistische Tendenz des Vereines nicht unterstützen könne . . .' The Community Board had several years earlier turned down a memorandum for financial help by the student society (dated 22 July 1884) which had complained about the 'cool attitude' and 'defensive stance' of the bulk of the Kultusgemeinde towards its activities; see Schoeps, p. 159.

[86] Schalit, 'Erinnerungen', 72; Otto Abeles, 'Dreissig Jahre Kadimah', *Die Welt*, no. 5 (1913), 146 ff.; and Schoeps, p. 165.

[87] Schalit, 'Erinnerungen', 72: 'Die erste "Kadimah" warb um die Seele der Juden, wir kämpften um diese Seele. Wir hatten eine andere Einstellung. Jene glaubten an die Macht des Geistes, wir, voll Trotz und überschäumender Lebenslust, vertrauten wohl der Macht der Idee, aber auch der Kraft unserer Fäuste.'

[88] See Gaisbauer, p. 136, Schoeps, p. 164.

[89] Ibid. (*bis*). Schalit, 'Erinnerungen', 72, also mentions the duels fought by students of Kadimah in 1891 with the Polish fraternity Ognisko.

[90] Schalit, 'Erinnerungen', 73.   [91] Ibid.

within the Jewish community as a whole but even among the nationalist students. Nathan Birnbaum deplored the practice as a form of 'national assimilation', an imitation of the most 'reactionary' feudal traditions of the German student movement.[92] He argued that the *Burschenschaft* tradition of duelling was alien to the character of Judaism, encouraging students to rowdiness, purely for the sake of displaying their physical prowess. Fencing sessions, duelling, and the wearing of peaked caps, instead of advancing Jewish self-awareness merely degraded 'our national feeling . . . through the aping of alien national superficiality'.[93] Dr Bloch was also extremely critical of what he regarded as an assimilationist 'translation of German into Jewish nationalism'.[94]

These criticisms stung Kadimah leaders to retort that duelling was an indispensable 'tactical device', necessary in order to win the respect of the general student body.[95] It was not merely an act of self-defence but a positive refutation of anti-Semitic charges concerning Jewish 'cowardice'.[96] Furthermore, a student who refused a challenge could not become an Austrian reserve officer. This circumstance might endanger his future status and career. More importantly, through their skill in swordmanship and readiness to protect the Jewish student body, Kadimah members greatly enhanced the prestige of their fraternity even among those Jews who were initially cool to Zionist ideology.

The deliberately provocative decision of the German nationalist fraternities at their Waidhofen conference on 11 March 1896, declaring that 'the Jewish students were without honour or character', underlined the importance of the issues at stake.[97] Theodor Herzl recorded in his diary on 14 March 1896:

Great excitement at the University of Vienna. The 'Aryan' duelling associations have decided that in the future they will deny satisfaction, with any weapons, to Jews on the grounds that all Jews are without honour or cowards.

My young friend Pollak and another Jew [members of *Kadimah*] have challenged two anti-Semitic reserve officers; and when they refused to fight,

---

[92] Nathan Birnbaum, 'Das assimilerte Nationaljudentum', *Selbstemanzipation*, no. 6/7 (1892), 53 ff.

[93] Ibid., 4 Mar. 1892.

[94] *Österreichische Wochenschrift*, 19 Nov. 1897, p. 942, claimed that '. . . das Gehaben der nationaltümelnden jüdischen Studenten mit ihren Schlägern, färbigen Bändern und Aufzügen ist durch und durch unjüdisch, eine Nachaffung fremder Sitte und Unsitte . . .'.

[95] ' "Przyszlosc" und Kadimah', *Jüdische Volkszeitung*, no. 34 (21 Aug. 1894), 3.

[96] Schalit, 'Erinnerungen', 77.   [97] Ibid. 74.

reported the matter to the General Command. The latter referred it to the District Command.

Much hangs upon the latter's decision—namely, the future position of Jews in the Austrian army. I steamed up Bacher about the matter and made it properly hot for Benedikt, whose son is at the University.[98]

Clearly this was an issue of great importance to Viennese Jewry as a whole. The Waidhofen resolution was immediately perceived as a serious infringement of Jewish legal and social equality. As Isidor Schalit recalled, the implications seemed profoundly disturbing, for 'the German national students were the coming teachers, judges and officials of the State'.[99] Together with the fraternities of Unitas and Ivria, Kadimah therefore passed a unanimous resolution indignantly repudiating 'the national arrogance of the German duelling fraternities' (*wehrhaften Studentschaft*) and dismissing with contempt the proposition that the concept of honour depended on 'belonging to the German people or the Aryan race'.[100] Kadimah even enjoyed the backing of the Kultusgemeinde Board which passed a resolution in its plenary sitting of 15 March 1896, expressing satisfaction at the dignified stand of the Jewish student fraternities.[101]

The protest movement against the Waidhofen resolution initiated by Kadimah and its student allies obliged the Rector of Vienna University and then the Government itself to intervene. On 19 May 1896 the Lower Austrian *Statthalterei* (Provisional Governor's office) officially dissolved all the German nationalist fighting fraternities which had participated in the Waidhofen resolution.[102] The results of this ban proved a disappointment. The dissolved fraternities simply changed their names or else merged with other student organizations. German nationalist students continued to insult and attack Jewish students with impunity. If anything, the level of violence at the University of Vienna increased during the first decade of the twentieth century.[103] The passive attitude of the Rector and the Senate of the

---

[98] *The Diaries of Theodor Herzl*, ed. and trans. Marvin Lowenthal (London, 1958), 104.

[99] Schalit, 'Erinnerungen', 74–5.

[100] Ibid. 75. Both Unitas and Ivria were duelling fraternities as were Libanonia and Hasmonea. After 1894 according to Schalit, 'fast die ganze jüdische Studentschaft das Schlagen aufgenommen hatte'. In that year, Kadimah alone had fought 30 student duels with the German nationalist fraternity Gothia with considerable success, a fact which encouraged other Jewish students. Nevertheless a considerable number of former members of Kadimah followed Sigmund Werner into the non-duelling Gamalah fraternity (founded in 1894) which was strongly socialist in orientation.

[101] Ibid. 75–6.   [102] Ibid. 77.

[103] See in this connection the interesting articles by Ber Borochov, the leading

University to these disturbances suggested a latent German nationalist bias behind the academic mask of dynastic patriotism.[104]

By the early 1890s, Kadimah had undoubtedly established itself in Jewish student constituency as the most reliable bulwark against the aggression of the German-national fraternities. Following its example, Josef Bierer established the Hasmonea in Czernowitz (1891). Former Kadimah members established three new Viennese fraternities in 1894: Unitas, whose membership was mainly Moravian, Libanonia, an association of Jewish veterinary medics, and the socialist Gamalah.[105] In 1895 the *Landsmannschaft* of Silesian university students changed its name to Ivria. It, too, was modelled on the Viennese Kadimah.

The proclamations of the various Jewish student nationalist societies which subsequently arose in Prague, Brünn, and the main cities of Galicia likewise manifested the seminal influence of the Viennese Kadimah. In June 1894 the Jewish student association Makkabea in Prague (which changed its name two years later to Verein der jüdischen Hochschuler in Prag, Bar Kochba) declared:

In the German and Bohemian schools of higher education in Prague, as is true for all those in Austria and Germany, there is a sharp demarcation between Jewish and non-Jewish students. Although the Jew always tried to be totally submerged in German and Slavic ways, though they paid homage to national chauvinism and did not want to bother with their own Jewish people, they were rejected by non-Jews with scorn and ridicule and ejected from societies which frequently they had themselves founded . . . However, the limits of humiliation and self-sacrifice [*Selbstpreisgebung*] were reached. Voices could be heard saying: 'Shall we force ourselves onto a society that does not want us in its midst? Have we really sunk so low as to be unable to stand on our own feet? Are we not despised precisely because we do not respect ourselves as Jews?' Constantly increasing anti-Semitism makes it easy to answer this question. That is why the Jewish national student associations came into being in Vienna, Czernowitz, Berlin, Heidelberg etc., for the purpose of raising Jewish national consciousness. This is also the aim of the Jewish national student society 'Maccabäa' of Prague.[106]

theoretician of the Marxist Poale-Zion (who lived in Vienna for several years before 1914), in vol. iii of *Ketavim* (Tel Aviv, 1955–66) on anti-Semitism in the German student fraternities and the Jewish response. In particular, 'Nochah Sin'at Yisrael bayn Kotlei ha-universita', pp. 122 ff., and 'Studentim Germanim ve-yehudim be-Vinah', pp. 165–75, both written in 1913 during his stay in Vienna.

[104] Schalit, 'Erinnerungen', 47–8.
[105] Ibid. 49–50. For a complete list of the Jewish fraternities established in Austria in this period, see Gaisbauer, pp. 138 ff.
[106] See Felix Weltsch (ed.), *Prag ve-Yerushalaim: Sefer le-Zekher Leo Herman*

The Prague society, like its Viennese prototype, proclaimed that 'the Jews have been and remain a unique people because of their origin, history, thinking and feeling'.[107] It, too, appealed to Jewish national history and to the Maccabean fight for freedom as the basis of its call to arms for Jewish youth. Like the Vienna Kadimah, its central message was the need to organize Jewish self-help, to reassert Jewish honour and dignity and positively to affirm pride in Jewish identity. The nationalism of these early Austrian Zionists aimed at 'the physical and spiritual regeneration of Jewry' and it was formulated in ethical, humanist, and universal terms.[108] It sought to synthesize the latent Jewish nationalism inspired by the Bible with the liberal ideals of the 1848 German Academic Legion. Nationalism, classical humanism, and cosmopolitanism in the Kadimah ideology were by no means contradictory concepts.

The activity of Kadimah during the first decade of its existence had been focused mainly on the university and on finding a response to the provocations of the anti-Semitic German National students. The Jewish nationalists nearly succeeded in capturing for their cause the *Jüdisch-Akademische Lesehalle* (Jewish-Academic Reading Hall), the central forum of cultural life for Jewish students at the University of Vienna. Kadimah still hoped at this stage to win over the majority of Jewish students to a militant struggle against anti-Semitism, if not to a fully-fledged nationalist politics.[109] But the *Lesehalle* preferred neutrality on political issues. Though it did become more 'Jewish', partly as a result of the campaign inaugurated by Kadimah, it continued to identify with the liberal Jewish establishment.[110] As Theodor Herzl noted in his diaries in May 1896, following a visit from two young members of Kadimah, Schalit and Neuberger: 'It appears that at the University the assimilationists have once again gained the upper hand. No one wants to hear about Zionism in the society.'

Excluded from an effective voice in the Kultusgemeinde, the Union,

(Jerusalem, n.d.), 48–9, from the article by N. M. Gelber, 'Kavim le-Kidmat Toldoteah shel Ha-Zionut be-Bohemia ve-Moravia'. The text is entitled 'Aufruf der Prager "Makabäa"' and was signed by the Special Representative Committee of the Jewish national student body in Prague.

[107] Ibid.

[108] Schalit, 'Erinnerungen', 81–2: 'Der Nationalismus, den wir für uns konstruierten, war ein ethischer Nationalismus, erfüllt von Sittlichkeit und Humanität . . .'

[109] Ibid. 69–70.

[110] *Jahresbericht der Jüdisch-Akademischen Lesehalle in Wien für des Verwaltungsjahr 1894/5, Central Archives of the History of the Jewish People, AW/1787*. The *Lesehalle* was subsidised by the IKG; see Archives, AW 1536/1.

and other established Jewish institutions, the nationalist youth had to create their own independent framework. *Kadimahianer* like Moritz Schnirer, Oskar Kokesch, and the engineer Johann Kremenetzky, along with Reuben Brainin and Saul Raphael Landau was closely involved in the Palestinian colonization association, Admath Jeschurun, founded in 1885 to replace Reuben Bierer's defunct Ahavath Zion.[111] In June 1892 Nathan Birnbaum travelled to Galicia and Bukovina on behalf of Admath Jeschurun in an effort to found similar organizations.[112] Birnbaum and his colleagues, encouraged by the independent growth of Zionist societies in Galician cities after 1890, hoped to form a national organization which would become the ideological clearing-house and focal point for the scattered Zionist clubs in the Austrian Empire. In 1892 Birnbaum even advocated the creation of a mass Zionist party but the effort failed for lack of funds and the kind of inspirational leadership later provided by Theodor Herzl.[113]

Kadimah none the less organized political meetings in the early 1890s in Viennese districts like the Leopoldstadt, Brigittenau, and Favoriten as well as sending agitators to the western Austrian provinces (Bohemia, Moravia, and Silesia) to help establish Zionist associations and fraternities.[114] In 1892, as a result of this activity, members of Kadimah and Admath Jeschurun organized a coalition of the different Ḥovevei Zion groups into *Zion: Verband der österreichischen Vereine für Colonisation Palästinas und Syriens* (Zion: Federation of Austrian Associations for the Colonisation of Palestine and Syria).[115] In the following year, the Viennese section of this umbrella organization was created. *Zion* was to provide an important nucleus for Theodor Herzl at the beginning of his political activity, for it was the only organization at his disposal before the Basle Congress of 1897.[116] No

---

[111] *Selbstemanzipation*, no. 6 (1890), 7.

[112] Kressel, 'Selbstemanzipation', 91; see also *Selbstemanzipation*, 15 May 1892.

[113] *Selbstemanzipation*, 23 Feb. 1892, pp. 39 ff., and 4 Mar. 1892, pp. 52–4.

[114] See Schalit, 'Erinnerungen', 71, who was specially involved in Zionist agitation in Prague, Brünn, and Silesian towns at this time.

[115] 'Statuten des Zion: Verband der österreichischen Vereine für Colonisation Palästinas und Syriens, 1892' (CAHJ, AW/2884); see also *Selbstemanzipation*, 1 June 1893, pp. 4–5.

[116] Schalit, 'Erinnerungen', 71. See the entry of 5 Apr. 1896 in *The Diaries of Theodor Herzl*, 108: 'Dr. Moses Schnirer and Dr. Kokesch of the Vienna Society "Zion" brought me its resolution to the effect that, relying upon the support of Zionists, I should go ahead with my work. Schnirer is in favour of circulating an appeal addressed to university-trained Jews throughout the world. A committee of fifteen or twenty persons is to be found in Vienna, each of whom would send the appeal to three of four friends in

less significant was the number of prominent *Kadimahianer* who collaborated with Herzl from the mid-1890s. They included Reuben Bierer, Nathan Birnbaum, Moritz Schnirer, Reuben Brainin, Johann Kremenetzky, Abraham Salz, Oskar Kokesch, Siegmund Werner, and Isidor Schalit. This experienced group of cadres would form the nodal-point of Austrian Zionism in its formative period.

Pre-Herzlian Zionism in Austria had been confined predominantly to the student milieu. For all its restless militancy and idealism it lacked a fully crystallized political idea or sense of organization. The publication of *Der Judenstaat* in February 1896 provided the missing spark to set alight the movement patiently prepared by Kadimah and its academic offshoots in the Austrian provinces. On first reading the proofs Dr Isidor Schalit literally raced to Herzl's home in the Pelikangasse to swear his allegiance to the author with characteristically breathless pathos: 'Herr Doktor, what you have written is our dream, the dream of many young people. What we have sought for and failed to find during all those years is the word that you have now pronounced: *der Judenstaat*. Come with us and lead us and we will create what is humanly possible.'[117] Herzl was undoubtedly moved by the effusive response which he had sparked in the student fraternities but did not allow the enthusiasm to go to his head.

On 21 February 1896 he recorded in his diaries:

Yesterday a *Kommers* social feast at the *Kadimah*. The students gave me a great ovation. I had to make a speech, but I spoke of moderation—and moderately. I didn't want to arouse any beer-inspired enthusiasm. I urged them to stick to their studies and warned them against unhealthy elation. Perhaps we shall never get to the physical Zion, and so we must strive in any case towards an inner Zion . . .[118]

A few months later, visited by Isidor Schalit and Neuberger from the Kadimah, he calmly noted in his diaries:

They also told me that a proposal was afoot to recruit a volunteer battalion of one or two thousand troops and attempt a landing at Jaffa. A few might pay with their lives, but Europe would be forced to take cognizance of Jewish aspirations. I advised them against this beautiful Garibaldian idea, for these one or two thousand, unlike the 'Ten Thousand' at Marsala, would not find a

other cities. Thus thousands of signatures will be collected. It would give me substantial backing.'

[117] Schalit, 'Erinnerungen', 84.
[118] *The Diaries of Theodor Herzl*, 100–1.

nationally prepared population awaiting them. The landing would be suppressed within twenty-four hours, like some schoolboy lark.[119]

The cool realism, political intuition, and worldly experience of Herzl clearly marked him off from the more hot-headed academic youth who had rallied to his banner. Fifteen years earlier he, too, had been an impetuous fraternity student (*Burschenschaftler*), who had returned his peaked cap and sashes to Albia, following the first manifestation of public anti-Semitism in its ranks. This was one of several bonds which linked him to the Jewish academic youth of Vienna. The collective response of Jewish nationalist students to his appeal reflected their common experience of wounded pride and the determination to reassert ethnic dignity in the face of racial insults. But it also expressed a burning aspiration for the freedom and independence, symbolized by statehood.

In the spring of 1896 all the Zionist student associations of the Monarchy, at the instigation of Schnirer and Kokesch, addressed Herzl in the following terms.

Dear Dr Herzl: The appeal which you have issued to the Jewish people in your *Judenstaat* is finding a mighty echo in the hearts of thousands of your fellow Jews. Our people's longing for freedom is as old as our exile. But there have only been isolated voices which have given audible expression to this desire. You, most honoured Herr Doktor, have had the courage to express these feelings in a clear and concise manner and to give a new and promising direction to the national aspirations of our people. For this you deserve the gratitude of the nation which the undersigned—intellectual workers of Jewry [*geistige Arbeiter des Judentums*]—can best document by hailing the renewed unfurling of our national banner and placing themselves devotedly at the service of the holy cause of the Jewish people.[120]

The signatories, containing thousands of members in their ranks, were Zion (Federation of Austrian Associations for the Colonization of Palestine and Syria); Kadimah (Vienna), the Jewish Student Association; Unitas (Vienna), the Association of Austrian-Silesian University students; Ivria (Vienna), the Student Association; Gamalah (Vienna), the Association of Jewish Students of Veterinary Medicine; Libanonia (Vienna), the Theological Association of Students at the Israelite Theological Academy (Vienna); the Student Association

---

[119] Ibid. 134 [Pentecost 1896].
[120] See A. Friedemann, *Das Leben Theodor Herzl's* (2nd edn., Berlin, 1919), 115–16.

Hasmonea (Czernowitz); and the Student Association Humanitas in Graz.[121]

On 4 March 1896 the non-duelling Viennese fraternity Gamalah also declared its 'enthusiastic approval' and 'heartfelt appreciation to Dr Theodor Herzl for the courage and resoluteness with which he is championing the Zionist idea'.[122] The Jewish students of Gamalah proclaimed their readiness to answer Dr Herzl's call and 'to fight at his side for the realization of his great and lofty idea'.[123] In May 1896 the Federation of Zion organizations and Kadimah issued signed sheets indicating their support for Herzl's leadership and approving his proposed solution to the 'Jewish question'. The statement argued that 'never before has the political regeneration of the Jewish people been promulgated in such a clear and concise manner, never before has such a detailed and attractive outline been presented as in Dr Theodor Herzl's recently published pamphlet *The Jewish State*'.[124]

These warm declarations of sympathy and support undoubtedly strengthened Herzl's resolve at a time when his future course was still far from certain. In Isidor Schalit's words: 'We surrounded him, guarded him, did not leave him alone for a single minute; we established contacts with Zionists in other countries, collected thousands of signatures, organized deputations, etc.'[125] Kadimah and other Zionist student associations in Vienna continued to play a crucial role as Herzl's lieutenants right up until the First Zionist Congress of 1897, held in Basle.[126] Schnirer, Kokesch, and Schalit played a central part in preparations for the Basle Congress, in which ten members of Kadimah participated.[127] This was an impressive figure for a student association that numbered approximately 150 members. The energy, oratorical skills, and militancy of this relatively small group made them particularly suited to the task of propagandizing the Zionist idea.

The special rapport which the students established with Herzl, the personal loyalty they felt towards him, and the fact that Vienna was at that time the headquarters of the world Zionist movement enhanced still more the importance of the Austrian student cadre. For example, during the First Zionist Congress, Abraham Salz from Austrian Galicia was Vice-President during the proceedings; Nathan Birnbaum

[121] Friedemann, *Das Leben Theodor Herzl's*, 115–16; complete list and text also in Schalit, 'Erinnerungen', 85.

[122] See *Zion: Monatsschrift für die nationalen Interessen des jüdischen Volkes* (Berlin), 2, no. 3, 31 Mar. 1896, pp. 101–2.   [123] Ibid.

[124] See Friedmann.   [125] Schalit, 'Erinnerungen', 84; Schoeps's Trans., p. 170.

[126] Schalit, 'Erinnerungen', 105–6.   [127] Ibid. 89–90, 93–4.

was elected General Secretary of the Zionist organization; Siegmund Werner was appointed editor-in-chief of *Die Welt* (the leading Zionist newspaper) in succession to the Cracow-born Saul Raphael Landau. Another member of Kadimah, Isidor Schalit, a Viennese who had been closely involved with *Die Welt*, was already one of Herzl's closest personal assistants.

Herzl's Viennese colleagues controlled the Inner Actions Committee (EAC) of the World Zionist Organization in the first years of its existence. Kokesch, Kremenetzky, Marmorek, Schalit—four of his most trusted colleagues—were regular members of the EAC, which was responsible for day-to-day management of affairs in the world Zionist movement. This inner sanctum was a source of constant irritation to the Russian Zionists who felt that Vienna tended at times to ignore their concerns. Describing the seven years of Herzl's ascendency within the Zionist movement, David Vital has written:

> Herzl and his men, the 'diplomats of Vienna' of whom Ahad Ha'am and many others complained, did hold the stage, as we have seen, for some years; and doing so, their immediate influence on the movement was tremendous and in certain, if limited ways—technical and organizational *modi operandi*, for example— lasting. But this leadership from the periphery was exceptional, of relatively brief duration, and always somewhat anomalous.[128]

Vienna maintained its hegemony in the World Zionist Organization as long as Herzl lived, though its true centre of gravity had already shifted to Russia. Following his unexpectedly early death in 1904 and the eclipse of *political* Zionism, it was never likely that his Viennese lieutenants could assume command.[129] They lacked the personal stature and mass base to prevail against Russian Zionism. Nevertheless, at least one of Herzl's Viennese intimates, the wealthy industrialist Johann Kremenetzky (1848–1934), who hailed from Odessa, was able to provide a bridge between Herzl and his Russian followers.[130] Originally trained as an engineer, Kremenetzky had settled in Vienna in 1879. He built the first factory for electric bulbs in Austria, became one of Herzl's closest friends, and remained a member of the Zionist executive until 1905. Kremenetzky's friendship with Moritz Schnirer and the Kadimah circle had first led him to the small Zionist group

---

[128] David Vital, *Zionism: The Formative Years* (Oxford, 1982), 166.

[129] Ibid. 418–19.

[130] See Mascha Hoff, *Johann Kremenezky und die Gründung des KKL* (Frankfurt, 1986), for the first biography of this fascinating personality who appears in Herzl's utopian novel *Altneuland* as the engineer and builder of the new society.

that met in the early 1890s in the rooms of the Café Louvre in Wipplingerstrasse. This Viennese circle subsequently became the nucleus of Herzl's inner Actions Committee.[131] Kremenetzky's fascination with technology, social organization and practical politics attached him to Herzl. As the first head of the Jewish National Fund, the Russian-born engineer was able to implement the primary goal of the 'practical Zionists'—the establishment of a viable economic infrastructure for Jewish settlement in Erez Israel.

For pragmatic realists like Kremenetzky, Herzlian Zionism provided not so much a doctrine as a well-structured organization and the political will which could transform Zionism into a concrete movement of Jewish self-help.

Herzl's major achievement had been to provide a sense of ethnic pride, strength and political direction to the diffuse activities of the Zionist fraternities, societies, and philanthropic groups scattered throughout the Austrian Empire. His charistmatic personality seemed to embody for contemporary observers all the smouldering national pride of the Jewish people. As the Austrian Jewish dramatist Richard Beer-Hofmann wrote in an enthusiastic letter to Herzl in mid-February 1896: 'Even more than the contents of the book I was attracted to its implications. At last there comes again a man who does not carry his Judaism with resignation like a burden or a misfortune, but is proud to be the legal inheritor of an immemorial culture.'[132]

The bold Herzlian assertion of Jewish honour and self-assurance had an immense appeal to Zionist youth in Vienna and through the Empire.[133] They immediately recognized in Herzl a figure of worldly position and social rank whose leadership provided Zionism with a prestige it could never hope to acquire while it remained essentially a student movement on the margins of Austrian public life. With Herzl's creation of the Zionist organization and the entry of the movement into the mainstream of history, the pioneering task of the students was largely fulfilled. Kadimah, the original torch-bearer of the Jewish

---

[131] *Hoff, Johann Kremenezky*, 13. Schnirer's *Gedenkworte* for Kremenetzky are in CZA M 23. On the Café Louvre circle see Tullo Nussenblatt (ed.), *Zeitgenossen über Herzl* (Brünn, 1899), 133; also Alex Bein, *Theodore Herzl* (Philadelphia, 1962), 210–11. Apart from Kremenetzky, this first battalion of political Zionism included the lawyer Kokesch, Moritz Schnirer, York-Steiner, and the Shakespearian scholar, Leon Kellner.

[132] Quoted in Bein, pp. 186–7.

[133] Schalit, 'Erinnerungen', 88: 'Die ersten und kräftigsten Mitarbeiter Herzls waren wir zionistischen Akademiker.'

national idea voluntarily receded into the background, though many of its members assumed important positions in the new organization.[134]

Although Kadimah's innovative period was over, Jewish student nationalism continued to be a significant force in Austrian universities during the first decades of the twentieth century.[135] At the University of Vienna, Jewish students vigorously affirmed the right of Austria Jews to be recognized as a fully-fledged nation in the Imperial framework. Only through such official recognition would the Jews of the Empire be fully accepted as equal citizens. Following the path blazed by Kadimah since the 1880s, the new generation of Jewish national students insisted that they were neither Germans, Czechs, nor Poles, but members of a separate Jewish nation. By the end of 1905 they had adopted the call for Jewish national autonomy within Austria to their specifically Zionist programme.

Isidor Schalit, as head of the Austrian Zionist organization, strongly supported the shift in emphasis to internal Austrian politics. He believed that this would be the most effective counter to assimilation and the best way to ensure the continuity of the Jewish national renaissance.[136] Other Austrian Zionist leaders also favoured adoption of the slogan of 'national autonomy' as part of their broad strategy of seeking hegemony over the organized Jewish community and control of its financial resources.[137] National autonomy had acquired a new relevance with the democratization of Austrian politics in 1906. The introduction of universal male suffrage increased the prospect that Jews might be politically mobilized on an ethnic basis and gain representation as a national minority in the Austrian Parliament. This

---

[134] Ibid. 100–1, 105–6.

[135] Borochov, 'Studentim Germanim ve-yehudim be-Vinah', *Ketavim*, iii. 165 ff.

[136] See CZA Z 2/433, 'Programm der zionistischen Partei der Juden in Österreich' and the letter of Isidor Schalit dated Mar. 1907 to the President of the World Zionist Organization, where he places great hopes on the coming parliamentary elections: 'Es ist unsere Pflicht bis dahin zu sorgen, dass die jüdische Bevölkerung in ihrer überwiegenden Mehrheit auch für sich die Autonomie verlange, sonst wird über das jüdische Volke sicherlich zu Tagesordnung übergangen, und die Juden unter die deutschen, polnischen, tschechischen etc., nationalen Gemeinschaften aufgetheilt werden.'

[137] On the Austrian socialist theories of cultural-national autonomy which influenced Jewish autonomists and Zionists in the first decade of the 20th cent., see Karl Renner, *Der Kampf der österreichischen Nationem um den Staat* (Leipzig and Vienna, 1902). The Austro-Marxist Otto Bauer in his classic study *Die Nationalitätenfrage und die Sozialdemokratie* (Vienna, 1907) denied the legitimacy of Jewish demands in Galicia for national autonomy. See Robert S. Wistrich, *Socialism and the Jews: The Dilemmas of Assimilation in Germany and Austria-Hungary* (Littman Library, London and Toronto, 1982), 335 ff.; also 'Marxism and Jewish Nationalism. The Theoretical Roots of Confrontation', *Journal of Jewish Sociology*, 17, no. 1 (June 1975), 43–54.

hope had led in July 1906 to a fusion of Zionists and Jewish national autonomists in the Jewish National Party. Its success in winning four seats in Galicia and Bukovina in the Reichsrat elections of 1907 seemed to vindicate the Austrian Zionist strategy. The electoral campaign was clearly seen by the Zionists in the context of their broader struggle to claim political leadership of the Jewish 'nationality' in Austria.[138]

The new Zionist politics aimed to convince the Austrian authorities of the need to establish national voting curias and proportional minority representation—demands which were vehemently opposed by the Jewish establishment in Vienna. The Zionists spoke out in defence of the cultural, economic, and political rights of the Jewish 'nation' in Austria, basing themselves on an extra-territorial autonomist programme. They were careful to present their demands as being fully compatible with the interests of the Austrian State and contemporary trends to rejuvenate the Dual Monarchy through broader mass participation and universal suffrage.[139] A historic opportunity had arrived, so the Austrian Zionist leadership believed in 1907, to break with the old assimilationist politics. Jews must end the traditional habit of self-renunciation whereby they sacrificed themselves for the interests of nationalities who in any event rejected them as an 'alien national minority'. In a democratized, federalist Austrian State based on national autonomy, there would be room for an independent Jewish political organization, committed Jewish parliamentary deputies, and a national programme to defend the interests of the Jewish minority.

The new orientation of the Austrian Zionist movement towards representing Austrian Jewry as an autonomous national entity found a particularly strong echo at the University of Vienna where there were more than twenty Jewish national groups in existence by 1910. Their campaign (like that of the Jewish National Party in the 1907 Austrian elections) focused increasingly on the recognition of Yiddish as an official language of the Jewish nationality, as a way of demarcating themselves from German, Polish, Czech, and other national groups.[140] Yiddish became a key issue for Jewish students under the influence of

---

[138] Schalit, CZA Z2/433: 'Als officielle Leiter ihrer Nation würden die Zionisten auf das Nationalselbstbewusstsein der 1½ Millionen Juden Oesterreichs, sowie der durchwegs national erzogenen Jugend unterstützt, den Zionismus leicht zur Ehrensache der ganzen Nation, zum Endziel aller nationalen Bestrebungen machen können.'

[139] Ibid., 'An Oesterreichs Judenschaft'.

[140] Rozenblit, 'The Assertion of Identity', 178 ff.

autonomist ideology—a means to obtain recognition of their 'nationality' by the university authorities. The Yiddish language was turned into a touchstone of Jewish national solidarity and a symbolic protest against the official policy of assimilating Yiddish-speaking Jews from Galicia and Bukovina as members of other nationalities.

Marsha Rozenblit has shown how this campaign to raise Jewish student consciousness at the University of Vienna gradually developed after the autumn of 1902, with the active support of Zionist duelling fraternities like Kadimah, Ivria, Unitas, Libanonia, and Maccabäa. In 1907 the campaign gained momentum and led to interpellations in the Reichsrat by Jewish deputies demanding the recognition of Jewish nationhood at institutions of higher education in Austria.[141] Jewish students were urged to register '*Judisch*' next to the category of 'mother tongue' on their registration forms as 'a point of honour' and identification with their own people. This call was increasingly heeded. Rozenblit has pointed out that the fact that 'half of the Jewish medical students, and 35% of all Jewish students at the University of Vienna in 1910 regarded themselves as members of the Jewish nation is an indication of the widespread and deep-seated extent of Jewish national feeling and self-awareness in the younger generation of educated Austrian Jewry'.[142]

The regional breakdown of the lands of origin of these Jewish national students shows that just over a third of the total number from Galicia (38 per cent). Jewish national feeling was also particularly strong among students from Bukovina and Russia. Among students from Silesia and Moravia, Jewish national identification was similarly marked. According to Rozenblit's statistical analysis, it was significantly lower among Hungarians, Bohemians, and Viennese-born Jewish students.[143] These statistical indicators are not surprising. They reflect the general pattern of Jewish assimilation in the Habsburg Monarchy, confirming that Westernized Austrian Jews in the student body were less 'Zionist' than the *Ostjuden*. These regional differences should not, however, obscure the remarkable extent to which Jewish national feelings had penetrated the entire student milieu in Austria on the eve of the First World War.

The seed sown by Kadimah in the early 1880s had clearly struck roots in the Jewish student body thirty years later. Its success can be attributed to the intensity of racial anti-Semitism in the universities,

---

[142] Ibid. 180.   [141] Ibid. 179.
[143] See Table III in Rozenblit's article, p. 186.

endemic nationality conflicts throughout the Empire, the growing number of immigrant *Ostjuden* in Vienna, and the general impact of the Austrian Zionist movement. The special mission of Kadimah as the first standard-bearer of the Jewish national idea may have ended with the emergence of Herzl and political Zionism. But the social conditions that originally gave rise to Jewish student nationalism at the University of Vienna persisted and ensured its continued growth.

12

The Metamorphoses of Nathan Birnbaum

Everywhere, where they are found, too numerous to be lost in the crowd and also too few to impress their neighbours—they [the Jews] offer the most dangerous pretext for persecution: powerlessness. This powerlessness is the cause for the unavoidability of the national friction between Jews and non-Jews and lends Jew-hatred that potency which forbids comparison to any other form of national hatred, gives it that notorious significance which has been manifested for centuries in incitement, slanders and repressions. This unavoidability and intensity joined together—a possibility that Engels appears not to have thought of at all—justifies the weighty anxiety that Jew-hatred might portend a serious danger for the social peace of the community.

Nathan Birnbaum, *Die nationale Wiedergeburt des jüdischen Volkes in seinem Lande, als Mittel zur Lösung der Judenfrage* (Vienna, 1893)

The individual Jew may have a fatherland but the Jewish people has none and that is its misfortune.

Nathan Birnbaum (1893)

What is Zionism? Zionism comprises the following factors: 1. Recognition of the Jewish people as an entity which by virtue of its cultural gifts has a natural right and obligation to continue to exist as an entity and to act as such. 2. The realization that the situation of the Jewish people is thoroughly degrading and unfortunate. 3. The conviction that it is necessary completely to transform the international legal and economic situation of the Jewish people by finding a territory that will be a shelter and a rallying place for Jews fleeing from the wrath of persecutors as well as a support and a centre for the entire Jewish people. 4. The view that only one country is suited to be this shelter and rallying place, this support and centre: Palestine, the ancient national home of the Jews.

Nathan Birnbaum, Address to the Admath Jeschurun Association, Vienna, 23 January 1892

> If all the Austrian peoples are to be guaranteed their basic national rights, then why not the Jews as well, who need this confirmation most urgently of all? This question, hitherto raised only by individuals in small circles, is now suddenly being aired on all sides.
>
> Nathan Birnbaum, *Ost und West* (January 1906)

> One may say without exaggeration that the Yiddish language places East European Jewry and with it the entire Jewish people before a turning-point in its national destiny. Only in the light of this despised Golus dialect can the people's full independence be restored and Jews win their second, higher national emancipation.
>
> Nathan Birnbaum (August 1908)
> at Yiddish Conference in Chernovtsy

Nathan Birnbaum (1864–1937), the founder of Austrian Zionism, was born in Vienna of parents who came from a West Galician and Hungarian religious background. His father, the son of Polish Hasidim, had arrived in Vienna from Cracow with the first wave of Galician immigration. On his mother's side, Nathan Birnbaum descended from an old and distinguished north Hungarian rabbinical family whose roots can be traced back to the medieval scholar Rashi.[1] Educated in Viennese elementary and secondary schools, Birnbaum soon became estranged from his moderately orthodox family background though he did not take the assimilationist path typical of most of his adolescent contemporaries.[2] Even at secondary school, in spite of the tremendous influence of German culture, Birnbaum shocked his peers by expressing the conviction that Austrian Jews were not German but belonged to a distinct nation whose destiny must lead it to regain the land of Palestine.[3] Building on the early training in Jewish studies he had received at home, Birnbaum steeped himself in Hebrew journals, especially Perez Smolenskin's *Ha-Shahar*, and avidly devoured

---

[1] Nathan Birnbaum, *The Bridge: Selected Essays* (London, 1956), 11.

[2] Birnbaum, 'Gegen die Selbstverständlichkeit', in L. Rosenhek (ed.), *Festschrift zur Feier des 100. Semesters der akademischen Verbindung Kadimah* (Mödling, 1933), 29, and 'Iberblik iber Mayn Lebn', *Yubileum-Bukh* (Warsaw, 1925) (in Yiddish), 10.

[3] 'Gegen die Selbstverständlichkeit', 29. Writing on 19 Apr. 1932, Birnbaum recalled that in his high-school days in Vienna it was unthinkable for any young Jew 'sich nicht der deutschen Nation zuzuzählen'. According to this autobiographical account, his Jewish nationalist revelation came in 1879/80 (in the fifth or sixth form). In a conversation with a friend he insisted that Jews should declare themselves as members of the Jewish nation with their own unique past and look to Palestine for their future.

literature about the Jewish national movement in Eastern Europe.[4] The firm belief that the Jews were an ethnic entity with a unique history and culture tied to Ereẓ Israel prompted the eighteen-year-old law student (then in his first year at the University of Vienna) to found Kadimah together with Reuben Bierer from East Galicia and Moritz Schnirer who came from Bucharest.[5]

In 1884 the twenty-year-old Birnbaum issued his first publication, a pamphlet provocatively entitled *Die Assimilationssucht: Ein Wort an die sogenannten Deutschen, Slaven, Magyaren etc. mosaischer Confession von einem Studenten jüdischer Nationalität* (The Mania of Assimilation. A Word to the so-called Germans, Slavs, Magyars, etc. of the Mosaic Persuasion by an Undergraduate of Jewish Nationality). It was the beginning of what was to be a remarkably volatile career as a publicist, editor, and agitator which in its metamorphoses spanned all the major ideological trends in *fin de siècle* Central European Jewish life. For nearly fifteen years Birnbaum was the leading Zionist ideologue in Austria-Hungary, the founder and editor of the first Jewish nationalist journal in the German language, *Selbstemanzipation*, in which he coined the term 'Zionism'.[6] After disagreements with Herzl which caused him to leave the newly created Zionist Organization, he became for a while a protagonist of 'cultural' as against 'political' Zionism.

[4] See J. Klausner, *Historiya shel ha-sifrut ha-ivrit ha-hadasha* (Tel Aviv, 1955), v. 14–231; Emmanuel S. Goldsmith, 'Nathan Birnbaum', in his *Architects of Yiddishism at the Beginning of the Twentieth Century: A Study in Jewish Cultural History* (London and New York, 1976), 100, who suggests that 'the various phases of Birnbaum's ideological odyssey, including his Diaspora nationalism, may be traced to aspects of Smolenskin's writings'. Goldsmith plausibly claims that Birnbaum was also influenced by Hebrew radical-socialist writers of the 1870s like Aron Lieberman (his periodical *Ha-Emet* was published in Vienna in 1877), Morris Winchevsky, and Moses Leib Lilienblum, as well as Smolenskin and Pinsker.

[5] 'Gegen die Selbstverständlichkeit', 30. Birnbaum recalled how difficult it was in the early 1880s to win over the 'Westerners' in Vienna to Kadimah since they had no living *Volksjudentum* to serve as their inspiration. The 'Easterners', on the other hand, came 'aus einem lebendigen jüdischen Volksmilieu . . . wo es auch schon eine Bewegung der Selbstemanzipation oder der nationalen Wiedergeburt gab . . .'.

[6] G. Kressel, 'Selbstemanzipation', *Shivat Zion*, 4 (1956), 58–62. The first issue of *Selbstemanzipation* appeared on the day Perets Smolenskin died, 1 Feb. 1885, with an appeal to brother Jews (*Stammesgenossen:*) that began: 'Die Lebenskraft, die im Körper des jüdischen Volkes wohnt, ist unvergänglich, unzerstörbar! Weder das hasserfüllte Walten des wildesten Rassenhasses, der von Aussen an unserem Untergange arbeitet, noch der innen fressende Wurm des nationalen Lebensüberdrusses werden je im Stande sein, die zähe Natur unseres ewigen Volkes zu erschüttern!' The second issue on 16 Feb. 1885 carried a glowing tribute to Smolenskin, which *inter alia* deplored the fact that 'In Wien selbst, wo der grosse Todte lebte und seine Zeitschrift herausgab, da war er freilich verhältnismässig wenig bekannt . . .'

After 1900 he turned increasingly to an autonomist philosophy of 'diaspora nationalism'. His advocacy of the national autonomy principle duly led to Birnbaum to develop a full-blown ideology of Yiddishism. In 1908 he was the initiator and architect of the first Yiddish Language Conference at Czernowitz (Bukovina), where he would live for the next three years.[7] Finally, in the closing years before the First World War, Birnbaum moved closer to Jewish religious tradition, eventually became an orthodox practising Jew, and in 1919 was appointed the first general secretary of the Agudat Israel World Organization.[8]

This extraordinary personal odyssey, bewildering in its sharp intellectual turns, marked Birnbaum off from his Viennese contemporaries. Like that other contemporary ideological nomad, the Russian Jewish revolutionary Chaim Zhitlovsky, he seemed almost predestined by such political inconsistency to become a forgotten figure.[9] Yet his sudden shifts, doubts, hesitations, and contradictions were in many ways a faithful mirror of the cultural dilemmas confronting Austrian Jewry. Birnbaum's individualism, his originality and breadth of intellectual interests, the prophetic strain in his writings and the intensity of his commitment to Jewish life gave him a special position in the eyes of contemporaries; one which even his touchy, difficult temperament and lack of political *savoir-faire* could not entirely erase. Birnbaum remains therefore, a particularly sensitive barometer for the

[7] See 'Eröffnungsrede auf der jüdischen Sprachkonferenz in Czernowitz', held on 30 Aug. 1908 (retrans. by Birnbaum himself from the original Yiddish version), in Dr Nathan Birnbaum, *Ausgewählte Schriften zur jüdischen Frage* (Chernovtsy, 1910), ii. 41–5. See also in the same collection 'Der "Jargon"', ibid. 46–51 and 'Zum Sprachenstreit. Entgegnung an Achad haam', ibid. 52–74.

[8] A. E. Kaplan und Max Landau (eds.), *Vom Sinn des Judentums: Ein Sammelbuch zu Ehren Nathan Birnbaums* (Frankfurt, 1924), documents this final metamorphosis or 'return' to Judaism; see esp. Samuel Rappaport, 'Der Gottsucher', pp. 34–43, and Joseph Carlebach, 'Stil und Persönlichkeit', pp. 70 ff. The latter regards Birnbaum as the embodiment of 'einen grandiosen Kampf gegen den neujüdischen Intellektualismus, gegen die jüdische "Aufklärungsperiode" . . .' (p. 70). Max Landau, 'Nathan Birnbaum und das Jüdische Volk', p. 83, also transforms the later Birnbaum into a crusader against 'die maskilsche Mentalität im jüdischen Volke' and its scornful arrogance towards the true spiritual values of Judaism.

[9] On Chaim Zhitlovsky, see Jonathan Frankel, *Prophecy and Politics: Socialism, Nationalism and the Russian Jews, 1862–1917* (Cambridge, 1981), 258–87. Like Zhitlovsky, Birnbaum could be described as a creature of transient mood who remained loyal to certain key concepts (anti-assimilationism, belief in the eternal and indestructible character of the Jewish spirit, in the uniqueness of the Jewish nation etc.), but applied them to reality in sharply different ways at different periods. Birnbaum was, however, at no time a *revolutionary* socialist in spite of his early sympathy for aspects of socialist teaching.

era of transition in which he lived. His various mutations seem to embody many of the central problems of the Jewish national renaissance in Central and Eastern Europe.

On one issue, at least, Birnbaum did remain faithful to the concepts he had first enunciated in 1884 as a twenty-year-old student. From the outset of his career as a young Zionist until its close as a *Ba'al tschuva*, he was adamantly opposed to the assimilation of Jews into the surrounding society and their adaptation to the practices of peoples whom he considered culturally inferior.[10] In *Die Assimilationssucht*, Birnbaum had denounced in ringing tones the 'suicidal' policy of Jewish Germanization, Magyarization, and Slavicization, based in his view on self-deception, self-abnegation, and an unnatural desire for self-dissolution.[11] This 'mania for amalgamation' with surrounding peoples deliberately ignored the national character and special features of a 4,000-year-old Jewish history;[12] it was a modern form of 'Hellenization' in which the servile imitation of alien cultures had come to assume pathological proportions which directly provoked the rise of political anti-Semitism in Central Europe.[13] According to Birnbaum, anti-Semites justifiably saw in this Jewish 'mimicry' and self-dissolution a clear sign of moral inferiority and an admission of weakness rather than an expression of equality.

The only antidote for post-emancipation Jewry against the anti-Semitic virus, Birnbaum argued, lay in the reawakening of national consciousness and the encouragement of Zionist colonization in Erez Israel. Jews must seek national equality as a group in order to regain their inner balance and the respect of other nations.[14] Beyond the issue of self-humiliation implicit in a policy of assimilation within nations that rejected them, Jews should recognize that they had never been merely a 'religious community' or an 'amorphous mass of individuals'. They were historically a nation with a heroic past and the most sublime intellectual creations to its name. They had the closest physical and spiritual ties with Erez Israel, the return to which had been the focus of their prayers and longings for 1,800 years. The love of the Holy Land must, however, assume a more activist and consciously national

---

[10] D. Vital, *The Origins of Zionism* (Oxford, 1975), 223.
[11] Birnbaum, *Die Assimilationssucht*, 8–9. In his obituary for Perez Smolenskin, *Selbstemanzipation*, 16 Feb. 1885, p. 1, Birnbaum again attacked 'die ganze Erbärmlichkeit der assimilatorischen Selbstmordstheorie', a formulation to which he was to return throughout countless variations.
[12] *Die Assimilationssucht*, 6.
[13] Ibid. 9–11. [14] Ibid. 14.

character. For Jews it represented their only salvation as 'a place of refuge for those weary of exile and a pillar in the moral and material sense for those who will remain in exile'.[15]

Once the Jews had regained their fatherland 'contemporary Jew-hatred in its specific form would disappear from the earth and the whole of Jewry breathe again after a long and fearful millenial nightmare'.[16] To strengthen his argument, the young Birnbaum pointed to the establishment of new Jewish settlements in Palestine, the growing number of Jewish national associations, clubs, and periodicals in the Diaspora, and the revival of the Hebrew language in Eastern Europe.[17] What was still lacking was a common national will to promote large-scale action on behalf of Jewish territorial concentration and agricultural settlement in the Holy Land.

Birnbaum devoted the next decade and a half of his doctrinal and propagandist activity in Central and Eastern Europe to the promotion of this Palestinocentric credo. Only a territorial centre in Erez Israel, would cure Jewry from the sickness of exile and dispersion, providing a secure home for the 'superfluous' Jews of Europe and bringing to an end the plague of anti-Semitism. This territorial centre would not run counter to the social, economic, and political interests of Diaspora Jewry. On the contrary, it would increase the loyalty of those who remained behind to their countries of domicile, reinforcing their security and self-confidence.

In an address delivered at a discussion evening sponsored by the Admath Jeschurun Association in Vienna on 23 January 1892, Birnbaum, expounding on 'The Principles of Zionism', explained:

We are a people without a land and a nation without soil, and that is our misfortune. Our best friends cannot help us when we are thrashed somewhere, for there is no interfering in the internal affairs of another state. We ourselves are even more impotent and the most that we can do is to stand at the border of the state in question and await our persecuted and expelled brethren with old and new clothes, with soup, coffee and ship tickets to America. This cannot suffice forever. A territory must be found which is truly ours, even if it is under

---

[15] *Die Assimilationssucht*, 14; also Birnbaum, 'Die Ziele der jüdisch-nationalen Bestrebungen, Pt. II', *Selbstemanzipation*, no. 4, 16 May 1890, pp. 1–2.

[16] *Die Assimilationssucht*, 15.

[17] Ibid. Birnbaum already considered in 1884 that the diffusion of Hebrew was such in Eastern Europe 'dass ihr zu einer vollständigen Nationalsprache sehr wenig fehlt und dies Wenige würde und musste eine territoriale Concentration alsbald nachholen. Ein von Hebräern bevölkertes Judäa schüfe auch ein von Juden gesprochenes Hebräisch.'

the modest title of international law. This land must become the focal point for our people which is scattered all over the earth—a focal point and support. All of our fellow Jews [*Stammesgenossen*], whether they go to that country or not, should enjoy its protection; some will benefit from the material gain of a home for themselves, others from the moral gain of a homeland [*Heimat*] for the people as a whole. With a Jewish fatherland the position of Israel among the nations would at once become normal and respected one, based on the principle of mutuality.[18]

In his concluding remarks, Birnbaum emphasized that the new movement was not 'unpatriotic' any more than it was 'reactionary', 'anti-religious', 'dangerous', or 'impracticable'. Zionism would actually reinforce feelings of local patriotism which Jews already felt for their adoptive fatherlands.

A person who sincerely loves his people has truer patriotic feelings [*Vaterlandsgefühl*] than an opportunist. Whoever lightheartedly can abandon his people is not reliable. The Zionist seeks a fatherland for the whole Israelite people [*das ganze Israelitische Volk*] because the facts demand it: but he also loves the fatherland in which he was born, because he lives in it and is more or less protected. The interests of his particular fatherland and of the longed-for fatherland of the Jewish nation do not collide in any way.[19]

Birnbaum's Zionism in these early years found expression through the Jewish nationalist student fraternity Kadimah and above all in his editorship of *Selbstemanzipation* (the first Zionist journal in any West European language) dedicated to 'the national, social and political interests of the Jewish people'.[20] Always lacking money and hampered by a small circulation, the journal stopped publication after fifteen months; renewed in 1890, it continued for four more years in Vienna, then moved to Berlin for publication purposes under a new name (*Jüdische Volkszeitung*). It was still edited by Birnbaum who remained in the Austrian capital. *Selbstemanzipation* took up most of Birnbaum's time since he served not only as editor but also as publisher, chief contributor, bookkeeper, typist, and office boy. During the first years it was published at his own expense and at one point his mother even sold her shop of kitchen utensils to help cover the costs. Several times

---

[18] 'Die Prinzipien des Zionismus', *Selbstemanzipation*, no. 5, 4 Mar. 1892, p. 53. Birnbaum's important lecture was published in three issues on 1 Feb., 4 Mar., and 7 Apr. 1892.

[19] Ibid., p. 58.

[20] See Kressel, 'Selbstemanzipation', 79–89, for the history of the journal and its difficulties.

manicipation
Zan. 1891

Stammesgenossen!

Gegen die neuen Leiden des jüdischen Volkes erweisen sich die bisher angewendeten Mittel als ungenügend. In der bedingungslosen Unterlehnung an die Völker fand Israel nicht das geträumte Glück; dagegen genügten die bloßen Versuche, um es seiner Selbstachtung zu berauben.

In sich selbst muß unser Stamm seine Rettung finden!

Daher muß ein wahrhaft jüdisches Geschlecht erzogen werden, welches seine Religion, Geschichte und Sprache kennend, zugleich mit dem Geiste der modernen Civilisation den Geist des classisch-hebräischen Alterthums in sich aufgenommen hat. Jüdische Schulen sollen dieses Ziel erreichen helfen, und zwar durch jüdische Rabbiner und Lehrer, welche nicht eine wenig geachtete und unsichere Stellung, wie heute, in ihrem Wirken beengt.

Daher müssen an der Spitze jüdischer Gemeinden Männer treten, welche Herz und Sinn für das Judenthum haben.

Dies allein, nicht Rücksicht auf Vermögen, hat uns zu entscheiden.

Daher müssen wir das Vertrauen der Völker nach Möglichkeit durch aufrichtiges und offenes Gebahren im socialen wie im politischen Leben zu gewinnen suchen. Wir dürfen uns nicht über das durch Patriotismus und unser jüdisches Interesse bedingte Maß in ihre eigensten Angelegenheiten mengen.

Daher müssen wir die in moralischer und wirthschaftlicher Hinsicht schädliche Berufseinseitigkeit der Juden zu beheben und an die Stelle eines fast ausschließlichen Handelsbetriebes die Lust und Liebe zur physischen Arbeit zu setzen trachten.

Daher müssen wir einen jüdischen Bauernstand gründen!

Daher müssen wir diesem Bauernstande Boden, den heimatlosen Stammesgenossen Grundbesitz, den Opfern europäischer Verfolgung eine Zufluchtsstätte, dem zersprengten und durch seine Zersplitterung ohnmächtigen jüdischen Volke einen Mittel- und Einigungspunkt schaffen!

Wir müssen daher die Colonisation Palästina's, welche in acht Jahren tausende unglückliche Juden aus Rußland und Rumänien zu glücklichen Bauern in 12 blühenden Colonien gemacht hat, thatkräftig unterstützen!

So ist denn unser Programm:

Solidarität des Gesammtjudenthums, Wiedergeburt altisraelitischer Art und Sitte, Schaffung eines jüdischen Bauernstandes, d. i. Colonisation Palästina's.

Für dieses Programm wollen wir, wie bisher, mit unentwegter Treue eintreten. An Euch, Gesinnungsgenossen, liegt es, uns in unserem Streben zu unterstützen. Wer von Euch die kleine Ausgabe nicht zu scheuen braucht, abonnire die "Selbst-Emancipation", denn mit dem Lesen allein hat er seiner Pflicht nicht Genüge gethan. Es gilt, das Blatt, welches, das einzige in deutscher Sprache, die oben angeführten Ideen vertritt, nicht nur zu erhalten, sondern auch zu vergrößern.

Editorial in *Selbstemanzipation* (2 January 1892)

Birnbaum was on the point of bankruptcy and fellow-students would bring him bread to keep him from starving.[21]

Poverty would continue to be the bane of his existence. Though he had qualified as a lawyer at the University of Vienna in 1885, Birnbaum never succeeded in law practice, partly because his pronounced 'Semitic' features discouraged clients in the increasingly virulent anti-Jewish atmosphere of the Habsburg metropolis. Abandoning a legal career, Birnbaum decided in the early 1890s to devote himself wholly to journalism and Zionist affairs. He adopted the pen name Mathias Acher, to symbolize his radical break with religious tradition and the espousal of a new synthesis between European modernism, Jewish nationalism, and a moderate socialism.[22]

Throughout its chequered existence *Selbstemanzipation* was devoted to the didactic propagation of the idea of Jewish renaissance. In early issues attention was focused on the challenge of anti-Semitism and the war against all forms of assimilationism within the Jewish camp.[23] Birnbaum contended that the efforts of liberalism to neutralize the 'Jewish question' and to dilute the 'national, social and religious opposition between the Jews and Europeans' were futile.[24] He maintained that not only a millennial Jewish history but even the natural sciences and political economy supported his hypothesis of deeply rooted racial differences.[25] Birnbaum certainly believed in a

---

[21] See J. Fraenkel, 'Halifat Hamikhtavim Beyn Nathan Birnbaum leveyn Siegmund Werner', *Shivat Tsion*, 2–3 (Jerusalem, 1953), 275 (in Hebrew); also by the same author, 'Mathias Acher's Fight for the Crown of Zion', *Jewish Social Studies* (Apr. 1954), pp. 115–34.

[22] Mathias Acher was the pseudonym taken by Birnbaum in 1891 at a Seder evening of the Kadimah students' fraternity in Vienna where he made a speech denouncing the *Yavneh* tradition. The name Mathias recalled the Hasmonean uprising against Hellenism; Acher was the Hebrew name meaning 'a stranger' given by the rabbis to an admired sage and heretic in the Jewish tradition, Elisha ben Avuya, a 2nd-cent. scholar who became an adherent of the gnostic dualism derived from Greek philosophy and who later renounced Judaism. This combination of zealotry, idealism, and heresy revealed in the choice of pen-name seems appropriately to capture the psychological ambivalence behind many of Birnbaum's ideological positions.

[23] See 'Antisemiten, Assimilanten, Nationaljuden', *Selbstemanzipation*, 3 April 1885, pp. 2–3, with its sharp attack on the von Schoenerer movement: 'jene unsaubere, fanatisch blinde Partei', for distorting the inextinguishable 'racial differences between Jews and the Aryan peoples' in such a way as to defame an entire nation.

[24] 'Ist Wahrhaftigkeit Zugeständnis?', ibid., no. 5, 2 Mar. 1886, pp. 1–2. See also other early articles by Birnbaum which relate to this theme: 'Verjudung–Entjudung', ibid., no. 7, 1 May 1885; 'Der Judenhass', no. 1, 1 Jan. 1886; 'Antisemitismus und Nationaljudenthum', 3, no. 2, 16 Apr. 1890.

[25] 'Nationalität und Sprache', ibid., 16 Feb. 1886. In this article Birnbaum claimed: 'Vermöge des Rassengegensatzes denkt und fühlt auch der Deutsche oder Slave anders als der Jude.'

Jewish race. Indeed, in these early years, race seemed to him the central concept of human existence, responsible for creating the *Volksgeist* (folk-spirit) with all its national peculiarities. For example, just as the 'Aryan' race-spirit created the *Nibelungenlied*, so in Birnbaum's view the ancient Jewish *Volksgeist* had brought forth the Bible.[26]

This early Zionist race-thinking was founded on biological concepts that had become fashionable in an age of positivism, which naturally favoured ideologies based on the natural sciences. It sought to ground Jewish identity in secular and 'scientific' concepts that owed little to the religious heritage, or on the liberal abstract Judaism of the post-emancipation era. The fact that modern anti-Semites also exploited racial arguments did not deter Zionist ideologues like Birnbaum from using similar notions to refute their claims. Inevitably, they were accused by liberal Jews of encouraging anti-Semitism. Birnbaum, however, argued that it was the Jewish assimilationist *refusal* to recognize a primordial national individuality which had provoked *völkisch* anti-Semitism.[27] The undignified effort to dejudaize Jewry in order to achieve social acceptance at all costs had merely exacerbated an irresolvable national antipathy.[28] The vain attempt to suppress Jewish messianic hopes, to stifle Jewish self-criticism, and to reject anti-Semitism *tout court* without considering that it might reflect (though in vulgar, distorted form) certain realities of Jewish life in Europe, was harmful.[29] Recalling in 1902 his earlier feelings about anti-Semitism, Birnbaum made a rather revealing confession:

There was a time when I regarded Jew-hatred with a certain benevolence. I observed its activity with a kind of pleasure, I was almost happy with its successes and progress. If I did not always express these feelings freely, this was only out of a kind of tactical discretion which I had to impose upon myself so as not to offend too much those whom I wished to win over to Jewish national aspirations. How gladly I would have rather vexed them with the whole truth by calling out: the wicked anti-Semitic rascals are completely right, their insults you might prefer not to listen to and they are certainly inappropriate in their absolute form, yet they are but the stammering

[26] See 'Volkstum und Weltbürgertum', ibid., 16 April 1890, p. 1, where Birnbaum postulates an unbridgeable chasm between the Jewish and German *Volksgeist*.

[27] 'Ist Wahrhaftigkeit Zugeständnis?,' pp. 1–2.

[28] 'Erlöschung–Erlösung', ibid., no. 1, 1 Feb. 1885, p. 2: 'Dieser instinctive Ekel vor der moralischen Unselbständigkeit eines Stammes, der von dem merkwürdigen Wahne befallen ist, sich selbst vernichten zu wollen, ist der Keim des modernen Antisemitismus.'

[29] 'Unsere Mängel', ibid., pp. 2–3.

expressions of a very correct feeling that an unbridgeable gulf yawns between Jews and non-Jews—that both have antithetical ideals of beauty and morality. They are right and we are right and it is good that they storm so. At least we now know where we are.[30]

Birnbaum evidently saw a certain justification in Central European anti-Semitism, looked at from a Zionist standpoint. This was not surprising given that classical Zionism aimed at the physical and moral regeneration of the decadent *Golusjude*. From the beginning there had been a powerful element of Jewish self-criticism in Zionist polemics which betrayed a certain affinity to anti-Semitic argumentation. The attacks on Jewish 'mammonism', parvenu characteristics, *schnorrering*, and vulgar mannerisms provided some common ground between Zionists and anti-Semites. Soo, too, did the critique of assimilation in general. Zionism was, however, primarily concerned with changing these negative characteristics through the creation of a new, more harmonious environment. In their own homeland Jews would become productivized, recovering both their moral and physical balance. Unlike the anti-Semites, Birnbaum and other early Zionist thinkers in Central Europe certainly did *not* believe in the 'eternity' of racial characteristics, or in a hierarchy of higher and lower races, let alone in the permanent degeneration of the Jews. On the contrary, they assumed that Zionism as a doctrine of national self-help must lead to a dramatic transformation in the way of life and thought prevalent among Diaspora Jews. It would thereby provide a radical therapy for the sickness of *Galut* (exile).

Nathan Birnbaum was convinced that until this national redemption came about, anti-Semitism would remain an ineradicable historical phenomenon which neither revolution, reform, or enlightenment could uproot.[31] Birnbaum emphasized that, in spite of its obvious socio-economic components, 'Jew-hatred is not primarily an economic but a national phenomenon'. It was essentially a form of national friction and even of 'pure racial antipathy' exacerbated by the dispersion of the Jews and their fundamental powerlessness.[32] Hence the absurdity of efforts at *Abwehr* engaged in by Jewish community

---

[30] Birnbaum in *Ost und West*, 2, no. 8 (Aug. 1902), 517–18; repr. as 'Einige Gedanken über den Antisemitismus', in *Ausgewählte Schriften*, i. 154.

[31] See the remarks of Sanford Ragins, *Jewish Responses to Anti-Semitism in Germany, 1870–1914* (Cincinnati, 1980), 125 ff.

[32] Birnbaum, *Die nationale Wiedergeburt des jüdischen Volkes in seinem Lande* (Vienna, 1893 repr. in *Ausgewählte Schriften*, i. 41.

leaders ('social conservatives' as Birnbaum liked to call them) in Vienna and elsewhere in the Diaspora. In vain they tried to change the emotional bias of the masses through rational argument and to counter by enlightened propaganda their congenital 'need to hate'. Jewish self-defence was basically a still-born idea: '*Abwehr* could only emerge in rationalistic brains, among men who want to explain history armed solely with logic, and who overlook the fullness of influences from the life of the instincts and emotions . . . A movement which is based on such pre-instinctual philosophical foundations cannot succeed and therefore it is understandable, that *Abwehr* has suffered setback after setback . . .'[33]

Birnbaum's disparagement and open ridicule of Jewish defence against anti-Semitism was characteristic of early Zionist thinkers immersed in the issues of national revival, emigration, and territorial concentration. Already in February 1885 Leo Pinsker in a letter to Birnbaum had advised him to deal less with the anti-Semites and to focus more on the moral values, the productivization, and the national health of the Jewish people.[34] Significantly, after the third issue, *Selbstemanzipation* did include a section on Erez Israel, its climate, conditions, and the development of agricultural settlements during the First Aliya.[35] The journal began to place greater emphasis on the virtues of manual labour, the need to regenerate the Jewish masses, and on the return to the soil as the key concepts of Zionism. In his 1892 lecture to the Admath Jeschurun association, Birnbaum explained:

Land is the magic charm that arouses in nations a feeling of proud strength, guards them against unnaturalness and utter demoralization, and gives them physical and moral strength. Israel will have to cultivate its soil again; it will develop a peasantry that will enjoy its work and its life. The marrow of this class will rejuvenate the entire body of the Jewish people; the nervousness and distraction that are so frequently found in educated Jews will decrease and the idolatry of money will become less intense.[36]

Both *Selbstemanzipation* and its successor, the *Jüdische Volkszeitung*, stressed the need for Zionists to encourage more actively the

[33] Birnbaum, *Ausgewählte Schriften*, i. 26. From Birnbaum's lecture entitled *Die jüdische Moderne* (Vienna, 1896) delivered before the academic society Kadimah in June 1896.
[34] Kressel, 'Selbstemanzipation', 64–5.
[35] See Birnbaum, 'Die Colonisation Palästinas', *Selbstemanzipation*, 2, no. 4, 16 Feb. 1886; 'Colonisationspläne', 5, no. 10, 15 May 1892; 'Organisation der Colonisations-tätigkeit', 6, no. 6, 18 May 1893.
[36] 'Die Prinzipien des Zionismus', ibid., no. 5, 4 Mar. 1892, p. 53.

settlement of Palestine, praised the fertility of soil, and provided detailed information on the progress of its Jewish colonies.[37] Birnbaum himself set off for a lecture tour of Galicia and Bukovina in May 1892, designed to promote a more energetic settlement programme.[38] As part of this campaign, *Selbstemanzipation* also fought vigorously against the alternative colonization plans developed by Baron Hirsch in Argentina and by other philanthropists for furthering Jewish settlement in the United States.[39]

In this propaganda for Zionism as a programme of national redemption, Nathan Birnbaum underlined that 'the emotions of a whole people are a force' which should be used to mobilize the Jewish masses.

The cry 'Zion' arouses a world of such emotions in the hearts of our fellow Jews and brings out hosts of enthusiastic fighters, whereas the cry of 'America' (if, for instance, one wished to found the new home for Israel there), leaves the Jewish national soul [*die jüdische Volksseele*] cold . . . It is also not easy to make a people of farmers [*ein Ackerbauvolk*] out of a people of traders [*Handelsvolk*]. Only enthusiasm can overcome this Herculean task; it cannot be undertaken with business-like sobriety. The Jewish farmer will derive this enthusiasm from the soil of his ancestors, whereas the smallest failure will drive him from a foreign soil which means nothing to him.[40]

To this quasi-mystical view of the link between land and people, tinged with an agrarian romanticism, Birnbaum added another consideration. Palestine was after all a 'Semitic country' located in the Orient. 'The Jews are an oriental people. This is where they will feel at home and be able to undertake a cultural mission which, in line with the entire course of their history, belongs to them and to them alone . . . they are qualified to rouse the Orient from its lethargy, restore it to history, and do great work in the service of mankind.'[41]

Birnbaum was convinced that only when the Jewish nation was reconnected to its 'natural' surroundings in the Orient could its creative energies be fully released and radiate outwards throughout 'Semitic' Asia, helping to bring its backward peoples into the orbit of

[37] 'Osten oder Westen', ibid., 17 Oct. 1890, pp. 1–3.
[38] 'Colonisationspläne', ibid., 15 May 1892; also Kressel, 'Selbstemanzipation', 91.
[39] 'Die wichtigste Frage', *Jüdische Volkszeitung*, 30 Jan. 1894, pp. 4–5; see also 'So lange es Zeit ist!', ibid., 3 Apr. 1894, p. 2.
[40] 'Die Prinzipien des Zionismus', *Selbstemanzipation*, 7 Apr. 1892.
[41] Ibid. Birnbaum also saw an advantage in the fact that Palestine was 'easily and quickly accessible from the major countries of the Jewish Diaspora' and that the Turkish government and people 'are very favourably disposed to the Jews'.

Europe. The 'civilizing mission' of the Jews did not, however, consist merely in becoming an agent of Europeanism. Rather Israel was to be a true mediator between East and West.[42] A consistently sharp critic of the materialistic culture of Europe (which he opposed to the idealism of the 'Jewish spirit') Birnbaum prophesied its future regeneration through the return of Jews to Palestine. The Jews would become the avant-garde of a renewed European civilization in its most modern form. Zionism would provide the ideal East–West synthesis following the exodus of idealistic Jews from Europe. Jewry would reinvigorate and purify the best of modern culture through its renewed encounter with the 'Semitic' Orient.[43]

In order to achieve this visionary goal, Birnbaum recognized that the Zionist movement would have to win the confidence of the Turkish government. In the 1890s the Sublime Porte showed no signs of accepting large-scale Jewish settlement, let alone political independence in Palestine-Syria. The Ottoman Turks must therefore be persuaded that there would be cultural, material, and political benefits in encouraging Jewish colonization within their Empire. Birnbaum consequently argued that the incoming Jewish settlers would bring with them the blessings of industry, prosperity, and education. They would help the Orient to resist the constant humiliations incurred at the hands of the Western powers.[44] Ottoman Turkey would thereby obtain a zealous defender of its leadership in the Orient as well as a bulwark against recurring European violations of its sovereignty.[45] The European Powers, for their part, would find in the Jews ideal middlemen between themselves and the Orient.[46]

Birnbaum's nationalist philosophy, developed in Vienna in the early

[42] Shmuel Almog, *Zionut ve-historia* (Jerusalem, 1982), 104–5, 109.

[43] ' "Die Heilung des jüdischen Volkes", Vortrag von N. Birnbaum in Lemberg', *Selbstemanzipation*, 15 Nov. 1892, p. 202.

[44] 'Die Türkei und die Palästina-Colonisation', ibid., no. 17 (1891), repr. in annexe to his *Nationale Wiedergeburt*, 38–40.

[45] Ibid. 40. Birnbaum suggested that the instinct of self-preservation would oblige the Jews 'ein übrigens friedliches und im versöhnenden Geiste wirkender Gegenwicht gegen das Araberthum abzugeben, und für den osmanischen Staatsgedanken immer und überall einzutreten'.

[46] *Ausgewählte Schriften*, i. 18. Birnbaum, like Moses Hess before him, liked to quote from the futurist vision of the French Gentile Zionist, Ernst Laharanne, whose *La Nouvelle Question d'Orient: Reconstitution de la nation Juive* (Paris, 1860) spoke of the great calling of the Jews 'to be a living channel of communication between three continents'. Birnbaum's notion of Jewry as mediators between Europe and the Orient probably owed something both to Laharanne's cultural imperialism and Hess's secular Jewish messianism.

1890s, anticipated many features of Herzl's Zionist programme as announced in *Der Judenstaat* only a few years later. Like Herzl he held that a gradual process of Jewish emigration from Europe would end the pressure of anti-Semitism on the remaining Jews and moderate the relentless economic struggle for existence.[47] In addition to the demographic factor, the establishment of a Jewish *Heimat* in Palestine would 'enoble and civilize, strengthen and harden the Jews of the Diaspora', normalizing their position. In the long run, it would make possible far more effective protests on behalf of persecuted Jewry.[48] Once the Jews had their own national centre, it would automatically become their advocate and defender in international affairs. Jews would no longer be despised outlaws (*vogelfrei*), whose powerlessness virtually invited anti-Semitic persecution.[49]

Like Herzl after him, Birnbaum also insisted that Zionism was consonant with the universalist traditions of the Enlightenment. The purity of their national idea would enable Jews to make a fuller contribution to human civilization, once they were free from the bitter yoke induced by anti-Semitism.[50] Jewish nationalism did not contradict the idea of humanity (*Menschheit*) since it was devoid of the aggressive spirit of earlier European epochs. Indeed, it was in harmony with the most advanced trends of social development.[51] In an independent Jewish homeland, the Jews would be free to develop their distinctive social and ethical genius for the greater welfare and redemption of mankind.[52]

Unlike Herzl or most of the other leading Zionists in Central Europe, Birnbaum had been markedly influenced in his youth by socialist teachings. Hence he devoted considerable attention to the challenge of Social Democracy, regarding it as the most serious rival

---

[47] *Die nationale Wiedergeburt* (1893), in *Ausgewählte Schriften*, i. 9, where Birnbaum writes that once the percentage of Jews falls *below* the saturation point at which intolerance becomes manifest 'das würde natürlich eben so sehr ein beträchtliches Nachlassen der antisemitischen Spannung, als eine Milderung des Daseinskampfes der jüdischen—und übrigens auch der nichtjüdischen—Volksmassen bedeuten'.

[48] Ibid. 9.

[49] Ibid. 10: 'Ein Volk ohne völkerrechtliche Geltung ist vogelfrei. Je rascher und gründlicher die zivilisierte Welt diese Vogelfreiheit bezüglich der Juden aufheben will, desto früher und radikaler wird sie von dem Judenhasse . . . befreit werden.'

[50] Ibid. 15.   [51] Ibid. 18–20.

[52] Birnbaum struck a secular messianic note with his prophecy: 'In eigenen Heim wird die jüdische Nation wieder ihre gewaltigen sittlichen, d. i. sozialen Anlagen entfalten und kraft derselben die endliche soziale Erlösung des Meschengeschlechtes herbeiführen helfen. Der seiner Ketten ledige jüdische Genius wird den Weg zum allgemeinen Menschheitsglück verkürzen.' (Ibid. 20).

for the hearts and minds of Jewish youth.[53] Already in his seminal lecture on the 'principles of Zionism' on 23 January 1892, Birnbaum had polemicized with those Social Democrats who viewed Zionism as a narrow-minded, reactionary form of nationalism:

The Zionists are nationalists in that they want to help their people to engage in cultural competition with other nations on an equal footing. Nationalistic in this non-aggressive sense, a Zionist may even espouse socialistic principles in the realm of economics, but he will never be able to accommodate himself to official socialism which decrees that existing national differences and the consequent differences in morality and temperament should be disregarded and the social question should therefore be solved in a stereotyped way. This error of official socialism become especially glaring with regard to the Jewish question, which is supposed to be solved automatically along with the social question.[54]

Birnbaum firmly rejected the optimistic claim of the German Social Democratic leader August Bebel that the victory of socialism was imminent. There was no basis to the Marxist belief that anti-Semitism was merely a product of the crisis in the capitalist system or that under socialism it would simply evaporate.

It is not true because the peculiarities, weaknesses, whims, sympathies and antipathies of the nations will naturally persist even in a socialist society, and thus Jew-hatred will not be buried either, for it is deeply ingrained in the psyche of the peoples. In fact, the Jews will be even worse off in a socialistic society unless their specific Jewish question is solved first. Only the national rebirth of the Jewish people can prevent anti-Semitism from being dragged into the socialist era where it would be even more dangerous because of the omnipotence of the people's will as represented by public officials.[55]

In his lecture, *Die jüdische Moderne*, delivered in 1896 to the students of Kadimah in Vienna, Birnbaum elaborated on this theme at

[53] Letter of Dr Solomon Birnbaum (son of Nathan Birnbaum) to the author on 24 Feb. 1980. Dr Birnbaum writes that 'during his Zionist phase he [N. B.] was influenced by Socialism' but 'never belonged to a Socialist Party'. Solomon Birnbaum also reminded me that his father was highly critical of the Austrian Social Democrats for expelling the newly founded Jewish Social Democratic Workers' Party of Galicia from its ranks in 1905. For this episode, which occurred during Birnbaum's Diaspora Nationalist phase, see Robert S. Wistrich, 'Austrian Social Democracy and the Problem of Galician Jewry 1890–1914', *Leo Baeck Yearbook*, 26 (1981), 89–124.

[54] 'Die Principien des Zionismus', *Selbstemanzipation*, no. 5, 4 Mar. 1892, p. 54.

[55] Ibid. For a similarly prophetic formulation, see *Ausgewählte Schriften*, i. 21: 'Greift der Zionismus nicht durch, so wird nach einem allfälligen, scheinbar völligen Siege der Gleichheitsidee die Judenfrage als ungelöstes Residuum, der Judenhass als ein verhängnisvoller Keil im Fleische der neuen Gesellschaft zurückbleiben.'

greater length. While acknowledging the importance of Karl Marx's historical materialism for the understanding of society, economics, and human evolution in general, Birnbaum argued that it ignored 'the history of man as a racial being'.[56] Nationality and race were historical factors no less potent than social and class conflicts. Birnbaum insisted that 'the firm foundation of nationality is always and everywhere race, whether a pure or mixed race [*einheitliche oder Mischrasse*]'.[57] In the course of development, races became 'ennobled' and attained the level of a 'nationality', which had 'nothing to do with the state of language'.[58] Hence, there was no scientific basis to socialist denials of Jewish nationality on the grounds that the Jews lacked a state, territory, or a unified national language. For the proof of Jewish national existence was rooted precisely in its 'racial quality'.[59] Birnbaum even claimed that the Jews had 'the strongest national feeling of all peoples, which is natural enough from the materialistic standpoint, since it is racially the most strongly distinct nationality'.[60] Basing himself on these *völkisch* premisses, Birnbaum insisted that anti-Semitism would not disappear in a new socialist order since its underlying roots lay in national tensions, racial antipathies, and the dispersion of the Jews. Social Democracy could offer no practical solution to the 'Jewish question' except to wait for the promised revolution. But the Jews manifestly required an immediate remedy for their plight.

In the 1890s Birnbaum regarded himself as a quasi-socialist within the Zionist movement, primarily concerned with the economic and social regeneration of the Jewish people. He strongly identified himself with the hostility of most socialists in Central Europe towards feudal values, clericalism, free-trade liberalism, and the materialist ethos of bourgeois society. It was self-evident for Birnbaum that there could be no room for Stock Exchange Jews, private enterprise, or 'profiteering' in the settlement of Ereẓ Israel.[61] Adapting the views of agrarocentric

---

[56] '*Die jüdische Moderne*. Vortrag gehalten im Akademischen Vereine "Kadimah" in Wien von Mathias Acher (Vienna and Leipzig, 1896), 10: 'Die landläufige materialistische Geschichtsauffassung vernachlässigt die Geschichte des Menschen als Rassewesens und berücksichtigt ausschliesslich die Geschichte des Menschen als Gattungswesens.'

[57] Ibid. 13.   [58] Ibid.

[59] Ibid. 13–14. 'Gehören nun aber Staat und Sprache nicht zum eisernen Bestände der Nationalität, dann gibt es keinen Zweifel an der gegenwärtigen Existenz der jüdischen Nationalität. Denn ihre Rassequalität kann ihr Niemand bestreiten.'

[60] Ibid. 24.

[61] Birnbaum's anti-capitalist vision led to differences of opinion with the Galician Zionist Abraham Salz who did not share his emotional affinities with socialist thought; see A. Salz, 'Socialismus oder Colonisation Palästinas', *Selbstemanzipation*, no. 9 (1891), p. 2.

nineteenth-century radicals like Fourier, Louis Blanc, Henry George, or even the German 'socialists of the chair', he looked to Palestine not only as a refuge from anti-Semitism but as the nucleus for building up a new class of free and independent Jewish farmers. The creation of a healthy peasant stock was regarded by Birnbaum and many early Zionists as indispensable for an organic national development that would free Jewry from the curse of 'mammonism' and the commercial, speculative spirit.[62]

Birnbaum's moralistic critique of the assimilationist Jewish upper classes for their vulgar materialism and parvenu lack of tact owed much to the prevailing anticapitalist and anti-urban values of the Central European intelligentsia.[63] But there was still a considerable gap between this populist anti-mammonism tinged with 'socialism' and the doctrines of class-war advocated by the Marxist labour movement.[64] Still greater was the gulf between Social Democratic internationalism and Birnbaum's unshakeable conviction that ethnic differences were primordial. His 'socialism' was firmly predicated on the primacy of national liberation. This led him to regard Social Democracy as a particularly dangerous rival for the Zionist movement. Aware of the charismatic appeal which revolutionary radicalism exercised on Jewish youth in Eastern Europe, Birnbaum sought to incorporate its more rational elements such as the need for social reform and greater economic equality. At the same time he adamantly rejected its 'cosmopolitanism' and predilection for a violent overthrow of the capitalist system.[65] The *Zukunftsmusik* of the Social Democrats, especially their promise of imminent universalist redemption, awakened a palpable echo in Jewish hearts attuned by centuries of suffering to messianic chords. For this very reason Birnbaum feared that the

[62] 'Die Ziele der jüdisch-nationalen Bestrebungen, Pt. II', ibid., no. 4, 16 May, 1890, p. 2. For Birnbaum, the epitome of this capitalist profiteering spirit was the United States. His opposition to Jewish settlement in America derived as much from 'social' as it did from national considerations.

[63] 'Die Ziele der jüdisch-nationalen Bestrebungen, Pt. III, Ethischer Teil', ibid., 2 June 1890.

[64] There was a certain parallel between Nathan Birnbaum's view of socialism and that of Theodor Hertzka, editor of the *Wiener Allgemeine Zeitung*. See Birnbaum's long report on a lecture that Hertzka delivered before the Oesterreichisch-Israelitische Union on 14 Jan. 1893, published in *Selbstemanzipation*, no. 3, 28 Feb. 1893, pp. 2–4, under the title 'Arischer und semitischer Geist'. Birnbaum remarked that 'Dr. Hertzka sprach als socialist—ein Wort, das man nicht mit der Parteibezeichnung Socialdemocrat verwechseln darf—und als Jude. Er ist ein Mann, der die Eigenart des jüdischen Wesens erkannt hat und diese Eigenart vollständig und mit Bewusstsein in sich verkörpert.'

[65] 'Die Socialdemokratie und die Juden', ibid., no. 6, 16 June 1890, pp. 1–2.

socialist dream might prove even more destructive to Jewry than the liberal mirage of assimilation.[66]

The inroads of Social Democratic propaganda among impoverished Jewish workers in Galicia seemed to confirm the 'assimilationist' danger to the young Zionist movement coming from this source. The Polish socialists led by Ignacy Daszyński, sought to encourage class-consciousness among the Galician Jewish proletariat as a step towards their eventual absorption in the Polish nation. Both Birnbaum and the Cracow-born socialist Zionist, Saul Raphael Landau, opposed this campaign as detrimental to the national interests of Galician Jewry.[67] Jews had bled long enough in the social and national-liberation struggles of other peoples. It was an illusion to believe that such participation would lead to the elimination of anti-Semitism or that it could end the isolation of the Jews among the nations of Eastern Europe; equally naïve was the assumption that the abolition of states, nations, or religious communities would eliminate social inequalities, economic exploitation, or mass poverty.[68]

Zionism, on the other hand, aspired to a synthesis of Jewish patriotic and religious traditions with progressive, democratic ideals that sought to overcome 'the materialistic and egoistic mode of thinking of European society'.[69] It sought the national redemption of all classes of Jewry in an independent homeland, an ideal for which internationalist Social Democrats displayed little sympathy. In impoverished regions like Galicia the ideologies of proletarian and Jewish solidarity stood indeed in glaring antithesis to one another in the early 1890s.[70] The strike of the tallith weavers in Galicia during the summer of 1892 was a case in point. The cause of the strikers, who worked fifteen hours a day in appalling conditions for wages of one to three gulden a week, was eagerly taken up by Austrian and Polish socialists who organized collections on their behalf.[71] *Selbstemanzipation* acknowledged their

[66] Ibid., p. 1. See also the report on 'Der internationale Arbeitercongress in Brüssel', ibid., no. 17, 2 Sept. 1891, p. 3, which pointed to the ambivalence of the Socialist International on the 'Jewish question' and criticized the extreme assimilationist position adopted by the Austrian socialist leader, Victor Adler.

[67] Saul Raphael Landau, 'Der Socialismus und die Juden in Galizien,' ibid., no. 6 and 7, 7 Apr. 1892, pp. 54–6.

[68] Birnbaum, 'Zum ersten Mai', ibid., no. 9, 1 May 1892, pp. 79–81.

[69] Ibid., p. 80.

[70] Birnbaum, 'Die Tallisweber von Kolomea', ibid., no. 16 and 17, 29 Aug. 1892, pp. 166–7.

[71] 'Der jüdische Weberstreik', *Arbeiterzeitung*, 5 Aug. 1892, also 'Zum Kolomaer Weberstreik', ibid., 16 Sept. 1892; and Max Zetterbaum, 'Klassengegensätze bei den Juden', *Die Neue Zeit*, ii (1892–3), 39.

efforts to better the conditions of the Galician proletariat but pointed to the danger that Social Democracy could gain a firmer foothold among their co-religionists, unless Zionists devoted more concern to the solution of the social problem.[72] At the same time, it warned its readers against the chimera of the class-struggle, emphasizing that as long as Jews remained in *Galut* (exile) they would continue to be 'a dependent and unprotected minority'.[73]

Birnbaum remained sceptical at this time of efforts by some Jewish nationalists to organize Jews as an independent political factor in Galicia.[74] As a Zionist he still believed that only an independent territorial centre for the Jewish people as a whole could provide a long-term solution to the problem of Jewish poverty. Local Jewish political activity in a national framework could at best constitute a useful adjunct to colonization in Palestine.[75] The impressive growth of Galician Zionism as a result of favourable local conditions in the Polish province led him, however, to modify this standpoint. Already in 1891 the Lemberg Zionists had developed a detailed programme and began publishing their own Zionist newspaper *Przyszlosc* ('Future') in Polish. This paper would exercise a considerable influence on Jewish public opinion in Galicia. In the summer of 1892 Birnbaum himself travelled through many cities in Galicia and Bukovina, helping to found new Zionist clubs and promoting the idea of unifying Hovevei Zion groups in one national organization. Hence he was eager to avoid further tensions with the Galicians.[76]

Together with Dr Abraham Salz, chairman of the executive committee of the Galician Zionists, Birnbaum convened a unity conference in Cracow on 1 November 1893.[77] The conference clarified the principles, the means of information, and the methods of

---

[72] 'Die Tallisweber . . .', 167: 'Der Strike [*sic*] der Tallisweber von Kolomea kann der Socialdemokratie die schönste Gelegenheit geben, sich unter der galizischen Judenheit einzunisten.'

[73] Ibid.: '. . . auch im sozialistischen Zukunftsstaate wird die Judenhetze nicht aufhören, wenn die Juden wie heute und damals allerwärts die abhängige und schutzlose Minorität sein werden.'

[74] See Nathan Gelber, *Toldot Ha-Tnuah ha-Ziyyonit be-Galitsiah*, (Tel Aviv, 1958), 15.

[75] N.B., 'Parteiprogramme', *Selbstemanzipation*, 21 June 1892, p. 116; 'Die Zionistische Partei', 23 Feb. 1892, p. 41.

[76] The first conference of Jewish nationalists had been convened on 23–5 Apr. 1893 and was attended by representatives from all the existing Zionist societies in Galicia. Nathan Birnbaum, who represented the Austrian Zionists, was elected honorary chairman of the conference.

[77] See *Selbstemanzipation*, no. 18, 15 Nov. 1893, pp. 3–5.

propaganda to be adopted by the 'Organization of Austrian Zionists'.[78] The Austrian Zionist party declared as its first basic principle, the striving 'for the resurrection [*Wiedergeburt*] of the Jewish nation and ultimately the reconstruction of Jewish communal life [*der Wiederherstellung des jüdischen Gemeinwesens*] in Palestine'. At the same time it also recognized the 'duty of guarding the political, social and economic interests of Jews in Austria'. In addition, resolutions were adopted to demand the 'abolition of the present guild system in Austria', the abrogation of the *numerus clausus*, and the abolition of Sunday as an obligatory day of rest for Jews. The conference also called for the participation by Zionists in elections, the publication (in Yiddish) of a pamphlet to enlighten the masses about electoral reforms, and for the submission of a petition to the authorities for the recognition as literates (*Alphabeten*) 'of those individuals who read and write Hebrew'.[79]

Birnbaum had by now already crystallized a programme of political Zionism which sought to combine legal guarantees for a Jewish home in Palestine with participation in Austrian politics in order to strengthen the Zionist movement.[80] The Zionist cause would have to put on the international agenda in order to overcome the obstacles placed by the Turkish government in the way of Jewish settlement in Palestine. No less importantly, Zionism had to propagandize and organize among the Jewish masses as a political movement; it had to become more involved in Austrian electoral activity without losing sight of the 'final goal'.

The fight of Austrian Jews for their national rights and their liberation from the illusion that anti-Semitism might be definitively eradicated, were objectives considered attainable by political agitation;[81] broader cultural aims of developing the Hebrew language, knowledge of Jewish history, and encouraging the settlement of Palestine were a

[78] See 'Corporationen und Versammlungen', ibid., no. 20, 15 Dec. 1893, p. 7, for the change in the name of the organization to 'The Austrian Jewish National Party', which was proposed by Birnbaum.

[79] *Selbstemanzipation*, 15 Nov. 1893; also Kressel, 'Selbstemanzipation', 90. At this stage in his career, Birnbaum, possibly influenced by the Hebrew writer Reuben Brainin (1862–1939) who had recently settled in Vienna, attached great importance to the role of the Hebrew language for Western Jews, in promoting the national renaissance. Yiddish, on the other hand, he still regarded as the language of the ghetto and *Galut*, unfit for a civilized nation seeking its auto-emancipation.

[80] N.B., 'Politischer Zionismus', *Selbstemanzipation*, no. 23, 19 Dec. 1892; 'Jüdische Politik', no. 8, 15 June 1893: 'Die Wahlreform und die Zionisten'. no. 16, 15 Oct. 1893; no. 17, 1 Nov. 1893. Also *Die nationale Wiedergeburt des jüdischen Volkes* (Vienna, 1893).

[81] N.B., 'Der neue Cours' ('Ein Wort an aller Zionisten'), ibid., no. 21, 2 Nov. 1891, pp. 1–2.

matter of education and enlightenment. In the pursuit of these purposes, Birnbaum regarded Vienna as an ideal centre for the Zionist movement:

Vienna lies on the frontier between East and West in Europe. It lies in the midst of a Jewish population numbering millions; it is the point where German and Russo-Polish, Ashkenazi and Sephardi Jewry meet and can best be united in common work; it is as if born to be the centre of Jewish national agitation— which for a long time will have to be the chief preoccupation of our movement. Vienna is moreover a German city, which is of the greatest significance for the winning over of the very important German Jewish element in Austria and Germany. Finally, Vienna is the capital of a nationalities' state, and hence incomparably more suitable for our movement, then for example, Berlin.[82]

Vienna was indeed better placed than Paris, Berlin, London, or New York to be the bridge between Russian and Western Jewry, since its geo-political position gave it close proximity to the heartland of the Jewish masses. It was irrelevant, Birnbaum insisted, that the bulk of Viennese Jewry did not support the movement. Zionism could in any case expect no sympathy from the millionaire Stock Exchange Jews, the liberal rabbis (*Seelsorger*), or journalists of the *Neue Freie Presse*, who ' hate every national movement of an oppressed people and grudgingly surrender only in the face of success'.[83] Nor did it matter that Vienna was no longer the centre of world politics and that it lacked a tradition of supporting movements for national self-determination comparable to London or Paris. Zionism, at this early stage in its development, had to concentrate on education, internal consolidation, and the centralizing of its meagre resources rather than achieving diplomatic successes.[84]

Birnbaum was well aware that the assimilationist leaders of Viennese Jewry and the owners of the great liberal newspapers feared Zionism as a 'danger' to their position, almost on a par with socialism and anarchism. Though the Zionists in Vienna were still only a *Privatpartei*, limited to a relatively narrow circle, the Jewish leadership fulminated against them as unwelcome disturbers of the 'sweet tranquility and comfortable prosperity of Viennese Jewry'.[85] They were seen as

---

[82] B., 'Die zionistische Partei', ibid., no. 4, 23 Feb. 1892, p. 40.

[83] Ibid. 41. Birnbaum contrasted here the opposition of the *Neue Freie Presse* to the Slav and Irish national movements and their reluctant capitulation before Hungarian demands.

[84] Ibid.: '. . . die Politik, die wir wünschen, soll eben mehr eine innere, als eine äussere, mehr Selbsterziehung als Diplomatik sein.'

[85] 'Der gegenwärtige Stand unserer Sache in Oesterreich', ibid., no. 21, 15 Nov. 1892, pp. 1–2.

rebellious trouble-makers whose aims, argumentation, and methods seemed to reinforce those of the anti-Semites. Their ideology and agitation threatened to undermine the hard-earned status of the 'Mosaic Germans'.[86] Against this challenge the Jewish notables and Press barons would seek to employ the time-honoured Viennese tactic of *todtschweigen* (to kill the movement by silence).

Birnbaum none the less remained confident that this strategy would not succeed. In the Austrian provinces, especially in Galicia, the Zionist movement had already encountered a receptive public opinion which argued well for the future.[87] But Vienna remained 'the key to the Jewry of Austria', for even in far-off Galicia, the magic of the *Kaiserstadt* exercised a remarkable spell over provincial Jews. Hence the crucial importance for the Zionist movement of increasing its strength in the Habsburg capital.[88] Viennese Zionists would have to extend their appeal beyond student circles and reach out to all classes of Austrian Jewry. They would have to counteract 'the lack of idealism among Austrian Jews' and the indifference of the assimilationists to Jewish history and literature by energetically promoting associations whose goal was the cultivation of 'Jewish science and consciousness'.[89] Along with the creation of *Colonisationsvereine* that encouraged the settlement of Palestine, such Jewish cultural associations were potentially a most important avenue for the percolation of Jewish national feeling into wider strata of the population. So, too, were the religious organizations of the Jewish community. Zionists could not remain indifferent, as a 'national-social Party' within Jewry, to key institutions such as the Viennese Kultusgemeinde, which, based though it might be on 'the fairy-tale of a de-nationalized "Mosaic confession"', still provided a nucleus for preserving the national character and traditional solidarity within Jewry. Hence, the task of Zionism must be to transform these 'confessional communities' into

[86] Ibid.

[87] Ibid. 1. Birnbaum acknowledged that, outside Galicia, the situation was much less promising for Zionism. He blamed this primarily on the entanglement of Jews in the struggle between Germans and Slavs, which had led to 'such a high level of estrangement from their own nationality'.

[88] Ibid.: 'Das Wort Wien hat einen guten Klang bei den österreichischen Juden, man muss ihn daher den Leuten vorspielen können.'

[89] B., 'Pflege der geistigen Güter unseres Volkes', ibid., no. 7, 1 June 1893, pp. 1–2, for Birnbaum's critique of 'die materialistische Trockenheit des österreichischen Judenthums', which he compared unfavourably with the achievements of German Jewry in the domain of Jewish *Wissenschaft*.

autonomous foci of Jewish national life, culture, and science, into working centres for 'the future of our people'.[90]

A new strategy was also required at the more general Austrian level where the intensification of national conflicts, various proposals for electoral reform, and the crisis of the parliamentary system were obliging the Zionists to rethink their indifference to everyday politics.[91] Already in February 1891 Birnbaum argued that as patriotic Austrian citizens and as Jews, Zionists could not remain neutral to the outcome of Reichsrat elections. Though the *final* goals of the movement lay beyond the Dual Monarchy, as Austrian citizens the Zionists should place the interests of the Habsburg State before those of 'blind party fanaticism'.[92] It was in their interest to support political parties which defended the cause of civic equality and rejected anti-Semitism. In Viennese districts, the Zionists clearly preferred Liberal to anti-Semitic candidates. As a general principle, they favoured the 'democratic' orientation in the capital and the provinces. In mixed nationality areas, Jews would have to decide according to their own national interests whether to back Germans or Czechs, Poles or Ukrainians, Italians or Slavs.

Birnbaum realized that the Zionist movement was still too disorganized and ill-prepared to directly engage on its own account in Austrian electoral politics. Moreover, he constantly emphasized that electoral politics could provide no panacea for the ills of the Diaspora, which could only be cured by territorial concentration in a Jewish homeland.[93] At most, electoral participation could be considered a palliative to ease the sufferings of the *Galut* and raise the national consciousness of the Jewish masses.[94] Birnbaum still remained adamantly opposed to a 'Jewish politics' based solely on self-defence against anti-Semitism. This trend, adopted increasingly by community leaders, had been forced upon them by the bankruptcy of German liberalism. But the

[90] 'Das neue Statut der Wiener jüdischen Gemeinde', ibid., no. 17, 1 Nov. 1893, pp. 1–2. Birnbaum was especially critical of the inadequacy of Hebrew language instruction in the educational programme of the Vienna Kultusgemeinde.

[91] Almog, p. 133.

[92] B., 'Zu den Reichsrathswahlen', *Selbstemanzipation* 16 Feb. 1891, pp. 2–3.

[93] Ibid., p. 2. 'Nur die Schaffung eines Heims für unser Volk kann dessen Unglück beheben; alle andern Versuche sind Flickwerk.' See also *Die jüdische Moderne*, 26.

[94] See 'Die Wahlreform und die Zionisten', *Selbstemanzipation*, no. 16, 15 Oct. 1893, p. 5, where Birnbaum remarked that '. . . die zu erwartende Wahlen müssen wenigstens benützt werden, um der Todtschweigerei, welche von der deutsch geschriebenen Tagespresse gegenüber unseren Bestrebungen betrieben wird und unsere Fortschritte bedeutend verlangsamt, entgegenzuwirken.'

community leadership remained as inimical as ever to the collective aspirations of the Jewish nation as a whole.[95]

By the mid-1890s Birnbaum had built up a small circle of disciples in Vienna, Berlin, and Galicia as well as establishing contacts with leaders of Ḥovevei Zion in many European countries. An excellent speaker and a tireless champion of the Zionist cause for nearly fifteen years, he had clearly emerged as the most distinguished intellectual among the Jewish nationalists in Austria and Germany. His lecture to Kadimah on 'Jewish Modernism' (*Die jüdische Moderne*), delivered in Vienna on 7 May 1896, was widely considered to be an outstanding exposition of the Zionist cause. Elaborating on the common German distinction between the particularism of *Kultur* and the universal features of civilization, Birnbaum argued that emancipation had not brought in its wake a genuine Jewish assimilation to the specific national cultures in Europe:

When we compare the so-called assimilated Jews with their surroundings, we find a similarity between them only in that circle of ideas and emotions common to all civilized European peoples [*Culturvölkern*]—but this similarity is almost completely absent when it comes to the national peculiarities of individual nations. The assimilated Jew has more or less the same extensive needs, social conscience, political maturity, bold scientific outlook, refined epicureanism and purified artistic taste . . . of the cultured European. But he does not possess, or at least only to a very small degree, the robust defiance and formal pedantry of the German, the élan and frivolity of the Frenchman, the elemental simplicity and melancholy of the Slav.[96]

The universalistic Europeanization of the Jews had not led to genuine 'national assimilation', but instead had merely increased anti-Semitism and Jewish insecurity. Only through Zionism, Birnbaum told his student audience, could the Jews become integral and authentic *Culturmenschen*.

But the mid-1890s Birnbaum had become increasingly preoccupied with the cultural and spiritual dimensions of the Jewish problem rather than with Palestinian colonization programmes or party-political Zionism.[97] He none the less welcomed the publication of Theodor Herzl's *Judenstaat*, sympathizing with its clarion call for Jewish

[95] Birnbaum, 'Jüdische Politik', ibid., no. 8, 15 June 1893, pp. 1–2.

[96] Mathias Acher, *Die jüdische Moderne*, 3.

[97] See ibid. 31 for Birnbaum's rejection of political 'Partei-Zionismus' as a pure abstraction and the inadequacy of small-scale colonization in Palestine in the face of Turkish resistance.

sovereignty and admiring the bold organizational plan to achieve this goal. Birnbaum and Herzl shared a common vision in 1896 of the international dimensions of the 'Jewish question'. Both men believed passionately in the need for a comprehensive legal-political solution that would finally end the pariah status of the Jews and normalize their position.[98] Herzl's watchword of Jewish political independence in a separate sovereign State seemed to complement and confirm everything that Birnbaum had been arguing for over a decade.

Hence it was only natural that Birnbaum should be invited by Herzl to deliver an address on 'Zionism as a Cultural Movement' at the First Zionist Congress in Basle (1897). In this speech, Birnbaum elaborated the critique of 'abstract Europeanism' which he had earlier expressed in *Die jüdische Moderne*.[99] He envisaged Zionism as a synthetic movement of national renaissance that would breathe the spirit of Western progress into the ghetto Jewry of Eastern Europe while reviving the 'dead Europeanism' of Western Jewry.[100] Only through possession of their own land would the 'Europeanism' of Western Jews become fruitful and the national culture of the *Ostjuden* emerge from its stagnation;[101] only in Erez Israel would Western Jews be liberated from the curse of 'ruthless Mammonism' and the *Ostjuden* from the blight of endemic pauperism. The ghetto culture of the East would be transformed with the help of Western Jews into a progressive national culture. It would integrate the highest political, technical, and aesthetic achievements of Europe with the prophetic teachings of social justice that were the unique historic legacy of Israel.[102] No people were better suited than the Jews, with their inherited 'oriental' character and European education, to act as mediators between East and West; no land was better predestined for this role than Palestine, at the confluence of three continents and in closest proximity to the Suez Canal.[103]

[98] See his review of Herzl's *Der Judenstaat* in Hermann Bahr's periodical *Die Zeit*, 6, no. 873 (Vienna), 22 Feb. 1896; also *Die jüdische Moderne*, 31–8.

[99] Mathias Acher, *Zwei Vorträge über den Zionismus* (Berlin, 1898), 1–12: 'Der Zionismus als Culturbewegung: Referat, gehalten auf dem Zionisten-Congress in Basel am 29. August 1897.'

[100] Ibid. 5. Birnbaum stressed in this speech the indissoluble bond between Zionism, the future of the Jewish people, and European civilization. Zionism could not have blossomed in the 'ghetto'. 'Erst als durch den Massenaufstieg zum Europäismus im Westen, wie im Osten eine Generation erstand, die von der abendländischen Civilisation mit ihren grossen thatkräftigen Nationen das Wollen erlernt hatte, war die Bahn für den Zionismus geebnet' (ibid. 5–6).

[101] Ibid. 6.   [102] Ibid. 9.   [103] Ibid. 10–11.

At the First Congress in 1897 Birnbaum was elected Secretary-General of the Zionist Organization, yet within a year he had left the movement once Herzl opposed his re-election. The frictions between the two men which made their further co-operation impossible were both personal and political, rooted in differences of social background, material circumstances, temperament, and outlook.[104] Birnbaum undoubtedly felt betrayed when members of Kadimah and other Zionist groups in Vienna pledged unconditional loyalty to Herzl, a complete newcomer to the cause and in many ways a stranger to Jewish life. He rapidly came to see in Herzl a power-hungry tyrant and usurper who sought the 'crown of Zion' while propagating ideas which Birnbaum himself had been preaching for years.[105]

Birnbaum clearly had no desire to play the role of a lieutenant rather than a general in the movement which he had done so much to initiate. As touchy and sensitive as Herzl in matters of personal prestige, his envy was doubtless aroused by the lightning speed with which his rival succeeded in capturing the imagination of the Jewish masses and Zionist youth in Central and Eastern Europe. Birnbaum's painstaking efforts during fifteen years of activity in the cause of Jewish nationalism seemed forgotten.[106] Too impulsive, inconsistent, and self-critical to play the role of a *Führerpersönlichkeit*, Birnbaym was unceremoniously thrust into the background by Herzl's meteoric rise. Too much a wanderer in the realm of ideas to feel at home even in his own mental constructions, he gradually turned his back on Zionism—the movement which in Austria he had done so much to create.

A valuable glimpse into the animosity which pervaded his relations with Herzl on the eve of their rupture is provided in Birnbaum's correspondence with Dr Siegmund Werner (1867–1928). The first member of Kadimah to engage in a duel, Werner had subsequently founded the non-duelling Jewish socialist fraternity Gamalah in 1894. Birnbaum saw in Werner a natural ally in his efforts to establish a radical Zionism to the left of Herzl and tried hard to win him over. But all the major Jewish national fraternities (Kadimah, Ivria, Gamalah, Libanonia), fascinated by Herzl's personality and ideas, had already declared their support for his brand of political Zionism. In a letter to Werner on 21 July 1897 Birnbaum conceded that it was impossible to counter Herzl's influence by 'open resistance'. To win support for the

---

[104] Alex Bein, *Die Judenfrage: Biographie eines Weltproblems* (Stuttgart, 1980), ii. 280.
[105] Josef Fraenkel, *Mathias Achers Kampf um die 'Zionskrone'* (Basle, 1959), 10.
[106] Ibid. 12–13.

leftist trend, calm and patient work within the ranks of Austrian Zionism would be required.[107] At the same time, Birnbaum proclaimed his backing for the convening of the First Zionist Congress. This would be a major step towards transforming the Jews into a national entity with an organized will of their own.[108] In 1897 he still identified with Herzl's diplomatic orientation more than with the 'practical Zionists' in Berlin like Hirsch Hildesheimer and Willy Bambus who advocated a strategy of gradual 'infiltration' as the best method of advancing Jewish settlement in Palestine.

Nevertheless, Birnbaum continued to hope for a common 'leftist' front against Herzl at the First Congress. On 28 July 1897 Werner, writing from Vienna to Birnbaum (who had moved for financial reasons to Berlin), informed him that the *Kadimahianer* were solidly behind Herzl. There was no support among the Viennese Zionists for more leftist positions, apart from Saul Raphael Landau (1869–1946), the first editor-in-chief of *Die Welt*.[109] In another letter from Vienna on 5 August 1897 Dr Werner explicitly mentioned Landau's plans to create a 'social-Zionist group' within the movement which would be centred around Birnbaum and the Swiss socialist Zionist Dr David Farbstein.[110] Landau, like Birnbaum, hoped to win backing for his radical views from the Galician Zionists.[111]

Any hopes that Werner could line up 'leftist' support in Austria for Birnbaum's brand of 'social Zionism' were rapidly dispelled as the movement came under Herzl's influence.[112] Replying to Werner on 15 August 1897, Birnbaum now described Herzl as 'a real bourgeois and opportunist despite his radical tendencies', who would soon turn further to the Right. 'This would drive us Leftists into open opposition and we would stand no chance for the time being. We can only make headway if people regard us as the closest allies of Herzl.'[113]

Birnbaum declared in the same letter, that though Zionism had nothing directly to do with internal Austrian politics, '. . . Zionists, who

---

[107] Fraenkel, *Mathias Achers Kampf*, 22: 'Wir können uns gegen den Wagen nicht stemmen. Es heisst allenfalls in der Partei Platz und Einfluss gewinnen. Dann wird sich alles geben.'

[108] See *Zion*, 31 May 1897, p. 382. This Zionist monthly, founded in Berlin in 1895, was edited by Birnbaum with the help of collaborators like Dr Oskar Kokesch, Dr Hirsch Hildesheimer, Dr Heinrich Loewe, and some other leading Berlin Zionists. Birnbaum, whose financial situation was desperate, had left Vienna for Berlin to assume the editorship in 1896.

[109] Fraenkel, *Mathias Achers Kampf*, 31–6.   [110] Ibid. 41–2.   [111] Ibid. 46.

[112] See also Werner's letter of 13 Aug. 1897 to Birnbaum, in ibid. 49 ff.

[113] Ibid. 55.

after all are also human beings and Jews, should participate in political life—if possible, within a social Jewish *Volkspartei* . . .'.[114] Like Landau, he clearly recognized the importance of the 'social question' for Zionism and the need to liberate the Jewish proletariat from the terrible conditions endemic in the *Galut*. Birnbaum was still convinced that if socialism triumphed, it would also be adopted in the Jewish State. But he was not yet prepared to lead a social-political faction at the First Zionist Congress in open opposition to Herzl. The same reluctance was exhibited by Saul Raphael Landau, Isidor Schalit, David Farbstein, and Nachman Syrkin, despite their opposition to 'bourgeois Zionism'.

Birnbaum's miserable material circumstances undoubtedly acted as a serious brake to his fading hopes of challenging Herzl for the leadership of the Zionist movement. Theodor Herzl was able to finance the newspaper *Die Welt*, the Zionist Congress, the wages of his collaborators, and most of his political work largely from his own pocket. Birnbaum was frequently unable even to buy bread and medicines for his children.[115] This material discrepancy aggravated still further Birnbaum's resentment of Herzl. Bitterly he complained to Dr Werner: 'If Dr. Herzl—who with his strong character and capacity for enthusiasm possesses a very hard, un-Jewish heart—had to spend only one day as I have been living in the past years . . . I feel sure that he would sing a different tune. But then, he would not have become so famous . . .'[116] Birnbaum unconsciously seemed to blame his own dire straits on Herzl and 'die Herren in Wien'. He speculated that his financial plight might never have arisen, had he not devoted his abilities ('which are certainly not inferior to Herzl') to Zionism.[117] The one solution that might have straightened out his financial affairs would have been a properly remunerated position in the Zionist movement. Birnbaum privately appealed to Dr Werner and his Galician colleagues to intercede to this end at the Basle Congress— out of 'humanity, Party feeling and perhaps also to compensate me for an old injustice'.[118]

---

[114] Ibid. 56.

[115] Ibid. 60–1. See also Birnbaum's letter of 19 Aug. 1897 to Werner, pp. 66–7: 'Ich lebe seit Jahren in den furchbarsten Verhältnissen. Deshalb ging ich ja auch aus Wien weg. In Berlin ging's noch ärger.'

[116] Ibid. 67. Birnbaum went on to describe the desperate situation of his family, with a chronically sick wife and his young children suffering from bronchitis: 'five persons in one room, and my wife, with her lung trouble, doing the washing without any help . . .' (ibid. 69).   [117] Ibid. 69–70.   [118] Ibid. 70.

Already a 'veteran' of the Jewish national cause, at the age of thirty-three, Birnbaum had not yet abandoned his hopes of controlling Zionist policy. In a letter from Vienna on 23 August 1897, Dr Werner sought to lower his expectations and to dissuade Birnbaum from placing his hopes of a secured financial existence on becoming a paid official of the Zionist organisation.[119] He strongly advised Birnbaum to secure the good graces of influential individuals in the movement rather than to rely on the Viennese leadership. They had no resources to spare and were preoccupied with more important matters. As a close collaborator of Herzl, Dr Werner was doubltess aware of the Zionist leader's deep distrust of Birnbaum's personality and political motives. Herzl's diaries record the mutual sense of antagonism and dislike. As early as 1 March 1896, he noted:

Birnbaum is unmistakably jealous of me. What the baser sort of Jews put into vulgar or sneering language, namely that I am out for my personal advantage, is what I catch in the intimations of this cultivated gentleman . . . I judge Birnbaum to be an envious, vain, and obstinate man. I hear that he had already turned away from Zionism and gone over to Socialism, when my appearance led him back again to Zion.[120]

Three days later Herzl expressed his growing irritation at the *schnorrering* requests from Berlin.

Dr. Birnbaum wrote me today a letter bemoaning his financial straits. I gave him twenty florins, which I herewith duly record, because I am certain he is inimical to me and will grow more so.

In conversation he spoke slightingly to me about Landau. During the evening, at the meeting convened by Landau, he made a socialistic speech; and from Landau's report I gather that it contained an argument against a discussion of my pamphlet, which was on the agenda. These are discouraging signs. Landau further writes that Birnbaum wants to become the Socialist leader in Palestine. We haven't got the country, and they already want to tear it apart.[121]

Matters came to a head at the First Zionist Congress in Basle, with a motion proposed by Isidor Schalit that the Secretary-General [Birnbaum] be elected by the Congress that he have a vote and also a

[119] Fraenkel, *Mathias Achers Kampf*, 75–8.
[120] *The Diaries of Theodor Herzl*, ed. and trans. Marvin Lowenthal (London, 1958), 102.
[121] Ibid. 103.

seat on the Actions Committee.[122] The motion implied that the Secretary-General, as trustee for the Congress, could in Herzl's words 'counter-balance the other twenty-two members of the Executive Committee!' It was voted down.[123] Birnbaum was indeed elected to the Viennese *Aktionskommittee* (along with Herzl, Schnirer, Kokesch, and Johann Kremenetzky), but could not retain this top leadership position under Congress rules and at the same time remain Secretary-General. His inevitable resignation from the Actions Committee provoked, however, a demonstration by his friends. Dr Malz publicly declared: 'Dr Birnbaum must have the mandate. We should not accept his resignation. Without Birnbaum there would be no Herzl, no Zionist movement in Austria.'[124]

Malz recalled that Birnbaum had no means of financial support because of his sacrifices for the Zionist cause. This statement aroused some stormy, tumultuous reactions which obliged Malz to leave the platform. Herzl himself had no doubt that Birnbaum had orchestrated the whole scene. He contemptuously noted in his diary on 3 September 1897:

Another critical moment—when the Birnbaum business occurred. This Birnbaum, who had dropped Zionism for Socialism three years before I appeared on the scene, poses himself and imposes himself as my 'predecessor'. In shameless begging-letters, written to me and others, he represents himself as the discoverer and founder of Zionism, because he had written a pamphlet like many another since Pinsker (of whom too, I had of course been unaware.) He now induced a few young people to put forward a motion that the secretary-general of the Executive Committee be directly appointed and paid by the Congress. And this fellow, who at the First National Assembly of the Jewish people has no other thought but to get himself voted a stipend, dares to draw comparisons between himself and me. Here too, as in his begging-letters, he adds audacity to his beggary.[125]

Herzl could not be expected to work for long with such a resentful rival as Secretary-General. Within a year Birnbaum had left the movement. He ceased to attend Zionist Congresses or to contribute

---

[122] Fraenkel, *Mathias Achers Kampf*, 83. Schalit argued that 'Bei den Sozialdemokraten ist es auch so. Wir sind keine Bourgeois-Partei', a phrase repeated by a number of delegates, which particularly irritated Herzl.

[123] *The Diaries of Theodor Herzl*, 226–7, described the motion as 'the only discordant note at the Congress; and instigated by Schalit, a young man whom I had overwhelmed by kindness'.

[124] Fraenkel, *Mathias Achers Kampf*, 83–4.

[125] *The Diaries of Theodor Herzl*, 226.

under his own name to *Die Welt*, the new Zionist newspaper founded in Vienna by Herzl. Nathan Birnbaum still saw himself at this stage as a Jewish nationalist. Like Ahad Ha'am, one of the leading ideological opponents of Herzl within Russian Zionism, Birnbaum attacked 'Charter Diplomacy' as a dead end for the movement. Similarly he now emphasized that the purpose of the Jewish national renaissance was to provide a solution for the 'problem of Judaism' rather than the 'problem of Jewry'.[126] Birnbaum began to criticize sharply the Zionist 'negation of the Diaspora', proclaiming instead that *Israel geht vor Zion* (Israel comes before Zion). The needs of the Jewish people would have to take precedence over the creation of a national centre in Palestine. The *Galut* could no longer be downgraded 'simply as valuable cultural manure for just one potential culture in a soil which is not yet ours'.[127] Jewish nationalism had to become more concerned with the here-and-now. It had to develop a new understanding and appreciation of the central core of the Diaspora experience—the everyday lives of the East European Jewish masses.

Already at the First Zionist Congress in 1897, Birnbaum had acknowledged the 'national individuality' and 'unique culture of this Eastern Jewry' (three-quarters of the world Jewish population), 'expressed in costumes and language, literature and art, customs and traditions, in religious, social and legal life . . .'.[128] But in his earlier Zionist phase he was highly critical of the self-enclosed culture of the ghetto and pessimistic about its future. Having left the Zionist movement he had changed his mind about the *Ostjuden*, moving steadily towards an ideology of *Golus* nationalism based on the centrality of their language, culture, and history.

When I found them to be a people with all the signs of a live, separate nation, it became more and more clear to me that a nation that already exists does not have to be created again *de novo*, and that what is of principal importance is preserving its life. Thus I developed my Golus-Nationalism. In Western Europe I stood up for Eastern European Jews, pointing out their lively folk existence and I requested of the latter that they guard what they possess and especially that they do not destroy it for the sake of dreams of the future.[129]

Birnbaum called his theory of non-Zionist nationalism, worked out between 1902 and 1905, *Alljudentum* (Pan-Judaism), since it sought to

---

[126] Goldsmith, p. 105.   [127] Ibid. 106.
[128] 'Der Zionismus als Kulturbewegung: Referat, gehalten auf dem Zionisten-Kongress in Basel am 29. August 1897', in *Ausgewählte Schriften*, i. 70.
[129] *Yubileum-Bukh*, 13; Goldsmith, p. 107.

embrace Jewish cultural life throughout the Diaspora and to secure the recognition by the great Powers of world Jewry as a 'nationality'. Reversing his earlier views concerning the inevitability of assimilation outside Palestine, Birnbaum now argued that the demographic, socio-economic, cultural, and political factors which had led to the disintegration of Jewish identity in the West did not apply to the *Ostjuden*. They still lived in dense physical concentrations, imbued with a strong national consciousness and Jewish folk tradition. Their culture was undergoing a remarkable renaissance, symbolized by the creative flowering of Yiddish literature.[130]

Birnbaum was convinced that the prospect of the *Ostjuden* being able to obtain the right of cultural-national autonomy had increased as a result of the political crisis overtaking the multinational Imperial structures of Russia and Habsburg Austria. After 1900 these Empires seemed to be in the process of losing their legitimacy as centralized states. Federalism was increasingly discussed as a solution to their intractable nationality problems. Birnbaum's espousal of Diaspora nationalism and adoption of autonomism as a realistic political programme for the mass of Austrian Jewry was thus part of a wider trend in both the Jewish and non-Jewish worlds. It was no accident that the first decade of the twentieth century saw the blossoming of theories of national autonomy developed by thinkers as diverse as the Austro-Marxists, Karl Renner, and Otto Bauer, the Russian-Jewish historian Simon Dubnow, or the popularist revolutionary Chaim Zhitlovsky. More significant still, was their adoption as electoral programmes by Jewish political parties and by various national minorities in both Russia and Austria-Hungary.[131]

Nathan Birnbaum was well aware of the more favourable climate of opinion towards cultural-national autonomism which had developed across the political spectrum in Habsburg Austria. In an editorial

[130] 'Ostjüdische Aufgaben: Vortrag, gehalten am 8. Juli 1905 in der akademischen Verbindung "Zephirah" in Czernowitz', in *Ausgewählte Schriften*, i. 260–75; also 'Etwas über Ost- und Westjuden', ibid. 276–82, first publ. in *Jüdische Volkskalander für das Jahr 5665* (1904–5).

[131] On the theory and practice of autonomism, see Simon Dubnow, *Nationalism and History: Essays on Old and New Judaism*, ed. and introd. K. S. Pinson (Philadelphia, 1958); Oscar Janowsky, *The Jews and Minority Rights, 1898–1919* (New York, 1933); Kurt Schillsweig, 'Nationalism and Autonomy among East European Jewry: Origin and Historical Development up to 1939', *Jewish Social Studies* (Apr. 1944), pp. 27–68; Robert S. Wistrich, *Socialism and the Jews: The Dilemmas of Assimilation in Germany and Austria-Hungary* (London and Toronto, 1982), 299–348; and Frankel, *Politics*, pp. 162–7, 217–24.

published in the *Neue Zeitung* on 9 August 1907, Birnbaum insisted
that national autonomy was an idea whose time had come. It had
supporters in all Austrian political camps, among young and old,
conservatives and revolutionaries, bourgeois and workers, Germans
and Slavs.[132] The old dualistic system in Austria-Hungary and the
centralist constitution were both bankrupt. The Habsburg Monarchy
could survive only if it abandoned its anachronistic national and
confessional structures in favour of socially progressive, democratic,
and autonomist principles. Austria would thereby transform itself into
a federation of nations bound together by common economic and
cultural interests.[133] Birnbaum demanded that the reconstitution of the
Monarchy on a democratic basis of cultural-national autonomy should
include official recognition of the Jews as a nationality. As a
preliminary step towards this goal he proposed a reorientation of
Austrian Jewish politics towards seeking alliances with other ethnic
groups willing to support Jewish aspirations.[134]

In the heat of the electoral campaign of 1906 this ethnic strategy
seemed to present a promising option. In the Austrian Reichsrat the
Ukrainian leader, Romanchuk, even advocated (as a counterweight to
Polish 'assimilation' of the Jewish minority) public recognition of the
Jews as an independent nationality.[135] Birnbaum, like other Jewish
nationalists, favoured the proposed Ukrainian alliance against the
Polish landowning aristocracy, advanced by Romanchuk.[136] In the
general elections of 1907 the three successful Zionist candidates in
Galicia were indeed elected, thanks to the electoral agreement reached
with the Ukrainians.[137]

Birnbaum himself was, however, unsuccessful in his personal
campaign to be elected in an East Galician constituency during the
same elections[138] This bitter disappointment probably accounts for his

[132] 'Nationale Autonomie', *Neue Zeitung*, 2, no. 9, 9 Aug. 1907, p. 1. Birnbaum had
founded this weekly in 1906 to further his autonomist political objectives.
[133] Dr Kadisch, 'Rück- und Ausblicke', ibid., 1, no. 11, 16 Nov. 1906, p. 1: 'Jede
Nation und jede Religion hat wohl das unveräusserliche Recht auf Autonomie, keine
aber kann das Recht auf Herrschaft über alle anderen beanspruchen . . .'
[134] Ibid.: 'Eine Einigung aller auf national-sozialem Boden fussenden österreichischen
Juden und weiters eine Verständigung mit den nationalen Autonomisten der übrigen
Völken, welche die Juden als gleichberechtigte Nation anerkennen, ist unbedingt
notwendig.'
[135] Goldsmith, p. 108.
[136] 'Jüdische Polen', *Neue Zeitung*, 1, no. 7, 19 Oct. 1906, pp. 2–3; 'Juden und
Ruthenen', ibid., 1, no. 4, 28 Sept. 1906, p. 2; also, ibid., 28 June 1907, p. 1.
[137] 'Galizische Wahlen',*Arbeiterzeitung*, 11 June 1907, pp. 1–3; Janowsky, pp. 136–40.
[138] See 'Wie eine strahlende Welt!' (first pub. 7 June 1907), in*Ausgewählte Schriften*, ii.

increasing disillusion with electoral politics and his turning to Yiddish language and culture as the source of authentic Jewish values. In the multinational environment of Czernowitz (Chernovtsy) (where Benno Straucher had been elected as a Jewish National Party deputy to the Reichsrat in 1907) Birnbaum discovered a Yiddish-speaking culture which had retained its vitality.[139] During the three years spent in Czernowitz between 1908 and 1911, Birnbaum began to propagandize energetically on behalf of the Yiddish language, literature, and drama. He organized 'Yiddish evenings' in Vienna, established Yidishe Kultur (a student organization for the promotion of Yiddish culture), and translated the works of outstanding Yiddish writers like Sholom Aleichem, Scholem Asch, and Y. L. Peretz into German.[140] Not only did he conduct an unremitting crusade to raise its prestige among Jews and non-Jews, but he worked hard to master the language himself so as to become a more effective propagandist of the new cause. Yiddish became the vehicle of his *Golus* nationalism, the symbol of the pan-Judaist consciousness which he now sought to instil in the Jewish masses throughout the Diaspora.

Birnbaum fiercely rejected the superiority complex of assimilated German Jews towards the mongrel 'jargon' as well as Zionist contempt directed at the servile language of the *Galut*. He glowingly portrayed Yiddish as the mirror of a proud, creative tradition. As the language of no less than nine million Jews dispersed throughout the world, it had to be considered a major factor of national cohesion. Without Yiddish as their living *Umgangssprache*, Eastern European Jewry would soon sink to the level of their Western co-religionists. As a result, the organic unity of Jewish *Volkstum* in the East would rapidly disintegrate.[141]

During his Czernowitz period, Nathan Birnbaum began to develop

3–5, Birnbaum's personal account of his electoral experience, full of lyrical enthusiasm for the courage and self-sacrifice of the Galician *Ostjuden*. On the electoral chicanery, see B., 'Die galizischen Raubwahlen', *Neue Zeitung*, 2, 12 June 1907, pp. 1–2. Goldsmith, p. 109, claims however: 'Many Jews declined to vote for him because they were afraid that, if he were elected, his Jewish physiognomy would set off a new wave of anti-Semitic ridicule and slander.'

[139] 'Die Sprachenfrage in der Bukowina und die Juden', *Neue Zeitung*, 2, 26 July 1907, pp. 1–2. On the Jewish national movement in Bukowina, see the fine article by Gerald Stourzh, 'Galten die Juden als Nationalität Altösterreichs?', *Studia Judaica Austriaca* x, *Prag–Czernowitz–Jerusalem* (Eisenstadt, 1984), 73–98; on Birnbaum's role in this movement, see ibid. 80.

[140] See 'Für die jüdische Sprache' (29 Nov. 1907), and 'Der "Jargon"', in *Ausgewählte Schriften*, ii. 34–40, 46–51; also Goldsmith, pp. 109–18.

[141] 'Zum Sprachenstreit. Eine Entgegnung an Achad Ha'am', in *Ausgewählte Schriften*, ii. 71.

a complete theory of Yiddishism in order to demonstrate its indispensability to Jewish national life and consciousness. Yiddish, he argued, was the vehicle of uniquely Jewish cultural values. Its intimacy, elasticity, and hybrid character testified to the genius of adaptation displayed by Diasporic Jewry throughout its long exile. Jewish intellectuals who denounced Yiddish as a semi-barbaric 'Jargon', merely demonstrated their total estrangement from Jewish life and the soul of the Jewish people.

Birnbaum's radical break with Enlightenment stereotypes of Yiddish should be seen as part of his general revision of conventional Western notions concerning the *Ostjuden*. They had become for him the cultural measure of Jewish integrity, whose wholeness and authenticity had to be defended at all costs from the incursions of the West. By 1909 Birnbaum was openly calling for the emancipation of the *Ostjuden* from the yoke of Western Jewry, even if this entailed shattering what he now considered to be a fictitious unity of the Jewish people.[142] The call for separation was motivated less by hatred of the West than by a defensive feeling that only through such insulation could the *Ostjuden* preserve their distinctiveness and cultural originality from the forces of decomposition.[143]

Birnbaum's advocacy of autonomism and Yiddishism placed him in opposition to the two central warring camps within Austrian Jewry at the turn of the century—the Zionists and the assimilationists. But despite his own desertion of Zionism, Birnbaum was still closer to their camp than to that of the Jewish establishment. Increasingly, Zionists and Diaspora nationalists found that they could co-operate on a range of issues. Both agreed that the Jewish masses should establish their own autonomous institutions; that they must develop an independent national life and *Sozialpolitik* in the Diaspora (what the Zionists after 1905 called *Gegenwartsarbeit*); that they should freely use their own national language (i.e. Yiddish) and seek official recognition as a nationality (*Volksstamm*) within the Empire.[144]

---

[142] 'Die Emanzipation des Ostjudentums vom Westjudentum' (Herbst 1909), ibid. 13–33.

[143] Ibid. 30: '. . . nicht Sympathieen und Antipathieen, nicht vorgefasste Meinungen uber "faulen Westen" und "gesunden Osten" liegen dem Wunsche und der Hoffnung zugrunde, dass sich das Ostjudentum gegenüber dem Westjudentum durchsetze; sondern die Einsicht in die Todesgefahr des ganzen jüdischen Volkstums, wenn dies nicht geschieht.'

[144] See Schillsweig, pp. 30 ff.; also Max Rosenfeld, 'Die jüdische Gemeinden in Oesterreich', *Der Jude* (1916/17), pp. 152–62, for the Zionist view.

The struggle for the official acknowledgement of Yiddish as a minority language that could be used in schools, offices, and public life provided another common denominator between Zionists and auto-nomists. This pursuit of Jewish national politics, especially in Galicia—where it aroused the vehement opposition of the Polish aristocracy and the assimilationist 'Poles of the Mosaic faith'—reinforced the links within the national camp.[145]

On the other hand, autonomism clearly differed from Zionism in so far as it waged the national struggle exclusively in the Diaspora. The autonomists divorced nationality from statehood, defining it primarily in terms of language and culture. National affiliation was to be expressed in personal rather than territorial terms. In this way, autonomism sought to provide an extraterritorial solution to the problem of the dispersed Jewish minority in the multinational Monarchy.[146] The cultural autonomy favoured by Nathan Birnbaum intended to integrate the Jews along with other Austrian minorities as a distinct national unit within a federative state organism. Birnbaum believed that this would finally equalize the status of the Jews and thereby undercut the basis of anti-Semitism. In 1905 Birnbaum even insisted that anti-Semitism could be uprooted only if Austrian Jews voted in separate electoral curias for their own lists.[147] Once they ceased to act as electoral cannon-fodder for the nationalist bourgeois parties (Germans, Poles, Czechs, Hungarians, etc.) or for the Social Democrats, the road to a full normalization of relations between Jews and Gentiles in Austria-Hungary would be clear.

During these years Birnbaum became genuinely convinced that national autonomy provided the best hope for the future of the eight million Jews who lived in Russia, Austria-Hungary, and the Balkans.[148] In 1907 he affirmed that the full development of the Jewish nation and

[145] Leila P. Everett, 'The Rise of Jewish National Politics in Galicia, 1905–1907', in Andrei S. Markovits and Frank E. Sysyn (eds.), *Nationbuilding and the Politics of Nationalism: Essays on Austrian Galicia* (Harvard, 1982), 149–77.

[146] Nathan Birnbaum, 'Der nationale Autonomie der Juden', *Der Weg*, 1, no. 14, 30 Dec. 1905, in J. Fraenkel (Ed.), *The Jews of Austria: Essays on their Life, History and Destruction* (London, 1967), 134.

[147] Ibid. 135. In this article Birnbaum polemicized against assimilationist critics who suggested that the recognition of the Jewish nationality meant a return to the ghetto and the acceptance of anti-Semitic theories. Against this claim he retorted: 'Kein Ghetto kann geschlossener sein als diese Atmosphäre von Zwielicht und Zweideutigkeit . . .'—i.e. than the new ghetto produced by the failure of assimilation.

[148] 'Judische Autonomie', *Ost und West*, 6, no. 1 (1906), in Fraenkel, *Jews of Austria*, 146.

of its cultural creativity was perfectly feasible within a federalist Austrian State based on universal suffrage. Such a democratic solution would also help resolve a fundamental problem facing contemporary Jewry—the achievement of equal status without surrendering national individuality. Birnbaum firmly believed that national autonomy within Austria based on the extension and flourishing of Yiddish culture offered the best prospect of reinforcing the distinctive identity of the *Ostjuden* and holding back the forces of assimilation.[149]

This obsession with the implacable erosion of authentic Jewish identity by the 'mania of assimilation' had characterized Nathan Birnbaum's approach to Jewish questions since his earliest Zionist involvement. By the turn of the century he no longer believed that the ravages of assimilation could be resisted by Palestinian colonization and the abandonment of *Golus*. He had turned his back on the dream of building a modernist culture in the Orient if this entailed the negation of an already existing, vibrant East European Jewish national culture in the present. After 1900 he was convinced that the real *Kulturjuden* were to be found in the ghettoes of Eastern Europe. But he was soon afflicted by doubts whether this world of secular *Yiddishkeit* could survive the intrusions of Western modernity. National autonomy, which seemed such a promising option in 1907, paled into insignificance with the continued decay of the Habsburg State and its disintegration during the First World War. The affirmation of the East European *Golus* was losing its credibility unless it could somehow be anchored to that oldest of Jewish sacred missions—preserving the monotheistic faith of Israel.[150]

Nathan Birnbaum's metamorphosis from political to cultural Zionist, from Pan-Judaist and Yiddishist to *Agudas Yisroel* gave expression to his lifelong search for the roots of Jewish being.[151] Birnbaum had always been preoccupied by the 'essence of Judaism' and remained faithful to this stubborn search for an authentic identity in spite of apparent contradictions and paradoxes. Alienated in his youth by the liberal assimilated rootlessness and hedonistic materialism of Viennese Jewry, his prophetic passion had first been inflamed by the Jewish national idea. For nearly twenty years he had carried its torch in Central Europe.

---

[149] 'Die Autonomiebestrebungen der Juden in Österreich', ibid. 143: 'Die nationale Autonomie wird uns den neuen Juden schaffen helfen, nach dem unsere Seelen so lechzen.'   [150] See Nathan Birnbaum, *Gottes Volk* (Vienna and Berlin, 1918).
[151] *Vom Sinn des Judentums*, 9.

Austrian Zionism was largely a creation of Nathan Birnbaum. Theodor Herzl's meteoric rise to prominence unexpectedly drove Birnbaum to the periphery. His self-exclusion then led him to rediscover the national life and unique culture of the *Ostjuden* at first hand. As a result of this encounter, Nathan Birnbaum became the first German-speaking intellectual to transmute the image of these despised *Schacherjuden* and *Schnorrers* into a counter-myth of vibrant folk creativity. Like Martin Buber (another Viennese-born intellectual with Galician roots), Birnbaum came to see in the *Ostjuden* the best hope for the regeneration of the Jewish nation. In his writings they became the incarnation of true *Geist* and *Kultur*. Their maligned Yiddish language was the embodiment and repository of Jewish traditions and spiritual values.

Birnbaum's rediscovery of the grandeur of the Jewish Diaspora, of its martyrdom and creativity, brought him to a deeper sense of the mystery of Jewish survival. The search of the alienated intellectual for the roots of his own people and the definition of its specific genius led him to a new appreciation of the peculiar spiritual uniqueness of the Jews. Birnbaum abandoned the pagan idols of land and *Volk*, turning his back on the resurgent temptations of modern secular nationalism. His final metamorphosis led him to the religious sources of the Jewish experience—the Sinaitic revelation, the God of Israel, and the 'inner faith' of the eternal people.[152]

Birnbaum lived with a rare intensity the dilemmas and the tensions of all the major ideologies which helped to shape modern Jewish history in Central and Eastern Europe. Zionism, Socialism, and autonomism, Yiddishism, and Orthodoxy were only the outer garments of this odyssey which reflected both the restless personal quest and the socio-cultural dynamics behind the Jewish national renaissance. Birnbaum's odyssey with its myriad ideological collages 'made of fragments of modernity, glimpses of futurity and resurrected remnants of a half-forgotten past' (to borrow Schorske's striking image from another context) was a typically *fin de siècle* intellectual adventure.[153] In the best romantic tradition, Birnbaum had once sought the secrets of Jewish existence in the soul of the *Volk*. In the striving of Jewish messianism to realize the 'Kingdom of God' he would ultimately find the key to its *Volksgeist*, once he had abandoned the materialist and positivistic doctrines of race which he had imbibed in his youth.

[152] Ibid. 41 ff.
[153] Carl Schorske, *Fin-de-siècle Vienna: Politics and Culture* (London, 1980), 120.

Looking back on his 'conversion' from secular materialist nationalism to an idiosyncratic orthodox Judaism, Birnbaum denounced his own past as nothing but an immersion in idolatry. Indeed the whole of nationalist and socialist 'freethinking modernity' was sunk in error and illusion.[154] The mystery and survival of Jewish peoplehood was not accessible to the 'natural laws' of economics, sociology, or history.[155] Secular ideologies like Zionism or Marxism were remote from the essence of the Jewish nation as a holy people.[156] Revelation, Law, and tradition alone were authentic. The false gods of European progress and of 'emancipated humanity' merely represented 'the masquerade of little people' playing at god even as they were sinking in the mire.[157] The Viennese Jew, Nathan Birnbaum, had finally 'returned home', to the world of the Torah, the Prophets, and traditional Judaism.

[154] Nathan Birnbaum, 'From Freethinker to Believer' (1927), in Lucy S. Dawidowicz (ed.), *The Golden Tradition: Jewish Life and Thought in Eastern Europe* (London, 1967), 213–24.
[155] Ibid. 217.
[156] Ibid. 219.
[157] Ibid. 222.

13

Theodor Herzl: The Making of a Political Messiah

The only way to solve the Jewish question is to promote a general improvement of the physical and metaphorical profile of the nation. The cross-breeding of the western races with the so-called oriental, on the basis of a common state religion—that is the great, the to-be-desired solution!

Theodor Herzl (February 1882)

About two years ago I wanted to solve the Jewish question, at least in Austria, with the help of the Catholic Church. I wished to gain access to the Pope . . . and say to him: Help us against the anti-Semites and I will start a great movement for the free and honourable conversion of Jews to Christianity.

Theodor Herzl (1896)

The sentiment of solidarity with which we have been reproached so frequently and acrimoniously was in the process of disintegration at the very time we were being attacked by anti-Semitism. And anti-Semitism served to strengthen it anew. We returned home, as it were. For Zionism is a return to the Jewish fold even before it becomes a return to the Jewish land . . .

Theodor Herzl, First Zionist Congress
(29 August 1897)

And then one night I had a wonderful dream. The King-Messiah came, a glorious and majestic old man, took me in his arms, and swept off with me on the wings of the wind. On one of the shining clouds we encountered the figure of Moses. The features were familiar to me out of my childhood from the statue of Michelangelo. The Messiah called to Moses: 'It is for this child that I have prayed!' And to me he said: 'Go and declare to the Jews that I shall come soon and perform great wonders and great deeds for my people and for the whole world!'

A boyhood dream of Theodor Herzl,
recounted to Reuben Brainin (1904)

'When Herzl comes into my office to report on the manuscripts that have come in,' said his editor-in-chief Moritz Benedikt, 'I never know whether it is my literary editor or the Messiah after all.' He said this with a smile; but he really didn't know. Nobody did.

Raoul Auernheimer (1948)

Theodor Herzl (1860–1904), creator of political Zionism and first Jewish statesman of the modern age, reflected in his cultural background much of the colourful multi-ethnic complexity of the Austro-Hungarian Monarchy. Born into a middle-class merchant family in Budapest, he grew up in a social milieu which cultivated a deep love of German language and literature while retaining a residual loyalty to Jewish traditional values. Herzl's Hungarian background was not unimportant for his future development though he rarely mentioned it except in a casual, offhand manner. In a short autobiography, written in January 1898 for the London *Jewish Chronicle*, he recalled:

I was born in 1860 in Budapest in a house next to the synagogue where lately the rabbi denounced me from the pulpit in very sharp terms because, forsooth, I am trying to obtain for the Jews more honour and greater freedom than they enjoy at present. On the front door of the house in the Tabakgasse where I first saw the light of this world, 20 years hence a 'notice' will be posted up with the words—'This house to let.'[1]

Between 1866 and 1870 Herzl attended the primary school of the Budapest Jewish community, where he studied Hebrew for four years in addition to the usual secular and religious subjects.[2] Excelling in Hungarian, German, arithmetic, and science, he received only 'good' for his efforts in *lashon haKodesh* (the holy tongue). In his autobiographical sketch, the Zionist leader ironically observed:

My earliest recollection of that school consists of the caning which I received from the master because I did not know the details of the Exodus of the Jews from Egypt. At the present time a great many schoolmasters want to give me a caning because I recollect too much of the Exodus from Egypt.[3]

[1] *Jewish Chronicle* (London), 14 Jan. 1898.
[2] See Joseph Patai, 'Herzl's School Years', *Herzl Year Book*, 3 (New York, 1960), 54, who notes that Solomon Kohn, the headmaster of this school, 'sympathized with the Hebrew renascence movement and sent enthusiastic greetings when the journals *Hatzefirah* and *Havatzelet* were launched in Jerusalem'.
[3] *Jewish Chronicle*, 14 Jan. 1898.

In the autumn of 1870 Theodor Herzl joined the Realschule, a secondary school which emphasized the sciences and modern languages rather than classical studies. His marks in mathematical and technical subjects were disappointing, ending his dream of becoming an engineer like his boyhood hero, Ferdinand de Lesseps. Alienated by the mechanical learning-by-rote of the Scriptures, Herzl's results in religious studies were lower than average.

His youthful imagination was sparked, however, by a book of Jewish legends which he had received as a Bar-Mitzvah gift in May 1873. Shortly before he died, Herzl confessed to Reuben Brainin that it was the Messiah legend which had excited him the most at the time—'the coming of the Messiah whose arrival is awaited daily by many Jews even in this generation'.[4] As a thirteen-year-old he dreamed that the 'King-Messiah' had taken him up in his arms into the heavens where they encountered Moses.[5] The Messiah in the dream repeated the words of the biblical Hannah to her son Samuel, calling to Moses: 'It is for this child I have prayed.' To the young Herzl, the 'King-Messiah' declared: 'Go proclaim to the Jews that I shall come soon and perform great wonders and great deeds for my people and for the whole world.'[6] Since Herzl kept this dream secret until he was a dying man, its precise effect on his future political path is impossible to assess. But the possibility of an unconscious early identification with a Moses-like figure who would lead the Jews from slavery to freedom, cannot be excluded. From the age of thirteen, however, the attentions of the increasingly ambitious youngster turned to literature. At that age, the adolescent Herzl founded a pupil's literary society called *Wir* ('We') in Budapest—'to enrich our knowledge, to make progress in the use of the language, and to perfect our style'—of which he was the President and also the most prolific author. He could write in fluent Hungarian as well as in German on subjects as diverse as Napoleon, Savonarola, Muhammad, about Hungarian patriots and poets, Greek mythology, religion, and heroism.[7] Herzl's adolescent essays included sympathetic reviews of the works of Hungarian poets like János Arany (1817–82), who penned the great national epic *Toldi*, as well as Mihály Vörösmarty

[4] Reuben Brainin, *Heyye Herzl* (New York, 1919), 17–18.
[5] For a Jungian psychoanalytic interpretation, see Grete Mahrer, 'Herzl's Return to Judaism', *Herzl Year Book*, 2 (New York, 1959), 28–33.
[6] Brainin; also quoted in Alex Bein, *Theodor Herzl: A Biography* (Philadelphia, 1962), 13–14.
[7] Patai, p. 60.

(1800–55), author of the Hungarian national anthem.[8] It is, however, unlikely that Herzl was ever a Magyar chauvinist. Even in post-emancipation Hungary, discrimination had by no means disappeared and it was still difficult for Jews to obtain jobs in government service.[9] In 1875 (the same year he entered the evangelical Gymnasium which was attached to Budapest's main Protestant church), anti-Semitism was first placed on the political map by Gyözö von Istóczy's speech in the Hungarian Parliament. Von Istóczy claimed that the Jews were an aggressive, socially exclusive, cosmopolitan caste who had tenaciously resisted assimilation for nearly 4,500 years. Their 'liberalism' was merely a cunning fraud to deceive the Gentiles. The true aim of these nomadic alien invaders was universal economic domination.[10]

Herzl did not leave any comment on von Istóczy's violent speech against Hungarian Jewry—a community whose members had swollen eightfold from 75,000 in 1785 to 552,000 by 1870. Thus we do not know whether he followed von Istóczy's extraordinary declaration, on 24 June 1878 in the Hungarian Diet, in favour of restoring a Jewish State in Palestine. This speech was made at the same time that the eighteen-year-old Herzl was sitting his final exams in Budapest. But there are some curious parallels between Herzl's later arguments for Zionism and those made by the Hungarian anti-Semite two decades earlier. Von Istóczy's 'Zionist' speech took as its point of departure the existence of a national emergency in Hungary, provoked in his eyes by Jewish 'domination' of the country. 'It may very well be that in no other land in Europe does the Jewish Question necessitate a more urgently radical solution than in our monarchy [i.e. empire] and especially in Hungary.'[11] According to von Istóczy the solution to this question entailed a Pan-European diplomacy which would reconnect the Jews

---

[8] Patai, 68; see also Andrew Handler, *Dori: The Life and Times of Theodor Harzl in Budapest (1860–1878)* (Univ. of Alabama, 1983), p. xii, who credits Herzl with 'great enthusiasm and profound understanding of Hungarian nationalism, its literary bases and its political objectives'.

[9] In his newspaper autobiography (see *Jewish Chronicle*, 14 Jan. 1898) Herzl gave anti-Semitism as a reason for his poor marks and for his leaving the technical school. 'But I soon lost all my former love for logarithms and trigonometry, because at the time a very pronounced anti-Jewish tendency prevailed at the *Realschule*.' Herzl decided to become a classical scholar instead, adding: 'At the *gymnasium* which was called the *Evangelisches Gymnasium*, the Jewish boys formed the majority, and therefore we had not to complain of any *Judenhetze*.'

[10] On von Istóczy, see Jacob Katz, *From Prejudice to Destruction: Anti-Semitism, 1700–1933* (Cambridge, Mass., 1982), 238–42: also N. Katzburg, *Ha-Antishemiut be-Hungaria, 1867–1914* (Tel Aviv, 1969), and Handler, pp. 114–15.

[11] Handler, p. 115.

to Palestine where they would help restore financial stability to the ailing Turkish Empire. Above all they would find constructive outlets in the Holy Land for their mobility, restless energy, diligence, and frustrated national ambitions.

In the Middle East, von Istóczy believed that political conditions were now ripe for a return of the Jews to Palestine and the restoration of the State 'from which they have remained expelled for 1800 years'. Von Istóczy looked to European statesmen and politicians like Disraeli, Gambetta, Lasker, Glaser, and Unger ('the souls of the Austrian Cabinet')—all of whom he insisted on labelling as Jews by 'race'—to take the initiative in implementing his proposals in the interests of public welfare.[12] This mystical racist appeal to 'Jewish patriots' to begin rebuilding their ancestral home was accompanied by the anti-Semitic demand that their 'cosmopolitan' brethren should cease to form a 'state within a state'. They should assimilate fully with non-Jews and make 'an honest peace with Christian civilization'. There is no evidence that von Istóczy's speech was read by Herzl or that it influenced in any direct manner his own path to Zionism.[13] But he was certainly aware of the Hungarian deputy's pivotal role in the Tisza-Eszlár blood libel of 1882. To what degree the burgeoning popular anti-Semitism in his native land may have marked him must remain an open question.

The young Herzl had left Budapest with his parents for Vienna in 1878 before Hungarian anti-Semitism had fully developed or spread to other parts of the Austrian Monarchy. His rejection of Magyar culture and the scarcity of his references to Hungary is striking, though not uncommon for middle-class Germanized Jews of his generation. Certainly his earlier bilingual and bicultural background was rapidly repressed once he had settled in Vienna where Hungarians were not especially popular. This suspicion was particularly evident in the German nationalist student milieu at the University of Vienna into which Herzl sought integration. As a Hungarian as well as a Jew, Herzl

---

[12] Ibid.

[13] This similarity probably explains the enthusiastic reception of Herzl's *Judenstaat* by the Hungarian anti-Semitic deputy, Ivan von Simonyi (1836–1904), one of von Istóczy's closest collaborators. Author of *Die Wahrheit über die Judenfrage* (1882), von Simonyi had co-founded the *Westungarischer Grenzbote* seven years earlier. It was to a 'chivalrous' editorial in this newspaper that Herzl referred in his diary of 26 Feb. 1896. See *The Diaries of Theodor Herzl*, ed. and trans. Marvin Lowenthal (London, 1958), 101. On 4 Mar. 1896, Herzl conceded: 'My warmest adherent so far is the Pressburg antisemite, Ivan v. Simonyi, who bombards me with flattering editorials and sends me two copies of each issue' (*Diaries, 103*).

may have felt doubly an outsider and therefore driven to overcompensate by adopting an intense German nationalism during his student years. No doubt his passionate interest in German literature, history, and politics—evident in Budapest—did make this transition easier than it might otherwise have been. Already in the 1870s he had absorbed from his Germanophile mother a fervent admiration for German *Kultur*, characteristic of many middle-class Budapest Jews.[14] Like their co-religionists in Prague, these westernized Jews saw themselves as a minority within a minority who represented the vanguard of *German* language and culture in Hungary. Thus it is not altogether surprising that the young law-student Theodor Herzl should have been drawn towards German nationalism. His social marginality in Vienna encouraged the adoption of a Prussian model of *Deutschtum* increasingly in vogue among the generation of university students in revolt against traditional liberal values.[15] Nevertheless, Herzl appears to have retained a certain strain of cosmopolitan humanism even in his Pan-German phase of student militancy that owed something to his Hungarian Jewish background.

In this respect, Herzl resembled other prominent Germanized Jews from Budapest such as Adolf Fischof, Theodor Hertzka, and Max Nordau. It is perhaps significant that this group of Hungarian-born Jewish intellectuals was politically far more activist in temperament than their Viennese-born counterparts.[16] Herzl's moral fervour, his

[14] Amos Elon, *Herzl* (New York, 1975), 24 ff. Also Handler, pp. 65–6, who argues that Magyarization had already gripped Hungary in the immediate post-*Ausgleich* period of Herzl's childhood and adolescence. Handler admits that Herzl loved and admired German culture from afar but maintains that he had adjusted well to the fervently patriotic Hungarian institutions of his Budapest years.

[15] For Herzl's deeply rooted pro-Prussian feelings there is a great deal of evidence from his diaries and in his diplomatic orientation as a Zionist statesman. See the entry of 22 June 1895 for his hero-worship of Bismarck's political genius (*Diaries*, 52); also his letter to Rabbi Moritz Güdemann, 22 Aug. 1895, ibid. 65, and 5 July 1895, ibid. 55: 'if there is one thing I should like to be', Herzl noted in this entry, 'it is a member of the old Prussian nobility.' In a diary entry dated Berlin, 8 Oct. 1898, ibid. 252, he wrote the following panegyric to the Wilhelminian Empire: 'To live under the protection of this strong, great, moral, splendidly governed and thoroughly organized Germany is certain to have the most salutary effects upon the national character of the Jews.' In his novel, *Altneuland* (Vienna, 1902), the central figure Friedrich Loewenberg (i.e. Herzl himself) sails to the South Pacific as the devoted companion of a Junker aristocrat, called Koenigshoff ('King's Court'). Significantly, not one of Herzl's heroic fantasy-figures or role-models was Austrian, though quite a number were Prussians.

[16] See William M. Johnston, *The Austrian Mind: An Intellectual and Social History, 1848–1938* (Berkeley and Los Angeles, 1983), 356–61, who treats Herzl briefly under the category 'Utopians from Hungary', and points to the parallels with Hertzka and Nordau.

gift for improvization and readiness to gamble, his original combination of diplomatic flair and imaginative utopianism, also seem more obviously Hungarian than Austrian characteristics. Similarly, the emphasis on national identity and patriotic consciousness was more highly developed in Hungary than in Habsburg Austria with its supranational traditions of universal Empire. Despite these influences, it is none the less evident that German rather than Hungarian nationalism provided the most relevant paradigm for Herzl's political Zionism.[17]

Herzl's Jewish identity is in some respects no less complicated than the possible Magyar influences on his later evolution. Only one generation separated him from the religious orthodoxy of eastern and south-east Europe. His paternal grandfather Simon Loeb Herzl (1805–79) who lived in Semlin, a small Austro-Hungarian frontier town near Belgrade, remained a pious, strictly orthodox Jew to the end of his days.[18] The son of a rabbi, he sometimes led the religious services in the small congregation in his home town. More important still, he was a follower of one of the pioneers of religious Zionism, the rabbi of Semlin, Yehuda Alkalai (1798–1878). As early as 1834, Alkalai had proposed the establishment of Jewish colonies in Ereẓ Israel as a prelude to the coming Redemption.[19] Simon Loeb Herzl, who visited his family in Budapest annually, always spoke enthusiastically of Alkalai's ideas. It is more than possible that it was from his lips that Theodor Herzl first heard about the idea of Jews colonizing the Holy Land.

Theodor's father, Jacob Herzl (1835–1902), a successful bank director and timber merchant, who had grown up in Semlin, had also been a pupil of Rabbi Yehuda Alkalai. Later, in Budapest, he became a supporter of the Hungarian proto-Zionist rabbi, Joseph Natonek

---

[17] Ibid. 360. For Herzl's attitude to German national feeling, see his letter to Baron de Hirsch on 3 June 1895: 'Do you know out of what the German Empire sprang? Out of reveries, songs, fantasies, and black-red-and-gold ribbons—and in short order. Bismarck merely had to shake the tree which the visionaries planted.' (*Diaries*, 22).

[18] Desmond Stewart, *Theodor Herzl: Artist and Politician* (London, 1974), 26–7.

[19] See Yehuda Alkalai, *The Third Redemption* (1843), extracts repr. in A. Hertzberg (ed.), *The Zionist Idea: A Historical Analysis and Reader* (New York, 1973), 105–7. Alkalai emphasized that the redemption must begin 'with efforts by the Jews themselves', who 'must organize and unite, choose leaders and leave the lands of exile'. He advocated the creation of an international Jewish organization, of a company that would 'appeal to the Sultan to give us back the land of our ancestors in return for an annual rent'. Alkalai immigrated to Palestine and settled in Jerusalem in 1874, when Theodor Herzl was fourteen years old.

(1813–92).[20] Thus not only paternal devotion but also ideological conviction may have determined Jacob Herzl's strong moral and financial support for his son's efforts to maintain the momentum of the struggling Zionist movement after 1897.[21] Theodor Herzl was also encouraged in his Zionist project by his strong-willed possessive mother, Jeannette, whose love of the German classics and commitment to the values of middle-class *Bildung* by no means excluded loyalty to Jewish national traditions.[22] It was from this handsome, self-willed woman that Theodor Herzl inherited his strong sense of aesthetic form, sartorial elegance, social etiquette, and deportment. His extraordinarily close attachment to her was to exercise a powerful grip on his whole personality.[23] It clearly affected his shaky marriage to Julie Naschauer and most probably shaped his curiously desensualized view of women. The possible impact of Jeanette Herzl on her son's conversion to the idea of redeeming a lost motherland is probably best left to the speculations of psycho-history.[24]

During Herzl's early years in Vienna, he studied law and in his own words 'took part in all the stupid student's farces, including the wearing of a coloured cap of a *Verbindung*, until this Association one fine morning passed a resolution that no Jews should henceforth be received as members'.[25] This humiliating episode of social rejection deeply wounded Herzl's sense of personal and ethnic pride. His allegiance to the semi-feudal values and German nationalism of the

---

[20] Handler, pp. 32–3. Natonek negotiated with the Turkish government in Constantinople (1867) to obtain a charter for Jewish settlement in Palestine. In 1872 he became the pioneer publicist of the Zionist idea in Budapest with his magazine *Das einige Israel* ('The United Israel'), advocating Jewish national emancipation. See Zev. Y. Zahavi, *Me-ha-Ḥatam Sofer ve-ad Herzl* (Jerusalem, 1966), 196–215, in Hebrew.

[21] Another pre-Herzlian 'Zionist' in the family was Samuel Bilitz (1796–1885), brother of Herzl's paternal grandmother, whose activities on behalf of Palestine went back to the 1850s. An Austrian consular official in various Balkan cities, he settled in Jerusalem towards the end of his life (*Encyclopaedia Judaica* (Jerusalem, 1971), viii. 421.)

[22] Ludwig Lewisohn (ed.), *Theodor Herzl: A Portrait for This Age* (New York, 1955), 34–5, overstates in my view the assimilationist drives of Jeannette Herzl and the tepidness of the family's Judaism. So, too, have Alex Bein and all Herzl's subsequent biographers, who present German *Bildung* in too dramatic a contrast with the Jewish world of that period; see, e.g., Stewart, p. 26.

[23] See Alex Bein, *Theodore Herzl* (Philadelphia, 1962), 64, 68–9. For the psycho-sexual dynamics, see Peter Loewenberg, 'Theodor Herzl: A Psychoanalytic Study in Charismatic Political Leadership', in Benjamin B. Wolman (ed.), *The Psycho-analytic Interpretation of History* (New York, 1971), 150–91.

[24] Loewenberg, pp. 176, 179, 183–4. See also David Litwak's moving tribute to his mother at the end of *Altneuland*, trans. Paula Arnold (Haifa, 1960), 216–17.

[25] 'Theodor Herzl, An Autobiography', *Jewish Chronicle*, 14 Jan. 1898.

Austrian *Burschenschaften* was shaken to the roots.[26] There is little doubt that he enjoyed the romantic ritual of the Teutonic student fraternities, the sporting of glamorous swords, coloured caps, and ribbons. He had unreservedly identified with the ardent pro-Prussian and Germanocentric nationalism of his fellow students in rebellion against the decadent *Schlamperei* of the old Austrian Monarchy.[27] Arthur Schnitzler recalled in his memoirs:

One of the Jewish students who belonged to a German-national fraternity before the changes just mentioned, was Theodor Herzl. I can remember seeing him with his blue student's cap and black walking-stick with the ivory handle and F.V.C. (*Floriat Vivat Crescat*) engraved on it, parading in step with his fraternity brothers. That they eventually expelled him, or, as the students called it, 'bounced' him, was undoubtedly the first motivation that transformed this German-national student and spokesman in the Academic Debating Hall (where we had stared at each other contemptuously one evening at a meeting, without however knowing each other personally), into the perhaps more enthusiastic than convinced Zionist, as which he lives on in posterity.[28]

The somewhat diffident Schnitzler had been unfavourably struck in the early 1880s by what he regarded as Herzl's snobbish condescension and effortless superiority. There is at the same time an element of admiration mixed with envy in his evocation of Herzl's precocious *savoir-faire*, his elegance, self-possession, and abilities as a speaker, graphically demonstrated in the *Akademische Lesehalle*.[29] In reality, the young Herzl's aristocratic pose of confident nonchalance disguised an underlying self-doubt, insecurity and proneness to fits of acute depression.

Herzl had joined the nationalistic duelling fraternity Albia in 1881. Only four years earlier the fraternity had adopted the black, red, and gold ensign of German nationalism in opposition to the loyalist *schwarzgelb* (black-yellow) colours of Austria.[30] Theodor's *nom de*

---

[26] Elon, p. 54. This identification was also true at the time of other Jewish contemporaries such as Heinrich Friedjung, Victor Adler, Sigmund Freud, Gustav Mahler, and Siegfried Lipiner who were later to become Austrian luminaries; see William J. McGrath, 'Student Radicalism in Vienna', *Journal of Contemporary History*, 2, no. 3 (July 1967), 183–202.

[27] On the implications of the illiberal backlash of the early 1880s for Viennese culture, see Carl E. Schorske, 'Generational Tension and Cultural Change: Reflections on the case of Vienna', *Daedalus* (Fall 1978), 111–22.

[28] Arthur Schnitzler, *Jugend in Wien: Eine Autobiographie* (Frankfurt, 1981), 153.

[29] 'Excerpts from the Correspondence between Schnitzler and Herzl, *Midstream*, 6, no. 1 (1960), 48–9 (Schnitzler to Herzl, 5 Aug. 1892).

[30] Stewart, pp. 84–5.

combat in the fraternity was Tancred, recalling the aristocratic young hero of a novel by Great Britain's Prime Minister, Benjamin Disraeli, which had first been published in 1847. In *Tancred*, the convert Disraeli had expressed a visionary, romantic Toryism, looking to re-establish the harmony of English society and to revitalize the Church as a moral and religious force by restoring its Jewish foundations. *Tancred* was also a vehicle for Disraeli's proto-Zionism. There are passages in the novel which speak out vigorously in favour of restoring national independence to the Jews and sharply criticize Jewish assimil-ationists, afraid of revealing their race.[31] Was the young Herzl already attracted to this Judaeo-Christian strain of messianism at an uncon-scious level? There is no direct evidence to validate this hypothesis but the exotic figure of Disraeli clearly exerted its fascination on the young Herzl.[32]

On 11 May 1881 Herzl fought his obligatory student's duel. He appeared to have readily adapted to the aristocratic code of honour on which the ethos of the Austro-German student corporations was based. But with the rise of racial anti-Semitism in the Austrian *Burschenschaften*, the position of the twenty-two-year-old Herzl became increasingly untenable. The death of Richard Wagner on 13 February 1883 and the memorial celebration in the composer's honour by the Union of German Students in Vienna rapidly degenerated into a pro-Bismarckian, Pan-German, and anti-Semitic demonstration. Herzl wrote an indignant letter of condemnation to the Albia fraternity leadership offering to resign. As 'a lover of freedom' (*freiheitsliebender*) and as a Jew, he felt outraged by the new turn of events. His protest

---

[31] A characteristic example of Disraeli's 'Zionism' can be found in *Tancred*: 'The vineyards of Israel have ceased to exist, but the eternal law enjoins the children of Israel still to celebrate the vintage. A race that persists in celebrating their vintage, although they have no fruits to gather, will regain their vineyards.' The novel also unfolds an entire Middle East policy including the revival of Palestine-Syria under British influence, the defence of Eastern Jewry, the crowning of Queen Victoria as Empress of India, and the British annexation of Cyprus. See Benjamin Jaffe, 'A Reassessment of Benjamin Disraeli's Jewish Aspects', *Transactions of the Jewish Historical Society of England* (1975), pp. 115–23.

[32] Herzl was certainly well aware of Disraeli's Zionism. see his *Diaries*, 210, 15 May 1897: 'I urged Kellner to write a series of character studies on leading exponents of the Zionist idea: Disraeli, George Eliot, Moses Hess, etc. He waxed enthusiastic and will begin with Disraeli in the first number.' On 21 June 1900 Herzl noted in a letter to the great Hungarian Jewish scholar, adventurist, and unofficial diplomat, Arminius Vambéry (1832–1913): 'Disraeli once said to a young Jew "You and I belong to a race who can do everything but fail".' (*Diaries*, 329.)

letter was coldly accepted and terminated his relationship with Albia.[33]

The Wagnerian demonstration was not Herzl's first encounter with the 'Jewish question'. Comments in his diary entry of 8 February 1882 on the novel, *The Jews of Cologne*, by the popular and prolific German writer, Wilhelm Jensen, indicated that the young Herzl was by no means free of Jewish self-hatred. He was deeply concerned and repulsed by the physical and moral effects of the ghetto on the Jews. In his view, their despised physique and mentality was essentially the result of a lack of cross-breeding with other races. The 'gloomy ghetto' whose influence still endured 'long after its material walls have fallen' had cramped the outlook of many educated Jews. The ghetto was directly responsible for the 'misshapen' historical development of Jewry. It had acted like a tight ring tormenting and paralysing the fingers, preventing creative activity, initiative, and free movement in the Jewish life.[34]

Herzl's reading of Eugen Dühring's *Die Judenfrage als Racen, Sitten und Culturfrage* (The Jewish Question as a Question of Race, Morals and Civilization) provoked a more forthright response.[35] 'This rogue— the teeth past which his villanies gush should be bashed in!—turns up his eyes with odious mock-libertarian piety to say: To all men, the most boundless freedom; but for the Jews, "a law of exception" [*Ausnahms-gesetz*]: the new phrase for the medieval ghetto.'[36] Dühring was nothing but a malicious, hypocritical *Freiheitsjesuit*, (an 'infamous freedom-cleric'). His so-called 'solution' of the Jewish question combined a restoration of the ghetto with 'a modern systematic dejudaizing [*Entjudung*] of the press and usury . . .', of law, medicine, and the other free professions.[37] The real motive for this policy of 'dejudaization' was to destroy Jewish economic competition. But as Herzl observed, a new rationale was required for the 1880s. It was this need which the Berlin philosopher had provided. The German Jew-baiters clearly realized that accusations of ritual murder and well-poisoning were inadequate in a more rationalistic, secularized society.

They recognize, as does Herr Dühring, that religious attacks on the Jews no long work. Now race must step forward! The faggots of the middle ages have

[33] Alex Bein, *Theodor Herzl: Biographie* (Vienna, 1934), 66–7; Stewart, pp. 94–5; Elon, pp. 60–1.

[34] *Jugendtagebuch*, 8–9 Feb. 1882, in Tullo Nussenblatt (ed.), *Theodor Herzl Jahrbuch* (Vienna, 1937), 22 ff.

[35] Ibid., 9 Feb. 1882; see also Leon Kellner, *Theodor Herzls Lehrjahre (1860–1895)* (Vienna, 1920), 127–34.

[36] Kellner, p. 133.   [37] Ibid. 132.

become damp; they refuse to ignite. Modern fuel is needed for them to blaze jollily, for spluttering Jew-fat to send up its savoury smell to the straight noses of Protestants, of those free-thinkers who replace the Dominicans, who in medieval times supervised such matters. From fire to loot—or vice versa— Herr Dühring and company hunt for loot and find it . . . Greed is the low, stinking motive of all movements against the Jews . . . the only change has been more sophistication, erudition, intelligence . . .[38]

Herzl's rage did not blind him to the qualities of Dühring's German prose-style. Indeed, he even felt that Jews had something to learn from the pitiless exposure of their faults to be found in the book.[39] But Herzl had no doubt that Dühring was ultimately an enemy, a cruel and vengeful slanderer of the Jews. Racial prejudices had led the German anti-Semite to exaggerate and also to overlook the historical conditioning of Jewish qualities.[40] In 1882, the young Herzl still remained confident that enlightened tolerance would eventually win the day. 'Yet despite new nursery tales against the modern Jews, one hopes for a brighter future in which humane, unimpassioned men will look back upon contemporary anti-Jewish movements as educated people, even educated anti-Semites, today look back at those of the Middle Ages.'[41]

The shock of Dühring's racist assault on Jewry, followed by his traumatic experience with the Albia fraternity, were not yet enough to transform Herzl into a Zionist. The new Teutonic racialism pioneered in Berlin and perfected in Vienna troubled him, wounded his pride, and forcefully reminded him that he was a Jew without making him a nationalist. Throughout the 1880s he remained unaware of the Zionist critique of assimilation undertaken by Moses Hess, Perez Smolenskin, Leon Pinsker, and Nathan Birnbaum. He knew nothing of Pinsker's *Autoemancipation* nor even of the student society Kadimah, established in 1883 at the University of Vienna. It almost seemed as if Herzl was deliberately evading the 'Jewish question' at the very moment that it became a major issue of contention in Austria.[42] There are no further references during his writings of the 1880s to the striking growth of

[38] Kellner, 132.

[39] Ibid. 128.

[40] Ibid. 131.

[41] Ibid. 134. Lewisohn in *Theodor Herzl: A Portrait for This Age*, somewhat unfairly regards this comment as an echo of 'the babble of the Enlightenment' (p. 39).

[42] However in his short autobiography, Herzl laconically describes his brief period in Salzburg as a judicial clerk, during 1884, in the following terms: 'I would have liked to have stayed in this beautiful town, but, as a Jew, I could never have advanced to the position of a Judge. I therefore bade goodbye to Salzburg and to the law business at the same time.'

political anti-Semitism in Russia, France, Germany, Hungary, Poland, and the Czech lands.

After obtaining a law degree at the University of Vienna in 1884, Herzl travelled widely throughout Europe. He turned out some thirty plays and sketches of plays, innumerable articles, travelogues, and short stories. Newspapers in Vienna and Berlin opened their columns to his witty *feuilletons*, a fragile and evanescent art-form in which Herzl displayed consummate mastery.[43] In 1887 he briefly became literary editor of Hertzka's *Wiener Allgemeine Zeitung*. Four years later he would be invited to fill the highly prestigious post of Paris correspondent of the *Neue Freie Presse*. Throughout his formative period during which he established his reputation as a popular dramatist, journalist, and litterateur, Herzl *publicly* avoided the 'Jewish question'. This should not however be taken as proof that it had ceased to preoccupy him.

In his 'Zionist' diary, begun in Paris around Pentecost 1895, Herzl noted that in the years following his first observations on Dühring, 'the question gnawed and tugged at me, tormented me and rendered me profoundly unhappy. In fact, I always came back to it whenever my own personal experiences—their joys and sorrows—lifted me to a higher plane.'[44] By his own admission, still bitterly vexed by the 'Jewish question', Herzl occasionally fantasized about slipping over 'into some corner of the Christian world'. But when the historian Dr Heinrich Friedjung, editor of the nationalist *Deutsche Wochenschrift*, advised him 'to adopt a pen name less Jewish than my own', he flatly refused.[45] Early in 1891, before arriving in Paris, Herzl had even thought of writing a 'Jewish' novel about his close friend Heinrich Kana, who had committed suicide in Berlin that February. He had intended to contrast the sufferings of poor Jews with the comfortable complacency of their richer brethren.

The four years which Herzl spent in Paris (1891–5) would change all this by providing a new perspective on the world and the causes of modern anti-Semitism.

In Paris I came into close contact with politics—at least as an observer. I saw how the world is governed. I stared, too, at the phenomenon of the crowd—for a long time without understanding it. I also attained here a freer and more detached attitude toward anti-Semitism, from which I did not suffer, at least in any direct manner. In Austria or Germany I constantly have to fear that

[43] Carl E. Schorske, *Fin-de-siècle Vienna: Politics and Culture* (London, 1980), 9–10.
[44] *Diaries*, 4.   [45] Ibid. 4–5.

someone will shout 'Hep, Hep!' at my heels. But here I pass through the crowd 'unrecognized'. In this 'unrecognized' lies a terrible reproach against the antisemites.[46]

Herzl had been aware of anti-Semitism throughout his life, whether as a schoolboy, a university student, or a young adult. He had encountered it in Hungary, in Germany, and especially on his 'home' soil in Austria. But only in Paris did he begin to see it as a universal phenomenon, to 'understand it historically and to pardon'. At the beginning of September 1892 he had published his first article on the subject, sparked by the killing of Captain Mayer (a young Jewish officer in the French army) by the aristocratic anti-Semite, the Marquis de Morès. Despite the sardonic humour, Herzl's report still maintained a degree of optimism.

Until recently there was a measure of decency in French anti-Semitism, one could almost say: courtesy . . . Even when it burst out against the Jews directly, it did not deny that they were human beings. For one coming here from other countries this was very surprising. In France the particular sin with which the Jews were charged was that they came from Frankfurt; the injustice is plain to see for some are from Mainz and even from Speyer. They are often called *Israélites*, which must be seen as expressing a more relaxed attitude. However, the Jews have been most fortunate of all in their death. When their brilliant lives, the object of so much envy, duly came to a successful end, these Jewish humans are buried among the Christian humans.[47]

This ironic distance was typical of Herzl's sketches on French public life—whether the subject was parliamentary politics, financial corruption, class warfare, anarchist terror, or the rise of anti-Semitism. But gradually an identifiable pattern began to emerge that reflected the parallels between the crises of the French Republic and the collapse of liberal ideals in his Austrian homeland. The rise of a mass politics on the Right and the Left, the loss of faith in the parliamentary system, the challenge to liberal rationalism in the arts and in philosophy were all symptoms of the crisis afflicting bourgeois Europe. Nowhere was the new irrationalism more visible than in the increasing prominence of the 'Jewish question'.[48] In 1893, Herzl momentarily thought that anti-Semitism might be contained by an even broader mass movement such as Social Democracy. In a long letter on the 'Jewish question' which he sent from Paris on 26 January 1893, Herzl informed Baron

---

[46] *Diaries*, 5–6.   [47] *Neue Freie Presse*, 3 Sept. 1892.
[48] Schorske, *Fin-de-Siècle Vienna*, 154–6.

Friedrich Leitenberger, a leading industrialist in Vienna: 'If one cannot suppress a movement, one reacts with another movement. By that I simply meant Socialism. It is my conviction that the Jews, pressed against the wall, will have no other alternative than Socialism.'[49]

Herzl was already convinced by 1892 of 'the emptiness and futility of trying to "combat" antisemitism' by establishing liberal Christian Leagues such as the Abwehrverein, presided over in Vienna by Baron Leitenberger.[50] The dramatic progress of the Lueger movement in Vienna and of increasingly visible anti-Semitic agitation in Paris, Berlin, and other European cities, would persuade him that universalist solutions of any kind to the 'Jewish question' were simply not viable.

There was a brief moment in 1893 when Herzl did flirt with the idea of solving the Jewish problem by personal combat. He even imagined himself challenging one of the leading Austrian anti-Semites—von Schoenerer, Lueger, or Prince Liechtenstein—to a duel. If he should lose his life he would become a martyr to 'the world's most unjust movement'. But should he win,

> then I would have delivered a brilliant speech which would have begun with my regrets for the death of a man of honor . . . Then I would have turned to the Jewish question and delivered an oration worthy of Lassalle. I would have sent a shudder of admiration through the jury. I would have compelled the respect of the judges, and the case against me would have been dismissed. Thereupon the Jews would have made me one of their representatives and I would have declined because I would refuse to achieve such a position by the killing of a man.[51]

From this 'affair of honour' Herzl passed to an even more archaic solution. He envisaged nothing less than the mass conversion of Austrian Jewry to Catholicism to be implemented in accordance with a bizarre code of chivalry. Baptism would be free and honourable, 'inasmuch as the leaders of this movement—myself in particular— would remain Jews, and as Jews would urge a conversion to the majority-faith. In broad daylight, on twelve o'clock of a Sunday, the exchange of faith would take place in St. Stephen's Cathedral, with solemn parade and the peal of bells.'[52]

[49] Chaim Bloch, 'Herzl's First Years of Struggle', *Herzl Year Book*, 3 (New York, 1960), 79.

[50] See ibid. 79–82; also *Diaries*, 6.

[51] Schorske, *Fin-de-siècle Vienna*, 160; Bein, *Theodore Herzl: A Biography*, 87–8.

[52] *Diaries*, 7. For Herzl's views on conversion, see Central Zionist Archives A, CZAJ HN III (305), letter of Herzl to Moritz Benedikt, 27 Dec. 1892, repr. in Theodor Herzl, *Briefe und Tagebücher: Briefe 1866–1895* (Frankfurt and Vienna, 1983), 507–8. 'Ich

The assimilationist editor of the *Neue Freie Presse*, Moritz Benedikt, vetoed this fantastic plan based on an approach by Herzl to the Pope in Rome through the Austrian Princes of the Church. His objection was moral as well as practical: 'For a hundred generations your race has clung fast to Judaism. You are proposing now to set yourself up as the man to end this stand. This you cannot do, and have no right to do. Besides, the Pope would never receive you.'[53]

Abandoning these childish fantasies, Herzl began to develop a new philosophical approach to anti-Semitism as a result of talks in Baden with the Austrian Jewish journalist and arts critic, Ludwig Speidel (1830–1906). The Jews had remained a foreign body among the nations, so Herzl reasoned with his Austrian friend, as a result of anti-social characterstics developed in the ghetto. The oppression and discrimination practised by the Catholic Church had forced them into usury and damaged their character. Even after emancipation they still remained 'ghetto Jews'. Concentrated in the liberal professions, they were creating 'a terrible pressure upon the earning powers of the middle classes, a pressure under which the Jews themselves really suffer most'.[54] Yet Herzl still believed that anti-Semitism would do the Jews no harm.

I hold it to be a movement useful for the development of Jewish character. It is the education of a group by the surrounding populations and will perhaps in the end lead to its absorption. We are educated only through hard knocks. A sort of Darwinian mimicry will set in. The Jews will adapt themselves.[55]

A few months later, while sitting for his bust in the studio in Paris of the Moravian-born Jewish sculptor, Samuel Friedrich Beer (1846–1912), Herzl conceived his last non-political attempt to overcome anti-Semitism. His play, *Das neue Ghetto* (1894), written at white heat in a mere seventeen days, depicted the familiar milieu of the assimilated Jewish bourgeoisie in Vienna. The main character, Dr Jacob Samuel, a high-minded Jewish lawyer, is married to Hermine, the spoiled, emotionally shallow daughter of a rich businessman.[56] The play begins

billige die Taufe jedes einzelnen Juden, der Kinder hat.' Herzl informed Benedikt that he would like to baptize his own son '. . . damit er die Kränkungen und Zurücksetzungen nicht habe, die ich hatte und noch haben werde aus dem Titel meiner Judenschaft'. What held him back was loyalty and gratitude to his father. Furthermore, he felt that as a matter of honour one should not abandon Jewry 'wenn es angefeindet ist' (p. 508).

[53] *Diaries*, 8.   [54] Ibid. 9–10.   [55] Ibid. 10.
[56] Herzl frequently depicted replicas of his wife Julie Naschauer in unflattering terms in his dramatic works. After Aug. 1891, his marriage on the rocks, Herzl was virtually separated from his wife and children. See *Diaries*, p. xv; Stewart, pp. 127–31, 147–51.

with his marriage and ends with Jacob's tragic death in a duel, shot by an anti-Semitic aristocrat and retired captain of cavalry, Count von Schramm; but not before he makes his dying statement onstage. 'O Jews, my brethren, they won't let you live again—until you . . . Why do you hold me so tight? (Mumbles) I want to—get—out! (Louder). Out—of—the—Ghetto!'[57]

In the play, Dr Samuel unashamedly confesses his debt of honour to his boyhood Gentile friend, Dr Franz Wurzlechner: 'I learned big things and little—inflections, gestures, how to bow without being obsequious, how to stand up without seeming defiant—all sorts of things.'[58] But Wurzlechner, who had taught his Jewish friend the code of gentlemanly conduct, decides to go into politics and promptly recognizes that with 'too many Jewish friends, brokers, speculators' he would automatically be labelled a *Judenknecht* (lackey of the Jews).

Dr Samuel's bourgeois milieu—the millionaire Bourse-Jew Rheinberg, the small stockbroker Wasserstein, the apostate physician Dr Bichler, and Rabbi Friedheimer—is scathingly depicted by Herzl as superficial, materialistic, and irredeemably warped by its 'ghetto' traits. Nevertheless, the market-playing Rabbi Friedheimer is permitted to defend the ghetto for its preservation of patriarchal family virtues. He warns Jacob: 'When there was still a real ghetto, we were not allowed to leave it without permission, on pain of severe punishment. Now the walls and barriers have become invisible, as you say. You are still rigidly confined to a moral ghetto. Woe to him who would desert it.'[59]

Jacob Samuel, escorting the Rabbi to the door, appears to express the playwright's view that 'the inner barriers we must clear away ourselves. We ourselves, on our own.' Escape from the ghetto involved much more than simply a struggle against Gentile anti-Semitism. It was above all a self-emancipation from negative Jewish qualities. The last thing Herzl had in mind was 'a defence of the Jews or a rescue-attempt on their behalf'. As he made clear in a letter to Arthur Schnitzler, rejecting the charge of misanthropy, he had no interest in presenting positive, sympathetic Jewish characters.[60]

Das neue Ghetto, which remained Herzl's favourite play, was not performed until 5 January 1898 at the Vienna Carl Theatre where it

[57] Theodor Herzl, *The New Ghetto*, trans. Heinz Norden (New York, 1955).
[58] Ibid.
[59] Ibid.; see also Stewart, pp. 149–50.
[60] See Olga Schnitzler, *Spiegelbild der Freundschaft* (Salzburg, 1962), 90 ff., for letters between Herzl and Schnitzler concerning the play.

ran for twenty-five performances. It marked an important stage in Herzl's movement towards a novel perception of the 'Jewish question'.[61] As in earlier plays, there was a marked element of social criticism, directed especially at the worship of money and the moral decadence of the Jewish and Gentile middle classes. Jacob Samuel at one point promises help to a coal miner in order to save workers' jobs and avoid a catastrophe in the mine, whose funds had been irresponsibly dissipated by its titled owner, Captain von Schramm. 'You are guilty', Samuel tells the owner (after the mine has been flooded and lives needlessly lost) 'because while pursuing your aristocratic pastimes, you permitted your slaves to drudge for you underground . . . for miserable starvation wages.'

Here, as elsewhere, Herzl expressed his objection to the tyrannical hold of money on society, a factor which strongly influenced his perception of the need to create a new type of Jew, free from any taint of egoistic materialism.[62] In 1894 he told Ludwig Speidel that the 'ruling powers forced us into the money-traffic' and as the Emperor's vassals (*Kammerknechte*), Jews had served as a medium for indirect taxation. 'We extracted from the people money which the rulers later robbed from us or confiscated. All of these sufferings rendered us odious and changed our character, which in former times had been proud and noble.'[63]

Zionism eventually became in Herzl's mind the way to overcome the corruption induced by this dominance of money-values in middle-class Jewish life. In a letter to Baron de Hirsch on 5 July 1895, he had complained that Jews seemed unable to understand 'that a man can act for other motives than money, that a man can refuse to be dominated by money without being a revolutionist'.[64] Herzl wanted to eradicate the unhealthy preoccupation with Mammon, along with other 'ghetto' traits of excessive restraint, timidity, and fear that were dysfunctional to the forging of an independent nation. For him, Zionism entailed a

---

[61] Lewisohn, pp. 46–9; Harry Zohn 'Three Austrian Jews in German Literature: Schnitzler, Zweig, Herzl', in J. Fraenkel (ed.), *The Jews of Austria: Essays on their Life, History and Destruction* (London, 1967), 79.

[62] Oskar K. Rabinowicz, 'Herzl the Playwright', *Jewish Book Annual*, 18 (1960–1), 100–15.

[63] *Diaries*, 9.

[64] Ibid. 26–7. Herzl liked to contrast himself, as the *condottiere* of the spirit, to Baron Hirsch as the *condottiere* of money. He knew how to distinguish none the less between great philanthropists like Hirsch and Baron Edmond de Rothschild, even when they refused to support his plans, and the rich parvenu class of upper middle-class Jews whom he detested.

radical transvaluation of values in the Nietzschean sense, the forging of 'a noble ideal of a new Jew, a man living by the myth of chivalry', who would be the antithesis of the old ghetto culture.[65] A diary entry of 8 June 1895, written after dining with some middle-class Jewish friends, revealed his awareness of the yawning gap between his own ego-ideal and that of his Viennese surroundings.

Well-to-do, educated, depressed people. They groaned under their breath against antisemitism . . . The husband expects a new St. Bartholomew's Night. The wife thinks that conditions could hardly be worse. They disputed whether it was good or bad that Lueger's election as mayor of Vienna had not been officially validated.

Their despondency took the heart out of me. They do not suspect it, but they are Ghetto creatures, quiet, decent, timorous. Most of our people are like that. Will they understand the call to freedom and manliness?[66]

Herzl's interview with the Baron de Hirsch in June 1895 revealed that he looked to Zionism to uplift the race, to make it strong for war, virtuous, and properly educated in the love of work.[67] The encouragement of deeds of 'great moral beauty', of *actions d'éclat*, must be part of the training in 'true manhood' that would liberate Jews from the legacy of the ghetto and its shabby occupations.[68] Herzl's emphasis on the importance of a flag ('with a flag you can lead men where you will'), of fantasy, visions, and imponderables in the organization of the masses was part of this same instinctive awareness of the psychological dynamics behind nationalist movements.[69] The aesthetic dimension, love of the dramatic gesture, and a feeling for the importance of liturgy, myth, and symbolism was perhaps the most obviously Viennese element in Herzl's politics.[70] In his collection of fragmentary thoughts for the *Judenstaat* Herzl confessed that 'in all this I am still the dramatist', taking 'poor, ragged fellows from the street', dressing them in beautiful garments, and allowing them to 'perform before the world a wonderful play which I have devised'.[71] Indeed it was in *fin-de-siècle*

---

[65] Loewenberg, pp. 169–71. See also A. Hertzberg's introd. to *The Zionist Idea*, 47–8, where he notes the 'Nietzschean strain in Herzl'—namely the Promethean overtones of his conception of mission, his will to change history, and his capacity to act alone.

[66] *Diaries*, 38–9.   [67] Ibid. 17.   [68] Ibid. 16–18.

[69] Ibid. 22. See also Schorske, *Fin-de-siècle Vienna*, 165, who points to Bismarck as Herzl's 'master and model' in the manipulation of the mysterious depths of the *Volksseele*.

[70] See Robert S. Wistrich, 'Theodor Herzl: Between Theatre and Politics', *Jewish Frontier* (July–Aug. 1982), pp. 12–13.

[71] Ibid. Herzl added: 'I do not operate anymore with individual people but with masses: clergy, army administration, academy, etc. all for me—mass-units'.

Vienna that he had perfected this art of dramatic orchestration, with which he captured the imagination of the Jewish masses and impressed Zionism as a political movement on the consciouslness of the outside world.

This ability to weave the illusion of power, to create the mood and then forge the will for nationhood in a demoralized and dispersed people, owed much to those theatrical talents that Herzl had developed in his pre-Zionist stage of development.[72] 'With nations', he once said, 'one must speak in a childish language: a house, a flag, a song are the symbols of communication.'[73] The same dramatic flair was apparent in his staging of the First Zionist Congress as an elegant, impressive, festive spectacle and in his stubborn insistence that delegates wear formal dress.[74] Peter Loewenberg has admirably summed up this gift: 'Herzl was a man of the theatre who brought the theatre into politics, making drama of politics. He had the capacity to pass from the unreal to the real, to mix the spheres of drama and politics, to transfer the enchantment of make-believe staging to the world of diplomacy and political power.'[75]

Herzl's passage to Zionism was not unrelated to an unconscious desire to turn politics into a more successful drama, with himself as stage-manager, director, and leading actor.[76] In the new play which he

[72] Carl Schorske's ingenious comparison of Herzl, von Schoenerer, and Lueger as Austrian masters of the political *Gesamtkunstwerk* (to which one could of course add Adolf Hitler) suffers from an unfortunate failure to distinguished between constructive and destructive goals. To place the pioneers of mass anti-semitism and of the Jewish national home on the same plane as 'political artists'—even if only by implication—is dangerously misleading. None the less, Schorske's insights into Herzl are many and stimulating; see *Fin-de-siècle Vienna*, 146–75.

[73] Quoted in Loewenberg, p. 167. See also *Diaries*, 36–8, 7 June 1895. Two days earlier, listening to Wagner's *Tannhäuser* at the Paris Opera, Herzl had been fascinated by the ability of a crowd to sit for hours 'tightly packed, motionless, bodily torture . . .', all for the sake of an imponderable—'for sounds, tones and pictures!' (*Diaries*, 33). This apparently confirmed his feelings about the importance of symbolism.

[74] Ibid. 224, 3 Sept. 1897: 'People must be brought to expect only the finest things from the Congress and the utmost solemnity.'

[75] Loewenberg, p. 166.

[76] Herzl planned the mass emigration of the Jews in dramatic terms, down to the last detail. See, e.g., *Diaries*, 40–1, 9 June 1895, where he declares: 'Therefore I shall transport over there genuine Vienna cafés. With these small expedients I ensure the desirable illusion of the old environment. Must give attention to these minute needs, they are very important.' On the other hand, in an entry of 4 June 1902, Herzl noted the irony that he had become a 'renowned propagandist' in an area that he felt to be peripheral to the real centre of his personality. 'And yet I feel, I know, that I am by instinct a great writer . . . who failed to yield his true harvest only because he became nauseated and discouraged.'

would stage, the theme was to be: 'the poignant salvation of a people, the plot was one man's vision and sacrifice, which would overcome all odds, the supporting cast was the rulers of the world's nations, and the backdrop was the grim tale of antisemitism and racial persecution in European history.'[77]

Herzl's conversion to Zionism clearly presupposed that the liberal project of assimilation in Central Europe had failed.[78] In *Der Judenstaat* (1896) he wrote:

We have everwhere tried sincerely to merge with the surrounding national community [*Volksgemeinschaft*], seeking only to maintain the faith of our fathers. It is not permitted us. In vain are we loyal patriots, even superloyal in some places; in vain do we make the same sacrifices of blood and property as our fellow citizens; in vain do we strive to increase the fame of our native lands in the arts and sciences or their wealth by trade and commerce. In our native lands, where we have lived for centuries we are still decried as aliens [*Fremdlinge*]; often by those whose ancestors had not yet arrived at a time when Jewish sighs had long been heard in the country. Who the alien is, that is something decideded by the majority; it is a matter of power [*eine Machtfrage*] like everything else in the relations between nations.[79]

The radical Zionist view that anti-Semitism had rendered liberal assimilationist objectives impossible has often been attributed to the impact on Herzl of the Dreyfus affair. Certainly, he had witnessed the degradation of Captain Alfred Dreyfus (a French-Jewish officer convicted of selling military secrets to the Germans) in Paris on 22 December 1894. His dispatches reveal that he was indeed shocked by the cry of the Parisian mob at the École Militaire: 'À mort! À mort les juifs!'[80] Nevertheless, Herzl's comments on Dreyfus's trial did not suggest any direct connection with his conversion to Zionism.[81] Only after the announcement of the second verdict of guilty against the

[77] Loewenberg, p. 167.

[78] Alain Boyer, 'Assimilation et sionisme chez Herzl', in *Aspects du Sionisme: Théorie—utopie—histoire* (Actes de l'Atelier International INALCO tenu au Collège de France, Paris, 1982), 66–77.

[79] Theodor Herzl, *Der Judenstaat* 11th edn., (Jerusalem, 1946), 11.

[80] See Benjamin Seff (Herzl's *nom de plume* based on his Hebrew name, Binyamin Ze'ev), 'Conditions in France', in Lewisohn, p. 210: 'The mob did not cry "Down with Dreyfus!" It howled "Down with the Jews!" That was the keynote from the first moment and that is the keynote today.'

[81] See, e.g., Herzl's article on the revision of the case in *Die Welt*, 3, no. 23, 9 June 1899; trans. in Lewisohn, pp. 212–16, where the affair is seen as a victory for the liberal banner of truth and justice. The universalistic conclusion is that 'all men are bidden to the table where humanity feasts'.

Jewish officer in September 1899, did Herzl publicly draw the
conclusion that Dreyfus's fate represented that of the Jew as a whole in
modern society: '. . . the Jew who tries to adapt himself to his
environment, to speak its language, to think its thoughts, to sew its
insignia on his sleeves—only to have them ruthlessly ripped away.'[82]

Nearly five years after the original trial, in an article for the *North
American Review* (1899), Herzl first wrote that the Dreyfus case had
made him into a Zionist.[83] It had not simply been a miscarriage of
justice but 'contained the wish of the overwhelming majority in
France, to damn a Jew, and in this one Jew, all Jews'.[84] Herzl now
concluded that it was the people itself who, 'in republican, modern,
civilized France, one hundred years after the Declaration of the Rights
of Man', had spontaneously revoked the edict of the Great Revolution.[85]

Even if we assume that the violence of French anti-Semitism during
the Dreyfus affair shocked him, the evidence does not substantiate the
widely held assumption that this was a decisive factor in making him
into a fully-fledged Zionist.[86] There is not a single word about Captain
Dreyfus in the early part of Herzl's Zionist Diaries, begun only four
months after the degradation scene which he had witnessed in the
École Militaire in Paris. Indeed, the subject is scarcely discussed in the
diaries. Similarly, in *Der Judenstaat* the case is altogether ignored,
while French anti-Semitism is seen as little more than a social
irritant.[87] This silence stands in marked contrast to the constant
preoccupation in Herzl's Diaries with Vienna and the growth of
Austrian anti-Semitism, scarcely surprising in view of Lueger's
crushing electoral victories back home.[88]

[82] Benjamin Seff, 'Five Against Two' (first pub. in *Die Welt*, 3, no. 37, 15 Sept.
1899), Lewisohn, p. 220.

[83] 'Zionismus', in his *Zionistische Schriften*, i (3rd edn., Tel Aviv, 1934), 374–6. 'Zum
Zionisten hat mich nämlich—der Prozess Dreyfus gemacht. Nicht der jetzige in Rennes,
sondern der ursprüngliche in Paris, dessen Zeuge ich 1894 war.'

[84] Ibid. 375.

[85] Ibid. 376: 'Das Volk, wenigstens ein sehr grosser Teil davon, will nicht mehr die
Menschenrechte für die Juden.'

[86] The arguments against attaching too great an importance to the Dreyfus case have
been well made by Henry J. Cohn, 'Theodor Herzl's Conversion to Zionism', *Jewish
Social Studies* (Apr. 1970), pp. 101–10.

[87] *Der Judenstaat*, 19, contrasts Austria where 'anti-Semites terrorise the whole of
public life' to Germany where Jews 'occasionally get a good beating' and France, where
Jews 'are shut out of the so-called best circles and excluded from clubs'. Even in his
Jewish Chronicle autobiography of 14 Jan. 1898, which recalls that 'during the last two
months of my residence in Paris I wrote the book "The Jewish State"', there is no
mention of Dreyfus or French anti-Semitism.

[88] For one of many examples, see *Diaries*, 69, 20 Sept. 1895, which *inter alia* also

Der Judenstaat should not therefore be attributed to any one cause but rather to a succession of political events in France and Austria during the 1890s and their interaction with Herzl's complex personality. The tract was in fact written in a semi-mystical state of ecstasy and possession.[89] Herzl was fully aware that his Zionist project might be taken as the extravagant imaginings of a madman and that (as he wrote to Bismarck), 'the first impulse of every rational human being must be to send me to the observation room—Department for Inventors of Dirigible Balloons'.[90]

In spite of his momentary self-doubt, Herzl's *Der Judenstaat* was essentially a sober, rational analysis of the 'Jewish question' with a detailed and practical plan of operation. In contrast to older liberal views of anti-Semitism as a vestigial relic of the Middle Ages, Herzl contended that it was a product of emancipation—even a consequence of its outward success. The Jews, he argued, had already become a bourgeois people in the ghetto. In the aftermath of emancipation, they had emerged as particularly dangerous economic competitors for the Gentile middle classes. Accelerated assimilation into the wider society and the growth of Christian envy at Jewish wealth had exacerbated anti-Semitism; so, too, had well-intentioned Jewish responses such as emigration—which merely spread anti-Semitism to the lands where Jews emigrated—or socialism, which had accentuated the exposed position of the Jews at the poles of capitalist society.[91] The causes of anti-Semitism were ineradicable and rooted in the very structure of Diasporic Jewish life:

We are what the ghetto made us. We have without doubt attained pre-eminence in finance because medieval conditions drove us to it. The same

contrasted 'the turmoil of popular agitation in Paris' with the more sinister calm and hostility of Vienna. 'In Vienna the City Council elections were held on the day before Erev Rosh Hashanah. The anti-Semites won all the vacancies. The mood among the Jews reflects despair. The Christians are in an inflammatory state . . . Towards evening I went to the Landstrasse district. A silent tense crowd before the polling station. Suddenly Dr Lueger appeared in the square. Wild cheering; women waving white kerchiefs from the windows. The police held the people back.' Herzl also recorded the loving fervour in the words, spoken by a man next to him in the crowd, who said: '*Das ist unser Führer.*'

[89] 'Theodor Herzl, An Autobiography', *Jewish Chronicle*, 14 Jan. 1898: 'I do not recall ever having written anything in such an elevated frame of mind as that book.' His only relaxation was listening to Wagner's music, especially the opera *Tannhäuser*, but this coincidence does not make Zionism into a Wagnerian *Gesamtkunstwerk*, in spite of Schorske's imaginative argument; see *Fin-de-siècle Vienna*, 163.

[90] Quoted in David Vital, *The Origins of Zionism* (Oxford, 1975), 245.

[91] *Der Judenstaat*, 20–1.

process is now being repeated. We are again being forced into money-lending—by being kept out of other occupations. But once on the stock exchange, we are again objects of contempt. At the same time we continue to produce an abundance of mediocre intellectuals [*mittlere Intelligenzen*] who find no outlet, and this is no less a danger to our social position than our increasing wealth. The educated and propertyless Jews are now rapidly becoming socialists. Hence we shall certainly suffer acutely in the social struggle [between classes] . . .[92]

Herzl regarded anti-Semitism as a highly complex movement containing 'elements of cruel sport, vulgar commercial rivalry [*gemeiner Brotneid*], inherited prejudice, religious intolerance' and even of Gentile self-defence.[93] He pointed out that 'the old prejudices against us are still deeply ingrained in the folk ethos' (*Volksgemüt*) and that 'folk wisdom and folkore are both antisemitic'.[94] These prejudices might theoretically be overcome through full assimilation (i.e. intermarriage). But this socio-historical process had been blocked in the Gentile middle classes where the 'Jewish question' was centred.[95] In any event, Herzl no longer believed that the Jews as a people could or should even wish to assimilate.

The distinctive nationality of the Jews neither can, will, nor must perish. It cannot, because external enemies consolidate it. It does not wish to as two thousand years of appalling suffering have proved. It need not as I am trying to prove in this pamphlet, in the wake of countless other Jews who did not give up hope. Whole branches of Jewry may wither and fall away. The tree lives on.[96]

Herzl made it clear that he now regarded the Jews as 'one people' (*ein Volk*) and the 'Jewish question' as pre-eminently a *national* question whose solution would have to be discussed 'by the civilized nations of the world in council'.[97] Since there was no reasonable hope for the disappearance of anti-Semitism, an orderly exodus of the Jews to their own homeland and the creation there of a sovereign Jewish State would have to be rapidly worked out in conjunction with the Great Powers. This exodus would permit 'an inner emigration of Christian citizens into the positions evacuated by the Jews . . .'. The voluntary departure of the Jews would not be accompanied by economic disturbances, crises, or persecutions but on the contrary remove the object of anti-Semitism and hence its motivation.

[92] *Der Judenstaat*, 20–1.
[93] Ibid. 11.   [94] Ibid. 12.   [95] Ibid. 13.
[96] Ibid. 14: 'Die Volkspersönlichkeit der Juden kann, will und muss aber nicht untergehen.'   [97] Ibid. 11.

Responsibility for the exodus would be assumed by a political body called the Society of Jews to be established in London. Their resettlement was to be assured by the Jewish Company, to which the longest chapter in Herzl's pamphlet is devoted.[98] On the crucial question of a territory, Herzl was still undecided in 1896 between Palestine or Argentina, though clearly leaning towards 'our unforgettable homeland'.

The very name [of Palestine] would be a force of extraordinary potency for attracting our people. If His Majesty the Sultan were to give us Palestine, we would in return undertake to regulate the finances of Turkey. There we should form a portion of a rampart for Europe against Asia, we would be an outpost of civilization [*Kultur*] against barbarism. We should as a neutral state remain in contact with all of Europe, which would have to guarantee our existence. The Holy Places of Christendom would be placed under some form of international extraterritoriality. We should form a guard of honour about these holy places . . . [which] would be the great symbol of the solution of the Jewish question after 1800 years of Jewish suffering.[99]

Der Judenstaat placed Zionism on the map of international politics, forcing a public discussion of the 'Jewish question', exactly as Herzl had hoped. It signalled the beginning of his seven-year involvement with the organization and diplomacy at the head of the world Zionist movement, which was institutionalized at the First Congress in Basle (29–31 August 1897).[100] This story has been told elsewhere and need not detain us here, except as it touches on the history of Viennese Jewry—a community with whose leadership Herzl was soon set on a collision course. Whatever personal respect and even admiration they might feel for Herzl, the movement he represented remained anathema in the eyes of the Kultusgemeinde.[101]

To understand better the bitterness which much of Jewish bourgeois Vienna came to feel towards Herzl one must recall the enthusiastic affection and esteem with which the pre-Zionist *feuille-*

---

[98] Ibid. 30–50. In this chapter, Herzl proposed a seven-hour working day, healthy housing, good schools, and restriction on women's labour, and emphasized that the *Judenstaat* must be based on advanced principles of social justice.

[99] Ibid. 28.

[100] See Vital, *The Origins of Zionism*, 267–375, *Zionism: The Formative Years* (Oxford, 1982) for the most authoritative account.

[101] See *Diaries*, 88, for the stunned reaction of Theodor Lieben, secretary of the Vienna Jewish community, to Herzl's 'Utopia'; also 'Die Wahlen in der österreichischen Cultusgemeinden', *Die Welt*, 9 Nov. 1900. See also 'Wiener Wahlen', *Die Welt*, no. 46, 14 Nov. 1902, pp. 1–2, and 'Die Wahlen in die Wiener Kultusgemeinde', no. 47, 21 Nov. 1902, pp. 1–2, for the Herzlian programme of democratizing communal life.

toniste of the *Neue Freie Presse* and the littérateur of *Jung Wien* had once been regarded by these same circles. Before 1896 they were fascinated by his brilliant sparkling essays with their pathos, lucidity, and charm, by the elegance of his aphorisms and the refinement of his ironic scepticism. As Stefan Zweig recalled:

None was better able to give unconsciously what the Viennese wanted. When, in collaboration with a colleague, he wrote a graceful comedy for the *Burgtheater*, it was just right, just what everyone wanted, a dainty morsel made of the finest ingredients and artistically served. Moreover, the man was strikingly handsome—courteous, obliging, entertaining; indeed, none was more beloved, better known or more celebrated than he among the entire bourgeoisie—and also the aristocracy—of old Austria.

This popularity, however, suddenly received a terrible blow. As the century approached its close there gradually penetrated a rumour . . . that this graceful, aristocratic, masterly *causeur* had, without warning, written an abstruse treatise which demanded nothing more nor less than that the Jews should leave their Ringstrasse homes and their villas, their businesses and their offices—in short, that they should emigrate, bag and baggage, to Palestine, there to establish a nation.[102]

The most serious personal consequence of this irritation, ridicule, and even hostility to which he was henceforth subjected lay its effect on his position in the *Neue Freie Presse*. The newspaper for which he had worked as literary editor since his return from Paris in 1895 remained as ever a stronghold of German-orientated liberalism and cosmopolitan Jewish intellectualism of the classic assimilationist variety. Its proprietor and editor-in-chief Moritz Benedikt (1849–1920) once told Raoul Auernheimer (1876–1948), a cousin of Herzl and a well-known member of the *Jung Wien* literary circle; 'I am not *pro*-Jewish; I am not *anti*-Jewish; I am *a*-Jewish.'[103]

The *Neue Freie Presse* had traditionally espoused a policy of passivity, silence, and *attentisme* towards radical, anti-liberal movements (including anti-Semitism), a strategy with which Herzl had decisively broken.

[102] Stefan Zweig, 'König der Juden', in *Theodor Herzl: A Memorial*, ed. Meyer W. Weisgal (New York, 1929), 55; repr. in *Herzl Year Book*, 3 (New York, 1960), 110.

[103] Raoul Auernheimer, 'Beard of the Prophet', *Herzl Year Book*, 6 (New York, 1964–5), 75. This article is a slightly abridged version of a chapter in Auernheimer's autobiography, *Das Wirtshaus zur verlorenen Zeit* (Vienna, 1948). Though Auernheimer was himself a believer in enlightened cosmopolitanism he saw Herzl's Zionism as a logical and realistic response to 19th-cent. European nationalisms, indeed 'the last link in the chain'. It was not surprising, he added, 'that this national movement of protest arose in Austria, where it had been preceded by Hungarian, Czech, Polish, Yugoslavian and Italian asserverations of national independence—not to mention the German ones'.

Even before his conversion to Zionism, Herzl's bold advice to Eduard Bacher (1846–1908), co-editor and proprietor of the newspaper, that the Austrian Liberals should support universal suffrage, had been unceremoniously rejected. In serious political matters Herzl was still considered by his superiors as a mere chatterer and *feuilletoniste*.[104] Nevertheless he had hoped for a sympathetic hearing from Bacher on his *Judenstaat* ideas. But following their first discussion of the issue in September 1895 it was clear that 'he [Bacher] would likely fight them tooth and nail'.[105] Bacher believed that anti-Semitism was an 'unpleasant' but essentially ephemeral movement.[106] Shortly afterwards, when Herzl brought up the subject with Moritz Benedikt, the editor-in-chief emphatically refused to open the columns of the *Neue Freie Presse* to a discussion of Zionism, arguing: 'Your idea is a powerful machine-gun and it may go off backwards.'[107]

Herzl realized that his determination to persist with Zionism was leading him to an inevitable collision with his Viennese employers in which his future with the newspaper might be at stake.[108] In a conversation on 3 February 1896, Bacher warned Herzl that anti-Semites everywhere would seize on his claim that Jews could not assimilate, picking out of his text whatever suited their purpose and quoting it 'forever after'.[109] The next day Benedikt strongly urged Herzl to desist from publishing the *Judenstaat* on the grounds that he was risking his established literary prestige and damaging the paper. Zionism, he emphasized, contradicted the liberal principles of the *Neue Freie Presse*. Benedikt further argued that it was wrong for Herzl to take upon himself 'the tremendous moral responsibility of setting this avalanche in motion—endangering so many interests'. As the

---

[104] *Diaries*, 7–8.

[105] Ibid. 66. In a letter to Rabbi Moritz Güdemann on 22 Aug. 1895, Herzl had said that he would explain everything to Bacher—and he must decide whether it calls for action or for novel-writing . . .'. In the entry of 20 Sept. 1895, ibid. 67, it was already evident that 'he [Bacher] would be absolutely closed to my ideas . . .'.

[106] Ibid. 67.

[107] Ibid. 70; also Bein, *Herzl: A Biography*, 153–6. Herzl had been offered the editorship of the old Vienna 'Presse' at this time (20 Sept. 1895) by the new Austrian Prime Minister, Count Casimir Badeni, a tempting, though more or less 'official' position which he ultimately rejected. His attempt to use this offer to soften the *Neue Freie Presse*'s line against Zionism failed. But the proprietors of the paper grudgingly agreed to give him a furlough to evaluate the whole Zionist plan, by setting up a 'Study Commission' in Paris or London.

[108] *Diaries*, 89, entry of 1 Feb. 1896: 'I already feel that, regardless of my able work, they consider me a liability.'

[109] Ibid.

editor-in-chief saw it: 'We shall no longer have our present fatherland, and shall not yet have the Jewish state.'[110] Herzl, who had already published a synopsis of the *Judenstaat* in the London *Jewish Chronicle*, refused to bow to this pressure.[111] Benedikt in turn threatened, cajoled, and flattered him—emphasizing that as 'one of our most distinguished collaborators, you are part and parcel of the *Neue Freie Presse*—all to no avail.[112]

The continuing duel with his employers became more acrimonious when in 1897 Herzl founded the Zionist weekly *Die Welt* and it transpired that a number of its leading writers were also on the staff of the *Neue Freie Presse*. On 18 June 1897 the authoritarian Benedikt warned that *Die Welt* must either disappear or else Herzl must sever all connections with it. Herzl recorded the clash as follows:

> Benedikt sought, as a friend, to dissuade me from my 'stubbornness'. Then a threat: I could not take my furlough until I had given him a definite answer, that is to say, stop the publication of *Die Welt*. Then a promise: he guaranteed I should not regret it if I complied with his wish . . . Furthermore, I must not play a prominent part at the [Zionist] Congress, I must not step to the fore.[113]

Having exerted 'all the weight of his superior position' Benedikt then disclaimed any intent to intimidate his literary editor: 'Of course I am not trying to coerce your conscience—only you must do nothing that may hurt the *Neue Freie Presse*.'[114]

Bacher, while echoing Benedikt's threat against *Die Welt* and forcefully advising him against becoming an 'itinerant Zionist preacher', was more amiable and paternalistic towards Herzl.[115] On one occasion, on 19 March 1897, Bacher even confessed that he would like to visit Palestine. Recounting an old Jewish legend relating to the origins of the *Altneuschul* (the famous Old-New synagogue) in Prague, Bacher remarked on the continuity in Jewish national consciousness through the centuries.[116]

---

[110] *Diaries*, 91–2, entry of 4 Feb. 1896.

[111] See Herzl, 'The Solution of the Jewish Question', *Jewish Chronicle*, 17 Jan. 1896. The German text first appeared in Dr Bloch's *Österreichische Wochenschrift*, 21 Feb. 1896.

[112] *Diaries*, 92. At one point Benedikt even exclaimed, 'You are in fact no Austrian at all, but a Hungarian'—to which Herzl firmly retorted, 'I am an Austrian citizen.'

[113] Ibid. 216–17.

[114] Ibid. 217. Herzl cooly noted the irony that it was liberals like Benedikt who wrote 'indignant editorials whenever a Minister restricts some freedom of opinion on the part of his officials'.

[115] Ibid. 219–20, entry of 23 Aug. 1897.   [116] Ibid. 203–4.

Herzl's superiors none the less remained adamant in refusing to publicize or even discuss Zionism in their powerful newspaper. They privately regarded Herzl's involvement in the Zionist movement as a foolish, inexplicable act verging on madness. But they were not prepared to dispense with his highly valued services as literary editor. Herzl, for his part, as a result of his heavy financial outlays in Zionism, had become more dependent than ever on his income at the *Neue Freie Presse*. On 24 August 1899 he wrote:

I have to tremble lest I be dismissed; I don't dare to take the holiday which my health requires, for I have already been away from my desk for six weeks—the whole of it spent on active service for Zionism. So, once more, I return today to the office, after having been a free and mighty lord at Basle, [the Third Zionist Congress] and enter my employer Bacher's room like a submissive clerk back from vacation. Cruel![117]

A wandering Jewish statesman without a state, Herzl was therefore obliged to lead a schizophrenic existence in Vienna after 1897. At one and the same time, he was the celebrated leader of an international movement and the 'wage slave' of the mighty *Neue Freie Presse*, in constant dread that neglect of his responsibilities might lose him an indispensable source of income. Moreover, his failure to persuade Benedikt to recognize the existence of Zionism seriously hampered the progress of the movement in Austria. In an interview on 30 April 1904 with the Polish-born Foreign Minister of Austria-Hungary, Count von Goluchowski, Herzl commented ironically on this disappointment.

Here in Austria, I said, our movement is relatively unknown, owing to the silence of the *Neue Freie Presse*. This in turn is due to the fact that Benedikt denies the existence of a Jewish people. I happen to affirm this with a simple proposition: The proof of their existence is that I am one of them.

And he? asked Goluchoswki, what is he? A Protestant? No. [Herzl answers]. He belongs to a species which I have never laid eyes on. He is an Austrian. I am acquainted with Germans, Poles, Czechs—but I've never yet seen an Austrian . . .[118]

[117] Ibid. 319, entry of 24 Aug. 1899.
[118] Ibid. 437–8, entry of 2 May 1904. Count von Goluchowski was sympathetic to Zionism but preferred another power to take the initiative, in particular England. He also advised Herzl that winning over the Hungarian government was indispensable. Von Goluchowski's positive response to Herzl derived largely from Russian governmental interest in Zionism. In that respect he was different from two earlier Austrian Prime Ministers, Count Badeni (1895–7) and Ernst von Körber (1900–4), who had sought Herzl's advice on *domestic* policy and hoped to use his journalistic services to break the monopoly of the *Neue Freie Presse* but were uninterested in Zionism. See Isaiah

The Diary records that 'the Austrian Minister for Foreign Affairs smiled in agreement'.

Another disappointment to Herzl in his adopted home of Vienna was the Rothschild family. *Der Judenstaat* had originally been prepared as a 20,000 word 'Address to the Rothschilds' and he tried hard to win them over to his project.[119] Herzl was convinced that with their help, the solution of the Jewish problem would be much easier and obviate the need for turning to the masses.[120] In the 'Address' he had sought to prove that the Jews, and especially the House of Rothschild, were seriously threatened by anti-Semitism. In Russia the property of the Jews would be confiscated, in Germany there would be anti-Jewish legislation, and in Austria a wave of pogroms would break out. The Jews would be expelled from all these countries and some of them killed in flight. Hence a Jewish State must be created to avoid this danger and the Rothschilds should invest their capital in this venture.[121] Herzl was persuaded that the Rothschild family should direct his proposed 'Society of Jews' and the 'Jewish Company', taking in hand the political work for the establishment of the new State. Neither his father Jacob (who from the outset disbelieved in the possibility of the Rothschilds' co-operation) nor Rabbi Güdemann, nor even his closest lieutenant, Max Nordau, could dissuade Herzl from this approach.[122]

Through Moritz Güdemann, Herzl hoped to set up a meeting with

Friedman, 'The Austro-Hungarian Government and Zionism: 1897–1918', *Jewish Social Studies* (July 1965), pp. 147–67.

[119] See Josef Fraenkel, 'Herzl and the Rothschild Family', *Herzl Year Book*, 3 (New York, 1960), 217–36. Herzl looked to the Chief Rabbi of Vienna, Güdemann, to approach Albert von Rothschild; Zadok Kahn (Chief Rabbi of France) and Nordau were to intercede with Edmond de Rothschild in Paris; while Joseph Cowen, J. L. Greenberg, and Zangwill were to see Nathan Meyer Rothschild in London.

[120] *Diaries*, 188, entry of 19 July 1896, recounting 'two hours of hot and heavy argument' with Baron Edmond de Rothschild in Paris. Herzl told the Baron that, he was the 'keystone of the entire combination' and that he had wanted 'to hand over the direction of the whole enterprise to you, the philanthropic Zionist, and eliminate myself'. He declared that Rothschild's refusal would force him 'to set the masses in motion by indiscriminate agitation', exactly what he had wished to avoid.

[121] Fraenkel, 'Herzl and the Rothschild Family', 218–19.

[122] See, however, the conclusion to Herzl's entry of 18 Aug. 1895, after he had read his 'Address' to Rabbi Güdemann and the Berlin philanthropist, Heinrich Meyer-Cohn, in a Munich restaurant. 'We came to the conclusion that the "Address" should not be laid before the Rothschilds, who are vulgar and contemptuous egotists. The idea must be carried immediately to the people, and in the form of a novel . . . I have to believe Güdemann and Meyer-Cohn when they tell me that the "Big Jews" are not to be had.' (*Diaries*, 64.)

Albert von Rothschild (1844–1911), the head of the Vienna branch of the family, in order to read him the 'Address'. Impatient of the delays, Herzl wrote a long personal letter to Albert Rothschild on 28 June 1895, declaring his readiness to travel from Paris to Vienna to explain his ideas. Herzl informed the Viennese Rothschild:

I am only trying to overcome anti-Semitism, where it originated and where its main source still remains—in Germany. I consider the Jewish question as extremely grave. Whoever believes that Jew-hatred is merely a passing phase is greatly mistaken. It must continually worsen until the inevitable revolution breaks out . . .[123]

Albert Rothschild did not deign to answer this letter or care to listen to the 'Address', a deeply wounding rebuff that finally prompted Herzl to publish his outline as *Der Judenstaat*, after deleting some passages in it specifically addressed to the Rothschild family. To his chagrin, he was to discover that it was easier to obtain an invitation from the Turkish Sultan, the German Emperor, from Russian Imperial statesmen, British Cabinet Ministers, and even his Holiness the Pope than from the Rothschild family. Herzl did not, however, abandon his efforts to win over the English and French Rothschilds even though Albert Rothschild was henceforth beyond the pale. In Herzl's novel *Altneuland* (1902), he is evoked in unflattering terms through the character of Baron von Goldstein.

Herzl's dealings with wealthy, influential Jews like the Rothschilds and Baron de Hirsch reflected a certain ambiguity in his attitudes to financial power. Evidently he believed that he was providing the Rothschilds and Hirsch with a great historical mission—to organize the Jewish exodus from Europe.[124] Their capital resources were an essential part of his strategy of persuasion aimed at gaining the support of the Turkish Sultan and the European Great Powers for the resettlement of the Jews in Palestine. When they failed to respond, Herzl immediately threatened to mobilize the Jewish masses against the plutocracy.[125] The warnings he issued against the rich Jews had a

[123] Fraenkel, 'Herzl and the Rothschild Family', 219.
[124] See *Diaries*, 35, 7 June 1895: 'I bring to the Rothschilds and the big Jews their historical mission, *J'accueillerai toutes les bonnes volontés*—we *must* be united—*et écraserai les mauvaises* (I warn the Rothschild family council).'
[125] See *Diaries*, 193, for Herzl's letter of 26 July 1896 to the Chief Rabbi of France, Zadok Kahn. 'I am an opponent of the House of Rothschild because I consider it to be a national misfortune for the Jews.' In London on 11 July 1896 Herzl had said that he did not want a demagogic movement, but 'if the gentry should prove too genteel', he was willing to set the masses in motion.

somewhat intimidatory and demagogic ring. Nevertheless, Herzl was no socialist wolf in sheep's clothing. He recognized, for example, the utility and indispensability of the Stock Exchange. But he also tended to blame the 'Bourse-Jews' for the growth of anti-Semitism.[126] Like Theodor Hertzka, his distinguished Viennese contemporary, he sought a middle road between liberalism and Marxism that would maintain private enterprise while guaranteeing the welfare of the poor through an enlightened *Sozialpolitik*.

Herzl's pronounced sensitivity to human suffering and the economic inequalities of bourgeois society preceded his conversion to Zionism. In 1893 he proposed a plan of *assistance par le travail* (help through work) to the Austrian government based on a West European model of restoring the unemployed masses to productive labour.[127] In Vienna he supported the strike of the exploited streetcar workers for a shortening of their working day, even though Jews were among the stockholders in the streetcar company.[128] In his notes and jottings in June 1895 concerning the *Judenstaat*, he wrote: 'No women or children shall work in our factories. We want a vigorous race. The State shall take care of needy women and children.'[129]

On 11 June 1895 the thought struck Herzl that he was solving not only the Jewish question but '*tout bonnement*, the social question!' The key lay in the creation of new economic conditions on virgin soil, which would demonstrate how to free humanity from 'ancient abuses, habitual inertia, and inherited or acquired wrongs'.[130] The reproach of toying with state socialism did not disconcert Herzl, provided 'the State aims at the right things'—i.e. not the advantages of a group or caste 'but the gradual ascent of everyone towards its distant lofty goals of humanity'.[131]

Der Judenstaat had been inspired by modern secular ideals rather than any messianic dream of restoring the ancient Kingdom of David and its sacral splendour. It envisaged an open, pluralist society free from nationalist or clerical pressures. At the same time Herzl had broken with the classical liberalism of *laissez-faire* economics. He

---

[126] See Benjamin Seff in *Die Welt*, 12 Nov. 1897, for an article that analyses Stock Exchange misery as 'part of the general misery of the Jews'.

[127] See Moshe Schaerf, 'Herzl's Social Thinking', *Herzl Year Book*, 3 (New York, 1960), 199–206.

[128] See the column 'Die Woche' in *Die Welt*, 11 June 1897, repr. as 'The Vienna Streetcar Strike', in Theodor Herzl, *Zionist Writings: Essays and Addresses* (New York, 1973), i. 85.

[129] *Diaries*, 41, entry of 11 June 1895.   [130] Ibid. 45.   [131] Ibid.

sketched out in some detail the role of the State in organizing work-battalions for the unemployed, destroying urban slums, taking responsibility for old-age insurance, public health, and the integrity of the family.[132] Like other Austrian thinkers, Herzl was influenced by the Central European *étatiste* tradition of political thought which modified his legalistic liberalism and even gave an anti-democratic tinge to some of his writings.[133]

There was also an anti-statist aspect to Herzl's social thought, manifest in his utopian novel *Altneuland*, with its vision of a 'mutualist', co-operative society that would function without state control or the rule of professional politicians.[134] In Herzl's utopia, the state has truly 'withered away';[135] there is no government but rather a 'Council of administration'; there is no ministry of defence, no 'high policy' or borders dividing people from one another. Economic and technological considerations in the best Saint-Simonian tradition have supplanted military and political affairs. In *Altneuland* the new society is wholly preoccupied with the development of industry, commerce, education, housing, welfare, and technical inventions. Its pioneers have applied and realized the utopian socialist ideals of Fourier, Cabet, Proudhon, Louis Blanc, Bellamy, and Theodor Herzka;[136] they have implemented in practical form the co-operative experiments of the nineteenth-century Rochdale pioneers and absorbed the lessons of the model Irish village of Rahaline.[137]

In Herzl's new society, all the land is in public ownership. Industries, banks, and newspapers are co-operatively owned by workers and consumers who live in clean, well-planned cities.[138] The new society is secular, cosmopolitan, and pluralist. It enjoys a seven-

[132] *Der Judenstaat*, 32-9.

[133] Joachim Doron, 'Social Concepts Prevalent in German Zionism: 1883–1914', *Studies in Zionism*, no. 5 (Apr. 1982), 1–31. For a discussion of Herzl's views, see pp. 25 ff.

[134] *Altneuland* (Haifa, 1960), 59.

[135] Ibid. 210. *Altneuland* is defined here as a 'commonwealth in a new form', 'a very large co-operative society, within which there are many small co-operatives for sundry aims'.

[136] Ibid. 114.

[137] Ibid. 115–18: 'The New Society is founded on an idea which is the common product of all civilized nations' (p. 117).

[138] Ibid. 67–72. The Zionist hero of the New Society, David Litwak, emphasizes that there is no regimentation of the individual. 'With us the individual is neither ground between the millstones of capitalism, nor beheaded by the levelling-down process of socialism. We know the values of the development of the individual, just as we respect and protect its economic foundation, private property.'

hour workday, female suffrage and scrupulously observes full equality between Jews and non-Jews.[139] Reshid Bey, the Moslem Arab protagonist, is, for example, a full member of the New Society, and explains to Mr Kingscourt, his incredulous Prussian questioner: 'Jewish immigration was a blessing for all of us. Naturally first of all for the landowners who either sold their acres to the Jewish company at high prices, or kept them in wait for even higher ones. As regards myself, I've sold my land to the New Society because I find myself better off that way.'[140]

The Arab fellahin in Herzl's utopia have benefited no less than the landowners from the general economic and technical progress created by the new society. With the draining of swamps, building of canals, planting of eucalyptus groves and avenues, a veritable transformation of living conditions takes place. 'These people [the Arabs] are far better off than before; they are healthy, they have better food, their children go to school. Nothing has been done to interfere with their customs or their faith—they have only gained by welfare.'[141] Thus the co-operative vision of Zion in Herzl's *Altneuland* synthesizes the best traditions of humanist universalism—it describes a tolerant, progressive society that 'could very well exist anywhere, in any country of the world'.[142]

In spite of its woodenness as literature *Altneuland* is also a revealing personal document. Its central figure, the young Viennese Jewish lawyer Friedrich Loewenberg (transparently a self-portrait) turns his back on Europe after a disappointment in love. Together with his Prussian officer friend, Kingscourt, he sets out for the South Seas, visiting a decaying Ottoman Palestine *en route*, as Herzl had done in 1898. Returning twenty years later to a flourishing model society, Loewenberg finds the family of the poor beggar boy from the Brigittenau district, David Litwak, whom he had saved from starvation in Vienna. The enterprising, hardworking Litwaks—Herzl's ideal Jewish family—have been reborn in Palestine. David Litwak is about

---

[139] The villain in the novel, an opportunist rabbi called Dr Geyer, is harshly depicted as a superpatriot, 'the truly nationalist Jew' who seeks to discriminate and incite against 'the stranger within our gates' (p. 108).

[140] Ibid. 94–5.   [141] Ibid. 95.

[142] Ibid. 215. Cultural Zionists like Ahad Ha'am and Nathan Birnbaum criticized Herzl for precisely this reason claiming that his 'New Society' had no authentic Jewish content and naïvely transplanted to Palestine the humanistic ideals of the Westernized Jewish middle-class intelligentsia. See Nathan Birnbaum, 'Altneuland', in *Ausgewählte Schriften zur jüdischen Frage* (Chernovitsy, 1910), ii. 272–6.

to be elected president of the Pioneer society. As foils to their honesty and simplicity, Herzl depicts typical Viennese Jewish bourgeois families like the Loefflers and Laschners, with their gaudy wealth and empty lives, prototypes of the self-seeking materialism he detested; cynics like Gruen and Blau, 'the two wittiest men of Vienna', who in the early part of the novel had ridiculed Zionism; and spoiled, overdressed, coquettish women like Ernestine Loeffler, who had broken Friedrich Loewenberg's heart in Vienna.

In this circle money was everything, for it bought pleasures and profits, the only thing worth having. And he, Friedrich, was tied to this circle, to the Jewish bourgeoisie, since they were his future clients, and he depended on them for his livelihood—worse luck! He would be fortunate if he became counsel for Baron Goldstein. The Gentile world was closed to him as surely as if it were bolted and barred. So what was left to him? Either to accomodate himself to the Loefflers' circle, share their mean ideal of life, act on behalf of doubtful moneyed people . . . Or, if this was too unpalatable, loneliness and poverty.[143]

Friedrich Loewenberg's escape from this rotten middle-class world eventually transports him into the dream of utopian future in Palestine. The tone is no longer set by parvenu Jewish types, like the Loefflers, the Laschners, the Schiffmanns, and their friends. To be sure, they also live in the new Palestine, still as cynical and materialistic as ever, but their role is no longer significant. Their place has been taken by ideal human beings like David and Miriam Littwak, modest, unpretentious, and dignified, who epitomize a new kind of Jew. They represent to Herzl the antithesis of the Viennese Jewish bourgeoisie of his own time and place.

In the New Society there is no more place for arranged marriages, crooked business deals, Stock Exchange speculation, and beggary, or the careerist politicians that Herzl had satirized in his Viennese plays and journalism. The reborn Jewish nation in Erez Israel was more than simply a transplantation of Austro-liberalism to Zion. It was premissed upon a radical restructuring of the values and behaviour-patterns of the middle-class Jewish society which Herzl had known in Vienna.

This dramatic change in ethos reflected something of Herzl's own personality, which combined a regal and chivalric bearing, the gift for political leadership, and an idealism that deeply impressed the Jewish masses of Eastern Europe. It was ultimately their desperate misery and longing for a saviour which transmuted Herzl into the King-Messiah

[143] *Altneuland*, 18.

E. M. Lilien, Illustration for the Fifth Zionist Congress, 1902

figure of which he had dreamed in his own child-like fantasies. His first encounter with the Jewish masses showed a subtle awareness of this dialectical process between leader and led. After a meeting in the East End of London in July 1896 he wrote in his Diaries:

As I sat on the platform of the Working Men's stage last Sunday I underwent a curious experience. I saw and heard my legend being made. The people are sentimental, the masses do not see clearly. I believe that by now they no longer have a clear image of me. A faint mist is beginning to rise and envelop me, and may perhaps become the cloud in which I shall walk.

But even if they no longer see my features distinctly, still they sense that I mean truly well by them and that I am the little people's man.[144]

In sophisticated, cosmopolitan Jewish Vienna the resistance to political Messiahs was much stronger. The epithet 'King of Zion', coined by the satirist Karl Kraus, stuck to Herzl like the mark of Cain, provoking satire, mockery, and the malaise of those who could not fathom what had happened 'to this otherwise intelligent, witty and cultivated writer'.[145] But for the mass of poor Jews in Eastern Europe and throughout the world, the unexpected death of Herzl on 3 July

[144] *Diaries*, 182.
[145] Stefan Zweig, *The World of Yesterday* (New York, 1943), 103.

1904, at the age of only forty-four, had a radically different meaning. None was to capture the scene with greater artistry than Herzl's youthful protégé, the Viennese writer, Stefan Zweig.

Suddenly, to all the railroad stations of the city, by day and by night, from all realms and lands, every train brought new arrivals. Western, Eastern, Russian, Turkish Jews; from all the provinces and all the little towns they hurried excitedly, the shock of the news still written on their faces; never was it more clearly manifest what strife and talk had hitherto concealed—it was a great movement whose leader had now fallen. The procession was endless. Vienna, startled, became aware that it was not just a writer or a mediocre poet who had passed away, but one of those creators of ideas who disclose themselves triumphantly in a single country, to a single people at vast intervals . . . All regulation was upset through a sort of elementary and ecstatic mourning such as I had never seen before nor since at a funeral. And it was this gigantic outpouring of grief from the depths of millions of souls that made me realize for the first time how much passion and hope this lone and lonesome man had borne into the world through the power of a single thought.[146]

[146] Ibid. 109.

14

Zionism and its Jewish Critics

Do you really expect me to accept all your propositions, premisses, and conclusions and to join with you in raising up the sky-blue flag of a Jewish State and political nation? In such a case I should have to deny my entire past and retract all the sermons I have delivered and published in more than thirty years. From the days of Moses Mendelsohn and particularly since the great French Revolution the Jews have sent out their best men to fight for their recognition and civic equality in European states . . . Have they done all this to abandon, in this year of 1882, everything that they have achieved, to give up all they have fought for and gained, to acknowledge that they are strangers without a fatherland . . . and, with the wanderer's staff in hand, to set out for an uncertain new fatherland?

> Adolf Jellinek to Leon Pinsker,
> Vienna (1882)

. . . this time the Jews will not arrive dry-shod in the promised land; another Red Sea, social democracy, will bar their way.

> Karl Kraus, *Eine Krone für Zion* (1898)

At the beginning of the new century this sarcastic city [Vienna] perhaps derided no one more than Theodor Herzl, unless it was that other man, who at that same time, alone and unaided, set up another great universal concept: his fellow-Jew, Sigmund Freud . . .

> Stefan Zweig, 'King of The Jews'

He did not mind recognizing Zionism as a moral principle and a social movement, if it could honestly be regarded in that light, but the idea of the foundation of a Jewish State on a religious and national basis struck him as a nonsensical defiance of the whole spirit of historical evolution.

> Heinrich Bermann, a character in Arthur Schnitzler's novel
> *Der Weg ins Freie* (1907)

And if all the Jews of the world were united in a free community in Palestine, this would mean no more to Judaism as a religion than would the gathering of all friends of truth and enlightenment on a desert island.

Chief Rabbi Moritz Güdemann to the writer Kamilla Theimer
(19 December 1907)

The opposition to Zionism within the Jewish community of Vienna came from many directions, religious and atheist, assimilationist and autonomist, fron conservatives, liberals, and socialists. Some Jews regarded Zionism as merely illusory and unrealizable, for some it was undesirable on principle, while for others it seemed positively harmful and even dangerous.[1] Religious critics, whether orthodox or reform, perceived Zionism as essentially a secular movement, contrary to the essence of the Jewish religion. They argued that it contradicted the messianic promises of divine Redemption and the traditional loyalty of Jews to their Diasporic fatherlands.[2] Not only did Zionism deny the accepted self-definition of Jewry as a religious community but its demand for radical changes in the character and structure of Jewish life openly challenged the authority of the Torah, of the Jewish establishment and its rabbis.[3] For the ultra-orthodox, Zionism represented a profanation and blasphemy against Torah Judaism. In the eyes of the reformers it was a parochial retreat from the universalist Jewish 'mission' of *Weltbürgertum* to an anachronistic mode of tribal nationalism.[4]

[1] See Walter Laqueur, *A History of Zionism* (New York, 1976), 384 ff., for a useful summary of the varieties of anti-Zionist argumentation that existed in Europe before the creation of the Jewish State.

[2] Michael Selzer (ed.), *Zionism Reconsidered: The Rejection of Jewish Normalcy* (New York, 1970), contains a number of early religious texts condemning Zionism, such as the statement by the Holy Gerer Rebbe (1901); by the Lubavicher Rebbe, Rabbi Shalom Dov Baer Schneersohn (1903); and by Nathan Birnbaum (1919). Birnbaum's text 'In Bondage to our Fellow Jews', pp. 1–9, which attacked Zionists for being completely estranged from Torah Judaism and impelled by an 'evil craving to remould us on the European model, to "make men of us", . . .', is especially interesting in view of his pioneering role in the creation of Austrian Zionism.

[3] For a summary of the orthodox position, see Emile Marmorstein, *Heaven at Bay* (London, 1969), 79–80, who quotes a letter of Rabbi Joseph Hayyim Sonnenfeld (1848–1932), written in 1898, claiming that Zionists believed that 'the whole difference between Israel and the nations lies in nationalism, blood and race, and that the faith and the religion are superfluous . . . Dr. Herzl comes not from the Lord, but from the side of pollution . . .'.

[4] For classic examples of the universalist interpretation of Judaism in an anti-Zionist spirit, see Hermann Cohen, *Religion and Zionismus* (Crefeld, 1916), and C. G.

Liberal critics in Vienna, as elsewhere, contended that Zionism stood in open defiance to the whole trend of historical evolution which was tending towards assimilation and the fusion of the Jewish minority with the surrounding nations. Liberals did not necessarily deny the existence of a 'Jewish question' in Vienna, in the Dual Monarchy, or in Europe as a whole. But they generally felt that Zionism would merely aggravate anti-Semitism instead of providing a cure. Moreover, for many secular Viennese Jews there was the fear that a militant assertion of Jewish nationalism would endanger their civic status and economic prosperity. Martin Freud summed up this assimilationist reflex as follows: 'Emigrate? Who dreamed of leaving beautiful Austria, where they flourished under the protection of a benign and powerful Emperor? Give up their positions as bank presidents, as leaders of rich commercial and industrial concerns? No! They wanted to maintain their wealth and bequeath it to their children.'[5]

The 'utopian' character of the Zionist project before 1914 reinforced such practical objections. The prospects of immigration to Palestine—then a decaying backwater of the Turkish Empire—were decidedly unappealing except to a handful of impoverished idealists, most of them angry young men and women from Eastern Europe. The impracticability of Zionism was also a useful auxiliary argument in the socialist arsenal, reinforcing more weighty ideological considerations. Most socialist Jews in Austria believed that Jewish nationalism was an outworn relic from the ghetto past. According to Marxist prognoses the classless society of the future would definitively eradicate anti-Semitism. In its wake, the 'Jewish question' would finally disappear.[6] The anti-Zionist critique from the Left, like that of the liberal assimilationists, either rejected the existence of a separate 'Jewish nation' or claimed that it was doomed to rapid dissolution. From this perspective, Zionism could only appear as marginal, irrelevant, or as a harmful diversion from the social and political struggles of the working classes in Central Europe.[7]

Montefiore, *Liberal Judaism and Jewish Nationalism* (London, 1917). Theodor Herzl had already dealt with many of these objections in the early days of political Zionism. See his article on the 'Protest Rabbis' in *Die Welt*, 16 July 1897, and his criticism of Claude Montefiore's views, 6 May 1898.

[5] Martin Freud, 'Who was Freud?', in J. Fraenkel (ed.), *The Jews of Austria: Essays on their Life, History and Destruction* (London, 1967), 207.

[6] Robert S. Wistrich, *Socialism and the Jews: The Dilemmas of Assimilation in Germany and Austria-Hungary* (Littman Library, London and Toronto, 1982), 299 ff.

[7] Otto Bauer, *Die Nationalitätenfrage und die Sozialdemokratie* (Vienna, 1907), 366 ff.

The first public reactions to Zionism in Vienna had been prompted by the trauma of the 1881 Russian pogroms. Thousands of destitute Jews swarming from the towns of Southern Russia and the Ukraine into Brody, Lemberg, Tarnopol, and the overcrowded ghettos of Austrian Galicia testified to the need to regulate and channel Jewish emigration in a more orderly manner. In the Habsburg capital as in other cities of Western Europe Jewish emergency committees sprang up to organize relief, with the Vienna Israelitische Allianz playing an important role. Its President, Joseph Ritter von Wertheimer, was, however, quick to emphasize that Palestine, under existing social and political conditions, would be the least suitable of countries to provide penniless Jewish emigrants with a livelihood. While praising the efforts of Charles Netter and the Alliance Israélite Universelle in Paris to develop agriculture and crafts among indigenous Palestinian Jewish youth, Wertheimer argued that it would be altogether misguided to propose the Holy Land as a refuge for the Russian and Romanian refugees.[8] Not only was Palestine backward in industry, commerce, and the sciences but the majority of its Jews lived off the *chaluka* (charity), in a state of degrading, semi-beggary; the 'chimerical' idea of sending European Jews to this miserable Ottoman backwater 'to found a great new ghetto' could have been conceived only by anti-Semites and blind zealots in the ranks of Jewry.[9] Wertheimer proposed instead the co-ordination of efforts by the Alliance Israélite and related organizations in London, Paris, Berlin, and Vienna to direct Jewish emigration to Texas, Canada, and Australia. In these great open spaces they would find ample opportunity to put their skills to constructive use.[10]

Proposals for the Jewish colonization of Palestine were even more harshly dismissed in *Die Neuzeit* as an anti-Semitic conspiracy to reinforce the negative image of Jewry as 'alien' outsiders in European society.[11] It was pointed out as early as 1882 that one of the most fervent apostles of Palestinian Jewish colonization was the Hungarian anti-Semitic leader, Gyózó von Istóczy.[12] It seemed the height of folly

---

[8] Joseph Ritter von Wertheimer, *Zur Emancipation unserer Glaubensgenossen* (Vienna, 1882), 9.

[9] Ibid. 8. [10] Ibid. 10–11.

[11] 'Mystères de Vienne' (Der israelitischen Allianz zur Beachtung empfohlen), *Die Neuzeit*, 6 Jan. 1882, p. 2: 'Es unterliegt keinem Zweifel, dass von jenen Antisemiten, welche die Juden gerne als fremde Element verschreien möchten, ein Verein zur Deportation unserer Glaubensbrüder nach Palästina mit Jubel begrüsst werden würde.'

[12] Ibid. 2.

for wealthy Jewish philanthropists or for the Allianz to provide money for settlements in Palestine which would only make the fight against anti-Semitism in Europe more difficult.[13] The chorus of East European 'Hebraists', neo-romantics, and neo-orthodox wiseacres who noisily advocated a return to Zion in the wake of the Russian persecutions, were simply playing into the hands of the worse enemies of Jewry.[14]

Perhaps the most sophisticated critic of the Ḥovevei Zion movement in the early 1880s was the Viennese preacher Adolf Jellinek. During a historic meeting with Jellinek in Vienna in March 1882 Pinsker had eloquently presented the desire of persecuted Russian Jews to settle as free human beings on 'our own national soil, to found a communal and political commonwealth and to show the nations that we have not degenerated but that we are a race of indestructible vitality, gifted and capable of founding a state, no matter how small'. Jellinek, though moved by Pinsker's despair, firmly rejected his assumption that Jews were being turned into vagrants by the wave of anti-Semitism agitating Europe. To undertake a new Exodus 'would mean accepting the view of our implacable foes who deny that we have any true patriotic feelings for Europe'.[15]

Jellinek assured Pinsker that Viennese Jewry was doing everything possible for their Russian co-religionists as were the more enlightened rulers of Europe on whose moral support they could count. In Jellinek's view the causes of the Russian pogroms were rooted not in hereditary Judaeophobia but in the overcrowding of the Pale of Settlement.

It is not good for Jews to concentrate anywhere in a great number. This weakens their expansive force and promotes prejudice, jealousy, ill will, and religious bias against them. England, France, Italy and Belgium, where our brethren have the most freedom, have relatively few Jews in their midst, so few,

---

[13] *Die Neuzeit*, 6 Jan. 1882, p. 3. *Die Neuzeit* singled out for particular condemnation 'unberufene hebraistische Phrasenhelden, die von dem literarischen Schacher—oder was daselbe ist, *Schachar-Geiste* besessen sind . . .' The reference was clearly aimed at the Perez Smolenskin's agitation on behalf of Palestine in the Viennese *Ha-Shahar*.

[14] 'Das 'heilige' Land', *Die Neuzeit*, 9 Sept. 1881, p. 1. This editorial claimed that the chief sponsors of Zionism were Christian missionary societies, who saw the return of the Jews to 'the so-called land of their fathers' as a prelude to their conversion to Christianity.

[15] See *Die Neuzeit*, 31 Mar., 7 Apr., 14 Apr. 1882, for the dialogue between Pinsker (described as 'the physician Dr. X, from Russia') and Jellinek; also Adolf Jellinek, *Aus der Zeit: Tagesfragen und Tagesbegebenheiten* (Budapest, 1886), 20–81.

in fact that in Warsaw and Vilna alone there are at least as many Jews as in all the above-mentioned countries combined . . .

In my view, this circumstance has contributed a great deal to the sad and bleak situation of our Russian brethren. This situation must be remedied, and that can be done only through a large-scale, prudently planned, and well-organized emigration. Your compatriots should emigrate to a free country and found splendid settlements there rather than to Asia, to an oriental semi-Russia [Turkish Palestine] where the open hands of the pashas smell of Russian leather, where property is rendered insecure by brutal hordes and religious fanaticism is heated up by the rays of an oriental sun. The most respected Jews of Europe and America are concerning themselves with such an emigration at this very moment. Without intending to do so, the Russian government has aroused a feeling of solidarity, cohesiveness, kinship and community of faith among the Jews of Europe and America in a way unprecedented in world history.[16]

Jellinek's rejection of Ottoman Palestine as a land of emigration, outlined in a newspaper editorial on 9 January 1885, derived mainly from its lack of freedom, physical security, or the basic infrastructure of modern civilization.[17] It remained a country dominated by the arbitrary whims of Turkish pashas and marauding Bedouin robbers, in the thrall of barbaric superstition and fanaticism. Jewish ultra-orthodoxy in particular, which Jellinek denounced as a 'demonic force hostile to civilization', constituted the greatest obstacle to a prosperous and successful colonization.[18]

The special place of Palestine in Jewish religious history and its undeniable emotional appeal to Russian Jews were, admittedly, positive factors in favour of a return to the land of the fathers. The agricultural nature of the Palestinian settlements might also contribute to reawakening the will to redemptive labour and the productivization of the Jews. None the less, Jellinek insisted that only a colonization of Palestine based on purely humanitarian and economic considerations could be realistically contemplated. Any attempt to give a national or messianic dimension to the return to Zion, whether by Russian Jews or by the Jewish student nationalists in Vienna, would have to be categorically repudiated.[19] The 'romantic enthusiasts of New Judea' with their 'mindless phrases about a Jewish nationality' were merely providing new pretexts for anti-Semites to brand Western Jews as

[16] Ibid.
[17] J. 'Jüdische Colonial-Politik', *Die Neuzeit*, 9 Jan. 1885, p. 12.　　[18] Ibid.
[19] Ibid. A reference to Jellinek's ongoing polemic against the Maccabbean strivings of Kadimah.

'aliens' in their own fatherlands.[20] But the Jews were manifestly *not* a political nation and the future of Zion was 'an open question of high policy' whose outcome a handful of Russian Jewish zealots could not hope to influence.[21]

The Maccabean celebrations of Kadimah held in Vienna in December 1891 inspired Jellinek to define more precisely his ideological position with regard to assimilation and Jewish nationalism.

There is no Jewish nation. The Jews form, it is true, a separate stock [*Stamm*], a special religious community. They should cultivate the ancient Hebrew language, study their rich literature, know their history, cherish their faith and make the greatest sacrifices of it; they should hope and trust in the wisdom of Divine Providence, the promises of their prophets and the development of mankind so that the sublime ideas and truths of Judaism may gain the day. But for the rest, they should amalgamate with the nations whose citizens they are, fight in their battles and promote their institutions for the welfare of the whole.[22]

Jellinek acknowledged that the rehabilitation of Zion was a sublime Jewish ideal. But in the language of the Hebrew prophets, it belonged to '*Achrith Hayamim*' (the end of days), to the Kingdom of God which neither a neo-pagan cult of Maccabean heroism nor glorious deeds in battle could help to bring about.[23] There was no objection to Jews being permitted to settle in Zion, in order to buy land, engage in agriculture or trade. However, the final dispensation of Jerusalem and of Palestine must be left to the advent of a messianic age of universal peace.

This anti-Zionist stance prompted a sharp retort from Nathan Birnbaum in *Selbstemanzipation*. Indignantly, he rejected Jellinek's strictures against the 'un-Jewish' character of the Maccabean cult encouraged by Kadimah.[24] According to Birnbaum, the object of

---

[20] *Die Neuzeit*, 9 Jan. 1885, p. 12.

[21] Ibid. Jellinek's formula, 'Emigration, Colonisation aber keine Restauration oder Restauration-Phantasieen!', accurately summed up his position on Palestine. See also M. Rosenmann, *Dr Adolf Jellinek: sein Leben und Schaffen* (Vienna, 1931), 215, who records Jellinek's conversation with Nathan Birnbaum and Kadimah members in the spring of 1883, in which he affirmed his opposition to Zionism but declared: 'Ich glaube, dass Zion einmal aufgebaut werden wird.'

[22] A.J., 'Weihfest oder Makkabäerfest?', *Die Neuzeit*, 18 Dec. 1891.

[23] Ibid. 'Was die Erfüllung der höchsten jüdischen ideale, die Zukunft des jüdischen Stammes, die Ehrenrettung Zions betrifft, so können auch eine Million Makkabäer nichts dazubeitragen.'

[24] Birnbaum, 'Angriff und Abwehr', *Selbstemanzipation*, no. 1, 5 Jan. 1892, pp. 3–6. Birnbaum pointed to the irony that the religious reformer Jellinek was now piously

Zionism was not to glorify martial successes or individual heroes but to uphold 'the principle of active love for one's own nation and its ideals'.[25] The Maccabees had been a model of national self-help, not of sabre-rattling militarism; contemporary Jewish nationalism was concerned not so much with the 'messianic age' but with saving the Jews from material and moral disintegration by securing an inalienable homeland.[26] Only in this way would they be able to create an independent culture and represent authentically Jewish ideals. The continuity of the Jewish people could not be assured through fusion with 'Aryan' peoples whose mode of thinking was fundamentally different.[27]

Birnbaum vehemently repudiated Jellinek's charge that the Jewish nationalists were youthful 'enthusiasts without any political under-standing'. He reminded the Viennese rabbi that within Russian Zionism alone there were hundreds of able, experienced men whose social and scientific standing was by no means inferior to that of Jellinek himself.[28] He believed that the longing for Zion was a powerful sentiment shared by millions of East European Jews and by a significant part of central European Jewry;[29] it still flickered 'beneath the ashes of the *autodafé* which assimilation was preparing' and which Zionism resolutely sought to avert. Moreover, as Birnbaum had already pointed out to the Christian Verein zur Abwehr des Antisemitismus in Vienna, the creation of a Jewish fatherland (*Patria*) had nothing to do with anti-Semitic calls for a 'repatriation' of Jews to Palestine. This did not, however, prevent the argument from being endlessly repeated by Jewish anti-Zionists.[30]

---

defending the appellation Ḥanukkah against that of *Hag Ha-Maccabiyim* (Festival of the Maccabees), in the name of tradition!

[25] Ibid. 4.   [26] Ibid. 5.

[27] Ibid. Birnbaum also noted that the very qualities which Jellinek wished to nurture were specifically national, making his denial of Jewish 'nationality' somewhat quixotic.

[28] Ibid. 6. See also the article by Gustav Seidemann, 'Unsere Legitimation', *Selbstemanzipation*, no. 5, 4 Mar. 1892, pp. 54–5, for a polemic directed at Jellinek's arguments against the Jewish national cause.

[29] See 'Die Antwort der Zionisten an das "Freie Blatt "', *Selbstemanzipation*, 6, no. 4, 20 Mar. 1893, pp. 1–2. The *Freies Blatt* was the weekly organ of the Christian Verein zur Abwehr des Antisemitismus in Vienna. On 12 Mar. 1893 it had published an article critical of Zionism. Birbaum's response exposed the superficiality of its arguments and affirmed: '. . . auch in Westeuropa und dem westlichen Mittleuropa ist die Erlösungshoffnung im jüdischen Volke noch nicht todt . . .' (ibid., p. 2).

[30] Ibid., p. 2: 'Die Quelle des Antisemitismus ist der Hass gegen das jüdische Volk, die des Zionismus die Liebe zu demselben; das Ziel des Antisemitismus ist das Unglück Israels, dasjenige des Zionismus das Glück unseres Stammes.'

Die Neuzeit continued its polemics in the early 1890s against the idea of a 'Jewish nationality', whether promoted by Jews or Christians.[31] Jellinek insisted that a dispersed people like the Jews, lacking territory or a sovereign state of its own, let alone a common history, language, or culture, was at most a race or stock (*Stamm*). 'A king without land is no sovereign, a *Stamm* without independent political and cultural life can never more appear as a nation.'[32] The ethnic cohesion of Jewry proclaimed by the Zionists was therefore artificial. It ignored the only historic unity to which Judaism could genuinely aspire—that of professing a pure monotheistic faith which had withstood the persecutions of centuries.[33]

Jellinek's evocation of the *Kiddush ha-Shem* (sanctification of the name) as a theological support for his anti-Zionism provoked another polemical reply from Nathan Birnbaum. The founder of Austrian Zionism declared that this medieval willingness to defy death for the sake of the faith was scarcely present among the young generation of European Jews. Hebrew monotheism had become irrelevant for those Jewish bourgeois who frequented the Viennese ballrooms and racing tracks, for the *Konfessionslos* workers of the Leopoldstadt, or for Jewish students seeking to advance in their professional careers.[34] Piety and martyrdom were not exactly the defining characteristics of contemporary Central European Jewry. Traditional bonds of group solidarity had been steadily disintegrating over the years. Nor could religious belief restore what had been torn asunder by the forces of modern materialism and social assimilation. Since modern Jewish youth had already lost its religious faith, 'religious sentimentality' could no longer be an effective argument against secular Jewish nationalism.[35] Only Zionism still had the power to bring about a moral rebirth of Israel,

[31] J. 'Das Judenthum—eine Nationalität', ibid., no. 10, 10 Mar. 1893, p. 1. This polemic was prompted not by Zionism but by the memorandum of Cardinal Vaszary at a Hungarian Bishops' conference in Budapest, 'in welchem das Judenthum nicht bloss als eine Religion, sondern auch als eine Nationalität bezeichnet wird . . .'. Jellinek saw this declaration as damaging to Hungarian Jewry, whose ardent Magyar patriotism he glowingly praised.

[32] Ibid.

[33] J., 'Die Einheit des Judenthums', ibid., no. 32, 11 Aug. 1893, p. 1. See the response of Birnbaum entitled 'Einheit', in *Selbstemanzipation*, no. 13, 1 Sept. 1893, pp. 1–3.

[34] Birnbaum, ibid. 2.

[35] Ibid.: 'Die jüdische Jugend lacht heute nicht mehr allein über die frommen Juden von alten Schlag, sie spottet auch über den "Mosaismus". Auch der steht der Assimilation im Wege.'

restoring its national unity and reviving the spirit of patriotic sacrifice for a visionary ideal.[36]

With the death of Adolf Jellinek in 1893 the hostility of *Die Neuzeit* became somewhat tempered. For instance, Herzl's *Der Judenstaat* received a lengthy and not unsympathetic review in its columns. The sober circumspection and practical sense of the tract attracted particular attention.[37] Indeed, the reviewer seemed pleasantly suprised at the businesslike formulation of the Herzlian project. With some puzzlement he noted the lack of any messianic enthusiasm for the Holy Land of the patriarchs or for the Holy City of Jerusalem in *Der Judenstaat*. Biblical prophecies of return played no visible role in the new political Zionism espoused by Theodor Herzl. *Die Neuzeit* seemed on balance to be relieved that Herzl had carefully avoided any suggestion that he might be second Moses or the 'promised Messiah'.[38]

An editorial of 25 June 1897 publicly welcomed the fact that the Zionist movement had revived Jewish ethnic consciousness (*Stammesgefühl*) in the hearts of Jewish academic youth. The renewed interest in Jewish history and in the literary treasures of Judaism was seen as a positive gain, attributable to the impact of Zionism in Vienna.[39] Favourable mention was given to Zionist efforts to provide a new source of hope for alleviating the misery of millions of impoverished *Stammesgenossen* in Eastern Europe through planned colonization in Palestine. The same editorial even spoke in complementary terms of secular Zionist leaders like Herzl and Nordau—men whose education, intelligence, and public standing could not be denied.[40] *Die Neuzeit* for the first time emphasized the fact that Zionism was an age-old Jewish aspiration which had been revived in modern times in order to provide a concrete solution to the problem of mass pauperism among the Jewish masses in Eastern Europe.[41] It printed articles sympathetic to national-religious Zionism by Herzl's close collaborator in Sofia, the physician Reuben Bierer, and by the Chief Rabbi of France, Zadoc Kahn;[42] even declarations by orthodox Polish rabbis in favour of a

[36] Ibid.
[37] D. Löwy, 'Literarische Nachrichten', *Die Neuzeit*, 28 Feb. 1896, p. 89: 'Dennoch aber ist sein nüchtern entworfener und gesunder Grundlage combinirter Plan beachtens—u. schätzenswerth . . .'   [38] Ibid.
[39] D. Löwy, 'Zionismus', ibid., 25 June 1897, pp. 265–6.
[40] Ibid., p. 266: '. . . beide Männer vom Licht und Glanze ausgezeichneter Bildung, klaren Denkens, Umsicht, Einsicht und Vorsicht umstrahlt . . .'
[41] 'Judenstaat und Zukunftsstaat', ibid., 20 Aug. 1897, p. 346.
[42] Dr. Rubin Bierer, 'Vom dem Congress', ibid., 27 Aug. 1897, p. 353; also 'Zadoc Kahn über den Zionismus', 8 Oct. 1897, pp. 412–14.

synthesis between Torah and Zionism were published in its columns.[43]
Die Neuzeit also began to report speeches at the Zionist Congresses, to
provide information on the progress of the Palestinian colonies and on
new developments within the movement in a tone almost approaching
benevolent neutrality.[44]

Such changes notwithstanding, *Die Neuzeit* was by no means
converted to the Zionist cause. Like the Viennese Jewish establishment
whose views it frequently reflected, its editors sharply disapproved of
the Zionist proposition that the Jews should constitute a 'political
nation'. *Die Neuzeit* repudiated no less firmly the notion that Zionism
might provide a global solution to the 'Jewish question' or that it would
eventually eradicate anti-Semitism. Like the community leaders in
Vienna, it could not see any realistic prospect of the Jews acquiring
Palestine in the foreseeable future.[45] Nevertheless, there was a much
greater willingness to recognize the educational value of the Zionist
movement and its contribution towards the organization of Jewish self-
help. In particular, the weekly sympathized with any programme
orientated towards material assistance for Russian and Romanian
Jews. Philanthropic Zionism did not conflict in any way with the civic
status of Western Jewry.

An interesting pointer to the gradual moderation of anti-Zionism in
Die Neuzeit during the late 1890s was the critical review it published of
Chief Rabbi Güdemann's *Nationaljudenthum*. This uncompromising
polemic against Herzl's political Zionism had been written from an
orthodox-conservative religious standpoint.[46] After carefully sum-
marizing the Chief Rabbi's arguments and welcoming his belated foray
into the public domain, the reviewer contested his central assumption
that Jewish national independence was contrary to the spirit of Judaism
and its cosmopolitan 'mission'. The Jews had prayed and suffered in
the hope of returning to Zion for nearly 2,000 years. This dream could
not be reduced to a mere 'symbol' relating to a pie-in-the-sky
messianic future which would eventually embrace all of mankind. The
physical ingathering of the exiles in the land of Israel was no less a part
of Hebrew prophetic teaching than the universalist vision of social

---

[43] 'Thora und Zionismus', ibid., 13 Jan. 1899, pp. 13–14.
[44] 'Aus dem heiligen Lande', ibid., 10 Mar. 1899, p. 99; S. Fl., 'Die jüdische
Colonialbank', ibid., 31 Mar. 1899; 'Die Zionisten—Congress in London', ibid., 24
Aug. 1900.
[45] See Lucien Brunner, 'Die Noth des jüdischen Volkes', III, ibid., 14 Sept. 1900, p.
388.
[46] R., 'National judenthum', ibid., 30 Apr. 1897, pp. 183–4.

justice or of the brotherhood of man. The Jewish 'mission' neither began nor would it end with the Diaspora. Equally, the creation of a Jewish State did not necessarily entail the final end of the dispersion.[47]

Rabbi Gudemann's relations with Herzl were in fact considerably more ambiguous and complex than his anti-Zionist pamphlet of 1897 might suggest. Despite their apologetic tone, his Memoirs, begun in 1899 (at the age of 64) and completed only in 1913, offer an interesting insight into his attitude towards Zionism.[48] No less revealing are the letters written by Güdemann to Herzl between June 1895 and February 1896. Contact between the two men had originally been initiated at Herzl's request to secure the Chief Rabbi's co-operation in a campaign on behalf of the Jews. In a letter from Paris Herzl had proposed that Güdemann help to draft a memorandum dealing with the situation of the Jews in the world, their occupational distribution, and the problem of anti-Semitism.[49] Rabbi Güdemann was impressed by the rather unusual occurrence that a prestigious and worldly journalist in Vienna should display such concern for his co-religionists.[50] In reply he pointed out that Dr Bloch was far better equipped than himself to provide an overview of anti-Semitism in contemporary Europe.[51]

On 16 June 1895 Herzl wrote a second letter to the Chief Rabbi, boldly informing him that he had 'found the solution [of the Jewish problem] but it no longer belongs to me. It belongs to the world.'[52] Herzl asked Güdemann to act as his intermediary in establishing contact with Albert Rothschild in Vienna. He requested that the Chief Rabbi read the 'Address to the Rothschilds' to the head of the Viennese branch of the family. Unfortunately, nothing was to come of this approach to the Viennese Rothschilds.

On 17 July 1895 Güdemann, responding to another letter from Herzl, enthusiastically affirmed that he 'had not anticipated such an

[47] Ibid. p. 184.
[48] Moritz Güdemann, 'Aus meinem Leben', 4 vols. (n.d.), in Archives of the Leo Baeck Institute, New York, ii. 142; iii. 118 ff., 128 ff., 185–95. The section entitled 'Meine Stellung zum Zionismus' is also reproduced by Mordechai Eliav, 'Herzl und der Zionismus aus der Sicht Moritz Güdemanns', *Bulletin des Leo Baeck Instituts*, no. 56/7 (1980), 160–8.
[49] Herzl Archives, CZA H VIII 309, Güdemann to Herzl, letter of 14 June 1895. Güdemann declared himself to have been most pleasantly surprised 'als ich bei Ihnen ein so warmes Interesse für *unsere* Sache wahrnehme'.
[50] J. Fraenkel, 'The Chief Rabbi and the Visionary', *The Jews of Austria*, 119.
[51] M. Güdemann, 'Meine Stellung zum Zionismus', 161.
[52] Fraenkel, 120.

interest on your side' in Jewish affairs and then launched into a bitter complaint about current Jewish tribulations in Vienna.

It is truly a calamity. I am at my wit's end. I cannot read the newspaper anymore, all those parliamentary reports and the daily news on the anti-Semitic excesses. Every time I feel the urge to smash something. I have lived for almost thirty years in Vienna and like every renegade became an enemy of my previous fatherland, that is to say Germany, on account of the anti-Semitism which originated from there. I became enamoured of Austria, my adopted fatherland, and especially of Vienna and whenever I came back to my *Heimat* . . . I would enthuse about Vienna . . . But now I must tell you that this is no people and this is no city. Both the state and city are a dungheap, a pighouse [*Schweinerei*]. Look at Hungary: . . . it is a joy to have lived to see how Hungary has secreted out this *materia peccans* of anti-Semitism. Germany too is strong and there are men in its Parliament whose presence is edifying and Liberalism was after all capable of breaking the heads of scoundrels like Hammerstein. The Jews of Berlin act accordingly . . .

Here, however, there is nobody, not even a *single* man in Parliament on whom one would not like to spit. How much [. . .] was wasted by the *Neue Freie Presse* on Plener [the liberal leader] who never found a warm word for the Jews, how sugary are [Professor] Süss and *tuttiquanti*! And, so too, are the Jews over here. There is truly *not one* with whom one could mount guard . . .[53]

Güdemann even suggested that this communal passivity might be a divine punishment for the dependence of the Kultusgemeinde on the wealthy notables who no longer moved in Jewish circles. Indeed, he strongly urged Herzl not to rely on the rich Jews to support his plans. In his letter, Güdemann clearly advocated a more militant stance and a courageous personal example as the only thing that might lighten the darkening gloom created by anti-Semitism.

They spit often enough in our faces, why not openly spit back. Unfortunately the newspapers, which really are Jewish papers [*Judenzeitungen*], are also dull and lifeless. Nothing but decorum and objectivity, as if when it matters, they mix their ink with rose-water. Perhaps from the present Jewish fighting fraternities a few fine fellows will one day emerge . . .

Güdemann reminded Herzl[54] that this militant spirit, had been incarnated in Austria by the Reichsrat deputy, Rabbi Joseph Bloch. But 'the terrorism of a Schneider and consorts had obliged the Polish club to sacrifice him' and Dr Bloch would have to resign his mandate. Güdemann pointed out to Herzl that failure to re-elect his friend

[53] Herzl Archives, CZA H VIII 309, Güdemann to Herzl, 17 July 1895.
[54] Ibid.

Bloch 'would be a great victory for the anti-Semites and a disgrace for us'. Unfortunately, Rabbi Bloch's services were not appreciated by the wealthy Viennese Jews. 'They think that he brings about anti-Semitism. But one must learn from one's adversaries. In reality he is the only Jew who is taken seriously and feared by them. He must in any event be re-elected but the Jews of his constituency, though they constitute a majority, are as useless as the rest and they want money, which Bloch doesn't have . . . he is the only one, who could and has stood up to the slanders of a Rohling, Schneider, etc. with the weapon of science.'[55]

Güdemann concluded that Austrian Jewry was confronted by a clear choice: either they were resigned to accepting without rebuttal the constant flood of anti-Semitic abuse or they were prepared to fight for their faith and honour. The Chief Rabbi fervently hoped that the decision could be influenced by the *Neue Freie Presse*. If it supported Bloch's campaign then perhaps the rich Jews might also intervene on his behalf.

Güdemann's next letter, dated 23 July 1895, reinforces the impression that he regarded Herzl above all as an unexpected ally in the immediate fight against Austrian anti-Semitism. He reminded Herzl that through 'your relationship to the *Neue Freie Presse* you have the possibilities and connections in which you can be useful to the Jews in unforeseeable ways'.[56] Above all, the Chief Rabbi wanted to make sure that Herzl did nothing rash to endanger his relations with the owners and editors of the great Liberal newspaper. This concern was prompted not only by Güdemann's solicitude for Herzl's wife and children but by the interests of the Jewish cause as he understood it.

At this stage during their correspondence, the Chief Rabbi was not above using conventional flattery, ardently praising Herzl's 'genuine, warm, flaming Jewish heart' and his readiness to sacrifice himself on behalf of the Jews. He informed Herzl that, since Ignaz Kuranda, he had never encountered such enthusiasm for Jewish affairs in an Austrian journalist. Such a passionate commitment was refreshing in the cynical atmosphere of Viennese Jewish journalism and, as he admitted in a letter of 3 August 1895, far more important to him than the nature of Herzl's private religous beliefs. Güdemann at this time even cast himself in the role of a political adviser. He warned Herzl against a premature approach to the German Emperor Wilhelm II

[55] Ibid.
[56] CZA H VIII 309, Güdemann to Herzl, 23 July 1895.

which might arouse anti-Semitic suspicions and allusions to the intrigues of 'international Jewry'. He also advised against any hasty steps which were not synchronized with Benedikt and Bacher at the *Neue Freie Presse*.

The Chief Rabbi was clearly unaware as yet of the sweeping scope of Herzl's project. He interpreted Herzl's reference to having found a 'solution' for the 'Jewish question' as relating essentially to the local conditions in Vienna and to the fight against anti-Semitism.[57] The ensuing correspondence was directed to arranging a tripartite meeting on neutral ground between the Paris-based Herzl, Güdemann (whose rabbinical duties tied him to Vienna), and the wealthy Berlin banker, Dr Heinrich Meyer-Cohn—a personal friend of the Chief Rabbi. It was finally decided that the three men should meet in Munich where Herzl would reveal the full details of his plan.

On 17 August 1895, in a small Jewish restaurant in Munich, Herzl finally read his 'Address to the Rothschilds' before his two startled listeners. The elderly Güdemann was evidently moved by Herzl's charismatic personality, though whether he had been intellectually convinced must remain an open question. He suggested that Herzl should 'incorporate his ideas in a novel, as had been done in the book *Freiland* [by Theodor Herzka], which had appeared at the time. That would prove whether his idea could produce practical results.'[58]

Herzl optimistically believed that he had won over the previously 'anti-Zionist' Chief Rabbi, whose moral support he regarded as crucial to gaining the confidence of the rich Jews in Vienna and elsewhere in Western Europe. According to Herzl, Güdemann told him:

If you are right, what I have hitherto believed falls to pieces. And yet I am wishing that you are right. Up till now I have believed that we are not a nation—but more than a nation. I believed that we have the historic mission of being the exponents of universalism among the nations and therefore were more than a people identified with a specific land.[59]

As they prepared to leave for supper that same evening in Munich,

[57] Güdemann, 'Meine Stellung zum Zionismus', 162 insisted in his memoirs that all along he had never interpreted Herzl's intentions as anything other than 'eine den Wiener Juden, die damals gerade unter den aufkommenden Antisemitismus heftig zu leiden hatten, hilfreiche journalistische Aktion'.

[58] Ibid. 163. But this explanation remains difficult to credit after their meeting in Munich.

[59] *The Diaries of Theodor Herzl*, ed. and trans. Marvin Lowenthal (London, 1958), 63, entry of 18 Aug. 1895; also Alex Bein, *Theodor Herzl: A Biography* (Philadelphia, 1962), 150.

Güdemann reportedly remarkedly: 'I could think you were Moses'—a comparison which Herzl (in his diary entry) 'laughingly rejected'. The messianic allusion recurred when Herzl accompanied Güdemann to the Munich railway station. In the Herzlian version, the Chief Rabbi of Vienna fervently implored him: 'Remain as you are! Perhaps you are called of God!'[60] Güdemann categorically denied this account iin his own memoirs, quoting a letter he had written from Munich in August 1895 to his wife where he had described Herzl as 'a poet' but called his proposals 'unrealizable'.[61] The discrepancy between the two versions is not altogether surprising given the different expectations and premisses of the protagonists.

Herzl was evidently concerned by the criticism voiced in Munich that his Zionist project might be 'utopian'. In another letter to Rabbi Güdemann on 22 August 1895 he contrasted his plan with Theodor Hertzka's utopian tract *Freiland*, which the Chief Rabbi had urged him to read:

... *Freiland* depicts a complicated piece of machinery, with many cogs and wheels but nothing about it persuades me that it could be set in motion.

As against this, my own plan consists of utilizing a genuine and existing driving force.

What is that force? The misery, the tragedy, the crying need of the Jewish people.

Who dares to deny that this force exists?

We are all familiar with the power of steam which, when generated by boiling water in a tea-kettle, lifts the kettle lid. This tea-kettle phenomenon may be seen in the Zionist experiments and a hundred other organized efforts to 'combat anti-Semitism'. But I say that the force is now strong enough to drive a great machine and set a people in motion.[62]

Güdemann became, however, more sceptical once he was safely ensconced in Vienna and no longer 'under the immediate impression of your [i.e. Herzl's] personality as in Munich'. In a letter on 30 August 1895 he informed Herzl that 'it is all the time clearer to me that the

---

[60] *Diaries*, 63–4.

[61] Güdemann, 'Meine Stellung zum Zionismus', 163: 'Herzl ist ein Poet, aber die Sache, so interessant sie ist, undurchführbar'.

[62] See *Diaries*, 64–6, and Bein, pp. 151–2, for Herzl's letter of 22 Aug. 1895 to Güdemann.

moment is not yet ripe and that many good Jews still have no understanding of your intentions. The idea of emigration will be rejected by the best and most pious Jews in Central Europe.'[63] He therefore advised Herzl to delay any personal initiatives intended to implement his proposals practically. Once again, he recalled the precedent of Theodor Hertzka who had 'destroyed his plan through precipitate action'. Güdemann insisted that the support of Eduard Bacher and the *Neue Freie Presse* would be decisively important in preparing the ground and diffusing Herzl's ideas to a wider public. Should this backing be refused Herzl was advised by the Chief Rabbi to write a novel elaborating his Zionist concept in artistic form.

Herzl's Diaries present a similar picture of the Viennese Chief Rabbi, blowing alternately hot and cold to his blandishments.[64] Yet as late as 26 December 1895 Güdemann had warmly complemented Herzl. He had read the first draft of *Der Judenstaat* 'with great composure', observing that it made 'a truly uplifting impression' upon him. Güdemann predicted that many of Herzl's comments would arouse the 'mockery of the Jews and the persecutory hatred of our enemies'. But he still believed that the pamphlet as a whole and especially its enthusiastic conclusion would stir the hearts of even the most 'tepid' co-religionists.

Güdemann seemed to sense intuitively the whole gamut of emotions—stunned surprise, ironic laughter, and a tinge of sympathy —which Herzl's tract was to produce in Viennese Jewry. With remarkable equanimity, he endorsed Herzl's argumentation, proposing only minimal corrections to the text. For example, he objected to Herzl's formulation that the Jews were no longer 'assimilable'. Güdemann also suggested eliminating an isolated remark that might be interpreted as offensive to the rabbis. However, there was no hint in his comments of any fundamental contradiction between Judaism and Jewish nationalism. Even the truly dramatic possibility that Herzl's tract might inaugurate the end of the millennial Diaspora did not unduly arouse Güdemann. He was still fixated on Herzl's links with the *Neue Freie Presse*:

Possibly, a serious person will always have doubts, but be that as it may, the

---

[63] Herzl Archives, CZA H VIII 309, Güdemann to Herzl, 30 Aug. 1895.
[64] See *Diaries*, 72 entry of 3 Nov. 1895. Herzl angrily told Güdemann that he was a *Schutzjude* (a protected Jew), when the Chief Rabbi reproached him for not accepting Prime Minister Badeni's offer to edit a government newspaper.

Word will strike like a bombshell or like a storm, which will be followed by lightning, perhaps not immediately, but in powerful pulsations.

The most important thing in any case is that this is being said by you, a poet and a journalist of the *Neue Freie Presse*; in short this is being stated by one of that company which has derided Judaism more than all the others. That a renowned member of this guild speaks of the 'faith of the fathers' and wants to realise this dream, will seem fantastic to all Jews. Even if perhaps you will be of no service to the Jews you will have been tremendously useful to your guild. They should be grateful when they know how the Jews think of you.[65]

Güdemann's comments, which hoped for a positive effect first and foremost on 'Jewish' journalism (especially on the un-Jewish Jews of the *Neue Freie Presse*) scarcely announced the rupture that would occur a year later. On 27 January 1896 he was still assuring Herzl with apparent satisfaction that the tract would 'strike like a bombshell and work wonders'.[66] As late as 2 February 1896, returning the final proofs to Herzl, he could write that he had read *Der Judenstaat* right through and 'find nothing to criticize'. The same day, encountering Herzl in Vienna's Prater, he again reiterated his enthusiasm.[67] Güdemann even approved Herzl's refusal to submit to the pressure of his employers at the *Neue Freie Presse* to delay publication of the pamphlet.[68]

Despite this support, Herzl became increasingly doubtful whether Güdemann would be able to resist community pressures to declare himself against Zionism.[69] In January 1897 he already referred very bitterly to the Chief Rabbi as an 'unctuous creature' without any backbone, on whom it was pointless to waste any more words. Following a chance encounter with Güdemann in the Schottenring, he noted in his Diary on 18 March 1897:

He had a number of absurd notions: he would rather let himself be killed in front of the Seitenstettegasse synagogue than yield to the anti-Semites. He will 'not take to flight' and other familiar pleasantries. He also spoke about the 'mission of the Jews', which consists of their being dispersed throughout the world. Every Jew who does nicely in the place where he happens to be dispersed talks about this 'mission'—but none of the others.[70]

[65] Herzl Archives, CZA H VIII 309 (20), Güdemann to Herzl, 26 Dec. 1895.

[66] *Diaries*, 88 entry of 27 Jan. 1896; also Herzl Archives, CZA H VIII, 309, Güdemann to Herzl, 27 Jan. 1896.

[67] *Diaries*, 89, 2 Feb. 1896. 'I was just thinking of you', he said. 'You don't realize at all what a big thing you have done.' Also Herzl Archives, CZA H VIII 309, 2 Feb. 1896. Güdemann wrote to Herzl: 'ich habe alles gelesen und finde nichts zu monieren.'

[68] *Diaries*, 92, 4 Feb. 1896.

[69] Ibid. 107, 26 Mar. 1896: '. . . he is afraid of the rich Jews who oppose it [i.e. the Jewish State] . . .' [70] Ibid. 203.

A diary entry of 17 April 1897, following Güdemann's 'malicious attack' on Zionism, anticipated the final settling of accounts.[71] 'He confines himself to vague cowardly ambiguities, but he wishes, it is clear, to provide ammunition for bolder warriors. I shall answer him— and, following the Machiavellian formula, it will be a crusher.'[72] Six days later he set about demolishing Güdemann's *Nationaljudentum*—a detailed rebuttal that appeared in Dr Bloch's *Österreichische Wochenschrift*.

Before considering Herzl's response, it is important to look at Güdemann's own version of these events and the reasons for his public adoption of an anti-Zionist position in April 1897. In his memoirs, Rabbi Güdemann recalled that at the end of December 1895 he had visited Herzl's home in the Pelikangasse. To his great surprise and consternation, the Chief Rabbi found 'a huge Christmas tree' in the drawing-room. 'Imagine my dismay. Soon Herzl entered, together with Oppenheim, also an editor of the *Neue Freie Presse*. Our conversation—in the presence of the Christmas tree—was rather cumbersome, and I soon took my leave. As far as I can recall, we paid no more visits to each other's homes.'[73]

Despite the cooling of their relations, Güdemann admitted in his memoirs to having congratulated Herzl on the appearance of *Der Judenstaat*. At the same time, he somewhat ingenuously claimed that he never imagined that Herzl could be serious about *implementing* the Zionist programme. Güdemann conceded that he had not in the least objected in 1896 to the secular, free-thinking standpoint of *Der Judenstaat*. But who could possibly imagine that as an orthodox rabbi he approved it?[74]

What had provoked the change in Rabbi Güdemann's initially benign view of Zionism was the enthusiastic embrace of Herzl's ideas by Jewish student circles and their noisy, provocative agitation in Vienna, of which he wanted no part. Güdemann could never understand how an assimilated Jew like Herzl with his superior

[71] *Diaries*, 208. For Herzl it was self-evident that Güdemann's pamphlet *Nationaljudentum* had been written 'at the behest of the local "upper (-class)" Jews'. He sarcastically noted that as soon as it appeared, 'Rothschild sent for thirty copies'.

[72] Ibid. 208. Herzl's reply appeared in Dr Bloch's *Österreichische Wochenschrift* on 23 Apr. 1897; in Herzl's *Zionist Writings: Essays and Addresses* (New York, 1973), i. 62–70.

[73] Güdemman, 'Meine Stellung zum Zionismus', 164. In fact, Herzl called several times on Güdemann after this encounter to discuss Zionism, and their relations remained friendly for a few months.

[74] Ibid. 166.

German *Bildung* suddenly desired to 'uproot himself from this native soil' (*sich aus diesem Mutterboden selbst auszuroden*)—encouraging Jewish youth to follow suit.[75] He also resented being pressurized by Herzl to preach in the Temple in favour of Zionism. According to Güdemann, at their last meeting in March 1897 on the Vienna Schottenring Herzl half in jest told him that he would in any event be forced to collaborate with the Zionists. Güdemann had angrily replied:

You are not a Jew at all. In the Talmud it is written: Vengeance is great, for it appears between two names of God: 'A God of vengeance is God.' You do not seem to be aware of this at all. I should go away from here, where the name of Jew and all those who bear it are constantly abused and cursed—I should clear the way for our enemies in order to grow vegetables in Palestine? No, not even ten thousand horses could drag me away from here, until I experience my revenge and satisfaction at the downfall of the anti-Semites [*Judenfeinde*].[76]

It was in this defiant mood that he had written his *Nationaljudenthum* and not, as Herzl scathingly suggested, at the behest of the Community Board. According to Güdemann, not a single member of the Kultusgemeinde leadership had read his pamphlet before publication or sought to influence him against Zionism.[77]

Güdemann's tract presented modern Jewish nationalism essentially as an indignant, defiant response against anti-Semitism and its proscription of the Jews as 'aliens'.[78] The Zionists insisted that the Jews constituted a 'nationality' even though they no longer possessed their own national territory. The nationalist movement sought to turn an age-old religious aspiration into a *political* programme. But they ignored the teachings of Judaism which alone in Güdemann's eyes could be the decisive arbiter.[79] Economic and political considerations of the moment were altogether secondary. The central issue was whether contemporary Zionism corresponded to the eternal truths of Judaism and its history.

Güdemann argued that the biblical Israelites had indeed been a nation (*Volk*) until the destruction of the Second Temple, though not in the pagan sense. Unlike the peoples of Antiquity, the Israelites had not glorified wars of conquest or depicted their military heroes as divine figures.[80] The victory hymns of ancient Israel had praised and magnified the Lord alone. The peoplehood of Israel was therefore

---

[75] Ibid.   [76] Ibid.   [77] Ibid. 166–7.
[78] Dr M. Güdemann, *Nationaljudenthum* (Leipzig and Vienna, 1897), 3.
[79] Ibid. 5.   [80] Ibid. 7 ff.

inseparable from its monotheistic concept of God.[81] The biblical Israelites repudiated from the beginning of their history the pagan nationalism of the Gentiles. They had renounced the prevailing cult of blood and iron in favour of a Divine lordship over heaven and earth.

Hence, Israel was not bound to a particular soil and its spiritual purpose was independent of rootedness in its own clod of earth. Mosaic teaching had prevented the emergence of an ideology of 'nativism' and expressly warned against a xenophobic rejection of the 'stranger' in the gates.[82] The individuality of Israel had above all been expressed by its yearning for transcendence, by its independence of territorial and national boundaries, and by its universal mission to be a light to the Gentiles.[83] After the Babylonian exile, Judah had become transformed into Diasporic Jewry. The State had been dissolved into a 'church' and the nation into a religous community. Its 'chosenness' lay in the dedicated fulfilment of its unique spiritual task. The prophetic teachings, which had preserved the distinctiveness of the Jewish people through the centuries of Dispersion, stood irrevocably opposed to any form of 'exclusivist, nativist consciousness of nationality'.[84] Thus, according to Gümemann, Jewish nationality and Judaism were fundamentally antithetical ideas.[85] The Jewish Diaspora embodied the vision of a united humanity beyond nationalism, worshipping the one true God. The Diaspora was not therefore the 'degenerated branch of an old stock' but the historic realization of the prophetic legacy, directed towards the Kingdom of God and the ideal fatherland of all mankind.

Modern Jewish nationalism contradicted this sublime historical mission. It proposed the abandonment of a future-orientated messianism, the sacrifice of its cosmopolitan ideal to the temporary needs of the moment.[86] Contemporary Zionism blindly attacked the 'assimilationist aspirations' of Jewry. In so doing, it had forgotten that 'the standard-bearers of Judaism'—philosophers like Philo, Maimonides, and Mendelssohn—had been an integral part of the cultural history of their times.[87] Jews had adapted, acclimatized, and assimilated themselves to surrounding cultures throughout their Diaspora history. In

---

[81] Gümemann, *Nationaljudenthum*, 13–14.

[82] Ibid. 19.　　　　　　　　[83] Ibid. 20.　　　　　　　　[84] Ibid. 23.

[85] Ibid. 27: 'Wir glauben gezeigt zu haben, dass die jüdische Religion geradezu antinational ist.' Gümemann quoted Theodor Mommsen's famous formula that the Jews were a ferment of national decomposition in the ancient world but reproached him for failing sufficiently to understand the positive side of the concept of *Weltbürgertum*.

[86] Ibid. 35.　　　　　　　　[87] Ibid. 37.

the nineteenth century they had continued this meritorious tradition. Only an exaggerated 'assimilationism' which advocated the 'self-dissolution' (*Selbstaufgebung*) of Judaism could be legitimately condemned.

Rabbi Güdemann believed that Zionism itself aspired to a far-reaching collective assimilation in so far as it 'transferred the national chauvinism of the present to Jewry'. In that sense the Jewish nationalists and not their critics contravened the biblical injunction against worshipping false gods. A nationalist Judaism based on canon and bayonets, which 'exchanged the roles of David and Goliath', would be a pathetic travesty of itself;[88] it would merely confirm the judgement of those who regarded the 2,000-year-old history of the Dispersion as 'a work of our depravity'. On the other hand, the Diaspora represented 'one of the most glorious parts of the history of Jewry' and its indestructibility was a sign that the future belonged to a universalistic Judaism.

Like Jellinek before him, Rabbi Güdemann did not object to colonization in the Holy Land as a means of bettering the miserable plight of impoverished Russian Jews. But such settlements should be sharply divorced from nationalist goals based on prophetic promises of redemption.[89] National restoration and independent statehood in Palestine were fundamentally irrelevant to 'true Zionism'; for the Zion of the Bible was inseparable from the moral perfection and brotherhood of all mankind.[90] The attempted conquest of Palestine would be no less than 'an encroachment on the leadership of God', a distortion of the teachings of the Torah, the prophets, the psalms, and the lessons of Jewish history. This profane Zionism was liable to prejudice the civil rights of Jews in their European fatherlands.

Güdemann maintained that there was no reason for Jews to cease regarding themselves as German, Magyars, or Frenchmen simply because the anti-Semites denied them this right. Judaism would long since have perished, had it depended for its survival on the definition of others or if it had imitated the nationalism of the Gentiles. Jews must therefore reject the principle of 'nationality' as being contrary to their fundamental interests and to their entire spiritual heritage. Quoting the Austrian national poet, Franz Grillparzer ('from humanity through nationality to bestiality'), the Chief Rabbi of Vienna concluded

---

[88] Ibid. 38.   [89] Ibid. 39.

[90] Ibid. 41: 'Zion galt und gilt den Juden als das Symbol ihrer eigenen, aber auch die ganze Menschheit umfassenden Zukunft.'

his anti-Zionist tract by asserting that Jews must hold fast to their faith and fight for their rights rather than abandon the struggle.[91]

Herzl's reply was a skilful, elegant, and effective polemic though it scarcely dealt with the deeper philosophical issues raised by Rabbi Güdemann. Herzl insisted that the Zionist movement was 'political through and through' and that religious objections were therefore beside the point. But he also pointed to a recent pamphlet by the orthodox Hasidic scholar, Ahron Marcus of Podgorze-Cracow, and to the opinions of highly respected rabbis to show that even from a religious standpoint Zionism could be easily defended by appropriate quotations from sacred texts.[92] The real strength of Zionism lay in its inclusiveness, in its ability to join freethinkers with orthodox Jews, and in its capacity to unite *all* members of the Jewish people. Zionism allowed its adherents 'complete freedom of conscience'.

Herzl took issue with Güdemann's definition of national consciousness as being based on a common fatherland, language, jurisprudence, and customs. He argued that in the modern world 'all peoples live in the Diaspora, as it were'—the specific *privilegium odiosum* of the Jews residing in the tragic fact that 'we are everywhere colonists without a mother country'—an anomaly which Zionism now sought to correct. In Herzl's understanding, the Jews were indisputably a nation because they corresponded to his bottom-line definition of constituting 'a historical group of people who recognizably belong together and are held together by a common foe'.[93] To ignore this simple truth in the name of a so-called Jewish 'mission' was a luxury only sated, comfortable philistines could afford.

Herzl was particularly scathing about Güdemann's interpretation of the traditional prayers for Zion which the Chief Rabbi had described as being 'anything but national in intent'.[94]

Are we, then, to believe that when people pray for a return to Zion they mean just the opposite? Are we to believe that the words of the prayer do not have the meaning which the congregation, faithfully adhering to these words, associates with them? At the very moment when the course of world affairs—the definitive kind of anti-Semitism which arose after the emancipation, re-awakening Jewish nationalism, the situation in the Orient, and the achievements of technology—all combine to render the return to Zion an imminent

---

[91] Güdemann, *Nationaljudenthum*, 42.

[92] 'Dr. Güdemann's National-Judentum', in Herzl's *Zionist Writings*, trans. H. Zohn (New York, 1973), i. 64–5.

[93] Ibid. 67.   [94] Ibid. 68.

possibility, at that moment there is a Chief Rabbi who says 'Never mind all that—it is just a 'symbol'![195]

For Herzl it was clear that the good-natured Güdemann had simply 'allowed himself to be used by wirepullers'. The Chief Rabbi was being manipulated by rich Jews who were 'clever enough to bribe their own way out of anti-Semitism—with favours, money and the sacrifice of their convictions . . .'.[96] Contrary to Güdemann's assertions, there was no contradiction between Zionism 'with its social reforms (the seven-hour working day, etc.), its tolerance, and its love for the poorest among the outcasts' and the future of mankind envisaged by prophetic Judaism. The Zionist vision, Herzl dreamed would harness 'the productive streams of humanity' which it fertilized, to the ancient soil of Palestine, thereby reawakening the Jewish nation to new life. This utopia of social engineering was manifestly destined to be 'the Zion of the poor, of the young and also that of the pious'.[97]

In his Memoirs Güdemann did not mention Herzl's rejoinder. He had been deeply hurt by a much cruder assault published by Max Nordau in *Die Welt* (11 July 1897) against his notion of a cosmopolitan Jewish 'mission'[98] He regarded Herzl as being much too refined to stoop to this level. Indeed, in retrospect he seemed to regret deeply the public conflict which had opposed him to Herzl.[99] Moritz Güdemann did acknowledge, for example, one important merit of Herzlian Zionism in the Viennese context. It had revived the traditional prayers for Zion 'like a bolt from the blue', even in the hearts of those 'educated Jews' who had sought to delete them from the prayer books thirty years earlier. 'What a blessing Zionism could have been', Güdemann concluded in his Memoirs, 'had it been content to allow this idea to pursue its original religious course instead of diverting it into nationalism. But they [the Zionists] wanted to be Jews and free-thinkers, i.e. Jews and non-Jews, at the same time, a *contradictio in adjecto*.'[100]

Güdemann's anti-Zionism was not motivated solely by religious considerations. An important factor was his tenacious refusal to allow the anti-Semites to deny his 'inalienable right' to German nationality.

---

[95] Ibid. 69.   [96] Ibid. 70.   [97] Ibid.
[98] Güdemann, 'Meine Stellung zum Zionismus', 167.
[99] Ibid. 'Herzl hatte eine zu feine Natur, als dass er sich zum Haudegen geeignet hätte. Ich glaube auch, dass diese Ausartung seiner Umgebung ihm Kummer bereitete und mit zu seinem frühzeitigen Tode beigetragen hat. Ehre seinem Andenken!'
[100] Ibid. 168.

A letter written by Güdemann on 19 December 1907 to the authoress Kamilla Theimer expressed his deep revulsion at the 'unclean' distinction between German and Jew proposed by demagogues in Berlin and Vienna. After a few barbs directed at Bismarck ('the first to bring forth this wickedness'), at his midwife Adolf Stoecker, and against the Austrian anti-Semite Ernst Schneider, Güdemann diagnosed the inner contradiction within Christianity that lay at the heart of Judaeophobia.

The Christian kneels before the image of a Jew, wrings his hands before the image of a Jewess; his Apostles, Festivals, and Psalms are Jewish. Only a few are able to come to terms with this contradiction—most free themselves by anti-Semitism. Obliged to revere a Jew as God, they wreak vengeance upon the rest of the Jews by treating them as devils.[101]

Unlike the Zionists, Güdemann sincerely believed that the 'Aryan' people would become ashamed of anti-Semitism, though he admitted the possibility of periodic relapses. More importantly, for the Jews to despair in the face of this 'vile thing' would mean to abandon the positive civilizing influence they had exercised for centuries on mankind. Güdemann regarded Zionism as precisely such a retreat into national separatism. 'Would such isolation satisfy their innate urge and call to influence humanity? For centuries the Christians have accused the Jews of isolating themselves. And suddenly such isolation is to be a panacea? The poison is now to serve as an antidote? That is no sensible cure.'[102]

Similar views were undoubtedly held by most leaders of the Viennese Kultusgemeinde and other major Jewish organizations such as the Allianz or the Austrian Israelite Union. The President of the Union, Sigmund Mayer, a long-standing assimilationist, had un-equivocally asserted that the Jews were not a nation since they lacked a common land, language, or culture of their own. In his view, Yiddish culture was an empty phrase. Even more fantastic was the notion of creating a Hebrew-speaking 'nationality' in Palestine or in the Habsburg Empire. Mayer indignantly protested against the main goal of the Jewish National party in Austria 'to constitute the Jews as a political nation, similar to the Czechs and Germans, the Poles and

---

[101] 'Aus einem Briefe von Sr. Ehrw, Ob-Rabbiner Dr. Güdemann an Frau Kamilla Theimer v. 19. December 1907', in Central Archives of the History of the Jewish People, A/W 731.5. The letter has also been printed in J. Fraenkel's article 'The Chief Rabbi and the Visionary', *Jews of Austria*, 115–17.
[102] Ibid.

Ruthenians [Ukrainians], Slovenes, Rumanians, etc.'.[103] This auto-nomist goal was no less of an impractical utopia in Austrian conditions than the more far-reaching Zionist objective of a Jewish national restoration to Palestine. Far from counteracting anti-Semitism, Zionism and Jewish national autonomism would merely focus all the hatred of the surrounding Austrian nationalities against the Jewish people.[104]

For Mayer, as for the liberal Jewish establishment and the Austrian Social Democratic Party, Jewish nationalism constituted a return to the ghetto. It stood in flagrant contradiction to general historical trends, to the economic interest of Jewry in the unity of the Dual Monarchy, and to the legal-political basis of emancipation. Like Rabbi Güdemann, though for slightly different reasons, Sigmund Mayer held that it was a Jewish mission to oppose the forces of nationalism. In so doing, the Jews were the true heralds of a cosmopolitan future for Austria and the whole of mankind.[105] Mayer's classical liberal critique of Jewish nationalism combined fervent loyalty to German culture with belief in a strong supranational Austria.

This integrationist ideology was shared by the Austro-Marxists, whose anti-Zionism echoed widely-held liberal-assimilationist pre-misses with regard to the 'Jewish question'. Thus, Austro-Marxist theoreticians like Karl Renner and Otto Bauer advocated a programme of cultural-national autonomy within a federalist Austrian State from which they explicitly excluded the Jews. Jewish Marxists frequently turned out to be among the fiercest critics of Zionism and rising Jewish autonomism in the Habsburg Empire.[106]

Both Austrian Liberals and Social Democrats of Jewish origin believed that assimilation was an inevitable and positive social process. They generally shared the same distaste for Yiddish and Hebrew, for the culture of the ghetto, and for the social backwardness of the Galician Jewish masses. Hence, any national demands put forward in the name of Eastern Jews in Galicia and Bukovina were invariably decried as clerical, divisive, and reactionary. The spectre of a Jewish *Volkstum* in the hinterlands of the Monarchy and on its eastern borders

---

[103] Sigmund Mayer, *Die Wiener Juden: Kommerz, Kultur, Politik, 1700–1900*; (Vienna and Berlin, 1917), 465.

[104] Ibid. 492.

[105] Ibid. 493: 'Die Juden als Gegner der Nationalismus waren sozusagen die frühesten Bürger der kommenden politischen Welt.'

[106] See Robert S. Wistrich, 'Austrian Social Democracy and the problem of Galician Jewry 1890–1914', *Leo Baeck Yearbook*, 26 (1981), 89–124.

was something that seemed particularly to disturb the Marxists, perhaps because it called into question their own position as Germanized intellectuals and leaders of the labour movement.[107] The most prominent Jews in the Austrian Social Democracy—Victor Adler, Wilhelm Ellenbogen, Friedrich Austerlitz, Otto Bauer, Robert Danneberg, and Max Adler—were imbued with a deep attachment to German culture. Their attachment to the multinational framework of the Austrian Empire and their belief in the superiority of socialist ideals, tended to intensify their negation of Jewish nationalism.[108] In this attitude they were joined by outstanding Jewish leaders of the Polish Social Democratic Party (PPSD) in Galicia like Hermann Diamand and Hermann Liebermann, who were both elected to the Austrian Parliament in 1907.[109] Their critique of Zionism was probably sharpened by the fact that it undoubtedly had a significant electoral appeal to Galician Jewry.[110]

It was no accident that some of the harshest attacks against Zionism published in *fin de siècle* Marxist journals came from the pens of Jewish Social Democrats in Galicia and other parts of Eastern Europe. For example, in 1896, Max Zetterbaum, a leading propagandist of the PPSD, denounced Herzl's *Judenstaat* as a shameless imposture by the polished, elegant, and worldly *feuilletoniste* of the *Neue Freie Presse*. It was obviously the work of a man totally ignorant of Jewish religious tradition. Devoid of the poetry and mysticism in authentic Judaism, everything in Herzl's tract was 'modern' in the most artificial sense. Political Zionism was a typically vacuous product of *fin-de-siècle*

---

[107] Nathan Birnbaum, *Ausgewählte Schriften zur jüdischen Frage* (Chernovtsy, 1910), i. 298: 'Oder schreckt sie etwa schon der Gedanke, sich in Zukunft mit ihrem Judentum nicht mehr so gut verbergen zu können wie bisher? Dass der Sturm aus dem Osten den Nebel zereissen könnte und sie dann nackt dastehen müssten vor aller Welt, in der von ihnen gehasstesten, eigenen, in der Haut der Juden.'

[108] Wistrich, 'Austrian Social Democracy', 116 ff.

[109] See David Balakan, *Die Sozialdemokratie und das jüdische Proletariat* (Chernovtsy, 1905), written from a Bundist standpoint and highly critical of both the Austrian and Galician Socialists for their negation of Jewish autonomist demands. Also Mathias Acher (Nathan Birnbaum), *Das Stiefkind der Sozialdemokratie* (Vienna, 1905). On Diamand, see Wistrich, 'Austrian Social Democracy', 105 ff.

[110] See Wistrich, *Socialism and the Jews*, 314 ff., for the competition between Polish Social Democrats and Zionists in Galicia to gain the support of the Jewish masses. The labour Zionists, organized by one of Herzl's aides, Saul Raphael Landau, began to make progress in disseminating Zionist ideas among Jewish workers in the 1890s. See S. R. Landau, *Sturm und Drang im Zionismus: Rückblicke eines Zionisten* (Vienna, 1937), 147–58. In Vienna, too, there were clashes between Social Democrats and Zionists in 1898–9.

Viennese Judaism, motivated mainly by frustrated ambition and expressing a purely imitative nationalism.[111]

Other socialist critics of Jewish origin drew ignominious comparisons between Zionist student agitation at the University of Vienna and the rowdy antics of the beer-swilling, arrogant Pan-German fraternities.[112] An Austro-Marxist intellectual like Gustav Eckstein maintained that 'the representatives of the nationality principle in Jewry' relied on 'the same racial principle that was used against them by their bitterest enemies, the Pan-Germans'.[113] The liberal hypothesis that anti-Semitism and Zionism were two sides of the same coin was eagerly taken up by Jewish Marxists. Did not both ideologies insist on branding the Jews as an alien 'nationality' (or *Gastvolk*) and doggedly seek to repatriate them to Palestine?[114]

Like their liberal forerunners, socialist Jews tended to regard Zionism as a reactionary and artificial attempt to separate Jews from other peoples on the basis of a non-existent Jewish 'nationality'. Friedrich Austerlitz, editor of the Viennese *Arbeiterzeitung*, campaigning as a socialist candidate in the Leopoldstadt during the 1907 elections, was reported as saying: 'The Zionists canvass for votes from the very people who they want to shut up ghettoes again. They exploit the concealed affliction of the Jews, namely that they do not have equal rights, and direct their secret pride towards a false goal.'[115]

When the Eleventh Zionist Congress opened in Vienna on 3 September 1913, the *Arbeiterzeitung* devoted a full-length article to exposing the pretensions of its leaders. Zionism, it declared, was rooted in the self-deception of Herzl and his followers that anti-Semitism could be eradicated by an exodus of *Ostjuden* from Europe to a 'land of milk and honey'. For all its 'free-thinking pretensions' it was nothing but 'the old Jewish orthodoxy dressed up in modern costume',

---

[111] Max Zetterbaum's review appeared in Karl Kautsky's influential German Marxist periodical *Die Neue Zeit* at the beginning of 1896. The text is partly reproduced in a French version by Michael Pollak, *Vienne 1900: une identité blessée* (Paris, 1984), 94–5.

[112] 'Eine Studentenprügelei', *Arbeiterzeitung* (Vienna), 18 Nov. 1898, p. 4; also 'ein zionistischer Gänsemarsch', ibid, 23 Feb. 1899, p. 6.

[113] See Gustav Eckstein's review of Ignaz Zollschan's massive treatise, *Das Rassenproblem unter besonderer Berücksichtigung der theoretischen Grundlagen der jüdischen Rassenfrage* (Vienna, 1909) in *Neue Zeit* (Stuttgart, 1910–11), i. 60. Zollschan was an Austrian Jewish anthropologist sympathetic to Zionism, who had been influenced by contemporary race-thinking in Central Europe, though he challenged its conclusions regarding the physical and intellectual 'degeneration' of Jewry.

[114] 'Der Zionismus—staatsgefährlich', *Arbeiterzeitung*, 29 Dec. 1900, p. 5.

[115] 'Wiener Wahlversammlung in der Leopoldstadt', ibid., 28 Mar. 1907, p. 6.

a pseudo-nationalism trying desperately to resurrect Hebrew, 'though this has never been the everyday language of the Jews, not even 2,000 years ago'.[116] There was something pathetic about the determined Zionist pride in national characteristics which 'strike other people as Jewish eccentricity of not always the pleasantest kind'.[117]

Above all, Zionism appeared to be wholly utopian and impracticable. The Jews of Turkish Palestine numbered no more than 100,000 and most of these inhabitants had been resident well before the beginning of Zionist colonization. There was little prospect that rich Jews would invest in this lost cause, since they had better uses for their millions than to settle their impoverished brethren in the Holy Land.[118] The whole project was therefore an 'unrealizable dream' in stark contradiction to economic, political, and geographical realities.

Who is likely to believe that Turkey is going to give up its rule over a country of whose 700,000 inhabitants four-fifths are Muslims, simply because the Jews wish to return to their 'Promised Land'? Who is likely to believe that the 'Christian States' are going to put themselves out to create a Jewish State? . . . Who can be so naïve as to believe the city-dwellers can be turned into small farmers in a distant and now almost uncivilized country?[119]

Similar objections to Zionism were also raised by conservative and liberal Jewish assimilationists in Vienna. What specifically differentiated Marxist hostility to Jewish nationalism from its rivals was the attempt to portray political Zionism as the class ideology of the Jewish bourgeoisie and the economically declining *Mittelstand* in the Austrian provinces. This petty bourgeoisie was being driven by impoverishment to seeking quack remedies for their desperate plight. No less typical of the Marxist critique was the assumption that modern industrialism had begun decisively to erode Jewish 'national' characteristics. Capitalism was supposedly breaking down ethnic and religious barriers, thereby preparing the path for a classless socialist society in which Jewry would eventually disappear as a distinct entity. This was the central premise of the case presented by the Austro-Marxist Otto Bauer (1881–1938) against Jewish cultural-national autonomy in a monumental work of 1907 on the Austrian nationality question. Otto Bauer did not directly polemicize against Zionism. But he did provide the theoretical underpinning for socialist theories of assimilation that denied any national future to the Jewish people. According to Otto Bauer, the

---

[116] 'Die Zionisten Kongress in Wien', *Arbeiterzeitung*, 4 Sept. 1913, pp. 6–7.
[117] Ibid.   [118] Ibid.   [119] Ibid.

Jews would not be able to survive as a nation without a territorial centre. Capitalist society was relentlessly stripping away their ethnic characteristics by obliterating their specific economic function as middlemen and money-lenders. Bauer concluded: 'It would perhaps be too much to say even in Western and Central Europe that the Jews are not a nation. But one can certainly assert that they are ceasing to be a nation.'[120]

Even in Russia and Eastern Europe, where the non-assimilated Jewish masses formed the core of the Jewish nation, modern capitalism was beginning to break down the social, cultural, and economic barriers between Jews and Gentiles. The aim of the Social Democrats must be to encourage this natural development. They wished to bring Eastern Jewish proletarians into a common class-struggle with the German and Slavic working classes. Hence Socialists strongly opposed any perpetuation of traditional ghetto habits, of 'the culture of a people totally isolated from the mainstream of European civilization, a people held together by the heritage of an outmoded system of thought and by the dead weight of observances transmitted from generation to generation'.[121] Otto Bauer regarded cultural assimilation as the *sine qua non* for preparing the Jewish worker to participate in the general class-struggle: '. . . only then will his special Jewish misery disappear and he will be left with nothing but the common proletarian misery which he will fight and conquer in the common battle, shoulder to shoulder with his Aryan [sic] colleagues.'[122]

Within this Marxist perspective, both Zionism and Jewish national autonomy were generally depicted as unwelcome and reactionary diversions from the internationalist character of the proletarian cause. At the turn of the century a handful of socialist Zionists began to challenge these ideological assumptions. Their leading theorist, the Russian radical *émigré* Nachman Syrkin (1867–1924), suggesting that Jewish assimilationist leaders in the international labour movement were imitating the Jewish bourgeoisie by throwing off their Judaism as an unwanted burden.[123] Syrkin claimed in 1898 that there was no other nation, whose revolutionary avant-garde had gone to such lengths to 'preach assimilation to a dominant nationality'. Such

---

[120] Otto Bauer, *Die Nationalitätenfrage und die Sozialdemokratie* (Vienna, 1907), 370.
[121] Ibid. 379.   [122] Ibid.
[123] See Syrkin's article in the Austrian periodical *Deutsche Worte*, edited by the Social Democrat Engelbert Pernerstorfer, 18 July 1898, pp. 298–313; also extracts from his classic tract 'The Jewish Problem and the Socialist-Jewish State' (1898), in A. Hertzberg (ed.), *The Zionist Idea: A Historical Analysis and Reader* (New York, 1973), 340 ff.

socialist cosmopolitanism was based on false premises. Echoing earlier Austrian Zionist thinkers and publicists like Nathan Birnbaum and Saul Raphael Landau, Syrkin insisted that international Social Democracy should not suppress the national character of any people. On the contrary, it must encourage all struggles for national liberation including that of the Jewish people. Jews had been attracted to socialism because of their oppressed economic condition and their messianic traditions of defending human freedom and social justice. But they also required Zionism since their singular social position excluded an effective struggle in contemporary conditions. Moreover, socialism could 'solve the Jewish problem only in the remote future'.[124] Like Pinkser, Birnbaum, and Herzl, Syrkin saw the acquisition of a national territory as the only immediate remedy to this plight. Zionism was therefore a movement that necessarily affected all classes of Jewry and stood beyond the class struggle as a central creative task of national regeneration.

Such arguments made little or no impression on the Jewish intellectuals in the Austrian labour movement before 1914. Nor did Zionism win many adherents among the leading writers and artists of *fin-de-siècle* Vienna, including those who were more immediately concerned with the problems posed by Jewish identity.[125] Among the most militant of the anti-Zionist critics was the satirist Karl Kraus (1874–1936), who in 1898 published a malevolent pamphlet against Herzl and Zionism, sarcastically entitled *Eine Krone für Zion*. Kraus was a young Bohemian-born Jew from a middle-class background who had already demonstrated his contempt for the fashionable Viennese literary establishment in his first important work, *Die demolierte Literatur* (Literature Demolished). He reacted no less vehemently towards the new Zionist movement.[126]

There were many reasons for Kraus's hostility, some of them merely aesthetic such as his mocking the Zionists for their regressive 'Assyrian' beards and hair-styles. In certain respects his anti-Zionist

[124] Syrkin, 'The Jewish Problem', 345.

[125] A rare exception was the writer and poet Richard Beer-Hofmann (1866–1945), friend of Hofmannstahl and Schnitzler, whose pride in his ancestral heritage led him to support ardently Herzl's Zionism. Beer-Hofmann suggested as early as 1896 that the Palestinian experiment begin with the founding of a great medical university to improve health conditions in the Orient. See the entry of 9 Apr. 1896 in *The Diaries of Theodor Herzl*, 108; also Sol Liptzin, 'Richard Beer-Hofmann', in J. Fraenkel (ed.), *Jews of Austria*, 213–19.

[126] *Eine Krone für Zion* (Vienna, 1898) repr. in Karl Kraus, *Frühe Schriften, 1892–1900*, ii. *1897–1900* (Münich, 1979), 298 ff.

positions had become reminiscent of precisely those Jewish liberals whom he had consistently pilloried in his satirical journalism. Like the liberals, he was also an unconditional advocate of assimilation, regarding Zionism as an ephemeral reaction against anti-Semitism— one which was more likely to exacerbate rather than cure the disease. At the same time, his assault on the decadent Viennese bourgeoisie and modish *Jung Wien* littérateurs including Theodor Herzl (whom he primarily attacked as the *feuilletoniste* of the *Neue Freie Presse*) contained a more radical accent. It was a position which in 1898 seemed close to the Social Democrats. Indeed, Karl Kraus maintained in his pamphlet that Socialism, rather than Western bourgeois Zionism, would save the Jewish masses of Eastern Europe.[127]

One of the more disturbing features in the Krausian polemic was the obsessive harping on the mutual interdependence between Viennese anti-Semites and the Zionists. Both were accused of seeking to keep the 'Jewish question' alive and constantly at the centre of public attention. Indeed, Herzl and the Jewish nationalist students were nothing if not 'Jewish anti-Semites' in the eyes of Karl Kraus.[128] The rallying-cry 'Hinaus mit den Juden!' had been nurtured in his view by the irresponsible Zionist agitation in Vienna designed to further their 'depraved aims'. Fortunately, these objectives had no chance of being realized.[129] In Western Europe, where assimilated Jews lived a satiated life, the Zionist slogan of 'the millennial suffering of Jewry' was a wholly artificial fiction which Kraus was convinced would find little resonance. Admittedly, in Eastern Europe, where an obscurantist orthodoxy prevented poor Jews from joining up with their proletarian class-comrades, Zionism had begun to make headway and sought to enclose them in a new national ghetto.[130] In place of the decaying religious ties of solidarity, the Zionist organization hoped to link the Jewish weavers of Lodz with the wealthy Israelites of the

[127] Ibid. 314.

[128] Ibid. 298–9. Kraus referred in passing at this point to Herzl's article 'Mauschel' which had appeared in *Die Welt* on 15 Oct. 1897. *Mauschel* (from the German word *mauscheln* referring to the garbled German, spoken with a Yiddish accent and associated with Jewish petty traders from the East) was the name given by Herzl to his anti-Zionist opponents. The article had been a vitriolic assault on these critics, not without its own anti-Semitic tinge. However, the *Mauschel* type depicted by Herzl seemed to anticipate uncannily the mocking, denunciatory tone of Kraus's own pamphlet.

[129] Ibid. 299.

[130] Ibid. 301: 'Die den Hunger gemeinsam haben sollten, werden nach nationalen Merkmalen getrennt und gegeneinander ausgespielt.'

Ringstrasse. This was one of the many illusions which Kraus was determined to prick.

Kraus caricatured the Zionist Congress in Basle with particular gusto. The sight of delegates 'of the chosen people' enthusing over the Jewish flag and dreaming of a homeland on the banks of the Jordan was guaranteed to provoke his scorn.[131] With remorseless irony he knocked the self-congratulatory publicity of the Zionists, who were delighted that no voices had been publicly raised against their assembling in a Swiss city. Christians had even expressed sympathy for the new movement. According to Kraus, this fraternity was indeed well-founded:

It is known that the Zionists record every rumpus against the Jews with a certain satisfaction. They rejoiced over the pillaging in Galicia [the 1898 pogroms] as if this had been exclusively their success though one cannot deny the Polish Club a certain merit in the affair. No special mention is necessary here that the confessional school is not lacking in the Zionist programme. The Jewish nationalist journalists no less than the [anti-Semitic] Vienna city council have promoted the decree that will introduce segregation in primary school classes . . .[132]

Not content with this malicious false symmetry. Kraus went so far as to claim that 'the innate sensibility of the poets of *Jung Wien* [Young Vienna] had shown itself to be a particularly fertile ground for the new philosophy'.[133] According to Kraus: '. . . only philistine Zionism permitted these gentlemen, hitherto preoccupied by their nerves to feel themselves contemporaries. With astounding rapidity they have overcome the millennial suffering of Judaism, which now enables them to adopt a thousand new and unimaginable poses.'[134]

Through Zionism, these coffee-house literati (whom Kraus heartily detested) had acquired a *Weltanschauung* which went beyond lacquered finger-nails and the inflated bombast of the bourgeois salons; in place of effete and world-weary aestheticism, these Ringstrasse dandies (Hermann Bahr, Schnitzler, Beer-Hofmann, Herzl, Salten) had found a new cause—the transformation of Jewry into an agriculturally productive nation. But the revival of *Jung Wien* was only one aspect of the 'metamorphosis' produced by Zionism.

For more robust natures, the new Zionist faith takes the form of a fanaticized Jewish consciousness. I am thinking of the headstrong students who look East,

---

[131] Kraus, *Frühe Schriften* ii, 303–4.   [132] Ibid. 304.   [133] Ibid.   [134] Ibid. 305.

the shocktroops of an eventual holy war. They have succeeded in convincing Christians, including those who previously displayed not the slightest predilection for anti-Semitism, of the salutary nature of the idea of segregation . . .'[135]

Jewish nationalist students, determined to exhibit their self-assertiveness 'in all its grotesque obtrusiveness', proposed to transform unappetizing physical traits, stigmatized by vulgar anti-Semitism, into a source of pride. On no account would they permit the Pan-Germans to concern themselves solely with the fight against clericalism and the Slavs. Zionism would not allow the 'Jewish question' to fade quietly. But Kraus maintained that he could see no virtue in a philosophy which in his view consisted of trying to make 'hooked noses meritorious'.

Having thus exposed the inanities of the Zionist students with their demonstratively provocative behaviour, Kraus passed on to a brief critique of the utopian romanticism contained in the Zionist economic programme. But the development of Palestine interested him far less than the linguistic Babel at the Basle Congress which not even the literary gifts of Dr Herzl had been able to overcome. Discussions in Basle concerning the possibilities of a new Jewish 'national' culture based on the Hebrew language sounded no less fantastic to Kraus than the proposition that a Jewish State might be forged out of the divergent interests of German, English, French, Slavic, or Turkish Jews.[136]

Despite his anti-Zionism, Kraus did not wish to be seen as 'an advocate of the assimilated Jews' though he shared their belief in the extraordinary adaptability of Jewry.[137] He recognized that the centre of Zionist agitation in Austria must inevitably be focused in Galicia where economic misery had made the Jewish masses more receptive. But money collected for Zionist goals in Galicia would be better spent—so Kraus argued—on creating a decent educational network. Like the Liberals, Kraus wanted to restrict orthodox influence, to persuade Galician Jews to abandon their anachronistic hairstyles (*payot*), their outmoded clothing, and Yiddish speech. Colonization in Galicia itself, he ironically observed, would certainly be far less expensive and utopian than 'the planned radical cure of an Exodus'.[138]

---

[135] Ibid. 306. [136] Ibid. 308–9.

[137] Ibid. 309: 'Bestimmt, in allen umgebenden Culturen unlösbar aufzughen und dem noch immerdar Ferment zu bleiben, erweist sich diese Wesensart stärker als ihre übereifrigen Verkünder.'

[138] Ibid. 310.

Kraus was evidently convinced that Zionism would prove to be nothing more than an ephemeral *fin de siècle* fad. To his mind it defied both reason and reality. The prospects of social change and betterment within European civilization—including the gradual decline of anti-Semitism—seemed decidedly more favourable and likely than the return of the Jews to Palestine.[139] Humanitarian phraseology could not disguise the reactionary ghetto character of the Zionist enterprise.

Even if one abstracts from all the political dangers, good taste still has every right to protest, that the wit of a drunken old man in Hernals [a suburb of Vienna] shouting 'Out with the Jews!' finds its simple repetition in Zionism. Apart from its more pompous tone, the reply 'Yes, out with us, Jews!' offers precious little difference.[140]

Kraus's arguments seem remarkably similar to those of the wealthy assimilated Viennese Jews, whom he detested no less than the Zionists. Nevertheless, while rejecting the snobbery of these 'feudal Jews' and of the great Jewish financial dynasties, he manifestly sympathized with their refusal to accept the 'Zionist imposture'. The social and economic gulf between these patricians and the Galician plebs was too great to be bridged by resounding proclamations about 'Jewish solidarity'. Kraus concluded

. . . the propertied classes, feudal as well as bourgeois Jews will reply to Zionist solicitations with broad laughter. But in the weary heart of the Galician proletarians, Zionism will stir a corrupting flame. Nostalgia only warms the heart so long as the ignorance of realities persists. The creation of illusions is not social reform, but a deliberate deception and every mirage can only prolong the suffering of those who cross the desert. And this time one can scarcely assume that the Jews will arrive dry-shod in the promised land; another Red Sea, Social Democracy, will bar their way.[141]

Kraus's parting barbs were directed at Max Nordau and Theodor Herzl—the 'King of Zion'—as he sarcastically nicknamed him.

Certain gentlemen feel a certain uneasiness confronted with the sluggishness that reigns in their environment; these sensitive natures, surfeited by the premature success with which their talent and good fortune have overwhelmed them, urgently require a new meaning and seriousness in their lives. Without doubt this deserves the attention of the public. It is indeed worth troubling oneself about the development of Dr Theodor Herzl, the distinguished Viennese prose writer. But it was certainly not inscribed in the order of this world that the need to pass from the *feuilleton* to leading article should

---

[139] Kraus, *Frühe Schriften* ii, p. 311   [140] Ibid. 312.   [141] Ibid. 313–14.

condemn hundreds of thousands of men to sinking back into their old misery from the heights of a delusive brilliance.[142]

As for Max Nordau (the *Literaturarzt* who so obtrusively felt the pulse of the *fin de siècle*, searching for its tiniest anomalies), it was only fitting that this expert on 'degeneration' should be the chairman of the Zionist Congress. Nordau's notes on Zionism show that his feelings about Karl Kraus were scarcely more complementary.

Kraus ridicules the national reawakening of the Jews and labels it assimilation. When all is said and done, his article reflects blind rage and his own fear of the reawakening of the Jews. He accuses Herzl (and the Zionists) of stopping at nothing to stir up base instincts and hostilities. Kraus is a past master at invective.[143]

Although Karl Kraus was something of a literary outsider, his invective was not without influence in Vienna. The epithet, *Der König von Zion*, which he had used to mock Herzl, achieved a wide currency. Stefan Zweig recalled:

When he [Herzl] entered the theatre, a handsome, bearded personage, grave and compellingly aristocratic in his demeanor, a sibilation arose on all sides: *Der König von Zion*, or 'His Majesty has arrived'. This ironic title peered at him through every conversation, through every glance. The papers vied with one another in ridiculing the new idea—that is, those in which it was not prohibited, as it was in Herzl's own *Neue Freie Presse*, to mention the word *Zionismus* altogether.[144]

Fin de siècle Vienna was not especially kind to its most creative sons, whether Jew or Gentile—least of all to those who felt the prophetic call. Herzl's confession to Stefan Zweig in 1904 was most telling in this respect:

It was abroad that I learned everything I know. Only there do we become used to think in broad perspective. I feel sure that here [in Vienna] I would never have had the courage for that first idea; they would have destroyed it with their irony before it was fully developed. But, thank God, it had matured before I brought it here, so that they could do nothing to harm it.[145]

[142] Ibid. 314.
[143] 'Notes on Zionism by Max Nordau' (sel. Chaim Bloch), *Herzl Year Book*, 8 (New York, 1971), 34.
[144] Stefan Zweig, 'King of the Jews', *Herzl Year Book*, 3 (New York, 1960), 110–11.
[145] Ibid. 115.

PART IV

CULTURE AND IDENTITY

15

Prophets of Doom:
Karl Kraus and Otto Weininger

There are two beautiful things in the world: to belong to the *Neue Freie Presse* or to despise it. I did not hesitate for a moment which choice I should make.

> Karl Kraus, *Die Fackel* (1899)

Judaism, at the present day, has reached its highest point since the time of Herod. Judaism is the spirit of modern life. Sexuality is accepted, and contemporary ethics sing the praises of pairing . . . It is the Jew and the woman who are the apostles of pairing to bring guilt on humanity.

> Otto Weininger, *Geschlecht und Charakter* (1903)

To defeat Judaism, the Jews must first understand himself and war against himself. So far, the Jew has reached no further than to make and enjoy jokes against his own peculiarities. Unconsciously he respects the Aryan more than himself. Only steady resolution, united to the highest self-respect, can free the Jew from Jewishness. This resolution, be it ever so strong, ever so honourable, can only be understood and carried out by the individual, not by the group. Therefore the Jewish question can only be solved individually; every single Jew must try to solve it in his proper person.

> Otto Weininger, *Geschlecht und Charakter* (1903)

The anti-Semitism of the Jews bears testimony to the fact that no one who has had experience of them considers them lovable—not even the Jew himself; the anti-Semitism of the Aryans grants us an insight no less full of significance: it is that the Jew and the Jewish race must not be confounded. There are Aryans who are more Jewish than Jews, and real Jews who are more Aryan than certain Aryans.

> Otto Weininger, *Geschlecht und Charakter* (1903)

I believe I can say this about myself, that I go along with the

development of Judaism up to the Exodus, but that I don't
participate in the dance around the Golden Calf—and from that
point on share only in those characteristics which were also found
in the defenders of God and in the avengers of a people gone
astray.

Karl Kraus, *Die Fackel* (1913)

Fin de siècle Vienna, perhaps more than any other intellectual and
artistic centre of European civilization, demonstrated the Janus-face of
modernity: the combining of a profoundly liberating and emancipatory
message with an agonizing exploration of its dark, daemonic aspects.
But it was above all the sombre dimension, the sense of malaise
and uncertainty exhibited by its cultural élite in the face of political
decline, rapid social and economic change, and turbulent ethnic
conflicts which gave Vienna its peculiar character and originality: that
restless search for identity and intellectual-aesthetic innovativeness
which broke through time-honoured conventions and taboos of
Western Christian civilization. Within this creative fermentation,
the Jewish preponderance was a phenomenon that forcefully struck
most contemporary observers and not only the fabricators of anti-
Semitic mythologies. Names like Freud, Adler, Schnitzler, Mahler,
Schoenberg, Altenberg, Kraus, Weininger, Broch, and Stefan Zweig,
not to mention those of Jewish extraction like Hugo von Hofmannstahl
and Ludwig Wittgenstein, remind one of the centrality of Jews among
the leading innovators within the Viennese cultural élite.

In this city renowned for its superficial gaiety and Strauss waltzes,
personal traumas and collective anxieties fused to produce such
diverse movements as psychoanalysis, Austro-Marxism, Zionism, anti-
Semitic mass parties, logical positivism, and the Viennese secession
which were to change the face of the twentieth century. Jews by virtue
of their special place in the urban intelligentsia inevitably stood in the
forefront of this fermentation and change. Doubly alienated, both as
intellectuals and Jews, from other sectors of the ruling élite, their
avant-garde role in the development of radically new paradigms,
myths, and cultural values was frequently decisive. Not surprisingly,
the crisis of liberal rationalism and the disillusionment with politics
that characterized the Austrian *fin de siècle* as a whole was experienced
by Jewish intellectuals with particular intensity; for the defeat of
political liberalism had coincided with the rise of a triumphant mass
anti-Semitism that threatened their mental equilibrium and the very

foundations of Jewish existence. The modern cultural crisis that overtook Austria thus became inextricably bound up with fundamental questions involving Jewish identity in the personal and collective sense.

This intellectual crisis could sometimes assume an extreme form, (as in the examples of Karl Kraus and Otto Weininger) involving the radical negation of both the Viennese and Jewish components in an individual identity. In both these cases, self-negation was part of a broader, more far-reaching critique of modernity *per se*. Feelings of *Angst* and insecurity, the inclination to self-criticism and the related striving for moral absolutes, encouraged an apocalyptic mood of cultural pessimism and despair. In Karl Kraus this revolt was directed outward to a bitter, satirical denunciation of prevailing aesthetic and cultural norms in Viennese society; for the more introverted and introspective Weininger, the ethical reckoning with the vices of the age produced a self-destructive struggle with the demons of the self, leading ultimately to suicide.

For both Kraus and Weininger, the assault on *fin de siècle* superficiality and decadence in all its literary and artistic manifestations involved a sharp reaction against the Jewish milieu from which they had originated and whose values they ultimately rejected. In their broader repudiation of the Viennese *Moderne* and the world of the coffee-house literati in which they moved, in their struggle against aestheticism and ethical relativism or against philistinism of the big city press and the hypocrisy of prevailing sexual mores, Kraus and Weininger were both prophets swimming against the tide. Essentially as unpolitical as the ethos of the Viennese intelligentsia against which it revolted, the *Kulturkritik* of Kraus and Weininger reverted to older and intensely individualist values of integrity, authenticity, and moral purity. Both of these anti-Jewish Jews, in their own original and distinctive way, embodied and wrestled with the central dilemmas of the age; each of them in their personal biography thereby revealed an important facet of the crisis of Jewish identity in early twentieth-century Vienna.

Karl Kraus, one of the great stylists of modern German literature and Vienna's master satirist, was born on 28 April 1874, the second youngest of ten children, in the little Bohemian town of Jicin. When the boy was three years old, his father, a prosperous Jewish paper manufacturer, had moved with the family to Vienna, where Kraus attended school and then, briefly, the university. After a short-lived and unsuccessful attempt to make an acting career he turned to journalism and in spite of his youth was offered a leading position on the *Neue Freie Presse* as a possible successor to its deceased *feuilleton* editor, Daniel Spitzer. Having rejected this enticing prospect he founded his own periodical, *Die Fackel* (The Torch) on 1 April 1899, which he was to edit through 922 numbers, until his death from heart-failure in 1936.

Until 1911 the pages of *Die Fackel* still included occasional contributions from such prominent contemporaries as August Strindberg, Franz Wedekind, H. S. Chamberlain, Georg Brandes, Else Lasker-Schüler, and fellow Austrians like the composer Arnold Schoenberg, the writer Franz Werfel, and the poet Georg Trakl. Subsequently *Die Fackel* was written entirely by Karl Kraus himself. The début of this little red booklet, in which Kraus was to carry on a lonely guerrilla-war against the Austrian press and literary establishment for thirty-seven years, was described by a contemporary Viennese author in the following terms:

One day as far as the eye could see, everything was red. Never again has Vienna experienced a day like that. What murmuring, what whispering and excitement! Everyone reading from a red journal, on the street, in the tram, in the City Park . . . It was crazy . . . And the entire issue, written by a single person, packed so full of wit that one had to read it closely . . . so as not to miss any of its sparkling pearls.[1]

Most of Kraus's literary works had their origin in *Die Fackel*, which combined essays, drama, poetry, and cultural criticism with biting attacks on the morals of Viennese society. The chief object of its often brilliant and stinging polemics was the mendacity, pomposity, and hypocrisy of the Austrian press, especially as exemplified by the *Neue Freie Presse*.[2] *Die Fackel* was, however, far more than an exercise in alternative journalism of purely Viennese significance. In its pages a far-reaching reassessment of the relationship between texts and the

---

[1] Robert Scheu, *Karl Kraus* (Vienna, 1909), 4–6. An excerpt is quoted in Sidney Rosenfeld's stimulating article, 'Karl Kraus: the Future of a Legacy', *Midstream* (Apr. 1974), pp. 71–2.

[2] Henry Wickham Steed, *The Habsburg Monarchy* (London, 1913), 184 ff. Steed described the Austrian press as 'a semi-private, semi-public institution, worked chiefly by Jews under a dual control exercised through official press bureaux and the public prosecutor'. This leading reporter of the London *Times* considered the *Neue Freie Presse* to be 'a journal that embodies in concentrated form and, at times, with demonic force, the least laudable characteristics of Austro-German Jewry'. Rather like Karl Kraus, he felt that its excessive influence had been a key factor in the growth of Austrian political anti-Semitism.

facts, between language and the world, between words and deeds, was undertaken—one which transcended the immediate objects of its satirical concern.[3] Through its columns, Kraus gave voice to an intensely existential view of literature, of its moral and political function and its vital importance as a seismograph of the times, that was unrivalled by any of his contemporaries.

For Kraus, corruption of language entailed corruption of thought and hence of action, whether public or private.[4] Indeed, throughout his life Kraus was obsessed with language as the source of truth.[5] He regarded it not merely as an instrument of expression, but as a kind of revealed essence of the world.[6] A true *Sprachmystiker*, Kraus saw in language 'the divining rod that finds sources of thought'.[7] Language was 'the mother of thought not its handmaiden', the source from which he had drawn 'many a thought which I do not have and which I could not put into words'.[8] It was this sacred well of inspiration which the new journalism was busily debasing in the interests of mass circulation and profit.[9]

Kraus's bitterness towards the Viennese press was not only a reaction to its venality and subordination to commercial influence. What particularly aroused his resentment was the constant mingling of opinion and fact, subjective reactions and objective information epitomized by the *feuilleton*—a genre whose cultural role in *fin de siècle* Vienna was pre-eminent. For Kraus, the *feuilleton* symbolized that mixing of literary modes which undermined the moral and artistic integrity of the writer, subjectively distorting facts while reducing creative fantasy to the level of word-manipulation removed from any ethical content.[10]

[3] See J. P. Stern, 'Karl Kraus and the Idea of Literature', *Encounter* (Aug. 1975), pp. 37–48, for an interesting analysis of the pertinence of Kraus's literary critique of modern civilization and a dissection of his satirical method. Also the essay by Erich Heller in his seminal *The Disinherited Mind* (London, 1952), 183–201.

[4] D. J. Enright, 'Pure poison and blunt instruments', *Times Literary Supplement*, 5 Oct. 1984.

[5] See ch. 3, 'Language and Society. Karl Kraus and the Last Days of Vienna', in Allan Janik and Stephen Toulmin, *Wittgenstein's Vienna* (New York, 1973), 67–91, for a valuable account of Kraus's view of language and its impact on other Viennese intellectuals.

[6] Karl Kraus, *Werke*, ed. Heinrich Fischer, 14 vols. (Munich, 1952–67), vii. 83, iii. 134, 326. Also *Half-Truths and One-and-a-Half Truths. Karl Kraus: Selected Aphorisms*, ed. and trans. Harry Zohn (Montreal, 1976), 63–9.

[7] *Half-Truths*, 63.   [8] Ibid. 68.

[9] Ibid. 69; see also Nike Wagner, 'Karl Kraus', in *Critique* (août–sept 1975) pp. 998–1010, which touches on the erotic dimension in Kraus's attitude to language.

[10] Janik and Toulmin, pp. 79 ff. The prototype and pioneer of this genre in the

In his crusade for a purified culture, Kraus declared war not only on the press but on the corruption of expression and taste which had infected all levels of Viennese society. He turned with particular ferocity on the aesthetes of *Jung Wien*. In Kraus's view they exalted the life of refined feeling and beauty while ignoring what a recent critic has called 'the masculine virtues of Reason, ethics, and the honest truths contained in ordinary language, whether in words or in things'.[11] In adopting this puritanical stand, Kraus found an important ally in his architect friend, Adolf Loos (1870–1933). Loos's pioneer functionalist building on the Michaelerplatz, opposite the Imperial Residence, had been denounced in 1910 as a threat to the traditional aesthetic values of the Dual Monarchy. Kraus defended Loos and summed up their common revolt against the ornamental, decorative culture of Vienna with the famous remark: 'All that Adolf Loos and I did—he literally, I linguistically—was to show that there is a difference between an urn and a chamberpot, and that in this difference there is leeway for culture. But the others, the "positive ones," are divided into those who use the urn as a chamberpot and those who use the chamberpot as an urn.'[12]

Carl Schorske has recently described Kraus as 'a kind of anti-bourgeois bourgeois, upholding the traditional moral values of his class' against its practices—especially in the two paramount arenas of Viennese liberal culture—the press and the theatre.[13] There is much in this remark. Against the decadence prevailing in the public realm Kraus proposed a return to older more private virtues of veracity and individual integrity, along with a reassertion of moral absolutes. Characteristic of this attempt to rescue the moral force and truth of language was his *Theater der Dichtung*. These famous one-man readings of his own works (but also those of Shakespeare, Hauptmann, and early nineteenth-century Austrian dramatists like Raimund or Nestroy) dispensed with the scenic props, technological gimmicks, and

German language was Heinrich Heine, against who Kraus wrote a withering polemic. In one of his epigrams, Kraus observed: 'Heinrich Heine so loosed the corsets of the German language that today every little salesman can fondle her breasts.' See *Half-Truths*, 65.

[11] See Carl Schorske, 'Revolt in Vienna', *The New York Review of Books*, 29 May 1986, p. 25.

[12] *Half-Truths*, 69. See also Hermann Czech and Wolfgang Mistelbauer, *Das Looshaus* (Vienna, 1977). Kraus had been the first to spring to Loos's defence in the furore over the Michaelerplatz house; see *Die Fackel*, no. 313–14, 1 Dec. 1910.

[13] Schorske, p. 25.

cult of the actor which had in his view debased the tastes of the Viennese theatrical public.[14]

Since the late 1890s social criticism had played an important role in Kraus's polemical journalism. With withering scorn he had assailed the corruption of Habsburg officialdom, the abuses of an antiquated judicial system, court intrigues, the corrosive pathology of Austrian politics, double standards of sexual morality, and the coffee-house decadence of Viennese literary modernism.[15] In these apprentice years the young Kraus developed an uncompromising contempt for the 'immoral' hedonistic culture of Vienna, the provincialism and hypocrisy of its political and literary establishment.[16] In his essay *Sittlichkeit und Kriminalität* (1902) he singled out for special derision the false morality and duplicity of the law, the courts, and society as a whole in matters of sexuality. Kraus thoroughly despised the piggishness of a male chauvinist culture which denied the sensuality of women while at the same time encouraging a brutish licentiousness in men.[17]

However, while mercilessly exposing and satirizing the ugly side of Austrian life and culture, Kraus was far from wholly identifying himself with the Social Democratic critique of bourgeois society. Despite his low opinion of the Habsburgs (including the ageing Emperor Franz Joseph) and their chief pillars of support—the army, clergy, and Imperial bureaucracy—he remained a cultural conservative, suspicious of all ideologies, political movements, and collective solutions.[18] Kraus had never seen the goal of satire as changing the world; rather its central task was to unmask through an exposure of linguistic abuses the crimes and perversions of an era which stood condemned out of its own mouth. Kraus's autopsy of what appeared to him as an already moribund culture—that of Austria-Hungary—was a highly personal history which avoided even the hint of adhesion to any

[14] Ibid., Stern, p. 41. See also Elias Canetti, *Das Gewissen der Worte* (Munich and Vienna, 1975), 39–49, 234–56 for an evocation of the extraordinary power of these readings. 'Es hat, zu meinem Lebzeiten, nie einen solchen Sprecher gegeben, in keinem der europäischen Sprachbereiche, die mir vertraut sind.'

[15] See Karl Kraus, *Frühe Schriften, 1892–1900*, 2 vols. (Munich, 1979).

[16] Nike Wagner, 'Flegeljahre eines Moralisten', *Die Zeit* (Hamburg), 6 Apr. 1979, p. 11.

[17] For Kraus's view of female sensuality as the prime source of male creativity see, in addition, the aphorisms in Karl Kraus, *Dits et Contredits* (Paris, 1975), 13–41—a French translation from his *Sprüche und Widersprüche* (1909). Also Michael Pollak, *Vienne 1900: Une identité blessé* (Paris, 1984), 179–82.

[18] *Die Fackel*, no. 400–3 (1914), p. 92. Kraus declared himself not only against the bourgeoisie but also against the Rights of Man, the right to vote, the liberty of the press, psychoanalysis, the Jews, and the telephone!

social or political group. His highly-tuned antennae sensed all too lucidly the exhaustion and bankruptcy of the obsolescent political structure into which he had been born and the over-refinement of its culture against which he reacted with the rage of a prophet.[19]

Kraus came to regard this declining Empire as a 'proving ground for world destruction', already containing within itself the seeds of the catastrophic European disintegration in the First World War. This tragedy he was to capture with searing intensity in his apocalyptic drama, *Die letzten Tage der Menschheit* (The Last Days of Mankind). No other work of Central European literature was able to document the horror and anguish of modern war and give artistic form to visions of doom on such a gigantic scale.[20] Kraus's wartime masterpiece constitutes a nightmarish photomontage of all the clichés, platitudes, and lies that were reported, editorialized, consumed, and transformed into deeds by statesmen, generals, and other merchants of mechanized death.[21] Beyond the guilt of the militarists, profiteers, demagogues, churchmen, and war propagandists, the supreme villains were in his eyes the ladies and gentlemen of the press—desecrators of humanity who through 'the black magic of printer's ink' had manufactured that lack of imaginativeness which had allowed mankind blindly to exterminate itself.[22]

Kraus's indictment of the Viennese press as a poisoner of the human spirit and as an unparalleled agent of dissolution and decay was not devoid of an anti-Semitic animus. Many of the literary 'corrupters' of language whom he flayed without mercy were Jews, as were a

[19] Harry Zohn, 'The Stature of Karl Kraus', *Midstream* (Mar. 1986), pp. 42–8.

[20] Karl Kraus, *Die letzten Tage der Menschheit: Tragödie in fünf Akten mit Vorspiel und Epilog* (Vienna and Leipzig, 1922). Approaching nearly 800 pages and totalling 209 scenes, the work is virtually unperformable, as Kraus himself realized. In the prologue, the author in the guise of a character called 'Grumbler' announced: 'This play, which by earthly standards would take ten evenings to perform, is intended for a theatre on Mars. Earthly audiences could not endure it. For it is blood of their blood, and its content is the content of those unreal, unthinkable years beyond the reach of waking memory, preserved only in a bloody dream where clowns acted out the tragedy of mankind.'

[21] See Frank Field, *The Last Days of Mankind: Karl Kraus and his Vienna* (London, 1967); Hans Weigel, *Karl Kraus oder die Macht der Ohnmacht* (Vienna, 1968); and the Karl Kraus reader ed. Harry Zohn, *In These Great Times* (Montreal, 1976) which includes selections in English from *The Last Days of Mankind*, 157–258.

[22] Karl Kraus's essays from 1908 to the First World War were incorporated into a book entitled *Untergang der Welt durch schwarze Magie* (Vienna, 1922), which depicted the press as a prime cause of the coming disaster, which Kraus had long foreseen. In his essay 'Apokalypse' (1908) he had warned that 'the dung gases are rising from the world brain at all corners; culture is unable to catch a breath and in the end a dead humanity will lie next to the works which cost it so much ingenuity to invent . . .', Rosenfeld, p. 74.

significant proportion of the war profiteers, editors, and journalists whom he attacked. Many of his worst feuds were with the Viennese Jewish newspaper bosses like Moritz Benedikt and Imré Bekessy, with prominent Berlin publicists and critics of Jewish origin like Maximilien Harden and Alfred Kerr, or with the Austrian war correspondent Alice Schalek. Already in his first important work, *Die demolierte Literatur* (1897), Kraus had ferociously satirized the literary circle of 'Young Vienna' centred on the legendary Café Griensteidl. Among this group some of the most prominent targets of his critical pen were Jewish-born writers like Arthur Schnitzler, Richard Beer-Hoffman, Felix Salten, and Theodor Herzl, whom he reproached for irresponsible literary dilettantism, easy-going superficiality, and pandering to the clichés of modernistic fashion.[23]

On the other hand, Kraus in his self-appointed role as destroyer of inflated reputations could be no less vehement and explicit in his criticism of Christians than he was of Jews. Such leading 'Catholic' representatives of *Jung Wien* as Hermann Bahr, Leopold von Andrian, and the outstanding poet-dramatist Hugo von Hofmannstahl (admittedly of Jewish decent) were censured and ridiculed with equal severity. The Austrian landed aristocracy came in for harsh criticism much like the Jewish financial aristocracy; the German 'Aryan' bourgeoisie was castigated along with its Jewish counterparts; Viennese dialect speech was satirized almost in equal measures to the Viennese Jewish jargon which Kraus jeered at all his life.[24] Thus, one can partially subscribe to Werner Kraft's opinion that Kraus 'was against the Jews and Christians of his time, as he was for the Jews and Christians of his time; he was for the world and the salvation of the world.'[25]

Kraft, however, argued rather more controversially that Kraus 'always spoke in the name of Judaism, even when he spoke most critically against the Jews of his time'.[26] Like other Jewish admirers of

[23] See Harry Zohn, 'Karl Kraus: "Jüdischer Selbsthasser" oder "Erzjude"?', *Modern Austrian Literature*, 8, no. 1/2 (1975), 1–15; and Robert S. Wistrich, 'Karl Kraus: Jewish Prophet or Renegade?', *European Judaism*, 9, no. 2 (Summer 1975), 32–8.

[24] Rosenfeld, p. 79, argues on these grounds that there was 'no imbalance' in his attacks on individual Jews or on the Jewish role in Viennese public life.

[25] Werner Kraft, *Franz Kafka: Durchdringung und Geheimnis* (Frankfurt, 1968), 199 ff. See also *Karl Kraus: Beiträge zum Verständnis seines Werkes* (Salzburg, 1956), by the same author, a passionate admirer of Kraus, who lives in Jerusalem. Harry Zohn, 'Karl Kraus', 9, notes the interesting fact that the most positive assessments of Kraus's work in recent years have been written by Jews.

[26] Kraft, *Karl Kraus*, 81 ff.

Kraus, Werner Kraft saw in the Viennese satirist a descendant of the
Hebrew prophets condemning the decadent Judaism of his age. Karl
Kraus in this perspective emerges as prototype of the idealistic
nonconformist Jew—a 'high priest of truth' rebelling against dogma
and prejudice.[27] The fanatic Krausian insistence on moral absolutes
and artistic truth also led other admirers like the poet Berthold Viertel
to regard their idol as an *Erzjude* (arch-Jew) in the Old Testament
tradition, whose 'heresy' had consisted in rejecting the profane
ambitions and cult of material success of his co-religionists as a sin
against the 'spirit'.[28] Kraus had courageously taken on his own
shoulders the responsibility of Jewry for the decadence of the age,
assuming, in the words of another sympathizer, 'the stance of Jeremiah
and Isaiah' in his call for social justice and compassion for his fellow-
man.[29] Nevertheless, the manifest excesses of tone and argument in
Kraus's castigation of Jews and Judaism and his tendency to generalize
from individual failings have continued to trouble even some of his
most sympathetic critics.[30]

The alternative option of classifying Karl Kraus as a Jewish self-
hater is by no means new. Writers like Max Brod long ago regarded
him as a prime example of the eternally dissatisfied, anti-Semitic Jew
who had rejected Jewish elements in his personality, unconsciously
projecting them outwards in harsh and unfair diatribes against his co-
religionists.[31] Theodor Lessing in his controversial study *Der jüdische
Selbsthass* (1930) evoked Karl Kraus as a particularly tragic instance of
moralistic, puritanical self-hatred, indeed as the 'most serious' and
uncompromising of contemporary German Jew-haters.[32] Pointing to

[27] See, e.g., Caroline Kohn, *Karl Kraus, le polémiste et l'ecrivain: Défenseur des droits de
l'individu* (Paris, 1962), 100–1.

[28] Berthold Viertel, 'Karl Kraus: Ein Charakter und die Zeit', in his *Dichtungen und
Dokumente*, ed. Ernst Ginsberg (Munich, 1956), 261–2.

[29] Paul Neumarkt, 'Kraus, Tucholsky, F. Mendelssohn: A Trio of Apostates', *Jewish
Currents XXVII*, 11 Dec. 1973, pp. 39 ff.; also Erich Heller in *New York Review of Books*,
9 Aug. 1973, p. 37: 'Kraus's "anti-Semitism" in all its problem-ridden complexity, was a
new form of the prophet's indignation at the worshippers of the Golden Calf.'

[30] Even Rosenfeld, p. 79, who takes a benevolent view of Kraus, admits that he was
prone 'to interpret what he saw as Jewish transgressions as though they were expressions
of an unalterable character rather than consequences of a specific social-historical
development in the Diaspora'.

[31] Max Brod, *Une Vie combative* (Paris, 1964), 76–7. A contemporary of Kraus, Brod
particularly reproached him for the malice of his attacks on the *Ostjuden* in Vienna.

[32] Theodor Lessing, *Der jüdische Selbsthass* (Berlin, 1930), 43–4: 'Wohl in keiner
zweiten Gestalt des gegenwärtigen Deutschland offenbart sich der geniale Selbsthass
des sittlichen Menschen in gleich unerlösbarer Tragik, denn hier ward eine schöne und

Kraus's obsession with the sacredness of language and the spirituality of the 'Word'—regarded by some enthusiasts as a Jewish mystical trait—Lessing ironically commented: 'He hates the sacrilege of the Word and uses millions of words to praise the chaste bliss of holy Silence.'[33]

Other critics have emphasized Kraus's estrangement from his Jewish origins and his alleged inability 'to grow roots in non-Jewish soil' as the main cause of his anti-Semitic tendencies.[34] The Austrian Jewish historian Hans Tietze related this estrangement and 'self-hatred' to Diasporic rootlessness, which had found an especially fertile soil in *fin-de-siècle* Vienna under the impact of a loosening Jewish tradition, the strength of assimilationist influences, and the pressures of an anti-Semitic environment.[35] For Tietze, self-hatred was, however, a legitimate form of Jewish self-consciousness which had not emerged by chance alongside Zionism, psychoanalysis, and other Jewish modes of response to modernity, in an age of split identity.[36] Kraus had sought to find a concrete target for his apocalyptic despair in the evils of modern journalism, yet ended up focusing his wrath on specifically Jewish responsibilities because they were the closest to home and the most emotionally distressing to such an uncompromising moralist. Hence the tragic-comic spectacle of a satirical war conducted against the Austrian press which ultimately expressed a highly dramatic mode of self-flagellation.[37]

Modern assessments of Kraus's attitude to Jewishness, whether positive or negative, cannot however be divorced from the context of

reine Naturkraft an ein zu guter letzt völlig fruchtloses Werk vertan, von dem nach zwei, drei Geschlechtern nichts übrigbleiben kann als ein Berg bedrücktes Papier.'

[33] Ibid. Lessing interpreted Kraus's 'self-hatred', his more general *Menschenhass*, and 'keuschendem Hasse gegen Literatur' as perverse expressions of an 'unerbittlichen und puritanischen, Sittlichkeitseifers . . .'.

[34] Sol Liptzin in *Jewish Spectator*, Oct. 1972, pp. 14–15, refers to the 'masochistic antisemitism' which led Kraus 'to vilify Heine, to applaud Otto Weininger, to attack the defenders of Dreyfus, and to refuse to speak out against Hitler in 1933'.

[35] Hans Tietze, *Die Juden Wiens* (Vienna and Leipzig, 1933), 269–70. See also Robert S. Wistrich, *Revolutionary Jews from Marx to Trotsky* (London, 1976) for an interpretation of modern Jewish radicalism in Vienna and in 19th-cent. and 20th-cent. European history as a whole.

[36] Tietze, pp. 269–70.

[37] See Zohn, 'Karl Kraus', 6, for a quotation from Marcel Reich-Ranicki's *Über Ruhestörer* (Munich, 1973): 'Der stets verbissene und zuweilen tragikomische Krieg, den Karl Kraus ein Leben lang gegen die österreichische Presse geführt hat, erweist sich bei näherer Betrachtung als sein geheimer Kampf gegen das Jüdische oder, richtiger gesagt, gegen das, was er für das Jüdische hielt. Dieser Kampf war nich anderes als eine schmerzhafte und hochdramatische Selbstauseinandersetzung.'

time and place.[38] Karl Kraus did not invent the *Judenfrage* or even the distorted but widely held opinion that in Vienna 'all public life was dominated by Jews'.[39] It must be remembered that even Socialists of Jewish origin like Friedrich Austerlitz, editor of the Viennese *Arbeiterzeitung*, could uninhibitedly assert in 1900:

The Jews possess pretty well all the means of power in the modern State: the banks (of greater significance in Austria which was always struggling with more financial difficulties than elsewhere) were controlled by Jews, as were the chairs at the universities; in the sciences, in the arts, in politics, the Jewish coterie held sway. Nothing however advanced anti-Semitism in Vienna more than the fact that for a long time the Viennese press was owned by Jews.[40]

Indeed, Austerlitz, though not a racial or clerical anti-Semite in the sense of Schoenerer or Lueger, found it easy enough to explain and justify these movements in terminology that clearly echoed that of his political adversaries.

It was a conspiracy in favour of the Jews; the legend of the solidarity of all members of the people of Israel was at that time a reality. How many Austrian politicians later confessed that they were driven to anti-Semitism only by the callow intolerance of the Viennese Press, which pursued every word that anyone dared to utter against the Jews with the jealous hatred of their god Jehovah into the fourth generation.[41]

These words, to which Karl Kraus would most probably have subscribed, can be properly understood only in the context of late nineteenth-century Austrian conditions. They utilized a language tainted by anti-Semitism even though they expressed the views of a leading figure in the labour movement, which was in practice the firmest opponent of racialist tendencies and open anti-Jewish discrimination in the Habsburg Empire.[42] The disturbing ambiguity of this discourse suggests the need to differentiate between anti-Jewish prejudices on a personal and cultural level (including those internalized

[38] See Wistrich, 'Karl Kraus' 32 ff., and Wilma Abeles Iggers, *Karl Kraus: A Viennese Critic of the Twentieth Century* (The Hague, 1967), 180 ff., for attempts to deal with this problem in a historical context.

[39] Jakob Wassermann, *My Life as German and Jew* (New York, 1933), 186.

[40] Friedrich Austerlitz, 'Karl Lueger', *Neue Zeit*, ii (Stuttgart, 1900–1), 40.

[41] Ibid. 40–1.

[42] See J. W. Bruegel, 'The Antisemitism of the Austrian Socialists, A Reassessment', *The Wiener Library Bulletin*, 25 (1971/2), nos. 3/4, NS no. 24 pp. 39–43, and the reply by Avraham Barkai, ibid. 43–5. For a comprehensive treatment of the issue see Robert S. Wistrich, *Socialism and the Jews: The Dilemmas of Assimilation in Germany and Austria-Hungary* (London and Toronto, 1982), 242–98.

by Jews themselves) and the readiness to make concrete political demands to exclude Jews which was officially part of the programme of the anti-Semitic parties. Neither Karl Kraus nor the Austrian socialists, in spite of their unpleasant verbal attacks on 'Jewish finance' and the 'rule of the Jewish press', ever considered translating their diffuse prejudices against Jews as individuals or even as a group into political action against the civil rights of the Jewish minority. Nevertheless, in such problematic cases, hostility to the liberal-capitalist establishment and the so-called 'Jewish' press led at times to a surprising readiness to minimize the seriousness of anti-Semitism and even to flirt with its rhetoric.

Karl Kraus's initial reactions to Viennese anti-Semitism had in fact been very critical, not say contemptuous. The successes of the clerical anti-Semites in the 1897 elections confirmed his already low opinion of the mental capacities of the Viennese common man and the pathological backwardness of Austrian politics. The anti-Semitic deputies who gave 'popular expression to this basest of all political ideas' were undoubtedly a true reflection of the people's will.[43] Acknowledging the spell which Lueger exerted over the Viennese, Kraus anticipated that the simple-minded 'aversion to Jews' which had hitherto formed the core of his platform must inevitably give way to a more democratic tendency which would be scarcely more edifying.[44] The young Kraus did not minimize the personal corruption of Lueger's subordinates like Ernst Vergani, editor of the anti-Semitic scandal-sheet, the *Deutsches Volksblatt*, who had been publicly tried for embezzlement;[45] nor did he fail to castigate the bone-headed crudity of the new Christian-Social deputies like Gregorig, Schneider, Axmann, and Bielohlawek or the disastrous consequences he expected from anti-Semitic mismanagement of municipal affairs. Lueger, he concluded, was surrounded by a miserable collection of forgers, pick-pockets, and liars who had rapidly succeeded in depressing the already debased level of Austrian parliamentarism to new depths. It seemed

---

[43] See 'Wiener Brief', *Breslauer Zeitung*, 78, no. 202, 21 Mar. 1897, in Kraus, *Frühe Schriften*, ii. 31–2.

[44] Article in *Wiener Rundschau*, no. 12, 1 May 1897, ibid. 53 ff.: 'Er nähert sich insoferne dem socialdemokratischen Programme, als die Geistesarmuth fortan nicht mehr ein Privilegium gewisser bevorzügter Classen sein soll, vielmehr die allgemeine Dummheit auf der Grundlage der Gleichberechtigung angestrebt wird.'

[45] Ibid. 65–6; also 'Wiener Brief', 19 Aug. 1897, ibid. 92–3: '... der Antisemitismus, dieser irregeleitete Sozialismus der Beschränkten, dessen höchste geistige Quintessenz in dem Ausruf "Jud" gegeben ist, er hat auch Herrn Ernst Vergani zu einer Persönlichkeit gemacht ...'

inconceivable to Kraus that the Christian Socialists could continue for long to make a 'business' out of the sham anti-Semitism, which had temporarily masked their political incompetence.[46]

But Kraus's undisguised contempt for the 'socialism of the fools of Vienna' (Ferdinand Kronawetter's classic definition of this plebeian anti-semitism) led him dangerously to underrate its staying-power and long-term corrosive effects on public opinion. In his opinion, especially after the founding of *Die Fackel* in 1899, the 'Jewish' Liberal press and above all the *Neue Freie Presse* was a far more formidable and sophisticated enemy, against which he would consistently direct his most vituperative attacks. The *Neue Freie Presse* came to embody for Kraus all the evils of Austrian society and of the bourgeois-materialist civilization he loathed. He constantly blamed it for the subordination of culture to profit, for its kotowing to financial interests, for crude sensationalism, lack of principle, chauvinism, and war-mongering.[47] To his mind the Liberal-progressive allure of this newspaper was merely a mask for the selfishness of the 'officious representatives of capitalism'.[48]

Kraus's enmity towards Moritz Benedikt, the powerful editor of the *Neue Freie Presse*, and his loathing for the cultural snobbery and pretentiousness of Austro-liberalism, brought him some strange bedfellows. They included Jörgen Lanz von Liebenfels, the mystical prophet of Austrian racism who influenced the young Hitler and who publicly admired Kraus as a 'blond Jew': von Liebenfels subscribed to *Die Fackel* and his praise for its author was even printed in its pages.[49] Kraus also published a number of articles by the high priest of Germanic racial superiority, Houston S. Chamberlain, then living in Vienna, with those anti-Semitic allusions he appeared to sympathize.[50]

---

[46] Kraus, *Frühe Schriften* ii. 99: 'Auf die Dauer wird mit der Konstatirung, dass ein anderer Mensch israelitischer Abstammung ist, kein Geschaft zu machen sein . . .'

[47] Iggers, pp. 107–9.   [48] *Die Fackel*, May 1899.

[49] See ibid., 19 Sept. 1913, for a token of von Liebenfels's esteem for Karl Kraus, whom he elevated to the rank of honorary Aryan. A curious footnote to this admiration is the fact that Kraus's writings were not included in the Nazi burning of the books in 1933. Neumarkt, p. 39, writes: 'he, in an ironical twist of fate, became Hitler's "decent Jew", whose writings were spared because he had exposed the international conspiracy of world Jewish finance.'

[50] For H. S. Chamberlain's articles on Mommsen and on Catholic universities, see *Die Fackel*, Nov./Dec. 1901, and no. 92, Jan. 1902, pp. 1–32. On the close relationship between Kraus and Chamberlain, see now Edward Timms, *Karl Kraus: Apocalyptic Satirist* (New Haven and London, 1986), 238–40. Kraus clearly accepted Chamberlain's identification of Jewry as a world-historical force undermining Christian-Germanic culture and traditional European civilization as a whole.

Though no racial ideologue himself, Kraus shared a common antipathy towards liberalism with these prophets of Teutonic 'Aryanism' and openly declared that 'Jewish' corruption in the Stock Exchange and the press was the real cause of Viennese anti-Semitism.

Kraus's anti-liberalism even brought him momentarily closer to Karl Lueger, the anti-Semitic Catholic Mayor of Vienna, who he still hoped might sweep away the social abuses of 'Jewish' capitalism and venal press. This brief caprice led, like all Kraus's political flirtations, to rapid disillusionment. Lueger by 1900 had clearly cooled his earlier confrontational posture towards Viennese Jewry and sought an accommodation with its prosperous business class.[51] This truce confirmed to Kraus that the Viennese anti-Semites did not in the least mean what they said on the 'Jewish question', any more than they intended to weed out capitalist corruption in general.[52] In February 1900 he sarcastically observed:

Some obscure Jews have been beaten up, a few teachers have not been promoted—but Rothschild's profits from municipal business grow. And since Herr Benedikt has for the last twenty years successfully persuaded the Viennese Jews that they have no real interest other than the balance-sheet of Wittkowitz [the Rothschild-owned iron works] it is therefore no surprise that the readers of the *Neue Freie Presse* feels very comfortable under Lueger's regime. The impartial observer finally discovers that there is only one partisan anti-Semitic lie: namely that all Jews are clever people . . .[53]

Kraus was similarly disillusioned with the Viennese Social Democrats for whose policies he had felt a certain sympathy at the end of the 1890s. After 1900 he already considered them as unreliable allies in his uncompromising struggle against the *Neue Freie Presse* and the 'egoistic' liberal press, whose rottenness they had come to underestimate in the wake of Lueger's triumph.[54] Social Democratic *embourgeoisement* was characteristically symbolized for Kraus by the fact that the Viennese *Arbeiterzeitung* had found favour in Jewish middle-class homes ever since it began to attack clerical anti-Semitism.[55]

Kraus's attitude to the Dreyfus affair was largely shaped by his overriding contempt for the *Neue Freie Presse* and the 'Jewish' liberal

[51] *Die Fackel*, no. 32, Feb. 1900, pp. 22–3.

[52] Ibid. 12 ff.   [53] Ibid. 22–3.   [54] Ibid., no 40, May 1900, p. 5.

[55] Ibid.: 'Wahr ist, dass in jenen Haüsern, in denen die Arbeiter-Zeitung" seit ihren täglichen Beschimpfungen der Antisemiten gerne gelesen wird, die "Fackel" keinen Zutritt hat.'

Viennese press. Their pro-Dreyfus campaign induced him to launch a vituperative onslaught on the partiality of Jewish journalists in Austria. He accused the 'schmocks' of Viennese journalism of having invented the fairytale of a Jesuit-military conspiracy in France against Captain Dreyfus, in order to defend their own venal Stock Exchange interests.[56] They were nothing but hypocritical, hired scribblers who, while mobilizing Viennese opinion against the French army, knowingly whitewashed the barbarities of the Austro–Hungarian ruling-class. Kraus concluded that '. . . even the brutal disregard of an individual's fate in the name of a higher goal, will always show itself more humane than the rage for truth of agitated frequenters of the Stock Exchange'.[57]

It was no accident that *Die Fackel* was the one European journal to publish the anti-Dreyfusard articles of the German Social Democrat, Wilhelm Liebknecht. Like Kraus, he was convinced that the Dreyfusard agitation was a calculated conspiracy by dubious financial circles and the liberal press to save a guilty officer. The most likely consequence of this campaign would be to increase anti-Semitism.[58] Kraus's position was not in itself anti-Jewish since he disagreed with the implication of the Viennese clerical and nationalist anti-Semites that Dreyfus's guilt was inherent in his blood. Nor did he suggest that a 'Jewish international conspiracy' on racial lines had been explicitly mobilized in favour of Dreyfus.[59] Equally, Kraus was far removed from any attempt to advocate the cleansing of Jews from the ranks of the French army and civil administration.[60] But his polemical stance implying not only that Dreyfus was guilty, but that any campaign in his favour must be motivated and tainted by selfish Jewish financial interests, came very close indeed to mainstream anti-Semitic opinion.

[56] For similarly hostile socialist comments in Vienna, see 'Vom Tage', *Arbeiterzeitung*, 25 Jan. 1898, pp. 1 f.: 'Das ganze Gelichter von der mehr oder weniger jüdischen Finanz kämpft mit für Dreyfus und hofft, mit dieser guten Sache seine schlechte Sache zu retten, und erwartet, wenn die Unschuld von Dreyfus erwiesen wäre, von den Verbrechen des Wuchers und der Ausbeutung freigesprochen zu werden.' Like Kraus, the Viennese Social Democrats suspected that behind der Dreyfusard campaign 'die ganze verdächtige Bände der jüdischen Schmarotzer' was seeking rehabilitation.

[57] *Die Fackel*, no. 14, Aug. 1899, p. 3.

[58] Wilhelm Liebknecht, 'Nachträgliches zur "Affaire"', ibid. no. 18, Sept. 1899, pp. 1–10; no. 19, Oct. 1899, pp. 11–20; no. 21, Dec. 1899, pp. 1–12; and June 1900.

[59] For the reactions of Vienna's anti-Semitic press, see 'Zum Dreyfus-Scandale', *Deutsches Volksblatt*, 13 Jan. 1898, pp. 1 f.; 'Der Dreyfus-Rummel', *Ostdeutsche Rundschau*, 26 Jan. 1898; 'Die Juden und Zola als Vertheidiger des Dreyfus', *Reichspost*, 15 Jan. 1898, pp. 1 f.

[60] 'Der Prozess Esterhazy und das Judentum', *Deutsches Volksblatt*, 12 Jan. 1898, p. 1.

With a barely disguised glee, Kraus noted that Theodor Herzl was too busy with the Zionist Congress in Basle to report on the retrial of Dreyfus by a military court at Rennes in the autumn of 1899. In *Die Fackel* he ironized: 'Between Basle and Rennes surges the thousand-year-old affliction of Jewry, and both here and there, prophets lie in wait, who calculate the pathos of this world by the line.'[61] Kraus, as we have already noted, regarded Zionism as being based on the absurd premiss that the Jewish nation could be re-created. In July 1899 he derisively observed in *Die Fackel*: 'Zionism may seem a less ridiculous aspiration when propagated amonst Eastern Jews or when it sends its victims from the puddle of Galician culture directly to the Palestinian settlements. But in Central Europe it offers the unpleasant spectacle of clumsy hands scratching at the 2000-year-old grave of an extinct people.'[62]

Nor did Theodor Herzl, the Zionist leader busy attempting to revive this 'corpse', escape Kraus's satiric attentions in *Die Fackel*: 'The King of the Jews', as he was mockingly referred to, found himself portrayed as a perfumed Ringstrasse dandy and a pathetic caricature of a Jewish messianic leader: '. . . the clothes which he rents out of grief for his people, have been ordered from the most worldly tailor.'[63]

For Kraus it seemed self-evident that not Zionism, but only a conscious, determined effort by the Jews to strip off their undesirable ghetto characteristics, could solve the 'Jewish question'. Despite occasional expressions of compassion for the poor Jews of Galicia, Kraus, like most assimilated German Jews in Vienna, had little time for what he disparagingly dismissed as the *Ghettomensch*. By this un-appetizing term he meant those traditional Jews who stubbornly clung to their religion, customs, and Yiddish language, refusing to integrate with the Catholic Germanic culture of whose values he felt himself to be the self-appointed guardian. In July 1899 he summed up his attitude toward the *Ostjuden* as follows: '. . . despite every respect for the equality of all faiths: oriental enclaves in European civilization are a nonsense.'[64]

Kraus's antipathy to the *Ostjuden* was closely linked to his aesthetic repugnance for Yiddish. Any traces of 'Jewish' linguistic usage in a German sentence inevitably aroused his ire, constituting the intrusion

---

[61] *Die Fackel*, no. 14, Aug. 1899, p. 3.   [62] Ibid., no. 11, July 1899, p. 6.

[63] Ibid., Apr. 1899; also 'Achtung vor dem König von Zion', ibid., no. 80, June 1901, and no. 91, Jan. 1902, pp. 11–12.

[64] Ibid., no. 11, July 1899, p. 5.

of an alien element in the purity of the language. Kraus was convinced like most assimilationists that the persistence of such immediately recognizable linguistic characteristics, and the obtrusive Jewish mannerisms that generally accompanied them, was a major cause of anti-Semitism.[65] When anti-Jewish riots broke out in Bohemia in 1899 he was quick to blame the ghetto and Stock Exchange Jews for provoking popular wrath. His solution was the classic policy of extreme assimilation, namely the rapid self-dissolution of the Jews as a group. 'Only a courageous purge of the ranks and the laying aside of the characteristics of a race, which through many centuries of dispersion has long ceased to be a nation, can bring the torment to a stop. Through dissolution to redemption!'[66]

The ethnic death-wish of the twenty-four-year-old Kraus had been personally realized a year earlier (1898), when he formally left the Jewish community, declaring himself *Konfessionslos*. In 1911 he *secretly* converted to Catholicism, though twelve years later he ostentatiously left the Church without ever returning to Judaism. This 'arch-Jew' stood therefore beyond even the periphery of Jewish communal life. Yet he never denied his origins, which in any event would have been exceedingly difficult and ultimately futile in the atmosphere of early twentieth-century Vienna. Condemned by social and political circumstances into a purely negative identification, Kraus responded by onesidedly identifying the 'Jewish spirit' with the shallow materialism and cultural philistinism of the age.

This largely explained his favourable attitude to Karl Lueger, whom he continued to regard with respect as a significant and vital personality, even though in his early days Kraus had satirized the mindless anti-Semitism of the Catholic Mayor's more plebeian followers. Indeed, Kraus's main reproach against Lueger remained the fact that he had not pressed the Christian-Social fight against the Stock Exchange and the 'Jewish' liberal press more energetically.[67]

Kraus's profound amibivalence towards anti-Semitism and his tendency to trivialize its effects was revealed not only in his sympathy for Lueger but in his attitude to dramatic episodes like the Hilsner affair in Bohemia.[68] As in the case of Dreyfus, Kraus was apparently unconcerned by the fate of an individual victim of injustice,

[65] *Die Fackel*, no. 11, July 1899, p. 5.   [66] Ibid. no. 23, Nov. 1899, pp. 5 ff.
[67] Iggers, pp. 136–7.
[68] See Frantisek Cervinka, 'The Hilsner Affair', *Leo Baeck Yearbook*, 18 (1968), 142–61.

particularly when he happened to be a Jew. Nor was he unduly perturbed by the fact that the agitation around Hilsner—a Jewish shoemaker's assistant who had been wrongly condemned to death (later commuted to life-imprisonment) in 1899 for the alleged 'ritual murder' of a young Christian girl—had provoked an ugly pogromist mood in the Czech lands. What did, however, attract his righteous indignation was the campaign of the liberal press to expose the mendacity of the blood libel and to free Hilsner. Kraus's response was maliciously to accuse the *Neue Freie Presse* of having implied that any Jew convicted by an Austrian court must automatically be innocent![69]

Such was Kraus's enmity towards Benedikt's newspaper that he turned it into a scapegoat for a vast range of social abuses which it had merely reported and systematically opposed any cause which it championed. Thus Kraus's cleansing operation, for all its ruthless exposé of the literary, social, and political venality of a decaying Empire and its resourceful unmasking of stock clichés and taboos, tended to suffer from the monomaniac one-sidedness of his own private obsessions.

It is admittedly true that this Viennese prophet of doom spared no institution, no political party of privileged clique from the scornful arrows of his uncompromising critique. But the emotional imbalance that was ultimately rooted in his seemingly unlimited capacity for moral indignation and a pronounced streak of intellectual sadism led to frequent distortions, of which his stance on the 'Jewish' question but was but one illustration. Like his younger, more tragic contemporary, Otto Weininger, Kraus's war on the 'Jewish spirit' which had allegedly corrupted the purity of German language, culture, and social values was all too readily diverted into anti-Semitic channels.[70] This deflection was not only a question of personal psychology but also reflected the pressures of an anti-Semitic society and the proclivities of a Central European anti-modernist tradition of cultural criticism which Kraus had absorbed and of which he became a supreme exponent. Kraus's conservative identification with the politics, philosophy, and aesthetic values of pre-1848 Austria, together with his pessimistic view of modern man and of the new techno-logical civilization, can perhaps best explain his animus against

---

[69] *Die Fackel*, Nov. 1899, pp. 5 ff.; Nov. 1900, p. 62; Apr. 1901.
[70] Iggers, pp. 188–90.

liberal–capitalist Jewry.[71] Opposition to emancipatory movements, to liberalism, and to secular modernity frequently went together in Austria, as elsewhere in Europe, with antipathy towards Jews; Karl Kraus like Otto Weininger exemplified this intellectual syndrome in his own specifically 'Jewish' variation on *Kulturantisemitismus*.[72]

Kraus's spirited defense of Otto Weininger (1880–1903), the highly gifted Viennese Jewish philosopher who committed suicide in the house where Beethoven had died on 4 October 1903, was another aspect of this syndrome and throws an interesting light on their respective attitudes to the 'Jewish question'. Nine months after Weininger's tragic death, Kraus wrote in his periodical:

It is true that I declared in *Die Fackel*, whose fight against corruption cannot easily be accused of being 'Jewish,' that the philosopher Weininger, converted by conviction to Christianity and representing German idealism, was far more 'German' than many Germans of Jewish spirit . . . what obviously surpasses the understanding of narrow and partisan minds is the fact that one can radically criticize the Judaism of a Disraeli and company, while admiring the authentically German culture of a Heine and a Ferdinand Lassalle; and that one should not confuse the absolute rejection of Judaism (i.e. scientific and intellectual anti-Semitism) with the anti-Semitism of brawlers generally moved by nothing but material envy or reactionary clericalism. The Jewish party sees things more lucidly: it is not plebeian anti-Semitism which it fears . . . but the intellectual and higher anti-Semitism of a Houston Stewart Chamberlain.[73]

Kraus's positive evocation of Houston Chamberlain (1855–1927) in the context of defending Weininger was indeed appropriate. For the seeds of the hostile treatment of Jewry and Judaism in Weininger's celebrated book *Geschlecht und Charakter* (1903) had been sown by the English-born prophet of Teutonic racism. Weininger, partly under the influence of Chamberlain's theories, which he frequently quoted as a source and inspiration, had found what he believed to be an important 'scientific' support for his view that Judaism was hateful and inferior. It

---

[71] See Pollak, *Vienne 1900*, for an overview of the traditions of cultural pessimism in Austria; also Iggers, pp. 204 ff.

[72] The similarity and the difference between Kraus and Weininger is provocatively touched on by Hans Mayer in his classic study *Aussenseiter* (Frankfurt, 1976), 124: 'Gemeinsam der jüdische Selbsthass. Sehr ähhliche Intonationen der konkreten Kulturkritik. Moralische Kantianer sind sie beide. Allein die Metaphysik bei Kraus ist eine solche des *Untergang*, während Weininger immer noch das Bild einer emanzipierten Humanität im Sinne des 18 Jahrhunderts entwirft . . .'

[73] *Die Fackel*, no. 165, July 1904.

must be remembered that Chamberlain's *Foundations of the Nineteenth Century*, with its pseudo-philosophical and encyclopaedic pretensions, its claim to have created a new *Weltanschauung*, its metaphysical style and lyrical irrationalism, exercised a mesmeric effect on many of Weininger's contemporaries.[74] Moreover, there was a more direct parallel. Chamberlain, like Weininger after him, had graduated from biologistic positivism to a quasi-mystical world view that sought to synthesize the racial theories of Richard Wagner with the ethics of Immanuel Kant.[75]

Nevertheless there were significant differences between the condemnations of Jewish existence as rootless and 'immoral' made by Kraus or Weininger and the anti-Semitic utterances of Germanic racists, although they frequently used a similar terminology.[76] The objective of even the most radically self-critical Jews was ultimately to purge negative Jewish characteristics in order to accelerate rather than to prevent assimilation to the dominant German culture. Moreover, both Kraus and Weininger, when they attacked the 'false' morality of contemporary Judaism, always left open the possibility, however remote, of self-improvement, transcendence, and ultimate redemption from this negativity in the wake of merciless self-criticism.

In the case of Otto Weininger this self-reproach admittedly turned into a radical form of Jewish anti-Semitism inextricably linked to his extreme anti-feminism.[77] But even Weininger emphasized that in spite

[74] Chamberlain's best-selling *Die Grundlagen des neunzehnten Jahrhunderts* (Munich, 1899/1900) had already been published in Vienna, where the author lived, at the time when Weininger began working on his doctorate. The two had met at meetings of the Viennese philosophical society; see Jacques Le Rider, *Le Cas Otto Weininger: Racines de l'antiféminisme et de l'antisémitisme* (Paris, 1982), 200–1.

[75] Weininger's attraction to racial thinking was by no means exceptional among intellectual Jews in *fin de siècle* Vienna. See Hans Kohn, *Karl Kraus, Arthur Schnitzler, Otto Weininger: Aus dem jüdischen Wien der Jahrhundertwende* (Tübingen, 1962), 69: 'Mann kann von dem Wien der Jahrhundertwende und der Stellung jüdischer Menschen in ihm nicht sprechen, ohne zu betonen, wie sie alle von dem National- und Rassedenken, das um jene Zeit in Mittleuropa und gerade in Wien überhand nahm beeindrückt und bedrängt wurden . . .'

[76] Dennis B. Klein, *Jewish Origins of the Psychoanalytic Movement* (Chicago and London, 1985), 29–30.

[77] See Le Rider, *Le Cas Otto Weininger*, pp. 137–66, for the background to anti-feminism in the *fin de siècle*. For the rather different position on sexuality adopted by Kraus (who none the less saw Weininger as an ally in his fight against the hypocritical morality of bourgeois Vienna), see ibid. 144 ff., and *Die Fackel*, no. 157, Mar. 1904. Kraus's enigmatic response to *Geschlecht und Charakter*, was to subscribe enthusiastically to Weininger's arguments in favour of misogyny, while remaining an 'admirer of women'. See also Nike Wagner, *Geist und Geschlecht: Karl Kraus und die Erotik der Wiener*

of his low estimate of the Jew, 'nothing could be further from my intention than to lend the faintest support to any practical or theoretical persecution of Jews'.[78] Indeed for Weininger, slogans like 'Buy only from Christians' themselves had a 'Jewish taint': '. . . they have a meaning only for those who regard the race and not the individual, and what is to be compared with them is the Jewish use of the word "Goy", which is now almost obsolete. I have no wish to boycott the Jew, or by any such immoral means to attempt to solve the Jewish question.'[79]

Otto Weininger's *jüdischer Selbsthass* had in fact nothing directly to do with the Pan-German anti-Semitism that exalted German *Volkstamm* or with the economic and religious resentment behind Christian-Social agitation against the Jews.[80] His searing diatribes against Judaism and Jewry were in reality far more closely connected with profoundly personal problems of identity and sexual *Angst* than with the social or political issues of the age.[81] In this respect the biographical indications which we possess concerning his short life are important indicators.[82]

Otto Weininger was born in Vienna on 3 April 1880 into a well-educated and liberally-minded, assimilated Viennese Jewish family. His father Leopold, to whom Otto was strongly attached, was a gifted goldsmith with a passion for the arts (especially for the music of Richard Wagner) and a self-taught mastery of languages. Leopold Weininger's statuettes and ornate cups of gold, platinum, and enamel were widely sought after by museums in Europe, and Emil Lucka, a

Moderne (Frankfurt, 1982), 168, who, in spite of Weininger's misogyny, praises the many subtle psychological observations on women in his book.

[78] Otto Weininger, *Sex and Character* (London and New York, 1906), authorized trans. from the 6th German edn., 311–12.

[79] Ibid. 312.

[80] Le Rider, p. 193. This apolitical character of Weininger's reflections was very typical of the late 19th-cent. Viennese intelligentsia, whether Jewish or Christian.

[81] Weininger's social position as a Jewish intellectual in Vienna none the less played a role in the *direction* which his moral indignation assumed. See Michael Pollak, 'Otto Weiningers Antisemitismus—eine gegen sich selbst gerichtete moralische Verurteilung des intellektuellen Spiels' in Jacques Le Rider and Norbert Leser (eds.), *Otto Weininger: Werk und Wirkung* (Vienna, 1984), 120.

[82] See Karl Kraus in *Die Fackel*, no. 144, Oct. 1903, pp. 1–3, 15–22; and the books by his close friends, Emil Lucka, *Otto Weininger: Sein Werk und seine Persönlichkeit* (Vienna, 1905), and Hermann Swoboda, *Otto Weiningers Tod* (Leipzig, 1910); also Carl Dallago, *Otto Weininger und sein Werk* (Innsbruck, 1912) and the very valuable study by the Norwegian psychiatrist David Abrahamsen, *The Mind and Death of a Genius* (New York, 1946).

friend of his son, described him as 'one of the last in Austria—perhaps the last—masters of this art'.[83] He had introduced his son when still very young to the music of Wagner and he visted Bayreuth several times to listen with reverent awe to the German composer's operas.[84] The romantic cult of Wagner in the Weininger household was to have a profound impact on Otto's world-view, especially with regard to women and Jews.

Leopold Weininger for all his aesthetic sensibility was an austere, rigid, and puritanical personality who had personally supervised his children's education and maintained a severe discipline in the home. There was something profoundly gloomy and secretive in his temperament which seems to have been transmitted to his son. Emil Lucka wrote on this score: 'I think Otto received a greater heritage from his father. He loved him more than he did his mother; the deep, dark inner life was common to them.'[85] Otto Weininger would have appeared to have absorbed from his patriarchial father not only his austere and sensitive temperament, his love of music, and his extraordinary ability for languages but also a strong though ambivalent antipathy toward Jews.[86] Rosa Weininger, Otto's sister, wrote to the psychiatrist David Abrahamsen on 27 August 1938: 'My father was Jewish, as was my mother. My father was highly anti-semitic, but he thought as a Jew and was angry when Otto wrote against Judaism.'[87] Otto Weininger was far less close to his mother Adelheid, described by Rosa as 'a fine, good, simple woman' who was 'overshadowed by the stronger personality of her husband'.[88] His resentment and possibly

[83] Letter of Emil Lucka from Vienna, dated 10 Sept. 1938, repr. in Abrahamsen, pp. 204–5.

[84] See Abrahamsen, pp. 214–15, for the letter from Bayreuth of Leopold Weininger to his daughter Rosa, dated 20 Aug. 1902, in which he writes that to him Richard Wagner 'will always be, above everyone else, the great tone poet!' In the same letter, the father observes: 'I have from your earliest years educated you so that you should learn only that which was beautiful and noble, and I acknowledge with pleasure that Otto is an aesthetic human being.'

[85] Emil Lucka, 'Erinnerungen an Leopold Weininger', *Der Tag* (Vienna), 3 Jan. 1923; also Abrahamsen, pp. 14–15.

[86] At the age of eighteen, Otto Weininger spoke English, French, and Italian as well as German, was fluent in Spanish and Norwegian (which he learnt in order to read Ibsen in the original), and knew Latin and Greek. His knowledge of Judaism was, however, minimal (Abrahamsen, p. 14).

[87] Letter VI, in Appendix to ibid. 204. In another letter of 27 June 1939, Rosa remarked: 'Our name always was Weininger, and we always were Jews.' Otto Weininger's conversion to Protestantism on 21 July 1902 was, however, approved by his father. The whole family later converted to Christianity.

[88] Letters of 27 Aug. 1938 and 27 June 1939, ibid. 204, 208.

even hatred of his mother may well have contributed to his highly jaundiced view of both women and Jews.[89]

At the Gymnasium in Vienna Weininger proved to be a precocious and outstanding student, though not particularly popular with his teachers.[90] From 1898 to 1902 he studied at the University of Vienna under Professor Friedrich Jodl (1849–1914), working on a dissertation originally entitled 'Eros and Psyche' which became the basis of his sensational book, *Geschlecht und Charakter*. At the University he was initially an anti-metaphysical positivist, influenced by Richard Avenarius's *Kritik der reinen Erfahrung* (Critique of Pure Experience), by the philosophy of Kant and Nietzsche, and also by the experimental sciences.[91] Around 1900 the gifted young student began to move towards a philosophical orientation in psychology against the prevailing dominance in Vienna of biology, physiology, and empirical methods of laboratory investigation.[92]

In October 1900, through the intermediary of his friend Hermann Swoboda (a patient of Sigmund Freud), Weininger first heard of the notion of bisexuality.[93] The theory, then being developed by Freud's Berlin collaborator Wilhelm Fliess, changed the whole course of his research, leading him to believe that all differences between man and woman could be reduced to a single principle, the sex difference. Man and woman, as Weininger later expounded the theory, were not separated distinctively from each other. Rather there was in every individual a mixture of masculine and feminine substance.

During the period from the autumn of 1900 to the summer of 1901 Weininger feverishly gathered material relating to the topic of bisexuality for his doctoral thesis. Little interested in social problems and indifferent to politics, his mental energy was entirely devoted to

---

[89] Abrahamsen, p. 184: 'Basically the denial of his mother religion was also directed against his mother, whom he hated.' There is, however, no direct evidence for this assertion.

[90] William M. Johnston, *The Austrian Mind: An Intellectual and Social History, 1848–1938* (Berkeley and Los Angeles, 1983), 159.

[91] Le Rider, *Le Cas Otto Weininger*, 15–16.   [92] Ibid. 20–1.

[93] See H. Swoboda, *Die gemeinnützige Forschung und der eigennützige Forscher* (Vienna, 1906), 6–7. Also the letter of Freud dated 11 June 1939, in Abrahamsen, pp. 207–8: 'Weininger was never my patient, but one of his friends was. Through this means Weininger became acquainted with the views on bisexuality which I had already applied in my analysis prompted by Fliess.' On Fliess, see Sigmund Freud, *The Origins of Psychoanalysis: Letters to Wilhelm Fliess. Drafts and Notes, 1887–1902* trans. Eric Mosbacher and James Strachey (New York, 1977), 41, 241, 324. Fliess accused Weininger and Swoboda of plagiarizing his theory of bisexuality. Freud's own relationship with Fliess was adversely affected by this scandal.

the world of philosophy, psychology, and music—especially the work of Richard Wagner whom he regarded as the quintessential artistic genius. In the autumn of 1901 he went to Sigmund Freud (whose works on hysteria he admired) with a draft of his thesis, which as yet contained 'no depreciatory words about the Jews and much less criticism of women'.[94] Freud was sharply critical of its boldly speculative and deductive method, telling Weininger that he acted 'like a robber in a room of treasures—picking up what he could carry and destroying the rest . . .'.[95]

Weininger was not, however, unduly discouraged. He had broken once and for all with the experimental psychology of Mach and Avenarius and turned now increasingly to ethical-philosophical subjects. By 21 February 1902 he wrote to Hermann Swoboda that he was in the process of discovering the key to universal history, and in another letter in March concluded, 'Let us return to Kant!' He claimed also to have 'made great progress on the Jewish question and ethics'.[96] Weininger's doctoral thesis was presented in June 1902 and shortly after its successful defence he ostentatiously converted to Protestantism, the minority Christian religion in Austria. This option clearly signified in Weininger's case not only a break with his detested Jewish origins and with the Catholic Baroque traditions of Viennese culture but also a positive identification with the austere Protestant faith of his favourite German philosopher, Immanuel Kant.[97]

Weininger's return to Kant and the traditions of German idealism was an integral part of his new inward preoccupation with metaphysics, with the defence of an extreme rationalism and an ascetic, individualist morality.[98] Kant's categorical imperative doubtless served him as a

[94] Abrahamsen, pp. 52 ff.

[95] Ibid. 54–5, 208; Swoboda, pp. 21–22. The words Freud used were: 'Sie haben das Schloss geöffnet mit einem gestohlenen Schlüssel' (You have opened the lock with a stolen key). None the less Weininger made a strong personal impression on Freud: 'A slender, grown-up youth with grave features and a veiled, quite beautiful look in his eyes; I could not help feeling that I stood in front of a personality with a touch of genius' (Abrahamsen, p. 55).

[96] Le Rider, *Le Cas Otto Weininger*, 23.

[97] Pollak, *Vienne 1900*, 103: 'La conversion de Weininger au protestantisme, choix d'assimilation rare dans l'Autriche catholique, se propose comme une sorte de rattachement spirituel à l'esprit prussien et à la philosophie de Kant, étrangère à la tradition culturelle viennoise.'

[98] Leopold Thaler, 'Weininger's Weltanschauung im Lichte der Kantischen Lehre' (Univ. of Vienna diss., 1923), p. 75: 'Mit Kant hat er also gemein die Ethizität der Weltanschauung, das Primat der praktischen Vernunft . . . Kant war ihm ein innerer Imperativ, der Kritizismus ein Ideal der Forschung und der Philosophie . . . Kant war der *innere Richter* seines Denkens.'

yardstick with which to measure and reject the sensuous, plastic culture of Vienna and its frivolous sexual mores. Modern notions of sexuality and the moral relationship between man and women were henceforth judged by Weininger in the light of the conception of humanity pervading the philosophy of Kant and were found to be catastrophically defective. Woman, the young philosopher portentously declared, must cease to be a sexual object for man and wholly renounce her femininity if she was to become truly human. Chastity had become for Weininger the only possible road to inner female emancipation.[99]

Weininger's distortion of the Kantian moral law into an instrument for rationalizing his gnostic-Manichean view of the feminine sex was clearly a reflection of his own increasingly desperate efforts to master a disturbed sexuality.[100] In the philosophic part of his doctoral thesis, Weininger had already postulated Masculinity and Feminity as opposite poles, positive and negative. The principle of Maleness (understood as a Platonic Idea) represented Being, Femaleness was non-Being. Woman was nothing but man's expression and projection of his own sexuality. Her qualities depended on her essential lack of character and individuality, her non-existence as a human being. Woman represented guilt, negation, embodiment of man's lower self; yet she was no less eternal than existence itself. 'Man created woman, and will always create her afresh, as long as he is sexual. Just as he gives woman consciousness, so he gives her existence. Woman is the sin of man.'[101]

In his book *Geschlecht und Charakter*, Weininger developed *ad absurdum* this bitterly tragic, dualistic conception of the universe, drawing freely on Platonism and the self-hating traditions of Christianity from Augustine, Origen, and Tertullian through Pascal to such modern misogynists as the great German philosophers, Kant, Schopenhauer, and Nietzsche. Biological and physiological data from his thesis were integrated with new ethico-philosophical chapters to demonstrate the sombre, bellicose thesis that woman, as the incarnation of sexuality, symbolized the principle of Nothingness in the cosmos. Her 'acceptance of the Phallus' was immoral, she bowed down to it as 'her supreme Lord and welcome master', thereby perpetuating

---

[99] David Luft, 'Otto Weininger als Figur des fin de siècle', in Le Rider and Leser, *Otto Weininger*, 74–5.

[100] Paul-Laurent Assoun, 'Der perverse Diskurs über die Weiblichkeit', in ibid. 189–90.

[101] Weininger, *Sex and Character*, 299.

through the sexual act a universe of negation.[102] Yet ultimately this curse on woman was the responsibility of man himself, whose evil will had been imposed on her and whose guilt she epitomized.[103]

Weininger's Faustian ethic of self-overcoming explicitly postulated that man must defeat the 'negative' feminine part of himself by warring against his own sexual drives. He was only too aware that this demand derived from a profound and unrelenting self-hatred. In a brilliant essay in 1902 on his favourite dramatist, the Norwegian Henrik Ibsen, he had even classified humanity into two groups—those who loved and those who hated themselves.[104] The self-haters pursued the Pascalian principle that 'le moi est haïssable' and were therefore incapable of loving another person or communicating with those who loved them. In such philosophers as Pascal, Schopenhauer, and above all Friedrich Nietzsche, Weininger diagnosed supreme case-studies in autophobia.[105] But it could be demonstrated that self-hatred was 'the best foundation for self-examination' and for profound insight into the human condition. In a text dating from 3 April 1902 Otto Weininger analysed his own crisis of self-hatred, relating it to the very nature of philosophy.

The artist always loves himself; the philosopher hates himself. A glorious love is created in the artist by the least sign of love and respect, while the philosopher as such is never loved. But when one is misjudged and still loved, then one becomes hard, hard until one is compassionate with oneself! All this self-examination is a phenomenon typical of the self-hater.[106]

Weininger's morbid thoughts were pitilessly revealed in the closing paragraph of this text which compared his state of mind with that of 'a house where the shutters are forever closed'. Inside this house, all was sullen, angry, bitter. 'A wild, desperate activity, a slow, terrifying realization in the dark, an eternal clearing out of things—inside! Do not ask how it looks inside the house—but the light shines on, and amazed, it knocks on the door over and over again. Yet the windows close ever tighter from within.'[107]

Weininger's remorseless self-examination led him to the insight that

---

[102] Ibid.

[103] Ibid. 299–300.

[104] See 'Essai sur Henrik Ibsen et son "Peer Gynt" (à l'occasion du 75ᵉ anniversaire de la naissance de l'écrivain)', in Weininger, *Des fins ultimes* (Lausanne, 1981), 57–66. Weininger was strongly attracted to Scandinavian writers like Ibsen, Strindberg, and Kurt Hamsun.

[105] Ibid. 63–5.

[106] The full text is reproduced in Abrahamsen, p. 215.   [107] Ibid.

all hatred was a projected phenomenon, including his personal animosity towards women—the confession of an inability to overcome his own sexuality.[108] Similarly, with hatred of the Jews: '. . . whoever detests himself: that he should persecute it in others is merely his endeavour to separate himself in this way from Jewishness; he strives to shake it off and to localise it in his fellow-creatures and so for a moment to free himself of it.'[109]

In the closing chapters of *Geschlecht und Charakter* Weininger sought to apply his theories regarding Masculinity and Feminity to the Jewish problem, one which he recognized to be 'of the deepest significance for the study of all races, and in itself . . . intimately bound up with many of the most troublesome problems of the day'.[110] Weininger's definition of Judaism was neither racial-anthropological, national, nor religious.[111] 'I mean neither a race nor a people nor a recognized creed. I think of it as a tendency of the possibility for all mankind, but which has become actual in the most conspicuous fashion only amongst the Jews.'[112]

Weininger first of all illustrated his point by a characterological analysis of the anti-Semite. He argued that the purest Aryans by descent were generally 'philosemites' even though they might be 'unpleasantly moved by some of the peculiar Jewish traits'. Aggressive anti-Semites, on the other hand, nearly always displayed 'certain Jewish characters' and their hatred derived from this recognition of undesirable qualities in themselves from which they desired to be free. The commoner natures among the Aryans were actively anti-Semitic precisely because they never sat in judgement on themselves.[113] This

[108] Otto Weininger, *Taschenbuch und Briefe an einen Freund* (Vienna, 1919), 66: 'Der Hass gegen die Frau ist immer nur noch nicht überwundener Hass gegen die eigene Sexualität.'

[109] Weininger, *Sex and Character*, 304.   [110] Ibid. 303.

[111] A racial definition, as Weininger clearly recognized, would have foreclosed the possibility of escape from one's origins and was therefore unacceptable to him. A national definition also seemed unconvincing 'since the Jews of his acquaintance claimed to be part of the German people'. Moreover, Weininger regarded Zionism as the negation of Judaism, at least in his understanding of that term. Solomon Liptzin in his illuminating book, *Germany's Stepchildren* (Philadelphia, 1961), 186, suggested that Weininger could not define Judaism as a creed, 'since the Viennese Jews were on the whole no more religious than he himself'.

[112] Weininger, *Sex and Character*, 303.

[113] Ibid. 304. In a footnote Weininger also claimed, however, that the greatest geniuses (Tacitus, Pascal, Voltaire, Herder, Goethe, Kant, Jean Paul, Schopenhauer, Grillparzer, Wagner) 'have nearly always been anti-Semites' since 'they have something of everything in their natures, and so can understand Judaism'.

psychology of projection also explained why 'the bitterest Antisemites are to be found amongst the Jews themselves'.[114] The object of hatred was that person alone 'who reminds one unpleasantly of oneself'.

Even Richard Wagner, whose music was in Weininger's estimation 'the most powerful in the world' and who had captured more than any other artist the essence of the German race, illustrated the truth of his psychological law. Wagner's Siegfried might be 'the most un-Jewish type imaginable' and the music of *Parsifal* forever inaccessible to 'genuine Jews', yet the composer could only attain these artistic heights by first overcoming the Jewishness in himself. It was no accident, therefore, that Wagner's music produced the greatest impression 'not only on Jewish anti-Semites, who had never completely shaken off Jewishness, but also on Indo-Germanic anti-Semites'.[115] Wagner's achievement was the product of a great inner struggle for self-transcendence and it was indeed 'the immense merit of Judaism that it, and nothing else, leads the Aryan to a knowledge of himself and warns him against himself'.[116]

Weininger's analysis of the founders of religion, 'the greatest of the geniuses', proceeded along similar lines. Their impulse to regenerate man through faith derived from a mighty struggle to overcome the evil, guilt, and original sin within themselves. This was above all true of Jesus Christ, 'the man who conquered in Himself Judaism, the greatest negation, and created Christianity, the strongest affirmation and the most direct opposite of Judaism'.[117] Unlike Houston Stewart Chamberlain, Weininger did not believe that the birth of Christ in Palestine was an accident nor did he accept the racist theory of an 'Aryan' Jesus.

Christ was a Jew, precisely that He might overcome the Judaism within Him, for he who triumphs over the deepest doubt reaches the highest faith; he who has raised himself above the most desolate negation is the most sure in his position of affirmation. Judaism was the peculiar, original sin of Christ; it was His victory over Judaism that made Him greater than Buddha or Confucius. Christ was the greatest man because He conquered the greatest enemy. Perhaps He was, and will remain, the only Jew to conquer Judaism. The first of the Jews to become wholly the Christ was also the last who made the transition.[118]

Weininger speculated that the possibility of producing another

[114] Ibid. Weininger explicitly excluded 'the quite Jewish Jews' like the 'completely Aryan Aryans' from this categorization.
[115] Ibid. 305.   [116] Ibid. 306.   [117] Ibid. 327–8.   [118] Ibid. 328.

Christ lay dormant in Jewry and that this might well be the historic meaning of Judaism. Indeed, the survival of the Jewish people must somehow be linked to the idea of Messiah, 'of one who shall save them from Judaism'. Though he did not explicitly say as much, it would seem that Weininger saw his own mission in this messianic light, following his conversion to Christianity.[119] *He* was destined to be the liberator of the dawning twentieth century who would free humanity from the yoke of a daemonic world of Femininity and Judaism; he would be the new Redeemer who had come to deliver the hedonistic, frivolous, and sensual world of *fin-de-siècle* Vienna from the devils of earthy corruption. Weininger's apocalyptic vision of a doomed civilization was the counterpoint to his own idealized vision of purified, virile intellect, of a new immanent God of self, a bizarre kind of Dionysian neo-Kantianism embodied in his own spiritual strivings. Weininger's indictment of the age and its decadence was even more total than that of Karl Kraus:

Our age is not only the most Jewish but the most feminine. It is a time when art is content with daubs and seeks its inspiration in the sports of animals; the time of a superficial anarchy, with no feeling for Justice and the State; a time of communistic ethics, of the most foolish of historical views, the materialistic interpretation of history; a time of capitalism and of Marxism; a time of economy and technical instruction; a time with no great artists and no great philosophers; a time without originality and yet with the most foolish craving for originality; a time when the cult of the Virgin has been replaced by that of the Demi-vierge. It is the time when pairing has not only been approved but has been enjoined as a duty.[120]

Weininger was convinced that as in the year One, mankind was impatiently waiting for a new founder of religion, one who might well come from the 'inferior' world of Judaism. Hence, the turn of the century was a time of decision between the two polarities of mankind:

The decision must be made between Judaism and Christianity, between business and culture, between male and female, between the race and the individual, between unworthiness and worth, between the earthly and the higher life, between negation and the God-like. Mankind has the choice to make. There are only two poles, and there is no middle way.[121]

Weininger's antitheses with their critique of decadence, their polarization of culture and civilization, *Geist* and *Geld*, soul and

[119] Liptzin, pp. 188–9.
[120] Weininger, *Sex and Character*, 329–30.   [121] Ibid. 330.

intellect, genius and talent, virility and femininity, Christianity and Judaism, reflect the commonplaces of a post-Nietzschean dilettantism in Central Europe. Along with the writings of Chamberlain, Klages, Theodor Lessing, and Walter Rathenau they provide a crucial link in the chain leading from Nietzsche to the Spenglerian vision of *Untergang*.[122] Neo-romantic, regressive, anti-capitalist and anti-Marxist, this Weiningerian *Kulturkritik* bizarrely fused Kantian enlightenment with an irrationalism mediated through Schopenhauer, Wagner, Nietzsche, and Chamberlain. In the light of a homoerotic world-view that substituted the battle of the sexes for the class-struggle and glorified the virility of idealistic German philosophy at the expense of 'feminine' psychology, Weininger's conceptions could be readily described as 'pre-fascist'.[123] Both German Nazis and Italian Fascists were not surprisingly attracted to the views of this renegade Jew.[124] For in Weininger's philosophy one could find in embryonic form many of the key themes of twentieth-century Fascist ideology: anti-Semitism, anti-feminism, Anglophobia, anti-liberalism, and anti-Communism, along with a cult of disciplined virility, individual heroism, moral austerity, and the romantic exaltation of genius.[125]

The reactionary character of Weininger's outlook was particularly evident in his negative association of Jews with communism and anarchism. Like the ideologists of the conservative Right in Europe, Weininger insisted that Jews had no inward relation to individual freedom, landed property, or to the State. Whereas co-operative socialism was supposedly 'Aryan' (Owen, Carlyle, Ruskin, Fichte), communism was thoroughly 'Jewish' (Marx). Modern social democracy had moved so far apart from earlier socialism, 'precisely because Jews have taken so large a share in developing it'.[126] Like women, Jews were incapable of a true ethical conception of the State, involving 'the

---

[122] Mayer, pp. 118–26.

[123] Le Rider, *Le Cas Otto Weininger*, 213–17.

[124] See Dietrich Eckart, 'Das Judentum in und ausser uns', *Auf gut deutsch* (Jan.–Apr. 1919), in Barbara Miller Lane and Leila J. Rupp, *Nazi Ideology before 1933: A Documentation* (Manchester, 1978), 18–26; also Adolf Hitler, *Monologue im Führerhauptquartier, 1941–1944*, ed. W. Jochmann (Hamburg, 1980), 148. Both Eckart and Hitler regarded Weininger as the prime example of a 'decent Jews' who had committed suicide out of recognition of the parasitic role which Jewry played among the peoples. For Weininger's influence in Italy, see Alberto Cavaglion, *Otto Weininger in Italia* (Rome, 1982), and his article (together with Michel David), 'Weininger und die italienische Kultur', in Le Rider and Leser, *Otto Weininger*, 37–48.

[125] Cavaglion, p. 47; Le Rider, *Le Cas Otto Weininger*, 215–16.

[126] Weininger, *Sex and Character*, 307.

aggregation of individual aims, the formation of and obedience to self-imposed laws'. Lacking any conception of a 'free intelligible ego' in the Kantian sense and incapable of even respecting each other's individuality, Jews could only regard the State as something irredeemably alien.

Like Herzl, Weininger evidently looked to the Prusso-German rather than the Austrian model as the 'ideal' form of State, with Kant rather than Bismarck as his spiritual guide.[127] But unlike the founder of political Zionism he was uninterested in the socio-economic or political aspects of the Jewish problem. What Herzl regarded as a *Machtfrage* that had to be solved on a collective basis by restoring Jewish honour and re-creating a territorial basis for the exercise of sovereignty, remained for Weininger essentially a metaphysical question. Ideas rather than power in his view determined the course of history. Politicians and statesmen were inherently incapable of creating genuine cultural values. They were at best great criminals, far lower on the scale of genius than artists, philosophers, or founders of religion.

There was, however, a more important reason, beyond this unflattering opinion of political man, which determined Weininger's rejection of Herzl's Zionist solution to the Jewish problem. Notwithstanding the fact that Zionism 'has brought together some of the noblest qualities of the Jews', it was in his view 'doomed to failure' because it negated the Diasporic essence of Judaism.[128] Quoting Houston S. Chamberlain, Weininger argued that 'since the destruction of the Temple at Jerusalem, Judaism has ceased to be national and has become a spreading parasite, straggling all over the earth and finding true root nowhere. Before Zionism is possible, the Jew must first conquer Judaism.'[129]

Since the Jew remained eternally bound to his soulless 'communist' nature and committed to the Diasporic conception of 'world-wide distribution of the Jews', he could hardly be mobilized for Zionism. This implicitly anti-Semitic theory, suitably adapted from Weininger by Nazi ideologists like Dietrich Eckart and Alfred Rosenberg and exploited by Adolf Hitler himself, led to the peculiarly pernicious proposition that Jews were inherently lacking in any State-building qualities. Since Jewry was a priori defined as a usurious Diasporic entity, incapable of creative endeavour in the fields of art, science,

---

[127] Pollak, *Vienne 1900*, 103, suggests that Weininger's remarks about the State be seen in the context of his '. . . mépris pour les traditions culturelles antiphilosophiques autrichiennes et son idolatrie pour la pensée issue des universités prussiennes'.

[128] Weininger, *Sex and Character*, 307.   [129] Ibid. 312.

economy, and politics, all efforts by Zionists to productivize this nation would later be condemned by the Nazis as doomed to failure.[130]

Having rejected Zionism, the portrait of the Jew that Weininger now proceeded to draw was one of an unrelieved negativity, consistent with his underlying identification of Judaism with Femininity. Thus, the Jew lacked innate good breeding and nobility. He had 'an inordinate love of titles' but unlike the Aryan no individual sense of ancestry. He was lacking in any conception of Supreme Good and Evil, unconcerned with God and the Devil, indifferent to either Heaven or Hell.[131] Like Woman, he had no sense at all of the greatness of morality or of 'radical evil' as expounded in Kantian philosophy. Moreover, in the Judaic world-view (as among women) the family loomed larger than State or society, the preservation of the race was more important than that of the individual. Like women, too, Jews were perpetually absorbed in sexual matters and 'habitual match-makers', organically incapable of comprehending asceticism. They were therefore primarily responsible for the disastrous victory of the 'pairing instinct' in modern life:

The pairing instinct is the great remover of the limits between individuals; and the Jew, *par excellence*, is the breaker down of such limits. He is the opposite pole from aristocrats, with whom the preservation of the limits between individuals is the leading idea. The Jew is an inborn communist. The Jew's careless manners in society and his want of social tact turn on this quality, for the reserves of social intercourse are simply barriers to protect individuality.[132]

The inferiority of the Jew was closely bound up with that of his religion. Thus, for Weininger 'Jewish' arrogance and bigotry derived from a slavish disposition embodied in the Ten Commandments, 'the most immoral book of laws in the universe, which enjoins on obedient followers, submission to the powerful will of an exterior, with the reward of earthly well-being and the conquest of the world'.[133] Following Kant and Schopenhauer, Weininger solemnly proclaimed that the Jew was devoid of soul, of any sense of the divine in man or the

---

[130] See Robert S. Wistrich, *Hitler's Apocalypse: Jews and the Nazi Legacy* (London, 1985), 155 ff., for an elaboration of Nazi anti-Zionism and anti-Semitism. Weininger's view of Zionism was more positive than that of the Nazis but he believed it to be wholly unrealizable. For a contemporary Israeli dramatization of the tension between Zionism and Judaism as reflected in Weininger's life, see Joshua Sobol's play, *Soul of a Jew: The Death of Otto Weininger* (trans. from the Hebrew text, *Nefesh Yehudi*, 1982).

[131] Weininger, *Sex and Character*, 309.

[132] Ibid. 311.

[133] Ibid. 313.

belief in immortality.[134] Incapable of true mysticism, he therefore lacked a true faith in God. Indeed, the Jew was the prototype of unbelievers, materialists, and freethinkers. In natural science his efforts were characteristically devoted to removing all transcendentalism or any hint of 'the secret and spiritual meaning of things'; the cosmos had to be made as flat and commonplace as possible.[135] Typically enough the Jews were beguiled by Darwinism and mechanical, materialistic theories of life.

Hence it was no accident for Weininger that Jews had embraced medical science in such numbers and become especially prominent in the study of chemistry, which reduced medicine to a mere matter of drugs. This soulless 'Judaistic' science was the antithesis of the noble 'Aryan' conception of Copernicus, Galileo, Kepler, Euler, Newton, Linnaeus, Lamarck, and Faraday.[136] In philosophy, too, the Jewish contribution had been superficial, slavish, and of course deterministic. Even Spinoza ('incomparably the greatest Jew of the last nine hundred years') lacked depth and only Goethe's high estimation of him could explain the exaggerated esteem in which he was held.[137] Indeed, the shallowness of Spinoza underlined to Weininger's satisfaction the truth of his thesis that Jews, like women, were congenitally incapable of 'Aryan' genius or seeking after transcendental truth.[138]

Of all the Germanic races, it was the English who resembled the Jews most closely. Following Richard Wagner, the young Viennese philosopher singled out for special criticism the 'soulless psychology' of the English, their religious orthodoxy and devotion to the Sabbath as well as their alleged lack of talent in architecture, music, and philosophy. The two greatest Englishmen, Shakespeare and Shelley, stood far from 'the pinnacle of humanity' and were notably inferior to Michelangelo and Beethoven. Only the Scots and the Irish were exempted from this diatribe.[139] The abiding sin of the English was

[134] Weininger, *Sex and Character*, 313–14.

[135] Ibid. 314. Weininger saw himself as applying at this point the theories of Richard Wagner's *Das Judentum in der Musik* (1850), to the allegedly antiphilosophical and profoundly materialistic 'Judaic' conception of science.   [136] Ibid. 315.

[137] According to Weininger, Spinoza's 'Jewishness' was revealed in his rejection of free will, his use of the mathematical method, and his failure to comprehend the State!

[138] Ibid. 317.

[139] Weininger's depiction of national character turned very largely on a subjective and romantic estimate of 'genius'. For him the greatest names in British philosophy were the Scotsmen Hume and Adam Smith. He also respectfully mentioned three other Scotsmen, Carlyle, Hamilton, and Robert Burns as well as the Irishmen Bishop Berkeley, Swift, and Sterne.

their notorious empiricism but they were none the less more capable of transcendence than the Jews and their sense of humour was at least superior.[140]

Though denying the Jews any quality of genius or individuality, Weininger did acknowledge their extreme adaptability, the 'mobility' of their minds, and their indisputable talent for mimicry. Unlike women, there was in the Jews an aggressive receptivity:

... he adapts himself to every circumstance and every race, becoming, like the parasite, a new creature in every different host, although remaining essentially the same. He assimilates himself to everything, and assimilates everything; he is not dominated by others, but submits himself to them. The Jew is gifted, the woman is not gifted, and the giftedness of the Jew reveals in many forms of activity, as for instance, in jurisprudence; but these activities are always relative and never seated in the creative freedom of the will.[141]

Weininger related the plasticity of the Jew to the fact that he was utterly without faith, that he believed 'in nothing, within him or without him'; whereas the woman at least believed in man, the Jew was completely irreligious, mocking, and frivolous.[142] Lacking the seriousness, reverence, and piety which constituted the foundations of true culture, the Jew was always a double or multiple personality, without any finality. Indeed, the essential idea of Judaism consisted in this multiplicity which derived from a want of reality, the lack of a fundamental relation to the Kantian thing-in-and-of itself.[143]

The Jew, therefore, stood outside reality, never making himself one with anything or entering into real relationships. A zealot without zeal, he had no share in the infinite, the unconditioned, the transcendent: 'He is without simplicity of faith, and so is always turning to each new interpretation, so seeming more alert than the Aryan. Internal multiplicity is the essence of Judaism, internal simplicity that of the Aryan.'[144] Bereft of true faith and inner identity, the Jew naturally excelled in money-making 'in which alone he can find his standard of value'; believing in nothing he took refuge in material things, the antithesis of all true culture and idealism.[145] The enigma of his character which was marked by its ambiguity and duplicity ultimately lay in the spiritual mediocrity and nothingness which guided all his actions.

Weininger did not, however, close all exits from Judaism, for his

[140] Ibid. 318–19.   [141] Ibid. 320.   [142] Ibid. 321.
[143] Ibid. 323–4.   [144] Ibid. 324.   [145] Ibid.

own conversion had been designed to show that through deep inner struggle the Jew could become not only a Christian but an 'Aryan':

The Jew, indeed, who has overcome, the Jew who has become a Christian, has the fullest right to be regarded by the Aryan in his individual capacity, and no longer be condemned as belonging to a race above which his moral efforts have raised him. He may rest assured that no one will dispute his well-founded claim.[146]

Weininger held that the solution of the 'Jewish question' resided in this 'holy baptism of the Spirit', in the conscious self-overcoming and metamorphosis of the Jew into an Aryan. Yet, within a few months of publishing his startling confession of the soul, he had fired a bullet into his breast, an act which was to transform his book into a best-seller and the virtually unknown Weininger into a *cause célèbre*.[147]

For a significant part of the *fin de siècle* generation of Austrian intellectuals and artists in revolt against their society and its vices, the martyred Weininger now became a legendary figure, whose philosophical extravagance and extremism did not prevent them from admiring his boldness.[148] Karl Kraus, Ludwig Wittgenstein, Hermann Broch, Robert Musil, Arnold Schoenberg, George Trakl, Hermann von Doderer, and the Brenner Circle in Innsbruck all praised Weininger's intellectual honesty and were influenced in some degree by his work. Like Carl Dallago, a leading member of the Brenner Circle, who wrote a monograph on Weininger in 1912, they saw in him 'a Nietzschean character who philosophized, not by reading books and writing learned articles, but from within the depths of his own personal experience of life'.[149]

Karl Kraus played a particularly important role in championing Weininger, deploring the critical stance of the *Neue Freie Presse* and the superficiality of the liberal press in discussing his sexual theories.

[146] Weininger, *Sex and Character*, 312.

[147] See Le Rider, *Le Cas Otto Weininger*, 39 ff., on the newspaper comment in Vienna surrounding his suicide. A second edition of his book appeared in Nov. 1903. By Dec. 1904 the sixth edition had already been published.

[148] A good example of this cult was perhaps the greatest of 20th-cent. 'Viennese' philosophers, Ludwig Wittgenstein (himself from a Protestant Jewish family), who wrote to G. E. Moore: 'I can quite imagine that you don't admire Weininger very much . . . It is true that he is fantastic, but he is *great* and fantastic' (Ludwig Wittgenstein, *Letters to Russell, Keynes and Moore*, ed. Georg Henrik von Wright (New York, 1974), 159).

[149] A. Janik and S. Toulmin, *Wittgenstein's Vienna* (New York, 1973), 73. See Dallago, pp. 3 ff., and the important article by Gerald Stieg, 'Otto Weiningers "Blendung". Weininger, Karl Kraus und der Brenner-Kreis', in Le Rider and Leser, *Otto Weininger*, 59–70.

Kraus also defended Weininger's memory against charges of plagiarism and attempts to depict both his book and his suicide as the acts of a megalomaniac or an insane mind.[150] It was moreover *Die Fackel* which first carried August Strindberg's enthusiastic tribute to this 'virile and intrepid thinker' who had dared to steal the fire of the gods and openly reveal for the first time the 'congenital inferiority' of the feminine sex.[151]

Nevertheless, Kraus did not share Weininger's exaltation of the rational as against the sensual elements in man, nor could he accept the total devaluation of the feminine principle as expounded in *Geschlecht und Charakter*. The 'feminine' elements of tender fantasy, which Kraus regarded as the emotional essence of Woman, were to his way of thinking a civilizing factor and source of artistic creativity. On the other hand, Weininger's 'heroic' moralism and revolt against Viennese triviality attracted Kraus as did his exhaustive discussion of sexuality.[152] Kraus also accepted in large measure the Weiningerian characterization of Woman as a purely sexual, alogical, and superficial creature.[153] Like Weininger, he sharply rejected the feminist movement.

Moreover, Kraus clearly sympathized with Weininger's caustic view of Judaism, though without really sharing either his obsession with religious questions of guilt and redemption or his morbidly pessimistic view of life.[154] Neither a Kantian philosopher nor a romantic Wagnerian, Kraus had no taste for metaphysical speculation or Faust-like efforts to unlock the keys to the universe. Nor, as a quintessentially Austrian satirist, could he embrace Weininger's cult of Prusso-German superiority, though he did identify with the young philosopher's disgust at Viennese coffee-house aestheticism.[155]

In contrast to Weininger, Kraus's more concrete perception of

---

[150] See *Die Fackel*, no. 152, Jan. 1904; no. 212, Nov. 1906; no. 216, Jan. 1907, for the accusations of plagiarism put forward by Wilhelm Fliess and Richard Pfennig against Weininger and his friend Swoboda over the issue of bisexuality.

[151] Ibid., no. 144, Oct. 1903. For the full text, see Le Rider, *Le Cas Otto Weininger*, 40–1.

[152] Ibid. no. 157, Mar. 1904.

[153] See Le Rider, *Le Cas Otto Weininger*, 148, who points out that Kraus celebrated polygamous sexuality as the supreme attribute of femininity and eroticism as the vocation of Woman.

[154] Hans Kohn, p. 34.

[155] Ibid. 43. Regarding Weininger, Hans Kohn observes: 'Von dem Wien der spielerischen Oberfläche, des Leichtseins, hatte er nichts, auch nichts von verbindlichem und verständnisvollem Leben mit Menschen. Seine Ethik war eine kriegerische, kompromisslose Forderung.'

social problems led him to focus his wrath against the empirical, identifiable vices of a pharisaic Austrian society and to see in the debasement of language the central symptom of European cultural decline. For all these reasons Kraus was much more closely tied to his Viennese surroundings and to the happenings of the moment, though his capacity for moral outrage was in many respects no less one-sided and extreme than that of Otto Weininger. Kraus, too, combined the fanaticism of the prophet with the demand for absolute integrity and the most rigorous moral standards. But his apocalyptic ethics did not exclude a fusion of spiritual and sensual or of 'masculine' and 'feminine' qualities, to borrow the language of Weininger. Self-hatred also played a far smaller role in his personality, shaped as it was by the vanity of the artist and the overweening confidence of a self-appointed *Censor Germaniae*.

Kraus's relentless campaign against Jewish mannerisms, literary cliques, financial corruption, and egoistic materialism did not, in contrast to Weininger, derive from a deep sense of sexual guilt or self-denial, though unconscious feelings of hatred and revenge doubtless played their part. Nor did Kraus's antipathy to Judaism lead him to place his hopes in a new Christianity or in a Messiah-redeemer who could point the way to human self-transcendence. In that sense Kraus was far less obsessed than Weininger with the 'essence' of Judaism as a religion or with the need to deliver Jews from its yoke.[156] His emotional aggression was directed against a very particular faction of Jews, against irritating mannerisms and linguistic characteristics rather than against the 'Jewish character' *per se*. Indeed, in Kraus's case the expression of hostility was so bound up with other motives that it is difficult to decide whether self-hatred was involved at all.[157]

Weininger, on the other hand, consciously expressed his philosophical self-hatred as an act of aggression against his own Jewish identity and against the inferior values of the Jews as a group. Admittedly his target was a Platonic ideal type identified as 'the Jew', who conceptually embodied the negativity of the cosmos, rather than Jewry as an ethnic or religious minority. Thus, Weininger could even

---

[156] Weininger's attempt to demonstrate the essential irreligiosity and inadequacy of Judaism as a faith was based on astonishing ignorance of its teachings. See the detailed review and rebuttal of his book in the *Österreichische Wochenschrift*, 31 July 1903, pp. 489–92.
[157] On the methodological problems of defining Jewish self-hatred, see Kurt Lewin's valuable article of 1941 in *Resolving Social Conflicts: Selected Papers on Group Dynamics*, ed. Gertrude Weiss (New York, 1948), 186–200.

claim that the 'Aryan' had a moral obligation not to persecute the Jew just as the male was expected to avoid mistreating the female. But this demand was frequently ignored or overlooked by those who read Weininger, especially the anti-Semites who drew comfort and sustenance from his views.[158] Moreover, Weininger's intensely personal anti-Semitism like his fear and hatred of women was far too unrelenting to be classified simply as a philosophical caprice.[159] Even on the last night of his life, his aphorisms were charged with an astonishing rage and animosity towards Jews and Judaism:

It is Jewish to blame the other (Christianity). Judaism means laying all the blame on someone else. The devil is the man who blames the faithful (God). In this respect Judaism is the radical evil. He is stupid who laughs frivolously at the question, who does not recognise the problem: The Parsifal Legend. The Jew takes no blame. 'How can I help it?' The Christian assumes all guilt. The Jew will accept no guilt (i.e., no problem either) . . . he is opposed to the will of God who wants evil.[160]

There is a great temptation to dismiss such irrational anti-Semitism as a simple expression of personal psychopathology. Such an interpretation overlooks, however, the long cultural conditioning that made Weininger's anti-Semitic paroxysms possible and it ignores the socio-political context of *fin de siècle* Vienna, which rendered them almost commonplace. Nevertheless, the more differentiated verdict of the founder of psychoanalysis, Sigmund Freud, the great Viennese contemporary of Weininger who also knew him slightly (and appreciated his talent while rejecting his theories), is certainly worth quoting:

The castration complex is the deepest unconscious root of anti-Semitism; for even in the nursery little boys hear that a Jew has something cut off his penis— a piece of his penis, they think—and this gives them a right to despise Jews. And there is no stronger unconscious root for the sense of superiority over women. Weininger (the young philosopher who, highly gifted but sexually deranged after producing his remarkable book, *Geschlecht und Charakter*

---

[158] It is interesting to note that a commentary on Weininger was published in the Third Reich to prove the validity of Nazi racial theories concerning the impossibility of Jewish assimilation. See the pamphlet by Dr Alexander Centgraf, *Ein Jude treibt Philosophie* (Berlin, 1943), who approvingly quoted Theodor Lessing's quasi-racist dictum: 'Kein Mensch hat sich je von dem Zwang seines Blutes befreit.'

[159] See Weininger, *Taschenbuch*, 39: 'Jüdisches Gemeinheit und Dummheit. Der Jude ist moralisch das, was die Dummheit intellektuel ist. Er ist die Fliege, die den Esel blütig schindet.' See also, p. 63 for a continuation of this diatribe.

[160] See Weininger, *Über die letzten Dinge* (Vienna and Leipzig, 1904), 183; Abrahamsen, p. 183.

[1903], in a chapter that attracted much attention, treated Jews and women with equal hostility and overwhelmed them with the same insults. Being a neurotic, Weininger was completely under the sway of his infantile complexes; and from that standpoint what is common to Jews and women is their relation to the castration complex.[161]

---

[161] 'Analysis of a Phobia in a Five-Year-Old Boy. "Little Hans"' (1909), in Sigmund Freud, *Case Histories I: 'Dora' and 'Little Hans'*, trans. Alix and James Strachey (London, 1980), 198 (footnote).

16

The Jewish Identity of Sigmund Freud

'When I was a young man' he [Jakob Freud] said, 'I went for a walk one Saturday in the streets of your birthplace; I was well dressed, and had a new fur cap on my head. A Christian came up to me and with a single blow knocked off my cap into the mud and shouted: 'Jew! get off the pavement!' 'And what did you do?' I asked. 'I went into the roadway and picked up my cap', was his quiet reply. This struck me as unheroic conduct on the part of the big strong man who was holding the little boy by the hand.

Sigmund Freud, *The Interpretation of Dreams* (1900)

But in any event I ask you to keep the book [*The Interpretation of Dreams*] as a token of the high esteem in which I—like so many others—have held for many years the poet and fighter for the human rights of our people.

Sigmund Freud to Theodor Herzl (28 September 1902)

. . . you are closer to my intellectual constitution because of racial kinship, while he [Carl Jung] as a Christian and a pastor's son finds his way to me only against great inner resistances. His association with us is the more valuable for that. I nearly said that it was only by his appearance on the scene that psychoanalysis escaped the danger of becoming a Jewish national affair.

Sigmund Freud to Karl Abraham (3 May 1908)

It was only to my Jewish nature that I owed the two qualities that have become indispensable to me throughout my difficult life. Because I was a Jew I found myself free of many prejudices which restrict others in the use of the intellect: as a Jew I was prepared to be in the opposition and to renounce agreement with the 'compact majority'.

Sigmund Freud, Address to the 'B'nai B'rith' (May 1926)

On the occasion of his seventieth birthday in 1926, Sigmund Freud wrote to his friend and disciple Marie Bonaparte with a characteristic touch of irony:

The Jewish societies in Vienna and the University of Jerusalem (of which I am a trustee), in short the Jews altogether, have celebrated me like a national hero, although my service to the Jewish cause is confined to the single point that I have never denied my Jewishness. The official world—the University [of Vienna], Academy, Medical Association—complete ignored the occasion. Rightly, I think; it was only honest. I could not have looked upon their congratulations and honours as sincere.[1]

In the same letter Freud singled out the celebration of the Jewish Lodge 'to which I have belonged for twenty years' and the speech in his honour made there by his private physician Professor Ludwig Braun (1867–1936), 'which cast a spell over the whole audience, including my family'.[2] Braun, who joined the Viennese Lodge of the B'nai B'rith in 1900 (three years after Freud) and had known the founder of psychoanalysis for nearly forty years, defined him in this celebrating speech as a *Ganzjude*.[3] Freud's quality of wholeness, his ability to recognize the unity of nature and mind behind discordant surface phenomena, his independence from religious dogma or conventional taboos and especially his courage in opposing the rest of society, had stamped him as a genuine Jew. In his spiritual 'optimism', tenacious persistence, dignity, and composure in the face of social rejection he had exhibited precisely those traits which explained why Jews had always been in the forefront of the fight for freedom.[4] It was these same characteristics, Professor Braun suggested, which had naturally drawn Freud to B'nai B'rith and its humanitarian ideals. They had also been expressed in his brainchild, the new science of psychoanalysis, which Braun described as an 'authentically Jewish conception of life' (*Lebensanschauung*), one devoted to seeking the general laws of nature and fearlessly exploring the depths of the mind.[5]

Freud's own address to the B'nai B'rith on 6 May 1926 with its strong affirmation of his 'Jewish nature', of the humanitarian goals of the Viennese lodge and its importance as a forum for independent-minded men of principle, amplified on Braun's remarks and demon-

---

[1] Sigmund Freud to Maria Bonaparte, 10 May 1926, in *Letters of Sigmund Freud*, sel. and ed. Ernst L. Freud (New York, 1961), 221 (henceforth designated as *Letters*).

[2] Ibid.

[3] Ludwig Braun, 'Die Persönlichkeit Freuds und seine Bedeutung als Bruder', *B'nai B'rith Mittheilungen für Österreich*, 26 (May 1926), 118–31.

[4] Ibid. 126 ff.   [5] Ibid. 128 ff.

strated his high regard for the ethical fraternity. Beyond that, it also provided an important testimony to his personal development, beliefs, and the nature of his Jewish identification. Freud recalled that his feeling of attraction to the lodge had crystallized in the years after 1895 when he had felt like a virtual pariah in Vienna.

On the one hand I had gained the first insight into the depth of human instinct, had seen many things which were sobering, at first even frightening; on the other hand the disclosure of my unpopular discoveries led to my losing most of my personal relationships at that time; I felt as though outlawed, shunned by all. This isolation aroused in me the longing for a circle of excellent men with high ideals who would accept me in friendship despite my temerity. Your Lodge was described to me as the place where I could find such men.

That you are Jews could only be welcome to me, for I was myself a Jew, and it has always appeared to me not only undignified, but outright foolish to deny it. What tied me to Jewry was—I have to admit it—not the faith, not even the national pride, for I was always an unbeliever, have been brought up without religion, but not without respect for the so-called 'ethical' demands of human civilization. Whenever I have experienced feelings of national exaltation, I have tried to suppress them as disastrous and unfair, frightened by the warning example of those nations among which we Jews live. But there remained enough to make the attraction of Jews and Judaism irresistible, many dark emotional powers [*Dunkelmächte*] all the stronger the less they could be expressed in words, as well as the clear consciousness of an inner identity, the familiarity of the same psychological structure [*die Heimlichkeit der gleichen seelischen Konstruktion*].[6]

According to Freud, this 'uncanny' primordial feeling of solidarity, with its particularist ethnic nexus and common psychic structure, had nothing to do with Jewish religious identity. Though he could not define it, these 'dark emotional powers' were in fact profoundly rooted in the Galician Jewish background from which he originated and to which he was to remain attached all his life in a typically ambivalent fashion.[7] His personality had indeed been formed in an East European

[6] *Letters*, 366–7; also repr. in the article by his son Martin, 'Who was Freud?', in J. Fraenkel (ed.), *The Jews of Austria: Essays on their Life, History and Destruction* (London, 1967), 197–9.

[7] See John Murray Cuddihy, *The Ordeal of Civility: Freud, Marx, Levi-Strauss, and the Jewish Struggle with Modernity* (New York, 1974), 17–108, for a bizarre but thought-provoking look at Freudianism as a modernizing strategy for 'shtetl' Jews seeking to 'pass' into middle-class Gentile society. According to Cuddihy, psychoanalysis was a specifically Jewish way of overcoming the 'ordeal of civility' by coming to terms with the pre-Emancipation Jewish self, the unruly 'id', whose vulgarity had been repressed and censored by bourgeois Christian respectability. Unfortunately the unhistorical approach and a number of gross exaggerations mar his interpretation.

Jewish home and then nurtured in the semi-proletarian Leopoldstadt district of Vienna to which Freud's parents had moved in 1859 from his birthplace in Příbor (Freiberg), Moravia.[8]

Freud's father Jakob, born in 1815 in the Galician *shtetl* of Tsymenitz, was originally an observant Jew, the son of a Hasidic rabbi. Steeped in Jewish learning and rituals he had remained strictly orthodox until the age of twenty when he moved to Freiberg. Replying to a correspondent in 1930, Sigmund Freud observed in this connection:

It may interest you to hear that my father did indeed come from a Chassidic background. He was forty-one when I was born and had been estranged from his native environment for almost twenty years. My education was so unJewish that today I cannot even read your dedication, which is evidently written in Hebrew. In later life I have often regretted this lack in my education [*dieses Stück meiner Unbildung*].[9]

This recollection is consistent with the fact that by the time the family had migrated to Vienna for economic reasons, Jakob Freud had already abandoned many of his earlier religious observances. But he still remained Jewish to the core, in his appearance (he had a long beard and dignified countenance), his ability to recite the Passover Seder service by heart, his diligent study of the Talmud, and his knowledge of Hebrew literature.[10] On his son's thirty-fifth birthday, his father proudly gave him a rebound copy of the Bible which Sigmund had read as a boy, with a special Hebrew dedication written in the spirit of Jewish religious tradition:

To my Dear Son, Solomon. [Freud's Hebrew name was Shlomo, in memory of his paternal grandfather.] It was in the seventh year of your life that the Spirit of God began to stir you and spake to you [thus] 'Go though and pore over the book which I wrote, and there will burst open for thee springs of understanding, knowledge and reason. It is indeed the book of books. Sages have delved into it and legislators have derived [from it] knowledge and law.'

---

[8] In a letter to the Mayor of Příbor (Freiberg) on 25 Oct. 1931, Freud wrote: 'I left Freiberg at the age of three, revisited it as a sixteen-year-old schoolboy on vacation as a guest of the family Fluss, and have never been here since . . . [but] deep within me, although overlaid, there continues to live the happy child from Freiberg, the first-born son of a youthful mother, the boy who received from this air, from this soil, the first indelible impressions.' (*Letters*, 407–8.)

[9] Letter of 20 Feb. 1930 to A. A. Roback, in *Letters*, 395.

[10] Judith Bernays Heller, 'Freud's Mother and Father', *Commentary* (May 1956), 418–21; Ernest Jones, *The Life and Work of Sigmund Freud*, i (London and New York, 1953), 19 and ii (New York, 1955), 409.

Thou has seen the vision of the Almighty. Thou hast listened and ventured and achieved, soaring on the wings of the wind.[11]

The gift, a token of his father's 'undying love', was clearly intended to impress upon Sigmund the continuing importance of the religious tradition in which he had been raised.[12] Yet Jakob Freud must surely have been aware that, in his son's eyes, the religious rituals of Judaism had long seemed to be empty and meaningless. Indeed, the vehemence of Sigmund Freud's antipathy to Judaism as a religion was almost certainly connected with his symbolic rejection of the father who could no longer properly observe or transmit to him fully intact the traditional Jewish way of life. Like so many other Jewish fathers of this transitional generation, the textile merchant Jakob Freud had brought to Vienna only fragments of the living tradition from his ghetto community in the countryside. But this residual loyalty to Judaism was no longer sufficient for the new generation, forced to live between two worlds and two cultures.[13] The inherent duplicity of their situation produced for a whole generation of socially and spiritually uprooted young Viennese Jews a sense of inner conflict, imposture, and despair—the kind of localized neuroses out of which Sigmund Freud was eventually to construct his universalist psychoanalytic typology. In that sense the Oedipus complex can indeed be seen, in Marthe Robert's terms, as the portrait writ large of the primordial 'murdered father', Jakob Freud, a lapsed Galician Hasid.[14]

[11] Abraham Aaron Roback, *Freudiana* (Cambridge, Mass., 1957), 92. At the time Jakob Freud wrote this dedication, Sigmund had already achieved much in his chosen professional field, though a major scientific discovery still eluded him.

[12] Ibid.

[13] See Franz Kafka, *Briefe, 1902–1924* (New York, 1958); Marthe Robert, *D'Œdipe à Moïse: Freud et la conscience juive* (Paris, 1974), 20 ff. Describing his own father complex and that of his generation, Kafka wrote that they wanted 'to break with Judaism, generally with the vague approval of their fathers (this vagueness is the revolting part of it). This is what they wanted, but their hindlegs were bogged down in the father's Judaism, and their front legs could find no new ground.' (Kafka, *Briefe*, 337.)

[14] Robert, p. 24: '. . . c'est Jakob le juif galicien, et non un roi grec de légende qui a été d'abord pour Freud le père assassiné.' But see also letter of 2 Nov. 1896, in Freud, *The Origins of Psychoanalysis: Letters to Wilhelm Fliess Drafts and Notes, 1887–1902*, trans. Eric Mosbacher and James Strachey (New York, 1977), 170–1, for Freud's immediate reaction to his father's death: 'By one of the obscure routes behind the official consciousness the old man's death affected me deeply. I valued him highly and understood him very well indeed, and with his peculiar mixture of deep wisdom and imaginative lightheartedness he meant a great deal in my life . . . I feel now as if I had been torn up by the roots.' By 15 Oct. 1897 Freud is, however, already telling Fliess: 'I have found love of the mother and jealousy of the father in my case too, and now believe it to be a general phenomenon of early childhood . . .' For Freud, this explained

Freud's father-complex, of which he became fully aware only during his own self-analysis following Jakob's death on 23 October 1896, was closely linked to an early childhood experience that concerned anti-Semitism. During one of their strolls together in Vienna when Sigmund was eleven or twelve years old, Jakob Freud had recounted to his son an incident that had occurred many years earlier during his own youth in Freiberg. A local Gentile had come up to him, knocked his *Streimel* (fur hat) into the mud, and ordered him off the pavement. Instead of resisting this impudent behaviour, Jakob Freud had calmly picked up his cap in the roadway. For Jakob the point of the anecdote was to illustrate how much the condition of Jews had improved since the 1830s. However, this 'unheroic' conduct by his father deeply shocked Freud and left an indelible trauma on his mind. 'I contrasted this situation, which did not please me, with another, more in harmony with my sentiments—the scene in which Hannibal's father, Hamilcar Barca, made his son swear before the household altar to take vengeance on the Romans. Ever since then Hannibal has had a place in my fantasies.'[15]

Freud recalled this incident in *The Interpretation of Dreams* (1900) but had not initially noticed that in the first edition he mistakenly gave the name 'Hasdrubal' (Hannibal's brother) in place of the Carthaginian General's real father, Hamilcar Barca. In the *Psychopathology of Everyday Life* he subsequently explained that he had been unable to forgive the lack of courage of his own father, Jakob Freud, towards 'the enemies of our people'. It was this stinging memory of paternal cowardice that cause Sigmund's 'astonishing' error with regard to Hasdrubal.[16]

Sigmund Freud is unlikely to have felt a similar shame with regard to his mother, a prime source of his unshakeable courage and self-confidence. This youthful and dominant woman, née Amalia Nathanson (1835–1930), who came originally from Brody in north-east Galicia, had arrived in Vienna when she was still a child (she actually witnessed the 1848 Revolution). She was a typical Polish Jewess—

the 'gripping' power of the *Oedipus Rex* drama, for every member of the audience was once 'a budding Oedipus in phantasy . . .'.

[15] *The Interpretation of Dreams*, in *Standard Edition of the Complete Psychological Works of Sigmund Freud*, trans. and ed. James Strachey, 24 vols. (London, 1953–74) (henceforth *S.E.*), iv. 196 ff. Also *The Basic Writings of Sigmund Freud*, trans. and ed. Dr A. A. Brill (New York, 1938), 260–1.

[16] Freud, *Zur Psychopathologie des Alltagslebens* (Frankfurt, 1976), 174; Eng. version, *Psychopathology of Everyday Life*, in *Basic Writings*, 143.

'impatient, self-willed, sharp-witted and highly intelligent'.[17] The centre of the family, full of tender concern and devotion towards her eldest son, Amalia Freud had never been fully acculturated. According to the recollections of her grandson Martin Freud, Amalia still retained the language, manners, and beliefs of her native environment. She belonged to a 'peculiar race' distinct not only from the Gentiles:

... but absolutely different from Jews who had lived in the West for some generations ... These Galician Jews had little grace and no manners; and their women were certainly not what we should call 'ladies'. They were highly emotional and easily carried away by their feelings ... They were not easy to live with, and grandmother [Amalia], a true representative of her race, was no exception. She had great vitality and much impatience.[18]

A similarly affectionate ambivalence towards the *Ostjuden* from whom he sprang was shown by Martin's father, Sigmund Freud. For years he fondly collected Galician Jewish anecdotes and jokes, some of which he used in his book *Der Witz und seine Beziehung zum Unbewussten* (1905) and regarded as being 'of deep significance'. Mostly they treated of Galician Jews' aversion to baths, the wiles of Jewish marriage brokers, the impudence of *schnorrers*, and the superstitions of the *Wunderrebbes* (miracle-rabbis).[19] Freud himself noted the prevalence of self-criticism in these jokes which 'have grown up on the soil of Jewish popular life'. Unlike jokes told about Jews by foreigners which rarely rose above the level of brutal derision, the anecdotes created by Jews themselves were based on a knowledge of 'their real faults as well as the connection between them and their good qualities'.[20] Whether cynical, merely sceptical, tendentious, or absurd, this humour realistically reflected, according to Freud, the 'manifold and hopeless miseries of the Jews', the ambiguous relationship between rich and poor, the 'democratic mode of thinking of Jews', and their ability to laugh at their own characteristics.[21] One Galician joke in particular tells us much about the behaviour patterns of *Ostjuden* in a modern civilized society, though its obvious sociological dimension was never discussed by Freud.

[17] Martin Freud, 'Who was Freud?', 202. See also Franz Kobler, 'Die Mutter Sigmund Freuds', *Bulletin des Leo Baeck Instituts*, no. 19 (1962), 149–70.
[18] Quoted in Cuddihy, pp. 100–1.
[19] Sigmund Freud, *Jokes and Their Relation to the Unconscious*, trans. James Strachey (London, 1978), 84–7, 92–3, 99–101, 112, 118, 157–161.
[20] Ibid. 157, 194.
[21] Ibid. 157, 160.

A Galician Jew is travelling in a train. He had made himself really comfortable, had unbuttoned his coat and put his feet up on the seat. Just then a gentleman in modern dress entered the compartment. The Jew promptly pulled himself together and took up a proper pose. The stranger fingered through the pages of a notebook, made some calculations, reflected for a moment and then suddenly asked the Jew: 'Excuse me, when is Yom Kippur (the Day of Atonement)?' 'Oho!' said the Jew, and put his feet up on the seat again before answering.[22]

The Polish train-joke reappears in the *Judenroman* published in Vienna two years after Freud's book on jokes, by his literary 'double', Arthur Schnitzler. In this novel, *Der Weg ins Freie* (1907), the Jewish intellectual protagonist Heinrich Bermann interprets the Galician anecdote as providing a bird's-eye view into the tragi-comic situation of contemporary Jewry.

It expresses the eternal truth that no Jew has any real respect for his fellow Jew, never. As little as prisoners in a hostile country have a real respect for each other, particularly when they are hopeless; envy, hate yes; frequently, admiration, even love; all that there can be between them but never respect, for the play of all their emotional life takes place in an atmosphere of familiarity, so to speak, in which respect cannot help being stifled.[23]

Freud, who ostensibly saw in the same Galician joke the expression of a 'democratic way of thought' did not comment on the element of Jewish self-contempt which had caught Schnitzler's eye. Quite possibly he was attracted to the warm, intimate folk Judaism that harkened back to the pre-Emancipation *Gemeinschaft* of the Galician *shtetl*. The familiarity provided by shared ethnicity did not in this particular case arouse his disapproval. The recognition of the primordial identity beneath the mask superimposed and artificially assumed by the assimilating Jew was something very important to Freud, whose attitude to modern 'civilized' refinement was to remain ambiguous. His own psychoanalytic solution to the neuroses of modernity could perhaps be seen as an ingenious compromise between the intimacies of the East European Jewish subculture from which he came and the formalized behavioural constraints of the middle-class

---

[22] Freud, *Jokes and Their Relation to the Unconscious*, 121. See the apt comment of Cuddihy, p. 21: 'The sudden disclosure of a shared ethnicity reconstitutes the premodern *Gemeinschaft* which knew no "public places" with their "situational proprieties", which encountered no strangers, which made no private–public cleavage.'

[23] Arthur Schnitzler, *Der Weg ins Freie* (Berlin, 1929), 173–4.

Viennese Jewry which he had joined.[24] Though a scathing critic and rebel against self-deceptive stratagems of civilized consciousness, Freud had been personally too scarred by childhood poverty, cultural deprivation, and humiliations of racial discrimination, to which lower-class Jews were especially exposed, to idealize his own family and ethnic milieu. But the hardships induced by his background also strengthened his determination not to show the presumed weakness and resignation of his father in the face of anti-Semitic hostility.

The childhood world of the Leopoldstadt in which Freud grew up in the 1860s, and its influence on his later attitudes to the social problems of assimilation and Jewish identity is an enigma to which he left precious few clues in his own writings. In the brief account given in his *Autobiographical Study*, Freud tersely wrote:

When I was a child of four I came to Vienna, and I went through the whole of my education there. At the 'Gymnasium' I was at the top of my class for seven years . . . Although we lived in very limited circumstances, my father insisted that, in my choice of profession, I should follow my own inclinations. Neither at that time, nor indeed in my later life, did I feel any particular predilection for the career of a physician. I was moved, rather by a sort of a curiosity, which was, however, directed more towards human concerns than towards natural objects . . . My early familiarity with the Bible story (at a time almost before I had learnt the art of reading) had, as I recognized much later, an enduring effect upon the direction of my interest.[25]

Freud's extensive knowledge of the Old Testament was in fact mediated through the popular Hebrew–German Bible with commentary by Ludwig Philippson (1811–89); this enlightened German scholar who sought to steer a middle course between Jewish Reform and Orthodoxy, similar to that of Adolf Jellinek in Vienna, had founded in 1837 the *Allgemeine Zeitung des Judentums* (a newspaper dedicated to Jewish emancipation) which he continued to edit until his death. As a boy, Sigmund Freud had been deeply engrossed in the Philippson Bible, whose presentation of text (in parallel Hebrew and German columns) and of German commentary perfectly embodied its

[24] Cuddihy, p. 29, puts Freud's unspoken premise in vulgar form as follows: 'the id of the "Yid" is hid under the lid of Western decorum (the "superego").' Psychoanalytic strategy meant transforming the *Judenfrage*, essentially 'a politico-social circumstance into a personal, individual problem' and a misfortune of history into a 'universalist science of man' (p.63). According to Cuddihy, Freud's ultimate position on Gentile efforts to 'civilize' the Jews was neutral. He was in favour of 'enlightenment' but against assimilation or conversion.

[25] Freud, *An Autobiographical Study*, trans. James Strachey (London, 1936), 13.

editor's liberal assimilationist outlook. In particular, the stories of Joseph and Moses left an indelible mark on his childhood imagination and later fantasy-life.[26] Joseph, the interpreter of dreams, was almost certainly his first hero, not least because of the obvious similarities between his family constellation and that of Freud himself. Moreover, the Joseph story must have had a special attraction in the liberal 1860s when Jewish hopes of assimilation in Austria were particularly high and the influence of the Catholic Church was on the decline.

It was during this neo-'Josephinist' period of enlightened reform (Freud like most Austrian Jews much admired the late eighteenth-century Habsburg Emperor, Joseph II) that his father had brought home portraits of the new ministers in the 'Bürger' Ministry. The house, as Freud recalled in his *Interpretation of Dreams*, had been illuminated in honour of these middle-class professional men—Herbst, Giskra, Ungar, Berger, and the rest.

There were even Jews among them. So henceforth every diligent Jewish schoolboy carried a Cabinet Minister's portfolio in his satchel. The events of that period no doubt had some bearing on the fact that up to a time shortly before I entered University it had been my intention to study law; it was only at the last moment that I changed my mind.[27]

It was also at this time that a wandering 'poet' had come to the table of the eleven-year-old Sigmund and his parents in a Prater restaurant, and 'been inspired to declare that I should probably grow up to be a Cabinet Minister'.[28] As William McGrath has recently pointed out, in dreaming of a ministerial career the young Freud could readily build on an element in the Joseph story, 'for Joseph had also become a minister'.[29] Beyond the themes of sibling rivalry, the wanderings of his own family, and his avowed interest in its ancestors,[30] Sigmund Freud (son of Jakob) could therefore look to the biblical Joseph as a role-

---

[26] William J. McGrath, *Freud's Discovery of Psychoanalysis: The Politics of Hysteria* (Cornell, 1986) 40 ff., convincingly demonstrates the centrality of the Joseph story in Freud's emotional life and the probable influence of Philippson's interpretation on his understanding of its meaning. See also Leonard Shengold, 'Freud and Joseph', in Mark Kanzer and Julius Glenn (eds.), *Freud and His Self-Analysis* (New York, 1979), 67–86.

[27] *The Interpretation of Dreams*, in *S.E. iv*. 193.

[28] Ibid.   [29] McGrath, p. 32.

[30] Freud, *An Autobiographical Study*, 12–13, begins with a brief evocation of these migrations: 'My parents were Jews, and I have remained a Jew myself. I have reason to believe that my father's family were settled for a long time on the Rhine (at Cologne), that, as a result of a persecution of the Jews during the fourteenth and fifteenth century, they fled eastwards, and that, in the course of the nineteenth century, they migrated back from Lithuania through Galicia to German Austria.'

model in successful acculturation and political achievement: as a profound dreamer, an inward-looking man of feelings, and a rational, statesmanlike figure who rose to high office in a strange land.[31]

During his years as a pupil of the Leopoldstadter Communal-Realgymnasium (1865–73), Freud had been an outstanding student and was duly made head boy. However, in his sixteenth year (1871) his conduct began to deteriorate as he passed through a typical crisis of rebellious adolescence. It was at this time that he became 'inseparable friends' with Heinrich Braun (1854–1927), subsequently to emerge as a prominent German Social Democrat and to be the future brother-in-law of Victor Adler (1852–1918), the founder of Austrian socialism.[32] Freud recorded that he had 'spent every hour not taken up by school with him' and already guessed that 'he possessed something which was more valuable than any success at school and which I have learned since to call "personality" '.[33] He had much admired Heinrich Braun's 'energetic behaviour' and independent judgement, secretly comparing him with a young lion; though Braun was no learner, Freud was 'deeply convinced that one day he would fill a leading position in the world'.[34] Heinrich Braun had first directed the young Freud's interest to 'progressive' books like Henry Thomas Buckle's *History of Civilization* and the *History of the Rise and Influence of the Spirit of Rationalism* by the Irish historian, W. E. H. Lecky (1838–1903).

Braun had also encouraged Freud in his growing aversion to school, 'aroused a number of revolutionary feelings within me', and directed him along the path of antiauthoritarian and anticlerical rebellion.[35] It was under his prodding that Freud originally planned to study law at

---

[31] McGrath, p. 47. In his *Interpretation of Dreams*, Freud observed that 'the name Joseph plays a great part in my dreams . . . My own ego finds it very easy to hide itself behind people of that name, since Joseph was the name of a man famous in the Bible as an interpreter of dreams.' See also Freud's letter of 29 Nov. 1936 to Thomas Mann, after the 'beautiful experience' of reading his new volume *Josef in Ägypten*. In this letter, Freud expounded in great detail 'the phantasy of Joseph as the secret daemonic motor' behind the life of Napoleon Bonaparte—another of his boyhood heroes (*Letters*, 286–8). The obsession speaks for itself as do the autobiographical elements in the identification.

[32] Heinrich Braun later became the co-founder of the leading Marxist theoretical review in Germany, *Die Neue Zeit*, and editor of the *Archiv für soziale Gesetzgebung und Statistik*. In the late 1870s he belonged for a while to the Pan-German radical student circle around Victor Adler and Pernerstorfer in Vienna. A convert, whose sister Emma subsequently married Victor Adler, he had ambivalent attitudes to anti-Semitism. See Robert S. Wistrich, *Socialism and the Jews: The Dilemmas of Assimilation in Germany and Austria-Hungary* (London and Toronto, 1982), 78, 84, 236, 332.

[33] Letter of Freud to Julie Braun-Vogelstein (Heinrich's wife), 30 Oct. 1927, in *Letters*, 231–3.

[34] Ibid. 232.   [35] Ibid.

university and 'engage in social activities'; a project he only abandoned in favour of medicine after hearing Goethe's beautiful essay on Nature read aloud at a popular lecture just before leaving school.[36] At university their paths had diverged. However on one occasion around 1883, following a chance encounter, Heinrich Braun invited Freud to lunch in the house of his brother-in-law Victor Adler, at 19 Berggasse in the Alsergrund district. These were the same rooms in which the founder of psychoanalysis was to live uninterruptedly from 1891 until his expulsion from Vienna in 1938.[37]

Freud's Jewish identity during his late school years and the period of his university studies was to become more ambivalent under the contradictory pressures of assimilation to German culture, social radicalism, and rising anti-Semitism. From 1873 to 1878 Freud was an active member of the Leseverein der deutschen Studenten Wiens, a radical student society wholly committed to the German nationalist cause.[38] Already an enthusiastic Darwinist and materialist, he was increasingly attracted to scientific modernism and anticlerical liberalism. The young Freud was particularly drawn to the North German physicalist school of Helmholtz whose foremost representative in Vienna was another Protestant German, his greatly admired teacher, Ernst Brücke. At this time he began to study the materialist German philosopher Ludwig Feuerbach, whose psychology of religion had a considerable impact on his radical views.[39]

Freud also reacted sharply like other members of the Leseverein to the Ritter von Ofenheim scandal which helped discredit Austro-liberalism in the eyes of a whole generation of nationalist German students.[40] But whereas the Ofenheim Affair politicized many of the

[36] *Letters*, 232. See also Freud, *An Autobiographical Study*, 13–14.
[37] Freud noted this strange coincidence in his letter to Julie Braun-Vogelstein, ibid. 232. In his *Interpretation of Dreams* Freud recalled a clash he had with Victor Adler in the German students' club on the relation between philosophy and the natural sciences: 'I was a green youngster, full of materialistic theories, and thrust myself forward to give expression to an extremely one-sided point of view. Thereupon someone who was my senior and my superior, someone who has since then shown himself as a leader of men and an organizer of large groups . . . stood up and gave us a good talking to.' Although Freud insulted Adler and refused to withdraw his remarks in spite of the general uproar, he remembered that the latter was 'too sensible to look upon the incident as a challenge and let the affair drop'. See *S.E.* iv. 212. Freud's attraction to Berggasse 19, where the much admired Adler had practised medicine before him, may not therefore have been accidental.
[38] See McGrath, pp. 97 ff.   [39] Ibid. 105–7.
[40] Ibid. 107–8. See also Heinz Stanescu, 'Young Freud's Letters to his Rumanian Friend Silberstein', *The Israel Annals of Psychiatry and Related Disciplines*, 9 (Dec. 1971),

Leseverein students, Freud began at precisely this point to lose his interest in politics and devote himself increasingly to science.[41] Philosophical and religious radicalism interested him far more after 1875 than political radicalism of the nationalist or social-democratic variety.[42] He now came under the decisive influence of the great medical teachers at the University of Vienna such as the Berlin-born physiologist Ernst Wilhelm Brücke (1819–92) in whose laboratory he learnt the act of detailed scientific observation between 1876 and 1882; the brilliant psychiatrist from Dresden, Theodor Meynert (1833–92) who specialized in the anatomy of the brain; and yet another German, Richard Krafft-Ebing (1840–1902), author of *Psychopathia sexualis: Eine klinisch-forensische Studie* (1886).[43]

The inspirational example of these great scientists from Germany helped to counteract the bitter disappointment which Freud felt at encountering rampant anti-Semitism in the Viennese student body on entering the University in 1873.[44]

In his *Autobiographical Study*, Freud openly confronted the issue:

Above all, I found that I was expected to feel myself inferior and an alien because I was a Jew. I refused absolutely to do the first of these things. I have never been able to see why I should feel ashamed of my descent or, as people were beginning to say, of my race. I put up, without much regret, with my non-acceptance into the community; for it seemed to me that in spite of this exclusion an active fellow-worker could not fail to find some nook or cranny in the framework of humanity. These first impressions at the University, however, had one consequence which was afterwards to prove important; for at any early age I was made familiar with the fate of being in the Opposition

---

195–209, and the previously unpublished correspondence with Silberstein in German with English translations provided in McGrath's excellent summary, pp. 95 ff.

   [41] McGrath, p. 109.

   [42] A strong philosophical influence on him at this time was the German-born Catholic Professor, Franz Brentano (1838–1917), who had written an important treatise on psychology which profoundly modified Freud's one-sided materialism. On Brentano's impact in Vienna after 1874, see William M. Johnston, *The Austrian Mind: An Intellectual and Social History, 1848–1938* (Berkeley and Los Angeles, 1983), 290 ff.

   [43] Johnston, pp. 229–33. See also Erna Lesky, *Die Wiener medizinische Schule* (Graz, 1965); Dora Stockert-Meynert, *Theodor Meynert und seine Zeit: Zur Geistesgeschichte Österreichs in der zweiten Hälfte des 19 Jahrhunderts* (Vienna, 1930); and Berta Szeps, *My Life and History* (New York, 1939), 164–6.

   [44] Freud, *An Autobiographical Study*, 15: 'At length, in Ernst Brücke's physiological laboratory, I found rest and satisfaction—and men, too, whom I could respect and take as my models.'

and of being put under the ban of the 'compact majority'. The foundations were thus laid for a certain degree of independence of judgement.[45]

Having grown up in the more tolerant, optimistic atmosphere of Austrian political liberalism in the 1860s and early 1870s when assimilation and social acceptance still seemed relatively painless, Freud's sense of shock was understandable. Nevertheless it had not been his first encounter with the new anti-Semitism. Already in the higher classes of the Sperl Gymnasium in the Leopoldstadt, the rapid influx of Jews had provoked a reaction which made him 'realize the consequences of belonging to an alien race' and he was forced by the 'anti-Semitic feeling among my classmates to take a definite stand . . .'[46] Indeed it was precisely this Catholic anti-Semitic backlash which had intensified his childhood cult of Hannibal, the great 'Semitic' commander who had dared to challenge the might of Rome.[47] 'Hannibal and Rome symbolized, in my youthful eyes, the struggle between the tenacity of the Jews and the organization of the Catholic Church. The significance for our emotional life which the anti-Semitic movement has since assumed helped to fix the thoughts and impressions of those earlier days.'[48]

Nevertheless Freud's response to Jews and Judaism during his late adolescence was marked by considerable equivocacy as his letters to a close Romanian friend, Eduard Silberstein (1857–1925), make plan. He was steadily moving away from the traditional customs, rituals, and pieties of his East European home environment. Not only did he proudly proclaim himself as 'godless', refusing to observe the Jewish festivals which his father still held sacred, but in letters to friends he indulged in open mockery of Jewish ritual observances.[49] Reminders of his own provincial background and ties with unassimilated Jews from Eastern Europe began to grate on his nerves. An encounter with just such a family on the return trip from Freiberg to Vienna in September

[45] Freud, *An Autobiographical Study*, 14–15.

[46] *The Interpretation of Dreams*, in *Basic Writings*, 260.

[47] Ibid. During Freud's years at Gymnasium, the percentage of Jews jumped from 44 per cent in 1865 to 73 per cent in 1873, the year of his graduation; see Dennis B. Klein, *Jewish Origins of the Psychoanalytic Movement* (Chicago and London, 1985), 48.

[48] *Basic Writings*, 260. In this self-analysis of 1899, Freud was of course probing the deeper roots of his obsessive desire to go to Rome and the reasons for his neurotic efforts to follow in Hannibal's footsteps. On the connection between Rome and the Catholic anti-Semitism of Austria, see Sebastiano Timpanaro, 'Freud's Roman Phobia', *New Left Review* (Sept./Oct. 1984), pp. 4–32.

[49] Stanescu, pp. 199–200; Freud, 'Some Early Unpublished Letters', trans. Ilse Scheier, *International Journal of Psychoanalysis*, 50, no. 4 (1969), 422–4; Klein, p. 45.

1872 prompted him to make some violently deprecatory remarks in a letter to his friend Emil Fluss:

Now this Jew talked the same way as I had heard thousands of others talk before, even in Freiberg. His face seemed familiar—he was typical. So was the boy with hom he discussed religion. He was cut from the cloth from which fate makes swindlers when the time is ripe: cunning, mendacious, kept by his adoring relatives in the belief that he is a great talent, but unprincipled and without character. I have enough of this rabble.[50]

The transparent desire to dissociate himself from such undesirable provincial Jewish characteristics coincided with Freud's growing aspirations to identify with liberal German *Kultur*.[51] By the time he had entered medical school in Vienna, Freud clearly regarded Jewish religious traditions as thoroughly anachronistic and looked to German-Austrian democratic ideals as the basis for social integration and assimilation. At the same time he was trying to sever his connections with the *Ostjuden*, the 'alien race' who were the initial target of German national anti-Semitism.[52]

In the Vienna medical school this backlash was directed first and foremost against poor Jewish students from Hungary and Galicia. It assumed public import when the eminent surgeon, Professor Theodor Billroth (1829–94), proposed a *numerus clausus* against the eastern Jews who were flooding the Vienna medical faculty.[53] Billroth did not confine his remarks merely to the need to maintain scientific standards or the objective difficulties in securing a livelihood that inevitably confronted immigrant Jews. He postulated a deep and fundamental cleavage 'between pure German and pure Jewish blood', denying that Jews could ever lose their national characteristics or 'participate in the national struggles like the Germans themselves'.[54] Billroth's book on

[50] Freud 'Some Early Unpublished letters', 420; Klein, p. 46.

[51] Freud's letter to Emil Fluss, dated 16 June 1873, in *Letters*, 3–6, where he boasts of his German style, suggests this assimilationist aspiration. Reproaching his friend for his sadness at leaving Freiberg, Freud wrote: 'Oh, Emil, why are you a prosaic Jew? Journeymen of Christian-Germanic disposition have composed the most beautiful poems under such circumstances.'

[52] Klein, pp. 46 ff., notes that already in 1869 or 1870 Freud formally assumed the German-sounding Christian name Sigmund in place of the Polish 'Sigismund' which his father had given him. This was in a sense a repudiation of his East European Jewish background, especially since the name 'Sigismund' was a favoured butt of anti-Semitic jokes.

[53] Theodor Billroth, *Über das Lehren und Lernen der medizinischen Wissenschaften an den Universitäten der deutschen Nation* (Vienna, 1876), 148–52.

[54] Ibid. 152–4.

the state of medical instruction in the universities, and the ensuing storm, unleashed German nationalist demonstrations and a sharp retort from Jewish students. Some assimilated Jewish leaders of the German Leseverein like Victor Adler challenged Billroth's racial assumptions and insisted that Jews were not only loyal to German nationalism but 'an important factor in the cultural development of the [German] nation'.[55] At the same time they disapproved of liberal Jewish agitation against Billroth and the criticisms expressed in the *Neue Freie Presse*.

Though this first wave of nationalist agitation eventually receded, the seed of racial intolerance had already been sown in the German-Austrian *Burschenschaften* by mid-1875, the exact moment that Freud began to turn away from radical politics to the pursuit of experimental science. This early disappointment of his hopes in a German democratic nationalism must have deeply shaken the young Freud and strengthened his resolve to reassert his somewhat insecure Jewish identity. This was apparent in the vigour of his responses to anti-Semitism in the early 1880s once he had graduated from medical school and begun his internship at Vienna's General Hospital.

Freud's letters from Vienna to his future wife Martha Bernays in Hamburg are a precious testimony to his maturing personality during this crucial formative period and throw much light on the complexity of his Jewish identity at this time. Martha was the granddaughter of the orthodox Sephardic Rabbi Isaac Bernays (1792–1848) of Hamburg and her parents were strictly observant Jews. Martha herself observed *Kashrut*, fasted on Yom Kippur (in spite of Freud's remonstrations), and at the outset of their long engagement never wrote to her fiancé on the Sabbath.[56]

In a remarkable letter to Martha which he composed in Hamburg, the twenty-six-year-old Freud, taking into account her sensitivities and curious about her family, recounted to her in great detail a meeting with a local Jewish stationer who had turned out to be a disciple of her grandfather, the Haham Bernays. This old Jewish shopkeeper, whose name was Nathan, had proved to be a mine of information about her family background; about the Haham ('a quite extraordinary person' who had 'taught religion with great imaginativeness and humaneness'); and about the profound pedagogical value of the Holy Scriptures.[57] In spite of his own intransigent atheism, Freud had been fascinated by

[55] Klein, pp. 51–2; Wistrich, *Socialism and the Jews*, 235.   [56] Jones, i. 116.
[57] Freud to Martha Bernays, 23 July 1882, in *Letters*, 17–22.

this Jewish stationer's exposition of Isaac Bernays' teachings. The whole encounter reminded him of Lessing's famous humanist drama, *Nathan the Wise*:[58]

Religion was no longer treated as a rigid dogma, it became an object of reflection for the satisfaction of cultivated artistic taste and of intensified logical efforts, and the teacher of Hamburg [Isaac Bernays] recommended it finally not because it happened to exist and had been declared holy, but because he was pleased by the deeper meaning which he found in it or which projected into it . . . His teacher, he continued, had been no ascetic. The Jew, he said, is the finest flower of mankind, and is made for enjoyment. Jews despise anyone who lacks the ability to enjoy . . . The law commands the Jew to appreciate every pleasure, however small, to say grace over every fruit which makes him aware of the beautiful world in which it is grown. The Jew is made for joy and joy for the Jew. The teacher illustrated this with the gradual importance of joy in the Holy Days [*Steigerung der Feste*].[59]

Freud declared to Martha that on taking his leave, he 'was more deeply moved than the old Jew could possibly guess' and ended his letter on a decidedly upbeat note: 'and as for us, this is what I believe: even if the form wherein the old Jews were happy no longer offers us any shelter, something of the core, of the essence of this meaningful and life-affirming Judaism will not be absent from our home.'[60]

Freud's view of Judaism as it emerges from this letter and other sources seems to indicate a curious paradox. On the one hand, he already regarded religion as a childish illusion and he was later to develop a theory that equated it with obsessional neurosis.[61] He would consistently reject any belief in a personal deity or in an abstract God of the philosophers as a form of dependence, beneath the dignity of reason. In the tradition of Enlightenment criticism and scepticism, Freud would consistently disparage the rhetoric of faith as at best a

[58] Ibid. 20.

[59] Ibid. 21.

[60] Ibid. 22. Not much of this 'life-affirming Judaism' appears to have been transmitted to Freud's children. See Martin Freud, 'Who was Freud?', 293–4: 'We were brought up without any traces of the Jewish ritual. Our festivals were Christmas, with presents under a candle-lit tree, and Easter, with gaily painted Easter eggs.' Before his marriage, Freud's son had never been in a synagogue, nor had his brothers or sisters. On the other hand they all remained Jewish, moved in Jewish circles, had exclusively Jewish friends and business partners.

[61] See Freud, *Totem and Taboo*, trans. James Strachey (London, 1960), 1st publ. Vienna, 1913, and *The Future of an Illusion* (London, 1928). In the latter book he insisted that 'scientific work is the only road which can lead us to a knowledge of reality outside ourselves'. Religion, on the other hand, was seen as an illusion rooted in the father-complex and the need for a defence against childish helplessness.

naïve regression to infantilism or at its worst as an instrument of mass manipulation.[62] At the same time, in contrast to his strong animus against Roman Catholicism, Freud could still recognize in Judaism both a method of teaching and a rational kernal which had contributed significantly to progress and the education of mankind.[63] The legalist-rationalist traditions of Judaism which Freud would later see as having been embodied in the figure of Moses, the educator, legislator, and destroyer of idols, appealed to his own iconoclastic temperament. Hence his identification with what he took to be the deep-rooted hostility of Judaism to mysticism, irrationality, and superstition.[64]

Freud's respect for the ethical and pedagogical value of Judaism had been strongly shaped during his adolescence by an able religious instructor, Samuel Hammerschlag, who had taught him Bible studies at the Leopoldstadt Gymnasium.[65] Hammerschlag, like the moderate reformers Ludwig Philippson and Adolf Jellinek, had aimed at a balanced synthesis of thought and feeling in religious instruction; this served him in Freud's words 'as a way of educating toward love of the humanities, and from the material of Jewish history he was able to find the means of tapping the sources of enthusiasm hidden in the hearts of young people'.[66] Freud saw in him, above all, a *teacher* who possessed 'the gift of leaving ineradicable impressions on the development of their pupils. A spark of the same fire which animated the spirit of the great Jewish seers and prophets burned in him.'[67]

Evidently Hammerschlag's method of appealing to the heart and

[62] See Philip Rieff, *Freud: The Mind of a Moralist* (Berkeley, 1959), ch. 8, 'The Religion of the Fathers', for Freud's psychology of religion as 'the last great formulation of nineteenth-century secularism'.)

[63] Robert, p. 56.

[64] It was precisely this uncompromising rationalist element which Freud later regarded as a central difference between himself and Carl Gustav Jung, who could not rid himself of the vestiges of religion and archaic images. For the same reason Freud believed that Jews initially found it less difficult than Gentiles to absorb psychoanalysis. See *A Psycho-Analytic Dialogue: The Letters of Sigmund Freud and Karl Abraham 1907–1926*, ed. Hilda C. Abraham and Ernst L. Freud trans. Bernard Marsh and Hilda C. Abraham (London and New York, 1965), 46. 'On the whole it is easier for us Jews', Freud wrote to Abraham, 'as we lack the mystical element.' Freud shared his Berlin colleague's view that 'our Talmudic mode of thought cannot disappear just like that'.

[65] Hammerschlag was the director of the religious school in the Kultusgemeinde between 1857 and 1873 and an outstanding pedagogue who sought to stimulate and awaken the imagination of youth by invoking the moral and spiritual side of biblical heroism; see Klein, pp. 43–4.

[66] Freud wrote an obituary for the *Neue Freie Presse*, Following Hammerschlag's death in 1904, repr. in *S.E.* ix. 255.

[67] Ibid.

spirit, his resolve to spark the imagination of the child through direct contact with biblical stories rather than demanding the mechanical memorization of facts and details, had deeply impressed the adolescent Freud.[68] In this inspired religious teacher he had found an ideal fusion of Jewish passion with German classical humanism, consonant with his own liberal outlook. Hammerschlag, rather like the preacher Adolf Jellinek, emphasized the progressive, humanitarian message of the Old Testament, seeking to combine Jewish group particularism with the universal truths of mankind.[69] This elevated ethical conception of the Bible mediated by German enlightened ideals had been clearly echoed in Freud's letter to his fiancée of 23 July 1882 and it continued to influence his views even though he thoroughly detested orthodox ritualism.

Moreover, Professor Hammerschlag remained for Freud not just a teacher, but the prototype of a Jewish *Mensch* and intimate family friend who throughout his university years had often helped him 'out of a difficult situation', even though he himself was poor.[70] In January 1884 Freud reported to Martha Bernays that Hammerschlag had given him a sum of money to assist his training at the General Hospital; he also mentioned how much he enjoyed the warm atmosphere in the Hammerschlag family 'quite apart from the deep-seated sympathy which has existed between myself and the dear old Jewish teacher ever since my schooldays'.[71]

No less important than Samuel Hammerschlag in shaping Freud's more positive feelings about his Jewish identity was his fellow-physician, collaborator on *Studies in Hysteria*, and close friend, Josef Breuer (1842–1925). Breuer's father had also been a religious instructor and colleague of Hammerschlag at the Kultusgemeinde school, and their two families lived in the same Viennese apartment building where Freud probably first encountered him.[72] Freud soon came to regard Josef Breuer as a father-figure to whom he could look for advice, scientific inspiration, and moral reinforcement. It was

[68] See Samuel Hammerschlag, 'Das Programm der Israel [it schen] Religionsschule in Wien', *Bericht der Religionsschule der Israelitischen Cultusgemeinde in Wien über die Schuljahre 1868 und 1869* (Vienna, 1869), for his views on religious instruction.

[69] Ibid. 11–12.

[70] Freud to Martha Bernays, 10 Jan. 1884, in *Letters*, 86–7.

[71] Ibid. 87. In the same letter Freud described the Professor's daughter, Anna Hammerschlag, as 'an admirable girl'. His own daughter, Anna Freud, was later named after her. Another daughter, Sophie Freud, was also named after Samuel Hammerschlag's niece.

[72] Jones, i. 223; Robert, p. 149.

Breuer who dissuaded his impetuous younger colleague from contemplating conversion to Protestantism rather than agreeing to an orthodox Jewish marriage ceremony with Martha Bernays in 1886![73] It was also under Breuer's quiet prompting that Freud came to appreciate the importance of fraternity, intimacy, and mutual trust among Jews in the increasingly hostile Viennese environment of the mid-1880s.[74]

Freud was none the less far from blind to the faults and weaknesses of the Viennese Jewish milieu in which he moved. An extraordinarily searching portrait of this environment was provided in a letter that he wrote to Martha Bernays in September 1883, following the suicide of his close friend Nathan Weiss, a *Dozent* at the General Hospital.[75] Weiss had hanged himself in a public bath in the Landstrasse following the collapse of his recent marriage. In a penetrating analysis, Freud demonstrated that his tragic death was 'by no means an accident' but rather 'a logical outcome of his temperament' combined with intolerable social and familial pressures.

Nathan was the son of the Talmudist Isaac Hirsch Weiss (1815–1905), described by Freud as a 'lecturer at the religious college of Vienna, a very brilliant scholar who, had he chosen to study Chinese instead of rabbinical law, would certainly have become a university professor'.[76] Despite this respectable background, the father was 'a very hard, bad, brutal man' whose colossal vanity had forced all his sons to study. 'In the home there was no love and bitter poverty, no education and endless demands.'[77]

As a result most of the sons 'went to the dogs' and six months earlier, one of them had shot himself. Nathan, the most gifted, had 'inherited all his father's talent' but felt pressured by his example incessantly to prove himself and succeed at all costs.[78] Vain, self-important, selfish, and often ruthless, Nathan Weiss seemed incapable of friendship or enjoyment of 'human and natural things'.

---

[73] Jones, i. 183. [74] Klein, pp. 58–9.

[75] See letter to Martha Bernays, 16 Sept. 1883, in *Letters*, 59–65.

[76] Ibid. 60. [77] Ibid.

[78] The Moravian-born Isaac Hirsch Weiss had been lecturer in Talmudic literature at the Vienna *Beth Hamidrash* since 1864. A *maskil* who sought to blend study of the Oral Law with critical scientific methods and secular culture, he angered both the conservative Hungarian and Galician rabbis and the radical German reformers by his approach to the Talmud. His major work, the five-volume *Dor Dor ve-Dorshav* (1871–91)—written in Hebrew like all his compositions—described the history of the Oral Law from its beginnings until after the expulsions from Spain. See *Encyclopaedia Judaica* (Jerusalem, 1971), xvi. 413–14.

His exhibitionist conduct seemed a mystery to Freud until Josef Breuer had reminded him 'of the story of the old Jew who asks his son: "My son, what do you want to be?" And the son answers: "Vitriol, the stuff that eats its way through everything." '[79] Freud now grasped that Weiss's compulsive behaviour, his self-destructive drive for worldly success and social acceptance was the outcome of a typically Jewish father–son conflict. For beneath the exterior of a restless, unhappy *arriviste* and the manic desire for self-assertion, there was ultimately a good-natured, vivacious, and warm human being hidden inside Nathan Weiss, who had been misshapen by his father's ambitions.[80] With his first excursion into romance, Weiss had come tragically unstuck, for he 'believed he could force love as he had forced all his other successes'.[81] The girl, put off by his arrogance and bad manners, had rebuffed him but under enormous familial pressure she finally consented to the wedding. Weiss, who 'could not bear the thought that a girl could refuse him, and sacrificed everything recklessly with the single object of not having to face the world as a failure', then plunged into what was a brief and disastrous marriage.[82]

The mutual recriminations of the two Jewish families at the funeral in Vienna profoundly shocked Freud. Isaac Weiss's colleague, Meir Friedmann (1831–1908), also a lecturer at the Vienna *Beth Hamidrash* and a great Talmud scholar, quoting the Old Testament, openly called for revenge:[83]

And it is written: 'If a corpse be found, and one does not know by whose hand he died, then one must turn to the next of kin; they are the murderers.' But we, his parents and brothers, have not shed his blood—And now in clear words he began to accuse the other family of having dealt the fatal blow. And all this he spoke with the powerful voice of the fanatic, with the ardour of the savage, merciless Jew.

We were all petrified with horror and shame in the presence of the Christians who were among us. It seemed as though we had given them reason to believe that we worship the God of Revenge, not the God of Love.[84]

This emotionally shattering story of Vienese Jewish life in the 1880s,

---

[79] *Letters*, 60.   [80] Ibid. 62.   [81] Ibid. 64.   [82] Ibid.

[83] On Friedmann (pen-name *Ish-Shalom*), see *Encyclopaedia Judaica*, vii. 191–2. A traditionalist who maintained that 'the Talmud is the foundation of Judaism and whoever abandons it is abandoning life', Friedmann, who originated from Slovakia, was considered an exceptionally erudite Jewish scholar. After 1894 he taught at the rabbinical seminary in Vienna, where his students included Solomon Schechter and the future Chief Rabbi of Vienna, Zvi Chajes.

[84] *Letters*, 65.

as recounted by the young Freud, contained many of the themes that
continued to preoccupy him in coming years: the conflict between
fathers and sons (Nathan had personally described his father as a
'monster'); between individual needs and social demands; the price of
ambition and success; the disorientation produced by the restless drive
for achievement and the unhappiness engendered by over-zealous
assimilation. Freud's concern with the reaction of the Christians present
at the funeral and his horror at Jewish religious fanaticism seemed to
indicate a continuing sense of malaise with regard to his own
Jewishness. Yet he must also have seen in Nathan Weiss's suicide a
warning against the unrestrained striving for social acceptance.

By the end of 1883 Freud already had few illusions concerning the
prospects or desirability of full assimilation to German-Austrian
society in Vienna, though he still felt uncomfortable as a Jew. Many
years later (in 1926) he told George Sylvester Viereck: 'My language is
German, my culture, my attainments are German. I considered myself
German intellectually, until I noticed the growth of anti-Semitic
prejudice in Germany and German Austria. Since that time, I prefer to
call myself a Jew.'[85] Freud did not precisely specify at what point in
time this transformation occurred but it cannot have happened only 'in
his late years' nor was it merely a reaction to anti-Semitic insults and
humiliations.[86] Racial anti-Semitism in Imperial Vienna undoubtedly
affronted Freud's sense of personal dignity. Moreover, it pervaded the
German national movement with which he had once sympathized, and
poisoned student relationships and university politics in the medical
faculty where he worked. But its importance was essentially that of a
catalyst in Freud's growing inner affirmation of Jewish identity during
the mid-1880s.[87]

A letter written by Freud from Leipzig on 16 December 1883,
recounting an anti-Semitic incident during his train journey through
Germany, already reveals a new self-assertiveness and defiant courage

[85] *S.E.* xxi. 169.

[86] Peter Gay, *Freud, Jews and other Germans: Masters and Victims in Modernist Culture*
(Oxford, 1979), 90–1. Gay mistakenly concludes from the Viereck interview that it was
only in 1926 that Freud chose 'to call himself a Jew rather than a German . . .'. In my
opinion Professor Gay insists rather too strongly on Freud's German self-definition and
underestimates the extent of his Jewish allegiance which was not just 'a kind of defiance'.

[87] See the letter to Martha Bernays of 23 Oct. 1883, in *Letters*, 71, describing the
career of Dr Benedikt Stillung (1810–79), a German Jewish anatomist who developed
the theory of the vasomotor nervous system. Freud saw in Stillung's determination, 'the
industry, the tenacious enthusiasm of the Jew', even if he lacked the 'talent normally
expected from Jews'.

in the face of deliberate abuse.[88] Freud had inadvertently disturbed some passengers by opening a window in the train which immediately provoked a shout in the background: 'He's a dirty Jew!' With this brutal intervention the whole situation had taken on a different complexion. Freud recounted the scene to Martha Bernays with obvious pride:

My first opponent also turned anti-Semitic and declared: 'We Christians consider other people, you'd better think less of your precious self', etc., and muttering abuses befitting his education, my second opponent announced that he was going to climb over the seats to show me, etc. Even a year ago I would have been speechless with agitation, but now I am different; I was not in the least frightened of that mob, asked the one to keep to himself his empty phrases which inspired no respect in me, and the other to step up and take what was was coming to him. I was quite prepared to kill hm, but he did not step up; I was glad I refrained from joining in the abuse, something one must always leaves to the others.[89]

Freud left that he had held his own rather well 'and used the means at my disposal courageously' without descending to the level of his opponents. His newly discovered self-confidence and resolve to respond firmly to anti-Semitism found further expression in his solidarity with a friend and fellow doctor Carl Koller, who had been insulted in the Vienna General Hospital.[90] Writing to Mertha Bernays on 6 January 1885 Freud described the incident which he recently provoked an uproar at the General Hospital in Vienna.

He [Koller] had a difference of opinion about some minor technical matter with the man who acts as a surgeon for Billroth's clinic, and the latter suddenly called Koller a 'Jewish swine'. Now you must try to imagine the kind of atmosphere we live in here, the general bitterness—in short, we would all have reacted just as Koller did: by hitting the man in the face.[91]

Since both men were reserve officers, the anti-Semitic surgeon was obliged to challenge Koller to a duel. Freud promptly sent his colleague a bottle of wine 'to fortify him for the fight' and rejoiced at Koller's subsequent triumph. 'We are all delighted, a proud day for us. We are going to give Koller a present as a lasting reminder of his victory.'[92]

---

[88] Ibid. 78. [89] Ibid.
[90] Dr Carl Koller (1858–1944) had gained fame for discovering the anaesthetic value of cocaine in eye operations at a time when Freud himself was doing experimental work on its properties; see Freud, *An Autobiographical Study*, 24.
[91] *Letters*, 131. [92] Ibid. 132.

Freud's undisguised feeling of Jewish pride and solidarity had been sparked by the hostile atmosphere he encountered at the Vienna Hospital but its deeper sources lay in his own maturing personality and desire for independence. Significantly, during his stay in Paris in the winter of 1885–6, Freud further consolidated this more positive sense of Jewish identity along with confidence in his own abilities and future path in life. His studies with the famous French neurologist Jean-Martin Charcot (after whom he named one of his sons) opened up new insights into the nature of hysterical repression and its connection with sexuality. In Charcot he saw not only a great scientist but a liberator and enlightened secularizer determined, in William McGrath's words, 'to free his patients from the oppressive weight of dogmatic misconceptions'.[93] Freud found the atmosphere in Charcot's clinic 'very informal and democratic'.[94] The French physician had inspired in him 'an entirely new idea about perfection' and a growing dissatisfaction with the Viennese scientific milieu which he had temporarily left.[95]

An introspective letter of 2 February 1886 suggested that, through the critical distance afforded by his stay in Paris, Freud was also coming to terms with the deeper conflicts in his own personality. He no longer felt a burning grievance that 'nature had not, in one of her benevolent moods, stamped my face with that mark of genius which now and again she bestows on men'. He was confident that capacity for work, strong character, and 'the absence of outstanding intellectual weaknesses' would be very conducive in the future to the 'slow success' he now envisaged for himself.[96] Freud felt that his inaccessibility and gruffness to strangers were 'the result of suspicion due to my having learned that common or bad people treat me badly'; but as he grew 'stronger and more independent' this trait would gradually disappear. He recalled that at school he had ever been 'the bold oppositionist, always on hand when an extreme had to be defended'; with scarcely concealed enthusiasm he linked this character trait to his Jewishness, recalling a remark of his friend Josef Breuer.

He told me he had discovered that hidden under the surface of timidity there lay in me an extremely daring and fearless human being. I had always thought

---

[93] For influence of the Charcot on Freud, see McGrath, pp. 152–70. For his response to Paris as 'a city of danger, of the questionable, of the irrational', see Carl E. Schorske, 'Freud: The Psycho-archaeology of Civilizations', *Proceedings of the Massachusetts Historical Society*, 92 (1980), 57–8.

[94] *Letters*, 176; written from Paris to Martha Bernays on 21 Oct. 1885.

[95] Letter of 24 Nov. 1885. ibid. 185.　　　　　　　　　　[96] Ibid. 202.

so, but never dared tell anyone. I have often felt as though I had inherited all the defiance and all the passions with which our ancestors defended their Temple and could gladly sacrifice my life for one great moment in history.[97]

In the same letter to Martha Bernays Freud mentioned a political conversation (which had taken place during a soirée at Charcot's house) concerning the imminent prospect of a new Franco-German war. Freud wrote to his fiancée: 'I promptly explained that I am a Jew, adhering neither to Germany nor Austria. But such conversations are always very embarrassing to me, for I feel stirring within me something German which I long ago decided to suppress.'[98]

The gradual shift in Freud's self-definition was further reinforced by the icy reception which his new ideas on hysteria received following his return to Vienna and appearance before the Gesellschaft der Aerzte (Society of Medicine) in the winter of 1886. In his *Autobiographical Study* Freud cryptically recalled:

The impression that the high authorities had rejected my innovations remained unshaken; and with my hysteria in men and my production of 'hysterical paralyses by suggestion', I found myself forced into the Opposition. As I was soon afterwards excluded from the laboratory of cerebral anatomy and for a whole session had nowhere to deliver my lectures, I withdrew from academic life and ceased to attend the learned societies. It is a whole generation since I have visited the *Gesellschaft der Aerzte*.[99]

Freud's bitterness towards the Medical Society derived not only from its authoritarian, dogmatic rejection of new scientific ideas but also from the socio-political pressures that were building up in Vienna. In a letter of February 1888 to the Berlin Jewish physiologist Wilhelm Fliess (1858–1928), who was soon to become his main solace and ego support, Freud reported on a terrible row at the Vienna Medical Society. 'They wanted to force us to subscribe to a new weekly which is intended to represent the pure, elevated and Christian views of certain dignitaries who have long since forgotten what work is like. They will naturally carry their proposal through; I feel very inclined to resign.'[100]

Freud's Jewish identity evidently thrived on this type of adversarial relationship with the 'compact majority' in Catholic Vienna, whose outlook he openly despised.[101] Disgusted by the whole atmosphere of

---

[97] Ibid.   [98] Ibid. 203.   [99] *An Autobiographical Study*, 26.
[100] Freud to Fliess, 4 Feb. 1888, in Freud, *The Origins of Psychoanalysis*, 55.
[101] See the unfavourable comparison of Vienna with Berlin in his letter of 29 Aug. 1888, ibid. 57; also his letter of 22 Sept. 1898, ibid. 264: 'It is a misery to live here, and it is no atmosphere in which the hope of completing anything difficult can survive.' On the complexities of his relationship with Vienna, see Marie-Louise Testenoire, 'Freud et Vienne en 1900', *Critique*, 31, nos. 339–40 (août–sept. 1975), 819–36.

fin de siècle Vienna and the anti-Semitic tendencies which had infiltrated the medical faculty, the academic administration, and municipal politics, he increasingly withdrew into his own therapeutic work with patients. As he informed Wilhelm Fliess in a letter on 11 March 1900: 'I hate Vienna with a positively personal hatred, and, just the contrary of the giant Antaeus, I draw fresh strength whenever I remove my feet from the soil of the city which is my home.'[102]

His correspondence with Fliess during the 1890s reveals a man virtually cut off from the wider society, living in and for his intimate family circle, his patients, and his Jewish friends, mainly doctors like Leopold Königstein and Oscar Rie (1863–1911) with whom he played tarot once a week. His scientific work was proceeding well but very much in splendid isolation.[103] By 1894 even his close contact with Breuer had ended and he was thrown back entirely on his own intellectual resources.[104] Politics barely interested him with the exception of the anti-Semitic successes in the Viennese municipal elections which prompted a few lapidary remarks to Fliess on 23 September 1895; '. . . the Liberals were beaten by 46 seats to nil, and in the second district by 32 seats to 14. I voted after all. Our district remained liberal.'[105]

Lueger's non-confirmation in office following an Imperial veto prompted Freud to light up a cigar in joy but can scarcely be taken as indicating a passionate interest in Austrian politics.[106] Nevertheless Freud was angry at one of Fliess's friends for his tolerant evaluation of Lueger. Writing to Fliess on 25 May 1899 he reported: 'I treated him badly because of this. D. [Dernburg] wanted to persuade us that here all is very well . . . and that we are unfair in complaining so bitterly. I still think we know better.'[107]

The popular successes of Lueger's Christian-Social movement could only have confirmed Freud in his low estimate of most Viennese non-Jews and of human nature in general. But the anti-Semitic triumph constituted a more immediate source of anxiety, for it directly affected his promotion prospects at the University. Since his appointment in 1885 as *Privatdozent* (the lowest rung on the academic ladder), Freud's professional ambitions and hopes for a professorship had been

---

[102] *The Origins of Psychoanalysis*, 311.
[103] Letter of 21 May 1894 to Fliess, ibid. 83: '. . . I am pretty well alone here in tackling the neuroses. They regard me rather as a monomaniac, while I have the distinct feeling that I have touched on one of the great secrets of nature.'
[104] Letter of 22 June 1894 to Fliess, ibid. 95.   [105] Ibid. 124.
[106] Letter of 8 Nov. 1895, ibid. 133.   [107] McGrath, p. 184.

thwarted—a source of deep frustration that constantly recurred in his recorded dreams.[108] On 8 February 1897 he wrote to Fliess that his friend Professor Hermann Nothnagel and Krafft-Ebing were going to propose him for the coveted professorship but the former had warned him that the chances were slim. 'You know the further difficulties. It may do no more than put you on the *tapis*'.[109]

Freud believed, not without reason, that the Minister of Education was highly unlikely to accept the proposal out of 'denominational consideration'.[110] One of his closest Jewish friends, Leopold König-stein, whose own promotion had been delayed for years, had already confirmed Freud's suspicions on this score. The existing political constellation in early 1897, following Lueger's confirmation as Mayor of Vienna and the dependence of Count Badeni's shaky government on Christian-Social support, made the promotion of Jews in the universities particularly difficult. It was against this depressing background that Freud's dream of the uncle with the yellow beard (February 1897) had taken place—a dream which directly related to his own professional ambitions. In the dream Freud found that he had stepped into the shoes of the Minister who refused to appoint him in order to ridicule two Jewish academics in a similar position to himself.[111] 'In mishandling my two learned and eminent colleagues because they were Jews, and in treating the one as a simpleton and the other as a criminal, I was behaving as though I were the Minister, I had put myself in the Minister's place.'[112]

The ruthless ambition reflected in some of his dreams was only one of many unpleasant surprises in store for Freud during the course of the searching self-analysis he undertook following his father's death. In a letter to Wilhelm Fliess of 10 July 1900, he vividly described the hidden depths of the unconscious which he had uncovered as 'an intellectual hell, layer upon layer of it, with everything fitfully gleaming

---

[108] In a letter of 24 Jan. 1892 to Fliess he mentioned incorrectly that he had been passed over in favour of a younger colleague. 'It leaves me quite cold, but perhaps it will hasten my final breach with the university.' (*The Origins of Psychoanalysis*, 190.)

[109] Ibid. 191.

[110] On the issue of anti-Semitism as a factor in delaying Freud's appointment as *Ausserordentliche Professor*, see Josef and Renée Gicklhorn, *Sigmund Freud's akademische Laufbahn* (Vienna, 1960), and the refutation by K. R. Eissler, *Sigmund Freud und die Wiener Universität* (Berne, 1966).

[111] See McGrath, pp. 176 ff., and Robert, pp. 159, 165–6, for interpretations of this dream.

[112] *The Interpretation of Dreams*, in *S.E.* iv. 193.

and pulsating; and the outline of Lucifer-Amor coming into sight at the darkest centre'.[113]

As he explored these darkest recesses of psychical life concealed beneath the civilized veneer of bourgeois society—the nature of infantile sexuality, neurotic symptoms, parricidal tendencies, and dream censorship—Freud had few doubts that his work would be 'odious to most people'. In Vienna one could write about sex as a vice or study its perversions and disorders but not deal with it in detail as part of everyday reality. This was the difference between Freud and Krafft-Ebing. Moreover, Freud's insistence that neurosis had psychic rather than physical causes increasingly irritated his academic colleagues; his emphasis on primordial sexual drives upset the conventions of bourgeois morality; his intransigent atheism angered the guardians of Catholic culture. Above all Freud was a Jew in a city where the social and political barriers of anti-Semitism virtually ensured that psychoanalysis would be contemptuously dismissed as a 'Jewish science'. As he complained to his fellow psychoanalyst, Karl Abraham; 'Rest assured that, if my name were Oberhüber, in spite of everything my innovations would have met with far less resistance.'[114]

At the same time this acute sense of exclusion, social marginality, and apartness from the Gentile Austrian majority (as Freud himself obscurely realised) was related to his creative originality. It could not be an accident, Freud insisted, that 'the first advocate of psychoanalysis was a Jew' for to 'profess belief in this new theory called for a certain degree of readiness to accept a position of solitary opposition with which no one is more familiar than a Jew'.[115] Precisely because of his status as a social pariah in the Gentile world, the Jew could afford to be less conformist and freer, even with regard to his own spiritual heritage. His mind was uncluttered by the vestiges of dogma and superstition, by the crushing burden of theological beliefs ingrown in Christian civilization. Hence, Freud suggested, only an absolutely irreligious Jew could have invented psychoanalysis.[116] His discoveries were in a paradoxical sense directly related to his Jewishness for it was from this unique tradition that he had inherited his nonconformism, his freedom from prejudice and the courage of rebellion.[117]

[113] *The Origins of Psychoanalysis*, 323.
[114] Freud to Karl Abraham, letter of 23 July 1908, in *A Psycho-Analytic Dialogue*, 46.
[115] Freud, 'The Resistances to Psycho-Analysis' (1925), in *S.E.* xix. 222.
[116] *Psycho-Analysis and Faith: The Letters of Sigmund Freud and Oskar Pfister*, trans. Eric Mosbacher (London and New York, 1963), 63.
[117] See *Letters*, 366–7; also in *S.E.* xx. 274.

This personal belief in a shared psychological structure among Jews, combined with his own ostracism in Viennese society, had attracted Freud to the B'nai B'rith lodge which he joined on 29 September 1897. The society provided him not only with a refuge from anti-Semitism, a congenial Jewish atmosphere, and a sympathetic forum for expounding his psychoanalytic hypotheses but also with a framework for sharing with others the humanitarian ideals which he had held since his youth.[118] The B'nai B'rith brotherhood in Vienna had been created in the winter of 1894 under the pressure of anti-Semitic hostility. Its declared ideals were to unite 'Israelites' in promoting their own interests and those of humanity; to develop their mental and moral character, to inculcate among them the principles of philanthropy, honour, and patriotism; to alleviate the sufferings of the poor and to aid the victims of persecution.[119]

Freud was sympathetic to these humanitarian interests, especially approving the appeal to Enlightenment ideals of universal brotherhood and equality and their attempted synthesis with the humanistic traditions of Judaism.[120] He was drawn to an ethical society which could provide an island of refuge within a hostile environment while not wholly severing relations with the non-Jewish world. The sense of uniqueness and moral superiority felt by B'nai B'rith members like Solomon Ehrmann, Freud's close friend from his student days, was not exclusivist but universalist. However, the mob anti-Semitism of the Vienna streets had taught Ehrmann and other lodge brothers that their contemporaries were not yet ready for progressive humanitarian ideals and social equality. Hence it was the function of Judaism to sustain these noble principles within small educated groups like B'nai B'rith who would work steadfastly and independently for the progress of mankind.

Dennis Klein has convincingly demonstrated the intensity of Freud's commitment to the fraternal and democratic currents within B'nai B'rith, his fundamental agreement with its cultural ideals, and joyful acknowledgement of his Jewish descent.[121] He identified

---

[118] See Letter to Wilhelm Fliess, 12 Dec. 1897, in *The Origins of Psychoanalysis*, 238, where Freud writes: 'I gave a lecture on dreams to my Jewish society (an audience of laymen) last Tuesday, and it had an enthusiastic reception. I shall continue it next Tuesday . . .'; also letter of 11 Mar. 1900, ibid. 312.

[119] Klein, 76 ff.

[120] See ibid. 78 ff. for a discussion of the different views within the society on how to reconcile the desire for a self-contained Jewish community with universal ideals.

[121] Ibid. 86 ff.

particularly with its conception of a Jewish ethical élite. This idea was to provide a kind of model for the creation of the psychoanalytic movement in 1902. Precisely during the period when Freud became a virtual pariah within the Viennese academic establishment (1897–1902) he had discovered in the B'nai B'rith a supportive forum and audience for his psychoanalytic ideas. During these six years he lectured to the brotherhood on scientific topics no less than eight times, offering his first public expositions of the *Interpretation of Dreams* and some of the theories embodied in *The Psychopathology of Everyday Life* (1901).[122] He also lectured twice to the society on the life and work of Émile Zola, the great French novelist whose impassioned intervention in the Dreyfus affair had inspired his fervent admiration.[123] Zola fascinated Freud both from the psychoanalytic point of view as a writer and in humanist terms as a fighter against authority, injustice, and the persecution of Jews.

Freud's most active participation in the B'nai B'rith society during 1901–2 immediately preceded his creation of the first Viennese psychoanalytic circle which was composed at the outset exclusively of Jews. Not until March 1907, when the Swiss psychiatrists Carl Gustav Jung (1875–1961) and Ludwig Binswanger (1881–1966) attended their first meeting in Vienna, did the psychoanalytic group include any Gentiles. This ethnic parochialism aroused deeply ambivalent feelings in Freud. On the one hand, he felt at home in this intimate Jewish circle of analysts who were linked not only by their common therapeutic concerns but also by a kind of unspoken ethnic bond. At the same time Freud strongly desired to universalize the mission and message of psychoanalysis. For this purpose the Swiss Gentile psychiatric establishment of Jung and his small group in Zurich was crucial to Freud who made considerable efforts to ensure their allegiance. Only through their presence in the leadership of the movement could be hope to overcome the anti-Semitic taunt that psychoanalysis was a 'Jewish science'. Hence his well-known plea to Karl Abraham (1877–1925) on 3 May 1908: '. . . please be tolerant and do not forget that it is really easier for you than it is for Jung to follow my ideals, for in the first place you are completely independent, and then you are closer to my intellectual constitution because of racial kinship.'[124]

---

[122] Klein, 87–8.
[123] See Letter of 9 Feb. 1898 to Wilhelm Fliess, in *The Origins of Psychoanalysis*, 245; 'Zola keeps us breathless. He is a fine fellow, a man with whom one could get on.'
[124] Freud to Karl Abraham, 3 May 1908, in *A Psycho-Analytic Dialogue*, 34.

Freud urged Abraham to show restraint in spite of what he felt to be Swiss 'deviations' in the direction of Christian spiritualism, for only through Jung's appearance on the scene had psychoanalysis 'escaped the danger of becoming a Jewish national affair'.[125] In reply, Karl Abraham confessed eight days later:

. . . I find it easier to go along with you rather than with Jung. I, too, have always felt this intellectual kinship. After all, our Talmudic way of thinking cannot disappear just like that. Some days ago a small paragraph in *Jokes* strangely attracted me. When I looked at it more closely, I found that, in the technique of apposition and in its whole structure, it was completely Talmudic.[126]

Writing from Berchtesgaden on 23 July 1908 Freud did not object to Abraham's conclusions. On the contrary he frankly admitted to his Jewish disciple: 'May I say that it is consanguineous Jewish traits that attract me to you? We understand each other.' Once again Freud declared his displeasure at the quarrel between Abraham and Jung; but he did not reproach him, emphasizing instead the necessity of suffering wrongs for the greater good of the psychoanalytic cause. 'I nurse a suspicion that the suppressed antisemitism of the Swiss that spares me is deflected in reinforced form upon you. But I think that we as Jews, if we wish to join in, must develop a bit of masochism, be ready to suffer some wrong. Otherwise there is not hitting it off.'[127]

In another letter to Abraham on 26 December 1908 Freud put the issue in slightly different but even more unequivocal terms: 'Our Aryan [*sic*] comrades are really completely indispensable to us, otherwise psychoanalysis would succumb to antisemitism.'[128]

In his correspondence with Jung, Freud expressed a similar preoccupation in more discreet and tactful language. He wrote to Jung on 2 September 1907:

For my peace of mind, I tell myself that it is better for psychoanalysis . . . that you will be spared a part of the opposition that would be awaiting me, that nothing but useless repetitions would be heard if I were to say the same things all over again, and that you are more suitable as a propagandist, for I have invariable found that something in my personality, my words and ideas strike people as alien, whereas to you all hearts are open.[129]

[125] Ibid.
[126] Abraham to Freud, 11 May 1908, ibid. 36.
[127] Ibid. 45.
[128] Ibid. 63.
[129] Freud to Jung, 2 Sept. 1907, in *Letters*, 256.

Freud clearly regarded Jung both as his bridge to the Gentile world and as the Joshua who would carry on and eventually complete his work of conquering the Promised Land of psychiatry.[130] In a letter to Jung on 13 August 1908 Freud was quite explicit in this regard. 'With your strong and independent character; with your Germanic blood which enables you to command the sympathies of the public more readily than I, you seem better fitted than anyone else I know to carry out this mission.'[131]

Determined to establish a broader basis for the new science than that offered by his own Viennese Jewish colleagues, Freud ignored their objections and at the Nuremberg Conference of 1910 made Jung President of the International Psycho-Analytical Association.[132] He defended this step by insisting that it was essential for him 'to form ties in the world of general science'; psychoanalysis could not remain a Jewish sectarian movement if it aspired to universal significance. Therefore, according to Freud, 'Jews must be content with the modest role of preparing the ground.'[133]

Freud's confidence in Jung who had seemed ready 'to give up, for my sake, certain race prejudices which he had so far permitted himself to indulge' and his belief that the Swiss psychiatrist was his obvious heir, turned out to be sadly mistaken.[134] Freud had of course long been aware of their divergences. Jung believed, for instance, that 'the sexual terminology should be reserved only for the most extreme forms of your "libido" and that a less offensive collective term should be established . . .';[135] He knew that Jung was struggling to free himself inwardly, as he had put it in a letter to Freud, 'from the oppressive sense of your [i.e. Freud's] paternal authority'.[136] Moreover, the two men disagreed no less fundamentally on the question of myth and religion than they did over the importance of sexuality. This difference came out openly in 1910 when Freud had proposed that the

[130] Jones, ii. 37.

[131] *The Freud–Jung Letters: The Correspondence between Sigmund Freud and C. G. Jung*, ed. William McGuire, trans. Ralph Manheim and R. F. C. Hull (Princeton, 1974), 168.

[132] Jones, ii. 48–9, remarks that the jealousy of the Viennese psychoanalytic circle towards Jung 'was accentuated by their Jewish suspicion of Gentiles in general with its rarely failing expectation of antisemitism. Freud himself shared this to some extent . . .'. See also ibid. 77.

[133] Fritz Wittels, *Sigmund Freud: His Personality, His Teachings and His School*, trans. Eden and Cedar Paul (New York, 1924), 140.

[134] Freud, 'The History of the Psychoanalytic Movement', in *Basic Writings*, 960.

[135] Jung to freud, letter of 31 Mar. 1907, in *The Freud–Jung Letters*, 25.

[136] Jung to Freud, letter of 2 Apr. 1909, ibid. 275.

Psychoanalytic movement join forces with an 'International Fraternity for Ethics and Culture' to fight for common progressive ideals of world improvement and practical reform while opposing the injustice practised by reactionary States and by the Catholic Church.[137] This proposal was consistent enough with the humanitarian mission that Freud had affirmed in his B'nai B'rith activities and subsequently transposed to psychoanalysis.

In a letter of 11 February 1910 Jung scathingly dismissed Freud's idea of an Ethical Fraternity as artificial, a mythical 'nothing', lacking any archaic-infantile driving force or rootedness in the deep instinct of the race.[138] Jung certainly did not think that 2,000 years of Christianity could be so easily replaced except by something equivalent in mass appeal that could reabsorb the 'ecstatic instinctual forces' inspired by its advent. The Swiss psychiatrist was not interested in practical ethics based on rationalistic presumptions but in the 'eternal truth of myth' which he believed that psychoanalysis should deliberately cultivate among intellectuals.[139] Jung even spoke of transforming Christ back 'into the soothsaying god of the vine . . .' (Dionysus) and rediscovering the infinite rapture and 'wantonness in our religion'.[140]

The gulf between the two men was clearly too deep to be bridged over for long, especially in view of Freud's scorn for half-measures, circumlocutions, or roundabout, non-committal phraseology on the role of sexuality in the life of the psyche. In Stefan Zweig's words, Freud was never prepared 'to hang a verbal fig-leaf in front of his convictions' so that they could be smuggled in through the back door 'without attracting disagreeable attention'.[141] He was simply not prepared to substitute polite words like 'eros' or 'love' for libido, as the Swiss would have preferred. Nor could he easily swallow Jung's latent Christian mysticism and myth-centred irrationalism which would have struck a death-blow to both the scientific and the materialist foundations of psychoanalysis.

Jung's defection in 1912/13 was none the less a bitter blow to Freud's hopes to make Zurich rather than Vienna the centre of psychoanalysis and, if that was possible, increased still further his

---

[137] Freud to Jung, 13 Jan. 1910, ibid. 288; see also Erich Fromm, *Sigmund Freud's Mission* (New York, 1972), 73.

[138] Jung to Freud, letter of 11 Feb. 1910, in *The Freud–Jung Letters*, 293–4.

[139] Ibid.

[140] Ibid. 294.

[141] Stefan Zweig, *Freud: La Guérison par l'esprit* (Paris, 1932), 134.

distrust of 'Aryans'.[142] In a letter on 8 June 1913 to one of his favourite Jewish disciples, the Hungarian Sandor Ferenczi, Freud acknowledged the existence of different racial outlooks but still sought to preserve science as a kind of neutral ground.

Certainly there are great differences between the Jewish and the Aryan spirit. We can observe that every day. Hence, there would assuredly be here and there differences in outlook on art and life. But there should not be such a thing as Aryan or Jewish science. Results in science must be identical, though the presentation of them may vary.[143]

But this Freudian regard for the universality of science should not blind one to the strong Jewish self-consciousness that existed in the psychoanalytic movement before the First World War. Not only Freud but also some of his closest followers like Otto Rank (1884–1939), Fritz Wittels (1880–1950), and Victor Tausk (1879–1919) believed that Jews were specially called to educate and redeem humanity from sexual neuroses and from the nefarious effects of a repressive civilized morality.[144] In an adolescent essay written on 13 December 1905, Otto Rank had observed that 'the Jews thoroughly understand the *radical* cure of neurosis better than any other people, even better than the artistically and sublimely talented Greeks with their powerful tragedies'.[145]

Rank was perhaps the closest to Freud of all his Viennese disciples. After initially repudiating his family, father, and the Jewish religion, he had come round to the view that Jews possessed special creative powers and were best qualified to be the 'physicians' of mankind. In view of his central importance in Freud's inner circle this fact was not without significance.[146] Like Otto Weininger, Rank held that the

---

[142] Jones, ii. 184. Jones, the most faithful Gentile disciple of Freud, declared himself astonished 'how extraordinarily suspicious Jews could be of the faintest sign of antisemitism . . .' and considered Ferenczi along with Hanns Sachs as the worst offenders in this regard. Freud stood somewhere in the middle on this issue, though he too was 'pretty sensitive'.

[143] Ibid. 168.

[144] On Otto Rank and Judaism, see Klein, pp. 103–33, for an excellent summary. Also the new biography by E. James Lieberman, *Acts of Will: The Life and Work of Otto Rank* (New York, 1985), 64–5, 93–4, 220–1, 407–8, touches on Rank's Jewishness.

[145] See Klein, pp. 170–3 (App. C), for a trans. of Rank's essay.

[146] Rank was not only secretary of Freud's psychoanalytic circle after 1906 but also founding co-editor with Hanns Sachs of *Imago* and together with Ferenczi and Jones of the *Internationale Zeitschrift für Psychoanalyse*. Extremely prolific, he was highly regarded by Freud but broke with him after his book *Das Trauma der Geburt* (1923) appeared. See Freud to Rank, letter of 25 Aug. 1924 at the time of the break, in *Letters*, 352–4.

'essence of Judaism' lay in its *'stress on primitive sexuality'*. But in contrast to Weininger, he turned this trait into positive expression of naturalness to which other peoples should aspire.[147]

Freud most probably did not share Rank's vision of the sexually unrepressed Jew as a potential saviour of humanity from a neurotic civilization. But implicit in his own work was a belief in the desirability of 'an infinitely freer sexual life', even though, as he told an American correspondent, he had 'made very little use of such freedom'.[148] Moreover, Freud had undoubtedly transmitted to his disciples a latent sense of chosenness, pride, and Jewish self-consciousness which encouraged them to believe in a psychoanalytic mission of universal redemption.[149]

Freud's own conception of this mission was in theory rationalist, enlightened, and anti-authoritarian. Rejecting both religion and secular ideologies like nationalism or socialism he looked to a fuller understanding of the mind as the guide to a better life. Psychoanalysis was in that sense not just a theory but a *movement* with a quasi-political and quasi-religious character that sought to save the world for an enlightened ideal.[150] It had its small, well-organized avant-garde, its own publications, central organization, hierarchies, rituals, and sectarian dogmas; it also had its witchhunts, heresies, and vendettas. In practice, the undisputed leader at the centre wanted corroborators rather than collaborators, a devoted band of apostles who would help establish his immortality and eventually carry his teachings to the wider society.[151]

These adherents in Vienna were virtually without exception urban middle-class Jewish intellectuals who shared Freud's sense of belonging to an embattled minority and had transferred this feeling to the equally hated and maligned psychoanalytic movement. As social pariahs who had no real anchor in a hostile Austrian society, these followers were all the more dependent on Freud and unwilling to risk his anger. Nevertheless deviations, dissensions, and splits frequently occurred with the brightest of Freud's pupils leaving the circle when the atmosphere became too constricting on their creativity.

[147] Klein, pp. 171, 173 n. 6 (App. C).

[148] See letter to James J. Putnam, dated 8 July 1915, which relates to questions of personal and social morality, in *Letters*, 308.

[149] See Klein, pp. 138 ff., who makes an interesting case for seeing psychoanalysis as a 'Jewish' movement.   [150] Fromm, p. 92.

[151] Wittels, p. 134. Speaking of Freud, Wittels wrote: 'What he wanted was to look into a kaleidoscope lined with mirrors that would multiply the images he introduced into it.'

The most damaging of these apostasies was that of Alfred Adler (1870–1937), born into a petty-bourgeois Jewish family in the Viennese suburb of Rudolfsheim, who largely socialized among Gentiles. His father, Leopold, an assimilated corn merchant from the Burgenland, had deliberately avoided the residential self-segregation of many immigrant Jews in Vienna.[152] The son had studied medicine under Meynert and Krafft-Ebing at the University of Vienna and received his doctorate in 1895. Two years later Alfred Adler married a radical Russian student, Raissa Epstein (1873–1962), and in 1900 he opened a private medical practice on the Praterstrasse in Vienna.

In 1902 Adler began to regularly partipate in the Wednesday discussion evenings in Freud's apartment and soon established himself as the most gifted, ambitious, and argumentative of his Viennese adherents. Adler was, significantly, the only member of Freud's early circle to join the Austrian Social Democratic Party. As early as 1909 he attempted to synthesize Marx and Freud under the influence of Leon Trotsky, then living in Vienna. In his *Studie über die Minderwertigkeit von Organen* (1907) Adler suggested that children with inferior physiques overcompensated for their weakness by exaggerating their intellectual strengths. Unlike Freud, Adler did not regard libidinal drives or the Oedipus Complex as decisive factors in understanding the psyche. Instead he emphasized far more the role of will-power, self-assertion, and the search for security.[153] The break which came in 1911 was sealed by Adler's treatise the following year entitled *Über den nervösen Charakter* (The Neurotic Constitution) and his creation of a new school of Individual Psychology.[154]

In sharp contrast to Freud, Adler was quintessentially Viennese in character. He spoke the natural, unabashed patois of the city and felt thoroughly at home in its environs.[155] Even though he was a socialist freethinker, Alfred Adler had converted to Protestantism as a young man, in order to complete his 'escape from Judaism'; his connection with the Jewish community was a burden which he desired to throw off. Through baptism, this radical atheist could reinforce his sense of belonging to Vienna, to the majority Christian community and the simple people he had grown up with in his youth.[156] For Freud, on the

---

[152] See Josef Rattner, *Alfred Adler in Selbstzeugnissen und Bilddokumenten* (Hamburg, 1972), 9–10.
[153] Ibid. 26–7.
[154] See Hertha Olger, *Alfred Adler: The Man and His Work* (4th edn., London, 1973).
[155] Manès Sperber, *Masks of Loneliness: Alfred Adler in Perspective* (New York, 1974), 31.
[156] Ibid. 30–1.

other hand, this was yet another reason to distrust Adler, for in later years the founder of psychoanalysis came to regard baptism as an act of betrayal, tantamount to joining the enemy camp.[157]

Adler had indeed committed a double apostasy in Freud's mind, for he had also betrayed psychoanalysis in return for greater social acceptance among non-Jews. This was the meaning of Freud's rather cruel remark in a letter to Arnold Zweig on 22 June 1937 upon hearing of Adler's sudden death of a heart attack in Scotland: 'I don't understand your sympathy for Adler. For a Jew boy [*ein Judenbub*] from a Viennese suburb a death in Aberdeen is an unheard-of career in itself and a proof of how far he had got on. The world really rewarded him richly for his service in having contradicted psychoanalysis.'[158]

Adler, like Jung, had apostasized by domesticating sexuality in order to make psychoanalysis more *salonfähig*, an act which to Freud was tantamount to prostituting its central truth. In addition to this apostasy, Adler was in Freud's eyes an assimilationist of the worst kind who had sold out his Jewish heritage for purely careerist reasons. His relatively smooth adaptation to the *fin de siècle* Viennese environment, in which Freud had always seen himself as alone and embattled, seemed to confirm this negative judgement.

Peter Gay has persuasively argued that 'Freud lived far less in Austrian Vienna than in his own mind'.[159] Even the medical Vienna from which he had acquired his first analytic training was 'a microcosm of German scientific talent', with many of its greatest teachers coming from the Protestant North. It was no accident that Freud himself rejected with scorn attempts to derive the origins of psychoanalysis from the Viennese milieu as if it were the theoretical projection of 'an atmosphere of sensuality and immorality not to be found in other cities . . .'.[160] Freud denied that Vienna was significantly different from other European cities in terms of sexual mores or the level of neuroses and nervous disturbances.[161] The fact of the matter for Freud was that Vienna, far from inspiring him, 'has done everything possible to deny her share in the origin of psychoanalysis', especially in learned and

---

[157] Ibid. 32.

[158] Sigmund Freud, *Briefwechsel mit Arnold Zweig* (Frankfurt, 1968), 155; Rattner, p. 32.

[159] Gay, p. 33.

[160] Freud, 'The History of the Psychoanalytic Movement', in *Basic Writings*, 956–7; also Gay, pp. 29–35; Jones, 323.

[161] Freud, 'Psychoanalytic Movement', 957.

cultured circles.[162] Moreover, he felt convinced that the negative linkage of psychoanalysis to Vienna was 'only a euphemistic substitution for another one which one did not care to bring up publicly'—namely that it was a 'Jewish' science.[163] On 24 April 1910 Freud had written along these lines to Ferenczi, following a violent attack on his theories at a meeting of the Medical Society of Hamburg. 'Viennese sensuality is not to be found anywhere else! Between the lines you can read further that we Viennese are not only swine but also Jews. But that does not appear in print.'[164]

Admittedly Vienna remained Freud's environment for seventy-eight years, a setting to which he was tied by the force of habit, inertia, and an evident dislike of uprooting himself. But he remained remote from its coffee-house literati, salons, and theatres, indifferent to its modernist culture, and disgusted by its 'politics in a new key'. Freud was, if anything, a supremely un-Viennese Jew, a stranger in his native city. Only in July 1914, following the declaration of war on Serbia by the Habsburg Empire, did Freud for a while acknowledge a positive sense of identification with his city, country, and German-Austrian nationality such as he had once felt in his youth. Writing to Karl Abraham he declared: '. . . for the first time in thirty years, I feel myself to be an Austrian and feel like giving this not very hopeful Empire another chance. Morale everywhere is excellent. Also the liberating effect of courageous action and the secure prop of Germany contributes a great deal to this.'[165]

This brief flurry of Austrian patriotic enthusiasm could not however be sustained and by 10 December 1917 Freud was confessing to Abraham: 'The only thing that gives me any pleasure is the capture of Jerusalem and the British experiment with the chosen people.'[166]

Freud's interest in Zionism was not new and in some ways his

---

[162] One of Freud's bitterest opponents was the satirist Karl Kraus, who coined the epigram: 'Psychoanalysis is that mental illness for which it regards itself as therapy.' Kraus regarded psychoanalysis as 'Jewish', frequently harping on its connection with the 'ghetto' and 'trading mentality'. Kraus's comment: 'They have the press, they have the stock exchange, and now they also have the subconscious!' could easily be construed as anti-Semitic. See Karl Kraus, *Selected Aphorisms*, ed. and trans. Harry Zohn (Montreal, 1976), 76–80.

[163] Freud, *Basic Writings*, 957.

[164] Jones, ii. 131.

[165] Letter to Abraham, 26 July 1914, in Jones, p. 171. By the end of the year, Freud could write to Ferenczi that he would not 'weep a single tear for the fate of Austria or Germany'.

[166] *A Psycho-Analytic Dialogue*, 264.

reactions to it epitomized the ambivalence of his Jewish identity. On the one hand he had long ago become sceptical towards nationalism and the negative reception of psychoanalysis had underlined to him the danger of a 'Jewish national' identification. At the same time Freud felt some sympathy for Zionism in so far as it was a defiant, fighting response to Jewish powerlessness and second-class status. He had always instructed his children not to tolerate insults and to defend themselves against indignity and injustice.[167] In contrast to the anti-Zionist outlook of many liberal Viennese Jews Freud was delighted when his son Martin joined Kadimah at the turn of the century and in 1936 at the age of eighty he himself was honoured by the Zionist corporation as one of their *Alte Herren*.[168] Freud had of course been well aware of the brutality of the German-national students at the University of Vienna, from his own student memories, the reading of the newspapers, and the everyday experience of his sons.[169]

Yet, curiously enough, the name of Theodor Herzl, his famous contemporary who lived in the same neighbourhood, was never mentioned in Freud's voluminous correspondence. His son Martin related this extraordinary anomaly to the 'conspiracy of silence about Zionism' cultivated by the Jewish liberal press of Austria, which feared that the new movement might undermine the civic status of Jewry.

Few of our Jewish friends had ever heard of Theodor Herzl, who had already gained international importance by this time. Nor did they know what he stood for. Even I, who came from a house without prejudices, knew only that Herzl was the father of Trude Herzl, who, as my sister's friend, frequently visited our house, and that he was the man who wrote those very nice articles in the *Neue Freie Presse*, which was read in our house as a matter of course. Of Zionism, I knew nothing.[170]

Freud never commented on the fact that Herzl had been chief Paris correspondent of the *Neue Freie Presse* at the time of Dreyfus's

---

[167] Martin Freud, 'Who was Freud?', 208.

[168] Ibid. 'A delegation of Kadimah members visited him at his home and brought him the coloured ribbon of the corporation, which, with their assistance, he fastened around his chest.'

[169] Ibid. 207. Martin Freud gives a vivid description of the rowdy anti-Semitic agitation at the turn of the century when he was a student in Vienna. The courage of the Kadimah members inspired him to join rather than be a 'mere spectator' of the constant fights within the university.

[170] Ibid. 207–8. In a personal interview given to the author in London in the summer of 1979, Anna Freud confirmed this account and her childhood friendship with Trude Herzl.

condemnation, in spite of his interest in Émile Zola and the Affair.[171] Nor is there any reference in his correspondence to the Zionist Congresses that Herzl was organizing at the very time that Freud was groping towards his epoch-making interpretation of dreams. Apparently Freud and Herzl never personally met in Vienna in spite of their living in such geographical proximity and the friendly relationship between their daughters.[172] Nevertheless Freud did send Herzl a copy of the *Interpretation of Dreams* in September 1902 in the hope of a review. 'But in any event', he told Herzl, 'I ask you to keep the book as a token of the high esteem in which I—like so many others—have held since many years the poet and the fighter for the human rights of our people.'[173]

Freud's reference to 'human rights' (*Menschenrechte*) rather than 'national rights' reflects the liberal-universalist perspective in which he felt able to admire Herzl's activity on behalf of the Jews. The letter thus confirms that Freud was indeed aware of and not unsympathetic to Herzl's Zionism but regarded it with a certain discretion and critical distance.

The psycho-historian Peter Loewenberg has convincingly demonstrated that the Herzlian idea of a Jewish homeland did indeed appear in veiled form in Freud's 'My son, the Myops . . .' dream of 1898. Freud finds himself in this strange dream sitting in the city of Rome on the edge of a fountain, 'greatly depressed and almost in tears'.

A female figure—an attendant or nun—brought two boys out and handed them over to their father, who was not myself. The elder of the two was clearly my eldest son; I did not see the other one's face. The woman who brought out the boy asked him to kiss her good-bye. She was noticeable for having a red nose. The boy refused to kiss her, but holding out his hand in farewell, said '*Auf Geseres*' to her, and then '*Auf Ungeseres*' to the two of us (or to one of us). I had the notion that this last phrase denoted a preference.[174]

Freud himself explained that this dream had been constructed 'on a

[171] Letter to Fliess mentioning Zola's role in the Dreyfus case, in *The Origins of Psychoanalysis*, 245.

[172] See Avner Falk, 'Freud and Herzl', *Midstream*, 28 (Jan. 1977), 3–24.

[173] Freud to Herzl, 28 Sept. 1902, Central Zionist Archives, Jerusalem. See Peter Loewenberg, 'Sigmund Freud as a Jew: A Study in Ambivalence and Courage', *Journal of the History of the Behavioral Sciences*, 7, no. 4 (Oct. 1971), 367, who first drew my attention to this letter.

[174] See *S.E. v. 441*; also *Basic Writings*, 420 ff., and Peter Loewenberg, 'A Hidden Zionist Theme in Freud's My Son, the Myops . . . Dream', *Journal of the History of Ideas*, 31. no. 1 (Jan.–Mar. 1970), 129–32.

tangle of thoughts provoked by a play which I had seen, called *Das neue Ghetto* [The New Ghetto]. The Jewish problem, concern about the future of one's children, to whom one cannot give a country of their own . . .'[175] Curiously enough, Freud did not evoke the name of Herzl, who was the author of this play which had clearly sparked off his own feelings of estrangement and depression in the face of Viennese anti-Semitism. But he did spontaneously link the biblical psalm of exile 'By the waters of Babylon we sat down and wept' to the Roman fountain in the dream and to the news that a Jew had recently been obliged to resign his position in a state asylum in Vienna. Moreover, the Hebrew word *Geseres* with its associations of suffering and persecution, the nun with a red nose (symbolizing both clericalism and drunken Gentiles), and the veiled references to emigration, all suggested the idea of an imminent Exodus in order to save his children from disaster. Nevertheless, Freud's dream was not of Zion but rather of a land like Victorian England (to which his two half-brothers had emigrated in 1859) which would be relatively free of anti-Semitism. Herzl's political solution of an exodus to Palestine was repressed for obscure reasons, whatever latent attractions it might have briefly held for Freud.[176]

According to Leo Goldhammer, Freud did however recount in a university lecture in Vienna around 1905 a dream which he had of Herzl. In this fantasy, the founder of political Zionism had appeared as 'a majestic figure, with a pale, dark-toned face framed by a beautiful, raven-black beard, with infinitely sad eyes. The apparition strove to explain to . . . [Freud] the necessity of immediate action if the Jewish people was to be saved.'[177]

These words astonished Freud 'by their logic and their pent-up emotion' but they appear to have exercised no immediate effect on his life. His attitude to political Zionism remained cautious, at times sympathetic and on other occasions decidedly equivocal. In 1913, for example, he cautioned Herzl's son Hans against following in his father's footsteps, remarking: 'Your father is one of those people who have turned dreams into reality. This is a very rare and dangerous

---

[175] *S.E.* v. 441.

[176] Loewenberg, 'A Hidden Zionist Theme', 132, suggests that Freud may have unconsciously envied Herzl in view of the repressed political ambitions of his own adolescence. At the same time his own new land 'was to be a far more universal realm in the mind of all mankind'. Freud's concept of redemption was 'through insight rather than by political action'.

[177] Leo Goldhammer, 'Herzl and Freud', *Herzl Year Book*, 1 (New York, 1958), 195.

breed. It includes the Garibaldis, . . . the Herzls . . . I would simply call them the sharpest opponents of my scientific work.'[178]

Whereas Freud saw his task as simplifying dreams through analysis and reducing them to ordinary proportions, the 'psychosynthesizers' like Theodor Herzl had confused the issue, turning fantasies upside down and commanding the world 'while they themselves remain on the other side of the psychic mirror'.[179] These 'robbers in the underground of the unconscious world', master-practitioners of the politics of fantasy, aroused in Freud both envy and a kind of fascinated horror.[180] Psychoanalysis among its many goals had also set itself the task of liberating mankind 'from a political world which seemed to threaten the very existence of freedom'.[181] Freud's ambiguous and rather negative evaluation of Herzl may well have reflected his intensely personal inner conflict with authority, with father-figures as well as his own fantasy identification with Moses and the Exodus story.[182] Herzl, who had opted to repeat the Mosaic epic through political action, must have struck a sensitive nerve in Freud which he preferred to repress.

None the less the presence of a latent 'Zionism' can be detected in Freud's outlook in spite of the fact that he was neither a practising Jew nor a conscious nationalist. Freud's hatred of Rome was a case in point, though it has usually been interpreted solely in terms of a reaction against the Catholic anti-Semitism he suffered in Austria.[183] Freud himself linked his youthful admiration for Hannibal's war against Rome with the ongoing struggle between 'the tenacity of Jewry and the organization of the Catholic Church'. Other boyhood heroes, like the Puritan revolutionary Oliver Cromwell (after whom he named his second son), Napoleon Bonaparte, and General Massena, had been either protectors or emancipators of the Jews. They could also be construed as enemies of Catholic Rome, historically the great persecutor and oppressor of the Jewish people.

But Freud's secret wish to 'conquer' Rome, while it certainly

---

[178] Falk, p. 19; see also the brief discussion in McGrath, pp. 314–16.

[179] Ibid. (*bis*).

[180] See Carl E. Schorske, 'Politics and Patricide in Freud's *Interpretation of Dreams*', *The American Historical Review*, 78, no. 2 (Apr. 1973), 328–47, for a masterly explication of Freud's attitudes to Austrian sociopolitical reality and their impact on the genesis of psychoanalysis. This aspect has now been thoroughly explored in McGrath's book.

[181] McGrath, p. 317.

[182] Ibid. 293 ff.; see also Martin S. Bergmann, 'Moses and the Evolution of Freud's Jewish Identity', *The Israel Annals of Psychiatry and Related Disciplines*, 14 (Mar. 1976), 3–26.

[183] Timpanaro, pp. 7 ff.

mirrored the deep Jewish–Catholic antagonism that embitterd his life in Austria, may also have had a hidden 'national' dimension. The ghosts of Hannibal and his own father which called for 'vengeance on the Romans' might have been motivated not only by revulsion against the Christian Middle Ages and the Catholic anti-Semitism whose bastion and symbol was the 'Eternal City';[184] they could also have contained a more atavistic and unconscious motif of resentment against the victorious power which had destroyed not only ancient Carthage but also Jerusalem, sacking the Temple and driving the Jewish people into exile.

The triumph of pagan Rome (even though Freud genuinely loved it as a centre of ancient culture) had also meant the temporary demise of the Jewish people, scattered to the winds and subjected to relentless persecution. Freud's adolescent identification with Hannibal, the tenacious 'Semitic' general who had fought this mighty power, and his reference to the bravery of his Hebrew ancestors in defending their Temple, suggest that in his unconscious mind hostility to Rome had deeper pre-Christian, ethnic roots.[185]

Freud's primordial, affective, and nationally tinged Jewishness was most strongly expressed in the 1920s. In a letter to Professor Friedrich Thieberger on 25 April 1926 he wrote: 'Towards Zionism I have only sympathy, but I make no judgement on it, on its chances of success and on the possible dangers to it.'[186]

Two months earlier he had responded with 'unreserved approval' to the pamphlet of an Italian Jew on the Zionist question, expressing his pleasure at 'the sympathy, humaneness and understanding' displayed by its author on a matter 'so distorted by human passions'.[187] He told his correspondent: 'Although I have been alienated from the religion of my ancestors for a long time, I have never lost the feeling of solidarity with my people and realize with satisfaction that you call yourself a pupil of a man of my race—the great Lombroso.'[188]

---

[184] See Schorske, 'Politics and Patricide', 336 ff., for this interpretation of Freud's Roman dreams.

[185] Robert Gordis, 'The Two Faces of Freud', *Judaism*, 24, no. 94 (Spring 1975), 194–200, touches on this neglected theme in his article.

[186] Letter quoted in Ernst Simon's valuable article, 'Sigmund Freud, The Jew', *Leo Baeck Yearbook*, 2 (1957), 275.

[187] Letter to Enrico Marselli, dated 18 Feb. 1926, in *Letters*, 365. Marselli was the author of *La Psicanalisi* (Turin, 1926) which claimed that psychoanalysis was a direct product of the Jewish mind. Freud emphasized that he would not 'be ashamed' if this were true, though he expressed no definite opinion.

[188] Ibid. 365.

Such responses were typical of Freud's emotional, atavistic sense of tribal solidarity which softened some of his reservations concerning Zionism.[189]

But even his interest in Palestine and the new Jewry was still riddled with typically enigmatic Freudian ambiguity. Thus in a special introduction to the Hebrew translation of his *Totem and Taboo*, Freud wrote:

No reader of [the Hebrew version of] this book will find it easy to put himself in the emotional position of an author who is ignorant of the language of holy writ, who is completely estranged from the religion of his fathers—as well as from every other religion—and who cannot take a share in nationalist ideals, but who has yet never repudiated his people, who feels that he is in his essential nature a Jew and who has no desire to alter that nature. If the question were put to him: 'Since you have abandoned all these characteristics of your countrymen, what is there left to you that is Jewish?' he would reply: 'A very great deal, and probably its very essence.' He could not now express that essence clearly in words; but some day, no doubt, it will become accessible to the scientific mind.[190]

Though he adopted no 'Jewish standpoint and made no exceptions in favour of Jewry', Freud concluded his preface by expressing the conviction that 'unprejudiced science cannot remain a stranger to the spirit of the new [Palestinian] Jewry'.[191]

But in the final analysis modern Palestine interested Freud far less than the world of classical antiquity which was his deepest passion outside of Psychoanalysis.[192] Indeed the scientific excavation of prehistoric remains and the exploration of Greek, Roman, and Egyptian sites provided Freud with a model for his own 'archaeological' probings of the unconscious mind. This was probably the closest that

---

[189] In this context Wilhelm Reich's negative view of Freud's Jewishness is revealing; see Wilhelm Reich, *Reich Speaks of Freud* (Harmondsworth, 1975), 64 ff. The most politically radical of his Jewish disciples, Reich insisted that in style, thinking and interests 'Freud was really German'. Nevertheless he also described Freud as a Zionist, who could not cut loose from a Jewishness which he detested to the core. Reich felt that 'characterologically, religiously or nationally' Freud was not at all Jewish. But this assessment may have been a projection of Reich's own radical assimilationism and anti-Jewish sentiments.

[190] Freud, *Totem and Taboo*, p. xi. This preface was written by Freud in Vienna in Dec. 1930.

[191] Ibid.

[192] Gay, pp. 41 ff., has rightly emphasized the addiction of Freud to classical archaeology, expressed in his collection of statuettes, bronzes, and terracottas as well as in his writings. His envy of the archaeologist Schliemann who uncovered ancient Troy layer by layer was symptomatic in this regard.

Freud ever came to indulging in religous rites, which in this case involved considerable material sacrifices and pilgrimages to the 'holy' cities of Rome and Athens. In his cult of antiquity, Freud found moreover a reinforcement of the European humanist ideals which he had imbibed at school and a neutral meeting-ground where cultivated Jews and Gentiles could momentarily enjoy the illusion of liberation from the tensions of the present. Yet even here, in the disinterested pursuit of scientific truth, the malaise of his Jewish origins came to haunt and pursue Freud without rest. For if the Joseph legend had inspired his early childhood, that of Moses came to obsess and torment his final years. Nowhere was this more apparent than in the startling hypothesis that underlay his last major work *Moses and Monotheism.*

In place of the historical Moses of Judaism, Freud drew the highly personal portrait of a Moses who had been born an Egyptian nobleman and whose presumed *murder* by his 'adopted' people, the Jews, had paradoxically created Hebrew monotheism.[193] This Moses was revered by Freud as a heroic lawmaker and creator of culture. Already in 1914, in his anonymously published essay on Michelangelo's statue of Moses in Rome, he had presented his hero as a supreme exemplar of self-control and the renunciation of powerful passions for the sake of his lawgiving mission.[194] In *Moses and Monotheism* he was transformed into the initiator of a repressive though ultimately beneficial revolution from above that laid the foundation of all civilized morality. In Freud's arbitrary construction, it was 'one man, the man Moses, who created the Jews'. They were his 'chosen people', their tenacity, obstinacy, and moralism were shapen by his character and will.[195]

Freud now believed that in this Mosaic doctrine of chosenness lay the deepest motive for hatred of the Jews, 'that jealousy of the people which declared itself the first-born, favourite child of God the Father . . .'.[196] He insisted that 'it was the man Moses who imprinted this trait—significant for all time—upon the Jewish people'.[197] The Egyptian Moses had given the self-esteem of the Jews a religious

---

[193] The theme of parricide and aggression against father figures was obsessive in Freud and long predated his interest in Moses. For its connection with Freud's uneasy and hostile relation to Judaism, see Léon Vogel, 'Freud's Judaism: An Analysis in the Light of his Correspondence', *Judaism*, 24, no. 94 (Spring 1975), 181–93, and David Aberbach, 'Freud's Jewish Problem', *Commentary* (June 1980), pp. 35–9. Marthe Robert's *D'Oedipe à Moïse* is the most detailed interpretation of his father-complex and the role it played in shaping his Jewish identity.

[194] Freud, 'The Moses of Michelangelo', in *S.E.* xiii. 108–36.

[195] *Moses and Monotheism*, in *S.E.* xxiii. 46.

[196] Ibid. 91.   [197] Ibid. 106.

anchorage and therefore it was solely to him that 'this people owes its tenacity of life but also much of the hostility it has experienced and still experiences'.[198] In Egypt the seed of monotheism had indeed failed to ripen but among the ancient Jews it had been constantly renewed through the Hebrew prophets and gave evidence 'of a peculiar psychical aptitude in the masses who had become the Jewish people . . .'.[199] They alone had assumed the exacting burdens of the monotheistic religion 'in return for the reward of being the chosen people'. From this exalted consciousness developed those character-traits of rational intellectuality, legalism, tenacity, separateness, and moral austerity which Freud admired in the Jewish people and which were indeed reflected in his own personality.

Moses and Monotheism, written under the dark shadow of Nazism, was at once the most controversial and personal of Freud's works. It must have cost him considerable emotional pain to deprive the Jews of the man 'they take pride in as the greatest of their sons', an action which he knew would profoundly offend Jewry for national as well as religious reasons.[200] Yet this iconoclastic book for all its obvious inadequacies was by no means the deed of a renegade seeking to denigrate his people at its moment of supreme crisis. It should rather be seen as the paradoxical response of a consistent freethinker and radical atheist who through most of his life had affirmed a stubborn identification with Jewry and with the figure of Moses in spite of negating all forms of religious self-definition and national intoxication. It was from this ancient source of inspiration that Freud, perhaps the most un-Viennese of all Viennese Jews, had derived his indomitable power of resistance and to which he had returned at the end of his days. Through the powerful image of Moses, indelibly impressed upon the historic character of Jewry, he expressed that overcoming of magic and mysticism, that enigmatic promise of inner freedom through the exercise of reason, which gave him the courage to explore the dark side of the psyche without succumbing to despair.

---

[198] *S.E.* xxiii. 106. See also the letter of Freud to Arnold Zweig on 30 Sept. 1934 which explained the external motivation that prompted the book. 'Faced with the renewed persecutions, one asks oneself again how the Jew came to be what he is and why he has drawn upon himself this undying hatred. I soon found the formula: Moses created the Jew.'

[199] *S.E.* xxiii. 111.

[200] See his letter to Charles Singer of 31 Oct. 1938, in *Letters*, 453.

17

Arthur Schnitzler's Road to the Open

It is certainly not true that in the ghetto which you have in mind, all Jews run around depressed or inwardly shoddy. *There are others*—and *they* are precisely the ones who are hated most by the anti-Semites.

Arthur Schnitzler, letter to Theodor Herzl
(17 November 1894)

I play with human souls. Meaning is found only by those who look for it. Dreaming and waking, truth and lies, coalesce. There is no security anywhere.

Arthur Schnitzler, *Paracelsus* (1897)

Assimilation . . . a word . . . yes, it will come some day . . . in the far, far distant future. It will not come in the way some wish and others fear. It will not be exactly assimilation . . . but, perhaps, something essentially similar. Do you know what the final conclusion will probably prove? That we, we Jews I mean, were, in a sense, a ferment of humanity—yes, that will, perhaps, be realized in a thousand or two thousand years.

Heinrich Bermann in Arthur Schnitzler's
Der Weg ins Freie (1907)

In these pages a lot will be said about Judaism and anti-Semitism, more than may at times seem in good taste, or necessary, or just. But when these pages may be read, it will perhaps no longer be possible to gain a correct impression (at least I hope so), of the importance, spiritually almost more than politically and socially, that was assigned to the so-called Jewish question when these lines were written.

Arthur Schnitzler,
Jottings for an Autobiography (1913)

Perhaps no writer of the Young Vienna circle captured so perfectly the prevailing atmosphere of Vienna at the turn of the century as the Jewish doctor and poet, Arthur Schnitzler (1862–1931). In his dramas, novels, and short stories he drew the Janus-faced and at times contradictory portrait of a city famed throughout Europe for its light-hearted hedonism and gaiety, yet constantly aware of its precarious existence as the capital of an Empire slowly approaching extinction. Under the surface of abandonment to eros and dance, comedy and light opera, there lay a darker mood of world-weary fatigue, disorientation, impotence and tragic tensions caught to perfection in Schnitzler's literary work.[1] A curious melancholy, a haunting sadness, lassitude, and resignation seemed to grip Schnitzler's characters in their constant search for happiness and pleasure. Their joys and sorrows were frequently overshadowed by a morbid preoccupation with sexual guilt and death or else by the loneliness accompanying the search for individual freedom and truth in a corrupt society.[2]

At the same time Schnitzler, for all the unmistakeable period flavour of his writings, was also a radical innovator in his frank explorations of sexual behaviour, his early experiments with novelistic stream-of-consciousness techniques, and the profundity of his psychological insight. It was no accident that Sigmund Freud wrote to him on 8 May 1906, observing with considerable satisfaction 'the far-reaching conformity existing between your opinions and mine on many psychological and erotic problems'.[3] Freud admitted: 'I have often asked myself in astonishment how you come by this or that piece of secret knowledge which I had acquired by a painstaking investigation of the subject, and I finally came to the point of envying the author whom hitherto I had admired.'[4]

In a further letter of 14 May 1922, celebrating the dramatist's sixtieth birthday, Freud made a more detailed 'confession' which he asked Schnitzler to keep to himself and 'share with neither friend nor strangers'. For a long time, Freud had apparently tormented himself with the question 'why in all these years I have never attempted to make your acquaintance and talk with you'.[5] The conclusion reached

---

[1] See Hans Kohn, 'Eros and Sorrow. Notes on the Life and Work of Arthur Schnitzler and Otto Weininger', *Leo Baeck Yearbook*, 6 (1961), 152 ff.

[2] See William M. Johnston, *The Austrian Mind: An Intellectual and Social History, 1848–1938* (Berkeley and Los Angeles, 1983), 171 ff., on Schnitzler, Viennese impressionism, and the fascination with death.

[3] Sigmund Freud to Arthur Schnitzler, 8 May 1906, in *The Letters of Sigmund Freud*, sel. and ed. E. L. Freud (New York, 1961), 251.

[4] Ibid. Freud added that he had been pleased and elated to learn that Schnitzler also derived inspiration from his writings.

[5] Ibid. 339.

by the father of psychoanalysis reveals much about Freud and Schnitzler:

I think I have avoided you from a kind of reluctance to meet my double [*Doppelgänger*]. Not that I am easily inclined to identify myself with another, or that I mean to overlook the difference in talent that separates me from you, but whenever I get deeply absorbed in your beautiful creations I invariably seem to find beneath their poetic surface the very presuppositions, interests, and conclusions which I know to be my own. Your determinism as well as your skepticism—what people call pessimism—your preoccupation with the truths of the unconscious and of the instinctual drives in man. your dissection of the cultural conventions of our society, the dwelling of your thoughts on the polarity of love and death; all this moves me with an uncanny familiarity. (In a small book entitled *Beyond the Pleasure Principle*, published in 1920, I tried to reveal Eros and the death instinct as the motivating powers whose interplay dominates all the riddles of life.) So I have formed the impression that you know through intuition—or rather through detailed self-observation—everything that I have discovered by laborious work on other people. Indeed, I believe that fundamentally your nature is that of an explorer of psychological depths, as honestly impartial and undaunted as anyone has ever been . . .[6]

Schnitzler undoubtedly shared with Freud a common recognition of the supremely important role in life played by the instincts and the conflict this inevitably engendered with the repressive moral values of bourgeois society. Both of these liberal Viennese Jews in their different ways were pioneers in the investigation of what Freud, in a letter to Schnitzler on 15 May 1912, had called the 'underestimated and much-maligned erotic'.[7] Both had derived creative inspiration from their dreams;[8] moreover, they both came to recognize that neurotics could achieve self-awareness through reliving their traumas.[9] Yet for all their fascination with neuroses, and the dark side of the psyche, neither Freud nor Schnitzler identified with neurotics nor did they succumb to the fashionable temptations of Central European irrationalism. In both

[6] Ibid.

[7] Quoted in the introd. to Kurt Bergel (ed.), *Georg Brandes und Arthur Schnitzler: Ein Briefwechsel* (Berne, 1956), 29: '. . . der thörichten und frevelhaften Geringschätzung, welche die Menschen heute für die Erotik bereit halten.'

[8] See Schnitzler's interview with George Sylvester Viereck in the latter's book, *Glimpses of the Great* (London, 1933), 333.

[9] It was no accident some of Freud's early followers appreciated Schnitzler's *œuvre*. See, in particular, Hanns Sach, 'Die Motivgestaltung bei Schnitzler', *Imago*, 2 (1913), 302–18, and the book by Theodor Reik, *Arthur Schnitzler als Psycholog* (Munich, 1913). For Schnitzler's critical response to Reik's analysis, see Nata Minor, 'Capitales de non-lieu: Vienne, Freud, Schnitzler', *Critique*, 31, nos. 339–40 (août-sept. 1975), 837–45.

Freud and Schnitzler one can find the same strong residues of a
moralistic humanism uneasily combined with the cool scepticism
engendered by the discovery of the unconscious, by the debasement of
mass politics and the 'civilized' double standards of *fin-de-siècle*
Austrian society.

Already as a medical student at the University of Vienna Schnitzler
had indeed been attracted to psychology and served like Freud as
assistant in the clinic of the great brain anatomist, Theodor Meynert.[10]
Like Freud, he had taken an unconventional early interest in
hypnotism, aroused above all by the pioneering research of the
Frenchmen Charcot and Hippolyte Bernheim, and in 1889 even
published a medical treatise *On Functional Aphonia and Its Treatment
with Hypnosis and Suggestion*.[11] Schnitzler's orientation toward hypnotism, psychotherapy, and telepathy during this medical phase of his
career thus showed remarkable parallels with that of Freud. Indeed,
the similarities went back beyond their experiences as medical
students, for both Freud and Schnitzler were the first-born sons of
relatively liberal Jewish families, had received their first education
from Catholic nurses, and experienced as young children the death of
a sibling.[12]

Unlike Freud, Schnitzler had however grown up in a typical
Viennese Jewish upper middle-class home. His father, Johann
Schnitzler, was a self-made man—a distinguished Hungarian-born
laryngologist from Gross-Kanizsa who counted some of Vienna's
leading stage performers among his clients and friends. Johann's
professional standing was to give his eldest son an entrée in later years
into two privileged spheres: medicine and the theatre.[13] In contrast to
the many references to his father in his autobiography, Arthur
Schnitzler had noticeably little to say about his mother (née Louise
Markbreiter), though he did describe in rather greater detail her
relatives, who were long established in Vienna and belonged to the
grossbürgerlich milieu.[14] Thus we learn that his maternal grandfather,

---

[10] Meynert had disparaged Freud's experiments with cocaine and his enthusiasm for
hypnosis and French psychiatry; see Johnston, p. 232.

[11] Arthur Schnitzler, *My Youth in Vienna*, trans. Catherine Hutter (New York, 1970),
270.

[12] Minor, p. 843.

[13] Schnitzler, *My Youth in Vienna*, 9, demonstrated little interest in his father's
provincial Hungarian background: '. . . neither longing nor home sickness ever tempted
me to return to Gross-Kanizsa.' See ibid. 14 for his first memories of the theatre.

[14] Hartmut Scheible, *Arthur Schnitzler in Selbstzeugnissen und Bilddokumenten* (Hamburg, 1976), 13–14, regards the invisibility of his mother in Schnitzler's autobiography

Philip Markbreiter, 'son or grandson of a Viennese court jeweller, doctor of medicine and philosophy, had been a popular physician in his day and in his leisure hours an excellent pianist. With his education and talents he could certainly have gone further in every respect, or at least have achieved a *niveau* worthy of him, if he hadn't fallen victim, incurably as the years went by, to the vice of gambling.'[15]

Schnitzler's grandmother, Amalia, born in the German-Hungarian town of Guns, not far from the Lower Austrian border, was a member of the eminent Schey family, which had prospered 'thanks to highly astute financial transactions with debt-ridden Hungarian aristocrats'.[16] Schnitzler described the rich variety of Jewish types in this assimilated upper middle-class milieu (which reappeared in his novel *Der Weg ins Freie*) with a characteristic touch of irony:

Some members moved to the big cities; the family branched out and intermarried, often advantageously. Bankers, officers, scholars and farmers may be counted among them; and the family tree shows no lack of eccentrics in whom the Jewish patriarch and aristocrat, the entrepreneur and the cavalier are curiously intermingled. Some of the youngest members differ from the older aristocracy only by a little more wit and the racial idiosyncrasy of an irony directed against oneself. Among the women and girls, besides those who because of their appearance and mannerisms can't deny their origin or don't want to, we find some who indulge in sport and fashion, and it is self-explanatory that snobbery—the world ailment of our times—found exceptionally favourable conditions for development during the epoch I touch upon fleetingly here.[17]

Schnitzler vividly recalled the family gatherings on the Day of Atonement in Amalia Markbreiter's home when 'we could look longingly for the glitter of the evening star on the horizon which would herald the end of fasting'. His grandmother Amalia had been the one truly devout member of the family, who went to the synagogue on Yom Kippur.

Her children and grandchildren, as long as they continued to celebrate the Day of Atonement, did so mainly for her sake and after her death solely out of a feeling of reverence for her. Yet even for my grandmother this fasting on the Day of Atonement, as well as the eating of unleavened bread on Passover (which incidentally is delicious when crumbled in coffee), was the one tradition to which she adhered strictly, however, only insofar as she was

as a reflection of the patriarchial social norms in which he was brought up rather than as indicative of a troubled relationship.

[15] *My Youth in Vienna*, 10.   [16] Ibid. 11–12.   [17] Ibid. 12.

concerned. The Feast of Tabernacles, even the Sabbath, was not celebrated in my grandparents' house; and the generation which followed, in spite of all stubborn emphasis on racial solidarity, tended to display indifference to the spirit of Jewish religion, and opposition, sometimes even a sarcastic attitude, to its formalities.[18]

Thus although Schnitzler initially grew up in the largely Jewish area of the Leopoldstadt (then 'still a fashionable and distinguished district') the comfortable social position and religious indifference of his parents did not initially encourage much interest in Jewish affairs. Interestingly enough, in his first jottings for an autobiography, written down in 1901, Schnitzler recalled rather critically the naïve optimism of his childhood and adolescence which had been 'determined by the so-called liberalism of the 1960's and 1870's'; '. . . a false belief was aroused in young people, who were supposed to strive on a prescribed way towards clearly defined goals, and then forthwith be able to build their house and their world on a stable foundation. In those days we thought we knew what was true, good and beautiful; and all life lay ahead of us in grandiose simplicity.'[19] This world of solid bourgeois values, embodied by his father's professional success as a physician and social connections with celebrities in the arts, profoundly shaped the optimistic outlook of the Schnitzler family.[20] Not surprisingly his father's view on public and artistic matters 'conformed on the whole with those of the compact majority who in those days were represented by the *Neue Freie Presse*, and who were not always wrong'.[21]

In 1871 Arthur Schnitzler had entered the prestigious Viennese Akademisches Gymnasium. At this secondary school he showed little diligence in academic studies, least of all any talent for the natural sciences though through his father's example, he 'seemed destined inexorably and hopefully for a medical career'. His history teacher,

---

[18] *My Youth in Vienna*, 13.   [19] Ibid. 3.

[20] See ibid. 22–3 on his father's career and friendships. As a student in Gymnasium, Johann Schnitzler had written a few plays and one of his teachers even prophesied that 'the little Jew boy' would one day be 'Hungary's Shakespeare'. Later, when his son Arthur revealed the urge to a similar literary vocation, Johann Schnitzler strongly opposed his intentions. But he went often to the theatre 'if for no other reason than to please his patients, whom he liked to visit in their dressing rooms and treat, if they needed it.'

[21] Ibid. 24. The tolerance and understanding in this and other Schnitzlerian judgements exemplifies the difference between his attitudes to middle-class society and Viennese Jewry, and those of Karl Kraus or Otto Weininger. Schnitzler did not radically reject his milieu or conditions of life, though he was often highly critical of his contemporaries. What interested him were the complexities and contradictions in human behaviour. See Kohn, pp. 154–5.

Ludwig Blume, was as he recalled a staunch nationalist whose favourite question was: 'Who can list the German Kaisers?' Schnitzler's practised skill in answering this question ensured his exemption from the history finals. Professor Blume, an enthusiastic Wagnerian, had been attracted as much to the German composer's racist politics as to his aesthetic predilections:

Similarly, his [Blume's] antipathy to all things Jewish was rooted more in conviction than in emotion. For even if it amused him to pronounce the names of his pupils with a certain tendentious emphasis, this did not prevent him from writing the 'excellent' he deserved into Spitzer, Samuel's report card; and Kohn, Isidor got what he deserved when, unlike diligent Kohn, Richard or Lowry, Ernst, he failed.[22]

In the mid-1870s, the late bloom period of Austro-liberalism, anti-Semitism, in Schnitzler's words, 'existed, as it had always done, as an emotion in the numerous hearts so inclined and an idea with great possibilities of development, but it did not play an important role politically or socially'.[23] In the Gymnasium there was a certain separation of Jews and Gentiles into groups, but Jew-hatred was still relatively harmless and frowned upon. This situation began to change, however, by autumn 1879 when Schnitzler enrolled in the faculty of medicine at the University of Vienna. He had joined the German-Austrian Reading Society with its monarchist tendencies rather than the German nationalist Akademischer Leseverein—less for political reasons than because of certain advantages (such as cheap theatre tickets) which went with membership. The violent nationalist speeches made at the large student gatherings did not interest him at all 'except insofar as they included antisemitism which had just begun to develop and which filled me with anxiety and bitterness'.[24] Characteristically it was the *psychological*, not the political, religious, or social aspects of the 'Jewish question' which attracted the young Schnitzler's interest.[25]

In accordance with my whole nature it was predominantly the psychological viewpoint that absorbed me. The religious factor played little or no part. I was

---

[22] Ibid. 63.
[23] Ibid.: 'The word hadn't even been invented; and one was satisfied to call those who were particularly inimical toward Jews, almost contemptuously, *Judenfresser*, or "Jew devourers".'
[24] Ibid. 77.
[25] Ibid. Schnitzler insisted that his reaction was 'not rooted solely in the fact that I was Jewish, nor was it the result of any personal experiences'. Attacks on Schnitzler as a Jew, he would not 'suffer in full measure until later', when he was an established playwright.

repulsed by all dogma, from whichever pulpit it was preached or at whatever school it was taught. I found the subject, in the true sense of the word, undiscussable. I had as little relationship to the so-called beliefs of my fathers—to that which was *truly* belief and not merely memory, tradition and atmosphere—as to any other religion.[26]

In October 1882 Schnitzler joined the medical student corps for a year of military service. Here he found Hungarian and Polish Jews whose military bearing and appearance 'left much to be desired'; but also other co-religionists who in their officers' uniform behaved from the first day in such a martial and swashbuckling fashion, as if they had been at least cadets or veteren officers in a hussar regiment'.[27] One of Schnitzler's closest companions during his first year in the army was his second cousin, Louis Mandl, whose younger brother Ignatz had already become a Vienna councillor and ally of Karl Lueger, then a rising municipal politician. Schnitzler's view of the so-called 'anti-corruption democratic party' led in the early 1880s by Lueger and Mandl was unreservedly caustic. The 'democrats' turned into anti-Semites 'not because more corrupt elements were to be found among the Jewish population than among those of other faiths, but because it seemed more easily explicable to the masses, and therefore promised a quicker political success, to denounce as corrupt a strictly defined group of human beings, especially the Jews, who seemed destined for the role even without the 'yellow mark' they once had to wear. This seemed preferable to the more troublesome method of ferreting out a few suspicious creatures from various other classes and religions and delivering them up case by case to the morally indignant.'[28]

Once the anti-Semitic wing had clearly prevailed among the so-called 'anti-corruptionists', Lueger immediately sacrificed his Jewish mentor and comrade-in-arms Ignatz Mandl for the sake of his own political ambitions. Schnitzler noted that even at the height of his popularity, Lueger was no more anti-Semitic 'than he had been in the days when he had played tarot at the home of Dr. Ferdinand Mandl, with his brother Ignatz and other Jews'. But Schnitzler sharply rejected the familiar argument that Lueger's private convictions somehow made his public anti-Semitism less objectionable: 'There were and still are people', Schnitzler observed 'who thought it was to his credit

---

[26] *My Youth in Vienna*, 77. Schnitzler's negative view of Judaism stemmed from the same free-thinking rationalist premises of the Enlightenment as that of Freud. His resentment of the zealotry of the Catholic clergy was, however, far more bitter.

[27] Ibid. 114.   [28] Ibid. 119.

that even during the period of his most pronounced anti-Semitism he preserved a certain preference for a great many Jews and didn't try to conceal it, but as far as I am concerned, this has always seemed to me the strongest evidence of his moral questionability.'[29]

It was during his student days that Schnitzler, like so many young Austrian Jews, first became aware of the insidious spread of anti-Semitism.

The German-national associations, or *Burschenschaften*, had already started to expel all Jews and Jewish descendants; and conflicts during the so-called 'promenade' on Saturday mornings, and during student carousels, also street fights, were not rare in those days between anti-Semitic student corps and the radical-liberal *Landsmannschaften*, formed by those coming from the same native areas, some of which were predominantly Jewish.[30]

As a result of the daily provocations in lecture halls, corridors, and laboratories, Jews began to defend themselves, becoming 'exceptionally expert and dangerous fencers'. Anti-Semitism even began to invade student societies whose purpose was purely humanitarian and which had nothing to do with philosophy or politics, 'nor with the phantom of the honour of rank'. This agitation was directed primarily at needy, industrious Jewish medical students from Hungary who received a monthly subsidy of two to five gulden (which came mainly from Jewish pockets) from one of the university clubs.[31] The German nationalists now sought to exclude Hungarian and Slav students (i.e. mainly Jews) from this financial aid and despite Schnitzler's efforts eventually succeeded in obtaining a decisive victory. They were helped by a baptized Jew, who 'with the false objectivity of the renegade knew so cleverly how to defend the viewpoint of his wretched but, in all probability, sincerely convinced fellow members . . . that he became the butt of a slogan that was popular at the time: "Anti-Semitism did not succeed until the Jews began to sponsor it." '[32]

Even during his army service, Schnitzler observed that there was a clear-cut division between Gentiles and Jews and private socializing was very narrowly circumscribed. Nevertheless, there was far less German national militancy permitted in the Imperial Army than in the universities and the young Schnitzler did not suffer open discrimination.

---

[29] Ibid. 120.   [30] Ibid. 128.   [31] Ibid. 129.

[32] Ibid. 130. Schnitzler's animus against baptized Jews was frequently expressed in his writings. Like Freud, he regarded them as opportunist turncoats whose attempts to curry favour with the 'compact majority' disgusted him.

Coming as he did from a comfortable upper middle-class background, it was still difficult for him to grasp the socio-economic and political impact of anti-Semitism or its full destructive potential. He could perceptively register the pervasiveness of prejudice without really comprehending its social dynamics or as yet feeling personally affected.[33]

In September 1885, shortly after his graduation, Schnitzler became an assistant doctor in the Vienna General Hospital and in his father's Polyclinic. Apart from his routine medical work he would go regularly to the theatre, concerts, parties, and coffee-houses, acquiring a reputation as a dandy, a wit, and a womanizer. Since the beginning of 1887 he had none the less become editor of the *Internationale Klinische Rundschau*, which his father had founded and continued to direct behind the scenes. But his heart was in literature not medical journalism, in individual self-gratification rather than positivistic science, in the restless, unceasing pursuit of women rather than the great questions of history and politics.[34] The debonair playboy and sensualist of the late 1880s was preoccupied above all with the problems of the self rather than society, with the compulsions and delusions of Eros rather than those of civilization as a whole. By 1890, when he first made contact with the literary circle of Young Vienna, Schnitzler had already opted for a literary career. It was at this time that he began to establish enduring friendships with its most prominent members, Hermann Bahr (1863–1934), Richard Beer-Hofmann (1866–1945), Felix Salten (1869–1947), and the schoolboy prodigy, Hugo von Hofmannstahl (1874–1929).[35]

Schnitzler's Anatol cycle (1888–92), seven loosely knit one-act plays illustrating episodes from an elegant, easy-going, philanderer's life, made him the talk of Vienna.[36] Portraying an ageless Narcissus flitting from one woman to the next, whose deceptions in love were matched only by his self-deceptions, Schnitzler laid bare, in playful form, the hypocrisy and flippancy of sexual dalliance as well as hinting

[33] Scheible, p. 29.
[34] *My Youth in Vienna*, 234–5: '. . . homeland was a place to cavort in, wings and backdrop for one's private fate; fatherland was a creation of chance, a totally indifferent administrative affair; and the weaving and working of history penetrated one's ears . . . only in the cacophony of politics to which one didn't like to listen . . .'
[35] Scheible, pp. 37 ff.
[36] See Hellmut Andics, *Luegerzeit: Das schwarze Wien bis 1918* (Vienna, 1984), 159 ff., for the impact of Anatol as a 'Symbolfigur' of bourgeois society in Vienna at the beginning of the 1890s.

at the dilemmas of a vacuous aestheticism.[37] In his later cyclical masterpiece, *Das Reigen*, written in the late 1890s but first published only in 1903, Schnitzler unmasked the naked brutality, mendacity, and selfish lust behind the sexual act in ten short scenes constructed with great delicacy and intricate psychology. As a result of this and other writings which exposed a sick society, whose outmoded conventions were out of joint with actual sexual behaviour, Schnitzler suffered much abuse as a Jew, a decadent sensualist, and 'subverter of morality'.[38] Similarly, his masterly short story *Leutnant Gustl* (1900), with its implied critique of Austrian militarism and the code of honour which enforced duelling, cost Schnitzler his officer rank for allegedly bringing the Imperial-Royal Army into disrepute.[39] Significantly, in this controversial short story, Schnitzler already demonstrated a growing understanding of the social function of anti-Semitism in providing an expression for the *ressentiment* of the Austrian petty bourgeoisie and its fear of proletarization.[40]

Since the mid-1890s Schnitzler's literary work had taken on a more critical tenor, unconsciously influenced perhaps by the collapse of political liberalism. In his satirical playlet of 1898, *Der grüne Kakadu* (The Green Cockatoo), Schnitzler used the French Revolution 'as a vehicle for irony about contemporary Austrian society in its current crisis'.[41] The decadent aristocrats in a low-class Parisian cabaret, watching a group of comedians on the stage pretending to have commited all kinds of crimes, are suddenly confronted by the masses who erupt into the bar from the streets, drunk from the storming of the Bastille. The aristocrats, unable to distinguish dream from real life, initially assume that the terror is still part of the play until they are overwhelmed by the irrationality of political reality.

In *Paracelsus* (1899), a drama about the Renaissance physician and psychologist, the same disorienting confusion of dream and reality is

---

[37] Rolf-Peter Janz and Klaus Laermann, *Arthur Schnitzler: Zur Diagnose des Wiener Bürgertums im Fin de Siècle* (Stuttgart, 1977), 1–16.

[38] Ibid. 55–75; Scheible, pp. 65–70. *Das Reigen* was banned in Vienna before the First World War and in many other cities it was denounced by the clergy as the embodiment of immorality and by the German nationalists as 'Jewish' pornography.

[39] See Janz and Laermann, pp. 110–54, for an analysis of *Leutenant Gust* and of the sociology of the duel in *fin de siècle* Austria. The short story was first published in the *Neue Freie Presse*.

[40] See ibid. 121, 125 on Schnitzler's depiction of Gustl's anti-Semitism as a reaction to status anxiety.

[41] See Carl E. Schorske, 'Politics and Psyche in *fin de siècle* Vienna: Schnitzler and Hofmannstahl', *The American Historical Review*, 66 (1960–1), 930–40.

expressed by the central character in lines which epitomized the essence of Schnitzler's art.

It was a play! What should it be otherwise? Everything we do on earth is play, even if it seems great and profound. One plays with wild armed troops, another with mad superstitious men, someone perhaps with sun or stars,—I play with human souls. Only those who look for a meaning will find it. Dreaming and waking, truth and lie mingle. Security exists nowhere. We know nothing of others, nothing of ourselves. We always play. Wise is the man who knows it.[42]

Sicherheit ist nirgends ('Security exists nowhere'), this famous line of Schnitzler expressed to perfection the *fin de siècle* mood of helplessness in the face of political irrationality; the uncanny sense of an approaching demise which threatened both the Austrian Monarchy and one of its most important and vulnerable constituent parts—the Jewish community of Vienna.

In Schnitzler's 'gay' Vienna, the themes of dying and death were never far from the surface. They suffused his feeling and thinking in creations like the novel *Sterben* (1894), the playlets *Das Vermächtnis* (1898) and *Letzte Masken* (1902) and longer plays like *Liebelei* (1895), the haunting tragi-comedy *Das weite Land* (1911) or later prose works such as *Fräulein Else* (1924). The merging of love and death, of dream and reality, the incomprehensibility of human relationships, the bewildering unforeseeability of life, and the chaos within the psyche as well as external reality, gave to Schnitzler's work a profoundly disillusioning quality belied by its elegant, playful surface. This melancholy, bitter-sweet hue of his work with its depressing consciousness of the transience of all human existence, was quintessentially Viennese.[43] At the same time, Schnitzler's masterly psychological insights into the decadent spirit and manners of that same Vienna with its casual sexual mores and outmoded code of honour, were not unconnected with his exposed social situation as a Jewish liberal outsider.

It must be remembered that as Schnitzler matured in the 1890s, he had begun, like his friends Beer-Hofmann and Hofmannsthal, to repudiate aestheticism as a way of life and to discard its slogan, 'Art for art's sake'. Increasingly, like Freud, he sought to reaffirm the enlightened rationalist values of his paternal inheritance in spite of their evident conflict with the primacy of the instinctual drives he had

[42] See Kohn, p. 159, for the translation from the German text.
[43] Ibid. 158; see also Johnston, pp. 169 ff.

discovered in the psyche.[44] Paradoxically, for all the subversive radicalism of their respective explorations of established sexual morality and interpersonal relationships, neither Freud nor Schnitzler desired to revolutionize the still secure framework of bourgeois culture, let alone the more fragile structure of the Imperial polity. In an Austrian society increasingly torn by political and ideological factionalism, they sought refuge in the traditional liberal values of objectivity, disinterested rational judgement, and a tolerant pluralism. In the case of Schnitzler this inclination found expression in a sceptical individualism and deep detestation of political fanaticism which enabled him to preserve a modicum of integrity and serenity in his beleaguered world. In this respect Schnitzler's response was indeed representative of many cultivated Viennese Jewish intellectuals confronted by the triumphs of reactionary clericalism and rabid anti-Semitism.

In his jottings for an autobiography in 1912, Schnitzler bitterly recalled the traumatic psychological and spiritual impact of the 'Jewish question' on the intellectuals and artists of his generation:

It was not possible, especially not for a Jew in public life, to ignore the fact that he was a Jew; nobody else was doing so, not the Gentiles and even less the Jews. You had the choice of being counted as insensitive, obtrusive and fresh; or of being oversensitive, shy and suffering from feelings of persecution. And even if you managed somehow to conduct yourself so that nothing showed, it was impossible to remain completely untouched; as for instance a person may not remain unconcerned whose skin has been anesthetized but who has to watch, with his eyes open, how it is scratched by an unclean knife, even cut into until the blood flows.[45]

With his growing fame as a writer, Schnitzler was to feel ever more acutely the perfidy of Viennese anti-Semitism and the powerlessness of Jews to change or even to modify it. At almost every point he would find that his literary work, like that of other Jewish-born artists whom he admired, such as the composer Gustav Mahler, was attacked or dismissed on purely racist grounds.[46]

This inescapable social and political stigma embittered his existence all the more, since Schnitzler felt no inner connection to Jewish

---

[44] Schorske, p. 936.　　　　　[45] *My Youth in Vienna*, pp. 6–7.

[46] In his diaries one finds entries which reflect this helplessness in the face of anti-Semitic irrationality: e.g., 'Die Antisemiten sind straflos, unangreifbar', or the remark on 4 Nov. 1904, 'Wie schön ist es ein Arier zu sein, man hat sein Talent so ungestört'. See the interesting article by Egon Schwarz in the *Frankfurter Allgemeine Zeitung*, no. 112, 14 May 1977, on the then unpublished diaries of Arthur Schnitzler.

national traditions or religious beliefs. As in the case of Freud anti-Semitism reinforced his low opinion of human nature, bordering at times on misanthropy.[47] None the less, for all his pessimism he felt a powerful need to exact revenge through the only effective means available to him—a literary work which would describe 'the tragedy of the Jews'.[48] Thus, Schnitzler's rage at the unscrupulous mendacity and wild demagogy of the Austrian anti-Semites had reawakened in him by the late 1890s a latent feeling of solidarity with other Jews despite his distrust of any form of collective identity. The baseness of Viennese anti-Semitism provoked in this liberal humanist the same instinctive *Trotzgefühl* that it had in Freud, though this defiance was at times tempered by Schnitzler's congenital scepticism and attempts to preserve an outward stand of detached objectivity.

Schnitzler, it must be said, was far from being an 'assimilationist' as his life-long contempt for Jewish *Renegaten* indicated. Both baptized Jews and those who ostentatiously sought to behave or pass as German nationalists struck him as foolish, cowardly, and irresponsible opportunists.[49] Like his close friend, the poet and writer Richard Beer-Hofmann, who was no less allergic to the self-negation of converts and Teutomaniac Jews, Schnitzler regarded an affirmation of Jewish ethnic identity as the only dignified response in the face of anti-Semitism. But in contrast to Beer-Hofmann, Schnitzler remained critical of the Zionist solution to the 'Jewish question', in spite of his growing sense of social isolation in *fin-de-siècle* Vienna.

Schnitzler's awareness of Zionism has been sparked by his burgeoning friendship with Theodor Herzl after 1892. Herzl's sharpness in debate, his sartorial elegance and *savoir-faire*, had already made an impression on the young Schnitzler in the Akademische Lesehalle during the late 1870s when the future Zionist leader actively

[47] See Schnitzler's letter to Olga Waissnix on 29 Mar. 1897, pub. in their correspondence *Liebe, die starb vor der Zeit: Ein Briefwechsel* (Vienna, 1970), 319: 'In der letzten Zeit verstimmt mich auch der Antisemitismus sehr stark—man sieht doch eigentlich mit merkwürdiger Ruhe zu, wie man einfach aus dem Geburtsgrunde von Millionen Menschen nicht für voll genommen wird.' Also in Schnitzler, *Briefe, 1875–1912* (Frankfurt, 1981), 316.

[48] Schnitzler, *Briefwechsel*, 319: 'Es wird bald wieder Zeit, die Tragödie der Juden zu schreiben.'

[49] See diary entry of 13 Nov. 1902 referring to the obsequious, grovelling servility of Jews who mocked the allegedly 'un-German' elements in the writer Jacob Wassermann: 'Juden, die in kriecherisch stinkend Weise sich bei den Antisemiten anbiedern und mit vornehmen Spott über das "undeutsche" bei Wassermann losziehen.' Quoted in Norbert Abels, *Sicherheit ist nirgends: Judentum und Aufklärung bei Arthur Schnitzler* (Königstein/Ts., 1982), 98.

participated in German student meetings.[50] Their more intimate relationship dated, however, from Herzl's Paris days as correspondent of the *Neue Freie Presse*. In July 1892 Herzl took the initiative and suddenly wrote to Schnitzler from France congratulating him on a recent novella, *Das Märchen* and bewailing his own failures as a writer: 'The pieces in which I believed, and into which I put true artistic effort, never saw the light of day. When, desperate, I manufactured something for the stage, I was produced—and despised. When I pause to reflect on my place in German literature—which I do but seldom—I am moved to laughter.'[51]

Praising Schnitzler's blossoming dramatic talent, Herzl dismissed his own efforts as those of a mere *Literat*—in other words, 'a narrowhearted, intolerant, jealous, spiteful rogue'.[52] Writing again to Schnitzler in January 1893 Herzl regretted that political journalism was stunting his literary ambitions and pessimistically predicted a new revolution in France. 'If I do not beat a hasty retreat to Brussels, in all probability they'll shoot me as a bourgeois, a German spy, a Jew or a capitalist.'[53] The best political solution for the French people, Herzl concluded, would be *un bon tyran*.

In November 1894 Herzl wrote to Schnitzler once more, this time in connection with the new play he had just completed, *Das neue Ghetto*, asking him for his frank opinion and help in finding a producer. Herzl did not yet want to be known as the author, proposing instead the pseudonym Albert Schnabel and solemnly swearing Schnitzler to 'keep silence' as to the real identity of the playwright.[54]

On 17 November 1894 Schnitzler wrote back, complimenting Herzl on having discovered a new milieu for the stage and new forms which other writers had not yet attempted.[55] Certain Jewish characters in the play he admired, notably Herr Wasserstein, though he felt that Herzl made some personages too explicit about themselves. More importantly, Schnitzler criticized Herzl's original ending, in which the dying hero Jacob Samuel had been made to say, 'Jews, brothers, they won't let you live again, until you've learnt how to die.' Schnitzler preferred a wordless death but more fundamentally he objected to the very premise of the last sentence in Herzl's play.

There was a time when Jews were burnt at the stake by the thousands. They

---

[50] See Schnitzler's correspondence with Herzl, in *Midstream*, 6, no. 1 (Nov. 1960); also Schnitzler, *Briefe, 1875–1912*, 237–9.
[51] Olga Schnitzler, *Spiegelbild der Freundschaft* (Salzburg, 1962), 83.
[52] Ibid. 84.   [53] Ibid.   [54] Ibid. 86–7.   [55] Ibid. 87.

had learnt how to die. But for all that they were not allowed to live. Thus your drama, after a good start, gets on the wrong track. A good character to introduce might be a Jewish fraternity student who had issued thirty challenges, since he is a Jew. You could oppose to him another student, a member of a Catholic guild, who for reasons of conscience does not fight and is therefore respected![56]

Schnitzler was no less dissatisfied with the presentation of Jacob Samuel as 'the Jew with the wounded sense of honour'—a character who seemed to lack inner freedom.

As he stands, he is unsympathetic because the conception does not hold up. Don't you agree? And here I see further still. The figure of the strong Jew is lacking throughout the play. It is certainly not true that in the ghetto which you have in mind, all Jews run around depressed or inwardly shoddy. *There are others*—and *they* are precisely the ones who are hated most by the anti-Semites. Your play is daring—I should like it to be defiant. Above all, don't make your heroes so resigned to die.[57]

Schnitzler clearly rejected Herzl's notion that the Viennese Jews were all frightened, cringing ghetto types. Herzl's reply did not seem, however, to grasp the motives or the point behind Schnitzler's critical reaction. He saw no reason to falsify his own 'misanthropy' and 'portray wonderfully noble and pure-hearted people even if I don't believe in their existence'.[58] Herzl manifestly misinterpreted Schnitzler's objections as a call 'to emasculate myself for the sake of a possible success'. Moreover, he emphasized that he had no intention of defending or rescuing the Jews (Schnitzler had found the play implicitly damaging to Jewry as a polemic) nor of being a 'sympathetic poet'.[59]

The New Ghetto, much to Herzl's chagrin, was turned down by a number of theatres and in his isolation he now felt more than ever the need for Schnitzler's friendship and encouragement.[60] On 23 June 1895, while *The New Ghetto* was being considered for staging in Prague, Herzl dramatically informed Schnitzler from Paris that 'something different, new, much greater' had now taken hold of him and on his return from France to Austria at the end of July he would provide more details.[61] When they finally met in Vienna in the autumn

---

[56] Schnitzler, *Spiegelbild der Freundschaft*, 88.   [57] Ibid. 89.   [58] Ibid. 90.
[59] Ibid.   [60] See ibid. 92 for his letter to Schnitzler of 14 Feb. 1895.
[61] Ibid. 94. Herzl did not indicate that the idea of the Jewish State had seized him but instead enigmatically wrote: 'Dieses Werk ist jedenfalls für mich und mein ferneres Leben von der grössten Bedeutung—vielleicht auch für andere Menschen.'

of 1895 Herzl greeted Schnitzler with characteristic bravado: 'I have solved the Jewish question!' he declared to his startled friend.[62] Several weeks later, after the appearance of *Der Judenstaat*, Schnitzler, answering its author's query as to whether he would be coming to Palestine, expressed doubts that Herzl himself would be going. When Herzl suggested that his plays would be better performed in Palestine than in Vienna's Burgtheater, Schnitzler remained sceptical: 'But in what language?' was his immediate retort.[63]

In his own eyes Schnitzler was unquestionably a German writer and dramatist, who resented any effort whether by Austro-German or Jewish nationalists to cast doubt on that status.[64] Only those authors whose language was Hebrew were in his opinion entitled either to call themselves or to be classified as Jewish writers. Regarding Zionism, as he later declared, he did not want to see it eliminated from the world political scene or from 'the soul economy of contemporary Jewry'. This qualified approval was, however, tinted with a touch of urbane scepticism as well as sympathy. 'As a spiritual element to elevate one's self-reliance, as a possibility for reacting against all sorts of dark hatreds, and especially as a philanthropic action of the highest rank Zionism will always retain its importance, even if it should some day prove to have been merely a historic episode.'[65]

A good part of Schnitzler's reservations about Zionism stemmed from a strong emotional attachment to Vienna and to Austrian soil.[66] This *Heimatgefühl* had nothing to do with conventional Austrian patriotism or the nationalist concept of a *Vaterland* with clearly defined geographical boundaries, which he firmly repudiated.[67] It was, however, connected with a deep feeling for the German language and the Austrian landscape. Abstract notions such as 'nation', 'race', or the

---

[62] Ibid. 95.

[63] Ibid. Herzl's reply was that the plays would be performed in all civilized languages. He thought that a linguistic federalism on the Swiss or Austrian model could be established in the Jewish State.

[64] See the undated letter quoted in Harry Zohn, 'Three Austrian Jews in German Literature', in J. Fraenkel (ed.), *The Jews of Austria: Essays on their Life, History and Destruction* (London, 1967), 73. Schnitzler regarded himself, Beer-Hofmann, Werfel, Wassermann, and dozens of others of Jewish origin as far more German than the anti-Semitic writers.

[65] Ibid.

[66] Even Herzl appears to have recognized this fact after his initial disappointment at his friend's hesitations. 'Schnitzler? He belongs here, on *this* soil [i.e. Austria]—as fully and as much as Schubert.' See Olga Schnitzler, p. 100.

[67] Abels, p. 69, quotes from a Schnitzlerian aphorism of 1904: 'Ich habe Heimatgefühl aber keinen Patriotismus.'

wider political community simply left him cold.[68] Schnitzler consistently distrusted all ideologies and collective political solutions which in his view inevitably usurped and distorted the complex inner reality of subjective experience and led to the elevation of the state at the expense of the individual. His negative response to a dogmatic, political Zionism was in tune with this individualist assertion of the supreme importance of personal feelings deriving from childhood, upbringing, and life-experience in the formation of identity.

Already in the opening pages of his autobiography, Schnitzler's impatience with the notion of Palestine as the 'land of the fathers' is patently manifest.

I don't know when my ancestors settled in Gross-Kanizsa, or for that matter in Hungary, where they may have wandered before that or settled down after having left their original home in Palestine two thousand years before . . . However I am tempted to come to grips at this point with the curious view that a person, born in a certain country, raised and active there, is supposed to recognize as his homeland another country, not the one in which his parents and grandparents lived decades ago but the one his ancestors called their native land thousands of years before, and this not solely for political, sociological or economic reasons—which would bear discussion—but also *emotionally*.[69]

Schnitzler's strong feelings on this issue were echoed in his long and complex novel, *Der Weg ins Freie* (The Road to the Open) by the Jewish writer, Heinrich Bermann. On an autumn cycling expedition to the hills just outside Vienna, Bermann becomes embroiled in an argument with the handsome Zionist, Leo Golowski—evidently the author's back-handed tribute to Theodor Herzl. Golowski's philosophical equanimity in the face of Austrian anti-Semitism had been expressed in a manner guaranteed to provoke the touchy and somewhat neurotic Bermann:

One really can't bear a grudge against these people if they regard themselves as the natives and you and me as the foreigners. After all, it is only the expression of their healthy instinct for an anthropological fact which is confirmed by history. Neither Jewish nor Christian sentimentalism can do anything against that and all the consequences which follow from it.[70]

[68] Olga Schnitzler, p. 96: 'Vaterland, das war ja überhaupt eine Fiktion, ein Begriff der Politik, schwebend, veränderlich, nicht zu fassen.'

[69] *My Youth in Vienna*, 9–10.

[70] Schnitzler, *The Road to the Open* (New York, 1923), 107, authorised trans. by Horace Samuel.

Leo Golowski's startling suggestion that the anti-Semites might have a point and his appeal to such dubious notions as 'healthy instinct' sparked a bitter retort.

My own instinct is at any rate quite as much a rule of conduct for me as the instinct of Herren Jalaudek Junior and Senior [Christian-Social anti-Semites], and that instinct tells me infallibly that my home is here, just here, and not in some Land which I don't know, the description of which doesn't appeal to me the least bit and which certain people want to persuade me is my fatherland on the strength of the argument that it was the place from which my ancestors some thousand years ago were scattered into the world. One might further observe on that point that the ancestors of the Herren Jalaudek and even of our friend Baron von Wergenthin were quite as little at home here as mine and yours.[71]

The Zionist protagonist responds by arguing that such sentiments represented a purely subjective, egoistic viewpoint. The fact, moreover, that Bermann happened to write in German about Austrian people and Austrian conditions was simply irrelevant; so, too, were 'secondary inconveniences' such as the non-promotion of a few Jewish officials, officers, or university lecturers in Vienna. The real issue was the overall material and psychological condition of the Jewish people, especially the East European Jews whom Leo had encountered at the Zionist Congress in Basle.

With these people, whom he saw at close quarters for the first time, the yearning for Palestine, he knew it for a fact, was no artificial pose. A genuine feeling was at work within them, a feeling that had never become extinguished and was now flaming up afresh under the stress of necessity. No one could doubt that who had seen, as he had, the holy scorn shine out in their looks when a speaker exclaimed that they must give up the hope for Palestine for the time being and content themselves with settlements in Africa and the Argentine.[72]

This passionate defence of Zionism spurred Bermann to exclaim that the new movement was perhaps 'the worst affliction that had ever burst upon the Jews'. Words like national feeling and religion simply embittered Bermann with 'their wanton, yes malignant, ambiguity'. The fatherland was nothing more than a fiction. Religious dogmas were 'all equally intolerable and repulsive'. Bermann felt no identification with anyone in the whole world: neither with 'the weeping Jews in Basle' nor with 'the bawling Pan-Germans in the Austrian

[71] Ibid.   [72] Ibid. 108–9.

Parliament'; with Jewish usurpers as little as with 'noble robber-knights', 'with a Zionist bar-keeper as little as with a Christian Socialist grocer'.[73] Common persecution and anti-Semitic hatred could not make him feel solidarity with those who wished to found a Jewish State in 'nonsensical defiance of the whole spirit of historical evolution'. Zionism might perhaps be acceptable in theory as a 'moral principle and a social movement' but in practice its goals were unattainable.[74] 'What is your home-country, Palestine? A geographical idea. What does the faith of your father mean to you? A collection of customs which you have now ceased to observe and some of which seem as ridiculous, and in as bad taste, to you as they do to me.'[75]

With characteristic impartiality, Schnitzler does not adopt a clear position in these intra-Jewish debates, which often take place in the presence of the Gentile artist-aristocrat, George von Wergenthin. At times in these discussions the Baron feels himself pulled towards Leo 'whose words seem to thrill with an ardent pity for the unfortunate members of his race, and who would turn proudly away from people who would not treat him as their equal'; at other times, he sympathized with Heinrich Bermann's scorn for the wild attempt 'to collect from all the corners of the world the members of a race whose best men had always merged in the culture of the land of their adoption'.[76]

In the novel it is this debate over the pros and cons of Zionism which first allows the Catholic Baron to glimpse something of the mysterious destiny of the Jews in a new and melancholy light; to sense the confusion of their existence 'tossed to and fro as they were between defiance and exhaustion, between the fear of appearing importunate and their bitter resentment at the demand that they must needs yield to an insolent majority, between the inner consciousness of being at home in the country where they lived and worked, and their indignation at finding themselves persecuted and insulted in that very place'.[77]

The Zionist road to freedom, advocated by the youthful Leo Golowski, is also briefly considered by another character, the millionaire cartridge-manufacturer Salomon Ehrenberg, whose salon provides a central focus for the action in the novel.[78] Ehrenberg, the

[73] Schnitzler, *The Road to the Open*, 109.   [74] Ibid. 110.   [75] Ibid.
[76] Ibid.   [77] Ibid. 111.
[78] For analyses of the social panorama in the novel, see Robert S. Wistrich, 'Arthur Schnitzler's "Jewish Problem"', *The Jewish Quarterly*, 22, no. 4 (82) (Winter 1975), 27–30; Willehad Paul Eckert, 'Arthur Schnitzler und das Wiener Judentum', *Emuna*, no. 2 (Mar./Apr. 1973), 120–6; and Janz and Laermann, pp. 155 ff.

patriarchial industrialist, is in constant conflict with the social climbing and assimilationist ambitions of his wife and children. He detests the Austrian feudal nobility whom his son Oskar, with his 'nonchalant aristocratic swagger' and upper-class accent, seeks to imitate, a fact which made their relationship increasingly unendurable. At the same time, whenever his father began to talk Yiddish, 'as he was most fond of doing in front of company, and with obvious malice, Oskar would bite his lips and make a point of leaving the room'.[79]

The proud, defiant Ehrenberg, one of Schnitzler's *Kraftjuden* from an older generation, is disgusted and appalled by the seeming indifference of his wife, son, and their blasé Jewish friends to Gentile anti-Semitism. In one of the early conversations in the novel, he informs the agnostic young writer Edmund Nürnberger that he is shortly planning to go on a trip to Egypt, Syria, and Palestine. 'Yes, it's perhaps only because one's getting older, perhaps because one reads so much about Zionism and so forth, but I can't help it, I should like to see Jerusalem before I die.'[80] Ehrenberg hastens to add that neither his wife nor children have any understanding for this wish but 'when one reads what's going on in the world it often makes one inclined to think that there's no other way out for us'. When the somewhat foppish Nürnberger objects that until now anti-Semitism had not prevented Ehrenberg from accumulating a vast fortune and criticizes his partiality, the old patriarch angrily retorts: 'If some one were to bash in your top hat in the Ringstrasse because, if you will allow me to say so, you have a somewhat Jewish nose, you'd pretty quick realize that you were insulted because you were a Yiddisher fellow. You take my word for it.'[81]

When Salomon Ehrenberg bitterly informs Nürnberger that his son Oskar is also an anti-Semite, his wife gently sighs that 'this was a fixed idea in his mind: he sees anti-Semites everywhere, even in his own family.'[82] According to Nürnberger this had indeed become 'the latest Jewish national disease'. Sarcastically the young dandy informs his host: 'I myself have only succeeded up to the present in making the acquaintance of one genuine anti-Semite. I am afraid I am bound to admit, dear Herr Ehrenberg, that it was a well-known Zionist leader.'[83]

In another striking scene, Ehrenberg clashes with Leo Golowski's sister, the young socialist agitator Thérèse, who had recently been imprisoned for her part in a Bohemian coal-miners' strike. He warns

[79] *The Road to the Open*, 187.
[80] Ibid. 67.   [81] Ibid. 68.   [82] Ibid. 69.   [83] Ibid.

her that 'exactly the same thing will happen to you Jewish Social Democrats as happened to the Jewish Liberals and German Nationalists'. Jews, Ehrenberg declared, had created both the liberal and Pan-German movements in Austria only to be betrayed, deserted, and spat on like dogs: '. . . and precisely the same thing will happen in the case of Socialism and Communism. As soon as you've drawn the chestnuts out of the fire they'll start driving you away from the table. It always has been so and always will be so.'[84]

Ehrenberg's tragicomic conflicts with his own son Oskar (an extreme case of the generational tensions depicted in the novel) over the issue of assimilation eventually culminate in a grotesque finale. His son, now a lieutenant in the reserve, is by chance observed by his father removing his hat in front of the Church of St Michael in Vienna, to please his young aristocratic and Catholic comrades.[85] Enraged by this action, his father boxes his ears on the spot, at midday at the centre of Vienna, a public humiliation that leads to a bungled attempt at Oskar to commit suicide. In the novel, the scandal is immediately inflated by the clerical and anti-Semitic press in Vienna who insist that the Ehrenbergs be brought before a jury for sacrilege or blasphemy.

Before this absurdist climax (which reflected accurately enough the Viennese atmosphere around 1900) Salomon Ehrenberg had already returned from his visit to Palestine, disillusioned by the scenery and the fatigue of the journey, without even seeing the new Jewish settlements.[86] Zionism, in the sense of emigration, could be no more of a personal solution for him than for the younger, upstanding Leo Golowski. Perhaps the last word on the 'Zionist' theme in the novel is given to the cynical Heinrich Bermann, who explains to the Gentile Baron that any definitive answer to the Jewish question was still very far away.

In our time there won't be any solution that's absolutely positive. No universal solution at any rate. It will rather be a case of a million different solutions. For it's just a question which for the time being every one had got to settle himself as best as he can. Everyone must manage to find an escape for himself out of his vexation or out of his despair or out of his loathing, to some place or other where he can breathe again in freedom. Perhaps there are really people who would like to go as far as Jerusalem to find it . . . I only fear that many of them, once they arrive at their official goal, would then begin to realize that they had made an utter mistake. I don't think for a minute that migrations like that into

---

[84] *The Road to the Open*, 78.   [85] Ibid. 219–20.   [86] Ibid. 134–5.

the open should be gone in for in parties . . . For the roads there do not run through the country outside but through our own selves. Every one's life simply depends on whether or not he finds his mental way out. To do that of course it is necessary to see as clearly as possible into oneself, to throw the searchlight into one's most hidden crannies, to have the courage to be what one naturally is . . .'[87]

Schnitzler's *Der Weg ins Freie* was, as a novel, far more than just a literary discussion of Zionism or for that matter of the wider dimensions of the Jewish problem in *fin-de-siècle* Vienna. The main action revolves around the love-affair of George von Wergenthin with Anna Rosner, daughter of a lower middle-class Gentile family. The narcissistic Baron plays with the idea of marriage but at heart desires neither wife nor child, since he is insufficiently capable of loving others. Anna's still-born child from their liaison leaves him feeling both guilty and relieved that he has been able to terminate the affair without any lasting ties. In his portrait of the Catholic Baron, a welcome guest in the upper middle-class salons of Jewish Vienna, Schnitzler conveys a powerful sense of isolation, aimless drift, and creative paralysis; unable to make a commitment in love, von Wergenthin's talent as a composer remains unfulfilled and he is unable to make any meaningful choices let alone to master his own conflicting drives.[88]

Like the manifold and varied Jewish characters in the novel, the Baron is in a sense a victim of the disintegration of Austrian liberal values and the distortions of the self, produced by the morass of a decadent society.[89] Drifting in and out of the Jewish salons he acts as a

---

[87] Ibid. 252. George von Wergenthin's reaction to Heinrich's musings on the 'Jewish question' is shown as one of uneasiness. 'He feels he has something in common with all Jews and he stands nearer to the meanest of them than he does to me.' Curiously enough Schnitzler's credo of seeking the road to freedom through the self was echoed in a 'Zionist' formulation in Herzl's diary entry of 16 June 1895: 'No one has ever thought of looking for the Promised Land in the place where it really is—and yet it lies so near. It is here: within ourselves!' (*The Diaries of Theodor Herzl*, ed. and trans. Marvin Lowenthal (London, 1958), 48.

[88] Schorske, p. 939, reads into the breaking of George's liaison 'the end of a half century's efforts to wed bourgeoisie and aristocracy through aesthetic culture'. In von Wergenthin he sees the collapse of the aristocratic ideal which can no longer control or understand the reality of an irrational society as well as the impotence of the artist 'in a bourgeois world spinning out of orbit'.

[89] Ibid. 938. Schorske rightly notes the generational conflict that pervades the novel and provides a kind of linkage between Jews and Gentiles. The older generation with its stability and faith in a purposive moral-scientific culture now represents anachronistic, dying values. On the other hand, the younger generation of aesthetes, aristocrats, and upper middle-class Jews lacks vitality and is completely disorientated by the rise of a

kind of seismograph registering with detached politeness the endless psychic conflicts engendered by the impact of anti-Semitism on the personal existence of Viennese Jews. Yet, in spite of his light-hearted aristocratic grace, some of the self-analytical introspection and *Weltschmerz* of his Jewish friends seem to rub off on the Baron, creating mixed feelings within him.[90] In an early conversation in the novel, he is already irritated at a reminder of distant family connections between the Ehrenbergs, Golowskis, and Staubers, originating as they did from Hungary and Galicia.

As a matter of fact it rather jarred on his nerves. There was no necessity at all, in his view, for Doctor Stauber as well officially to communicate to him his membership of the Jewish community. He already knew it and bore him no grudge at all for it; but why do they always begin to talk about it themselves? Wherever he went, he only met Jews who were ashamed of being Jews, or the type who were proud of it and were frightened of people thinking they were ashamed of it.[91]

Schnitzler's Gentile anti-hero is constantly perplexed by these anxiety-ridden attitudes among some of his Jewish acquaintances. 'Speaking broadly, he found their tone to each other now too familiar, now too formal, now to facetious, now too sentimental; not one of them seemed really free and unembarrassed with the others, scarcely indeed with himself.'[92] Later in the story the easy-going aristocrat finds his tolerance severely strained by Heinrich Bermann's 'persecution-mania'. His Jewish friend had been clearing through his father's posthumous papers. The older Bermann who came from a Bohemian small town had been a liberal Austrian patriot and parliamentary deputy driven out of his party by what his son now regarded as a 'thoroughly German' combination of intrigue, bigotry, and brutality.

A Jew who loves his country . . . I mean in the way my father did, with a real feeling of solidarity, with real enthusiasm for the dynasty, is without the slightest question a tragi-comic figure. I mean . . . he belonged to the Liberalising epoch of the seventies and eighties when even shrewd men were overcome by the catchwords of the age. A man like that today would certainly appear merely comic . . .[93]

Von Wergenthin's exasperated reply to this cynical but essentially

petty-bourgeois antiliberal mass politics symbolized in the novel by Anna Rosner's brother Josef—a committed Christian-Social anti-Semite.

[90] Wistrich, p. 27.
[91] Schnitzler, *The Road to the Open*, 33.   [92] Ibid. 91.   [93] Ibid. 249.

true observation was that Heinrich had lost 'the capacity of seeing anything else in the world except the Jewish question'. This inspires one of the bitterer statements in the novel. With a piercing look Heinrich Bermann asks his Catholic friend.

Do you think that there's a single Christian in the world, even taking the noblest, straightest and truest one you like, one single Christian who has not in some moment or other of spite, temper or rage, made at any rate mentally some contemptuous allusion to the Jewishness of even his best friend, his mistress or his wife, if they were Jews or of Jewish descent?[94]

As for the persecution mania he was being accused of, that was nothing but 'an extremely intense consciousness that has been kept continuously awake, of a condition in which we Jews happen to find ourselves'.[95]

In answer to the impatient Baron's suggestion that if he felt this way he should emigrate to Palestine with Leo Golowski, Bermann reaffirms his rejection of purely objective solutions to 'an essentially subjective problem'. Neither Zionism nor assimilation (except in the very distant future) could possibly solve the oppressive malaise of the Jews. The only hope lay in an inner freedom based on vigilant self-observation and affirmation of one's autonomous identity. Yet the morbidity and pessimism of Heinrich's utterances, his tortured feelings of guilt, bitterness, and resentment at both Gentiles and fellow Jews seemed to belie this credo.[96]

Every race as such is naturally repulsive, only the individual manages at times to reconcile himself to the repulsive elements in his race by reason of his personal qualities. But I will not deny that I am particularly sensitive to the faults of the Jews. Probably the only reason is that I, like all others—we Jews, I mean—have been systematically educated up to this sensitiveness. We have been egged on from our youth to look upon Jewish peculiarities as particularly grotesque or repulsive, though we have not been so with regard to the equally grotesque and repulsive peculiarities of other people. I will not disguise it—if a Jew shows bad form in my presence, or behaves in a ridiculous manner, I often have so painful a sensation that I should like to sink into the earth.[97]

Bermann's sense of shame, nervousness, and over-sensitivity at the behaviour of his co-religionists were not a Jewish form of anti-Semitism but an embittered reaction to the fact that Jews were always

---

[94] Ibid. 250.   [95] Ibid.

[96] At one point George remarks that Heinrich Bermann is 'a more bitter anti-Semite than most of the Christians I know' (ibid. 153).

[97] Ibid. 153–4.

being made collectively responsible for the faults of individuals. The only Jews whom Bermann (like Schnitzler himself) genuinely hated were the renegades 'who try to offer themselves to their enemies and despisers in the most cowardly and cringing fashion, and think that in that way they can escape from the eternal curse whose burden is upon them . . .'.[98]

At the same time, the precarious situation of being perpetually trapped like prisoners in a 'hostile country' (*Feindesland*) was precisely what had given Jews a superior gift of understanding. Only this analytic intensity of consciousness, so necessary for survival in enemy territory, enabled Jews partially to cure themselves of their endemic feeling of strangeness. Thus what appeared to the Baron merely as a persecution complex or even megalomania was really the expression of a historically conditioned defence-mechanism deriving from the insecurity of the Jewish minority in the Diaspora.[99]

Nevertheless, George von Wergenthin, for all his sympathetic openness, still feels a certain latent antipathy for the 'exaggerated Jewish smartness' and 'relentless psychology' of the Bermanns and Nürnbergers. They were a 'disagreeable lot', surprised by nothing in life and lacking altogether in kindness.[100] He sensed that he could never achieve the same relaxed intimacy with them as with Gentiles of hiw own upper-class milieu. This was a thought which aroused in the Baron a growing discomfort and the vague realization that natural relationships could not flourish in the poisoned atmosphere of 'folly, injustice and insincerity' that characterized *fin de siècle* Vienna. Through the filter of this good-natured aristocratic Gentile, Schnitzler thereby demonstrated that, though the external ghetto walls had fallen, the Jews still lived in what was virtually a self-contained 'mental' ghetto, in which even the Baron was ultimately a privileged outsider.[101]

Secondary Jewish characters in the novel like the passionate socialist agitator Thérèse Golowski also lash out against the oppressively hostile atmosphere, when they feel sufficiently provoked. Thus Thérèse strongly defends her Zionist brother Leo against the glib assertion of an upper-class Gentile acquaintance that he is morbidly oversensitive to anti-Semitism. After declaring that she hated Jewish bankers and orthodox rabbis no less than feudal landowners or Catholic priests,

[98] Schnitzler, *The Road to the Open*, 154.
[99] Solomon Liptzin, *Germany's Stepchildren* (Philadelphia, 1961), 126–7; Wistrich, p. 29.
[100] *The Road to the Open*, 266.   [101] Wistrich, p. 30.

Thérèse pointedly adds: 'but if a man feels himself superior to me because he belongs to another creed or another race than I do, and being conscious of his greater power makes me feel that superiority, I would . . . Well, I don't know what I would do to a man like that.'[102]

All the Jewish characters in Schnitzler's novel, irrespective of their economic class or political opinions, are affected in some way by the triumph of populist Catholic anti-Semitism in Vienna and the social ostracism engendered by the cult of German racial superiority. Though their reactions vary in intensity, the outraged sense of pariahood and defiant, though often ambiguous, assertion of Jewish identity is common to many, as a result of their similar historic situation. In the Zionist Leo Golowski—who eventually kills in a duel an anti-Semitic first lieutenant who had ragged him for a year during military service—the response is relatively simple and uninhibited. So, too, in a different way, is the self-assertiveness of Willy Eissler, whose strong temperament and iron will made him resemble a Hungarian feudal magnate more than an Austrian Jew. What distinguished this son of a Viennese antique collector in the Baron's eyes 'from other young people of similar race and ambition was the fact that he was accustomed to admit his origin, to demand explanation or satisfaction for every ambiguous smile, and to make merry himself over all the prejudices and vanities of which he was so often the victim'.[103]

More ambiguous and complex was the response to anti-Semitism of Dr Berthold Strauber, who had abandoned his father's profession of medicine for a career in politics. At the beginning of the novel we see him driven back to bacteriology not merely by the anti-Semitic taunts of his Christian-Social parliamentary opponents but by disgust at the shameless cynicism behind this rhetoric. Revolted by the sheer flippancy of Austrian politics, the young Strauber comments on this trait in terms that were surely close to Schnitzler's heart. 'Our indignation is as little genuine as our enthusiasm. The only things genuine with us are our malice and our hate of talent.'[104]

Schnitzler had worked on his *Diskussionsroman* for five years (between 1902 and 1907) and whatever its aesthetic defects he succeeded in depicting a colourful gallery of contemporary Austrian Jewish types confronted with the problems of Jewish identity under Catholic anti-Semitic rule.[105] The Ehrenbergs, the Bermanns, the

---

[102] *The Road to the Open*, 231.   [103] Ibid. 11.   [104] Ibid. 28.

[105] See the letter of the famous Danish literary critic Georg Brandes, a good friend of Schnitzler and an assimilated Jew, who complained at the end of June 1908 that there

Golowskis, the Eisslers, the Straubers, and the Nürnbergers represented a rich cross-section of middle- and upper-class Viennese
Jewry, excluding only the orthodox and the semi-proletarian East
European (i.e. Galician) Jews. Schnitzler did not seek to impose any
uniform thesis on these characters or to introduce an artificial unity
into the mass of contradictory arguments.[106] Almost every strand of
Viennese Jewish opinion was in fact expressed in the novel, thereby
paralleling its narrative method of constant shifts in perspective and
the wider theme of an imminent breakdown in the Austrian social
order.[107]

Nevertheless, Schnitzler's growing sense of alienation from Austrian
society and politics comes through clearly enough. His depiction of the
defensive psychology of Viennese Jews doomed by a hostile environment to attitudes of suspicion, fear, overassertiveness, or self-
contempt mirrored his own existential situation and that of many of his
co-religionists. For all his reservations concerning Zionism there was
no attempt to minimize the difficulties with which Austrian Jewry now
found itself confronted as an exposed and vulnerable minority group.
The 'security mania' of Heinrich Bermann and the sense of an
unbridgeable gulf of non-communication between Jews and Gentiles
were not feelings alien to Schnitzler's personal experiences. He had
seen with his own eyes how swiftly his Austrian fatherland could turn
into an 'enemy land' for the Jews, in spite of their economic prosperity
and civic equality. He had never believed that polemics, apologetics, or
political agitation by Jews could radically alter this situation. Yet he
remained stubbornly attached to Vienna and the liberal cosmopolitan
traditions of the late eighteenth-century German Enlightenment.[108]
Hence his sceptical individualism sought bravely to reaffirm the

---

was no necessary artistic connection between the Baron's love-affair and the Jewish
theme of the novel. 'Das Verhältnis der jungen Barons zu seiner Geliebten ist eine
Sache, und die neue Lage der jüdischen Bevölkerung in Wien durch den Antisemitismus
eine andere . . .' (*Georg Brandes und Arthur Schnitzler: Ein Briefwechsel*, 95.)

[106] Ibid. 97, Schnitzler to Brandes, letter of 4 July 1908: '. . . es kam mir ja schliesslich
nicht darauf an, irgendwas nachzuweisen, weder dass Christ und Jude sich nicht
vertragen—oder dass sie sich doch vertragen können—sondern ich wollte, ohne
Tendenz, Menschen und Beziehungen darstellen—die ich gesehn habe (ob in der Welt
draussen oder in der Phantasie bliebe sich gleich.)'

[107] This lack of epic totality and possibly even the Jewish subject-matter may explain
Hugo von Hofmannstahl's dislike for the novel, which contributed to a cooling of their
relationship; see Hofmannstahl to Schitzler, 19 Oct. 1910, in Hofmannstahl *Briefwechsel
mit Arthur Schnitzler*, ed. Therese Nickl and Heinrich Schnitzler (Frankfurt, 1964), 95.

[108] Abels, p. 76.

autonomy of the inner self in an age of collectivist ideologies such as nationalism, Darwinian racism, anti-Semitism, militaristic Imperialism, and even Zionism, which might threaten its integrity.[109]

It was essentially the specific weight and aggression of Austrian anti-Semitism which drew Schnitzler out of this quasi-solipsistic position into a closer identification with Jews as a persecuted group.[110] Thus in a letter to the liberal Austrian historian Richard Charmatz on 4 January 1913, Schnitzler expressed considerable resentment at those Jews who claimed not to suffer from anti-Semitism whether from 'lack of sensitivity, convenience, satiety, snobbery or obsequiousness.'[111] At the same time he emphasized that in spite of the great debt which he owed to the German people and to Austrian culture, *Deutschtum* itself had derived much from the cultural and ethical achievements of Jewry over the centuries. Thus Schnitzler felt no less grateful to the ancestral heritage of his race than to the German and Austrian components in his identity.[112] Like Freud, Schnitzler evidently valued the nonconformity and freedom from dogma that he associated with his Jewishness. He also had a similar perception of the Jews as a ferment in history and an intensely individualist people who had known how to defy persecution and oppression over the centuries. Hence he was not at all attracted to radical assimilationist solutions, least of all in an age of mounting racism which made such options seem morally suspect and politically impracticable.

Schnitzler's sensitivity to the pressures of anti-Semitic prejudice in Viennese life was most poignantly revealed in his powerful drama *Professor Bernhardi* (1912). More than anywhere else in his literary work, Schnitzler exposed in this play the irrationality, meanness, political intrigue, and intolerance that threatened the man of integrity in contemporary society. The play was constructed around one central incident: the refusal of Professor Bernhardi, the Jewish director of the Elisabethinum private hospital, to admit a Catholic priest to the bedside of a dying girl, for fear that his appearance would destroy her

---

[109] Ibid. 84.

[110] Ibid. 96. Schnitzler's intense suspicion of all modes of collective identification is revealed in the following aphorism: 'Ich fühle mich mit neimandem solidarisch, weil er zufällig derselben Nation, derselben Rasse, derselben Familie angehört wie ich.' His sympathy for Jews did not arise out of any innate obligation but rather from a community of suffering.

[111] Ibid. 97.

[112] See S. Melchinger, 'Das Jüdische in Professor Bernhardi', *Theater heute*, 5 (1964), 7–12, p. 33; and Schnitzler, *Briefe, 1913–31* (Frankfurt, 1984), 2–4.

hallucinatory state of euphoria.[113] As a doctor and as a human being, Bernhardi believed he had made the right decision in permitting the girl a moment of happiness in her brief and tragic life. But the incident is quickly blown up by clerical forces into a political issue, with Bernhardi accused of having displayed gross insensitivity to the religious sensibilities of the Catholic population of Vienna. At first, in Act II, he seems ready to make a public declaration that he had no desire to offend religious feelings until he learns of the manœuvrings and political intrigues of his deputy Dr Ebenwald, a loyal German nationalist and anti-Semite.[114] He promptly tears up the declaration he had begun to write and henceforth insists that he owes society no explanation of his behaviour—the affair is one of private morality alone.

Bernhardi rejects the notions of political expediency of the Minister of Education, Professor Flint, who at first seeks to help the cause of the hospital, only opportunistically to abandon its director under intense Christian-Social pressure in the Austrian Parliament.[115] Found guilty of sacrilege in the ensuing court case, Bernhardi, despite the urgings of some of his colleagues, prefers to go to prison rather than make any public commitment that might compromise his moral conscience. When he comes out of prison he is deeply embarrassed to discover that he has become a hero for the free-thinking public and repudiates any attempt to turn him into a martyr for political causes.[116] In the final scene of the play this stance of withdrawal is implicitly criticized by Councillor Winkler who reproaches him for having initiated the whole affair, if he were not ready to act in defence of his moral principles.[117] This rather hypocritical condemnation, which comes from the person perhaps least qualified to make it, highlights the devious self-irony

[113] As early as 1899 Schnitzler had jotted down the idea of a play concerned with the conflict between religious and scientific attitudes to the sick; see Sol Liptzin, 'The Genesis of Schnitzler's *Professor Bernhardi*', *Philological Quarterly* 10 (1931), 349.

[114] Schnitzler, *Professor Bernhardi: A Comedy in Five Acts*, trans. Hetty Landstone (London, 1927), 55–60.

[115] Ibid. 60–74, 95. Flint's parliamentary speech begins by emphasizing Bernhardi's virtues and defending the right to make public appointments on merit alone. By the end he has completely retreated as a result of anti-Semitic heckling and protests.

[116] Ibid. 134: 'As a legal question the whole thing was distasteful enough: now I am about to see it develop into a political storm. And from that I shall flee, to prison, if there is no refuge. My business is to cure people.'

[117] Ibid. 159–60. Winkler suggests that neither he nor Bernhardi have the temperament of reformers—hence they should not involve themselves in such matters. 'We have not the inner conviction to follow up our principles to the final consequences—to give up our lives, if necessary, for our convictions.'

and ambivalence that characterizes many of the protagonists in the play.[118]

In the course of the drama Schnitzler had skilfully revealed many of the anti-Jewish prejudices prevalent in pre-1914 Austrian society and the cynial opportunism of medical colleagues who hoped to bring about the Professor's removal as head of the clinic. Bernhardi's deputy, Dr Ebenwald, ignoring the question of individual talent, seeks to obtain the appointment of a German colleague from Graz to replace Dr Tugendvetter rather than the latter's inoffensive assistant, Dr Wenger, who happens to be a Jew.[119] His cousin, 'the leader of the Clerical Party', plays a key part in the parliamentary agitation against Bernhardi.

In his own student days, Dr Ebenwald had been a leader of the German Nationalists; as he reminds his baptized Jewish supporter Dr Schreimann, '. . . you know what that means—Watch on the Rhine—Bismarck's Oak—Waidhofen Resolution. No satisfaction given to Jews or anyone of Jewish extraction.'[120] The exchanges between Ebenwald and Schreimann in Act III convey something of the confused, ambiguous state of affairs, even in the German nationalist camp. Schreimann, speaking in a strikingly Austrian dialect sometimes mingled with an inadvertent Jewish accent, assures Ebenwald that even if he were a Nationalist Jew he would side against Bernhardi in this case. 'And permit me to remark, once more, that I am as much a German as you. And I can assure you it takes more courage at the present time for a man of my origin to declare himself a German and a Christian than to remain what he was at birth. I should have had an easier time as a Zionist.'[121] When Ebenwald fondly recalls the notorious Waidhofen resolution of 1896 which forbade German students to 'give satisfaction' to Jews as members of an 'inferior race', Schreimann points to his own scar obtained in a duel with a German fraternity student. 'It had to be given sometimes, though, in spite of the strictest observance. I received this scar as a Jew.' Ebenwald replies:

[118] See the perceptive introd. by Martin Swales to the German text, Schnitzler, *Professor Bernhardi* (Oxford, 1972), 16–17.

[119] *Professor Bernhardi*, Eng. edn., 17 ff. Later in the play Ebenwald complains that though most of the patients at the Institute are Catholic, the house-doctors are mainly Jewish. 'That sort of thing causes bad blood in certain quarters' (ibid. 100).

[120] Ibid. 79.

[121] Ibid. Ebenwald, much to Schreimann's annoyance, quips: 'Quite likely. You could have been sure of a Professorship in Jerusalem, at any rate.'

'Well, don't we live in muddle times? You are more proud today of your Jewish scar than of all your Germanism.'[122]

Schreimann is not the only convert at the clinic to oppose Bernhardi. The half-Jewish Dr Adler, lecturer in pathological anatomy, descended on his mother's side from an old Viennese burgher family, belongs to Ebenwald's camp even though in his student days he had occasion 'to shed blood for the other side'.[123] Dr Goldenthal, Bernhardi's lawyer, is also a convert and fails to defend him adequately for fear of creating doubts about the sincerity of his conversion. In Act IV of the play he pointedly asks Bernhardi how he can imagine 'that a servant of the Church would speak a deliberate untruth' and defends 'the much abused Clericals' as men of outstanding intellect, courage, and nobility.[124] He is sharply reproached by the Gentile Professor Pflugfelder, an old liberal warhorse of 1848 vintage and a supporter of Bernhardi:

On listening to you, Dr. Goldenthal, one must have obtained the impression that Bernhardi's behaviour towards the Priest caused the deepest offence to the religious feelings of the whole Catholic world, from his Holiness the Pope down to the pietist in the most remote village. And, instead of declaring quite simply that every doctor was bound to act as Bernhardi did . . . you found it necessary to depict what was his simple duty as a physician as an act of thoughtlessness needing an apology. You treated the malicious idiots on the jury, who had made up their minds from the first moment to find Bernhardi guilty, as the choicest brains of the Nation—and the judges who had, so to say, brought the term of imprisonment for Bernhardi with them in their dispatch cases, you treated as patterns of penetration and Justice . . . And you, you Dr. Goldenthal, acted as though you yourself, in your innermost soul, believed in the indispensability and power of that sacrament, against which Bernhardi is supposed to have offended, and hinted that our friend Bernhardi is really very much in the wrong in not sharing those beliefs.[125]

Towards the end of the play, Franz Reder, Priest of the Church of St Florian, whom Dr Bernhardi had barred from seeing the dying girl in the sickroom, visits the doctor and a frank conversation ensues. The priest explains that it was his duty to the Catholic Church which caused him to testify against Bernhardi in the courtroom.[126] In the course of their increasingly strained dialogue he accuses the doctor of

---

[122] *Professor Bernhardi*, Eng. edn., 79.
[123] Ibid. 26.   [124] Ibid. 114–17.   [125] Ibid. 118–19.
[126] Ibid. 123. The priest tells Bernhardi: 'I can admit of no higher truth, Professor, than my Church. And the most sacred commands of my Church are loyalty and submission.'

arrogance and a 'deep and insurmountable animosity, which a man of your type finds unconquerable against any of my calling'.[127] For Bernhardi, 'animosity' was however too small a word to express 'that which parts us and will probably part us for all time. It appears to me as something far deeper—and more hopeless.'[128]

Bernhardi's moral stance in the play is above all that of a doctor and scientist. His profession is to cure people and thereby to serve humanity and science. He is an iconoclast only in so far as he defends what seem to him self-evident values of truth, independent judgement, and humanist ethics. Nothing is further from his mind than a desire to solve any social problem.[129] Hence, he refuses to be the plaything of politicians and resists the pressure from Ebenwald and then from the Minister of Education to appoint a non-Jew to the staff in order to exculpate himself from his action against the priest. For the same reason he refuses to join his sympathizers in the fight against clericalism and anti-Semitism.[130] This aversion to political militancy in general, or even as a specific response to anti-Jewish intrigues, was thoroughly characteristic of Schnitzler's own position.

As a play *Professor Bernhardi*, in spite of its apolitical standpoint, nevertheless displays a keen awareness of the ideological cross-currents undermining Austrian society in the first decade of the twentieth century. The drama skilfully reveals the religious, social, and political dimensions of the anti-Semitism pervading that society, even though the action is strictly confined to the enclosed world of the Elisabethinum Hospital. The rivalries and jealousies within the medical profession which it explores had been inextricably affected by this anti-Jewish climate of opinion that had developed over a period of thirty years, as Schnitzler was well aware from his own experience and that of his father. Indeed, much of the material from which the play was drawn can be identified as autobiographical, dating back to 'the struggle between the professors of the College of Medicine and the general practitioners over the Polyclinic my father and several other young doctors had founded'.[131] In his autobiography Schnitzler described in some detail the central role which this Polyclinic had

---

[127] Ibid. 125.   [128] Ibid. 126.

[129] Ibid. 160. In the closing scene, Bernhardi tells Winkler that he had 'not the remotest intention of solving any problem whatever'. He had simply done what he held 'to be right in one specific instance'.

[130] Ibid. 133. 'Don't you understand yet, gentlemen, that I will have nothing whatsoever to do with people who wish to make a political affair out of my case.'

[131] Schnitzler, *My Youth in Vienna*, 23.

assumed in his father's life and the unscrupulous agitation which had been unleashed against it in the 1870s, following the Viennese Stock Market crash.[132] Even after this first defamatory campaign subsided, Johann Schnitzler had to parry not only the professional jealousy of less successful practitioners and the superstitious fear of the simple-minded but also 'the petty and miserable intrigues which had been hatched in the college of medical professors itself . . .'.[133]

The 'old guard' at the University had seen in his father's flourishing clinic, and the growing fame of its lecturers, a dangerous rival.[134] In 1886 Johann Schnitzler felt obliged to publish a sharp exposure in the *Medizinische Presse* of the 'spirit of intolerance that is spreading also in the medical faculty', an atmosphere that was clearly mixed up with the impact of anti-Semitism. Within a few years, this spirit of intolerance began to penetrate the Polyclinic itself (where Jewish doctors were in a majority as in the Elizabeth Institute of Schnitzler's play) and to affect his father's career, in spite of his brilliant professional reputation and popularity as a consultant in the wealthiest bourgeois circles. 'In the years to come', Schnitzler recalled, 'some of his patients, especially those in so-called high society, were to leave him, and the brightness of his name was to be somewhat dimmed.'[135] This was not simply due to age and the pressure of younger, more successful specialists but also to 'the rapidly increasing power of those currents of intolerance' which steadily penetrated into even the highest reaches of the medical world.[136]

The action in *Professor Bernhardi* distilled not only these sobering personal and family experiences but also the political viciousness beneath the thin veneer of Viennese gaiety and *Gemütlichkeit*. The drama takes place not only in the context of the Christian-Social administration in Vienna but also against the background of a permanently hostile anti-Semitic press and a parliament corrupted by shameless demagoguery. In this climate of opinion the incident that provoked the Bernhardi Affair could all too easily be distorted out of all proportion by the clerical and anti-Semitic parties.[137] In Schnitzler's play, the parliamentary question put forward by the clerical faction referred explicitly to Bernhardi's 'Mosaic religion' and asked what

[132] Schnitzler, *My Youth in Vienna*, 166.   [133] Ibid.
[134] Ibid. 167.   [135] Ibid. 169–70.   [136] Ibid. 170.
[137] See *Professor Bernhardi*, Eng. edn., 43. The militant Jewish medical student, Loewenstein, points out that if a Christian had done the same thing as the Jewish doctor, he 'would have been backed up by thousands and hundreds of thousands, who now not only do not move a finger, but on the contrary, will range themselves against Bernhardi.'

measures the Minister of Education intended to take 'to give satisfaction to the Christian population of Vienna, who have been offended in their deepest religious feelings'.[138] The interpellation further considered it advisable to 'exclude persons who, through origin, education and character are not in a position to have the necessary understanding for the religious feelings of the indigenous Christian populace'.[139] Thus, the campaign against Bernhardi belonged indeed to the sustained Christian-Social agitation against Viennese Jewry, one which had singled out the *Verjudung* (Jewification) of the medical profession for special opprobrium. Jewish doctors were consistently being accused by the anti-Semites of unfair competition, of unethical practices, and even of engaging in 'criminal' experiments against their Christian patients.[140]

Schnitzler had been intimately familiar with this contemptible anti-Semitism since his days as a medical student and as he confessed in an angry outburst to Olga Waissnix on 29 March 1897 he had 'so strong a need for revenge against this rabble, that I would myself readily hang them'.[141] On 12 January 1899 he wrote to his friend Georg Brandes, the famous Danish literary historian, asking whether he ever read the Viennese newspapers, or debates in the parliament and municipal council. 'It is astonishing what swine we live among here;—and I always think that it must strike even the anti-Semites themselves, that Antisemitism—apart from anything else—has at any rate the strange power to bring to light the most mendacious rottenness and develop it to the highest degree.'[142] In an earlier letter to Brandes on 27 March 1898 Schnitzler had already pointed to the 'unbelievable' denunciations in the local anti-Semitic press of his new play *Freiwild*.[143]

Consistently slandered as a cheap Jewish *Literat*, a trashy pornographer and scandalous immoralist by the Viennese anti-Semites,

---

[138] Ibid. 85.   [139] Ibid.

[140] See, e.g., *Deutsches Volksblatt* (Vienna), 20 Oct. 1898, pp. 1 ff., and 28 Oct. 1898, recording the words of deputy Schneider: 'Die Regierung soll der Schweinerei ein Ende machen, dass die Juden an arischen Leibern herumarbeiten; sie sollen die Juden nehmen zu Sezieren, aber es sollen nicht unsere Frauen und Mädchen der Sezierung durch diese Juden verfallen und dazu benützt werden, um Studien zu machen und noch andere Dinge zu vollführen.'

[141] *Liebe, die starb vor der Zeit*, 319.

[142] Letter S 13 in *Georg Brandes und Arthur Schnitzler: Ein Briefwechsel*, 71. Schnitzler added the following irony: 'Wie merkwürdig, dass sogar die offenbaren Mängel, Fehler, meinetwegen Verbrechen der Judenpresse, die man als so spezifisch jüdisch hinstellen wollte, von der Antisemitenpresse ins ungeheurliche ausgebildet worden sind.'

[143] Letter S 11, ibid. 68: 'Insbesondere die antisemitschen Blätter leisteten Unglaubliches in Denunziationen.'

Schnitzler had every reason to feel a sense of exasperated resentment.[144] His success with the educated theatre-going public of the capital, crowned by the prestigious Grillparzer prize in 1908, merely brought the anti-Semitic attacks on this 'son of an immigrant Hungarian Jew, born by chance in Vienna' to a new crescendo of racist slander.[145] This relentless campaign undoubtedly persuaded Schnitzler (who had begun working on *Professor Bernhardi* already in 1899) that the time had come to provide a serious dramatic treatment of Viennese anti-Semitism in which he could fully utilize his own medical experiences and those of this immediate circle.

Thus, it was no accident that the figure of Professor Bernhardi bears more than a passing resemblance to his father and the intrigues of the Elisabethinum Hospital to the very struggles that had occurred a generation earlier in Johann Schnitzler's Polyclinic. Characters like Professor Cyprian, Oskar Bernhardi (who resembles the young Schnitzler), and the anti-semitic Tyrolese medical student, Hochroitz-pointner, are readily identifiable with real life personages.[146] The impact of the Waidhofen Resolution (1896) and of rabid German nationalism in medical student circles emerges strongly as part of the social background to the play. Equally the conflicts between secular humanism and Catholic values, between science and religion, as depicted in the play, accurately reflect the atmosphere of *Kulturkampf* in Austria during the first decade of the twentieth century.[147] By weaving all these themes around the central social issue of the adversarial relationship between a Christian State and its Jewish minority, Schnitzler was able to provide a striking microcosm of the crisis afflicting Vienna and its Jews towards the end of the Habsburg Monarchy.[148]

[144] *Deutsches Volksblatt*, 2 Sept. 1900, p. 7.

[145] Ibid., 28 Jan. 1908. The German nationalist newspaper contrasted Grillparzer's purity with the lascivious writings of Schnitzler, 'der Pornograph, der die schlecht parfümierten Kanapeegeschichten und Sexualanekdoten seines "Reigens" aus ersichtlicher Lust am Gemeinen verfasste . . .'. It also denounced the 'schimpfliche Verletzung der Standesehre' in Schnitzler's short story, *Leutnant Gustl* and the 'jüdischen Erfindung des "süssen Mädels"' to be found throughout his work.

[146] See the convincing reconstruction by Adolf Gaisbauer, 'Der historische Hintergrund von Arthur Schnitzlers "Professor Bernhardi"', *Bulletin des Leo Baeck Instituts*, 13, no. 50 (1974), 139–52, of the parallels between the Elisabethinum Hospital and the Polyclinic of Johann Schnitzler.

[147] See ibid. 152–62 on the political struggle between the clericals and free-thinking forces in Austria (Liberals, Social Democrats, etc.) for control of educational institutions which peaked at the time Schnitzler was writing *Professor Bernhardi*.

[148] See *Professor Bernhardi*, Eng. edn., 66, where the Minister of Education reminds

Significantly, *Professor Bernhardi* was considered too subversive and disparaging of Austrian public institutions to be performed in Vienna before 1914.[149] Even the famous Berlin critic and impresario Otto Brahm, who was a close personal friend of Schnitzler, refused to accept the play in his theatre. Though he liked the characterizations and dialogue, he was evidently embarrassed by the honest and unsparing treatment of the 'Jewish question' in the drama. He even wrote to Schnitzler, speciously suggesting that 'Berlin Jewish physicians are not being persecuted as was the Viennese Dr Bernhardi; on the contrary, they occupy a dominant position; we are not Catholic . . . and thus the point of departure of this play as well as its plot development will fascinate us less here than in the land of the Eucharist Congress.'[150]

Professor Bernhardi, like the best of Schnitzler's literary work, exemplified the deep moral seriousness and psychological acumen that underlay the smooth, urbane irony and deceptively light touch of this Viennese writer. Blending typically Austrian aesthetic elements with the clinical precision of 'a pronouncedly Jewish intellect', he succeeded in encapsulating better than any of his contemporaries the conflicting value orientations of a slowly disintegrating society.[151] A product of the gradual atrophy of Austro-liberalism into passivity, scepticism, and world-weariness, he none the less clung tenaciously to the cosmopolitan values of the classical German Enlightenment. Without illusions as to the foibles and failings of his own class or of Austrian society as a whole, he sought to salvage what was best in that world from the ravages of political demagogy and religious intolerance: the integrity of the individual, the respect for reason and for freedom of choice.[152]

For all his indifference to Judaism as a religion and to any form of group identification, Schnitzler remained, like Freud, a defiant Jew profoundly conscious of what he owed to his background and heritage.

---

the Jewish doctor: '. . . you forgot one small matter in your behaviour towards the priest, namely, that we live in a Christian State.'

[149] The first performance in Vienna took place in 1920 at the Deutsche Volkstheater; see W. P. Eckert, 'Arthur Schnitzler und das Wiener Judentum', 129.

[150] *Der Briefwechsel Arthur Schnitzler–Otto Brahm*, ed. and introd. Oskar Seidlin (Schriften der Gesellschaft für Theatergeschichte, vol. 57, Berlin, 1953), 256.

[151] See the verdict of the Viennese critic Manfred Vogel, quoted in Zohn, p. 74.

[152] Scheible, p. 106, regards *Professor Bernhardi* as expressing the failure of Schnitzler's effort to save the private realm of freedom from the invasion of collectivist values.

Though anti-Semitism embittered his life, he sought to analyse its manifestations with that same impartiality and objectivity which he brought to all his literary creations. Growing up as he did in *fin de siècle* Austria, this was frequently a task beyond even the self-critical, diagnostic talents of such a born sceptic. Disgusted by Austrian politics and generally indifferent to social problems, Schnitzler's supreme gift as an artist lay in keen psychological observation. No other Austrian writer was able to anatomize with the same unerring analytical precision the psychic structure of the Viennese Jewish bourgeoisie from which he came and whose crisis of identity his work so faithfully described. Schnitzler's Jewish characters voice the mood of that class, its scepticism, self-doubt, and pessimism in an age of mounting anti-Semitism. Schnitzler did not believe in any universal solutions of panaceas for the Jewish question. Neither assimilation, Zionism, socialism, conversion, nor self-hatred would bring closer the day when Jews could breathe easily without fear of persecution. The road into the open had been closed off in an Austrian society that distorted, deformed, and repressed the individual needs of its members. Security was nowhere in sight but in the intimate knowledge of the self lay perhaps the beginning of wisdom.

18

Imperial Swan-Song: From Stefan Zweig to Joseph Roth

Over the life of those whose blood flowed in him, justice was ever present like a sun, whose rays never warmed them, whose light never shone for them, and yet before whose dazzling splendour they reverently shielded their pain-covered forehead with trembling hands.—Ancestors, who wandered from land to land, ragged and disgraced, the dust of all the highways in their hair and beards ... calling out in their suffering, not to a Lord of Mercy, but to the God of Justice.

Richard Beer-Hofmann, *Der Tod Georgs* (1900)

The past of his people is his personal memory, the future of his people is his personal task.

Martin Buber,
Drei Reden über das Judentum (1911)

Scatter your seeds, scatter your seeds,
In unknown lands,
Through numberless years.
Wander your wanderings, watered with tears.
On, people of God; for wherever ye roam,
Your road leads through the world to eternity, home.

Stefan Zweig, *Jeremias* (1916)

Every assimilation, however superficial, is a flight, or the attempt at a flight from the unhappy community of the persecuted; it is an attempt to compensate for the contradictions which nonetheless exist.

Joseph Roth, *Juden auf Wanderschaft* (1923)

You must believe in the spirit!
Directly, without emotion
and selfless,
You must, God's elect, must, if you wish to remain it!

Arnold Schoenberg, *Credo* (1926)

One day when I was discussing the problem of anti-Semitism with the eminent Austro-Jewish poet, Richard Beer-Hofmann, he said to me: 'I am not at all astonished at the fact that they hate us and persecute us. But what I cannot understand is, why they do not marvel at us more.'

Erich Kahler, 'What are the Jews?' (1950)

The illusory sense of prosperity and security felt by the Central European bourgeoisie in the period prior to the First World War has rarely been portrayed more vividly than by the Viennese-born Jew Stefan Zweig (1881–1942). The description of the Habsburg Empire with which he opened his autobiography has long since become a classic evocation of that 'Golden Age', made all the more poignant by its patent idealization and sense of nostalgic wish-fulfilment.

Everything in our almost thousand-year-old Austrian Monarchy seemed based on permanency, and the State itself was the chief guarantor of this stability. The rights which it granted to its citizens were duly confirmed by parliament, the freely elected representative of the people, and every duty was exactly prescribed. Our currency, the Austrian crown, circulated in bright gold pieces, an assurance of its immutability. Everyone knew how much he possessed or what he was entitled to, what was permitted and what was forbidden. Everything had its norm, its definite measure and weight.[1]

Prosperous families could look to the future with equanimity, officials and officers knew when they would be advanced and when they would be pensioned. Houseowners could regard their property as a secure domicile for their children and grandchildren; businesses and estates were handed down from generation to generation.

In this vast empire everything stood firmly and immovably in its appointed place, and at its head was the aged emperor; and were he to die, one knew (or believed) another would come to take his place, and nothing would change in the well-regulated order. No one thought of wars, of revolutions, or revolts. All that was radical, all violence, seemed impossible in an age of reason.[2]

This Zweigian nostalgia for the pre-war world of stability and reason was shared by a number of other Austrian writers, some of them of Jewish origin like the Galician-born Joseph Roth (1894–1939). After the collapse of the Monarchy, these writers constructed a post-1918 myth of Habsburg beneficence, a literary fiction which reflected their

[1] Stefan Zweig. *The World of Yesterday* (New York, 1943), 1.
[2] Ibid. 2.

understandable estrangement from the grimmer features of life in Central Europe between the wars.[3]

By no means all of these writers had shared Zweig's view of the nineteenth century as moving on 'the straight and unfailing path toward being the best of all worlds'.[4] As we have seen, some Jewish intellectuals like Karl Kraus had long before 1914 sharply rejected the positivist religion of progress, based on the advances in material production, science, and technology. Liberal humanists like Freud and Schnitzler were all too keenly aware that waiting to erupt beneath the thin veneer of bourgeois civilization lay powerful and destructive forces of the instinctual 'underworld'. Even Zweig himself clearly recognized 'the optimistic delusion of that idealistically blinded generation' who had naïvely believed in a 'rapid and continuous rise of humanity'.[5]

One of the most searching critics of this myth of liberal progress was the Viennese Jewish novelist, Hermann Broch (1886–1951), a metaphysical Platonist thinker, influenced by Otto Weininger, who had himself converted to Christianity in 1908.[6] Broch, who coined the ambiguous phrase 'gay apocalypse' to characterize what Zweig preferred to see as a 'golden Age of security', regarded *fin de siècle* Vienna as the European capital of kitsch and the metropolis *par excellence* of the 'value vacuum' in modern civilization.[7] Like the novelist Robert Musil, that other sharp-eyed demystifier of Imperial-Royal myths,[8] Broch stressed the self-deceptive character of life in the Habsburg metropolis; the lack of ethical substance, the artificial character of a pseudo-constitutional structure ultimately held together by the mystique of the Crown, and the bureaucratic life-style embodied by the ageing Emperor Franz Joseph I.[9]

For Hermann Broch, post-1880 Vienna with its hedonistic aestheticism, its sceptical pessimism and provincial, non-revolutionary ethos had been turned into a museum-like city of dreams, gripped by

---

[3] See Claudio Magris, *Der habsburgische Mythos in der österreichischen Literatur* (Salzburg, 1966), and the discussion by Wendelin Schmidt-Dengler, 'Habsburg myth, Republican reality', *The Times Literary Supplement*, 11 June 1976, pp. 712–13.

[4] Zweig, p. 3.   [5] Ibid. 4.

[6] See Manfred Durzak, *Hermann Broch: Der Dichter und seine Zeit* (Stuttgart, 1968), and Hermann Broch, *Schriften zur Literatur*, i (Frankfurt, 1975), 111–275 for the seminal essay, 'Hofmannstahl und seine Zeit'.

[7] See Broch, *Schriften*, i, section 4, pp. 145 ff.: 'Die fröhliche Apokalypse Wiens um 1880.'

[8] See Robert Musil, *The Man without Qualities*, 3 vols. (London, 1953–60), i. 32–3, for a brilliant exposé of the ambiguities and paradoxes of the late Habsburg Empire.

[9] Broch, 'Hofmannstahl und seine Zeit', 153 ff.

political paralysis.[10] In spite of its outwardly imposing bureacratic machine and the solid dynastic patriotism of the Viennese *Bürgertum*, this was virtually 'a stateless society', hopelessly fragmented into disparate and conflicting elements, united only in an essentially fraudulent 'democracy of style', the aimless pursuit of pleasure, and an eclectic cult of decorativeness.[11] In his study of the personality and work of Habsburg Austria's finest lyrical dramatist, Hugo von Hofmannstahl (1874–1929), Broch sought to depict one of the noblest if doomed efforts to transcend this Central European 'value-vacuum'.

Hugo von Hofmannstahl was the great-grandson of one of the founders and leaders of Vienna's Jewish community at the turn of the nineteenth century, Isaac Loew Hofmann (1759–1849).[12] Descended from a poor immigrant Bohemian family, Isaac Loew Hofmann had been permitted to reside in Vienna in 1788 as a wholesale merchant. Ten years later he had established the manufacture of silk in Austria, freeing it from dependence on Italian imports.[13] Loew Hofmann also helped to develop the Austrian potash industry. In 1835 he was knighted by Emperor Ferdinand I as Edler von Hofmannstahl. His coat of arms depicted the Decalogue along with a silkwork, a mulberry leaf, and a poor-box. Very active in the Jewish community, this ennobled philanthropist was one of the founders of the Vienna 'Temple', generally supporting the orthodox conservative viewpoint in religious affairs.[14] His son August Emil von Hofmann married Petronella von Rho (an Italian Catholic from a Milanese patrician family) in 1839 and their children were brought up in the Catholic faith and the social milieu of the Austrian lower nobility.

The poet's half-Jewish father, the lawyer and bank director Dr Hugo Hofmann von Hofmannstahl (1841–1915), also married a Catholic, from Austrian and Swabian peasant stock. Having lost most of the family fortune in the Viennese Stock Market crash of 1873, his father adopted the more modest life-style of a bourgeois patrician loyal to the Empire and orientated towards the classic Austrian values of aesthetic *Bildung*.[15] Thanks to his father's devotion, Hugo von

[10] Broch, 'Hofmannstahl und seine Zeit', 170.

[11] Ibid. 173–5. Broch's description of Vienna as the metropolis of kitsch was based on the presupposition that in this city a minimum of ethical values was masked by a maximum of 'aesthetic values'.

[12] On Isaac Loew Hofmann, see *Österreichische Wochenschrift*, no. 28 (1911), pp. 265–7; H. Schnee, *Die Hoffinanz und der moderne Staat* 3 vols. (Berlin, 1953–5), iv. 335; and Max Grunwald, *Vienna* (Philadelphia, 1936), 207–8.

[13] Grunwald, p. 208.   [14] Ibid. 374.   [15] Broch, pp. 179–80.

Hofmannstahl grew up in a family environment highly favourable to individual self-cultivation and the development of his precocious literary talent.

Though never explicitly denying his Jewish ancestry, Hofmannstahl's vague hints of it, whether in poetry or drama, betray a distinct malaise. Hermann Broch linked this uneasiness to the strange 'inner anti-Semitism' of assimilated Jewry, produced by identification with the collective narcissism of the ruling classes and the painful memory of distant humiliations.[16] Thus as a young reserve-officer serving in Galicia in 1896 in the poverty-stricken Jewish village of Tlumacz, Hofmannstahl was frankly appalled at the stench and misery that surrounded him. In a letter to his father on 5 May 1896 he complained bitterly of his living quarters 'full of stinking Jews and stinking small horses'.[17] Even in some of his finest literary work, including the post-war tragedy *Der Turm*, where there appears a converted Jewish character Simon who speaks in a caricatured Yiddish dialect, one can find conventional anti-Semitic stereotypes, linking Jews to money.[18] The depiction of marginal Jewish figures in some of Hofmannstahl's pre-war dramas like *Das gerettete Venedig* demonstrates the same tendency to rely on facile second-hand Christian stereotypes concerning Jewish occupations, manners, and linguistic peculiarities. In spite of Hofmannstahl's concern and compassion for the poor in general, he showed no sympathy for the specific nature of Jewish misery or the remotest interest in radical movements like Socialism and Zionism which sought to provide concrete solutions to the problems of Jewry. Though he corresponded with Herzl (who had warmly encouraged his poetic gifts) he never once hinted at his Zionist involvements, even in the letter of condolences which he sent to the *Neue Freie Presse*, following the latter's early death.[19]

More significantly, Hofmannstahl avoided as far as possible any discussion of the 'Jewish question' in his very extensive correspondence with two of his closest literary friends, Arthur Schnitzler and Richard

[16] Ibid. 186. Broch observed that the collective narcissim of an assimilated minority frequently exceeded that of the assimilating ruling class or nation, while retaining an element of knowing self-irony. '. . . der Assimilierte empfindet sich damit als ein Auserwählter höhern Grades; er ist aus dem auserwählten Volk auserwählt worden.'

[17] Hugo von Hofmannstahl, *Briefe, 1890–1901* (Vienna, 1937), i. 184–6, 4–5 May 1896.

[18] See the detailed and balanced assessment of Ernst Simon, 'Hugo von Hofmannstahl: seine jüdischen Freunde und seine Stellung zum Judentum', *Mitteilungsblatt* (Tel Aviv), no. 38, 14 Oct. 1977, pp. 3–5.

[19] Ibid. 4. Hofmannstahl's distaste for Zionism can be safely assumed.

Beer-Hofmann (1866–1945). Schnitzler's *Der Weg ins Freie* provided an obvious opportunity to express an opinion on this critical problem in Austrian society, one moreover which his friend had eagerly solicited but which was not forthcoming.[20] The frank, extended treatment of anti-Semitism in Schnitzler's novel obviously disconcerted Hofmann-stahl as it did his half-Jewish literary friend, Leopold von Andrian.[21] So, too, did the growing Jewish national self-assertion and religious motifs in the work of Richard Beer-Hofmann after 1900, especially since the latter had long served as a kind of aesthetic role-model for the young poet.[22] Beer-Hofmann's biblical play, *Jaakobs Traum* (Jacob's Dream) finally prompted Hofmannstahl to accuse his friend in April 1919 of succumbing to 'chauvinism' and misplaced 'national pride'.[23] A month later, in another letter of May 1919, he apologetically claimed that the experiences of the First World War had rendered him hypersensitive to the slightest evocation of national sentiment.[24] Only in 1924 did Hofmannstahl appear to have overcome these negative feelings, graciously acknowledging that Beer-Hofmann like Dostoevsky may have found God through returning to his own people.[25] The gulf between the aristocratic cosmopolitan Austrianism of Hofmannstahl and the intensely Jewish ethnic pride of Beer-Hofmann (whose frequent use of the chosen people motif had a symbolic rather than any politically nationalist intent) reflected a familiar tension of Viennese life. Not only relationships between Jews and Gentiles, but also those between fully assimilated Jews and those who still preserved a degree of ethnic particularism, or between religious and apostate Jews could not ultimately escape strain and distortion.[26]

Hofmannstahl's evident malaise with regard to his Jewish ancestry was not uncharacteristic of many distinguished Viennese culture-creators who had converted to Christianity. Gustav Mahler (1860–

[20] *Mitteilungsblatt*, no. 38, 14 Oct. 1977, p. 4.

[21] Hugo von Hofmannstahl, *Briefwechsel mit Leopold von Andrian* (Frankfurt, 1968), 176.

[22] For the intimate relations between them, see Hofmannstahl, *Briefwechsel mit R. Beer-Hofmann* (Frankfurt, 1972); Olga Schnitzler, *Spiegelbild der Freundschaft* (Salzburg, 1962); and Michael Pollak, *Vienne 1900: Une identité blessée* (Paris, 1984), 135, 146–7, 176–8.

[23] See Hofmannstahl's letter of 20 Apr. 1919, in *Briefwechsel mit Beer-Hofmann*, 145.

[24] Letter of 23 May 1919, ibid. 167.   [25] Ibid. 176.

[26] See Hans Tramer, 'Einiges über Hugo von Hofmannstahl', *Mitteilungsblatt*, no. 39, 21 Oct. 1977, p. 5, for confirmation that Schnitzler distrusted Hofmannstahl's 'an Verleugnung grenzende Nichtbeachtung seiner jüdischen Abstammung'—an attitude consistent with the latter's desire for social acceptance in aristocratic circles. My thanks to Dr Eva Reichmann (London) for this reference.

1911), for ten years director of the Imperial Opera in Vienna and perhaps the last great symphonist of the nineteenth century, was a case in point. Mahler came from an impoverished petty-bourgeois Jewish family in southern Bohemia, dominated by a cruel, ruthless father permanently at odds with his long-suffering mother to whom Mahler was closely attached.[27] In an intimate conversation with Sigmund Freud in 1910 he reported that as a young child he had once dashed out of the house during a specially painful parental row and heard the hurdy-gurdy in the street grinding out a popular Viennese air, *Ach, du lieber Augustin*.[28] This incident with its conjunction of personal tragedy and light entertainment, deep emotion and sheer triviality, seems to have left a powerful impression on his inner mind and probably contributed to one of the hallmarks of his musical style—the unique and daring blend of sublime and mundane elements.

Mahler's impoverished provincial background and the anti-Jewish hostility he had encountered since childhood, made all the more obsessive and intense his desire to escape into the creative world of high culture through his brilliant musical gifts. Sent by his father to the Vienna conservatory in 1875, he graduated three years later and in 1880 began what was to be a spectacular professional career as a conductor.[29] During these formative years Mahler had become a close personal friend of the socialist Victor Adler, then still an ardent German nationalist, who strongly encouraged his musical development.[30] A passionate Wagnerian like Adler himself, Mahler was especially influenced by the German composer's vision of the redemptive role of the musical artist as the Poet-Priest of his generation.[31] Nevertheless, like Victor Adler, he could hardly identify with the *völkisch* nationalism of the Wagnerites or with the vicious

[27] Alma Mahler, *Erinnerungen an Gustav Mahler* (Frankfurt, 1980), 30–2.
[28] See the introd. by Donald Mitchell, ibid. 10–11. Freud had been consulted by Mahler during the psychoanalyst's visit to Leiden in the Netherlands in the summer of 1910. He confirmed the impact of the composer's unhappy early childhood on his later life and work.
[29] As a young man Mahler was aided by the Austrian Catholic composer Anton Bruckner who quickly recognized his talent. When talking to the Jewish musicians in his circle, Bruckner would politely address them as '*die Herren Israeliten*' (ibid. 135).
[30] William J. McGrath, *Dionysian Art and Populist Politics in Austria* (New Haven and London, 1974), 89 ff. Mahler was a regular participant at meetings of the Adler–Pernerstorfer circle which discussed philosophical, religious, and aesthetic theories. McGrath's book shows the influence of Schopenhauer, Nietzsche, and Wagner on Mahler's thinking in this formative period.
[31] McGrath, pp. 156–7. See also Alma Mahler, p. 106: 'Mahler und wir alle kämpften für Wagner. Mahler liebte Wagner ohne Vorbehalt.'

anti-Semitism that increasingly accompanied the Wagner cult.[32]
It was no accident that the racist Cosima Wagner (whom he had once
respected) subsequently sought to prevent his appointment in 1897 as
director of the Vienna Court Opera, a position which virtually
necessitated his conversion.[33]

Though his baptism was undertaken primarily for careerist reasons
Mahler was strongly attracted by Catholic mysticism, its religious as
well as its aesthetic components.[34] This Christian religiosity did not
drive Mahler to deny his Jewish origins, although he had long felt
estranged from Judaism and continued to be embarrassed by Jewish
jokes, by 'uncultivated' Jewish mannerisms and vulgar gesticulations.[35]
Nor did his conversion to Catholicism succeed in easing this sense of
malaise and alienation which cut far deeper than that felt by the
patrician Hofmannstahl. 'I am thrice homeless,' Mahler liked to
declare, 'as a native of Bohemia in Austria, as an Austrian among
Germans, and as a Jew throughout the world. Everywhere an intruder,
never welcome.'[36] Forced to abandon the cultural Pan-Germanism of
his youth by the rise of Viennese anti-Semitism (from which he
suffered acutely even at the peak of his dazzling career), Mahler could
never fully overcome his sense of homelessness. By the same token,
the multiple elements in his background—whether Slavic, Jewish,
German, or Catholic—gave a universal, cosmopolitan, and distinctively
'Austrian' quality to his music, reminiscent of Hofmannstahl's poetry
and drama.[37]

Mahler's extraordinary capacity for fusing diverse musical traditions
ranging from Viennese classicism and German romanticism to
provincial Austrian, Slavic, and Jewish folk-melodies was perhaps a
testament to his restless search for a universally valid mode of
expression. At the same time there was a rebellious subversive side to

[32] McGrath, p. 161. Also Mahler's characteristic belief in an argument with the
Germanic nationalist composer, Hans Pfitzner, 'dass je grosser ein Künstler sei, er desto
höher über den Nationen stehen müsse' (Alma Mahler, p. 109).

[33] Alma Mahler, p. 129.

[34] Ibid. 45. His wife, a free-thinker who had been brought up as a Catholic, noted the
striking paradox that in one of their first conversations 'ein Jude einer Christin
gegenüber sich heftig für Christus ereiferte'. Elsewhere she wrote: 'Er war christgläubig.
Er war Juden-Christ und hatte es schwer. Ich war Heiden-Christin und hatte es leicht.'

[35] Ibid. 129: 'Niemals durfte man vor Mahler jüdische Witze erzählen; er konnte sich
darüber ernsthaft erbösen.'

[36] Ibid. 137.

[37] See Hans Redlich's conclusion: 'Mahler's art works are permeated in a completely
unprecedented way by all the spiritual elements of the total Austrian complex.' Quoted
in McGrath, p. 161.

Mahler's art which placed it in opposition to the prevailing musical ideology of German romanticism. By integrating bizarre, vulgar, even burlesque elements into his first *Lieder* and symphonies, he seemed to be protesting against the self-satisfied satiety of nineteenth-century German bourgeois philistinism that had turned music into a kind of *Ersatzreligion*.[38] Mahler had, after all, experienced in childhood the evils of poverty, deprivation, and discrimination. He had witnessed the sufferings of the Czech proletariat at first hand. During his early years he had also absorbed the folk-songs and military marches of his native Bohemian province. Irony, pastiche, black humour, social criticism, and a deep sensitivity to suffering and death—all traits in some way linked to his Diasporic Jewish heritage—were as important in his artistic work as Dionysian notions of the vitality of nature.[39]

Acutely aware like Hofmannstahl of the need for the artist to find a way back to identification with the real world and the wholeness of existence, Mahler became obsessed with the search for depth and truth of expression.[40] Nevertheless, in the gigantism of his last great symphonies there appears a jarring, even hysterical, note of Christian triumphalism, which might be interpreted as a kind of over-compensation for past humiliations and an unresolved sense of insecurity that went back to his Jewish origins.[41]

Mahler's tortured search for artistic truth and mystical transcendence still took place within a relatively secure world though one to whose social tensions, inner malaise, and melancholy forebodings of doom he was keenly sensitive. His greatest disciple and successor, Arnold Schoenberg (1874–1951), shared Mahler's restlessness, his need for a security in faith, and perhaps even more acutely the pain of social rejection as a composer and a Jew.[42] Born in Vienna's Leopoldstadt

[38] Ulrich Schreiber, 'Gustave Mahler: une musique des contradictions sociales', *Critique*, 31, nos. 339–40 (août–sept. 1975), 927 ff.

[39] See ibid. 929 on the blending of popular art with classicism in Mahler.

[40] Ibid. 932 ff. Schreiber suggests a connection between Hofmannstahl and Mahler's response at the end of the 1890s to the crisis of impressionist aestheticism. In both artists one finds a similar preoccupation with re-establishing the unity of all Creation and the search for ways of expressing ultimate values such as the meaning of life in a world where the medium of communication appears to have temporarily broken down.

[41] Ibid. 935–6. Schreiber, following Adorno's *Mahler: Eine musikalische Physiognomik* (Frankfurt, 1960), argues that the triumphalism and Promethean scale of Mahler's last symphonies betray a compromise with the official art of the Christian establishment, symbolizing power and grandeur: 'De fait, la monstruosité de cette œuvre atteste, si l'on considère l'effet produit, l'identification de Mahler avec la bourgeoisie aryenne et chrétienne aggressive.'

[42] See Willi Reich, *Arnold Schönberg oder Der konservative Revolutionär* (Vienna, 1968).

district, the eldest son of Samuel and Pauline Schoenberg (née Nachod), his parents came from a typically poor, provincial orthodox Jewish background. His father arrived in Vienna from Hungarian-ruled Pressburg (his traditionalist mother came from a family of Prague tradesmen and tailors) and had soon shed the orthodox Judaism of his youth. In 1898 Arnold Schoenberg converted to Lutheranism, for a combination of careerist and cultural motives, linked *inter alia* to his admiration for the north German musical tradition.[43]

Already in his pre-1914 expressionist period, Schoenberg was a pugnacious intellectual revolutionary, whose musical experiments enraged the intransigently conservative musical tastes of the Viennese public.[44] Schoenberg's central innovation in this period was the rejection of tonality or, as he preferred to call it, the 'emancipation of dissonance'.[45] Between 1908 and 1913 in a series of music texts of relentless and morbid intensity that breathe some of the macabre, controlled hysteria of the new expressionism, Schoenberg began to break down the established hierarchies of Western music. A passionate Wagnerian like his mentor Gustav Mahler, Schoenberg felt in these early years a similar attraction to German neo-romanticism, to its belief in the sacred mission of the artist and its commitment to the mystical unity of man and cosmos. In Schoenberg's pre-war Viennese period, the 'emancipation of dissonance' gave however a sharper, more critical edge to this romantic tradition. Not only did the rejection of tonality destroy harmonic order and structure, it became a remarkably effective means for expressing musically the disorders of the psyche with a new and terrifying precision.[46]

In works like *Erwartung* (1909) and *Pierrot lunaire* (1912) Schoenberg did not, however, simply explore 'the dark powers' for the sake of greater psychological expressiveness. He was also responding to an inner moral imperative to shake a satiated, self-deceiving society out of its bourgeois complacency and comfort.[47] Like his fellow Viennese—Hofmannsthal in the realm of drama, Adolf Loos in the field of architecture, Wittgenstein in philosophy, and Karl Kraus in the

[43] Walter Rimler, 'Arnold Schoenberg's Judaism', *Midstream* (Apr. 1982), pp. 43–5.

[44] Charles Rosen, 'Schoenberg et l'expressionisme', *Critique*, 31, nos. 339–40 (août-sept. 1975, 909–18.

[45] Ibid. 911.

[46] See 'Explosion in the Garden: Kokoschka and Schoenberg', in Carl Schorske, *Fin-de-Siècle Vienna: Politics and Culture* (London, 1980), 344–64.

[47] Arnold Schoenberg, *Harmonielehre* (Vienna, 1911), 281.

critique of language—Schoenberg resolutely assaulted the citadel of Viennese aestheticism, substituting for beauty his own austere conceptions of musical truth. A painter, essayist, self-taught philosopher and musical theorist as well as revolutionary composer, Schoenberg saw himself as breaking through the final limits of the obsolete logic of Viennese bourgeois aesthetics.[48] At the same time his intellectual revolution in music, following upon that of Mahler, emphasized the supremacy of integrity and authenticity over the making of beautiful sounds.[49]

Schoenberg's fundamentally mystical temperament could not in the long run remain satisfied with purely destructive cultural criticism. Already in December 1912 he informed Richard Dehmel that for a long time he had been wanting to write an oratorio that would deal with 'modern man, who has passed through materialism, socialism and anarchy', while still retaining residues of ancient faith 'and finally succeeds in finding God and becoming religious'.[50] Schoenberg's return to a prophetic Judaism, which began during his Austrian army service after 1914 and gathered momentum in the 1920s, continued this trend of thought which was perfectly consistent with his pre-war puritanical revolt against Viennese aesthetics.[51]

During the First World War Schoenberg first appears to have become intensely preoccupied with contemporary Jewish problems and doubtful whether assimilation could succeed. It was at this time that he wrote his musically incomplete oratorio, *Die Jakobsleiter*, which already pointed the way to later dramas like *Der biblische Weg* (1926) with its advocacy of a home for the Jewish nation and to *Moses und Aron* (1932), his extraordinarily powerful twelve-tone opera glorifying Hebraic monotheism. These later works display an astonishing insight into the meaning and message of biblical Judaism. They should also be seen as a characteristically defiant response to the rise of National Socialist anti-Semitism and to the whole pseudo-Christian tradition of Wagnerian opera and music to which Schoenberg had once been attracted and which he now firmly repudiated.

Schoenberg's return to the Jewish prophetic heritage was undoubtedly accelerated by the intensification of German and Austrian

---

[48] See A. Janik and S. Toulmin, *Wittgenstein's Vienna* (New York, 1973), 106–12.

[49] Ibid. 111.

[50] Letter to Richard Dehmel, 13 Dec. 1912 in Arnold Schoenberg, *Briefe*, ed. Erwin Stein (Mainz, 1958).

[51] Schorske, pp. 360–1, briefly touches on this theme in connection with the opera *Moses und Aron*, but neglects to discuss the Jewish theme in any depth.

anti-Semitism after 1918. An incident in the Austrian resort of Mattsee near Salzburg in 1922, when he was unexpectedly asked by the local council to produce a certificate of baptism, acted as a catalyst.[52] This traumatic episode seems to have finally confirmed to Schoenberg what he had suspected for some time—namely that assimilation was an imposture. Shortly afterwards, he wrote to his painter friend, Wassily Kandinsky: 'What I was forced to learn during the past year, I have now at last understood and shall never forget it again. Namely, that I am no German, no European, maybe not even a human being—at any rate the Europeans prefer the worst of their own race to me—but that I am a Jew.'[53] Schoenberg declared himself quite 'satisfied at this state of affairs' and assured his Russian friend (who was hardly a philo-Semite) that he did not wish to be treated as an an exceptional Jew any longer. In another combative letter to Kandinsky in May 1923, Schoenberg prophetically warned:

What is anti-Semitism to lead to if not acts of violence? Is it too difficult to imagine this? For you it may be sufficient to deprive the Jews of their rights. Then Einstein, Mahler, myself and many others will have to be got rid of. But one thing is certain; they will not be able to exterminate those much tougher elements thanks to whose powers of resistance Jewry has perpetuated itself unaided against the whole mankind for two thousand years. For they apparently are organized in such a way that they can fulfil the task God has given them: to preserve themselves in exile, pure and unbroken, till the hour of redemption will come![54]

Arnold Schoenberg's definitive return to the ancient teachings and history of Judaism as a source of musical and philosophic inspiration took place after the collapse of the Habsburg Empire. His conviction that a national renaissance, culminating in the political restoration of the Jewish people in the land of Israel, was an urgent necessity of the hour, crystallized only in the 1920s. But henceforth he would consistently advocate a return of the 'Chosen People' to its land, its way of life, ideals, ethics, and constititution as promulgated in ancient times.[55]

---

[52] Rimler, p. 44.

[53] Letter to Wassily Kandinsky, 20 Apr. 1923, in Schoenberg, *Briefe*, 90. Schoenberg, having heard that some of the leaders at the Weimer Bauhaus centre had made anti-Semitic pronouncements, declined Kandinsky's invitation to collaborate in the project.

[54] Letter of 4 May 1923, ibid. 91 ff.

[55] See Peter Gradenwitz, 'Gustav Mahler and Arnold Schoenberg', *Leo Baeck Yearbook*, 5 (1960), 269 ff. for a detailed elaboration of this later phase in Schoenberg's development which lies beyond the chronological scope of our analysis.

This adoption of the biblical road and the Mosaic mission was indeed unusual but by no means unparalleled for a Viennese Jewish artist and thinker before 1918. The most striking literary parallel for such an attempt to restate for modern man the Hebraic position on fundamental questions was afforded by the Austrian poet and playwright, Richard Beer-Hofmann. Like Schoenberg, Beer-Hofmann's biblical awakening was fully consummated only during and after the First World War but his return to Judaism had already taken place much earlier, at the end of the 1890s. The roots of his dramatic biblical trilogy, beginning with *Jaakobs Traum* (1918), later to be followed by *Der junge David* (1933) and a third play, *Vorspiel auf dem Theater zu Koenig David* (1936) which was never completed, belong therefore to the Viennese *fin de siècle*.[56]

Born in 1866 into a lawyer's family of Bohemian-Moravian origin which had moved to Vienna in the mid-nineteenth century, Richard Beer had lost his mother at birth and was brought up by his childless uncle, the Viennese industrialist Alois Hofmann, whose name he subsequently attached to his own.[57] Free from financial constraints as the sole heir of the family and allowed to develop his talents without hindrance, Beer-Hoffman studied law at the University of Vienna, from which he graduated with a Doctorate in Jurisprudence in 1890. He was immediately drawn into the 'Young Vienna' literary group, where he formed warm friendships with its leading lights, Hermann Bahr, Arthur Schnitzler, Hugo von Hofmannstahl, Felix Salten, Peter Altenberg, and Theodor Herzl.

The twenty-five-year-old Beer-Hofmann was affectionately regarded in this circle as an elegant dandy and sparkling, witty conversationalist. His early short stories published in the slim volume, *Novellen* (1893), attracted attention for their finely chiselled psychological perceptions, though Beer-Hofmann did not subsequently consider them worthy of inclusion in his collected works.[58] They revolved in the main around

---

[56] The best short summary of Beer-Hofmann's work in its relation to the Jewish rebirth is by Sol Liptzin in J. Fraenkel (ed.), *The Jews of Austria: Essays on their Life, History and Destruction* (London, 1967), 213–19. See also Liptzin's introductory biographical essay to the Eng. trans. of Beer-Hofmann's *Jacob's Dream: A Prologue* (Philadelphia, 1946), 1–26.

[57] The archives of the Beer-Hofmann family in the Leo Baeck Institute, New York, have been consulted by the author. They include letters to his wife beginning from 1896, photographs, personal documents, and other family correspondence. See Richard Beer-Hofmann Collection and also that of his daughter, Miriam Beer-Hofmann Lens, LBI New York, AR 7258.

[58] See Richard Beer-Hofmann, *Gesammelte Werke* (Frankfrut, 1963). Beer-

classic motifs of Viennese literary epicureanism—the problems posed
by casual liaisons and the dissatisfactions of a frivolous, irresponsible
existence without personal commitment. Yet already in his novelette
Das Kind (1893) Beer-Hofmann began to touch on themes like the
responsibility of the individual for his fate and the link between parents
and children which were to preoccupy him in later life.

Beer-Hofmann's marriage to an Austrian Catholic who converted to
Judaism and the birth of his first daughter in 1898 inspired a beautiful
and moving philosophic lullaby, *Schlaflied für Miriam*, whose poetic
version of the unity of generations was to mark a definite turning-point
in his creativity. The last stanza reverberated with echoes of his Jewish
ancestral past and the responsibility to transmit it intact to coming
generations.

> Asleep, my Miriam?—Miriam, my child,
> We are but banks of a river, and wild
> Flows through us blood of our past, rushing loud
> On to the morrow, unresting and proud.
> In us are all—none, none is alone.
> You are their life and their life is your own—
> Miriam—my life and my child—sleep on![59]

Beer-Hofmann's only novel, *Der Tod Georgs*, completed in 1900,
expressed in its concluding chapter a similar sense of the unity and
continuity of Jewish existence. In the novel, the hero Paul has hitherto
led a futile, decadent existence until the death of a friend shakes him
out of his morbidly empty pursuit of pleasure. 'Out of darkness and
confusion emerged before him a new life . . . He saw the life he had
lived until now sinking behind him. Only his destiny was real.'[60] This
destiny that he discovered was shared in common with all those whose
'blood flowed in him', whose victories were those of God and whose
defeats were God's judgement: 'they [his Jewish ancestors] appointed
themselves for the role of witness to His power—a people of

Hofmann's output was not large (a constant source of reproach from his friends
Schnitzler and Hofmannstahl) and there were long fallow periods between his carefully
crafted writings.

[59] See Liptzin, in Austria, 215.

[60] See *Gesammelte Werke*, 616, 621–2; also Hartmut Scheible, *Literarischer Jugendstil
in Wien* (Munich and Zurich, 1984), 104. Scheible describes the turn to the continuity of
the past through dreams and symbolic correspondences as an attempt of Young
Viennese writers to overcome the deep split between their self and external reality. In
Beer-Hofmann's case, the turn away from aesthetic self-criticism to a search for the
place of the individual within the 'totality of life', led to 'inner Zionism'.

saviours.'⁶¹ Thus it was through the Jewish blood in his veins, his proud consciousness of descent and of the powerful religious idea of Divine Justice that the hapless aesthete Paul was able to transcend his endemic alienation and disorientation.⁶² The discovery of Judaism had liberated him from narcissistic aestheticism, brought him to the realization of his true mission in life, embodied in that of generations of ancestors.

Ancestors, who wandered in rags and in disgrace, from country to country . . . every man's hand against them, despised by the lowest but never despising themselves, honouring their God but not as a beggar honours the giver of alms, calling out in their sufferings not to a Lord of Mercy, but to the God of Justice . . . And beyond these ancestors, a people which did not beg for grace but wrestled fiercely for the blessings of its Deity, a people wandering through seas, unimpeded by deserts, ever aware of a God of Justice as of the blood in its veins . . .⁶³

It was through these ancestors who had voluntarily chosen the agony of pain and the ecstasy of redemption that Paul and his creator Beer-Hofmann expressed their commitment to the prophetic message of the Bible. Beer-Hofmann's intuitive Zionism was inextricably linked to this belief in a common Jewish fate and responsibility, to the awareness of belonging to an ethnic group which had chosen to bear witness to the God of Justice. This belief gave meaning to the apparent chaos and inscrutability of existence and preserved Beer-Hofmann from the endemic pessimism that characterized so much of *fin-de-siècle* Viennese literature. Without this feeling of being 'chosen' to accomplish a divine mission, Beer-Hofmann once told Schnitzler, he could not live.⁶⁴ It was this same conviction drawn from the Bible that sparked his poetic imagination and gave a unique quality of timelessness to his religious dramas, especially *Jacob's Dream*.⁶⁵

---

⁶¹ Scheible, 157 ff. Hofmannstahl retrospectively criticized the 'chauvinist' theme in *Der Tod Georgs* after reading *Jaakobs Traum* in 1918. He was clearly rattled by Beer-Hofmann's evocation of the 'chosen people' motif. For the latters reply, see *Hofmannstahl–Beer-Hofmann: Briefwechsel*, 148 ff.

⁶² Scheible, pp. 160–1.

⁶³ Richard Beer-Hofmann, *Der Tod Georgs* (Berlin, 1900), 215–16; *Gesammelte Werke*, 621–2.

⁶⁴ See Olga Schnitzler, pp. 125–53, for an intimate portrait of Beer-Hofmann by Schnitzler's widow which casts much light on their relationship.

⁶⁵ Ibid. 147. Schnitzler, in spite of his scepticism and indifference to religion, was deeply impressed by Beer-Hofmann's personality and poetic gifts. 'Es gibt kaum einen Anderen, der als Mensch so leuchtet, so einleuchtet. Ich liebe ihn sehr.' On *Jacob's Dream*, he noted: '. . . ein edles reines hohes Werk, wie es nur ein Mensch höchsten

Beer-Hofmann's rediscovery of Judaism at the end of the 1890s had led to his immersion in Jewish history and in the biblical roots of his heritage. Henceforth all his works were to bear the imprint of this identification. Even in his first drama *Der Graf von Charolais* (1904), which won the prestigious *Volksschillerpreis*, he introduced an original Jewish character, the creditor Itzig, into a plot based on a post-Elizabethan English tragedy (*The Fatal Dowry*, 1632, by Philip Massinger and Nathan Field). The father of this medieval Jew had been burnt at the stake by the Inquisition, which made Itzig unyielding and misanthropic in character. Accused by the hero Charolais of being an 'evil man', he defiantly responds:

> And why should I be kind to you?
> Give me one reason—a single one!
> Or do you think I should be kind because all human beings
> should be kind to each other?
> First, my Lord, tear out this heart contracted and
> convulsed by the affliction of a thousand wrongs;
> Put out these eyes and give me other eyes
> That are not wounded by too much of weeping;
> Smooth out my back that's bent to crookedness
> With bowing down in enforced humbleness;
> And give me other feet unwearied
> by the eternal wandering of exile.[66]

Beer-Hofmann was acutely sensitive to the duality of Jewish 'chosenness', both the blessing and the curse, the pain and the glory in the burden that Israel had taken on itself in history. This theme was basic to *Jacob's Dream* (a prologue to the planned trilogy built around the life of King David) which Beer-Hofmann began in May 1909 and completed in July 1915. It was only published at the end of the First World War, at the very moment of Austria-Hungary's final collapse.[67]

The play contrasts the biblical Jacob, an eternal seeker and doubter, full of mysterious dreams and longings, with the hunter Edom/Esau, his twin brother, who is the earthly, practical realist sated with possessions, food, drink, and women. In Jacob's vision at Beth-El where he makes a Covenant with God, the archangel Michael

---

Ranges schreiben konnte.' In 1917 Olga Schnitzler reports: 'Er las das erste Bild Davids vor: schön. Ein wahrhaft adeliger Mensch. Wie viele gibt es noch neben ihm?'

[66] Quoted in Solomon Liptzin in his introd. to *Jacob's Dream*, 6–7, from a trans. by Ludwig Lewisohn.

[67] Liptzin, *Jacob's Dream*, 8–9.

promises him that from his loins a people will spring, who will be a light to the nations and bear the divine message to the world: but at the same time the angel of darkness warns him of the price of martyrdom to be born by the eternal people. They would become homeless, be driven from place to place, be surrounded by envy and hatred.

> Thou chosen one, thou blessing to all peoples—
> Where grows the shame, the insult unknown to you?
> Your body, your mind are a disgust for all!
> They spit upon thy face . . .[68]

Each nation to whom his descendants cling, the angel Samael warns Jacob, 'shall burn thee out like an ulcer—to the root!'. Israel would become God's sacrifice, his punishment, his alibi to the nations, 'by all the world more hated than plague or poisonous weed or raving brute!'[69]

Yet Jacob is not dissuaded from accepting the Covenant, even though it means accepting the fate of being God's whipping-boy, whose suffering back must bear the lash of godhood that it may be brought to the recalcitrant nations.

> Lord, what Thy will imposes soon or late—
> I'll bear it not as yoke—but as a crown!
> If Thou did'st choose my blood to be a torch
> Which flaming burns above the nations' ways,
> Let none that from my blood come forth
> forget, Ever forget, my God,
> Thy holy choice![70]

No other Viennese writer was so proudly to affirm his faith in the historic fate of the Jews; a faith which reached its apotheosis in his stirring drama of 1933, *Der junge David*, completed in the year of Nazi ascendancy in Germany. None would succeed in transmuting so movingly the cataclysmic events of the age into eternal symbols beyond the perturbations of the moment. The art of Beer-Hofmann was nationalist only in a visionary and messianic sense, predicated on the conviction that it was better to suffer injustice than to commit it, to triumph through the spirit rather than through the illusory might of the sword. At the same time the poet believed passionately in the Jewish cultural renaissance and in the return of Israel to its land as a great act of historic restitution and reconciliation. Though strongly attached to

---

[68] Beer-Hofmann, *Jacob's Dream*, 164.
[69] Ibid.   [70] Ibid. 172.

the atmosphere and colours of the Austrian landscape, Beer-Hofmann's whole outlook was always closer to the biblical prophets with their universal vision of the relation between God and man, suffering, and redemption.

A similar revival of Hebrew humanism can be found in the writings of the religious philosopher Martin Buber (1878–1965), also a native of Vienna, whose breadth of poetic vision and concept of dialogue would subsequently achieve universal resonance.[71] Despite his Viennese origins and his central role in the Jewish national renaissance during the twentieth century, Buber touches our story only tangentially. His spiritual centre of gravity even before 1914 lay in Germany rather than Austria-Hungary. Nevertheless, once he entered the University of Vienna in 1896 to study philosophy and art history, Buber began to absorb the distinctive cultural influences of the Habsburg metropolis. In particular, his involvement with the world Zionist movement was a direct outgrowth of his encounter in Vienna with Theodor Herzl.

Martin Buber's Austrian regional roots were even more significant since his early formative years between 1800 and 1892 were spent in the East Galician capital of Lemberg, at the home of his grandfather, Salomon Buber (1827–1906). Salomon Buber was not only a bank director and central community figure in Lemberg but a leading *maskil* and Midrashic scholar who spoke fluent Hebrew. From his Galician grandfather Martin Buber first acquired his fascination for philology, his knowledge of Hebrew, of Jewish traditions and Hasidic folklore. The fusion between his encounters with Hasidism in Galicia and Bukovina and the Western culture (Polish as well as German) imbibed at the Polish language Gymnasium in Lemberg, opened the road to Buber's unique role as a cultural intermediary between East and West. Thus his Austrian background provided the crucial formative experiences which explain why it was Martin Buber who, more than any other single individual, would help transform Western perceptions (whether Jewish or Gentile) of the *Ostjuden*.[72]

---

[71] See the chapter on Buber in Solomon Liptzin's *Germany's Stepchildren* (Philadelphia, 1961), 255 ff., which touches very briefly on some parallels with Beer-Hoffman. Significantly, Buber introduced Beer-Hofmann's *Gesammelte Werke*, and sensed the affinities in their approach to Jewish issues.

[72] See the chapter on Buber in Steven E. Aschheim, *Brothers and Strangers: The East European Jew in German and German Jewish Consciousness 1800–1923* (Madison, 1983), 121–38, and the instructive article by Paul Mendes-Flohr, '*Fin-de-siècle* Orientalism, the *Ostjuden* and the Aesthetics of Jewish Self-Affirmation', *Studies in Contemporary Jewry*, i (1984), 96–138.

However, Buber's first student year in Vienna (1896) coincided, ironically enough, with the peak of his estrangement from Jewish problems in spite of his reading Herzl's *Judenstaat*. It was at precisely this time that the young Buber made his literary début with four essays in Polish for readers of *Przegląd tygodniowy* (Polish weekly) on the leading authors of 'Young Vienna'.[73] Remarkably enough, in these short essays Buber never once mentioned or even hinted at the Jewishness of his subjects, Arthur Schnitzler and Peter Altenberg, or the Jewish origins of Hugo von Hofmannstahl. His admiration for these three writers (and for Hermann Bahr) is none the less apparent, revealing that for the young aesthete, Viennese impressionism was a significant, if passing phase in his evolving sensibility. In the poetry of Hofmannstahl, the nineteen-year-old Buber found a majestic, melodious sense of form, and 'an extraordinary subtle sense for minute psychic nuances' though he felt much less affinity for the 'soft, unmasculine lassitude' of his work. In Schnitzler, Buber detected a perfect mastery of theatrical form that uncannily erased the boundaries and dissonances between reality and illusion;[74] while in Peter Altenberg, Vienna's eccentric Bohemian poet, Buber singled out for attention his boundless compassion for all living beings, a moving warmth and spontaneity which bore the stamp of a strong, individual personality.

The young Buber, like Beer-Hofmann, could not long remain satisfied with this impressionist aestheticism. In 1898 while still a student he joined Herzl's Zionist movement, three years later accepting the editorship of *Die Welt*, though he was to resign after only a few months.[75] The central source of conflict arose over Buber's membership of the Democratic Fraction (an internal opposition to Herzl) and his advocacy of Aḥad Ha-am's *Kulturzionismus* against political Zionism. Like the Russian Zionist and his Austrian predecessor Nathan Birnbaum, Buber believed that the cultural renaissance of Judaism rather than anti-Semitism must be made the fountain and driving-force of Zionism. Education was more important than a

---

[73] See William M. Johnston, 'Martin Buber's Literary Debut: "On Viennese Literature" (1897)', in *The German Quarterly*, 47 (Nov. 1974), 556–66, for the Eng. trans. of these articles. I am grateful to Professor Johnston for drawing my attention to these interesting texts.

[74] Ibid. 565.

[75] See Martin Buber, *Briefwechsel aus sieben Jahrzehnten*, i, *1897–1918* (Heidelberg, 1972), 160–3, 166, 170–3, 192–3, 199–200, for correspondence between Buber and Herzl during the period between 1898 and 1903.

programme of propaganda. Moreover, Buber criticized Herzl for reducing a living movement to a mere party and the Jewish question to a matter of physical existence (*Judenheitsfrage*) instead of raising it to the status of a problem of Judaism (*Judentumsfrage*).

Herzl, with his failure to perceive the organic nature of the national movement in Eastern Europe, remained in Buber's eyes a typically rootless Western Jew without any sense of tradition and no 'Jewish' elements at all in his personality.[76] A letter from Herzl warning him against opposition and urging him to find his way back into the movement had left a bitter impression on the young Buber, which somewhat jaundiced his judgement.[77] Herzl, he was ready to concede, had given an organizational form to Zionism but Buber still wondered in 1904 whether the movement created by him had not been a 'premature birth'.[78] Only in 1910, six years after the founder's death, did a more balanced picture emerge with Buber acknowledging Herzl's greatness as a man of 'spontaneous action' (*Elementaraktiver*), one whose deficiencies were conditioned precisely by his over-whelming will to activism.[79]

Unlike Herzl, Buber's cultural Zionism had been significantly influenced by the then fashionable Central European vocabulary of blood and *Volk*, tempered by Enlightenment traditions of *Bildung* and an evident desire to humanize nationalism. Certainly, discriminatory racism in the Germanic sense was utterly remote from Buber's mind. In a manner more reminiscent of Beer-Hofmann, the young Buber saw the individual Jew as an organic part of a link in the chain of generations. There was a collective fate, a common folk substance, a supra-individual unity of Jewish destiny which, Buber argued, lived within each Jew; obscure, inherited forces within his own inner self helped to determine his personality and linked every Jew to the ancient past of Israel. Buber was convinced that the Jew had first to become conscious of this past, of his tribal roots and the deepest layers of the collective self that stemmed from his heredity, before he could become creative in the service of his community. This neo-romanticist appeal to Jewish wholeness and self-affirmation, to the overcoming of the 'deep cleft in our being' expressed above all in his *Drei Reden über*

[76] See Buber's cool, even arrogant obituary, 'Theodor Herzl' (1904), in Martin Buber, *Die jüdische Bewegung*, i, 1900–1914 (Berlin, 1920), 137–51; and the equally harsh criticisms in 'Herzl und die Historie' (1904), in ibid. 152–73.

[77] Ibid. 167.

[78] Ibid. 170: 'Fast will es mir erscheinen, dass es zu früh geschah.'

[79] Ibid. 195 ff.: 'Er und wir. Zu Theodor Herzls 50. Geburtstag.'

das Judentum (1911)—originally delivered to the Prague student organization, Bar-Kochba—exercised a strong attraction on Zionist youth in the Habsburg Monarchy. Linked to the search for an authentic community (*Gemeinschaft*) and to the revolt of the youth movements against urbanism, bourgeois materialism, and sterile rationalism, Buberian teachings also became an important influence in the early history of radical Zionist groups like the Galician (and Viennese) Hashomer Hatzair.[80]

Buber's impact on pre-war Jewish youth in the Monarchy derived from his ability to synthesize Zionism with modern intellectual currents and from his acknowledged status as a leading German thinker. No less important was Buber's revelation of the intense spirituality of East European Jewish life to the educated public in the West through his presentations of Hasidism. No single Jewish thinker in the first decade of the twentieth century did more than Martin Buber to transform the negative rationalist stereotypes of *Ostjuden* in the eyes of assimilated Western Jews. Clearly this transfiguration owed much to Buber's Austro-Galician roots, his sensitivity to mystical and neo-romantic currents in German culture, and his ability to package Hasidic religiosity in an aesthetically satisfying manner. Even the patrician Hugo von Hofmannsthal, so remote from the world of *Ostjudentum*, was profoundly moved by reading Buber's *Rabbi Nachmann* in 1906.[81] Buber's emphasis on the formative power of myth and mysticism in the search for the unity of life, and his evocation of a movement (Hasidism) that seemed to channel irrationalism into positive social action, must have struck a responsive chord in Hofmannsthal's own thinking.[82]

Long before reading Buber, Hugo von Hofmannsthal had grasped the devitalizing consequences of a purely aesthetic attitude to life in which the individual remained divorced from external reality and positive deeds. As early as 1893 in his playlet *Der Tor und der Tod* (The Fool and Death), which Buber much admired, Hofmannsthal had manifested his clear desire to escape from this threatening void of self-enclosed narcissistic sensibility. Like many other Austrian artists of his generation, he too recognized the claims of instinctual life but sought to channel them after 1900 through the more dynamic form of

---

[80] See Elkana Margalit, 'Social and Intellectual Origins of the Hashomer Hatzair Youth Movement, 1913–20', *Journal of Contemporary History*, 4, no. 2 (1969), 25–46.

[81] Letter of Hofmannsthal to Buber, 20 June 1906, in Buber, *Briefwechsel*, i. 243.

[82] Aschheim, p. 130.

historical and mythological dramas that would reconstitute the living reality of a culture that was already breaking into fragments.[83]

Working within the framework of Habsburg traditionalism, Hofmannstahl sought to find a way back to the spiritual unity of the Austrian *Volk* through the use of language, myths, symbols, and a quasi-mystical evocation of traditional, hierarchic order.[84] Obsessed like other conservative Austrian intellectuals with the prospect of fragmentation, disintegration, and collapse, he looked to art miraculously to reconstruct on a symbolic, dream-like level the unity of Emperor and people.[85] His supranational myth of a cosmopolitan Austrianism can be seen as a last desperate attempt 'to reconcile all the component parts of a disintegrating culture', to restore historic continuity, aesthetic cohesion, and a central focus of identification 'which alone could resist the tendency of things to "fall apart" '.[86] For this act of symbolic unification, Hofmannstahl went back not only to the Catholic-Baroque heritage of Vienna but also to cultural models from the Middle Ages, from Venice, Florence, Spain, the Low Countries and England as well as to the universalism of the Goethian Enlightenment.

Hofmannstahl displayed in his highly developed historical intuition a similar respect for the influence of the past to that found in the work of Beer-Hofmann and Martin Buber; the belief in a formative power that shapes not only culture and society but the life of each individual. But in Hofmannstahl's case alone was it also his sense of the State as the 'alliance of past generations with later ones, and vice versa' (Adam Müller) which brought him to serve the conservative cause of Habsburg supranationalism. For Hofmannstahl, attachment to his native land necessarily presupposed the prism of the Imperial Habsburg State and loyalty to a cosmopolitan Austrian culture whose unfolding retrospectively appeared to him as the product of a natural organic process.[87]

In 1917 his Austrian patriotism led him sharply to distinguish between the characteristics of his countrymen and those of their Prusso-German allies.[88] Austria was for Hofmannstahl the embodi-

---

[83] Schorske, 'Politics and Psyche in *Fin-de-siècle* Vienna: Schnitzler and Hofmannstahl', *The American Historical Review*, 66 (1960–1), 943 ff.

[84] Broch, pp. 208 ff. [85] Ibid. 232 ff., 253.

[86] *Hofmannstahl, Three Essays*, trans. Michael Hamburger (Princeton, 1972), 13.

[87] See introd. by Hermann Broch to Hugo von Hofmannstahl, *Selected Prose* (London, 1952), pp. xlii–xliii.

[88] See the table entitled 'Prussian and Austrian', drawn up by Hofmannstahl in 1917

ment of organic, instinctive qualities, held together by love of home, by supreme confidence in the Crown, and by a culture which, in spite of its pluralism, unified and shaped its dense social texture; whereas Prussian Germany remained an artificial structure bound together by an authoritarian State, a powerful army, imposed discipline, and a homogeneous officialdom that masked profound social and cultural divisions. In Hofmannstahl's comparison, the individual Austrian emerges as essentially traditional in his views, adaptable, balanced, and far more self-ironic that the Prussian. He rejects every abstract dialectic, avoids crisis, prefers to keep things vague, and quietly seeks the preponderance of the private realm.[89]

The strength of the Prussians, on the other hand, lay in their self-reliance, their functional, masculine qualities, love of logical abstractions, and their will to fight for their rights. They lacked, however, an organic sense of history; moreover, they displayed no capacity to enter other people's thoughts nor any openness to new impressions. Hence, they tended to be arrogant, self-righteous, hectoring and pushy—forcing crises instead of letting things go in true Austrian fashion. Not only this Prusso-Austrian antithesis but also Hofmannstahl's aphorisms reveal that he saw clearly enough all the character-defects of the Germans, the poverty of their social life, their gracelessness, inaptitude for politics, and the masculine brutality of their nationalism—traits alien to his more receptive Austrian temperament.

Hofmannstahl's aversion for the politics of nationalism was shared by most of the leading Austrian Jewish writers of his generation, including one of his staunchest admirers, Stefan Zweig.[90] In Zweig's work the Enlightenment belief in *Bildung*, humanity, the primacy of individual development and personal relationships reached its supreme apotheosis. Much more than with Hofmannstahl, the focus of his interest was always humanity as a whole and he devoted most of his adult life to the transcendence of artificial barriers between different nations and creeds.[91] There was something at once profoundly

when he already had second thoughts about the wartime alliance with Imperial Germany, in *Hofmannstahl, Three Essays*, 118–19.

[89] Ibid. 119.

[90] See Zweig, *The World of Yesterday*, 46 ff.: 'In universal literature I know no example of anyone, with the exception of Keats and Rimbaud, who at so early an age attained such a flawless mastery of speech, such elevation of ideals, or such saturation with the substance of poetry . . . as this majestic genius . . .' (translation adapted by author).

[91] See George L. Mosse, *German Jews beyond Judaism* (Hebrew Union College, 1985), 20; also Leon Botstein, 'Stefan Zweig and the Illusion of the Jewish European', in Marion Sonnenfeld (ed.), *Stefan Zweig* (Albany, NY, 1983), 90 ff.

Viennese and very Jewish in this cultural stance beyond religion and nationalism, which resolutely clung to an individualistic bourgeois humanism in the face of mounting currents of social and political barbarism.[92]

In his beautifully written autobiography, *The World of Yesterday* (the biography of an age even more than of a person), Zweig gave full play to both the Viennese and Jewish aspects in explaining his belief in the priority of culture over politics:

There is hardly a city in Europe where the drive towards cultural ideals was as passionate as it was in Vienna. Precisely because the monarchy, because Austria itself for centuries had been neither politically ambitious nor particularly successful in its military actions, the native pride had turned more strongly towards a desire for artistic supremacy.[93]

Zweig observed that Vienna was a capital where 'all the streams of European culture converged'; where German, Slavonic, Hungarian, Spanish, Italian, French, and Flemish blood had freely mixed, at court, among the nobility and the people. The *genius loci* of this city of music lay precisely in its ability harmoniously to dissolve these manifold contrasts and assimilate them into something specifically Austrian and Viennese. 'Hospitable and endowed with a particular talent for receptivity, the city drew the most diverse forces to it, loosened, propitiated, and pacified them. It was sweet to live here, in this atmosphere of spiritual conciliation, and subconsciously every citizen became supernational, cosmopolitan, a citizen of the world.'[94]

For all the obvious elements of idealization and unconscious self-projection in this picture, Zweig rightly puts his finger on the fact that 'fanaticism for art' (especially theatromania) touched all classes in Vienna.

Making music, dancing, the theatre, conversation, proper and urbane deportment, these were cultivated here as particular arts. It was not the military, nor the political, nor the commercial, that was predominant in the life of the individual and of the masses. The first glance of the average Viennese into his morning paper was not at the events in parliament, or world affairs, but at the repertoire of the theatre, which assumed so important a role in public life as was hardly possible in any other city.[95]

[92] Mosse, p. 25, unfortunately overlooks the Austrian roots of Zweig's attitude, treating him solely as the exemplar of a specific German-Jewish heritage of *Bildung*.
[93] Zweig, *The World of Yesterday*, 12.
[94] Ibid. 13.
[95] Ibid. 14–15.

The intuitive sense of form and celebration of artistic endeavour which characterized Vienna as a city had also been transmitted to its Jewish bourgeoisie who emerged by the end of the nineteenth century as the leading patrons, audience, and consumers of the capital's cultural life. Without this ceaselessly stimulating Jewish interest, Zweig observed, Vienna would have remained as far behind Berlin in artistic matters as Austria trailed politically behind the German Reich. 'Whosoever wished to put through something in Vienna, or came to Vienna as a guest from abroad and sought appreciation as well as an audience, was dependent on the Jewish bourgeoisie . . . nine-tenths of what the world celebrated as Viennese culture in the nineteenth century was promoted, nourished or even created by Viennese Jewry.'[96]

Zweig regarded this massive participation of Jews in Viennese culture as an expression of their ardent patriotism, their desire for adaptation and rapid assimilation, and their genuine love of the city. The Jews considered that 'their being Austrian was a mission to the world'; their love for Viennese art gave them the feeling of full citizenship, of having become truly Viennese. Excluded from the most privileged circles—the administration of the state, the aristocracy, the higher reaches of the army and officialdom—Jews felt genuinely equal, above all in the promotion and consumption of culture. 'They were the real audience, they filled the theatres and the concerts, they bought the books and the pictures, they visited the exhibitions, and with their more mobile understanding, little hampered by tradition, they were the exponents and champions of all that was new.'[97]

Zweig emphasized that the Jews regarded this promotion of culture as 'a personal task'. Through the success of the Austrian Jewish symbiosis in Vienna, Jewry was indeed able to achieve 'the highest artistic performance of their millennial spiritual activity'. Through their peculiar intellectual energy, they were able to nurture, revive, and renew the somewhat 'effete tradition' of an easy-going, conciliatory Austrian people who none the less shared 'the identical deep instinct for cultural and aesthetic values which was so important to the Jews themselves'.[98]

In the early pages of his autobiography Zweig had already

---

[96] Ibid. 22.

[97] Ibid. Zweig contrasted Jewish activity in these fields with 'the indolence of the court, the aristocracy, and the Christian millionaires, who preferred to maintain racing stables and hunts to fostering art . . .'.

[98] Ibid. 20.

commented on 'the determination of the Jew to rise to a higher cultural plane in the intellectual world', as a dominant character trait shared by Eastern orthodox Jewry no less than by highly assimilated Germanized families. The supremacy of the spiritual over the merely material, of intellect over riches, had to be seen as common to all classes of Jewry, who would spare no sacrifice 'to have someone in their midst, a professor, a savant, or a musician, who plays a role in the intellectual world'. Success in the free professions or in the domains of art and culture was the ultimate mark of liberation from all the limitations and sordidness of the ghetto that had been imposed upon Jewry over the centuries. It was at the same time an escape from 'the morally dubious, the distasteful, the petty, the unspiritual, which is attached to all trade, and all that is purely business'. The ascension to the world of culture, Zweig suggested, was an effort at auto-redemption in the Wagnerian sense, designed to redeem themselves and the entire race from the curse of money.[99] Perhaps, he added, it also expressed 'a secret longing to resolve the merely Jewish—through flight into the intellectual— into humanity at large'.[100]

This was indeed a temptation constantly felt by Zweig, the gifted, highly-strung son of a wealthy industrialist father whose family came from Moravia and exhibited those virtues of methodical sobriety, business enterprise, and tolerant liberalism with which Stefan partly identified and yet from which he sought to escape.[101] Towards his mother, too (she was born in Italy into a cosmopolitan Jewish banking family), Zweig exhibited marked ambivalence—attraction to the multilingual, international character of her familial connections and distaste for the overbearing snobbishness of the maternal relatives.[102] This was the type of an upper middle-class background highly conducive to the nurturing of artistic talent in *fin de siècle* Vienna and to the cultivation of a supranational outlook, but distinctly less favourable for encouraging a strong sense of Jewish identity.

Not surprisingly Zweig gravitated already in his youth towards a free-floating Pan-European humanism, reinforced by Viennese cultural cosmopolitanism, by his constant travels and his contacts with the

[99] Zweig, *The World of Yesterday*, 11–12.

[100] Ibid. 12.

[101] See ibid. 6 ff. for Zweig's brief sketch of Moravian Jewry, who 'were entirely free both of the sense of inferiority and of the smooth pushing impatience of the Galician or Eastern Jews'.

[102] See ibid. 9–10 for Zweig's view of the pseudo-aristocratic snobbery of his mother's family.

literary élite of Western Europe. Neither at Gymnasium nor at the University of Vienna was he much troubled or interested by the rise of mass movements such as Social Democracy and Christian Socialism or even by the noisy racist agitation of the Pan-Germans.[103] His retrospective portrait of Karl Lueger was remarkably benign and even sympathetic, though he did acknowledge that Hitler had seen in him a relevant prototype in the mobilization of the petty-burgeois masses and in the use of anti-Semitic catch-words. But for Zweig, Lueger definitely remained within the established confines of civilized respectability. He had after all been academically educated, he was handsome, witty, and above all decent.

Lueger was modest and above reproach in his private life. He always maintained a certain chivalry towards his opponents, and his official anti-Semitism never stopped him from being helpful and friendly to his former Jewish friends. When his movement had finally captured the Viennese town council . . . his city administration remained perfectly just and even typically democratic. The Jews, who had trembled at this triumph of the anti-Semitic party continued to live with the same rights and esteem as always. The poison of hatred, and the will to mutual and unsparing destruction, had not yet entered into the bloodstream of the time.[104]

Zweig undoubtedly exaggerated the benign quality of Lueger's movement and underestimated the malaise experienced by most Viennese Jews under Christian-Social rule. He had grown up in a society where prosperous families, even if they were Jews, could still contemplate the future with a certain equanimity as long as the old Emperor lived. But Zweig's picture of stability and buoyancy was overdrawn. Equally, his depiction of the more violent Schoenerite Pan-Germans suffered from an overly subjective perspective. Zweig recognized clearly enough that Hitler took over his racist programme from the Pan-German nationalist rowdies who had deliberately sought to destroy Austria before 1914 and ceaselessly assaulted Jews and Slavs in the universities. He even admitted that 'the war of all against all had already begun in Austria' by the end of the nineteenth century,

[103] Ibid. 60 ff., 93–5. His fellow author and journalist Felix Salten took a much more realistic view of Lueger. See Salten's spech at a rally in Dec. 1905 attacking Lueger's attitude to the Russian pogroms; quoted in Joel Raba, 'Reactions of the Jews of Vienna to the Russian pogroms of 1905', *Michael*, ii (1973), 140–1. (Diaspora Research Institute, Tel Aviv.)

[104] Zweig, *The World of Yesterday*, 63; see also p. 25: '. . . I personally must confess that neither in school nor at University, nor in the world of literature, have I ever experienced the slightest suppression or indignity as a Jew.'

with the violent German nationalist demonstrations against Count Badeni's language ordinances.[105] But Stefan Zweig could not bring himself to connect too closely the 'brutalization of present-day politics, the horrible decline of our century' with the 'Golden Age of Security' in which he had grown up. By his own admission, at the time he had been far too wrapped up in his literary ambitions to notice 'these dangerous changes in our homeland'.[106]

From the available evidence it seems clear that it was not anti-Semitism which first brought Zweig to an awareness of his Jewish identity. Nor was it his family background since, as he confessed in an interview with David Ewen in 1931, 'my mother and father were Jewish only through accident of birth'.[107] In the same interview he recalled, however, the decisive influence of Theodor Herzl which had made of him 'a Jew in heart and in soul, as well as through birth'. According to Zweig: 'He [Herzl] showed me the greatness of our race. From that friendship really stems my intense interest in Jewish affairs.'[108]

This account is reinforced by his admiring portrait of Herzl in *The World of Yesterday* where he describes him as 'the first man of world importance whom I had encountered in my life'.[109] The young Zweig had already published some short stories and a volume of verse (*Silberne Saiten*, 1901) when they first met during the same year in the offices of the *Neue Freie Presse*. Thanks to Herzl, his first *feuilleton* was duly published in the newspaper—an honour which Zweig compared to Napoleon pinning the Legion of Honour upon a young sergeant on the battlefield. The main factor which kept Zweig from joining the newly founded Zionist movement, apart from his endemic aversion to politics, was not disagreement with Herzl but repulsion from 'the quarrelling and dogmatic spirit, the constant opposition, the lack of honest, hearty subordination in his circle'.[110]

[105] Zweig, *The World of Yesterday*, 65.

[106] Ibid. 66: 'We did not have the slightest interest in politics and social problems: what did these shrill wranglings mean in our lives? The city was aroused at elections, and we went to the libraries. The masses rose, and we wrote and discussed poetry.'

[107] Quoted in Joseph Leftwich, 'Stefan Zweig and the World of Yesterday', *Leo Baeck Yearbook*, 3 (1958), 91.

[108] Ibid. Zweig explained in the interview that he had turned away from Zionism when he came to feel that Jews were 'greater as thinkers and artists when they lived amidst the clash of the outside world than when they were isolated in a Jewish land'. But he retained profound affection and admiration for Herzl, the man, and the universal scope of his work.

[109] Zweig, *The World of Yesterday*, 101.   [110] Ibid. 107.

Stefan Zweig also very friendly at this time with the Galician-born book illustrator and art editor of the *Jüdischer Almanach*, Ephraim Moses Lilien (1874–1925), and in 1903 even published a sumptuous illustrated volume on his work up to that time. Lilien, the first Austrian artist to be directly involved with the Zionist movement, took an active part in the efforts of the 'Democratic Fraction' to foster Jewish culture. He was, for example, intimately associated with the Berlin publishing house, *Juedischer Verlag*, as an illustrator, editor, and publicity agent. Moreover, Lilien collaborated closely with both Theodor Herzl and Martin Buber and in 1905 became a member of the founding committee of the Bezelel School of Art in Palestine, a country which he visited a number of times before 1914. Though Stefan Zweig evidently admired Lilien, the *Jugendstil* artist, more than he did the passionate Zionist, his friendship must have helped maintain his interest in Jewish affairs. In *The World of Yesterday*, Zweig cryptically mentioned in passing that through Lilien he had first encountered 'a Judaism which in its strength and stubborn fanaticism had hitherto been unknown to me'.[111]

Zweig's wartime correspondence with Martin Buber and above all his outstanding dramatic work, *Jeremias*, written in 1916, reveal a more sharply defined sense of Jewish identity than he is often credited with. In a letter to Buber on 8 May 1916 Stefan Zweig reported that he was working on 'a great Jewish tragedy,' one whose significance was timeless though its pacifist message would be obvious to all (except the censors), against the background of the mass slaughter in the trenches. Zweig characterized *Jeremiah* to Buber as 'the tragedy and hymn of the Jewish people as the chosen people—not in the sense of prosperity but in that of eternal suffering, eternal falling and eternal rising—and the strength deriving from such a fate—. . .'.[112]

Zweig went on to explain his reservations regarding any nationalist interpretation of this chosenness:

. . . I would not want to choose Judaism as an emotional prison with conceptual bars separating me from the world outside. I have an antipathy to everything in Judaism that tends to create antithesis [*Gegensätzlichkeit*]: but I know that I repose in it and will never become an apostate. I am not proud of being a Jew, because I reject pride in any achievement which did not come from my own

---

[111] See ibid. 117, and E. M. Lilien, *Briefe an seine Frau, 1905–1925*, ed. Otto M. Lilien and Eve Strauss, with introd. by Ekkehard Hieronimus (Königstein/Ts., 1985), 9–28.

[112] Stefan Zweig, *Briefe an Freunde*, ed. Richard Freudenthal (Frankfurt, 1978), 64.

efforts, just as I am not proud of Vienna although I was born there, or of Goethe because he is of my language, or of the victories by our armies, in which my blood did not flow.[113]

Zweig deplored the lack of self-assurance, the insecurity, the 'inverted anxiety' and 'twisted feeling of inferiority' (*ein gedrehtes Minderwertigkeitsgefühl*) which he detected in the bombastic proclamations of Jewishness that he came across so frequently.[114] He assured Buber: 'I am not burdened by my Jewishness. I am not inspired by it, it does not torment me and it does not sunder me; I feel it the same way as I feel my heart beat when I think about it and I don't feel it when I don't think of it.'[115]

Zweig's interest in Jewish affairs was by no means purely ethereal at this time. He was, for example, sensitive to the tragic situation of Polish Jewry during the First World War and the fact that the flight of Galician refugees to Vienna was already envenoming Austrian anti-Semitism.[116] In a letter to Abraham Schwadron in the summer of 1916 he expressed his conviction that, in the aftermath of the war, bitterness against those who had encouraged it would surely be deflected against the Jews.[117] He fully expected that they would be made a scapegoat by nationalist political parties in both Austria and Poland, and that Jews would undoubtedly suffer more than any other nation, without enjoying any recompense.[118] Indeed, it was precisely Zweig's sensitivity to the imminent Jewish tragedy which exacerbated his resentment at those Viennese and German Jewish writers, like Felix Salten for instance, who became enthusiastic for the Hohenzollern cause.[119]

[113] Zweig, *Briefe an Freunde*, 65.   [114] Ibid. 65–6.

[115] Ibid. 66: 'Es belastet das Judesein mich nicht, es begeistert mich nicht, es quält mich nicht und sondert mich nicht, ich fühle es ebenso wie ich meinen Herzschlag fühle, wenn ich daran denke, und ihn nicht fühle, wenn ich nicht daran denke.'

[116] Ibid. 66–7.

[117] Ibid. 'Ich bin fest überzeugt, dass die Erbitterung, die jetzt schon latent ist, nach dem Kriege sich nicht gegen die Kriegshetzer, die Reichspost-Partei, sondern gegen die Juden entladen wird. Ich bin überzeugt—felsenfest—dass nach dem Kriege der Antisemitismus die Zuflucht dieser "Grossösterreicher" sein wird, dass Polen und Wiener da endlich eine Form der Einigkeit haben werden.'

[118] Ibid. 67: '. . . dieser Krieg ist die Tragödie des Judentums in Polen . . . mehr als jedes andere Volk werden sie Leiden, ohne Triumphe zu haben wie jene. Sie *leiden* nur, ohne Leiden zu machen—und das ist heute in einer Welt der Gewalt die ärgste Sünde.'

[119] Ibid. 66–7. Zweig commented ironically on Salten's Zionism ('immer Privatsache') and the fact that in his countless journalistic articles he never openly identified himself as a Jew. They had become estranged before the war when Salten accused Zweig of being too pro-German: 'Jetzt ist er Brandenburger bis ins Herz hinab, das nur gelegentlich jüdische.' For Zweig's contempt for Prussianized Jewish super-patriots like Ernst Lissauer, see *The World of Yesterday*, 231–3.

Zweig's almost physical revulsion at the wartime 'nationalistic madness' surrounding him had in fact strengthened his sense of Jewish identity, as he admitted in a letter of January 1917 to Martin Buber. The one thing which none the less separated him from Buber's humanist Zionist circle was his love and affirmation of the Diaspora 'as the meaning of the Jews' idealism and as their cosmopolitan, universally human mission' (*allmenschliche Berufung*).[120] Zweig did not want the Jews 'to become a nation once more and thereby debase themselves in the competition of realities'.[121] He made it clear to Martin Buber that he desired a union in the spirit—'the only real element—never in a language, in a nation [*Volk*], or in customs—syntheses which are as beautiful as they are dangerous'.[122] Zweig now claimed that the existing dispersed condition of Jewry was the most splendid imaginable:

this oneness without language, without ties, without homeland [*Heimat*]—only through the atmosphere of their being [*das Fluidum des Wesens*]. Any closer, more real amalgamation would seem to me a diminution of this incomparable condition. And the one thing which we should strengthen would be not to regard this condition as a debasement but to experience it lovingly and consciously, as I do.[123]

In the same letter Zweig reproached Buber's Zionist friend from Prague, the writer Max Brod, for being too 'fanatical' and 'nationalist' in his desire to transform and eradicate millennial sufferings in the course of one decade.[124] The gap between the positions of Zweig and Buber was also touched on in another letter to Abraham Schwadron in spring 1917. Zweig insisted that for him the grandeur of Judaism lay in its supranational character, in its role as a ferment and a cement between the nations, and in its eternal striving for a *spiritual* homeland. Buber, on the other hand, was too much oriented in Zweig's view towards the physical return to Zion and towards a nationalism which, however humanist its intentions might be, still bore the danger of hubris, vanity, and narrow-minded separatism.[125]

On 25 May 1917 Zweig wrote again to Buber, elaborating in greater detail his opposition to Zionist reliance on *Realpolitik* and his rejection of the principle behind Jewish nationalism. He recalled that what he had dimly felt already before 1914 and put into practice during his

[120] *Briefe an Freunde*, 68, letter to Martin Buber, 24 Jan. 1917.
[121] Ibid.   [122] Ibid. 68–9.   [123] Ibid. 69.   [124] Ibid.
[125] Ibid. 71.

world travels—the absolute freedom of feeling everywhere 'as a guest, a participant, and a mediator'—had been his inner salvation in recent years.[126] He gratefully acknowledged that what had made possible this 'supra-national feeling of freedom from the madness of a fanatical world' was precisely his Jewishness.[127]

I consider nationalist conceptions, like the notion of any restriction, as dangerous, and see in the idea of the realization of Judaism a decline and an abandonment of its highest mission. Perhaps it is the purpose of Judaism to demonstrate through the centuries that community [*Gemeinschaft*] is possible without soil, only through blood and intellect [*Geist*], only through the Word and faith, and to give up this uniqueness means to me to renounce a high office that we accepted from history, to close a book written in a thousand pages that still has space for thousands more years of wandering.[128]

Zweig conceded that this conviction probably derived from 'a deep pessimism and distrust' of all practical realizations which abandoned the realm of ideals and of the spirit. He admitted that personally he had no faith 'in the realisation of a national community' (*Volksgemeinschaft*) or in the rebuilding of a new Jewish national home, though he respected those who were striving to do so with devotion and skill.[129] But Zweig was convinced that the human and social realization which Buber sought to achieve in the earthly Zion was still hundreds of years away and therefore remained no less of an idea than his own notion of a 'spiritual Jerusalem'.

At the beginning of February 1918, following the Balfour Declaration, Zweig's anxious warnings about Zionism were if anything intensified and assumed a more prophetic tone and character.

. . . the more the dream threatens to become real, the dangerous dream of a Jewish state with cannon, flags, and decorations, the more determined I become to love the painful idea of the Diaspora, to love Jewish destiny more than Jewish prosperity. In prosperity and fulfilment this people never represented a value—only under pressure does it find its strength, only in dispersion its unity. And if it lives together, then it will disperse of itself. What is a nation if not fate transformed [*ein verwandeltes Schicksal*]? And what will remain of it if it evades its destiny.[130]

The return of Zion would mean ultimately the closing of a historic circle, the end of a ceaseless wandering over centuries throughout

---

[126] *Briefe an Freunde*, 75.   [127] Ibid.
[128] Ibid.   [129] Ibid. 76.
[130] Ibid. 83–4.

Europe and the whole world. For Stefan Zweig, this could lead only to 'a tragic disappointment like every repetition'.[131]

In his powerful pacifist play, *Jeremias*, Zweig sought to give dramatic flesh and blood to his vision of Jewish destiny—to present 'the tragedy of a man who has only the word, the warning, and the insight to pit against the realities'.[132] In a letter to Buber, Zweig had described the play as a hymn to the tragedy of the Jews as 'the chosen people', as eternal wanderers and sufferers who had spiritually wrestled with their God through countless lands and numberless years. Through his poetic reworking of the biblical story, Zweig expressed all the pent-up feelings of rage, impotence, and anguish which he had experienced during the First World War. The figure of Jeremiah provided him with a powerful vehicle for protesting against the 'false heroism that prefers to send others to suffering and death, the cheap optimism of the conscienceless prophets, both political and military, who, boldly promising victory, prolong the war . . .'.[133]

Jeremias enabled Zweig to describe, in dramatic form, the tragic situation of 'defeatists' like himself, doomed to being prophets of catastrophe with no influence over events. Yet the play was by no means blackly pessimistic in its overall message, for it reaffirmed Zweig's faith in the 'spiritual superiority of the vanquished'. More significantly, perhaps, the choice of a biblical theme allowed him to rediscover 'that community with the Jewish destiny whether in my blood or darkly founded in tradition'.[134] Thus *Jeremias* consolidated Zweig's increasingly strong identification with his Jewish heritage.

Was it not my people that again and again had been conquered by all other peoples, again and again, and yet outlasted them because of some secret power—that power of transforming defeat through will, of withstanding it again and again? Had they not presaged, our prophets, this perpetual hunt and persecution that today again scatters us upon the highways like chaff, and had they not affirmed this submission to power, and even blessed it as a way to God?[135]

In a world drunk with war, Zweig had found a symbol of hope 'in the book of books, in the primal source of my race, in the figure of

---

[131] Ibid. 84. See however Zweig's letter from Salzburg to the painter Hermann Struck, dated 18 June 1930, in which he expresses admiration for his decision to settle in Palestine. 'Ich bin überzeugt, dass dies auf die jüngere Generation moralisch stärker gewirkt hätte als alle Reden, Worte, Bücher und Broschuren' (ibid. 207).

[132] Ibid. 64, letter to Martin Buber of 8 May 1916.

[133] Zweig, *The World of Yesterday*, 252.   [134] Ibid. 253.   [135] Ibid.

Jeremiah, sublimest among the adversaries of war, martyrized for his convictions'.[136] In the closing ninth scene of Zweig's drama, Jeremiah explains the meaning of the pain and suffering undergone by the chosen people.

God sends us this trial that we may know him to be God. To those of other nations, few signs are given and little recognition is vouchsafed. They fancy themselves able to see the face of the Eternal in images of wood and stone. Our God, the God of our fathers, is a hidden God; and not until we are bathed in sorrow are we able to discern him. He chooses only those whom he has tried, and to none but the suffering does he give his love. Let us therefore rejoice at our trials, brothers, and let us love the suffering God sends. He has broken us with affliction, that he may sink the deeper into the freshly ploughed ground of our hearts, and that we may be ready for the scattering of the seed.[137]

The prophet's message was essentially an affirmation of the Diaspora, such as Zweig had already expounded in his letters to Martin Buber. 'Wandering is our habitation, trouble our heritage, God our home.'[138] In *Jeremias*, the homeless, the vanquished, the exiled become the chosen of God; for their very affliction turns into the guarantee of freedom, their tribulations contain the seeds of redemption; their suffering the promise of eternity. Thus, Jeremiah becomes the prophet of exodus and never-ending return.

> Wanderers, sufferers, march in the name
> Of your forefather Jacob, who erstwhile with God,
> Having wrestled the livelong night,
> Strove till dawn for a blessing,
> March on in the morning light
> By a path like that which your forefathers trod,
> When from Mizraim by Moses led
> Towards the land of promise their way they sped.[139]

The third chorus of wanderers echoes Jermiah's theme of a perpetual pilgrimage through the changing world, 'eternally vanquished' and 'by none made welcome', towards the final goal of their desire, a spiritual Jerusalem. The fifth chorus of wanderers encapsulates the prophet's teaching in terms perhaps more Christian than Hebraic in their underlying tone.

---

[136] See Stefan Zweig's introd. of 1929 to the 2nd Eng. edn., trans. Eden and Cedar Paul, *Jeremiah* (New York, 1929), p. viii.
[137] Ibid. 316.   [138] Ibid. 317.   [139] Ibid. 331.

We wander down the road of suffering,
Through our trials we are purified,
Everlastingly vanquished, and everlastingly overthrown,
For ever enslaved, for ever enfranchised,
Unceasingly broken and unceasingly renewed,
The mock and sport of all nations on earth.
We wander through the eternities,
A remnant, a remnant,
And yet numberless.
We march onward to God,
To God who is the beginning and the end,
To God who is our home.[140]

The dramatic power and eloquence of Zweig's *Jeremias* showed how far he had matured since the bitter-sweet aestheticism of his *Jung Wien* days. But his Jewish identification remained somewhat vacillating and uncertain, clearly subordinate to his Pan-European perspectives and severely limited by his apolitical temperament.[141] During the grim years of Nazi ascendancy, after 1933, by a cruel irony of fate Zweig himself was forced into exile and into the unwelcome and tragic role of the weary, homeless wanderer that he had glorified in *Jeremias*. His periodic reaffirmations of Diasporic Judaism in the new context of Hitler's rise to power now had the rather hollow and unconvincing ring of a man bewildered by the final collapse of his previously secure world and Erasmian humanist ideals. As late as 1940 Zweig was still asserting in somewhat naïve terms the superiority of the aesthetic and spiritual commitments of Jewry, and enthusiastically praising its voluntary renunciation of 'conquest, expansion and military power for the delights of the intellect'.[142]

The problem with this stance was not so much that Zweig's basic values were wrong but rather that his non-political idealization of culture seemed utterly impotent in an increasingly brutalized world. Zweig's unconditional faith in reason, humanity, artistic and intellectual creation beyond all nationalism, and *raison d'État*, like his prophetic belief in the ultimate victory of the downtrodden, appeared

[140] Ibid. 335.
[141] For a somewhat hostile and at times unfair critique of Zweig's political *naïveté*, see Hannah Arendt's essay, 'Juden in der Welt von gestern', in *Die verborgene Tradition: Acht Essays*. (Frankfurt, 1976), 74–87. The most interesting part of Arendt's analysis is the discussion of Zweig's obsession with celebrity and the role this played in the life of Viennese Jewry.
[142] Quoted in Harry Zohn, 'Three Austrian Jews in German Literature', in J. Fraenkel (ed.), *The Jews of Austria: Essays on their Life, History and Destruction* (London, 1967), 77.

by 1942 to be doomed by Europe's remorselessly suicidal path. In a world now dominated by the cult of power for its own sake, by martial glory and material aggrandisement, the pan-humanist values espoused by this last great survivor of the golden Age of Viennese Jewry looked like the defunct relic of a bygone era. What could the ideals of culture and *Bildung*, of Europeanism or Enlightenment, mean in the face of Hitler and the Holocaust? Neither a sentimental Austrian patriotism nor a residual Judaic sense of moral mission offered much practical hope in the face of the Nazi juggernaut.[143] Zweig's fatalism and despair at this self-destruction of Europe left only one alternative. His suicide in Brazil early in 1942 appeared finally to close the curtain on seventy years of Austrian Jewish cultural symbiosis which, with the exception of medieval Spain, Zweig believed to have been the happiest and most fruitful in Jewish diasporic history.[144]

As we have seen throughout this study, Stefan Zweig was only one of many Austrian Jews (and Gentiles) before him, who had fervently believed in the ideal of a supranational freedom of the spirit, even in an age of growing fanaticism and the worship of brute force. This noble dream was also shared by his friend and contemporary, the brilliant Austrian Jewish novelist Joseph Roth, whose torn identity illustrates in striking fashion many of the ambiguities of Jewish existence in the Habsburg Monarchy.

The work of Joseph Roth cannot be properly understood except against the ethnic background and socio-political climate of pre-war Austrian Galicia.[145] Born in 1894 in the East Galician town of Brody, a city with the highest percentage of Jews in the Austro-Hungarian Monarchy, Roth throughout his life derived creative inspiration from the milieu, atmosphere, and human types with which he had grown up. More consistently than any other German-language writer he fought against the negative stereotypes of his home province, and in particular of Galician Jewry, which still prevailed in Western Europe. On one occasion he confided to a friend: 'The more Western the origin of a

---

[143] For a compassionate account of Zweig's wrestlings and anguish at the Jewish tragedy in the 1930s, see Leftwich, pp. 81–99.

[144] Zweig, *The World of Yesterday*, 20. For Zweig's personal role in cultural mediation on a Pan-European scale, see Harry Zohn, 'Stefan Zweig, the European and the Jew', *Leo Baeck Yearbook*, 27 (1982), 323–36.

[145] Helmut Nürnberger, *Joseph Roth* (Hamburg, 1981), 17–35. David Bronsen, *Joseph Roth: Eine Biographie* (Cologne, 1974) and Joseph Roth, *Werke*, ed. and introd. Hermann Kestern, 4 vols. (Cologne, 1975–6), are the most important sources of information concerning his life and work.

Jew, the more Jews there are for him to look down on. The Frankfurt Jew despises the Berlin Jew, the Berlin Jew despises the Viennese Jew, the Viennese Jew despises the Warsaw Jew. Then there are still the Jews from way back in Galicia, upon whom they all look down, and that's where I come from, the lowest of all Jews.'[146]

There is no doubt that the young Roth had desired to escape from the provinciality and narrowness of the East Galician *shtetl*; on the other hand, Roth's descriptions of his native Galician landscape, of the agrarian life-style, the natural simplicity and naïve innocence of its inhabitants, are full of nostalgia, pathos, and warmth. In his remarkably essay, *Juden auf Wanderschaft*, Roth paid tribute to the beauty of his homeland and the positive qualities of its Jewish population. Roth especially valued the pious religiosity and continuity of Jewish family traditions in Galicia and Eastern Europe, spiritual assets that he held to be far superior to the empty and false assimilationism of Western bourgeois Jews.[147] The lowly Eastern Jew was not only closer to divine inspiration in Roth's estimation but also more human than his 'flourishing assimilated cousin in the West'. The modernity of the Western Jew was fundamentally suspect to Roth and identified with a loss of both Jewish and human substance.

Like Martin Buber, Roth discovered the real soul of Jewry not in the liberal Westernized 'protestantism' of German Reform Judaism but in the Hasidic communities of East Galicia and the Russian Ukraine.[148] His sentimental affection for the cohesion and unity of this Hasidic Jewry was in some ways complementary to his post-war conservative longing for a restoration of the old Habsburg Monarchy, in which orthodox Jews had found so comfortable a niche.[149] Moreover, it ran parallel to his sympathetic portrayal of the more backward Slavonic peoples of the Monarchy. In Roth's estimation, they had been momentarily spared the march of modernity and progress with its falsification of familial ties and erosion of the warm, primitive solidarity exuded by the *Gemeinschaft*.

In Roth's conservative transvaluation of values, the world of the *shtetl* re-emerged as the ideal embodiment of a lost intimacy and

[146] Quoted in David Bronsen, 'Austrian versus Jew: The Torn Identity of Joseph Roth', *Leo Baeck Yearbook*, 18 (1973), 223.

[147] Joseph Roth, *Juden auf Wanderschaft* (Amsterdam and Cologne, 1985), 22–39, 'Das jüdische Städtchen'.

[148] Ibid. 26–34.

[149] See Philip Manger, '*The Radetzky March*: Joseph Roth and the Habsburg Myth', in Mark Francis (ed.), *The Viennese Enlightenment* (London and Sydney, 1985), 40–62.

innocence; the materialist values of the Western *Bürgertum* (Jewish and Gentile) represented its self-alienated antithesis. In the inherited traditions, hopes, and fears of the *Ostjuden*, Roth found a more convincing metaphor for an authentically human universalism than in the sublimated sophistication of Western *Bildung*. Hence his alarm at the mass migration and growing assimilation of *Ostjuden* in the West, his regret and distaste for their efforts at achieving national integration in America, the Soviet Union, and Central or Western Europe.[150] The exodus to the West was for Roth an odyssey in the desert, leading ever farther *away* from the Promised Land of the *shtetl* into the sterilized anonymity of urban bourgeois existence with all its superficial cleanliness, comforts, and technological appliances.[151] Admittedly, the *Ostjude* was in many respects homeless and alien in the societal landscape of Eastern Europe, still subject to the bleak misery, economic uncertainties, oppression, and narrow-mindedness of the ghetto. But at least he had remained true to his own identity, his tradition, his ceaseless dialogue with God, and his sense of belonging to an unbroken chain of generations.

In his novel *Hiob* (Job), Roth embodied this ethos in the central figure of Mendal Singer, a 'pious, God-fearing and ordinary, an entirely commonplace Jew . . .' a *melamed*, who finds the ancestral continuity of his existence threatened by the loss of his closest family and by imminent emigration to America.[152]

In Roth's work the dignity of man was invariably rooted in the maintenance of traditions and the recognition of an all-embracing, generally recognized source of authority. Since his youth in Brody and especially during his wartime service in the Austro-Hungarian army, the homeless, fatherless Roth had found this anchor of existence in unconditional loyalty to the Emperor and his multinational Empire.[153]

---

[150] *Juden auf Wanderschaft*, 39–73. The section 'Die westlichen Gettos', pp. 39–60, begins with a few memorable pages on the settlement of *Ostjuden* in Vienna after 1914 which Roth witnessed at first hand.

[151] Ibid. 11, 'Ostjuden im Westen'.

[152] Joseph Roth, *Job: The Story of a Simple Man* trans. Dorothy Thompson (London, 1983). This novel, 1st pub. 1930, was warmly praised by Stefan Zweig and Thomas Mann. See also Sidney Rosenfeld, 'The Chain of Generations—A Jewish Theme in Joseph Roth's Novels', *Leo Baeck Yearbook*, 18 (1973), 228 ff.

[153] See Nürnberger, pp. 20–3. Roth's father Nachum came from West Galicia and grew up among the Hasidim. In 1892 he married Maria Grübel (Roth's mother) in Brody but soon became mentally sick. His son never met him and grew up in impoverished circumstances. Roth's relationship with his mother was painful and difficult.

After the collapse of this Empire (perhaps the greatest trauma of his adult life), Roth became the epic myth-maker of the Habsburgs, in addition to his role as a chronicler of the sufferings of the *Ostjuden*. Both in his personal life and his work, Roth sought to synthesize and combine these commitments, eloquently pleading the case for Austrian supranationalism and the mutual interdependence of the Habsburgs, the Jews, and the Slav national minorities. The Habsburg–Jewish–Slavic symbiosis was particularly evoked in his *Radetzkymarsch* (1932); in a masterly scene Roth described a congregation of pious Galician village Jews doing obeisance to Franz Joseph I (one of whose many titles was King of Jerusalem):

The black crowd of Jews eddied toward him. Their backs rose and fell. Their coal-black, flame-red, and silver-white beards waved in the gentle breeze. The patriarch stopped three paces from the Emperor. In his arms he bore a large purple Torah scroll decorated with a gold crown, its little bells softly jingling. Then the Jew lifted the Torah scroll towards the Emperor. And his widely bearded, toothless mouth gabbled in an incomprehensible language the blessing which Jews utter in the presence of an emperor. Francis Joseph inclined his head. The delicate haze of an Indian summer drifted above his black cap, ducks screeched in the air, a cock crowed in the distant farmyard. All else was quiet. A sombre muttering rose from the crowd of the Jews. Their backs bent lower still. 'Blessed art thou', said the Jew to the Emperor, 'who shall not see the end of the world.' I know it, Francis Joseph thought. He offered the old man his hand. He turned. He mounted his white horse.[154]

Roth not only underlined and sympathetically portrayed the affinity between the pious Catholic Emperor and his loyal Jewish orthodox subjects. He also came to believe fervently in the universal mission of the Habsburgs, in their divine legitimacy and special fitness to rule over the multitude of Christian peoples in the Empire. These peoples, in their turn, especially the more primitive Slavs, felt a special bond of loyalty to the Catholic, supranational Emperor. Hence, it was no coincidence that the officer hero of the *Radetzkymarsch*, Carl Joseph von Trotta, came from a family of Slovenian border peasants, whose special covenant with the Emperor had been established in 1859 when his grandfather had saved Franz Joseph's life at Solferino. Nor, that Trotta constantly seeks to return to the home and the traditional ways of his Slovenian ancestors. Eventually, after leaving the army, Trotta settles among Ukrainian peasants, Poles and Jews in East Galicia (on

---

[154] Joseph Roth, *The Radetzky March*, rev. trans. Eva Tucker (London 1984), 215.

the Russian border) only to fall in combat during the first days of the First World War.[155]

Through this epic novel of Habsburg Austria and its decline, as well as in the sequel, *Die Kapuzinergruft* (1939), Roth shows himself to be acutely aware of the centrifugal tendencies within the Monarchy, slowly but surely working towards disintegration. His mouthpiece against this trend in both novels was the sophisticated wealthy Polish Count Chojnicki, who every time he returned from Vienna would give his listeners an ominous lecture along the following lines:

The monarchy is bound to end. The minute the Emperor is dead, we shall splinter into a hundred fragments. The Balkans will be more powerful than we are. Each nation will set up its own dirty little government, even the Jews will proclaim a King in Palestine. Vienna's begun to stink of the sweat of democrats—I can't stand the Ringstrasse any more. The workers all wave red flags and don't want to work any more. The mayor of Vienna is a pious shopkeeper. Even the parsons are going red, they've started preaching in Czech in the churches. At the Burgtheater all the performances are filthy Jewish plays. And every week another Hungarian water-closet manufacturer is made a baron. I tell you, gentlemen, if we don't start shooting pretty soon, it'll be the end.[156]

In *Die Kapuzinergruft* Roth described in greater and more anguished detail the decline of the Monarchy, whose restoration had still appeared to him in the 1930s as the one remaining chance for Central European stability and the only possible bulwark against Nazi barbarism. In the novel, Roth sought to convey the power, greatness, and beauty of old Austria, the last truly *universal* State and legitimate successor to the Holy Roman Empire. But in fact the dismemberment had already happened, together with the descent into fanatical nationalism. In *Die Kapuzinergruft* Count Chojnicki explains that the instigators and instruments of this betrayal of the Habsburg Empire were the so-called 'master races', the German nationalists of Vienna, Bohemia, Moravia, and the Alpine lands and the Hungarian rulers who continued ruthlessly to oppress their Slovak, Romanian, Serbo-Croat, Ukrainian, and German minorities.

The only genuinely loyal Austrians, on the other hand, were to be found on the periphery of the Monarchy, among the Poles, the Ukrainians, the Slovenes, the caftaned Jews, and even among the Czechs, etc. In these crownlands, among the poorer, more backward,

---

[155] Roth, *The Radetzky March*, 309.   [156] Ibid. 129.

suffering national minorities beat the true heart of the Monarchy and not amidst the dazzling wealth, social graces, and cultural genius of Vienna. 'The traitors are not our Czechs, not our Serbs, not our Poles or Ukrainians', Count Chojnicki reminds Trotta, 'but only our Teutons, the official nationality.'[157] They could no longer grasp that Imperial Austria was the prototype of a universalist supranation, far superior in its historical significance and mission to the grotesque, narrow-minded, racist mythology of German nationalism.[158]

Joseph Roth identified himself completely in later years with the Austrian imperial mystique, with the Habsburgs and Roman Catholicism (to which he converted) even though, since his twenty-fifth year, the Empire had existed only in his imagination. He maintained this idealized fidelity in spite of his difficult experiences in Vienna between 1913 and 1916 (and again between 1918 and 1920) when anti-Semitism was particularly rampant in the city.[159] In his *Juden auf Wanderschaft* he wrote: 'It is terribly hard to be an *Ostjude*; there is no harder lot than that of a foreign *Ostjude* in Vienna.'[160] But this xenophobic anti-Semitism which he thoroughly despised did not diminish his regard for the aristocratic life-style and cultivated manners of the pre-war Viennese which he adopted and aped down to the elaborate hand-kissing and special Viennese accent.

Roth's identification with Vienna remained, however, secondary and essentially superficial. Admittedly, during his stay in Vienna he was led into such classic assimilationist contortions as the notorious falsifications of his real birthplace, and the downplaying of his Galician and Jewish origins.[161] But his later affirmation of his East European Jewish background and strong sense of identity with the age-old common fate and bond of blood shared over 4,000 years, was much more characteristic than occasional crises of self-hatred. In his negation of Western Jewish assimilation and self-alienation (almost as fierce as the condemnation by Franz Kafka and similarly tinged with intellectual anti-Semitism), one none the less feels the agony of a divided self.[162]

---

[157] Roth, *Werke*, iii. 400.
[158] See Wolf R. Marchand, *Joseph Roth und die völkisch-nationalistische Wertbegriffe* (Bonn, 1974) for Roth's anti-German views.
[159] *Juden Auf Wanderschaft*, 40: 'Die Christlichsozialen und Deutschnationalen haben den Antisemitusmus also wichtigen Programmpunkt. Die Sozialdemokraten fürchten den Ruf einen "jüdischen Partei." Die Jüdischnationalen sind ziemlich machtlos.'
[160] Ibid.
[161] Nürnberger, pp. 7 ff.; Bronsen, *Joseph Roth*, 12 ff.
[162] See Walter H. Sokel, 'Franz Kafka as a Jew', *Leo Baeck Yearbook* 18 (1973), 234–8, and the remarks of Bronsen on Roth, 'Austrian versus Jew', 224.

Roth's position towards Zionism was initially more ambiguous. He freely acknowledged its strong living roots in East European Jewry; he welcomed the achievements of the *ḥalutzim* in Palestine; and to some extent he sympathized with the logic of Jewish nationhood in the early 1920s, at a time of racial exlusivism, persecution, and discrimination against the Jewish minorities in the newly created Eastern European nation-states.[163] Roth noted that modern political Zionism had first developed in late Habsburg Austria in an atmosphere of bitter national struggles between Germans and Czechs, Magyars and Romanians, Poles and Ukrainians. The Jews had suffered because they lacked their own clearly defined territory. Trapped in the cross-fire of ethnic conflicts, their anomalous condition intensified the anti-Semitism of the Austrian peoples.[164]

Despite these considerations, the desire for a Jewish homeland ultimately seemed even more anachronistic to Roth than it did to anti-Zionist contemporaries like Arthur Schnitzler, Karl Kraus, or Stefan Zweig, though for different reasons. In part, Roth's anti-Zionist standpoint derived from his Habsburg mythology of supranationalism and his genuine revulsion against nationalism in general, as the scourge and plague of the twentieth century. In part he may also have been influenced by the Jewish orthodox view that the struggle for national freedom was irrelevant and even pernicious—the return to the Promised Land lay in the hands of God and could occur only when the Messiah appeared.[165]

Curiously enough, in the mid-1930s, under the impact of National Socialism, Roth's anti-Zionism became decidedly unbalanced, as the writer's world disintegrated into the bitterness and black despair engendered by hunger, exile, and alcoholism. In a letter to Stefan Zweig on 14 August 1935, he ruled out the idea of collaboration with Chaim Weizmann, or any other Nationalist Jews, against Hitler. Roth now claimed no more and no less than that 'a Zionist is a National Socialist, a Nazi is a Zionist'; he dwelt on the Zionist role in undermining the Jewish boycott of the Nazis, on 'connections' and

---

[163] *Juden auf Wanderschaft*, 20: 'Sie haben kein "Vaterland", die Juden, aber jedes Land, in dem sie wohnen und Steuern zahlen, verlangt von ihnen Patriotismus und Heldentod und wirft ihnen vor, dass sie nicht gerne sterben. In dieser Lage ist der Zionismus wirklich noch der einzige Ausweg: wenn schon Patriotismus, dann lieber einen für das eigene Land.'

[164] Ibid. 17.

[165] Ibid. 25. See Roth's remarks: 'Einem ostjüdischen Chassid und Orthodoxen ist ein Christ näher als ein Zionist.'

'sympathies' between the two nationalist movements. Roth even called Hitler 'a *stupid* brother of the Zionists'. He told Zweig: 'You may perhaps be able to protect Judaism in this way. But I am concerned to protect Europe and man in general, to protect them from Nazis and from Hitler-Zionists. I'm not concerned to protect the Jews except, possibly, as the most threatened avant-garde of mankind.'[166]

Roth's political position was by the 1930s thoroughly legitimist—i.e. Catholic, conservative, monarchist, and actively in favour of a Habsburg restoration. On 19 August 1935 he wrote to Zweig:

Your sensitivities may be outraged by the fact that a dirty Jew like me appears in print immediately after the Pope. But please believe that I am in deadly earnest. In fact, I see no road other than that which leads to Calvary, to Christ—no greater Jew. Indeed, perhaps I shall go even further and find the fortitude to enter an Order. Call it a kind of suicide. For me there is nothing but the Christian faith (no literature) and I do not believe in the world; I do not believe that it can be influenced.[167]

Roth's letters from this period are full of the deadly *morbus Austriacus*—resignation, melancholy, self-irony, and therapeutic nihilism. Yet for all his fatalism and Habsburg legitimist eccentricities, Roth was more perceptive than Zweig regarding the National-Socialist threat to Jewry. Indeed, he sharply reproached his friend in the same letter of 19 August 1935 for excessive optimism, naïvety, and escapism:

You underestimate, or do not appreciate, a number of obvious things: (1) The passion for humiliating the Jews did not begin today or yesterday; as all the world knows, it was an integral part of the programme of the Third Reich from its *very first day*. Streicher is no different from Hitler, and there's no need to wait till Streicher moves from Nuremberg to Berlin! The idea of national socialism, if it can be called such, contains nothing but contempt for the Jewish race! How is it that you can realize this only now? Why not two years ago? Two and three quarter years ago? This bestiality was inherent from the beginning. The shameful treatment of the Jews did not begin two months ago. We were insulted and humiliated from Hitler's first day.[168]

---

[166] Letter of Joseph Roth to Stefan Zweig from the Hotel Foyot, Paris, 14 Aug. 1935, in Roth, *Briefe, 1911–1939*, ed. Hermann Kesten (Cologne and Berlin, 1970), 419–22.

[167] Letter of 19 Aug. 1935 from same address to Stefan Zweig, ibid. 422–3. It is interesting to note that at this time Roth believed that Catholics alone were 'struggling heroically against the Third Reich'. On Roth's Paris years of exile (he commited suicide there in 1939, at the age of 44), see Henri Cellérier, 'Une Patrie pour une exilé: Joseph Roth', *Austriaca*, no. 19 (Nov. 1984), 49–68.

[168] *Briefe*, 423.

Joseph Roth and Stefan Zweig, it must be said, were poles apart in social background and as psychological types. Zweig, a true son of the Viennese patrician *Grossbürgertum*, clung to its liberal-humanist ideal of Europeanism, to which his Jewishness was on the whole subordinated. Joseph Roth, the rebellious East Galician and plebian *Ostjude*, turned to a reactionary Catholicism and Habsburg conservatism to protect his shattered world against the evils of modern nationalism, without ever abandoning his affection for orthodox, traditional Jews. Yet in spite of the obvious differences between Zweig and Roth, there was something in common in their nostalgia for the 'World of Yesterday' and their attempted syntheses of the best in European, German, and Jewish culture.[169] Roth, like Zweig, saw the Monarchy as a stabilizing and stable force, harmonizing different peoples and cultures. Both constructed their Habsburg 'myth' against the background of a fanatical post-war *völkisch* nationalism based on blood and race, which turned against the Jews with unprecedented ferocity. Moreover, both Zweig and Roth, like Hugo von Hofmannstahl, looked towards the legendary father-figure of Franz Joseph I as the protector of all his peoples. For the fatherless Joseph Roth in particular, the paternalistic figure of the old Emperor was to assume an extraordinary existential, symbolic, moral-political significance.[170] Far more than Stefan Zweig and in marked contrast to the majority of liberal Viennese Jews, Joseph Roth stressed the conservative values of order, aristocratic hierarchy, religiosity, and rural simplicity to be found in the Austrian Monarchy. He contrasted favourably the Latin universalism and supranationalism of the Habsburgs to the parvenu coarseness of the Hohenzollern dynasty. In the combination of Prussian militarism and the pagan mythology of Pan-Germanism, Roth discerned the historic roots of Hitlerism.[171] Both legacies were to his mind profoundly alien to the traditions of the House of Habsburg which had shaped the Austrian genius.

Roth's clear preference for the feudal, pre-modern values of

[169] *Briefe*, 257. Letter of Roth to Stefan Zweig, dated 22 Mar. 1933, ibid. 257: 'Man konnte das 6000jährige jüdische Erbe nicht verleugnen, aber ebensowenig kann man das 2000jährige nicht-jüdische verleugnen. Wir kommen eher aus der "Emanzipation," aus der Humanität, aus dem "Humanen," als aus Ägypten. Unsere Ahnen sind Goethe, Lessing, Herder nicht minder als Abraham, Isaac und Jakob.' See also, pp. 260, 263–4.

[170] David Bronsen, 'Der Jude auf der Suche nach einem Vaterland: Joseph Roth's Verhältnis zur habsburgischen Monarchie', *Wiener Tagebuch* (July/Aug. 1979), pp. 26–30.

[171] Joseph Roth, 'Die Juden und die Nibelungen', *Das Neue Tagebuch*, 2, no. 33, 18 Aug. 1934, pp. 786–8, discussed in Marchand, pp. 340–3.

Habsburg Austria found a parallel in his glorification of the more mystical, 'primitive' *Ostjuden* at the expense of bourgeois-rationalist Western Jewry. This inversion of familiar Enlightenment stereotypes is reminiscent of the *Gemeinschaft* passion to be found in the earlier writings of Martin Buber. In both Buber and Richard Beer-Hofmann, one finds too the same insistence as in Joseph Roth's writings, on the importance of blood ties, the legacy of ancestors, and the historic continuity embodied in the family chain of generations. These were themes common to a whole circle of younger artists and intellectuals in Central Europe at the turn of the century.

Hence Joseph Roth's work, despite its idiosyncratic character, can be interpreted as representative of a number of currents that were becoming influential among the Central European Jewish intelligentsia during the last years of the Habsburg Empire. Above all, his Habsburg dynastic patriotism and vindication of the *Pax Austriaca* in East-Central Europe were sentiments widely shared by Austrian Jews before 1914, irrespective of whether they were pariahs or parvenus, orthodox or reform, conservative, liberal, socialist, or Zionist.[172] In Vienna itself, the Imperial mystique was especially beguiling. Personally protected by the Emperor and the patriarchal order of the oldest reigning dynasty in Europe, prosperous, industrious, and at the peak of its creative power, Viennese Jewry in the main still felt confident in 1914 that it would ride out the anti-Semitic storm that had darkened its dramatic ascent. The struggle for Jewish emancipation had been victorious four decades before the outbreak of the First World War. Even Theodor Herzl did not seriously believe that it would be legally reversed. Nevertheless, the warning clouds were already on the horizon and in the work of the great political, religious, literary, and artistic figures of Habsburg Jewry we have found more than a trace of the coming catastrophe. Their visions, aspirations, tensions, and conflicts of identity were a faithful seismograph of the creative contradictions of Viennese Jewry whose achievements and failures were to exert a fateful impact on the course of twentieth-century history.

---

[172] Claudio Magris, p. 76, observed that '. . . gerade die jüdischen Dichter, von Werfel bis Roth und Zweig, mit der grössten Liebe an der Monarchie als ihrem geistigen Vaterland hängen'. As we have seen earlier, this dynastic patriotism existed in almost every stratum of Jewish society in Austria, especially after 1867.

Select Bibliography

This bibliography does not include the countless documents, newspaper articles, and reports read by the author in the course of his research, many of which are listed in the notes. Nor does it include articles in scholarly journals also listed in the notes, which were too numerous to be mentioned here. It is confined only to the most important books, memoirs, and correspondence (whether primary or secondary sources) explicitly cited in this work, which will be of value to the interested general reader.

PRIMARY SOURCES

ACHER, MATTHIAS (N. Birnbaum), *Die jüdische Moderne* (Vienna, 1896).

—— *Zwei Vorträge über den Zionismus* (Berlin, 1898).

—— *Das Stiefkind der Sozialdemokratie* (Vienna, 1905).

ADLER, VICTOR, *Aufsätze, Reden und Briefe*, 11 vols. (Vienna, 1922–9).

BALAKAN, DAVID, *Die Sozialdemokratie und das jüdische Proletariat* (Chernovtsy, 1905.

BAUER, OTTO, *Die Nationalitätenfrage und die Sozialdemokratie* (Vienna, 1907).

BEER-HOFMANN, RICHARD, *Der Tod Georgs* (Berlin, 1900).

—— *Jacob's Dream: A Prologue* (Philadelphia, 1946).

—— *Gesammelte Werke* (Frankfurt, 1963).

BERCHTHOLD, KLAUS (ed.), *Österreichische Parteiprogramme 1868–1966* (Munich, 1967).

BERGEL, KURT (ed.), *Georg Brandes und Arthur Schnitzler: Ein Briefwechsel* (Berne, 1956).

BILLROTH, THEODOR, *Über das Lehren und Lernen der medizinischen Wissenschaften an den Universitäten der deutschen Nation* (Vienna, 1876).

BIRNBAUM, NATHAN, *Die Assimilationssucht: Ein Wort an die sogenannten Deutschen, Slaven, Magyaren etc. mosaischer Confession von einem Studenten jüdischer Nationalität* (Vienna, 1884).

—— *Die nationale Wiedergeburt des jüdischen Volkes in seinem Lande als Mittel zur Lösung der Juden frage* (Vienna, 1893).

—— *Ausgewählte Schriften zur jüdischen Frage* (Chernovtsy, 1910).

—— *Gottes Volk* (Vienna and Berlin, 1918).

BLOCH, JOSEPH SAMUEL, *Aus der Vergangenheit für die Gegenwart* (Vienna, 1886).

668 *Select Bibliography*

BLOCH, JOSEPH SAMUEL, *Der nationale Zwist und die Juden in Österreich* (Vienna, 1886).
—— *Dokumente zur Aufklärung: Talmud und Judenthum in der Oesterreichischen Volksvertretung: Parliamentsreden* (Vienna, n.d.).
—— *My Reminiscences* (Vienna and Berlin, 1923).
—— *Israel and the Nations* (Berlin and Vienna, 1927).
BOROCHOV, BER. *Ketavim*, 3 vols. (Tel Aviv, 1955–66, in Hebrew).
BROCH, HERMANN, *Schriften zur Literatur*, i (Frankfurt, 1975).
BUBER, MARTIN, *Die jüdische Bewegung*, i, *1900–1914* (Berlin, 1920).
—— *Briefwechsel aus sieben Jahrzehnten*, i, *1897–1918* (Heidelberg, 1972).
CHAMBERLAIN, H. S. *Die Grundlagen des neunzehnten Jahrhunderts*, 2 vols. (Munich, 1899/1900).
CHARMATZ, RICHARD, *Oesterreichs innere Geschichte von 1848 bis 1907* (Leipzig, 1909).
—— *Adolf Fischof: Das Lebensbild eines österreichischen Politikers* (Stuttgart and Berlin, 1910).
DALLAGO, CARL, *Otto Weininger und sein Werk* (Innsbruck, 1912).
DECKERT, JOSEPH, *Der ewige Jude 'Ahasver'* (Vienna, 1894).
—— *Türkennoth und Judenherrschaft* (Vienna, 1894).
—— *Semitische und antisemitische Schlagworte in Doppelbeleuchtung* (Vienna, 1897).
DUBNOW, SIMON, *Nationalism and History: Essays on Old and New Judaism*, ed. and introd. K. S. Pinson (Philadelphia, 1958).
ELBOGEN, FRIEDRICH *Ein Mahnruf an das arbeitende Volk: Die Arbeiter und der Antisemitismus* (Vienna, 1885).
ENDLICH, JOHANN QUIRIN, *Der Einfluss der Juden auf unsere Civilisation mit besonderer Rücksicht auf Industrial-Anstalten in Österreich* (Vienna, 1848).
FRANZOS, KARL-EMIL, *Aus Halb-Asien: Culturbilder aus Galizien, der Bukowina, Süd-Russland und Rumanien*, i (Leipzig, 1876).
FREUD, SIGMUND, *The Future of an Illusion* (London, 1928).
—— *An Autobiographical Study*, trans. James Strachey (London, 1936).
—— *Basic Writings*, ed. and trans. A. A. Brill (New York, 1938).
—— *Standard Edition of the Complete Psychological Works*, trans. and ed. James Strachey, 24 vols. (London, 1953–74).
—— *Totem and Taboo*, trans. James Strachey (London, 1960).
—— *Letters*, sel. and ed. Ernst L. Freud (New York, 1961).
—— *Zur Psychopathologie des Alltagslebens* (Frankfurt, 1976).
—— *The Origins of Psychoanalysis: Letters to Wilhelm Fliess. Drafts and Notes, 1887–1902*, trans. Eric Mosbacher and James Strachey (New York, 1977).
—— *Jokes and their Relation to the Unconscious*, trans. James Strachey (London, 1978).
—— *Case Histories I: 'Dora' and 'Little Hans'*, trans. Alix and James Strachey (London, 1980).

—— *A Psycho-Analytic Dialogue: The Letters of Sigmund Freud and Karl Abraham 1907–1926*, ed. Hilda C. Abraham and Ernst L. Freud, trans. Bernard Marsh and Hilda C. Abraham (London and New York, 1965).

—— *Briefwechsel mit Arnold Zweig* (Frankfurt, 1968).

—— and JUNG, CARL, *The Freud–Jung Letters: The Correspondence between Sigmund Freud and C. G. Jung*, ed. William McGuire, trans. Ralph Manheim and R. F. C. Hull (Princeton, 1974).

FRIEDJUNG, HEINRICH, *Der Ausgleich mit Ungarn* (Vienna, 1877).

—— *The Struggle for Supremacy in Germany, 1859–1866*, trans. A. J. P. Taylor and W. C. McElwee (New York, 1966).

GEEHR, RICHARD S. (ed.), *'I Decide who is a Jew!' The Papers of Dr Karl Lueger* (Washington, DC, 1982).

GRUNWALD, MAX, *Samuel Oppenheimer und sein Kreis* (Vienna and Leipzig, 1913).

—— *Der Kampf um die Orgel in der Wiener israelitischen Kultusgemeinde* (Vienna, 1919).

GÜDEMANN, MORITZ, *Jerusalem: Die Opfer und die Orgel* (Vienna, 1871).

—— *Die Geschichte des Erziehungswesens und der Cultur der abendländischen Juden*, i (Vienna, 1880).

—— *Was bedeutet das Hebräische für den israelitischen Religions-Unterricht* (Vienna, 1893).

—— *Grabreden während der letzten fünfundzwanzig Jahre in der Wiener Israelitischen Kultusgemeinde* (Vienna, 1894).

—— *Nationaljudentum* (Leipzig and Vienna, 1897).

—— *Jüdische Apologetik* (Glogau, 1906).

—— 'Aus meinem Leben', 4 vols. (MS, Leo Baeck Institute Archives, New York, n.d.).

HERTZKA, THEODOR, *Freiland: Ein soziales Zukunftsbild* (Leipzig, 1890).

—— *Sozialdemokratie und Sozialliberalismus* (Dresden and Leipzig, 1891).

HERZL, THEODOR, *Briefe und Tagebücher: Briefe 1866–18995* (Frankfurt and Vienna, 1983).

—— *Der Judenstaat* (Vienna, 1896).

—— *Altneuland* (Vienna, 1902), Eng. trans. by Paula Arnold (Haifa, 1960).

—— *Zionistische Schriften*, i (3rd edn., Tel Aviv, 1934).

—— *The New Ghetto*, trans. Heinz Norden (New York, 1955).

—— *Diaries*, ed. and trans. Marvin Lowenthal (London, 1958).

—— *Zionist Writings: Essays and Addresses*, i, trans. Harry Zohn (New York, 1973).

—— *Zionist Writings: Essays and Addresses (1895–1899)* (enlarged Hebrew edn., Jerusalem, 1976).

HOFMANNSTAHL, HUGO VON, *Selected Prose*, introd. Hermann Broch (London, 1952).

—— *Three Essays*, trans. Michael Hamburger (Princeton, 1972).

HOFMANNSTAHL, HUGO VON, *Briefwechsel mit Arthur Schnitzler*, ed. Therese Nickl and Heinrich Schnitzler (Frankfurt, 1964).

—— *Briefwechsel mit Leopold von Adrian* (Frankfurt, 1968).

—— *Briefwechsel mit Richard Beer-Hofmann* (Frankfurt, 1972).

JACQUES, HEINRICH, *Denkschrift über die Stellung der Juden in Österreich* (Vienna, 1859).

JEITELES, ISRAEL, *Die Kultusgemeinde der Israeliten in Wien* (Vienna, 1873).

JELLINEK, ADOLF, *Predigten*, 2 vols. (Vienna, 1862–3).

—— *Schma Jisrael: Fünf Reden über das israelitische Glaubensbekenntnis* (Vienna, 1869).

—— *Studien und Skizzen. Der jüdische Stamm: Ethnograpische Studie* (Vienna, 1869).

—— *Bezelem Elohim: Fünf Reden über die israelitsiche Menschenlehre und Weltanschauung* (Vienna, 1871).

—— *Der israelitische Weltbund: Rede, am I. Tage des Hüttenfestes 5639 gehalten* (Vienna, 1878).

—— *Franzosen über Juden: Urteile und Aussprüche berühmter französischer Staatsmänner und Gelehrter über Juden und Judentum* (Vienna, 1880).

—— *Die hebräische Sprache: Ein Ehrenzeugnis des jüdischen Geistes* (Vienna, 1881).

—— *Der Talmudjude: Vier Reden* (Vienna, 1882).

—— *Aus der Zeit: Tagesfragen und Tagesbegenheiten* (Budapest, 1886).

—— *Denkrede auf Moses Mendelssohn am 4. Januar 1886 im israelitischen Bethause der innern Stadt Wien* (Vienna, 1886).

—— *Gedenkrede auf Herrn Josef Ritter von Wertheimer am 25. März 1887 im israelitischen Bethause der innern Stadt Wien* (Vienna, 1887).

—— *Das vierzigste Passahfest unter der Regierung Sr. Majestät Franz Joseph I.: Rede am I. Tage des Passahfestes im israelitschen Tempel der innern Stadt Wien gehalten* (Vienna, 1888).

—— *Dio, il mondo e l'uomo secondo le dottrine del giudaismo* (Trieste, 1890).

KAFKA, FRANZ, *Briefe, 1902–1924* (New York, 1958).

KAPLAN, A. E., and LANDAU, MAX (eds.), *Vom Sinn des Judentums: Ein Sammelbuch zu Ehren Nathan Birnbaums* (Frankfurt, 1924).

KAUFMANN, DAVID, *Samson Wertheimer, der Oberfaktor und Landesrabbiner (1658–1728) und seine Kinder* (Vienna, 1888).

—— *Die letzte Vertreibung der Juden aus Wien und Niederösterreich: Ihre Vorgeschichte (1625–1670) und ihre Opfer* (Vienna, 1889).

KLOPP, WIARD, *Die sozialen Lehren des Freiherrn von Vogelsang: Grundzüge einer christlichen Gesellschafts- und Volkswirtschaftslehre* (St. Pölten, 1894).

KOLMER, GUSTAV, *Parlament und Verfassung in Österreich*, 6 vols. (Leipzig, 1902–14).

KOMPERT, LEOPOLD, *Neue Geschichte aus dem Ghetto*, 2 vols. (Vienna, 1860).

KRALIK, RICHARD, *Karl Lueger und der christliche Sozialismus,* i (Vienna, 1925).

KRAUS, KARL, *Eine Krone für Zion* (Vienna, 1898).

—— *Die letzten Tage der Menschheit: Tragödie in fünf Akten mit Vorspiel und Epilog* (Vienna and Leipzig, 1922).

—— *Untergang der Welt durch schwarze Magie* (Vienna, 1922).

—— *Werke,* ed. Heinrich Fischer, 14 vols. (Munich, 1952–67).

—— *Frühe Schriften, 1892–1900,* 2 vols. (Munich, 1979).

LANDAU, SAUL RAPHAEL, *Unter jüdischen Proletariern: Reiseschilderungen aus Ostgalizien und Polen* (Vienna, 1898).

—— *Sturm und Drang im Zionismus: Rückblicke eines Zionisten* (Vienna, 1937).

LEWISOHN, LUDWIG (Ed.), *Theodor Herzl: A Portrait for This Age* (New York, 1955).

LILIEN, E. M., *Briefe an seine Frau, 1905–1925* ed. Otto M. Lilien and Eve Strauss, introd. by Ekkehard Hieronimus (Königstein/Ts., 1985).

LUCKA, EMIL, *Otto Weininger: Sein Werk und seine Persönlichkeit* (Vienna, 1905).

MAHLER, ALMA, *Erinnerungen an Gustav Mahler* (Frankfurt, 1980).

MASARYK, THOMAS G., *Die Notwendigkeit der Revision des Polnaer Prozesses* (Vienna, 1899).

MAYER, SIGMUND, *Ein jüdischer Kaufmann, 1831 bis 1911* (Leipzig, 1911).

—— *Die Wiener Juden: Kommerz, Kultur, Politik, 1700–1900* (Vienna and Berlin, 1917).

MÜLLER-TELLERING, EDUARD VON, *Freiheit und Juden. Zur Beherzigung an alle Volksfreunde* (Vienna, 1848).

NOSTITZ-RIENECK, GEORG (ed.), *Briefe Kaiser Franz Josephs an Kaiserin Elizabeth, 1859–1898,* ii (Vienna and Munich, 1966).

NUSSENBLATT, TULLO (ed.), *Zeitgenossen über Herzl* (Brünn, 1899).

OTRUBA GUSTAV (ed.), *Wiener Flugschriften zur sozialen Frage 1848* (Vienna, 1980).

PAPPENHEIM, BERTHA, and RABINOWITSCH SARA, *Zur Lage der jüdischen Bevölkerung in Galizien* (Frankfurt, 1904).

PLENER, ERNST VON, *Erinnerungen,* 3 vols. Stuttgart and Leipzig, (1911–1921).

POPPER-LYNKEUS, JOSEF, *Fürst Bismarck und der Antisemitismus* (Vienna and Leipzig, 1886; 2nd edn., 1925).

PRIBRAM, A. F. (ed.), *Urkunden und Akten zur Geschichte der Juden in Wien* (Vienna and Leipzig, 1918).

REIK, THEODOR, *Arthur Schnitzler als Psycholog* (Munich, 1913).

RENNER, KARL (Rudolf Springer), *Staat und Nation* (Vienna, 1899).

—— *Der Kampf der österreichischen Nationen um den Staat* (Leipzig, 1902).

—— *Das Selbstbestimmungsrecht der Nationen* (Vienna, 1918).

ROSENHEK, LUDWIG (ed.), *Festschrift zur Feier des 100. Semesters der akademischen Verbindung Kadimah (Mödling, 1933).*

ROSENMANN, M., *Zwei Jubiläums-Reden gehalten am 2. December 1898 anlässlich der Feier der 50 jährigen Regierung Sr. Majestät des Kaisers Franz Joseph I.* (Vienna, 1898).

ROSENMANN, M., *Jüdische Realpolitik in Oesterreich* (Vienna, 1900).

ROTH, JOSEPH, *Briefe, 1911–1939*, ed. Hermann Kesten (Cologne and Berlin, 1970).

—— *Werke*, ed. and introd. Hermann Kesten, 4 vols. (Cologne, 1975–6).

—— *Job: The Story of a Simple Man*, trans. Dorothy Thompson (London, 1983).

—— *The Radetzky March*, rev. trans. Eva Tucker (London, 1984).

—— *Juden auf Wanderschaft* (Amsterdam and Cologne, 1985).

RULF, ISAAK, *Aruchas Bas-Ammi. Israels Heilung: Ein ernstes Wort an Glaubens- und Nichtglaubensgenossen* (Frankfurt, 1883).

SCHALIT, ISIDOR, *'Kadimah: Aus meinen Erinnerungen'* (MS, Central Zionist Archives, Jerusalem, n.d.). (Also in Rosenhek.)

SCHEU, ROBERT, *Karl Kraus* (Vienna, 1909).

SCHNITZLER, ARTHUR, *The Road to the Open*, authorized trans. Horace Samuel (New York, 1923).

—— *Professor Bernhardi: A Comedy in Five Acts*, trans. Hetty Landstone (London, 1927).

—— *My Youth in Vienna*, trans. Catherine Hutter (New York, 1970).

—— *Briefe, 1875–1912* (Frankfurt, 1981).

—— *Briefe, 1913–1931* (Frankfurt, 1984).

SCHOENBERG, ARNOLD, *Harmonielehre* Vienna, 1911).

—— *Briefe*, ed. Erwin Stein (Mainz, 1958).

—— *Letters*, sel. and ed. Erwin Stein, trans. Eithne Wilkins and Ernst Kaiser (London, 1964).

SINGER, ISIDORE, *Berlin, Wien und der Antisemitismus* (Vienna, 1882).

STEED, HENRY WICKHAM, *The Habsburg Monarchy* (London, 1913).

SWOBODA, HERMANN, *Die gemeinnützige Forschung und der eigennützige Forscher* (Vienna, 1906).

—— *Otto Weiningers Tod* (Leipzig, 1910).

THON, JACOB, *Die Juden in Österreich* (Berlin, 1908).

WAENTIG, HEINRICH, *Gewerbliche Mittelstandspolitik: Eine rechtshistorisch-wirtschaftspolitische Studie auf Grund österreichischer Quellen* (Leipzig, 1898).

WEININGER, OTTO, *Geschlecht und Charakter* (Vienna, 1903).

—— *Über die letzten Dinge* (Vienna and Leipzig, 1904).

—— *Sex and Character* (London and New York, 1906).

—— *Taschenbuch und Briefe an einen Freund* (Vienna, 1919).

WERTHEIMER, JOSEPH VON, *Die Juden in Österreich*, 2 vols. (Leipzig, 1842).

—— *Die Stellung der Juden in Österreich* (Vienna, 1853).

—— *Zur Emancipation unserer Glaubensgenossen* (Vienna, 1882).

WIESINGER, ALBERT, *Arme Christen und Hungerleider, jüdische Kapitalisten und Geldvergeuder* (Vienna, 1870).

WOLF, GERSON, *Vom ersten bis zum zweiten Tempel: Geschichte der israelitischen Cultusgemeinde in Wien (1820–1860)*, (Vienna, 1861).
—— *Isak Noa Mannheimer, Prediger: Eine biographische Skizze* (Vienna, 1863).
—— *Die Juden in der Leopoldstadt im 17. Jahrhundert in Wien* (Vienna, 1864).
—— *Joseph Wertheimer: Ein Lebens- und Zeitbild* (Vienna, 1868).
—— *Geschichte der Juden in Wien (1156–1876)* (Vienna, 1876).
ZOHN, HARRY (ed.), *In These Great Times: A Karl Kraus Reader* (Montreal, 1976).
ZOLLSCHAN, IGNAZ, *Das Rassenproblem unter besonderer Berücksichtigung der theoretischen Grundlagen der jüdischen Rassenfrage* (Vienna, 1909).
ZWEIG, STEFAN, *Jeremiah*, trans. Eden and Cedar Paul (2nd Eng. edn., New York, 1929).
—— *Freud: La Guérison par l'esprit* (Paris, 1932).
—— *The World of Yesterday* (New York, 1943).
—— *Briefe an Freunde*, ed. Richard Freudenthal (Frankfurt, 1978).

SECONDARY SOURCES

ABELS, NORBERT, *Sicherheit ist nirgends: Judentum und Aufklärung bei Arthur Schnitzler* (Königstein/Ts., 1982).
ABRAHAMSEN, DAVID, *The Mind and Death of a Genius* (New York, 1946).
ADORNO, T. W., *Mahler: Eine Musikalische Physiognomik* (Frankfurt, 1960).
ALMOG, SHMUEL, *Zionut ve-historia* (Jerusalem, 1982).
ALTMANN, ALEXANDER (ed.), *Studies in Nineteenth-Century Jewish Intellectual History* (Harvard, 1964).
ANDICS, HELLMUT, *Luegerzeit: Das schwarze Wien bis 1918* (Vienna, 1984).
ARENDT, HANNAH, *The Origins of Totalitarianism* (New York, 1958; rev. edn., London, 1967).
—— *Rahel Varnhagen: Lebensgeschichte einer deutschen Jüdin aus der Romantik* (Munich, 1959).
—— *Die verborgene Tradition: Acht Essays* (Frankfurt, 1976).
ARKEL, DIRK VAN, *Antisemitism in Austria* (Leiden, 1966).
ASCHHEIM, STEVEN E., *Brothers and Strangers: The East European Jew in German and German Jewish Consciousness, 1800–1923* (Madison, 1983).
BAREA, ILSA, *Vienna: Legend and Reality* (London, 1966).
BARON, SALO, *Die Judenfrage auf dem Wiener Kongress* (Vienna and Berlin, 1920).
BATO, LUDWIG, *Die Juden im alten Wien* (Vienna, 1928).
BEIN, ALEX, *Theodore Herzl: A Biography*, trans. Maurice Samuel (Philadelphia, 1962).
—— *Die Judenfrage: Biographie eines Weltproblems*, 2 vols. (Stuttgart, 1980).
BELKE, INGRID, *Die sozialreformerischen Ideen von Josef Popper-Lynkeus (1838–1921* (Tübingen, 1978).
BENEDIKT, HEINRICH (ed.), *Geschichte der Republik Österreich* (Vienna, 1954).

BLUM, KOPEL, 'Aufklärung und Reform bei den Wiener Juden' (University of Vienna diss., 1935).

BORKENAU, FRANZ, *Austria and After* (London, 1938).

BOYER, JOHN W., *Political Radicalism in Late Imperial Vienna: Origins of the Christian Social Movement, 1848–1897* (Chicago and London, 1981).

BROD, MAX. *Une Vie combative* (Paris, 1964).

BRONSEN, DAVID, *Joseph Roth: Eine Biographie* (Cologne, 1974).

—— (ed), *Jews and Germans from 1860 to 1933: The Problematic Symbiosis* (Heidelberg, 1979).

BUNZL, JOHN, *Klassenkampf in der Diaspora: Zur Geschichte der jüdischen Arbeiterbewegung* (Vienna, 1975).

CANETTI, ELIAS. *Das Gewissen der Worte* (Munich and Vienna, 1975).

CARSTEN, F. L., *Fascist Movements in Austria: From Schönerer To Hitler* (London, 1977).

CENTGRAF, ALEXANDER, *Ein Jude treibt Philosophie* (Berlin, 1943).

CLARE, GEORGE, *Last Waltz in Vienna: The Destruction of a Family, 1842–1942* (London, 1982).

COHEN, GARY B., *The Politics of Ethnic Survival: Germans in Prague, 1861–1914* (Princeton, 1981).

CORTI, EGON, *Der Aufstieg des Hauses Rothschild* (Vienna, 1953).

CUDDIHY, J. M., *The Ordeal of Civility: Freud, Marx, Levi-Strauss and the Jewish Struggle with Modernity* (New York, 1974).

DAWIDOWICZ, LUCY S. (ed.), *The Golden Tradition: Jewish Life and Thought in Eastern Europe* (London, 1967).

DORON, JOACHIM, 'The Impact of German Ideologies on Central European Zionism, 1885–1914' (University of Tel Aviv diss., 1977, in Hebrew).

EISSLER, K. R., *Sigmund Freud und die Wiener Universität* (Berne, 1966).

ELON, AMOS, *Herzl* (New York, 1975).

EVANS, R. J. W., *The Making of the Habsburg Monarchy, 1550–1700* (Oxford, 1979).

FIELD, FRANK, *The Last Days of Mankind: Karl Kraus and his Vienna* (London, 1967).

FRAENKEL, JOSEF, *Mathias Achers Kampf um die 'Zionskrone'* (Basle, 1959).

—— (ed.), *The Jews of Austria: Essays on their Life, History and Destruction* (London, 1967).

FRANKEL, JONATHAN. *Prophecy and Politics: Socialism, Nationalism and the Russian Jews, 1862–1917* (Cambridge, 1981).

FRANZ, GEORG, *Liberalismus: Die deutschliberale Bewegung in der Habsburgischen Monarchie* (Vienna and Munich, 1955).

FROMM, ERICH, *Sigmund Freud's Mission* (New York, 1972).

FUCHS, ALBERT, *Geistige Strömungen in Österreich 1867–1918* (Vienna, 1949).

FUNDER, FRIEDRICH, *Von Gestern ins Heute* (Vienna, 1952).

GAY, PETER, *Freud, Jews and other Germans: Masters and Victims in Modernist Culture* (Oxford, 1979).

GELBER, N. M., *Aus zwei Jahrhunderten* (Vienna and Leipzig, 1924).

—— *Toldot Ha-Tnuah ha-Ziyyonijt be-Galitsia*, 2 vols. (Tel Aviv, 1958).

GICKLHORN, JOSEF and RENÉE, *Sigmund Freuds akademische Laufbahn* (Vienna, 1960).

GLETTLER, MONIKA, *Die Wiener Tschechen um 1900: Strukturanalyse einer nationalen Minderheit in der Grossstadt* (Munich and Vienna, 1972).

GOLD, HUGO (ed.), *Die Juden and Judengemeinden Mährens in Vergangheit und Gegenwart* (Brünn, 1929).

—— (ed.), *Geschichte der Juden in der Bukowina*, 2 vols. (Tel Aviv, 1958–62).

—— *Geschichte der Juden in Wien* (Tel Aviv, 1966).

GOLDHAMMER, LEO, *Die Juden Wiens: Eine statistiche Studie* (Vienna, 1927).

GOLDSMITH, EMMANUEL, *Architects of Yiddishism at the Beginning of the Twentieth Century: A Study in Jewish Cultural History* (London and New York, 1976).

GRUNWALD, KURT, *Türkenhirsch: A Study of Baron Maurice de Hirsch, Entrepreneur and Philanthropist* (Jerusalem, 1966).

GRUNWALD, MAX, *Vienna* (Philadelphia, 1936).

HAMANN, BRIGITTE, *Rudolf: Kronprinz und Rebell* (Vienna, 1978).

—— (ed.), *Kronprinz Rudolf: Schriften* (Vienna and Munich, 1979).

HANDLER, ANDREW, *Dori: The Life and Times of Theodor Herzl in Budapest (1860–1878)* (Univ., Alabama, 1893).

HANISCH, ERNST, *Der kranke Mann an der Donau: Marx und Engels über Österreich* (Vienna, Munich, and Zurich, 1978).

HÄUSLER, WOLFGANG, *Das galizische Judentum in der Habsburgermonarchie: Im Lichte der zeitgenössischen Publizistik und Reiseliteratur von 1772–1848* (Vienna, 1979).

HELLER, ERICH, *The Disinherited Mind* (London, 1952).

HELLWING, I. A., *Der konfessionelle Antisemitismus im 19. Jahrhundert in Österreich* (Vienna, 1972).

HERTZBERG, ARTHUR (ed.), *The Zionist Idea: A Historical Analysis and Reader* (New York, 1973).

HITLER, ADOLF, *Mein Kampf*, trans. Ralph Manheim (Boston, Mass., 1943).

HOFF, MASCHA, *Johann Kremenezky und die Gründung des KKL* (Frankfurt, 1986).

HOLLEIS, EVA, *Die Sozialpolitische Partei: Sozialliberale Bestrebungen in Wien um 1900* (Vienna, 1978).

IGGERS, WILMA A., *Karl Kraus: A Viennese Critic of the Twentieth Century* (The Hague, 1967).

ISRAEL, JONATHAN I., *European Jewry in the Age of Mercantilism, 1500–1750* (Oxford, 1985).

JANIK, ALLAN, and TOULMIN, STEPHEN, *Wittgenstein's Vienna* (New York, 1973).

JANOWSKY, OSCAR, *The Jews and Minority Rights, 1898–1918* (New York, 1933).

JANZ, ROLF-PETER and LAERMANN, KLAUS, *Arthur Schnitzler: Zur Diagnose des Wiener Bürgertums in Fin de Siècle* (Stuttgart, 1977).

JÁSZI, OSCAR, *The Dissolution of the Habsburg Monarchy* (Chicago and London, 1971).

JENKS, WILLIAM A., *The Austrian Electoral Reform of 1907* (New York, 1950).

—— *Austria under the Iron Ring, 1879–1983* (Charlottesville, Va., 1965).

JOHNSTON, WILLIAM M., *The Austrian Mind: An Intellectual and Social History, 1848–1938* (Berkeley and Los Angeles, 1983).

JONES, ERNEST. *The Life and Work of Sigmund Freud*, 3 vols. (London and New York, 1953–7).

KANN, ROBERT A., *The Multinational Empire*, 2 vols. (New York, 1950).

—— *A Study in Austrian Intellectual History: From Late Baroque to Romanticism* (London, 1960).

KATZ, JACOB, *From Prejudice to Destruction: Anti-Semitism, 1700–1933* (Cambridge, Mass., 1982).

KATZBURG, NATHANIEL, *Ha-Antishemiut be-Hungaria, 1867–1914* (Tel Aviv, 1969).

KESTENBERG-GLADSTEIN, RUTH, *Neuere Geschichte der Juden in den böhmischen Ländern, i, Das Zeitalter der Aufklärung, 1780–1830* (Tübingen, 1969).

KISCH, GUIDO, *In Search of Freedom* (London, 1949).

KLEIN, DENNIS B., *Jewish Origins of the Psychoanalytic Movement* (New York, 1981; rev. edn. Chicago and London, 1985).

KOHN, CAROLINE, *Karl Kraus, le polémiste et l'ecrivain: Défenseur des droits de l'individu* (Paris, 1962).

KOHN, HANS, *Karl Kraus, Arthur Schnitzler, Otto Weininger: Aus dem jüdischen Wien der Jahrhundertwende* (Tübingen, 1962).

KRAFT, WERNER, *Karl Kraus: Beiträge zum Verständnis seines Werkes* (Salzburg, 1956).

LANDAU, MOSES, '*Der Zionismus in Österreich-Ungarn*' (University of Vienna Ph.D. diss., 1932).

LAQUEUR, WALTER, *A History of Zionism* (New York, 1976).

LE RIDER, JACQUES, *Le Cas Otto Weininger: Racines de l'antiféminisme et de l'antisémitisme* (Paris, 1982).

—— and LESER, NORBERT (eds.), *Otto Weininger: Werk und Wirkung* (Vienna, 1984).

LESKY, ERNA, *Die Wiener medizinische Schule* (Graz, 1965).

LESSING, THEODOR, *Der jüdische Selbsthass* (Berlin, 1930).

LIEBERMAN, E. JAMES, *Acts of Will: The Life and Work of Otto Rank* (New York, 1985).

LIPTZIN, SOLOMON, *Germany's Stepchildren* (Philadelphia, 1961).

MACARTNEY, C. A., *The Habsburg Empire, 1790–1918* (London, 1969).

McCAGG, WILLIAM O., JUN., *Jewish Notables and Geniuses in Modern Hungary* (New York, 1972).

McGRATH, WILLIAM J., *Dionysian Art and Populist Politics in Austria* (New Haven and London, 1974).

—— *Freud's Discovery of Psychoanalysis: The Politics of Hysteria* (Cornell, 1986).

MAGRIS, CLAUDIO, *Der habsburgische Mythos in der österreichischen Literatur*, trans. from the Italian by Madeleine von Pasztory (Salzburg, 1966).

MAHLER, RAPHAEL, *A History of Modern Jewry, 1780–1815* (London, 1971).

MARCHAND, WOLF R., *Joseph Roth und die völkisch-nationalistische Wertbegriffe* (Bonn, 1974).

MARKOVITS, ANDREI S., and SYSYN, FRANK E. (eds.), *Nationbuilding and the Politics of Nationalism. Essays on Austrian Galicia* (Harvard, 1982).

MAY, ARTHUR J., *The Habsburg Monarchy, 1867–1914* (Cambridge, Mass., 1951).

MAYER, HANS, *Aussenseiter* (Frankfurt, 1976).

MICHEL, BERNARD, *Banques et banquiers en Autriche au début du XXe siècle* (Paris, 1976).

MITIS, OSKAR FREIHERR VON, *Das Leben des Kronprinzen Rudolf* (Vienna, 1928).

MOLISCH, PAUL, *Die deutschen Hochschulen in Österreich und die politisch-nationale Entwicklung nach 1848* (Munich, 1922).

—— *Geschichte der deutsch-national Bewegung in Österreich von ihren Anfängen bis zum Zerfall der Monarchie* (Jena, 1926).

MOSSE, GEORGE L. *German Jews beyond Judaism* (Hebrew Union College, Cincinnati, 1985).

MOSSE, WERNER, PAUCKER, ARNOLD, and RÜRUP, REINHARD (eds.), *Revolution and Evolution: 1848 in German-Jewish History* (Tübingen, 1981).

MUSIL, ROBERT, *The Man Without Qualities*, 3 vols. (London, 1953–60).

NÜRNBERGER, HELMUT, *Joseph Roth* (Hamburg, 1981).

OLGER, HERTHA, *Alfred Adler: The Man and His Work* (4th edn., London, 1973).

PALMON, AVRAHAM, 'The Jewish Community of Vienna between the Two World Wars, 1918–1938: Continuity and Change in Internal Political Life' (Hebrew University, Jerusalem, Ph.D. diss., 1985, in Hebrew).

PICHL, E., *Georg von Schoenerer und die Entwicklung des Alldeutschtums in der Ostmark* (Oldenburg, 1938).

POLLACK, MICHAEL, *Vienne 1900: Une identité blessée* (Paris, 1984).

PULZER, P. G. J., *The Rise of Political Antisemitism in Germany and Austria* (New York and London, 1964).

RAGINS, SANFORD, *Jewish Responses to Anti-Semitism in Germany, 1870–1914* (Cincinnati, 1980).

RATH, JOHN, *The Viennese Revolution of 1848* (New York, 1969).

RATTNER, JOSEF, *Alfred Adler in Selbstzeugnissen und Bilddokumenten* (Hamburg, 1972).

REICH, WILLI, *Arnold Schönberg oder der Konservative Revolutionär* (Vienna, 1968).

ROBACK, A. A., *Freudiana* (Cambridge, Mass., 1957).

ROBERT, MARTHE, *D'Œdipe à Moïse: Freud et la conscience juive* (Paris, 1974).

ROSENMANN, MOSES, *Isak Noa Mannheimer: Sein Leben und Wirken, zugleich ein Beitrag zur Geschichte der israeliten Kultusgemeinde in Wien in der ersten Hälfte des 19. Jahrhundert* (Vienna and Berlin, 1922).

—— *Dr Adolf Jellinek: Sein Leben und Schaffen* (Vienna, 1931).

ROZENBLIT, MARSHA, *The Jews of Vienna, 1867–1914: Assimilation and Identity* (Albany, NY, 1983).

SCHEIBLE, HARTMUT, *Arthur Schnitzler in Selbstzeugnissen und Bilddokumenten* (Hamburg, 1976).

—— *Literarischer Jugendstil in Wien* (Munich and Zurich, 1984).

SCHNEE, HEINRICH, *Die Hoffinanz und der moderne Staat*, 3 vols. (Berlin, 1953–5).

SCHNITZLER, OLGA, *Spiegelbild der Freundschaft* (Salzburg, 1962).

SCHORSKE, CARL E., *Fin-de-siècle Vienna: Politics and Culture* (London, 1980).

SIEGHART, RUDOLF, *Die letzten Jahrzehnte einer Grossmacht* (Berlin, 1932).

SKALNIK, KURT, *Dr. Karl Lueger: Der Mann zwischen den Zeiten* (Vienna and Munich, 1954).

SONNENFELD, MARION (ed.), *Stefan Zweig* (Albany, NY, 1983).

SPERBER, MANÈS, *Masks of Loneliness: Alfred Adler in Perspective* (New York, 1974).

SPIEL, HILDE, *Fanny von Arnstein oder die Emanzipation: Ein Frauenleben an der Zeitwende, 1758–1818* (Frankfurt, 1978).

STERN, FRITZ, *Gold and Iron: Bismarck, Bleichröder and the Building of the German Empire* (London, 1977).

STEWART, DESMOND, *Theodor Herzl: Artist and Politician* (London, 1974).

STOCKERT-MEYNERT, DORA, *Theodor Meynert und seine Zeit: Zur Geistesgeschichte Österreichs in der zweiten Hälfte des 19. Jahrhunderts* (Vienna, 1930).

SZEPS, BERTA. *My Life and History* (London, 1938; New York, 1939).

TAYLOR, A. J. P. *The Habsburg Monarchy, 1809–1918* (London, 1981).

TIETZE, HANS, *Die Juden Wiens* (Vienna, and Leipzig, 1933).

TIMMS, EDWARD, *Karl Kraus: Apolcalyptic Satirist* (New Haven and London, 1986).

TOURY, JACOB, *Turmoil and Confusion in the Revolution of 1848* (Merhavia, 1968, in Hebrew).

—— *Die jüdische Presse im österreichischen Kaiserreich, 1802–1918* (Tübingen, 1983).

VAGO, BELA (ed.), *Jewish Assimilation in Modern Times* (Boulder, Colo., 1981).

—— and MOSSE, G. L. (eds.), *Jews and Non-Jews in Eastern Europe, 1918–1945* (Jerusalem, 1974).

VITAL, DAVID, *The Origins of Zionism* (Oxford, 1975).

—— *Zionism: The Formative Years* (Oxford, 1982).

WACHSTEIN, BERNHARD, *Hebräische Publizistik in Wien* (Vienna, 1930).

WAGNER, NIKE, *Geist und Geschlecht: Karl Kraus und die Erotik der Wiener Moderne* (Frankfurt, 1982).

WANDRUSZKA, ADAM, *Geschichte einer Zeitung: Das Schicksal der 'Presse' und der 'Neuen Freien Presse' von 1848 zur Zweiten Republik* (Vienna, 1958).

—— and URBANWITSCH, PETER (eds.), *Die Habsburgermonarchie, 1848–1918*, 4 vols. (Vienna, 1981–).

WANGERMANN, ERNEST, *The Austrian Achievement, 1700–1800* (London, 1973).

WASSERMANN, JAKOB, *My Life as German and Jew*, trans. S. N. Brainin (New York, 1933).

WEIGEL, HANS, *Karl Kraus oder die Macht der Ohnmacht* (Vienna, 1968).

WEISL, WOLFGANG VON, *Die Juden in der Armee Österreich-Ungarns* (Tel Aviv, 1971).

WHITESIDE, A. G., *The Socialism of Fools: Georg Ritter von Schoenerer and Austrian Pan-Germanism* (Berkeley and Los Angeles, 1975).

WISTRICH, ROBERT SOLOMON, *Revolutionary Jews from Marx to Trotsky* London, 1976).

—— *Socialism and the Jews: The Dilemmas of Assimilation in Germany and Austria-Hungary* (Littman Library London and Toronto, 1982).

—— *Hitler's Apocalypse: Jews and the Nazi Legacy* (London, 1985).

WITTELS, FRITZ, *Sigmund Freud: His Personality, His Teachings and His School*, trans. Eden and Ceolar Paul (New York, 1924).

ZAHAVI, ZEV. Y., *Me-ha-Ḥatam Sofer ve-ad Herzl* (Jerusalem, 1966).

ZOHN, HARRY (ed.), *In These Great Times: A Karl Kraus Reader* (Montreal, 1976).

Glossary of Terms not explained in the text

Abwehr: Defence.

Abwehrvereine: Defence organizations against anti-Semitism, of which there were a growing number—both Jewish and Christian—in Central Europe in the years before the First World War.

Aggadah: That part of the Oral Law distinct from the Halakhah, a repository of allegorical material including stories, chronicles, sayings of the wise, and admonitions of the prophets.

Agudas Yisroel: Religious-orthodox, non-Zionist (originally anti-Zionist) political movement founded in 1912.

Ausgleich: The Compromise with Hungary of 1867 which transformed the Habsburg Empire into the Dual Monarchy.

Ba'al Tschuva: Term for one who has sinned and returns to the path of righteous living as prescribed by orthodox Judaism.

Berufsumschichtung: Vocational or professional regrouping. Term used by Zionists who advocated the productivization of the Jewish people through return to the land and manual labour.

Besitzbürgertum: Propertied bourgeoisie.

Beth Hamidrash: House of Study.

Bezirksrabbiner: Local district rabbi.

Bildung: Education, culture, formation of personality. A key term of the German *Aufklärung* in the late eighteenth century.

Bildungshass: Hatred of education, anti-intellectualism.

Chewra-Kadisha: Literally 'sacred society'. Title applied to Jewish confraternities who visited the sick, buried the dead, and comforted the bereaved.

Geist: Spirit, Mind, Intellect.

Gemeinderat: Municipal council.

Golusjude: A Diaspora Jew. From the Hebrew 'Galuth' meaning exile.

Grossbürgertum: The wealthiest segment of the bourgeoisie.

Grossdeutsch: Greater German. Later identified with programme of expansion to include all ethnic Germans within the borders of a Greater Germany.

Grundgesetz: Fundamental Law of 1867 which guaranteed the equality of all citizens in the Austrian Empire regardless of religion or nationality.

Haham (Ḥakham): Literally 'Wise man'. The officiating rabbi in Sephardi communities.

Halakhah: The legal system of Judaism based on accumulated jurisprudence and the decisions of the sages.

Halizah: Biblically prescribed ceremony, performed when a man refuses to marry his brother's childless widow.

Halutzim: Pioneers. Term referring to the agricultural labourers who built up Jewish settlements in Palestine after the turn of the century and were committed to a communitarian, socialist idea of co-operation.

Haskalah: The Hebrew term for Enlightenment.

Hausherren: Landlords.

Hazzan: Cantor officiating in a synagogue.

Heder: Jewish primary school of orthodox-religious character.

Heimatgefühl: Feeling or sentiment for one's native land and landscape.

Hetzreden: Inflammatory speeches of a demagogic nature.

Judenrein: Cleansed or 'free' of Jews. A term which became part of official Nazi language applied in the 'Final Solution of the Jewish Question'.

Judenzählung: Notorious census of Jews serving in the German Army ordered by the War Ministry in 1916 which cast unjustified doubts on the patriotism of German Jews.

Kaisertreu: Loyal to the Emperor and to the supranational Habsburg dynasty—an attitude especially characterstic of conservative and orthodox Jews in the Austrian Monarchy.

Kashrut: Regulations governing the Jewish Dietary Laws.

Krämergeist: Shopkeeper or mercantile mentality.

Kulturkampf: Struggle for culture. A term used by nineteenth-century liberals to describe their fight to separate the spheres of Church and State, religion and society, faith and science.

Landsmannschaften: Societies or associations (especially of East European Jewish immigrants) whose membership was composed of people from the same town or province in the country of origin.

Luftmensch: A rootless person. A term popularized by the Zionist thinker Max Nordau and applied to East European Jews without 'productive' occupations who engaged in peddling and petty commerce.

Machzike Hadath: A Jewish society in Galicia and Bukovina, founded in 1879 to unite orthodox Jews for political action, especially against secular or 'progressive' trends considered inimical to community traditions.

Maskilim: Adherents or supporters of the *Haskalah* or Jewish Enlightenment.

Melamed: A teacher of elementary Hebrew to young boys. Not a high-status occupation. Subsidiary meaning, a *shlemiel* or well-meaning drip.

Mittelstand: German term for the rather broad and diffuse social stratum which felt distinct from both the wealthy capitalists and the working classes. In Germany and Austria it included not only small tradesmen, artisans, and peasants but also civil servants, professional people, and salaried employees.

Piyyutim: Hebrew liturgical poetry.

Prediger: Preacher.

Rechtsschutzbureau: Legal aid office.

Schlamperei: Laxity or muddle. The Austrian answer to Prussian efficiency. Victor Adler once defined Habsburg Government as 'despotism softened by *Schlamperei*'.

Schnorrers: Professional Jewish beggars. A common occupation in Eastern Europe, especially in Galicia, and a constant source for Jewish jokes, many of them reflecting the impudence of this class of indigents.

Shtadlanim: Intercessors, advocates, and representatives of the Jewish community who used their access to high dignitaries, to State and Church authorities, in order to protect their co-religionists from arbitrary acts. They were the unofficial diplomats of a stateless community in the pre-modern era.

Shtetl: A small town, city, or village in Eastern Europe with its own unique Ashkenazic Jewish socio-cultural pattern.

Shulḥan Arukh: The authoritative code of Jewish Law composed by Joseph Caro in the sixteenth century, in the city of Safed in northern Israel.

Spiessbürger: Bourgeois, philistine.

Tashlich: New Year ritual of observant Jews who cast off their sins by praying near a stream or body of water.

Völkisch: Ethnic. Deriving from Volk, meaning people or nation. Associated with authoritarian and racist ideology.

Weltbürger, Weltbürgertum: Citizen of the world, Cosmopolitanism.

Wissenschaft des Judentums: The Science of Judaism.

Yeshivah: Traditional Jewish school devoted to the study of the Talmud and rabbinical literature.

Index